D1154870

Farnsworth & Young Cs.Cont. 3rd Ed. UCB—1

University Casebook Series

March, 1986

ACCOUNTING AND THE LAW, Fourth Edition (1978), with Problems Pamphlet (Successor to Dohr, Phillips, Thompson & Warren)

George C. Thompson, Professor, Columbia University Graduate School of Business.
Robert Whitman, Professor of Law, University of Connecticut.
Ellis L. Phillips, Jr., Member of the New York Bar.
William C. Warren, Professor of Law Emeritus, Columbia University.

ACCOUNTING FOR LAWYERS, MATERIALS ON (1980)

David R. Herwitz, Professor of Law, Harvard University.

ADMINISTRATIVE LAW, Seventh Edition (1979), with 1983 Problems Supplement (Supplement edited in association with Paul R. Verkuil, Dean and Professor of Law, Tulane University)

Walter Gellhorn, University Professor Emeritus, Columbia University.
Clark Byse, Professor of Law, Harvard University.
Peter L. Strauss, Professor of Law, Columbia University.

ADMIRALTY, Second Edition (1978), with Statute and Rule Supplement

Jo Desha Lucas, Professor of Law, University of Chicago.

ADVOCACY, see also Lawyering Process

AGENCY, see also Enterprise Organization

AGENCY—PARTNERSHIPS, Third Edition (1982)

Abridgement from Conard, Knauss & Siegel's Enterprise Organization, Third Edition.

ANTITRUST: FREE ENTERPRISE AND ECONOMIC ORGANIZATION, Sixth Edition (1983), with 1983 Problems in Antitrust Supplement and 1985 Case Supplement

Louis B. Schwartz, Professor of Law, University of Pennsylvania.
John J. Flynn, Professor of Law, University of Utah.
Harry First, Professor of Law, New York University.

BANKRUPTCY (1985)

Robert L. Jordan, Professor of Law, University of California, Los Angeles.
William D. Warren, Professor of Law, University of California, Los Angeles.

BUSINESS ORGANIZATION, see also Enterprise Organization

BUSINESS PLANNING, Temporary Second Edition (1984)

David R. Herwitz, Professor of Law, Harvard University.

BUSINESS TORTS (1972)

Milton Handler, Professor of Law Emeritus, Columbia University.

CHILDREN IN THE LEGAL SYSTEM (1983)

Walter Wadlington, Professor of Law, University of Virginia.
Charles H. Whitebread, Professor of Law, University of Southern California.
Samuel Davis, Professor of Law, University of Georgia.

CIVIL PROCEDURE, see Procedure

CLINIC, see also Lawyering Process

COMMERCIAL LAW (1983) with 1986 Bankruptcy Supplement

Robert L. Jordan, Professor of Law, University of California, Los Angeles.
William D. Warren, Professor of Law, University of California, Los Angeles.

COMMERCIAL LAW, CASES & MATERIALS ON, Fourth Edition (1985)

E. Allan Farnsworth, Professor of Law, Columbia University.
John Honnold, Professor of Law, University of Pennsylvania.

COMMERCIAL PAPER, Third Edition (1984)

E. Allan Farnsworth, Professor of Law, Columbia University.

COMMERCIAL PAPER (1983) (Reprinted from COMMERCIAL LAW)

Robert L. Jordan, Professor of Law, University of California, Los Angeles.
William D. Warren, Professor of Law, University of California, Los Angeles.

COMMERCIAL PAPER AND BANK DEPOSITS AND COLLECTIONS (1967), with Statutory Supplement

William D. Hawkland, Professor of Law, University of Illinois.

COMMERCIAL TRANSACTIONS—Principles and Policies (1982)

Alan Schwartz, Professor of Law, University of Southern California.
Robert E. Scott, Professor of Law, University of Virginia.

COMPARATIVE LAW, Fourth Edition (1980)

Rudolf B. Schlesinger, Professor of Law, Hastings College of the Law.

COMPETITIVE PROCESS, LEGAL REGULATION OF THE, Third Edition (1986), with Selected Statutes Supplement

Edmund W. Kitch, Professor of Law, University of Virginia.
Harvey S. Perlman, Dean of the Law School, University of Nebraska.

CONFLICT OF LAWS, Eighth Edition (1984)

Willis L. M. Reese, Professor of Law, Columbia University.
Maurice Rosenberg, Professor of Law, Columbia University.

CONSTITUTIONAL LAW, Seventh Edition (1985), with 1985 Supplement

Edward L. Barrett, Jr., Professor of Law, University of California, Davis.
William Cohen, Professor of Law, Stanford University.

CONSTITUTIONAL LAW, CIVIL LIBERTY AND INDIVIDUAL RIGHTS, Second Edition (1982), with 1985 Supplement

William Cohen, Professor of Law, Stanford University.
John Kaplan, Professor of Law, Stanford University.

CONSTITUTIONAL LAW, Eleventh Edition (1985), with 1985 Supplement (Supplement edited in association with Frederick F. Schauer, Professor of Law, University of Michigan)

Gerald Gunther, Professor of Law, Stanford University.

CONSTITUTIONAL LAW, INDIVIDUAL RIGHTS IN, Fourth Edition (1986), (Reprinted from CONSTITUTIONAL LAW, Eleventh Edition), with 1985 Supplement (Supplement edited in association with Frederick F. Schauer, Professor of Law, University of Michigan)

Gerald Gunther, Professor of Law, Stanford University.

CONSUMER TRANSACTIONS (1983), with Selected Statutes and Regulations Supplement

Michael M. Greenfield, Professor of Law, Washington University.

CONTRACT LAW AND ITS APPLICATION, Third Edition (1983)

The late Addison Mueller, Professor of Law, University of California, Los Angeles.
Arthur I. Rosett, Professor of Law, University of California, Los Angeles.
Gerald P. Lopez, Professor of Law, University of California, Los Angeles.

CONTRACT LAW, STUDIES IN, Third Edition (1984)

Edward J. Murphy, Professor of Law, University of Notre Dame.
Richard E. Speidel, Professor of Law, Northwestern University.

CONTRACTS, Fourth Edition (1982)

John P. Dawson, Professor of Law Emeritus, Harvard University.
William Burnett Harvey, Professor of Law and Political Science, Boston University.
Stanley D. Henderson, Professor of Law, University of Virginia.

CONTRACTS, Third Edition (1980), with Statutory Supplement

E. Allan Farnsworth, Professor of Law, Columbia University.
William F. Young, Professor of Law, Columbia University.

CONTRACTS, Second Edition (1978), with Statutory and Administrative Law Supplement (1978)

Ian R. Macneil, Professor of Law, Cornell University.

COPYRIGHT, PATENTS AND TRADEMARKS, see also Competitive Process; see also Selected Statutes and International Agreements

COPYRIGHT, PATENT, TRADEMARK AND RELATED STATE DOCTRINES, Second Edition (1981), with 1985 Case Supplement, 1986 Selected Statutes Supplement and 1981 Problem Supplement

Paul Goldstein, Professor of Law, Stanford University.

COPYRIGHT, Unfair Competition, and Other Topics Bearing on the Protection of Literary, Musical, and Artistic Works, Fourth Edition (1985), with 1985 Statutory Supplement

Ralph S. Brown, Jr., Professor of Law, Yale University.
Robert C. Denicola, Professor of Law, University of Nebraska.

CORPORATE ACQUISITIONS, The Law and Finance of (1986)

Ronald J. Gilson, Professor of Law, Stanford University.

CORPORATE FINANCE, Second Edition (1979), with 1984 Supplement

Victor Brudney, Professor of Law, Harvard University.
Marvin A. Chirelstein, Professor of Law, Columbia University.

CORPORATE READJUSTMENTS AND REORGANIZATIONS (1976)

Walter J. Blum, Professor of Law, University of Chicago.
Stanley A. Kaplan, Professor of Law, University of Chicago.

CORPORATION LAW, BASIC, Second Edition (1979), with 1983 Case and Documentary Supplement

Detlev F. Vagts, Professor of Law, Harvard University.

CORPORATIONS, see also Enterprise Organization

CORPORATIONS, Fifth Edition—Unabridged (1980), with 1984 Supplement

The late William L. Cary, Professor of Law, Columbia University.
Melvin Aron Eisenberg, Professor of Law, University of California, Berkeley.

CORPORATIONS, Fifth Edition—Abridged (1980), with 1984 Supplement

The late William L. Cary, Professor of Law, Columbia University.
Melvin Aron Eisenberg, Professor of Law, University of California, Berkeley.

CORPORATIONS, Second Edition (1982), with 1982 Corporation and Partnership Statutes, Rules and Forms

Alfred F. Conard, Professor of Law, University of Michigan.
Robert N. Knauss, Dean of the Law School, University of Houston.
Stanley Siegel, Professor of Law, University of California, Los Angeles.

CORPORATIONS COURSE GAME PLAN (1975)

David R. Herwitz, Professor of Law, Harvard University.

CORRECTIONS, SEE SENTENCING

CREDITORS' RIGHTS, see also Debtor-Creditor Law

CRIMINAL JUSTICE ADMINISTRATION, Third Edition (1986).

Frank W. Miller, Professor of Law, Washington University.
Robert O. Dawson, Professor of Law, University of Texas.
George E. Dix, Professor of Law, University of Texas.
Raymond I. Parnas, Professor of Law, University of California, Davis.

CRIMINAL LAW, Third Edition (1983)

Fred E. Inbau, Professor of Law Emeritus, Northwestern University.
James R. Thompson, Professor of Law Emeritus, Northwestern University.
Andre A. Moenssens, Professor of Law, University of Richmond.

CRIMINAL LAW AND APPROACHES TO THE STUDY OF LAW (1986)

John M. Brumbaugh, Professor of Law, University of Maryland.

CRIMINAL LAW, Second Edition (1986)

Peter W. Low, Professor of Law, University of Virginia.
John C. Jeffries, Jr., Professor of Law, University of Virginia.
Richard C. Bonnie, Professor of Law, University of Virginia.

CRIMINAL LAW, Third Edition (1980)

Lloyd L. Weinreb, Professor of Law, Harvard University.

CRIMINAL LAW AND PROCEDURE, Sixth Edition (1984)

Rollin M. Perkins, Professor of Law Emeritus, University of California, Hastings College of the Law.
Ronald N. Boyce, Professor of Law, University of Utah.

CRIMINAL PROCEDURE, Second Edition (1980), with 1985 Supplement

Fred E. Inbau, Professor of Law Emeritus, Northwestern University.
James R. Thompson, Professor of Law Emeritus, Northwestern University.
James B. Haddad, Professor of Law, Northwestern University.
James B. Zagel, Chief, Criminal Justice Division, Office of Attorney General of Illinois.
Gary L. Starkman, Assistant U. S. Attorney, Northern District of Illinois.

CRIMINAL PROCESS, Third Edition (1978), with 1985 Supplement

Lloyd L. Weinreb, Professor of Law, Harvard University.

DAMAGES, Second Edition (1952)

Charles T. McCormick, late Professor of Law, University of Texas.
William F. Fritz, late Professor of Law, University of Texas.

DEBTOR–CREDITOR LAW (1984) with 1986 Supplement

Theodore Eisenberg, Professor of Law, Cornell University.

DEBTOR–CREDITOR LAW, Second Edition (1981), with Statutory Supplement

William D. Warren, Dean of the School of Law, University of California, Los Angeles.
William E. Hogan, Professor of Law, New York University.

DECEDENTS' ESTATES (1971)

Max Rheinstein, late Professor of Law Emeritus, University of Chicago.
Mary Ann Glendon, Professor of Law, Boston College.

DECEDENTS' ESTATES AND TRUSTS, Sixth Edition (1982)

John Ritchie, Emeritus Dean and Wigmore Professor of Law, Northwestern University.
Neill H. Alford, Jr., Professor of Law, University of Virginia.
Richard W. Effland, Professor of Law, Arizona State University.

DOMESTIC RELATIONS, see also Family Law

DOMESTIC RELATIONS, Successor Edition (1984) with 1985 Supplement

Walter Wadlington, Professor of Law, University of Virginia.

ELECTRONIC MASS MEDIA, Second Edition (1979)

William K. Jones, Professor of Law, Columbia University.

EMPLOYMENT DISCRIMINATION (1983) with 1985 Supplement

Joel W. Friedman, Professor of Law, Tulane University.
George M. Strickler, Professor of Law, Tulane University.

ENERGY LAW (1983)

Donald N. Zillman, Professor of Law, University of Utah.
Laurence Lattman, Dean of Mines and Engineering, University of Utah.

ENTERPRISE ORGANIZATION, Third Edition (1982), with 1982 Corporation and Partnership Statutes, Rules and Forms Supplement

Alfred F. Conard, Professor of Law, University of Michigan.
Robert L. Knauss, Dean of the Law School, University of Houston.
Stanley Siegel, Professor of Law, University of California, Los Angeles.

ENVIRONMENTAL POLICY LAW 1985 Edition, with 1985 Problems Supplement (Supplement in association with Ronald H. Rosenberg, Professor of Law, College of William and Mary)

Thomas J. Schoenbaum, Professor of Law, University of Georgia.

EQUITY, see also Remedies

EQUITY, RESTITUTION AND DAMAGES, Second Edition (1974)

Robert Childres, late Professor of Law, Northwestern University.
William F. Johnson, Jr., Professor of Law, New York University.

ESTATE PLANNING, Second Edition (1982), with 1985 Case, Text and Documentary Supplement

David Westfall, Professor of Law, Harvard University.

ETHICS, see Legal Profession, and Professional Responsibility

ETHICS AND PROFESSIONAL RESPONSIBILITY (1981) (Reprinted from THE LAWYERING PROCESS)

Gary Bellow, Professor of Law, Harvard University.
Bea Moulton, Legal Services Corporation.

EVIDENCE, Fifth Edition (1984)

John Kaplan, Professor of Law, Stanford University.
Jon R. Waltz, Professor of Law, Northwestern University.

EVIDENCE, Seventh Edition (1983) with Rules and Statute Supplement (1984)

Jack B. Weinstein, Chief Judge, United States District Court.
John H. Mansfield, Professor of Law, Harvard University.
Norman Abrams, Professor of Law, University of California, Los Angeles.
Margaret Berger, Professor of Law, Brooklyn Law School.

FAMILY LAW, see also Domestic Relations

FAMILY LAW Second Edition (1985)

Judith C. Areen, Professor of Law, Georgetown University.

FAMILY LAW AND CHILDREN IN THE LEGAL SYSTEM, STATUTORY MATERIALS (1981)

Walter Wadlington, Professor of Law, University of Virginia.

FEDERAL COURTS, Seventh Edition (1982), with 1985 Supplement

Charles T. McCormick, late Professor of Law, University of Texas.
James H. Chadbourn, late Professor of Law, Harvard University.
Charles Alan Wright, Professor of Law, University of Texas.

FEDERAL COURTS AND THE FEDERAL SYSTEM, Hart and Wechsler's Second Edition (1973), with 1981 Supplement

Paul M. Bator, Professor of Law, Harvard University.
Paul J. Mishkin, Professor of Law, University of California, Berkeley.
David L. Shapiro, Professor of Law, Harvard University.
Herbert Wechsler, Professor of Law, Columbia University.

FEDERAL PUBLIC LAND AND RESOURCES LAW (1981), with 1983 Case Supplement and 1984 Statutory Supplement

George C. Coggins, Professor of Law, University of Kansas.
Charles F. Wilkinson, Professor of Law, University of Oregon.

FEDERAL RULES OF CIVIL PROCEDURE, 1984 Edition

FEDERAL TAXATION, see Taxation

FOOD AND DRUG LAW (1980), with Statutory Supplement

Richard A. Merrill, Dean of the School of Law, University of Virginia.
Peter Barton Hutt, Esq.

FUTURE INTERESTS (1958)

Philip Mechem, late Professor of Law Emeritus, University of Pennsylvania.

FUTURE INTERESTS (1970)

Howard R. Williams, Professor of Law, Stanford University.

FUTURE INTERESTS AND ESTATE PLANNING (1961), with 1962 Supplement

W. Barton Leach, late Professor of Law, Harvard University.
James K. Logan, formerly Dean of the Law School, University of Kansas.

GOVERNMENT CONTRACTS, FEDERAL, Successor Edition (1985)

John W. Whelan, Professor of Law, Hastings College of the Law.

GOVERNMENT REGULATION: FREE ENTERPRISE AND ECONOMIC ORGANIZATION, Sixth Edition (1985)

Louis B. Schwartz, Professor of Law, University of Pennsylvania.
John J. Flynn, Professor of Law, University of Utah.
Harry First, Professor of Law, New York University.

HINCKLEY JOHN W., TRIAL OF: A Case Study of the Insanity Defense

Peter W. Low, Professor of Law, University of Virginia.
John C. Jeffries, Jr., Professor of Law, University of Virginia.
Richard C. Bonnie, Professor of Law, University of Virginia.

INJUNCTIONS, Second Edition (1984)

Owen M. Fiss, Professor of Law, Yale University.
Doug Rendleman, Professor of Law, College of William and Mary.

INSTITUTIONAL INVESTORS, 1978

David L. Ratner, Professor of Law, Cornell University.

INSURANCE, Second Edition (1985)

William F. Young, Professor of Law, Columbia University.
Eric M. Holmes, Professor of Law, University of Georgia.

INTERNATIONAL LAW, see also Transnational Legal Problems, Transnational Business Problems, and United Nations Law

INTERNATIONAL LAW IN CONTEMPORARY PERSPECTIVE (1981), with Essay Supplement

Myres S. McDougal, Professor of Law, Yale University.
W. Michael Reisman, Professor of Law, Yale University.

INTERNATIONAL LEGAL SYSTEM, Second Edition (1981), with Documentary Supplement

Joseph Modeste Sweeney, Professor of Law, Tulane University.
Covey T. Oliver, Professor of Law, University of Pennsylvania.
Noyes E. Leech, Professor of Law, University of Pennsylvania.

INTRODUCTION TO LAW, see also Legal Method, On Law in Courts, and Dynamics of American Law

INTRODUCTION TO THE STUDY OF LAW (1970)

E. Wayne Thode, late Professor of Law, University of Utah.
Leon Lebowitz, Professor of Law, University of Texas.
Lester J. Mazor, Professor of Law, University of Utah.

JUDICIAL CODE and Rules of Procedure in the Federal Courts with Excerpts from the Criminal Code, 1984 Edition

Henry M. Hart, Jr., late Professor of Law, Harvard University.
Herbert Wechsler, Professor of Law, Columbia University.

JURISPRUDENCE (Temporary Edition Hardbound) (1949)

Lon L. Fuller, Professor of Law Emeritus, Harvard University.

JUVENILE, see also Children

JUVENILE JUSTICE PROCESS, Third Edition (1985)

Frank W. Miller, Professor of Law, Washington University.
Robert O. Dawson, Professor of Law, University of Texas.
George E. Dix, Professor of Law, University of Texas.
Raymond I. Parnas, Professor of Law, University of California, Davis.

LABOR LAW, Tenth Edition (1986), with 1986 Statutory Supplement

Archibald Cox, Professor of Law, Harvard University.
Derek C. Bok, President, Harvard University.
Robert A. Gorman, Professor of Law, University of Pennsylvania.

LABOR LAW, Second Edition (1982), with Statutory Supplement

Clyde W. Summers, Professor of Law, University of Pennsylvania.
Harry H. Wellington, Dean of the Law School, Yale University.
Alan Hyde, Professor of Law, Rutgers University.

LAND FINANCING, Third Edition (1985)

The late Norman Penney, Professor of Law, Cornell University.
Richard F. Broude, Member of the California Bar.
Roger Cunningham, Professor of Law, University of Michigan.

LAW AND MEDICINE (1980)

Walter Wadlington, Professor of Law and Professor of Legal Medicine, University of Virginia.
Jon R. Waltz, Professor of Law, Northwestern University.
Roger B. Dworkin, Professor of Law, Indiana University, and Professor of Biomedical History, University of Washington.

LAW, LANGUAGE AND ETHICS (1972)

William R. Bishin, Professor of Law, University of Southern California.
Christopher D. Stone, Professor of Law, University of Southern California.

LAW, SCIENCE AND MEDICINE (1984)

Judith C. Areen, Professor of Law, Georgetown University.
Patricia A. King, Professor of Law, Georgetown University.
Steven P. Goldberg, Professor of Law, Georgetown University.
Alexander M. Capron, Professor of Law, Georgetown University.

LAWYERING PROCESS (1978), with Civil Problem Supplement and Criminal Problem Supplement

Gary Bellow, Professor of Law, Harvard University.
Bea Moulton, Professor of Law, Arizona State University.

LEGAL METHOD (1980)

Harry W. Jones, Professor of Law Emeritus, Columbia University.
John M. Kernochan, Professor of Law, Columbia University.
Arthur W. Murphy, Professor of Law, Columbia University.

LEGAL METHODS (1969)

Robert N. Covington, Professor of Law, Vanderbilt University.
E. Blythe Stason, late Professor of Law, Vanderbilt University.
John W. Wade, Professor of Law, Vanderbilt University.
Elliott E. Cheatham, late Professor of Law, Vanderbilt University.
Theodore A. Smedley, Professor of Law, Vanderbilt University.

LEGAL PROFESSION, THE, Responsibility and Regulation (1985)

Geoffrey C. Hazard, Jr., Professor of Law, Yale University.
Deborah L. Rhode, Professor of Law, Stanford University.

LEGISLATION, Fourth Edition (1982) (by Fordham)

Horace E. Read, late Vice President, Dalhousie University.
John W. MacDonald, Professor of Law Emeritus, Cornell Law School.
Jefferson B. Fordham, Professor of Law, University of Utah.
William J. Pierce, Professor of Law, University of Michigan.

LEGISLATIVE AND ADMINISTRATIVE PROCESSES, Second Edition (1981)

Hans A. Linde, Judge, Supreme Court of Oregon.
George Bunn, Professor of Law, University of Wisconsin.
Fredericka Paff, Professor of Law, University of Wisconsin.
W. Lawrence Church, Professor of Law, University of Wisconsin.

LOCAL GOVERNMENT LAW, Second Revised Edition (1986)

Jefferson B. Fordham, Professor of Law, University of Utah.

MASS MEDIA LAW, Second Edition (1982), with 1985 Supplement

Marc A. Franklin, Professor of Law, Stanford University.

MENTAL HEALTH PROCESS, Second Edition (1976), with 1981 Supplement

Frank W. Miller, Professor of Law, Washington University.
Robert O. Dawson, Professor of Law, University of Texas.
George E. Dix, Professor of Law, University of Texas.
Raymond I. Parnas, Professor of Law, University of California, Davis.

MUNICIPAL CORPORATIONS, see Local Government Law

NEGOTIABLE INSTRUMENTS, see Commercial Paper

NEGOTIATION (1981) (Reprinted from THE LAWYERING PROCESS)

Gary Bellow, Professor of Law, Harvard Law School.
Bea Moulton, Legal Services Corporation.

NEW YORK PRACTICE, Fourth Edition (1978)

Herbert Peterfreund, Professor of Law, New York University.
Joseph M. McLaughlin, Dean of the Law School, Fordham University.

OIL AND GAS, Fourth Edition (1979)

Howard R. Williams, Professor of Law, Stanford University.
Richard C. Maxwell, Professor of Law, University of California, Los Angeles.
Charles J. Meyers, Dean of the Law School, Stanford University.

ON LAW IN COURTS (1965)

Paul J. Mishkin, Professor of Law, University of California, Berkeley.
Clarence Morris, Professor of Law Emeritus, University of Pennsylvania.

PATENTS AND ANTITRUST (Pamphlet) (1983)

Milton Handler, Professor of Law Emeritus, Columbia University.
Harlan M. Blake, Professor of Law, Columbia University.
Robert Pitofsky, Professor of Law, Georgetown University.
Harvey J. Goldschmid, Professor of Law, Columbia University.

PERSPECTIVES ON THE LAWYER AS PLANNER (Reprint of Chapters One through Five of Planning by Lawyers) (1978)

Louis M. Brown, Professor of Law, University of Southern California.
Edward A. Dauer, Professor of Law, Yale University.

PLANNING BY LAWYERS, MATERIALS ON A NONADVERSARIAL LEGAL PROCESS (1978)

Louis M. Brown, Professor of Law, University of Southern California.
Edward A. Dauer, Professor of Law, Yale University.

PLEADING AND PROCEDURE, see Procedure, Civil

POLICE FUNCTION, Fourth Edition (1986)

Reprint of Chapters 1–10 of Miller, Dawson, Dix and Parnas's CRIMINAL JUSTICE ADMINISTRATION, Third Edition.

PREPARING AND PRESENTING THE CASE (1981) (Reprinted from THE LAWYERING PROCESS)

Gary Bellow, Professor of Law, Harvard Law School.
Bea Moulton, Legal Services Corporation.

PREVENTIVE LAW, see also Planning by Lawyers

PROCEDURE—CIVIL PROCEDURE, Second Edition (1974), with 1979 Supplement

The late James H. Chadbourn, Professor of Law, Harvard University.
A. Leo Levin, Professor of Law, University of Pennsylvania.
Philip Shuchman, Professor of Law, Cornell University.

PROCEDURE—CIVIL PROCEDURE, Fifth Edition (1984)

Richard H. Field, late Professor of Law, Harvard University.
Benjamin Kaplan, Professor of Law Emeritus, Harvard University.
Kevin M. Clermont, Professor of Law, Cornell University.

PROCEDURE—CIVIL PROCEDURE, Fourth Edition (1985)

Maurice Rosenberg, Professor of Law, Columbia University.
Hans Smit, Professor of Law, Columbia University.
Harold L. Korn, Professor of Law, Columbia University.

PROCEDURE—PLEADING AND PROCEDURE: State and Federal, Fifth Edition (1983), with 1985 Supplement

David W. Louisell, late Professor of Law, University of California, Berkeley.
Geoffrey C. Hazard, Jr., Professor of Law, Yale University.
Colin C. Tait, Professor of Law, University of Connecticut.

PROCEDURE—FEDERAL RULES OF CIVIL PROCEDURE, 1986 Edition

PRODUCTS LIABILITY (1980)

Marshall S. Shapo, Professor of Law, Northwestern University.

UNIVERSITY CASEBOOK SERIES—Continued

PRODUCTS LIABILITY AND SAFETY (1980), with 1985 Case and Documentary Supplement

W. Page Keeton, Professor of Law, University of Texas.
David G. Owen, Professor of Law, University of South Carolina.
John E. Montgomery, Professor of Law, University of South Carolina.

PROFESSIONAL RESPONSIBILITY, Third Edition (1984), with 1986 Selected National Standards Supplement

Thomas D. Morgan, Dean of the Law School, Emory University.
Ronald D. Rotunda, Professor of Law, University of Illinois.

PROPERTY, Fifth Edition (1984)

John E. Cribbet, Dean of the Law School, University of Illinois.
Corwin W. Johnson, Professor of Law, University of Texas.

PROPERTY—PERSONAL (1953)

S. Kenneth Skolfield, late Professor of Law Emeritus, Boston University.

PROPERTY—PERSONAL, Third Edition (1954)

Everett Fraser, late Dean of the Law School Emeritus, University of Minnesota.
Third Edition by Charles W. Taintor, late Professor of Law, University of Pittsburgh.

PROPERTY—INTRODUCTION, TO REAL PROPERTY, Third Edition (1954)

Everett Fraser, late Dean of the Law School Emeritus, University of Minnesota.

PROPERTY—REAL AND PERSONAL, Combined Edition (1954)

Everett Fraser, late Dean of the Law School Emeritus, University of Minnesota.
Third Edition of Personal Property by Charles W. Taintor, late Professor of Law, University of Pittsburgh.

PROPERTY—FUNDAMENTALS OF MODERN REAL PROPERTY, Second Edition (1982), with 1985 Supplement

Edward H. Rabin, Professor of Law, University of California, Davis.

PROPERTY—PROBLEMS IN REAL PROPERTY (Pamphlet) (1969)

Edward H. Rabin, Professor of Law, University of California, Davis.

PROPERTY, REAL (1984)

Paul Goldstein, Professor of Law, Stanford University.

PROSECUTION AND ADJUDICATION, Third Edition (1986)

Reprint of Chapters 11–26 of Miller, Dawson, Dix and Parnas's CRIMINAL JUSTICE ADMINISTRATION, Third Edition.

PSYCHIATRY AND LAW, see Mental Health, see also Hinckley, Trial of

PUBLIC REGULATION OF DANGEROUS PRODUCTS (paperback) (1980)

Marshall S. Shapo, Professor of Law, Northwestern University.

PUBLIC UTILITY LAW, see Free Enterprise, also Regulated Industries

REAL ESTATE PLANNING (1980), with 1980 Problems, Statutes and New Materials Supplement

Norton L. Steuben, Professor of Law, University of Colorado.

REAL ESTATE TRANSACTIONS, Second Edition (1985), with 1985 Statute, Form and Problem Supplement

Paul Goldstein, Professor of Law, Stanford University.

RECEIVERSHIP AND CORPORATE REORGANIZATION, see Creditors' Rights

REGULATED INDUSTRIES, Second Edition, 1976

William K. Jones, Professor of Law, Columbia University.

REMEDIES (1982), with 1984 Case Supplement

Edward D. Re, Chief Judge, U. S. Court of International Trade.

RESTITUTION, Second Edition (1966)

John W. Wade, Professor of Law, Vanderbilt University.

SALES, Second Edition (1986)

Marion W. Benfield, Jr., Professor of Law, University of Illinois.
William D. Hawkland, Chancellor, Louisiana State Law Center.

SALES AND SALES FINANCING, Fifth Edition (1984)

John Honnold, Professor of Law, University of Pennsylvania.

SALES LAW AND THE CONTRACTING PROCESS (1982)

Reprint of Chapters 1–10 of Schwartz and Scott's Commercial Transactions.

SECURED TRANSACTIONS IN PERSONAL PROPERTY (1983) (Reprinted from COMMERCIAL LAW)

Robert L. Jordan, Professor of Law, University of California, Los Angeles.
William D. Warren, Professor of Law, University of California, Los Angeles.

SECURITIES REGULATION, Fifth Edition (1982), with 1985 Cases and Releases Supplement and 1985 Selected Statutes, Rules and Forms Supplement

Richard W. Jennings, Professor of Law, University of California, Berkeley.
Harold Marsh, Jr., Member of California Bar.

SECURITIES REGULATION (1982), with 1985 Supplement

Larry D. Soderquist, Professor of Law, Vanderbilt University.

SECURITY INTERESTS IN PERSONAL PROPERTY (1984)

Douglas G. Baird, Professor of Law, University of Chicago.
Thomas H. Jackson, Professor of Law, Stanford University.

SECURITY INTERESTS IN PERSONAL PROPERTY (1985) (Reprinted from Sales and Sales Financing, Fifth Edition)

John Honnold, Professor of Law, University of Pennsylvania.

SENTENCING AND THE CORRECTIONAL PROCESS, Second Edition (1976)

Frank W. Miller, Professor of Law, Washington University.
Robert O. Dawson, Professor of Law, University of Texas.
George E. Dix, Professor of Law, University of Texas.
Raymond I. Parnas, Professor of Law, University of California, Davis.

SOCIAL SCIENCE IN LAW, Cases and Materials (1985)

John Monahan, Professor of Law, University of Virginia.
Laurens Walker, Professor of Law, University of Virginia.

SOCIAL WELFARE AND THE INDIVIDUAL (1971)

Robert J. Levy, Professor of Law, University of Minnesota.
Thomas P. Lewis, Dean of the College of Law, University of Kentucky.
Peter W. Martin, Professor of Law, Cornell University.

TAX, POLICY ANALYSIS OF THE FEDERAL INCOME (1976)

William A. Klein, Professor of Law, University of California, Los Angeles.

TAXATION, FEDERAL INCOME, Successor Edition (1985)

Michael J. Graetz, Professor of Law, Yale University.

TAXATION, FEDERAL INCOME, Fifth Edition (1985)

James J. Freeland, Professor of Law, University of Florida.
Stephen A. Lind, Professor of Law, University of Florida.
Richard B. Stephens, Professor of Law Emeritus, University of Florida.

TAXATION, FEDERAL INCOME, Volume I, Personal Income Taxation, Second Edition (1986), Volume II, Taxation of Partnerships and Corporations, Second Edition (1980), with 1985 Legislative Supplement

Stanley S. Surrey, late Professor of Law, Harvard University.
Paul R. McDaniel, Professor of Law, Boston College Law School.
Hugh J. Ault, Professor of Law, Boston College Law School.
Stanley A. Koppelman, Boston University

TAXATION, FEDERAL WEALTH TRANSFER, Second Edition (1982) with 1985 Legislative Supplement

Stanley S. Surrey, late Professor of Law, Harvard University.
William C. Warren, Professor of Law Emeritus, Columbia University.
Paul R. McDaniel, Professor of Law, Boston College Law School.
Harry L. Gutman, Instructor, Harvard Law School and Boston College Law School.

TAXATION, FUNDAMENTALS OF CORPORATE, Cases and Materials (1985)

Stephen A. Lind, Professor of Law, University of Florida.
Stephen Schwarz, Professor of Law, University of California, Hastings.
Daniel J. Lathrope, Professor of Law, University of California, Hastings.
Joshua Rosenberg, Professor of Law, University of San Francisco.

TAXATION, FUNDAMENTALS OF PARTNERSHIP, Cases and Materials (1985)

Stephen A. Lind, Professor of Law, University of California, Hastings.
Stephen Schwarz, Professor of Law, University of California, Hastings.
Daniel J. Lathrope, Professor of Law, University of California, Hastings.
Joshua Rosenberg, Professor of Law, University of San Francisco.

TAXATION, PROBLEMS IN THE FEDERAL INCOME TAXATION OF PARTNERSHIPS AND CORPORATIONS, Second Edition (1986)

Norton L. Steuben, Professor of Law, University of Colorado.
William J. Turnier, Professor of Law, University of North Carolina.

TAXATION, PROBLEMS IN THE FUNDAMENTALS OF FEDERAL INCOME, Second Edition (1985)

Norton L. Steuben, Professor of Law, University of Colorado.
William J. Turnier, Professor of Law, University of North Carolina.

TAXES AND FINANCE—STATE AND LOCAL (1974)

Oliver Oldman, Professor of Law, Harvard University.
Ferdinand P. Schoettle, Professor of Law, University of Minnesota.

TORT LAW AND ALTERNATIVES, Third Edition (1983)

Marc A. Franklin, Professor of Law, Stanford University.
Robert L. Rabin, Professor of Law, Stanford University.

UNIVERSITY CASEBOOK SERIES—Continued

TORTS, Seventh Edition (1982)

William L. Prosser, late Professor of Law, University of California, Hastings College.
John W. Wade, Professor of Law, Vanderbilt University.
Victor E. Schwartz, Professor of Law, American University.

TORTS, Third Edition (1976)

Harry Shulman, late Dean of the Law School, Yale University.
Fleming James, Jr., Professor of Law Emeritus, Yale University.
Oscar S. Gray, Professor of Law, University of Maryland.

TRADE REGULATION, Second Edition (1983), with 1985 Supplement

Milton Handler, Professor of Law Emeritus, Columbia University.
Harlan M. Blake, Professor of Law, Columbia University.
Robert Pitofsky, Professor of Law, Georgetown University.
Harvey J. Goldschmid, Professor of Law, Columbia University.

TRADE REGULATION, see Antitrust

TRANSNATIONAL BUSINESS PROBLEMS (1986)

Detlev F. Vagts, Professor of Law, Harvard University.

TRANSNATIONAL LEGAL PROBLEMS, Third Edition (1986) with Documentary Supplement

Henry J. Steiner, Professor of Law, Harvard University.
Detlev F. Vagts, Professor of Law, Harvard University.

TRIAL, see also Evidence, Making the Record, Lawyering Process and Preparing and Presenting the Case

TRIAL ADVOCACY (1968)

A. Leo Levin, Professor of Law, University of Pennsylvania.
Harold Cramer, of the Pennsylvania Bar.
Maurice Rosenberg, Professor of Law, Columbia University, Consultant.

TRUSTS, Fifth Edition (1978)

George G. Bogert, late Professor of Law Emeritus, University of Chicago.
Dallin H. Oaks, President, Brigham Young University.

TRUSTS AND SUCCESSION (Palmer's), Fourth Edition (1983)

Richard V. Wellman, Professor of Law, University of Georgia.
Lawrence W. Waggoner, Professor of Law, University of Michigan.
Olin L. Browder, Jr., Professor of Law, University of Michigan.

UNFAIR COMPETITION, see Competitive Process and Business Torts

UNITED NATIONS LAW, Second Edition (1967), with Documentary Supplement (1968)

Louis B. Sohn, Professor of Law, Harvard University.

WATER RESOURCE MANAGEMENT, Second Edition (1980), with 1983 Supplement

Charles J. Meyers, Dean of the Law School, Stanford University.
A. Dan Tarlock, Professor of Law, Indiana University.

WILLS AND ADMINISTRATION, Fifth Edition (1961)

Philip Mechem, late Professor of Law, University of Pennsylvania.
Thomas E. Atkinson, late Professor of Law, New York University.

WORLD LAW, see United Nations Law

University Casebook Series

V7204—15g

CASES AND MATERIALS
ON
CONTRACTS

THIRD EDITION

By

E. ALLAN FARNSWORTH
Alfred McCormack Professor of Law, Columbia University

WILLIAM F. YOUNG
James L. Dohr Professor of Law, Columbia University

Mineola, N. Y.
THE FOUNDATION PRESS, INC.
1980

Printed in the United States of America

Library of Congress Cataloging in Publication Data

Farnsworth, Edward Allan.
Cases and materials on contracts.

(University casebook series)
Includes index.
1. Contracts—United States—Cases. I. Young, William Franklin, 1925- joint author. II. Title. III. Series.
KF801.A7F37 1980 346.73'02 80-15040
ISBN 0-88277-009-8

Farnsworth & Young Cs.Cont.3rd Ed. UCB

5th Reprint—1986

PREFACE

The course in Contracts serves a twofold purpose in the first year curriculum. It is the law school's first course in commercial transactions and so must provide the necessary foundation for advanced courses and seminars in this area and ultimately for professional practice. In American legal education, however, the first year Contracts course has always had an additional and more ambitious function. Law teachers have long believed—rightly we think—that contract law offers a body of precepts and problems exceptionally well suited to development of the student's "legal mind": respect for sources, skepticism toward easy generalizations, and disciplined creativity in the use of legal materials for the accomplishment of practical professional tasks. In the selection and arrangement of the materials in this casebook, we have tried to take account of both the specific and the more general objectives served by Contracts courses.

We have tried, where possible, to ease the task of learning. Text is used for introductory exposition and for background on business practices. Notes and problems spotlight topics of current interest (such as those affecting consumers) and suggest how timely counseling and thoughtful drafting may avoid later litigation. They also call attention to relevant statutes such as the Uniform Commercial Code, and to the formulations of the common law contained in the Restatement of Contracts. But this, like its predecessors, is still essentially a casebook-with-notes rather than a professor's notebook-with-cases. A law school casebook is not an encyclopedia or treatise and is designed for very different purposes. Although we have tried to indicate recurring questions of policy, no effort has been made to provide approved answers. We have tried to caution against the false assumption, to which beginning law students may be inclined, that questions of policy are somehow extrinsic and "nonlegal." In contracts, as elsewhere in the legal order, law and policy are inextricable.

We continue in the debt of our distinguished predecessors and co-workers, Edwin Patterson, George W. Goble and Harry W. Jones, to whose casebooks this volume is the successor. Our indebtedness to many other distinguished scholars is evident throughout. Less evident, but no less real, is our obligation to the imaginative and energetic law students whom we have been privileged to meet in the classroom. We are especially grateful for the help of the student assistants who have worked with us—Timothy Alvino and Leslie Bogen in particular.

E. ALLAN FARNSWORTH
WILLIAM F. YOUNG

New York
June, 1980

INTRODUCTION

This is a book about legally enforceable promises, or what lawyers call "contracts." What function do contracts serve in our society? What needs are met by private agreements among its members?

As a beginning, imagine taking an inventory of all the contracts made on a typical business day in a city with which you are familiar. How many businesses were sold? How many buildings? Cars? Television sets? How many people got jobs? Rented apartments? Opened bank accounts? Went to movies or ball games? Rode busses? What other transactions should be counted? As these questions suggest, the institution of contract is a vehicle through which the daily needs of ordinary people for goods and services are met. It is also, of course, a vehicle for mammoth enterprises in which governments and their agencies and great corporate bodies engage. Indeed, a large share of the wealth of any developed nation is embodied in contract rights.

The name "contract" is shared by printed forms distributed at counters (e.g., travel and insurance papers), and by agreements negotiated at arm's length by parties taking advice of counsel at every step. Countless contracts are formed daily by telephone, hand signal, or other informal means. The subjects of contracts, and the objects they advance, are even more diverse, if possible, than the means of their creation. Sometimes they are used to settle disputes. Sometimes they are used to establish long-term arrangements under which thousands of individual transactions are to be conducted. Sometimes they are used to vary the effects that certain rules of law would otherwise have on the parties and their dealings. And it is largely through contracts that interests in property are created and altered.

What does this diversity signify about the character of the law of contracts? A first inference might be that the law is largely instrumental. Much of it consists of specifying means for unstated and undetermined ends. To what purposes the power to contract will be put is left very largely to the choice of those who exercise it. Within the domain of contract, as it has been said, "the liberties recognized by law block out a sphere of social life which is left to be controlled, in the absence of further group action, by the process of *autonomous legal ordering*." [a] When organized commercial activity takes place within this sphere, it is commonly described as a "market." The law of contracts has a vital supporting function in relation to markets, as has been described by a distinguished American legal historian, Professor Willard Hurst, in the context of a study of the lumber industry in nineteenth-century Wisconsin: "Because marketing cannot go on save

---

a. Hart and Sacks, The Legal Process 147–48 (Tent. ed. 1958). See also Jones, the Jurisprudence of Contracts, 44 U.Cin.L.Rev. 43 (1975).

in a context of reasonably assured expectations, the legal order as a whole was, of course, indispensable to the existence of a market. But it was the law of contract which supplied the assurances and the procedures and tools necessary for the immediate operation and steadily expanding energy of the institution. . . . Law did not bring the market into being. But law provided essential conditions for its existence. . . . For the timber industry as for other business, contract law provided a framework of reasonably assured expectations within which men might plan and venture. The availability of the forms and procedures of contract thus helped the expansion of the market. . . . [The law] provided a framework of delegated power within which private decisions might operate. . . . The nature of contract was to disperse decision making widely. . . ." [b]

As the character and institutions of a society change, the functions of contract making and enforcement change with it. The dispersion of decision-making power in private hands may lose its attractiveness as an ideal, in competition either with anarchy or with more official forms of decision making.[c] Even if it does not, conditions may change so that contracts become instruments of concentrating power in large business units. The backing of legal force given to private agreements by contract law shows to best advantage in a community, market, or society, in which bargaining power is rather widely and evenly distributed. Professor Kessler expressed the point this way: "The individualism of our rules of contract law, of which freedom of contract is the most powerful symbol, is closely tied up with the ethics of free enterprise capitalism and the ideals of justice of a mobile society of small enterprisers, individual merchants and independent craftsmen." [d]

Well before the present century it was perceived that "enterprisers" of this type were sometimes overmatched in bargaining power by firms in monopoly positions. Then, and increasingly in this

---

b. W. Hurst, Law and Economic Growth: The Legal History of the Lumber Industry in Wisconsin 1936-1915, 285, 294, 297, 333 (1964).

c. Would it not be possible to dispense with contracts entirely by dispensing with the need for private ordering? An attempt was made in the Soviet Union in the early revolutionary years to administer the economy without the institution of contract, to base centralized distribution of wealth on administrative norms. The experiment ended in failure, and Lenin wrote in 1921 that "we must now admit . . . if we do not want to hide our heads under our wings . . . [that] the private market proved to be stronger than we and . . . we ended up with ordinary purchase and sale, trade." Contracts were reintroduced and contract law was codified, largely along traditional lines. Loeber, Plan and Contract Performance in Soviet Law in LaFave (ed.), Law in the Soviet Society 128-29 (1965). You may take it from this that contract is at least a durable institution and it is a safe generalization that few societies have been able to develop far without recognizing at least some promises as enforceable. See Farnsworth, The Past of Promise: A Historical Introduction to Contract, 69 Colum.L.Rev. 576, 578-82 (1969).

d. Kessler, Contracts of Adhesion—Some Thoughts About Freedom of Contract, 43 Colum.L.Rev. 629, 640 (1943).

century, the law has responded with restraints on the process of private ordering. Lately such restraints have been addressed especially to the position of consumers, as they have become increasingly involved in consensual transactions. Their participation in contract making commonly takes the form of routine assent, or "adhesion," to a standard form contract, whether in dealings with great corporations or in dealings with neighborhood merchants. Many contract forms are like statutes, having uniform application to large classes of persons. Through such forms, the draftsman may exercise positions of authority, in the name of contract, without the necessity of debate and democratic validation that limits legislation. So exercised, it often appears oppressive. Under what circumstances should the law refuse to allow the dominant party to invoke official sanctions for the breach of such agreements? Through statutes and judicial decisions, the law of contracts is moving to answer this question by placing new controls on the manner of contracting and the allowable terms of agreement. It is coming to place a higher value on what Professor Patterson called the freedom *from* contract.[e]

No one imagines that, when promises are kept, it is ordinarily because the promisor is conscious of the rules of contract law. Far from it: both social and business engagements are generally kept for other reasons, including the sense of honor and the concern for community standing. The standards of mutual assistance that apply in conscience and in the market place are sometimes higher, sometimes lower, than those that contract law attaches to a bargain. On the other hand, painstaking attention is regularly paid to contract rules in setting out the terms of a business transaction. There is a skill in drafting agreements that ranks high in legal accomplishments, and you should attempt in this course to grasp it.

It has already been suggested that contract law is useful for supporting market transactions. But its value runs beyond this, in a way hard to measure. Contract is the principal mechanism for allocating and distributing financial risks. This is the object of guarantee and insurance contracts, in particular. If agreements could not be defined with some degree of precision, as a skilled draftsman can do, the costs of uncertainty would stifle many an enterprise, and the affliction of insecurity would be uncontrolled. In addition, if there were no means of enforcing promises, those who keep them for reasons of conscience might be at such a disadvantage, as compared with the unscrupulous, that few of us would be willing and able to pay the price of honoring our undertakings.

Organization. The first five chapters of this book are concerned with the law relating to the enforceability of promises. Chapter 1

---

e. Patterson, An Apology for Consideration, 58 Colum.L.Rev. 929, 949 (1958).

examines possible bases for determining enforceability and concludes (not surprisingly in the light of the excerpt from Hurst) that bargained-for exchange is the principal basis in our law. Chapter 2 deals with when a writing is necessary to the enforceability of a promise. Chapter 3 explores the bargaining process through the traditional analysis of offer and acceptance. Chapter 4 presents in depth five particularly troublesome problems that arise in connection with the bargaining process. Chapter 5 concerns the restraints that are placed on the terms of bargains and on the bargaining process to prevent social evils such as overreaching and sharp practice.

Chapter 6 turns to a different theme. It is concerned with the remedies available to the aggrieved party when, assuming that there is a contract, the other party does not perform it.

The next four chapters are concerned with the nature and extent of the parties' obligations under the contract. As draftsmen of documents, lawyers have played a major part in this aspect of private ordering. In the words of Professor Llewellyn: "It was . . . the lawyer who devised the mortgage, who made possible the giving of security in goods or land, while leaving the beneficial use of the borrower during the period for which the security was needed; made possible, therefore, the secured production loan whereby a debtor had the chance of financing a new venture out of whose own profits he might hope to meet the debt. . . . It was the lawyer who devised the long-term lease for real estate improvement, and the collateral trust for real estate financing, or for financing new equipment for a mortgaged railroad. And, greatest perhaps of an single line of growth within our law, it was the lawyer who from the outset has shaped the thousand uses of the law of trusts. . . ."[f] Some of the materials in this book are designed to help you develop the skills in drafting that are essential to this facet of professional activity. Chapter 7 inquires into the processes, notably that of interpretation, that define the parties' obligations and repair deficiencies in their expressions, when courts are required to give them effect. Chapter 8 takes up the effects of one party's failure of performance, or prospective failure, on the other party's obligations. Chapter 9 deals with when impossibility of performance or frustration of purpose relieves a party of an obligation. And Chapter 10 considers when a party's obligation extends to a third person, as distinguished from the other party to the contract.

The final chapter, Chapter 11, looks at contract rights as a kind of property, and treats of their transfer

f. Llewellyn, The Bramble Bush 146–47 (1960).

SUMMARY OF CONTENTS

TABLE OF CONTENTS

TABLE OF CASES

The principal cases are in italic type. Cases cited or discussed are in roman type. References are to Pages.

NOTE ON EDITING

The editors' restatements of facts and insertions within opinions (except for corrections of obvious typographical errors) are enclosed in brackets. Footnotes in opinions and quoted texts have sometimes been omitted and the remaining ones renumbered in sequence. Footnotes inserted by the editors are lettered rather than numbered.

When a problem is accompanied by a reference to a case, the facts presented are sometimes abbreviated from those before the court, but may be markedly different. In any event, the reference is only intended to support a line of thought, or an analogy, and not to supply "the answer" to the problem.

In citation, the Restatement of Contracts (1932) and the Restatement Second of Contracts (1980) are referred to simply as "Restatement" and "Restatement Second." The Uniform Commercial Code is cited as "UCC." A. Corbin on Contracts (1950-1964) is cited as "Corbin," and S. Williston on Contracts (3d ed. by Jaeger 1957-1979) as "Williston."

CASES ON CONTRACTS

Chapter 1

BASIS FOR ENFORCING PROMISES

SECTION 1. THE MEANING OF "ENFORCE"

Books on the law of contracts often begin by explaining what lawyers mean by the word "contract." Sometimes lawyers use the word, as it is used in common speech, simply to refer to a writing containing terms on which the parties have agreed. But they often use "contract" in a more technical sense to mean a *promise*, or a set of promises, that the law will *enforce* or at least recognize in some way. See Restatement Second § 1.

Some idea of what the word "contract" means in practice can be gleaned from the cotton cases of 1973. That year saw a spectacular rise in the price of cotton on the American market. The causes were said to include large shipments to China, high water and flood conditions in the cotton belt, late plantings forced by heavy rains, and the devaluation of the dollar. In the early months of the year, before planting, a cotton farmer will make a "forward" sale contract for delivery to the buyer of all cotton to be raised and harvested on a specified tract at a fixed price per pound, without guarantee of quantity or quality. The farmer can then use this contract to finance the raising of his crop. Early in 1973, cotton farmers made such contracts to sell at a price roughly equal to the price on the market at that time, some 30 cents a pound. By the time the cotton had been raised and was ready for delivery, however, the market price had risen to about 80 cents a pound. The farmers felt, as one judge later put it, "sick as an old hound dog who ate a rotten skunk." Many refused to perform the "forward" contracts that they had made at the lower price, and scores of lawsuits resulted throughout the cotton belt.[a] Not only were the farmers universally unsuccessful, but the decisions evoked little attention. One court put it simply, "The criti-

a. This summary is taken largely from one of those cases, Bolin Farms v. American Cotton Shippers Ass'n, 370 F.Supp. 1353 (W.D.La.1974).

cal issue is whether . . . there was an enforceable promise to buy for each promise to sell. We believe there was."[b]

We are about to ask: What promises will the law enforce? But in answering that question it is helpful to have an idea of how courts enforce promises. Although the intricacies of this subject are reserved until later (see Chapter 6, Remedies for Breach), some insight into its fundamentals will be of use, even at this early stage.

LAREDO HIDES CO., INC. v. H & H MEAT PRODUCTS CO., INC.

Court of Civil Appeals of Texas, 1974.
513 S.W.2d 210.

BISSETT, Justice. This is a breach of contract case. Laredo Hides Company, Inc., the buyer, sued H & H Meat Products Company, Inc., the seller, to recover damages for breach of a written contract for the sale of cattle hides. Trial was to the court without a jury. A take nothing judgment in favor of defendant was rendered. Plaintiff has appealed.

The controlling facts of the case are undisputed. H & H Meat Products Company, Inc. (H & H) is a meat processing and packing corporation, located in Mercedes, Texas. It sells cattle hides as a byproduct of its business. Laredo Hides Company, Inc. (Laredo Hides) is a corporation, located in Laredo, Texas. It purchases cattle hides from various meat packers in the United States and ships them to tanneries in Mexico.

A written contract dated February 29, 1972, was executed whereby Laredo Hides agreed to buy H & H's entire cattle hide production during the period March through December, 1972. . . . [After two deliveries of hides, a $9,000 check sent by Laredo Hides to H & H in payment for the second shipment was delayed in the mail. Before it arrived, H & H gave Laredo Hides an ultimatum demanding payment within a few hours. When the demand was not met, H & H notified Laredo Hides on March 30, 1972, that H & H regarded this as a breach justifying cancellation of the contract and that it would deliver no more hides. In an omitted part of the opinion, the court held that H & H's precipitous action was unjustified, that its refusal to deliver more hides was itself a breach by repudiation of the contract that relieved Laredo Hides of tendering performance during the remaining months of the contract, and that the trial court's disposition of the case was error.]

Laredo Hides, on March 3, 1972, had contracted with a Mexican tannery for the sale of all the hides which it expected to purchase

b. J. L. McEntire & Sons, Inc. v. Hart Cotton Co. Inc., 256 Ark. 937, 943, 511 S.W.2d 179, 183 (1974). Citations to cases are collected at 15 UCC Rep. 20, 28.

from H & H under the February 29, 1972, contract. Following the cancellation by H & H of the contract, Laredo Hides, in order to meet the requirements of its contract with the tannery, was forced to purchase hides on the open market in substitution for the hides which were to have been delivered to it under the contract with H & H.

H & H's total production during the months April through December, 1972, was 17,218 hides. Under the contract with H & H, the price was $9.75 per hide for bull, steer and heifer hides, and $9.75 per hide for cow hides if the shipment was under 5% cow hides. In the event the shipment was more than 5% cow hides, the price on the excess of cow hides over 5% was reduced to $7.50 per cow hide. The market price for hides steadily increased following the execution of the contract in question. By December 31, 1972, the average cost of bull hides was about $33.00 each and the average cost of cow, heifer and steer hides was about $22.00 each. The total additional cost to Laredo Hides of purchasing substitute hides from other suppliers was $142,254.48. The additional costs (transportation and handling charges) to Laredo Hides which resulted because of the purchases from third parties amounted to $3,448.95. . . .

Since this case must be reversed, we now confront the issue of damages. The guidelines for determining a buyer's remedies in a case where there is a breach of a contract for the sale of goods by a seller are found in Chapter 2 of the Texas Business and Commerce Code. Among other remedies afforded by the Code, when there is a repudiation of the contract by the seller or a failure to make delivery of the goods under contract, the buyer may cover under § 2.711. He may have damages under § 2.712 "by making in good faith and without unreasonable delay any reasonable purchase of or contract to purchase goods in substitution for those due from the seller", and "may recover from the seller as damages the difference between the cost of cover and the contract price together with any incidental or consequential damages" provided by the chapter; or, he may, under § 2.713, have damages measured by "the difference between the market price at the time when the buyer learned of the breach and the contract price together with any incidental and consequential damages" provided by the chapter.

Laredo Hides instituted suit in May, 1972, and filed its amended petition (its trial pleading) on October 24, 1972, when performance was still due by H & H under the contract. It prayed for specific performance, or in the alternative " . . . damages at least in the amount of one hundred thousand dollars ($100,000), the same being the damages proximately caused by defendant's breach of the contract . . . " There was never a trial amendment of this petition. There were no exceptions by H & H to Laredo Hides' pleadings. Trial commenced on February 28, 1973, was recessed on March 2, 1973, resumed on May 15, 1973, and ended May 16, 1973. Judgment was signed and rendered on August 6, 1973.

Laredo Hides offered uncontroverted evidence of the hide production of H & H from April to December, 1972. It also established the price for the same number of hides which it was forced to buy elsewhere. There was testimony that purchases had to be made periodically throughout 1972 since Laredo Hides had no storage facilities, and the hides would decompose if allowed to age. Furthermore, White, a C.P.A., testified as to statistical summaries which he made showing the cost of buying substitute hides. These summaries were made from invoices which are also in evidence. All of this evidence was admitted without objection. Clearly, Laredo Hides elected to pursue the remedy provided by § 2.712 of the Code, and by its pleadings and evidence brought itself within the purview of the "cover" provisions contained therein.

It is not necessary under § 2.712 that the buyer establish market price. Duesenberg and King, Sales and Bulk Transfers under the U.C.C. § 14.04 Matthew Bender (1974). Where the buyer complies with the requirements of § 2.712, his purchase is presumed proper and the burden of proof is on the seller to show that "cover" was not properly obtained. Spies, Sales, Performance and Remedies, 44 Tex. L.Rev. 629, 638 (1966). There was no evidence offered by H & H to negate this presumption or to "establish expenses saved in consequence of the seller's breach", as permitted by § 2.712.

The difference between the cover price and the contract price is shown to be $134,252.82 for steer hides and $8,001.66 for bull hides, or a total of $142,254.48. In addition, Laredo Hides offered evidence of increased transportation costs of $1,435.77, and increased handling charges of $2,013.18. These are clearly recoverable as incidental damages where the buyer elects to "cover". §§ 2.715(a); 2.712(b).

. . .

There is no evidence that Laredo Hides, in any manner, endeavored to increase its damages sustained when H & H refused to deliver any more hides to it. Laredo Hides, in purchasing the hides in substitution of the hides which should have been delivered under the contract, acted promptly and in a reasonable manner. The facts of this case regarding the issue of liability of H & H and the issues pertaining to damages suffered by Laredo Hides, have been fully and completely developed in the court below. The facts upon which judgment should have been rendered for Laredo Hides by the trial court are conclusively established. It, therefore, becomes the duty of this Court to render judgment which the trial court should have rendered.

. . .

Applying the rules announced by the above cited cases and authorities to the instant case, we hold that the record does not support the findings of fact made by the trial judge and there is no legal justification for the conclusion of law reached by the court. Accordingly, the judgment of the trial court is reversed, and judgment is here rendered for Laredo Hides in the amount of $152,960.04, together with interest thereon at the rate of 6% per annum from August 6, 1973, the date judgment was rendered by the trial court, until paid.

Reversed and rendered.

NOTES

(1) *The Uniform Commercial Code.* Contracts for the sale of goods, such as H & H cattle hides, have a special significance for the law of contracts because they are the subject of Article 2 of the Uniform Commercial Code, which contains some of the most innovative contemporary thinking on contracts. See the Editors' Note to the Code in the Supplement. The Texas Business and Commerce Code is the Uniform Commercial Code as enacted in Texas. The rule on "cover" in UCC 2–712 is an example of such an innovation. It has no antecedent in prior law. Had this case arisen before the Code, Laredo Hides would have had to prove damages based on the difference between market price and contract price under the common law rule which in Texas was the antecedent of UCC 2–713. What disadvantages would that have had for Laredo Hides? Consider the type of evidence needed to prove cover price and market price for cattle hides. See UCC 2–723, 2–724. Consider the possibility that Laredo Hides' cover price might differ from market price.

(2) *Fundamental Assumptions.* Three fundamental assumptions are implicit in the court's opinion and in the Code provisions on which it is based.

The first is that the law is concerned with relief of *promisees* to *redress breach* and not with *punishment* of promisors to *compel performance.* Is the court's function to determine a sum of money that will make buyers like Laredo Hides "whole" or that will prevent sellers like H & H from breaking their contracts? Would it make any difference in the measure of damages if Laredo Hides' check had not been delayed in the mail and H & H had refused to deliver more hides because it had found another buyer who would pay more? (Why do you suppose H & H acted so precipitously if, as we are told in an omitted part of the opinion, it had dealt with Laredo Hides since the middle 1960's?) What answers does UCC 1–106(1) give?

The second assumption is that the law of contract remedies is designed to give the disappointed promisee relief based on his *expectation,* or the "benefit of the bargain," as measured by the net gain that he would have enjoyed had the contract been performed. The object is to put the disappointed promisee in the position in which he would have been had the promise been performed. See UCC 1–106(1). The interest that is protected in this way has been called the *expectation interest* to distinguish it from the reliance and restitution interests. The promisee has a *reliance* interest if he has changed his position to his detriment in reliance on the promise. (He may, for example, have incurred expenses in preparing to perform or have lost opportunities to make other contracts.) The law might protect this interest by putting the plaintiff back in the position in which he would have been had the promise not been made. The promisee has a *restitution interest* if he has not only relied on the promise but has conferred a benefit on the promisor. (He may, for example, have rendered some performance in return for the broken promise.) The law might protect this interest by putting the promisor back in the position in which he would have been had the promise not been made. How do damages based on cover protect Laredo Hides' expectation interest? See UCC 2–712. How would damages to protect that interest be measured if comparable hides were unavailable? How would damages based on Laredo Hides' reliance and restitution interests be measured? For more on the three interests, see Fuller and Perdue, The Reliance Interest in Contract Damages, 46 Yale L.J. 52, 53–57 (1936).

The third assumption is that the appropriate form of relief is *substitutional,* in the form of a judgment awarding money damages to be paid by H & H to Laredo Hides, rather than *specific,* in the form of an order to H & H to deliver the cattle hides to Laredo Hides. Note that Laredo Hides "prayed for specific performance" as an alternative to damages. Would it have been proper to grant specific performance instead of damages? See UCC 2–716(1) and the cases below.

(3) *The Case of the Missing Masterpiece.* In 1932 the Menzels bought a painting by Marc Chagall in Brussels for about $150. When the Germans invaded Belgium in 1940, the Menzels fled, leaving the Chagall in their apartment. When they returned six years later, the Chagall was gone, and a receipt by the German authorities had been left in its place. In 1955, the Perls, who ran an art gallery in New York, bought the Chagall from a Paris art gallery for $2,800, unaware of its history and relying on the reputation of the Paris gallery as to title. Later that year, the Perls sold it to List for $4,000. In 1962, Mrs. Menzel noticed a reproduction of the missing Chagall in an art book, together with List's name, and demanded its return. When List refused, she sued him for replevin, and he impleaded the Perls, claiming liability for breach of an implied warranty of title. Mrs. Menzel had judgment against List, who returned the Chagall to her. List had judgment against the Perls for $22,500, the value of the Chagall at the time of the trial. The Perls appealed and the Appellate Division reduced the judgment to $4,000, the amount List had paid. List appealed to the Court of Appeals. *Held:* Order of the Appellate Division reversed and judgment of the trial court reinstated. "The Perls support their position by reference to the damages recoverable for the breach of the warranty of quiet possession as to real property. [See Note, p. 13 infra.] However this rule has been severely criticized by [Williston who characterizes it as] ' . . . a violation of general principles of contracts to deny him in an action on the contract such damages *as will put him in as good a position as he would have occupied had the contract been kept.*' . . . Clearly, List can only be put in the same position he would have occupied if the contract had been kept by the Perls if he recovers the value of the painting at the time when . . . he was required to surrender the painting . . . ." Menzel v. List, 24 N.Y.2d 91, 246 N.E.2d 742 (1969).

SULLIVAN v. O'CONNOR

Supreme Judicial Court of Massachusetts, 1973.
363 Mass. 579, 296 N.E.2d 183.

KAPLAN, Justice. The plaintiff patient secured a jury verdict of $13,500 against the defendant surgeon for breach of contract in respect to an operation upon the plaintiff's nose. The substituted consolidated bill of exceptions presents questions about the correctness of the judge's instructions on the issue of damages.

The declaration was in two counts. In the first count, the plaintiff alleged that she, as patient, entered into a contract with the defendant, a surgeon, wherein the defendant promised to perform plastic surgery on her nose and thereby to enhance her beauty and improve her appearance; that he performed the surgery but failed to achieve the promised result; rather the result of the surgery was to disfigure and deform her nose, to cause her pain in body and mind, and to subject her to other damage and expense. The second count, based on the same transaction, was in the conventional form for malpractice, charging that the defendant had been guilty of negligence in performing the surgery.[a] Answering, the defendant entered a general denial.

On the plaintiff's demand, the case was tried by jury. At the close of the evidence, the judge put to the jury, as special questions, the issues of liability under the two counts, and instructed them accordingly. The jury returned a verdict for the plaintiff on the contract count, and for the defendant on the negligence count. The judge then instructed the jury on the issue of damages.

As background to the instructions and the parties' exceptions, we mention certain facts as the jury could find them. The plaintiff was a professional entertainer, and this was known to the defendant. The agreement was as alleged in the declaration. More particularly, judging from exhibits, the plaintiff's nose had been straight, but long and prominent; the defendant undertook by two operations to reduce its prominence and somewhat to shorten it, thus making it more pleasing in relation to the plaintiff's other features. Actually the plaintiff was obliged to undergo three operations, and her appearance was worsened. Her nose now had a concave line to about the midpoint, at which it became bulbous; viewed frontally, the nose from bridge to midpoint was flattened and broadened, and the two sides of the tip had lost symmetry. This configuration evidently could not be improved by further surgery. The plaintiff did not demonstrate, however, that her change of appearance had resulted in loss of employment. Payments by the plaintiff covering the defendant's fee and hospital expenses were stipulated at $622.65.

a. Interviews with counsel reveal that Sullivan's lawyer thought that the contract claim "simply gave the jury an easy means of deciding the case without 'embarrassing' the doctor." O'Connor's lawyer "did not originally consider the contract count in Mrs. Sullivan's declaration seriously. It was unusual in Massachusetts at that time to include a contracts claim in a medical case (he did not know of any prior case in which it had been done), and he thought plaintiff's counsel had thrown it in as an afterthought." Later research "convinced him that liability on that count would be limited to Mrs. Sullivan's medical expenses." See R. Danzig, The Capability Problem in Contract Law 5–43 (1978), which contains extensive background material on this case.

The judge instructed the jury, first, that the plaintiff was entitled to recover her out-of-pocket expenses incident to the operations. Second, she could recover the damages flowing directly, naturally, proximately, and foreseeably from the defendant's breach of promise. These would comprehend damages for any disfigurement of the plaintiff's nose—that is, any change of appearance for the worse—including the effects of the consciousness of such disfigurement on the plaintiff's mind, and in this connection the jury should consider the nature of the plaintiff's profession. Also consequent upon the defendant's breach, and compensable, were the pain and suffering involved in the third operation, but not in the first two. As there was no proof that any loss of earnings by the plaintiff resulted from the breach, that element should not enter into the calculation of damages.

By his exceptions the defendant contends that the judge erred in allowing the jury to take into account anything but the plaintiff's out-of-pocket expenses (presumably at the stipulated amount). The defendant excepted to the judge's refusal of his request for a general charge to that effect, and, more specifically, to the judge's refusal of a charge that the plaintiff could not recover for pain and suffering connected with the third operation or for impairment of the plaintiff's appearance and associated mental distress.

The plaintiff on her part excepted to the judge's refusal of a request to charge that the plaintiff could recover the difference in value between the nose as promised and the nose as it appeared after the operations. However, the plaintiff in her brief expressly waives this exception and others made by her in case this court overrules the defendant's exceptions; thus she would be content to hold the jury's verdict in her favor.

We conclude that the defendant's exceptions should be overruled.

It has been suggested on occasion that agreements between patients and physicians by which the physician undertakes to effect a cure or to bring about a given result should be declared unenforceable on grounds of public policy. See Guilmet v. Campbell, 385 Mich. 57, 76, 188 N.W.2d 601 (dissenting opinion). But there are many decisions recognizing and enforcing such contracts, see annotation, 43 A.L.R.3d 1221, 1225, 1229–1233, and the law of Massachusetts has treated them as valid, although we have had no decision meeting head on the contention that they should be denied legal sanction. Small v. Howard, 128 Mass. 131; Gabrunas v. Miniter, 289 Mass. 20, 193 N.E. 551; Forman v. Wolfson, 327 Mass. 341, 98 N.E.2d 615. These causes of action are, however, considered a little suspect, and thus we find courts straining sometimes to read the pleadings as sounding only in tort for negligence, and not in contract for breach of promise, despite sedulous efforts by the pleaders to pursue the latter theory. See Gault v. Sideman, 42 Ill.App.2d 96, 191 N.E.2d 436; annotation, supra, at 1225, 1238–1244.

It is not hard to see why the courts should be unenthusiastic or skeptical about the contract theory. Considering the uncertainties of medical science and the variations in the physical and psychological conditions of individual patients, doctors can seldom in good faith promise specific results. Therefore it is unlikely that physicians of even average integrity will in fact make such promises. Statements of opinion by the physician with some optimistic coloring are a different thing, and may indeed have therapeutic value. But patients may transform such statements into firm promises in their own minds, especially when they have been disappointed in the event, and testify in that sense to sympathetic juries.[1] If actions for breach of promise can be readily maintained, doctors, so it is said, will be frightened into practising "defensive medicine." On the other hand, if these actions were outlawed, leaving only the possibility of suits for malpractice, there is fear that the public might be exposed to the enticements of charlatans, and confidence in the profession might ultimately be shaken. See Miller, The Contractual Liability of Physicians and Surgeons, 1953 Wash.L.Q. 413, 416–423. The law has taken the middle of the road position of allowing actions based on alleged contract, but insisting on clear proof. Instructions to the jury may well stress this requirement and point to tests of truth, such as the complexity or difficulty of an operation as bearing on the probability that a given result was promised. See annotation, 43 A.L.R.3d 1225, 1225–1227.

If an action on the basis of contract is allowed, we have next the question of the measure of damages to be applied where liability is found. Some cases have taken the simple view that the promise by the physician is to be treated like an ordinary commercial promise, and accordingly that the successful plaintiff is entitled to a standard measure of recovery for breach of contract—"compensatory" ("expectancy") damages, an amount intended to put the plaintiff in the position he would be in if the contract had been performed, or, presumably, at the plaintiff's election, "restitution" damages, an amount corresponding to any benefit conferred by the plaintiff upon the defendant in the performance of the contract disrupted by the defendant's breach. See Restatement: Contracts § 329 and comment a, §§ 347, 384(1). Thus in Hawkins v. McGee, 84 N.H. 114, 146 A. 641, the defendant doctor was taken to have promised the plaintiff to convert his damaged hand by means of an operation into a good or perfect hand, but the doctor so operated as to damage the hand still further. The court, following the usual expectancy formula, would have

1. Judicial skepticism about whether a promise was in fact made derives also from the possibility that the truth has been tortured to give the plaintiff the advantage of the longer period of limitations sometimes available for actions on contract as distinguished from those in tort or for malpractice. See Lillich, The Malpractice Statute of Limitations in New York and Other Jurisdictions, 47 Cornell L.Q. 339; annotation, 80 A.L.R.2d 368.

asked the jury to estimate and award to the plaintiff the difference between the value of a good or perfect hand, as promised, and the value of the hand after the operation. (The same formula would apply, although the dollar result would be less, if the operation had neither worsened nor improved the condition of the hand.) If the plaintiff had not yet paid the doctor his fee, that amount would be deducted from the recovery. There could be no recovery for the pain and suffering of the operation, since that detriment would have been incurred even if the operation had been successful; one can say that this detriment was not "caused" by the breach. But where the plaintiff by reason of the operation was put to more pain than he would have had to endure, had the doctor performed as promised, he should be compensated for that difference as a proper part of his expectancy recovery. It may be noted that on an alternative count for malpractice the plaintiff in the *Hawkins* case had been nonsuited; but on ordinary principles this could not affect the contract claim, for it is hardly a defence to a breach of contract that the promisor acted innocently and without negligence. The New Hampshire court further refined the *Hawkins* analysis in McQuaid v. Michou, 85 N.H. 299, 157 A. 881, all in the direction of treating the patient-physician cases on the ordinary footing of expectancy. . . .

Other cases, including a number in New York, without distinctly repudiating the *Hawkins* type of analysis, have indicated that a different and generally more lenient measure of damages is to be applied in patient-physician actions based on breach of alleged special agreements to effect a cure, attain a stated result, or employ a given medical method. This measure is expressed in somewhat variant ways, but the substance is that the plaintiff is to recover any expenditures made by him and for other detriment (usually not specifically described in the opinions) following proximately and foreseeably upon the defendant's failure to carry out his promise. Robins v. Finestone, 308 N.Y. 543, 546, 127 N.E.2d 330 . . . . This, be it noted, is not a "restitution" measure, for it is not limited to restoration of the benefit conferred on the defendant (the fee paid) but includes other expenditures, for example, amounts paid for medicine and nurses; so also it would seem according to its logic to take in damages for any worsening of the plaintiff's condition due to the breach. Nor is it an "expectancy" measure, for it does not appear to contemplate recovery of the whole difference in value between the condition as promised and the condition actually resulting from the treatment. Rather the tendency of the formulation is to put the plaintiff back in the position he occupied just before the parties entered upon the agreement, to compensate him for the detriments he suffered in reliance upon the agreement. This kind of intermediate pattern of recovery for breach of contract is discussed in the suggestive article by Fuller and Perdue, The Reliance Interest in Contract Damages, 46 Yale L.J. 52, 373, where the authors show that, although not attaining the currency of the standard measures, a "reliance" measure has for special reasons been applied by the courts in a variety of settings, including noncommercial settings. See 46 Yale L.J. at 396–401.[2]

For breach of the patient-physician agreements under consideration, a recovery limited to restitution seems plainly too meager, if the agreements are to be enforced at all. On the other hand, an expectancy recovery may well be excessive. The factors, already mentioned, which have made the cause of action somewhat suspect, also suggest moderation as to the breadth of the recovery that should be permitted. Where, as in the case at bar and in a number of the reported cases, the doctor has been absolved of negligence by the trier, an expectancy measure may be thought harsh. We should recall here that the fee paid by the patient to the doctor for the alleged promise would usually be quite disproportionate to the putative expectancy recovery. To attempt, moreover, to put a value on the condition that would or might have resulted, had the treatment succeeded as promised, may sometimes put an exceptional strain on the imagination of the fact finder. As a general consideration, Fuller and Perdue argue that the reasons for granting damages for broken promises to the extent of the expectancy are at their strongest when the promises are made in a business context, when they have to do with the production or distribution of goods or the allocation of functions in the market place; they become weaker as the context shifts from a commercial to a noncommercial field. 46 Yale L.J. at 60–63.

There is much to be said, then, for applying a reliance measure to the present facts, and we have only to add that our cases are not unreceptive to the use of that formula in special situations. We have, however, had no previous occasion to apply it to patient-physician cases.[3]

2. Some of the exceptional situations mentioned where reliance may be preferred to expectancy are those in which the latter measure would be hard to apply or would impose too great a burden; performance was interfered with by external circumstances; the contract was indefinite. See 46 Yale L.J. at 373–386; 394–396.

3. In Mt. Pleasant Stable Co. v. Steinberg, 238 Mass. 567, 131 N.E. 295, the plaintiff company agreed to supply teams of horses at agreed rates as required from day to day by the defendant for his business. To prepare itself to fulfill the contract and in reliance on it, the plaintiff bought two "Cliest" horses at a certain price. When the defendant repudiated the contract, the plaintiff sold the horses at a loss and in its action for breach claimed the loss as an element of damages. The court properly held that the plaintiff was not entitled to this item as it was also claiming (and recovering) its lost profits (expectancy) on the contract as a whole. Cf. Noble v. Ames Mfg. Co., 112 Mass. 492. (The loss on sale of the horses is analogous to the pain and suffering for which the patient would be disallowed a recovery in Hawkins v. McGee, 84 N.H. 114, 146 A. 641, because he was claiming and recovering expectancy damages.) The court in the *Mt. Pleasant* case referred, however, to Pond v. Harris, 113 Mass. 114, as a contrasting situation where the expectancy could not be fairly determined. There the defendant had wrongfully revoked an agreement to

The question of recovery on a reliance basis for pain and suffering or mental distress requires further attention. We find expressions in the decisions that pain and suffering (or the like) are simply not compensable in actions for breach of contract. The defendant seemingly espouses this proposition in the present case. True, if the buyer under a contract for the purchase of a lot of merchandise, in suing for the seller's breach, should claim damages for mental anguish caused by his disappointment in the transaction, he would not succeed; he would be told, perhaps, that the asserted psychological injury was not fairly foreseeable by the defendant as a probable consequence of the breach of such a business contract. See Restatement of Contracts, § 341, and comment a. But there is no general rule barring such items of damage in actions for breach of contract. It is all a question of the subject matter and background of the contract, and when the contract calls for an operation on the person of the plaintiff, psychological as well as physical injury may be expected to figure somewhere in the recovery, depending on the particular circumstances. The point is explained in Stewart v. Rudner, 349 Mich. 459, 469, 84 N.W.2d 816. Cf. Frewen v. Page, 238 Mass. 499, 131 N.E. 475; McClean v. University Club, 327 Mass. 68, 97 N.E.2d 174. Again, it is said in a few of the New York cases, concerned with the classification of actions for statute of limitations purposes, that the absence of allegations demanding recovery for pain and suffering is characteristic of a contract claim by a patient against a physician, that such allegations rather belong in a claim for malpractice. See Robins v. Finestone, 308 N.Y. 543, 547, 127 N.E.2d 330; Budoff v. Kessler, 2 A.D.2d 760, 153 N.Y.S.2d 654. These remarks seem unduly sweeping. Suffering or distress resulting from the breach going beyond that which was envisaged by the treatment as agreed, should be compensable on the same ground as the worsening of the patient's condition because of the breach. Indeed it can be argued that the very suffering or distress "contracted for"—that which would have been incurred if the treatment achieved the promised result—should also be compensable on the theory underlying the New York cases. For that suffering is "wasted" if the treatment fails. Otherwise stated, compensation for this waste is arguably required in order to complete the restoration of the status quo ante.[4]

arbitrate a dispute with the plaintiff (this was before such agreements were made specifically enforceable). In an action for the breach, the plaintiff was held entitled to recover for his preparations for the arbitration which had been rendered useless and a waste, including the plaintiff's time and trouble and his expenditures for counsel and witnesses. The context apparently was commercial but reliance elements were held compensable when there was no fair way of estimating an expectancy. See, generally, annotation, 17 A.L.R.2d 1300. A noncommercial example is Smith v. Sherman, 4 Cush. 408, 413–414, suggesting that a conventional recovery for breach of promise of marriage included a recompense for various efforts and expenditures by the plaintiff preparatory to the promised wedding. . . .

4. Recovery on a reliance basis for breach of the physician's promise tends to equate with the usual recov-

In the light of the foregoing discussion, all the defendant's exceptions fail: the plaintiff was not confined to the recovery of her out-of-pocket expenditures; she was entitled to recover also for the worsening of her condition,[5] and for the pain and suffering and mental distress involved in the third operation. These items were compensable on either an expectancy or a reliance view. We might have been required to elect between the two views if the pain and suffering connected with the first two operations contemplated by the agreement, or the whole difference in value between the present and the promised conditions, were being claimed as elements of damage. But the plaintiff waives her possible claim to the former element, and to so much of the latter as represents the difference in value between the promised condition and the condition before the operations.

Plaintiff's exceptions waived.

Defendant's exceptions overruled.

NOTE

Choice of Expectation Interest. The law's initial choice of the expectation interest was not inevitable. In Flureau v. Thornhill, 2 Bl.W. 1078, 96 Eng.Rep. 635 (K.B.1776), the court chose to protect the promisee's reliance interest instead. That case announced the rule that recovery against a vendor who promised to convey land, but is unable without any bad faith to give a good title, is limited to the expense incurred by the purchaser in reliance on the promise, including any down payment. As DeGrey, C. J., stated, "I do not think that the purchaser can be entitled to any damages for the fancied goodness of the bargain, which he supposes he has lost." But the subsequent development of the law of damages did not follow this course. Although the rule has persisted in England as to contracts for the sale of land and has found its way into the law of a number of states, the tendency even in these jurisdictions has been to restrict its application.

ery for malpractice, since the latter also looks in general to restoration of the condition before the injury. But this is not paradoxical, especially when it is noted that the origins of contract lie in tort. See Farnsworth, The Past of Promise: An Historical Introduction to Contract, 69 Col.L. Rev. 576, 594–596; Breitel, J. in Stella Flour & Feed Corp. v. National City Bank, 285 App.Div. 182, 189, 136 N.Y.S.2d 139 (dissenting opinion). A few cases have considered possible recovery for breach by a physician of a promise to sterilize a patient, resulting in birth of a child to the patient and spouse. If such an action is held maintainable, the reliance and expectancy measures would, we think, tend to equate, because the promised condition was preservation of the family status quo. . . . It would, however, be a mistake to think in terms of strict "formulas." For example, a jurisdiction which would apply a reliance measure to the present facts might impose a more severe damage sanction for the wilful use by the physician of a method of operation that he undertook not to employ.

5. That condition involves a mental element and appraisal of it properly called for consideration of the fact that the plaintiff was an entertainer. Cf. McQuaid v. Michou, 85 N.H. 299, 303–304, 157 A. 881 (discussion of continuing condition resulting from physician's breach).

See 5 Corbin, § 1098. The dominant theme, then, is one of relief based on expectation.

WHITE v. BENKOWSKI

Supreme Court of Wisconsin, 1967.
37 Wis.2d 285, 155 N.W.2d 74.

[In 1962, the Whites bought a house that lacked its own water supply but was connected by pipes with a well on adjacent property occupied by the Benkowskis. The Whites made a written contract with the Benkowskis under which the Benkowskis promised to supply water to the Whites' home for ten years unless the municipality supplied it, the well became inadequate or the Whites drilled their own well. The Whites paid $400 for a new pump and an additional tank and promised to pay $3 a month and half the cost of any future repairs or maintenance. By 1964, what had begun as a friendly relationship between new neighbors had deterioriated and become hostile. In that year the Benkowskis shut off the water supply on nine occasions for periods that, according to Mrs. White's records, were well under an hour and occurred in the afternoon or early evening. Mr. Benkowski claimed that this was done either to allow accumulated sand in the pipes to settle or to remind the Whites that their use of water was excessive. The Whites sued the Benkowskis, seeking compensatory and punitive damages for breach of contract. The jury returned a special verdict that found that the Benkowskis had maliciously shut off the Whites' water supply to harass them. Compensatory damages were set at $10 and punitive damages at $2,000, but on motions after verdict the award was reduced to $1 compensatory damages and no punitive damages. The Whites appeal.]

WILKIE, Justice. Two issues are raised on this appeal.

1. Was the trial court correct in reducing the award of compensatory damages from $10 to $1?

2. Are punitive damages available in actions for breach of contract?

Reduction of Jury Award.

The evidence of damage adduced during the trial here was that the water supply had been shut off during several short periods. Three incidents of inconvenience resulting from these shut-offs were detailed by the plaintiffs. Mrs. White testified that the lack of water in the bathroom on one occasion caused an odor and that on two other occasions she was forced to take her children to a neighbor's home to bathe them. Based on this evidence, the court instructed the jury that:

" . . . in an action for a breach of contract the plaintiff is entitled to such damages as shall have been sustained by him which resulted naturally and directly from the breach if you find that the defendants did in fact breach the contract. Such damages include pecuniary loss and inconvenience suffered as a natural result of the breach and are called compensatory damages. In this case the plaintiffs have proved no pecuniary damages which you or the Court could compute. In a situation where there has been a breach of contract which you find to have damaged the plaintiff but for which the plaintiffs have proven no actual damages, the plaintiffs may recover nominal damages.

"By nominal damages is meant trivial—a trivial sum of money."

Plaintiffs did not object to this instruction. In the trial court's decision on motions after verdict it states that the court so instructed the jury because, based on the fact that the plaintiffs paid for services they did not receive, their loss in proportion to the contract rate was approximately 25 cents. This rationale indicates that the court disregarded or overlooked Mrs. White's testimony of inconvenience. In viewing the evidence most favorable to the plaintiffs, there was some injury. The plaintiffs are not required to ascertain their damages with mathematical precision, but rather the trier of fact must set damages at a reasonable amount. Notwithstanding this instruction, the jury set the plaintiffs' damages at $10. The court was in error in reducing that amount to $1.

The jury finding of $10 in actual damages, though small, takes it out of the mere nominal status. The award is predicated on an actual injury. This was not the situation present in Sunderman v. Warnken.[1] *Sunderman* was a wrongful-entry action by a tenant against his landlord. No actual injury could be shown by the mere fact that the landlord entered the tenant's apartment, therefore damages were nominal and no punitory award could be made. Here there was credible evidence which showed inconvenience and thus actual injury, and the jury's finding as to compensatory damages should be reinstated.

Punitive Damages.

"If a man shall steal an ox, or a sheep, and kill it, or sell it; he shall restore five oxen for an ox, and four sheep for a sheep." [2]

Over one hundred years ago this court held that, under proper circumstances, a plaintiff was entitled to recover exemplary or punitive damages.[3]

Kink v. Combs [4] is the most recent case in this state which deals with the practice of permitting punitive damages. In *Kink* the court

1. (1947), 251 Wis. 471, 29 N.W.2d 496.

2. Exodus 22:1.

3. McWilliams v. Bragg (1854), 3 Wis. 377 (*424).

4. (1965), 28 Wis.2d 65, 135 N.W.2d 789.

relied on Fuchs v. Kupper [5] and reaffirmed its adherence to the rule of punitive damages.

In Wisconsin compensatory damages are given to make whole the damage or injury suffered by the injured party. On the other hand, punitive damages are given

". . . on the basis of punishment to the injured party not because he has been injured, which injury has been compensated with compensatory damages, but to punish the wrongdoer for his malice and to deter others from like conduct." [6]

Thus we reach the question of whether the plaintiffs are entitled to punitive damages for a breach of the water agreement.

The overwhelming weight of authority supports the proposition that punitive damages are not recoverable in actions for breach of contract. In Chitty on Contracts, the author states that the right to receive punitive damages for breach of contract is now confined to the single case of damages for breach of a promise to marry.[7]

Simpson states:

"Although damages in excess of compensation for loss are in some instances permitted in tort actions by way of punishment . . . in contract actions the damages recoverable are limited to compensation for pecuniary loss sustained by the breach." [8]

Corbin states that as a general rule punitive damages are not recoverable for breach of contract.[9]

In Wisconsin, the early case of Gordon v. Brewster [10] involved the breach of an employment contract. The trial court instructed the jury that if the nonperformance of the contract was attributable to the defendant's wrongful act of discharging the plaintiff, then that would go to increase the damages sustained. On appeal, this court said that the instruction was unfortunate and might have led the jurors to suppose that they could give something more than actual compensation in a breach of contract case. We find no Wisconsin case in which breach of contract (other than breach of promise to marry) has led to the award of punitive damages.

Persuasive authority from other jurisdictions supports the proposition (without exception) that punitive damages are not available

5. (1963), 22 Wis.2d 107, 125 N.W.2d 360.

6. Malco, Inc. v. Midwest Aluminum Sales (1961), 14 Wis.2d 57, 66, 109 N.W.2d 516, 521.

7. 1 Chitty, Contracts (22d ed. 1961), p. 1339.

8. Simpson, Contracts, (2d ed. hornbook series), p. 394, sec. 195.

9. 5 Corbin, Contracts, p. 438, sec. 1077.

10. (1858), 7 Wis. 309 (* 355).

in breach of contract actions. This is true even if the breach, as in the instant case, is willful.

Although it is well recognized that breach of a contractual duty may be a tort, in such situations the contract creates the relation out of which grows the duty to use care in the performance of a responsibility prescribed by the contract. Not so here. No tort was pleaded or proved.

Reversed in part by reinstating the jury verdict relating to compensatory damages and otherwise affirmed. Costs to appellant.

NOTES

(1) *Availability of Punitive Damages.* Punitive damages are granted for tortious conduct that is sufficiently "outrageous" to justify them. See Restatement, Second, of Torts, § 908. But, as the Supreme Court of Wisconsin stated, "the overwhelming weight of authority supports the proposition that punitive damages are not recoverable in actions for breach of contract." In a leading English case that followed this proposition, however, Lord James of Hereford confessed "to some feeling of remorse, because during many years when I was a junior at the Bar, when I was drawing pleadings, I often strove to convert a breach of contract into a tort in order to recover a higher scale of damages." Addis v. Gramophone Co., [1909] A.C. 488, 492 (H.L.).

Some states have departed from the strict rule that denies punitive damages for breach of contract when the breach is accompanied by an "independent" tort that is sufficiently outrageous to justify punitive damages under tort law. Did the Benkowskis commit such a tort? In other states, punitive damages are imposed when the breach is accompanied by outrageous conduct that is "fraudulent," even in the absence of an independent tort that would justify punitive damages. Was this true of the Benkowskis' breach? See Restatement Second, § 355; Sullivan, Punitive Damages in the Law of Contract: The Reality and the Illusion of Legal Change, 61 Minn.L.Rev. 207 (1977). Courts have been especially willing to grant punitive damages against insurers for vexatious refusals to pay claims. See, e. g., Vernon Fire & Cas. Ins. Co. v. Sharp, 264 Ind. 599, 349 N.E.2d 173 (1976); Wright v. Public Sav. Life Ins. Co., 262 S.C. 285, 204 S.E.2d 57 (1974).

(2) *The Case of the Lemon and the Bad Apple.* Batchelor sued Hibschman Pontiac for compensatory and punitive damages for breach of a contract under which Batchelor had bought a Pontiac GTO. The jury awarded Batchelor $1,500 in compensatory damages and $15,000 in punitive damages. From a reversal of the award of punitive damages, Batchelor appeals. *Held*: Judgment of trial court affirmed, except that the case is remanded to the trial court with instructions to order a remittitur of $7,500 of the punitive damages. "Where the conduct of a party, in breaching his contract, independently establishes the elements of a common law tort, punitive damages may be awarded for the tort. Punitive damages may be awarded in addition to compensatory damages 'whenever the elements of fraud, malice, gross negligence or oppression mingle in the controversy.' . . . Here, the jury could reasonably have found elements of fraud,

malice, gross negligence or oppression mingled into the breach of warranty. The evidence showed that requested repairs were not satisfactorily completed although covered by the warranty and capable of correction. Some of these defects were clearly breaches of warranty. Paint was bubbled, the radio never worked properly, the hood and bumper were twisted and misaligned, the universal joints failed, the transmission linkage was improperly adjusted, the timing chain was defective causing improper tune-ups and the carburetor was defective, among other things. Batchelor took the car to the defendant with a list of defects on numerous occasions and picked up the car when told it was 'all ready to go.' It was reasonable to infer that the defendant's service manager represented repairs to have been made when he knew that the work had not been done and that in reliance on his representations, Batchelor drove the car on trips and had breakdowns. Before purchasing the car Batchelor was given special representations on the excellence of Hibschman's service department, and the jury could find that Batchelor relied on these in buying the car from the defendant. After having brought the car in on numerous occasions, Batchelor was told by Jim Hibschman, 'I would rather you would just leave and not come back. We are going to have to write you off as a bad customer.' And he was told by one of Hibschman's mechanics that, 'If you don't get on them and get this fixed, they will screw you around and you will never get it done.' From these statements the jury could infer that the defendant was attempting to avoid making certain repairs by concealing them during the period of the warranty. Batchelor gave the defendant numerous opportunities to repair the car and the defendant did not do so; instead he tried to convince Batchelor that the problems were not with the car, but rather with Batchelor. We are of the opinion that in this case the jury could have found there was cogent proof to establish malice, fraud, gross negligence and oppressive conduct." However, the court held that $15,000 was so large an amount as to violate the rule that punitive damages must not appear "at first blush" to be "outrageous or excessive." Hibschman Pontiac, Inc. v. Batchelor, 266 Ind. 310, 362 N.E.2d 845 (1977). Was there a "common law tort?" What tort?

(3) *The Case of the Sexagenarian Swinger.* Mrs. Syester, a widow in her sixties who worked in Des Moines as a "coffee girl," went to an Arthur Murray Dance Studio because of a gift from a friend. As the result of an "astoundingly successful selling campaign" in which the manager promised her that she "would be a professional dancer," she was sold over 4,000 hours of instruction (including three lifetime memberships), of which she used about 3,100 at a cost of nearly $30,000. She became dissatisfied when her 25 year-old instructor was dismissed, quit and, after protracted negotiations, sued the studio for fraud and misrepresentation. From a judgment on a jury verdict of $14,300 actual damages and $40,000 punitive damages, the defendant appealed. *Held:* Affirmed. There was sufficient "malice" to support an award of punitive damages. "The jury award of $40,000 was large. However, the evidence of greed and avariciousness on the part of defendants is shocking to our sense of justice as it obviously was to the jury. The allowance of exemplary damages is wholly within the discretion of the jury where there is a legal basis for the allowance of such damages." Syester v. Banta, 257 Iowa 613, 133 N.W.2d 666 (1965).[a] How did Mrs. Syes-

a. The report of this case should be consulted for its full flavor, including, for example, a reference to the revised edition of the studio's "Eight

ter's claim differ from one for "malicious" breach of contract? Is the "malicious" making of promises more culpable than the "malicious" breaking of promises?

Would the defendant's conduct have been criminal under an Iowa statute, enacted in 1965, which makes it a misdemeanor, punishable by a fine of up to $100 and imprisonment for up to 30 days, for anyone conducting a course of instruction for profit to "Falsely advertise or represent to any person any matter material to such course of instruction" or "to sell more than one lifetime contract to any one person." Iowa Code Ann. §§ 713A.1, 713A.4.

THE ECONOMICS OF BREACH

Suppose that a party, after having made a contract, discovers that it is less advantageous to him than he had supposed and considers breaking it. To what extent, if at all, should the law attempt to discourage him from doing so? On this question the economist has something to say.

From his competitive or free enterprise model, the economist has derived a set of decisional rules to enable individual economic units to make optimal allocations of their own resources. He has also derived a set of normative rules to guide society in the allocation of its resources. The economist's goal in formulating normative rules is that of "efficiency." The allocation of resources in a society is considered to be "efficient" if no alteration in that allocation will make some economic unit better off without making some other unit worse off. (Such an allocation is often called "Pareto optimal.")

In order to determine whether a unit is "better" or "worse" off, however, account must be taken of the preferences of that unit. The determination of these preferences is not a task for the economist. But given a set of individual preferences, the normative rules formulated by the economist will help society to achieve an efficient allocation of its resources in terms of those preferences.

Furthermore, the economist insists that, for the good of society, its resources be allocated efficiently at every point in time. It is therefore in the interest of society that each economic unit shift its resources whenever this would lead to an efficient allocation. But what if that unit is bound by a contract not to shift its resources? Should it break it and reallocate them?

The answer for each party to a contract is, of course, affected not only by his preferences but by the legal consequences that would follow from a breach of contract. (For present purposes, we will assume, somewhat unrealistically, that available legal remedies are always exacted, and that they are the only sanctions for breach.) The

Good Rules For Interviewing" with a part on "How to prevent a prospect from consulting his banker, lawyer, wife or friend."

law could, for example, provide such a large measure of recovery for breach that reallocation through breach would seldom be advantageous to a party. Or it could provide such a small measure of recovery that reallocation through breach would usually be advantageous to him. Normative economics suggests, however, that the measure of recovery should be the diminution in value to the injured party. Why?

Lowering the measure of recovery *below* the diminution in value caused him by the breach would not put him at the same level of satisfaction of his preferences that he expected and would fail to protect his expectations and preserve his planned allocation of resources. Raising the measure of damages *above* this level would discourage the breaking of contracts when society would want them broken and impair the efficient allocation of its resources. For it is in society's interest that each individual reallocate his resources whenever it makes him better off without making some other unit worse off. Since reallocation through breach will not make the injured party worse off if his expectations are protected by preserving his planned allocation of resources, and will, by hypothesis, make the party in breach better off, it is in society's interest that the contract be broken and the resources reallocated.

What does this suggest about the measure of damages for "wilful" breach? What does it suggest about the efficacy of the law of contracts in encouraging the performance of socially desirable promises? See generally, Barton, The Economic Basis of Damages for Breach of Contract, 1 J. Legal Stud. 277 (1972); Birmingham, Breach of Contract, Damage Measures, and Economic Efficiency, 24 Rutgers L.Rev. 273 (1970). For a brief survey of economics and contract law, see R. Posner, Economic Analysis of Law ch. 4 (2d ed. 1977).

NOTE

Examples. Does the preceding discussion on reallocation provide a convincing argument for the cotton farmers described at the beginning of this section? For H & H Meat Products Company? For the Benkowskis?

McCALLISTER v. PATTON

Supreme Court of Arkansas, 1948.
214 Ark. 293, 215 S.W.2d 701.

MILLWEE, Justice. A. J. McCallister was plaintiff in the chancery court in a suit for specific performance of an alleged contract for the sale and purchase of a new Ford automobile from the defendant, R. H. Patton. The complaint alleges:

"That on or about the 15th day of September, 1945, the Plaintiff entered into a contract with the Defendant, whereby the Plaintiff contracted to purchase and the Defendant to sell, one Ford super deluxe tudor sedan and radio.

"That the Defendant is an automobile dealer and sells Ford automobiles and trucks within the city of Jonesboro, Craighead County, Arkansas and that at the time this Plaintiff entered into this contract the Defendant had no new Ford automobiles in stock of any kind and was engaged in taking orders by contract, numbering the contracts in the order that they were executed and delivered to him. As the cars were received the Defendant would fill the orders as he had previously received the contracts. The Plaintiff's number was number 37.

"As consideration and as part of the purchase price the Plaintiff paid to this Defendant the sum of $25.00 and at all times stood ready, able and willing to pay the balance upon the purchase price in accordance with the terms of the contract. That a copy of this contract is hereto attached marked Exhibit 'A' and made a part of this Complaint, the original being held subject to the orders of this Court and the inspection of the interested parties.

"The Plaintiff is informed and verily believes and the Defendant has admitted to this Plaintiff that he has received more than 37 cars since the execution of this contract. The Defendant refuses to sell an automobile of the above make and description to this Plaintiff.

"Since the execution of this contract and to the present date, new Ford automobiles have been hard to obtain and this Plaintiff is unable to purchase an automobile at any other place or upon the open market of the description named in this contract and there is not an adequate remedy at law and the Court should direct specific performance of this contract."

The prayer of the complaint was that the defendant be ordered to sell the automobile to plaintiff in compliance with the contract, and for all other proper relief. Under the terms of the "New Car Order" attached to the complaint as Exhibit "A," delivery of the car was to be made "as soon as possible out of current or future production" at defendant's regularly established price. Plaintiff was not required to trade in a used car but might do so, if the price of such car could be agreed upon and, if not, plaintiff was entitled to cancel the order and to the return of his deposit. The deposit of $25 was to be held in trust for the plaintiff and returned to him at his option on surrender of his rights under the agreement. There was no provision for forfeiture of the deposit in the event plaintiff refused to accept delivery of the car.

Defendant demurred to the complaint on the grounds that it did not state facts sufficient to entitle plaintiff to the relief of specific performance, and that the alleged contract was lacking in mutuality of obligation and certainty of subject matter. There were further allegations in the demurrer constituting an answer to the effect that plaintiff was engaged in the sale of used cars and had contracted to resell whatever vehicle he obtained from the defendant; and that upon being so informed, defendant tendered and plaintiff refused to accept return of the $25 deposit. Plaintiff filed a motion to strike this part of the pleading.

The chancellor sustained the demurrer to the complaint and overruled the motion to strike. The plaintiff refused to plead further and his complaint was dismissed. This appeal follows.

In testing the correctness of the trial court's ruling in sustaining the demurrer we first determine whether the allegations of the complaint are sufficient to bring plaintiff within the rule that equity will not grant specific performance of a contract for the sale of personal property if damages in an action at law afford a complete and adequate remedy. Our cases on the question are in harmony with the rule recognized generally that, while equity will not ordinarily decree specific performance of a contract for the sale of chattels, it will do so where special and peculiar reasons exist such as render it impossible for the injured party to obtain adequate relief by way of damages in an action at law. In Cooper v. Roland, 95 Ark. 569, 130 S.W. 559, 560, the general rule and various exceptions thereto are discussed. It was there held that the trial court properly sustained a demurrer to a complaint in a suit for specific performance of a contract for the sale of county scrip notwithstanding an allegation that the scrip had no stable market value. Chief Justice McCulloch said in the opinion:

"The general rule, subject to some exceptions, undoubtedly is that courts of equity will not enforce specific performance of executory contracts for the sale of chattels, and this court has announced its adherence to that general rule. Collins v. Karatopsky, 36 Ark. 316. The rule established by the authorities is well stated in a note in volume 5 of American & English Annotated Cases, page 269: 'Courts of equity decree the specific performance of contracts, not upon any distinction between realty and personalty, but because damages at law may not, in the particular case, afford a plain, adequate and complete remedy. Therefore a court of equity will not, generally, decree performance of a contract in respect of personalty, not because of its personal nature, but because damages at law are as complete a remedy as the delivery of the property itself, inasmuch as with the damages like property may be purchased.' "

In Block v. Shaw, 78 Ark. 511, 95 S.W. 806, specific performance of an executory contract for the sale of cotton was denied on the ground that the purchaser had an adequate remedy at law in an action for damages for breach of the contract.

Among the various exceptions to the general rule are those cases involving contracts relating to personal property which has a peculiar, unique or sentimental value to the buyer not measurable in money damages. In Chamber of Commerce v. Barton, 195 Ark. 274, 112 S.W.2d 619, 625, this court held that the purchaser, Barton, was entitled to specific performance of a contract for the sale of Radio Station KTHS as an organized business. Justice Baker, speaking for the court, said:

"A judgment for a bit of lumber from which a picture frame might be made and also for a small lot of tube paint and a yard of canvas would not compensate one who had purchased a great painting.

"By the same token Barton would not be adequately compensated by a judgment for a bit of wire, a steel tower or two, more or less, as the mere instrumentalities of KTHS when he has purchased an organized business including these instrumentalities, worth perhaps not more than one-third of the purchase price. Moreover, he has also contracted for the good will of KTHS, which is so intangible as to be incapable of delivery or estimation of value. So the property is unique in character and, so far as the contract is capable of enforcement, the vendee is entitled to relief."

Exhaustive annotations involving many cases of specific performance of contracts for the sale of various types of personal property are found in L.R.A.1918E, 597 and 152 A.L.R. 4. Comparatively few cases involving suits for specific performance of contracts for the sale of new automobiles have reached the appellate courts. Plaintiff relies on the case of De Moss v. Conart Motor Sales, Inc., 72 N.E.2d 158, where an Ohio Common Pleas Court directed specific performance of a contract similar to the one under consideration on the ground that the purchaser was without an adequate remedy at law due to the fact that new automobiles were difficult to obtain.

A different result was reached in Kirsch v. Zubalsky, 139 N.J. Eq. 22, 49 A.2d 773, 775, where the court sustained defendant's motion to strike the bill of complaint for specific performance in which plaintiff alleged that he was unable to purchase an identical automobile elsewhere at regular O.P.A. price limitations because of the extreme scarcity of such cars and would be forced to pay an illegal bonus above O.P.A. regulations for any similar automobile available on the market. The court said: "The complainant mentions no characteristic which adds a special value to the automobile so as to put it in the category of an unique chattel; and he presents no facts which can be considered by this court as elements of value adding to the intrinsic worth of the automobile itself, so as to permit it to be classed as special or unique. While automobiles may be difficult to procure under the economic or industrial conditions of the present day, they are not in the category of unique chattels."

In Welch v. Chippewa Sales Co., 252 Wis. 166, 31 N.W.2d 170, 171, the plaintiff contended that the vehicle contracted for was invested with the quality of uniqueness due to a current shortage of automobiles and that a judgment for damages did not furnish an adequate remedy. In holding that the complaint did not state a cause of action for specific performance, the court cited Kirsch v. Zubalsky, supra, and said: "In spite of the failure of production fully to meet the demands of customers, automobiles, and indeed, the very make and type of automobile ordered by plaintiff in this case, are being produced by the thousands. There is no sentimental consideration worth while protecting that has to do with the particular make, color or style of automobile. Hence, the mere contention that plaintiff needs cars in his business is not impressive. . . . "

In the still more recent case of Poltorak v. Jackson Chevrolet Co., 322 Mass. 699, 79 N.E.2d 285, the plaintiff contracted for the purchase of a new passenger automobile and delivered to the dealer his automobile for which he was to be allowed a credit on the purchase price of a new car. It was held that plaintiff was not entitled to specific performance of the contract upon showing a scarcity of automobiles and in the absence of a showing of substantial harm of a character which could not be adequately compensated in an action at law for damages.

Efforts to obtain specific performance of similar contracts under Sec. 68 of the Uniform Sales Act, Act 428 of 1941, have been denied by the New York courts. This section provides that a court of equity may, "if it thinks fit," direct specific performance of a contract to deliver "specific or ascertained goods." In Kaliski v. Grole Motors, Inc., Sup., 69 N.Y.S.2d 645, the court held that a contract for the sale of a "New 1947 Studebaker two or four-door Champion automobile" was for the sale of an "unascertained" automobile and hence not specifically enforceable by the buyer. See also, Goodman v. Henry Caplan, Inc., 188 Misc. 242, 65 N.Y.S.2d 576; Cohen v. Rosenstock Motors, Inc., 188 Misc. 426, 65 N.Y.S.2d 481; Gellis v. Falcon Buick Co., Inc., 191 Misc. 566, 76 N.Y.S.2d 94.

Section 68 of the Uniform Sales Act, supra, follows Sec. 52 of the Sale of Goods Act of England. Some English courts, and a few courts of our own states which have adopted the uniform act, have construed this section as broadening the power of equity to grant relief by specific performance, while other courts in both countries have held that it merely recodified the law theretofore existing and did not give the remedy where it had not previously existed. Ann. 152 A.L.R. 45 et seq.; Williston on Sales, Rev.Ed., Vol. 3, Sec. 601. However, under all the decisions, a court of equity will not grant specific performance if a law action for damages affords an adequate remedy to the buyer.

Plaintiff says we will take judicial knowledge of the scarcity of new automobiles as a result of the recent world war. If so, we would also take judicial notice of the fact that large numbers of cars of the type mentioned in the alleged contract have been produced since 1945, and sold through both new and used car dealers in the open market. Although the complaint alleges inadequacy of the remedy at law, it does not set forth facts sufficient to demonstrate such conclusion. It is neither alleged nor contended that the car ordered has any special or peculiar qualities not commonly possessed by others of the same make so as to make it practically impossible to replace it in the market. While it is alleged that new Ford automobiles have been hard to obtain, no harm or inconvenience of a kind which could not be fully compensated by an award of damages in a law action is set forth in the complaint.

We conclude that the allegations of the complaint are insufficient to entitle plaintiff to equitable relief and that his remedy at law is adequate. The demurrer was, therefore, properly sustained. In view of this conclusion we do not find it necessary to examine the contention that lack of consideration and mutuality renders the contract specifically unenforceable.

The decree is affirmed.

NOTES

(1) *The Automobile Cases.* As the opinion indicates, McCallister v. Patton is typical of a number of cases that arose after the Second World War. In most of these the courts reached the same result as did the Arkansas court. But for a case allowing specific performance, see Heidner v. Hewitt Chevrolet Co., 166 Kan. 11, 199 P.2d 481 (1948). There the dealer had attempted to impose the additional requirement of a trade-in upon the buyer, and the trial court had found that "it was possible, but highly improbable, that plaintiff [buyer] could have bought in the open market, for cash alone, the type of automobile he [buyer] was willing to accept." Might the Arkansas court have allowed specific performance if additional facts had been alleged? What facts? Uniform Sales Act § 68 has been replaced by UCC 2–716(1) and (2). Would the Code have changed the result in the McCallister case?

(2) *The Case of the Cowboy's Lament.* Archie Sparrow, a cowboy, agreed to work on Chip Morris' cattle ranch for 16 weeks, in return for which Morris agreed to pay him $400 and give him a horse called Keno. When Sparrow went to work, Keno was practically unbroken, but during his spare time he trained him so that, with a little additional training, he would have been a first class roping horse. At the end of the 16 week term, Morris paid Sparrow the $400 but refused to give him the horse. Sparrow sued for specific performance. *Held:* For plaintiff. "Although it has been held that equity will not ordinarily enforce, by specific performance, a contract for the sale of chattels, it will do so where special and peculiar reasons exist which render it impossible for the injured party to obtain relief by way of damages in an action at law. McCallister v. Patton, 214 Ark. 293, 215 S.W.2d 701. . . . Certainly when one has made a roping horse out of a green, unbroken pony, such a horse would have a peculiar and unique value; if Sparrow is entitled to prevail, he has a right to the horse instead of its market value in dollars and cents." Morris v. Sparrow, 225 Ark. 1019, 287 S.W.2d 583 (1956).

EASTERN ROLLING MILL CO. v. MICHLOVITZ

Supreme Court of Maryland, 1929.
157 Md. 51, 145 A. 378.

[Since it began operation in 1920, Eastern Rolling Mill, a manufacturer of sheet steel in Baltimore, had sold its entire output of steel scrap, a by-product of its manufacture of sheet steel, to Michlovitz, dealers in scrap in Pennsylvania. At the end of 1922, the parties began to make periodic long-term contracts and, in September of 1927, Eastern contracted through Jones, its president, to sell to Michlovitz its entire output of scrap for a period of five years. Michlovitz was to take delivery at Eastern's Maryland plant. The contract price was $3 per ton less than the prices quoted as the Philadelphia market in "Iron Age," a trade publication, at the beginning of every quarter. The deduction was to cover a freight rate which was a minimum of $2.27 a ton to Michlovitz' yards and to every market within the Philadelphia market area except for the Bethlehem Steel plant, together with overhead, transportation costs, and a net profit to Michlovitz. There was a chance that Bethlehem Steel might take the scrap from Michlovitz, which would have increased its profit because the freight rate to Bethlehem's plant was only 90 cents per ton. There was also the chance that if Bethlehem did not take the scrap Michlovitz' costs might have been so high that it would have sustained a loss. In November of 1927, Jones died, and Hazlett, the new president, objected to the duration and prices and tried to get Michlovitz to agree to different terms. When Michlovitz declined, Eastern refused to make deliveries after June of 1928. Prior to that time, Bethlehem Steel had taken the scrap and Michlovitz had made a handsome profit. Michlovitz sued Eastern for specific performance, and, from a decree in favor of Michlovitz, Eastern appealed.]

PARKE, J. . . . In the present case section 246 of article 16 of the Code [a] has no application, since the defendant's proof satisfactorily showed that the defendant has property from which the plaintiffs may recover any damages and costs which might be adjudged for a breach of the contracts, therefore, apart from statute, Code, art. 83, § 89 [Uniform Sales Act § 68], the court, as a general rule, will refuse to decree specific performance in respect of chattels because damages are a sufficient remedy. This principle does not apply in all cases of chattels, so there are many exceptions to this rule,

a. This section, which is now Md.Ann. Code art. 16, § 169, provides: "No court shall refuse to specifically enforce a contract on the mere ground that the party seeking its enforcement has an adequate remedy in damages, unless the party resisting its specific enforcement shall show to the court's satisfaction that he has property from which such damages may be made, or shall give bond, with approved security, in a penalty to be fixed by the court, to perform the contract or pay all such costs and damages as may, in any court of competent jurisdiction, be adjudged against him for breach or nonperformance of such contract."

because, principally, of the inadequacy of the remedy at law in the particular case or of the special nature and value of the subject-matter of the contract. Passing by other illustrations of the exceptions to one more clearly in point, Pomeroy on Specific Performance (3d Ed.) § 15, puts it thus: "Again contracts for the delivery of goods will be specifically enforced, when by their terms the deliveries are to be made and the purchase price paid in installments running through a considerable number of years. Such contracts 'differ from those that are immediately to be executed.' Their profits depending upon future events cannot be estimated in present damages, which must, of necessity, be almost wholly conjectural. To compel a party to accept damages under such circumstances is to compel him to sell his possible profits at a price depending upon a mere guess." This statement of the law is supported by the Maryland decisions. . . .

Under the cases, the right to specific performance turns upon whether the plaintiffs can be properly compensated at law. The plaintiffs are entitled to compensatory damages, and, if an action at law cannot afford them adequate redress, equity will specifically enforce the contracts, which would not impose upon the court any difficulties in enforcement, as the subject-matter of the contracts is the accumulated scrap at the plant of the defendant. The defendant relied upon the case of Fothergill v. Rowland, L.R. 17 Eq. 132, but there the contract was one whose performance involved the working of a coal mine, which required personal skill, and this with its different facts distinguishes that case from the one at bar. The goods which the parties here had bargained for were not procurable in the neighborhood, and, moreover, they possessed a quality and concerntrated weight which could not be secured anywhere within the extensive region covered by the "Philadelphia Market." In addition, the delivery of the scrap at Baltimore was one of the valuable incidents of the purchase. It follows that the right to these specific goods is a consideration of great importance, and this and the difficulty of securing scrap of the same commercial utility are factors making for the inadequacy of damages.

The scrap is not to be delivered according to specified tonnage, but as it accumulates, which in the past has been at the rate of one and two, and occasionally three, carloads of scrap a day, so the quantities vary from quarter to quarter. If the plant should cease to operate or suffer an interruption, there would be no scrap accumulating for delivery under the contracts, and its deliveries would end or be lessened. Neither are the prices for the scrap constant during the period of the contracts, but change from quarter to quarter according to the quotations of two specified materials on the Philadelphia market whose quarterly prices are accepted as the standards upon which the contract prices are quarterly computed. The contracts run to September 30, 1932. By what method would a jury determine the future quarterly tonnage, the quarterly contract price, and quarterly market price during these coming years? How could it possibly arrive at any fair ascertainment of damages? Any estimate would be speculative and conjectural, and not, therefore, compensatory. It follows that the defendant's breach of its contracts is not susceptible of fair and proper compensation by damages; and that to refuse to compel the defendant to do merely what it bound itself to do, and to remit the plaintiffs to their action at law, is to permit the defendant to relieve itself of the contracts and to force the plaintiffs to sell their profits at a conjectural price. To substitute damages by guess for due performance of contract could only be because "there's no equity stirring."

The equitable remedy of specific performance is indicated by the facts and circumstances; and would seem to be authorized by section 89 of article 83 of the Code [Uniform Sales Act § 68], providing as follows:

"89. Where the seller has broken a contract to deliver *specific or ascertained goods*, a court having the powers of a court of equity may, if it thinks fit, on the application of the buyer, by its judgment or decree, direct that the contract shall be performed specifically without giving the seller the option of retaining the goods on payment of damages. The judgment or decree may be unconditional, or upon such terms and conditions as to damages, payment of the price and otherwise, as to the court may seem just."

[In the remainder of its opinion the court concluded that the scrap was "specific or ascertained goods."]

For the reasons given, the decree will be affirmed.

Decree affirmed, with costs.

NOTES

(1) *The Code.* What effect would UCC 2–716 have on this case? One obvious effect would be to relieve the court of the embarrassment caused by the words "specific or ascertained goods." Comments 1 and 2 to UCC 2–716 explain: "[W]ithout intending to impair in any way the exercise of the court's sound discretion in the matter, this Article seeks to further a more liberal attitude than some courts have shown in connection with the specific performance of contracts of sale. . . . In view of this Article's emphasis on the commercial feasibility of replacement, a new concept of what are 'unique' goods is introduced under this section. Specific performance is no longer limited to goods which are already specific or ascertained at the time of contracting. The test of uniqueness under this section must be made in terms of the total situation which characterizes the contract. Output and requirements contracts involving a particular or peculiarly available source or market present today the typical commercial specific performance situation, as contrasted with contracts for the sale of heirlooms or priceless works of art which were usually involved in the older cases. However, uniqueness is not the sole basis of the remedy under this section for the relief may also be granted 'in other proper circumstances'

and inability to cover is strong evidence of 'other proper circumstances.' "[a] If Michlovitz were limited to damages, how would his damages be calculated under the Code?

(2) *The Case of the Slowdown in Steel.* Bliss, a general contractor, contracted to expand and modernize Phoenix Steel's plant, which was spread over a 60-acre site, for $27,500,000. Work did not progress as rapidly as contemplated in the contract, and Phoenix sought a court order of specific performance to compel Bliss to comply with the contract by putting on the job the 300 more workmen required to make up a full second shift during the period that one of the mills had to be shut down because of the work. *Held:* Specific performance denied. "It is not that a court of equity is without jurisdiction in a proper case to order the completion of an expressly designed and largely completed construction contract, particularly where the undertaking is tied in with a contract for the sale of land and the construction in question is largely finished. . . . The point is that a court of equity should not order specific performance of any building contract in a situation in which it would be impractical to carry out such an order, . . . unless there are special circumstances or the public interest is directly involved. . . . I conclude that to grant specific performance . . . would be inappropriate in view of the imprecision of the contract provision relied upon and the impracticability if not impossibility of effective enforcement by the Court of a mandatory order designed to keep a specific number of men on the job at the site of a steel mill which is undergoing extensive modernization and expansion. If plaintiffs have sustained loss as a result of actionable building delays . . . , they may, at an appropriate time, resort to law for a fixing of their claimed damages." On a motion for reargument, Phoenix argued that it sought only an order "directing the performance of a ministerial act, namely, the hiring by defendant of more workers." The court denied the motion, relying on "the well established principle that performance of a contract for personal services, even of a unique nature, will not be affirmatively and directly enforced." Northern Delaware Industrial Development Corp. v. E. W. Bliss Co., 245 A. 2d 431 (Del.Ch.1968). See also Parev Products v. I. Rokeach & Sons, p. 725 infra. Consider the remark of Chancellor Walworth, in denying a decree of specific performance against an opera singer: "I am not aware that any officer of this court has that perfect knowledge of the Italian language, or possesses that exquisite sensibility in the auricular nerve which is necessary to understand, and to enjoy with a proper zest, the peculiar beauties of the Italian opera, so fascinating to the fashionable world." DeRivafinoli v.

a. For an entertaining opinion dealing with uniqueness, see American Brands, Inc. v. Playgirl, Inc., 498 F.2d 947 (2d Cir. 1974), in which the manufacturer of Tarryton cigarettes sought to enjoin Playgirl from breaking their contract by refusing to publish Tarryton advertisements and by publishing other advertisements on the back covers of eight issues of its magazine. The court rejected the manufacturer's contention that the back pages of other magazines of comparable circulation would not afford the manufacturer a suitable substitute, since "it would seem likely that its profits picture would be the same whether the tobacco consumers are malleable young ladies or more jaded aging males" and there "is nothing in the record . . . to indicate what segment of the populace is titillated by Playgirl and why in any event it is not susceptible to the lure of tobacco by . . . blandishment in other and more pedestrian periodicals."

Corsetti, 4 Paige 263, 270 (N.Y.1833). Are general contractors distinguishable from opera singers?

FARNSWORTH, LEGAL REMEDIES FOR BREACH OF CONTRACT, 70 Colum.L.Rev. 1145, 1149–56 (1970).[a] The relief available to the promisee is of two main kinds. It is said to be "specific" when it is intended to secure for the promisee the very benefit that he was promised, as where the court confers the promised benefit on the injured party or orders the defaulting promisor to do so. It is said to be "substitutional" when it is intended to provide him with something in substitution for that benefit, as where the court awards the injured party money damages.[1]

Although damages will, in some cases, permit the injured party to arrange an adequate substitute for the expected benefit, specific relief is clearly the form better suited to the objective of putting the promisee in the position in which he would have been had the promise been performed. Of course the passage of time may reduce the effectiveness even of specific relief. The benefit will at best usually be delayed since contract remedies are ordinarily not available until after breach has occurred.[2] And there are some situations in which specific relief is simply not possible at all. For example, the promise may have been one to deliver particular goods which turn out to be defective, or to have been destroyed, or to have been sold to a third person. But there remain many instances in which specific relief will be both timely and feasible. They can be put into two broad categories.

a. Reprinted by permission of the Columbia Law Review.

1. Substitutional redress need not be limited to money, but may be in kind. Isaac Schapera tells of a case among the Tswana in which a man who broke his promise to deliver a cow to another was obliged to deliver four cows, one in substitution for the cow he should have given and three in substitution for its offspring. Schapera, Contract in Tswana Case Law, 9 J. African L. 142, 148 (1965). Charles Wright notes the incidence of this in everyday dealing—"If I lose the ski poles I have borrowed from a friend, I buy a new pair and return them to him"—and suggests that legal sanctions of this sort might be considered. Wright, The Law of Remedies as a Social Institution, 18 U.Det.L.J. 376, 378 (1955). In a society with a market economy, however, the tendency is to assume that the injured party can procure a substitute himself and need only be compensated for the expense involved. In French law, for example, if the promisor fails to perform his duty to do work, as where a landlord fails to repair the leased premises, the court may authorize the promisee to have it done at the promisor's expense. P. Herzog, Civil Procedure in France 557 (1967). Cf. the buyer's remedy of "cover" under UCC 2–712 . . . .

2. In the exceptional case where a party repudiates his obligation in advance of the time for performance, specific relief might be given without delay. And where a declaratory judgment is granted before the time for performance, it at least reinforces the extra-legal compulsions to perform, although it adds no legal compulsion.

In one category of cases, specific relief does not require the cooperation of the defaulting promisor. If the promise is to deliver goods, an officer of the court may seize and deliver them; if it is to convey land, he may execute a binding conveyance; if it is to pay money, he may seize and sell enough of the promisor's assets to yield the required sum. In this category the practical impediments to specific relief are at a minimum. In the other category of cases, however, specific relief does require the cooperation of the promisor. Consider, for example, a promise to act in a play, to paint a house, or to build a building. To assure specific relief in each of these cases some form of coercion may be needed, so that the practical impediments are substantial.

The civil law systems, i. e., those descended from Roman law, have by and large proceeded on the premise that specific redress should be ordered whenever possible, not only for cases in the first category, but even for those in the second category as well, unless the disadvantages of the remedy outweigh its advantages. As Dawson has said of the German law,

> The main reservations are for cases where specific relief is impossible, would involve disproportionate cost, would introduce compulsion into close personal relationships or compel the expression of special forms of artistic or intellectual creativity. Presumably German courts, like French courts and our own, would not affirmatively order painters to paint pictures or singers to sing.[3]

The logic of the civil law is reenforced by practical considerations in communist countries that lack markets on which aggrieved parties can arrange substitute transactions. The task of manufacture imposed on a state enterprise by a government plan, for example, can only be accomplished if the enterprise receives the specific raw materials that it has been promised for production; money damages are not an adequate substitute.

The common law countries escape both the civil law's doctrinal logic and communism's practical need for compulsion. The early common law courts did know specific relief, for many of the first suits after the Norman Conquest were proprietary in nature, designed to regain something of which the plaintiff had been deprived. Even the action of debt was of this character, since it was based on the notion of an unjust detention of something belonging to the plaintiff. But it became the practice in these actions to allow money damages for the detention in addition to specific relief, and with the development of new forms of action, such as assumpsit, that were in no way proprietary, substitutional relief became the usual form.

3. Dawson, Specific Performance in France and Germany, 57 Mich.L.Rev. 495, 530 (1959).

The typical judgment at common law declared that the plaintiff recover from the defendant a sum of money, which in effect imposed on him a new obligation as redress for the breach of the old. The new obligation required no cooperation on his part for its enforcement since, if the sum was not paid, a writ of execution would issue empowering the sheriff to seize and sell so much of the defendant's property as was required to pay the plaintiff. The proprietary actions remained, so that there were a few instances where relief at common law was specific; for example, in an action by a buyer for replevin of goods sold to him but not delivered, the sheriff might first seize them from the seller and turn them over to the buyer, and the judgment would then declare that the buyer was entitled to them. And, of course, where the claim was to a sum of money that the defendant had promised to pay, the effect, as in the original action for debt, was to give the promisee specific relief; for example, in an action by the seller for the price of goods delivered but not paid for, judgment would be given against the buyer for the full amount of the price. But these instances were the exception rather than the rule, and even where the common law courts granted specific redress, they were unwilling to exert pressure directly on the defendant to compel him to perform. The judgment itself was seen as a mere declaration of rights as between the parties, and the process for its execution was directed not at the defendant but at the sheriff, ordering him to put the plaintiff in possession of real or personal property or to seize the defendant's property and sell such of it as was necessary to satisfy a money judgment.

The enforcement of promises in equity developed along very different lines. Prior to the development of assumpsit by the common law courts in the sixteenth century, most of the cases brought before the chancellor were based on promises that would not have been enforceable at common law, and the question was whether they would nevertheless be enforced in equity. After the development of assumpsit, equity accepted the test for enforcement that had been developed by the rival common law courts, and refused to enforce simple promises made without "consideration." To this extent its jurisdiction in contract became concurrent with that of the common law courts, and its concern shifted from the enforceability of the promise to the nature of its enforcement.

Under the influence of the canon law (for the early chancellors were usually clerics), decrees in equity came to take the form of a personal command to the defendant to do or not to do something. His cooperation was assumed, and if he disobeyed he could be punished not only for criminal contempt, at the instance of the court, but also for civil contempt, at the instance of the plaintiff. This put into the plaintiff's hands the extreme sanction of imprisonment, which might be supplemented by fines payable to the plaintiff and sequestration of the defendant's goods.[4] So it was said that equity acted *in personam,* against the person of the defendant, while the law acted *in rem,* against his property. But it did not follow that the chancellor stood ready to order every defaulting promisor to perform his promise. Equitable relief was confined to special cases in light of both practical and historical limitations.

The practical limitations grew out of the problems inherent in coercion. Our courts, like those of civil law countries, will not undertake to coerce a performance that is personal in nature—to compel an artist to paint a picture or a singer to sing a song. (They have, to be sure, been ingenious in framing orders enjoining contracted parties from acting inconsistently with their promises as a substitute for orders directing them to perform them—the court that will not order the singer to sing may enjoin him from singing elsewhere.)[5] Our courts have also been reluctant to order specific performance where difficulties of supervision or enforcement are foreseen, e. g., to order a building contractor specifically to perform his contract to repair a house. It has been suggested that "in their origins these ideas carried a load of snobbery, expressed in distaste for menial tasks—'how can a Master judge of repairs in husbandry?'"[6] Today they are more often justified as a means of avoiding conflict and unfairness where no clear standards can be framed in advance. The practical exigencies of drafting decrees to guide future conduct under threat of contempt have also moved courts to require that contract terms be expressed with somewhat greater certainty if specific performance is to be granted than if damages are to be awarded. But these practical limitations are on the whole far less significant than the historical ones.

The most important of the historical limitations derives from the circumstance that, since the chancellor had first granted equitable relief in order to supply the deficiencies of the common law, equitable remedies were readily characterized as "extraordinary." When, dur-

4. The development of these supplementary sanctions is traced in C. A. Huston, The Enforcement of Decrees in Equity 76–83 (1915) . . . . Huston notes the measures required "to coerce obedience from the stubborn seventeenth-century Englishman. Thus in 1598, after one Walter had been already subjected in vain to close imprisonment for some time, the court ordered him to perform within a fortnight 'which if he shall not do . . . . then his Lordship mindeth without further delay not only to shut the defendant close prisoner but also to lay as many irons on him as he may bear.'" Id. at 79, citing Clerk v. Walter, Monro 718.

5. Lumley v. Wagner, 1 De G.M. & G. 618, 42 Eng.Rep. 687 (Ch.App.1852). A more extreme example is that of a suit for specific performance of a contract to run street cars to connect with the plaintiff's trains, in which the court enjoined the defendant from operating any cars unless it performed its contract. Prospect Park & Coney Island R. R. v. Coney Island & Brooklyn R. R., 144 N.Y. 152, 39 N.E. 17 (1894).

6. Dawson, supra note 3, at 537, quoting from Rayner v. Stone, 2 Eden 128, 130, 28 Eng.Rep. 845, 846 (1762). . . .

ing the long jurisdictional struggle between the two systems of courts, some means of accommodation were needed, an "adequacy" test was developed to prevent encroachment by the chancellor on the powers of the common law judges. Equity would stay its hand if the remedy at law was "adequate." To this test was added the gloss that the money damages awarded by the common law courts were ordinarily "adequate"—a gloss encouraged by the philosophy of free enterprise, since in a market economy money ought to enable an aggrieved promisee to arrange a substitute transaction. As one writer put it:

> The law, concerning itself more and more with merchandise bought or sold for money, with things having a definite and calculable exchange value, came to conceive that the money compensation, which was an entirely adequate remedy in the common case, and in many cases the only possible one when once the wrong complained of had been committed, was [generally] the only remedy available for their use . . . .[7]

So it came to be that, in sharp contrast to the civil law approach, money damages were regarded as the norm and specific relief as the deviation, even where the law could easily have provided specific relief without any cooperation from the defaulting promisor.

Land, which the common law viewed with particular esteem, was singled out for special treatment. Each parcel, however ordinary, was considered to be "unique," and from this it followed that if a vendor defaulted on his promise to convey land, not even money would enable an injured purchaser to find a substitute. The remedy at law being in this sense "inadequate," a decree of specific performance would ordinarily issue.[8] Although the case for allowing the vendor to have specific performance when the purchaser defaulted was less compelling, equity also granted him relief. But no such reason applied to the contract for the sale of goods, for in a market economy it was supposed that, with rare exceptions for such "unique" items as heirlooms and objects of art, substantially similar goods were available elsewhere. Some attempts have been made to liberalize this restriction. The draftsmen of the Uniform Commercial Code state in its Comments that it introduces "a new concept of what are 'unique'

7. C. A. Huston, supra note 4, at 74. Holmes, with some overstatement, wrote that "The duty to keep a contract at common law means a prediction that you must pay damages if you do not keep it—and nothing else." Holmes, The Path of the Law, 10 Harv.L.Rev. 457, 462 (1897).

8. E. g., Kitchen v. Herring, 42 N.C. 190 (1851) (principle in regard to land adopted, not because it was fertile or rich in minerals, or valuable for timber, but simply because it was land —a favorite and favored subject in England, and in every country of Anglo-Saxon origin). [For a rare exception, where the purchaser wanted the land to resell it at a profit, see Watkins v. Paul, 95 Idaho 499, 511 P.2d 781 (1973).]

goods," and they assert that "where the unavailability of a market price is caused by a scarcity of goods of the type involved, a good case is normally made for specific performance under this Article." But specific performance is still the exception, not the rule, and in contrast to the view held in socialist countries, it is to be justified on the basis of the peculiar needs of the aggrieved party and not the general welfare of society as a whole. Although a court, in determining the adequacy of an award of damages, may take account of such factors as the difficulty of their ascertainment (e. g., under a long-term "output" or "requirements" contract) and the improbability of their collection (e. g., against an insolvent defendant), the typical buyer of goods must still content himself with money as a substitute for the goods in the event of breach.

A second historical limitation, or group of limitations, is premised on the notion that equitable relief is "discretionary." Since the chancellor was to act according to "conscience" (a circumstance that prompted the famous charge that his conscience might vary with the length of his foot [9]), he might withhold relief where considerations of "fairness" or "morality" dictated. Some of the most renowned of these equitable restrictions are embodied in equity's colorful maxims: "he who seeks equity must do equity"; "he who comes into equity must come with clean hands"; and "equity aids the vigilant." One of the most troublesome is the now largely discredited "mutuality of remedy" rule, under which specific performance would not be granted to the aggrieved party unless it would have been available to the other party had the aggrieved party been the one in breach. It is one of the curious inconsistencies to arise out of the dual jurisdiction of law and equity that these restrictions operated to bar only equitable relief and did not prevent the award of damages at law.

The historical development of the parallel systems of law and equity may afford an adequate explanation of the reluctance of our courts to grant specific relief; it is scant justification for it. A more rational basis might be the severity of the sanctions available under the contempt power for their enforcement. In any event, the current trend is clearly in favor of the extension of specific relief. The fusion of law and equity into a single court system at least facilitates a major change in this direction, and commentators have urged such a change.

> Why not, as in both French and German law, give specific performance as to any physical object that can be found and is reachable by direct execution? It is true that whenever

9. "'Tis all one, as if they should make his foot the standard for the measure we call a Chancellor's foot; what an uncertain measure this would be! One Chancellor has a long foot, another a short foot, a third an indifferent foot; 'tis the same thing in the Chancellor's conscience." Selden, Table Talk, quoted in Gee v. Pritchard, 2 Swanst. 402, 414, 36 Eng.Rep. 670, 679, (Ch.1818).

> speed is a factor and markets reasonably organized, promisees will not often ask for it . . . . But why not leave this to the promisee's choice? [10]

Still, for the present, the promisee must ordinarily be content with money damages.

NOTES

(1) *The Game for Dough.* In recent years the world of professional athletics, with its warring leagues, has been more productive of litigation in this field than has the world of opera. The availability of injunction has been enhanced by the belief that the requirement "that the player be an athlete of exceptional talent . . . is met prima facie in cases involving professional athletes." [a] Nassau Sports v. Peters, 352 F.Supp. 870, 876 (E.D.N.Y.1972).

The requirement that "he who comes into equity must come with clean hands" has come under special scrutiny in these cases. Compare New York Football Giants, Inc. v. Los Angeles Chargers Football Club, Inc., 291 F.2d 471 (5th Cir. 1961) (Giants, who had kept contract with Charles Flowers secret so he could play in Sugar Bowl, lacked "clean hands" and could not have Flowers enjoined from playing with Chargers), with Houston Oilers v. Neely, 361 F.2d 36 (10th Cir.), cert. denied, 385 U.S. 840 (1966) ("if the rule announced in [the Flowers] case was intended to apply to every instance in which a contract is entered into with a college football player before a post-season game with an understanding that it will be kept secret to permit that player to compete in the game, then we must respectfully disagree"). See also New England Patriots Football Club, Inc. v. University of Colorado, 592 F.2d 1196 (1st Cir. 1979) (Patriots were not barred from enjoining University of Colorado from hiring Patriots' coach Charles Fairbanks. Court rejected Colorado's contention that Patriots had "unclean hands" as a result of having lured Fairbanks from the University of Oklahoma in 1973, inducing him to break his contract there. "Both parties may have done the University of Oklahoma dirt, but that does not mean unclean hands with respect to 'the controversy in issue.' ")

(2) *Problem.* Suppose that a buyer of cotton had come to you in 1973 and asked what his remedies were against a recalcitrant farmer under an enforceable contract like that described at the beginning of this section? What advice would you give?

In Mitchell-Huntley Cotton Co., Inc. v. Waldrep, 377 F.Supp. 1215 (N.D.Ala.1974), the court granted a declaratory judgment that a buyer who was "in the business of buying cotton from producers and others and selling and delivering same to textile mills and others" was "entitled to specific performance" of its contracts with farmers and enjoined the farmers from

10. Dawson, supra note 3, at 532. . . .

a. As one court admonished a quarterback, however, "some day your passes are going to wobble in the air, you are not going to find that receiver. If you keep . . . jumping your contracts . . . some day your abilities will be such that [your club] won't even send a twice disbarred attorney from Dogpatch to help you." Chicago Cardinals Football Club v. Ethcheverry, (unreported) (D.N.M. 1956), quoted in Detroit Football Co. v. Robinson, 186 F.Supp. 933 (E.D. La.1960).

violating them. "The cotton in question is unique and irreplaceable because of the scarcity of cotton . . . . The majority of all cotton to be produced in the United States in the 1973 crop year has been sold under contracts similar to those here at issue. There is no substantial carry-over of merchantable grades and classes of cotton from prior years in storage in the United States and there will be very little cotton available for purchase in the open market through the 1973 cotton season." Does it appear that the plaintiff's damage remedy was inadequate if, as the court found, "a drastic shortage of cotton developed and the price for same on the open market had increased [from an original contract price of $.30 per pound] to an amount in excess of $.80 per pound"?

For cases denying specific performance of cotton contracts, see Weathersby v. Gore, 556 F.2d 1247 (5th Cir. 1977); Duval & Co. v. Malcom, 233 Ga. 784, 214 S.E.2d 356 (1975).

(3) *Reasons for Breach.* Why does a party refuse to perform his promise? Professor Harold Havighurst offers "five circumstances contributing to such a result": "(1) The debtor dies . . . . (2) Evil men, without conscience and not responsive to any relevant social pressures, succeed in entering the circle of the trusted. This is usually attributable to the creditor's ignorance or poor judgment. (3) The debtor is subject to little competitive pressure . . . . (4) The debtor, because of insolvency or for some other reason, finds it impossible or difficult to perform. (5) Controversy develops . . . because one party does not measure up to the other party's expectation based upon past practices or upon evaluations of character, or because of a miscalculation with respect to events either before or after the making of the contract." H. Havighurst, The Nature of Private Contract 74–75 (1961). Do these categories cover the behavior of H & H Meat Products? The Benkowskis? R. H. Patton? Eastern Rolling Mill? Ask yourself the same question with respect to the cases in the next section of this chapter.

M. DOMKE, THE LAW AND PRACTICE OF COMMERCIAL ARBITRATION 1–3, 10–11 (1968).[a] Arbitration is a means of settling many of the disputes that arise in the daily course of the economic life of the nation. It is a process by which parties voluntarily refer their disputes to an impartial third person, an arbitrator, selected by them for a decision based on the evidence and arguments to be presented before the arbitration tribunal. The parties agree in advance that his determination, the award, will be accepted as final and binding upon them. "Broadly speaking, arbitration is a contractual proceeding, whereby the parties to any controversy or dispute, in order to obtain an inexpensive and speedy final disposition of the matter involved, select judges of their own choice and by consent submit their controversy to such judges

a. Reprinted by permission of Callaghan & Co.

for determination, in the place of the tribunals provided by the ordinary processes of law." [1]

An arbitration can validly take place only if the parties have specifically and expressly agreed to use this method for the settlement of their disputes. Parties may agree upon arbitration either when their contractual relationship begins (i. e., at the execution of the agreement) or at some later date after a controversy has arisen. Generally, arbitration is possible only if the parties can be deemed to have agreed among themselves to its use. This is a basic principle in the notion of voluntary arbitration based on an agreement free of compulsion by a third person. In many states (including most important commercial states) and in the federal area, statutes have been enacted which compel observance of the arbitration clause once it has been agreed to. This type of enactment may be considered as the specific enforcement of a contract clause. In other states, where such statutes have not been enacted, parties are free to reject the use of the arbitration clause. In such cases the arbitration clause receives less weight than other provisions in the contract between the parties.

Arbitration, which involves a final determination of disputes, has elements of the judicial process. Although an alternative to formal court litigation, it does not replace it in all aspects, but rather coexists with court procedure as an adjunct and part of the American system of administering justice. In court proceedings there is a permanent body of law which determines rights and obligations within a traditional legal framework. These proceedings are governed by long-established rules on evidence and review of both the facts and the law by higher courts. In arbitration there is no continuity of service of the arbitration tribunals. Arbitration tribunals are temporarily established for each specific case, even by agencies administering arbitration, and do not generally apply principles of substantive law or court-established rules of evidence. The arbitrators give no reason for their decision, and the award is generally not open to review by courts for any error in finding facts and applying law. Despite differences between court litigation and arbitration proceedings, principles of justice must be maintained, and it is in this area that court intervention in the arbitration process plays an important role.

. . .

Commercial arbitration, as used generally, is not confined to the typical trade arrangements for the sale and purchase of commodities and manufactured goods, and for controversies in the maritime field. It also comprises controversies arising out of building and engineering contracts, agency and distribution arrangements, close corporation and partnership relations, separation agreements, individual em-

1. Gates v. Arizona Brewing Co., 54 Ariz. 266, 269, 95 P.2d 49, 50 (1939).

ployment contracts, license agreements, leases, estate matters, contracts of government agencies and municipal bodies with private firms for construction work, stock exchange transactions and controversies in the broad insurance field, reinsurance arrangements, inter-insurance company subrogation claims, and the new development of arbitration of uninsured motorist accident claims. . . .

The business world has long recognized the need for removing delays and other impediments to the settlement of commercial disputes. It has resorted to an organized form of arbitration by administering arbitration facilities in many business organizations, chambers of commerce, exchanges and trade associations. Preestablished rules of procedure and the maintenance of panels of experts, from which the arbitrators may be chosen, provide for the various contingencies that may arise in commercial arbitration, especially when a party is unwilling to participate in the proceedings. Businessmen have resorted to established organizations since the early days of development of mercantile transactions. Through their administration of commercial arbitration, these business organizations play an important role in the self-regulation of the industries and trades they represent.

Institutional arbitration also serves to standardize business transactions and trade practices and to control the business ethics of the participants. Such trade arbitration has also been helpful in creating a uniform system of contract forms defining terms and conditions that previously were the source of frequent controversies. It was said: "The emphasis in these groups [trade associations and exchanges] is on the utilization of norms and standards of the trade for deciding without regard to their similarity to or difference from the norms or standards that would be imposed by substantive rules of law." [2] However, it is not so much legal implication in interpreting contractual provisions that is the basis of business conflicts; more often it is the ascertainment of certain facts that necessitates determination by a third party. These viewpoints had previously been voiced by Harlan F. Stone, late Chief Justice of the Supreme Court of the United States, when he said: "The very refinements and complexities of our court machinery often make it cumbersome and dilatory when applied to controversies involving simple issues of fact or law. This is especially true in the case when the issue of fact turns upon expert knowledge as to the nature or quality of merchandise or the damage consequent upon the failure to perform a contract for its delivery . . . which can be better determined by a layman having training and experience in a particular trade or business than by a judge and jury who have not had that training and experience." [3]

2. Mentschikoff, Commercial Arbitration, 61 Columbia L.Rev. 846, 859 (1961).

3. 10 Proceedings of the Academy of Political Science 197 (1923).

Similarly, the famous statement of Judge Learned Hand has often been repeated in court decisions, both federal and state: "In trade disputes one of the chief advantages of arbitration is that arbitrators can be chosen who are familiar with the practices and customs of the calling, and with just such matters as what are current prices, what is merchantable quality, what are the terms of sale, and the like." [4]

The trend to institutional arbitration by the business community, in various agencies administering commercial arbitration, is obviously based on the recognition of the value of preestablished rules and control of the procedure through such administrative measures of the agency. Thereby delays will be avoided and many other contingencies met, such as the failure of a party to appoint an arbitrator, the challenge of an arbitrator, and any misconduct during the proceedings. . . .

NOTES

(1) *AAA Standard Arbitration Clause.* The American Arbitration Association recommends the following arbitration clause for insertion in all commercial contracts:

> Any controversy or claim arising out of or relating to this contract, or the breach thereof, shall be settled by arbitration in accordance with the Rules of the American Arbitration Association, and judgment upon the award rendered by the Arbitrator(s) may be entered in any Court having jurisdiction thereof.

It recommends a somewhat different clause for the submission of existing disputes.

(2) *More on the Slowdown in Steel.* Suppose that in the construction contract involved in the case in Note 2, p. 29 supra, Bliss and Phoenix had included the arbitration clause recommended by the American Arbitration Association. Section 42 of the Rules of the Association, entitled Scope of Award, provides:

> The Arbitrator may grant any remedy or relief which he deems just and equitable and within the scope of the agreement of the parties, including, but not limited to, specific performance of a contract. . . .

Would the court have enforced an arbitral award granting the relief that it refused in the actual case? See Grayson-Robinson Stores, Inc. v. Iris Constr. Corp., 8 N.Y.2d 133, 202 N.Y.S.2d 303, 168 N.E.2d 377 (1960) (a 4–3 decision).

(3) *More on the Whites and Benkowskis.* Suppose that in White v. Benkowski, p. 14 supra, the contract had included the arbitration clause recommended by the American Arbitration Association. Would the court

4. American Almond Products Co. v. Consolidated Pecan Sales Co., 144 F. 2d 448 (CA 2nd, 1944), 154 A.L.R. 1205 (1945). See also Characteristics of Commercial Arbitration. Comments on a Bar Association Symposium, 19 Arb.J. 129 (1964).

have enforced an arbitration award granting the punitive damages that it held improper in the actual case? See Garrity v. Lyle Stuart, Inc., 40 N. Y.2d 354, 386 N.Y.S.2d 831, 353 N.E.2d 793 (1976).

(4) *Declaratory Judgments.* Courts may render declaratory judgments under statutes adopted in most jurisdictions and, in some instances, without the aid of statute. See Uniform Declaratory Judgments Act; Federal Declaratory Judgments Act, 28 U.S.C.A. §§ 2201, 2202. Such judgments declare the legal relations between the parties but do not award damages or other relief. They can be rendered even though no breach of contract has occurred. Declaratory judgments are of increasing importance in the resolution of contract disputes. See C. Wright, Law of Federal Courts 497–503 (3d ed. 1976).

SECTION 2. BENEFIT, DETRIMENT AND BARGAINED–FOR EXCHANGE

What promises will the law enforce? The answer to this question under early English law was closely tied to the common law actions of covenant, debt and assumpsit, and even today no adequate answer can ignore this aspect of legal history.

The first of these actions, covenant, was used to enforce contracts made under seal. Once a written promise was sealed and delivered, the action of covenant was available to enforce it, and it made no difference whether the promisor had bargained for or received anything in exchange for his promise, or whether the promisee had in any way changed his position in reliance on it. In medieval England, the seal was a piece of wax affixed to the document and bearing an impression identifying the person who had executed it. At first its use was confined to the nobility, but later it spread to the commonalty. With the growth of literacy and the use of the personal signature as a means of authentication, the requirement of formality was so eroded that a seal could consist of any written or printed symbol intended to serve as a seal. The word "Seal" and the letters "L. S." (*locus sigilli*) were commonly used for this purpose.

Two functions performed by such legal formalities as the seal have been described by Professor Fuller as "evidentiary," that is, providing trustworthy evidence of the existence and terms of the contract in the event of controversy, and "cautionary," that is, bringing home to the parties the significance of their acts—inducing "the circumspective frame of mind appropriate in one pledging his future." Fuller, Anatomy of the Law 36–37 (1968); Fuller, Consideration and Form, 41 Colum.L.Rev. 799, 800 (1941). With the erosion of the solemnity of the seal, it became doubtful that it performed either of these functions well. Consequently, the distinctive effect of the seal on the enforceability of promises has been abolished in roughly half of the states of the United States and seriously curtailed in the rest. The most recent of these assaults on the seal came in UCC 2–203, which, in the words of its draftsmen, "makes it clear that every effect of the seal which relates to 'sealed instruments' as such is wiped out insofar as contracts for sale are concerned." (Comment 1 to UCC 2–203). Where the seal still retains some effect, it is often limited to raising a rebuttable presumption of consideration or making applicable a longer period of limitations. A survey of the laws on the seal in the various states is contained in the Statutory Note at the beginning of Chapter 4, Topic 3, of the Restatement Second.

The second of the three actions, that of debt, could be used to enforce some types of unsealed promises to pay a definite sum of money, including a promise to repay money that had been loaned and a promise to pay for goods that had been delivered or for work that had been done. Since these were situations in which the contemplated exchange was completed on one side, they appealed to the primitive notion that the promisor (or debtor) had something belonging to the promisee (or creditor) which he ought to surrender. The proprietary element present in this notion is reflected in the popular expression that the depositor who is owed money by a bank "*has* money in the bank." What the promisee had given the promisor was sometimes called the "*quid pro quo*," and, as the underlying principles of contract law developed, the promisor's obligation in debt was considered to rest upon his receipt of a *benefit* from the promisee.

The third and ultimately the most important action, assumpsit, grew out of cases in which the promisee sought to recover damages for physical injury to person or property on the basis of a consensual undertaking. In one such case a ferryman who undertook to carry the plaintiff's horse across a river was held liable when he overloaded the boat and the horse drowned. In another a carpenter who undertook to build the plaintiff a house was held liable when he did so unskillfully. The underlying theme of these decisions was that of misfeasance—the promisor, having undertaken (*assumpsit*) to do something, had done it in a manner inconsistent with his undertaking to the detriment of the promisee. The decisions did not go so far as to impose liability for nonfeasance—where the promisor had done *nothing* in pursuance of his undertaking—for example, where the carpenter in the case just put had failed to build the house at all. It was not until the latter half of the fifteenth century that the common law courts began to make this extension. When they did, they imposed a requirement, analogous to that in the misfeasance cases, that the promisee must have incurred a *detriment* in reliance on the promise —as where the owner had changed his position by selling his old house in reliance on the carpenter's promise to build him a new one.

Finally, by the end of the sixteenth century, the courts made a second major extension of the action of assumpsit and held that a party who had given only a promise in exchange for the other's promise had incurred a detriment by having his freedom of action fettered, since he was bound in turn by his own promise. By this circular argument, the common law courts began to enforce exchanges of promises. Here is the opinion in what is said to be the earliest case recognizing that a promise, not even partly performed, could be consideration for a return promise:

> Note, That a promise against a promise will maintain an action upon the case, as in consideration that you do give me £10 on such a day, I promise to give you £10 such a day after.

Strangborough v. Warner, 4 Leo. 3 (Q.B.1588). See Holdsworth, Debt, Assumpsit and Consideration, 11 Mich.L.Rev. 347, 351 (1913).

Eventually, for reasons that need not be gone into here, the action of assumpsit was allowed to supplant that of debt for the enforcement of promises that would previously have been enforced in the latter action. Thus, by the beginning of the seventeenth century, the common law courts had succeeded in developing the action of assumpsit as a general basis for the enforcement of promises. By the same time, the term "consideration" had come to be used as a word of art to express the sum of the conditions necessary for such an action to lie. It was therefore a tautology that a promise, if not under seal, was enforceable only where there was "consideration," for this was to say no more than that it was enforceable only where the action of assumpsit would lie. Bound up in the concept of consideration were several elements. Most important, from the *quid pro quo* of debt came the idea that there must have been an exchange arrived at by way of bargain. To the extent that debt inspired the concept of consideration, there was the notion that there must be a *benefit* to the promisor. To the extent that assumpsit inspired it, there was the notion that there must be a *detriment* to the promisee. The interplay of these elements can be judged from the cases that follow and from Restatement Second, § 71. They lend at least some support to the claim of the English legal historian, F. W. Maitland, that "The forms of action we have buried, but they still rule us from their graves." Maitland, The Forms of Action at Common Law 2 (1936 ed.). For a thorough treatment of this historical background, see A. W. B. Simpson, A History of the Common Law of Contract (1975). See also P. Atiyah, The Rise and Fall of Freedom of Contract (1979); Farnsworth, The Past of Promise: An Historical Introduction to Contract, 69 Colum.L.Rev. 576 (1969).

NOTE

How could England have reached the end of the sixteenth century before giving, in Strangborough v. Warner, legal recognition to exchanges of promises that were not partly performed? Apparently this development was even slower in coming in America. According to one legal historian, "the primitive state of eighteenth century American contract law is underscored by the surprising fact that some American courts did not enforce executory contracts where there had been no part performance . . . . The pressure to enforce such contracts would not be great in a pre-market economy where contracts for future delivery were rare . . . ." Horwitz, The Historical Foundations of Modern Contract Law, 87 Harv.L.Rev. 917, 929–30 (1974), reprinted in M. Horwitz, The Transformation of American Law, 1780–1860, 169 (1977).

HAMER v. SIDWAY

Court of Appeals of New York, 1891.
124 N.Y. 538, 27 N.E. 256.

Appeal from an order of the general term of the supreme court in the fourth judicial department, reversing a judgment entered on the decision of the court at special term in the county clerk's office of Chemung county on the 1st day of October, 1889. The plaintiff presented a claim to the executor of William E. Story, Sr., for $5,000 and interest from the 6th day of February, 1875. She acquired it through several mesne assignments from William E. Story, 2d. The claim being rejected by the executor, this action was brought.

It appears that William E. Story, Sr., was the uncle of William E. Story, 2d; that at the celebration of the golden wedding of Samuel Story and wife, father and mother of William E. Story, Sr., on the 20th day of March, 1869, in the presence of the family and invited guests, he promised his nephew that if he would refrain from drinking, using tobacco, swearing, and playing cards or billiards for money until he became 21 years of age, he would pay him the sum of $5,000. The nephew assented thereto, and fully performed the conditions inducing the promise. When the nephew arrived at the age of 21 years, and on the 31st day of January, 1875, he wrote to his uncle, informing him that he had performed his part of the agreement, and had thereby become entitled to the sum of $5,000. The uncle received the letter, and a few days later, and on the 6th day of February, he wrote and mailed to his nephew the following letter:

Buffalo, Feb. 6, 1875.

"W. E. Story, Jr.:

"Dear Nephew—Your letter of the 31st ult. came to hand all right, saying that you had lived up to the promise made to me several years ago. I have no doubt but you have, for which you shall have five thousand dollars as I promised you. I had the money in the bank the day you was 21 years old that I intend for you, and you shall have the money certain. Now, Willie, I do not intend to interfere with this money in any way till I think you are capable of taking care of it and the sooner that time comes the better it will please me. I would hate very much to have you start out in some adventure that you thought all right and lose this money in one year. The first five thousand dollars that I got together cost me a heap of hard work. . . . It did not come to me in any mysterious way, and the reason I speak of this is that money got in this way stops longer with a fellow that gets it with hard knocks than it does when he finds it. Willie, you are 21 and you have many a thing to learn yet. This money you have earned much easier than I did besides acquiring good habits at the same time and you are quite welcome to the money; hope you will make good use of it. I was ten long years getting this together after I was your age. Now, hoping this will be satisfactory, I stop. . . .

Truly Yours,
"W. E. STORY.

"P.S.—You can consider this money on interest."

The nephew received the letter and thereafter consented that the money should remain with his uncle in accordance with the terms and conditions of the letters. The uncle died on the 29th day of January, 1887, without having paid over to his nephew any portion of the said $5,000 and interest.[a]

PARKER, J. The question which provoked the most discussion by counsel on this appeal, and which lies at the foundation of plaintiff's asserted right of recovery, is whether by virtue of a contract defendant's testator William S. Story became indebted to his nephew William E. Story, 2d, on his twenty-first birthday in the sum of five thousand dollars. The trial court found as a fact that "on the 20th day of March, 1869, . . . William E. Story agreed to and with William E. Story, 2d, that if he would refrain from drinking liquor, using tobacco, swearing, and playing cards or billiards for money until he should become 21 years of age, then he, the said William E. Story, would at that time pay him, the said William E. Story, 2d, the sum of $5000 for such refraining, to which the said William E. Story, 2d, agreed," and that he "in all things fully performed his part of said agreement."

The defendant contends that the contract was without consideration to support it, and, therefore, invalid. He asserts that the prom-

a. The opinion of the Supreme Court, from which this appeal was taken, recites further interesting facts: the uncle had long planned to make a gift of $5,000 to young William; the uncle later loaned $2,500 to William, who went into bankruptcy along with his father and listed no claim against his uncle among his assets; the uncle subsequently gave $11,000 worth of goods to William and his father, taking promissory notes and a general release from both that was broad enough to cover this claim; but it was claimed by the plaintiff on trial that, prior to William's bankruptcy, he had already assigned the $5,000 claim to his wife, so that it was no longer one of his assets and was not later affected by the release. See Hamer v. Sidway, 64 N.Y.Sup.Ct. (57 Hun.) 229, 11 N.Y.S. 182 (1890).

isee by refraining from the use of liquor and tobacco was not harmed but benefited; that that which he did was best for him to do independently of his uncle's promise, and insists that it follows that unless the promisor was benefited, the contract was without consideration, a contention which, if well founded, would seem to leave open for controversy in many cases whether that which the promisee did or omitted to do was, in fact, of such benefit to him as to leave no consideration to support the enforcement of the promisor's agreement. Such a rule could not be tolerated, and is without foundation in the law. The Exchequer Chamber, in 1875, defined consideration as follows: "A valuable consideration in the sense of the law may consist either in some right, interest, profit, or benefit accruing to the one party, or some forbearance, detriment, loss, or responsibility given, suffered, or undertaken by the other." Courts "will not ask whether the thing which forms the consideration does in fact benefit the promisee or a third party, or is of any substantial value to any one. It is enough that something is promised, done, forborne, or suffered by the party to whom the promise is made as consideration for the promise made to him." Anson's Prin. of Con. 63.

"In general, a waiver of any legal right at the request of another party is a sufficient consideration for a promise." Parsons on Contracts, 444.

"Any damage, or suspension or forbearance of a right, will be sufficient to sustain a promise." Kent, Vol. 2, 465, 12th Ed.[b]

Pollock, in his work on contracts, page 166, after citing the definition given by the Exchequer Chamber already quoted, says: "The second branch of this judicial description is really the most important one. Consideration means not so much that one party is profiting as that the other abandons some legal right in the present or limits his legal freedom of action in the future as an inducement for the promise of the first."

Now, applying this rule to the facts before us, the promisee used tobacco, occasionally drank liquor, and he had a legal right to do so.[c]

b. James Kent (1763–1847) began practice after three years as an apprentice and was active in Federalist politics. Hamilton introduced him to the writings of European authors on the civil law, which were to influence his later work. In 1793, largely through his Federalist connections, he was made Professor of Law in Columbia College. He attracted few students, and soon resigned to become a judge on the New York Supreme Court, then the highest court in the state. In 1814 he became Chancellor. Upon his retirement in 1823, he lectured again at Columbia for three years. Out of these lectures grew the "Commentaries on American Law," in four volumes, which became the most important American law book of the century. (It is the source of the quotation above.) Kent lived to prepare six editions; subsequent ones were revised by others. For his work on the Court of Chancery, he has been called practically the creator of equity in the United States.

c. The opinion of the trial court, which is unreported, adds that he "on one occasion . . . refused to use the same when suffering from fever and ague in the West."

That right he abandoned for a period of years upon the strength of the promise of the testator that for such forbearance he would give him $5000. We need not speculate on the effort which may have been required to give up the use of those stimulants. It is sufficient that he restricted his lawful freedom of action within certain prescribed limits upon the faith of his uncle's agreement, and now having fully performed the conditions imposed, it is of no moment whether such performance actually proved a benefit to the promisor, and the court will not inquire into it, but were it a proper subject of inquiry, we see nothing in this record that would permit a determination that the uncle was not benefited in a legal sense. Few cases have been found which may be said to be precisely in point, but such as have been support the position we have taken.

In Shadwell v. Shadwell, 9 C.B.N.S. 159, an uncle wrote to his nephew as follows:

"MY DEAR LANCEY—I am so glad to hear of your intended marriage with Ellen Nicholl, and as I promised to assist you at starting, I am happy to tell you that I will pay you 150 pounds yearly during my life and until your annual income derived from your profession of a chancery barrister shall amount to 600 guineas, of which your own admission will be the only evidence that I shall require.

"Your affectionate uncle,

"CHARLES SHADWELL."

It was held that the promise was binding and made upon good consideration.

In Lakota v. Newton, an unreported case in the Superior Court of Worcester, Mass., the complaint averred defendant's promise that "if you (meaning plaintiff) will leave off drinking for a year I will give you $100," plaintiff's assent thereto, performance of the condition by him, and demanded judgment therefor. Defendant demurred on the ground, among others, that the plaintiff's declaration did not allege a valid and sufficient consideration for the agreement of the defendant. The demurrer was overruled.

In Talbott v. Stemmons, 89 Ky. 222, the step-grandmother of the plaintiff made with him the following agreement: "I do promise and bind myself to give my grandson, Albert R. Talbott, $500 at my death, if he will never take another chew of tobacco or smoke another cigar during my life from this date up to my death, and if he breaks this pledge he is to refund double the amount to his mother." The executor of Mrs. Stemmons demurred to the complaint on the ground that the agreement was not based on a sufficient consideration. The demurrer was sustained and an appeal taken therefrom to the Court of Appeals, where the decision of the court below was reversed. In the opinion of the court it is said that "the right to use and enjoy the use of tobacco was a right that belonged to the plaintiff and not forbidden by law. The abandonment of its use may have saved him money or contributed to his health; nevertheless, the surrender of that right caused the promise, and having the right to contract with reference to the subject-matter, the abandonment of the use was a sufficient consideration to uphold the promise." Abstinence from the use of intoxicating liquors was held to furnish a good consideration for a promissory note in Lindell v. Rokes, 60 Mo. 249. The cases cited by the defendant on this question are not in point. . . .

[In an omitted part of the opinion the court held that the action was not barred by the statute of limitations because under the uncle's letter he held the money in trust and not merely as a debtor.] Order reversed and judgment of special term affirmed.

NOTES

(1) *Benefit and Detriment.* On what ground did the Court of Appeals hold that the uncle's promise was enforceable? Under the finding of the trial court, what was the consideration for that promise? Was the consideration arguably a benefit to the uncle? A detriment to the nephew? Did the Court of Appeals conclude that it was a benefit or a detriment? Did the circumstances under which the promise was made and the fact that it was reaffirmed play any role in that court's thinking?

(2) *"Bargain Theory" of Consideration.* What role do benefit and detriment play under Restatement Second, §§ 71, 79? Was there consideration for the uncle's promise under the Restatement Second? Holmes,[a] an early advocate of the "bargain theory" of consideration espoused by the Restatement, spoke of the "reciprocal conventional inducement": "It is said that consideration must not be confounded with motive. It is true that it must not be confounded with what may be the prevailing or chief motive in actual fact. A man may promise to paint a picture for five hundred dollars, while his chief motive may be a desire for fame. A consideration may be given and accepted, in fact, solely for the purpose of making a promise binding. But, nevertheless, it is the essence of a consideration, that, by the terms of the agreement, it is given and accepted as the motive or inducement of the promise. Conversely, the promise must be made and accepted as the conventional motive or inducement for furnishing the consideration. The root of the whole matter is the relation of reciprocal conventional inducement, each for the other, between consideration and promise." O. W. Holmes, The Common Law 293–94 (1881). "[T]he promise and the consideration must purport to be the motive each for the other, in whole or at least in part. It is not enough that the promise induces the detriment or that the detriment induces the promise if the other half is wanting." Holmes, J., in Wisconsin & Michigan Railway Co. v. Powers, 191 U.S. 379 (1903). Compare Restatement Second, § 71(2) with § 81(1). For a discus-

a. Oliver Wendell Holmes (1841–1935) practiced law in Boston, served briefly as professor of law at Harvard, and then for twenty years as justice and later chief justice of the Supreme Judicial Court of Massachusetts. In 1902 he was appointed an associate justice of the United States Supreme Court, where the quality of his dissenting opinions won him the title of the "Great Dissenter." He resigned because of his great age in 1932. His most famous work is The Common Law (1881), based on a series of lectures.

sion of Holmes' role in the development of the bargain theory, see G. Gilmore, The Death of Contract 19–21 (1974); but see Speidel, Book Review, 27 Stan.L.Rev. 1161 (1975). See also Braucher, Freedom of Contract and the Second Restatement, 78 Yale L.J. 598, 599–607 (1969).

(3) *Policing the Bargain.* It should be evident that the doctrine of consideration—whether viewed in terms of benefit, detriment or bargain—does not enable courts to police bargains to assure fairness, or at least the absence of unfairness, of the exchange. The doctrines under which courts do police bargains are explored in Chapter 5, Policing the Bargain.

(4) *Problem.* Thomas Hurley has worked as general superintendent for Marine Contractors for eight years, during which time Marine has made annual payments into an Employee Retirement Plan and Trust Fund, a legally separate entity whose sole trustee is also the president of Marine. Hurley now plans to leave Marine, and is entitled under the terms of the trust to payment of his vested share after a five year waiting period. Marine wants Hurley to make a binding promise to Marine not to compete with it after he leaves its employ. In return, Marine's president, as trustee, is willing to have the trust pay Hurley his vested share immediately. Will payment by the trust to Hurley be consideration for Hurley's promise to Marine? Does the answer depend on whether you are looking for a benefit, a detriment or a bargain? See Marine Contractors Co., Inc. v. Hurley, 365 Mass. 280, 310 N.E.2d 915 (1974).

GRATUITOUS PROMISES

Suppose that the uncle had given the nephew $5,000 in cash at the golden wedding anniversary and had told him that it was a gift which he could keep on condition that he refrained from drinking, smoking, swearing and gambling until he was twenty-one. Surely the nephew, having met the condition, could have kept the money if the uncle's executor had attempted to get it back. Why, if the law recognizes gratuitous transfers, should it not recognize gratuitous promises? Why did the court have to find that there was consideration? Is it arguable that gratuitous promises serve no useful economic function? That they raise dangers as to proof? What sorts of rules would you suggest if it were thought desirable to enable promisors, in appropriate cases, to make enforceable gratuitous promises? To what extent should those rules take account of such factors as the promisor's motives, the social utility of the promise, the formality with which it was made, and the availability of alternative means of making gifts? These questions will be considered again in Section 6, in connection with reform of the doctrine of consideration.

Every human society relies to some extent upon cooperation among its members to achieve social purposes. To what extent do the notion of consideration and the resulting unenforceability of gratuitous promises comport with the view that this cooperation can best be achieved by a system of "free enterprise"? Consider in this regard, and in connection with the following cases, these words of

Adam Smith, written in 1776: "[M]an has almost constant occasion for the help of his brethren, and it is vain for him to expect it from their benevolence only. He will be more likely to prevail if he can interest their self-love in his favour, and shew them that it is for their own advantage to do for him what he requires of them. Whoever offers to another a bargain of any kind, proposes to do this: Give me that which I want, and you shall have this which you want, is the meaning of every such offer; and it is in this manner that we obtain from one another the far greater part of those good offices which we stand in need of. . . . We address ourselves, not to their humanity but to their self-love, and never talk to them of our own necessities but of their advantages. Nobody but a beggar chooses to depend chiefly upon the benevolence of his fellow-citizens." A. Smith, An Inquiry into the Nature and Causes of the Wealth of Nations 11 (1811 ed., bk. 1, ch. II). Is it significant that a bargained-for exchange may serve the function of coordinating the use of economic resources, while a gratuitous promise merely changes the distribution of wealth?

In an analysis of the economics of gratuitous promises, Professor Richard Posner asks why "economic man" would ever make a promise without receiving in exchange something of value from the promisee. He answers that "a gratuitous promise, to the extent it actually commits the promisor to the promised course of action . . . , creates utility for the promisor over and above the utility to him of the promised performance . . . by increasing the present value of an uncertain future stream of transfer payments."

"To illustrate, suppose A promises to give $1000 a year for the next 20 years to the B symphony orchestra. The value of the gift to B is the discounted present value of $1000 to be paid yearly over a 20-year period in the future. Among the factors that will be used by B in discounting these expected future receipts to present value is the likelihood that at some time during the 20-year period A will discontinue the annual payments. Depending on B's estimation of A's fickleness, income prospects, etc., the present value of the gift of $1000 a year may be quite small; it may not be much more than $1000. But suppose the gift is actually worth more to B because A is certain to continue the payments throughout the entire period, though this fact is not known to B. If A can make a binding promise to continue the payments in accordance with his intention, B will revalue the gift at its true present worth. The size of the gift (in present-value terms) will be increased at no cost to A. Here is a clear case where the enforcement of a gratuitous promise would increase net social welfare.

"This can be seen even more clearly by considering A's alternatives if his promise is not enforceable. One possibility would be for A to promise a larger gift, the discounted value of which to B would equal the true value as known to A. The higher cost of the gift to A would be a measure of the social cost of the unenforceability of his promise. Another possibility would be for A to substitute for the promised series of future transfers a one-time transfer the present value of which would be the same as that of the series of enforceable future transfers. However, the fact that A preferred making a future gift to a present one suggests that they are not perfect substitutes; there are many reasons (including tax and liquidity considerations) why they might not be. Consequently, if A cannot bind himself to make a series of future gifts, he may be led to substitute a one-time transfer, the present value of which is less than that of the series of future gifts, although greater than that of a declared but unenforceable intention to make a series of future gifts. Thus, nonenforceability of gratuitous promises could tend to bias transfers excessively toward immediacy." [a] Posner, Gratuitous Promises in Economics and Law, 6 J. Legal Stud. 411, 411–13 (1977), reprinted in A. Kronman & R. Posner, The Economics of Contract Law 46–47 (1979).

NOTE

Consideration as Form. Under the bargain theory of consideration, can a gratuitous promise be made enforceable by a mere token payment, arranged by the parties for the sole purpose of satisfying the requirement of consideration? Holmes concluded that since courts would not in general "inquire into the amount of such consideration . . . , consideration is as much a form as a seal." Krell v. Codman, 154 Mass. 454, 28 N.E. 578 (1891). (The term "peppercorn" is often used to deride consideration that is of trifling value.) Will such a device be given effect?

There is some authority, most of it old, that it will be. E. g., Thomas v. Thomas, 2 Q.B. 851, 114 Eng.Rep. 330 (1842). Illustration 1 to the first Restatement § 84 reads:

> A wishes to make a binding promise to his son B to convey to B Blackacre, which is worth $5,000. Being advised that a gratuitous promise is not binding, A writes to B an offer to sell Blackacre for $1. B accepts. B's promise to pay $1 is sufficient consideration.

The Restatement Second takes the opposite view. Illustration 5 to § 71 reads:

> A desires to make a binding promise to give $1,000 to his son B. Being advised that a gratuitous promise is not binding, A offers to buy from B for $1,000 a book worth less than $1. B accepts the offer knowing that the purchase of the book is a mere pretense. There is no consideration for A's promise to pay $1,000.

For a case in support of this illustration, see Fischer v. Union Trust Co., 138 Mich. 612, 101 N.W. 852 (1904).

a. Reproduced by permission of the Journal of Legal Studies.

FIEGE v. BOEHM

Court of Appeals of Maryland, 1956.
210 Md. 352, 123 A.2d 316.

DELAPLAINE, Judge. This suit was brought in the Superior Court of Baltimore City by Hilda Louise Boehm against Louis Gail Fiege to recover for breach of a contract to pay the expenses incident to the birth of his bastard child and to provide for its support upon condition that she would refrain from prosecuting him for bastardy.

Plaintiff alleged in her declaration substantially as follows: (1) that early in 1951 defendant had sexual intercourse with her although she was unmarried, and as a result thereof she became pregnant, and defendant acknowledged that he was responsible for her pregnancy; (2) that on September 29, 1951, she gave birth to a female child; that defendant is the father of the child; and that he acknowledged on many occasions that he is its father; (3) that before the child was born, defendant agreed to pay all her medical and miscellaneous expenses and to compensate her for the loss of her salary caused by the child's birth, and also to pay her ten dollars per week for its support until it reached the age of 21, upon condition that she would not institute bastardy proceedings against him as long as he made the payments in accordance with the agreement; (4) that she placed the child for adoption on July 13, 1954, and she claimed the following sums: Union Memorial Hospital, $110; Florence Crittenton Home, $100; Dr. George Merrill, her physician, $50; medicines $70.-35; miscellaneous expenses, $20.45; loss of earnings for 26 weeks, $1,105; support of the child, $1,440; total, $2,895.80; and (5) that defendant paid her only $480, and she demanded that he pay her the further sum of $2,415.80, the balance due under the agreement, but he failed and refused to pay the same.

Defendant demurred to the declaration on the ground that it failed to allege that in September, 1953, plaintiff instituted bastardy proceedings against him in the Criminal Court of Baltimore, but since it had been found from blood tests that he could not have been the father of the child, he was acquitted of bastardy.[a] The Court sustained the demurrer with leave to amend.

Plaintiff then filed an amended declaration, which contained the additional allegation that, after the breach of the agreement by defendant, she filed a charge with the State's Attorney that defendant was the father of her bastard child; and that on October 8, 1953, the Criminal Court found defendant not guilty solely on a physician's testimony that "on the basis of certain blood tests made, the defendant

a. Such a demurrer was known at common law as a "speaking demurrer."

can be excluded as the father of the said child, which testimony is not conclusive upon a jury in a trial court."

Defendant also demurred to the amended declaration, but the Court overruled that demurrer.

Plaintiff, a typist, now over 35 years old, who has been employed by the Government in Washington and Baltimore for over thirteen years, testified in the Court below that she had never been married, but that at about midnight on January 21, 1951, defendant, after taking her to a moving picture theater on York Road and then to a restaurant, had sexual intercourse with her in his automobile. She further testified that he agreed to pay all her medical and hospital expenses, to compensate her for loss of salary caused by the pregnancy and birth, and to pay her ten dollars per week for the support of the child upon condition that she would refrain from instituting bastardy proceedings against him. She further testified that between September 17, 1951, and May, 1953, defendant paid her a total of $480.

Defendant admitted that he had taken plaintiff to restaurants, had danced with her several times, had taken her to Washington, and had brought her home in the country; but he asserted that he had never had sexual intercourse with her. He also claimed that he did not enter into any agreement with her. He admitted, however, that he had paid her a total of $480. His father also testified that he stated "that he did not want his mother to know, and if it were just kept quiet, kept principally away from his mother and the public and the courts, that he would take care of it."

Defendant further testified that in May 1953, he went to see plaintiff's physician to make inquiry about blood tests to show the paternity of the child; and that those tests were made and they indicated that it was not possible that he could have been the child's father. He then stopped making payments. Plaintiff thereupon filed a charge of bastardy with the State's Attorney.

The testimony which was given in the Criminal Court by Dr. Milton Sachs, hematologist at the University Hospital, was read to the jury in the Superior Court. In recent years the blood-grouping test has been employed in criminology, in the selection of donors for blood transfusions, and as evidence in paternity cases. The Landsteiner blood-grouping test is based on the medical theory that the red corpuscles in human blood contain two affirmative agglutinating substances, and that every individual's blood falls into one of the four classes and remains the same throughout life. According to Mendel's law of inheritance, this blood individuality is an hereditary characteristic which passes from parent to child, and no agglutinating substance can appear in the blood of a child which is not present in the blood of one of its parents. The four Landsteiner blood groups, designated as AB, A, B, and O, into which human blood is divided on the basis of the compatibility of the corpuscles and serum with the corpuscles and serum of other persons, are characterized by different combinations of two agglutinogens in the red blood cells and two agglutinins in the serum. Dr. Sachs reported that Fiege's blood group was Type O, Miss Boehm's was Type B, and the infant's was Type A. He further testified that on the basis of these tests, Fiege could not have been the father of the child, as it is impossible for a mating of Type O and Type B to result in a child of Type A.

Although defendant was acquitted by the Criminal Court, the Superior Court overruled his motion for a directed verdict. In the charge to the jury the Court instructed them that defendant's acquittal in the Criminal Court was not binding upon them. The jury found a verdict in favor of plaintiff for $2,415.80, the full amount of her claim.

Defendant filed a motion for judgment n. o. v. or a new trial. The Court overruled that motion also, and entered judgment on the verdict of the jury. Defendant appealed from that judgment.

Defendant contends that, even if he entered into the contract as alleged, it was not enforceable, because plaintiff's forbearance to prosecute was not based on a valid claim, and hence the contract was without consideration. . . .

It was originally held at common law that a child born out of wedlock is *filius nullius*, and a putative father is not under any legal liability to contribute to the support of his illegitimate child, and his promise to do so is unenforceable because it is based on purely a moral obligation. . . .

However, where statutes are in force to compel the father of a bastard to contribute to its support, the courts have invariably held that a contract by the putative father with the mother of his bastard child to provide for the support of the child upon the agreement of the mother to refrain from invoking the bastardy statute against the father, or to abandon proceedings already commenced, is supported by sufficient consideration. Jangraw v. Perkins, 77 Vt. 375, 60 A. 385; Beach v. Voegtlen, 68 N.J.L. 472, 53 A. 695; Thayer v. Thayer, 189 N.C. 502, 127 S.E. 553, 39 A.L.R. 428.

In Maryland it is now provided by statute that whenever a person is found guilty of bastardy, the court shall issue an order directing such person (1) to pay for the maintenance and support of the child until it reaches the age of eighteen years, such sum as may be agreed upon, if consent proceedings be had, or in the absence of agreement, such sum as the court may fix, with due regard to the circumstances of the accused person; and (2) to give bond to the State of Maryland in such penalty as the court may fix, with good and sufficient securities, conditioned on making the payments required by the court's order, or any amendments thereof. Failure to give such bond shall be punished by commitment in the jail or the House of

Correction until bond is given but not exceeding two years. Code Supp.1955, art. 12, § 8.

Prosecutions for bastardy are treated in Maryland as criminal proceedings, but they are actually civil in purpose. . . . Accordingly a contract by the putative father of an illegitimate child to provide for its support upon condition that bastardy proceedings will not be instituted is a compromise of civil injuries resulting from a criminal act, and not a contract to compound a criminal prosecution, and if it is fair and reasonable, it is in accord with the Bastardy Act and the public policy of the State.

Of course, a contract of a putative father to provide for the support of his illegitimate child must be based, like any other contract, upon sufficient consideration. . . .

In 1867 the Maryland Court of Appeals, in the opinion delivered by Judge Bartol in Hartle v. Stahl, 27 Md. 157, 172, held: (1) that forbearance to assert a claim before institution of suit, if not in fact a legal claim, is not of itself sufficient consideration to support a promise; but (2) that a compromise of a doubtful claim or a relinquishment of a pending suit is good consideration for a promise; and (3) that in order to support a compromise, it is sufficient that the parties entering into it thought at the time that there was a *bona fide* question between them, although it may eventually be found that there was in fact no such question.

We have thus adopted the rule that the surrender of, or forbearance to assert an invalid claim by one who has not an honest and reasonable belief in its possible validity is not sufficient consideration for a contract. 1 Restatement, Contracts, sec. 76(b). We combine the subjective requisite that the claim be *bona fide* with the objective requisite that it must have a reasonable basis of support. Accordingly a promise not to prosecute a claim which is not founded in good faith does not of itself give a right of action on an agreement to pay for refraining from so acting, because a release from mere annoyance and unfounded litigation does not furnish valuable consideration.

Professor Williston was not entirely certain whether the test of reasonableness is based upon the intelligence of the claimant himself, who may be an ignorant person with no knowledge of law and little sense as to facts; but he seemed inclined to favor the view that "the claim forborne must be neither absurd in fact from the standpoint of a reasonable man in the position of the claimant, nor, obviously unfounded in law to one who has an elementary knowledge of legal principles." 1 Williston on Contracts, Rev.Ed., sec. 135. We agree that while stress is placed upon the honesty and good faith of the claimant, forbearance to prosecute a claim is insufficient consideration if the claim forborne is so lacking in foundation as to make its assertion incompatible with honesty and a reasonable degree of intelligence. Thus, if the mother of a bastard knows that there is no foundation, either in law or fact, for a charge against a certain man that he is the father of the child, but that man promises to pay her in order to prevent bastardy proceedings against him, the forbearance to institute proceedings is not sufficient consideration.

On the other hand, forbearance to sue for a lawful claim or demand is sufficient consideration for a promise to pay for the forbearance if the party forbearing had an honest intention to prosecute litigation which is not frivolous, vexatious, or unlawful, and which he believed to be well founded. Snyder v. Cearfoss, 187 Md. 635, 643, 51 A. 2d 264; Pullman Co. v. Ray, 201 Md. 268, 94 A.2d 266. Thus the promise of a woman who is expecting an illegitimate child that she will not institute bastardy proceedings against a certain man is sufficient consideration for his promise to pay for the child's support, even though it may not be certain whether the man is the father or whether the prosecution would be successful, if she makes the charge in good faith. . . .

Another analogous case is Thompson v. Nelson, 28 Ind. 431. There the plaintiff sought to recover back money which he had paid to compromise a prosecution for bastardy. He claimed that the prosecuting witness was not pregnant and therefore the prosecution was fraudulent. It was held by the Supreme Court of Indiana, however, that the settlement of the prosecution was a good consideration for the payment of the money and it could not be recovered back, inasmuch as it appeared from the evidence that the prosecution was instituted in good faith, and at that time there was reason to believe that the prosecuting witness was pregnant, although it was found out afterwards that she was not pregnant. [The court's summary of a similar decision on similar facts in Illinois is here omitted. Heaps v. Dunham, 95 Ill. 583, 590.]

In the case at bar there was no proof of fraud or unfairness. Assuming that the hematologists were accurate in their laboratory tests and findings, nevertheless plaintiff gave testimony which indicated that she made the charge of bastardy against defendant in good faith. For these reasons the Court acted properly in overruling the demurrer to the amended declaration and the motion for a directed verdict.

[The court's discussion of alleged errors in the trial court's charge to the jury is here omitted.]

As we have found no reversible error in the rulings and instructions of the trial court, we will affirm the judgment entered on the verdict of the jury.

Judgment affirmed, with costs.

NOTES

(1) *The Objective Requisite.* What was the consideration for Fiege's promise? Boehm's forbearance to press a claim that later turned out to be

invalid? According to Restatement, § 76, "forbearance to assert an invalid claim . . . by one who has not an honest and reasonable belief in its possible validity" is not consideration. Examine Restatement Second, § 74(1). What has happened to the requirement of the first Restatement, that the forbearing party have a reasonable belief in his position? On a close reading of the main case, does it appear that the new Restatement rule is substantially identical to the rule of the case?

It is a commonplace observation in judicial opinions that the law favors private settlements of disputed claims, both to alleviate discord and to eliminate sources of uncertainty. One way to favor settlements, illustrated in Fiege v. Boehm, is to hold the promisor (Fiege), who promises to pay in settlement of the claim, bound to his promise. Another way is taken up at page 433 infra.

(2) *Other Questions.* Did Boehm fail to disclose any important fact at the time Fiege made his promise? Is it arguable that her failure amounted to a misrepresentation? Misrepresentation by non-disclosure is dealt with at page 413 infra. Could Boehm have enforced such promises against two men?

If Fiege had promised to pay for 21 years in consideration of Boehm's forbearance for that period of time, he might have argued that he could renege on his promise at any time before she had given *all* the consideration, that is, had foreborne for 21 years. (Could William E. Story have reneged on his promise at any time before his nephew turned 21?) This argument is considered in Chapter 4, Section 4. Note, however, that Boehm's lawyer avoided this argument by alleging, in effect, that Fiege promised to pay her for 21 years in consideration of her forbearance for "as long as he made the payments in accordance with the agreement." If that was his promise, she had given all of the consideration as of May, 1953, when he stopped making the payments.

(3) *The Case of the Church's Immunity.* Ralston suffered injuries, as she alleged, in a fall on a church stairway, which resulted from its negligence. An adjuster for the church's insurance company called on her and promised that it would pay all her expenses if she would refrain from suing the church or the insurer. Not being paid, she sued the insurer on its promise. The trial court sustained its demurrer to the plaintiff's petition alleging these facts, and she appealed. *Held:* Reversed. The insurer based its argument on holdings of the court that churches and charitable organizations are immune from liability for their torts. Referring to other holdings, however, the court concluded that a claim by the plaintiff, based on negligence, would not have been "obviously invalid or frivolous." If it promised to pay the plaintiff, the court said, the insurer was hardly in a position to make that contention. Ralston v. Mathew, 173 Kan. 550, 250 P. 2d 841 (1952).

Was the decision in this case parallel to that in Fiege v. Boehm? Of course there was this difference: the challenge to Boehm's claim was based on its factual weakness, whereas Ralston's claim was questioned on a legal ground. Should this make a difference in the standard applied? Should the viewpoint of a layman or that of a lawyer be used to answer the question whether or not a claim was "obviously invalid" in law?[a] Do you see any harmful result for the law of *torts* that may result from a decision like Ralston v. Mathew?

NEWMAN & SNELL'S STATE BANK v. HUNTER, 243 Mich. 331, 220 N.W. 665, 59 A.L.R. 311 (1928). [Lee Hunter died in January, 1926, owing $3,700 to Newman & Snell's State Bank. His note for that amount was secured by 50 shares of stock in the Hunter Company, which had been pledged to the bank. The company continued to do business as long as Hunter lived, but afterward it was liquidated, and its debts proved to be greater than its assets. Hunter's estate was also insolvent: there was not enough to pay his funeral expenses and the statutory allowance for his widow, Zennetta. On March 1 there was a transaction between Zennetta and the bank, on the basis of which it now sues her. The transaction was described as follows, in an agreed statement of facts: "the defendant gave the plaintiff the note described in the plaintiff's declaration in this cause, and the plaintiff surrendered to her therefor, and, in consideration thereof, the note of said Lee C. Hunter. The defendant also paid the plaintiff the earned interest due on the deceased's note." Apparently the bank retained the Hunter Company stock, as security for Zennetta's note. From judgment for the plaintiff, the defendant appealed.]

FELLOWS, J. [The court first considered the question whether or not the bank's surrender of Hunter's note was a "sufficient consideration" for Zennetta's note. Conceding a conflict in the precedents, the court ruled that it was not.] Here we have the widow's note given to take up the note of her insolvent husband, a worthless piece of paper. . . . [I]t seems clear to me that the transaction was without consideration. [Then the court considered and rejected the bank's contention that it had released a security interest in the pledged stock.] Stripped of all legal fiction, the cold facts are that, when the negotiations opened, plaintiff had this stock and the worthless note of defendant's husband. When they ended, the bank still had the stock and defendant's note.

[Reversed.]

NOTES

(1) *Questions.* Was this decision consistent with the rules stated in Restatement Second, §§ 71 and 79? Would the decision have been the same if Hunter's estate had been just large enough to pay the widow's allowance, all his debts, and a $1,000 bequest to Zennetta? If it had been large enough to pay a portion (say 10%) of his debts, but not all of them?

a. See Renney v. Kimberly, 211 Ga. 396, 86 S.E.2d 217 (1955), in which a deed of a non-existent interest in land was held not to be consideration for promises made by the grantees to the grantor. The court analyzed its prior decisions to determine that the deed conveyed no interest.

Suppose that when Zennetta gave the bank her note it had handed her, in exchange, a document releasing its claim against the estate. What result under Restatement Second, § 74? (The bank had a "valid" claim against Hunter's estate, be it noted, only there was nothing to pay it with.) Is the decision as it stands an example of "widow's law"?

(2) *"Sufficiency" of Consideration.* The first Restatement embodied a concept of the "sufficiency" of consideration. Although consideration did not have to be "adequate," it had to be "sufficient." See Restatement §§ 76–81. The Restatement Second abandons this concept. Under its terminology the question is simply whether there is "consideration," with no qualifying adjective.

FEINBERG v. PFEIFFER CO.

Saint Louis Court of Appeals, Missouri, 1959.
322 S.W.2d 163.

Action on alleged contract by defendant to pay plaintiff a specified monthly amount upon her retirement from defendant's employ. The Circuit Court, City of St. Louis, rendered judgment for plaintiff, and defendant appealed.

DOERNER, Commissioner. This is a suit brought in the Circuit Court of the City of St. Louis by plaintiff, a former employee of the defendant corporation, on an alleged contract whereby defendant agreed to pay plaintiff the sum of $200 per month for life upon her retirement. A jury being waived, the case was tried by the court alone. Judgment below was for plaintiff for $5,100, the amount of the pension claimed to be due as of the date of the trial together with interest thereon, and defendant duly appealed.

The parties are in substantial agreement on the essential facts. Plaintiff began working for the defendant, a manufacturer of pharmaceuticals, in 1910, when she was but 17 years of age. By 1947 she had attained the position of bookkeeper, officer manager, and assistant treasurer of the defendant, and owned 70 shares of its stock out of a total of 6,503 shares issued and outstanding. Twenty shares had been given to her by the defendant or its then president, she had purchased 20, and the remaining 30 she had acquired by a stock split or stock dividend. Over the years she received substantial dividends on the stock she owned, as did all of the other stockholders. Also, in addition to her salary, plaintiff from 1937 to 1949, inclusive, received each year a bonus varying in amount from $300 in the beginning to $2,000 in the later years.

On December 27, 1947, the annual meeting of the defendant's Board of Directors was held at the Company's offices in St. Louis, presided over by Max Lippman, its then president and largest individual stockholder. The other directors present were George L. Marcus, Sidney Harris, Sol Flammer, and Walter Weinstock, who, with

Max Lippman, owned 5,007 of the 6,503 shares then issued and outstanding. At that meeting the Board of Directors adopted the following resolution, which, because it is the crux of the case, we quote in full:

"The Chairman thereupon pointed out that the Assistant Treasurer, Mrs. Anna Sacks Feinberg, has given the corporation many years of long and faithful service. Not only has she served the corporation devotedly, but with exceptional ability and skill. The President pointed out that although all of the officers and directors sincerely hoped and desired that Mrs. Feinberg would continue in her present position for as long as she felt able, nevertheless, in view of the length of service which she has contributed provision should be made to afford her retirement privileges and benefits which should become a firm obligation of the corporation to be available to her whenever she should see fit to retire from active duty, however many years in the future such retirement may become effective. It was, accordingly, proposed that Mrs. Feinberg's salary which is presently $350.00 per month, be increased to $400.00 per month, and that Mrs. Feinberg would be given the privilege of retiring from active duty at any time she may elect to see fit so to do upon a retirement pay of $200.00 per month for life, with the distinct understanding that the retirement plan is merely being adopted at the present time in order to afford Mrs. Feinberg security for the future and in the hope that her active services will continue with the corporation for many years to come. After due discussion and consideration, and upon motion duly made and seconded, it was—

"Resolved, that the salary of Anna Sacks Feinberg be increased from $350.00 to $400.00 per month and that she be afforded the privilege of retiring from active duty in the corporation at any time she may elect to see fit so to do upon retirement pay of $200.00 per month, for the remainder of her life."

At the request of Mr. Lippman his sons-in-law, Messrs. Harris and Flammer, called upon the plaintiff at her apartment on the same day to advise her of the passage of the resolution. Plaintiff testified on cross-examination that she had no prior information that such a pension plan was contemplated, that it came as a surprise to her, and that she would have continued in her employment whether or not such a resolution had been adopted. It is clear from the evidence that there was no contract, oral or written, as to plaintiff's length of employment, and that she was free to quit, and the defendant to discharge her, at any time.

Plaintiff did continue to work for the defendant through June 30, 1949, on which date she retired. In accordance with the foregoing resolution, the defendant began paying her the sum of $200 on the first of each month. Mr. Lippman died on November 18, 1949, and was succeeded as president of the company by his widow. Because of an illness, she retired from that office and was succeeded in October, 1953, by her son-in-law, Sidney M. Harris. Mr. Harris testified that while Mrs. Lippman had been president she signed the monthly pension check paid plaintiff, but fussed about doing so, and considered the payments as gifts. After his election, he stated, a new accounting firm employed by the defendant questioned the validity of the payments to plaintiff on several occasions, and in the Spring of 1956, upon its recommendation, he consulted the Company's then attorney, Mr. Ralph Kalish. Harris testified that both Ernst and Ernst, the accounting firm, and Kalish told him there was no need of giving plaintiff the money. He also stated that he had concurred in the view that the payments to plaintiff were mere gratuities rather than amounts due under a contractual obligation, and that following his discussion with the Company's attorney plaintiff was sent a check for $100 on April 1, 1956. Plaintiff declined to accept the reduced amount, and this action followed. Additional facts will be referred to later in this opinion. . . .

Appellant's next complaint is that there was insufficient evidence to support the court's findings that plaintiff would not have quit defendant's employ had she not known and relied upon the promise of defendant to pay her $200 a month for life, and the finding that, from her voluntary retirement until April 1, 1956, plaintiff relied upon the continued receipt of the pension installments. The trial court so found, and, in our opinion, justifiably so. Plaintiff testified, and was corroborated by Harris, defendant's witness, that knowledge of the passage of the resolution was communicated to her on December 27, 1947, the very day it was adopted. She was told at that time by Harris and Flammer, she stated, that she could take the pension as of that day, if she wished. She testified further that she continued to work for another year and a half, through June 30, 1949; that at that time her health was good and she could have continued to work, but that after working for almost forty years she thought she would take a rest. Her testimony continued:

"Q. Now, what was the reason—I'm sorry. Did you then quit the employment of the company after you—after this year and a half? A. Yes.

"Q. What was the reason that you left? A. Well, I thought almost forty years, it was a long time and I thought I would take a little rest.

"Q. Yes. A. And with the pension and what earnings my husband had, we figured we could get along.

"Q. Did you rely upon this pension? A. We certainly did.

"Q. Being paid? A. Very much so. We relied upon it because I was positive that I was going to get it as long as I lived.

"Q. Would you have left the employment of the company at that time had it not been for this pension? A. No.

"Mr. Allen: Just a minute, I object to that as calling for a conclusion and conjecture on the part of this witness.

"The Court: It will be overruled.

"Q. (Mr. Agatstein continuing): Go ahead, now. The question is whether you would have quit the employment of the company at that time had you not relied upon this pension plan? A. No, I wouldn't.

"Q. You would not have. Did you ever seek employment while this pension was being paid to you—A. (interrupting): No.

"Q. Wait a minute, at any time prior—at any other place? A. No, sir.

"Q. Were you able to hold any other employment during that time? A. Yes, I think so.

"Q. Was your health good? A. My health was good."

It is obvious from the foregoing that there was ample evidence to support the findings of fact made by the court below.

We come, then, to the basic issue in the case. While otherwise defined in defendant's third and fourth assignments of error, it is thus succinctly stated in the argument in its brief: " . . . whether plaintiff has proved that she has a right to recover from defendant based upon a legally binding contractual obligation to pay her $200 per month for life."

It is defendant's contention, in essence, that the resolution adopted by its Board of Directors was a mere promise to make a gift, and that no contract resulted either thereby, or when plaintiff retired, because there was no consideration given or paid by the plaintiff. It urges that a promise to make a gift is not binding unless supported by a legal consideration; that the only apparent consideration for the adoption of the foregoing resolution was the "many years of long and faithful service" expressed therein; and that past services are not a valid consideration for a promise. Defendant argues further that there is nothing in the resolution which made its effectiveness conditional upon plaintiff's continued employment, that she was not under contract to work for any length of time but was free to quit whenever she wished, and that she had no contractual right to her position and could have been discharged at any time.

Plaintiff concedes that a promise based upon past services would be without consideration, but contends that there were two other elements which supplied the required element: First, the continuation by plaintiff in the employ of the defendant for the period from December 27, 1947, the date when the resolution was adopted, until the date of her retirement on June 30, 1949. And, second, her change of position, i. e., her retirement, and the abandonment by her of her opportunity to continue in gainful employment, made in reliance on defendant's promise to pay her $200 per month for life.

We must agree with the defendant that the evidence does not support the first of these contentions. There is no language in the resolution predicating plaintiff's right to a pension upon her continued employment. She was not required to work for the defendant for any period of time as a condition to gaining such retirement benefits. She was told that she could quit the day upon which the resolution was adopted, as she herself testified, and it is clear from her own testimony that she made no promise or agreement to continue in the employ of the defendant in return for its promise to pay her a pension. Hence there was lacking that mutuality of obligation which is essential to the validity of a contract. . . .

Consideration for a promise has been defined in the Restatement of the Law of Contracts, Section 75, as:

"(1) Consideration for a promise is

(a) an act other than a promise, or

(b) a forbearance, or

(c) the creation, modification or destruction of a legal relation, or

(d) a return promise,

bargained for and given in exchange for the promise."

As the parties agree, the consideration sufficient to support a contract may be either a benefit to the promisor or a loss or detriment to the promisee. . . .

[The rest of the opinion in this case, dealing with Feinberg's second contention, is at p. 96 infra.]

NOTES

(1) *The Missing Ingredient.* Why was not Feinberg's 37 years of service, prior to the resolution of December 27, 1947, consideration for Pfeiffer's promise? Why was not her 18 months of service, subsequent to the resolution, consideration? Why was not her retiring consideration?

(2) *Counselling.* Suppose that Mr. Lippman had called in his lawyer in December, 1947, and said, "I want you to draw up a resolution that will make it sure that Mrs. Feinberg will get a pension of $200 a month as long as she lives." Could the promise have been made enforceable under the doctrine of consideration? How? Would it have helped to have reworded the resolution to include the words, "*in consideration of* her many years of long and faithful service"? See Perreault v. Hall, 94 N.H. 191, 49 A.2d 812 (1946).

(3) *"Moral Obligation."* The contention that a promise is enforceable if it is made in satisfaction of a "moral obligation," such as the one that arguably arose out of Feinberg's "many years of faithful service," is considered at length in Section 6 of this chapter.

KIRKSEY v. KIRKSEY

Supreme Court of Alabama, 1845.
8 Ala. 131.

The plaintiff was the wife of defendant's brother, but had for some time been a widow, and had several children. In 1840, the plaintiff resided on public land, under a contract of lease, she had held over, and was comfortably settled, and would have attempted to secure the land she lived on. The defendant resided in Talladega County, some sixty or seventy miles off. On the 10th October, 1840, he wrote to her the following letter:

"Dear Sister Antillico,—Much to my mortification, I heard that brother Henry was dead, and one of his children. I know that your situation is one of grief and difficulty. You had a bad chance before, but a great deal worse now. I should like to come and see you, but cannot with convenience at present. . . . I do not know whether you have a preference on the place you live on or not. If you had, I would advise you to obtain your preference, and sell the land and quit the country, as I understand it is very unhealthy, and I know society is very bad. If you will come down and see me, I will let you have a place to raise your family, and I have more open land than I can tend; and on account of your situation, and that of your family, I feel like I want you and the children to do well."

Within a month or two after the receipt of this letter, the plaintiff abandoned her possession, without disposing of it, and removed with her family, to the residence of the defendant, who put her in comfortable houses, and gave her land to cultivate for two years, at the end of which time he notified her to remove, and put her in a house, not comfortable, in the woods, which he afterwards required her to leave.

A verdict being found for the plaintiff, for $200, the above facts were agreed, and if they will sustain the action, the judgment is to be affirmed, otherwise it is to be reversed.

ORMOND, J. The inclination of my mind is that the loss and inconvenience which the plaintiff sustained in breaking up and moving to the defendant's, a distance of sixty miles, is a sufficient consideration to support the promise to furnish her with a house, and land to cultivate, until she could raise her family. My brothers, however, think that the promise on the part of the defendant was a mere gratuity, and that an action will not lie for its breach. The judgment of the court below must therefore be reversed, pursuant to the agreement of the parties.

NOTES

(1) *Characterization of "If" Clauses.* How did the court read the words, "If you will come down and see me, I will let you have a place to

raise your family"? As words of bargain for an exchange or of condition to a gratuitous promise of a gift? Was not the benefit to the brother-in-law comparable to the benefit to the uncle in Hamer v. Sidway, p. 44 supra?

(2) *Reliance as a Basis.* Should "Sister Antillico" be allowed to recover on the ground that she relied on the promise, even though her reliance was not bargained for? This question will be taken up in the next section of this book.

(3) *Problem.* A father and a daughter became estranged after the mother had divorced the father, and the daughter refused to see the father. The father then wrote to his daughter: "If you will meet me at Tiffany's next Monday at noon, I will buy you the emerald ring advertised in this week's New Yorker." The daughter came to Tiffany's at the time specified, and met her father there, but he failed to buy her the promised ring. Bargained-for exchange or conditional gratuitous promise?

Williston [a] put this case: "If a benevolent man says to a tramp,—'if you go around the corner to the clothing shop there, you may purchase an overcoat on my credit,' no reasonable person would understand that the short walk was requested as the consideration for the promise, but that in the event of the tramp going to the shop the promisor would make him a gift." 1 Williston § 112. Is the situation of the daughter distinguishable from that of the tramp?

BROADNAX v. LEDBETTER

Supreme Court of Texas, 1907.
100 Tex. 375, 99 S.W. 1111.

[Action by Broadnax to recover a reward of $500 offered by Ledbetter for the recapture and return to the Dallas County jail of a prisoner, Vann, who had escaped therefrom. The defendant interposed demurrers on the ground that the petition stated no cause of action because it was not alleged that the plaintiff had knowledge or notice of the reward when the escaped prisoner was captured and returned to jail by the plaintiff.

[These demurrers were sustained and judgment was entered dismissing plaintiff's case. Plaintiff appeals. The following question was certified: Was notice or knowledge to plaintiff of the existence of the reward when the capture was made essential to his right to recover?]

a. Samuel Williston (1861–1963) joined the faculty of the Harvard Law School in 1890, after practicing law for a short period in Boston, and taught there until his retirement in 1938. His principal fields were contracts and sales. His multi-volume work, A Treatise on the Law of Contracts, was first published in 1920 and became one of the most widely used legal treatises in the United States. He was the Reporter for the Restatement of Contracts and the draftsman of several uniform laws, including the Uniform Sales Act.

WILLIAMS, J. . . . Upon the question stated there is a conflict among the authorities in other states. All that have been cited or found by us have received due consideration, and our conclusion is that those holding the affirmative are correct. The liability for a reward of this kind must be created, if at all, by contract. There is no rule of law which imposes it except that which enforces contracts voluntarily entered into. A mere offer or promise to pay does not give rise to a contract. That requires the assent or meeting of two minds, and therefore is not complete until the offer is accepted. Such an offer as that alleged may be accepted by anyone who performs the service called for when the acceptor knows that it has been made and acts in performance of it, but not otherwise. He may do such things as are specified in the offer, but, in so doing, does not act in performance of it, and therefore does not accept it, when he is ignorant of its having been made. There is no such mutual agreement of minds as is essential to a contract. The offer is made to anyone who will accept it by performing the specified acts, and it only becomes binding when another mind has embraced and accepted it. The mere doing of the specified things without reference to the offer is not the consideration for which it calls. . . .

Some of the authorities taking the opposite view seem to think that the principles of contracts do not control the question, and in one of them, at least, it is said that "the sum offered is but a boon, gratuity, or bounty, generally offered in a spirit of liberality, and not as a mere price, or a just equivalent simply for the favor or service requested, to be agreed or assented to by the person performing it, but, when performed by him, as justly and legally entitling him to a fulfillment of the promise, without any regard whatever to the motive or inducement which prompted him to perform it." Eagle v. Smith, 4 Houst., Del., 293. But the law does not force persons to bestow boons, gratuities, or bounties merely because they have promised to do so. They must be legally bound before that can be done. It may be true that the motive of the performer in rendering service is not of controlling effect as is said in some of the authorities above cited in pointing out the misapprehension of the case of Williams v. Carwardine, 6 English Ruling Cases 133, into which some of the courts have fallen. But this does not reach the question whether or not a contractual obligation is essential.

Other authorities say that it is immaterial to the offerer that the person doing that which the offer calls for did not know of its existence; that the services are as valuable to him when rendered without as when rendered with knowledge. Dawkins v. Sappington, 26 Ind. 199; Auditor v. Ballard, 9 Bush., Ky., 572, 15 Am.Rep. 728. But the value to the offerer of the acts done by the other party is not the test. They may in supposable cases be of no value to him, or may be no more valuable to him than to the person doing them. He is responsible, if at all, because, by his promise, he has induced another to do the specified things. Unless so induced, the other is in no worse position than if no reward had been offered. The acting upon this inducement is what supplies, at once, the mutual assent and the contemplated consideration. Without the legal obligation thus arising from contract there is nothing which the law enforces.

Reasons have also been put forward of a supposed public policy, assuming that persons will be stimulated by the enforcement of offers of rewards in such cases to aid in the detection of crime and the arrest and punishment of criminals. But, aside from the fact that the principles of law to be laid down cannot on any sound system of reasoning be restricted to offers made for such purposes, it is difficult to see how the activities of people can be excited by offers of rewards of which they know nothing. If this reason had foundation in fact, it would hardly justify the courts in requiring private citizens to minister to the supposed public policy by paying rewards merely because they have made offers to pay upon which no one has acted. Courts can only enforce liabilities which have in some way been fixed by the law. While we have seen no such distinction suggested, it may well be supposed that a person might become legally entitled to a reward for arresting a criminal, although he knew nothing of its having been offered where it is or was offered in accordance with law by the government. A legal right might in such a case be given by law without the aid of contract. But the liability of the individual citizen must arise from a contract binding him to pay.

The question is answered in the affirmative. [Judgment affirmed.]

NOTES

(1) *Knowledge of Offer.* Were Broadnax's acts "bargained for"? Could he have recovered if he had captured Vann while ignorant of the reward but had learned of it before returning him to jail? Is his solution to release the criminal and capture him again? See Restatement Second, § 51. Could Broadnax have recovered if he had known of the reward but had captured Vann and turned him in because he was a close friend and wished to save him from mob violence? See Restatement Second, § 81(2). Could he have recovered if he had said, when he turned Vann in, that he did not want the reward? See Corbin, § 58. For an interesting reward case, see Taft v. Hyatt, 105 Kan. 35, 180 P. 213 (1919).

The court's dictum that if the reward were "offered in accordance with law by the government . . . , [a] right might in such a case be given by law without the aid of contract," was followed in Choice v. City of Dallas, 210 S.W. 753 (Tex.Civ.App.1919), involving the offer of a reward by an ordinance of the city of Dallas, which the court characterized as "in the nature of a bounty." In some legal systems, including the German, a promise of reward is treated, "not as an offer which would require acceptance in order to ripen into a contract, but as a unilateral jural act which as such is effective and binding without acceptance." 1 R. Schlesinger (ed.), Formation of Contracts: A Study of the Common Core of Legal Systems 101–02

(1968). Would such a concept be a desirable one in our law? (Can a helpful analogy be found in a conditional promise under seal?)

(2) *Problem.* Diamond Jim III, a rock fish, was tagged and placed in the Chesapeake Bay on June 19 by the American Brewery in connection with its Third Annual American Beer Fishing Derby. Under the Derby's well-publicized rules, the person who caught Diamond Jim III would receive a cash prize of $25,000. On August 6, William Simmons set out to go fishing in the Bay. He had heard of the contest, but did not have it in mind on that day. He caught Diamond Jim III, and although he at first took little notice of the tag, he realized upon reexamining it a half hour later that he had caught the prize fish. Is Simmons legally entitled to the prize? See Simmons v. United States, 308 F.2d 160 (4th Cir. 1962); cf. "Industrial America" v. Fulton Industries, 285 A.2d 412 (Del.1971).

(3) *Who Can Accept?* Generally, an offer can be accepted only by one whom it invites to furnish the consideration. The classic case is Boulton v. Jones, 2 H. & N. 564 (1857). Jones, a regular customer of Brocklehurst, a pipe hose manufacturer with whom he had a running account, sent an order for leather hose addressed to Brocklehurst. Earlier the same day Boulton, Brocklehurst's foreman and manager, had bought the entire business including stock in trade. Boulton furnished the hose without notifying Jones of the change in ownership. When Jones refused to pay, Boulton sued for the price. *Held*: For Jones, Bramwell, B., noted that, "When a contract is made, in which the personality of the contracting party is or may be of importance, as a contract with a man to write a book, or the like, or where there might be a set-off, no other person can interpose and adopt the contract." If Jones had used or disposed of the goods, Boulton's remedy would be in quasi contract for their reasonable value, not the price. (See Section 5, Restitution as a Basis for Recovery.) Suppose, however, that Jones still had the goods and was able to return them, but did not offer to do so. Would there be a contract? This case is criticized in Williams, Mistake as to Party in the Law of Contract II, 23 Can.B.Rev. 380, 383 (1945).

SECTION 3. PROMISE FOR PROMISE

We have already seen how, in the historical development of the action of assumpsit as a general basis for the enforcement of promises, courts came to recognize that the consideration for a promise could be found in a return promise, even if not even partly performed (see p. 43 supra). But what rationale lies behind the enforcement of a promise when the promisee cannot show that he has conferred a benefit upon the promisor nor even that he has done anything in reliance on the promise? If one of the parties to an exchange of promises has second thoughts about the transaction the instant after the exchange has occurred, why should he not be allowed to retract his promise without liability?

Consider this simple example. W. O. Lucy met with A. H. Zehmer and his wife Ida and arranged for the sale to Lucy of a farm owned by the Zehmers. The Zehmers promised to convey the land, and Lucy promised to pay $50,000. When the Zehmers refused to convey, Lucy sued for specific performance. The Zehmers claimed that, before they had left Lucy after making the agreement, they had told him that they would not perform. Lucy claimed that the Zehmers had not told him this until three days after the agreement, and that in the meantime he had arranged to raise half of the money from his brother and had employed an attorney to examine the title. The Supreme Court of Appeals of Virginia held that Lucy was entitled to specific performance. Since there had been a bargained-for exchange of promises, the Zehmers' refusal came too late even on their version of the facts. (The opinion, which gives other salient facts, appears at p. 173 infra.)

Why should Lucy be allowed to enforce a promise when the Zehmers had in no way benefited and Lucy had, on the Zehmers' version of the facts, in no way relied to his detriment? Would it not be better to require Lucy to prove that his version of the facts was correct and that he had relied upon the Zehmers' promise? How much reliance would you require? Would it be enough if Lucy had testified, without contradiction, that he would have made an offer on another farm had the Zehmers not agreed to sell him theirs, and that the other farm had been sold before they told him that they would not perform? Would promisees such as Lucy be as safe in relying on promises if those promises were enforceable only on proof of reliance? For some answers to these questions, see Fuller and Perdue, The Reliance Interest in Contract Damages, 46 Yale L.J. 52, 61–62 (1936).

Restatement Second, § 71 makes it clear that the consideration for a promise can be found in a return promise. With some exceptions, "a promise which is bargained for is consideration if, but only if, the promised performance would be consideration." The following cases explore the exceptions.

NOTES

(1) *Unilateral and Bilateral Contracts.* A distinction between "unilateral" and "bilateral" contracts has long had currency. In a unilateral contract only one party makes promises; in a bilateral contract both parties make promises. The relationships between the parties in the two types of contract can be analyzed in terms of *right* and *duty*.

A is said to have a *right* that B shall do an act when, if B does not do the act, A can initiate legal proceedings against B, and B in such a situation is said to have a *duty* to do the act. *Right* and *duty* are therefore correlatives. In this strict sense there can never be a *right* without a *duty*, nor a *duty* without a *right*. The *right-duty* relationship is one between two parties. The *right* describes the relationship from one end and the *duty* from the other. Since, in a "unilateral" contract there is a promise on one side only, there is a *duty* on one side only, and a *right* on the other side; and since in a "bilateral" contract there is a promise on each side, there is a *right* and a *duty* on each side. The Restatement Second abandons the use of the terms "unilateral" and "bilateral," "because of doubt as to the utility of the distinction, often treated as fundamental, between the two types." Reporter's Note to Restatement Second, § 1.

For the precise use of terms such as *right* and *duty* the legal profession is indebted to the work of Professor Wesley Newcomb Hohfeld,[a] whose system of "Hohfeldian terminology" is set forth in Hohfeld, Fundamental Legal Conceptions (1923). In this terminology the offeree has, before the contract is made, a *power* to create a contract by means of acceptance. A *power* is the capacity to change a legal relationship. See Corbin, Legal Analysis and Terminology, 29 Yale L.J. 163 (1919); Goble, The Sanction of a Duty, 37 Yale L.J. 426 (1928).

(2) *Conditional Promises.* A promisor, such as Lucy, who seeks the other party's promise in return for his own promise is not, to be sure, unconcerned with the other party's performance of the return promise. The difference between Lucy's situation and that of a promisor, such as Ledbetter in Broadnax v. Ledbetter (p. 65 supra), of the variety encountered in the preceding section of the casebook, is that Lucy wants a return promise in *addition* to that performance. Both Ledbetter and Lucy want some assurance that they will get something for their money. Ledbetter's assurance that he will not have to pay the reward unless Vann is captured follows from the doctrine of consideration itself: his promise to pay the reward is not enforceable unless Vann is captured. If Lucy's promise to pay for the Zehmer's farm becomes enforceable merely on the Zehmer's making their promise in return, how is Lucy assured that he will not have to pay the price unless he gets the farm?[a] The solution to this problem involves aspects of the performance, as distinguished from the formation, of a contract and will not be considered in detail until Chapter 8. However, a brief discussion of the solution may be helpful, even at this early stage.

The solution involves the concept of a *condition.* Even though a promise is enforceable, it may still be conditional in that its performance will become due only if a particular event, known as a "condition," occurs. This does not mean that the promise is not enforceable until the event occurs, but only that the event must occur before the promisor must perform. Suppose that a home owner pays $1,000 to an insurance company in return for

a. Wesley Newcomb Hohfeld (1879–1918) practiced law briefly in San Francisco before joining the Stanford law faculty in 1905. In 1914 he left Stanford to teach at Yale until his death at the age of thirty-nine. He made a lasting contribution to legal literature through his development of the eight terms of "Hohfeldian terminology" in his book Fundamental Legal Conceptions. Corbin wrote, "He was a severe taskmaster, requiring his students to master his classification of 'fundamental conceptions' and to use accurately the set of terms by which they were expressed. They found this, in the light of the usage of the other professors [at Yale], almost impossible." Their resistance resulted in a petition to the President of Yale that Hohfeld's appointment not be extended. The petition was ignored and generations of law studests have continued to master Hohfeld's terms.

a. It is clear that if he paid the price and did not get the farm he would have a claim for damages against the Zehmers for breach of contract and probably, since the subject of the contract is land, one for specific performance as well. But such claims may not be as satisfactory to Lucy as a right to withhold payment until he gets a deed to the farm.

the company's promise to pay the owner $100,000 if his house is destroyed by fire. If the house burns, performance of the company's promise to pay becomes due. If it does not burn, performance does not become due. The burning of the house was not the acceptance of an offer: there was a contract—an enforceable promise by the company—before the house burned. The burning of the house was a condition of the company's promise to pay, an event that had to occur before performance of that promise was due.

Where a party makes a promise in exchange for a return promise, he can be protected by making his own promise conditional on performance by the other party, so that he is under no duty to perform until the other party has performed. Even if the contract does not so provide, the court may impose such "constructive conditions of exchange" by the process of implication. (See Wood v. Lucy, Lady Duff-Gordon, p. 81 infra.) In the case of the contract for the sale to Lucy of the Zehmers' farm, since both parties could perform simultaneously,[b] a court would protect both parties by making it a condition of Lucy's duty to pay that the Zehmers tender a deed and a condition of the Zehmers' duty to tender a deed that Lucy tender the price.[c] Further discussion must be left to Chapter 8.

(3) *Dominance of Bilateral Contracts.* Bilateral contracts are much more common and much more economically significant than unilateral contracts. Why do you suppose this is?

STRONG v. SHEFFIELD

Court of Appeals of New York, 1895.
144 N.Y. 392, 39 N.E. 330.

[Action on a promissory note. A judgment for plaintiff, Benjamin B. Strong, against defendant, Louisa A. Sheffield, was reversed by the General Term of the Supreme Court. The facts are stated in the opinion.]

ANDREWS, C. J. The contract between a maker or endorser of a promissory note and the payee forms no exception to the general rule that a promise, not supported by a consideration, is nudum pactum. The law governing commercial paper which precludes an inquiry into the consideration as against bona fide holders for value before maturity, has no application where the suit is between the original parties to the instrument. It is undisputed that the demand note upon which the action was brought was made by the husband of the

b. If simultaneous performance is not possible or is contrary to the agreement of the parties, the promise of the party who is to perform later is regarded as conditional on earlier performance by the other party. If a home owner promises a painter to pay him $1,000 in return for the painter's promise to paint his house, it will be assumed in the absence of a contrary agreement that the painter is to go first so that painting the house is a condition of the owner's duty to pay.

c. It is generally regarded as enough if a party makes an offer to perform, accompanied with manifested present ability to make it good, even if he does not go so far as to actually tender what he is to deliver by holding it out. See Comment *b* to Restatement Second, § 238; UCC 2–503(1).

defendant and endorsed by her at his request and delivered to the plaintiff, the payee, as security for an antecedent debt owing by the husband to the plaintiff. The debt of the husband was past due at the time, and the only consideration for the wife's endorsement, which is or can be claimed, is that as part of the transaction there was an agreement by the plaintiff when the note was given to forbear the collection of the debt, or a request for forbearance, which was followed by forbearance for a period of about two years subsequent to the giving of the note. There is no doubt that an agreement by the creditor to forbear the collection of a debt presently due is a good consideration for an absolute or conditional promise of a third person to pay the debt or for any obligation he may assume in respect thereto. Nor is it essential that the creditor should bind himself at the time to forbear collection or to give time. If he is requested by his debtor to extend the time, and a third person undertakes in consideration of forbearance being given to become liable as surety or otherwise, and the creditor does in fact forbear in reliance upon the undertaking, although he enters into no enforceable agreement to do so, his acquiescence in the request, and an actual forbearance in consequence thereof for a reasonable time, furnishes a good consideration for the collateral undertaking. In other words, a request followed by performance is sufficient, and mutual promises at the time are not essential unless it was the understanding that the promisor was not to be bound, except on condition that the other party entered into an immediate and reciprocal obligation to do the thing requested. . . . The note in question did not in law extend the payment of the debt. It was payable on demand, and although being payable with interest it was in form consistent with an intention that payment should not be immediately demanded, yet there was nothing on its face to prevent an immediate suit on the note against the maker or to recover the original debt. . . .

In the present case the agreement made is not left to inference, nor was it a case of request to forbear, followed by forbearance, in pursuance of the request, without any promise on the part of the creditor at the time. The plaintiff testified that there was an express agreement on his part to the effect that he would not pay the note away, nor put it in any bank for collection, but (using the words of the plaintiff) "I will hold it until such time as I want my money, I will make a demand on you for it." And again: "No, I will keep it until such time as I want it." [a] Upon this alleged agreement the de-

a. The record on appeal indicates that Benjamin Strong was Louisa Sheffield's uncle. He had sold his business on credit to Louisa's husband, Gerardus, and then sought Gerardus' note with Louisa's endorsement as security for the debt. Louisa was reluctant to endorse her husband's note because she had her own successful business and did not want to hurt her credit by having it known that she had undertaken a debt of her husband. Strong testified that he told Gerardus at a gymnasium, "Rard, I will give you my word as a man . . . that if you will give

fendant endorsed the note. It would have been no violation of the plaintiff's promise if, immediately on receiving the note, he had commenced suit upon it. Such a suit would have been an assertion that he wanted the money and would have fulfilled the condition of forbearance. The debtor and the defendant, when they became parties to the note, may have had the hope or expectation that forbearance would follow, and there was forbearance in fact. But there was no agreement to forbear for a fixed time or for a reasonable time, but an agreement to forbear for such time as the plaintiff should elect. The consideration is to be tested by the agreement, and not by what was done under it. It was a case of mutual promises, and so intended. We think the evidence failed to disclose any consideration for the defendant's endorsement, and that the trial court erred in refusing so to rule.

The order of the General Term reversing the judgment should be affirmed, and judgment absolute directed for the defendant on the stipulation with costs in all courts.

Ordered accordingly.

NOTES

(1) *Questions.* The Restatement Second, § 77, mentions the "illusory" or "apparent" promise as a type that is not consideration. Did the plaintiff, Strong, make any promise of substance to the Sheffields, or either of them? Was his promise alternative in any sense? See the Restatement section cited.

Suppose Mrs. Sheffield had written to Strong: "I will be responsible for my husband's debt if you will not bother him about it for two years." Would she have been accountable to Strong if he had done nothing about the note for that period? What difference is there between this situation and the case as it stands?

(2) *Statutory Change.* The precise rule of this case is reversed by UCC 3–408, and may have been reversed by the enactment of the Negotiable Instruments Law, soon after the decision. See First National City Bank v. Valentine, 61 Misc.2d 554, 306 N.Y.S.2d 227 (Sup.Ct.1969), rearg. denied 62 Misc.2d 719, 309 N.Y.S.2d 563 (1970). However, inasmuch as these statutes purport to apply only to negotiable instruments, the principle of the case is presumably still viable in the absence of such an instrument.

(3) *The Bonus Case.* For a case in which the conception of illusory promise was used in favor of a consumer, see Sentinel Acceptance Corp. v.

me a note, with your wife's endorsement, as further security for what you owe me, that I will not pay that note away; I will not put it in any bank for collection, but I will hold it until such time as I want my money, I will make a demand on you for it." Strong also testified that when Gerardus turned over the note, Gerardus asked, "You won't pay this note away?" and Strong replied, "No, I will keep it until such time as I want it." Record pp. 12–13.

Colgate, 162 Colo. 64, 424 P.2d 380 (1967). The defendant, a buyer on credit of home fire- and burglar-alarm systems, had been promised a bonus for a list of names of twenty prospects, provided the seller's agent succeeded in making a full presentation to each of them. The seller was made the sole judge of compliance with the condition. In an action for the unpaid purchase price, the doctrine of mutuality was applied to excuse the buyer.

(4) *Extensions of Time.* Many contracts involve a more or less continuous exchange of values between the parties. Contracts of employment and lease contracts are examples. If there is an agreement for the term of such a contract to be extended, without other change, it can be understood that each party makes a further commitment, and there is scarcely a problem of consideration.

The same analysis can be applied to the extension of an interest-bearing debt.[b] But suppose the creditor promises the debtor an extra year to pay, and authorizes the debtor to stop the running of interest by making payment anytime during the year when he is ready. Is the creditor bound to the extension? After some part of the year has elapsed, the debtor may contend that the accumulated interest for that period serves as consideration for the creditor's promise of forbearance. But is that plausible? Does Strong v. Sheffield tend to refute such a contention?[c]

Consult Restatement Second, § 74(2). If a debtor renews, in writing, his promise to pay, and in exchange the creditor agrees to extend the time for payment, is the creditor bound under this rule?

DI BENEDETTO v. DI ROCCO

Supreme Court of Pennsylvania, 1953.
372 Pa. 302, 93 A.2d 474.

HORACE STERN, Chief Justice. In this action for specific performance of a contract for the sale of real estate the court below—in our opinion erroneously—held that the agreement was lacking in mutuality of obligation; accordingly it sustained preliminary objections and dismissed plaintiff's bill in equity.

In the written agreement between the parties, dated March 11, 1949, defendants, the owners of premises 6441 Haverford Avenue, Philadelphia, agreed to sell that property to plaintiff for the sum of $8,500, of which $100 was to be paid, and was paid, at the time of the

b. See Adamson v. Bosick, 82 Colo. 309, 259 P. 513 (1927); Rogers v. First National Bank, 282 Ala. 379, 211 So.2d 796 (1968).

c. "The law is well settled that the extension of a note must be for a definite period in order to be enforceable as an extension agreement." Shepherd v. Erickson, 416 S.W.2d 450 (Tex.Civ.App.1967).

signing of the agreement, and the balance of $8,400 in cash at the settlement; by written addition to the agreement made June 21, 1949, plaintiff was to pay a further sum of $602. There were two provisions in the agreement which have given rise to the present controversy. The one was that "In the event that the buyer *cannot* make the settlement, he may cancel this agreement, without any further liability on his part, and deposit money returned." The other was that "It is hereby further agreed that the purchaser will give to the seller six (6) months notice prior to July 1, 1951, of his intention to exercise the herein agreement to purchase, ..." Settlement was to be made on or before July 1, 1951, said time to be the essence of the agreement. The agreement was signed by plaintiff and by one P. DiBenedetto as agent for defendants, but defendants themselves added: "we hereby approve the above contract," and signed the agreement with seals opposite to their names.

On December 7, 1950, plaintiff's attorneys, acting on his behalf, wrote to defendants advising them that, in accordance with the clause as to the giving of six months' notice prior to July 1, 1951 of plaintiff's "intention to exercise the agreement to purchase," they thereby gave notice of his intention to make settlement on that date or the nearest legal date thereto. On June 20, 1951, the same attorneys wrote to defendants, enclosing settlement certificate and informing them that arrangements had been made for settlement at the Broad Street Trust Company on Friday, June 29, 1951, at 3 p. m. On that day and at that time plaintiff appeared at the Trust Company, ready, willing and able to carry out the terms of the agreement on his part to be performed, but defendants failed to appear and have ever since refused to convey title.

The first question in the case is whether plaintiff, by reason of the first of the two clauses above quoted, had an absolute, arbitrary right to cancel the agreement without any further liability on his part. We think that he had no such right. The determinative, crucial word in that regard is "*cannot*". "Cannot" connotes, not unwillingness, but inability. Cf. Hannock v. Tope & Tope, 77 Pa.Super. 101, 104; Wilker v. Jenkins, 88 Pa.Super. 177. If defendants had brought action against plaintiff to compel performance of his agreement to purchase the property he could have successfully defended only by proving that he was *unable* to complete the transaction, not merely that he did not *desire* to do so. Plaintiff, however, by notifying defendants more than six months prior to the time fixed for settlement that it was his intention to make settlement at the time specified, admitted thereby that he was *not unable* to make settlement and therefore that he had no *right* to cancel the agreement. The agreement constituted, therefore, a contract binding on both parties alike, and did not lack mutuality of obligation.

Even were we to assume, however, that the agreement did not obligate plaintiff from the very beginning but should be interpreted as the mere grant of an *option* to him to purchase the property, he certainly became bound when the notice of December 7, 1950, was given. The agreement being under seal, and accompanied by the payment of $100 at the time of its execution, there was consideration sufficient to entitle him to the right to exercise the option, and even had there been no consideration the exercise of the option before any revocation of it by defendants converted it into a contract with mutuality of obligation. Driebe v. Fort Penn Realty Co., 331 Pa. 314, 200 A. 62, 117 A.L.R. 1091. . . .

Defendants question the legal sufficiency of the notice of December 7, 1950, on the ground that it was not shown that the agents who wrote the letter were authorized so to do by plaintiff in writing. This overlooks the well established principle that the Statute of Frauds does not require an agreement for the sale of real estate to be signed by the purchaser but only by the "parties making or creating" the interest in the land. Stevenson v. Titus, Administrators, 332 Pa. 100, 2 A.2d 853.

Decree reversed and the record remanded with a procedendo; costs to abide the event.

NOTES

(1) *The Concealed Offer.* Seller promises to fill all the orders for sand, at a stated price, that Buyer cares to send him, and Buyer promises to pay for any sand he orders. There is no contract on the face of this "exchange." However, if Buyer orders five carloads of sand before Seller retracts his promise or it lapses, there is a contract for that number. What the parties may have *thought* was a contract did at least amount to an offer by Seller.

Similarly, if there were no contract of sale in the main case, there was at least an offer to sell, and an acceptance occurred before revocation. As the court says, "even had there been no consideration the exercise of the option before any revocation of it by defendants converted it into a contract. . . ." Compare the analysis of a check-credit agreement in First Wis. National Bank v. Oby, 52 Wis.2d 1, 188 N.W.2d 454 (1971).

(2) *Questions.* The court mentions the deposit of $100 as binding an option. Is that view tenable, in view of the provision, "deposit money to be returned" if the buyer cannot make settlement? Is it possible that the owner bargained for the use of $100 for some months, as the consideration for an option? Cf. Kowal v. Day, 20 Cal.App.3d 720, 98 Cal.Rptr. 118 (1971).

Consult Restatement Second, § 87. As a test of the rule stated in subsection (1)(a), consider the following changes in the main case: no deposit money is paid, the agreement permits the buyer to cancel if he desires to do so, and the seller repudiates shortly after signing. Does the rule apply to bind the seller?

(3) *"Satisfaction."* Suppose that Di Rocco's obligation to buy the premises had been conditioned on his obtaining a lessee for the premises under a lease "satisfactory to" him? Would his promise then have been il-

lusory? In Mattei v. Hopper, 51 Cal.2d 119, 330 P.2d 625 (1958), the promise of a buyer of land for a shopping center was conditioned on his obtaining leases for future occupancy that were "satisfactory" to him. The court read his promise as requiring him "to exercise his judgment in good faith" so that it was not illusory.

(4) *Problem.* North, the owner of a going business, wishes to live in a warmer climate. He finds a similar business in a southern state, owned by South, who wishes to sell. South's business is in rented quarters. North and South come to terms, which they put in writing. The "sale contract" provides for closing in six months, "but only if North is able to sell his present business for $50,000 cash within that time." It also provides: "The agreement is conditioned upon North getting a five-year extension of South's current lease." If South repudiates the agreement soon after signing it, does North have a contract claim against him? If South does not repudiate, and North does nothing about selling his business, does South have a contract claim against him? Compare Paul v. Rosen, 3 Ill.App.2d 423, 122 N.E.2d 603 (1954), with Carlton v. Smith, 285 Ill.App. 380, 2 N.E. 2d 116 (1936).

McMICHAEL v. PRICE

Supreme Court of Oklahoma, 1936.
177 Okl. 186, 58 P.2d 549.

Action by Harley T. Price, doing business as the Sooner Sand Company, against W. M. McMichael, wherein defendant filed a counterclaim. From a judgment for plaintiff, defendant appeals.

Affirmed.

OSBORN, Vice Chief Justice. This action was instituted in the district court of Tulsa county by Harley T. Price, doing business as Sooner Sand Company, hereinafter referred to as plaintiff, against W. M. McMichael, hereinafter referred to as defendant, as an action to recover damages for the breach of a contract. The cause was tried to a jury and a verdict returned in favor of plaintiff for $7,512.51. The trial court ordered a remittitur of $2,500, which was duly filed. Thereafter the trial court rendered judgment upon the verdict for $5,012.51, from which judgment defendant has appealed.

The pertinent provisions of the contract, which is the basis of this action, are as follows: . . .

"Now, therefore, in consideration of the mutual promises herein contained, the said second party [defendant, McMichael] agrees to furnish all the sand of various grades and qualities which the first party can sell for shipment to various and sundry points outside of the City of Tulsa, Oklahoma, and to load all of said sand in suitable railway cars . . . for delivery to said Frisco Railway Company as said initial carrier. Said second party agrees to furnish the quantity and quality of sand at all and various times as the first party [Price] may designate by written or oral order, and agrees to furnish and load same within a reasonable time after said verbal or written order is received.

"In consideration of the mutual promises herein contained, first party agrees to purchase and accept from second party all of the sand of various grades and quality which the said first party can sell, for shipment to various and sundry points outside of the City of Tulsa, Oklahoma, provided that the sand so agreed to be furnished and loaded by the said second party shall at least be equal to in quality and comparable with the sand of various grades sold by other sand companies in the City of Tulsa, Oklahoma, or vicinity. First party agrees to pay and the second party agrees to accept as payment and compensation for said sand so furnished and loaded, a sum per ton which represents sixty per cent (60%) of the current market price per ton of concrete sand at the place of destination of said shipment. . . .

"This contract and agreement shall cover a period of ten years from the date hereof, . . ."

Defendant contends that the contract between the parties was a mere revocable offer and is not a valid and binding contract of purchase and sale for want of mutuality. The general rule is that in construing a contract where the consideration on the one side is an offer or an agreement to sell, and on the other side an offer or agreement to buy, the obligation of the parties to sell and buy must be mutual, to render the contract binding on either party, or, as it is sometimes stated, if one of the parties, not having suffered any previous detriment, can escape future liability under the contract, that party may be said to have a "free way out" and the contract lacks mutuality. Consolidated Pipe Line Co. v. British American Oil Co., 163 Okl. 171, 21 P.2d 762. Attention is directed to the specific language used in the contract binding the defendant to "furnish all of the sand of various grades and qualities which the first party can sell" and whereby plaintiff is bound "to purchase and accept from second party all of the sand of various grades and qualities which the said first party (plaintiff) can sell." It is urged that plaintiff had no established business and was not bound to sell any sand whatever and might escape all liability under the terms of the contract by a mere failure or refusal to sell sand. In this connection it is to be noted that the contract recites that plaintiff is "engaged in the business of selling and shipping sand from Tulsa, Oklahoma, to various points." The parties based their contract on this agreed predicate. . . .

At the time the contract involved herein was executed, plaintiff was not the owner of an established sand business. The evidence shows, however, that he was an experienced salesman of sand, which fact was well known to defendant, and that it was anticipated by both parties that on account of the experience, acquaintances, and connections of plaintiff, he would be able to sell a substantial amount of sand to the mutual profit of the contracting parties. The record discloses that for the nine months immediately following the execution of the contract plaintiff's average net profit per month was $516.88.

By the terms of the contract the price to be paid for sand was definitely fixed. Plaintiff was bound by a solemn covenant of the contract to purchase all the sand he was able to sell from defendant and for a breach of such covenant could have been made to respond in damages. The argument of defendant that the plaintiff could escape liability under the contract by going out of the sand business is without force in view of our determination, in line with the authorities hereinabove cited, that it was the intent of the parties to enter into a contract which would be mutually binding. . . .

The judgment is affirmed.

NOTES

(1) *Sand v. Glue.* Peter Cooper's Glue Factory wrote to a jobber in glue, agreeing to supply "your requirements of 'Special BB' glue for the year 1916, price to be 9¢ per lb." The jobber was misleadingly named Schlegel Manufacturing Company; in fact it had no manufacturing business in which glue was used. During 1916 the jobber ordered about five times as much glue as it had ordered in any of the preceding five years. The Glue Factory supplied less than half of the amount ordered, and Schlegel sued it. From a judgment for the plaintiff, the defendant appealed. *Held:* Reversed. The court remarked: "The price of glue having risen during the year 1916 from nine to twenty-four cents per pound, it is quite obvious why orders for glue increased correspondingly." In ruling that consideration was lacking for the defendant's promise, the court made these observations about the agreement: "there is no standard mentioned by which the quantity of glue to be furnished can be determined with any approximate degree of accuracy. . . . [T]here was no obligation on the part of the plaintiff to sell any of the defendant's glue, to make any effort towards bringing about such sale, or not to sell other glues in competition with it." Schlegel Manufacturing Co. v. Cooper's Glue Factory, 231 N.Y. 459, 132 N.E. 148 (1921).

In what respects was the glue agreement like the sand agreement in the main case? In what respects different? What was the decisive difference?

(2) *Requirements Contracts.* The contract in McMichael v. Price is known as a "requirements" contract, in that the quantity of sand to be supplied was to be determined by the needs of Price in supplying his customers.[a] A contract which calls on the seller to deliver and the buyer to take all of the goods, or all of a certain sort, that may be produced by a seller is known as an "output" contract. A contract for the sale of all the cotton to be raised and harvested on a specified tract of land (see p. 1 su-

a. For another example, see HML Corp. v. General Foods Corp., p. 731 infra.

pra) is an output contract. Output and requirements contracts are commonly bracketed together in discussion, as presenting common problems. In this note output contracts will not be further noticed, but what is said about requirements contracts may be understood as bearing on output contracts as well. For an examination of the difficulties faced in drafting such contracts and some solutions, see Note, 78 Harv.L.Rev. 1212 (1965).

An initial problem as to requirements contracts is the one addressed in the main case: does the buyer have a "free way out"? Though there are some older precedents to the contrary,[b] the consensus now is that the requirement of mutuality is satisfied without a commitment by the buyer to take a fixed quantity of goods. Comment 2 to UCC 2–306 explains that such a contract does not "lack mutuality of obligation since, under this section, the party who will determine quantity is required to operate his plant or conduct his business in good faith and according to commercial standards of fair dealing in the trade so that his output or requirements will approximate a reasonably foreseeable figure. Reasonable elasticity in the requirements is expressly envisaged by this section and good faith variations from prior requirements are permitted even when the variation may be such as to result in discontinuance. A shutdown by a requirements buyer for lack of orders might be permissible when a shut-down merely to curtail losses would not. The essential test is whether the party is acting in good faith." Would the contract for "Special BB" glue in Note 1 supra be enforceable under the Code? Would it make a difference if only Peter Cooper made glue under that name?

If requirements contracts are generally to be enforced, a question arises of how to limit the demands that a buyer can make in the event of a market rise during the term of a fixed-price requirements contract. UCC 2–306(1) attempts to provide an answer by precluding the buyer from demanding a "quantity unreasonably disproportionate to any stated estimate or to any normal or otherwise comparable . . . requirements." For a case in which this was applied to a fixed-price requirements contract for fuel oil, see Orange & Rockland Utilities, Inc. v. Amerada Hess Corp., 59 A.D.2d 110, 397 N.Y.S.2d 814 (1977). Could this standard be applied to Price's contract for sand, considering that he had no established sand business? Would the limitation to "good faith" requirements be helpful?

Although the language of UCC 2–306(1) is not entirely clear, the better view seems to be that the "unreasonably disproportionate" language imposes only an upper limit and does not prevent a buyer under a requirements contract from going out of business or otherwise reducing his requirements, as long as he does so in good faith. See R. A. Weaver & Associates, Inc. v. Asphalt Constr., Inc., 587 F.2d 1315 (D.C.Cir. 1978); Weistart, Requirements and Output Contracts: Quantity Variations under the UCC, 1973 Duke L.J. 599.

Requirements and output contracts will be considered again in Chapter 7, Section 3.

b. See Miami Butterine Co. v. Frankel, 190 Ga. 88, 8 S.E.2d 398 (1940); Miami Coca-Cola Bottling Co. v. Orange Crush Co., 296 Fed. 593 (5th Cir. 1924).

WOOD v. LUCY, LADY DUFF-GORDON

Court of Appeals of New York, 1917.
222 N.Y. 88, 118 N.E. 214.

Appeal from Supreme Court, Appellate Division, First Department.

Action by Otis F. Wood against Lucy, Lady Duff-Gordon. From a judgment of the Appellate Division (177 App.Div. 624, 164 N.Y. Supp. 576), which reversed an order denying defendant's motion for judgment on the pleading, and which dismissed the complaint, plaintiff appeals. Reversed.

CARDOZO, J.[a] The defendant styles herself "a creator of fashions." Her favor helps a sale. Manufacturers of dresses, millinery, and like articles are glad to pay for a certificate of her approval. The things which she designs, fabrics, parasols, and what not, have a new value in the public mind when issued in her name. She employed the plaintiff to help her to turn this vogue into money. He was to have the exclusive right, subject always to her approval, to place her indorsements on the designs of others. He was also to have the exclusive right to place her own designs on sale, or to license others to market them. In return she was to have one-half of "all profits and revenues" derived from any contracts he might make. The exclusive right was to last at least one year from April 1, 1915, and thereafter from year to year unless terminated by notice of 90 days. The plaintiff says that he kept the contract on his part, and that the defendant broke it. She placed her indorsement on fabrics, dresses, and millinery without his knowledge, and withheld the profits. He sues her for the damages, and the case comes here on demurrer.[b]

a. Benjamin Nathan Cardozo (1870–1938) practiced in New York City after law school. He served as judge and later chief judge of the Court of Appeals of New York, and was appointed an associate justice of the Supreme Court of the United States in 1932 to fill the vacancy left by Holmes. Of his contribution to the law of contracts, Professor Corbin has written: "It cannot be said that he made any extensive changes in the existing law of contract. To state the facts of the cases, the decision, and the reasoning of his opinion will not show the overthrow of old doctrine or the establishment of new. Instead, it will show the application of existing doctrines with wisdom and discretion; an application that does not leave those doctrines wholly unaffected, but one that carries on their evolution as is reasonably required by the new facts before the court. When Cardozo is through, the law is not exactly as it was before; but there has been no sudden shift or revolutionary change." Cardozo's best known jurisprudential work is a series of lectures entitled The Nature of the Judicial Process (1921).

b. In dismissing the complaint, the Appellate Division explained that "the plaintiff by this contract promises to collect the revenues derived from the indorsements, sales and licenses and to pay the cost of collecting them of his half thereof and to account to the defendant each month. But this promise on his part is not binding on him unless he places indorsements, makes sales or grants licenses, and nowhere in the contract has he bound himself to get these in-

The agreement of employment is signed by both parties. It has a wealth of recitals. The defendant insists, however, that it lacks the elements of a contract. She says that the plaintiff does not bind himself to anything. It is true that he does not promise in so many words that he will use reasonable efforts to place the defendant's indorsements and market her designs. We think, however, that such a promise is fairly to be implied. The law has outgrown its primitive stage of formalism when the precise word was the sovereign talisman, and every slip was fatal. It takes a broader view today. A promise may be lacking, and yet the whole writing may be "instinct with an obligation," imperfectly expressed (Scott, J., in McCall Co. v. Wright, 133 App.Div. 62, 117 N.Y.S. 775; Moran v. Standard Oil Co., 211 N. Y. 187, 198, 105 N.E. 217). If that is so, there is a contract.

The implication of a promise here finds support in many circumstances. The defendant gave an exclusive privilege. She was to have no right for at least a year to place her own indorsements or market her own designs except through the agency of the plaintiff. The acceptance of the exclusive agency was an assumption of its duties. Phoenix Hermetic Co. v. Filtrine Mfg. Co., 164 App.Div. 424, 150 N. Y.S. 193; W. G. Taylor Co. v. Bannerman, 120 Wis. 189, 97 N.W. 918; Mueller v. Mineral Spring Co., 88 Mich. 390, 50 N.W. 319. We are not to suppose that one party was to be placed at the mercy of the other. Hearn v. Stevens & Bro., 111 App.Div. 101, 106, 97 N.Y.S. 566; Russell v. Allerton, 108 N.Y. 288, 15 N.E. 391. Many other terms of the agreement point the same way. We are told at the outset by way of recital that:

"The said Otis F. Wood possesses a business organization adapted to the placing of such indorsements as the said Lucy, Lady Duff-Gordon, has approved."

The implication is that the plaintiff's business organization will be used for the purpose for which it is adapted. But the terms of the defendant's compensation are even more significant. Her sole compensation for the grant of an exclusive agency is to be one-half of all the profits resulting from the plaintiff's efforts. Unless he gave his efforts, she could never get anything. Without an implied promise, the transaction cannot have such business "efficacy, as both parties must have intended that at all events it should have." Bowen, L. J., in The Moorcock, 14 P.D. 64, 68. But the contract does not stop there. The plaintiff goes on to promise that he will account monthly

dorsements, or make the sales or grant the licenses. . . . It is quite apparent that in this respect the defendant gives everything and the plaintiff nothing and there is a lack of mutuality in the contract. . . . In fact the plaintiff in the nature of the case could not perform any of his various dependent agreements unless he placed indorsements, made sales or granted licenses to manufacture. And as the contract did not bind him to do any of these things, there is no provision of the contract which the defendant could enforce against him." 177 App.Div. at 626, 164 N.Y.S. at 577.

for all moneys received by him, and that he will take out all such patents and copyrights and trademarks as may in his judgment be necessary to protect the rights and articles affected by the agreement. It is true, of course, as the Appellate Division has said, that if he was under no duty to try to market designs or to place certificates of indorsement, his promise to account for profits or take out copyrights would be valueless. But in determining the intention of the parties the promise has a value. It helps to enforce the conclusion that the plaintiff had some duties. His promise to pay the defendant one-half of the profits and revenues resulting from the exclusive agency and to render accounts monthly was a promise to use reasonable efforts to bring profits and revenues into existence. For this conclusion the authorities are ample. [Ten citations omitted.]

The judgment of the Appellate Division should be reversed, and the order of the Special Term affirmed, with costs in the Appellate Division and in this court.

CUDDEBACK, McLAUGHLIN, and ANDREWS, JJ., concur. HISCOCK, C. J., and CHASE and CRANE, JJ., dissent.

NOTES

(1) *Rationale.* What is the rationale for the implication of a promise? To what extent is it an application of the maxim *ut res magis valeat quam pereat* (that the thing may rather have effect than be destroyed)? To what extent does it turn on the fact that Lady Duff-Gordon gave Wood "an exclusive privilege"? To what extent does it turn on other of the "many circumstances" referred to by Cardozo? What answers are suggested by the statement of the rule in UCC 2–306(2)?

(2) *Problem.* About Christmastime one year, Tim's employment was terminated by the Scrooge Company, a small firm that he had served as a bookkeeper since its inception several years before. About a year before his discharge, the directors of Scrooge had "Voted, That Scrooge Company does contract to pay monthly to Tim not less than $200 beginning January 1, for such services as he, in his sole discretion may render. The term of this contract to be not less than five years." How would you argue that Scrooge committed a breach of contract in firing Tim? See Griswold v. Heat Incorporated, 108 N.H. 119, 229 A.2d 183 (1967); cf. Pacific Pines Constr. Corp. v. Young, 257 Or. 192, 477 P.2d 894 (1970).

SYLVAN CREST SAND & GRAVEL CO. v. UNITED STATES, 150 F.2d 642 (2d Cir. 1945). [Sylvan Crest bid on a United States government contract to supply trap rock for an airport using government forms. Under the terms of the government's invitation for bids typed on the forms, the rock was "To be delivered to project as required. Delivery to start immediately . . . . Cancellation by the Procurement Division may be effected at any time." A printed clause on the backs of the forms provided that "if the contractor refuses or fails to make deliveries . . . within the time specified

. . . the Government may by written notice terminate the right of the contractor to proceed with deliveries . . . ." Sylvan Crest's bids were accepted by the government on June 29, 1937. After some deliveries had been made and paid for, the government gave notice of cancellation on July 11, 1939. Sylvan Crest sued the United States for breach of contract. From summary judgment for the United States, plaintiff appeals.]

SWAN, Circuit Judge . . . . No one can read the document as a whole without concluding that the parties intended a contract to result from the Bid and the Government's Acceptance. If the United States did not so intend, it certainly set a skillful trap for unwary bidders. No such purpose should be attributed to the government. . . . In construing the document the presumption should be indulged that both parties were acting in good faith. . . .

Beyond question the plaintiff made a promise to deliver rock at a stated price; and if the United States were suing for its breach the question would be whether the "acceptance" by the United States operated as a sufficient consideration to make the plaintiff's promise binding. Since the United States is the defendant the question is whether it made any promise that has been broken. Its "acceptance" should be interpreted as a reasonable business man would have understood it. Surely it would not have been understood thus: "We accept your offer and bind you to your promise to deliver, but we do not promise either to take the rock or pay the price." The reservation of a power to effect cancellation at any time meant something different from this. We believe that the reasonable interpretation of the document is as follows: "We accept your offer to deliver within a reasonable time, and we promise to take the rock and pay the price unless we give you notice of cancellation within a reasonable time." Only on such an interpretation is the United States justified in expecting the plaintiff to prepare for performance and to remain ready and willing to deliver. Even so, the bidder is taking a great risk and the United States has an advantage. It is not "good faith" for the United States to insist upon more than this. It is certain that the United States intended to bind the bidder to a "contract," and that the bidder thought that the "acceptance" of his bid made a "contract." A reasonable interpretation of the language used gives effect to their mutual intention. Consequently we cannot accept the contention that the defendant's power of cancellation was unrestricted and could be exercised merely by failure to give delivery orders. The words "cancellation may be effected at any time" imply affirmative action, namely, the giving of notice of intent to cancel. The defendant itself so construed the clause by giving notice of cancellation on July 11, 1939, as alleged in its answer. While the phrase "at any time" should be liberally construed, it means much less than "forever." If taken literally, it would mean that after the defendant had given instructions for delivery and the plaintiff had tendered delivery in accordance therewith, or even after delivery had actually been made, the defendant could refuse to accept and when sued for the price give notice of cancellation of the contract. Such an interpretation would be not only unjust and unreasonable, but would make nugatory the entire contract, contrary to the intention of the parties, if it be assumed that the United States was acting in good faith in accepting the plaintiff's bid. The words should be so construed as to support the contract and not render illusory the promises of both parties. This can be accomplished by interpolating the word "reasonable", as is often done with respect to indefinite time clauses. See Starkweather v. Gleason, 221 Mass. 552, 109 N.E. 635. Hence the agreement obligated the defendant to give delivery instructions or notice of cancellation within a reasonable time after the date of its "acceptance." This constituted consideration for the plaintiff's promise to deliver in accordance with delivery instructions, and made the agreement a valid contract. . . .

[Reversed and remanded.]

NOTES

(1) *Termination Clauses and Mutuality of Obligation.* If the contractor (plaintiff in the principal case) had refused to deliver gravel under the contract, would he have been liable for damages for breach of contract? What was the government's side of the exchange, that is, the consideration for the contractor's promise to deliver gravel as called for?

(2) *Interpretation of Termination Clauses.* With the problem in the Sylvan Crest case, compare UCC 2–309(3). What if a termination clause explicitly negates any duty of notification? As to this, Comment 8 to UCC 2–309 includes the following statement: "An agreement dispensing with notification or limiting the time for the seeking of a substitute arrangement is, of course, valid under this subsection unless the results of putting it into operation would be the creation of an unconscionable state of affairs." For more on this question, see the Corenswet case, p. 521 infra; see also Chapter 7, Section 3.

(3) *Good Faith.* An illustration based on the facts of this case appears in Restatement, Second, § 205, under the following rule: "Every contract imposes upon each party a duty of good faith and fair dealing in its performance and its enforcement." According to the illustration, good faith requires the buyer to order and accept the rock within a reasonable time unless he has given the seller notice of intent to cancel. Is this proposition essential to the decision in the actual case? Are the two logically related? For more on good faith, see Note 1, p. 730 infra.

SECTION 4. RELIANCE AS AN ALTERNATIVE BASIS FOR ENFORCEMENT

RICKETTS v. SCOTHORN

Supreme Court of Nebraska, 1898.
57 Neb. 51, 77 N.W. 365.

SULLIVAN, J. In the District Court of Lancaster county, the plaintiff, Katie Scothorn, recovered judgment against the defendant, Andrew D. Ricketts, as executor, of the last will and testament of John C. Ricketts, deceased. The action was based upon a promissory note, of which the following is a copy: "May the first, 1891. I promise to pay to Katie Scothorn on demand, $2,000 to be at 6 per cent. per annum. J. C. Ricketts." In the petition the plaintiff alleges that the consideration for the execution of the note was that she should surrender her employment as bookkeeper for Mayer Bros., and cease to work for a living. She also alleges that the note was given to induce her to abandon her occupation, and that, relying on it, and on the annual interest, as a means of support, she gave up the employment in which she was then engaged. These allegations of the petition are denied by the administrator.

The material facts are undisputed. They are as follows: John C. Ricketts, the maker of the note, was the grandfather of the plaintiff. Early in May—presumably on the day the note bears date—he called on her at the store where she was working. What transpired between them is thus described by Mr. Flodene, one of the plaintiff's witnesses: "A. Well, the old gentleman came in there one morning about nine o'clock, probably a little before or a little after, but early in the morning, and he unbuttoned his vest, and took out a piece of paper in the shape of a note; that is the way it looked to me; and he says to Miss Scothorn, 'I have fixed out something that you have not got to work any more.' He says, 'none of my grandchildren work, and you don't have to.' Q. Where was she? A. She took the piece of paper and kissed him, and kissed the old gentleman, and commenced to cry." It seems Miss Scothorn immediately notified her employer of her intention to quit work, and that she did soon after abandon her occupation. The mother of the plaintiff was a witness, and testified that she had a conversation with her father, Mr. Ricketts, shortly after the note was executed, in which he informed her that he had given the note to the plaintiff to enable her to quit work; that none of his grandchildren worked, and he did not think she ought to. For something more than a year the plaintiff was without an occupation, but in September, 1892, with the consent of her grandfather, and by his assistance, she secured a position as bookkeeper with Messrs. Funke & Ogden. On June 8, 1894, Mr. Ricketts died. He had paid one year's interest on the note, and a short time before his death expressed regret that he had not been able to pay the balance. In the summer or fall of 1892 he stated to his daughter, Mrs. Scothorn, that if he could sell his farm in Ohio he would pay the note out of the proceeds. He at no time repudiated the obligation.

We quite agree with counsel for the defendant that upon this evidence there was nothing to submit to the jury, and that a verdict should have been directed peremptorily for one of the parties. The testimony of Flodene and Mrs. Scothorn, taken together, conclusively establishes the fact that the note was not given in consideration of the plaintiff pursuing, or agreeing to pursue, any particular line of conduct. There was no promise on the part of the plaintiff to do, or refrain from doing, anything. Her right to the money promised in the note was not made to depend upon an abandonment of her employment with Mayer Bros., and future abstention from like service. Mr. Ricketts made no condition, requirement, or request. He exacted no quid pro quo. He gave the note as a gratuity, and looked for nothing in return. So far as the evidence discloses, it was his purpose to place the plaintiff in a position of independence, where she could work or remain idle, as she might choose. The abandonment by Miss Scothorn of her position as bookkeeper was altogether voluntary. It was not an act done in fulfillment of any contract obligation assumed when she accepted the note.

The instrument in suit, being given without any valuable consideration, was nothing more than a promise to make a gift in the future of the sum of money therein named. Ordinarily, such promises are not enforceable, even when put in the form of a promissory note. . . . But it has often been held that an action on a note given to a church, college, or other like institution, upon the faith of which money has been expended or obligations incurred, could not be successfully defended on the ground of a want of consideration. . . . In this class of cases the note in suit is nearly always spoken of as a gift or donation, but the decision is generally put on the ground that the expenditure of money or assumption of liability by the donee on the faith of the promise constitutes a valuable and sufficient consideration. It seems to us that the true reason is the preclusion of the defendant, under the doctrine of estoppel, to deny the consideration. . . .

Under the circumstances of this case, is there an equitable estoppel which ought to preclude the defendant from alleging that the note in controversy is lacking in one of the essential elements of a valid contract? We think there is. An estoppel in pais is defined to be "a right arising from acts, admissions, or conduct which have induced a change of position in accordance with the real or apparent intention of the party against whom they are alleged." . . . According to the undisputed proof, as shown by the record before us, the plaintiff was a working girl, holding a position in which she earned a salary of $10 per week. Her grandfather, desiring to put her in a position of independence, gave her the note, accompanying it with the remark that his other grandchildren did not work, and that she would not be obliged to work any longer. In effect, he suggested that she might abandon her employment, and rely in the future upon the bounty which he promised. He doubtless desired that she should give up her occupation, but, whether he did or not, it is entirely certain that he contemplated such action on her part as a reasonable and probable consequence of his gift. Having intentionally influenced the plaintiff to alter her position for the worse on the faith of the note being paid when due, it would be grossly inequitable to permit the maker, or his executor, to resist payment on the ground that the promise was given without consideration. The petition charges the elements of an equitable estoppel, and the evidence conclusively establishes them. If errors intervened at the trial, they could not have been prejudicial. A verdict for the defendant would be unwarranted. The judgment is right, and is

Affirmed.

NOTES

(1) *Kirksey Revisited.* Would the reasoning of the court in the principal case support a recovery by the plaintiff promisee in Kirksey v. Kirksey, p. 64 supra?

(2) *Estoppel: New Wine in an Old Bottle.* Decisions like the one in the principal case involve far more than routine application of established estoppel theory. The conventional estoppel case concerns a representation of fact made by one party and relied on by the other; the estopped party is prohibited from alleging or proving facts that would contradict the truth of his own earlier representation if the other party has taken action in reliance on that representation. Cases like Ricketts v. Scothorn concern not a factual representation but a promise, and the estoppel idea is used affirmatively as the legal basis of a claim.[a]

(3) *Bargained-For Exchange as an Alternative.* Might another court have found a bargained-for exchange in the principal case, and so have enforced the note to Katie Scothorn as a promise supported by consideration? Compare, particularly, Hamer v. Sidway, p. 44 supra.

"PROMISSORY ESTOPPEL"

Holmes said, "It would cut up the doctrine of consideration by the roots, if a promisee could make a gratuitous promise binding by subsequently acting in reliance on it." Commonwealth v. Scituate Savings Bank, 137 Mass. 301, 302 (1884). Nevertheless, Ricketts v. Scothorn is one of a number of cases that, even prior to the promulgation of the Restatement of Contracts in 1932, recognized reliance

a. That the claimant has no right to a trial by jury of such a claim because "the doctrine of promissory estoppel is essentially equitable in nature," see C & K Engineering Contractors v. Amber Steel Co., Inc., 23 Cal.3d 1, 151 Cal.Rptr. 323, 587 P.2d 1136 (1978).

as a basis for the enforcement of promises. For the most part, these cases fall into four categories.

1. *Family Promises.* One category consisted of cases, like Ricketts v. Scothorn itself, in which the promise was made by one member of a family to another. Is there a possible connection between the growth of this category and the fact that the pattern of bargained-for exchange, so common in a commercial setting, ordinarily seems out of place in a family setting? Contrast Ricketts v. Scothorn with Hamer v. Sidway, p. 44 supra.

2. *Promises to Convey Land.* Another category consisted of cases involving promises to convey land, on which the promisee had relied by moving onto the land and making improvements. An early example is Freeman v. Freeman, 43 N.Y. 34 (1870). Would the facts in Kirksey v. Kirksey, p. 64 supra, have brought that case within this category?

3. *Promises Coupled With Gratuitous Bailments.* A third category was made up of cases in which a bailor sought to enforce a promise made by the bailee in connection with a gratuitous bailment. The leading case is Siegel v. Spear & Co., 234 N.Y. 479, 138 N.E. 414 (1923). Siegel bought furniture on credit from Spear, giving Spear a mortgage on it and agreeing not to remove it from his apartment in New York City without Spear's consent until it was paid for. When he decided to leave the city for the summer, he saw Spear's credit man, McGrath, who agreed to store it free of charge. McGrath then said, "You had better transfer your insurance policy over to our warehouse," to which Siegel answered that he had no insurance but would get some through his agent. McGrath replied, "That won't be necessary to get that from him; I will do it for you; it will be a good deal cheaper; I handle lots of insurance; when you get the next bill —you can send a check for that with the next installment." In May, Siegel sent the furniture to Spear's storehouse. About a month later it was destroyed by fire. It had not been insured. Siegel sued Spear, had judgment, and Spear appealed. The Court of Appeals affirmed. Although the gratuitous bailment itself imposed no duty on Spear to insure the furniture, such a duty arose from McGrath's promise followed by the delivery of the furniture by Siegel. The court distinguished an old New York case, Thorne v. Deas, 4 Johns. 84 (N.Y.Sup.Ct.1809), in which the court had refused to hold one of two joint owners of a ship to his promise made to the other owner to insure the ship, when he had failed to do so and the ship had been lost. There, in contrast to Siegel, the promisee "parted with nothing . . . gave up possession of none of his property" to the promisor. This category will be considered further in connection with the next case.

4. *Charitable Subscriptions.* The fourth category of cases involves charitable subscriptions. The enforceability of such gratu-

itous promises may be regarded as particularly desirable as a means of allowing decisions about the distribution of wealth to be made at an individual level. See the discussion of gratuitous promises at p. 49 supra. As one court put it, "This promise was made to a charitable corporation, and for that reason we are not confined to the same orthodox concepts which once were applicable to every situation arising within a common law jurisdiction. There can be no denying that the strong desire on the part of the American courts to favor charitable institutions has established a doctrine which once would have been looked upon as legal heresy." Danby v. Osteopathic Hospital Ass'n of Delaware, 34 Del.Ch. 427, 104 A.2d 903 (1954). It is sometimes possible to enforce such a promise by finding an exchange among subscribers of promises for the benefit of (and enforceable by) the charitable organization, particularly where one subscriber appears as the "bellwether" of the flock and promises a large sum on condition that other subscribers raise a specified amount. See Congregation B'Nai Sholom v. Martin, 382 Mich. 659, 173 N.W.2d 504 (1969). (How could you draft a pledge form to help your favorite charity take advantage of this possibility?) It is also sometimes possible to enforce such a promise by finding that the charity has done or has promised to do something in exchange for the subscriber's promise.

It is perhaps curious that the most widely known and influential decision on charitable subscriptions goes off on this last ground and contains only dictum concerning the effect of reliance. It is Allegheny College v. National Chautauqua County Bank of Jamestown, 246 N.Y. 369, 159 N.E. 173 (1927). Mary Yates Johnston promised to pay $5,000 to Allegheny College by a writing denoted an "Estate Pledge" that stipulated that "this gift shall be known as the Mary Yates Johnston memorial fund, the proceeds from which shall be used to educate students preparing for the ministry." The sum was not payable until 30 days after her death, but $1,000 was paid while she was alive and set aside by the college for the specified purpose. She later repudiated her promise, and on the expiration of 30 days following her death the college brought an action against her executor for the unpaid balance. Cardozo, C. J., writing for the New York Court of Appeals, found consideration for her promise in the return promise of the college to set up the memorial fund which arose "by implication" from its acceptance of the $1,000. "The college could not accept the money and hold itself free thereafter from personal responsibility to give effect to the condition." But in the course of his opinion, Cardozo went out of his way to speak to the effect of reliance. "[T]here has grown up of recent days a doctrine that a substitute for consideration or an exception to its ordinary requirements can be found in what is styled 'a promissory estoppel'. . . . Whether the exception has made its way in this state to such an extent as to permit us to say that the general law of consideration has been modified accordingly, we do not now attempt to say. Cases such as Siegel v. Spear & Co. . . . may be signposts on the road. Certain, at least, it is that we have adopted the doctrine of promissory estoppel as the equivalent of consideration in connection with our law of charitable subscriptions."

Restatement, § 90. Cardozo's dictum in the Allegheny College case was surely influenced by what was to become Restatement, § 90, the text of which had been considered at the annual meeting of the American Law Institute in 1926. It reads:

> **§ 90. Promise Reasonably Inducing Definite and Substantial Action**
>
> A promise which the promisor should reasonably expect to induce action or forbearance of a definite and substantial character on the part of the promisee and which does induce such action or forbearance is binding if injustice can be avoided only by enforcement of the promise.

Although it avoids the use of the term "promissory estoppel," it states in general terms the principle that had been applied in the four categories of cases just described. See Boyer, Promissory Estoppel: Principle from Precedents, 50 Mich.L.Rev. 639, 873 (1952). Its remarkable impact is suggested by the fact that it is quoted in both of the following cases.

NOTE

Measure of Recovery. During the discussion of Restatement § 90 on the floor of the American Law Institute, Professor Williston, as Reporter, made the following statement: "Either the promise is binding or it is not. If the promise is binding it has to be enforced as it is made. As I said to Mr. Coudert, I could leave this whole thing to the subject of quasi contracts so that the promisee under those circumstances shall never recover on the promise but he shall recover such an amount as will fairly compensate him for any injury incurred; but it seems to me you have to take one leg or the other. You have either to say the promise is binding or you have to go on the theory of restoring the status quo." 4 American Law Institute Proceedings, Appendix, 103–04 (1926). Does not the etymology of "promissory estoppel" (although neither version of § 90 uses that term) support Williston?

EAST PROVIDENCE CREDIT UNION v. GEREMIA

Supreme Court of Rhode Island, 1968.
103 R.I. 597, 239 A.2d 725.

KELLEHER, Justice. This is a civil action to collect from the defendants the balance due on a promissory note. The defendants filed a counterclaim. The case was heard by a justice of the superior court. He dismissed the plaintiff's complaint and found for the defendants on their counterclaim. The case is before us on the plaintiff's appeal.

On December 5, 1963, defendants, who are husband and wife, borrowed $2,350.28 from plaintiff for which they gave their promissory note. The payment of the note was secured by a chattel mortgage on defendants' 1962 ranch wagon. The mortgage contained a clause which obligated defendants to maintain insurance on the motor vehicle in such amounts as plaintiff required against loss by fire, collision, upset or overturn of the automobile and similar hazards. This provision also stipulated that if defendants failed to maintain such insurance, plaintiff could pay the premium and ". . . any sum so paid shall be secured hereby and shall be immediately payable." The defendants had procured the required insurance and had designated plaintiff as a loss payee on its policy. The premium therefor was payable in periodic installments.

On October 11, 1965, defendants received a notice from the insurance carrier informing them that the premium then payable was overdue and that, unless it was paid within the ensuing twelve days, the policy would be cancelled. A copy of this notice was also sent by the insurer to plaintiff who thereupon sent a letter to defendants. The pertinent portion thereof reads as follows:

"We are in receipt of a cancellation notice on your Policy.

"If we are not notified of a renewal Policy within 10 days, we shall be forced to renew the policy for you and apply this amount to your loan."

Upon receiving this communication, defendant wife testified that she telephoned plaintiff's office and talked to the treasurer's assistant; that she told this employee to go ahead and pay the premium; that she explained to the employee that her husband was sick and they could not pay the insurance premium and the payment due on the loan; and that the employee told her her call would be referred to plaintiff's treasurer. The employee testified that she told defendant to contact this officer. We deem this difference in testimony insignificant. It is clear from the record that defendants communicated their approval of and acquiescence in plaintiff's promise to pay the insurance due on the car and that this employee notified the treasurer of such fact.

On December 17, 1965, defendants' motor vehicle was demolished in a mishap the nature of which cannot be learned from the record. It is obvious, however, that the loss was within the coverage of the policy. The automobile was a total loss. The evidence shows that at the time of the loss, the outstanding balance of the loan was $987.89 and the value of the ranch wagon prior to the loss exceeded the balance due on the loan.

Sometime after this unfortunate incident, all the parties became aware that the insurer would not indemnify them for the loss because the overdue premium had not been paid and defendants' policy had been canceled prior to the accident.

The defendants had on deposit with plaintiff over $200 in savings shares. The plaintiff, in accordance with the terms of the note, had deducted therefrom certain amounts and applied them to defendants' indebtedness so that at the time this litigation was instituted defendants allegedly owed plaintiff $779.53.

In finding for defendants on their counterclaim, the trial justice awarded them all the moneys which plaintiff had applied after the date of defendants' accident to the then outstanding balance of the loan.[1] The justice, at the conclusion of the evidence, made certain findings which were in accordance with the testimony as set forth above. He found from the evidence that plaintiff, in pursuance of its right under the mortgage contract and its letter to defendants, had agreed to renew the policy and charge any premiums paid by it on behalf of defendants to the outstanding balance on their loan.

In reaching this conclusion, the trial justice made the following observation: ". . . it seems to me quite clear that the defendants, having been given notice that the plaintiff would do this [pay the overdue premium], and calling the plaintiff's attention to the fact that they weren't going to renew and that the plaintiff had better do this to protect everybody, seems to me at that point there was agreement on the part of the plaintiff that it would procure this insurance. Or, put it another way, that they are estopped from denying that they were exercising the right that they had under the original mortgage." The superior court further found that defendants were justified in believing in plaintiff's assurance that it would pay the overdue premium.

The sole issue raised by this appeal is whether or not plaintiff is precluded from recovering on its loan contract by reason of its failure to fulfill a promise to defendants to pay the overdue insurance premium. In urging that the trial justice erred in finding for defendants, plaintiff directs our attention to Hazlett v. First Fed. Sav. & Loan Assn., 14 Wash.2d 124, 127 P.2d 273, in which the court refused to apply the doctrine of promissory estoppel to enforce a gratuitous promise made by a mortgagee to procure fire insurance for mortgaged property even though the mortgagor suffered serious detriment in reliance on the mortgagee's promise.[a]

1. Included in this amount are the moneys deducted from the savings shares, $80 received from a junkyard as the salvage value of the wrecked automobile and a $10 payment made by defendants on December 28, 1965.

a. The Hazlett case, in which the court held that the reliance had to take the form of affirmative conduct rather than mere forbearance, has been "overruled *sub silentio*" by a later case in the Supreme Court of Washington, according to Hellbaum v. Burwell and Morford, 1 Wash.App. 694, 463 P.2d 225 (1969), which cited with approval the Geremia case.

Until recently it was a general rule that the doctrine of estoppel was applied only to representations made as to facts past or present. Anderson v. Polleys, 54 R.I. 296, 173 A. 114; Croce v. Whiting Milk Co., R.I., 228 A.2d 574. This doctrine is commonly known as "equitable" estoppel. Over the years, however, courts have carved out a recognized exception to this rule and applied it to those circumstances wherein one promises to do or not to do something in the future. This latter doctrine is known as "promissory" estoppel. See Southeastern Sales & Service Co. v. T. T. Watson, Inc., Fla.App., 172 So.2d 239. See also Berarducci v. Diano, 60 R.I. 305, 198 A. 351.

[The court quoted Restatement § 90.] Although this court has not yet applied the doctrine of promissory estoppel as it is expressed in the Restatement, we have in Mann v. McDermott, 77 R.I. 142, 73 A.2d 815, implied that in appropriate circumstances we would.

Traditionally, the doctrine of promissory estoppel has been invoked as a substitute for a consideration, rendering a gratuitous promise enforceable as a contract. 28 Am.Jur.2d, Estoppel and Waiver, § 48 at 657–658; note 20 S.W. Law Journal 656, "Extension of the Doctrine of Promissory Estoppel into Bargained-for Transactions." Viewed in another way, the acts of reliance by the promisee to his detriment provided a substitute for consideration. Hoffman v. Red Owl Stores, Inc., 26 Wis.2d 683, 133 N.W.2d 267.

While the doctrine was originally recognized and most often utilized in charitable subscription cases, it presently enjoys a much wider and more expanded application. See 1 Williston, Contracts (3d Jaeger), § 140; 1A Corbin, Contracts, §§ 193–209; 48 A.L.R.2d 1069–1088. Relative to the problem presented in this case, we have discovered several cases in which the theory of promissory estoppel has been invoked. In these cases, courts have held that a gratuitous promise made by one to procure insurance on the promisee's property is made enforceable by the promisee's reliance thereon and his forbearance to procure such insurance himself. Graddon v. Knight, 138 Cal.App.2d 577, 292 P.2d 632; see also 1A Corbin, Contracts, § 208 at 265 and cases cited therein. Our research indicates, therefore, that the contrary view expressed in Hazlett v. First Fed. Sav. & Loan Assn., supra, and relied upon by plaintiff, is a minority viewpoint on the issue before us and we are disinclined to follow it.

In the instant case, however, after a careful review of the facts, we are of the opinion that plaintiff made more than a mere gratuitous or unrecompensed promise. Instead, we believe that the promise by plaintiff to pay the insurance premium on defendants' car was one made in exchange for valid consideration. The mortgage contract provided that in the event plaintiff paid a premium for defendants, it would add such expended sums to the outstanding balance of defendants' loan. We are satisfied from a close examination of plaintiff's reply to defendants' interrogatories and of the chattel mortgage agreement that plaintiff intended to compute interest on any money it expended in keeping the insurance on defendants' car active. Hence, in our opinion, the interest due on any sums paid out by plaintiff on behalf of defendants for insurance represents valid consideration and converts their promise into a binding contract. The plaintiff's failure to successfully carry out its promise must be deemed a breach of that contract entitling defendants to assert a right of action which would at the very least offset any amount of money found owing to plaintiff on their loan.

We would point out that, even if it could be shown by plaintiff that it never intended to compute any interest on amounts paid by it for insurance premiums on defendants' car and that its promise was truly a pure gratuitous undertaking, we believe such a showing would be of no avail to it since we would not hesitate in finding from this record evidence sufficient to establish a case for the application of promissory estoppel. The conditions precedent for the invocation of this doctrine are well set forth by Dean Boyer in his oft-cited article, "Promissory Estoppel: Requirements And Limitations Of The Doctrine," 98 U.Pa.L.Rev. 459. He enumerates the conditions as follows:

"(1) Was there a promise which the promisor should reasonably expect to induce action or forbearance of a definite and substantial character on the part of the promisee?

"(2) Did the promise induce such action or forbearance?

"(3) Can injustice be avoided only by enforcement of the promise?"

After a study of the facts in this case, our reply to each of the above inquiries is a definite "yes." Promissory estoppel as a legal theory is gaining in prominence as a device used by an increasing number of courts to provide a much needed remedy to alleviate the plight of those who suffer a serious injustice as a result of their good-faith reliance on the unfulfilled promises of others. As the Arkansas supreme court has so appropriately commented in Peoples Nat'l Bank of Little Rock v. Linebarger Constr. Co., 219 Ark. 11, at 17, 240 S.W.2d 12, at 16, the law of promissory estoppel exhibits ". . . an attempt by the courts to keep remedies abreast of increased moral consciousness of honesty and fair representations in all business dealings . . . ." We subscribe to those sentiments.

The plaintiff's appeal is denied and dismissed and the judgment appealed from is affirmed.

NOTE

Case Comparison. What was the consideration for the Credit Union's promise? Does the discussion of promissory estoppel in the principal case go beyond Siegel v. Spear, p. 89 supra? On somewhat similar facts, a lower New York court denied recovery, explaining that Siegel v. Spear applied only to "misfeasance" as distinguished from "nonfeasance," and that the Allegheny College case "extended the doctrine of promissory estoppel only to the law relating to charitable subscriptions." A lower court, therefore, "should go no further." Comfort v. McCorkle, 149 Misc. 826, 268 N.Y.S. 192 (1933). (No assessment of the New York law in this area can ignore Spiegel v. Metropolitan Life Insurance Co., 6 N.Y.2d 91, 160 N.E.2d 40 (1959), although, because of the court's failure to deal with the precedents, that case raises more questions than it answers.)

FEINBERG v. PFEIFFER CO.

Saint Louis Court of Appeals, Missouri, 1959.
322 S.W.2d 163.

[The facts and the first part of the opinion in this case are at p. 59 supra. The court there rejected Mrs. Feinberg's contention that her continuation in the employ of Pfeiffer Co. from December 27, 1947, the date of the resolution, until the date of her retirement, June 30, 1949, was consideration for Pfeiffer's promise to pay her $200 per month for life upon her retirement. In the portion of the opinion below, the court considers Mrs. Feinberg's second contention, that the promise was enforceable because of her reliance on it, "i. e., her retirement, and the abandonment by her of her opportunity to continue in gainful employment."]

DOERNER, Commissioner. . . . But as to the second of these contentions we must agree with plaintiff. By the terms of the resolution defendant promised to pay plaintiff the sum of $200 a month upon her retirement.

[The court quoted Restatement, § 90.] Was there such an act on the part of plaintiff, in reliance upon the promise contained in the resolution, as will estop the defendant, and therefore create an enforceable contract under the doctrine of promissory estoppel? We think there was. One of the illustrations cited under Section 90 of the Restatement is: "2. A promises B to pay him an annuity during B's life. B thereupon resigns a profitable employment, as A expected that he might. B receives the annuity for some years, in the meantime becoming disqualified from again obtaining good employment. A's promise is binding." This illustration is objected to by defendant as not being applicable to the case at hand. The reason advanced by it is that in the illustration B became "disqualified" from obtaining other employment *before* A discontinued the payments, whereas in this case the plaintiff did not discover that she had cancer and thereby became unemployable until *after* the defendant had discontinued the payments of $200 per month. We think the distinction is immaterial. The only reason for the reference in the illustration to the disqualification of A is in connection with that part of Section 90 regarding the prevention of injustice. The injustice would occur regardless of when the disability occurred.

Would defendant contend that the contract would be enforceable if the plaintiff's illness had been discovered on March 31, 1956, the day before it discontinued the payment of the $200 a month, but not if it occurred on April 2nd, the day after? Furthermore, there are more ways to become disqualified for work, or unemployable, than as the result of illness. At the time she retired plaintiff was 57 years of age. At the time the payments were discontinued she was over 63 years of age. It is a matter of common knowledge that it is virtually impossible for a woman of that age to find satisfactory employment, much less a position comparable to that which plaintiff enjoyed at the time of her retirement.

The fact of the matter is that plaintiff's subsequent illness was not the "action or forbearance" which was induced by the promise contained in the resolution. As the trial court correctly decided, such action on plaintiff's part was her retirement from a lucrative position in reliance upon defendant's promise to pay her an annuity or pension. [The court quoted from Ricketts v. Scothorn, supra.]

The Commissioner therefore recommends, for the reasons stated, that the judgment be affirmed.

PER CURIAM. The foregoing opinion by DOERNER, C., is adopted as the opinion of the court. The judgment is, accordingly, affirmed.

NOTE

Case Comparison. How would the court that decided the principal case have decided the case of Kirksey v. Kirksey, p. 64 supra?

RESTATEMENT SECOND, § 90

In view of the great influence that § 90 of the first Restatement has had, § 90 of the Restatement Second set out below, merits a particularly careful reading. Note the addition of the second sentence of Subsection (1). Comment *d* to § 90 suggests that in some situations, relief may be "measured by the extent of the promisee's reliance rather than by the terms of the promise." In what kinds of situations would this be appropriate? Note too the deletion in the first sentence of the requirement that the reliance be of "a definite and substantial character." Is this change related to the addition of the second sentence? Finally, note the liberalization in Subsection (2) of the rule as to charitable subscriptions.[a]

§ 90. Promise Reasonably Inducing Action or Forbearance

(1) A promise which the promisor should reasonably expect to induce action or forbearance on the part of the

a. For a case following the rule stated in Subsection (2), see Salsbury v. Northwestern Bell Telephone Co., 221 N.W.2d 609 (Iowa, 1974). Contra: Mount Sinai Hospital of Greater Miami, Inc. v. Jordan, 290 So.2d 484 (Fla.1974).

promisee or a third person and which does induce such action or forbearance is binding if injustice can be avoided only by enforcement of the promise. The remedy granted for breach may be limited as justice requires.

(2) A charitable subscription or a marriage settlement is binding under Subsection (1) without proof that the promise induced action or forbearance.

NOTES

(1) *Case Analysis.* Assuming that each of the following plaintiffs had been allowed to recover under the rule stated in Restatement Second, § 90, which of them might appropriately have been limited to recovery based on the reliance interest? Katie Scothorn? The Geremias? Anna Feinberg? Antillico Kirksey? Why?

(2) *Rewards: Reprise.* Does the rule of Restatement Second, § 90(2) on charitable subscriptions afford a helpful analogy for the proposition that a promise of a reward ought to be enforceable by one who does the requested act in ignorance of the promise? See Note 1, p. 67 supra.

(3) *"The Death of Contract."* In a little book with the provocative title "The Death of Contract," Professor Grant Gilmore describes the "decline and fall" of "the general theory of contract," as espoused by Langdell, Holmes and Williston. He refers to "the Restatement's schizophrenia" and quotes § 75 of the first Restatement.

"This is, of course, pure Holmes. The venerable Justice took no part in the Restatement project. It is unlikely that he ever looked at the Restatement of Contracts. If, however, § 75 was ever drawn to his attention, it is not hard to imagine him chuckling at the thought of how his revolutionary teaching of the 1880s had become the orthodoxy of a half-century later."

He then quotes § 90 of the first Restatement. "And what is that all about? We have become accustomed to the idea, without in the least understanding it, that the universe includes both matter and anti-matter. Perhaps what we have here is Restatement and anti-Restatement or Contract and anti-Contract. We can be sure that Holmes, who relished a good paradox, would have laughed aloud at the sequence of § 75 and § 90. The one thing that is clear is that these two contradictory propositions cannot live comfortably together: in the end one must swallow the other up.

"A good many years ago Professor Corbin gave me his version of how this unlikely combination came about. When the Restaters and their advisors came to the definition of consideration, Williston proposed in substance what became § 75. Corbin submitted a quite different proposal. To understand what the Corbin proposal was about, it is necessary to backtrack somewhat. Even after the Holmesian or bargain theory of consideration had won all but universal acceptance, the New York Court of Appeals had, during the Cardozo period, pursued a line of its own. There is a long series of Cardozo contract opinions, scattered over his long tenure on that court. Taken all in all, they express what might be called an expansive theory of contract. Courts should make contracts wherever possible, rather than the other way around. Missing terms can be supplied. If an express promise is lacking, an implied promise can easily be found. In particular Cardozo delighted in weaving gossamer spider webs of consideration. There was consideration for a father's promise to pay his engaged daughter an annuity after marriage in the fact that the engaged couple, instead of breaking off the engagement, had in fact married. There was consideration for a pledge to a college endowment campaign (which the donor had later sought to revoke) in the fact that the college, by accepting the pledge, had come under an implied duty to memorialize the donor's name: 'The longing for posthumous remembrance is an emotion not so weak as to justify us in saying that its gratification is a negligible good.' Evidently a judge who could find 'consideration' in DeCicco v. Schweizer or in the *Allegheny College* case could, when he was so inclined, find consideration anywhere: the term had been so broadened as to have become meaningless. We may now return to the Restatement debate on the consideration definition. Corbin, who had been deeply influenced by Cardozo, proposed to the Restaters what might be called a Cardozoean definition of consideration—broad, vague and, essentially, meaningless—a common law equivalent of causa, or cause. In the debate Corbin and the Cardozoeans lost out to Williston and the Holmesians. In Williston's view, that should have been the end of the matter.

"Instead, Corbin returned to the attack. At the next meeting of the Restatement group, he addressed them more or less in the following manner: Gentlemen, you are engaged in restating the common law of contracts. You have recently adopted a definition of consideration. I now submit to you a list of cases—hundreds, perhaps or thousands?—in which courts have imposed contractual liability under circumstances in which, according to your definition, there would be no consideration and therefore no liability. Gentlemen, what do you intend to do about these cases?

"To understand Corbin's point we must backtrack and digress again. I have made the point that Holmesian consideration theory had, as Holmes perfectly well knew, not so much as a leg to stand on if the matter is taken historically. Going back into the past, there was an indefinite number of cases which had imposed liability, in the name of consideration, where nothing like Holmes's 'reciprocal conventional inducement' was anywhere in sight. Holmes's point was that these were bad cases and that the range of contractual liability should be confined within narrower limits. By the turn of the century, except in New York, the strict bargain theory of consideration had won general acceptance. But, unlike Holmes, many judges, it appeared, were not prepared to look with stony-eyed indifference on the plight of a plaintiff who had, to his detriment, relied on a defendant's assurances without the protection of a formal contract. However, the new doctrine precluded the judges of the 1900 crop from saying, as their predecessors would have said a half-century earlier, that the 'detriment' itself was 'consideration.' They had to find a new solution, or, at least, a new terminology. In such a situation the word that comes instinctively to the mind of any judge is, of course, 'estoppel'—which is simply a way of saying that, for reasons which the court does not care to discuss, there must be judgment for plaintiff. And in the contract cases after 1900 the word 'estoppel,' modulating into such phrases as 'equitable estoppel' and 'promissory estoppel,' began to appear with increasing frequency. Thus Corbin, in his submission to the Restaters, was plentifully supplied with new, as well as with old, case material.

"The Restaters, honorable men, evidently found Corbin's argument unanswerable. However, instead of reopening the debate on the consideration definition, they elected to stand by § 75 but to add a new section—§ 90—incorporating the estoppel idea although without using the word 'estoppel.' The extent to which the new section § 90 was to be allowed to undercut the underlying principle of § 75 was left entirely unresolved. The format of the Restatement included analytical, discursive, often lengthy comments, interspersed with illustrations—that is, hypothetical cases, the facts of which were frequently drawn from real cases. Section 90 is almost the only section of the Restatement of Contracts which has no Comment at all. Four hypothetical cases, none of them, so far as I know, based on a real case, are offered as 'illustrations,' presumably to indicate the range which the section was meant to have. An attentive study of the four illustrations will lead any analyst to the despairing conclusion, which is of course reinforced by the mysterious text of § 90 itself, that no one had any idea what the damn thing meant. . . .

"[Now] the unwanted stepchild of Restatement (First) has become 'a basic principle' of Restatement (Second) which, the comment seems to suggest, prevails, in case of need, over the competing 'bargain theory' of § [71]. The Comment and the new Illustrations are entirely clear that the principle of § 90 is applicable in commercial contexts as well as in noncommercial ones—thus disposing of one of the suggested limitations on the use of original § 90. No doubt wisely, the draftsman of the Comment refrains from taking any position on the suggestions in some recent cases that a § 90 recovery is not a contract recovery at all.

"Clearly enough the unresolved ambiguity in the relationship between § 75 and § 90 in the Restatement (First) has now been resolved in favor of the promissory estoppel principle of § 90 which has, in effect, swallowed up the bargain principle of § [71]. The wholly executory exchange where neither party has yet taken any action would seem to be the only situation in which it would be necessary to look to § [71]—and even there, as the Comment somewhat mysteriously suggests, the 'probability of reliance' may be a sufficient reason for enforcement without inquiring into whether or not there was any 'consideration.' . . .

"Speaking descriptively, we might say that what is happening is that 'contract' is being reabsorbed into the mainstream of 'tort.' Until the general theory of contract was hurriedly run up late in the nineteenth century, tort had always been our residual category of civil liability. As the contract rules dissolve, it is becoming so again. It should be pointed out that the theory of tort into which contract is being reabsorbed is itself a much more expansive theory of liability than was the theory of tort from which contract was artificially separated a hundred years ago." G. Gilmore, The Death of Contract 61–65, 72, 87 (1974).[a]

SECTION 5. RESTITUTION AS A BASIS FOR RECOVERY

Courts have, with reason, regarded with suspicion claims to recover for benefits voluntarily conferred. The Restatement of Restitution § 112, Comment a, gives this rather obvious illustration:

> During A's absence and in the belief that A will be willing to pay for the work, B improves A's land, which is worth and is offered for sale at $5000, to such an extent that upon A's return he sells the land for $8000. B is not entitled to restitution from A.

It has been suggested that the proposition "that no one should be required to pay for benefits that were 'forced' upon him . . . is often stated with more than the needed vigor, perhaps in an effort to neutralize the beguiling effect of the unjust enrichment principle, which postulates that gains produced through another's loss are unjust and should be restored."[a] The following cases pose difficult problems in drawing the line between the "officious intermeddler" or the "volunteer" and the deserving claimant. The subject of restitution is explored in detail in the four-volume work, G. Palmer, Law of Restitution (1978).

CALLANO v. OAKWOOD PARK HOMES CORP.

Superior Court of New Jersey, 1966.
91 N.J.Super. 105, 219 A.2d 332.

COLLESTER, J. A. D. Defendant Oakwood Park Homes Corp., (Oakwood) appeals from a judgment of $475 entered in favor of plaintiffs Julia Callano and Frank Callano in the Monmouth County District Court.

The case was tried below on an agreed stipulation of facts. Oakwood, engaged in the construction of a housing development, in December 1961 contracted to sell a lot with a house to be erected thereon to Bruce Pendergast, who resided in Waltham, Massachusetts. In May 1962, prior to completion of the house, the Callanos, who operated a plant nursery, delivered and planted shrubbery pursuant to a contract with Pendergast. A representative of Oakwood had knowledge of the planting.

Pendergast never paid the Callanos the invoice price of $497.95. A short time after the shrubbery was planted Pendergast died.

a. Dawson, The Self-Serving Intermeddler, 87 Harv.L.Rev. 1409 (1974).

Thereafter, on July 10, 1962 Oakwood and Pendergast's estate cancelled the contract of sale. Oakwood had no knowledge of Pendergast's failure to pay the Callanos. On July 16, 1962 Oakwood sold the Pendergast property, including the shrubbery located thereon, to Richard and Joan Grantges for an undisclosed amount.

The single issue is whether Oakwood is obligated to pay plaintiffs for the reasonable value of the shrubbery on the theory of *quasi*-contractual liability. Plaintiffs contend that defendant was unjustly enriched when the Pendergast contract to purchase the property was cancelled and that an agreement to pay for the shrubbery is implied in law. Defendant argues that the facts of the case do not support a recovery by plaintiffs on the theory of *quasi*-contract.

Contracts implied by law, more properly described as *quasi* or constructive contracts, are a class of obligations which are imposed or created by law without regard to the assent of the party bound, on the ground that they are dictated by reason and justice. They rest solely on a legal fiction and are not contract obligations at all in the true sense, for there is no agreement; but they are clothed with the semblance of contract for the purpose of the remedy, and the obligation arises not from consent, as in the case of true contracts, but from the law or natural equity. Courts employ the fiction of *quasi* or constructive contract with caution.[a] C.J.S. Contracts § 6, pp. 566–570 (1963).

In cases based on *quasi*-contract liability, the intention of the parties is entirely disregarded, while in cases of express contracts and contracts implied in fact the intention is of the essence of the transaction. In the case of actual contracts the agreement defines the duty, while in the case of *quasi*-contracts the duty defines the contract. Where a case shows that it is the duty of the defendant to pay, the law imparts to him a promise to fulfill that obligation. The duty which thus forms the foundation of a *quasi*-contractual obligation is frequently based on the doctrine of unjust enrichment. It rests on the equitable principle that a person shall not be allowed to enrich himself unjustly at the expense of another, and on the princi-

a. "Quasi contract" is a useful term for describing a ground for recovering money in an action at common law, when the claim is not based either on principles of tort law or on a true contract. Together with such equitable remedies as those discussed in Note, p. 111, infra, it serves to redress unjust enrichment. "Restitution" is a broader term, propagated by American scholars in this century, to embrace all of the remedies having that function. It refers also to the theory on which they are based. "Quantum meruit" (as much as he deserved) is an older term, narrower, and less useful in current discourse about contract law. It describes a form of action, or short-form pleading, used for centuries in enforcing duties of payment for services. A related action for the worth of goods was "quantum valebant" (as much as they were worth).

Inexact uses of these terms are common. In particular, the term "quantum meruit" is often used interchangeably with "quasi-contract."

ple of whatsoever it is certain a man ought to do, that the law supposes him to have promised to do. St. Paul Fire, etc., Co. v. Indemnity Ins. Co. of No. America, 32 N.J. 17, 22, 158 A.2d 825 (1960).

The key words are *enrich* and *unjustly*. To recover on the theory of *quasi*-contract the plaintiffs must prove that defendant was enriched, *viz.*, received a benefit, and that retention of the benefit without payment therefor would be unjust.

It is conceded by the parties that the value of the property, following the termination of the Pendergast contract, was enhanced by the reasonable value of the shrubbery at the stipulated sum of $475. However, we are not persuaded that the retention of such benefit by defendant before it sold the property to the Grantges was inequitable or unjust.

Quasi-contractual liability has found application in a myriad of situations. See Woodruff, Cases on Quasi-Contracts (3d ed. 1933). However, a common thread runs throughout its application where liability has been successfully asserted, namely, that the plaintiff expected remuneration from the defendant, or if the true facts were known to plaintiff, he would have expected remuneration from defendant, at the time the benefit was conferred. See Rabinowitz v. Mass. Bonding & Insurance Co., 119 N.J.L. 552, 197 A. 44 (E. & A. 1937); Power-Matics, Inc. v. Ligotti, 79 N.J.Super. 294, 191 A.2d 483 (App.Div.1963); Shapiro v. Solomon, 42 N.J.Super. 377, 126 A.2d 654 (App.Div.1956). It is further noted that *quasi*-contract cases involve either some direct relationship between the parties or a mistake on the part of the person conferring the benefit.

In the instant case the plaintiffs entered into an express contract with Pendergast and looked to him for payment. They had no dealings with defendant, and did not expect remuneration from it when they provided the shrubbery. No issue of mistake on the part of plaintiffs is involved. Under the existing circumstances we believe it would be inequitable to hold defendant liable. Plaintiffs' remedy is against Pendergast's estate, since they contracted with and expected payment to be made by Pendergast when the benefit was conferred. . . . A plaintiff is not entitled to employ the legal fiction of *quasi*-contract to "substitute one promisor or debtor for another." Cascaden v. Magryta, 247 Mich. 267, 225 N.W. 511, 512 (Sup.Ct.1929).

Plaintiffs place reliance on De Gasperi v. Valicenti, 198 Pa.Super. 455, 181 A.2d 862 (Super.Ct.1962), where recovery was allowed on the theory of unjust enrichment. We find the case inapposite. It is clear that recovery on *quasi*-contract was permitted there because of a fraud perpetrated by defendants. There is no contention of fraud on the part of Oakwood in the instant case.

Recovery on the theory of *quasi*-contract was developed under the law to provide a remedy where none existed. Here, a remedy exists. Plaintiffs may bring their action against Pendergast's estate.

We hold that under the facts of this case defendant was not unjustly enriched and is not liable for the value of the shrubbery.

Reversed.

NOTES

(1) *The Case of Contractor's Claim.* Paschall's built a bathroom onto the Doziers' house at the request and on the credit of their daughter, Mrs. Best, who lived with them, and with the knowledge and consent of the Doziers. Paschall's was unsuccessful in collecting from Mrs. Best, who was subsequently adjudicated a bankrupt, and sued the Doziers on a theory of restitution. The trial court sustained the Doziers' demurrer and dismissed the complaint, and Paschall's appealed. *Held*: Reversed and remanded "to the trier of facts to determine whether or not the defendant has been so unjustly enriched at the detriment of the complainant so as to require him to make compensation therefor." The court granted that it may be "the general rule" that "an implied undertaking cannot arise against one benefitted by the work performed, where the work is done under a special contract with another. . . . However, the situation is dissimilar where a person furnishes materials and labor under a contract for the benefit of a third party, and that contract becomes unenforceable or invalid. . . . [W]e think that before recovery can be had against the landowner on an unjust enrichment theory, the furnisher of the materials and labor must have exhausted his remedies against the person with whom he had contracted, and still has not received the reasonable value of his services." Paschall's, Inc. v. Dozier, 219 Tenn. 45, 407 S.W.2d 150 (1966).

Can this case be distinguished from the Callano case? One writer suggests: "Where benefit is conferred on a stranger through performance of one's own contract various intermediate solutions could be thought of. The most plausible would be to permit restitution of the benefit to the stranger when the remedy of the gain-producer against his own obligor had failed or was certain to fail. Restitution would then serve as a surrogate, being held in reserve to insure the gain-producer against deficits in the return promised him." Dawson, The Self-Serving Intermeddler, 87 Harv.L. Rev. 1409, 1457–58 (1974). To what extent are the Callano and Paschall's cases consistent with this suggestion? For an analysis in economic terms, see A. Kronman and R. Posner, The Economics of Contract Law 59–64 (1979).

(2) *Subcontractors and Mechanics' Liens.* An application of the problem considered in the preceding case that is of great practical importance concerns the rights of subcontractors on construction jobs. Typically two separate contracts are involved, one between the owner and the general contractor, and another between the general contractor and the subcontractor. It is clear that if, after the subcontractor has performed, he is not paid by the general contractor, the subcontractor has no contractual rights against the owner. It is also clear, under reasoning like that in the Callano case, that even though the subcontractor has benefitted the owner by improving his property, he cannot recover in restitution. "If he has not availed himself of his lien rights under the statutes, and is unable to now collect from the general contractor, the loss must be borne by him and not by the owner, who has the right to rely upon his agreement with the principal contractor." Gebhardt Brothers, Inc. v. Brimmel, 31 Wis.2d 581, 586, 143 N.W.2d 479,

482 (1966); see also Pendleton v. Sard, 297 A.2d 889 (Me.1972); Annot., 62 A.L.R.3d 288 (1975).

The statutes to which the court refers in the preceding quotation provide for what are historically known as "mechanics' liens." Now in effect in all states, these statutes began to be enacted in the late eighteenth century to spur construction in a young and growing country. They protect laborers, materialmen, subcontractors, contractors and the like, who make improvements on real property by giving them a lien, i. e., a security interest, in that property to secure payment for those improvements. Public property is generally exempt. The subcontractor's lien is limited to the reasonable value of what he has done, and in some states it may not exceed the amount then due from the owner to the general contractor. Typically the lien must be perfected by serving notice on the owner and filing a statement in a public office within prescribed times. Although the lien does not create any personal obligation from the owner to the subcontractor, it is enforceable through sale of the owner's property in foreclosure proceedings, with the debt owed by the general contractor to the subcontractor payable out of the proceeds.[a]

COTNAM v. WISDOM

Supreme Court of Arkansas, 1907.
83 Ark. 601, 104 S.W. 164.

Appeal from Circuit Court, Pulaski County; R. J. Lea, Judge.

Action by F. L. Wisdom and another against T. T. Cotnam, administrator of A. M. Harrison, deceased, for services rendered by plaintiffs as surgeons to defendant's intestate. Judgment for plaintiffs. Defendant appeals. Reversed and remanded.

Instructions 1 and 2, given at the instance of plaintiffs, are as follows: "(1) If you find from the evidence that plaintiffs rendered professional services as physicians and surgeons to the deceased, A. M. Harrison, in a sudden emergency following the deceased's injury in a street car wreck, in an endeavor to save his life, then you are instructed that plaintiffs are entitled to recover from the estate of the said A. M. Harrison such sum as you may find from the evidence is a reasonable compensation for the services rendered. (2) The character and importance of the operation, the responsibility resting upon the surgeon performing the operation, his experience and professional training, and the ability to pay of the person operated upon, are elements to be considered by you in determining what is a reasonable charge for the services performed by plaintiffs in the particular case."

a. Why did not the Callanos and Paschalls have liens? The New Jersey statute provides for a lien on property for improvements including "planting thereon any shrubs," but only for "debts contracted by the owner" of the property. N.J.Stat.Ann. § 2A:44–66. Oakwood, not Pendergast, was the "owner" of the property. Similarly, the Tennessee statute provides for a lien where improvements have been made on a house but only by "contract with the owner or his agent." Tenn.Code Ann. §§ 64–1102.

HILL, C. J. (after stating the facts). . . . . . The first question is as to the correctness of [the first] instruction. As indicated therein the facts are that Mr. Harrison, appellant's intestate, was thrown from a street car, receiving serious injuries which rendered him unconscious, and while in that condition the appellees were notified of the accident and summoned to his assistance by some spectator, and performed a difficult operation in an effort to save his life, but they were unsuccessful, and he died without regaining consciousness. The appellant says: "Harrison was never conscious after his head struck the pavement. He did not and could not, expressly or impliedly, assent to the action of the appellees. He was without knowledge or will power. However merciful or benevolent may have been the intention of the appellees, a new rule of law, of contract by implication of law, will have to be established by this court in order to sustain the recovery." Appellant is right in saying that the recovery must be sustained by a contract by implication of law, but is not right in saying that it is a new rule of law, for such contracts are almost as old as the English system of jurisprudence. They are usually called "implied contracts." More properly they should be called "quasi contracts" or "constructive contracts." See 1 Page on Contracts, sec. 14; also 2 Page on Contracts, sec. 771.

The following excerpts from Sceva v. True, 53 N.H. 627, are peculiarly applicable here: "We regard it as well settled by the cases referred to in the briefs of counsel, many of which have been commented on at length by Mr. Shirley for the defendant, that an insane person, an idiot, or a person utterly bereft of all sense and reason by the sudden stroke of an accident or disease may be held liable, in assumpsit, for necessaries furnished to him in good faith while in that unfortunate and helpless condition. And the reasons upon which this rests are too broad, as well as too sensible and humane, to be overborne by any deductions which a refined logic may make from the circumstances that in such cases there can be no contract or promise, in fact, no meeting of the minds of the parties. The cases put it on the ground of an implied contract; and by this is not meant, as the defendant's counsel seems to suppose, an actual contract—that is, an actual meeting of the minds of the parties, an actual, mutual understanding, to be inferred from language, acts, and circumstances by the jury—but a contract and promise, said to be implied by the law, where, in point of fact, there was no contract, no mutual understanding, and so no promise. The defendant's counsel says it is usurpation for the court to hold, as a matter of law, that there is a contract and a promise, when all the evidence in the case shows that there was not a contract, nor the semblance of one. It is doubtless a legal fiction, invented and used for the sake of the remedy. If it was originally usurpation, certainly it has now become very inveterate, and firmly fixed in the body of the law. Illustrations might be multiplied, but enough has been said to show that when a contract or promise implied by law is spoken of, a very different thing is meant from a contract in fact, whether express or tacit. The evidence of an actual contract is generally to be found either in some writing made by the parties, or in verbal communications which passed between them, or in their acts and conduct considered in the light of the circumstances of each particular case. A contract implied by law, on the contrary, rests upon no evidence. It has no actual existence. It is simply a mythical creation of the law. The law says it shall be taken that there was a promise, when in point of fact, there was none. Of course this is not good logic, for the obvious and sufficient reason that it is not true. It is a legal fiction, resting wholly for its support on a plain legal obligation, and a plain legal right. If it were true, it would not be a fiction. There is a class of legal rights, with their correlative legal duties, analogous to the obligations quasi ex contractu of the civil law which seem to lie in the region between contracts on the one hand, and torts on the other, and to call for the application of a remedy not strictly furnished either by actions ex contractu or actions ex delicto. . . ."

In its practical application it sustains recovery for physicians and nurses who render services for infants, insane persons, and drunkards. . . . And services rendered by physicians to persons unconscious or helpless by reason of injury or sickness are in the same situation as those rendered to persons incapable of contracting, such as the classes above described. . . . The court was therefore right in giving the instruction in question. . . .

There was evidence in this case proving that it was customary for physicians to graduate their charges by the ability of the patient to pay, and hence, in regard to that element, this case differs from the Alabama case [Morrissett v. Wood, 123 Ala. 384, 26 So. 307]. . . . This could not apply to a physician called in an emergency by some bystander to attend a stricken man whom he never saw or heard of before; and certainly the unconscious patient could not, in fact or in law, be held to have contemplated what charges the physician might properly bring against him. In order to admit such testimony, it must be assumed that the surgeon and patient each had in contemplation that the means of the patient would be one factor in determining the amount of the charge for the services rendered. While the law may admit such evidence as throwing light upon the contract and indicating what was really in contemplation when it was made, yet a different question is presented when there is no contract to be ascertained or construed, but a mere fiction of law creating a contract where none existed in order that there might be a remedy for a right. This fiction merely requires a reasonable compensation for the services rendered. The services are the same be the patient prince or pauper, and for them the surgeon is entitled to fair compensation for his time, service, and skill. It was therefore error to admit this evidence, and to instruct the jury in the second instruction that in determining what was a reasonable charge they could consider the "ability to pay of the person operated upon."[a]

It was improper to let it go to the jury that Mr. Harrison was a bachelor and that his estate was left to nieces and nephews. This was relevant to no issue in the case, and its effect might well have been prejudicial. While this verdict is no higher than some of the evidence would justify, yet it is much higher than some of the other evidence would justify, and hence it is impossible to say that this was a harmless error.

Judgment is reversed, and cause remanded.

BATTLE and WOOD, JJ., concur in sustaining the recovery, and in holding that it was error to permit the jury to consider the fact that his estate would go to collateral heirs; but they do not concur in holding that it was error to admit evidence of the value of the estate, and instructing that it might be considered in fixing the charge.

NOTES

(1) *Question.* Would the result have been different if Dr. Wisdom had treated Harrison in response to a call from Harrison's daughter, who had said, "Give him the best care you can and I will pay you for it"? See p. 128 infra.

(2) *Gratuitousness.* Where one's life or property is imperiled by storm, fire, accident or other casualty, and another renders assistance, the law presumes, in accordance with the mores of our society, that the services were intended to be gratuitous. Thus where a passing motorist finds an injured pedestrian on the highway, administers first aid and takes him to a hospital, there is a presumption of gratuity which will ordinarily bar recovery. However, the presumption may be rebutted if the services are excessively expensive or burdensome to the person rendering them, as where he goes out of his way a hundred miles to take the injured person to a hospital, or where his services continue for days or weeks. The presumption that services rendered in an emergency are gratuitous may also be overturned if the person rendering them does so in a business or professional capacity, as where a passing ambulance removes the injured person to the hospital or where, as in Cotnam v. Wisdom, a passing physician treats the injured person. The law of salvage in admiralty affords some interesting comparisons with land rules concerning services rendered in an emergency. See Wade, Restitution for Benefits Conferred Without Request, 19 Vand.L. Rev. 1183, 1208–11 (1966).

(3) *Amount of Recovery.* What is the proper measure of recovery in quasi contract? In Hill v. Waxberg Constr. Co., 237 F.2d 936 (9th Cir. 1956), the court gave the following answer: "An 'implied in fact' contract is essentially based on the intentions of the parties. It arises where the court finds from the surrounding facts and circumstances that the parties intended to make a contract but failed to articulate their promises and the

a. For a case rejecting Cotnam v. Wisdom on this point, see In re Agnew's Estate, 132 Misc. 811, 231 N.Y.S. 4 (1928).

court merely implies what it feels the parties really intended. It would follow then that the general contract theory of compensatory damages should be applied. Thus, if the court can in fact imply a contract for services, the compensation therefor is measured by the going contract rate. An 'implied in law' contract, on the other hand, is a fiction of the law which is based on the maxim that one who is unjustly enriched at the expense of another is required to make restitution to the other. The intentions of the parties have little or no influence on the determination of the proper measure of damages. In the absence of fraud or other tortious conduct on the part of the person enriched, restitution is properly limited to the value of the benefit which was acquired. The distinction is based on sound reason, too, for where a contract is all but articulated, the expectations of the parties are very nearly mutually understood, and the Court has merely to protect those expectations as men in the ordinary course of business affairs would expect them to be protected, whereas in a situation where one has acquired benefits, without fraud and in a non-tortious manner, with expectations so totally lacking in such mutuality that no contract in fact can be implied, the party benefited should not be required to reimburse the other party on the basis of such party's losses and expenditures, but rather on a basis limited to the benefits, which the benefited party has actually acquired." [a]

Thus in Michigan Central R. Co. v. State, 85 Ind.App. 557, 155 N.E. 50 (1927), the railroad company delivered to the State of Indiana a carload of coal under the mistaken belief that it was the consignee. On discovering its error, the railroad company paid the proper consignee for the coal at the market price of $6.85 a ton and then sued the State for reimbursement based on that price. The evidence showed that the State was buying the same kind of coal at $3.40 a ton. The trial court gave judgment for the railroad company based on $3.40 per ton and this was affirmed. The railroad company may recover in quasi contract only the expense saved the State ($3.40 a ton) and not the outlay of the railroad ($6.85 a ton).

(4) *Duty of Another.* Particularly troublesome problems of "officiousness" and "gratuitousness" are posed where a claimant seeks restitution from one whose duty he has, in some measure, performed. Some of the most common instances arise in connection with duties owed to other members of one's family. If a husband fails to furnish his wife with necessaries, a third party who, without the husband's request, does so may generally recover their reasonable value from the husband. Similarly, if a father fails to furnish a minor child with necessaries, a third party who does so, without the father's request, may generally recover their reasonable value from the father. Such problems are more fully considered in courses in

a. One important consequence of the distinction between "implied in fact" and "implied in law" arises under the Tucker Act, in which the federal government has consented to be sued in the Court of Claims on claims "founded . . . upon any express or implied contract with the United States" (28 U.S.C.A. § 1491). In Schillinger v. United States, 155 U.S. 163 (1894), the Supreme Court held that this did not confer jurisdiction upon the Court of Claims over a claim by a patentee whose patent had been used by the government without his consent since "there is no statement tending to show a coming together of minds in respect to anything." The case has given rise to the proposition that the Court of Claims has no jurisdiction over a claim based on a contract implied in law. Merritt v. United States, 267 U.S. 338 (1925).

family law. For an interesting case on the liability of parents for medical services rendered to their child after they had refused to provide them, see Greenspan v. Slate, 12 N.J. 426, 97 A.2d 390 (1953).

LIABILITY FOR APPROPRIATION OF IDEAS

Claims of liability for appropriation of ideas have provided fertile ground for the development of the law relating to unjust enrichment. Schott v. Westinghouse Electric Corp., 436 Pa. 279, 259 A.2d 443 (1969), is illustrative. Schott, an employee of Westinghouse, twice submitted a suggestion concerning the construction of circuit breaker panels pursuant to a program under which Westinghouse invited its employees to submit suggestions for cash awards from $5.00 up to $15,000. On the suggestion form, above the line for the employee's signature, appeared the stipulation, "I agree that the decision of the local Suggestion Committee on all matters pertaining to this suggestion . . . will be final." The Committee twice rejected Schott's suggestion, stating that it would require heavy preliminary expenditures but would be reconsidered if circuit breaker redesign was undertaken for other reasons. Schott sued Westinghouse alleging that it had appropriated his idea by making the suggested change within the next year but had refused to pay him, giving the excuse that it had been made as "the result of independent action taken without knowledge of your suggestion."

He pleaded causes of action in both contract and unjust enrichment, but the trial court dismissed the complaint. The Supreme Court of Pennsylvania reversed as to the cause of action in unjust enrichment. The stipulation on the form precluded a claim in contract, but the allegations that the use of his "basic idea" resulted in savings to Westinghouse stated a cause of action in unjust enrichment since it did not appear that he "expected no payment or intended to confer a gratuity, nor in the context of the suggestion program . . . that the benefit was conferred officiously." Schott's case was distinguished from those in which recovery had been denied on the ground that "the 'idea' . . . was neither concrete in form nor novel in nature." Two judges concurred on the ground that Schott had stated a cause of action in contract, but had relinquished any claim in unjust enrichment when he signed the form, and one judge dissented.

Courts have dealt with claims for the use of ideas in terms of breach of a contract implied in fact, restitution to prevent unjust enrichment, and breach of a fiduciary duty arising out of disclosure. Although recovery may be had regardless of whether the idea was solicited or not, courts have generally insisted that the idea "appropriated" be "concrete" and "novel" and that its disclosure be "in confidence." On the difficulty of proving "novelty," as well as "appropriation," see C. P. Flemming v. Ronson Corp., 107 N.J.Super. 311, 258

A.2d 153 (1969). For more on the use of ideas, including practices adopted by corporations to protect themselves, see Havighurst, The Right to Compensation for an Idea, 49 Nw.U.L.Rev. 295 (1954); Note, 65 Harv.L.Rev. 673 (1952).

NOTE

Constructive Trust and Subrogation. The common law action for damages to prevent unjust enrichment is supplemented by several types of equitable relief. The most important of these are the constructive trust and subrogation. See, generally, Dawson, Restitution or Damages?, 20 Ohio St.L.J. 175, 181–85 (1959). The "constructive trust" is a method of giving the plaintiff restitution where the defendant has acquired title to property from him or through disposition of his property. The court impresses the property with a constructive trust and will compel its transfer to the plaintiff, subject to the rights of intervening good faith purchasers. See Restatement of Restitution § 160. "Subrogation" is a method of giving the plaintiff restitution where his property has been used in fully discharging another's obligation or a security interest on another's property. The court allows the plaintiff to be subrogated to the position which the creditor or securityholder had occupied prior to the discharge. See Restatement of Restitution § 162. These kinds of equitable relief will not be dealt with in detail here.

SECTION 6. REFORM OF THE DOCTRINE OF CONSIDERATION: THE CASE OF "MORAL OBLIGATION"

As long ago as 1765, Lord Mansfield[a] declared that "The ancient notion about the want of consideration was for the sake of evidence only: for when it is reduced into writing . . . there was no objection to the want of consideration. . . . In commercial cases amongst merchants, the want of consideration is not an objection." Pillans and Rose v. Van Mierop and Hopkins, 3 Burr. 1663, 97 Eng. Rep. 1035 (K.B.1765). His rule was short lived, for three years later it was rejected by the House of Lords, which concluded that, "All contracts are, by the laws of England, distinguished into agreements by specialty [i. e., agreements under seal], and agreements by parol; nor is there any such third class as some of the counsel have endeavored to maintain, as contracts in writing. If they be merely written

a. William Murray, first Earl of Mansfield (1705–1793), was a rival of the elder Pitt in school, in Parliament and in politics. He favored strict measures with the American rebels. His friend Alexander Pope helped him practice advocacy and later praised his eloquence in verse. Dr. Johnson said of him, "much can be made of a Scot if caught young." Mansfield achieved greatness as a judge, being Lord Chief Justice from 1756 to 1788. One of his chief services was in rationalizing mercantile law. In commercial cases he made effective use of special "juries" of merchants, whose advice about their practices was sometimes instrumental in transforming custom into law.

and not specialties, they are parol, and a consideration must be proved." Rann v. Hughes, 7 T.R. 350n, 101 Eng.Rep. 1014n (1778). Mansfield's heresy did not, however, remain quiescent. The view that the formality of putting a promise in writing should operate as an alternative to consideration continued to have appeal, and gained new vitality when the abolition of the seal raised the doctrine of consideration to even greater prominence.

The civil law countries (those whose legal systems are derived from Roman law) commonly have procedures involving the appearance of the promisor before a notary (a lawyer who holds an appointment from the state and who has no counterpart in common law countries), by which irrevocable gratuitous promise may be made. See von Mehren, Civil Law Analogues to Consideration: An Exercise in Comparative Analysis, 72 Harv.L.Rev. 1009, 1057–62 (1959). A few states have general statutes that facilitate the making of binding gratuitous promises by recognizing some form of writing as a substitute for a seal. One such statute, the Model Written Obligations Act, proposed by the National Conference of Commissioners on Uniform State Laws, provides:

> A written release or promise hereafter made and signed by the person releasing or promising shall not be invalid or unenforceable for lack of consideration, if the writing also contains an additional express statement, in any form of language, that the signer intends to be legally bound.

Only Pennsylvania has adopted this act, and a 1937 recommendation of the English Law Revision Commission that a similar statute be adopted in that country has not been followed.[b] A New Mexico statute provides:

> Every contract in writing hereafter made shall import a consideration in the same manner and as fully as sealed in-

b. See the 1937 Report of the [English] Law Revision Committee on the Statute of Frauds and the Doctrine of Consideration (Sixth Interim Report, Cmd. No. 5449 (1937).) This fourteen-member Committee concurred in a Report on Consideration, which took the bargain concept as the meaning of "consideration," and then gave an historical summary of the doctrine which reflected the highly critical attitude of Holdsworth. Thus it was stated that the origin of consideration was "more or less" fortuitous and that the reasons which gave rise to the requirement have "ceased to be of importance at the present day." The Committee's conclusion in principle was as follows:

"If the view is accepted that all that is necessary in order to render an agreement enforceable is that there should be evidence that the parties intend to create a relationship binding in law, then it seems to follow that this requirement can be satisfied equally well either by consideration regarded as evidence of that intention or by some other evidence of that intention. On this basis, it becomes possible to frame proposals which will carry into effect this purpose, and will, while doing as little violence as possible to any long-established theories, remove hardships arising from the technical applications of the doctrine which have crept into the law of contracts."

struments have heretofore done. (N.M.Stat.Ann. § 20–2–8 (1953).)

A more common variety of general legislation is typified by a California statute that makes a writing "presumptive evidence of consideration" (Cal.Civ.Code § 1614 (West 1954)). The specific provisions of the Uniform Commercial Code and of New York statutes, none of which applies to the simple promise of a gift, will be dealt with later at appropriate points.

For a modest exercise that may show at least some of the difficulties inherent in reform of the doctrine of consideration, we turn to the problem of the enforceability of a promise made in recognition of a "moral obligation." First, however, review Feinberg v. Pfeiffer Co., p. 59 supra.

MILLS v. WYMAN

Supreme Judicial Court of Massachusetts, 1825.
3 Pick. 207.

This was an action of assumpsit brought to recover a compensation for the board, nursing, etc. of Levi Wyman, son of the defendant, from the 5th to the 20th of February, 1821. The plaintiff then lived at Hartford, in Connecticut; the defendant at Shrewsbury, in this state. Levi Wyman, at the time when the services were rendered, was about 25 years of age, and had long ceased to be a member of his father's family. He was on his return from a voyage at sea, and being suddenly taken sick at Hartford, and being poor and in distress, was relieved by the plaintiff in the manner and to the extent above stated. On the 24th of February, after all the expenses had been incurred, the defendant wrote a letter to the plaintiff, promising to pay him such expenses. There was no consideration for this promise, except what grew out of the relation which subsisted between Levi Wyman and the defendant, and Howe, J., before whom the case was tried in the Court of Common Pleas, thinking this not sufficient to support the action, directed a nonsuit. To this direction the plaintiff filed exceptions.

PARKER, C. J. General rules of law established for the protection and security of honest and fair-minded men, who may inconsiderately make promises without any equivalent, will sometimes screen men of a different character from engagements which they are bound *in foro conscientiae* to perform. This is a defect inherent in all human systems of legislation. The rule that a mere verbal promise, without any consideration, cannot be enforced by action, is universal in its application, and cannot be departed from to suit particular cases in which a refusal to perform such a promise may be disgraceful.

The promise declared on in this case appears to have been made without any legal consideration. The kindness and services towards the sick son of the defendant were not bestowed at his request. The son was in no respect under the care of the defendant. He was twenty-five years old, and had long left his father's family. On his return from a foreign country, he fell sick among strangers, and the plaintiff acted the part of the good Samaritan, giving him shelter and comfort until he died. The defendant, his father, on being informed of this event, influenced by a transient feeling of gratitude, promised in writing to pay the plaintiff for the expenses he had incurred. But he has determined to break this promise, and is willing to have his case appear on record as a strong example of particular injustice sometimes necessarily resulting from the operation of general rules.

It is said a moral obligation is a sufficient consideration to support an express promise; and some authorities lay down the rule thus broadly; but upon examination of the cases we are satisfied that the universality of the rule cannot be supported, and that there must have been some pre-existing obligation, which has become inoperative by positive law, to form a basis for an effective promise. The cases of debts barred by the Statute of Limitations, of debts incurred by infants, of debts of bankrupts, are generally put for illustration of the rule. Express promises founded on such pre-existing equitable obligations may be enforced; there is a good consideration for them; they merely remove an impediment created by law to the recovery of debts honestly due, but which public policy protects the debtors from being compelled to pay. In all these cases there was originally a *quid pro quo,* and according to the principles of natural justice the party receiving ought to pay; but the legislature has said he shall not be coerced; then comes the promise to pay the debt that is barred, the promise of the man to pay the debt of the infant, of the discharged bankrupt to restore to his creditor what by the law he had lost. In all these cases there is a moral obligation founded upon an antecedent valuable consideration. These promises, therefore, have a sound legal basis. They are not promises to pay something for nothing; not naked pacts, but the voluntary revival or creation of obligations which before existed in natural law, but which had been dispensed with, not for the benefit of the party obliged solely, but principally for the public convenience. If moral obligation, in its fullest sense, is a good substratum for an express promise, it is not easy to perceive why it is not equally good to support an implied promise. What a man ought to do, generally he ought to be made to do whether he promise or refuse. But the law of society has left most of such obligations to the interior forum, as the tribunal of conscience has been aptly called . . . .

Without doubt there are great interests of society which justify withholding the coercive arm of the law from these duties of imperfect obligation, as they are called; imperfect, not because they are less binding upon the conscience than those which are called perfect, but because the wisdom of the social law does not impose sanctions upon them.

A deliberate promise in writing, made freely and without any mistake, one which may lead the party to whom it is made into contracts and expenses, cannot be broken without a violation of moral duty. But if there was nothing paid or promised for it, the law, perhaps wisely, leaves the execution of it to the conscience of him who makes it. It is only when the party making the promise gains something, or he to whom it is made loses something, that the law gives the promise validity. And in the case of the promise of the adult to pay the debt of the infant, of the debtor discharged by the statute of limitations or bankruptcy, the principle is preserved by looking back to the origin of that transaction, where an equivalent is to be found . . . .

For the foregoing reasons we are all of opinion that the nonsuit directed by the Court of Common Pleas was right, and that judgment be entered thereon for costs for the defendant.

NOTES

(1) *The Case Against "Moral Obligation."* Mills v. Wyman accurately reflects the traditional common law view that a promise made in recognition of a "moral obligation" arising out of a benefit previously received is not enforceable. A benefit conferred before a promise is made can hardly be said to have been given in "exchange" for the promise. Williston says: "However much one may wish to extend the number of promises which are enforceable by law, it is essential that the classes of promises which are so enforceable shall be clearly defined. The test of moral consideration must vary with the opinion of every individual. Indeed, as has been said, since there is a moral obligation to perform every promise, it would seem that if morality was to be the guide, every promise would be enforced and if the existence of a past moral obligation is to be the test, every promise which repeats or restates a prior gratuitous promise would be binding." Williston, § 148.

(2) *Recognized Exceptions.* In some exceptional situations the common law did enforce a promise on the ground that it was made in recognition of what could be viewed as a "moral obligation." Leading examples include those mentioned by the court in Mills v. Wyman: a promise to pay a debt that is no longer legally enforceable because of the running of the period of limitations or because of the discharge of the debtor in bankruptcy proceedings, and a promise by an adult to perform a duty imposed by a promise that he made as an infant and that he could have avoided on that ground. See Restatement Second, §§ 82, 83. Does the court in Mills v. Wyman adequately distinguish these examples? [a]

a. In 1782 Lord Mansfield, whose earlier bout with the doctrine of consideration is discussed at p. 111 supra, derived from such exceptions the dictum, "Where a man is under a moral obligation, which no Court of Law or Equity can inforce, and promises, the honesty and rectitude of the thing is

(3) *Reaffirmation of Debt Discharged in Bankruptcy.* The enforceability of a promise to pay a debt that is no longer legally enforceable because of the discharge of the debtor in bankruptcy proceedings is now governed by the Bankruptcy Reform Act of 1978. While that law was being drafted, a staff attorney of the Federal Trade Commission (Bureau of Consumer Protection) reported to Congress on his investigation of consumer finance practices, including case histories reflecting "many hundreds of induced reaffirmations [that is, promises by bankrupts to pay their debts]. An endless variety of techniques was employed to obtain these agreements. Common inducements were threats to property, threats to reputation and standing, and offers of additional cash." His recommendation was for a measure that would invalidate all such agreements,[b] and such a proposal was embodied in the report of the National Bankruptcy Commission created by Congress to review the bankruptcy laws. It would have "abrogated," with modest exceptions, the law that a debtor's promise to pay a discharged debt is enforceable.[c] Congress did not, however, accept his proposal, and the Bankruptcy Reform Act of 1978 contains much more complex protections for the consumer. For the enforceability of a "reaffirmation" of debt it may be required, according to the circumstances, (a) that the bankruptcy court "inform the debtor [*inter alia*] of the legal effect and consequences" of the agreement, and (b) with respect to certain consumer debts, that the court approve the agreement as being "in the best interest of the debtor" and "not imposing an undue hardship" on him or a dependent. Even so, the statute permits the debtor to rescind the agreement within a 30-day period. It does not change any nonbankruptcy rule by which the agreement would be otherwise *un*enforceable. 11 U.S.C.A. § 524(c), (d). As the Bankruptcy Commission pointed out, a discharged debtor remains free to "exercise any motivation to make voluntary payments, in the nature of gifts, to the creditor of an extinguished debt." [d]

WEBB v. McGOWIN

Court of Appeals of Alabama, 1935.
27 Ala.App. 82, 168 So. 196.
Certiorari denied 232 Ala. 374, 168 So. 199 (1936).

Action by Joe Webb against N. Floyd McGowin and Joseph F. McGowin, as executors of the estate of J. Greeley McGowin, deceased. From a judgment of nonsuit, plaintiff appeals.

BRICKEN, Presiding Judge. This action is in assumpsit. The complaint as originally filed was amended. The demurrers to the complaint as amended were sustained, and because of this adverse ruling by the court the plaintiff took a nonsuit, and the assignment of

a consideration." Hawkes v. Saunders, 1 Cowp. 289, 98 Eng.Rep. 1091 (1782). The dictum never became the law.

b. Statement of David A. Williams, reprinted in H.R.Doc. No. 95–595, 95th Cong., 1st Sess. (1977) at 166, 172–73.

c. Report of the Commission on the Bankruptcy Laws, Part 2 (House Doc. No. 93–137, at p. 143).

d. Id.

errors on this appeal are predicated upon said action or ruling of the court.

A fair statement of the case presenting the questions for decision is set out in appellant's brief, which we adopt.[a]

"On the 3d day of August, 1925, appellant while in the employ of the W. T. Smith Lumber Company, a corporation, and acting within the scope of his employment, was engaged in clearing the upper floor of Mill No. 2 of the company. While so engaged he was in the act of dropping a pine block from the upper floor of the mill to the ground below; this being the usual and ordinary way of clearing the floor, and it being the duty of the plaintiff in the course of his employment to so drop it. The block weighed about 75 pounds.

"As appellant was in the act of dropping the block to the ground below, he was on the edge of the upper floor of the mill. As he started to turn the block loose so that it would drop to the ground, he saw J. Greeley McGowin, testator of the defendants, on the ground below and directly under where the block would have fallen had appellant turned it loose. Had he turned it loose it would have struck McGowin with such force as to have caused him serious bodily harm or death. Appellant could have remained safely on the upper floor of the mill by turning the block loose and allowing it to drop, but had he done this the block would have fallen on McGowin and caused him serious injuries or death. The only safe and reasonable way to prevent this was for appellant to hold to the block and divert its direction in falling from the place where McGowin was standing and the only safe way to divert it so as to prevent its coming into contact with McGowin was for appellant to fall with it to the ground below. Appellant did this, and by holding to the block and falling with it to the ground below, he diverted the course of its fall in such way that McGowin was not injured. In thus preventing the injuries to McGowin appellant himself received serious bodily injuries, resulting in his right leg being broken, the heel of his right foot torn off and his right arm broken. He was badly crippled for life and rendered unable to do physical or mental labor.

"On September 1, 1925, in consideration of appellant having prevented him from sustaining death or serious bodily harm and in con-

a. We are grateful to counsel for the McGowin estate for the following version of the controversy. After Webb's injury, he received workmen's compensation payments from the company. When these benefits ran out, McGowin, as president, had the company continue the payments "purely out of the kindness of his heart." (It was therefore the estate's position that McGowin never made the promise alleged in Webb's complaint.) By the time the controversy arising from the demurrer was decided by the Alabama Supreme Court, the estate was ready for final settlement and to avoid further expense and delay, the executors agreed to settle the claim. Counsel later concluded that, in view of the notoriety achieved by the decision, "it would probably have been better to have had the record clarified by following up the case after reversal and requiring the plaintiff to prove the averments of his complaint."

sideration of the injuries appellant had received, McGowin agreed with him to care for and maintain him for the remainder of appellant's life at the rate of $15 every two weeks from the time he sustained his injuries to and during the remainder of appellant's life; it being agreed that McGowin would pay this sum to appellant for his maintenance. Under the agreement McGowin paid or caused to be paid to appellant the sum so agreed on up until McGowin's death on January 1, 1934. After his death the payments were continued to and including January 27, 1934, at which time they were discontinued. Thereupon plaintiff brought suit to recover the unpaid installments accruing up to the time of the bringing of the suit.

"The material averments of the different counts of the original complaint and the amended complaint are predicated upon the foregoing statement of facts." . . .

The action was for the unpaid installments accruing after January 27, 1934, to the time of the suit. . . .

1. The averments of the complaint show that appellant saved McGowin from death or grievous bodily harm. This was a material benefit to him of infinitely more value than any financial aid he could have received. Receiving this benefit, McGowin became morally bound to compensate appellant for the services rendered. Recognizing his moral obligation, he expressly agreed to pay appellant as alleged in the complaint and complied with this agreement up to the time of his death; a period of more than 8 years.

Had McGowin been accidentally poisoned and a physician, without his knowledge or request, had administered an antidote, thus saving his life, a subsequent promise by McGowin to pay the physician would have been valid. Likewise, McGowin's agreement as disclosed by the complaint to compensate appellant for saving him from death or grievous bodily injury is valid and enforceable.

Where the promisee cares for, improves, and preserves the property of the promisor, though done without his request, it is sufficient consideration for the promisor's subsequent agreement to pay for the service, because of the material benefit received. . . .

In Boothe v. Fitzpatrick, 36 Vt. 681, the court held that a promise by defendant to pay for the past keeping of a bull which had escaped from defendant's premises and been cared for by plaintiff was valid, although there was no previous request, because the subsequent promise obviated that objection; it being equivalent to a previous request. On the same principle, had the promisee saved the promisor's life or his body from grievous harm, his subsequent promise to pay for the services rendered would have been valid. Such service would have been far more material than caring for his bull. Any holding that saving a man from death or grievous bodily harm is not a material benefit sufficient to uphold a subsequent promise to pay for the service, necessarily rests on the assumption that saving life and preservation of the body from harm have only a sentimental value. The converse of this is true. Life and preservation of the body have material, pecuniary values, measurable in dollars and cents. Because of this, physicians practice their profession charging for services rendered in saving life and curing the body of its ills, and surgeons perform operations. The same is true as to the law of negligence, authorizing the assessment of damages in personal injury cases based upon the extent of the injuries, earnings, and life expectancies of those injured.

In the business of life insurance, the value of a man's life is measured in dollars and cents according to his expectancy, the soundness of his body, and his ability to pay premiums. The same is true as to health and accident insurance.

It follows that if, as alleged in the complaint, appellant saved J. Greeley McGowin from death or grievous bodily harm, and McGowin subsequently agreed to pay him for the service rendered, it became a valid and enforceable contract.

2. It is well settled that a moral obligation is a sufficient consideration to support a subsequent promise to pay where the promisor has received a material benefit, although there was no original duty or liability resting on the promisor. [Cases cited.]

The case at bar is clearly distinguishable from that class of cases where the consideration is a mere moral obligation or conscientious duty unconnected with receipt by promisor of benefits of a material or pecuniary nature. . . . . Here the promisor received a material benefit constituting a valid consideration for his promise.

3. Some authorities hold that, for a moral obligation to support a subsequent promise to pay, there must have existed a prior legal or equitable obligation, which for some reason had become unenforceable, but for which the promisor was still morally bound. This rule, however, is subject to qualification in those cases where the promisor having received a material benefit from the promisee, is morally bound to compensate him for the services rendered and in consideration of this obligation promises to pay. In such cases the subsequent promise to pay is an affirmance or ratification of the services rendered carrying with it the presumption that a previous request for the service was made. . . .

4. The averments of the complaint show that in saving McGowin from death or grievous bodily harm, appellant was crippled for life. This was part of the consideration of the contract declared on. McGowin was benefited. Appellant was injured. Benefit to the promisor or injury to the promisee is a sufficient legal consideration for the promisor's agreement to pay. . . .

5. Under the averments of the complaint the services rendered by appellant were not gratuitous. The agreement of McGowin to

pay and the acceptance of payment by appellant conclusively shows the contrary. . . .

From what has been said, we are of the opinion that the court below erred in the ruling complained of; that is to say in sustaining the demurrer, and for this error the case is reversed and remanded.

Reversed and remanded.

SAMFORD, Judge (concurring). The questions involved in this case are not free from doubt, and perhaps the strict letter of the rule, as stated by judges, though not always in accord, would bar a recovery by plaintiff, but following the principle announced by Chief Justice Marshall in Hoffman v. Porter, Fed.Cas.No.6,577, 2 Brock. 156, 159, where he says, "I do not think that law ought to be separated from justice, where it is at most doubtful," I concur in the conclusions reached by the court.

[Part of the short opinion of the Supreme Court of Alabama, denying certiorari, is set out below.]

FOSTER, Justice. . . . The opinion of the Court of Appeals here under consideration recognizes and applies the distinction between a supposed moral obligation of the promisor, based upon some refined sense of ethical duty, without material benefit to him, and one in which such a benefit did in fact occur. We agree with that court that if the benefit be material and substantial, and was to the person of the promisor rather than to his estate, it is within the class of material benefits which he has the privilege of recognizing and compensating either by an executed payment or an executory promise to pay. The cases are cited in that opinion. The reason is emphasized when the compensation is not only for the benefits which the promisor received, but also for the injuries either to the property or person of the promisee by reason of the service rendered.

Writ denied.

NOTES

(1) *Restitution.* Did Webb have a claim against McGowin in restitution? If so, the release of that claim in exchange for McGowin's promise could serve as consideration for that promise. Does this appear to have been the basis for the decision in the case?

(2) *The Case for "Moral Obligation."* "Courts have frequently enforced promises on the simple ground that the promisor was only promising to do what he ought to have done anyway. These cases have either been condemned as wanton departures from legal principle, or reluctantly accepted as involving the kind of compromise logic must inevitably make at times with sentiment. I believe that these decisions are capable of rational defense. When we say the defendant was morally obligated to do the thing he promised, we in effect assert the existence of a substantive ground for enforcing the promise. . . . The court's conviction that the promisor ought to do the thing, plus the promisor's own admission of his obligation,

may tilt the scales in favor of enforcement where neither standing alone would be sufficient. If it be argued that moral consideration threatens certainty, the solution would seem to lie, not in rejecting the doctrine, but in taming it by continuing the process of judicial exclusion and inclusion already begun in the cases involving infants' contracts, barred debts, and discharged bankrupts." Fuller, Consideration and Form, 41 Colum.L.Rev. 799, 821, 822 (1941). See also Grosse, Moral Obligation as Consideration in Contracts, 17 Vill.L.Rev. 1 (1971); Henderson, Promises Grounded in the Past: The Idea of Unjust Enrichment and the Law of Contracts, 57 Va.L. Rev. 1115 (1971).

Compare the following analysis. "The facts of a leading rescue past-consideration case, Webb v. McGowin, illustrate the benefits that may accrue to the promisor in such cases if the promise is legally enforceable, over and above the benefits of the transfer itself. The rescued person promised to pay his rescuer $15 every two weeks for the rest of the rescuer's life. This was a generous gift to the extent that the promise was enforceable but a much less generous one to the extent it was not. Had the promisor believed that such a promise was unenforceable, he might have decided instead to make a one-time transfer that might have had a much lower present value than that of the annuity which he in fact promised. Both parties would have been made worse off by this alternative. Hence, it is not surprising that the court held the promise to be enforceable.

"Lon Fuller in a well-known article suggested a different rationale for the past-consideration doctrine. Proceeding from the premise that the requirement of consideration is designed in part to prevent people from making promises on the spur of the moment—promises they do not really mean to make and therefore should not be forced to honor (the 'cautionary' function of consideration)—he argues that where the promise is to do what the promisor is morally obligated to do anyway, we need not worry whether he is acting deliberately or not—he *should* have made the promise and that is all that is important. This paternalistic approach is both difficult to square with the basic premises of contract law and an unnecessary embellishment to a theory of the enforcement of gratuitous promises. Fuller is aware of the relevance of economic considerations in explaining the pattern of enforcement and only fails to see that economic analysis can also explain the past-consideration cases." Posner, Gratuitous Promises in Economics and Law, 6 J. Legal Stud. 411, 419 (1977), reprinted in A. Kronman and R. Posner, The Economics of Contract Law 52–53 (1979).

(3) *The Case of the Spared Spouse.* Lee Taylor assaulted his wife in Lena Harrington's house, where she had taken refuge from a previous assault. The wife knocked him down with an axe, and was about to cut his head open when Lena Harrington deflected the axe, mutilating her hand badly but saving Lee Taylor's life. Later, he orally promised her to pay her damages, but paid only a small sum. She sued him on his promise. *Held:* for defendant. "[H]owever much the defendant should be impelled by common gratitude to alleviate the plaintiff's misfortune, a humanitarian act of this kind, voluntarily performed, is not such consideration as would entitle her to recover at law." Harrington v. Taylor, 225 N.C. 690, 36 S.E.2d 227 (1945).

(4) *Reform by Statute.* New York does not recognize "moral obligation" as an equivalent of consideration, but a New York statute enacted in

1941 and now found in General Obligations Law § 5–1105 provides: "A promise in writing and signed by the promisor or by his agent shall not be denied effect as a valid contractual obligation on the ground that consideration for the promise is past or executed, if the consideration is expressed in the writing and is proved to have been given or performed and would be a valid consideration but for the time when it was given or performed."

California Civil Code § 1606, enacted in 1872, provides: "An existing legal obligation resting upon the promisor, or a moral obligation originating in some benefit conferred upon the promisor, or prejudice suffered by the promisee, is also a good consideration for a promise, to an extent corresponding with the extent of the obligation, but no further or otherwise."

How would these statutes have affected the results in the preceding cases? Would the common recital "for value received" satisfy the New York statute? Would you favor the adoption of either statute by other states? Would you favor the adoption of a statute enacting Restatement, Second, § 86? [a] What kind of active support would you expect such proposals for reform to muster?

THE "ZEALOUS" ADVOCATE AND "TECHNICAL" DEFENSES

Is any ethical question raised when a lawyer is asked to represent a client who has a "technical" defense to the legal enforcement of a "moral" obligation?

An extreme position on the zeal of the advocate is reflected in the famous statement of Lord Brougham, in his defense of Queen Caroline before the House of Lords, in the case of her divorce from George IV:

> I once before took occasion to remind your lordships . . . that an advocate, by the sacred duty which he owes his client, knows in the discharge of that office but one person in the world, that client and none other. To save that client by all expedient means, to protect that client at all hazards and costs, to all others, and among others to himself, is the highest and most unquestioned of his duties; and he must not regard the alarm, the suffering, the torment, the destruction which he may bring upon any other. Nay, separating even the duties of a patriot from those of an advocate, and casting them, if need be, to the wind, he must go on reckless of the consequences, if his fate it should

a. The Reporter who drafted Restatement Second, § 86 has expressed the belief that "this statement of principle is more useful than the statutory formula drafted by the New York Law Revision Commission. . . . [The latter] is too broad in scope and too restrictive in formal requirements; it does not seem to have had any significant effect." Braucher, Freedom of Contract and the Second Restatement, 78 Yale L.J. 598, 605 (1969).

unhappily be to involve his country in confusion for his client's protection.[a]

Canon 7 of the American Bar Association's Code of Professional Responsibility says, with more moderation, "A lawyer should represent a client zealously within the bounds of the law," and Disciplinary Rule 7–101(A) adds that he shall not intentionally "[f]ail to seek the lawful objectives of his client through reasonably available means permitted by law and the Disciplinary Rules, except as provided by DR 7–101(B)." Disciplinary Rule 7–101(B) says that a lawyer may, "[w]here permissible, exercise his professional judgment to waive or fail to assert a right or position of his client." Although Ethical Consideration 7–7 says that, except for "certain areas of legal representation not affecting the merits of the cause or substantially prejudicing the rights of a client . . . the authority to make decisions is exclusively that of the client," Ethical Consideration 7–8 says that in "assisting his client to make a proper decision, it is often desirable for a lawyer to point out those factors which may lead to a decision that is morally just as well as legally permissible." What position should he take as to his client's defense of lack of consideration for his promise to perform his "moral" obligation?

In practice, the ethical problems implicit in the use of a "technical" defense may be presented in quite another way. "Is it proper to use surprise tactics to defeat on a technical ground a claim or defense that you consider unjust upon grounds that you may not be able to establish? Does it make a difference whether the grounds that you consider meritorious but difficult to prove are factual or legal? It is in some such 'intermediate' form that the problem of professional responsibility usually arises. Most cases are settled; in the smaller percentage going to trial, each lawyer generally feels that the other party is at least seeking more than is justly due, if not making a wholly unjustified claim or defense. Probably the answer implicit in prevailing practice is that it is permissible to use any legally supportable ground of claim or defense, though it is a surprise move, to uphold a position you believe just, whatever the basis of your belief may be." R. Keeton, Trial Tactics and Methods 5 (2d ed. 1973).

NOTE

Canon Buttle's Case. Canon Buttle's case may shed some light on the problem. Trustees under a trust of land for sale orally agreed to sell it to Mrs. Simpson for £6,000 and the matter had proceeded so far that one copy of the contract had been signed by Mrs. Simpson and the other by one, but

a. For a fascinating account of Brougham's defense of the Queen and of his fidelity "to his own somewhat peculiar conception of an advocate's duty," see J. B. Atlay, 1 The Lives of the Victorian Chancellors chs. 10, 11 (1906). For discussion of his conception, see S. Thurman, E. Phillips and E. Cheatham, Cases and Materials on the Legal Profession 280–81 (1970). On zealous advocacy and the public interest, see M. Freedman, Lawyers' Ethics in an Adversary System 9–26 (1975).

only one, trustee. Canon Buttle, one of the beneficiaries of the trust, then offered £6,500 on behalf of a charity. The trustees indicated that they felt "in honour bound" to complete the sale to Mrs. Simpson. Canon Buttle and other beneficiaries sought an order restraining the trustees, and the trustees asked for the direction of the court. Wynn-Parry, J., of the Chancery Division said:

> It is true that persons who are not in the position of trustees are entitled, if they so desire, to accept a lesser price than that which they might obtain on the sale of property. . . . It redounds to the credit of a man who acts like that in such circumstances. Trustees, however, are not vested with such complete freedom. They have an overriding duty to obtain the best price which they can for their beneficiaries. . . . The only consideration which was present to their minds was that they had gone so far in the negotiations with Mrs. Simpson that they could not properly, from the point of view of commercial morality, resile from these negotiations. That being so, they did not, to any extent, probe Canon Buttle's offer as, in my view, they should have done. . . . There being a serious purchaser, I shall give the trustees liberty to sell to Mrs. Simpson for £6,600, that being the highest price offered.

Buttle v. Saunders, [1950] 2 All.E.R. 193 (Ch.). Does a lawyer have "complete freedom" to act according to his sense of "commercial morality," or does he have an "overriding duty" to his client?

Chapter 2

THE REQUIREMENT OF A WRITING FOR ENFORCEABILITY: THE STATUTE OF FRAUDS

SECTION 1. THE HISTORY OF THE STATUTE

Most legal systems require a writing for the enforcement of some sorts of promises. In this country the most important requirement of this kind is derived from the British Statute of Frauds enacted by Parliament in 1677 (The Statute of Frauds, An Act for Prevention of Frauds and Perjuries, Stat. 29, Car. II, c. 3). We shall be concerned with four major categories of contracts that are subjected to this requirement in nearly every state: (1) contracts to answer for the duty of another; (2) contracts not to be performed within one year; (3) contracts for the sale of an interest in land; and (4) contracts for the sale of goods. The New Jersey version of the statute below is representative of contemporary American statutes of frauds. The first three categories enumerated above are found in paragraphs (b), (e) and (d), respectively. Contracts for the sale of goods, which even in the original English version were covered by a separate section, are dealt with in New Jersey as elsewhere in UCC 2–201.

"No action shall be brought upon any of the following agreements or promises, unless the agreement or promise, upon which such action shall be brought or some memorandum or note thereof, shall be in writing, and signed by the party to be charged therewith, or by some other person thereunto by him lawfully authorized:

a. A special promise of an executor or administrator to answer damages out of his own estate;

b. A special promise to answer for the debt, default or miscarriage of another person;

c. An agreement made upon consideration of marriage;

d. A contract for sale of real estate, or any interest in or concerning the same; or

e. An agreement that is not to be performed within one year from the making thereof." (N.J.Stat.Ann. § 25:1–5 (West).)

The requirement of a writing is not an alternative to the requirement of consideration but an addition to it. As to its justification, consider the discussion of the "evidentiary" and "cautionary" functions of legal formalities at p. 41 supra. See Perillo, The Statute of Frauds in the Light of the Functions and Dysfunctions of Form, 43 Fordham L.Rev. 39 (1974).

NOTES

(1) *Other Categories.* Some state statutes include other categories of contracts.[a] Two of the most important of these are contracts not to be performed within a lifetime and brokerage contracts. The California statute below includes both (see paragraphs 5 and 6).

> The following contracts are invalid, unless the same, or some note or memorandum thereof, is in writing and subscribed by the party to be charged or by his agent:
>
> 1. An agreement that by its terms is not to be performed within a year from the making thereof;
>
> 2. A special promise to answer for the debt, default, or miscarriage of another . . . ;
>
> 3. An agreement made upon consideration of marriage other than a mutual promise to marry;
>
> 4. An agreement for the leasing for a longer period than one year, or the sale of real property, or of an interest therein; and such agreement, if made by an agent of the party sought to be charged, is invalid, unless the authority of the agent is in writing, subscribed by the party sought to be charged;
>
> 5. An agreement authorizing or employing an agent or broker to purchase or sell real estate for compensation or a commission;
>
> 6. An agreement which by its terms is not to be performed during the lifetime of the promisor, or an agreement to devise or bequeath any property, or to make any provision for any person by will;
>
> 7. An agreement by a purchaser of real property to pay an indebtedness secured by a mortgage or deed of trust upon the property purchased, unless assumption of said indebtedness by the

a. Some writing requirements are not ordinarily regarded as related to the statute of frauds.

One example is the requirement of a writing for an agreement to arbitrate disputes. California Code of Civil Procedure § 1281, for example, provides: "A written agreement to submit to arbitration an existing controversy or a controversy thereafter arising is valid, enforceable and irrevocable, save upon such grounds as exist for the revocation of any contract." Note that, in contrast to the statute of frauds, this statute does not state that the writing must be signed.

Another example is the requirement of a writing for a security interest. UCC 9–203(1) provides that, with some exceptions, "a security interest is not enforceable . . . unless . . . the debtor has signed a security agreement which contains a description of the collateral."

purchaser is specifically provided for in the conveyance of such property. (West's Ann.Cal.Civ.Code § 1624.)

(2) *Repeal of the Statute in England.* In 1954, after 277 years, the British Parliament repealed all of the Statute of Frauds except those provisions requiring a writing for promises to answer for the debt of another and contracts for the sale of land (Act, 1954, 2 & 3 Eliz. 2, c. 34). Why do you suppose these exceptions were made?

Among the reasons for repeal given by the English Law Revision Committee were these: the classes of contracts that are within the statute "seem to be arbitrarily selected and to exhibit no relevant common quality"; the requirement of a writing is "out of accord with the way in which business is normally done" and " 'promotes more frauds than it prevents' "; and the statute was the product of a time when "essential kinds of evidence were excluded (e. g., the parties could not give evidence), and objectionable types of evidence were admitted (e. g., juries were still in theory entitled to act on their own knowledge of the facts in dispute)" and is "an anachronism" in a time "when the parties can freely testify." Law Revision Committee, Sixth Interim Report, Cmd. No. 5449, pp. 6–7 (1937).

The situation in England may, however, be distinguishable from that in this country in several respects. Chief among these are: first, the fact that in England trial by jury in contract actions is within the discretion of the judge, makes it possible to keep from the jury a case formerly within the statute; and second, the fact that in England counsel's fees are included in the costs assessed against the losing party, makes it more likely that the technicalities and uncertainties of the statute will discourage litigants from suing on otherwise meritorious claims. See 68 Harv.L.Rev. 383 (1954).

SECTION 2. WHAT CONTRACTS ARE WITHIN THE STATUTE

Contracts to Answer for the Duty of Another. One of the most important of the provisions of the statute of frauds is that which requires a writing for a promise "to answer for the debt, default, or miscarriage of another." The provision is directed generally at suretyship contracts. Suretyship is defined in Restatement of Security, § 82 as "the relation which exists where one person has undertaken an obligation and another person is also under an obligation or other duty to the obligee, who is entitled to but one performance, and as between the two who are bound, one rather than the other should perform."

As a simple example, suppose that A wishes to obtain services on credit from C. In order to induce C to extend credit, A not only promises to pay the price but has B add his own promise to pay C the price. Both A and B are under obligation to pay the full amount to C; C is entitled to but one performance; and as between A and B, A rather than B should perform. The relation thus fits the Restatement definition of suretyship: A is the *principal*, B is the *surety*, and C is the *creditor*. B's promise is one to answer for the duty of A and so comes within the statute of frauds.

"Why should such promises, more than others, be subject to that requirement? Doubtless because the promisor has received no benefit from the transaction. This circumstance may make perjury more likely, because while in the case of one who has received something the circumstances themselves which are capable of proof show probable liability, in the case of a guaranty nothing but the promise is of evidentiary value. Moreover, as the lack of any benefit received by the guarantor increases the hardship of his being called upon to pay, it also increases the importance of being very sure that he is justly charged." 3 Williston, § 452. Consider also the "evidentiary" and "cautionary" functions of formalities discussed at p. 41 supra. Which of them applies here?

Suppose, however, that instead of the tripartite agreement described above, B and C agree that C will perform services to A in return for which B will repay C the price at a later time. This is not a suretyship relation. B's promise is not one to answer for the debt of A, because A is under no obligation to C, and so B's promise to C is not within the statute.[a] But do not all of the reasons just given for requiring a writing apply with equal force to this situation?

Much litigation has been devoted to characterizing specific transactions to determine whether the promise in suit is one to answer for the duty of *another*. Suppose, for example, that in Cotnam v. Wisdom, p. 105 supra, Dr. Wisdom had treated Harrison in response to a call from Harrison's daughter, who had said, "Give him the best care you can and I will pay you for it." Does the statute apply to the daughter's promise? The Supreme Court of Vermont said in Lawrence v. Anderson, 108 Vt. 176, 184 A. 689 (1936): "Such a promise is not collateral or secondary, but primary and original. . . . To such a contract the Statute of Frauds does not apply, for the simple reason that it is not a promise to pay the debt of another, but is a promise to pay the debt of the promisor—one that he makes his own by force of his engagement."[b] The court, however, went on to hold that the doctor by first charging the patient, billing his estate, and engaging a lawyer to proceed against the estate, "elected to accept the [daughter's] engagement as collateral" to the father's, so that when he sued the daughter a year and a half after the accident "he could not hold the defendant, though she had tendered an engagement direct, in form." Would it have been better to say that the daughter was not bound because the doctor did not accept her offer? Was

a. As will be seen in Chapter 10, A may, as a third party beneficiary, be entitled to enforce the promise that C made to B.

b. For a conflicting interpretation of similar language, see City of Highland Park v. Grant-Mackenzie Co., 366 Mich. 430, 115 N.W.2d 270 (1962).

there any way out of the doctor's dilemma? If he had first pressed a claim against the daughter, without success, could he then have recovered from the estate? See Note 1, p. 104 supra and Note 1, p. 108 supra.

NOTES

(1) *"Main Purpose" or "Leading Object" Rule.* Even where the promise is plainly one to answer for the duty of another, some courts have made an exception if the promisor's "main purpose" or "leading object" is to further his own economic advantage. An example is a promise by the controlling shareholder in a corporation to repay a loan made to the corporation if it does not repay it, where the purpose of the promise is to further the shareholder's economic advantage by obtaining the loan. What is the reason for this exception? Compare Howard M. Schoor Associates, Inc. v. Holmdel Heights Constr. Co., 68 N.J. 95, 343 A.2d 401 (1975), with Burlington Industries v. Foil, 284 N.C. 740, 202 S.E.2d 591 (1974).

(2) *Novation.* If A is already under an obligation to C, and C agrees to release A from liability in exchange for B's promise to pay, the transaction is known as a *novation.* The statute of frauds is construed so as not to apply to B's promise in such a case. Why? Is it not a promise to answer for the debt of A?

(3) *Promise Made to Debtor.* A promise made to the debtor is not within the statute. For a promise to come within the statute it "must be one to pay the debt of another, and while 'another' might have been construed to mean merely another than the promisor, it has been construed to mean another than either the promisee or the promisor, and, therefore, the statute applies only to promises made to the person or persons to whom another is answerable. . . . That is seemingly due to the notion that the mischief sought to be remedied by the statute was perjured claims by creditors that promises had been made to them." G. Costigan, Cases on Contracts 913 (3d ed. 1934). If, therefore, B promises A that he will pay A's debt to C, the statute does not apply. This is so even though, as will be seen in Chapter 10, Third Party Beneficiaries, C may recover from B as a creditor beneficiary of B's promise.

Contracts Not to be Performed Within One Year. Of all the classes of contracts brought within the original statute of frauds, the most difficult of rationalization is that consisting of contracts "not to be performed within the space of one year from the making thereof." If the one-year limitation is based upon the tendency of memory to fail and evidence to grow stale with the passage of time, it is ill-contrived: for the one-year period is not between fact and proof of that fact, but between the making of the contract and completion of performance. Suppose, for example, that an oral contract that cannot be performed within a year is broken the day after its making. No action can be maintained upon it, although its terms are still fresh in the minds of the parties. But suppose that an oral contract that can be performed within a year is broken, and suit is not brought until nearly six years (the usual statute of limitations for contract) after the breach. The action can be maintained upon it although its terms are no longer fresh in the minds of the parties.

If the one-year limitation is an attempt to separate significant contracts of long duration for which writings should be required from insignificant contracts of short duration for which writings are unnecessary, it is equally ill-contrived: for the one-year period is not between the commencement of performance and the completion of performance, but between the making of the contract and the completion of performance. Suppose, for example, that an oral contract to work for one day, thirteen months from now, is broken. No action can be maintained upon it, although its duration is only one day. But suppose that an oral contract to work for a year beginning today [a] is broken. An action can be maintained upon it although its duration is a full year.

Perhaps because of the difficulty in justifying the one-year provision, it has been subjected to a number of judicial limitations. The most important of these is that in most states in order to fall within the statute, the contract must be one which *cannot* be performed within a year. The mere possibility that performance may take less than a year is ordinarily sufficient to take the contract out of the statute. For example, if A agrees to work for B for A's life, the contract is not within the statute because it *could* be completely performed within a year in the event that A should die within that time. See Restatement Second, § 130, Illustration 2.[b]

NOTES

(1) *Applicability of One-Year Provision.* To which of the following oral agreements does the one-year clause of the statute of frauds apply?

(a) A agrees to work for B for 5 years.

a. Where the contract is to be performed over the term of a year beginning on the day of the making of the contract, the statute is clearly inapplicable. Where the contract is to be performed over the term of a year beginning on the day following the day of the making of the contract, there is disagreement as to the applicability of the statute. Some courts have been willing to disregard fractions of a day and have held the statute inapplicable; others have calculated the period exactly and have held the statute applicable. See 3 Williston, § 502.

b. An illustration is Freedman v. Chemical Constr. Corp., 43 N.Y.2d 260, 401 N.Y.S.2d 176, 372 N.E.2d 12 (1977), which involved an agreement to procure for a contractor a contract to build a chemical plant in Saudi Arabia in return for a fee to be paid on completion of the plant. Although it took over three years to procure the contract and another six to build the plant, the court concluded that the agreement was not within the one year provision. "It matters not . . . that it was unlikely or improbable that a $41 million plant would be constructed within one year. The critical test, instead, is whether 'by its terms' the agreement is not to be performed within a year."

(b) A agrees to work for B for A's life.

(c) A agrees to work for B for A's life, but not exceeding 5 years.

(d) A agrees to work for B for 5 years, if A lives that long.[c]

(e) A agrees to work for B for 5 years, but if A dies the contract is to be terminated.[d]

(f) A agrees to work for B for 5 years, but A can cancel the agreement at the end of one year.[e]

Is there a rational basis for requiring a writing in some of these cases and not in others?

(2) *Lifetime Provision.* The New York act requires a writing for an agreement that "is not to be performed within one year from the making thereof or the performance of which is not to be completed before the end of a lifetime." New York Gen.Oblig.L. § 5–701. In addition to the one-year provision, the California version requires a writing for an agreement

c. In Silverman v. Bernot, 218 Va. 650, 239 S.E.2d 118 (1977), Marietta Bernot claimed that Joseph Silverman had orally promised that if she remained in his employ as office manager and housekeeper until she reached the age of 62 or until his death, whichever occurred first, she would receive a pension of $300 a month and a residence for the rest of her life. Bernot sued Silverman for wrongful discharge and for anticipatory repudiation of the pension agreement. The court held that her claim was not barred by the statute of frauds "since the death of the employer could have occurred within the first year of the agreement." The court distinguished Gilliam v. Kouchoucos, infra note d. There is a "distinction between termination (defeasance) by operation of law . . . and completion by performance" and here "the parties have expressly delineated the duration of the contract in terms of the life of the employer."

d. In Gilliam v. Kouchoucos, 161 Tex. 299, 340 S.W.2d 27 (1960), Kouchoucos had a written contract with Gilliam to serve as manager of a motel. Kouchoucos claimed that he then made an oral contract with Gilliam to serve as manager of a club for the same term. That term was set forth in the written contract as a "term of ten years from the date of completion of the premises . . . . This contract and agreement shall, however, terminate on the death of the operator . . . ." Kouchoucos sued Gilliam for breach of their oral agreement. The court held that Kouchoucos' claim was barred by the statute of frauds. "The statute relates to a contract 'not to be performed within the space of one year from the making thereof.' It thus has application only to contracts which are terminated by performance, and does not apply to contracts which may be terminated within a year by some means other than performance. All personal service contracts are terminated by death. Therefore, the addition of the words 'but the agreement shall terminate on the death of the operator', added nothing."

e. In Hopper v. Lennen & Mitchell, 146 F.2d 364 (9th Cir. 1944), Hedda Hopper, a columnist and radio personality, claimed that she had an oral contract with Lennen & Mitchell, an advertising agent, to do weekly radio broadcasts over a term of five years, which was broken down into ten twenty-six week periods. Lennen & Mitchell had the right to cancel by written notice four weeks before the end of any period. When Lennen & Mitchell refused to perform, she sued for damages. The court held that her claim was not barred by the statute of frauds. It recognized that a "rather sharp cleavage in decision has resulted in a 'majority' and a 'minority' rule," but that under the law of California, which applied to the contract, the contract could be performed within a year because Lennen & Mitchell "were to be bound for a longer period than twenty-six weeks only at their discretion."

"which by its terms is not to be performed during the lifetime of the promisor, or an agreement to devise or bequeath any property, or to make any provision for any person by will." Cal.Civ.Code § 1624(6), set out in Note 1, p. 126 supra. How would the questions in the preceding note be answered under these provisions? Is this a desirable modification of the statute?

(3) *Promises Not to Compete.* Dixon sold his grocery business to Doyle and orally promised Doyle that he would not go into the grocery business in Chicopee for five years. Doyle sued for breach of that promise and Dixon set up the defense of the statute of frauds. From a judgment for the plaintiff, the defendant appealed. *Held*: Affirmed. "[I]f the death of the promisor within the year would merely prevent full performance of the agreement, it is within the statute; but if his death would leave the agreement completely performed and its purpose fully carried out, it is not. It has accordingly been repeatedly held by this court that an agreement not hereafter to carry on a certain business at a particular place was not within the statute, because, being only a personal engagement to forbear doing certain acts, not stipulating for anything beyond the promisor's life, and imposing no duties upon his legal representatives, it would be fully performed if he died within the year." Doyle v. Dixon, 97 Mass. 208 (1867).

Professor Williston has criticized this decision: "It is obvious, however, that the contract would not be fully performed under the circumstances; it would merely have become certain that the contract would be performed since the promisor being dead could not longer break a negative promise; but no one can refrain from competition for [five] years within a year." 3 Williston, § 497.

Suppose that Dixon, in his contract to sell his business, had promised not to engage in the grocery business in Chicopee for five years, in return for which Doyle had promised to pay him $5,000 at the end of that time. If Dixon had died in six months, could his executor have maintained an action against Doyle for $5,000, either then or at the end of the five years, on the ground that there had been complete performance?

(4) *The Commission Cases.* Zupan, a freelance advertising solicitor, was promised orally by Blumberg that he would receive a 25% commission on any account that he brought in so long as the account remained active. When Blumberg stopped paying commissions, Zupan sued and Blumberg set up the statute of frauds. From judgment for the plaintiff, the defendant appealed. *Held*: Reversed. "It was within the contemplation of the parties to the contract that the customer might give orders for years, as actually occurred." And "a salesman's right to commissions cannot be defeated by the arbitrary refusal of his employer to accept orders from the procured customer." Zupan v. Blumberg, 2 N.Y.2d 547, 141 N.E.2d 819 (1957). Does this mean that a seller's oral promise to pay a salesman a 5% commission on all sales that he may make is also unenforceable? Compare Nat Nal Service Stations v. Wolf, 304 N.Y. 332, 107 N.E.2d 473 (1952), with Burkle v. Superflow Manufacturing Co., 137 Conn. 488, 78 A.2d 698 (1951). What of a brewer's promise to make a distributor "the exclusive wholesale distributor in Queens County of Schmidt beer . . . for as long as Schmidt sold beer in the New York metropolitan area"? See North Shore Bottling Co. v. C. Schmidt & Sons, 22 N.Y.2d 171, 239 N.E.2d 189 (1968).

(5) *Effect of Performance on One Side.* A wholly executory oral contract that is performable within a year on one side but not on the other is within the statute and is unenforceable on both sides. It is generally held, however, that if the one party who could do so had actually completely performed within a year, the contract is no longer within the statute and is enforceable. Some courts have extended this exception to cases in which the plaintiff has performed without regard to whether his performance took place within a year. Professor Corbin has argued that it is the "fact that full performance has been rendered that affords a reason for enforcement." 2 Corbin, § 457. Indeed, in Professor Corbin's view, where the restitutionary remedy is inadequate, a *part* performance by one party should be sufficient to remove the bar of the statute in contracts not to be performed within a year. 2 Corbin, § 459; see Note 1, p. 162 infra. Are these incursions into the one-year provision best explained on logical grounds or on the basis of hostility to the provision?

(6) *Problem.* Carl Coan, a first-year law student, entered into an oral agreement with Victor Orsinger, under which Coan was to be resident manager of an apartment development owned by Orsinger "until [Coan] completed his law studies as a student duly matriculated in Georgetown University Law Center, Washington, D. C. or was obliged to discontinue these studies." Five weeks after Coan undertook his duties, he was fired. Does the statute of frauds bar recovery by Coan? See Coan v. Orsinger, 265 F. 2d 575 (D.C.Cir. 1959).

Contracts for the Sale of an Interest in Land. The original statute of frauds provides that "no action shall be brought . . . upon any contract or sale of lands, tenements or hereditaments, or any interest in or concerning them" unless the contract is in writing. An interest in land includes, among other interests, a lease, a mortgage, an easement, and sometimes it includes trees, buildings, or other things attached to the soil. Under what circumstances these and other interests are "land" within the meaning of the statute may be considered in courses in the field of real property.

Suppose that S orally agrees with B to convey to him land, for which B orally promises to pay $10,000. The failure of either S or B to perform this agreement does not give the other a cause of action, either at law for damages or in equity for specific performance. Even if B pays $500 down to "bind the bargain" the agreement will not be enforceable. But, although the statute makes no express exception, if S makes the agreed transfer he is allowed to recover the purchase price on the rather tenuous ground that the part of the transaction that brought it within the statute has been performed. And in some cases involving the sale of land the contract may be "taken out" of the statute by what is called "part performance."

The doctrine of part performance originated in suits in equity for specific performance. Its basis has been stated as follows: "The ground upon which a court, notwithstanding the statute of frauds, may compel the complete performance of an oral contract for the sale of real estate which has been partly performed is that such a decree may be necessary in order to avoid injustice toward one who in reliance upon the agreement has so altered his position that he cannot otherwise be afforded adequate relief. His mere entry into possession with the consent of the owner does not in and of itself meet this condition. . . . True, whenever he has made permanent improvements upon the property the courts are ready to order a conveyance, even though it might be possible to provide compensation in damages. A sufficient reason for this is that alterations in the artificial features of real estate are so largely a matter of individual taste that the loss to their designer in being deprived of their benefit might not be adequately measured either by the increased value of the property, or by his expenditures in making them. And whenever possession is taken under such circumstances that its relinquishment involves a disadvantage apart from the mere loss of the benefits of the bargain, a case may be presented for equitable relief, dependent upon the special circumstances. Nothing having been shown here beyond the bare fact of possession, we think the court erred in [allowing specific performance]." Baldridge v. Centgraf, 82 Kan. 240, 108 P. 83 (1910).

There is considerable difference of opinion as to what constitutes a sufficient part performance to take the contract out of the statute. See Wilson v. La Van, 22 N.Y.2d 131, 238 N.E.2d 738 (1968). Restatement Second, § 129.

Contracts for the Sale of Goods. The original requirement of a writing for contracts "for the sale of any goods, wares and merchandizes, for the price of ten pounds sterling or upwards" was contained in a separate section, section seventeen, rather than in section four, which listed the other classes of contracts that came within the statute.

Although the separate section of the British Statute of Frauds that dealt with the sale of goods was repealed by Parliament in 1954, the draftsmen of the Uniform Commerical Code concluded that the requirement of a writing for contracts for the sale of goods should be retained in the United States. "[T]he spread of literacy, the rise of metropolitan living, the drive toward internal records, and the Code's removal of those unwise misinterpretations which so largely influenced the English decision, leave reasonable room for some Statute of Frauds in the sales area." Supplement No. 1 to the 1952 Official Draft of Text and Comments of the Uniform Commercial Code, p. 98 (1955). The Code's version of the statute for the sale of goods is found in UCC 2–201. See also UCC 1–206. For an empirical study of the statute as it applies to the sale of goods, see Note, 66 Yale L.J. 1038(1957).

One of the problems in defining the scope of this branch of the statute has been in distinguishing contracts for the sale of goods from contracts for services. The distinction is significant because the statute of frauds does not apply to contracts for services unless, of course, they happen to fall within the one-year provision. The difficulty is most acute where the contract involves both the supplying of goods and the furnishing of services. Consider, for example, a contract for a set of false teeth to be made by a dentist, for a portrait to be painted by an artist,[a] for a suit to be made to measure by a tailor, for a machine to be designed and produced by an engineering firm.[b] Note that although UCC 2–201 applies to specially manufactured goods (see UCC 2–105(1)), subsection (3)(a) makes an exception for such goods if they are not suitable for sale to others in the ordinary course of the seller's business.

A similar problem has arisen in distinguishing between the sale of goods and the sale of land. Here the distinction is significant because, although the statute of frauds applies to both, its requirements as to the sale of goods are considerably less exacting than as to the sale of land. The problem may arise in a contract for the sale of timber as it stands, of minerals to be extracted, or of a building to be removed. For the Code solution to such problems, see UCC 2–107.

SECTION 3. HOW THE STATUTE CAN BE SATISFIED

We have been concerned with determining what contracts are within the statute of frauds. We now turn to how the statute can be satisfied, assuming that the contract comes within it. Here it is important to keep in mind that the sale of goods was the subject of a special section, section seventeen, in the original British version, while all of the other classes of contracts within the statute were dealt with in section four. The latter and its statutory progeny provide for satisfaction of the statute only by a writing. The former and its statutory progeny (notably UCC 2–201) provide for satisfac-

a. In National Historic Shrines Foundation v. Dali, 4 UCC Rep. 71 (N.Y. Sup.Ct.1967), an oral agreement by Salvador Dali with a non-profit corporation to paint a picture of the Statue of Liberty on a television program and give the completed painting to the corporation for sale to the public was held not to be within UCC 2–201.

b. In Robertson v. Ceola, 225 Ark. 703, 501 S.W.2d 764 (1973), it was held that a contract for "purchase and installation" of tile during the construction of a home was not within UCC 2–201, even though the homeowner was to pay "$12 per hour for labor plus 15% of the cost of . . . materials." However, in Huyler Paper Stock Co. v. Information Supplies Corp., 117 N.J.Super. 353, 284 A.2d 568 (1971), it was held that a contract to collect and purchase the output of paper waste from a processor of data information cards was within UCC 2–201. As to whether computer programs are goods, see Note, 77 Mich.L.Rev. 1149 (1979).

tion not only by a writing, but in the alternative by acceptance and receipt of goods and by part payment. Furthermore, as will be seen, there are important differences in the kind of writing required under the present-day versions of these two original sections of the statute.

In the case of the statutes derived from section four, the writing must state "with reasonable certainty the essential terms and conditions." Restatement Second, § 137. The attitude of courts toward this requirement is suggested by the opinion of Cardozo in Marks v. Cowdin, 226 N.Y. 138, 123 N.E. 139 (1919), in which he said: "The statute must not be pressed to the extreme of a literal and rigid logic. . . . The memorandum which it requires, like any other memorandum, must be read in the light of reason."

Marks went to work as sales manager for Cowdin's ribbon business, under a contract that ran from 1911 to 1913. Cowdin sent out notices to salesmen describing him as "sales-manager." In 1913 the contract was orally renewed for three years, at a larger compensation. Later that year, after a disagreement with Cowdin, Marks asked for and received a memorandum signed by Cowdin and reciting that the arrangement made earlier that year for Marks' employment at a salary of $15,000 per year plus a stated share of gross profits "continues in force until Jan. 1st, 1916," but omitting any mention of his title or duties. When, in 1914, Cowdin told Marks that he was to work under a new sales manager, McLaren, Marks refused and was fired. Marks sued Cowdin, who raised the one-year provision of the statute as a defense. The Court of Appeals rejected this defense. The contract had been made in January; the memorandum had been signed the following December. "It assumes the existence of a position that the plaintiff is then filling. It says that the employment shall be continued for a term and at a salary prescribed . . . . We are not left to gather the relation between the parties from executory promises. We are informed that the relation existing is the one to be maintained . . . . In this case the plaintiff does not need the aid of one spoken word of promise to identify his place. His first contract was for two years, from January 1, 1911, to January 1, 1913. During that period, writings subscribed by the defendants attest the nature of his position. The memorandum exacted by the statute does not have to be in one document. It may be pieced together out of separate writings, connected with one another either expressly or by the internal evidence of subject matter and occasion."

CRABTREE v. ELIZABETH ARDEN SALES CORP.

Court of Appeals of New York, 1953.
305 N.Y. 48, 110 N.E.2d 551.

Action for damages for breach of employment contract employing plaintiff as sales manager of defendant corporation.

FULD, Judge. In September of 1947, Nate Crabtree entered into preliminary negotiations with Elizabeth Arden Sales Corporation, manufacturers and sellers of cosmetics, looking toward his employment as sales manager. Interviewed on September 26th, by Robert P. Johns, executive vice-president and general manager of the corporation, who had apprised him of the possible opening, Crabtree requested a three-year contract at $25,000 a year. Explaining that he would be giving up a secure well-paying job to take a position in an entirely new field of endeavor—which he believed would take him some years to master—he insisted upon an agreement for a definite term. And he repeated his desire for a contract for three years to Miss Elizabeth Arden, the corporation's president.[a] When Miss Arden finally indicated that she was prepared to offer a two-year contract, based on an annual salary of $20,000 for the first six months, $25,000 for the second six months and $30,000 for the second year, plus expenses of $5,000 a year for each of those years, Crabtree replied that that offer was "interesting". Miss Arden thereupon had her personal secretary make this memorandum on a telephone order blank that happened to be at hand:

"EMPLOYMENT AGREEMENT WITH
NATE CRABTREE Date Sept. 26–1947

At 681—5th Ave. 6: P.M.

* * *

Begin	20000.
6 months	25000.
6 "	30000.

5000.—per year, Expense money
[2 years to make good]

"Arrangement with Mr. Crabtree, By Miss Arden, Present Miss Arden, Mr. John, Mr. Crabtree, Miss OLeary"

A few days later, Crabtree 'phoned Mr. Johns and telegraphed Miss Arden; he accepted the "invitation to join the Arden organization", and Miss Arden wired back her "welcome". When he reported for work, a "pay-roll change" card was made up and initialed by Mr. Johns, and then forwarded to the payroll department. Reciting that it was prepared on September 30, 1947, and was to be effective as of October 22d, it specified the names of the parties, Crabtree's "Job

a. Elizabeth Arden, who was born Florence Nightingale Graham, was a legendary tyrant who built a million dollar cosmetics business out of a jar of cleansing cream. According to her biographers, she was much given to firing employees. Once, on firing her male auditor, she assured a female employee, "Don't you worry dear. Remember, these men come and go. But you girls are here forever." When molested by a total stranger on the roof of the St. Regis Hotel, her response was to order one of her executives to "Fire him." A. Lewis and C. Woodworth, Miss Elizabeth Arden 96, 307 (1972).

Classification" and, in addition, contained the notation that "This employee is to be paid as follows:

" First six months of employment	$20,000.	Per annum
Next six months of employment	25,000.	" "
After one year of employment	30,000.	" "

Approved by RPJ [initialed]"

After six months of employment, Crabtree received the scheduled increase from $20,000 to $25,000, but the further specified increase at the end of the year was not paid. Both Mr. Johns and the comptroller of the corporation, Mr. Carstens, told Crabtree that they would attempt to straighten out the matter with Miss Arden, and, with that in mind, the comptroller prepared another "pay-roll change" card, to which his signature is appended, noting that there was to be a "Salary increase" from $25,000 to $30,000 a year, "per contractual arrangements with Miss Arden". The latter, however, refused to approve the increase and, after further fruitless discussion, plaintiff left defendant's employ and commenced this action for breach of contract.

At the ensuing trial, defendant denied the existence of any agreement to employ plaintiff for two years, and further contended that, even if one had been made, the statute of frauds barred its enforcement. The trial court found against defendant on both issues and awarded plaintiff damages of about $14,000, and the Appellate Division, two justices dissenting, affirmed. Since the contract relied upon was not to be performed within a year, the primary question for decision is whether there was a memorandum of its terms, subscribed by defendant, to satisfy the statute of frauds, Personal Property Law, § 31.

Each of the two payroll cards—the one initialed by defendant's general manager, the other signed by its comptroller—unquestionably constitutes a memorandum under the statute. That they were not prepared or signed with the intention of evidencing the contract, or that they came into existence subsequent to its execution, is of no consequence, see Marks v. Cowdin, 226 N.Y. 138, 145, 123 N.E. 139, 141; Spiegel v. Lowenstein, 162 App.Div. 443, 448–449, 147 N.Y.S. 655, 658; see, also, Restatement, Contracts, §§ 209, 210, 214; it is enough, to meet the statute's demands, that they were signed with intent to authenticate the information contained therein and that such information does evidence the terms of the contract. See . . . 2 Corbin on Contracts [1951], pp. 732–733, 763–764; 2 Williston on Contracts [Rev. ed., 1936], pp. 1682–1683. Those two writings contain all of the essential terms of the contract—the parties to it, the position that plaintiff was to assume, the salary that he was to receive—except that relating to the duration of plaintiff's employment. Accordingly, we must consider whether that item, the length of the contract, may be supplied by reference to the earlier unsigned office memorandum, and, if so, whether its notation, "2 years to make good", sufficiently designates a period of employment.

The statute of frauds does not require the "memorandum . . . to be in one document. It may be pieced together out of separate writings, connected with one another either expressly or by the internal evidence of subject-matter and occasion." . . . Where each of the separate writings has been subscribed by the party to be charged, little if any difficulty is encountered. . . . Where, however, some writings have been signed, and others have not—as in the case before us—there is basic disagreement as to what constitutes a sufficient connection permitting the unsigned papers to be considered as part of the statutory memorandum. The courts of some jurisdictions insist that there be a reference, of varying degrees of specificity, in the signed writing to that unsigned, and, if there is no such reference, they refuse to permit consideration of the latter in determining whether the memorandum satisfies the statute. . . . That conclusion is based upon a construction of the statute which requires that the connection between the writings and defendant's acknowledgment of the one not subscribed, appear from examination of the papers alone, without the aid of parol evidence. The other position—which has gained increasing support over the years—is that a sufficient connection between the papers is established simply by a reference in them to the same subject matter or transaction. . . . The statute is not pressed "to the extreme of a literal and rigid logic", Marks v. Cowdin, supra, 226 N.Y. 138, 144, 123 N.E. 139, 141, and oral testimony is admitted to show the connection between the documents and to establish the acquiescence, of the party to be charged, to the contents of the one unsigned. . . .

The view last expressed impresses us as the more sound, and, indeed—although several of our cases appear to have gone the other way, . . . —this court has on a number of occasions approved the rule, and we now definitively adopt it, permitting the signed and unsigned writings to be read together, provided that they clearly refer to the same subject matter or transaction. . . .

The language of the statute—"Every agreement . . . is void, unless . . . some note or memorandum thereof be in writing, and subscribed by the party to be charged", Personal Property Law, § 31—does not impose the requirement that the signed acknowledgment of the contract must appear from the writings alone, unaided by oral testimony. The danger of fraud and perjury, generally attendant upon the admission of parol evidence, is at a minimum in a case such as this. None of the terms of the contract are supplied by parol. All of them must be set out in the various writings presented to the court, and at least one writing, the one establishing a contractual relationship between the parties, must bear the signature of the party to be charged, while the unsigned document must on its face refer to the same transaction as that set forth in the one that was signed. Parol evidence—to portray the circumstances surrounding the making of the memorandum—serves only to connect the separate documents and to show that there was assent, by the party to be charged, to the contents of the one unsigned. If that testimony does not convincingly connect the papers, or does not show assent to the unsigned paper, it is within the province of the judge to conclude, as a matter of law, that the statute has not been satisfied. True, the possibility still remains that, by fraud or perjury, an agreement never in fact made may occasionally be enforced under the subject matter or transaction test. It is better to run that risk, though, than to deny enforcement to all agreements, merely because the signed document made no specific mention of the unsigned writing. . . .

Turning to the writings in the case before us—the unsigned office memo, the payroll change form initialed by the general manager Johns, and the paper signed by the comptroller Carstens—it is apparent, and most patently, that all three refer on their face to the same transaction. The parties, the position to be filled by plaintiff, the salary to be paid him, are all identically set forth; it is hardly possible that such detailed information could refer to another or a different agreement. Even more, the card signed by Carstens notes that it was prepared for the purpose of a "Salary increase per contractual arrangements with Miss Arden". That certainly constitutes a reference of sorts to a more comprehensive "arrangement," and parol is permissible to furnish the explanation.

The corroborative evidence of defendant's assent to the contents of the unsigned office memorandum is also convincing. Prepared by defendant's agent, Miss Arden's personal secretary, there is little likelihood that that paper was fraudulently manufactured or that defendant had not assented to its contents. Furthermore, the evidence as to the conduct of the parties at the time it was prepared persuasively demonstrates defendant's assent to its terms. Under such circumstances, the courts below were fully justified in finding that the three papers constituted the "memorandum" of their agreement within the meaning of the statute.

. . . Only one term, the length of the employment, is in dispute. The September 26th office memorandum contains the notation, "2 years to make good". What purpose, other than to denote the length of the contract term, such a notation could have, is hard to imagine. Without it, the employment would be at will, see Martin v. New York Life Ins. Co., 148 N.Y. 117, 121, 42 N.E. 416, 417, and its inclusion may not be treated as meaningless or purposeless. Quite obviously, as the courts below decided, the phrase signifies that the parties agreed to a term, a certain and definite term, of two years, after which, if plaintiff did not "make good", he would be subject to discharge. And examination of other parts of the memorandum supports that construction. Throughout the writings, a scale of wages, increasing plaintiff's salary periodically, is set out; that type of arrangement is hardly consistent with the hypothesis that the employment was meant to be at will. The most that may be argued from defendant's standpoint is that "2 years to make good", is a cryptic and ambiguous statement. But, in such a case, parol evidence is admissible to explain its meaning. . . . Having in mind the relations of the parties, the course of the negotiations and plaintiff's insistence upon security of employment, the purpose of the phrase—or so the trier of the facts was warranted in finding—was to grant plaintiff the tenure he desired.

The judgment should be affirmed, with costs.

NOTES

(1) *Reason and the Statute of Frauds.* How many of the following propositions involving the statute of frauds make sense to you?

(a) When a writing satisfying the statute is signed by only one party, it makes the contract enforceable *against* that party even though it is not enforceable *by* that party.[a] See 2 Corbin, § 282.

(b) The printed firm name of the defendant appearing in the letterhead at the top of a writing is a sufficient signature if it is adopted by the defendant with the intention of authenticating the writing. See 2 Corbin, § 522; UCC 1–201(39) and Comment 39.[b]

(c) If a writing satisfying the statute of frauds has been lost, the statute may be satisfied by parol evidence of its making and contents. See 2 Corbin, § 529.

(d) Parol evidence may be used to show that a memorandum, complete on its face, is not a correct representation of all the terms of the agreement and is, for this reason, insufficient. See 2 Corbin, §§ 288, 498. On reformation, see 3 G. Palmer, Law of Restitution §§ 13.13–13.15 (1978), based on Palmer, Reformation and the Statute of Frauds, 65 Mich.L.Rev. 421 (1967).

(2) *The Case of the Careless Cancellation.* On October 16, a salesman for Varnish Company took an oral order from Lorick & Lowrance for paint and varnish, noted it in his memorandum book and sent a copy to Varnish Company. On October 17, Lorick & Lowrance wrote Varnish Company, "Gents: Don't ship paint ordered through your salesman. We have con-

a. "The operation of the [Statute] is often lopsided and partial. A and B contract: A has signed a sufficient note or memorandum, but B has not. In these circumstances B can enforce the contract against A, but A cannot enforce it against B." Law Revision Committee, Sixth Interim Report, Cmd. No. 5449, pp. 6–7 (1937), discussed in Note 2, p. 127 supra.

b. Should a tape recording satisfy the Statute of Frauds? Should it make a difference if the taping was approved for this purpose by the party later sought to be charged? See Ellis Canning Co. v. Bernstein, 348 F.Supp. 1212 (D.Colo.1972); Swink & Co., Inc. v. Carroll McEntee & McGinley, Inc., 266 Ark. 279, 584 S.W.2d 393 (1979); Misner, Tape Recordings, Business Transactions via Telephone, and the Statute of Frauds, 61 Iowa L.Rev. 941 (1976).

cluded not to handle it." Varnish Company shipped the goods before this letter was received. Lorick & Lowrance refused to take them and Varnish Company sued. From a nonsuit based on the statute of frauds, the plaintiff appealed. *Held*: Reversed. The letter clearly referred to the order, which, although unsigned, was in writing and otherwise satisfied the statute of frauds. "We have, then, an admission in writing that an order for the goods in question through the salesman had been given, and we have the order referred to, likewise in writing, and the two together fully satisfy the requirements of the statute." Louisville Asphalt Varnish Co. v. Lorick & Lowrance, 29 S.C. 533, 8 S.E. 8 (1888).[c]

For a different conclusion, see Grant v. Auvil, 39 Wash.2d 722, 238 P. 2d 393 (1951), in which the court held that a postal card saying "I have decided to not raise any turkeys this year, so will you please cancel my order" did not sufficiently refer to a memorandum signed only by the salesman, even though that memorandum used the term "order."

Reconsider the agreement described in paragraph (f) of Note 1, p. 130 supra, under which A agreed to work for B for 5 years but can cancel the agreement at the end of one year. If A is uncertain whether the agreement is within the statute, how should he word his notice of cancellation?

(3) *The Case of the Chary Chanteuse.* George Scheck had for many years been the manager of Connie Francis, a popular singer. About a year after an earlier employment agreement had expired, they began negotiations for a new agreement. After the final negotiation session, her lawyer mailed Scheck four copies of a new five-year contract with a covering letter, signed by the lawyer on her behalf, asking Scheck to "sign all copies" and "have Connie sign them." Scheck signed them, but Francis did not. He continued to work for Francis until about a year later, when a dispute arose and he sued Francis for damages. From dismissal of his complaint on the ground that it was barred by the statute of frauds, he appealed, arguing that the statute was satisfied by the contract (unsigned by Francis) when read together with the letter (signed on her behalf). *Held:* Affirmed. "The plaintiff's reliance upon the Crabtree case . . . is misplaced . . . . In the present case, unlike Crabtree, the letter signed by the defendants' attorney . . . does not serve to establish a contractual relationship between the parties . . . . Quite obviously, it was written for the sole purpose of forwarding the documents to the parties for signature . . . . The signatures which would authenticate the existence of the contracts within the meaning of the statute were to be made later after the parties read and approved the terms set forth in the proposed documents." Scheck v. Francis, 26 N.Y.2d 466, 260 N.E.2d 493 (1970).

(4) *Ethics and the Statute of Frauds.* In a thoughtful article, Dean Stevens pointed out that, "It is probably a prevailing practice automatically to plead the Statute of Limitations to a stale claim and the Statute of Frauds when there is known to be no writing signed by the defendant, or his agent, evidencing the contract sued upon. The statutes are there, they

c. That a car dealer's order to the manufacturer designating the car described as "sold" and naming the "customer" satisfies the statute, see Thomaier v. Hoffman Chevrolet, Inc., 64 A.D.2d 492, 410 N.Y.S.2d 645 (1978).

supply the defenses, and the attorney would not be giving full and competent service to his client if he did not advise him of them and advance them for him." As to the Statute of Frauds, Dean Stevens saw a problem of ethics in which "the lawyer's conscience may be in conflict, not merely with a custom of the profession habitually to plead the defense, as in the case of the Statute of Limitations, but with judge-made law, that is all but unanimously adopted, to the effect that the defendant can admit an honest obligation and yet defeat its enforcement by pleading that the agreement was only oral and that there is no written evidence of the obligation as required by the Statute of Frauds. In the conflict between conscience and judicially approved practice, what is the lawyer to do? Conscience tells him that the practice is wrong, but the literature from insurance companies reminds him of liability for malpractice." Stevens, Ethics and the Statute of Frauds, 37 Cornell L.Q. 355 (1952).

What effect will UCC 2–201(3)(b) have upon this problem? Does it include an involuntary admission resulting from a failure to deny the allegations of the complaint? See Alaska Code § 09.25.020(4); Yonge, The Unheralded Demise of the Statute of Frauds, Welsher . . ., 33 Wash. & Lee L.Rev. 1 (1976); Comment, 65 Calif.L.Rev. 150 (1977).

SOUTHWEST ENGINEERING CO. v. MARTIN TRACTOR CO.

Supreme Court of Kansas, 1970.
205 Kan. 684, 473 P.2d 18.

FONTRON, Justice. This is an action to recover damages for breach of contract. Trial was had to the court which entered judgment in favor of the plaintiff. The defendant has appealed.

Southwest Engineering Company, Inc., the plaintiff, is a Missouri corporation engaged in general contracting work, while the defendant, Martin Tractor Company, Inc., is a Kansas corporation. The two parties will be referred to hereafter either as plaintiff, or Southwest, on the one hand and defendant, or Martin, on the other.

We glean from the record that in April, 1966, the plaintiff was interested in submitting a bid to the United States Corps of Engineers for the construction of certain runway lighting facilities at McConnell Air Force Base at Wichita. However, before submitting a bid, and on April 11, 1966, the plaintiff's construction superintendent, Mr. R. E. Cloepfil, called the manager of Martin's engine department, Mr. Ken Hurt, who at the time was at Colby, asking for a price on a standby generator and accessory equipment. Mr. Hurt replied that he would phone him back from Topeka, which he did the next day, quoting a price of $18,500. This quotation was re-confirmed by Hurt over the phone on April 13.

Southwest submitted its bid on April 14, 1966, using Hurt's figure of $18,500 for the generator equipment, and its bid was accepted. On April 20, Southwest notified Martin that its bid had been accepted. Hurt and Cloepfil thereafter agreed over the phone to meet in Springfield on April 28. On that date Hurt flew to Springfield, where the two men conferred at the airfield restaurant for about an hour. Hurt took to the meeting a copy of the job specifications which the government had supplied Martin prior to the letting.

At the Springfield meeting it developed that Martin had upped its price for the generator and accessory equipment from $18,500 to $21,500. Despite this change of position by Martin, concerning which Cloepfil was understandably amazed, the two men continued their conversation and, according to Cloepfil, they arrived at an agreement for the sale of a D353 generator and accessories for the sum of $21,500. In addition it was agreed that if the Corps of Engineers would accept a less expensive generator, a D343, the aggregate price to Southwest would be $15,000. The possibility of providing alternative equipment, the D343, was suggested by Mr. Hurt, apparently in an attempt to mollify Mr. Cloepfil when the latter learned that Martin had reneged on its price quotation of April 12. It later developed that the Corps of Engineers would not approve the cheaper generator and that Southwest eventually had to supply the more expensive D353 generator.

At the conference, Mr. Hurt separately listed the component parts of each of the two generators on the top half of a sheet of paper and set out the price after each item. The prices were then totaled. On the bottom half of the sheet Hurt set down the accessories common to both generators and their cost. This handwritten memorandum, as it was referred to during the trial, noted a 10 per cent discount on the aggregate cost of each generator, while the accessories were listed at Martin's cost. The price of the D353 was rounded off at $21,500 and D343 at $15,000. The memorandum was handed to Cloepfil while the two men were still at the airport. We will refer to this memorandum further during the course of this opinion.

On May 2, 1966, Cloepfil addressed a letter to the Martin Tractor Company, directing Martin to proceed with shop drawings and submittal documents for the McConnell lighting job and calling attention to the fact that applicable government regulations were required to be followed. Further reference to this communication will be made when necessary.

Some three weeks thereafter, on May 24, 1966, Hurt wrote Cloepfil the following letter:

"MARTIN TRACTOR
COMPANY, INC.
Topeka Chanute Concordia Colby

CATERPILLAR *

"P. O. Box 1698
Topeka, Kansas
May 24, 1966

Mr. R. E. Cloepfil
Southwest Engineering Co., Inc.
P. O. Box 3314, Glenstone Station
Springfield, Missouri 65804

Dear Sir:

Due to restrictions placed on Caterpillar products, accessory suppliers, and other stipulations by the district governing agency, we cannot accept your letter to proceed dated May 2, 1966, and hereby withdraw all verbal quotations.

Regretfully,
/s/ Ken Hurt
Ken Hurt, Manager
Engine Division"

On receipt of this unwelcome missive, Cloepfil telephoned Mr. Hurt who stated they had some work underway for the Corps of Engineers in both the Kansas City and Tulsa districts and did not want to take on any other work for the Corps at that time. Hurt assured Cloepfil he could buy the equipment from anybody at the price Martin could sell it for. Later investigation showed, however, that such was not the case.

In August of 1966, Mr. Cloepfil and Mr. Anderson, the president of Southwest, traveled to Topeka in an effort to persuade Martin to fulfill its contract. Hurt met them at the company office where harsh words were bandied about. Tempers eventually cooled off and at the conclusion of the verbal melee, hands were shaken all around and Hurt went so far as to say that if Southwest still wanted to buy the equipment from them to submit another order and he would get it handled. On this promising note the protagonists parted.

After returning to Springfield, Mr. Cloepfil, on September 6, wrote Mr. Hurt placing an order for a D353 generator (the expensive one) and asking that the order be given prompt attention, as their completion date was in early December. This communication was returned unopened.

A final effort to communicate with Martin was attempted by Mr. Anderson when the unopened letter was returned. A phone call was placed for Mr. Martin, himself, and Mr. Anderson was informed by the girl on the switchboard that Martin was in Colorado Springs on a vacation. Anderson then placed a call to the motel where he was told Mr. Martin could be reached. Martin refused to talk on the call, on learning the caller's name, and Anderson was told he would have to contact his office.

Mr. Anderson then replaced his call to Topeka and reached either the company comptroller or the company treasurer who responded by cussing him and saying "Who in the hell do you think you are? We don't have to sell you a damn thing."

Southwest eventually secured the generator equipment from Foley Tractor Co. of Wichita, a company which Mr. Hurt had one time suggested, at a price of $27,541. The present action was then filed, seeking damages of $6,041 for breach of the contract and $9,000 for loss resulting from the delay caused by the breach. The trial court awarded damages of $6,041 for the breach but rejected damages allegedly due to delay. The defendant, only, has appealed; there is no cross-appeal by plaintiff.

The basic disagreement centers on whether the meeting between Hurt and Cloepfil at Springfield resulted in an agreement which was enforceable under the provisions of the Uniform Commercial Code (sometimes referred to as the Code), which was enacted by the Kansas Legislature at its 1965 session. K.S.A. 84–2–201(1), being part of the Code, provides:

"Except as otherwise provided in this section a contract for the sale of goods for the price of $500 or more is not enforceable by way of action or defense unless there is some writing sufficient to indicate that a contract for sale has been made between the parties and signed by the party against whom enforcement is sought or by his authorized agent or broker. A writing is not insufficient because it omits or incorrectly states a term agreed upon but the contract is not enforceable under this paragraph beyond the quantity of goods shown in such writing."

Southwest takes the position that the memorandum prepared by Hurt at Springfield supplies the essential elements of a contract required by the foregoing statute, i. e., that it is (1) a writing signed by the party sought to be charged, (2) that it is for the sale of goods and (3) that quantity is shown. In addition, the reader will have noted that the memorandum sets forth the prices of the several items listed.

It cannot be gainsaid that the Uniform Commercial Code has effected a somewhat radical change in the law relating to the formation of enforceable contracts as such has been expounded by this and other courts. In the Kansas Comment to 84–2–201, which closely parallels the Official UCC Comment, the following explanation is given:

"Subsection (1) relaxes the interpretations of many courts in providing that the required writing need not contain all the material terms and that they need not be stated precisely. All that is required is that the writing afford a basis for believing that the offered oral evidence rests on a real transaction. Only three definite and invariable requirements as to the writing are made by this subsection. First, it must evidence a contract for the sale of goods; second, it must be 'signed,' a word which includes any authentication which identifies the party to be charged; and third, it must specify quantity. Terms relating to price, time, and place of payment or delivery, the general quality of goods, or any particular warranties may all be omitted."

From legal treatises, as well, we learn that the three invariable requirements of an enforceable written memorandum under 84–2–201 are that it evidence a sale of goods, that it be signed or authenticated and that it specify quantity. In Vernon's Kansas Statutes Annotated, Uniform Commercial Code, Howe and Navin, the writers make this clear:

"Under the Code the writing does not need to incorporate all the terms of the transaction, nor do the terms need to be stated precisely. The Code does require that the writing be broad enough to indicate a contract of sale between the parties; that the party against whom enforcement is sought, or his agent, must have signed the writing; and that the quantity dealt with must be stated. Any error concerning the quantity stated in the memorandum prevents enforcement of the agreement beyond the precise quantity stated." (p. 116.)

The defendant does not seriously question the interpretation accorded the statute by eminent scriveners and scholars, but maintains, nonetheless, that the writing in question does not measure up to the stature of a signed memorandum within the purview of the Code; that the instrument simply sets forth verbal quotations for future consideration in continuing negotiations.

But on this point the trial court found there *was* an agreement reached between Hurt and Cloepfil at Springfield; that the formal requirements of K.S.A. 84–2–201 *were* satisfied; and that the memorandum prepared by Hurt contains the three essentials of the statute in that it evidences a sale of goods, was authenticated by Hurt and specifies quantity. Beyond that, the court specifically found that Hurt had apparent authority to make the agreement; that both Southwest and Martin were "merchants" as defined in K.S.A. 84–2–104; that the agreement reached at Springfield included additional terms not noted in the writing: (1) Southwest was to install the equipment; (2) Martin was to deliver the equipment to Wichita and (3) Martin was to assemble and supply submittal documents within three weeks; and that Martin's letter of May 24, 1966, constituted an anticipatory breach of the contract.

We believe the record supports all the above findings. With particular reference to the preparation and sufficiency of the written memorandum, the following evidence is pertinent:

Mr. Cloepfil testified that he and Hurt sat down at a restaurant table and spread out the plans which Hurt had brought with him; that they went through the specifications item by item and Hurt wrote each item down, together with the price thereof; that while the specifications called for a D353 generator, Hurt thought the D343 model might be an acceptable substitute, so he gave prices on both of them and Southwest could take either one of the two which the Corps of Engineers would approve; that Hurt gave him (Cloepfil) the memorandum "as a record of what we had done, the agreement we had arrived at at our meeting in the restaurant at the airport."

We digress at this point to note Martin's contention that the memorandum is not signed within the meaning of 84–2–201. The sole authentication appears in hand-printed form at the top left-hand corner in these words: "Ken Hurt, Martin Tractor, Topeka, Caterpillar." The court found this sufficient, and we believe correctly so. K.S.A. 84–1–201(39) provides as follows:

" 'Signed' includes any symbol executed or adopted by a party with present intention to authenticate a writing."

The official U.C.C. Comment states in part:

"The inclusion of authentication in the definition of 'signed' is to make clear that as the term is used in this Act a complete signature is not necessary. Authentication may be printed, stamped or written; . . . . It may be on any part of the document and in appropriate cases may be found in a billhead or letterhead. . . . The question always is whether the symbol was executed or adopted by the party with present intention to authenticate the writing."

Hurt admittedly prepared the memorandum and has not denied affixing his name thereto. We believe the authentication sufficiently complies with the statute.

[The rest of the opinion in this case is at p. 245 infra.]

NOTES

(1) *Question.* Even if the court had not regarded Hurt's memorandum at the airport as sufficient to satisfy UCC 2–201, would not Hurt's letter of May 24 have satisfied it? See Note 2, p. 141 supra.

Although the opinion does not quote Cloepfil's May 2 letter, the record on appeal, p. 6, shows that it read in part: "We hereby authorize you to proceed with the preparation of shop drawings and submittal documents for the engine generator set for McConnell AFB lighting job. . . . If we furnish [the] cabinet, how will it affect the $705.00 price you showed on your sheet to me? . . . 'You are required to follow the provisions of DMS Reg. 1 and all other applicable regulations and orders of BDSA in obtaining controlled materials and other products and materials need [sic] to bill this order.' "

(2) *Quantity Term Under the Code.* As we saw earlier, contracts for the sale of goods were the subject of a special section in the original statute of frauds. This passed into Uniform Sales Act § 4, and then into UCC 2–201. Although the draftsmen of the Code did not abolish the requirement of a writing, they relaxed it very considerably. The original statute spoke of "some note or memorandum in writing of the said bargain," and the Uniform Sales Act of "some note or memorandum in writing of the contract or sale." But UCC 2–201(1) requires only "some writing sufficient to indicate that a contract for sale has been made between the parties," but couples this with an insistence on the quantity term.[a] Why must the writing specify the *quantity* but not the *price*? Comment 1 to UCC 2–201 gives this answer:

> In many valid contracts for sale the parties do not mention the price in express terms, the buyer being bound to pay and the seller to accept a reasonable price which the trier of fact may well be trusted to determine. Again, frequently the price is not mentioned since the parties have based their agreement on a price list or catalogue known to both of them and this list serves as an efficient safeguard against perjury. Finally, "market" prices and valuations that are current in the vicinity constitute a similar check. Thus if the price is not stated in the memorandum it can normally be supplied without danger of fraud.

How convincing is the argument that the market is a check on perjury as to price, in view of the fact that the relief sought by the injured party usually consists of damages based on the difference between the contract

a. What is the "quantity" in the case of a requirements or output contract? In the case of a contract for exclusive dealing? See UCC 2–306.

In Kubik v. J & R Foods of Oregon, 282 Or. 179, 577 P.2d 518 (1978), the court held that the quantity term was stated under a contract giving the buyer the exclusive right to buy barbecue sauce since "the 'quantity' the seller is obligated to supply is that amount which proof shows his best effort would have produced; the 'quantity' a buyer is obligated to purchase is that amount which proof shows he would have used or required if he exercised his best efforts to utilize the product."

That description in terms of output is sufficient, see R. L. Kimsey Cotton Co., Inc. v. Ferguson, 233 Ga. 962, 214 S.E.2d 360 (1975).

price and a real or hypothetical transaction on the market? (Will not relatively small increments in price bulk large in the calculation of damages?)[b]

(3) *Acceptance of Payment or Goods.* The insistence of the draftsmen on some evidence of the quantity term is carried over to the provisions on acceptance of payment or of the goods. The original statute could be satisfied not only by a writing, but also if "the buyer shall accept part of the goods . . . sold, and actually receive the same, or give something in earnest to bind the contract, or in part payment." A comparable provision was inserted in the Uniform Sales Act. Its application is illustrated by Helen Whiting v. Trojan Textile Corp., 307 N.Y. 360, 121 N.E.2d 367 (1954), in which the seller orally agreed to sell the buyer 83,000 yards of three different kinds of cloth goods. The seller then sent the buyer five yards of each kind of cloth with a separate writing covering each kind. The buyer kept the cloth, but signed only one of the writings and repudiated the other two. It was held that there was a sufficient acceptance and receipt to satisfy the statute as to all three kinds of cloth. "[T]he three five-yard pieces were not samples sent for approval but were 'part of the goods' accepted and received by the buyer. . . . Of course they were very small deliveries, but they were billed as deliveries under the contracts." The draftsmen of the Code dealt with this problem in UCC 2–201(3)(c). Note the language, "with respect to goods for which payment has been made and accepted, or which have been received and accepted." Comment 2 to that section explains that, "If the court can make a just apportionment, therefore, the agreed price of any goods actually delivered can be recovered without a writing or, if the price has been paid, the seller can be forced to deliver an apportionable part of the goods."[c] And what if it cannot make a just apportionment as, for example, in the case of acceptance and receipt of some but not all the parts of a dismantled machine, or part payments against an indivisible unit of goods?[d] Compare Thomaier v. Hoffman Chevrolet, Inc., 64 A.D.2d 492, 410 N.Y.S.2d 645 (1978) (statute satisfied by such part payment), with Williamson v. Martz, 11 Pa.D. & C.2d 33 (1956) (statute

b. Professor Williston, who drafted the Uniform Sales Act, attacked the provisions of UCC 2–201, as, with one exception, "the most iconoclastic in the Code." With regard to the relaxation in the requirements of the writing he wrote: "No such inaccuracy is permitted under existing law, and the value of a memorandum open to such contradiction is questionable." Williston, The Law of Sales in the Proposed Uniform Commercial Code, 63 Harv.L.Rev. 561, 573, 574 (1950). Do you agree?

c. Professor Corbin has written: "The present writer would have preferred to leave unchanged the old provisions as to part payment and acceptance and receipt. This is for two reasons . . . : first, he believes that the statutory provisions should be wholly abandoned because they increase litigation, greatly promote dishonest repudiation, and do not greatly aid our judicial system to frustrate fraud and perjury; and secondly, because a true apportionment of the goods or the price can not be made without first proving the terms of the contract, and having proved them the contract should be enforced in full." Corbin, The Uniform Commercial Code—Sales; Should It be Enacted?, 59 Yale L.J. 821, 831 n. 7 (1950).

d. If part payment is by check, a notation on the check may satisfy the requirement of a writing so that this question does not arise. See Cohn v. Fisher, 118 N.J.Super. 286, 287 A.2d 222 (1972) ("deposit on aux. sloop, D'Arc Wind, full amount $4,650"). For a case holding that part payment may be by check, see Anthony v. Tidwell, 560 S.W.2d 908 (Tenn.1977).

not satisfied by such part payment); see Note, 20 U.Kan.L.Rev. 538 (1972). Which result is more consistent with the Code's emphasis on the quantity term?

(4) *Multiple Application of the Statute.* Where more than one provision of the statute of frauds applies to a contract, all the applicable provisions must be satisfied if the contract is to be enforceable. So, for example, if the contract is one for the sale of goods which cannot be performed within one year, both the sale of goods and the one year provisions must be satisfied. As a result, acceptance and receipt of part of the goods or part payment will not make the contract enforceable because these do not satisfy the one year provision.

(5) *Oral Rescission and Modification.* Generally, a written contract that comes within the statute of frauds may be completely rescinded or abrogated orally. E. g., ABC Outdoor Advertising v. Dolhun's Marine, 38 Wis.2d 457, 157 N.W.2d 680 (1968). But in the case of a modification or variation, the statute of frauds must be satisfied if the contract as modified comes within its provisions. Where the contract as modified is not within the statute, however, even though the original contract was, an oral modification has been held effective. The Code rule is set out in UCC 2–209(3).

(6) *Economics of Breach (Reprise).* In what respect, if any, was Martin's officer correct in telling Anderson, "We don't have to sell you a damn thing"? Suppose that in May of 1966 Martin had decided to phase out its production of D353 generators as uneconomical, and that it would have cost Martin $35,000 to have produced a generator for Southwest. What would you have advised Martin to do? To produce a D353 generator and deliver it to Southwest? To offer to deliver to Southwest a generator acquired from Foley Tractor? To refuse to deliver a generator to Southwest? See the discussion of the economics of breach at p. 19 supra.

SATISFACTION BY "A WRITING IN CONFIRMATION"

The most innovative provision in UCC 2–201, and the most provocative of litigation, is subsection (2). Although subsection (1) incorporates the traditional requirement that the writing be "signed by the party sought to be charged," subsection (2) provides a mechanism by which a party may be precluded from raising the defense of the statute merely by a failure to object to "a writing in confirmation of the contract." It is the subject of the following opinion.[a]

a. Of UCC 2–201(2) Professor Williston wrote, "This provision, though entirely novel, would be desirable if it were not for the permission of extreme inaccuracy in the memorandum. . . . Furthermore, the provision, if acceptable between merchants, should be applied also where only one party or neither party is a merchant." Williston, The Law of Sales in the Proposed Uniform Commercial Code, 63 Harv.L.Rev. 561, 575 (1950). Do you agree? Consider, in this connection, the following quotation: "The advice of Wm. Randolph Hearst, 'Throw [it] in the wastebasket. Every letter answers itself in a couple of weeks.' Koenigsberg, King News, 273 (1941), is not a safe legal principle." Gateway Co. v. Charlotte Theatres, 297 F.2d 483, 486 (5th Cir. 1961).

HARRY RUBIN & SONS v. CONSOLIDATED PIPE CO.

Supreme Court of Pennsylvania, 1959.
396 Pa. 506, 153 A.2d 472.

BENJAMIN R. JONES, Justice. This is an appeal from the action of the Court of Common Pleas No. 1 of Philadelphia County, which sustained, in part, the appellees' preliminary objections to the appellants' complaint in assumpsit.

Rubin-Arandell, in their complaint, alleged that on three different dates—August 22nd, 25th and 28th, 1958—they entered into three separate oral agreements, all for the sale of goods in excess of $500, with one Carl Pearl, an officer and agent of Consolidated-Lustro, for the purchase of plastic hoops and materials, for use in assembling plastic hoops, and that Consolidated-Lustro failed to deliver a substantial portion of the hoops and material as required by the terms of the oral agreements. The court below, passing upon Consolidated-Lustro's preliminary objections, held that two of the alleged oral agreements violated the statute of frauds provision of the Uniform Commercial Code and were unenforceable. Rubin-Arandell contend that certain memoranda[1] (attached as exhibits to the complaint) were

---

1. "Purchase Order . . .

"Lustro Plastic Tile Company No. 2859
General Office & Warehouse
1066 Home Avenue
AKRON 10, OHIO
POrtage 2–8801

"Ordered From
Consolidated Tile Co.
Date
Ship to
Ship when Route Via FOB

Quantity	Number	Description	Price
30,000		Hoops Te-Vee Red, Green, Blue as per sample From Lengths 8′–10″ to 9′–3″ So they can nest	36½¢

"Lustro Plastic Tile Co.
By /s/ Harry Rubin & Sons Inc.
Leonard R. Rubin, V. Pres."

"Consolidated Pipe Co. "August 25, 1958
1066 Homes Ave.
Akron, Ohio
Att: Mr. Carl Pearl
"Dear Carl,

"As per our phone conversation of today kindly enter our order for the following:

60,000 Tee-Vee Hoops made of rigid polyethylene tubing from lengths of 8′ 10″ to 9′ 2″; material to

sufficient to take both oral agreements out of the statute of frauds. . . .

The statute of frauds provision of the Uniform Commercial Code, supra, states: ". . . (2) Between merchants if within a reasonable time a writing in confirmation of the contract and sufficient against the sender is received and the party receiving it has reason to know its contents, it satisfies the requirements of subsection (1) against such party unless written notice of objection to its contents is given within ten days after it is received."

As between merchants, the present statute of frauds provision (i. e. under Section 2–201(2), supra) significantly changes the former law by obviating the necessity of having a memorandum signed by the party sought to be charged. The present statutory requirements are: (1) that, within a reasonable time, there be a writing in confirmation of the oral contract; (2) that the writing be sufficient to bind the sender; (3) that such writing be received; (4) that no reply thereto has been made although the recipient had reason to know of its contents. Section 2–201(2) penalizes a party who fails to "answer a written confirmation of a contract within ten days" of the receipt of the writing by depriving such party of the defense of the statute of frauds.[2]

The memoranda upon which Rubin-Arandell rely consist of the purchase order on the Lustro form signed by Rubin stating the quantity ordered as 30,000 hoops with a description, the size and the price of the hoops listed and the letter of August 25th from Rubin to Consolidated requesting the entry of a similar order for an additional 60,000 hoops at a fixed price: "As per our phone conversation of today." This letter closes with the significant sentence that: "It is our understanding that these [the second order for 60,000 hoops] will be produced upon completion of the present order for 30,000 hoops."

Consolidated-Lustro's objection to the memoranda in question is that by employment of the word "order" rather than "contract" or "agreement", the validity of such memoranda depended upon acceptance thereof by Consolidated-Lustro and could not be "in confirmation of the contract[s]" as required by Section 2–201(2). We believe,

---

weigh 15 feet per lb., colors red, green and yellow
packed 2 Dozen per carton
39¢ each

"It is our understanding that these will be produced upon comp[l]etion of the present order for 30,000 hoops.

"Very truly yours,
Harry Rubin & Sons, Inc.
/s/ Leonard R. Rubin, Vice-pres."

---

2. Comment to Section 2–201, 12A P.S. p. 87.

however, that the letter of August 25th sufficiently complies with Section 2–201(2) to remove both oral contracts from the statute of frauds. The word "order" as employed in this letter obviously contemplated a binding agreement, at least, on the part of the sender, and, in all reason, should have been interpreted in that manner by the recipient. The sender in stating that "It is our understanding that these will be produced upon completion of the present order for 30,000 hoops," was referring to the initial order as an accomplished fact, not as an offer depending upon acceptance for its validity. Any doubt that may exist as to the sender's use of the word "order" is clearly dispelled by its use in the communication confirming a third contract.[3] This letter of August 28th, 1958, states: "Pursuant to our phone conversation of yesterday, *you may enter our order* for the following [number, description and price]. . . . *This order is to be entered* based upon our phone conversation, in which you *agreed* to ship us your entire production of this Hoop material at the above price . . . ." (Emphasis supplied.) The letter of August 25th was a sufficient confirmation in writing of the two alleged oral contracts, and, in the absence of a denial or rejection on the part of the recipient within ten days, satisfied the requirements of Section 2–201(2) of the Uniform Commercial Code.

Under the statute of frauds as revised in the Code "All that is required is that the writing afford a basis for believing that the offered oral evidence rests on a real transaction."[4] Its object is the elimination of certain formalistic requirements adherence to which often resulted in injustice, rather than the prevention of fraud. The present memoranda fulfill the requirement of affording a belief that the oral contracts rested on a real transaction and the court below erred in holding otherwise. Nor are Consolidated-Lustro harmed by such a determination since Rubin-Arandell must still sustain the burden of persuading the trier of fact that the contracts were in fact made orally prior to the written confirmation.[5] . . .

The order of the court below, as modified, is affirmed and the record remanded for proceedings consistent with this opinion.

NOTES

(1) *Question.* What result if the letter had read: "As per our telephone conversation of today we are pleased to offer . . ."? See Alice

3. As to this alleged oral contract, the court below held Consolidated-Lustro's defense of the statute of frauds provision was without merit.

4. See "Uniform Commercial Code Comment" under "Purpose of Changes 1", 12A P.S. § 2–201.

5. Appellees also argue that parties not named in the communications cannot be bound. Oral testimony to establish that the addressee of the letter was an agent of the unnamed appellees is admissible and does not violate the Statute of Frauds. See Penn Discount Corp. v. Sharp, 125 Pa.Super. 171, 189 A. 749.

v. Robett Mfg. Co., 328 F.Supp. 1377 (N.D.Ga.1970), aff'd per curiam, 445 F.2d 316 (5th Cir. 1971).

(2) *What is "in Confirmation"?* Not all courts have agreed with the interpretation of "in confirmation" in the Harry Rubin case. In Trilco Terminal v. Prebilt Corp., 167 N.J.Super. 449, 400 A.2d 1237 (1979), a buyer relied on its purchase orders, sent after the alleged oral agreement. Each order bore on its face the typewritten word "CONFIRMATION" and the printed language "THIS ORDER NOT VALID WITHOUT RETURN ACKNOWLEDGMENT." The court held that the orders did not satisfy UCC 2–201(2).

"According to my reading of the written confirmation proviso, it is satisfied only when a writing refers to the prior agreement in language that should make it clear to the recipient that such an agreement is relied upon. This is not to say that the confirmation must 'expressly state that it is sent in confirmation of [a] prior transaction,' but rather that it must at least 'indicate that a binding or completed transaction has been made.' 1 Anderson, Uniform Commercial Code (2 ed. 1970), § 2.201:51. In other words, if an ordinary merchant could not surmise from a writing that its sender was asserting the existence of a contractual relationship between the parties, the writing is not 'in confirmation of the contract.'

"This analysis differs from that employed by the *Rubin* court in that it does not assume that subsection 2's requirement of a writing in confirmation of a contract is interchangeable with the requirement common to both subsections of 'a writing sufficient to indicate that a contract for sale has been made between the parties.' It has been pointed out that a more stringent writing requirement under subsection 2 can be justified by the statutory language and the fact that its effect is to bind a merchant to a writing that he did not sign. See Dusenberg and King, 3 Bender's Uniform Commercial Code Service, § 2.04[2] (1978). In addition, this approach recognizes that since subsection 1 will be applied frequently in situations not involving subsection 2, its writing requirement will be developed in large part without regard to the peculiar role that a writing must play under this latter subsection.

"Whether more is required of a writing under subsection 2 than under subsection 1 is not yet clear. As previously mentioned, only one case has been reported in this jurisdiction discussing subsection 1's writing requirement, while no cases have been reported discussing subsection 2. In the context of the present case, it is not necessary to reach this perplexing issue because none of the writings advanced is, in any sense, a clear written confirmation of a prior oral agreement. No writing refers to any previous agreement or indicates that a binding or completed transaction has been entered into between the parties. In sum, the purchase orders are ambiguous and confusing, if viewed as anything more than routine purchasing documents. Therefore, I conclude that these purchase orders are not writings in confirmation of a contract." But see R. S. Bennett & Co. v. Economy Mechanical Industries, 606 F.2d 182 (7th Cir. 1979), in which the court rejected the argument "that section 2–201(2) . . . sets forth a less stringent requirement than 2–201(1)." With the holding in the Trilco Terminal case, compare Perdue Farms, Inc. v. Motts, Inc. of Mississippi, 459 F.Supp. 7 (N.D. Miss.1978), in which a buyer's "CONFIRMATION OF PURCHASE" was not deprived of its effect as a confirmation by the word "order" in a clause reading, "The terms and conditions on the reverse side of this Confirmation are an integral part of this order." (That case also contains a helpful discussion of how the sender can prove that his writing was "received.")

(3) *Seller's Invoice.* It is a common practice for a seller who has made an oral agreement over the telephone to send the buyer an invoice that is on the seller's letterhead but that does not bear a handwritten signature. Does such an invoice satisfy UCC 2–201(2)? For authority that it does, see Associated Hardware Supply Co. v. Big Wheel Distributing Co., 355 F.2d 114 (3d Cir. 1966); Automotive Spares Corp. v. Archer Bearings Co., 382 F. Supp. 513 (N.D.Ill.1974).

(4) *What is "Objection to Its Contents"?* What would have amounted to "notice of objection to its contents" by Consolidated? Would it have been enough if Consolidated had written, "Credit terms are not available because of your default on your earlier contract"? See Perdue Farms, Inc. v. Motts, Inc. of Mississippi, 459 F.Supp. 7 (N.D.Miss.1978). Could a communication sent before receipt of the "writing in confirmation" amount to "notice of objection to its contents"? See Continental-Wirt Electronics Corp. v. Sprague Electric Co., 329 F.Supp. 959 (E.D.Pa.1971).

AZEVEDO v. MINISTER, 86 Nev. 576, 471 P.2d 661 (1970). [In early November, 1967, Azevedo, a rancher who was licensed to buy and sell hay, made an agreement over the telephone to buy hay from Minister, a rancher who raised and sold large quantities of hay. The price was to be $26.50 per ton for the first and second cuttings and $28 per ton for the third cutting. After depositing $20,000 in a designated escrow account to secure payment, Azevedo began hauling hay from the Minister Ranch. As he did so, Minister furnished him with periodic accountings, beginning on December 4, that specified dates, bale count and weight, and names of truckers. Minister added the following statement to his January 21 accounting:

> From your original deposit of $20,000.00 there is now a balance of $1819.76. *At this time there remains* [*sic*] *approximately 16,600 bales of hay yet to be hauled on your purchase,* about 9200 of which are first crop, 7400 of which are second crop. We would appreciate hearing when you plan to haul the *balance of the hay.* Also please make a deposit to cover the hay, sufficient in amount to pay for the hay you will be currently hauling. At this time you have only about *$2.25 deposit per ton on the remaining balance of the hay,* and we cannot permit a lower deposit per ton and still consider the hay as being sold. [Emphasis added.]

Azevedo made no reply, deposited an additional $3,000 in the escrow account and continued hauling hay. In the accounting of February 22, Minister added:

> Balance of deposit on approximately 14000 bales remaining to be hauled—$1635.26.

Again, Azevedo made no reply. In the latter part of March, 1968, Azevedo refused to buy any more hay, claiming that there had never been an agreement as to quantity. Minister, claiming that Azevedo agreed over the telephone to buy 1,500 tons, sued for breach of contract. From a judgment for Minister, Azevedo appealed, arguing that the agreement was unenforceable under UCC 2–201.]

MOWBRAY, Justice . . . The parties agree that they are "merchants" within the meaning of that term as defined in the Code. . . . Appellant urges that the January and February accountings do not meet the standards of [UCC 2–201(2)] because neither memorandum makes reference to any oral agreement between the parties. A fair reading of the memoranda shows otherwise. . . . Although neither the January nor the February memorandum refers to the previous November agreement by telephone, the language clearly demonstrates that the referred-to agreement between the parties was not an *in futuro* arrangement, but a pre-existing agreement between Azevedo and Minister. As the court said in Harry Rubin & Sons, Inc. v. Consolidated Pipe Co., 396 Pa. 506, 153 A.2d 472, 476 (1959), in ruling on a case involving subsection (2) of section 2–201: "Under the statute of frauds as revised in the Code [,] 'All that is required is that the writing afford a basis for believing that the offered oral evidence rests on a real transaction.'" . . . The district judge found that it did so in the instant case, and the record supports his finding. . . .

Appellant argues that the delay of 10 weeks (November 9 to January 21) as a matter of law is an unreasonable time. We do not agree. What is reasonable must be decided by the trier of the facts under all the circumstances of the case under consideration. . . . In this case, the parties commenced performance of their oral agreement almost immediately after it was made in early November. Azevedo deposited $20,000 in the designated escrow account and began hauling hay. Minister commenced sending his periodic accounting reports to Azevedo on December 14. It is true that the accounting containing the confirming memorandum was not sent until January 21. It was at that time that Azevedo's deposit of $20,000 was nearing depletion. Minister so advised Azevedo in the January memorandum. Azevedo responded by making an additional deposit. He did not object to the memorandum, and he continued to haul the hay until the latter part of March. Under "the nature, purpose and circumstances" of the case, we agree with the district judge that the delay was not unreasonable.

[Affirmed.]

NOTES

(1) *Farmer as Merchant.* Is it clear that both parties were merchants under UCC 2–201(2)? Whether a farmer is a merchant for this purpose has been much disputed. See Comment, 13 Creighton L.Rev. 325 (1979); Note, 59 Utah L.Rev. 59 (1977). According to the Supreme Court of South Dakota, "the average farmer . . . with no particular knowledge or experience in selling, buying, or dealing in future commodity transactions, and who sells only the crops he raises to local elevators for cash or who places

his grain in storage under one of the federal loan programs, is not a 'merchant'" under UCC 2–201(2). Terminal Grain Corp. v. Freeman, — S.D. —, 270 N.W.2d 806, 812 (1978). But according to the Supreme Court of Texas, a farmer who "is knowledgeable about the business of growing and selling crops, and . . . has made it his usual practice . . . to determine the best price obtainable for his crops [and] stays abreast of the current market prices by listening to the market reports on the radio and by telephoning various grain dealers to get the current price quotations," is a "merchant" under UCC 2–201(2). Nelson v. Union Equity Co-op. Exchange, 548 S.W.2d 352, 355 (Tex.1977).

(2) *What is a "Reasonable Time"?* Compare Azevedo v. Minister with Cargill, Inc. v. Stafford Elevator, 553 F.2d 1222 (10th Cir. 1977). The court there upheld a finding that a confirmation of a contract to sell wheat was not received "within a reasonable time" where it was not received for nearly four weeks because it had been improperly addressed.

(3) *Southwest Engineering Case (Reprise).* In the Southwest Engineering case, p. 143 supra, even if the court had not regarded Hurt's memorandum as sufficient to satisfy UCC 2–201(1), would not Hurt's silence in the face of Cloepfil's letter of May 2 have satisfied UCC 2–201(2)? See Note 1, p. 149 supra.

SECTION 4. MITIGATING DOCTRINES

What alternatives are open to the injured party who has already done something in performance of, or at least in preparation for, an agreement that later turns out to be unenforceable because of the statute of frauds? Can he have a recovery based on his restitution interest, or perhaps even his reliance interest, although he is barred from a recovery based on his expectation interest? Many cases recognize the right of such a plaintiff to recover the reasonable value of his performance, to the extent that it has benefitted the defendant, and evidence of the unenforceable oral agreement is admissible on the question of the value of the plaintiff's performance. Cf. Campbell v. Tennessee Valley Authority, 421 F.2d 293 (5th Cir. 1969).

Where, however, there has been only reliance, without benefit, courts have traditionally denied relief. As the court put it in the leading case of Boone v. Coe, 153 Ky. 233, 154 S.W. 900 (1913), "Having received no benefit, no obligation to pay is implied." The following cases explore this proposition.

NOTE

Brokerage Contracts. California is typical of many states in having a special provision requiring a writing for an agreement "authorizing or employing an agent, broker or any other person to purchase or sell real estate . . . for compensation or a commission." See Note 1, p. 126 supra. How would the reasonable value of the broker's services to his principal, if he were allowed restitution, differ from the amount provided in the unenforceable contract? On the assumption that it would differ little, if at all, it is usually held that the broker cannot have restitution because it would circumvent the statute. E. g., Baugh v. Darley, 112 Utah 1, 184 P.2d 335 (1947).

MONARCO v. LO GRECO

Supreme Court of California, 1950.
35 Cal.2d 621, 220 P.2d 737.

TRAYNOR, Justice.[a] Natale and Carmela Castiglia were married in 1919 in Colorado. Carmela had three children, John, Rosie and Christie, by a previous marriage. Rosie was married to Nick Norcia. Natale had one grandchild, plaintiff Carmen Monarco, the son of a deceased daughter by a previous marriage. Natale and Carmela moved to California where they invested their assets, amounting to approximately $4,000, in a half interest in agricultural property. Rosie and Nick Norcia acquired the other half interest. Christie, then in his early teens, moved with the family to California. Plaintiff remained in Colorado. In 1926, Christie, then 18 years old, decided to leave the home of his mother and step-father and seek an independent living. Natale and Carmela, however, wanted him to stay with them and participate in the family venture. They made an oral proposal to Christie that if he stayed home and worked they would keep their property in joint tenancy so that it would pass to the survivor who would leave it to Christie by will except for small devises to John and Rosie. In performance of this agreement Christie remained home and worked diligently in the family venture. He gave up any opportunity for further education or any chance to accumulate property of his own. He received only his room and board and spending money. When he married and suggested the possibility of securing some present interest to support his wife, Natale told him that his wife should move in with the family and that Christie need not worry, for he would receive all the property when Natale and Carmela died. Natale and Carmela placed all of their property in joint tenancy and in 1941 both executed wills leaving all their property to Christie with the exception of small devises to Rosie and John and $500 to plaintiff. Although these wills did not refer to the agreement, their terms were agreed upon by Christie, Natale and Carmela. The venture was successful, so that at the time of Natale's death his and Carmela's in-

a. Roger Traynor (1900–) was a member of the law faculty of the University of California at Berkeley from 1930 to 1940 and specialized in tax law. He served from 1940 to 1964 as associate justice of the Supreme Court of California and from 1964 to 1970 as its chief justice. Some of his opinions on contract law are discussed in Macaulay, Mr. Justice Traynor and the Law of Contracts, 13 Stan.L.Rev. 812 (1961).

terest was worth approximately $100,000. Shortly before his death Natale became dissatisfied with the agreement and determined to leave his half of the joint property to his grandson, the plaintiff. Without informing Christie or Carmela he arranged the necessary conveyances to terminate the joint tenancies and executed a will leaving all of his property to plaintiff. This will was probated and the court entered its decree distributing the property to plaintiff. After the decree of distribution became final, plaintiff brought these actions for partition of the properties and an accounting. By cross-complaint Carmela asked that plaintiff be declared a constructive trustee of the property he received as a result of Natale's breach of his agreement to keep the property in joint tenancy. On the basis of the foregoing facts the trial court gave judgment for defendants and cross-complainant, and plaintiff has appealed.

The controlling question is whether plaintiff is estopped from relying upon the statute of frauds (Civil Code § 1624; Code Civ. Proc. § 1973) to defeat the enforcement of the oral contract.[a] The doctrine of estoppel to assert the statute of frauds has been consistently applied by the courts of this state to prevent fraud that would result from refusal to enforce oral contracts in certain circumstances. Such fraud may inhere in the unconscionable injury that would result from denying enforcement of the contract after one party has been induced by the other seriously to change his position in reliance on the contract, . . . or in the unjust enrichment that would result if a party who has received the benefits of the other's performance were allowed to rely upon the statute. . . . In many cases both elements are present. Thus, not only may one party have so seriously changed his position in reliance upon, or in performance of, the contract that he would suffer an unconscionable injury if it were not enforced, but the other may have reaped the benefits of the contract so that he would be unjustly enriched if he could escape its obligations. . . .

In this case both elements are present. In reliance on Natale's repeated assurances that he would receive the property when Natale and Carmela died, Christie gave up any opportunity to accumulate property of his own and devoted his life to making the family venture a success. That he would be seriously prejudiced by a refusal to enforce the contract is made clear by a comparison of his position with that of Rosie and Nick Norcia. Because the Norcias were able to make a small investment when the family venture was started, their interest, now worth approximately $100,000, has been protected. Christie, on the other hand, forbore from demanding any present interest in the venture in exchange for his labors on the assurance that Natale's and Carmela's interest would pass to him on their death. Had he invested money instead of labor in the venture on the same oral un-

a. See the lifetime provision set out in Note 1, p. 126 supra.

derstanding, a resulting trust would have arisen in his favor. Byers v. Doheny, 105 Cal.App. 484, 493–495, 287 P. 988; see, Restatement, Trusts, § 454, comment j. illus. 12. His twenty years of labor should have equal effect. On the other hand, Natale reaped the benefits of the contract. He and his devisees would be unjustly enriched if the statute of frauds could be invoked to relieve him from performance of his own obligations thereunder.

It is contended, however, that an estoppel to plead the statute of frauds can only arise when there have been representations with respect to the requirements of the statute indicating that a writing is not necessary or will be executed or that the statute will not be relied upon as a defense. This element was present in the leading case of Seymour v. Oelrichs, 156 Cal. 782, 108 P. 88, 134 Am.St.Rep. 154, and it is not surprising therefore that it has been listed as a requirement of an estoppel in later cases that have held on their facts that there was or was not an estoppel. . . . Those cases, however, that have refused to find an estoppel have been cases where the court found either that no unconscionable injury would result from refusing to enforce the oral contract, . . . or that the remedy of quantum meruit for services rendered was adequate. . . . In those cases, however, where either an unconscionable injury or unjust enrichment would result from refusal to enforce the contract, the doctrine of estoppel has been applied whether or not plaintiff relied upon representations going to the requirements of the statute itself. . . . Likewise in the case of partly performed oral contracts for the sale of land specific enforcement will be decreed whether or not there have been representations going to the requirements of the statute, because its denial would result in a fraud on the plaintiff who has gone into possession or made improvements in reliance on the contract. . . . In reality it is not the representation that the contract will be put in writing or that the statute will not be invoked, but the promise that the contract will be performed that a party relies upon when he changes his position because of it. Moreover, a party who has accepted the benefits of an oral contract will be unjustly enriched if the contract is not enforced whether his representations related to the requirements of the statute or were limited to affirmations that the contract would be performed.

It is settled that neither the remedy of an action at law for damages for breach of contract nor the quasi-contractual remedy for the value of services rendered is adequate for the breach of a contract to leave property by will in exchange for services of a peculiar nature involving the assumption or continuation of a close family relationship. . . . The facts of this case clearly bring it within the foregoing rule. . . .

The judgments are affirmed.

NOTES

(1) *Estoppel by Performance.* Does estoppel "swallow up" the doctrine of part performance as applied to contracts for the sale of land (p. 133 supra) and of full performance on one side as applied to contracts not to be performed within one year (Note 5, p. 133 supra)? See McIntosh v. Murphy, 52 Haw. 29, 469 P.2d 177 (1970), in which the court relied on Monarco v. Lo Greco to permit an automobile sales manager to enforce an oral one-year employment contract after he had moved 2,200 miles from Los Angeles to Honolulu and worked for two and a half months. See also Lucas v. Whittaker Corp., 470 F.2d 326 (10th Cir. 1972), in which the court, applying California law, relied on Monarco v. Lo Greco to permit a general manager of a battery manufacturer to enforce an oral two-year employment contract after he had resigned from his previous job, moved from Missouri to Colorado and worked for thirteen months.

Monarco v. Lo Greco is discussed, approvingly, in Traynor, Unjustifiable Reliance, 42 Minn.L.Rev. 11, 18 (1957). See Notes, 66 Mich.L.Rev. 170 (1967); 53 Calif.L.Rev. 590 (1965); Annot., 54 A.L.R.3d 715 (1973).

(2) *The Case of the Venal Vendor.* Roberts agreed over the telephone to sell Caplan heavy construction equipment located at a site in Montana for $35,000. During the next ten months Caplan sent an agent from California to Montana to inspect the equipment and had a number of conversations that confirmed his belief that such an agreement was in effect. In reliance, Caplan negotiated to resell the equipment to five separate buyers, anticipating profits of $30,500, and refrained from obtaining similar equipment from four other sellers. When Caplan demanded delivery, he was told that Roberts had sold the equipment to several other firms, one of them a firm with which Caplan had negotiated a resale agreement. Similar equipment was no longer available. Caplan sued for breach of contract, asking $30,500 damages. From summary judgment for Roberts, Caplan appealed. *Held:* Affirmed. The contract was governed by California law and was unenforceable under UCC 2–201. Monarco v. Lo Greco did not apply because there was no unjust enrichment since appellant had not performed and would not "suffer unconscionable injury if appellee were allowed to assert the bar of the statute of frauds and thereby prevent the enforcement of the oral agreement. . . . [T]he only injury appellant, as the buyer under the oral contract, might have suffered from the seller's refusal to deliver, is the loss of the profit he was to make on the resale of the equipment. And . . . the mere 'loss of bargain, and damage resulting therefrom, do not themselves estop a seller from relying upon the Statute of Frauds.'" Caplan v. Roberts, 506 F.2d 1039 (9th Cir. 1974).

WARDER & LEE ELEVATOR, INC. v. BRITTEN

Supreme Court of Iowa, 1979.
274 N.W.2d 339.

McCORMICK, Justice. The question in this action for breach of an oral contract to sell grain is whether the trial court erred in holding defendant's statute of frauds defense under the Uniform Commercial Code was defeated by promissory estoppel. We affirm the trial court. . . .

Plaintiff Warder & Lee Elevator, Inc., operates a grain elevator in the town of Webster. The corporation president, Francis Lee, managed the elevator for many years until he suffered a slight stroke in November 1974. He was succeeded as manager by his son James who had been an elevator employee since 1964. The Lees were the only witnesses at trial.

We recite the evidence in the light most favorable to the judgment. Francis Lee was alone in the elevator office on July 4, 1974. Defendant John W. Britten, a farmer in the area, came to the office during the morning with a friend. The elevator had purchased Britten's grain for years, and he and Lee were well acquainted. At Britten's request Lee quoted him the price the elevator would pay for new-crop corn and soybeans for fall delivery based on market prices of the prior day.

Britten offered to sell and Lee agreed for the elevator to purchase from Britten 4000 bushels of corn at $2.60 per bushel and 2000 bushels of beans at $5.70 per bushel for October-November delivery.

The elevator did not at that time require a seller to sign a memorandum or other writing to show the agreement. Instead, the only writing consisted of notes showing the terms of sale made by Lee for internal bookkeeping purposes. All of the elevator's prior purchases from Britten had been upon oral agreement, and Britten had kept his promises on each occasion. In fact, no seller had previously refused to perform an oral agreement with the elevator.

It was the custom of the elevator not to speculate in grain but to act essentially as a broker. Thus on July 5, 1974, the elevator sold the same quantities of corn and beans as were involved in the Britten purchase for fall delivery to terminal elevators at Muscatine for a few cents more per bushel.

Grain prices increased substantially during July. On July 29, 1974, Britten called Francis Lee and said he wished to "call the deal off". Lee told him: "You cannot call it off. We sold this grain, and we expect delivery this fall." Britten said he would not deliver the grain.

In an effort to mitigate its loss and to enable it to meet its commitment to sell the grain, the elevator purchased appropriate quantities of new-crop corn and beans from other farmers on and shortly after July 29.

In August 1974, James Lee met Britten on a street in Webster. Britten initiated a conversation in which he said he would not fulfill his agreement and offered $500 in settlement. Although counsel for Britten objected to the admissibility of the evidence at trial, the objection was untimely and no motion to strike was made. Lee rejected the offer. He told Britten the elevator had sold the grain and expected him to perform under his contract.

Britten sold his 1974 crop elsewhere.

The elevator brought this action against Britten for breach of the oral agreement, seeking as damages the loss it sustained in covering its delivery obligation under the July 5 contracts by which it sold the quantity of grain purchased from Britten. See § 554.2712, The Code. That loss was $6478.34, which was the amount, plus interest, for which the trial court entered judgment.

Britten offered no evidence at trial. He relied solely on the statute of frauds in § 554.2201, The Code. The elevator urged promissory estoppel in bar of the defense.

The statute of frauds applicable to the sale of crops is § 554.-2201. Under this statute an oral contract for the sale of goods for a price of $500 or more is unenforceable, with certain stated exceptions. The elevator does not contend any of those exceptions is applicable. Promissory estoppel is not among them.

Authority for use of promissory estoppel to defeat the statute of frauds, if it exists, must be found under § 554.1103. It provides:

> Unless displaced by the particular provisions of this chapter, the principles of law and equity, including the law merchant and the law relative to capacity to contract, principal and agent, estoppel, fraud, misrepresentation, duress, coercion, mistake, bankruptcy, or other validating or invalidating cause shall supplement its provisions.

We have not had occasion to decide whether the provisions of § 554.2201 displace the doctrine of estoppel which would otherwise be available in accordance with § 554.1103. However, other courts which have considered the question have held the doctrine is available. Several of those decisions involved grain sales in circumstances analogous to those in the present case. See Decatur Cooperative Association v. Urban, 219 Kan. 171, 547 P.2d 323 (1976); Jamestown Terminal Elevator, Inc. v. Hieb, 246 N.W.2d 736 (N.D.1976); Farmers Elevator Company of Elk Point v. Lyles, 238 N.W.2d 290 (S.D. 1976).

When other courts have refused to apply the doctrine they have done so because of a different view of the doctrine of promissory estoppel rather than because of any perceived statutory bar to its use. . . .

We have long recognized promissory estoppel as a means of defeating the general statute of frauds in § 622.32, The Code. . . . We see nothing in § 554.2201 which purports to require a different rule under the Uniform Commercial Code.

The listing of exceptions to the statute of frauds in § 554.2201 is plainly definitional. The provision does not purport to eliminate equitable and legal principles traditionally applicable in contract actions. Therefore it does not affect the viability of defenses to application of the rule of evidence which it defines. See White and Summers, Handbook of the Law Under the Uniform Commercial Code § 2–6 at 59 (1972) ("There is every reason to believe these remain good law, post-Code.").

If § 554.2201 were construed as displacing principles otherwise preserved in § 554.1103, it would mean that an oral contract coming within its terms would be unenforceable despite fraud, deceit, misrepresentation, dishonesty or any other form of unconscionable conduct by the party relying upon the statute. No court has taken such an extreme position. Nor would we be justified in doing so. Despite differences relating to the availability of an estoppel defense, courts uniformly hold "that the Statute of Frauds, having been enacted for the purpose of preventing fraud, shall not be made the instrument of shielding, protecting, or aiding the party who relies upon it in the perpetration of a fraud or in the consummation of a fraudulent scheme." 3 Williston on Contracts § 553A at 796 (Third Ed. Jaeger, 1960). The estoppel defense, preserved on the same basis as the fraud defense by § 554.1103, developed from this principle. "The Statute was designed as the weapon of the written law to prevent frauds; the doctrine of estoppel is that of the unwritten law to prevent a like evil." Id. at 797–798.

We have found no reported decision in any jurisdiction holding that the statute of frauds in the Uniform Commercial Code, defined as it is in § 554.2203, displaces principles preserved in § 554.1103. We do not believe that our legislature intended for it to do so.

We hold that the provisions of § 554.2201 do not displace the doctrine of estoppel in relation to the sale of goods in Iowa. . . .

Specific circumstances which justify use of the doctrine as a means of avoiding a statute of frauds defense are now expressed in Restatement Second of Contracts § 139,[a] as follows:

> (1) A promise which the promisor should reasonably expect to induce action or forbearance on the part of the promisee or a third person and which does induce the action or forbearance is enforceable notwithstanding the Statute of Frauds if injustice can be avoided only by enforcement of the promise. The remedy granted for breach is to be limited as justice requires.

a. In the editing of this opinion, the court's references to this section have been changed to conform to the final numbering system of the Restatement Second.

(2) In determining whether injustice can be avoided only by enforcement of the promise, the following circumstances are significant:

(a) the availability and adequacy of other remedies particularly cancellation and restitution;

(b) the definite and substantial character of the action or forbearance in relation to the remedy sought;

(c) the extent to which the action or forbearance corroborates evidence of the making and terms of the promise, or the making and terms are otherwise established by clear and convincing evidence;

(d) the reasonableness of the action or forbearance;

(e) the extent to which the action or forbearance was foreseeable by the promisor.

This section complements Restatement Second of Contracts § 90, the predecessor of which we previously approved. . . . We now approve and adopt the standard in § 139. Of course, it also obviates any distinction based upon whether the promise is unilateral or bilateral. Restatement § 139, comment a. ("This Section is complementary to § 90, which dispenses with the requirement of consideration if the same conditions are met, but it also applies to promises supported by consideration.").

In order to obtain the benefit of the doctrine of promissory estoppel to defeat a statute of frauds defense, the promisee must show more than the nonperformance of an oral contract. See 3 Williston on Contracts § 553A (Third Ed. Jaeger, 1960). Under § 139 the defense cannot be overcome, when it is otherwise applicable, unless the promisee proves (1) the promisor should reasonably have expected the agreement to induce action or forbearance, (2) such action or forbearance was induced, and (3) enforcement is necessary to prevent injustice.

In determining whether injustice can be avoided only by enforcement of the promise, the circumstances listed in § 139(2) must be considered. In this manner, § 139(2) provides a means of deciding whether the equities support enforcement of the agreement.

We must now decide whether the trial court erred in applying the doctrine of promissory estoppel in this case.

Britten contends the elevator should not have the benefit of the doctrine because it . . . did not prove he knew it would rely on the oral agreement. [We find that this contention] is without merit. We do so because we believe substantial evidence supports the inference he expected or reasonably should have expected the agreement to induce action by the elevator. It was not necessary for the elevator to prove he actually knew it would rely on his promise. He should have known his prior dealings with the elevator gave the elevator manager every reason to believe he would keep his word. Furthermore, it is reasonable to believe that a farmer who sells grain regularly to country elevators knows they may immediately sell the grain which they purchase. In this case, Britten expressed no surprise when the elevator refused to allow him to rescind because of its sales in reliance on the agreement. Instead he sought to buy his way out of the transaction.

We conclude that the elements of promissory estoppel were supported by substantial evidence. In keeping with the standard in Restatement § 139, we hold that injustice could be avoided only by enforcement of Britten's promise. The trial court did not err in holding the agreement was enforceable despite the statute of frauds defense.

Affirmed.

All Justices concur except REYNOLDSON, C. J., and ALLBEE, J., who dissent.

REYNOLDSON, Chief Justice (dissenting).

I respectfully dissent. The contract in issue falls squarely within the language and intent of the statute of frauds, § 554.2201 . . . The lead sentence in § 554.2201 now provides: "Except as otherwise provided *in this section* . . ." The limiting language of § 554.2201 at least ought to displace a doctrine which would gut the legislative intent of the statute. Distilled to its essence, § 139, as interpreted by the majority, provides that if one contracting party should know the other contracting party will rely on the contract and injustice will result if the oral contract is not enforced, the statute of frauds will be ignored. It is a rare case when either promisor in a bilateral contract does not rely on the contract. . . . Any party to a contract should realize such reliance occurs. Most situations in which such an oral contract is breached result in injustice.

But the § 554.2201 statute of frauds obviously is designed to suffer these injustices in isolated oral contract cases in favor of the general public policy to reduce fraud and perjury, curtail litigation and controversy, and encourage written contracts in sales of goods for a price of $500 or more. It is significant that by trial time the plaintiff corporation in the case at bar was using written sales contracts with its customers.

Adopting §§ 90 and 139 as an unwritten exception to § 554.2201 will not only encourage oral contracts, it will bring a massive infusion of litigation to our overloaded courts. Trial courts will be compelled to determine, on an *ad hoc* basis, whether there was a contract, whether the promisor could "reasonably expect" the other party to rely on it, whether reasonable action or forbearance resulted, whether "justice requires" a remedy, and otherwise engage in the delicate balancing maneuvers mandated by § 139(2).

In the final analysis, the majority opinion means written contracts are unnecessary in initial purchases of agricultural products, probably Iowa's largest economic marketplace and involving almost three billion dollars worth of goods each year. We should proceed down that road with great caution. . . .

Finally, it should be noted the facts in this case would not warrant application of § 139 of the Restatement.

Imposition of § 139 would require proof the defendant seller in this case "should reasonably expect" that the plaintiff corporation would promptly resell the grain. There is no evidence in the transcript in this case to show defendant either knew this was plaintiff's practice or that it was a custom in the industry. . . .

NOTES

(1) *The Grain Cases of 1973.* A rash of grain cases grew out of contracts made in 1973. "During the summer of 1973 the commodities market, especially the wheat, corn and soybean markets, experienced unprecedented price increases. Major factors contributing to these increases included the Russian wheat sale, unusually large exports of grain and soybeans, unfavorable harvesting weather and transportation shortages. Under these conditions several marketing practices, including the widespread use of oral contracts, proved inadequate.

"The grain marketing system, in addition to reducing seasonal price fluctuations,[1] had also served the purpose of transferring the risk of loss (and gain) from farmers and grain elevators to those willing to speculate in the commodities futures markets. This was accomplished through the grain elevators' nonspeculative trading in the commodities futures markets known as "hedging." [2] Because of the fast pace and wide price variations during a

1. Under normal conditions, prices dropped by harvest time because of the large supply. See, e. g., R. Kohls, Marketing of Agricultural Products 192–93, 202 (1955); S. Kroll & I. Shishko, The Commodity Futures Market Guide 5–6, 63–66 (1973).

2. This transfer of risk was typically accomplished in the following manner: The farmer, wishing to avoid the likelihood of a decline in the market price at harvest time, negotiated a "forward contract" with a local grain elevator several months prior to harvest. The forward contract contained an agreed price for a specified amount to be delivered at a specified time in the future. The local elevator, typically a small operation unable to bear the risk of a lower market price at harvest and delivery time, immediately sold the same amount of grain to a regional elevator for future delivery. The regional elevator (and occasionally the local elevator), also wishing to avoid the same risk, used the futures markets for nonspeculative trading known as "hedging." In hedging, the regional elevator would sell a futures contract in the commodities exchange for the same quantity of grain for delivery at the same time it expected to resell the grain purchased from the local elevator. This procedure worked on the assumption that the prices for futures contracts follow the cash prices for the grain, so that if the regional elevator lost money on its grain purchase from the local, it would gain a similar amount on its futures contracts. [Continued on next page.]

single day of trading on the commodities exchange, all of the parties typically relied upon oral telephone agreements rather than written contracts when buying and selling grain.[a]

"Under usual conditions, the grain elevator lost money on its purchase from farmers but gained a similar amount from its hedging in the commodities futures markets. In 1973, however, when prices had risen instead of dropped at harvest time, elevators lost money on their hedging. When some farmers refused to perform their prior contracts the elevators did not make the expected gain to offset their hedging losses. . . .

"In the rash of cases which followed the 1973 upheaval in the commodities market, the courts were presented with a variety of theories under which the oral contracts between grain elevators and farmers could be enforced despite the statue of frauds." Note, Promissory Estoppel, Equitable Estoppel and Farmer as a Merchant: The 1973 Grain Cases and the UCC Statute of Frauds, 1977 Utah L.Rev. 59, 61–63.[b]

(2) *Restatement Second.* Restatement Second, § 139 had no counterpart in the first Restatement. How does the rule that it states compare with that of Monarco v. Lo Greco? How does promissory estoppel differ from equitable estoppel under the statute of frauds? See 44 Fordham L. Rev. 114 (1975).

OZIER v. HAINES, 411 Ill. 160, 103 N.E.2d 485 (1952). [Ozier, who ran a grain elevator, sued Haines, alleging that Haines had orally sold Ozier 5,000 bushels of corn at $1.24 a bushel, and that relying on this Ozier had immediately resold the corn over the telephone to a broker while Haines was still in Ozier's office. Ozier also alleged that it was the custom of the grain trade to buy and sell on oral contracts. He claimed $4,450, the difference between the price

---

2 Continued

The hedging procedure of a regional elevator is exemplified as follows:

	Grain purchased from local elevator	Futures Market
Day of purchase from local elevator for future delivery	Buys 100,000 bu. at $2.00 for future delivery	Sells 100,000 bu. contract at $2.10
Day of sale of grain received from local elevator	Sells 100,000 bu. at $1.95	Buys 100,000 bu. contract at $2.05
	Loss of 5¢/bu.	Gain of 5¢/bu.

See R. Kohls, supra note 1, at 209.

---

a. That "exceptions to the Statute of Frauds cannot be enlarged by usage in the trade, such as a consistent failure of grain dealers to utilize written agreements in their dealings with farmers," see Farmers Cooperative Ass'n v. Cole, 239 N.W.2d 808, 814 (N.D.1976); see also Ozier v. Haines, infra.

b. Reproduced by permission of the Utah Law Review.

which he had to pay for the corn on the open market and the contract price. The complaint was dismissed on the ground that the contract was unenforceable under the statute of frauds, and the plaintiff appealed.]

DAILEY, Chief Justice. . . . [One of the elements of equitable estoppel is:] "Words or conduct by the party against whom the estoppel is alleged amounting to a misrepresentation or concealment of material facts. . . ." [Ozier's] position is that the promisee's reliance upon an unenforcible promise will validate the promise. To adopt such a view would render the Statute of Frauds useless and unmeaning. It is true that harsh results, or moral fraud as plaintiffs choose to term it, may occur where one has changed his position in reliance on the oral promise of another, but it is a result which is invited and risked when the agreement is not reduced to writing in the manner prescribed by law. The present case is a patent example, for although the parties were in each other's presence and in a business office, no attempt was made to reduce their agreement to the simplest writing . . . . [Furthermore,] the customs pleaded could not render nugatory the provision of the Statute of Frauds. . . .

[Affirmed.]

NOTE

Traditional View. Ozier v. Haines represents the traditional view. Does the decision in Warder & Lee Elevator "render the Statute of Frauds useless and unmeaning," as the court in Ozier v. Haines expressed it? See Note, 1977 Utah L.Rev. 59, 67–72; see also Edwards, The Statute of Frauds of the Uniform Commercial Code and the Doctrine of Estoppel, 62 Marquette L.Rev. 205 (1978).

Chapter 3
THE BARGAINING PROCESS

SECTION 1. THE NATURE OF ASSENT

What kind of assent to a bargain is necessary to bind a party? Different answers are given by two contrasting theories of contract, commonly described as "objective" and "subjective." They are illustrated by these excerpts from Judge Learned Hand [a] and his colleague Judge Jerome Frank,[b] concurring in a case in which Hand wrote the opinion of the court.

According to Hand: "A contract has, strictly speaking, nothing to do with the personal, or individual, intent of the parties. A contract is an obligation attached by the mere force of law to certain acts of the parties, usually words, which ordinarily accompany and represent a known intent. If, however, it were proved by twenty bishops that either party when he used the words intended something else than the usual meaning which the law imposes upon them, he would still be held, unless there were some mutual mistake or something else of the sort." Hotchkiss v. National City Bank of New York, 200 F. 287, 293 (S.D.N.Y.1911).

According to Frank: "In the early days of this century a struggle went on between the respective proponents of two theories of contracts, (a) the "actual intent" theory—or 'meeting of the minds' [c] or

a. Learned Hand (1872–1961) was admitted to the practice of law in New York in 1897, appointed to the United States District Court for the Southern District of New York in 1909 and to the United States Court of Appeals for the Second Circuit in 1924. He retired in 1951, after having sat on the bench longer than any other federal judge. Justice Cardozo called him "the greatest living American jurist," and he was so regarded by many of his contemporaries. His extrajudicial utterances may be sampled in The Spirit of Liberty (1952) and The Bill of Rights (1958).

b. Jerome New Frank (1889–1957) practiced in Chicago and New York for more than twenty years before going to Washington in 1933, where he served first as a government lawyer and then as a member and later chairman of the Securities and Exchange Commission. In 1941 he was appointed to the United States Court of Appeals for the Second Circuit. He also lectured at the Yale Law School and was associated with the philosophy of law known as "legal realism." One of his best known books is Law and the Modern Mind (1930).

c. For the curious origin of the term "meeting of the minds," see Farnsworth, "Meaning" in the Law of Contracts, 76 Yale L.J. 939, 943–44 (1967). It has remained a popular metaphor, e. g., "Any greater 'meeting of the minds' would require them to bump their heads together." Turner v. Worth Insurance Co., 106 Ariz. 132, 472 P.2d 1 (1970).

'will' theory—and (b) the so-called 'objective' theory.[1] Without doubt, the first theory had been carried too far: Once a contract has been validly made, the courts attach legal consequences to the relation created by the contract, consequences of which the parties usually never dreamed—as, for instance, where situations arise which the parties had not contemplated. As to such matters, the 'actual intent' theory induced much fictional discourse which imputed to the parties intentions they plainly did not have.

"But the objectivists also went too far. They tried (1) to treat virtually all the varieties of contractual arrangements in the same way, and (2), as to all contracts in all their phases, to exclude, as legally irrelevant, consideration of the actual intention of the parties or either of them, as distinguished from the outward manifestation of that intention. The objectivists transferred from the field of torts that stubborn anti-subjectivist, the 'reasonable man'; so that, in part at least, advocacy of the 'objective' standard in contracts appears to have represented a desire for legal symmetry, legal uniformity, a desire seemingly prompted by aesthetic impulses. Whether (thanks to the 'subjectivity' of the jurymen's reactions and other factors) the objectivists' formula, in its practical workings, could yield much actual objectivity, certainty, and uniformity may well be doubted. At any rate, the sponsors of complete 'objectivity' in contracts largely won out in the wider generalizations of the Restatement of Contracts and in some judicial pronouncements." Ricketts v. Pennsylvania R. Co., 153 F.2d 757 (2d Cir. 1946).

Does either theory adequately explain the decision in the following case? For a recent discussion of the two theories, see Kabil Developments Corp. v. Mignot, 279 Or. 151, 566 P.2d 505 (1977).

NOTES

(1) *Criticism of Objective Theory.* Over half a century ago, one of the critics of the objective theory suggested that courts are too zealous in protecting the expectations of a party who mistakenly, although reasonably, believes that the other has assented. He thought it unfortunate that one party "is bound to the contract though the other party is notified of the mistake before the latter has changed his position or suffered any damage,"

1. "The 'actual intent' theory, said the objectivists, being 'subjective' and putting too much stress on unique individual motivations, would destroy that legal certainty and stability which a modern commercial society demands. They depicted the 'objective' standard as a necessary adjunct of a 'free enterprise' economic system. In passing, it should be noted that they arrived at a sort of paradox. For a 'free enterprise' system is, theoretically, founded on 'individualism'; but, in the name of economic individualism, the objectivists refused to consider those reactions of actual specific individuals which sponsors of the 'meeting-of-the-minds' test purported to cherish. 'Economic individualism' thus shows up as hostile to real individualism. This is nothing new: The 'economic man' is of course an abstraction, a 'fiction.' "

and suggested that contractual liability be limited to situations where there was subjective agreement and that liability in tort be imposed for the negligent use of language where a misunderstanding prevented such agreement. Whittier, The Restatement of Contracts and Mutual Assent, 17 Calif.L.Rev. 441 (1929). This would have an important effect on the amount of damages, since tort liability would protect only the promisee's reliance interest, while contractual liability would protect his expectation interest.

Take the case of a seller who misspeaks and offers to sell "fifty thousand" boxes at a stated price when he means to say "fifteen thousand." If the buyer accepts, neither knowing nor having reason to know of the seller's mistake in expression, can he recover his loss in expectation if the seller refuses to deliver more than fifteen thousand? Would it make a difference if the seller notified the buyer of the mistake immediately after the buyer's acceptance? See Note 4, p. 265 infra.

(2) *Mistake in Transmission.* Suppose that the seller sends his offer by telegram and the telegraph company makes an error in transmitting it so that it reads "fifty thousand" boxes rather than "fifteen thousand" as the seller instructed it. There is authority that the seller is bound by a contract for fifty thousand. Ayer v. Western Union Telegraph Co., 79 Me. 493, 10 A. 495 (1887). Contra: Western Union Telegraph Co. v. Cowin & Co., 20 F.2d 103 (8th Cir. 1927).

Does this carry the objective theory too far? Can the imposition of the risk on the sender of the telegram be justified on the ground that the sender has a contractual relationship with the telegraph company?

(3) *Relief for Mistake.* The possibility that a party may be relieved of a contractual obligation on the ground that his assent was the result of mistake is considered at several points in this book. See, in particular, Chapter 4, Section 1 infra.

LUCY v. ZEHMER

Supreme Court of Appeals of Virginia, 1954.
196 Va. 493, 84 S.E.2d 516.

BUCHANAN, Justice. This suit was instituted by W. O. Lucy and J. C. Lucy, complainants, against A. H. Zehmer and Ida S. Zehmer, his wife, defendants, to have specific performance of a contract by which it was alleged the Zehmers had sold to W. O. Lucy a tract of land owned by A. H. Zehmer in Dinwiddie county containing 471.6 acres, more or less, known as the Ferguson farm, for $50,000. J. C. Lucy, the other complainant, is a brother of W. O. Lucy, to whom W. O. Lucy transferred a half interest in his alleged purchase.

The instrument sought to be enforced was written by A. H. Zehmer on [Saturday,] December 20, 1952, in these words: "We hereby agree to sell to W. O. Lucy the Ferguson Farm complete for $50,000.-00, title satisfactory to buyer," and signed by the defendants, A. H. Zehmer and Ida S. Zehmer.

The answer of A. H. Zehmer admitted that at the time mentioned W. O. Lucy offered him $50,000 cash for the farm, but that he, Zehmer, considered that the offer was made in jest; that so thinking, and both he and Lucy having had several drinks, he wrote out "the memorandum" quoted above and induced his wife to sign it; that he did not deliver the memorandum to Lucy, but that Lucy picked it up, read it, put it in his pocket, attempted to offer Zehmer $5 to bind the bargain, which Zehmer refused to accept, and realizing for the first time that Lucy was serious, Zehmer assured him that he had no intention of selling the farm and that the whole matter was a joke. Lucy left the premises insisting that he had purchased the farm.

Depositions were taken and the decree appealed from was entered holding that the complainants had failed to establish their right to specific performance, and dismissing their bill. The assignment of error is to this action of the court. . . .

The defendants insist that the evidence was ample to support their contention that the writing sought to be enforced was prepared as a bluff or dare to force Lucy to admit that he did not have $50,000; that the whole matter was a joke; that the writing was not delivered to Lucy and no binding contract was ever made between the parties.

It is an unusual, if not bizarre, defense. When made to the writing admittedly prepared by one of the defendants and signed by both, clear evidence is required to sustain it.

In his testimony Zehmer claimed that he "was high as a Georgia pine," and that the transaction "was just a bunch of two doggoned drunks bluffing to see who could talk the biggest and say the most." That claim is inconsistent with his attempt to testify in great detail as to what was said and what was done. It is contradicted by other evidence as to the condition of both parties, and rendered of no weight by the testimony of his wife that when Lucy left the restaurant she suggested that Zehmer drive him home. The record is convincing that Zehmer was not intoxicated to the extent of being unable to comprehend the nature and consequences of the instrument he executed, and hence that instrument is not to be invalidated on that ground. C.J.S. Contracts, § 133, b., p. 483; Taliaferro v. Emery, 124 Va. 674, 98 S.E. 627. It was in fact conceded by defendants' counsel in oral argument that under the evidence Zehmer was not too drunk to make a valid contract.

The evidence is convincing also that Zehmer wrote two agreements, the first one beginning "I hereby agree to sell." Zehmer first said he could not remember about that, then that "I don't think I wrote but one out." Mrs. Zehmer said that what he wrote was "I hereby agree," but that the "I" was changed to "We" after that night. The agreement that was written and signed is in the record and indicates no such change. Neither are the mistakes in spelling that Zehmer sought to point out readily apparent.

The appearance of the contract, the fact that it was under discussion for forty minutes or more before it was signed; Lucy's objection to the first draft because it was written in the singular, and he wanted Mrs. Zehmer to sign it also; the rewriting to meet that objection and the signing by Mrs. Zehmer; the discussion of what was to be included in the sale, the provision for the examination of the title, the completeness of the instrument that was executed, the taking possession of it by Lucy with no request or suggestion by either of the defendants that he give it back, are facts which furnish persuasive evidence that the execution of the contract was a serious business transaction rather than a casual, jesting matter as defendants now contend. . . .

If it be assumed, contrary to what we think the evidence shows, that Zehmer was jesting about selling his farm to Lucy and that the transaction was intended by him to be a joke, nevertheless the evidence shows that Lucy did not so understand it but considered it to be a serious business transaction and the contract to be binding on the Zehmers as well as on himself. The very next day he arranged with his brother to put up half the money and take a half interest in the land. The day after that he employed an attorney to examine the title. The next night, Tuesday, he was back at Zehmer's place and there Zehmer told him for the first time, Lucy said, that he wasn't going to sell and he told Zehmer, "You know you sold that place fair and square." After receiving the report from his attorney that the title was good he wrote to Zehmer that he was ready to close the deal.

Not only did Lucy actually believe, but the evidence shows he was warranted in believing, that the contract represented a serious business transaction and a good faith sale and purchase of the farm.

In the field of contracts, as generally elsewhere, "We must look to the outward expression of a person as manifesting his intention rather than to his secret and unexpressed intention. 'The law imputes to a person an intention corresponding to the reasonable meaning of his words and acts.'" First Nat. Exchange Bank of Roanoke v. Roanoke Oil Co., 169 Va. 99, 114, 192 S.E. 764, 770.

At no time prior to the execution of the contract had Zehmer indicated to Lucy by word or act that he was not in earnest about selling the farm. They had argued about it and discussed its terms, as Zehmer admitted, for a long time. Lucy testified that if there was any jesting it was about paying $50,000 that night. The contract and the evidence show that he was not expected to pay the money that night. Zehmer said that after the writing was signed he laid it down on the counter in front of Lucy. Lucy said Zehmer handed it to him. In any event there had been what appeared to be a good faith offer and a good faith acceptance, followed by the execution and apparent delivery of a written contract. Both said that Lucy put the writing in his pocket and then offered Zehmer $5 to seal the bargain. Not until then, even under the defendants' evidence, was anything said or done to indicate that the matter was a joke. Both of the Zehmers testified that when Zehmer asked his wife to sign he whispered that it was a joke so Lucy wouldn't hear and that it was not intended that he should hear.

The mental assent of the parties is not requisite for the formation of a contract. If the words or other acts of one of the parties have but one reasonable meaning, his undisclosed intention is immaterial except when an unreasonable meaning which he attaches to his manifestations is known to the other party. Restatement of the Law of Contracts, Vol. I, § 71, p. 74. . . .

An agreement or mutual assent is of course essential to a valid contract but the law imputes to a person an intention corresponding to the reasonable meaning of his words and acts. If his words and acts, judged by a reasonable standard, manifest an intention to agree, it is immaterial what may be the real but unexpressed state of his mind. C.J.S. Contracts, § 32, p. 361; 12 Am.Jur., Contracts, § 19, p. 515.

So a person cannot set up that he was merely jesting when his conduct and words would warrant a reasonable person in believing that he intended a real agreement. . . .

Whether the writing signed by the defendants and now sought to be enforced by the complainants was the result of a serious offer by Lucy and a serious acceptance by the defendants, or was a serious offer by Lucy and an acceptance in secret jest by the defendants, in either event it constituted a binding contract of sale between the parties. . . .

The complainants are entitled to have specific performance of the contract sued on. The decree appealed from is therefore reversed and the cause is remanded for the entry of a proper decree requiring the defendants to perform the contract in accordance with the prayer of the bill.

Reversed and remanded.

NOTES

(1) *Jesting and Bluffing.* What result if the price had been $50 rather than $50,000? See Note, p. 51 supra. In Keller v. Holderman, 11 Mich. 248 (1863), Holderman, as a "frolic and banter," gave Keller a $300 check for a watch worth about $15. Holderman had no money in the bank and intended to insert a condition in the check rendering him not liable. This he neglected to do. Keller sued Holderman on the check and had judgment. Holderman appealed. *Held*: Reversed. "When the Court below found as a fact that 'the whole transaction between the parties was a frolic and a banter, the plaintiff not expecting to sell, nor the defendant intending to buy the

watch at the sum for which the check was drawn,' the conclusion should have been that no contract was ever made by the parties. . . ."

Note that the Zehmers, in addition to contending that "the whole matter was a joke," contended that the writing "was prepared as a bluff or dare to force Lucy to admit that he did not have $50,000." What result if the offer had been so intended by the Zehmers and if Lucy, knowing this, had "called their bluff" by raising the money from his brother through transferring a half interest to him? Should a distinction be made between jesting and bluffing in this situation?

(2) *Statute of Frauds (Review).* Was the contract in Lucy v. Zehmer within the statute of frauds? Was the statute satisfied?

SULLIVAN v. O'CONNOR

[For the report of this case see p. 6 supra.]

NOTES

(1) *Statute.* Would you favor enactment in Massachusetts of a statute like the following one, enacted in Ohio in 1976?

> No action shall be brought to charge a person licensed . . . to practice medicine or surgery, osteopathic medicine or surgery, or podiatric medicine and surgery in this state, upon any promise or agreement relating to a medical prognosis unless the promise or agreement is in writing and signed by the party to be charged therewith. (Ohio Rev.Code Ann. § 1335.05.)

For a similar statute, see Mich.Comp. Laws Ann. § 566.132.

(2) *Problem.* Father consulted Doctor about an operation to remove scar tissue from Son's hand which had resulted from a severe burn nine years before. Father asked Doctor, "How long will the boy be in the hospital," and Doctor replied, "Three or four days, not over four; then the boy can go home and it will be just a few days when he will go back to work with a good hand." Son's hand was not healed for a month after the operation. Is Doctor liable to Father for breach of contract? Would your answer be different if Doctor added, "I will guarantee to make the hand a hundred percent perfect hand"? How much would Father recover if Doctor were liable? See Hawkins v. McGee, 84 N.H. 114, 146 A. 641 (1929).

"GENTLEMEN'S AGREEMENTS"

Can the parties to an agreement, by express provision, prevent the machinery of government from enforcing their promises? Consider this question in connection with two significant situations where such "gentlemen's agreements" have been used.

One arises in "firm-commitment underwriting" of corporate stock, a transaction in which the corporate issuer sells an entire issue of stock outright to a group of underwriters, who in turn sell to a larger group of dealers, who then sell to the public. Under the Securities Act of 1933, a registration statement containing specified information about the stock, the issuer and the underwriters must be filed with the Securities and Exchange Commission before the stock is offered to either the dealers or the public. Before going to the substantial trouble and expense of preparing and printing a registration statement, the issuer wants some assurance of the availability of the underwriters. The underwriters, however, are not willing to make an enforceable promise to purchase the stock, since that would subject them to the risk of an adverse change in the market during the time before the registration statement takes effect. The solution has been found in having the underwriters write to the issuer a "letter of intent," which is then signed by the issuer, and which sets out, often in considerable detail, the terms of the proposed underwriting, but states that "no liability or obligation of any nature whatsoever is intended to be created as between any of the parties hereto." Such a clause was given effect in Dunhill Securities Corp. v. Microthermal Applications, Inc., 308 F.Supp. 195 (S.D.N.Y.1969).

Bonus and death benefit plans afford a second situation in which gentlemen's agreements are used. The employer may want to disclose the plan in order to take advantage of the resulting incentive, but may want to keep its administration within his uncontrolled discretion. In Mabley & Carew Co. v. Borden, 129 Ohio St. 375, 195 N.E. 697 (1935), an employer gave an employee a certificate promising that a specified death benefit would be paid to her designated beneficiary if she was still employed at the time of her death, but stating that "it carries no legal obligation whatsoever or assurance or promise of future employment, and may be withdrawn or discontinued at any time by this Company." The court held that, in spite of this language, the employer was liable to the beneficiary. Why should this language be treated differently from that of the "letter of intent"? Cf. Spooner v. Reserve Life Ins. Co., 47 Wash.2d 454, 287 P.2d 735 (1955), distinguishing bonus plans from death benefit plans.

NOTE

Family and Social Agreements. There are many promises made in a family setting for which the machinery of the government's judicial process is not ordinarily available. In Balfour v. Balfour, [1919] 2 K.B. 571, denying a wife recovery on her husband's promise to pay her an allowance of £30 a month, Lord Atkin expressed the prevailing judicial attitude toward such promises: "[T]hey are not contracts because the parties did not intend that they should be attended by legal consequences. To my mind it would be of the worst possible example to hold that agreements such as this resulted in legal obligations which could be enforced in the Courts. . . . Agreements such as these are outside the realm of contracts altogether. . . . In respect of these promises each house is a domain into which the King's writ does not seek to run, and to which his officers do not seek to be admitted." What assumptions might justify this attitude?

Could the same have been said of the promises in Hamer v. Sidway, p. 44 supra, Kirksey v. Kirksey, p. 64 supra, and Ricketts v. Scothorn, p. 86 supra? Would it make a difference if the husband and wife put their agreement in writing? Stated that they intended it to be legally enforceable? See Note, 79 Harv.L.Rev. 1650 (1966); McDowell, Contracts in the Family, 45 B.U.L.Rev. 43 (1965). Difficult problems arise in connection with claims of implied contracts for services in the family, where courts have been prone to find that the services were gratuitous. See Havighurst, Services in the Home—A Study of Contract Concepts in Domestic Relations, 41 Yale L.J. 386 (1932); Wilhoite v. Beck, 141 Ind.App. 543, 230 N.E.2d 616 (1967).

Would you expect a court to enforce a promise made in a social setting, such as a promise to be a guest at a dinner party? Would it make a difference if the host had gone to considerable expense to make elaborate preparations? [a]

SECTION 2. THE OFFER

The process by which the parties arrive at a bargain will vary widely according to the circumstances. It is common to assume that it involves two distinct steps: first, an offer by one party and, second, an acceptance by the other. A discussion of whether this is inevitably the case can be deferred until later. It is helpful to begin, at least, with this assumption.

What is an offer? Corbin[a] gives this answer: "An offer is . . . an act whereby one person confers upon another the power to create contractual relations between them. . . . [T]he act of

a. Such disputes seldom reach the courts. A rare exception is Horsley v. Chesselet, decided in the Municipal Court of San Francisco in 1978 (Small Claims Action No. 346278), in which Mr. Horsley sued Miss Chesselet for $32 "that he expended . . . for gasoline and for theatre tickets in order to perform his promise to escort Defendant for an evening at the theatre." The court found "that the promise to engage in a social relationship for one evening" was unenforceable and ordered returned to plaintiff his "Exhibit 'A' for identification, a cardboard object in the shape of a broken heart, . . . with the Court mindful of Lord Byron's admonition, 'Maid of Athens, ere we part, Give, oh give me back my heart!' "

As to the applicability of contract principles to plea bargaining, see Cooper v. United States, 594 F.2d 12 (4th Cir. 1979).

a. Arthur Linton Corbin (1874–1967) practiced law in Colorado for four years after his graduation from law school in 1899. He taught at the Yale Law School from 1903 until his retirement in 1943, and became a leading authority on the law of contracts. His eight-volume treatise, Corbin on Contracts, which began to appear in 1950, ranks as one of the great legal treatises in any field of law in this country. He also served as Special Advisor and as Reporter for the Chapter on Remedies for the Restatement of Contracts.

the offeror operates to create in the offeree a power . . . ; thereafter the voluntary act of the offeree alone will operate to create the new relations called a contract. . . . What kind of act creates a power of acceptance and is therefore an offer? It must be an expression of will or intention. It must be an act that leads the offeree reasonably to believe that a power to create a contract is conferred upon him. . . . It is on this ground that we must exclude invitations to deal or acts of mere preliminary negotiation, and acts *evidently* done in jest or without intent to create legal relations. All these are acts that do not lead others reasonably to believe that they are empowered 'to close the contract.'" Corbin, Offer and Acceptance, and Some of The Resulting Legal Relations, 26 Yale L.J. 169, 181–82 (1917). See also Restatement Second, § 24.

NOTE

Agreement Without Offer and Acceptance? In the traditional conception, a contract is formed at a determinable moment through the process of offer and acceptance. Consider, however, these examples given in 2 Schlesinger (ed.), Formation of Contracts: A Study of the Common Core of Legal Systems 1584–86 (1968): "Especially when large deals are concluded among corporations and individuals of substance, the usual sequence of events is not that of offer and acceptance; on the contrary, the businessmen who originally conduct the negotiations, often will consciously refrain from ever making a binding offer, realizing as they do that a large deal tends to be complex and that its terms have to be formulated by lawyers before it can be permitted to become a legally enforceable transaction. Thus the original negotiators will merely attempt to ascertain whether they see eye to eye concerning those aspects of the deal which seem to be most important from a business point of view. Once they do, or think they do, the negotiation is then turned over to the lawyers, usually with instructions to produce a document which all participants will be willing to sign. . . . When the lawyers take over, again there is no sequence of offer and acceptance, but rather a sequence of successive drafts. These drafts usually will not be regarded as offers, for the reason, among others, that the lawyers acting as draftsmen have no authority to make offers on behalf of their clients. After a number of drafts have been exchanged and discussed, the lawyers may finally come up with a draft which meets the approval of all of them, and of their clients. It is only then that the parties will proceed to the actual formation of the contract, and often this will be done by way of a formal 'closing' . . . or in any event by simultaneous execution or delivery, in the course of a more or less ceremonial meeting, of the document or documents prepared by the lawyers.

"In the usual negotiation of a large-scale transaction there is thus no room for offer and acceptance (except where options are involved). If the writers on contract law nevertheless continue to analyze the formation of contracts almost exclusively in terms of offer and acceptance, they may be right insofar as they speak of the majority of personal and business transactions of modest or medium size; but in the world of truly large-scale dealings, the traditional analysis is no longer in tune with present-day practice. . . .

"In the field of corporate finance, many important transactions are settled by signing and exchanging identical documents. The typical 'closing' in a financial transaction involves more than two parties, often as many as half a dozen—a factor which in itself tends to attenuate the concepts of offer and acceptance since there may be as many independent interests involved as there are parties. It is customary for the attorneys at a closing to verify that all documents are in order and that all conditions precedent have been met (or are waived). When they are satisfied, the documents are then signed and exchanged by and among all the parties. Even though the signing may not be completely simultaneous, the exchange often is. Similarly where the documents have in fact been signed previously but held 'in escrow' by the attorneys for the signers pending verification of all details, they are simultaneously exchanged."[a] Is there no offer and acceptance in such cases?

OWEN v. TUNISON

Supreme Judicial Court of Maine, 1932.
131 Me. 42, 158 A. 926.

Action by W. H. Owen against R. G. Tunison for breach of contract.

BARNES, J. This case is reported to the law court, and such judgment is to be rendered as the law and the admissible evidence require.

Plaintiff charges that defendant agreed in writing to sell him the Bradley block and lot, situated in Bucksport, for a stated price in cash, that he later refused to perfect the sale, and that plaintiff, always willing and ready to pay the price, has suffered loss on account of defendant's unjust refusal to sell, and claims damages.

From the record it appears that defendant, a resident of Newark N. J., was, in the fall of 1929, the owner of the Bradley block and lot.

With the purpose of purchasing, on October 23, 1929, plaintiff wrote the following letter:

"Dear Mr. Tunison:

"Will you sell me your store property which is located on Main St. in Bucksport, Me. running from Montgomery's Drug Store on one corner to a Grocery Store on the other, for the sum of $6,000.00?"

Nothing more of this letter need be quoted.

On December 5, following, plaintiff received defendant's reply apparently written in Cannes, France, on November 12, and it reads:

"In reply to your letter of Oct. 23rd which has been forwarded to me in which you inquire about the Bradley Block, Bucksport, Me.

a. Reprinted by permission of Rudolf B. Schlesinger.

"Because of improvements which have been added and an expenditure of several thousand dollars it would not be possible for me to sell it unless I was to receive $16,000.00 cash.

"The upper floors have been converted into apartments with baths and the b'l'dg put into first class condition.

"Very truly yours,

"[Signed] R. G. Tunison."

Whereupon, and at once, plaintiff sent to defendant, and the latter received, in France, the following message:

"Accept your offer for Bradley block Bucksport Terms sixteen thousand cash send deed to Eastern Trust and Banking Co Bangor Maine Please acknowledge."

Four days later he was notified that defendant did not wish to sell the property, and on the 14th day of January following brought suit for his damages.

Granted that damages may be due a willing buyer if the owner refuses to tender a deed of real estate, after the latter has made an offer in writing to sell to the former, and such offer has been so accepted, it remains for us to point out that defendant here is not shown to have written to plaintiff an offer to sell.

There can have been no contract for the sale of the property desired, no meeting of the minds of the owner and prospective purchaser, unless there was an offer or proposal of sale. It cannot be successfully argued that defendant made any offer or proposal of sale.

In a recent case the words, "Would not consider less than half" is held "not to be taken as an outright offer to sell for one-half." Sellers v. Warren, 116 Me. 350, 102 A. 40, 41.

Where an owner of millet seed wrote, "I want $2.25 per cwt. for this seed f. o. b. Lowell," in an action for damages for alleged breach of contract to sell at the figure quoted above, the court held: "He [defendant] does not say, 'I offer to sell to you.' The language used is general, and such as may be used in an advertisement, or circular addressed generally to those engaged in the seed business, and is not an offer by which he may be bound, if accepted, by any or all of the persons addressed." Nebraska Seed Co. v. Harsh, 98 Neb. 89, 152 N. W. 310, 311, and cases cited in note L.R.A.1915F, 824.

Defendant's letter of December 5 in response to an offer of $6,000 for his property may have been written with the intent to open negotiations that might lead to a sale. It was not a proposal to sell.

Judgment for defendant.

NOTES

(1) *Analysis of Communications.* Did Tunison by his letter of November 12 indicate an intention to empower Owen "to close the contract"? Or did he indicate that he expected the offer to come from Owen? A useful technique in analyzing the language used by the parties is to redraft it twice, staying as faithful to the original as possible, so that it would clearly require a decision, first for one party, then for the other. Take, for example, the language "it would not be possible for me to sell it unless I was to receive $16,000 cash." What result if Tunison had said instead, "I will sell for $16,000"? What result if he had said, "I will not entertain an offer for less than $16,000"? Which comes closer to the meaning of the language that he used? Is the fact that there is a considerable disparity between $6,000 and $16,000 relevant? The interpretation of contract language is the subject of Chapter 7, Section 2. On how this differs from the interpretation of communications to determine whether a contract exists in the first place, see Note 2, p. 683 infra.

(2) *Problem.* In May, Joseph Oliver spoke to several neighbors about his plans to dispose of his ranch. On June 13, one of them, J. W. Southworth, asked Oliver if his plans for selling "continued to be in force," to which he responded that he expected soon to be able to put a price on the property. Southworth then said that he had the money available, that Oliver "didn't have to worry," and that "everything was ready to go." Four days later, Oliver sent a letter to four neighbors, including Southworth, enclosing "the information that I had discussed with you," as follows:

> Selling [ranch as described] at the assessed market value of . . . $324,419. Terms available—29% down—balance over 5 years at 8% interest. Negotiate sale date for December 1, 1976 or January 1, 1977 . . . .

Has Oliver made an offer to sell his ranch? See Southworth v. Oliver, 284 Or. 361, 587 P.2d 994 (1978).

HARVEY v. FACEY, [1893] A.C. 552 (P.C.) (Jamaica). [Harvey and another, solicitors in Kingston, were interested in a piece of property known as Bumper Hall Pen. Facey, the owner, had been engaged in negotiations for its sale to the town of Kingston for £900. Harvey telegraphed Facey, who was on a journey, "Will you sell us Bumper Hall Pen? Telegraph lowest cash price—answer paid." Facey replied by telegram, "Lowest price for Bumper Hall Pen £900." Harvey answered, "We agree to buy Bumper Hall Pen for the sum of nine hundred pounds asked by you." Harvey sued for specific performance of this agreement and for an injunction to restrain the town of Kingston from taking a conveyance of the property. The trial court dismissed the action on the ground that the agreement did not disclose a concluded contract; the Supreme Court of Jamaica reversed; the defendants appealed to the Judicial Committee of the Privy Council.]

LORD MORRIS. . . . [T]heir Lordships concur in the judgment of Mr. Justice Curran that there was no concluded contract between the appellants and L. M. Facey to be collected from the aforesaid telegrams. The first telegram asks two questions. The first question is as to the willingness of L. M. Facey to sell to the appellants [i. e. Harvey]; the second question asks the lowest price, and the word "telegraph" is in its collocation addressed to that second question only. L. M. Facey replied to the second question only, and gives his lowest price. The third telegram from the appellants treats the answer of L. M. Facey stating his lowest price as an unconditional offer to sell to them at the price named. Their Lordships cannot treat the telegram from L. M. Facey as binding him in any respect, except to the extent it does by its term, viz., the lowest price. Everything else is left open, and the reply telegram from the appellants cannot be treated as an acceptance of an offer to sell to them; it is an offer that required to be accepted by L. M. Facey. The contract could only be completed if L. M. Facey had accepted the appellants' last telegram. It has been contended for the appellants that L. M. Facey's telegram should be read as saying "yes" to the first question put in the appellants' telegram, but there is nothing to support that contention. L. M. Facey's telegram gives a precise answer to a precise question, viz., the price. The contract must appear by the telegrams, whereas the appellants are obliged to contend that an acceptance of the first question is to be implied. Their Lordships are of opinion that the mere statement of the lowest price at which the vendor would sell contains no implied contract to sell at that price to the persons making the inquiry. . . . [Reversed and the judgment of the trial court restored.]

NOTE

More Analysis of Communications. Redraft Facey's telegram so that it clearly would have required a decision for Harvey. Redraft it so that it clearly would have required a decision for Facey. Which seems closer to the meaning of the language that he used? Is it significant that Harvey presumably knew that he was not the only potential buyer for Bumper Hall Pen? Could Harvey's first telegram have been more skillfully drafted? What result if it had read, "What is the lowest price at which you will sell me Bumper Hall Pen?" See, in criticism of Harvey v. Facey, Russell, 1 Can.Bar Rev. 392, 398–403 (1923); in approval, MacLeod, 1 Can.Bar Rev. 694 (1923); and in rejoinder, Russell, 1 Can. Bar Rev. 713 (1923).

FAIRMOUNT GLASS WORKS v. CRUNDEN–MARTIN WOODENWARE CO.

Court of Appeals of Kentucky, 1899.
106 Ky. 659, 51 S.W. 196, 21 Ky.Law Rep. 264.

Action by the Crunden-Martin Woodenware Company against the Fairmount Glass Works to recover damages for breach of contract. Judgment for plaintiff, and defendant appeals. Affirmed.

HOBSON, J. On April 20, 1895, appellee wrote appellant the following letter:

"St. Louis, Mo., April 20, 1895. Gentlemen: Please advise us the lowest price you can make us on our order for ten car loads of Mason green jars, complete, with caps, packed one dozen in a case, either delivered here, or f. o. b. cars your place, as you prefer. State terms and cash discount. Very truly, Crunden-Martin W. W. Co."

To this letter appellant answered as follows:

"Fairmount, Ind. April 23, 1895. Crunden-Martin Wooden Ware Co., St. Louis, Mo.—Gentlemen: Replying to your favor of April 20, we quote you Mason fruit jars, complete, in one-dozen boxes, delivered in East St. Louis, Ill.: Pints, $4.50, quarts, $5.00, half gallons, $6.50 per gross, for immediate acceptance, and shipment not later than May 15, 1895; sixty days' acceptance, or 2 off, cash in ten days. Yours truly, Fairmount Glass Works.

"Please note that we make all quotations and contracts subject to the contingencies of agencies or transportation delays or accidents beyond our control."

For reply thereto, appellee sent the following telegram on April 24, 1895:

"Fairmount Glass Works, Fairmount, Ind.: Your letter twenty-third received. Enter order ten car loads as per your quotation. Specifications mailed. Crunden-Martin W. W. Co."

In response to this telegram, appellant sent the following:

"Fairmount, Ind., April 24, 1895. Crunden-Martin W. W. Co., St. Louis, Mo.: Impossible to book your order. Output all sold. See letter. Fairmount Glass Works."

Appellee insists that, by its telegram sent in answer to the letter of April 23d, the contract was closed for the purchase of 10 car loads of Mason fruit jars. Appellant insists that the contract was not closed by this telegram, and that it had the right to decline to fill the order at the time it sent its telegram of April 24. This is the chief question in the case. The court below gave judgment in favor of appellee, and appellant has appealed, earnestly insisting that the judgment is erroneous.

We are referred to a number of authorities holding that a quotation of prices is not an offer to sell, in the sense that a completed contract will arise out of the giving of an order for merchandise in accordance with the proposed terms. There are a number of cases holding that the transaction is not completed until the order so made is accepted. 7 Am. & Eng.Enc.Law (2d Ed.) p. 138; Smith v. Gowdy, 8 Allen, Mass., 566; Beaupre v. Telegraph Co., 21 Minn. 155. But each case must turn largely upon the language there used. In this case we think there was more than a quotation of prices, although appellant's letter uses the word "quote" in stating the prices given. The true meaning of the correspondence must be determined by reading it as a whole. Appellee's letter of April 20th, which began the transaction, did not ask for a quotation of prices. It reads: "Please advise us the lowest price you can make us on our order for ten carloads of Mason green jars. . . . State terms and cash discount." From this appellant could not fail to understand that appellee wanted to know at what price it would sell ten car loads of these jars; so when, in answer, it wrote: "We quote you Mason fruit jars . . . pints $4.50, quarts $5.00, half gallons $6.50, per gross, for immediate acceptance; . . . 2 off, cash in ten days,"—it must be deemed as intending to give appellee the information it asked for. We can hardly understand what is meant by the words "for immediate acceptance," unless the latter was intended as a proposition to sell at these prices if accepted immediately. In construing every contract, the aim of the court is to arrive at the intention of the parties. In none of the cases to which we have been referred on behalf of appellant was there on the face of the correspondence any such expression of intention to make an offer to sell on the terms indicated. . . . The expression in appellant's letter, "for immediate acceptance," taken in connection with appellee's letter, in effect, at what price it would sell it the goods, is, it seems to us, much stronger evidence of a present offer, which, when accepted immediately, closed the contract. Appellee's letter was plainly an inquiry for the price and terms on which appellant would sell it the goods, and appellant's answer to it was not a quotation of prices, but a definite offer to sell on the terms indicated, and could not be withdrawn after the terms had been accepted.

It will be observed that the telegram of acceptance refers to the specifications mailed. These specifications were contained in the following letter: "St. Louis, Mo., April 24, 1895. Fairmount Glass-Works Co., Fairmount, Ind.—Gentlemen: We received your letter of 23rd this morning, and telegraphed you in reply as follows: 'Your letter 23rd received. Enter order ten car loads as per your quotation. Specifications mailed,'—which we now confirm. We have accordingly entered this contract on our books for the ten cars Mason green jars, complete, with caps and rubbers, one dozen in case, delivered to us in East St. Louis at $4.50 per gross for pint, $5.00 for quart, $6.50 for one-half gallon. Terms, 60 days' acceptance, or 2 per cent. for cash in ten days, to be shipped not later than May 15, 1895. The jars and caps to be strictly first-quality goods. You may ship the first car to us here assorted: Five gross pint, fifty-five gross quart, forty gross one-half gallon. Specifications for the remaining 9 cars we will send later. Crunden-Martin W. W. Co." It is insisted for appellant that this was not an acceptance of the offer as made; that the stipulation, "The jars and caps to be strictly first-quality goods," was not in their offer; and that, it not having been accepted as made, appellant is not bound. But it will be observed that appellant declined to furnish the goods before it got this letter, and in the correspondence with appellee it nowhere complained of these words as an addition to the contract. Quite a number of other letters passed, in which the refusal to deliver the goods was placed on other grounds, none of which have been sustained by the evidence. Appellee offers proof tending to show that these words, in the trade in which parties were engaged, conveyed the same meaning as the words used in appellant's letter, and were only a different form of expressing the same idea. Appellant's conduct would seem to confirm this evidence.

Appellant also insists that the contract was indefinite, because the quantity of each size of the jars was not fixed, that ten car loads is too indefinite a specification of the quantity sold, and that appellee had no right to accept the goods to be delivered on different days. The proof shows that "ten car loads" is an expression used in the trade as equivalent to 1,000 gross, 100 gross being regarded as a car load. The offer to sell the different sizes at different prices gave the purchaser the right to name the quantity of each size, and, the offer being to ship not later than May 15th, the buyer had the right to fix the time of delivery at any time before that. . . . The petition, if defective, was cured by the judgment, which is fully sustained by the evidence.

Judgment affirmed.

NOTES

(1) *The "Battle of the Forms" (Opening Skirmish).* The pattern of communications illustrated in the Fairmount Glass Works case remains an important one, even today. Commercial contracts for the sale of goods are often the result of an exchange of several documents by the buyer and seller rather than a single document signed by both. In routine transactions most of these documents are standardized printed forms with blanks filled in to fit the particular transaction. Typically the buyer will begin by sending his "request for quotation" form, comparable to Crunden-Martin's letter of April 20. The seller will answer by sending his "quotation" form, comparable to Fairmount's letter of April 23. The buyer will reply by sending his "purchase order" form, comparable to Crunden-Martin's telegram of April 24. Finally the seller will send his "sales acknowledgement" form, and then the goods will be shipped by the seller and received by the buyer. These final steps did not, of course, take place in the Fairmount Glass Works case. This pattern of bargaining by communication on standard forms has come to be known as the "battle of the forms." Each party strives to make a contract on the terms of *his* form. Other problems that this raises will be taken up in the next chapter. See Chapter 4, Section 3, infra. For the present, the problem is the characterization of Fairmount's "quotation" of April 23.

(2) *Offer or Not?* Suppose Fairmount's letter of April 23 had not been in response to a preliminary letter from Crunden-Martin. Would the result have been the same? What significance should be attached to the use of the expression "we quote you" in Fairmount's letter of April 23? What facts make "quote" mean "offer"? Is the second paragraph of Fairmount's

letter significant in this connection? In answering these questions, consider the following case.

Kershaw wrote Moulton, "In consequence of a rupture in the salt trade we are authorized to offer Michigan fine salt in full car load lots of 80 to 95 barrels, delivered at your city at 85 cents per barrel to be shipped per C. & N. W. R. R. Co. only. At this price it is a bargain as the price in general remains unchanged. Shall be pleased to receive your order." Moulton immediately wired Kershaw, "Your letter of yesterday received and noted. You may ship me two thousand barrels Michigan fine salt as offered in your letter." Kershaw failed to ship the salt, and Moulton sued for breach of contract. The trial court overruled Kershaw's demurrer and Kershaw appealed. *Held:* Reversed. "The language is not such as a business man would use in making an offer to sell . . . a definite amount of property." Moulton v. Kershaw, 59 Wis. 316, 18 N.W. 172 (1884). Suppose Kershaw's communication to Moulton had read, "we are authorized to offer two thousand barrels Michigan fine salt," etc. Would the result have been different? What would be the objection to construing Kershaw's communication as an offer to sell any reasonable quantity of salt—say one to twenty-five car load lots—leaving it to the offeree to name the precise quantity? Has not Kershaw committed himself in advance to supply any reasonable quantity? What result if Kershaw's communication had read, "we are authorized to offer you all the Michigan fine salt you will order," etc.?

"FORMAL CONTRACT CONTEMPLATED"

Not infrequently the parties, particularly following complex negotiations, agree on what they consider the essential terms and leave details to be worked out, often by their lawyers, in connection with the preparation of a formal document which they both expect to sign. The process is more fully described in Note, p. 180 supra. (See also the discussion of "letters of intent" at p. 178 supra.) If one of the parties refuses to sign the formal document, can the other enforce the agreement? Consider the following case.

Dohrman, who was in Florida, reached an agreement, through an exchange of letters, with the Sullivans for the sale to them of Dohrman's home in Kentucky. In the course of this exchange, he had written to them: "If the answers are to our satisfaction, we will immediately forward the sales contract which we have prepared which contains the terms of the agreement. This of course would act as a confirmation of the sale. If a sale is confirmed, I shall forward the deed." A week later he wrote his real estate agent a letter enclosing three copies of a formal sales contract for the "prospective purchasers" to sign. The contract stated that he had "bargained and sold" the property to the Sullivans. The letter said that when the Sullivans had signed the acceptance on the contract, "we will sign them, retain one for ourselves and return to you a copy for them and a copy for your company's record." The Sullivans signed, but Dohrman did not. The Sullivans sued Dohrman for specific performance. A judgment for the Sullivans was affirmed. Dohrman's letter enclosing the contract was an offer which the Sullivans accepted. "Where all the substantial terms of a contract have been agreed on and there is nothing left for future settlement, the fact alone that the parties contemplated execution of a formal instrument as a convenient memorial or definitive record of the agreement does not leave the transaction incomplete and without binding force in the absence of a positive agreement that it should not be binding until so executed." Dohrman v. Sullivan, 310 Ky. 463, 220 S.W.2d 973 (1949).[a]

NOTE

A Case for Contrast. Massee, who lived in Minnesota, reached an agreement through an exchange of letters with Gibbs, who lived in Illinois, on the terms under which he would sell Gibbs a farm in Minnesota. Massee then wrote: "If you wish I can draw contract covering terms as planned and send it to you. . . . If contract and terms are agreeable you do not need to come up." Gibbs wrote back his approval, and Massee then sent an initial draft of the contract, which Gibbs returned unsigned with "the changes that seemed right to complete our deal for the land," adding, "Have another copy made, and if satisfactory to you forward the two copies with your signature. . . . I see no reason why we can't close it right up." Massee had the contract redrawn as requested, signed it in duplicate, and sent both copies to Gibbs, who refused to sign. Massee sued Gibbs for damages. *Held*: For Gibbs. "The correspondence makes it clear that all through defendant did not intend to be bound, and never expressed his assent to become bound, without the formal execution of the contract. . . . This is not a case where there has been a 'mere reference to a future contract in writing' wanted by one or more of the parties as a memorial of something already finally agreed upon, but is rather one where the 'reduction of the agreement to writing and its signature' has been made a condition precedent to its completion." Massee v. Gibbs, 169 Minn. 100, 210 N.W. 872 (1926).[b]

Can the Dohrman and Massee cases be distinguished?

CRAFT v. ELDER & JOHNSTON CO.

Court of Appeals of Ohio, Montgomery County, 1941.
38 N.E.2d 416.

[Action by Craft against Elder & Johnston Co. for alleged breach of contract. From a judgment of dismissal plaintiff appeals.]

BARNES, Judge. . . . On or about January 31, 1940, the defendant, the Elder & Johnston Company, carried an advertisement

a. For similar results on more complex facts, see Lambert Corp. v. Evans, 575 F.2d 132 (7th Cir. 1978); Field v. Golden Triangle Broadcasting, Inc., 451 Pa. 410, 305 A.2d 689 (1973), cert. denied, 414 U.S. 1158 (1974).

b. For a similar result on more complex facts, see G. H. Lindekugel & Sons, Inc. v. Brezina Constr. Co., 83 S.D. 404, 160 N.W.2d 121 (1968).

in the Dayton Shopping News, an offer for sale of a certain all electric sewing machine for the sum of $26 as a "Thursday Only Special". Plaintiff in her petition, after certain formal allegations, sets out the substance of the above advertisement carried by defendant in the Dayton Shopping News. She further alleges that the above publication is an advertising paper distributed in Montgomery County and throughout the city of Dayton; that on Thursday, February 1, 1940, she tendered to the defendant company $26 in payment for one of the machines offered in the advertisement, but that defendant refused to fulfill the offer and has continued to so refuse. The petition further alleges that the value of the machine offered was $175 and she asks damages in the sum of $149 plus interest from February 1, 1940. . . .

The trial court dismissed plaintiff's petition as evidenced by a journal entry, the pertinent portion of which reads as follows: "Upon consideration the court finds that said advertisement was not an offer which could be accepted by plaintiff to form a contract, and this case is therefore dismissed with prejudice to a new action, at costs of plaintiff."

Within statutory time plaintiff filed notice of appeal on questions of law and thus lodged the case in our court. . . .

It seems to us that this case may easily be determined on well-recognized elementary principles. The first question to be determined is the proper characterization to be given to defendant's advertisement in the Shopping News. . . .

"It is clear that in the absence of special circumstances an ordinary newspaper advertisement is not an offer, but is an offer to negotiate—an offer to receive offers—or, as it is sometimes called, an offer to chaffer." Restatement of the Law of Contracts, Par. 25, Page 31.

Under the above paragraph the following illustration is given, " 'A', a clothing merchant, advertises overcoats of a certain kind for sale at $50. This is not an offer but an invitation to the public to come and purchase."

"Thus, if goods are advertised for sale at a certain price, it is not an offer and no contract is formed by the statement of an intending purchaser that he will take a specified quantity of the goods at that price. The construction is rather favored that such an advertisement is a mere invitation to enter into a bargain rather than an offer. So a published price list is not an offer to sell the goods listed at the published price." Williston on Contracts, Revised Edition, Vol. 1, Par. 27, Page 54.

"The commonest example of offers meant to open negotiations and to call forth offers in the technical sense are advertisements, circulars and trade letters sent out by business houses. While it is possible that the offers made by such means may be in such form as to become contracts, they are often merely expressions of a willingness to negotiate." Page on the Law of Contracts, 2d Ed., Vol. 1, Page 112, Par. 84.

"Business advertisements published in newspapers and circulars sent out by mail or distributed by hand stating that the advertiser has a certain quantity or quality of goods which he wants to dispose of at certain prices, are not offers which become contracts as soon as any person to whose notice they may come signifies his acceptance by notifying the other that he will take a certain quantity of them. They are merely invitations to all persons who may read them that the advertiser is ready to receive offers for the goods at the price stated." Corpus Juris 289, Par. 97. . . .

We are constrained to the view that the trial court committed no prejudicial error in dismissing plaintiff's petition.

The judgment of the trial court will be affirmed and costs adjudged against the plaintiff-appellant.

NOTES

(1) *Advertisements as Offers.* If advertisements such as that in the Craft case were held to be offers, what would be the position of the store if the demand were to exceed its supply? Would it arise if "first come, first served" were read into every advertisement? This last approach appears to be that of French law, under which "the great majority of authorities consider such a proposal to be an offer, even if it can be accepted only by one of those to whom it is addressed. But such an offer is subject to the condition, as to each offeree, that it has not already been accepted by a quicker-acting offeree." 1 Schlesinger (ed.), Formation of Contracts: A Study of the Common Core of Legal Systems 359 (1968). Can you see any difficulties that might arise under this approach? What if the personal qualities (e. g., integrity) of the other party will play an important role under the contract?

(2) *Ohio Legislation on "Bait-and-Switch."* The term "bait-and-switch" is used to describe advertising that seeks to attract customers by advertising at a spectacularly low price a product, used as "bait," that the seller does not intend to sell, so that the seller can then try to "switch" the customer to another product on which his profit is greater. Would a rule similar to that of French law, under which advertisements were offers unless they provided otherwise, afford substantial protection to persons who are now victimized by this practice?

In 1969 Ohio adopted the Uniform Deceptive Trade Practices Act, promulgated by the National Conference of Commissioners on Uniform State Laws in 1964. Among the things that it makes a "deceptive trade practice" is the advertising of goods or services "with intent not to sell them as advertised" or "with intent not to supply reasonably expectable public demand unless the advertisement discloses a limitation of quantity." The principal remedy under the act is an injunction by any person "likely to be damaged."

Proof of "monetary damage or loss of profits" is not required.[a] Ohio Rev. Code Ann. §§ 4165.02(I)(K), 4165.03. See also Ohio Rev. Code Ann. § 119.-061, which provides for suspension of the license of one who engages in such a deceptive trade practice. For an Ohio case imposing liability at common law for fraudulently advertising an auction sale, see Schwartz v. Capital Savings & Loan Co., 56 Ohio App.2d 83, 381 N.E.2d 957 (1978).

(3) *Federal Trade Commission.* In addition to state legislation of the type described in the preceding note, Section 5 of the Federal Trade Commission Act has since 1938 declared "unfair or deceptive acts or practices in or affecting commerce" to be unlawful. The act provides for enforcement by the Federal Trade Commission, which consists of five members. If a violation of the act is found, the Commission may issue a cease-and-desist-order, which may be reviewed by a federal court of appeals. Once such an order has become final, the violator is subject to civil penalties of up to $10,000 for each violation, with each day of continuing disobedience constituting a separate offense. An order restraining a respondent from false and deceptive advertising does not, of course, provide the kind of individual relief sought by Mrs. Craft.

The Commission also publishes industry guides giving its advice on the legality of specific conduct in selected areas, renders advisory opinions in response to individual inquiries concerning the legality of a proposed course of action, promulgates rules on which it may rely in future proceedings,[b] and accepts assurances that objectionable practices will be discontinued. In recent years a growing number of state and local governments have established special agencies for consumer protection.

LEFKOWITZ v. GREAT MINNEAPOLIS SURPLUS STORE, 251 Minn. 188, 86 N.W.2d 689 (1957). [The Great Minneapolis Sur-

a. The comparable language of the uniform act, § 3(a), reads "monetary damage, loss of profits, or intent to deceive." On the uniform act and the Ohio amendments, see Dole, Merchant and Consumer Protection: The Uniform Deceptive Trade Practices Act, 76 Yale L.J. 485 (1967); Carpenter, Consumer Protection in Ohio Against False Advertising and Deceptive Practices, 32 Ohio St.L.J. 1 (1971).

b. In 1971, for example, the Commission promulgated a rule making it "an unfair or deceptive act or practice" for a retail foodstore, without appropriate disclosure, to offer "food and grocery products or other merchandise . . . at a stated price, by means of any advertisement disseminated in an area served by any of its stores which are covered by the advertisement which do not have such products in stock, and readily available to customers during the effective period of the advertisement," or to fail "to make the advertised items conspicuously and readily available for sale at or below the advertised prices." A retailer who does not have the products in stock is given a defense if he "maintains records sufficient to show that [they] were ordered in adequate time for delivery and delivered to the stores in quantities sufficient to meet reasonably anticipated demands." 16 C.F.R. § 424.-1.

plus Store published the following advertisement in a Minneapolis newspaper:

"SATURDAY 9 A. M.
2 BRAND NEW PASTEL
MINK 3-SKIN SCARFS
Selling for $89.50
Out they go
Saturday. Each $1.00
1 BLACK LAPIN STOLE
Beautiful,
worth $139.50 ....$1.00
FIRST COME
FIRST SERVED"

Lefkowitz was the first to present himself on Saturday and demanded the Lapin stole for one dollar. The store refused to sell to him because of a "house rule" that the offer was intended for women only. Lefkowitz sued the store and was awarded $138.50 as damages. The store appealed.]

MURPHY, Justice. . . . The defendant relies principally on Craft v. Elder & Johnston Co. . . . On the facts before us we are concerned with whether the advertisement constituted an offer, and, if so, whether the plaintiff's conduct constituted an acceptance. There are numerous authorities which hold that a particular advertisement in a newspaper or circular letter relating to a sale of articles may be construed by the court as constituting an offer, acceptance of which would complete a contract. . . . The test of whether a binding obligation may originate in advertisements addressed to the general public is "whether the facts show that some performance was promised in positive terms in return for something requested." 1 Williston, Contracts (rev. ed.) § 27. The authorities above cited emphasize that, where the offer is clear, definite and explicit, and leaves nothing open for negotiation, it constitutes an offer, acceptance of which will complete the contract. . . . Whether in any individual instance a newspaper advertisement is an offer rather than an invitation to make an offer depends on the legal intention of the parties and the surrounding circumstances. . . . We are of the view on the facts before us that the offer by the defendant of the sale of the Lapin fur was clear, definite, and explicit, and left nothing open for negotiation. . . . The defendant contends that the offer was modified by a "house rule" to the effect that only women were qualified to receive the bargains advertised. The advertisement contained no such restriction. This objection may be disposed of briefly by stating that, while an advertiser has the right at any time before acceptance to modify his offer, he does not have the right, after acceptance, to impose new or arbitrary conditions not contained in the published offer. . . .

Affirmed.[a]

NOTES

(1) *Rationale.* Can the Craft and Lefkowitz cases be distinguished? In what respect was the advertisement in the latter more "clear, definite and explicit" than that in the former? Were the words "First Come First Served" significant?

(2) *Competitive Bidding.* A party seeking to set a contract price may fix it himself, may leave it to private negotiation or may determine it by competitive bidding. If he determines it by competitive bidding, he may invite open bids at an auction, as is often done in the sale of goods or land, or may invite sealed bids, as is common in the letting of building contracts.

If he invites competitive bids, is this an offer to be accepted by the highest bidder when the bid is made? Or is it merely an invitation for offers by bids that can then be accepted or rejected by the one who has invited them? The law has taken the latter view, that it is the bidder who makes the offer. Can you see why?

This is the general rule stated in UCC 2–328 with respect to the sale of goods by auction. Under that section the auctioneer may, however, make an offer if he chooses to do so, and the usual way of doing this is by advertising the sale to be "without reserve." Note that if the sale is "without reserve," the auctioneer is bound not to withdraw after a bid is made, but the bidder is not similarly bound. Local statutes may also govern auction sales.

The rather elaborate provisions of UCC 2–328 are, of course, expressly applicable only to the sale of goods. UCC 2–102. Might they be extended by analogy to the sale of land? Comment 1 to UCC 1–102 recognized the possibility of reasoning from the Code by analogy: "[Courts] have recognized the policies embodied in an act as applicable in reason to subject-matter which was not expressly included in the language of the act . . . . They have done the same where reason and policy so required, even where the subject-matter had been intentionally excluded from the act in general. . . . Nothing in this Act stands in the way of the continuance of such action by the courts." See Hoffman v. Horton, 212 Va. 565, 186 S.E.2d 79 (1972), a land auction case in which the court reasoned by analogy to UCC 2–328.

(3) *Auctions and the Statute of Frauds.* What is to prevent the bidder at an auction from backing out after the hammer has fallen and setting up the statute of frauds? Some states have statutes that give the auctioneer the power to bind the bidder by making a memorandum of the sale. See, e. g., Cal.Civ.Code § 2363; N.Y.Gen.Obl.L. § 5–701(6).

a. In an omitted part of the opinion, the court discusses the fact that Lefkowitz had answered a similar advertisement of Great Minneapolis Surplus Store only a week before the publication of the advertisement in question. At that time the store had also refused to sell to him, explaining that by a "house rule" the offer was intended for women only and sales would not be made to men. Considering this additional fact, do you agree with the court's decision that he could recover under the later advertisement See Note 3, p. —— supra.

(4) *Problem.* Chicago Medical School distributed a bulletin for prospective students that stated that it selected its students "on the basis of scholarship, character, and motivation" after evaluation "on the basis of academic achievement, Medical College Admission Test results, personal appraisals by a pre-professional advisory committee or individual instructors, and the personal interview, if requested." Robert Steinberg received such a bulletin, applied for admission and paid a $15 fee, which the school accepted. He has been rejected and wants to sue the school on the ground that in breach of a contract with him it failed to evaluate his application according to the stated criteria and relied instead on the ability of the applicant or his family to pledge or pay large sums of money to the school. Can you state a theory under which the school had a contract with Steinberg? Who made the offer? Steinberg v. Chicago Medical School, 69 Ill.2d 320, 13 Ill.Dec. 699, 371 N.E.2d 634 (1977).

SECTION 3. THE ACCEPTANCE

What is an acceptance? Corbin gives this answer: "An acceptance is a voluntary act of the offeree whereby he exercises the power conferred upon him by the offer, and thereby creates the set of legal relations called a contract. What acts are sufficient to serve this purpose? We must look first to the terms in which the offer was expressed, either by words or by other conduct. . . . The offeror has, in the beginning, full power to determine the acts that are to constitute acceptance. After he has once created the power, he may lose his control over it, and may become disabled to change or to revoke it; but the fact that, in the beginning, the offeror has full control of the immediately succeeding relation called a power, is the characteristic that distinguishes contractual relations from non-contractual ones. After the offeror has created the power, the legal consequences thereof are out of his hands, and he may be brought into numerous consequential relations of which he did not dream, and to which he might not have consented. These later relations are nevertheless called contractual." Corbin, Offer and Acceptance, and Some of the Resulting Legal Relations, 26 Yale L.J. 169, 199 (1917).

Assuming that there has been an offer, the offeree by exercising his power of acceptance "thereby creates," as Corbin puts it, "the set of legal relations called a contract." One of the most important consequences of this "set of legal relations" is that the offeror is no longer free to change his mind and withdraw from the relationship without incurring liability. By what means, then, may the offeree exercise this power of acceptance? If, as Corbin says, the offeror has "full power to determine the acts that are to constitute acceptance," the first step in answering this question is to look at the offer to see what sort of acceptance it invited.

We already know from Chapter 1 that the offeror may either have been bargaining for a performance or for a promise. As will be seen more clearly from the cases that make up the bulk of this book, the economically significant transactions in our society usually involve the latter sort of bargain, in which the offeror seeks the assurance of another promise in return for his own. (Why should this be so? If bargaining for performance was good enough for William E. Storey in Hamer v. Sidway, p. 44 supra, and for A. L. Ledbetter in Broadnax v. Ledbetter, p. 65 supra, why should it not be good enough for any offeror?) In these economically significant transactions, in which the offeror invites a promise as acceptance, what will suffice as a promise? Are words essential? Or may a promise be inferred from other conduct? And, if so, what conduct? Preparation for performance? Beginning performance? Other acts? Mere silence? This section considers these and related questions. The problems that arise when the offer seeks performance as acceptance are postponed until Chapter 4, Section 4 infra.

INTERNATIONAL FILTER CO. v. CONROE GIN, ICE & LIGHT CO.

Commission of Appeals of Texas, 1925.
277 S.W. 631.

Action by the International Filter Company against the Conroe Gin, Ice & Light Company. Judgment for defendant was affirmed in 269 S.W. 210, and plaintiff brings error. Reversed and remanded.

NICKELS, J. Plaintiff in error, an Illinois corporation, is a manufacturer of machinery, apparatus, etc., for the purification of water in connection with the manufacture of ice, etc., having its principal office in the city of Chicago. Defendant in error is a Texas corporation engaged in the manufacture of ice, etc., having its plant, office, etc., at Conroe, Montgomery county, Tex.

On February 10, 1920, through its traveling solicitor, Waterman, plaintiff in error at Conroe, submitted to defendant in error, acting through Henry Thompson, its manager, a written instrument, addressed to defendant in error, which (with immaterial portions omitted) reads as follows:

"Gentlemen: We propose to furnish, f. o. b. Chicago, one No. two Junior (steel tank) International water softener and filter to purify water of the character shown by sample to be submitted. . . . Price: Twelve hundred thirty ($1,230.00) dollars. . . . This proposal is made in duplicate and becomes a contract when accepted by the purchaser and approved by an executive officer of the International Filter Company, at its office in Chicago. Any modification can only be made by duly approved supplementary agreement signed by both parties.

"This proposal is submitted for prompt acceptance, and unless so accepted is subject to change without notice.

"Respectfully submitted,

"International Filter Co.
"W. W. Waterman."

On the same day the "proposal" was accepted by defendant in error through notation made on the paper by Thompson reading as follows:

"Accepted Feb. 10, 1920.

"Conroe Gin, Ice & Light Co.,
"By Henry Thompson, Mgr."

The paper as thus submitted and "accepted" contained the notation, "Make shipment by Mar. 10." The paper, in that form, reached the Chicago office of plaintiff in error, and on February 13, 1920, P. N. Engel, its president and vice president, indorsed thereon: "O. K. Feb. 13, 1920, P. N. Engel." February 14, 1920, plaintiff in error wrote and mailed, and in due course defendant in error received, the following letter:

"Feb. 14, 1920.

"Attention of Mr. Henry Thompson, Manager.

"Conroe Gin, Ice & Light Co., Conroe, Texas—Gentlemen: This will acknowledge and thank you for your order given Mr. Waterman for a No. 2 Jr. steel tank International softener and filter, for 110 volt, 60 cycle, single phase current—for shipment March 10th.

"Please make shipment of the sample of water promptly so that we may make the analysis and know the character of the water before shipment of the apparatus. Shipping tag is inclosed, and please note, the instructions to pack to guard against freezing.

"Yours very truly,

"International Filter Co.
"M. B. Johnson."

By letter of February 28, 1920, defendant in error undertook to countermand the "order," which countermand was repeated and emphasized by letter of March 4, 1920. By letter of March 2, 1920 (replying to the letter of February 28th), plaintiff in error denied the right of countermand, etc., and insisted upon performance of the "contract." The parties adhered to the respective positions thus indicated, and this suit resulted.

Plaintiff in error sued for breach of the contract alleged to have been made in the manner stated above. The defense is that no contract was made because: (1) Neither Engel's indorsement of "O. K.," nor the letter of February 14, 1920, amounted to approval "by an executive officer of the International Filter Company, at its office in Chicago." (2) Notification of such approval, or acceptance, by plaintiff in error was required to be communicated to defendant in error;

it being insisted that this requirement inhered in the terms of the proposal and in the nature of the transaction and, also, that Thompson, when he indorsed "acceptance" on the paper stated to Waterman, as agent of plaintiff in error, that such notification must be promptly given; it being insisted further that the letter of February 14, 1920, did not constitute such acceptance or notification of approval, and therefore defendant in error, on February 28, 1920, etc., had the right to withdraw or countermand, the unaccepted offer. Thompson testified in a manner to support the allegation of his statement to Waterman. There are other matters involved in the suit which must be ultimately determined, but the foregoing presents the issues now here for consideration.

The case was tried without a jury, and the judge found the facts in favor of defendant in error on all the issues indicated above, and upon other material issues. The judgment was affirmed by the Court of Civil Appeals, 269 S.W. 210.

We agree with the honorable Court of Civil Appeals upon the proposition that Mr. Engel's indorsement of "O. K." amounted to an approval "by an executive officer of the International Filter Company, at its office in Chicago," within the meaning of the so-called "proposal" of February 10th. The paper then became a "contract," according to its definitely expressed terms, and it became then, and thereafter it remained, an enforceable contract, in legal contemplation, unless the fact of approval by the filter company was required to be communicated to the other party and unless, in that event, the communication was not made.

We are not prepared to assent to the ruling that such communication was essential. There is no disposition to question the justice of the general rules stated in support of that holding, yet the existence of contractual capacity imports the right of the offerer to dispense with notification; and he does dispense with it "if the form of the offer," etc., "shows that this was not to be required." 9 Cyc. 270, 271; Carlill v. Carbolic Smoke Ball Co., 1 Q.B. 256 (and other references in note 6, 9 Cyc. 271). . . .

The Conroe Gin, Ice & Light Company executed the paper for the purpose of having it transmitted, as its offer, to the filter company at Chicago. It was so transmitted and acted upon. Its terms embrace the offer, and nothing else, and by its terms the question of notification must be judged, since those terms are not ambiguous.

The paper contains two provisions which relate to acceptance by the filter company. One is the declaration that the offer shall "become a contract . . . when approved by an executive officer of the International Filter Company, at its Chicago office." The other is thus stated: "This proposal is submitted for prompt acceptance, and unless so accepted is subject to change without notice." The first provision states "a particular mode of acceptance as sufficient to make the bargain binding," and the filter company (as stated above) followed "the indicated method of acceptance." When this was done, so the paper declares, the proposal "became a contract." The other provision does not in any way relate to a different method of acceptance by the filter company. Its sole reference is to the time within which the act of approval must be done; that is to say, there was to be a "prompt acceptance," else the offer might be changed "without notice." The second declaration merely required the approval thereinbefore stipulated for to be done promptly; if the act was so done, there is nothing in the second provision to militate against, or to conflict with, the prior declaration that, thereupon, the paper should become "a contract."

A holding that notification of that approval is to be deduced from the terms of the last-quoted clause is not essential in order to give it meaning or to dissolve ambiguity. On the contrary, such a construction of the two provisions would introduce a conflict, or ambiguity, where none exists in the language itself, and defeat the plainly expressed term wherein it is said that the proposal "becomes a contract . . . when approved by an executive officer." There is not anything in the language used to justify a ruling that this declaration must be wrenched from its obvious meaning and given one which would change both the locus and time prescribed for the meeting of the minds. The offerer said that the contract should be complete if approval be promptly given by the executive officer at Chicago; the court cannot properly restate the offer so as to make the offerer declare that a contract shall be made only when the approval shall have been promptly given at Chicago and that fact shall have been communicated to the offerer at Conroe. In our opinion, therefore, notice of the approval was not required.

The letter of February 14th, however, sufficiently communicated notice, if it was required. . . . Here the fact of acceptance in the particular method prescribed by the offerer is established aliunde the letter—Engel's "O. K." indorsed on the paper at Chicago did that. The form of notice, where notice is required, may be quite a different thing from the acceptance itself; the latter constitutes the meeting of the minds, the former merely relates to that pre-existent fact. The rules requiring such notice, it will be marked, do not make necessary any particular form or manner, unless the parties themselves have so prescribed. Whatever would convey by word or fair implication, notice of the fact would be sufficient. And this letter, we think, would clearly indicate to a reasonably prudent person, situated as was the defendant in error, the fact of previous approval by the filter company. If the Gin, Ice & Light Company had acted to change its position upon it as a notification of that fact, it must be plain that the filter company would have been estopped to deny its sufficiency. . . .

We recommend that the judgment of the Court of Civil Appeals be reversed, and that the cause be remanded to that court for its disposition of all questions not passed upon it by it heretofore and properly before it for determination.

CURETON, C. J.[a] Judgment of the Court of Civil Appeals reversed, and cause remanded to the Court of Civil Appeals for further consideration by that court, as recommended by the Commission of Appeals.

NOTES

(1) *Control of Representatives.* Where a seller is a large organization with salespersons who are expected to use a carefully prepared standard form for all contracts, there is a risk that the salespersons will make written changes on the form itself during their negotiations with customers. Does a home-office-approval clause protect against that risk?[b] Does the clause expose the seller to any other risk? A home-office-approval clause is also useful if the buyer's credit must be checked.

(2) *Notice.* Can you distinguish the position of International Filter from that of the offeree who merely says "I accept" to himself? See Restatement Second, §§ 54, 56. For a case holding that the mere signing of the contract by the offeree was not acceptance even though the contract said that it would be binding "when . . . signed by both parties," see Kendel v. Pontious, 261 So.2d 167 (Fla.1972).

In the opinion below, the Court of Civil Appeals reasoned that International Filter's letter of February 14 "did not constitute an acceptance of appellee's proposal, nor a notification of the acceptance made by Mr. Engel in Chicago." International Filter Co. v. Conroe Gin, Ice & Light Co., 269 S.W. 210, 215 (Tex.Civ.App.1925). It relied on Courtney Shoe Co. v. E. W. Curd & Son, 142 Ky. 219, 134 S.W. 146 (1911). In that case a manufacturer wrote, "Your order . . . is at hand and will receive our prompt and careful attention," but sent a second letter eight days later rejecting the order on the ground that the salesman had made the sale without authority. It was held that this was not an acceptance.[c] Do you agree with the Court of Civil Appeals?

(3) *Problem.* Rio Grande Pickle Co. employed George Fujimoto as supervisor of planting and growing operations and Jose Bravo as labor recruiter. When both men threatened to quit unless their remuneration was sub-

a. Chief Justice of the Supreme Court of Texas.

b. See Restatement Second of Agency § 167 as to the effect of such language as: "No agent of seller has authority to change the terms hereof."

c. For a different result, see Hill's Inc. v. William B. Kessler Inc., 41 Wash. 2d 42, 246 P.2d 1099 (1952). On May 16 a Seattle retailer ordered men's fall suits through the manufacturer's salesman on a printed form, supplied by the salesman, providing that the manufacturer was not bound until acceptance by one of its officers in New Jersey. On May 23 the manufacturer, by form letter advised the retailer that, "You may be assured of our very best attention to this order."

On July 18, however, after the time for placing orders for fall suits had passed, and at the instigation of one of the retailer's large competitors in Seattle, the manufacturer wrote to "cancel" the order. The retailer sued the manufacturer and had judgment in the trial court, which found that the manufacturer's form letter had been an acceptance. The Supreme Court of Washington affirmed. Are the cases distinguishable?

stantially increased, the president of Rio Grande orally offered a salary plus a bonus of ten percent of the company's annual profits. Bravo insisted on an agreement in writing, and, in October of 1965, Rio Grande sent each man a written offer that did not specify how it was to be accepted. Both men signed but neither returned the writing to the company. They continued to work for Rio Grande with no further discussion of salary until November of 1966. Is Rio Grande bound by the writings? See Fujimoto v. Rio Grande Pickle Co., 414 F.2d 648 (5th Cir. 1969).

(4) *Problem.* J. I. Case Credit Corporation owned a repossessed tractor located in some woods. In a telephone conversation in the middle of February, Case offered to sell the tractor to Thompson for $1,000 "as is, where is." If Thompson decided to buy the tractor, he was to pick it up in the woods and pay the price in cash. Thompson picked up the tractor on March 1 but did not tell Case this for several weeks. In the meantime, on March 12, Case sold the tractor to another buyer. Is Case bound by a contract with Thompson? See UCC 2–206(2), 2–204(2); Petersen v. Thompson, 264 Or. 516, 506 P.2d 697 (1973).

WHITE v. CORLIES AND TIFT

Court of Appeals of New York, 1871.
46 N.Y. 467.

Appeal from judgment of the General Term of the first judicial district, affirming a judgment entered upon a verdict for plaintiff.

The action was for an alleged breach of contract.

The plaintiff was a builder, with his place of business in Fortieth Street, New York City.

The defendants were merchants at 32 Dey Street.

In September, 1865, the defendants furnished the plaintiff with specifications for fitting up a suite of offices at 57 Broadway, and requested him to make an estimate of the cost of doing the work.

On September 28th, the plaintiff left his estimate with the defendants, and they were to consider upon it, and inform the plaintiff of their conclusions.

On the same day the defendants made a change in their specifications, and sent a copy of the same, so changed, to the plaintiff for his assent under his estimate, which he assented to by signing the same and returning it to the defendants.

On the day following the defendants' bookkeeper wrote the plaintiff the following note:

"New York, September 29.

"Upon an agreement to finish the fitting up of offices 57 Broadway in two weeks from date, you can begin at once.

"The writer will call again, probably between 5 and 6 this p. m.

"W. H. R.
For J. W. Corlies & Co.,
32 Dey St."

No reply to this note was ever made by the plaintiff; and on the next day the same was countermanded by a second note from the defendants.

Immediately on receipt of the note of September 29th, and before the countermand was forwarded, the plaintiff commenced a performance by the purchase of lumber and beginning work thereon.

And after receiving the countermand, the plaintiff brought this action for damages for a breach of contract.[a]

The court charged the jury as follows: "From the contents of this note which the plaintiff received, was it his duty to go down to Dey Street (meaning to give notice of assent), before commencing the work?

In my opinion it was not. He had a right to act upon this note and commence the job, and that was a binding contract between the parties."

To this defendants excepted. . . .

FOLGER, J. We do not think that the jury found, or that the testimony shows, that there was any agreement between the parties, before the written communication of the defendants of September 30th was received by the plaintiff. This note did not make an agreement. It was a proposition, and must have been accepted by the plaintiff before either party was bound, in contract, to the other. The only overt action which is claimed by the plaintiff as indicating on his part an acceptance of the offer, was the purchase of the stuff necessary for the work, and commencing work, as we understand the testimony, upon that stuff.

We understand the rule to be, that where an offer is made by one party to another when they are not together, the acceptance of it by that other must be manifested by some appropriate act. It does not need that the acceptance shall come to the knowledge of the one making the offer before he shall be bound. But though the manifestation need not be brought to his knowledge before he becomes bound,

a. Some additional facts, taken from the record on appeal of White's testimony may be helpful. Corlies' initial request was to have the office done in black walnut, a hard wood, within 21 days. White replied that he could not do the job in a hard wood in that time. Corlies then requested an estimate for white pine, a soft wood. White left the estimate on September 28, but did not indicate the time within which he would finish. Corlies made a change in the specifications to which White assented. There followed the letter of September 29 from Corlies. The countermand from Corlies said that it had decided to do the office in black walnut and requested an estimate for that in place of pine. Record, pp. 7–12.

he is not bound, if that manifestation is not put in a proper way to be in the usual course of events, in some reasonable time communicated to him. Thus a letter received by mail containing a proposal may be answered by letter by mail, containing the acceptance. And in general, as soon as the answering letter is mailed, the contract is concluded. Though one party does not know of the acceptance, the manifestation thereof is put in the proper way of reaching him.

In the case in hand, the plaintiff determined to accept. But a mental determination not indicated by speech, or put in course of indication by act to the other party, is not an acceptance which will bind the other. Nor does an act, which in itself, is no indication of an acceptance, become such, because accompanied by an unevinced mental determination. Where the act uninterpreted by concurrent evidence of the mental purpose accompanying it, is as well referable to one state of facts as another, it is no indication to the other party of an acceptance, and does not operate to hold him to his offer.

Conceding that the testimony shows that the plaintiff did resolve to accept this offer, he did no act which indicated an acceptance of it to the defendants. He, a carpenter and builder, purchased stuff for the work. But it was stuff as fit for any other like work. He began work upon the stuff, but as he would have done for any other like work. There was nothing in his thought, formed but not uttered, or in his acts that indicated or set in motion an indication to the defendants of his acceptance of their offer, or which could necessarily result therein.

But the charge of the learned judge was fairly to be understood by the jury as laying down the rule to them, that the plaintiff need not indicate to the defendants his acceptance of their offer; and that the purchase of stuff and working on it after receiving the note, made a binding contract between the parties. In this we think the learned judge fell into error.

Judgment reversed, and new trial ordered.

NOTES

(1) *Means of Acceptance.* One who wants a contractor to do work ordinarily seeks a promise from the contractor. Can you see why? Assuming that Corlies' offer sought a promise, what means of acceptance by promise did it invite? What does the language of the offer and the nature of the transaction suggest? What answer if Corlies had written, "If you want to do the work, let me know by return mail and you can begin work at once"? See Restatement Second, §§ 30, 50, 60, 62.

In argument on appeal, counsel for Corlies argued that "the defendants did not instruct the plaintiff to go to work *upon the receipt of the note;* but to go to work upon *an agreement to finish* the work in two weeks from date. . . . The question of time had not been agreed upon. . . . [T]he defendants had a right to put the question of assent at rest by demanding an agreement . . . and thus avoid the doubts and difficulties of spelling out an assent from the acts of the plaintiff. . . ." They also argued that "in case the plaintiff had broken off the performance after purchasing lumber, the defendants could have no redress . . . , as Mr. White could show that the purchase of lumber by him was a daily occurrence." (Appellant's Brief, pp. 3–4.) How much of this argument was accepted by the court?

(2) *Problem.* As a shopper in a supermarket was lifting a soft drink bottle from the shelf to place it in a shopping cart, the bottle exploded, seriously injuring the shopper. Was there a "contract for . . . sale" giving rise to an implied warranty of merchantability under UCC 2–314? See Barker v. Allied Supermarket, 596 P.2d 870 (Okla.1979).

EVER–TITE ROOFING CORPORATION v. GREEN, 83 So.2d 449 (La.App.1955). [The Greens wished to have Ever-Tite Roofing re-roof their residence, and signed a document that set out the work in detail and the price in monthly installments. This document was also signed by Ever-Tite's sales representative who, however, had no authority to bind Ever-Tite. The document contained a provision that, "This agreement shall become binding only upon written acceptance hereof, by the principal or authorized officer of the Contractor, or upon commencing performance of the work." As the Greens knew, since the work was to be done entirely on credit, it was necessary for Ever-Tite to get credit reports and obtain the approval of the lending institution that was to finance the contract. When this was accomplished, about nine days after execution of the agreement, Ever-Tite loaded two trucks and sent them with its workmen some distance to the Green's residence. Upon their arrival they found that others had been engaged two days before, and they were not permitted to work. Ever-Tite sued the Greens for breach of contract. From a judgment for defendant, plaintiff appealed.]

AYRES, Judge. . . . The basis of the judgment appealed was that defendants had timely notified plaintiff before "commencing performance of work". The trial court held that notice to plaintiff's workmen upon their arrival with the materials that defendants did not desire them to commence the actual work was sufficient and timely to signify their intention to withdraw from the contract. With this conclusion we find ourselves unable to agree. . . . Defendants evidently knew this work was to be processed through plaintiff's Shreveport office. The record discloses no unreasonable delay on plaintiff's part in receiving, processing or accepting the contract or in commencing the work contracted to be done. No time limit was specified in the contract within which it was to be accepted or within which the work was to be begun. It was nevertheless understood between the parties that some delay would ensue before the acceptance of the contract and the commencement of the work, due to the necessity of compliance with the requirements relative to financing the job through a lending agency. The evidence as referred to hereinabove shows that plaintiff proceeded with due diligence.[a] . . . . [S]ince the contract did not specify the time within which it was to be accepted or within which the work was to have been commenced, a reasonable time must be allowed therefor in accordance with the facts and circumstances and the evident intention of the parties. A reasonable time is contemplated where no time is expressed. What is a reasonable time depends more or less upon the circumstances surrounding each particular case. The delays to process defendants' application were not unusual. The contract was accepted by plaintiff by the commencement of the performance of the work contracted to be done. This commencement began with the loading of the trucks with the necessary materials in Shreveport and transporting such materials and the workmen to defendants' residence. Actual commencement or performance of the work therefore began before any notice of dissent by defendants was given plaintiff. The proposition and its acceptance thus became a completed contract.

[Reversed.]

NOTE

Questions. Why did Ever-Tite use a home-office-approval clause? What was the purpose of the words "or upon commencing performance of the work"? Could the court have read this language more favorably to the Greens?

ALLIED STEEL AND CONVEYORS, INC. v. FORD MOTOR CO.

United States Court of Appeals, Sixth Circuit, 1960.
277 F.2d 907.

[On August 19, 1955, Ford ordered machinery from Allied on Ford's printed form, Purchase Order No. 15145, which provided that if Allied was required to perform work of installation on Ford's premises, Allied would be responsible for all damages caused by the negligence of its own employees. Attached to and made a part of the Purchase Order was another printed form, Form 3618, which included a much broader indemnity provision requiring Allied to assume full responsibility not only for the negligence of its own employees, but also for the negligence of Ford's employees in connection with Allied's work, but this provision was marked "VOID." The Purchase Order was accepted by Allied and the contract performed.

a. In an omitted part of the opinion the court set out several articles of the Louisiana Civil Code. Under article 1809, the most relevant here, the offeror "may therefore revoke his offer or proposition before such acceptance, but not without allowing such reasonable time as from the terms of the offer he has given, or from the circumstances of the case he may be supposed to have intended to give to the party to communicate his determination."

Subsequently, on July 26, 1956, Ford submitted to Allied Amendment No. 2 to Purchase Order 15145, by which Ford proposed to purchase additional machinery. The Amendment provided:

> This purchase order agreement is not binding until accepted. Acceptance should be executed on acknowledgment copy which should be returned to buyer.

The copy of Ford's Form 3618 attached to the Amendment was identical to that attached to Purchase Order No. 15145, but the broad indemnity provision of Form 3618 was not marked "VOID." The acknowledgment copy of the Amendment was executed by Allied on November 10 and reached Ford on November 12, 1956. At that time Allied had already begun installation and on September 5, 1956, Hankins, an employee of Allied, had sustained personal injuries as a result of the negligence of Ford's employees in connection with Allied's work. Hankins later brought suit against Ford and Ford in turn impleaded Allied, relying on the indemnity provision of Form 3618. The trial resulted in a verdict for Hankins against Ford and for Ford against Allied. Allied's motion for judgment notwithstanding the verdict was denied and judgment was entered against it. Allied appealed.]

MILLER, District Judge. . . . Allied first says that the contractual provisions evidenced by Amendment No. 2 were not in effect at the time of the Hankins injury because it had not been accepted at that time by Allied in the formal manner expressly required by the amendment itself. It argues that a binding acceptance of the amendment could be effected only by Allied's execution of the acknowledgment copy of the amendment and its return to Ford.

With this argument we cannot agree. It is true that an offeror may prescribe the manner in which acceptance of his offer shall be indicated by the offeree, and an acceptance of the offer in the manner prescribed will bind the offeror. And it has been held that if the offeror prescribes an exclusive manner of acceptance, an attempt on the part of the offeree to accept the offer in a different manner does not bind the offeror *in the absence of a meeting of the minds on the altered type of acceptance.* Venters v. Stewart, Ky.App., 261 S.W.2d 444, 446; Shortridge v. Ghio, Mo.App., 253 S.W.2d 838, 845. On the other hand, if an offeror merely suggests a permitted method of acceptance, other methods of acceptance are not precluded. Restatement, Contracts, Sec. 61; Williston on Contracts, Third Ed. Secs. 70, 76. Moreover, it is equally well settled that if the offer requests a return promise and the offeree without making the promise actually does or tenders what he was requested to promise to do, there is a contract if such performance is completed or tendered within the time allowable for accepting by making a promise. In such a case a tender operates as a promise to render complete performance. Restatement, Contracts, Sec. 63; Williston on Contracts, Third Ed. Sec. 75.[a]

Applying these principles to the case at bar, we reach the conclusion, first, that execution and return of the acknowledgment copy of Amendment No. 2 was merely a suggested method of acceptance and did not preclude acceptance by some other method; and, second, that the offer was accepted and a binding contract effected when Allied, with Ford's knowledge, consent and acquiescence, undertook performance of the work called for by the amendment. The only significant provision, as we view the amendment, was that it would not be binding until it was accepted by Allied. This provision was obviously for the protection of Ford, Albright v. Stegeman Motorcar Co., 168 Wis. 557, 170 N.W. 951, 952, 19 A.L.R. 463, and its import was that Ford would not be bound by the amendment unless Allied agreed to all of the conditions specified therein. The provision for execution and return of the acknowledgment copy, as we construe the language used, was not to set forth an exclusive method of acceptance but was merely to provide a simple and convenient method by which the assent of Allied to the contractual provisions of the amendment could be indicated. The primary object of Ford was to have the work performed by Allied upon the terms prescribed in the amendment, and the mere signing and return of an acknowledgment copy of the amendment before actually undertaking the work itself cannot be regarded as an essential condition to completion of a binding contract.

It is well settled that acceptance of an offer by part performance in accordance with the terms of the offer is sufficient to complete the contract. . . .

Other authorities are to the effect that the acceptance of a contract may be implied from acts of the parties. Malooly v. York Heating & Vent. Corp., 270 Mich. 240, 253, 258 N.W. 622; and may be shown by proving acts done on the faith of the order, including shipment of the goods ordered, Petroleum Products Distributing Co. v. Alton Tank Line, 165 Iowa 398, 403, 146 N.W. 52. Cf. Texas Co. v. Hudson, 155 La. 966, 971, 99 So. 714, 716. It would seem necessarily to follow that an offeree who has unjustifiably led the offeror to believe that he had acquired a contractual right, should not be allowed to assert an actual intent at variance with the meaning of his acts.

a. It is curious that the court relies, even as an alternative ground, on the rule that full performance or a tender of full performance may operate as an acceptance of an offer that invites acceptance by a promise only. Allied had not fully performed and could not, since its performance was to extend over a substantial period of time, have tendered full performance. This rule is, perhaps fortunately, of limited practical importance and is not carried forward by the Restatement Second (see §§ 53(1), 62). See Note, 52 So.Cal.L.Rev. 1917 (1979). Of course the offer may give the offeree a choice between acceptance by promise and acceptance by performance, but that is not what the court suggests here.

It has been argued on behalf of Allied, by way of analogy, that Ford could have revoked the order when Allied began installing the machinery without first having executed its written acceptance. If this point should be conceded, cf. Venters v. Stewart, supra, it would avail Allied nothing. For, after Allied began performance by installing the machinery called for, and Ford acquiesced in the acts of Allied and accepted the benefits of the performance, Ford was estopped to object and could not thereafter be heard to complain that there was no contract. Sparks v. Mauk, 170 Cal. 122, 148 P. 926. . . .

Affirmed.

NOTES

(1) *Case Comparison.* Can the Ever-Tite and Allied Steel cases be distinguished from White v. Corlies and Tift? What is the critical language of the offer in each case? What reason did Ford have for putting the clause on its form? See Note 1, p. 187 supra. Consider, in this connection, the 1970 revision of Ford's purchase order, which reads:

> ACCEPTANCE—Unless otherwise provided herein, it is understood and agreed that the written acceptance by Seller of this purchase order or the commencement of any work or the performance of any services hereunder by Seller (including the commencement of any work or the performance of any services with respect to samples) shall constitute acceptance by Seller of this purchase order and of all of its terms and conditions, and that such acceptance is expressly limited to such terms and conditions.

(2) *The "Moment of Its Making."* According to UCC 2–204(2), "An agreement sufficient to constitute a contract for sale may be found even though the moment of its making is undetermined." Does this mean that a contract may be found even though there is no such thing as a "moment of its making" at all? Or merely that a contract may be found even though it is impossible to determine the "moment of its making"? Or merely that a contract may be found even though the "moment of its making" has not in fact been determined?

The Comment to the section explains that it is "directed primarily to the situation where the interchanged correspondence does not disclose the exact point at which the deal was closed, but the actions of the parties indicate that a binding obligation has been undertaken." Is it relevant that in the 1952 Official Edition of the Code, UCC 2–204(2) read: "Conduct by both parties which recognizes the existence of a contract is sufficient to establish a contract of sale even though the moment of its making cannot be determined"? Could the moment be determined in the Ever-Tite case? In the Allied Steel case? If so, when was it?

(3) *Statute of Frauds (Review).* Was the contract in the Allied Steel case within the statute of frauds? Was the statute satisfied? (Did Allied's execution of the acknowledgement copy on November 10 satisfy the statute as to it? Did *Ford's* receipt and acceptance of the goods satisfy the statute as to *Allied*? Did Allied's *delivery* of the goods?

(4) *Problem.* Owner invited Builder to submit alternative bids for a construction job, one at a fixed price and the other at cost plus a percentage

of cost. Builder did so. Owner did not indicate acceptance of either bid, but Builder did the work with Owner's acquiescence. What are builder's rights against Owner? See Peter Lind & Co. v. Mersey Docks and Harbour Board, [1972] 2 Lloyd's List L.R. 234.

SHIPMENT OF GOODS AS ACCEPTANCE

A recurring question of considerable practical importance is whether the seller's shipment of goods, in response to a buyer's order, is acceptance. The question usually arises when the buyer attempts to revoke his order after the seller has placed the goods on board a carrier in response to the order. UCC 2–206(1)(b) provides that such an order "for prompt or current shipment shall be construed as inviting acceptance either by a prompt promise to ship or by the prompt or current shipment of conforming or non-conforming goods." Under the Code the buyer's revocation comes too late if the seller has promptly shipped.

But the question can arise in another way. Suppose that the seller ships non-conforming goods. Has he bound himself to deliver goods that conform to the buyer's order? The answer under the Code must be that he has. This is clear from the provision that the seller can avoid this result if he "seasonably notifies the buyer that the shipment is offered only as an accommodation to the buyer." If the seller follows this course, his shipment is not an acceptance of the buyer's offer, but is a counter-offer to the buyer. What means of acceptance does that counter-offer invite? See the following case. See generally Restatement Second, §§ 32, 62, which are not limited to contracts for the sale of goods.

NOTE

(1) *Preparation for Shipment of Goods as Acceptance.* What if the buyer attempts to revoke his order when the seller has incurred expense in preparing to ship the goods but has not actually shipped them? In Doll & Smith v. A & S Sanitary Dairy Co., 202 Iowa 786, 211 N.W. 230 (1926), the buyer, through the seller's agent, ordered advertising material from the seller. After the seller had paid its agent his commission and had incurred some expense, the buyer sent the seller a cancellation of the order. The court held that since the seller had not sent the buyer an acceptance of the order, the revocation was effective. Can this decision be reconciled with the Ever-Tite case, supra?

(2) *Notice as a Condition.* Even where the offeree's performance, in whole or in part, amounts in itself to acceptance, he may be expected to notify the offeror that he has accepted. UCC 2–206(2) imposes such a requirement, stating that the consequence of the requirement is that the "offeror who is not notified of acceptance within a reasonable time may treat the offer as having lapsed before acceptance." A more conventional formulation of the consequence is that notice within a reasonable time is an implied condition of the offeror's duty to perform under the contract that is

formed by the acceptance. If the offeree does not give notice within a reasonable time, the offeror's performance under the contract does not become due and his duty is discharged. Note that notice is not part of the acceptance under either formulation, so that the offeror is bound even before notice is given, as long as it is subsequently given within a reasonable time. For more on notice of acceptance, where acceptance is by performance see p. 303 infra.

INDIANA MFG. CO. v. HAYES

Supreme Court of Pennsylvania, 1893.
155 Pa. 160, 26 A. 6.

Assumpsit for goods sold and delivered.

Plaintiff's claim on the trial, before Hemphill, J., was for the price of sixty-four refrigerators. Defendant claimed that he had never given the order for the refrigerators, and that it had been wrongfully sent in his name by a salesman of plaintiff.

Plaintiff introduced evidence tending to show that the refrigerators were accepted by defendant in the manner stated in the opinion of the Supreme Court. . . .

[The court instructed] "We say to you, gentlemen of the jury, there is no question of intention involved here to be submitted to you. There is no disputed question of fact. The goods were shipped to Mr. Hayes in his name, and when he took control of them by ordering the railroad company to turn them over to his agent, Mr. Cooper, the carter, the law implied an intention on his part to accept, and so far as the plaintiffs here are concerned he became the owner, and we instruct you to that effect, and must so qualify their points. . . .

"If the defendant gave no order to the plaintiffs for the goods sued for, and made no contract with them for furnishing him with refrigerators, it was his duty, when the said goods came to him, to decline to receive them from the railroad company. . . .

"If the sixty-four refrigerators were shipped to Robert L. Hayes by the plaintiffs, relying upon his order, and he received the same from the railroad company at West Chester, thereby discharging the said railroad company from liability to the shippers, the plaintiffs, the defendant, Robert L. Hayes, is bound to pay for the same, whether he authorized the sending of the order or not. . . ." [Verdict for the plaintiff.]

PER CURIAM, . . . Conceding that the defendant did not order the goods in question, yet when they arrived, and he was notified that they were upon the car, it was his duty to notify the plaintiffs of the alleged mistake. Instead of doing so he took the property out of the possession of the railroad company and had it hauled to his own place of business, and after having been fully informed of the shipment and consignment to him he sent a check to the plaintiff company for other merchandise purchased of it, without any reference to the goods in controversy. The case was submitted to the jury under proper instructions.

Judgment affirmed.[a]

NOTES

(1) *Questions.* What result if Hayes had told the railroad company, when he ordered the delivery of the refrigerators to Cooper, that he did not intend to pay for them?[b] See Restatement Second, § 69. What result if he had taken thirty-two of the refrigerators and left the other thirty-two with the railroad company? Are UCC 2–305(4), 2–601, 2–607(1) helpful? What result if the refrigerators had been delivered to Hayes' place of business and left there while he was away?

(2) *Exercise of Dominion over Check.* If a check accompanies an offer, one who exercises dominion over the check by cashing it or depositing it in a bank is generally held, on principles analogous to those applied in Indiana Mfg. Co. v. Hayes, to have accepted the offer. For a case in which this rule was applied although the check was deposited by mistake, see Hotz v. Equitable Life Assur. Soc., 224 Iowa 552, 276 N.W. 413 (1937). Football fans will also want to consult Los Angeles Rams Football Club v. Cannon, 185 F.Supp. 717 (S.D.Cal.1960) (Cannon's retention of checks from Rams was not acceptance of Rams' offer where acceptance would have made him ineligible for Sugar Bowl). But cf. Hoffman v. Ralston Purina Co., 86 Wis.2d 445, 273 N.W.2d 214 (1979) (retention of check for seven months was acceptance).

SILENCE NOT ORDINARILY ACCEPTANCE

The general rule is that silence alone is not acceptance. See Restatement Second, § 69. The offeror who appends to his offer, "Unless I hear from you within 48 hours, you will be deemed to have accepted my offer," cannot hold the offeree if he fails to reject.

In Hobbs v. Massasoit Whip Co., 158 Mass. 194, 33 N.E. 495 (1893), however, the court concluded that a silent retention amounted to an acceptance. A seller sued for $108.50, the price of 2,350 eelskins that he had sent to the buyer, a manufacturer of whips. Holmes wrote: "The plaintiff was not a stranger to the defendant, even if there was no contract between them. He had sent eelskins in the same way four or five times before, and they had been accepted and

a. If the defendant took possession of refrigerators he had not ordered, is he not liable in tort for conversion? Ordinarily the offeree cannot avoid liability in contract on this ground, and under the "waiver of tort" doctrine the offeror may have his choice of suing in tort or in contract. See Restatement Second, § 69, Comment e.

b. Cf. Russell v. Texas Co., 238 F.2d 636 (9th Cir. 1956) ("To put the problem in homely terms, may an offeree accept all of the benefits of a contract and then declare that he cannot be held liable for the burdens because he secretly had said 'King's Ex'? We think not.")

paid for. . . . [S]ending them [imposed] on the defendant a duty to act about them; and silence on its part, coupled with a retention of the skins for an unreasonable time, might be found by the jury to warrant the plaintiff in assuming that they were accepted, and thus to amount to an acceptance." What, beyond mere silence, was there in this case?

But what if the parties are reversed and it is the *buyer* who asserts that the seller has accepted by silent retention of his *order?* Ammons v. Wilson & Co., 176 Miss. 645, 170 So. 227 (1936), is such a case. On August 23, Wilson's travelling salesman, Tweedy, took an order from Ammons for 43,916 pounds of shortening at 7½ cents a pound, for prompt shipment. Wilson's form made it clear that Tweedy had no authority to make contracts and that the order was "taken subject to acceptance by seller's authorized agent at point of shipment." Wilson waited until September 4 before refusing to ship. By that time the price of shortening had risen to 9 cents a pound. The court reversed a judgment for Wilson entered on a directed verdict, and held that whether the delay of twelve days, "in view of the past history of such transactions between the parties, including the booking, constituted an implied acceptance," was a jury question. Tweedy had represented Wilson in the territory for six or eight months and during that time he had taken several orders from Ammons, "which orders in every case had been accepted and shipped not later than one week from the time they were given." What, beyond mere silence, was there in this case?

NOTES

(1) *Acceptance by Insurer's Silence.* Similar problems arise in connection with solicitation by insurance agents. In American Life Insurance Co. v. Hutcheson, 109 F.2d 424 (6th Cir. 1940), Hutcheson, who had a life insurance policy with Lincoln National Life, was solicited by an agent of American Life, to purchase insurance with that company instead. Hutcheson applied to American and paid his first premium on October 10. On the same day his policy with Lincoln lapsed. On the following day he had a medical examination and because his blood pressure was too high he was asked to take a second examination on October 14. The results reached American on October 21 and showed that his blood pressure was still too high. No notice was sent of this fact and Hutcheson was killed by accident on October 26. American Life tendered back the first premium and refused to pay under the policy. Hutcheson's wife, as beneficiary, sued American. From an adverse judgment based on a jury verdict the defendant appealed. *Held:* Affirmed. "It is the general rule that mere delay in passing upon an application for insurance is not sufficient in and of itself to amount to acceptance even though the premium is retained. . . . But an acceptance may be implied from retention of the premium and failure to reject within a reasonable time. . . . Having accepted and retained the premium paid upon an application solicited by its agent, the company was bound to act with reasonable promptitude." The jury could find that it did not and that therefore there was a contract. On the alternative of liability in tort for

unreasonable delay in acting on an application, see p. 346 infra. Cf. Freimuth v. Glens Falls Ins. Co., 50 Wash.2d 621, 314 P.2d 468 (1957).

(2) *Unsolicited Merchandise.* A persistent consumer complaint concerns the practice of sending unsolicited merchandise, often coupled with the suggestion that the recipient will be liable for the price if it is not returned. As you might suppose, this suggestion is not the law. Although the recipient who lays the merchandise on a shelf and does not use it incurs no liability, the practice is at best irritating and at worst deceptive, and a number of states have enacted statutes dealing with it. For example, a New York statute provides that no one shall "offer for sale goods . . . where the offer includes the voluntary and unsolicited sending of goods . . . not actually ordered or requested by the recipient, either orally or in writing. The receipt of any such unsolicited goods . . . shall for all purposes be deemed an unconditional gift to the recipient who may use or dispose of the same in any manner he sees fit without any obligation on his part to the sender." A sender who continues to request payment may be enjoined from doing so. (N.Y.Gen.Bus.Law § 396(2)(a).)

The practice of sending unsolicited merchandise has also been the target of regulation on the federal level. The Postal Reorganization Act of 1970 makes the mailing of "unordered merchandise" and "dunning communications" for such merchandise "an unfair method of competition and an unfair trade practice" in violation of Section 5 of the Federal Trade Commission Act. See Note 3, p. 192 supra. Free samples "clearly and conspicuously marked as such" and "merchandise mailed by a charitable organization soliciting contributions" are excepted. The act provides that merchandise mailed in violation of it "may be treated as a gift by the recipient," and requires, somewhat curiously, that it have attached to it "a clear and conspicuous statement" to this effect. 39 U.S.C.A. § 3009. For a discussion of these and other measures to deal with the problem, see Note, 1970 Duke L. J. 991.

(3) *Unsolicited Credit Cards.* A successful bank credit card system requires both a large number of cardholders and a large number of merchants who honor their cards. In order to launch the BankAmerica (now Visa) and Interbank systems, over 100 million unsolicited BankAmericards and Master Charge cards were mailed in the years from 1967 through 1970. The result was some 10 million active cardholders for each system. In 1970, Congress amended the Truth in Lending Act to add a new section 132:

> No credit card shall be issued except in response to a request or application therefor. This prohibition does not apply to the issuance of a credit card in renewal of, or in substitution for, an accepted credit card.

What was the reason behind the amendment? How could a recipient of an unsolicited credit card have incurred any liability if he neither used nor signed the card? Can you think of any disadvantages that might result from the amendment? (Senator William Proxmire of Wisconsin pointed out that . . . "two bank credit card systems . . . now account for 95 percent of the bank credit card market. A prohibition of unsolicited cards would make it difficult for new systems to compete against these two giants." Hearings on S. 721 before Subcommittee on Financial Institutions of the Senate Committee on Banking and Currency, 91st Cong., 1st Sess. 2 (1969).) See Weistart, Consumer Protection in The Credit Card Industry: Federal Legislative Controls, 70 Mich.L.Rev. 1476 (1972).

SECTION 4. TERMINATION OF THE POWER OF ACCEPTANCE

After one party has made an offer, conferring on the other party a power of acceptance, that power can be terminated in several ways: (1) revocation; (2) death or incapacity; (3) lapse; and (4) rejection. They will be considered in that order.[a]

REVOCATION OF AN OFFER

It is taken as a commonplace in common law countries that the offeror is free to revoke his offer at any time before the offeree has accepted it. Grotius, the great seventeenth-century Dutch jurist, favored the same rule. But this freedom to revoke is not inevitable, as is shown by the law of Germany and some other civil law countries where an offer is irrevocable for a reasonable time unless the offeror expresses a different intention. See 1 Schlesinger (ed.), Formation of Contracts: A Study of the Common Core of Legal Systems 780–83 (1968). Which rule seems preferable? One disadvantage of the German rule is that during the period of irrevocability, the offeree can take advantage of changing economic conditions to speculate at the expense of the offeror. Although Germany and the other countries that have this rule have experienced much greater economic upheavals than has the United States, they have been able to live with the rule, at least in part, because it can easily be avoided by expressly reserving the power to revoke or providing that the communication is not an offer at all. The extent to which the offeror in the United States can avoid the common law rule by expressly relinquishing the power to revoke is discussed at p. 223 infra.

HOOVER MOTOR EXPRESS CO. v. CLEMENTS PAPER CO.

Supreme Court of Tennessee, 1951.
193 Tenn. 6, 241 S.W.2d 851.

TOMLINSON, Justice. On November 19, 1949 Hoover Motor Express Company, Inc. made and delivered to Clements Paper Company a written offer with reference to the purchase of certain real estate. There was no consideration paid for the offer. On January

a. The problems raised by revocation and rejection in connection with contracts by correspondence, however, are not dealt with until Chapter 4, Section 2.

20, 1950 Clements Paper Company made a written acceptance of that offer. Hoover refused to go forward with the transaction and Clements Paper Company brought suit for specific performance or, in the alternative, for damages. Hoover defended on the ground that it had withdrawn the offer before its acceptance. The Chancellor and the Court of Appeals concurred in sustaining the bill of Clements Paper Company and ordered a reference to the master for ascertainment of damages. The controversy was then presented to this Court by Hoover's petition for certiorari. . . .

All are agreed that in order to convert into a contract an offer for which no consideration was paid there must be an acceptance of that offer before it is withdrawn. . . . [W]e must look to the evidence most favorable to Clements and determine from it whether there is therein any material evidence in support of this concurrent finding or any testimony that reasonably supports an inference or conclusion that the offer had not been withdrawn before its acceptance on January 20.

Clements was represented in this transaction by its Vice-President, Mr. Williams. He wrote the letter of January 20, 1950 accepting the offer. It is not contended in behalf of Clements that there was any acceptance prior to that date. Williams closes that letter with this statement: "We are ready to comply with our part of this agreement and are calling on you to do the same." The statement just quoted suggests the thought that its author, Mr. Williams, realized at the time he wrote the letter that something previously had occurred which caused him to anticipate that Hoover might not "comply" by going forward with its prior offer, Mr. Williams' letter of acceptance notwithstanding. This is important in that it throws light upon the construction placed by Williams upon a phone conversation had on January 13, 1950 by him with Hoover.

Williams had been authorized by Clements Paper Company some time in December to accept the written offer made by Hoover on November 19. It would, therefore, have been a simple matter for him then to have written the letter of acceptance which he finally wrote on January 20. The record leaves no doubt of the fact that Williams intended to accept the offer provided he could not get from Hoover a substantially better trade that he, Williams, had in mind. He, therefore, withheld acceptance and undertook on several occasions to get in touch with Hoover for the purpose of procuring, if he could, that better trade. Fortunately for Williams, in so far as the keeping alive of the offer is concerned, he never got around to conveying to Hoover the changes or additions he had in mind. But he did take a step to that end on January 13, 1950 by phoning Hoover with the idea of promoting his proposition. It is upon the legal effect that must be given that phone conversation, *as testified to by Williams,* that the outcome of this case must depend. If it can be given a construction which reasonably supports the concurrent finding mentioned that construction must be given.

Mr. Williams testified that he got Mr. Hoover on the phone on January 13 and "told him that we were ready to go through with it and I would like to discuss it with him". The matter which he testifies that he wanted to discuss with Mr. Hoover was whether Hoover would permit Clements to retain an easement for certain purposes through the property which Hoover had offered to buy.

Williams testifies that in reply to Williams' statement that he, Williams, wanted to discuss the offer with Hoover that Hoover replied "Well, I don't know if we are ready. We have not decided, we might not want to go through with it".

Williams made several other statements in his testimony as to what Hoover said in this phone conversation. The following are quotations from Williams' testimony: "He said he thought they might not go through with it."

"Q. After you had talked to him on January 13, on the telephone, that is Mr. Eph Hoover, Jr., he indicated to you that he had made other plans or in some way 'indicated' to you that the company had made other plans? A. Yes."

. . .

"Q. You had been told that they had made other plans? A. No, I had not been told. He said that he didn't think they were going through with the proposal and that he would call me on January 17."

(Hoover did not call Williams after the January 13 phone conversation.)

. . .

"A. That they had other plans in mind and he would let me know. He was not sure if he was going through with the original proposition.

"Q. Did he definitely refuse to positively commit himself on January 13 that he would go through with it? A. That is right."

. . .

"It was a very short discussion. Frankly, I was very much shocked when I heard from him that they didn't plan to go through with it. I had made my plans and had gone to the extent of having this elevation made."

The interpretation which Mr. Williams placed upon what Hoover said to him in the phone conversation of January 13 is stated in Clements' bill of complaint as follows: "This was the first information, suggestion or intimation that complainant had received that the defendant would not or might not carry out its agreement or offer."

Our problem is reduced to answering the question as to whether there can reasonably be placed upon the above quoted testimony of

Williams a construction that prevents the statement of Hoover, as testified to by Williams, from amounting to a withdrawal on January 13 of the offer before it was attempted on January 20 to accept it. This is true because "the continued existence of the offer until acceptance is, however, necessary to make possible the formation of the contract." 12 American Jurisprudence, page 531.

Although there is no Tennessee case deciding the point, in so far as we can find, the general rule is that express notice, in so many words, of withdrawal before acceptance of an offer of the character we have here is not required. In 55 American Jurisprudence, page 488, under a discussion of "Termination of Offer", there appears in the text, supported by reference to decisions, this statement: "It is sufficient to constitute a withdrawal that knowledge of acts by the offerer inconsistent with the continuance of the offer is brought home to the offeree."

The same principle is declared to be the law in the text of 17 Corpus Juris Secundum, Contracts, § 50, page 398 in this language: "it being sufficient that the person making the offer does some act inconsistent with it, as, for example, selling the property, and that the person to whom the offer was made has knowledge of such act."

Re-statement of the Law of Contracts, Section 41, page 49, has this to say: "Revocation of an offer may be made by a communication from the offeror received by the offeree, which states or implies that the offeror no longer intends to enter into the proposed contract, if the communication is received by the offeree before he has exercised his power of creating a contract by acceptance of the offer."

Re-statement of the Law of Agency, Section 88 expresses it thus: "Conduct manifesting to the agent or the principal that the third person no longer consents to the transaction constitutes a withdrawal."

. . .

Applying to the undisputed testimony as furnished by Williams the rule clearly stated in all the authorities from which we have above quoted—and we find none to the contrary—we think it must be concluded that Hoover's written offer of November 19 was withdrawn on January 13 thereafter prior to its attempted acceptance on January 20, and that the concurrent finding of the Chancellor and the Court of Appeals to the contrary is not supported by any material evidence. There can be no doubt as to it being a fact that on January 13 knowledge was brought home to Williams that Hoover no longer consented to the transaction. There was, therefore, no offer continuing up to the time of the attempted acceptance on January 20. . . .

The decree of the Court of Appeals and of the Chancellor will be reversed and the cause remanded for entry of a decree in keeping with this opinion. All costs in all Courts will be adjudged against Clements Paper Company.

NOTE

Language of Revocation. Compare the court's treatment of the claimed revocation in the Hoover case with the court's treatment of the claimed offers in Owen v. Tunison, p. 181 supra, and in Harvey v. Facey, p. 183 supra. Are they consistent?

DICKINSON v. DODDS

In the Court of Appeal, Chancery Division, 1876.
2 Ch.Div. 463.

On Wednesday, the 10th of June, 1874, the defendant John Dodds signed and delivered to the plaintiff, George Dickinson, a memorandum, of which the material part was as follows:

"I hereby agree to sell to Mr. George Dickinson the whole of the dwelling-houses, garden ground, stabling, and outbuildings thereto belonging, situate at Croft, belonging to me, for the sum of £800. As witness my hand this tenth day of June, 1874.

£800. [Signed] John Dodds."

"P. S.—This offer to be left over until Friday, 9 o'clock a. m. J.D. (the twelfth), 12th June, 1874. [Signed] J. Dodds."

The bill alleged that Dodds understood and intended that the plaintiff should have until Friday, 9 a. m., within which to determine whether he would or would not purchase, and that he should absolutely have until that time the refusal of the property at the price of £800, and that the plaintiff in fact determined to accept the offer on the morning of Thursday, the 11th of June, but did not at once signify his acceptance to Dodds, believing that he had the power to accept it until 9 a. m. on the Friday.

In the afternoon of the Thursday the plaintiff was informed by a Mr. Berry that Dodds had been offering or agreeing to sell the property to Thomas Allan, the other defendant. Thereupon the plaintiff, at about half past seven in the evening, went to the house of Mrs. Burgess, the mother-in-law of Dodds, where he was then staying, and left with her a formal acceptance in writing of the offer to sell the property. According to the evidence of Mrs. Burgess this document never in fact reached Dodds, she having forgotten to give it to him.

On the following (Friday) morning, at about seven o'clock, Berry, who was acting as agent for Dickinson, found Dodds at the Darlington Railway station, and handed to him a duplicate of the acceptance by Dickinson, and explained to Dodds its purport. He replied that it was too late, as he had sold the property. A few minutes later Dickinson himself found Dodds entering a railway carriage, and handed him another duplicate of the notice of acceptance, but Dodds declined to receive it, saying: "You are too late. I have sold the property."

It appeared that on the day before, Thursday, the 11th of June, Dodds had signed a formal contract for the sale of the property to the defendant Allan for £800, and had received from him a deposit of £40.

The bill in this suit prayed that the defendant Dodds might be decreed specifically to perform the contract of the 10th of June, 1874; that he might be restrained from conveying the property to Allan; that Allan might be restrained from taking any such conveyance; that, if any such conveyance had been or should be made, Allan might be declared a trustee of the property for, and might be directed to convey the property to, the plaintiff; and for damages.

The cause came on for hearing before Vice Chancellor Bacon on the 25th of January, 1876 [who decreed specific performance for the plaintiff. From this decision the defendants appeal].

JAMES, L. J., after referring to the document of the 10th of June, 1874, continued:

The document, though beginning "I hereby agree to sell," was nothing but an offer, and was only intended to be an offer, for the plaintiff himself tells us that he required time to consider whether he would enter into an agreement or not. Unless both parties had then agreed, there was no concluded agreement then made; it was in effect and substance only an offer to sell. The plaintiff, being minded not to complete the bargain at that time, added this memorandum: "This offer to be left over until Friday, 9 o'clock a. m. 12th June, 1874." That shows it was only an offer. There was no consideration given for the undertaking or promise, to whatever extent it may be considered binding, to keep the property unsold until 9 o'clock on Friday morning; but apparently Dickinson was of opinion, and probably Dodds was of the same opinion, that he (Dodds) was bound by that promise, and could not in any way withdraw from it, or retract it, until 9 o'clock on Friday morning, and this probably explains a good deal of what afterwards took place. But it is clear settled law, on one of the clearest principles of law, that this promise, being a mere nudum pactum, was not binding, and that at any moment before a complete acceptance by Dickinson of the offer, Dodds was as free as Dickinson himself. Well, that being the state of things, it is said that the only mode in which Dodds could assert that freedom was by actually and distinctly saying to Dickinson, "Now I withdraw my offer." It appears to me that there is neither principle nor authority for the proposition that there must be an express and actual withdrawal of the offer, or what is called a retraction. It must, to constitute a contract, appear that the two minds were as one, at the same moment of time, that is, that there was an offer continuing up to the time of the acceptance. If there was not such a continuing offer, then the acceptance comes to nothing. Of course it may well be that the one man is bound in some way or other to let the other man know that his mind with regard to the offer has been changed; but in this case, beyond all question, the plaintiff knew that Dodds was no longer minded to sell the property to him as plainly and clearly as if Dodds had told him in so many words, "I withdraw the offer." This is evident from the plaintiff's own statements in the bill.

The plaintiff says in effect that, having heard and knowing that Dodds was no longer minded to sell to him, and that he was selling or had sold to some one else, thinking that he could not in point of law withdraw his offer, meaning to fix him to it, and endeavoring to bind him: "I went to the house where he was lodging, and saw his mother-in-law, and left with her an acceptance of the offer, knowing all the while that he had entirely changed his mind. I got an agent to watch for him at 7 o'clock the next morning, and I went to the train just before 9 o'clock, in order that I might catch him and give him my notice of acceptance just before 9 o'clock, and when that occurred he told my agent, and he told me, 'You are too late,' and he then threw back the paper." It is to my mind quite clear that before there was any attempt at acceptance by the plaintiff, he was perfectly well aware that Dodds had changed his mind, and that he had in fact agreed to sell the property to Allan. It is impossible, therefore to say there was ever that existence of the same mind between the two parties which is essential in point of law to the making of an agreement. I am of opinion, therefore, that the plaintiff has failed to prove that there was any binding contract between Dodds and himself.

MELLISH, L. J. I am of the same opinion. . . . . Well, then, this being only an offer, and the law says—and it is a perfectly clear rule of law—that, although it is said that the offer is to be left open until Friday morning at 9 o'clock, that did not bind Dodds. He was not in point of law bound to hold the offer over until 9 o'clock on Friday morning. He was not so bound either in law or in equity. Well, that being so, when on the next day he made an agreement with Allan to sell the property to him, I am not aware of any ground on which it can be said that that contract with Allan was not as good and binding a contract as ever was made. Assuming Allan to have known (there is some dispute about it, and Allan does not admit that he knew of it, but I will assume that he did) that Dodds had made the offer to Dickinson, and had given him till Friday morning at 9 o'clock to accept it, still in point of law that could not prevent Allan from making a more favorable offer than Dickinson, and entering at once into a binding agreement with Dodds.

Then Dickinson is informed by Berry that the property has been sold by Dodds to Allan. Berry does not tell us from whom he heard it, but he says that he did hear it, that he knew it, and that he informed Dickinson of it. Now, stopping there, the question which arises is this: If an offer has been made for the sale of property, and before that offer is accepted the person who has made the offer enters into a binding agreement to sell the property to somebody else, and the person to whom the offer was first made receives notice in some way that the property has been sold to another person, can he after that make a binding contract by the acceptance of the offer? I am of opinion that he cannot. The law may be right or wrong in saying that a person who has given to another a certain time within which to accept an offer is not bound by his promise to give that time; but, if he is not bound by that promise, and may still sell the property to some one else, and if it be the law that, in order to make a contract, the two minds must be in agreement at some one time, that is, at the time of the acceptance, how is it possible that when the person to whom the offer has been made knows that the person who has made the offer has sold the property to someone else, and that, in fact, he has not remained in the same mind to sell it to him, he can be at liberty to accept the offer and thereby make a binding contract? It seems to me that would be simply absurd. If a man makes an offer to sell a particular horse in his stable, and says, "I will give you until the day after to-morrow to accept the offer," and the next day goes and sells the horse to somebody else, and receives the purchase money from him, can the person to whom the offer was originally made then come and say, "I accept," so as to make a binding contract, and so as to be entitled to recover damages for the non-delivery of the horse? If the rule of law is that a mere offer to sell property, which can be withdrawn at any time, and which is made dependent on the acceptance of the person to whom it is made, is a mere nudum pactum, how is it possible that the person to whom the offer has been made can by acceptance make a binding contract after he knows that the person who has made the offer has sold the property to some one else? It is admitted law that, if a man who makes an offer dies, the offer cannot be accepted after he is dead; and parting with the property has very much the same effect as the death of the owner, for it makes the performance of the offer impossible. I am clearly of opinion that, just as when a man who has made an offer dies before it is accepted it is impossible that it can then be accepted, so when once the person to whom the offer was made knows that the property has been sold to someone else, it is too late for him to accept the offer, and on that ground I am clearly of opinion that there was no binding contract for the sale of this property by Dodds to Dickinson; and, even if there had been, it seems to me that the sale of the property to Allan was first in point of time. However, it is not necessary to consider, if there had been two binding contracts, which of them would be entitled to priority in equity, because there is no binding contract between Dodds and Dickinson.

BAGGALLAY, J. A. I entirely concur in the judgments which have been pronounced.

JAMES, L. J. The bill will be dismissed, with costs.

NOTES

(1) *Indirect Communication of Revocation.* Few courts have had occasion to pass on "the rule of Dickinson v. Dodds." For a rare example, see Watters v. Lincoln, 29 S.D. 98, 135 N.W. 712 (1912), which also involved an offer to sell land. How would you state the rule? What did Berry tell Dickinson? That Dodds had made an *offer* to sell the property or that he had made a *contract* to sell the property?

In view of the paucity of cases, the Restatement formulation of the rule takes on a special significance. Does the following formulation of the first Restatement in § 42 strike you as a broad or narrow one?

> Where an offer is for the sale of an interest in land or in other things, if the offeror, after making the offer, sells or contracts to sell the interest to another person, and the offeree acquires reliable information of that fact, before he has exercised his power of creating a contract by acceptance of the offer, the offer is revoked.

Compare this with its successor, Restatement Second, § 43. Are there significant changes?

(2) *Capriciousness of the Law of Offer and Acceptance.* Suppose that Dodd's offer had not been revoked on Thursday. A contract would then have resulted when Berry handed Dodds the acceptance at the railway station on Friday. But if Dodds had seen Berry approaching and, guessing his purpose, had first called out "that it was too late, as he had sold the property," no contract would have resulted. Is it possible to defend a system of contract law in which the existence of a contract might depend on whether Berry handed the acceptance to Dodds an instant before or an instant after Dodds spoke? See Farnsworth, Mutuality of Obligation in Contract Law, 3 Dayton L.Rev. 271 (1978).

(3) *Revocation of General Offers.* In the case of a general offer, such as one addressed to the general public by an advertisement, it will ordinarily be impossible for the offeror actually to communicate a revocation to all of the persons who are aware of the offer. Illustrative are the offers in the Broadnax case, p. 65 supra, and the Lefkowitz case, p. 192 supra. The offeror can, of course, be required to give his notice of revocation publicity equal (and usually similar) to that given the offer. But having done this, is he nevertheless bound by the acceptance of an offeree who was aware of the offer but missed the notice of revocation? The answer is that he is not bound, in spite of the general requirement that a revocation be actually communicated to the offeree. See Restatement Second, § 46; Corbin, § 41; Williston, §§ 59, 59A. How would you revoke an offer of a reward posted on a bulletin board? Would taking it down be sufficient? When would the revocation take effect? See Carr v. Mahaska County Bankers Ass'n, 222 Iowa 411, 269 N.W. 494 (1936). For an entertaining example of revocation by publication, involving a reward issued by Secretary of War Stanton for Suratt, one of Booth's accomplices in the assassination of President Lincoln, see Shuey v. United States, 92 U.S. 73 (1875).

(4) *Problem.* A offered in writing to sell B Blackacre for $1,000, offer to remain open five days. On the fourth day B received information from the county recorder of deeds that he had received for recording a deed of Blackacre from A to C. This information being reliable, B believed it,

but thinking there might be some chance for error, notified A of his acceptance on the fifth day. The information given by the recorder proved to be erroneous, but A refused to perform. Contract?

OPTION CONTRACTS

Not only did the common law give the offeror the power to revoke his offer subject only to the offeree's exercise of his power of acceptance, but, as Dickinson v. Dodds indicates, a promise not to revoke, "being a mere nudum pactum, was not binding." Some means then had to be found to make that promise enforceable if the offeror's power to revoke were to be limited. A promise that effectively limits the offeror's power to revoke is called an "option contract" in the Restatement Second, in preference to the more traditional term "option." Restatement Second, § 25. In the early common law, of course, an option contract could be made by making the promise under seal. With the abolition of the seal, the doctrine of consideration became the exclusive means to this end. What would have been the result if Dickinson had paid Dodds £1 and the postscript had been changed to read, "In consideration of £1 paid, this offer is left over until Friday, 9 o'clock a. m."? [a] This technique may be adequate for offers for the sale of land, where the parties might be expected to foresee the possibility of revocation and deal with it in this rather elaborate way. It is less satisfactory for more informal transactions such as those for the sale of goods, where the offeror is less likely to clothe his promise in the trappings of consideration.

The Uniform Commercial Code therefore contains an important provision on "firm offers," which enables an offeror to make an irrevocable offer "to buy or sell goods" by means of a signed writing. UCC 2–205. In addition, New York has the following comprehensive statute, first enacted in 1941 (along with the statute on "moral obligation" in Note 4, p. 121 supra), and later amended to take account of the Code:

> Except as otherwise provided in section 2–205 of the uniform commercial code with respect to an offer by a merchant to buy or sell goods, when an offer to enter into a contract is made in a writing signed by the offeror, or by his agent, which states that the offer is irrevocable during a period set forth or until a time fixed, the offer shall not be re-

a. It can be argued that Dickinson's remedy against Dodds on such a "collateral" promise would be only for breach of that promise and not for breach of the promise to sell the land, so that he could not have specific performance. But both Corbin and Williston reject this view. See Corbin, § 44; Williston, § 61C. The point would not arise if the letter read: "In consideration of £1 paid, I hereby agree to sell to Mr. George Dickinson the whole of the dwelling-houses . . . situate at Croft, belonging to me, for the sum of £800, on condition that he notify me of his acceptance and tender the £800 by Friday, 9 o'clock a. m."

vocable during such period or until such time because of the absence of consideration for the assurance of irrevocability. When such a writing states that the offer is irrevocable but does not state any period or time of irrevocability, it shall be construed to state that the offer is irrevocable for a reasonable time. (New York General Obligations Law, § 5–1109.)

How could the form that Ever-Tite gave the Greens to sign, in the case at p. 204 supra, have been redrafted to take advantage of this provision if Ever-Tite were doing business in New York? Is the New York consumer under a contract for re-roofing, which is not governed by the Code, in any different position than the consumer under a contract for the sale of goods, which is? Which statute is preferable in this respect?

NOTES

(1) *Recitals.* If a sum of money is paid as consideration for an option, this fact is usually recited. What is the effect of such a recital if no payment is made? Some courts have held it to be of no effect. See Bard v. Kent, 19 Cal.2d 449, 122 P.2d 8 (1942) (no consideration in spite of a false recital that $10 had been paid). Others have held that it makes the offer irrevocable, either as a binding acknowledgement of payment or as a promise to pay. See Real Estate Co. of Pittsburgh v. Rudolph, 301 Pa. 502, 153 A. 438 (1930) (false recital that $1 had been paid "can only mean that [the offeror] acknowledges the receipt of that sum"); Smith v. Wheeler, 233 Ga. 166, 210 S.E.2d 702 (1974) (although the dollar had not been paid as recited, the recital created an obligation to pay that sum that amounted to consideration). Restatement Second, § 87 favors the former view, with the qualification that the proposed exchange be fair. Comment *b* to that section explains, "The signed writing has vital significance as a formality, while the ceremonial manual delivery of a dollar or a peppercorn is an inconsequential formality."

(2) *Consideration Other Than Money.* A promise not to revoke an offer may be supported by consideration other than money. An option may, for example, be part of a larger transaction, as where an option to renew a lease or to purchase the premises is given the lessee as part of the lease. Even where the option is not part of a larger transaction, something other than the payment of money, such as some action by the offeree in preparation for consummating the transaction may be consideration. But the difficulty of convincing the court that action of this kind was bargained for by the offeror counsels resort to the conventional device of payment of money. See Bard v. Kent, 19 Cal.2d 449, 122 P.2d 8 (1942) (lessee's checking figures and having an architect do sketches was not consideration for option to extend a lease); Friedman v. Tappan Development Corp., 22 N.J. 523, 126 A.2d 646 (1956) (neither buyer's prepayment of $400, refundable if sale was not consummated, nor his expenditure of $505 for title search was consideration for seller's promise not to revoke).

(3) *English Proposal.* In England, The Law Commission has suggested that it would be desirable to reform the law so that: "An offeror who has promised that he will not revoke his offer for a definite time should be

bound by the terms of that promise for a period not exceeding six years, *provided that* the promise has been made 'in the course of a business' . . . ." The promise would not have to be in writing. The Law Commission, Working Paper No. 60, Law of Contract, Firm Offers (1975). Would you favor such legislation in your state?

DEATH OF AN OFFEROR

Restatement Second, § 48 sets out the generally accepted rule in this country that an offeree's power of acceptance is terminated by the offeror's death or supervening incapacity. Professor Corbin said of this rule that there is not "any compelling necessity for its existence. It may be said that you cannot contract with a dead man; but neither can you force a dead man to pay his debts contracted before his death. Yet the law has no difficulty, in the latter case, in creating legal relations with the dead man's personal representative, and there would be no greater difficulty in declaring the power of acceptance to survive as against the offeror's representative or in favor of the offeree's representative." Corbin, Offer and Acceptance, and Some of the Resulting Legal Relations, 26 Yale L.J. 169, 198 (1917).

Jordan v. Dobbins, 122 Mass. 168 (1877), illustrates the rule. In February Jordan, Marsh & Co. had Dobbins guarantee the prompt payment of all sums owed by Moore to Jordan, Marsh as a result of sales of merchandise that Jordan, Marsh might make to Moore. In August Dobbins died. From the following January through May Jordan, Marsh sold Moore merchandise in ignorance of Dobbins' death. When Moore did not pay, Jordan, Marsh sued Dobbins' estate. The Supreme Judicial Court of Massachusetts denied recovery. "The agreement which the guarantor makes with the person receiving the guaranty is not that I now become liable to you for anything, but that if you sell goods to a third person, I will then become liable to pay for them if such third person does not. . . . Such being the nature of a guaranty, we are of opinion that the death of the guarantor operates as a revocation of it, and that the person holding it cannot recover against his executor or administrator for goods sold after the death. . . . It is no hardship to require traders, whose business it is to deal in goods, to exercise diligence so far as to ascertain whether a person upon whose credit they are selling is living."

Under the original draft of the first Restatement, as written by Professor Williston and his advisers, the unknown death of the offeror did not revoke the offer, but the Council of the American Law Institute changed the rule. Professor Williston concluded that "though the amount of actual authority is not impressive, there is a very general opinion among lawyers that death, even though unknown, does revoke an offer and does revoke an agency," and it was vital that the Restatement rule for contracts coincide with that for agency. 3 Proceedings of the American Law Institute 198 (1925). The Restatement Second preserves the rule, admitting that it "seems to be a relic of the obsolete view that a contract requires a 'meeting of the minds,' and it is out of harmony with the modern doctrine that a manifestation of assent is effective without regard to actual mental assent. . . . In the absence of legislation, [however,] the rule remains in effect." Comment *a* to Restatement Second, § 48. Should the application of the rule be limited to situations in which the offeree has not relied on the assumed contract in ignorance of the fact of the offeror's death?

Legislation changing the rule has been adopted in India, where Section 6(4) of the Indian Contract Act provides that a revocable offer is revoked "by the death or insanity of the proposer, if the fact of his death or insanity comes to the knowledge of the acceptor before acceptance." Would you favor enactment of such a statute in your state? Why do you suppose one has not already been enacted?

Death or incapacity of the offeree has the same effect as that of the offeror under Restatement Second, § 48. The death or incapacity of the offeror does not terminate the offeree's power of acceptance under an option contract.

NOTES

(1) *The Case of the Insane Guarantor.* In 1962, in order to induce Swift & Co. to sell provisions to the Pine Haven Nursing Home & Sanitarium, Joseph Smigel, one of the owners of Pine Haven, signed a "continuing guaranty" that Pine Haven would pay for goods delivered to it by Swift until ten days after receipt of notice of withdrawal of the guaranty. No such notice was ever given. In 1966, Smigel was adjudicated an incompetent. From January to October of 1967, Swift delivered goods to Pine Haven that were not paid for. Smigel died in November and Pine Haven went into bankruptcy in December of 1967. Swift sued Smigel's executor on the guaranty for the unpaid price. From a judgment dismissing Swift's complaint, Swift appeals. *Held:* Reversed. "In view of the . . . criticisms of the conventional approach, which strike us as persuasive, we are not disposed, in determination of this first-instance litigation . . . . routinely to follow existing standard formulations on the subject . . . . It would seem to us that if plaintiff neither knew nor had any reason to know of decedent's later adjudication as an incompetent during any portion of the time it was making the deliveries which gave rise to the debts here sued on, plaintiff's reasonable expectations based on decedent's original continuing promise would be unjustifiably defeated by denial of recovery. If the situation is judged in terms of relative convenience, it would seem easier and more expectable for the guardian of the incompetent to notify at least those people with whom the incompetent had been doing business of the fact of adjudication than for the holder of a guaranty such as here to have to make a specific inquiry as to competency of the guarantor on each occasion of an advance of credit to the principal debtor." Swift & Co. v. Smigel, 115 N.J.Super. 391, 279 A.2d 895 (1971), aff'd per curiam, 60 N.J. 348, 289 A.2d 793 (1972).

(2) *Problem.* You are a Philadelphia lawyer. A client, Benjamin Earle, comes to see you with the following story. "About four years ago I had a conversation with my aunt, Mary Dewitt, who lived in Massachusetts, and she said to me something like this, as best I can remember: 'Ben there are few left to come to my funeral. I have thought a great deal of you for coming to your uncle's funeral and bringing that large box of flowers in the terrible snowstorm we had, when our friends could not reach here from Boston, and you coming from Philadelphia. I want you to attend my funeral, Ben, if you outlive me, and I think you will, and I will pay all expenses and I will give you five thousand dollars. I want you to come.' I replied that I would come if I was living and if they informed me in time to get there and if I was able. We talked about it a little more on the occasion of my mother's funeral two years later. Aunt Mary died a few months ago and I went to Massachusetts for her funeral. Soon after the funeral, I received in the mail this paper, bearing the date of our conversation and signed by Aunt Mary." The paper reads, "If Benjamin A. Earle should come to my funeral, I order my executor to pay him the sum of five thousand dollars. Mary Dewitt." The executor has refused to pay and Mr. Earle wants to know whether he has a claim against the estate for $5,000 and his expenses. Advise him. Do you need more facts? How should those facts be elicited? Would it be well to begin by explaining some elementary contract law to Mr. Earle?[a] See Earle v. Angell, 157 Mass. 294, 32 N.E. 164 (1892).

The American Bar Association's Code of Professional Responsibility says, in Disciplinary Rule 7–102 (Representing a Client Within the Bounds of the Law), that a lawyer shall not "Participate in the creation . . . of evidence when he knows or it is obvious that the evidence is false." Ethical Consideration 7–6 adds: "Often a lawyer is asked to assist his client in developing evidence relevant to the state of mind of the client at a particular time. He may properly assist his client in the development and preservation of evidence of existing motive, intent, or desire; obviously, he may not do anything furthering the creation or preservation of false evidence. In many cases a lawyer may not be certain as to the state of mind of his client, and in those situations he should resolve reasonable doubts in favor of his client." Does this give you adequate guidance?

For a discussion of "whether it is proper to give your client legal advice when you have reason to believe that the knowledge you give him will tempt him to commit perjury," see Freedman, Professional Responsibility of the Criminal Defense Lawyer: The Three Hardest Questions, 64 Mich. L.Rev. 1469, 1478–82 (1966). According to Dean Freedman: "If the lawyer is not certain what the facts are when he gives the advice, the problem is substantially minimized, if not eliminated. It is not the lawyer's function to prejudge his client as a perjurer. He cannot presume that the client will make unlawful use of his advice. . . . Before he begins to remember essential facts, the client is entitled to know what his own interests are." Do you agree? Or is there "a point . . . at which it becomes brute rationalization to claim that the legal advice tendered to a client is meant to contribute to wise and informed decision-making." Noonan, The

a. For an example from fiction, see Paul Biegler's interview of his client, Lieutenant Manion, in Traver, Anatomy of a Murder 44–47 (1958).

Purposes of Advocacy and the Limits of Confidentiality, 64 Mich.L.Rev. 1485, 1488 (1966). If so, has that point been reached here?

Dean Freedman later revised his view to admit that the lawyer may be "giving the client more than just 'information about the law' [and] actively participating in—indeed, initiating—a factual defense that is obviously perjurious." He maintained, "at least at the earlier stages of eliciting the client's story, that the attorney should assume a skeptical attitude, and that the attorney should give the client legal advice that might help in drawing out useful information that the client, consciously or unconsciously, might be withholding. To that extent—but on a different, and more limiting, rationale—I adhere to my earlier position that there are situations in which it may be proper for the attorney to give the client legal advice even though the attorney has reason to believe that the advice may induce the client to commit perjury. There does come a point, however, where nothing less than 'brute rationalization' can purport to justify a conclusion that the lawyer is seeking in good faith to elicit truth rather than actively participating in the creation of perjury." M. Freedman, Lawyers' Ethics in an Adversary System 73, 75 (1975).

LAPSE OF AN OFFER

After some period of time, an offer lapses. If no period is specified in the offer, it lapses after a reasonable time. What is a reasonable time depends, of course, on the circumstances. Take an offer to buy or sell. If the subject matter undergoes rapid fluctuation in price, as is often the case for goods, this will shorten the time. If the subject matter does not undergo rapid fluctuations in price, as is generally the case for land, this will lengthen the time. The following two cases illustrate some other factors used in determining what is a reasonable time for this purpose.

In Akers v. J. B. Sedberry, 39 Tenn.App. 633, 286 S.W.2d 617 (1955), Akers, while in a conference with his employer, Sedberry, orally offered to resign. Sedberry ignored his offer and continued the conference. A few days later she wired her acceptance. He sued for breach of contract, and a decree in his favor was affirmed. "Ordinarily, an offer made by one to another in a face to face conversation is deemed to continue only to the close of their conversation, and cannot be accepted thereafter." But cf. Caldwell v. E. F. Spears & Sons, 186 Ky. 64, 216 S.W. 83 (1919).

In Loring v. City of Boston, 7 Metc. (Mass.) 409 (1844), the City of Boston had run in the daily papers an advertisement offering a $1,000 reward for the apprehension and conviction of any person setting fire to any building within the city limits. The advertisements continued for about a week in May, 1837, and did not appear again. In January, 1841, there was a fire in Boston, and Loring, with the reward in mind, pursued the incendiary to New York, arrested him, returned him to Boston, had him indicted and prosecuted, produced evidence that convicted him, and then sued the city for the reward. There was evidence that fire alarms had been frequent before the advertisements but much less so from that time until the end of 1841. Loring sued to recover the reward. The Supreme Judicial Court of Massachusetts denied recovery. Since the purposes of such an offer are to excite the vigilance of the public and, perhaps, to alarm offenders, the offer of the reward must be notorious in order to be effective. Three years and eight months was not a reasonable time under the circumstances. "In that length of time, the exigency under which it was made having passed, it must be presumed to have been forgotten by most of the officers and citizens of the community, and cannot be presumed to have been before the public as an actuating motive to vigilance and exertion on this subject; nor could it justly and reasonably have been so understood by the plaintiffs." But cf. Carr v. Mahaska County Bankers Ass'n, 222 Iowa 411, 269 N.W. 494 (1936).

NOTE

Questions. What is the effect of an expression of acceptance that arrives too late to operate as an acceptance? Can the offeror, if he chooses, simply disregard the delay and treat it as an acceptance? Or is it a counter-offer that must in turn be accepted by the original offeror in order to create a contract?

REJECTION OF AN OFFER

There is no doubt that rejection of an offer by the offeree terminates his power of acceptance so that he cannot thereafter accept the offer. But why should this be so? It can be argued that it would be unjust to allow an offeree who has rejected an offer to change his mind and accept it if the offeror has already substantially relied on the rejection. But how can this explain the application of the rule where no reliance by the offeror has been shown? Does the discussion of the enforceability of exchanges of promises at p. 68 supra suggest an answer?

MINNEAPOLIS & ST. LOUIS RAILWAY CO. v. COLUMBUS ROLLING-MILL CO.

Supreme Court of the United States, 1886.
119 U.S. 149, 7 S.Ct. 168, 30 L.Ed. 376.

This was an action by a railroad corporation established at Minneapolis in the State of Minnesota against a manufacturing corporation established at Columbus in the State of Ohio. The petition alleged that on December 19, 1879, the parties made a contract by which the plaintiff agreed to buy of the defendant, and the defendant sold to the plaintiff, two thousand tons of iron rails of the weight of fifty pounds per yard, at the price of fifty-four dollars per ton gross, to be delivered free on board cars at the defendant's rolling mill in the month of March, 1880, and to be paid for by the plaintiff in cash when so delivered. The answer denied the making of the contract. It was admitted at the trial that the following letters and telegrams were sent at their dates, and were received in due course, by the parties, through their agents.

December 5, 1879. Letter from plaintiff to defendant: "Please quote me prices for 500 to 3,000 tons 50 lb. steel rails, and for 2,000 to 5,000 tons 50 lb. iron rails, March 1880 delivery."

December 8, 1879. Letter from defendant to plaintiff: "Your favor of the 5th inst. at hand. We do not make steel rails. For iron rails, we will sell 2,000 to 5,000 tons of 50 lb. rails for fifty-four ($54.00) dollars per gross ton for spot cash, F.O.B. cars at our mill, March delivery, subject as follows: In case of strike among our workmen, destruction of or serious damage to our works by fire or the elements, or any causes of delay beyond our control, we shall not be held accountable in damages. If our offer is accepted, shall expect to be notified of same prior to Dec. 20th, 1879."

December 16, 1879. Telegram from plaintiff to defendant: "Please enter our order for twelve hundred tons rails, March delivery, as per your favor of the eighth. Please reply."

December 16, 1879. Letter from plaintiff to defendant: Yours of the 8th came duly to hand. I telegraphed you to-day to enter our order for twelve hundred (1,200) tons 50 lb. iron rails for next March delivery, at fifty-four dollars ($54.00) F.O.B. cars at your mill. Please send contract. Also please send me templet of your 50 lb. rail. Do you make splices? If so, give me prices for splices for this lot of iron."

December 18, 1879. Telegram from defendant to plaintiff, received same day: "We cannot book your order at present at that price."

December 19, 1879. Telegram from plaintiff to defendant: "Please enter an order for two thousand tons rails, as per your letter of the sixth. Please forward written contract. Reply." (The word "sixth" was admitted to be a mistake for "eighth.")

December 22, 1879. Telegram from plaintiff to defendant: "Did you enter my order for two thousand tons rails, as per my telegram of December nineteenth? Answer."

After repeated similar inquiries by the plaintiff, the defendant, on January 19, 1880, denied the existence of any contract between the parties.

The jury returned a verdict for the defendant, under instructions which need not be particularly stated; and the plaintiff alleged exceptions, and sued out this writ of error.

Mr. Justice GRAY, after making the foregoing statement of the case delivered the opinion of the court.

The rules of law which govern this case are well settled. As no contract is complete without the mutual assent of the parties, an offer to sell imposes no obligation until it is accepted according to its terms. So long as the offer has been neither accepted nor rejected, the negotiation remains open, and imposes no obligation upon either party; the one may decline to accept, or the other may withdraw his offer; and either rejection or withdrawal leaves the matter as if no offer had ever been made. A proposal to accept, or an acceptance, upon terms varying from those offered, is a rejection of the offer, and puts an end to the negotiation, unless the party who made the original offer renews it, or assents to the modification suggested. The other party having once rejected the offer, cannot afterwards revive it by tendering an acceptance of it. . . . If the offer does not limit the time for its acceptance, it must be accepted within a reasonable time. If it does, it may, at any time within the limit and so long as it remains open, be accepted or rejected by the party to whom, or be withdrawn by the party by whom, it was made. . . .

The defendant, by the letter of December 8, offered to sell to the plaintiff two thousand to five thousand tons of iron rails on certain terms specified, and added that if the offer was accepted the defendant would expect to be notified prior to December 20. This offer, while it remained open, without having been rejected by the plaintiff or revoked by the defendant, would authorize the plaintiff to take at his election any number of tons not less than two thousand nor more than five thousand, on the terms specified. The offer, while unrevoked, might be accepted, or rejected by the plaintiff at any time before December 20. Instead of accepting the offer made, the plaintiff on December 16, by telegram and letter, referring to the defendant's letter of December 8, directed the defendant to enter an order for twelve hundred tons on the same terms. The mention, in both telegram and letter, of the date and the terms of the defendant's original offer, shows that the plaintiff's order was not an independent proposal, but an answer to the defendant's offer, a qualified acceptance of that offer, varying the number of tons, and therefore in law a rejection of the offer. On December 18, the defendant by telegram declined to fulfil the plaintiff's order. The negotiation between the parties was thus closed, and the plaintiff could not afterwards fall back on the defendant's original offer. The plaintiff's attempt to do so, by the telegram of December 19, was therefore ineffectual and created no rights against the defendant.

Such being the legal effect of what passed in writing between the parties, it is unnecessary to consider whether, upon a fair interpretation of the instructions of the court, the question whether the plaintiff's telegram and letter of December 16 constituted a rejection of the defendant's offer of December 8 was ruled in favor of the defendant as a matter of law, or was submitted to the jury as a question of fact. The submission of a question of law to the jury is no ground of exception if they decide it aright. Pence v. Langdon, 99 U.S. 578, 25 L.Ed. 420. . . .

Judgment affirmed.

NOTES

(1) *Drafting.* Can you draft a telegram for the railroad, in answer to the rolling mill's letter of December 8, that would have been an offer to buy 1,200 tons of rails but not a rejection of the rolling mill's offer? See Restatement Second, §§ 38, 39.

(2) *Problem.* Suppose that the rolling mill's telegram of December 18 had read: "Cannot reduce quantity. We cannot book your order at present at that price." Would the result in the case have been the same? See Livingstone v. Evans, [1925] 4 D.L.R. 769 (Alberta Sup.Ct.).

SECTION 5. THE REQUIREMENT OF DEFINITENESS

The preceding sections of this chapter have explored the question: Did both parties *assent* to be bound? This section explores the question: Is there agreement *definite* enough to be enforced? Both questions must be answered in the affirmative for there to be a contract.

The requirement of definiteness is implicit in the principle that the promisee's expectation interest is to be protected. In calculating the damages that will put the promisee in the position in which he would have been had the promise been performed, a court must determine the scope of that promise with some precision. In the less usual case where the court orders specific performance or enjoins a threatened breach, it must know the scope of the promise with even greater precision to frame a decree because failure to obey subjects the promisor to the court's contempt power. If recovery on a broken promise were limited to the promisee's restitution or reliance interest, it would often be unnecessary to inquire into the scope of the promise, as long as it was clear that the promise had been broken. See the statements of the requirement of definiteness in UCC 2–204(3) [a] and in Restatement Second, § 33.

a. Williston would have deleted the last twelve words of this Code provision and inserted "minor" before "terms." "If parties choose to leave important terms open and nevertheless 'intend a contract,' I think their only reliance should be on business honor." Williston, The Law of Sales in the Proposed Uniform Commercial Code, 63 Harv.L.Rev. 561, 576 (1950).

The impact of the requirement of definiteness can be seen from Varney v. Ditmars, 217 N.Y. 223, 111 N.E. 822 (1916), in which an architectural draftsman sued his employer on the employer's promise to pay "a fair share of my profits" in addition to a stated salary. The court denied recovery of profits on the ground that their amount was a matter of "pure conjecture" and "may be any amount from a nominal sum to a material part according to the particular views of the person whose guess is considered. Such an executory contract must rest for performance upon the honor and good faith of the parties making it."

Before concluding that an agreement is too indefinite to enforce, however, a court must first interpret it. Often it can piece together enough terms to satisfy the requirement from preliminary negotiations, including prior communications, from references to external sources of terms, including trade and other standard terms, or from usages to which the parties are subject, a course of dealing between the parties prior to the transaction, or a course of performance between them after their agreement. Indefiniteness may also be cured by the addition of such implied terms as will be supplied by law, in the same manner in which the duty to use reasonable efforts was supplied in Wood v. Lucy, p. 81 supra. The processes by which language is interpreted and such terms are supplied are explored in detail in Chapter 7.

Terms such as "reasonable efforts" are regarded as sufficiently definite if their content can be determined by reference to some external standard. This would have been done in Wood v. Lucy had it been necessary, in an action by Lady Duff-Gordon against Otis Wood, to have determined what efforts would have been reasonable in his circumstances. Corthell v. Summit Thread Co., 132 Me. 94, 167 A. 79 (1933), is an extreme case. There an employer promised its employee "reasonable recognition" in return for his promise to turn over rights to his future inventions. The court held that the employer was liable under the agreement even though it had taken the precaution of going on to provide "the basis and amount of recognition to rest entirely 'with the employer, the agreement' to be interpreted in good faith on the basis of what is reasonable and intended and not technically." [b] Contrast Varney v. Ditmars, supra. Courts have also generally found "good faith" to be sufficiently definite under similar reasoning. The meaning of "reasonable efforts" and "good faith" is taken up in detail in Chapter 7, Section 3.

Furthermore, it is enough if the agreement provides the means for making its terms sufficiently definite by the time that perform-

b. For a more recent exceptional case, see Rutcosky v. Tracy, 89 Wash.2d 606, 574 P.2d 382, cert. denied, 439 U.S. 930 (1978), in which, when the plaintiff asked for extra compensation in the form of a percentage of the revenue from a program he was to develop, he was told merely that he would be "taken care of."

ance is called for. For example, in the cotton cases of 1973, discussed at p. 1 supra, the quantity of cotton was not determined until the cotton was harvested, but the agreements were not unenforceable on that ground. The same is true of output and requirements contracts generally. For another example, in the Fairmount Glass case, p. 184 supra, the seller argued "that the contract was indefinite, because the quantity of each size of the jars was not fixed," but the court held that the agreement was not unenforceable on this ground because the buyer had "the right to name the quantity of each size" before shipment. The same is true of contracts that have particulars of performance to be specified by one of the parties. See UCC 2–311. (Note that in the Fairmount Glass case the buyer, who was to specify the particulars, was the injured party. Would the agreement have been sufficiently definite if the buyer had been the party in breach and had refused not only to take and pay for the jars but even to make a specification?)

NOTES

(1) *Causes of Indefiniteness.* Why are parties not more precise in setting out the terms of their agreements? Consider the following possible answers.

(a) They do not want to take the time or trouble to do so, but prefer to rely on the terms that a court will supply in case a dispute arises.

(b) They are reluctant to raise difficult issues for fear that the deal may fall through.

(c) They do not foresee the problem that happens to arise.

Are there other answers? Might the answer in a particular case affect the court's willingness to overlook some indefiniteness?

(2) *Arbitration and Indefiniteness.* Reread the arbitration clause in Note 1, p. 40 supra. Under such a broadly worded clause, the very enforceability of the "contract," in the face of a claim of indefiniteness, is for the arbitrators to determine. Would you expect arbitrators to be more or less tolerant of indefiniteness than judges?

(3) *Restitution.* A party who has performed under an agreement that is unenforceable for indefiniteness is entitled to restitution. For example, in Varney v. Ditmars, supra, the court suggested that if the architectural draftsman's work was worth more than his salary, he would have a right to restitution measured by the difference. See also Note 1, p. 344 infra.

(4) *The Cotton Cases of 1973.* In one of the cotton cases of 1973, discussed at p. 1 supra, Riegel Fiber had made in March contracts on its own forms with ginning companies for delivery to Riegel of cotton that the ginners had contracted to buy from farmers. A typical quantity term of one of Riegel's contracts read:

> On the terms and conditions and at the prices set forth below, Buyer agrees to purchase and take delivery from Seller, and Seller agrees to sell and deliver to Buyer, all the acceptable cotton pro-

duced during the crop year 1973 on the following acreage, and none other:

No. of Acres	Farm No.	County	Allotment in Name Of	Projected Yield 1973
4,222		Cherokee & Calhoun Counties, Alabama	Various	500 Lbs. Per Acre

The ginner under this contract testified that he had no specific fields in mind when he signed the contract and that he never designated specific fields. After the sharp rise in cotton prices, Riegel sued the ginners to have the contracts declared valid and to have them specifically enforced. From an adverse judgment, Riegel appealed. *Held*: Reversed and remanded. The trial court erred in holding that UCC 2–201 precluded enforcement. Since "the writings . . . contained a quantity term . . ., the real issue . . . is not whether these contracts satisfy § 2–201, but whether the quantity term . . . is too indefinite to support judicial enforcement . . . . We need not reach the question whether these contracts fall within the reach of § 2–306 . . . ., because we think appellant presented ample evidence that the quantity terms . . .—viewed as requiring delivery of various pounds of cotton—meet the standards of definiteness required by the Code . . . . The district court relied heavily on the impossibility of determining from the face of the . . . contracts the specific fields covered by the agreements . . . . Yet we find no evidence that any of the parties believe that such specificity is *commercially* necessary or even desirable. For its part, Riegel is apparently willing to rely to a large extent on the farmers' good faith and commercial reasonableness in choosing which of their acres are to be used to grow contract cotton. Likewise, the record contains no hint of why the individual farmers or the ginners might prefer as a normal practice to contract as to rigidly specified fields." Riegel Fiber Corp. v. Anderson Gin Co., 512 F.2d 784 (5th Cir. 1975). What was the quantity? Was it 2,111,000 pounds of cotton? If so, why did not the contract simply say so? If not, what was it?

LEE v. JOSEPH E. SEAGRAM & SONS, INC.

United States Court of Appeals, Second Circuit, 1977.
552 F.2d 447.

GURFEIN, Circuit Judge: This is an appeal by defendant Joseph E. Seagram & Sons, Inc. ("Seagram") from a judgment entered by the District Court, Hon. Charles H. Tenney, upon the verdict of a jury in the amount of $407,850 in favor of the plaintiffs on a claim asserting common law breach of an oral contract. . . . The plaintiffs are Harold S. Lee (now deceased) and his two sons, Lester and Eric ("the Lees"). Jurisdiction is based on diversity of citizenship. We affirm.

The jury could have found the following. The Lees owned a 50% interest in Capitol City Liquor Company, Inc. ("Capitol City"), a wholesale liquor distributorship located in Washington, D.C. The other 50% was owned by Harold's brother, Henry D. Lee, and his nephew, Arthur Lee. Seagram is a distiller of alcoholic beverages. Capitol City carried numerous Seagram brands and a large portion of its sales were generated by Seagram lines.

The Lees and the other owners of Capitol City wanted to sell their respective interests in the business and, in May 1970, Harold Lee, the father, discussed the possible sale of Capitol City with Jack Yogman ("Yogman"), then Executive Vice President of Seagram (and now President), whom he had known for many years. Lee offered to sell Capitol City to Seagram but conditioned the offer on Seagram's agreement to relocate Harold and his sons, the 50% owners of Capitol City, in a new distributorship of their own in a different city.

About a month later, another officer of Seagram, John Barth, an assistant to Yogman, visited the Lees and their co-owners in Washington and began negotiations for the purchase of the assets of Capitol City by Seagram on behalf of a new distributor, one Carter, who would take it over after the purchase. The purchase of the assets of Capitol City was consummated on September 30, 1970 pursuant to a written agreement. The promise to relocate the father and sons thereafter was not reduced to writing.

Harold Lee had served the Seagram organization for thirty-six years in positions of responsibility before he acquired the half interest in the Capitol City distributorship. From 1958 to 1962, he was chief executive officer of Calvert Distillers Company, a wholly-owned subsidiary. During this long period he enjoyed the friendship and confidence of the principals of Seagram.

In 1958, Harold Lee had purchased from Seagram its holdings of Capitol City stock in order to introduce his sons into the liquor distribution business, and also to satisfy Seagram's desire to have a strong and friendly distributor for Seagram products in Washington, D.C. Harold Lee and Yogman had known each other for 13 years.

The plaintiffs claimed a breach of the oral agreement to relocate Harold Lee's sons, alleging that Seagram had had opportunities to procure another distributorship for the Lees but had refused to do so. The Lees brought this action on January 18, 1972, fifteen months after the sale of the Capitol City distributorship to Seagram. They contended that they had performed their obligation by agreeing to the sale by Capitol City of its assets to Seagram, but that Seagram had failed to perform its obligation under the separate oral contract between the Lees and Seagram. The agreement which the trial court permitted the jury to find was "an oral agreement with defendant which provided that if they agreed to sell their interest in Capitol

City, defendant in return, within a reasonable time, would provide the plaintiffs a Seagram distributorship whose price would require roughly an amount equal to the capital obtained by the plaintiffs for the sale of their interest in Capitol City, and which distributorship would be in a location acceptable to plaintiffs." No specific exception was taken to this portion of the charge. By its verdict for the plaintiffs, we must assume—as Seagram notes in its brief—that this is the agreement which the jury found was made before the sale of Capitol City was agreed upon.[2]

Appellant urges several grounds for reversal. It contends that, as a matter of law, (1) plaintiffs' proof of the alleged oral agreement is barred by the parol evidence rule; and (2) the oral agreement is too vague and indefinite to be enforceable. Appellant also contends that plaintiffs' proof of damages is speculative and incompetent. [The parts of the opinion that deal with the parol evidence rule and the proof of damages are at pp. 637 and 669 infra.]

II

Appellant contends . . . that the jury verdict cannot stand because the oral agreement was so vague and indefinite as to be unenforceable. First, appellant argues that the failure to specify purchase price, profitability or sales volume of the distributorship to be provided, is fatal to the contract's validity. The contention is that, because the oral agreement lacks essential terms, the courts cannot determine the rights and obligations of the parties. See 1 Corbin on Contracts § 95, at 394. Second, appellant contends that the agreement is unenforceable because there were no specific limits to plaintiffs' discretion in deciding whether to accept or reject a particular distributorship; and hence the agreement was illusory.[6]

2. The complaint alleged that Seagram agreed to "obtain" or "secure" or "provide" a "similar" distributorship within a reasonable time, and plaintiffs introduced some testimony to that effect. Although other testimony suggested that Seagram agreed merely to provide an opportunity for the Lees to negotiate with third parties, and Judge Tenney indicated in his denial of judgment n. o. v. that Seagram merely agreed "to notify plaintiffs as they learned of distributors who were considering the sale of their businesses," 413 F.Supp. at 698–99, the jury was permitted to find that the agreement was in the nature of a commitment to provide a distributorship. There was evidence to support such a finding, and the jury so found.

6. Appellant makes two other contentions in this regard, which may be disposed of summarily. It argues that the evidence introduced by plaintiffs was so contradictory and confusing that the jury could not ascertain Seagram's obligations with any definiteness. Although plaintiffs apparently did not try their case on a single coherent theory, see note 2 supra, the short answer is that, by its verdict, the jury gave credence to some of the evidence, discounted the remainder, and drew its inferences accordingly. Id. Second, appellant suggests that the evidence demonstrates at best Seagram's friendly willingness to *help* the Lees in their efforts to relocate, but no commitment to undertake any legal obligation. The short answer again is that there was contrary testimony which the jury chose to believe.

The alleged agreement, as the jury was permitted to find, was to provide the Lees with a liquor distributorship of approximately half the value and profit potential of Capitol City, within a reasonable time. The distributorship would be "in a location acceptable to plaintiffs," and the price would require roughly an amount equal to the plaintiffs' previous investment in Capitol City. The performance by plaintiffs in agreeing to the sale of Capitol City caused the counter-performance of the oral promise to mature.

Once the nature of the agreement found by the jury is recognized, it becomes clear that appellant's contentions are without merit. As for the alleged lack of essential terms, there was evidence credited by the jury, which did establish the purchase price, profitability and sales volume of the distributorship with reasonable specificity. In addition to the direct testimony of the Lees there was evidence that distributorships were valued, as a rule of thumb, at book value plus three times the previous year's net profit after taxes. Between this industry standard and the reference to the Capitol City transaction, there was extrinsic evidence to render the parties' obligations reasonably definite. Professor Corbin has observed that a court should be slow to deny enforcement "if it is convinced that the parties themselves meant to make a 'contract' and to bind themselves to render a future performance. Many a gap in terms can be filled, and should be, with a result that is consistent with what the parties said and that is more just to both of them than would be a refusal of enforcement." Corbin on Contracts § 97, at 425–26. New York courts are in accord in hesitating to find that a contract is too indefinite for enforcement. . . . The requirement that the alleged oral agreement be performed within a reasonable time is particularly unobjectionable, . . . especially in light of the fact, which Seagram knew, that plaintiffs would have to reinvest the proceeds from the sale of Capitol City within one year or suffer adverse tax consequences.[7]

As for the alleged unbridled discretion which the oral agreement conferred on the plaintiffs, we similarly conclude that there is no fatal defect. We note at the outset that the requirement that the new distributorship be "acceptable" to the Lees did not render the agreement illusory in the sense that it is not supported by consideration; the Lees' part of the bargain was to join in the sale of Capitol City's assets and assignment of its franchise, which they had already per-

7. Seagram also appears to contend that a promise to "relocate" is insufficiently specific. We disagree. Aside from the ordinary meaning of the word, the jury could rely on evidence, which was introduced, of other efforts by Seagram to "provide" a distributorship for other distributors —including Seagram's successful effort to provide Chet Carter with the Capitol City distributorship by purchasing it on his behalf, cf. Borden v. Chesterfield Farms, Inc., 27 A.D.2d 165, 277 N.Y.S.2d 494 (1st Dep't 1967), and Harold Lee's own experience in his original purchase of the 50% interest in Capitol City directly from Seagram.

formed. More importantly, we do not agree that the Lees had "unbridled" discretion. New York courts would in all events impose an obligation of good faith on the Lees' exercise of discretion, see e. g., Wood v. Lucy, Lady Duff-Gordon, 222 N.Y. 88, 118 N.E. 214 (1917), and there was also extrinsic evidence of what would constitute an "acceptable distributorship," and hence constitute reasonable performance by Seagram. Seagram appears to contend that if it had tendered reasonable performance, by offering an acceptable distributorship to the Lees, that the Lees nevertheless could have found it not "acceptable." This is not correct. It is true that Seagram could not have forced the Lees to take a distributorship, because they had not promised to do so. But Seagram's tender of reasonable performance would discharge its obligations under the oral agreement, whether or not the Lees "accepted." See 15 Williston on Contracts §§ 1808–10 (3d ed. 1972). The Lees could not prevent Seagram from fulfilling its obligations by unreasonably refusing an acceptable distributorship. Since the obligations of the parties under the contract therefore were ascertainable, it was not void for indefiniteness. Cf. Mason v. Rose, 176 F.2d 486, 489 (2d Cir. 1949). . . .

Affirmed.

NOTE

Questions. Why do you suppose the parties were not more precise in defining their obligations in connection with the new distributorship? To what sources did the court look in defining those obligations?

WALKER v. KEITH, 382 S.W.2d 198 (Ky.1964). [Walker leased a small lot to Keith for ten years at $100 a month, with an option in Keith to extend the lease for another 10-year term under the same terms except as to rental. The renewal option provided:

> rental will be fixed in such amount as shall actually be agreed upon by the lessors and the lessee with the monthly rental fixed on the comparative basis of rental values as of the date of the renewal with rental values at this time reflected by the comparative business conditions of the two periods.

Keith sought to exercise the option and, when the parties were unable to agree on the rent, brought suit against Walker.[a] Based upon the

a. We understand from counsel for Keith that the lot in controversy amounted to about one acre on the corner of an undeveloped tract of about 20 acres, and that the lessor was the partnership of Barnard and Walker. Keith used the property for a new business dealing in monuments and memorials, adding structures, driveways and walkways. After about six years, Barnard, who had engaged in the negotiations with Keith (although he later testified that the method for fixing the renewal rental had been proposed by Walker), sold his interest to Walker. After verdict of an advisory jury, the Chancellor fixed the new rent at $125 per month, and Walker appealed.]

CLAY, Commissioner. . . . On the face of the rent provision, the parties had not agreed upon a rent figure. They left the amount to future determination. If they had agreed upon a specific method of making the determination, such as by computation, the application of a formula, or the decision of an arbitrator, they could be said to have agreed upon whatever rent figure emerged from utilization of the method. This was not done.

It will be observed the rent provision expresses two ideas. The first is that the parties agree to agree. The second is that the future agreement will be based on a comparative adjustment in the light of "business conditions". . . .

The lease purports to fix the rent at such an amount as shall "actually be agreed upon". It should be obvious that an agreement to agree cannot constitute a binding contract. . . .

This proposition is not universally accepted as it pertains to renewal options in a lease. . . . We have examined the reasons set forth in those opinions and do not find them convincing. The view is taken that the renewal option is for the benefit of the lessee; that the parties intended something; and that the lessee should not be deprived of his right to enforce his contract. This reasoning seems to overlook the fact that a party must have an enforceable contract before he has a right to enforce it. We wonder if these courts would enforce an *original* lease in which the rent was not fixed, but agreed to be agreed upon.

Surely there are some limits to what equity can or should undertake to compel parties in their private affairs to do what the court thinks they should have done. . . . In any event, we are not persuaded that renewal options in leases are of such an exceptional character as to justify emasculation of one of the basic rules of contract law. An agreement to agree simply does not fix an enforceable obligation.

As noted, however, the language of the renewal option incorporated a secondary stipulation. Reference was made to "comparative business conditions" which were to play some part in adjusting the new rental. It is contended this provides the necessary certainty. . . .

It is true courts often must *imply* such terms in a contract as "reasonable time" or "reasonable price". This is done when the parties fail to deal with such matters in an otherwise enforceable contract. Here the parties were undertaking to fix the terms rather

about eight years Walker was approached to lease the entire tract for the construction of a shopping center, with the inclusion of the lot occupied by Keith as a condition. Should facts such as these have affected the outcome of the case?

than leave them to implication. Our problem is not what the law would imply if the contract did not purport to cover the subject matter, but whether the parties, in removing this material term from the field of implication, have fixed their mutual obligations.

We are seeking what the agreement actually was. When dealing with such a specific item as rent, to be payable in dollars, the area of possible agreement is quite limited. If the parties did not agree upon such an unequivocal item or upon a definite method of ascertaining it, then there is a clear case of nonagreement. The court, in fixing an obligation under a nonagreement, is not enforcing the contract but is binding the parties to something they were patently unable to agree to when writing the contract. . . .

It has been suggested that rent is not a material term of a lease. . . . Nothing could be more vital in a lease than the amount of rent. It is the price the lessee agrees to pay and the lessor agrees to accept for the use of the premises. Would a contract to buy a building at a "reasonable price" be enforceable? Would the method of determining the price be a matter of "form" and "incidental and ancillary" to the transaction? In truth it lies at the heart of it. This seems to us as no more than a grammatical means of sweeping the problem under the rug. It will not do to say that the establishment of the rent agreed upon is not of the essence of a lease contract. . . .

What the law requires is an adequate key to a mutual agreement. If "comparative business conditions" afforded sufficient certainty, we might possibly surmount the obstacle of the unenforceable agreement to agree. This term, however is very broad indeed. Did the parties have in mind local conditions, national conditions, or conditions affecting the lessee's particular business? . . .

Stipulations such as the one before us have been the source of interminable litigation. Courts are called upon not to enforce an agreement or to determine what the agreement was, but to write their own concept of what would constitute a proper one. Why this paternalistic task should be undertaken is difficult to understand when the parties could so easily provide any number of workable methods by which rents could be adjusted. As a practical matter, courts sometimes must assert their right not to be imposed upon. . . .

[Reversed.]

NOTES

(1) *Causes of Indefiniteness (Reprise).* Why did not Walker and Keith fix the rental in case of renewal in 1951? For one of the reasons suggested in Note 1, p. 234 supra?

(2) *Problem.* Standard Oil terminated the contract of Schmieder, one of its distributors. Schmieder owned equipment, including tanks and

pumps, that he had loaned to his customers. The contract gave Standard Oil the option to purchase this equipment at a price equal to Schmieder's "costs, minus such depreciation as may be mutually agreed upon." Is the option enforceable? See UCC 2–305; Schmieder v. Standard Oil Co. of Indiana, 69 Wis.2d 419, 230 N.W.2d 732 (1975).

GREENE v. LEEPER, 193 Tenn. 153, 245 S.W.2d 181 (1951). [Leeper leased property to Greene for five years with a clause providing: "The parties of the second part have a right to renew this lease for another term of five years at a rental to be agreed on according to business conditions at that time." Greene sought a declaratory judgment to determine his rights under the clause. The Chancellor held that the clause was too indefinite and dismissed the complaint. Greene appealed.]

PREWITT, Justice. . . . A renewal provision in a lease providing for an additional term of five years and leaving the amount of rent to be agreed on according to business conditions at the time of renewal is valid and enforceable. Stone v. Martin, 185 Tenn. 369, 206 S.W.2d 388, 389. In the case cited, the lease contract provided "at the monthly value of like property at time of expiration."

We think the equitable rule is that the primary and essential agreement is that renewal of the original lease and stipulations as to the amount of rent and methods of determining that amount are ancillary to the primary contract and matters of form rather than substance. In Stone v. Martin, supra, this Court said: "Real estate experts, with a knowledge of local conditions, would have no difficulty in fixing the rental value under those directions."

No doubt a part of the consideration of the original lease was the provision therein contained as to renewal. In the present case, complainant had an established business and his five year contract was about to run out, and complying with the renewal provision, he notified the property owner of his desire to exercise his option. We see no reason why, in fairness to lessor and lessee, the fair value of the property could not be determined with reasonable accuracy. . . .

In Stone v. Martin, supra, this Court, quoting from the conclusions of the Chancellor, said: "The lease is normally drawn by the lessor, as was true herein, and should be construed most strongly against him. The lessee's option to renew, being only an option, is purely for the lessee's benefit and must be taken as a part of the inducing consideration for his contract, a thing for which he has paid in part. To deprive him of it would be a detriment solely to him, the lessor losing nothing for which he has bargained."

Being of the opinion that the monthly rental can be determined with reasonable certainty by disinterested parties, we think the fair conclusion is that the lessee has a right to hold the premises for the additional five years provided he pays a reasonable rental to be determined as heretofore indicated.

[Reversed and remanded.]

NOTE

Agreements to Agree. Is there a difference between a situation in which the parties have agreed that a term, such as the compensation or the time for performance, shall be "reasonable," and one in which they have agreed that they shall negotiate in a "reasonable" manner to fix that term? Does UCC 2–204(3) recognize such a distinction? Does UCC 2–305(1)? Do these provisions invite a court to "make a contract for the parties"? According to the official comment to UCC 2–204, "the fact that one or more terms are left to be agreed upon [is not] enough of itself to defeat an otherwise adequate agreement." Does the comment go beyond the text of the Code? To what extent may such rules have desirable or undesirable effects on the parties during the bargaining process?

FLEXIBLE PRICING

Suppose that over a long term a seller wants to be assured of an outlet for a fixed quantity of his product and that a buyer wants to be assured of a source of supply for the same quantity. But neither wants to take the risk of a shift in the market: the seller does not want the risk of a rise in prices before delivery, and the buyer does not want the risk of a fall. How can they make an agreement that will be legally enforceable and yet will allow the price of the goods to fluctuate?

One possibility is to leave the price term "open," so that under UCC 2–305 the price will then be "a reasonable price at the time for *delivery*." The opportunities for dispute over what is "reasonable" may make this solution unattractive.[a] (Would it be useful to designate a third party to fix the price if the parties disagreed? See UCC 2–305.) Another possibility is to use an "escalator clause" under which the price will be fixed according to a formula tied in some way to the market. Would it be easier to draft such an agreement if there were an ascertainable market price for the raw materials required by the seller to produce his product? An ascertainable market price for the product itself? (On ascertainable market price, see UCC 2–723, 2–724.) Would prices charged by competing sellers or to competing buyers be useful?[b] Helpful analogies can be found in

a. That a market price is not necessarily a "reasonable" price, see Spartan Grain & Mill Co. v. Ayers, 517 F. 2d 214 (5th Cir. 1975) ("Spartan's prices [for chicken feed] were not necessarily unreasonable simply because they were higher than those charged by the other sellers, since it also committed itself to purchase" all the buyers' eggs).

b. The impact of the antitrust laws on this question must be left for a later course.

clauses in leases tied to gross profits, in clauses in collective bargaining agreements tied to the cost of living, and in clauses in construction contracts tied to costs ("cost-plus" contracts).[c] On flexible pricing, see Rosenn, Protecting Contracts from Inflation, 33 Bus.Law. 729 (1978); Note, 36 Va.L.Rev. 627 (1950).

Suppose that you succeeded in devising a *perfect* formula for tying the price to the buyer's market. Would it make any difference if the agreement were legally enforceable or not? (For what loss could the buyer recover damages if he could purchase the goods for the same price on the market?)

Some of the difficulties that parties have encountered at the hands of the courts are illustrated by Sun Printing & Publishing Ass'n v. Remington Paper & Power Co., 235 N.Y. 338, 139 N.E. 470 (1923). Sun Printing agreed to buy and Remington Paper to sell 1,000 tons of paper per month over a 16-month period. The agreement fixed the price for the first four months and provided: "For the balance of the period of this agreement the price of the paper and the length of terms for which such price shall apply shall be agreed upon by and between the parties hereto fifteen days prior to the expiration of each period for which the price and length of term thereof have been previously agreed upon, said price in no event to be higher than the contract price for newsprint charged by the Canadian Export Paper Company to the large consumers, the seller to receive the benefit of any differentials in freight rates." Prices rose and after the first four months Sun Printing offered to pay the Canadian Export price, but Remington Paper refused and Sun Printing sued for damages. The New York Court of Appeals held (5–2), in an opinion by Cardozo, that the complaint did not state a cause of action since there were "two subjects to be settled in the middle of December and at unstated intervals thereafter. One was the price to be paid. The other was the length of time during which such price was to govern. . . . . Seller and buyer understood that the price to be fixed in December for a term to be agreed upon would not be more than the price then charged by the Canadian Export Paper Company to the large consumers. They did not understand that, if during the term so established the price charged by the Canadian Export Paper Com-

An interesting variant is patterned after the "most favored nation" clause found in treaties. See, for example, Reynolds Metals Co. v. United States, 438 F.2d 983 (Ct.Cl.1971), in which the United States promised Reynolds to amend their contract "if later agreements with the Aluminum Company of America and/or the Kaiser Aluminum and Chemical Company are, in your opinion, more favorable than the agreement which has been executed with you."

c. Such clauses may, particularly in an inflationary period, have an adverse effect on the economy. (Is this necessarily so, if the clause is a substitute for a higher initial price?) Should this be of concern to the lawyer drafting an agreement for his client?

pany was changed, the price payable to the seller would fluctuate accordingly. . . . While the term was unknown, the contract was inchoate." What result under the Code? See UCC 2–305.

NOTE

Cardozo on Cardozo. Not long after the decision, Cardozo gave a series of lectures in which he said of this case: "The court subordinated the equity of a particular situation to the overmastering need of certainty in the transactions of commercial life. . . . The loss to business would in the long run be greater than the gain if judges were clothed with power to revise as well as to interpret. Perhaps, with a higher conception of business and its needs, the time will come when even revision will be permitted if it is revision in consonance with established standards of fair dealing, but the time is not yet." B. Cardozo, Growth of the Law 110–11 (1924).

What are the "needs" of business? "The standard contract used by manufacturers of paper to sell to magazine publishers has a pricing clause which is probably sufficiently vague to make the contract legally unenforceable. The house counsel of one of the largest paper producers said that everyone in the industry is aware of this because of a leading New York case concerning the contract, but that no one cares." Macaulay, Non-Contractual Relations in Business: A Preliminary Study, 28 Am.Sociological Rev. 55, 60 (1963).

SOUTHWEST ENGINEERING CO. v. MARTIN TRACTOR CO.

Supreme Court of Kansas, 1970.
205 Kan. 684, 473 P.2d 18.

[The facts and the first part of the opinion in this case, in which the court held that the airport memorandum satisfied UCC 2–201, are at p. 148, supra.]

The evidence already cited would be ample to sustain the trial court's finding that an agreement was reached between Hurt and Cloepfil in Springfield. However, Cloepfil's testimony is not the only evidence in support of that finding. In a pretrial deposition, Mr. Hurt, himself, deposed that "we agreed on the section that I would be quoting on, and we came to some over-all general agreement on the major items." At the trial Hurt testified he did not wish to change that statement in any way.

Hurt further testified that in his opinion the thing which stood in the way of a firm deal was Martin's terms of payment—that had Southwest agreed with those terms of payment, so far as he was concerned, he would have considered a firm deal was made. Mr. Hurt acknowledged while on the stand that he penned the memorandum and that as disclosed therein a 10 per cent discount was given Southwest on the price of either of the generators listed (depending on which was approved by the Corps of Engineers), and that the accessories common to both generators were to be net—that is, sold without profit.

It is quite true, as the trial court found, that terms of payment were not agreed upon at the Springfield meeting. Hurt testified that as the memorandum was being made out, he said they wanted 10 per cent with the order, 50 per cent on delivery and the balance on acceptance, but he did not recall Cloepfil's response. Cloepfil's version was somewhat different. He stated that after the two had shaken hands in the lobby preparing to leave, Hurt said their terms usually were 20 per cent down and the balance on delivery; while he (Cloepfil) said the way they generally paid was 90 per cent on the tenth of the month following delivery and the balance on final acceptance. It is obvious the parties reached no agreement on this point.

However, a failure on the part of Messrs. Hurt and Cloepfil to agree on terms of payment would not, of itself, defeat an otherwise valid agreement reached by them. K.S.A. 84–2–204(3) reads:

"Even though one or more terms are left open a contract for sale does not fail for indefiniteness if the parties have intended to make a contract and there is a reasonably certain basis for giving an appropriate remedy."

The official U.C.C. Comment is enlightening:

"Subsection (3) states the principle as to 'open terms' underlying later sections of the Article. If the parties intend to enter into a binding agreement, this subsection recognizes that agreement as valid in law, despite missing terms, if there is any reasonably certain basis for granting a remedy. The test is not certainty as to what the parties were to do nor as to the exact amount of damages due the plaintiff. Nor is the fact that one or more terms are left to be agreed upon enough of itself to defeat an otherwise adequate agreement. Rather, commercial standards on the point of 'indefiniteness' are intended to be applied, this Act making provision elsewhere for missing terms needed for performance, open price, remedies and the like.

"The more terms the parties leave open, the less likely it is that they have intended to conclude a binding agreement, but their actions may be frequently conclusive on the matter despite the omissions."

The above Code provision and accompanying Comment were quoted in Pennsylvania Co. v. Wilmington Trust Co., 39 Del.Ch. 453, 166 A.2d 726, where the court made this observation:

"There appears to be no pertinent court authority interpreting this rather recent but controlling statute. In an article entitled 'The Law of Sales In the Proposed Uniform Commercial Code,' 63 Harv. Law Rev. 561, 576, Mr. Williston wanted to limit omissions to 'minor' terms. He wanted 'business honor' to be the only compulsion where 'important terms' are left open. Nevertheless, his recommendation was rejected (see note on p. 561). This shows that those drafting the statute intended that the omission of even an important term does not prevent the finding under the statute that the parties intended to make a contract." (pp. 731, 732.)

So far as the present case is concerned, K.S.A. 84–2–310 supplies the omitted term. This statute provides in pertinent part:

"Unless otherwise agreed

"*(a)* payment is due at the time and place at which the buyer is to receive the goods even though the place of shipment is the place of delivery;"

In our view, the language of the two Code provisions is clear and positive. Considered together, we take the two sections to mean that where parties have reached an enforceable agreement for the sale of goods, but omit therefrom the terms of payment, the law will imply, as part of the agreement, that payment is to be made at time of delivery. In this respect the law does not greatly differ from the rule this court laid down years ago. . . .

We do not mean to infer that terms of payment are not of importance under many circumstances, or that parties may not condition an agreement on their being included. However, the facts before us hardly indicate that Hurt and Cloepfil considered the terms of payment to be significant, or of more than passing interest. Hurt testified that while he stated his terms he did not recall Cloepfil's response, while Cloepfil stated that as the two were on the point of leaving, each stated their usual terms and that was as far as it went. The trial court found that only a brief and casual conversation ensued as to payment, and we think that is a valid summation of what took place.

Moreover, it is worthy of note that Martin first mentioned the omission of the terms of payment, as justifying its breach, in a letter written by counsel on September 15, 1966, more than four months after the memorandum was prepared by Hurt. On prior occasions Martin attributed its cancellation of the Springfield understanding to other causes. In its May 24 letter, Martin ascribed its withdrawal of "all verbal quotations" to "restrictions placed on Caterpillar products, accessory suppliers, and other stipulations by the district governing agency." In explaining the meaning of the letter to Cloepfil, Hurt said that Martin was doing work for the Corps of Engineers in the Kansas City and Tulsa districts and did not want to take on additional work with them at this time.

The entire circumstances may well give rise to a suspicion that Martin's present insistence that future negotiations were contemplated concerning terms of payment, is primarily an afterthought, for use as an escape hatch. Doubtless the trial court so considered the excuse in arriving at its findings.

We are aware of Martin's argument that Southwest's letter of May 2, 1966, referring to the sale is evidence that no firm contract had been concluded. Granted that some of the language employed might be subject to that interpretation, the trial court found, on what we deem to be substantial, competent evidence, that an agreement of sale *was* concluded at Springfield. Under our invariable rule those findings are binding upon this court on appeal even though there may have been evidence to the contrary. (See cases in 1 Hatcher's Kansas Digest [Rev.Ed.] Appeal & Error, §§ 507, 508.)

The defendant points particularly to the following portion of the May 2 letter, as interjecting a new and unacceptable term in the agreement made at Springfield.

". . . We are not prepared to make a partial payment at the time of placing of this order. However, we will be able to include 100% of the engine-generator price in our first payment estimate after it is delivered, and only 10% will have to be withheld pending acceptance. Ordinarily this means that suppliers can expect payment of 90% within about thirty days after delivery."

It must be conceded that the terms of payment proposed in Southwest's letter had not been agreed to by Martin. However, we view the proposal as irrelevant. Although terms of payment had not been mutually agreed upon, K.S.A. 84–2–310 supplied the missing terms, i. e., payment on delivery, which thus became part of the agreement already concluded. In legal effect the proposal was no more than one to change the terms of payment implied by law. Since Martin did not accept the change, the proposal had no effect, either as altering or terminating the agreement reached at Springfield. . . . [The court concluded that UCC 2–207 was not applicable.]

We find no error in this case and the judgment of the trial court is affirmed.

NOTE

Questions. The opinion states that "as the trial court found, . . . terms of payment were not agreed upon at the Springfield meeting." Does this mean that the parties did not discuss terms of payment or that they discussed them but disagreed? If it means the latter, is the problem that the terms agreed on by the parties were not sufficiently *definite*? Or is it that they did not *assent* to be bound by the same terms?

Chapter 4

SOME TROUBLE SPOTS IN THE BARGAINING PROCESS

This chapter presents in depth five particularly troublesome problems that arise in connection with the bargaining process. It builds directly on the preceding chapter and involves the application, in more complex situations, of principles developed there.

Section 1 looks into the possibility that, in spite of the objective theory, an offeror may be relieved from a contract on the ground that he made a mistake in formulating his offer. This problem is explored in the context of a mistaken bid by a general contractor. Section 2 takes up the question of when an acceptance of an offer takes effect if the parties are at a distance. This problem is discussed in the context of a contract by mail. Section 3 inquires into when, in the face of the rule that an acceptance must give unequivocal assent to the offer, there is a contract even though the purported acceptance varies the terms of the offer. This problem is taken up in the context of the formation of a contract for the sale of goods under the Uniform Commercial Code. Sections 4 and 5 both deal with the effect of reliance on the revocability of an offer. In Section 4 the offer is one that seeks performance and the context is that of an owner's listing of property with a real estate broker. In Section 5 the offer is one that seeks a promise and the contexts are those of a subcontractor's bid to a general contractor and a franchisor's proposal to a franchisee.

SECTION 1. MISTAKE: BIDS BY GENERAL CONTRACTORS

AMERICAN INSTITUTE OF ARCHITECTS, HANDBOOK OF ARCHITECTURAL PRACTICE III 7.02–7.03 (1958).[a] Under the system of competitive bidding *on private work* each contractor *invited* submits a proposal to execute the work for a definite sum. The list of bidders is subject to the control of owner and architect and can be as limited or open as they may desire. For *public work* any contractor may bid provided he has met prequalification requirements; and can furnish either a certified check in the amount specified or a

a. Reprinted by permission of The American Institute of Architects. Further reproduction is not authorized.

bidder's bond to guarantee his acceptance of and ability to perform the contract if it is awarded him. Competitive bidding at first sight appears to have every advantage. The owner has before him proposals, the desirability of which would seem to be in inverse ratio to their amount. If the list of eligible bidders has been carefully screened he is in position to make the award because the bidders are of approximately equal responsibility and competence. If such screening has not been done, the best builder of a given locality may be pitted against the worst, and the lowest figure is apt to outweigh in the owner's mind the less obvious advantages afforded by the more competent bidder. For public work the law requires an award to the "lowest responsible bidder." [b] This is a condition scarcely capable of exact definition, but it leaves the awarding authority slight chance in court if an award is made to other than the low bidder. Thus the award is not always made to the best and most capable of the bidders.

In competitive bidding each contractor concentrates his effort to keep the price down. This reacts to the benefit of the owner and assures a reasonable and economical purchasing price. This is particularly true of those parts of the work which are performed by the contractor's own forces. For the remainder of the work a *general contractor* must depend upon *subcontractors* whose number varies directly with the complexity and diversity of the work to be bid upon. The *general contractor* invites a number of *subcontractors* to bid to him on the various branches of the work. Normally he has previously done business with most of them or knows their reputations. If he uses their bids in making up his own bid and he is the successful bidder, he is expected to award the subcontracts to those whose bids he has used. The architect may exercise some control over the selection of subcontractors by requiring evidence of their experience, reputation and financial responsibility. . . .

Unless care has been taken to include in the invitation only the *general contractors* with skill, responsibility and integrity, the lowest bid may come from a contractor who does not inquire closely into the honesty or competence of the lowest subbidders, or who discounts their bids in the hope that if awarded the contract, he can shop around among the subbidders and secure a lower price. Such contractors have little interest in the work and their selection increases the burden of the architect by drawing him into difficulties with in-

b. For example, subject to specific exceptions, contracts for military procurement under the Armed Services Procurement Act of 1947 "shall be made by formal advertising in all cases in which the use of such method is feasible and practicable under the existing conditions and circumstances." 10 U.S.C.A. § 2304(a). "Awards shall be made with reasonable promptness by giving written notice to the responsible bidder whose bid conforms to the invitation and will be the most advantageous to the United States, price and other factors considered." 10 U.S.C.A. § 2305(c).

competent *subcontractors* who are operating at a loss. Such results of competitive bidding from unselected and unscreened lists of *general contractors* are detrimental to the best interests of the owner. Fortunately this type of *general contractor* is becoming less common, and for involved and specialized building construction, contractors who are responsible trained engineers and business administrators are essential.

There are several ways by which an owner, unless compelled to advertise for bids, may avoid some of these difficulties of the competitive system:

(a) He may, with the advice of his architect, confine his list of bidders to the most reputable and competent. He should be made to see the importance of a well-chosen list, and be warned against offering a chance to bid to any indifferently qualified contractor in the hope that his bid will not be the lowest. He should be made to understand that the architect can not by supervision force a contractor to build properly, or better than he is able to. When bids are restricted to qualified contractors, the award should be to the lowest bidder.

(b) He may emphasize the clauses in instructions to bidders stating that "in the award of the contract not only the amount of the bid but the reputation and competence of the bidder will be taken into consideration," and that "the owner reserves the right to accept or reject any or all bids." Thus, without a restricted list, the obligation to award the work to the low bidder does not apply.

(c) He may reserve some of the more important branches of the work to be bid upon separately. . . .

(d) He may carry on the whole work under the separate contract system . . . thus attempting through his architect, to perform many of the expert duties of the *general contractor*.

(e) He may avoid the competitive system altogether and let his contract by the "Cost-plus-fee" system as explained below. Both architect and owner should recognize the considerable service of the bidders in estimating the construction cost of a project, and should not reject all bids and proceed to build by means of the separate contract system or by the direct employment of labor and purchase of materials.

NOTES

(1) *"Bid Shopping."* The preceding exerpt suggests the possibility that the general contractor may "shop around among the subbidders and secure a lower price." The construction industry regards such "bid shopping" with opprobrium, whether it occurs before or after the award.[c]

c. The Recommended Guide for Bidding Procedures and Contract Awards published jointly by the American Institute of Architects and the Associated General Contractors of America states:

"It is unethical, unwise and detrimental to the best interests of the

Subcontractors regard it with particular distaste when it occurs after the successful general contractor's bargaining position has been strengthened by the award.

It is objected, on the one hand, that bid shopping results in an undesirable decrease in competition, because subcontractors will pad their bids so that they can lower them later when bid shopping occurs, inflating the general contractor's bid to the ultimate disadvantage of the owner. Is this objection convincing if, as the exerpt suggests, there is a countervailing tendency among general contractors to discount their estimates on subcontractor's bids in anticipation of bid shopping?

It is objected, on the other hand, that bid shopping results in an undesirable increase in competition—that subcontractors will be driven to bid so low that they will be "operating at a loss" and tempted to use substandard work and materials, again to the ultimate disadvantage of the owner. Is this risk greater in the construction industry than in other areas of the economy?

The owner may combat post-award bid shopping by requiring that general contractors list their prospective subcontractors in their bids. This requirement is more common, however, in government than in private contracts. Why do not more private owners require listing if bid shopping is to their ultimate disadvantage? Subcontractors, whose self-interest is clearer, have attempted to combat bid shopping by organizing themselves into "bid depositories," although such concerted efforts raise serious problems under the antitrust law. See, e. g., Mechanical Contractors Bid Depository v. Christiansen, 352 F.2d 817 (10th Cir. 1965), cert. denied, 384 U.S. 918 (1966). They have also tried to combat pre-award bid shopping by waiting until the last possible moment to submit their bids. The resulting haste with which the general contractor must then prepare his own bid may, of course, cause him to make the kinds of errors that gave rise to the next two cases.[d] For more background, see Schultz, The Firm Offer Puzzle: A Study of Business Practice in the Construction Industry, 19 U.Chi. L.Rev. 237 (1952), an illuminating study of bidding practices in the construction industry in Indiana, based on questionaires returned by eighty general contractors and ninety-three subcontractors. For a similar survey in Virginia, see Note, 53 Va.L.Rev. 1720 (1967). See also Schueller, Bid Depositories, 58 Mich.L.Rev. 497 (1960); Notes, 18 U.C.L.A.L.Rev. 389 (1970); 39 N.Y.U.L.Rev. 816 (1964).

construction industry for a general contractor, prior to the award of the Contract, to disclose to the Architect, Owner, or others the amounts of sub-bids or quotations obtained in confidence for the purpose of preparing his bid."

The practice of subcontractors reducing their bids in order to get a subcontract from the successful general contractor is known as "bid chopping" or "bid peddling." See Christiansen v. Mechanical Contractors Bid Depository, 230 F.Supp. 186, 190 n. 10 (D. C.Utah 1964), affirmed in the opinion cited in the text below; Constructors Supply Co. v. Bostrom Sheet Mètal Works, Inc., 291 Minn. 113, 121, 190 N.W.2d 71, 76 (1971).

d. The Guide cited in footnote c supra also states:

"It is imperative that general contractors receive sub-bids sufficiently in advance of the time for submitting their bids to permit adequate analysis and compilation."

(2) *Offer or Not?* Is the owner's invitation for bids or the contractor's bid the offer? By analogy to the rule as to auctions, the contractor's bid is the offer. See Note 2, p. 194 supra. But it is possible to word the invitation so as to make it an offer. In Jenkins Towel Service v. Fidelity-Philadelphia Trust Co., 400 Pa. 98, 161 A.2d 334 (1960), the Supreme Court of Pennsylvania concluded that in the circumstances of that case the following letter from a trustee of real estate was an offer:

> We wish to acknowledge your letter . . . submitting an offer for the purchase of the group of properties . . . As you already know, several offers have been submitted for the purchase of these properties which offers are approximately of the same amount and on the same terms and conditions. . . . In order to give each and every prospect an equal chance and in order to secure the highest and best price . . . it has been decided to ask for sealed bids from all interested parties. It is suggested, therefore, that you forward to this office on or before Wednesday, June 24, 1959, your highest offer for the properties. At that time the bids will be opened and an Agreement of Sale tendered to the highest acceptable bidder provided the offer is in excess of $92,000, cash. [The letter also contained details as to the bid deposit and a provision on broker's commissions to be included in the Agreement of Sale.] The Trustees of course, reserve the right to approve of any and all offers, or to withdraw the properties from the market.

What language from the letter would you rely on in arguing that it was not an offer? What authorities from this chapter would you cite in support of your argument?

CRENSHAW COUNTY HOSPITAL BOARD v. ST. PAUL FIRE & MARINE INSURANCE CO.

United States Court of Appeals, Fifth Circuit, 1969.
411 F.2d 213.

AINSWORTH, Circuit Judge. This appeal is from a judgment in the amount of $10,000 (the maximum amount recoverable under a bid bond) in favor of Crenshaw County Hospital Board, a participant in federal Hill-Burton funds, for damages sustained by it as the result of appellant's alleged breach of the bond conditions. The bond, furnished by appellant St. Paul Fire and Marine Insurance Company as surety for Waller Construction Company, provided for payment to the Hospital Board in the event of a contract award to, and subsequent failure to perform by, its principal.[a]

a. The standard form of bid bond promulgated by the American Institute of Architects obligates the surety to pay "the difference not to exceed the penalty hereof [i. e., the amount of the bond] between the amount specified in said bid and such larger amount for which the Obligee may in good faith contract with another party to perform the Work covered by said bid."

The Hospital Board advertised for public bids in connection with certain construction work. The bid invitation announced that the lowest bid made by a responsible bidder would be accepted, and restricted withdrawal of bids for a period of thirty days after their having been opened. Waller Construction Company submitted its bid in the sum of $285,837.50. The bid opening was attended by W. A. Waller, one of the partners of the construction company. Waller's bid, which was $24,793.50 below the next bid, was announced by the Board to be the low bid. Two Board resolutions were passed accepting the bid of Waller and awarding to it the construction contract. On the following day these resolutions were signed by the Board Chairman and mailed to Waller. In the interim, Mr. Waller discovered that a $35,000 error had been made in the amount of the bid offer as the result of an inadvertent clerical mistake. He informed the Chairman of the Hospital Board of the error that same evening by telephone, requesting that his offer be rejected, and confirmed this by letter the following day. The Hospital Board considered Waller's request but later declined it upon advice of the Director in charge of allocating Hill-Burton funds in Alabama that the Federal Government could furnish a pro rata of the construction cost on the basis of the lowest bid only.[b] Consequently, the Board declined to release Waller from its offer. Waller failed to perform, and the contract was awarded to the next low bidder. The Board then initiated this action against Waller's surety for breach of contract, claiming the difference between the amount shown in the Waller bid and the higher amount it was obliged to pay as a result of Waller's failure to perform, subject to the limitation contained in the bond of $10,000.

Although the District Court specifically found that the bid was entered into in good faith, that the error was inadvertent, committed without gross negligence, and promptly communicated to the Board, it nevertheless held that there was a breach of contract. We affirm.

At the trial the insurance company argued that Waller's request to be excused from the contract was not tantamount to rejecting the contract and that the company stood ready to perform once the formal contract was tendered. The District Court rejected this contention, however, and found that Mr. Waller's conduct and remarks to the Board Chairman that the company "was not able to do, and could not do, the construction for the price of the bid which it had submitted" constituted a breach of the conditions of the bond sued on, which breach was subsequent to acceptance by the Hospital Board of the Waller bid.

b. Could it not be argued that the Director's advice was wrong? Would Waller's have been the "lowest bid" for the purpose of the federal requirement even if Alabama law had afforded him relief on the ground of mistake? Should it make a difference whether the Director's advice was correct?

The resolution adopted by the Board on the day of the bid opening states in pertinent part:

"BE IT FURTHER RESOLVED THAT, Mr. S. T. Windham is hereby authorized to execute said contract after final approval of the project by the State Board of Health and the U. S. Public Health Service and upon official notification thereof from the Bureau of Health Facilities Construction, Alabama State Department of Public Health."

Appellant contends that there was no binding contract inasmuch as acceptance by the Hospital Board of Waller's bid was conditional only, acceptance thereof being predicated upon final approval of the public health agencies, which approval was not forthcoming until approximately three weeks subsequent to Waller's alleged refusal to perform. Appellant urges, as it did at the trial, that under these circumstances the case is controlled by our holding in Peerless Casualty Company v. Housing Authority, 5 Cir., 1955, 228 F.2d 376. The District Court found the *Peerless* case to be inapposite. We agree with the District Court's analysis in distinguishing the two sets of fact.

In *Peerless*, starting with the common law premise that "an offer may be withdrawn at any time before it is accepted," thus aborting the creation of a binding contract, we held that a condition of approval of the Public Housing Administration which was annexed by an offeree to its attempted acceptance had the effect of delaying that acceptance, and that the withdrawal of the offer prevented a subsequent attempted acceptance from creating a contract. Id. at 378, 379. In *Peerless*, a bid bond for construction work had been entered into between Ivey, a building contractor, and its surety Peerless Casualty Company. The Housing Authority of Hazelhurst, Georgia, advertised for bids and stipulated therein that no bid was to be withdrawn without its consent for a period of thirty days subsequent to the opening of bids. Ivey's bid was low, and a motion was adopted by the local Authority to accept the bid. On the same night a clerical mistake was discovered by Ivey which had resulted in the submission of a bid lower than intended. On the following day he sent a telegram to the local Authority advising of the error. There, however, the factual similarity between the two cases ends. In reversing a verdict directed in favor of the Housing Authority, we found that there was no enforceable contract because *acceptance of the bid* was subject to approval of another agency. The resolution was to award the contract to Ivey "subject to the approval of the Public Housing Administration," which agency subsequently approved the acceptance.

In the instant case, the bid was unconditionally accepted by the Board. Subsequent approval by the other agencies of the "*project*" was a formality insofar as the contract between the parties was concerned.

We are not persuaded by appellant's "equitable" defense based on the District Court's findings of good faith and a promptly communicated, inadvertent error committed without gross negligence. While it is true that Alabama recognizes an equitable exception to the general rule that a unilateral error does not avoid a contract, where excessive hardships flow to the party responsible for an error, nevertheless, rescission based on such a mistake may be had only where no prejudice results to the other party. Ex Parte Perusini Const. Co., 1942, 242 Ala. 632, 7 So.2d 576, 578. A review of the evidence substantiates the District Court's finding that Waller's failure to perform in accordance with its bid resulted in damage to the Hospital Board in at least the amount sued for. Equity will also step in where a party through mistake names a consideration entirely disproportionate to the value of the subject involved and the other party is cognizant of the mistake. Townsend v. McCall, 1955, 262 Ala. 554, 80 So.2d 262, 266; Board of Water & Sewer Com'rs of City of Mobile v. Spriggs, 1962, 274 Ala. 155, 146 So.2d 872, 876. The consideration named by Waller was not out of all proportion to the value of the subject. It was $27,000 in excess of the projected cost of the job. An expert who had supervised more than three hundred hospital projects testified that there was not an unusual disparity between the Waller bid and the next lowest bid.[1] Also it appears that Waller had figured $25,000 profit in the job and that some of the subcontractors had offered to cut their prices to help him out of his difficulty. Thus to enforce the contract as made was not unconscionable. Townsend v. McCall, supra; Board of Water & Sewer Com'rs of City of Mobile v. Spriggs, supra; Ex Parte Perusini Const. Co., supra.

Affirmed.

NOTES

(1) *Restatement Second.* The Reporter's Note to Restatement Second, § 153 states that that section "liberalizes the rule stated in former § 503 . . . to take account of the trend of allowing avoidance although only one party has been mistaken."[a] How would the preceding case have been decided under that section?

1. Compare Townsend v. McCall, 1955, 262 Ala. 554, 80 So.2d 262, in which the estimated cost of the project was $350,000, the bid of the contractor claiming justifiable mistake was $183,000 and the next lowest bid was $356,000.

a. The Guide cited in footnote c, p. 251 supra, agrees:

"If, after bids are opened, the low bidder claims he has made an appreciable error in the preparation of his bid and can support such claim with evidence satisfactory to the Owner and the Architect, he should be permitted to withdraw his bid. His bid guarantee should be returned and he should be disqualified from again bidding on the Project in the event additional bids are requested."

It has, however, been argued that "The proof of whether he has made a mistake is so completely within his control and power that the [Owner] is helpless to refute it." Carter, J., dissenting in M. F. Kemper Constr. Co. v. City of Los Angeles, 37 Cal.2d 696, 706–07, 235 P.2d 7, 13 (1951).

(2) *Knowledge of Mistake.* If the offeree knows or has reason to know of the offeror's material mistake when he accepts, the offeror is not bound. "One cannot snap up an offer or bid knowing that it was made in mistake." Tyra v. Cheney, 129 Minn. 428, 152 N.W. 835 (1915). Difficulty arises when the offeror claims that the magnitude of the mistake was such that it should have been apparent from the face of the offer.

Heifetz Metal Crafts, Inc. v. Peter Kiewit Sons' Co., 264 F.2d 435 (8th Cir. 1959), is a good example. There Kiewit was preparing a bid for the construction of a hospital and Heifetz offered to do the kitchen work for $99,500, $52,000 less than Kiewit's next lowest quotation. Kiewit lowered his bid by $52,000, which made it $17,942,200, the lowest by $9,000. After Kiewit was awarded the contract and had accepted the Heifetz offer, Heifetz discovered that in preparing its quotation it had overlooked some subsidiary kitchen installations required by the plans. It sought rescission and argued that since its quotation was one-third less than the next lowest, Kiewit should have realized that there had been a mistake. The court rejected this contention and held that the contract was enforceable. It relied upon testimony by Kiewit's employees that they were ignorant of the mistake, upon Kiewit's lack of familiarity with the kitchen equipment field, and upon "testimony indicating that at times some contractor would have a special reason for desiring to obtain a particular job and would submit a figure controlled by that consideration." It noted that "the figures submitted by subcontractors on the electrical work for the project has varied from $1,400,000 to $1,850,000 and on the lathing and plastering work from $672,000 to $1,028,000; and the 'mechanical spread' had been between $3,647,000 and $6,000,000."

For a case holding that a bid of $7,751.51 for a government surplus lathe was not so out of line as to create a "suspicion of error," where the other bids were $3,441, $2,429.99, $1,511 and $288, see Wender Presses v. United States, 343 F.2d 961 (Ct.Cl.1965). Would it make a difference, in cases such as those cited above, if the offeree had asked the offeror to check his bid for a possible mistake? See Appleway Leasing, Inc. v. Tomlinson Dairy Farms, Inc., 22 Wash.App. 781, 591 P.2d 1220 (1979); Illustration 2 to Restatement Second, § 157. See also the next case.

Is it of any significance that a general contractor will sometimes pass over a low bid to accept one from a subcontractor with which he has a personal or business connection, and that subcontractors sometimes deliberately make losing bids to break up such combinations? Is it of any significance that subcontractors sometimes bid low in the expectation that changes will later be made to provide for profitable extra work?

In the rare case where the offeree not only knows or has reason to know that the offeror has made a mistake, but knows or has reason to know exactly what the mistake is (as where a decimal point has been misplaced), can the offeror hold the offeree, who has "snapped up" his offer, to a contract on the terms that the offer *would* have contained had the mistake not been made? Would the offeror be in a better position to make this argument in the unlikely event that the mistake was not discovered until performance had proceeded so far that rescission was no longer possible? For such a rare case in which the court gave an affirmative answer, see Chernick v. United States, 372 F.2d 492 (Ct.Cl.1967).

(2) *Problem.* Lee Calan Imports instructed the Chicago Sun-Times to advertise a used Volvo for sale at $1,795. The Sun-Times, by mistake, advertised it for $1,095. O'Brien went to look at the car and said that he wanted to buy it for $1,095. The salesman refused to sell it at the erroneous price. Is Lee Calan liable to O'Brien? Is the Sun-Times liable to Lee Calan? See O'Keefe v. Lee Calan Imports, 128 Ill.App.2d 410, 262 N.E.2d 758 (1970).

ELSINORE UNION ELEMENTARY SCHOOL DIST. v. KASTORFF

Supreme Court of California, 1960.
54 Cal.2d 380, 6 Cal.Rptr. 1, 353 P.2d 713.

SCHAUER, Justice. Defendants, who are a building contractor and his surety, appeal from an adverse judgment in this action by plaintiff school district to recover damages allegedly resulting when defendant Kastorff, the contractor, refused to execute a building contract pursuant to his previously submitted bid to make certain additions to plaintiff's school buildings. We have concluded that because of an honest clerical error in the bid and defendant's subsequent prompt rescission he was not obliged to execute the contract, and that the judgment should therefore be reversed.

Pursuant to plaintiff's call for bids, defendant Kastorff secured a copy of the plans and specifications of the proposed additions to plaintiff's school buildings and proceeded to prepare a bid to be submitted by the deadline hour of 8 p. m., August 12, 1952, at Elsinore, California. Kastorff testified that in preparing his bid he employed worksheets upon which he entered bids of various subcontractors for such portions of the work as they were to do, and that to reach the final total of his own bid for the work he carried into the right-hand column of the work sheets the amounts of the respective sub bids which he intended to accept and then added those amounts to the cost of the work which he would do himself rather than through a subcontractor; that there is "a custom among subcontractors, in bidding on jobs such as this, to delay giving . . . . their bids until the very last moment"; that the first sub bid for plumbing was in the amount of $9,285 and he had received it "the afternoon of the bid-opening," but later that afternoon when "the time was drawing close for me to get my bids together and get over to Elsinore" (from his home in San Juan Capistrano) he received a $6,500 bid for the plumbing. Erroneously thinking he had entered the $9,285 plumbing bid in his total column and had included that sum in his total bid and realizing that the second plumbing bid was nearly $3,000 less than the first, Kastorff then deducted $3,000 from the total amount of his bid and entered the resulting total of $89,994 on the bid form as his bid for the school construction. Thus the total included no allowance whatsoever for the plumbing work.

Kastorff then proceeded to Elsinore and deposited his bid with plaintiff. When the bids were opened shortly after 8 p. m. that evening, it was discovered that of the five bids submitted that of Kastorff was some $11,306 less than the next lowest bid. The school superintendent and the four school board members present thereupon asked Kastorff whether he was sure his figures were correct, Kastorff stepped out into the hall to check with the person who had assisted in doing the clerical work on the bid, and a few minutes later returned and stated that the figures were correct. He testified that he did not have his worksheets or other papers with him to check against at the time. The board thereupon, on August 12, 1952, voted to award Kastorff the contract.

The next morning Kastorff checked his worksheets and promptly discovered his error. He immediately drove to the Los Angeles office of the firm of architects which had prepared the plans and specifications for plaintiff, and there saw Mr. Rendon. Mr. Rendon testified that Kastorff "had his maps and estimate work-sheets of the project, and indicated to me that he had failed to carry across the amount of dollars for the plumbing work. It was on the sheet, but not in the total sheet. We examined that evidence, and in our opinion we felt that he had made a clerical error in compiling his bill. . . . In other words, he had put down a figure, but didn't carry it out to the 'total' column when he totaled his column to make up his bid. . . . He exhibited . . . at that time . . . his worksheets from which he had made up his bid." That same morning (August 13) Rendon telephoned the school superintendent and informed him of the error and of its nature and that Kastorff asked to be released from his bid. On August 14 Kastorff wrote a letter to the school board explaining his error and again requesting that he be permitted to withdraw his bid. On August 15, after receiving Kastorff's letter, the board held a special meeting and voted not to grant his request. Thereafter, on August 28, *written notification* was given to Kastorff of award of the contract to him.[1] Subsequently plaintiff submitted to Kastorff a contract to be signed in accordance with his bid, and on September 8, 1952, Kastorff returned the contract to plaintiff with a letter again explaining his error and asking the board to reconsider his request for withdrawal of his bid.

Plaintiff thereafter received additional bids to do the subject construction; let the contract to the lowest bidder, in the amount of $102,900; and brought this action seeking to recover from Kastorff the $12,906 difference between that amount and the amount Kastorff

1. On the bid form, provided by plaintiff, the bidder agreed "that if he is notified of the acceptance of the proposal within forty-five (45) days from the time set for the opening of bids, he will execute and deliver to you within five (5) days after having received *written notification* a contract as called for in the 'Notice to Contractors.'" (Italics added.)

had bid.[2] Recovery of $4,499.60 is also sought against Kastorff's surety under the terms of the bond posted with his bid.

Defendants in their answer to the complaint pleaded, among other things, that Kastorff had made an honest error in compiling his bid; that "he thought he was bidding, and intended to bid, $9500.00 more making a total of $99,494.00 as his bid"; that upon discovering his error he had promptly notified plaintiff and rescinded the $89,994 bid. The trial court found that it was true that Kastorff made up a bid sheet, which was introduced in evidence; that the subcontractor's bids thereupon indicated were those received by Kastorff; that he "had 16 subcontracting bids to ascertain from 31 which were submitted"; and that Kastorff had neglected to carry over from the left-hand column on the bid sheet to the right-hand column on the sheet a portion of the plumbing (and heating) subcontractor's bid. Despite the uncontradicted evidence related hereinabove, including that of plaintiff's architect and of its school superintendent, both of whom testified as plaintiff's witnesses, the court further found, however, that "it is not true that the right hand column of figures was totaled for the purpose of arriving at the total bid to be submitted by E. J. Kastorff. . . . . It cannot be ascertained from the evidence for what purpose the total of the right hand column of figures on the bid sheet was used nor can it be ascertained from the evidence for what purpose the three bid sheets were used in arriving at the total bid." And although finding that "on or about August 15, 1952," plaintiff received Kastorff's letter of August 14 explaining that he "made an error of omitting from my bid the item of Plumbing," the court also found that "It is not true that plaintiff knew at any time that defendant Kastorff's bid was intended to be other than $89,994.00 . . . . . It is not true that the plaintiff knew at the time it requested the execution of the contract by defendant Kastorff that he had withdrawn his bid because of an honest error in the compilation thereof. It is not true that plaintiff had notice of an error in the compilation of the bid by defendant Kastorff and tried nevertheless to take advantage of defendant Kastorff by forcing him to enter a contract on the basis of a bid he had withdrawn. . . . . It is not true that it would be either inequitable or unjust to require defendant Kastorff to perform the contract awarded to him for the sum of $89,994.00, and it is not true that he actually intended to bid for said work the sum of $99,494.00." [3] Judgment was given for plaintiff in the amounts sought, and this appeal by defendants followed.

2. Plaintiff's original published call for bids contained the following statement: "No Bidder may withdraw his bid for a period of forty-five (45) days after the date set for the opening thereof." Whether upon Kastorff's rescission for good cause prior to expiration of the 45 day period plaintiff could have accepted the next lowest bid is not an issue before us.

3. Other findings that Kastorff "in the company of his wife and another couple left San Juan Capistrano for Elsinore . . . at 6:00 P.M. on August 12, 1952, a distance of 34 miles by

In reliance upon M. F. Kemper Const. Co. v. City of Los Angeles (1951), 37 Cal.2d 696, 235 P.2d 7, and Lemoge Electric v. County of San Mateo (1956), 46 Cal.2d 659, 662, 664, 297 P.2d 638, defendants urged that where, as defendants claim is the situation here, a contractor makes a clerical error in computing a bid on a public work he is entitled to rescind.

In the Kemper case one item on a worksheet in the amount of $301,769 was inadvertently omitted by the contractor from the final tabulation sheet and was overlooked in computing the total amount of a bid to do certain construction work for the defendant city. The error was caused by the fact that the men preparing the bid were exhausted after working long hours under pressure. When the bids were opened it was found that plaintiff's bid was $780,305, and the next lowest bid was $1,049,592. Plaintiff discovered its error several hours later and immediately notified a member of defendant's board of public works of its mistake in omitting one item while preparing the final accumulation of figures for its bid. Two days later it explained its mistake to the board and withdrew its bid. A few days later it submitted to the board evidence which showed the unintentional omission of the $301,769 item. The board nevertheless passed a resolution accepting plaintiff's erroneous bid of $780,305, and plaintiff refused to enter into a written contract at that figure. The board then awarded the contract to the next lowest bidder, the city demanded forfeiture of plaintiff's bid bond, and plaintiff brought action to cancel its bid and obtain discharge of the bond. The trial court found that the bid had been submitted as the result of an excusable and honest mistake of a material and fundamental character, that plaintiff company had not been negligent in preparing the proposal, that it had acted promptly to notify the board of the mistake and to rescind the bid, and that the board had accepted the bid with knowledge of the error. The court further found and concluded that it would be unconscionable to require the company to perform for the amount of the bid, that no intervening rights had accrued, and that the city had suffered no damage or prejudice.

On appeal by the city this court affirmed, stating the following applicable rules (at pages 700–703 of 37 Cal.2d, at pages 10, 11 of 235 P.2d):

"Once opened and declared, the company's bid was in the nature of an irrevocable option, a contract right of which the city could not be deprived without its consent unless the requirements for rescission were satisfied. [Citations.] . . . the city had actual notice of the error in the estimates before it attempted to accept the bid, and

way of California State Highway . . . Kastorff had ample time and opportunity after receiving his last subcontractor's bid to extend the figures on his bid sheet from one column to the other, to check and recheck his bid sheet figures and to take his papers to Elsinore and to check them there prior to close of receipt of bids at 8:00 P.M."

knowledge by one party that the other is acting under mistake is treated as equivalent to mutual mistake for purposes of rescission. [Citations.] Relief from mistaken bids is consistently allowed where one party knows or has reason to know of the other's error and the requirements for rescission are fulfilled. [Citations.]

"Rescission may be had for mistake of fact if the mistake is material to the contract and was not the result of neglect of a legal duty, if enforcement of the contract as made would be unconscionable, and if the other party can be placed in statu quo. [Citations.] In addition, the party seeking relief must give prompt notice of his election to rescind and must restore or offer to restore to the other party everything of value which he has received under the contract. [Citations.]

"Omission of the $301,769 item from the company's bid was, of course, a material mistake. . . . [E]ven if we assume that the error was due to some carelessness, it does not follow that the company is without remedy. Civil Code section 1577, which defines mistake of facts for which relief may be allowed, describes it as one not caused by 'the neglect of a legal duty' on the part of the person making the mistake. It has been recognized numerous times that not all carelessness constitutes a 'neglect of legal duty' within the meaning of the section. [Citations.] On facts very similar to those in the present case, courts of other jurisdictions have stated that there was no culpable negligence and have granted relief from erroneous bids. [Citations.] The type of error here involved is one which will sometimes occur in the conduct of reasonable and cautious businessmen, and, under all the circumstances, we cannot say as a matter of law that it constituted a neglect of legal duty such as would bar the right to equitable relief.

"The evidence clearly supports the conclusion that it would be unconscionable to hold the company to its bid at the mistaken figure. The city had knowledge before the bid was accepted that the company had made a clerical error which resulted in the omission of an item amounting to nearly one third of the amount intended to be bid, and, under all the circumstances, it appears that it would be unjust and unfair to permit the city to take advantage of the company's mistake. There is no reason for denying relief on the ground that the city cannot be restored to status quo. It had ample time in which to award the contract without readvertising, the contract was actually awarded to the next lowest bidder, and the city will not be heard to complain that it cannot be placed in statu quo because it will not have the benefit of an inequitable bargain. [Citations.] Finally, the company gave notice promptly upon discovering the facts entitling it to rescind, and no offer of restoration was necessary because it had received nothing of value which it could restore. [Citation.] We are satisfied that all the requirements for rescission have been met."

In the Lemoge case (Lemoge Electric v. County of San Mateo (1956), supra, 46 Cal.2d 659, 662, 664), 297 P.2d 638, the facts were similar to those in Kemper, except that plaintiff Lemoge did not attempt to rescind but instead, after discovering and informing defendant of inadvertent clerical error in the bid, entered into a formal contract with defendant on the terms specified in the erroneous bid, performed the required work, and then sued for reformation. Although this court affirmed the trial court's determination that plaintiff was not, under the circumstances, entitled to have the contract reformed, we also reaffirmed the rule that "Once opened and declared, plaintiff's bid was in the nature of an irrevocable option, a contract right of which defendant could not be deprived without its consent unless the requirements for rescission were satisfied. [Citation.] Plaintiff then had the right to rescind, and it could have done so without incurring any liability on its bond." . . .

Further, we are persuaded that the trial court's view, as expressed in the finding set forth in the margin,[4] that "Kastorff had ample time and opportunity after receiving his last subcontractor's bid" to complete and check his final bid, does not convict Kastorff of that "neglect of legal duty" which would preclude his being relieved from the inadvertent clerical error of omitting from his bid the cost of the plumbing. (See Civ.Code, § 1577; M. F. Kemper Const. Co. v. City of Los Angeles (1951), supra, 37 Cal.2d 696, 702[6], 235 P.2d 7.) Neither should he be denied relief from an unfair, inequitable, and unintended bargain simply because, in response to inquiry from the board when his bid was discovered to be much the lowest submitted, he informed the board, after checking with his clerical assistant, that the bid was correct. . . .

If the situations of the parties were reversed and plaintiff and Kastorff had even executed a formal written contract (by contrast with the preliminary bid offer and acceptance) calling for a fixed sum payment to Kastorff large enough to include a reasonable charge for plumbing but inadvertently through the *district's* clerical error omitting a mutually intended provision requiring Kastorff to furnish and install plumbing, we have no doubt but that the district would demand and expect reformation or rescission. In the case before us the district expected Kastorff to furnish and install plumbing; surely it must also have understood that he intended to, and that his bid did, include a charge for such plumbing. The omission of any such charge was as unexpected by the board as it was unintended by Kastorff. Under the circumstances the "bargain" for which the board presses (which action we, of course, assume to be impelled by advice of counsel and a strict concept of official duty) appears too sharp for law and equity to sustain.

4. See footnote 3, supra.

Plaintiff suggests that in any event the amount of the plumbing bid omitted from the total was immaterial. The bid as submitted was in the sum of $89,994, and whether the sum for the omitted plumbing was $6,500 or $9,285 (the two sub bids), the omission of such a sum is plainly material to the total. In Lemoge (Lemoge Electric v. County of San Mateo (1956), supra, 46 Cal.2d 659, 661–662, 297 P.2d 638) the error which it was declared would have entitled plaintiff to rescind was the listing of the cost of certain materials as $104.52, rather than $10,452, in a total bid of $172,421. Thus the percentage of error here was larger than in Lemoge, and was plainly material.

The judgment is reversed.[a]

NOTES

(1) *Revocability.* Ordinarily a general contractor's bid on a construction contract is an offer that is revocable before acceptance. Where, however, the owner is a state or local government, statutes or ordinances usually provide that the general contractor may not withdraw his bid after the bids have been opened. Where the owner is the federal government, the same result has been reached on the basis of federal regulation. See Keys, Consideration Reconsidered—The Problem of the Withdrawn Bid, 10 Stan. L.Rev. 441, 448–53 (1958). Is there any reason to treat a bid made subject to such a rule any differently from a bid that has been accepted?

(2) *"Clerical" Errors.* Courts that have granted bidders relief for mistake have often characterized the mistake as "clerical" rather than as one in "judgment." What is the justification for such a distinction? See Restatement Second, § 154 and Illustration 6. It has been argued that from the bidder's standpoint, "his mistake is far more inexcusable when it is in computation rather than judgment. School boys have been disciplined for stupidity in that field." Carter, J., dissenting in M. F. Kemper Constr. Co. v. City of Los Angeles, 37 Cal.2d 696, 710, 235 P.2d 7, 15 (1951).

(3) *Bid Bonds and Deposits.* If the general contractor retains the power to revoke his offer, that power cannot be simply circumvented by the

a. In 1971, California enacted a statute under which:

> A bidder [on a public contract] shall not be relieved of his bid unless by consent of the awarding authority nor shall any change be made in his bid because of mistake, but he may bring an action against the public entity in a court of competent jurisdiction in the county in which the bids were opened for the recovery of the amount forfeited, without interest or costs.
>
> . . .

The bidder shall establish to the satisfaction of the court that:

> (a) A mistake was made.
>
> (b) He gave the public entity written notice within five days after the opening of the bids of the mistake, specifying in the notice in detail how the mistake occurred.
>
> (c) The mistake made the bid materially different than he intended it to be.
>
> (d) The mistake was made in filling out the bid and not due to error in judgment or to carelessness in inspecting the site of the work, or in reading the plans or specifications.

Cal. Gov't Code §§ 4201, 4203.

use of a bid bond. For, if the general contractor is free to withdraw his bid, the surety on his bid bond incurs no liability. A deposit may stand on a different footing. Comment a to Restatement Second, § 44 states that subject to the rules governing liquidated damages and penalties (discussed in Chapter 6, Section 4 infra): "The agreement may be valid as a provision for liquidated damages, or as a provision of security for the payment of actual damages. In either case, the offer is treated as irrevocable for the purpose of determining rights in the deposit, but the offeror's power of revocation is not otherwise impaired. In cases of bids on government contracts, statutes often authorize forfeiture without regard to the distinction between liquidated damages and penalty." Having a deposit also gives the owner an obvious practical advantage.

(4) *The Case of the Leftover Labels.* Alan Tromer, vice-president of Reed's Photo Mart began filling out a purchase order for five different kinds of labels which Reed's desired to buy from the Monarch Marking System Company. After writing "2M" to indicate two thousand in the quantity column for each of the first four, he was interrupted by a customer. When he later finished the order, he mistakenly wrote "4MM" rather than "4M" in the quantity column for the fifth kind. The purchase order provided for delivery "At once" and for shipment by parcel post. In accord with the usage in the label trade, Monarch's representative understood "4MM" to mean four million. He had the first four kinds printed and shipped immediately by parcel post and arranged for special printing and shipment of the four million labels of the fifth kind. Since they weighed 622 pounds, shipment by parcel post was impractical. When the four million labels were delivered by motor freight, Tromer refused to accept them and called Monarch to say that "a terrible mistake had been made." Monarch sued Reed's for the price of the labels, $2,680. The jury refused to find that Monarch knew of Tromer's mistake, and the trial court gave judgment for Monarch. On appeal by Reed's, the Court of Civil Appeals reversed because the trial court had not asked the jury whether Monarch should have known of the mistake. Monarch appealed on the ground that this was immaterial. *Held:* Reversed and judgment of trial court affirmed. "The mistake was a unilateral one; it was made by Reed's, and Monarch fully performed its part of the contract. The Texas rule has long been that relief from a unilateral mistake depends upon the ability of the party mistaken to put the other party into the same situation as he was prior to the transaction in question. . . . We have in this case a fully executed contract on the part of Monarch and the record is devoid of proof of any effort on the part of Reed's to restore Monarch to the status quo even to the extent that circumstances would permit." Monarch Marking System Co. v. Reed's Photo Mart, 485 S.W.2d 905 (Tex.1972).

SECTION 2. THE "MAILBOX RULE": CONTRACTS BY CORRESPONDENCE

This subsection deals with the problems that arise when distant parties bargain by mail, although similar problems arise when the parties bargain by telegraph or similar means of communication.

Suppose, for example, that one party has sent the other an offer, and that the offeree has dispatched an acceptance which has not yet been received by the offeror. Is is too late for the offeror to change his mind and revoke the offer? Is it too late for the offeree to change his mind and reject the offer? And is there a contract if the acceptance is lost and is never received by the offeror?

As will be seen, the tendency of the common law has been to answer such questions as these on the assumption that dispatch of the acceptance is ordinarily the crucial point at which the contract is made—after which the offeror's power to revoke is terminated, the offeree's power to reject is ended, and the risks of transmission are on the offeror. Because the early cases involved acceptance by post, this came to be known as the "mailbox rule." As will also be seen, the wisdom of making so many consequences flow from the same event is at least questionable.

POWER TO REVOKE

In 1818 the Court of King's Bench decided one of the most celebrated cases in the field of contracts, Adams v. Lindsell, 1 B. & Ald. 681, 106 Eng.Rep. 250 (K.B.1818). A firm of wool dealers had mailed an offer to sell "eight hundred tods of wether fleeces" to a firm of woolen manufacturers and the manufacturers had put a letter of acceptance in the post. While this letter was in transit, the dealers attempted to revoke their offer and sold the wool to another buyer.[a] When the manufacturers sued for breach of contract, the dealers argued that, "Till the plaintiffs' answer was actually received, there could be no binding contract between the parties." The court rejected this argument and upheld recovery.

> The Court said, that if that were so, no contract could ever be completed by the post. For if the defendants were not bound by their offer when accepted by the plaintiffs till the answer was received, then the plaintiffs ought not to be bound till after they had received the notification that the defendants had received their answer and assented to it. And so it

a. One of the curious features of the case is that although the dealers had sold the wool while the letter of acceptance was in transit, they had taken no steps to notify the manufacturers of their revocation until after it had been received. It would seem, therefore, under cases like Dickinson v. Dodds, p. 218, supra, that revocation had come too late in any event. The explanation appears to lie in Cooke v. Oxley, 3 T.R. 653, 100 Eng. Rep. 785 (K.B.1790), a confusing relic of the subjective theory of contracts, which evidently stood for the proposition that a person after having offered to sell goods could by a mere change of mind, as by a sale to another, prevent acceptance by the offeree. At the hearing in Dickinson v. Dodds, Cooke v. Oxley was distinguished as going solely on the pleadings by Vice Chancellor Bacon, who found it "not so clearly and satisfactorily reported as might be desired."

might go on ad infinitum. The defendants must be considered in law as making, during every instant of the time their letter was traveling, the same identical offer to the plaintiffs; and then the contract is completed by the acceptance of it by the latter.

The overwhelming weight of authority in the United States supports the "mailbox rule" of Adams v. Lindsell. See Restatement Second, § 63. The court's reasoning, however, is less than convincing. The Restatement Second, in Comment a to § 63 gives a different rationale.

> It is often said that an offeror who makes an offer by mail makes the post office his agent to receive the acceptance, or that the mailing of a letter of acceptance puts it irrevocably out of the offeree's control. Under United States postal regulations, however, the sender of a letter has long had the power to stop delivery and reclaim the letter. A better explanation of the rule that the acceptance takes effect on dispatch is that the offeree needs a dependable basis for his decision whether to accept. In many legal systems such a basis is provided by a general rule that an offer is irrevocable unless it provides otherwise. [See p. 214 supra.] The common law provides such a basis through the rule that a revocation of an offer is ineffective if received after an acceptance has been properly dispatched.

The following case is a rare departure from the prevailing rule.

NOTE

The Case of Protester's Postmark. On March 30, 1978, the adjutant general of the State of New Hampshire received an application from R. R. Cushing, Jr. for the use of the Portsmouth armory to hold a dance on the evening of April 29. On March 31, the adjutant general mailed a signed contract offer to Cushing agreeing to rent the armory for that evening. It required acceptance by the renter signing a copy of the agreement and returning it within five days of receipt. Cushing, who was acting on behalf of the Portsmouth Clamshell Alliance, an anti-nuclear group, received it and signed it on Monday, April 3. At 6:30 p.m. on Tuesday, Cushing received a telephone call from the adjutant general advising him that Governor Meldrim Thompson, Jr. had ordered that the offer be withdrawn. Cushing replied that he had already signed the contract. On April 5, the adjutant general mailed a written confirmation of the withdrawal. On April 6, he received by mail the signed contract dated April 3, postmarked April 5. Cushing and other members of the Alliance sued Thompson and the adjutant general seeking specific performance. From a grant of specific performance, the defendants appealed. Held: Affirmed. "Neither party challenges the applicable law. . . . Withdrawal of the offer is ineffectual once the offer has been accepted by posting in the mail. . . . Plaintiffs introduced the sworn affidavit of Mr. Cushing in which he stated that on April

3, he executed the contract and placed it in the outbox for mailing. Moreover plaintiffs' counsel represented to the court that it was customary office practice for outgoing letters to be picked up from the outbox daily and put in the U.S. mail. No testimony was submitted in this informal hearing, and the basis for the court's order appears to be in part counsels' representations, a procedure which was not objected to by the parties. . . . Thus the representation that it was customary office procedure for the letters to be sent out the same day that they are placed in the office outbox, together with the affidavit, supported the implied finding that the completed contract was mailed before the attempted revocation. . . . Because there is evidence to support it, this court cannot say as a matter of law that the trial court's finding that there was a binding contract is clearly erroneous, and therefore it must stand." Cushing v. Thompson, 118 N.H. 292, 308, 386 A.2d 805, 807 (1978).

RHODE ISLAND TOOL CO. v. UNITED STATES

United States Court of Claims, 1955.
130 Ct.Cl. 698, 128 F.Supp. 417.

[The United States invited bids from suppliers for a number of items. Its invitation read: "The successful bidder will *receive* Notice of Award at the earliest possible date, and such Award will *thereupon* constitute a binding contract between the bidder and the Government without further action on the part of the bidder." (Italics supplied by the court.) On September 10, Tool Company submitted a bid to supply fifteen lots of bolts, but in calculating the bid its sales manager failed to notice that the specifications for three of the lots had been changed from cheaper stud bolts to more expensive machine bolts, and mistakenly based the bid on the cost of stud bolts. On October 4 the government mailed to Tool Company an acceptance of its bid as to these three lots. On the same day Tool Company, having discovered its mistake, telephoned the government's representative withdrawing its bid as to these lots. The record did not show whether the government's acceptance had been mailed at this time, but the acceptance was not received by Tool Company until after the revocation. At the government's insistence Tool Company supplied machine bolts and then sued for an additional $1,640.60 over its bid.]

JONES, Chief Justice. . . . Under the old post office regulations when a letter was deposited in the mail the sender lost all control of it. It was irrevocably on its way. After its deposit in the mail the post office became, in effect, the agent of the addressee. Naturally the authorities held that the acceptance in any contract became final when it was deposited in the post office, since the sender had lost control of the letter at that time. That was the final act in consummating the agreement.

But some years ago[a] the United States Postal authorities completely changed the regulation [to permit the sender to withdraw his letter from the mail]. When this new regulation became effective, the entire picture was changed. The sender now does not lose control of the letter the moment it is deposited in the post office, but retains the right of control up to the time of delivery. The acceptance, therefore, is not final until the letter reaches destination, since the sender has the absolute right of withdrawal from the post office, and even the right to have the postmaster at the delivery point return the letter at any time before actual delivery. We have so held. Dick v. United States, 82 F.Supp. 326, 113 Ct.Cl. 94, and authorities therein cited. . . .

Does any one believe that if the mistake had been the other way, that is, if the machine bolts had been listed first and the stud bolts as later items, and that through oversight the defendant had mailed an acceptance for too high a price and the same day had wired withdrawing and cancelling the acceptance before it left the sending post office the defendant would nevertheless have been held to an excessive price? Or again, if after mailing such an acceptance the defendant, discovering its mistake, had gone to the sending post office and withdrawn the letter, the plaintiff on hearing of it, could have enforced an excessive contract on the ground that the acceptance actually had been posted and became final and enforceable, notwithstanding its withdrawal and nondelivery? We cannot conceive of such an unjust enforcement. No, under the new regulation, the Post Office Department becomes, in effect, the agency of the sender until actual delivery.

We are living in a time of change. The theories of yesterday, proved by practice today, give way to the improvements of tomorrow. To apply an outmoded formula is not only unjust, it runs counter to the whole stream of human experience. It is like insisting on an oxcart as the official means of transportation in the age of the automobile. The cart served a useful purpose in its day, but is now a museum piece. The old rule was established before Morse invented the telegraph as a means of communication. Commerce must have a breaking point upon which it may rely for the completion of a contract. At that time no faster mode of communication was known. But in the light of the faster means of communication the Post Office Department wisely changed the rule. The reason for the old rule had disappeared. This does not change any principle, it simply changes the practice to suit the changed conditions, but leaves unchanged the

a. Postal Laws and Regulations had been changed as early as 1885 to permit the sender of a letter to have it returned even after it had left the mailing post office by application to the post master of that office. United States Official Postal Guide 697 (1885). The practical problems of attempting to retrieve a letter are suggested in Macneil, Time of Acceptance: Too Many Problems for a Single Rule, 112 U.Pa.L.Rev. 947, 959 (1964).

principle of finality, which is just as definite as ever, though transferred to a different point by the new regulation. . . .

Manifestly a mistake was made. The defendant is not injured by permitting its correction. It only forbids defendant's unjust enrichment by preventing its taking technical advantage of an evident mistake.

Plaintiff is allowed to recover its actual losses, if any, in furnishing the machine bolts, limited, however, to the difference between its bid and that of the next lowest bidder on these particular items, that amount being not a yardstick, but a ceiling on any losses it may be able to prove; or, in the alternative, the reasonable value of the items furnished, subject to the same limitation.

The case is remanded to a commissioner of this court for the purpose of hearing evidence as to such losses, if any, or as to the reasonable value of the items furnished.

It is so ordered.

[LARAMORE and LITTLETON concurred. WHITAKER dissented in an opinion in which MADDEN concurred.]

NOTES

(1) *Mistake and the "Mailbox Rule."* How does this case differ from the Kastorff case, p. 258 supra? Could the court have based its decision on a narrower ground than the change in postal regulations? Would Rhode Island Tool have prevailed if it had made no mistake but had simply decided that it could get a better price elsewhere? See Morrison v. Thoelke, 155 So.2d 889 (Fla.App.1963). How great is the danger that an offeror, in the position of Rhode Island Tool, will make a false claim of mistake? Is it significant in this regard that Rhode Island Tool's bid was irrevocable (see Note 1, p. 264 supra)? See Macneil, Time of Acceptance: Too Many Problems for a Single Rule, 112 U.Pa.L.Rev. 947, 955–56 (1964).

(2) *Limits of the "Mailbox Rule."* The Restatement Second, § 63 makes the mailbox rule applicable only where the acceptance is "made in a manner and by a medium invited by [the] offer." See also UCC 2–206(1)(a). In Henthorn v. Fraser, [1892] 2 Ch. 27, the offeror at its office in Liverpool, handed to the offeree an offer to sell land in Birkenhead, where the offeree resided. The offeree took the offer to Birkenhead and posted an acceptance from there. While it was in transit, he received a letter from the offeror saying that the offer was "cancelled." The court held that the "mailbox rule" applied and there was a contract, even though the offer had not been by post. "Where the circumstances are such that it must have been within the contemplation of the parties that, according to the ordinary usages of mankind, the post might be used as a means of communicating the acceptance of an offer, the acceptance is complete as soon as it is posted." What of an offer by mail and an acceptance by telegram? An offer by telegram and an acceptance by mail?

(3) *Revocation and the "Mailbox Rule."* As might be supposed from such cases as Dickinson v. Dodds, p. 218 supra, a revocation is effective

only on receipt, not on dispatch. See Restatement Second § 42. The leading case is Byrne v. Van Tienhoven, 5 C.P.D. 344 (1880), in which the court rejected the argument that the rule laid down in Adams v. Lindsell for acceptance should be applied to revocation as well. "If [this] contention were to prevail no person who had received an offer by post and had accepted it would know his position until he had waited such a time as to be quite sure that a letter withdrawing the offer had not been posted before his acceptance of it." Nevertheless, California, Montana, North Dakota and South Dakota have statutes providing that a revocation as well as an acceptance is effective when dispatched.

(4) *Counselling.* Could the offeror avoid the "mailbox rule" and preserve his power of revocation until his receipt of the acceptance? Could he make his revocation effective on dispatch? How? That many of the problems in this subsection can be disposed of by careful draftsmanship is suggested in Farnsworth, Formation of International Sales Contracts: Three Attempts at Unification, 110 U.Pa.L.Rev. 305 (1962).

POWER TO REJECT

It has generally been assumed that the "mailbox rule," laid down by Adams v. Lindsell in connection with the termination of the offeror's power to revoke, applies as well in connection with the termination of the offeree's power to reject. In other words, once the offeree has dispatched an acceptance, it is too late for him to change his mind and reject the offer. See Restatement Second, § 63. This is, of course, not a necessary assumption, since it would be possible to frame a rule which would deprive the offeror of his power to revoke his offer upon dispatch of the acceptance by the offeree, but leave the offeree free to reject the offer, at least as long as the offeror receives the rejection before he receives the acceptance. The two rules can best be contrasted by considering the case of the overtaking rejection.

Suppose that on Monday Buyer receives by mail an offer from Seller of goods. On Tuesday Buyer mails Seller a letter of acceptance which arrives on Friday. On Wednesday Buyer calls Seller and tells him that he wants to revoke his acceptance and reject the offer. If the "mailbox rule" is applied, it is too late for Buyer to change his mind and Seller can hold him to a contract. If the other rule is applied, Buyer remains free to change his mind while the letter is in transit, and Seller cannot hold him to a contract. The disadvantage of this rule is that while the letter is in transit, although Seller is unable to revoke, Buyer is free to watch the market and speculate, having in effect an "option contract" for that period.

But does not the "mailbox rule" also have a disadvantage? Suppose that the rejection does not mention the letter of acceptance, as where Buyer on Wednesday sends an overtaking telegram which is received on Thursday and says simply, "Reject your offer." May not application of the "mailbox rule" to find a contract in such a case prejudice Seller if he relies on the telegram of rejection and sells the goods to another buyer before receiving the letter of acceptance on Friday? Might Buyer be estopped to enforce the contract in such a case? See Comment c and Illustration 7 to Restatement, Second, § 63.

NOTES

(1) *More on Mistake and the Mailbox Rule.* One of the few cases to balk at applying the "mailbox rule" to a rejection is Dick v. United States, 82 F.Supp. 326 (Ct.Cl.1949), which was relied upon in the Rhode Island Tool case, p. 268 supra. After preliminary negotiations, the Coast Guard mailed to Dick an offer to buy two sets of propellers for icebreaking vessels at Dick's proposed price of $63,775. On March 15, Dick mailed his acceptance. He then discovered that he had mistakenly assumed that the government wanted and the offer called for only one set of propellers, and on March 16 he telegraphed the Coast Guard calling attention to the mistake and saying that the price should be doubled. On March 21, his acceptance reached the Coast Guard. At the government's insistence Dick furnished the two sets of propellers and sued the United States to recover for the second set. In overruling the government's demurrer the Court of Claims pointed out that "some years ago the Post Office Department changed its regulation and provided that anyone depositing a letter in the mail might reclaim it," and concluded that even if the government was not "charged with knowledge" of Dick's mistake, he was not precluded from withdrawing his letter of acceptance by means of his later telegram.

Note that the Dick case, like the Rhode Island Tool case, involved a mistake. Is that fact significant? Had the government relied on the mistaken figure? Could the decision have been rested on any other ground? See the discussion of the problem in the Dick case in Macneil, Time of Acceptance: Too Many Problems for a Single Rule, 112 U.Pa.L.Rev. 947, 957–62 (1964).

(2) *Power to Accept.* In the case of the overtaking rejection, it is unnecessary to decide whether it is the dispatch or the receipt of the rejection that terminates the offeree's power to accept, since both dispatch and receipt of the rejection take place after the dispatch of the acceptance and before its receipt. Restatement Second, § 40 says that, in most cases, the power to accept ends at the time of receipt of the rejection. Consider the case of the overtaking acceptance.

Suppose again that on Monday Buyer receives by mail from Seller an offer to sell goods. On Tuesday Buyer mails Seller a letter of rejection, which arrives on Friday. On Wednesday Buyer sends Seller a telegram of acceptance, which overtakes the letter and arrives on Thursday. Under the Restatement Second rule there is a contract. This protects Seller if he has, for example, relied on the telegram of acceptance and passed up an opportunity to sell the goods to another buyer.

Suppose, however, that Buyer's telegram of acceptance does not overtake his letter of rejection, but arrives later on Friday. Is there still a contract, since the telegram of acceptance was *dispatched* before the letter of rejection was *received?* To so hold would be unfair to Seller if he had relied on the earlier arriving rejection and sold the goods to another buyer before he received the later arriving acceptance. What answer does the Restatement Second give in this situation?

RISKS OF TRANSMISSION

The third problem that the "mailbox rule" has been called upon to solve concerns the risks of transmission of the acceptance.[a] Household Fire and Carriage Accident Insurance Co. v. Grant, 4 Exch.Div. 216 (C.A.1879), is a leading case. Grant had paid £5 as a deposit and handed to the company's agent an offer to buy 100 shares of its stock, and it had posted its acceptance, addressed to him at his residence, but it had never arrived. The company then went into liquidation and suit was brought for the balance due on the shares. The Court of Appeal held that Grant was liable. According to Thesiger, L. J., the offer was made "under circumstances from which we must imply that he authorized the company" to send the acceptance by post.

> To me it appears that in practice a contract completed upon the acceptance of an offer being posted, but liable to be put an end to by an accident in the post, would be more mischievous than a contract only binding upon the parties to it upon the acceptance actually reaching the offeror. . . .

BRAMWELL, L. J., dissented:

> It is said that a contrary rule would be hard on the would-be acceptor, who may have made his arrangements on the footing that the bargain was concluded. But to hold as contended would be equally hard on the offeror, who may have made his arrangements on the footing that his offer was not accepted; his nonreceipt of any communication may be attributable to the person to whom it was made being absent. What is he to do but to act on the negative, that no communication has been made to him?

And so the battle has raged. Professor Langdell[b] sided with Bramwell:

> Adopting one view, the hardship consists in making one liable on a contract which he is ignorant of having made; adopting the other view, it consists in depriving one of the

a. On the risks of transmission of the offer, see Note 2, p. 173 supra.

b. Christopher Columbus Langdell (1826–1906) was a New York lawyer who became professor of law at Harvard Law School in 1870. His principal achievement as professor and later dean was the introduction of the case method of instruction through the publication in 1871 of his casebook on contracts. He believed that instruction should be of such a character that the students "might at least derive a greater advantage from attending it than from devoting the time to private study."

benefit of a contract which he supposes he has made. Between these two evils the choice would seem to be clear: the former is positive, the latter merely negative; the former imposes a liability to which no limit can be placed, the latter leaves everything *in statu quo.* As to making provision for the contingency of the miscarriage of a letter, this is easy for the person who sends it, while it is practically impossible for the person to whom it is sent.

Langdell, Summary of the Law of Contracts 21 (2d ed. 1880). Professor Llewellyn [c] sided with Thesiger:

> As between hardship on the offeror, which is really tough, and hardship on the offeree which would be even tougher, the vital reason for throwing the hardship of an odd delayed or lost letter upon the offeror remains this: the offeree is already relying, with the best reason in the world, on the deal being on; the offeror is only holding things open; and, in view of the efficiency of communication facilities, we can protect the offerees in *all* these deals at the price of hardship on offerors in very few of them. . . . [The] ingrained usage of business is to answer letters which look toward deals, but the usage is not so clear about acknowledging letters which close deals. The absence of an answer to a letter of offer is much more certain to lead to an inquiry than is the absence of an answer to a letter of acceptance, so that the party bitten by the mischance has under our rule a greater likelihood of being aware of uncertainty and of speedily discovering his difficulty.

Llewellyn, Our Case-Law of Contract: Offer and Acceptance, II, 48 Yale L.J. 779, 795 (1939). The Restatement Second takes the same view, but with some diffidence:

> In the interest of simplicity and clarity, the rule has been extended to cases where an acceptance is lost or delayed in the course of transmission. The convenience of the rule is less clear than in cases of attempted revocation of the offer, however, and the language of the offer is often properly interpreted as making the offeror's duty of performance conditional on receipt of the acceptance.

c. Karl Nickerson Llewellyn (1893–1962) practiced law in New York for two years, and taught law at Yale for several years before becoming a member of the law faculty at Columbia in 1925, where he remained until he joined the law faculty at Chicago in 1951. He was well-known for his contributions to the field of jurisprudence, as one of the school of "legal realists," and also to the fields of commercial law and contracts. He was Chief Reporter of the Uniform Commercial Code, and the author of many books, including The Bramble Bush: On Our Law and Its Study, which was written especially for first-year law students.

Comment b to Restatement Second, § 63.

NOTES

(1) *Applicability of "Mailbox Rule" to Lapse.* Should the "mailbox rule" apply to problems involving the lapse of an offer? If the offeror provides that his offer must be accepted by a specified date or within a specified period of time, is it enough that the acceptance be dispatched within that time, or must it be received within that time? Of course the offeror can dispose of the question by express provision, but what if he does not? How would you interpret a clause in a letter offering to sell land that read, "will give you eight days in which to accept"? See Caldwell v. Cline, 109 W.Va. 553, 156 S.E. 55 (1930). Should the answer depend on whether the offer was revocable or irrevocable? See Restatement Second, § 63(b) and compare Reserve Insurance Co. v. Duckett, 249 Md. 108, 238 A.2d 536 (1968), with Chanoff v. Fiala, 440 Pa. 424, 271 A.2d 285 (1970). How would you have drafted the clause?

(2) *"Mailbox Rule" Not Applicable to Performance.* Absent agreement to the contrary the "mailbox rule" does not apply to problems related to the performance, as distinguished from the formation, of a contract. If, for example, a contract requires a debtor to pay $1,000 to a creditor by June 1, payment must ordinarily reach the creditor by that date. It is not enough for the debtor to mail the payment on June 1, and if the payment is lost in the mail and never reaches the creditor, there is no performance. However, in Laredo Hides Co. v. H & H Meat Products Co., p. 2 supra, the court said (513 S.W.2d at 218, an omitted part of the opinion): "where the creditor expressly directs that the money owed be mailed to him, payment of such debt is made when a letter containing the agreed remittance . . . is deposited in the mail."

In Livesey v. Copps Corp., 90 Wis.2d 577, 280 N.W.2d 339 (1979), the court held that an option to buy land that expired on midnight of November 15 had not been accepted by a notice of exercise of the option that was mailed on November 15 but not received until November 16. "The majority rule is that notice to exercise an option is effective only upon its receipt by the party to be notified unless the parties otherwise agree."

SECTION 3. ACCEPTANCE VARYING OFFER: THE "BATTLE OF THE FORMS" IN THE SALE OF GOODS

The pattern of communications in a typical contract for the sale of goods was described briefly in Note 1, p. 187 supra. Here is a more extensive description by Professor Macaulay, based on a study of Wisconsin businessmen. In reading the cases that follow, consider what account, if any, should be taken of such findings in formulating legal rules applicable to the transactions described.

MACAULAY, NON-CONTRACTUAL RELATIONS IN BUSINESS: A PRELIMINARY STUDY, 28 Am.Sociological Rev. 55, 57–60 (1963).[a] A firm will have a set of terms and conditions for purchases, sales, or both printed on the business documents used in these exchanges. Thus the things to be sold and the price may be planned particularly for each transaction, but standard provisions will further elaborate the performances and cover the other subjects of planning. Typically, these terms and conditions are lengthy and printed in small type on the back of the forms. For example, 24 paragraphs in eight point type are printed on the back of the purchase order form used by the Allis Chalmers Manufacturing Company. The provisions: (1) describe, in part, the performance required, e. g., "DO NOT WELD CASTINGS WITHOUT OUR CONSENT"; (2) plan for the effect of contingencies, e. g., " . . . . in the event the Seller suffers delay in performance due to an act of God, war, act of the Government, priorities or allocations, act of the Buyer, fire, flood, strike, sabotage, or other causes beyond Seller's control, the time of completion shall be extended a period of time equal to the period of such delay if the Seller gives the Buyer notice in writing of the cause of any such delay within a reasonable time after the beginning thereof"; (3) plan for the effect of defective performances, e. g., "The buyer, without waiving any other legal rights, reserves the right to cancel without charge or to postpone deliveries of any of the articles covered by this order which are not shipped in time reasonably to meet said agreed dates"; (4) plan for a legal sanction, e. g., the clause "without waiving any other legal rights," in the example just given.

In larger firms such "boiler plate" provisions are drafted by the house counsel or the firm's outside lawyer. In smaller firms such provisions may be drafted by the industry trade association, may be copied from a competitor, or may be found on forms purchased from a printer. In any event, salesmen and purchasing agents, the operating personnel, typically are unaware of what is said in the fine print on the back of the forms they use. Yet often the normal business patterns will give effect to this standardized planning. For example, purchasing agents may have to use a purchase order form so that all transactions receive a number under the firm's accounting system. Thus, the required accounting record will carry the necessary planning of the exchange relationship printed on its reverse side. If the seller does not object to this planning and accepts the order, the buyer's "fine print" will control. If the seller does object, differences can be settled by negotiation.

This type of standardized planning is very common. Requests for copies of the business documents used in buying and selling were

a. Reprinted by permission of the American Sociological Review.

sent to approximately 6,000 manufacturing firms which do business in Wisconsin. Approximately 1,200 replies were received and 850 companies used some type of standardized planning. With only a few exceptions, the firms that did not reply and the 350 that indicated they did not use standardized planning were very small manufacturers such as local bakeries, soft drink bottlers and sausage makers.

While businessmen can and often do carefully and completely plan, it is clear that not all exchanges are neatly rationalized. Although most businessmen think that a clear description of both the seller's and buyer's performances is obvious common sense, they do not always live up to this ideal. The house counsel and the purchasing agent of a medium size manufacturer of automobile parts reported that several times their engineers had committed the company to buy expensive machines without adequate specifications. The engineers had drawn careful specifications as to the type of machine and how it was to be made but had neglected to require that the machine produce specified results. An attorney and an auditor both stated that most contract disputes arise because of ambiguity in the specifications.

Businessmen often prefer to rely on "a man's word" in a brief letter, a handshake, or "common honesty and decency"—even when the transaction involves exposure to serious risks. Seven lawyers from law firms with business practices were interviewed. Five thought that businessmen often entered contracts with only a minimal degree of advance planning. They complained that businessmen desire to "keep it simple and avoid red tape" even where large amounts of money and significant risks are involved. One stated that he was "sick of being told, 'We can trust old Max,' when the problem is not one of honesty but one of reaching an agreement that both sides understand." Another said that businessmen when bargaining often talk only in pleasant generalities, think they have a contract, but fail to reach agreement on any of the hard, unpleasant questions until forced to do so by a lawyer. Two outside lawyers had different views. One thought that large firms usually planned important exchanges, although he conceded that occasionally matters might be left in a fairly vague state. The other dissenter represents a large utility that commonly buys heavy equipment and buildings. The supplier's employees come on the utility's property to install the equipment or construct the buildings, and they may be injured while there. The utility has been sued by such employees so often that it carefully plans purchases with the assistance of a lawyer so that suppliers take this burden.

Moreover, standardized planning can break down. In the example of such planning previously given, it was assumed that the purchasing agent would use his company's form with its 24 paragraphs printed on the back and that the seller would accept this or object to any provisions he did not like. However, the seller may fail to read the buyer's 24 paragraphs of fine print and may accept the buyer's order on the seller's own acknowledgment-of-order form. Typically this form will have ten to 50 paragraphs favoring the seller, and these provisions are likely to be different from or inconsistent with the buyer's provisions. The seller's acknowledgment form may be received by the buyer and checked by a clerk. She will read the *face* of the acknowledgment but not the fine print on the back of it because she has neither the time nor ability to analyze the small print on the 100 to 500 forms she must review each day. The face of the acknowledgment—where the goods and the price are specified—is likely to correspond with the face of the purchase order. If it does, the two forms are filed away. At this point, both buyer and seller are likely to assume they have planned an exchange and made a contract. Yet they have done neither, as they are in disagreement about all that appears on the back of their forms. This practice is common enough to have a name. Law teachers call it "the battle of the forms."

Ten of the 12 purchasing agents interviewed said that frequently the provisions on the back of their purchase order and those on the back of a supplier's acknowledgment would differ or be inconsistent. Yet they would assume that the purchase was complete without further action unless one of the supplier's provisions was really objectionable. Moreover, only occasionally would they bother to read the fine print on the back of suppliers' forms. On the other hand, one purchasing agent insists that agreement be reached on the fine print provisions, but he represents the utility whose lawyer reported that it exercises great care in planning. The other purchasing agent who said that his company did not face a battle of the forms problem, works for a division of one of the largest manufacturing corporations in the United States. Yet the company may have such a problem without recognizing it. The purchasing agent regularly sends a supplier both a purchase order and another form which the supplier is asked to sign and return. The second form states that the supplier accepts the buyer's terms and conditions. The company has sufficient bargaining power to force suppliers to sign and return the form, and the purchasing agent must show one of his firm's auditors such a signed form for every purchase order issued. Yet suppliers frequently return this buyer's form *plus* their own acknowledgment form which has conflicting provisions. The purchasing agent throws away the supplier's form and files his own. Of course, in such a case the supplier has not acquiesced to the buyer's provisions. There is no agreement and no contract.

Sixteen sales managers were asked about the battle of the forms. Nine said that frequently no agreement was reached on which set of fine print was to govern, while seven said that there was no problem. Four of the seven worked for companies whose major customers are the large automobile companies or the large manufacturers of paper products. These customers demand that their terms and conditions govern any purchase, are careful generally to see that suppliers acquiesce, and have the bargaining power to have their way. The other three of the seven sales managers who have no battle of the forms problem, work for manufacturers of special industrial machines. Their firms are careful to reach complete agreement with their customers. Two of these men stressed that they could take no chances because such a large part of their firm's capital is tied up in making any one machine. The other sales manager had been influenced by a law suit against one of his competitors for over a half million dollars. The suit was brought by a customer when the competitor had been unable to deliver a machine and put it in operation on time. The sales manager interviewed said his firm could not guarantee that its machines would work perfectly by a specified time because they are designed to fit the customer's requirements, which may present difficult engineering problems. As a result, contracts are carefully negotiated.

A large manufacturer of packaging materials audited its records to determine how often it had failed to agree on terms and conditions with its customers or had failed to create legally binding contracts. Such failures cause a risk of loss to this firm since the packaging is printed with the customer's design and cannot be salvaged once this is done. The orders for five days in four different years were reviewed. The percentages of orders where no agreement on terms and conditions was reached or no contract was formed were as follows:

1953	75.0%
1954	69.4%
1955	71.5%
1956	59.5%

It is likely that businessmen pay more attention to describing the performances in an exchange than to planning for contingencies or defective performances or to obtaining legal enforceability of their contracts. Even when a purchase order and acknowledgment have conflicting provisions printed on the back, almost always the buyer and seller will be in agreement on what is to be sold and how much is to be paid for it. The lawyers who said businessmen often commit their firms to significant exchanges too casually, stated that the performances would be defined in the brief letter or telephone call; the lawyers objected that nothing else would be covered. Moreover, it is likely that businessmen are least concerned about planning their transactions so that they are legally enforceable contracts.

NOTE

Buyer as Offeror. In analyzing what Professor Macaulay refers to as "the battle of the forms," it is helpful to keep in mind that the most common situation is the one that he discusses in which the buyer is the offeror and the seller is the offeree. Why is this more common than the situation in the Fairmount Glass Works case, p. 184 supra, in which the seller was the offeror and the buyer was the offeree?

THE "MIRROR IMAGE" RULE AND THE CODE

Traditional contract doctrine insists that an acceptance must be on the terms proposed by the offer without the slightest variation. Anything else is a counter offer and a rejection of the original offer. See the Columbus Rolling Mill case, p. 229 supra. The offeror, "as master of his offer," thus enjoys freedom from contract except on his own terms. In Langellier v. Schaefer, 36 Minn. 361, 31 N.W. 690 (1887), an offeree who had received an offer of land for cash replied, "Your offer is accepted," and added, "please execute the enclosed deed . . . and send it to the Bank of Minnesota, St. Paul, with . . . instructions . . . to collect the amount due you, and deliver deed." When the offeror refused to convey the land, the offeree sued. He lost on the ground that an offer must be accepted "according to the terms" on which it was made, "without the introduction of any new terms." It is sometimes said that the acceptance must be the "mirror image" of the offer.

The rigors of the rule that an acceptance must be the "mirror image" of the offer may be mitigated in practice. First, a court may decide that what seemed to be an additional or different term in the acceptance was an "implied term" in the offer, so that language that at first appeared to vary the terms of the offer did not really do so. An example is the court's treatment of the buyer's addition, "the jars and caps to be strictly first-quality goods," near the end of the opinion in the Fairmount Glass Works case, p. 184 supra. See also Pickett v. Miller, 76 N.M. 105, 412 P.2d 400 (1966). Second, a court may conclude that the language of the acceptance relating to an additional or different term is only "precatory." Might not the court have read the language in Langellier v. Schaefer, just discussed, in this manner? This would have resulted in a contract on the terms of the offeror, who could then have decided whether or not to modify that contract by accepting the offeree's additional proposal. See Valashinas v. Koniuto, 308 N.Y. 233, 124 N.E.2d 300 (1954). Even where neither of these mitigating techniques is available and no contract has been made, parties often act on the assumption that their promises are binding and the transaction is carried out without incident. Disputes tend to rise in two kinds of cases.

In the first kind of case, one party claims that no contract was made while the other maintains the contrary. This was the situation in Langellier v. Schaefer, just discussed, where a seller of land seized on the variation to justify his refusal to convey. When the market rises, sellers are tempted to find such pretexts for getting out of their bargains, and when the market falls buyers are so tempted.[a] The more rigorous the application of the "mirror image" rule, the more readily available will be such pretexts.

In the second kind of case, some performance has taken place and it is clear that a contract has been made, but a dispute arises with respect to performance and the parties differ as to which terms control. Each party insists that a contract was made on his own terms. Under the "mirror image" rule, the party who sent the last form before performance began usually prevailed. This was because each later form operated as a rejection of any earlier offer by the other party and as a counter-offer. When the recipient of this last counter-offer performed, that was taken as his acceptance of that counter-offer. This made it advantageous to fire the "last shot" before performance began. In the typical contract for the sale of goods, it was the buyer who, by his purchase order, made the initial offer and the seller who, by his varying acknowledgement, fired the "last shot," rejecting the buyer's offer and making a counter-offer. When the buyer accepted the goods, he was taken to have accepted the seller's counter-offer and was bound by the seller's terms.

It was against this background that UCC 2–207 was drafted.

§ 2–207. Additional Terms in Acceptance or Confirmation

(1) A definite and seasonable expression of acceptance or a written confirmation which is sent within a reasonable time operates as an acceptance even though it states terms additional to or different from those offered or agreed upon, unless acceptance is expressly made conditional on assent to the additional or different terms.

(2) The additional terms are to be construed as proposals for addition to the contract. Between merchants such terms become part of the contract unless:

- (a) the offer expressly limits acceptance to the terms of the offer;
- (b) they materially alter it; or
- (c) notification of objection to them has already been given or is given within a reasonable time after notice of them is received.

(3) Conduct by both parties which recognizes the existence of a contract is sufficient to establish a contract for sale although the writings of the parties do not otherwise establish a contract. In such case the terms of the particular contract consist of those terms on

a. For a leading example, see Poel v. Brunswick-Balke-Collender Co., 216 N.Y. 310, 110 N.E. 619 (1915), in which the buyer took advantage of the "mirror image" rule in a falling market. The course of the market is discussed by the trial court in Poel v. Brunswick, Balke, Collender Co., 78 Misc. 311, 317, 139 N.Y.S. 602, 606 (1912).

which the writings of the parties agree, together with any supplementary terms incorporated under any other provisions of this Act.

NOTES

(1) *An Agenda.* The complexity of UCC 2–207 makes it useful to have a brief agenda of significant problems to consider. In reading the following materials, try to apply them to the situation in which the buyer sends a purchase order and the seller then sends an acknowledgement that is identical with the purchase order except:

(a) the acknowledgement contains an arbitration clause that the purchase order does not; or

(b) the acknowledgement contains a disclaimer of warranties that the purchase order does not; or

(c) the acknowledgement changes the delivery date from June 1 to July 1.

(2) *Counselling.* Should an offeree who receives an offer by telegram confirm the terms in his acceptance? Is there any risk in going beyond "I accept your offer" and adding a recital of the terms of the offer? What if there is a mistake in the recital? Consider Note 1, p. 172 supra, and see United States v. Braunstein, 75 F.Supp. 137 (S.D.N.Y.1947).

(3) *Problem.* On April 5, Westside gave Humble an option contract, irrevocable for 60 days, on a tract of land. On May 2, Humble wrote Westside, "Humble Oil & Refining Company hereby exercises its option to purchase . . . . The contract of sale is hereby amended to provide that Seller shall extend all utility lines to the property before the date of closing." On May 14, Humble wrote Westside, "Humble Oil & Refining Company hereby notifies you of its intention to exercise the option granted . . . . The exercise of said option is not qualified and you may disregard the proposed amendment to the contract suggested in the letter dated May 2 . . . ." Contract? See Humble Oil & Refining Co. v. Westside Investment Corp., 428 S.W.2d 92 (Tex.1968); Restatement Second, § 37.

MARLENE INDUSTRIES CORP. v. CARNAC TEXTILES, INC.

Court of Appeals of New York, 1978.
45 N.Y.2d 327, 380 N.E.2d 239.

GABRIELLI, Judge. This appeal involves yet another of the many conflicts which arise as a result of the all too common business practice of blithely drafting, sending, receiving, and filing unread numerous purchase orders, acknowledgments, and other divers forms containing a myriad of discrepant terms. Both parties agree that they have entered into a contract for the sale of goods; indeed, it would appear that there is no disagreement as to most of the essential terms of their contract. They do disagree, however, as to whether their agreement includes a provision for the arbitration of disputes arising from the contract.

Petitioner Marlene Industries Corp. (Marlene) appeals from an order of the Appellate Division which, one Justice dissenting, affirmed a judgment of Supreme Court denying an application to stay arbitration. There should be a reversal and arbitration should be stayed, for we conclude that the parties did not contract to arbitrate.

The dispute between the parties, insofar as it is relevant on this appeal, is founded upon an alleged breach by Marlene of a contract to purchase certain fabrics from respondent Carnac Textiles, Inc. (Carnac). The transaction was instituted when Marlene orally placed an order for the fabrics with Carnac. Neither party contends that any method of dispute resolution was discussed at that time. Almost immediately thereafter, Marlene sent Carnac a "purchase order" and Carnac sent Marlene an "acknowledgement of order". Marlene's form did not provide for arbitration; it did declare that it would not become effective as a contract unless signed by the seller, and that its terms could not be "superceded by a[n] unsigned contract notwithstanding retention". Carnac's form, on the other hand, contained an arbitration clause placed in the midst of some 13 lines of small type "boilerplate". It also instructed the buyer to "sign and return one copy of this confirmation". However, neither party signed the other's form. When a dispute subsequently arose, Carnac sought arbitration, and Marlene moved for a stay.

The courts below have denied the application to stay arbitration, the Appellate Division reasoning that "as between merchants where 'a writing in confirmation of the contract and sufficient against the sender is received and the party receiving it has reason to know its contents' written notice of objection should be given within 10 days after it is received" (59 A.D.2d 359, 360, 399 N.Y.S.2d 229, 231, quoting Uniform Commercial Code, § 2–201, subd. [2]). Since Marlene had retained without objection the form containing the arbitration clause, the court concluded that Marlene was bound by that clause. We disagree.

This case presents a classic example of the "battle of the forms", and its solution is to be derived by reference to section 2–207 of the Uniform Commercial Code, which is specifically designed to resolve such disputes. The courts below erred in applying subdivision (2) of section 2–201, for that statute deals solely with the question whether a contract exists which is enforceable in the face of a Statute of Frauds defense; it has no application to a situation such as this, in which it is conceded that a contract does exist and the dispute goes only to the terms of that contract. In light of the disparate purposes of the two sections, application of the wrong provision will often result in an erroneous conclusion. As has been noted by a recognized authority on the code, "[t]he easiest way to avoid the miscarriages this confusion perpetrates is simply to fix in mind that the two sections have nothing to do with each other. Though each has a special rule for merchants sounding very much like the other, their respective functions are unrelated. Section 2–201(2) has its role in the context of a challenge to the use of the statute of frauds to prevent proof of an alleged agreement, whereas the merchant rule of section 2–207(2) is for use in determining what are the terms of an admitted agreement" (Duesenberg, General Provisions, Sales, Bulk Transfers and Documents of Title, 30 Business Law 847, 853).[1]

Subdivision (2) of section 2–207 is applicable to cases such as this, in which there is a consensus that a contract exists, but disagreement as to what terms have been included in that contract. Subdivision (1) of section 2–207 was intended to abrogate the harsh "mirror-image" rule of common law, pursuant to which any deviation in the language of a purported acceptance from the exact terms of the offer transformed that "acceptance" into a counter-offer and thus precluded contract formation on the basis of those two documents alone (see Poel v. Brunswick-Balke-Collender Co., 216 N.Y. 310, 110 N.E. 619). Under subdivision (1) of section 2–207, however, an acceptance containing additional terms will operate as an acceptance unless it is "expressly made conditional on assent to the additional or different terms".[2] Having thus departed from the common-law doc-

1. The proper and rather limited role of subdivision (2), of section 2–201 has been graphically illustrated by Professors White and Summers, who consider it to be a partial exception to the Statute of Frauds which "merely ameliorates the writing requirement. A writing is still required, but it need not be signed by the party to be charged. The character of this exception is best understood in light of the form of fraud it was designed to combat. Assume that Orval Orfed and Len Lemhi orally agree over the telephone that Orfed will sell Lemhi 1000 bushels of wheat at $40 a bushel. Orfed, the seller, thereafter sends a signed confirmatory memorandum to Lemhi reciting the terms of the deal, a common practice in such transactions. Such a memo would be good against Orfed under 2–201 should Orfed back out and Lemhi sue him for damages. But absent 2–201(2) the confirmatory memo would not be good against Lemhi, for it is not signed by him as required by 2–201(1). Thus Lemhi would be free to sit back and 'play the market.' If at delivery date the cost of wheat had fallen to some level below $40 a bushel, and he wanted to buy elsewhere, he could back out, whereas Orfed could not back out, at least so far as the statute of frauds goes, should the market rise. Section 2–201(2) is designed to prevent the Lemhis of the world from taking advantage of the Orfeds. It says that a memo good against Orfed will also be good against Lemhi provided that (1) both are merchants, (2) the memo is sent by Orfed to Lemhi within a reasonable time (after the phone call?), (3) the memo by its terms 'confirms' the oral contract, (4) the memo is good against Orfed under 2–201(1), (5) Lemhi receives it, (6) Lemhi has 'reason to know its contents,' and (7) Lemhi does not object to its contents within ten days of receipt. This carefully circumscribed section thus seeks to combat one form of fraud which pre-Code versions of the statute of frauds actually facilitate. At the same time 2–201(2) itself encourages the common and wise business practice of sending memoranda confirming oral deals, for the section obviates a disadvantage to which the sender would otherwise be subject" (White & Summers, Uniform Commercial Code, § 2–3, pp. 47–48).

2. Assuming, *arguendo*, that Carnac's form was an acceptance rather than a confirmation, we would note that it did not expressly condition acceptance

trine, it became necessary for the code to make some provision as to the effect upon the contract of such additional terms in an acceptance. Subdivision (2) was designed to deal with that problem.

Before continuing, we would note that the section speaks of both acceptances and written confirmations. It is thus intended to include at least two distinct situations: one in which the parties have reached a prior oral contract and any writings serve only as confirmation of that contract; and one in which the prior dealings of the parties did not comprise actual formation of a contract, and the writings themselves serve as offer and/or acceptance. In either case, the writing or writings may contain additional terms, and in either case the effect of such additional terms under the code is the same. Thus, on this appeal, since the prior discussions of the parties did not reach the question of dispute resolution, it is unnecessary to determine whether those discussions rose to the level of contract formation, or whether no contract was created until the exchange of forms.[3] Therefore, whether Marlene's form is an offer and Carnac's an acceptance, or whether both are mere confirmations of an existing oral contract, the result in this case is the same, and that result is dependent upon the operation of subdivision (2) of section 2–207. . . .

The parties to this dispute are certainly merchants, and the arbitration clause is clearly a proposed additional term, whether Carnac's form be considered an acceptance of an oral or written offer or a written confirmation of an oral agreement. As such, it became a part of the contract unless one of the three listed exceptions is applicable. We hold that the inclusion of an arbitration agreement materially alters a contract for the sale of goods, and thus, pursuant to section 2–207 (subd. [2], par. [b]), it will not become a part of such a contract unless both parties explicitly agree to it.

It has long been the rule in this State that the parties to a commercial transaction "will not be held to have chosen arbitration as the forum for the resolution of their disputes in the absence of an express, unequivocal agreement to that effect; absent such an explicit commitment neither party may be compelled to arbitrate" (Matter of Acting Supt. of Schools of Liverpool Cent. School Dist. [United Liverpool Faculty Assn.], 42 N.Y.2d 509, 512, 399 N.Y.S.2d 189, 191, 369 N.E.2d 746, 748; . . . The reason for this requirement, quite simply, is that by agreeing to arbitrate a party waives in large part many of his normal rights under the procedural and substantive law

upon Marlene's assent to inclusion of an arbitration provision (but cf. Roto-Lith v. Bartlett & Co., 1 Cir., 297 F.2d 497).

3. It should be noted that in some cases, there may be no prior oral agreement, and the terms of the forms utilized may be so divergent as to preclude contract formation in the absence of further action upon the part of the parties (cf. Uniform Commercial Code, § 2–207, subd. [3]). This is not such a case.

of the State, and it would be unfair to infer such a significant waiver on the basis of anything less than a clear indication of intent. . . .

Since an arbitration agreement in the context of a commercial transaction "must be clear and direct, and must not depend upon implication, inveiglement or subtlety . . . [its] existence . . . should not depend solely upon the conflicting fine print of commercial forms which cross one another but never meet" (Matter of Doughboy Inds. [Pantasote Co.], 17 A.D.2d 216, 220, 233 N.Y.S.2d 488, 493). Thus, at least under this so-called "New York Rule" (Squillante, General Provisions, Sales, Bulk Transfers and Documents of Title, 33 Business Law 1875, 1881), it is clear that an arbitration clause is a material addition which can become part of a contract only if it is expressly assented to by both parties (see Matter of Doughboy Inds. [Pantasote Co.], supra; accord Frances Hosiery Mills v. Burlington Inds., 285 N.C. 344, 204 S.E.2d 834, see, also, Duesenberg, General Provisions, Sales, Bulk Transfers, and Documents of Title, 30 Business Law 847, 853). Applying these principles to this case, we conclude that the contract between Marlene and Carnac does not contain an arbitration clause; hence, the motion to permanently stay arbitration should have been granted.

Accordingly, the order appealed from should be reversed, with costs.

NOTES

(1) *What is an "Expression of Acceptance"?* Is every purported acceptance an "expression of acceptance" under UCC 2–207(1)? What if the seller says "I accept," but varies the price or quantity term?

The court faced such a question in one of the cotton cases of 1973, Duval & Co. v. Malcom, 233 Ga. 784, 214 S.E.2d 356 (1975). In March, the growers had tendered to the buyer a signed writing offering to sell their "entire crop of 1973 cotton of 729.6 acres plus any addition that may be leased prior to planting." Price and other terms were set out. The growers understood that the buyer would sign the document and give it back to them after lunch. When they returned, however, they discovered that the buyer had added language to the writing. On the front was added: "Projected yields and farm numbers on back." On the back were listed 15 farms by number and acreage and this language: "600 pounds per acre or approximately 875 b/c [bales of cotton]." (In 1971 this acreage had produced 756 bales and in 1972 only 380 bales.) The growers protested this addition and insisted that there was no contract. The buyer then added more language on the back: "Buyer will accept all of the cotton produced on this acreage regardless of whether it is more or less than the projected yield." The growers still insisted that there was no contract and left. When in the fall the growers refused to deliver, the buyer sued. The court reasoned that because of UCC 2–306(1), the buyer's insertion of a "stated estimate" that differed from the "prior output" was "a material alteration in the quantity term." It therefore concluded, after considering UCC 2–204 and 2–206 as well, that UCC 2–207 "is inapplicable because under the evidence adduced on the motions, no deal had in fact been closed . . . .

'Only where all the traditional criteria are met showing that a contract has been made should Section 2–207 be applied. . . .' "

(2) *Arbitration Clauses.* Not all courts would agree with the New York court's flat assertion that "it is clear that an arbitration clause is a material addition." In Dorton v. Collins & Aikman Corp., 453 F.2d 1161, 1169 (6th Cir. 1972), the court said: "We believe that the question of whether the arbitration provision materially altered the oral offer under Subsection 2–207(2)(b) is one which can be resolved only by the District Court on further findings of fact in the present case." Would it be relevant under this view that both parties were in an industry, such as in the textile industry, where arbitration clauses are widely used?[a] See Furnish, Commercial Arbitration Agreements and the Uniform Commercial Code, 67 Calif.L.Rev. 317 (1979).

AIR PRODUCTS & CHEM., INC. v. FAIRBANKS MORSE, INC., 58 Wis.2d 193, 206 N.W.2d 414 (1973). [In 1964, Air Products purchased from Fairbanks ten large electric motors under several contracts. In each case, after preliminary negotiations that resulted in an oral agreement, Air Products issued a purchase order confirming its oral orders and Fairbanks returned an executed copy of this purchase order together with Fairbanks' acknowledgement of order form. At the bottom of this form was the following language in bold face type:

> WE THANK YOU FOR YOUR ORDER AS COPIED HEREON, WHICH WILL RECEIVE PROMPT ATTENTION AND SHALL BE GOVERNED BY THE PROVISIONS ON THE REVERSE SIDE HEREOF UNLESS YOU NOTIFY US TO THE CONTRARY WITHIN 10 DAYS OR BEFORE SHIPMENT WHICHEVER IS EARLIER. BEFORE ACCEPTING GOODS FROM TRANSPORTATION COMPANY SEE THAT EACH ARTICLE IS IN GOOD CONDITION. IF SHORTAGE OR DAMAGE IS APPARENT REFUSE SHIPMENT UNLESS AGENT NOTES DEFECT ON TRANSPORTATION BILL. ACCEPTANCE OF SHIPMENT WITHOUT COMPLYING WITH SUCH CONDITIONS IS AT YOUR OWN RISK.
>
> THIS IS NOT AN INVOICE. AN INVOICE FOR THIS MATERIAL WILL BE SENT YOU WITHIN A FEW DAYS.

a. See Gaynor-Stafford Industries, Inc. v. Mafco Textured Fibers, 52 A.D.2d 481, 384 N.Y.S.2d 788 (1976) (Where "the parties . . . were merchants who have had long experience in the textile industry and in fact had dealt with each other for seven months," the addition of an arbitration clause was not a "material alteration."). That case was, however, decided before the Marlene case.

ACKNOWLEDGMENT OF ORDER

On the back of the form were six provisions under the following heading:

> The following provisions form part of the order acknowledged and accepted on the face hereof, as express agreements between Fairbanks, Morse & Co. ("Company") and the Buyer governing the terms and conditions of the sale, subject to modification only in writing signed by the local manager or an executive officer of the Company:

The sixth provision read:

> 6.—The Company nowise assumes any responsibility or liability with respect to use, purpose, or suitability, and shall not be liable for damages of any character, whether direct or consequential, for defect, delay, or otherwise, its sole liability and obligation being confined to the replacement in the manner aforesaid or defectively manufactured guaranteed parts failing within the time stated.

Air Products and its insurer, Hartford, later sued Fairbanks, alleging that six of the motors failed to perform satisfactorily, causing them substantial damages. Fairbanks relied on the sixth provision as an affirmative defense, to which Air Products and Hartford demurred. From an order overruling this demurrer, they appealed.]

HANLEY, Justice. . . . Because the reverse side of Fairbanks' Acknowledgement of Order states that the provisions contained there " . . . form part of the order acknowledged and accepted on the face hereof . . . " it would seem that Air Products could have "reasonably" assumed that the parties "had a deal." Since there is no express provision in the purchase orders making assent to different or additional terms conditioned upon Air Products' assent to them, the second requirement of coming under UCC 2–207 is also met. . . . At this point a contract does in fact exist between the parties under (1). Subsection (2) must now be resorted to to see which of the "variant" terms will actually become part of the contract.

At this juncture, Air Products and Hartford argue that 2–207(2) only applies to "additional terms" while Fairbanks' limitation of liability provisions were "different." To this extent they contend terms are "additional" if they concern a subject matter that is not covered in the offer and "different" if the subject matter, although covered in the offer, was covered in a variant way. Hartford and Air Products' argument seems to expressly contradict Official U.C.C. Comment #3 which unequivocably starts "Whether or not *additional or different* terms will become part of the agreement depends upon the provisions of subsection (2)." (Emphasis added). . . . The thrust of the "additional-different" dichotomy as averred for by Air Products and Hartford is that their offer as effectuated by a purchase order includes not only those terms which are expressly stated therein, but also those which are implied by law (e. g. warranty and damage) that will become a part of the contract formed by the sellers acceptance of the offer. Therefore, Fairbanks' limitation of liability terms are different since they are at variance with the implied warranty and damage terms in Air Products' offer [under Sections 2–314, 2–315 and 2–714].[a]

Air Products and Hartford next contend that if the added terms of the "acknowledgment of order" were "additional" terms they still do not become part of the contract because the prerequisites to their becoming a part of the contract which are contained in subsection (2) were not satisfied . . . . The language employed by Air Products in its "terms and conditions" was not express enough to bring into play the provisions of either subsection 2–207(2)(a) or (c). The ultimate question to be determined, therefore, is whether the disclaimer contained in Fairbanks' "acknowledgement of order" materially altered the agreement between the parties pursuant to sec. 2–207(2)(b). If they materially alter what would otherwise be firmed by the acceptance of an offer, they will not become terms unless the

a. In Steiner v. Mobil Oil Corp., 20 Cal.3d 90, 141 Cal.Rptr. 157, 569 P.2d 751, 759 n. 5 (1977), the Supreme Court of California addressed itself to this aspect of the Air Products case:

"Section 2207, subdivision (1), refers to acceptances in which terms are either 'additional to or different from' the terms of an offer. Section 2207, subdivision (2), however, expressly concerns itself with only 'additional terms.' Noting this difference, several courts and commentators have concluded that section 2207, subdivision (2), applies if an acceptance *adds* terms to an offer, but does not apply if an acceptance *alters* the terms of an offer. . . . Other courts and commentators, however, suggest that section 2207, subdivision (2), applies without regard to whether the varying terms of an acceptance differ from or add to an offer.

"We conclude that the applicability of section 2207, subdivision (2), should not turn upon a characterization of the varying terms of an acceptance as 'additional' or 'different.' First, Uniform Commercial Code comment 3 specifically states that '[w]hether or not additional *or different* terms will become part of the agreement depends upon the provisions of subsection (2).' (Italics added; see also UCC com. 2.) Second, the distinction between 'additional' and 'different' terms is ambiguous. Since an offer's silence with respect to a particular issue may indicate an intent to adopt the code's gap-filling provisions, even an acceptance term which at first glance appears to be plainly 'additional' is at least arguably 'different.' (See Air Products & Chem., Inc. v. Fairbanks Morse, Inc. (1973), 58 Wis.2d 193, 206 N.W.2d 414, 424.) Third, the distinction between additional and different terms serves no clear purpose. If additional and different terms are treated alike for purposes of section 2207, subdivision (2), an offeror does not, as some contend, lose 'the ability to retain control over the terms of his offer.' (Duesenberg & King [Sales & Bulk Transfers under the Uniform Commercial Code (1976) § 3.02], at p. 3–37.) Under section 2207, subdivision (2), if the offeror wishes to retain such control, he may do so by framing his offer so that it 'expressly limits acceptance to the terms of the offer . . . .' (§ 2207, subd. (2)(a).)"

buyer expressly agrees thereto. "If, however, they are terms which would not so change the bargain they will be incorporated unless notice of objection to them has already been given or is given within a reasonable time." Comment #3 to sec. 2–207. Hartford and Air Products contend that the eradication of a multi-million dollar damage exposure is *per se* material. . . . While the comment #4 clearly indicates that a disclaimer of an implied warranty of merchantability is material, there is no good reason to hold that a disclaimer that has the effect of eliminating millions of dollars in damages should become a part of a contract by operation of law. We conclude that the disclaimer for consequential loss was sufficiently material to require express conversation between the parties over its inclusion or exclusion in the contract. It follows that the order overruling the demurrers of Air Products and Hartford must be reversed.

NOTES

(1) *Air Products Narrowed.* The same court expressed some further thoughts on the Air Products case in Koehring Co. v. Glowacki, 77 Wis.2d 497, 253 N.W.2d 64 (1977). In that case a seller had circularized possible buyers advertising surplus machinery on an "as is, where is" basis. One of these prospective buyers telegraphed an offer for $16,500 "FOB, our truck, your plant, loaded," to which the seller had responded with a telegram "accepting" the bid but stating the condition that the machinery was sold on an "as is, where is" basis. The buyer subsequently claimed that there was no contract and the Supreme Court of Wisconsin agreed. It distinguished the Air Products case on the ground that "that case dealt with an exchange of printed forms, not an exchange of telegrams which represented bargaining positions as in the instant case. Thus the full language of sec. 402.207(1) applied in the Air Products Case, whereas in the instant case we elect to apply only the language after the comma of sec. 402.207(1) which provides: 'unless acceptance is expressly made conditional on assent to the additional or different terms.' Additionally, in the case before us, there was no prior oral agreement between the parties. If that were the situation and the exchanged telegrams merely confirmed that fact, then we would look to sec. 402.207(2), . . . as was done in Air Products, to determine whether to include the additional or different terms."

(2) *Disclaimers Contrasted with Arbitration Clauses.* An arbitration clause may be regarded as advantageous by a buyer as well as a seller. Therefore, even if, as in the Marlene case, an arbitration clause added by the seller-offeree is regarded as a mere proposal "for addition to the contract" that does not "become part of the contract" by the silence of the buyer-offeror, the buyer might choose expressly to assent to the seller's proposal to add the clause. A disclaimer of warranties, however, is advantageous only to the seller. Therefore, if as in the Air Products case, a disclaimer added by the seller-offeree is regarded as such a mere proposal for addition to the contract, it is most unlikely that the buyer would choose expressly to assent to the seller's proposal to add the clause.

This distinction was relied on in Roto-Lith, Ltd. v. F. P. Bartlett & Co., 297 F.2d 497 (1st Cir. 1962), one of the earliest and most notorious of the cases interpreting UCC 2–207. The question in that case was whether a disclaimer added by the seller-offeree had become part of the contract. The court held that it had. "It would be unrealistic to suppose that when an offeree replies setting out conditions that would be burdensome only to the offeror he intended to make an unconditional acceptance of the original offer, leaving it simply to the offeror's good nature whether he would assume the additional restrictions. To give the statute a practical construction, we must hold that a response which states a condition materially altering the obligation solely to the disadvantage of the offeror is an 'acceptance . . . expressly . . . conditional on assent to the additional . . . terms.' Plaintiff [buyer] accepted the goods with knowledge of the conditions specified in the acknowledgment. It became bound." The decision has been much criticized, both for its reading of subsection (1) and for its failure to consider the application of subsection (3).[b]

SOUTHERN IDAHO PIPE & STEEL CO. v. CAL–CUT PIPE & SUPPLY, INC.

Supreme Court of Idaho, 1977.
98 Idaho 495, 567 P.2d 1246.[a]

DONALDSON, Justice. This case involves a contract action under the Uniform Commercial Code. Appellant Cal-Cut Pipe & Supply, Inc. (hereinafter referred to as Cal-Cut) is a California based corporation dealing in used steel pipe. It has operated in the State of Idaho for a number of years. It is undisputed that respondent Southern Idaho Pipe & Steel Co. has dealt with Cal-Cut for the last ten years. Cal-Cut does not maintain sales offices or agents in the state, however. Its method of operation is to advertise in Idaho by mail or telephone. Deliveries are made in California as are the contracts of sale. The buyer is responsible for transporting the steel pipe.

On June 23, 1973, Southern Idaho received in the mail a publication advising that Cal-Cut wished to negotiate the sale of used steel pipe under specified terms. Several phone conversations ensued culminating in Cal-Cut's making of a formal written offer to sell to Southern Idaho. This occurred on August 7, 1973. The offer was accepted by mail, but Southern Idaho changed the final delivery date from October 15, 1973 to December 15, 1973. Southern Idaho enclosed a $20,000 check along with its acceptance, which check was deposited in Cal-Cut's bank account. It is disputed by the parties whether the change in the delivery date was discussed in subsequent

b. The Roto-Lith case was cited without criticism but was distinguished by a federal district court in the same circuit in Scott Brass, Inc. v. C & C Metal Products Corp., 473 F.Supp. 1124 (D.R.I.1979).

a. Appeal dismissed and cert. denied, 434 U.S. 1056 (1978).

communications. But both parties agree that they negotiated a change in the minimum amount of steel pipe that had to be sold to Southern Idaho from 40,000 to 30,000 feet. On August 20, 1973, Cal-Cut sent the written confirmation to Southern Idaho. The confirmation included the changed minimum requirement of 30,000 feet of steel and the *original* final delivery date of October 15. At the bottom of this confirmation was the postscript, "We will work it out." Southern Idaho did take delivery of 12,937 feet of pipe in California between September 8, 1973 and October 5, 1973.

Sometime in October, Cal-Cut refused to make any more pipe available. The parties disagreed as to when this occurred. Cal-Cut said it was October 17, 1973, Southern Idaho maintains that it was around the first of October and that the reason given by Cal-Cut was that the sale was not profitable. It is undisputed that the supply of steel pipe was in short supply and that market prices rose sharply during the latter part of 1973 and during 1974.

[The court first decided that the trial court had in personam jurisdiction over Cal-Cut under Idaho's long-arm statute.] Having resolved the threshold issue of jurisdiction, we now proceed to the question of whether the sales forms exchanged between the two parties resulted in a binding contract. The transaction in question involved a sale of goods as defined in I.C. § 28–2–105 so it is within the scope of the Uniform Commercial Code. I.C. § 28–2–102. The relevant code section that determines the validity of an acceptance when it includes different or additional terms is I.C. § 28–2–207. . . .

Section 28–2–207 of the Uniform Commercial Code was designed primarily to render equity in cases where an acceptance added additional or different terms and performance had not yet begun. At common law an acceptance had to mirror an offer; an ostensible acceptance that contained even a frivolous variation from the original terms of an offer was construed as a counteroffer. The draftsmen of § 28–2–207 had cases like Poel v. Brunswick Balke-Collender Co., 216 N.Y. 310, 110 N.E. 619 (1915) in mind.

In most sales transactions the sales contract is not bargained for in the usual meaning of the term. In lieu of comprehensive bargaining, the seller and the buyer exchange form contracts, each prepared by the party's respective counsel and each drafted to give advantage to its holder. The end result is that the two sets of forms usually diverge.

The parties to the transaction in *Brunswick* followed this procedure. The seller initiated the transaction sending the buyer an offer. The buyer sent back its own order form which happened to coincide with that of the seller except in one minor respect—it added "The acceptance of this offer you must in any event promptly acknowledge." The seller failed to acknowledge and the buyer for independent business reasons backed out of the contract. When the seller sued the buyer, the court, following the traditional common law approach, held that the buyer's order form did not constitute an acceptance, but was a counteroffer; a contract never came into being and the seller had no remedy. Section 28–2–207 changes the results in cases such as these. Its net effect is to lock the welsher into the contract; it rejects the common law mirror image rule and converts the common law counteroffer into an acceptance.

In this context, the dictates of § 28–2–207 are unambiguous. Unfortunately, the far more typical situation which courts have had to deal with is a dispute as to the terms of a contract which arises after the parties exchange documents, perform, or start to perform. Section 28–2–207 is less suited to this terrain. As one commentator has stated it, "This is not only a different but also a more difficult problem for the law than that of keeping the welsher in. The law as to terms must be sophisticated enough to nullify the efforts of fine-print lawyers, it must be sufficiently reliance-oriented to protect the legitimate expectations of the parties, and it must be fair and even-handed." J. White and R. Summers, Uniform Commercial Code § 1–2 (1972). Insofar as Section 28–2–207 was drafted primarily to create a contract where one did not exist under the common law, it does not furnish unambiguous answers to the varied problems that emerge when the legal dispute arises as to the terms of a contract after performance has begun.

In the present case, we have an acceptance that contains not additional terms, but contradictory terms. Southern Idaho in its acceptance changed the delivery date from October 15, 1975, to December 15, 1975. We also have partial performance of the contract.

The presence of contradictory terms does not present a problem as to the validity of the acceptance. The Uniform Commercial Code clearly envisions that a contract came into being under the facts of this case. Section 28–2–207(1) provides that a "definite and seasonable expression of acceptance . . . operates as an acceptance even though it states terms *additional to or different* from those offered or agreed upon, unless acceptance is expressly made conditional on assent to the additional or different terms." (emphasis added)

Although it is conceivable that a purported acceptance can be so different from the terms of an offer that it would not create a binding contract,[1] we do not believe that the acceptance in the case at bar

1. Section 28–2–204 of the Uniform Commercial Code establishes the general proposition that a "contract for the sale of goods may be made in any manner sufficient to show agreement." A purported acceptance that differs radically from the terms of an offer arguably does not manifest sufficient agreement to the offer to create a contractual obligation. Given the language and history of the Uniform Commercial Code this would be the exception, however. A document can qualify as an acceptance under § 2–207(1) and yet differ substantially from the offer. J. White and R.

diverged so radically from the terms of the offer to warrant this result. There are several indications in the record that the altered final delivery date did not constitute a radical change. Cal-Cut apparently acquiesced in the new delivery date when it added the postscript "we will work it out" to the confirmation form and when it began performance. In fact, Archie Langdon, president of Southern Idaho, testified that Cal-Cut orally agreed to the final delivery date. Cal-Cut also failed to establish the urgency of the October 15th as opposed to December 15th final delivery date. We therefore hold that Southern Idaho's response to Cal-Cut's offer created a binding contractual relationship between the parties.

The Uniform Commercial Code establishes the existence of a contract, but what terms it embodies is problematic.[2] Section 207(2) provides guidelines for the incorporation of additional terms, but it is silent as to the reconciliation of different terms. Section 207(3) states that the "terms of a particular contract consist of those terms on which the writings of the parties agree, together with any supplementary terms incorporated under any other provisions of this act," but it applies only to contracts that are actualized by the conduct of the parties in the absence of a written agreement. Here, we have already held that the written communications of the parties establish a contract.

Cal-Cut makes the argument that since its document was the offer, Southern Idaho's expression of acceptance was an acceptance of all the terms on this form, including the October 15th delivery date. Under this argument, the first party to a sales transaction will always get his own terms. In most commercial transactions, which party processes its form first is purely fortuitous. To allow the contents of a contract to be determined on this basis runs contrary to the underlying purposes of the Uniform Commercial Code of modernizing the law governing commercial transactions. I.C. § 28–1–102. We cannot accept such an arbitrary solution.

Nor can we accept the solution offered in Roto-Lith, Ltd. v. F. P. Bartlett & Co., 297 F.2d 497 (1st Cir. 1962). In that case the buyer sent a purchase order to the seller for a quantity of cellophane adhesive manufactured by the latter. Subsequently the seller returned an acknowledgment that contained a disclaimer of all warranties on the products. The buyer was silent as to the disclaimer; he neither as-

Summers, Uniform Commercial Code 1–2 (1969).

2. Cal-Cut's offer allowed an October 15, 1975 final delivery date while Southern Idaho's acceptance set the final delivery date as December 15, 1975. What the final delivery date was is significant not only because of its bearing on damages, but also because it is relevant to the issue of breach. The record contains contradictory evidence as to when Cal-Cut ceased deliveries. Cal-Cut contends that it was October 17, 1973, while Southern Idaho sets the date as October 1, 1973.

sented nor objected to it. The emulsion was shipped thereafter and was received and paid for by the buyer. The problem arose when the emulsion failed to adhere and the buyer instituted an action for damages. The First Circuit Court held that a responding document "which states a condition materially altering the obligation solely to the disadvantage of the offeror" was "expressly conditional" within the meaning of § 2–207(1).[3] The seller's supposed acceptance was therefore a counteroffer which was accepted when the buyer received and used the goods.

Under this approach, the party who fortuitously sends the responding form, will get all of his terms. *Roto-Lith* also undermines the purposes of § 28–2–207(1) in that it effectively reinstates the common law mirror image rule whenever, as would usually be the case, a responding document states a condition solely advantageous to the party proposing it.[4]

The solution we choose to adopt is one suggested by Comment 6 to § 28–2–207. "6. If no answer is received within a reasonable time after additional terms are proposed, it is both fair and commercially sound to assume that their inclusion has been assented to. Where clauses on confirming forms sent by both parties conflict each party must be assumed to object to a clause of the other conflicting with one on the confirmation sent by himself. As a result the requirement that there be notice of objection which is found in subsection (2) is satisfied and the conflicting terms do not become a part of the contract. The contract then consists of the terms originally expressly agreed to, terms on which the confirmations agree, and terms supplied by this Act, including subsection (2)." We acknowledge that this comment is confusing in that it refers both to conflicting terms and to § 28–2–207(2) which deals exclusively with additional terms. We believe, however, that the draftsmen of the Uniform Commercial Code must have intended Comment 6 to be relevant to the resolution of the present controversy. Section 28–2–207(1) allows a responding document containing different terms to function as an acceptance, but except for Comment 6 nothing in the Uniform Commercial Code broaches the subject of how the conflicting terms are to be incorporated into one contract. Section 28–2–207(2) details under what circumstances additional terms are incorporated into a contract. Section 28–2–207(3) determines the contents of a contract formed by conduct evidencing a contract. Comment 6 is the only explanation the draftsmen provide for the problem of conflicting terms.

3. Idaho Code § 28–2–207(1) provides that a responding document containing additional or different terms operates as an acceptance unless the "acceptance is expressly made conditional on assent to the additional or different terms."

4. *Roto-Lith* involved a responding document that contained an additional term, but its reasoning would be equally applicable to a response containing different terms. We reject it in both cases.

We hold on its authority that where a contract is formed by conflicting documents, the conflicting terms cancel out. The contract then consists of the terms that both parties expressly agree to with the contested terms being supplied by other sections of the Uniform Commercial Code.

Comparing this solution with other alternative solutions, White and Summers have said: "This outcome favors neither party. But if the buyer-offeror's argument be accepted, the offeror will almost always get his own terms. If on the other hand, the *Roto-Lith* decision be followed, and the second document is not an acceptance or is expressly conditional and therefore cannot 'operate' as an acceptance, the second party will almost always get his own terms because the second document will constitute a counteroffer accepted by performance. We believe that neither of these results is sound. . . . We recognize that the Code may then provide a term substantially identical to one of those rejected. So be it. At least the term so supplied has the merit of being a term that the draftsmen considered fair." J. White and R. Summers, Uniform Commercial Code § 1–2 (1972).

In the present case, the parties final delivery date of October 15, 1973 and December 15, 1973 cancel out and we must look to I.C. § 28–2–309(1) to supply the contested term. That section provides that the "time for shipment or delivery or any other action under a contract if not provided in the chapter or agreed upon shall be a reasonable time."

When addressing the issue of reasonability, courts have considered such factors as the nature of the goods to be delivered, the extent of the seller's knowledge of the buyer's intention, transportation conditions, and the nature of the market. J. White and R. Summers, Uniform Commercial Code § 3–5 (1972). In short, in accordance with Comment 1 to I.C. § 28–2–309 they have looked "to what constitutes acceptable commercial conduct in view of the nature, purpose, and circumstances of the action to be taken."

The trial court found that December 15th was a reasonable termination date. The record includes evidence that supports this conclusion. Southern Idaho had to haul steel pipe from California to Idaho, the pipe was being unearthed over a forty-five mile distance, transfer commenced in early September, and 30,000 feet of pipe had to be transported. Cal-Cut knew that Southern Idaho was depending upon a December 15, 1975 termination date as is evidenced by its confirmation letter stating that "we will work it out." We, therefore, adhere to the oft-quoted maxim that findings of the trial court which are supported by substantial and competent evidence will not be disturbed on appeal.

Given a December 15, 1973, termination date, Cal-Cut breached the contract when it declined to make further deliveries before that date. Southern Idaho is entitled to damages. [The court concluded that the trial court had properly awarded Southern Idaho damages for its loss of profits.]

Judgment affirmed. Costs to respondent.

NOTES

(1) *"Knock-Out Doctrine."* In their second edition, Professors White and Summers disagree over whether conflicting terms in an offer and an acceptance knock each other out. White and Summers differ as to the applicability of Comment 6 to UCC 2–207. "One of us (White) would turn to the foregoing comment and find that the two terms cancel one another. . . . The other of us (Summers) believes that Comment 6 . . . applies only to variant terms on *confirming* forms," not in an offer and an acceptance. J. White and R. Summers, Law under the Uniform Commercial Code § 1–2 (2d ed. 1980). Accord: Bosway Tube & Steel Corp. v. McKay Machine Co., 65 Mich.App. 426, 237 N.W.2d 488 (1975) (conflict as to warranties). Does an interpretation of UCC 2–207(1) that turns on whether the term in the "expression of acceptance" is "different" (in the sense of "conflicting") or merely "additional" seem sound?

The "knock-out doctrine" has not escaped criticism. "Surely this reasoning is wrong on just about all counts . . . . [W]here in the Code is there any hint at the proposition that an offeror has been defrocked of his prime common law prerogative, that of determining the basis on which he is willing to contract? . . . The Code would not have stood the chance for passage of the proverbial snowball in hell had the legal profession been instructed that it was intended to jettison so fundamental a legal principle as that which for centuries has given to offerors the right to fashion the basis of their sanctionable bargains. True, section 2–207 gives to offerees an ability to modify those terms unilaterally, but only under very limited circumstances. This is part of the trade-off for holding offerees to deals into which they inject an ambiguity, an ambiguity which the mirror image rule of the common law allowed as an escape from the normal expectations of the parties. The principal condition of this power is that the variance be immaterial. Short of this, . . . the terms of the offer control." Furthermore, reliance on Comment 6 is misplaced because it purports to explain only subsection (2) and not subsection (3), because it "lacks desired clarity" even in this, and because a "comment which is at odds with the section it purports to explain should . . . be ignored." A comment that might be useful is Comment 3, "which suggests that subsection (2) covers different as well as additional terms." Duesenberg, Contract Creation: The Continuing Struggle with Additional and Different Terms under Uniform Commercial Code Section 2–207, 34 Bus.Law 1477, 1484–86 (1979).[a]

(2) *Problem.* Idaho Power asked Westinghouse its price for a three-phase voltage regulator. Westinghouse responded with an offer to sell at a stated price on a form that excluded liability for "consequential damages" and that provided that its terms "and such others as may be accepted by Westinghouse in writing, constitute the entire agreement for the sale of the

a. Reproduced by permission of The Business Lawyer.

product." Idaho Power then sent its purchase order, which referred to Westinghouse's offer and provided, "acceptance of this order shall be deemed to constitute an agreement upon the part of the seller to the conditions named hereon and supersedes all previous agreements." After the regulator was delivered and installed, it failed, causing a fire. Idaho Power sues Westinghouse in a federal district court. How should the court decide under Idaho law? See Idaho Power Co. v. Westinghouse Electric Corp., 596 F.2d 924 (9th Cir. 1979).

CONSTRUCTION AGGREGATES CORP. v. HEWITT-ROBINS, 404 F.2d 505 (7th Cir. 1968). [Construction Aggregates Corp. (CAC) was the successful bidder on a contract to construct dikes enclosing some 60 square miles of the Dead Sea in Israel in order to form "evaporation pans" for the extraction of minerals. CAC then began negotiations with Hewitt-Robins (H-R) on a cost-plus contract for conveyors. On June 30, 1962, CAC sent H-R a letter "to set forth the final agreement" between the two companies and asking H-R to send its confirmation. On July 3 CAC sent H-R its purchase order. On July 20, H-R sent CAC a letter enclosing the executed acceptance copy of CAC's purchase order but stating that H-R's acceptance was "predicated on the following clarifications, additions or modifications to the order," including a substitute warranty clause which disclaimed liability for engineering design or component parts manufactured by others. CAC made no objection, except to telephone H-R on July 31 and get agreement, in a letter from H-R on that date, to a change in the terms of payment. CAC had difficulties with the conveyor system, which did not operate satisfactorily, and sued H-R for breach of implied warranties of fitness as to engineering design and component parts manufactured by others. From judgment for defendant on a jury verdict, plaintiff appealed.]

CUMMINGS, Circuit Judge. . . . Since H-R's acceptance was "expressly made conditional on assent to the additional or different terms" contained in its July 20th letter, the exception in the last clause of Section 2–207(1) of the Uniform Commercial Code was clearly applicable. Hence the district court was justified in permitting the jury to treat that letter as a counter-offer.

Section 2–207(3) recognizes that the subsequent conduct of the parties can establish a contract for sale. Since CAC's July 3 purchase order and H-R's July 20 counter-offer did not in themselves create a contract, Section 2–207(3) would operate to create one because the subsequent performance by both parties constituted "conduct by both parties which recognizes the existence of a contract." Such a contract by operation of law would consist only of "those terms on which the writings of the parties agree, together with any supplementary terms incorporated under other provisions of this Act." There having been no agreement on the warranty terms, the implied warranties provided in Sections 2–314 and 2–315 . . .

would then ordinarily become applicable. . . . Here, however, there is no occasion to create a contract by operation of law in default of further actions by the negotiating parties, for CAC can be said to have accepted the terms of H-R's counter-offer. CAC sought a change only in the payment terms of the counter-offer, raising no objection to H-R's other modifications of the original purchase order. H-R granted CAC's requested change in a letter of July 31 and could reasonably have assumed that CAC's single objection was an acquiescence in the remaining terms of the counter-offer. CAC did not object to this implication in H-R's July 31st letter reference to the terms of its counter-offer and therefore CAC could appropriately be held to the terms of the July 20th letter. . . .

[Affirmed.]

NOTE

"Expressly Made Conditional." What language in the offeree's form will satisfy the requirement of the proviso of UCC 2–207(1) that acceptance be "expressly made conditional on assent to the additional or different terms"? The Seventh Circuit later had this to say of its decision in the preceding case. "In Construction Aggregates Corp. v. Hewit-Robins, Inc., 404 F.2d 505, 509 (7th Cir. 1968), this court held that where a letter advised that acceptance was 'predicated on the following clarifications, additions or modifications' to a purchase order, acceptance was 'expressly made conditional on assent to the additional or different terms' and § 2–207(1) was therefore applicable. Although the writing did not state that acceptance was predicated on *assent* to the new terms, it was clear from the circumstances leading up to and surrounding this letter that such was the case. We do not read Construction Aggregates to say that the mere statement in a writing that it is subject to the terms included therein, along with the inclusion of additional or different terms, disqualifies the writing as an acceptance under § 2–207(1)." Luria Bros. & Co. Inc. v. Pielet Bros. Scrap Iron & Metal, Inc., 600 F.2d 103, 113 n. 12 (7th Cir. 1979).

C. ITOH & CO. (AMERICA) INC. v. JORDAN INT'L CO., 552 F.2d 1228 (7th Cir. 1977). [Itoh sent Jordan a purchase order for steel coils. Jordan sent back its acknowledgement form, which contained the following provision:

> Seller's acceptance is, however, expressly conditional on Buyer's assent to the additional or different terms and conditions set forth below and printed on the reverse side. If these terms are not acceptable, Buyer should notify Seller at once.

One of the provisions on the reverse side of Jordan's form was an arbitration clause that had no counterpart in Itoh's purchase order. After the steel had been delivered and paid for, Itoh sued Jordan claiming that the steel was defective and had been delivered late.

Jordan moved to stay the proceedings pending arbitration. From a denial of its motion, Jordan appealed.]

SPRECHER, Circuit Judge. . . . The instant case . . . involves the classic "battle of the forms" . . . . [Since] it is clear that the statement contained in Jordan's acknowledgement form comes within the Section 2–207(1) proviso . . . , the exchange of forms between Jordan and Itoh did not result in the formation of a contract under Section 2–207(1), and Jordan's form became a counteroffer. Thus, "[s]ince . . . [Itoh's] purchase order and . . . [Jordan's] counter-offer did not in themselves create a contract, Section 2–207(3) would operate to create one because the subsequent performance by both parties constituted 'conduct by both parties which recognizes the existence of a contract.'" Construction Aggregates, . . . at 509.

What are the terms of a contract created by conduct under Section 2–207(3) rather than by an exchange of forms under Section 2–207(1)? As noted above, at common law the terms of the contract between Jordan and Itoh would be the terms of the Jordan counter-offer. However, the Code has effectuated a radical departure from the common law rule. The second sentence of Section 2–207(3) provides that where, as here, a contract has been consummated by the conduct of the parties, "the terms of the particular contract consist of those terms on which the writings of the parties agree, together with any supplementary terms incorporated under any other provisions of this Act." Since it is clear that the Jordan and Itoh forms do not "agree" on arbitration, the only question which remains *under the Code* is whether arbitration may be considered a supplementary term incorporated under some other provision of the Code.

We have been unable to find any case authority shedding light on the question of what constitutes "supplementary terms" within the meaning of Section 2–207(3) and the Official Comments to Section 2–207 provide no guidance in this regard. We are persuaded, however, that the disputed additional terms (i. e., those terms on which the writings of the parties do not agree) which are necessarily excluded from a Subsection (3) contract by the language, "terms on which the writings of the parties agree," cannot be brought back into the contract under the guise of "supplementary terms." . . . Accordingly, we find that the "supplementary terms" contemplated by Section 2–207(3) are limited to those supplied by the standardized "gap-filler" provisions of Article Two. . . . Since provision for arbitration is not a necessary or missing term which would be supplied by one of the Code's "gap-filler" provisions unless agreed upon by the contracting parties, there is no arbitration term in the Section 2–207(3) contract which was created by the conduct of Jordan and Itoh in proceeding to perform even though no contract had been established by their exchange of writings.

We are convinced that this conclusion does not result in any unfair prejudice to a seller who elects to insert in his standard sales acknowledgement form the statement that acceptance is expressly conditional on buyer's assent to additional terms contained therein. Such a seller obtains a substantial benefit under Section 2–207(1) through the inclusion of an "expressly conditional" clause. If he decides after the exchange of forms that the particular transaction is not in his best interest, Subsection (1) permits him to walk away from the transaction without incurring any liability so long as the buyer has not in the interim expressly assented to the additional terms. Moreover, whether or not a seller will be disadvantaged under Subsection (3) as a consequence of inserting an "expressly conditional" clause in his standard form is within his control. If the seller in fact does not intend to close a particular deal unless the additional terms are assented to, he can protect himself by not delivering the goods until such assent is forthcoming. If the seller does intend to close a deal irrespective of whether or not the buyer assents to the additional terms, he can hardly complain when the contract formed under Subsection (3) as a result of the parties' conduct is held not to include those terms. Although a seller who employs such an "expressly conditional" clause in his acknowledgement form would undoubtedly appreciate the dual advantage of not being bound to a contract under Subsection (1) if he elects not to perform and of having his additional terms imposed on the buyer under Subsection (3) in the event that performance is in his best interest, we do not believe such a result is contemplated by Section 2–207. Rather, while a seller may take advantage of an "expressly conditional" clause under Subsection (1) when he elects not to perform, he must accept the potential risk under Subsection (3) of not getting his additional terms when he elects to proceed with performance without first obtaining buyer's assent to those terms. Since the seller injected ambiguity into the transaction by inserting the "expressly conditional" clause in his form, he, and not the buyer, should bear the consequence of that ambiguity under Subsection (3). . . .

Affirmed.

NOTES

(1) *Possibility of Rejection.* Would the result have been the same if Jordan had enclosed its form together with a letter saying, "We reject your offer to buy steel coils but enclose our own offer to sell steel coils"? (Does subsection (3) apply even if there is no "expression of acceptance" under subsection (1)?) Would a clause to the same effect on Jordan's form be as likely to succeed?

(2) *Strategy in the "Battle."* How should the parties draft their forms to win the "battle of the forms" under the Code? Is it better to be the offeror or the offeree? What clauses should be included in the buyer's "request for quotation," the seller's "quotation," the buyer's "purchase order," and the seller's "sales acknowledgement" forms? Would it not make

sense, at least where the buyer and seller have a continuing relationship, to negotiate an overriding agreement to govern all sales between them, rather than to engage in the "battle of the forms" each time? Would you so advise a client whose bargaining position is weak? Another possibility, of course, is for a trade association to work out standard terms to which both parties can adhere.

For advice on strategy, see Apsey, The Battle of the Forms, 34 Notre Dame Law. 556 (1959); Lipman, On Winning the Battle of the Forms: An Analysis of Section 2–207 of the Uniform Commercial Code, 24 Bus.Law. 789 (1969). On the battle in general, see Murray, Section 2–207 of the Uniform Commercial Code: Another Word about Incipient Unconscionability, 39 U.Pitt.L.Rev. 597 (1978); Murray, Intention Over Terms: An Exploration of UCC 2–207 and New Section 60, Restatement of Contracts, 37 Fordham L.Rev. 317 (1969); Taylor, U.C.C. Section 2–207: An Integration of Legal Abstractions and Transactional Reality, 46 U.Cin.L.Rev. 419 (1977); Notes, 57 Nw.U.L.Rev. 477 (1962); 30 U.Chi.L.Rev. 540 (1963); 32 U.Pitt.L.Rev. 209 (1970).

(3) *Business Practices and the "Battle of the Forms."* Macaulay concludes, on the basis of his study, p. 276 supra, that although businessmen sometimes make carefully planned contracts, in most situations contract is not needed, both because there is usually little room for honest misunderstandings or good faith differences of opinion about the seller's performances, and because there are many effective non-legal sanctions. The detailed planning required for contract may even be undesirable, as opposed to a more flexible relationship. Furthermore, resort to litigation, or the threat of litigation, has both monetary and non-monetary costs. Are such conclusions helpful in formulating legal rules applicable to the transactions described?

(4) *A Canadian Version.* In 1979 the Ontario Law Reform Commission published a draft bill to revise the Ontario Sale of Goods Act. In many respects the Commission looked to the Uniform Commercial Code for inspiration. It concluded, however, "that section 2–207 is not well drafted and that it raises as many issues as it solves . . . and that more than cosmetic changes are necessary in order to find acceptable solutions to the great variety of problems endemic in the 'battle of the forms' phenomenon." It therefore incorporated in its draft only "an almost verbatim version of UCC 2–207(3). 1 Ontario Law Reform Comm'n, Report on Sale of Goods 81–86 (1979). Would you agree?

SECTION 4. RELIANCE ON AN OFFER THAT SEEKS PERFORMANCE: REAL ESTATE BROKERS

Not since the series of cases that began with Hamer v. Sidway (Chapter 1, Section 2) have we explored the "unilateral" contract, in which the consideration is a performance rather than another promise. How do the rules of offer and acceptance apply to such a contract? According to Professor A. W. B. Simpson, an English legal historian, it was only in the nineteenth century that the idea grew up "that acceptance made a promise binding—it was consideration which did that . . . . All this changed in nineteenth-century law, when a doctrine of offer and acceptance was superimposed upon the sixteenth-century requirement of consideration and made to perform some of the same functions and some new ones generated principally by the problem of written contracts by correspondence . . . . The application of the offer and acceptance analysis to [offers of unilateral contracts] has never been happy; it only became canonical late in the nineteenth century in the celebrated case of Carlill v. Carbolic Smoke Ball Co. (1892)." [a] Simpson, Innovation in Nineteenth Century Contract Law, 91 L.Q.Rev. 247, 258, 262 (1975).

Requirement of Notice. That celebrated case involved the requirement of notice of acceptance of an offer of a unilateral contract.[b] It arose out of the following advertisement: "£100 reward will be paid by the Carbolic Smoke Ball Company to any person who contracts the increasing epidemic influenza, colds or any disease caused by taking cold, after having used the ball three times daily for two weeks according to the printed directions supplied with each ball. £1000 is deposited with the Alliance Bank, Regent Street shewing our sincerity in the matter. . . ." On the faith of this advertisement, Carlill used one of the balls as directed. When she contracted influenza, she sued the Company and was awarded £100 damages. The Company's appeal was dismissed. As Lindley, L. J., explained, the advertisement was not "a mere puff" but an offer under which "the reward is offered to any person who contracts the epidemic or other disease within a reasonable time after having used the smoke ball." The fact that she had not notified the Company of her acceptance was not fatal to her claim.[c] According to Bowen, L. J., "One cannot doubt that, as an ordinary rule of law, an acceptance of an offer made ought to be notified to the person who makes the offer, in order that the two minds may come together. . . . But there is this clear gloss to be made upon that doctrine, that as notification of acceptance is required for the benefit of the person who makes the

a. [1893] 1 Q.B. 256 (C.A.1892).

b. As White v. Corlies and Tift, p. 201 supra, suggests, where an offeror proposes a "bilateral" contract and invites acceptance by means of a promise it is ordinarily understood that the offeree must at least take steps to see that his promise is, in the words of the opinion in that case, "in some reasonable time communicated to him." See also Restatement Second, § 56. That this is not always so, however, see the International Filter case, p. 196 supra.

c. Was the acceptance of the Carbolic Smoke Ball Company's offer: (1) the purchase of the smoke ball; (2) its use in accordance with directions; (3) the plaintiff's contracting influenza; or (4) all three? Which of these acts was bargained for? Recall that a promise may be conditional, so that its performance becomes due only if a specified event occurs. See Note 2, p. 70 supra. Was there a conditional promise in the Carbolic Smoke Ball case?

offer, the person who makes the offer may dispense with notice to himself, if he thinks it desirable to do so, and I suppose there can be no doubt that where a person in an offer made by him to another person, expressly or impliedly intimates a particular mode of acceptance as sufficient to make the bargain binding, it is only necessary for the other person to whom such offer is made to follow the indicated method of acceptance; and if the person making the offer, expressly or impliedly intimates in his offer that it will be sufficient to act on the proposal without communicating acceptance of it to himself, performance of the condition is a sufficient acceptance without notification. . . . Now, if that is the law, how are we to find out whether the person who makes the offer does intimate that notification of acceptance will not be necessary in order to constitute a binding bargain? In many cases you look to the offer itself. In many cases you extract from the character of the transaction that notification is not required, and in the advertisement cases it seems to me to follow as an inference to be drawn from the transaction itself that a person is not to notify his acceptance of the offer before he performs the condition, but that if he performs the condition notification is dispensed with. It seems to me that from the point of view of common sense no other idea could be entertained."

A leading American case on the necessity of notice of acceptance of a unilateral offer is Bishop v. Eaton, 161 Mass. 496, 37 N.E. 665 (1894). In that case Frank Eaton, in Nova Scotia, had written to Bishop, in Illinois, that if he would help his brother, Harry Eaton, to get money, "I will see that it is paid." Bishop did help Harry get money by signing his note as surety when he got a loan. When Harry did not repay the loan, Bishop did, and sued Frank on his promise. The court thought that this was a case in which notice should have been given, since the loan was made in Illinois and Frank was in Nova Scotia. "Ordinarily there is no occasion to notify the offeror of the acceptance of such an offer, for the doing of the act is a sufficient acceptance, and the promisor knows that he is bound when he sees that action has been taken on the faith of his offer. But if the act is of such a kind that knowledge of it will not quickly come to the promisor, the promisee is bound to give him notice of his acceptance within a reasonable time after doing that which constitutes the acceptance." However, the court concluded that notice had been given.

Would notice have been required in these two cases under the rule stated in Restatement Second, § 54? What is the consequence of a requirement of notice? Take the facts of Bishop v. Eaton. Such a requirement can be framed so that Bishop does not accept Frank's offer until he both signs Harry's note and sends the notice to Frank. Or it can be framed so that Bishop accepts Frank's offer when he signs the note, but Frank's obligation is discharged if Bishop does not send a notice within a reasonable time. Would it make any difference? Suppose (putting the case in a modern context) that the day after Bishop signs the note, and before he has sent the notice to Frank, Frank telephones Bishop and tells him that he revokes. Is the revocation effective? See Restatement Second, § 54; UCC 2–206(2); Dole, Notice Requirements of Guaranty Contracts, 62 Mich.L.Rev. 57 (1963).

The Brooklyn Bridge Hypothetical. Professor Simpson's misgivings about the application of offer and acceptance analysis to offers of unilateral contracts can be illustrated by a notorious hypothetical put by Professor Wormser early in this century: "Suppose A says to B, 'I will give you $100 if you walk across the Brooklyn Bridge' . . . . B starts to walk across the Brooklyn Bridge and has gone about one-half of the way across. At that moment A overtakes B and says to him, 'I withdraw my offer.' Has B then any rights against A? Again, let us suppose that after A has said, 'I withdraw my offer,' B continues to walk across the Brooklyn Bridge and completes the act of crossing. Under these circumstances, has B any rights against A?" Wormser concluded that he had none. "What A wanted from B, what A asked for, was the act of walking across the bridge. Until that was done, B had not given to A what A had requested. The acceptance by B of A's offer could be nothing but the act on B's part of crossing the bridge. It is elementary that an offeror may withdraw his offer until it has been accepted. It follows logically that A is perfectly within his rights in withdrawing his offer before B has accepted it by walking across the bridge—the act contemplated by the offeror and the offeree as the acceptance of the offer." [d] Wormser, The True Conception of Unilateral Contracts, 26 Yale L.J. 136–137 (1916).

Restatement Second, § 45 states a rule, based on former Restatement, § 45 [e] and couched in language of "option contract," that supports a different result. It is set out below. (It is helpful in reading this section to understand that one cannot "tender" a performance that is to extend over a period of time, such as the crossing of the

d. Some courts have held that it also follows that such a contract is not within the one-year provision of the statute of frauds even if the offeree's performance cannot be completed within a year. They reason that "the making" of the contract does not occur until performance is completed. Hartung v. Billmeier, 243 Minn. 148, 66 N.W.2d 784 (1954); Auerbach's, Inc. v. Kimball, 572 P.2d 376 (Utah, 1977). However, in Hamer v. Sidway, p. 44 supra, the court said (124 N.Y. at 548, 27 N.E. at 258, an omitted part of the opinion) that the contract there was within the one-year provision, although the uncle was precluded from asserting it.

e. **§ 45. Revocation of Offer for Unilateral Contract; Effect of Part Performance or Tender**

If an offer for a unilateral contract is made, and part of the consideration requested in the offer is given or tendered by the offeree in response thereto, the offeror is bound by a contract, the duty of immediate performance of which is conditional on the full consideration being given or tendered within the time stated in the offer, or, if no time is stated therein, within a reasonable time.

Brooklyn Bridge.) Indeed, thirty-four years after Wormser first wrote of the Brooklyn Bridge hypothetical, he admitted: "Since that time I have repented, so that now, clad in sackcloth, I state frankly, that my point of view has changed. I agree, at this time, with the rule set forth in the Restatement . . . ." Book Review, 3 J.Legal Ed. 145 (1950).

§ 45. Option Contract Created by Part Performance or Tender

(1) Where an offer invites an offeree to accept by rendering a performance and does not invite a promissory acceptance, an option contract is created when the offeree tenders or begins the invited performance or tenders a beginning of it.

(2) The offeror's duty of performance under any option contract so created is conditional on completion or tender of the invited performance in accordance with the terms of the offer.

NOTES

(1) *Objections to "Option Contract."* Are there any objections to the "option contract" notion? May it not, in a rapidly fluctuating market, give the offeree an unfair chance to speculate during the time when the offeror is bound but the offeree is not? Judging from the kinds of situations in which the problem of the Brooklyn Bridge hypothetical actually arises, how great is this danger likely to be?

Would there be any advantage in limiting recovery by B in the Brooklyn Bridge hypothetical to damages based on his reliance rather than his expectation interest? See Fuller and Perdue, The Reliance Interest in Contract Damages: 2, 46 Yale L.J. 373, 410–17 (1937).

(2) *The Case of the Move to Maine.* Mrs. Hodgkin was a widow who lived alone on her farm in Lewiston, Maine. On February 8, 1915, she wrote Mrs. Brackenbury, one of her six children, in Independence, Missouri. She offered the Brackenburys the use and income of the farm if they would move to Maine and take care of Mrs. Hodgkin there during her life. The letter closed, "you to have the place when I have passed away." The Brackenburys moved to Maine late in April and began performance. But after a few weeks trouble developed, relations between the parties grew most disagreeable, and a suit was brought to force the Brackenburys to leave. They in turn sued to enforce their rights and prevailed in the trial court. *Held:* Affirmed. "The offer was the basis, not of a bilateral contract, requiring a reciprocal promise, a promise for a promise, but of a unilateral contract requiring an act for a promise . . . . The plaintiffs here accepted the offer by moving from Missouri to the mother's farm in Lewiston and entering upon the performance of the specified acts, and they have continued performance since that time so far as they have been permitted by the mother to do so. The existence of a completed and valid contract is clear." Brackenbury v. Hodgkin, 116 Me. 399, 102 A. 106 (1917).[f]

f. It is reported that even after this litigation, the Brackenburys and Mrs. Hodgkin continued to live together until Mrs. Hodgkin's death in Janu-

(3) *Is Promise or Performance Sought?* The whole problem can be avoided, of course, if the offer seeks a promise as acceptance and either a promise is given in so many words or one can be spelled out from the offeree's conduct. (Suppose, for example, that Mrs. Hodgkin's letter had read: "If you will agree to move to Lewiston and care for me on the home place. . . .") In Davis v. Jacoby, 1 Cal.2d 370, 34 P.2d 1026 (1934), the court held that an offer somewhat similar to that in Brackenbury v. Hodgkin invited a promise as acceptance, relying in part on the offeror's language: "Will you let me hear from you as soon as possible. . . ." In case of doubt, Restatement Second, § 32 gives the offeree an opportunity to treat the offer as inviting a promise as acceptance and thus to avoid Professor Wormser's argument simply by giving his promise. Would such an opportunity have been of any advantage to the Brackenburys? What if Mrs. Hodgkin had died after they had sold their home and liquidated their business in Missouri and begun the journey to Maine?

Are there circumstances in which an offeree might find an offer that invites a promise as acceptance *less* appealing than one which invites performance as acceptance? Suppose that the offeree's risk of failure is considerable, e. g., that A is seeking to get B to climb a flagpole rather than cross the Brooklyn Bridge. (Consider also the offer of a reward as in Broadnax v. Ledbetter, p. 65 supra.) How might an offeror frame an offer to make it appealing to the offeree under circumstances involving *both* substantial preparation for performance by the offeree *and* considerable risk of failure on his part, e. g., calling for him to deliver a piece of technologically sophisticated equipment which he might not be able to develop according to the required specifications?

(4) *The Case of the Maleficent Mortgagee.* Pattberg held a mortgage on Petterson's house on which $5,450 was due. On April 4, he wrote Petterson: "I hereby agree to accept cash for the mortgage. . . . It is understood and agreed as a consideration that I will allow you $780 providing said mortgage is paid on or before May 31. . . ." Late in May Petterson knocked at Pattberg's door with the cash. Pattberg demanded the name of his caller. Petterson replied: "It is Mr. Petterson. I have come to pay off the mortgage." Pattberg then said he had sold the mortgage. Petterson was obliged to pay the full amount to the purchaser. His widow sued Pattberg for $780. From a judgment for the plaintiff the defendant appealed. *Held:* Reversed. "[I]t clearly appears that the defendant's offer was withdrawn before its acceptance had been tendered. It is unnecessary to determine, therefore, what the legal situation might have been had tender been made before withdrawal." Speaking for himself, the writer of the opinion, Kellogg, J., thought the result would be the same since "the act requested to be performed was the complete act of payment, a thing incapable of performance unless assented to by the person paid." Lehman, J., dissented. "In unmistakable terms the defendant agreed to accept payment. . . . I recognize that in this case only an offer of payment and not a formal tender of payment was made. . . . Even so, under the fair con-

ary, 1921, that "the relations were unpleasant to the end," and that Mr. Brackenbury obtained a transcript of the record in the case and "would, from time to time, read from it to the old lady." J. Dawson and W. Harvey, Cases on Contracts 356 (3d ed. 1977).

struction of the words of the letter, I think the plaintiff had done the act which the defendant requested as consideration for his promise. . . . A formal tender is seldom made in business transactions, except to lay the foundation for subsequent assertion in a court of justice of rights which spring from refusal of the tender." Petterson v. Pattberg, 248 N.Y. 86, 161 N.E. 428 (1928).[g]

In 1937 New York enacted a statute providing that a written and signed offer to accept a performance in satisfaction of a claim, followed by a tender of performance before revocation, shall not be denied effect by reason of refusal of the tender. N.Y.Gen.Obl.L. § 15–503. Would this statute affect the result in Petterson v. Pattberg? In the Brooklyn Bridge hypothetical?

BROKERS AND THE BROOKLYN BRIDGE

The reader whose sense of relevance requires an example from the world of business may prefer to look at these problems through the optic of the real estate broker. Suppose that an owner of real property lists the property with a broker under an exclusive sale arrangement, promising the broker a commission if he arranges a sale and promising not to sell it himself or through another broker. Is the owner liable if, after the broker has incurred expenses in attempting to procure a buyer, he terminates their relationship, or sells the property himself or through another broker?

Most owners, in listing their property with a broker, use an "open" listing, under which the property is listed with more than one broker and the one who is fortunate enough to effect the sale claims his commission much as the bounty hunter claims his reward. The incentive for any one broker to make a substantial effort may, however, be small under an open listing. An owner who wants to encourage a particular broker to use more diligent efforts may give him the exclusive right to sell the property for a period of time under either an "exclusive agency" or an "exclusive right to sell." These differ in that the owner retains the right to sell the property himself under an "exclusive agency" but not under an "exclusive right to sell." [a] See Wallace, Promissory Liability Under Real Estate Brokerage Contracts, 37 Iowa L.Rev. 350 (1952); Note, 23 S.D.L.Rev. 478 (1978).

g. For a suggestion, based on the record on appeal, "that the mortgagor knew of the previous sale of the mortgage; since he brought $4,000 in cash with him, and was accompanied by his wife and a notary public as witnesses," see Note, 14 Cornell L.Q. 81, 84 n. 18 (1928).

a. There is also an arrangement called a "multiple listing" that attempts to combine the virtues of open and exclusive listings by having the owner list his property with a member of the local real estate board who promises to use his best efforts and, in turn, to sublist the property with other members of the board. He splits his commission if another broker arranges a sale.

What is the broker's situation if, after he has spent time and effort in trying to arrange a sale under an exclusive arrangement, the owner attempts to revoke? [b]

NOTES

(1) *Performance by Broker.* What amounts to performance by a broker of a listing agreement? Unless the agreement provides otherwise, the broker is generally considered to have earned his commission if he arranges a contract of sale between the seller and a buyer, even if it is not on terms as favorable to the seller as those that he stated in the listing agreement. (The seller will often be forced to sell at a lower price than that in the agreement and to accept a term conditioning the buyer's duty on his ability to obtain financing.) Absent a provision to the contrary, the broker is entitled to his commission even if the buyer later refuses to perform in breach of the contract of sale. It is not, however, necessary for the broker to arrange a contract of sale, for he is generally considered to have earned his commission if he produces a buyer "ready, willing and able" to buy on the terms stated by the seller in the listing agreement.

(2) *Problem.* John Smith listed his apartment building in Wisconsin with Clark Mansfield, a local real estate broker, at a cash price of $430,000 or at any other price or upon any other terms accepted by the seller during the term of the contract. Mansfield got an offer from Clarence McFadden in California for $412,000. Smith rejected it as too low, but later told Mansfield that he would accept it if Mansfield would reduce his commission from 5% of the sales price to a flat $15,000. Smith signed a contract of sale at $412,000 and it was mailed to McFadden in California, who signed it and mailed it back to Mansfield. Before Mansfield received it, however, he received a telegram from McFadden saying that he would not go through with the sale. McFadden did not buy the property and Smith, who believed that no contract for sale had been made, brought no action against him. Is Mansfield entitled to his $15,000 commission? See Mansfield v. Smith, 88 Wis.2d 575, 277 N.W.2d 740 (1979).

MARCHIONDO v. SCHECK

Supreme Court of New Mexico, 1967.
78 N.M. 440, 432 P.2d 405.

WOOD, Judge, Court of Appeals. The issue is whether the offeror had a right to revoke his offer to enter a unilateral contract.

Defendant, in writing, offered to sell real estate to a specified prospective buyer and agreed to pay a percentage of the sales price as a commission to the broker. The offer fixed a six-day time limit for acceptance. Defendant, in writing, revoked the offer. The revoca-

b. As to what happens if the buyer reneges after signing a contract, see Tristram's Landing v. Wait, 367 Mass. 622, 327 N.E.2d 727 (1975), following the "growing minority of states who have adopted the rule of Ellsworth Dobbs, Inc. v. Johnson, 50 N.J. 528, 236 A.2d 843 (1967)."

tion was received by the broker on the morning of the sixth day. Later that day, the broker obtained the offeree's acceptance.

Plaintiff, the broker, claiming breach of contract, sued defendant for the commission stated in the offer. On the above facts, the trial court dismissed the complaint.

We are not concerned with the revocation of the offer as between the offeror and the prospective purchaser. With certain exceptions (see C.J.S. Brokers § 95(2), pp. 223–224), the right of a broker to the agreed compensation, or damages measured thereby, is not defeated by the refusal of the principal to complete or consummate a transaction. Southwest Motel Brokers, Inc. v. Alamo Hotels, Inc., 72 N.M. 227, 382 P.2d 707 (1963).

Plaintiff's appeal concerns the revocation of his agency. As to that revocation, the issue between the offeror and his agent is not whether defendant had the power to revoke; rather, it is whether he had the right to revoke. 1 Mechem on Agency, § 568 at 405 (2d ed. 1914).

When defendant made his offer to pay a commission upon sale of the property, he offered to enter a unilateral contract; the offer was for an act to be performed, a sale. 1 Williston on Contracts, § 13 at 23 (3rd ed. 1957); Hutchinson v. Dobson-Bainbridge Realty Co., 31 Tenn.App. 490, 217 S.W.2d 6 (1946).

Many courts hold that the principal has the right to revoke the broker's agency at any time before the broker has actually procured a purchaser. See Hutchinson v. Dobson-Bainbridge Realty Co., supra, and cases therein cited. The reason given is that until there is performance, the offeror has not received that contemplated by his offer, and there is no contract. Further, the offeror may never receive the requested performance because the offeree is not obligated to perform. Until the offeror receives the requested performance, no consideration has passed from the offeree to the offeror. Thus, until the performance is received, the offeror may withdraw the offer. Williston, supra, § 60; Hutchinson v. Dobson-Bainbridge Realty Co., supra.

Defendant asserts that the trial court was correct in applying this rule. However, plaintiff contends that the rule is not applicable where there has been part performance of the offer.

Hutchinson v. Dobson-Bainbridge Realty Co., supra, states:

"A greater number of courts, however, hold that part performance of the consideration may make such an offer irrevocable and that where the offeree or broker manifests his assent to the offer by entering upon performance and spending time and money in his efforts to perform, then the offer becomes irrevocable during the time stated and binding upon the principal according to its terms. . . ."

Defendant contends that the decisions giving effect to a part performance are distinguishable. He asserts that in these cases the offer was of an exclusive right to sell or of an exclusive agency. Because neither factor is present here, he asserts that the "part performance" decisions are not applicable.

Many of the decisions do seem to emphasize the exclusive aspects of the offer. See Garrett v. Richardson, 149 Colo. 449, 369 P.2d 566 (1962); Geyler v. Dailey, 70 Ariz. 135, 217 P.2d 583 (1950); S. Blumenthal & Co. v. Bridges, 91 Ark. 212, 120 S.W. 974, 24 L.R.A.,N.S., 279 (1909); Williston, supra, § 60A, note 6, and cases there cited. See also Manzo v. Park, 220 Ark. 216, 247 S.W.2d 12 (1952), where a listing agreement for a definite period of time was held to imply an exclusive right to sell within the time named.

Such emphasis reaches its extreme conclusion in Tetrick v. Sloan, 170 Cal.App.2d 540, 339 P.2d 613 (1959), where no effect was given to the part performance because there was neither an exclusive agency, nor an exclusive right to sell.

Defendant's offer did not specifically state that it was exclusive. Under § 70–1–43, N.M.S.A.1953, it was not an exclusive agreement. It is not the exclusiveness of the offer that deprives the offeror of the right to revoke. It is the action taken by the offeree which deprives the offeror of that right. Until there is action by the offeree—a partial performance pursuant to the offer—the offeror may revoke even if his offer is of an exclusive agency or an exclusive right to sell. Levander v. Johnson, 181 Wis. 68, 193 N.W. 970 (1923).

Once partial performance is begun pursuant to the offer made, a contract results. This contract has been termed a contract with conditions or an option contract. This terminology is illustrated as follows: [the court quoted Restatement, § 45 and Restatement Second, § 45].

Restatement (Second) of Contracts, § 45, . . . , comment (g), says:

"This Section frequently applies to agency arrangements, particularly offers made to real estate brokers. . . ."

See Restatement (Second) of Agency § 446, comment (b).

The reason for finding such a contract is stated in Hutchinson v. Dobson-Bainbridge Realty Co., supra, as follows:

"This rule avoids hardship to the offeree, and yet does not hold the offeror beyond the terms of his promise. It is true by such terms he was to be bound only if the requested act was done; but this implies that he will let it be done, that he will keep his offer open till the offeree who has begun can finish doing it. At least this is so where the doing of it will necessarily require time and expense. In such a case it is but just to hold that the offeree's part performance furnishes the 'acceptance' and the 'consideration' for a binding subsidiary promise not to revoke the offer, or turns the offer into a presently binding contract conditional upon the offeree's full performance."

We hold that part performance by the offeree of an offer of a unilateral contract results in a contract with a condition. The condition is full performance by the offeree. Here, if plaintiff-offeree partially performed prior to receipt of defendant's revocation, such a contract was formed. Thereafter, upon performance being completed by plaintiff, upon defendant's failure to recognize the contract, liability for breach of contract would arise. Thus, defendant's right to revoke his offer depends upon whether plaintiff had partially performed before he received defendant's revocation. In re Ward's Estate, 47 N.M. 55, 134 P.2d 539, 146 A.L.R. 826 (1943), does not conflict with this result. Ward is clearly distinguishable because there the prospective purchaser did not complete or tender performance in accordance with the terms of the offer.

What constitutes partial performance will vary from case to case since what can be done toward performance is limited by what is authorized to be done. Whether plaintiff partially performed is a question of fact to be determined by the trial court.

The trial court denied plaintiff's requested finding concerning his partial performance. It did so on the theory that partial performance was not material. In this the trial court erred.

Because of the failure to find on the issue of partial performance, the case must be remanded to the trial court. State ex rel. Reynolds v. Board of County Comm'rs., 71 N.M. 194, 376 P.2d 976 (1962). We have not considered, and express no opinion on the question of whether there is or is not substantial evidence in the record which would support a finding one way or the other on this vital issue. Compare Geeslin v. Goodno, Inc., 75 N.M. 174, 402 P.2d 156 (1965).

The cause is remanded for findings on the issue of plaintiff's partial performance of the offer prior to its revocation, and for further proceedings consistent with this opinion and the findings so made.

It is so ordered.

NOTES

(1) *"Option Contract."* Under the option-contract reasoning of Restatement Second, § 45, what acts by the broker will suffice to bind the seller? Is it enough to advertise the property along with other properties in a newspaper? Must the broker find a buyer even after the owner has repudiated in order to earn his commission? Is he likely to be able to do this?[a] Would it be enough if he could show that he could have found a

a. If the agreement gives an exclusive right to sell, it commonly provides that the commission is payable if the property is sold during the term of the agreement, whether or not the broker arranges the sale.

buyer if the seller had not repudiated? Is he likely to be able to do this? See Brady v. East Portland Sheet Metal Works, 222 Or. 584, 352 P.2d 144 (1960).

(2) *Is Promise or Performance Sought? (Reprise).* Marchiondo v. Scheck is unusual, as the court itself acknowledges, in applying the option contract reasoning to a listing that was not exclusive. (Was there anything unusual about the listing with Marchiondo that facilitated this?) If the listing is exclusive, however, is the option contract reasoning necessary to protect the broker? Is there not consideration for the seller's promise in an implied promise by the broker to use best efforts under Wood v. Lucy (p. 81 supra)? Would it make a difference in this connection whether the listing gave the broker an exclusive agency or an exclusive right to sell?

(3) *Brokers and the Statute of Frauds.* As was mentioned earlier, many states have a special provision of the statute of frauds applicable to brokerage agreements, and it is usually held that such a provision bars restitution as well as recovery on the agreement. See Note, p. 159 supra. Should reliance by the broker make the agreement enforceable? See Note, 26 Hastings L.J. 1503 (1975).

SECTION 5. RELIANCE ON AN OFFER THAT SEEKS A PROMISE: SUBCONTRACTING AND FRANCHISING

When an offer seeks performance that extends over time, as in the situations discussed in the preceding section, the offeree cannot avoid acting in reliance before he has accepted and must thereby expose himself to the threat of revocation after reliance. When an offer seeks a promise, however, the offeree can ordinarily be expected to protect himself against the risk of revocation after reliance by making the return promise before doing anything in reliance. See White v. Corlies & Tift, p. 201 supra.

A court has, to be sure, some discretion in determining from all the circumstances whether the return promise has been made and may use this discretion to protect an offeree who has arguably accepted before revocation. Furthermore, a party whose reliance has conferred a benefit on the other may have a claim to restitution to prevent unjust enrichment even though no contract has resulted.

To take a simple example, the prospective buyer of land who makes a down payment during negotiations that fail to result in a contract is entitled to the return of his down payment. But unjust enrichment is often harder to show. So in Cronin v. National Shawmut Bank, 306 Mass. 202, 27 N.E.2d 717 (1940), National Shawmut Bank invited brokers to submit proposals for fire and theft insurance on specified property, involving premiums of about $850,000 and broker's commissions of between $30,000 and $40,000. Cronin submitted a proposal and, at the request of McCarthy, one of the bank's officers, he revised it several times until it was "the precise proposal that McCarthy wanted." The bank then gave the contract to another firm that submitted a proposal identical to Cronin's except for the names of the broker and the insurer, because a partner in that firm was a friend of one of McCarthy's superiors. Cronin sued the bank, including a claim in restitution. The Supreme Judicial Court of Massachusetts affirmed judgment for the bank. The bank "never actually availed itself of any proposal made by the plaintiff." The contract made was with a different insurer and serviced by a different broker. "To be sure the defendant got the benefit of the rates proposed by the plaintiff, and this may have been important; but what the rates would have been if they had not been the plaintiff's rates remains speculative. It has been held in a number of cases that deriving benefit from the broker's work does not lead to liability where there has been no employment." See also Gould v. American Water Works Service Co., 52 N.J. 226, 245 A.2d 14 (1968), cert. denied, 394 U.S. 943 (1969).

A contrasting case on restitution is Hill v. Waxberg, 237 F.2d 936 (9th Cir. 1956). Hill asked Waxberg, a contractor, to help him make preparations for the construction of a building on Hill's lot in Fairbanks, Alaska. It was understood that if the financing could be arranged through the Federal Housing Authority as contemplated, Waxberg would be awarded the building contract. Waxberg then made several trips to Seattle at Hill's request to confer with the architects, hired a third party to secure a drill log on the property, surveyed the property, and was instrumental in getting the data for the F.H.A. He expected to be compensated for this out of the profits from the contemplated contract. When the F.H.A. issued the commitment, Hill and Waxberg began negoiations for the building contract, but were unable to agree. Hill then made a contract with another contractor, and Waxberg sued to recover the reasonable value of his services and the expenditures made by him. The evidence showed that Waxberg's plans, ideas and efforts were of some value to Hill, and the trial court entered judgment for him on a jury verdict for $11,167.46. On Hill's appeal the Court of Appeals explained that it is a general principle of Anglo-American jurisprudence that "something in the nature of an implied contract results where one renders services at the request of another with the expectation of pay therefor, and in the process confers a benefit on the other. . . . It makes no difference whether the pay expected is in the form of an immediate cash payment, or in the form of profits to be derived from a contract, the consummation of which would or should be anticipated by reasonable men, and it follows *a fortiori* that such a rule obtains where the contract is in fact contemplated by *both* parties." The contract may be "implied in fact," in which case the general contract theory of compensatory damages applies, compensation for services being measured at "the going contract rate." Or it may be "implied in law," in which case a restitution measure of damages applies and recovery is limited to "the value of the benefit which was acquired." (This portion of the opinion is quoted in full in Note 3, p. 108 supra.) Because the trial judge did not adequately instruct the jury on this distinction, its judgment was reversed, unless the parties should agree to a reduction in its amount to $5,896.88, the asserted reasonable value of Waxberg's services plus his claimed expenses. Would not this court's reasoning have required a decision for Cronin on his claim against the bank? If so, for how much? Are the two cases distinguishable? Are the cases on liability for appropriation of ideas, discussed at p. 110 supra, relevant?

However, a claim to restitution leaves the claimant uncompensated for reliance that resulted in no benefit to the other party. To what extent might such reliance afford an independent ground for recovery? The following cases deal with this question.

NOTE

Contract "Implied in Fact." A party can, of course, make an enforceable promise to pay for work done in anticipation of the making of a later contract, and the promise need not be in words. In Bastian v. Gafford, 98 Idaho 324, 563 P.2d 48 (1977), Gafford asked Bastian if he would be interested in building an office building on Gafford's land. Bastian orally agreed to do so and began drafting plans. When it proved impossible to finance the project on a cost-plus basis, Bastian withdrew and Gafford went ahead and built the building using a different set of plans. Bastian sued "alleging an implied-in-fact contract to compensate him for his services," but the trial court entered judgment for Gafford "on the ground that he had not been unjustly enriched" because he had not used Bastian's plans. On appeal, the judgment was reversed and the case remanded for a new trial. "In basing its decision on unjust enrichment, the trial court failed to distinguish between a quasi-contract and a contract implied in fact. Although unjust enrichment is necessary for recovery based upon quasi-contract, it is irrelevant to a contract implied in fact. . . . For appellant to recover under the latter theory, it is not necessary that respondent either use the plans or derive any benefit from them. . . . It is enough that he requested and received them under circumstances which imply an agreement that he pay for appellant's services."

JAMES BAIRD CO. v. GIMBEL BROS.

United States Circuit Court of Appeals, Second Circuit, 1933.
64 F.2d 344.

Action by the James Baird Company against Gimbel Brothers, Incorporated. From a judgment dismissing the complaint, plaintiff appeals.

L. HAND, Circuit Judge. The plaintiff sued the defendant for breach of a contract to deliver linoleum under a contract of sale; the defendant denied the making of the contract; the parties tried the case to the judge under a written stipulation and he directed judgment for the defendant. The facts as found, bearing on the making of the contract, the only issue necessary to discuss, were as follows: The defendant, a New York merchant, knew that the Department of Highways in Pennsylvania had asked for bids for the construction of the public building. It sent an employee to the office of a contractor in Philadelphia, who had possession of the specifications, and the employee there computed the amount of the linoleum which would be required on the job, underestimating the total yardage by about one-half the proper amount. In ignorance of this mistake, on December twenty-fourth the defendant sent to some twenty or thirty contractors, likely to bid on the job, an offer to supply all the linoleum required by the specifications at two different lump sums, depending upon the quality used. These offers concluded as follows: "If successful in being awarded this contract, it will be absolutely guaranteed, . . . and . . . we are offering these prices for reasonable" (sic), "prompt acceptance after the general contract has been awarded." The plaintiff, a contractor in Washington, got one of these on the twenty-eighth, and on the same day the defendant learned its mistake and telegraphed all the contractors to whom it had sent the offer, that it withdrew it and would substitute a new one at about double the amount of the old. This withdrawal reached the plaintiff at Washington on the afternoon of the same day, but not until after it had put in a bid at Harrisburg at a lump sum, based as to linoleum upon the prices quoted by the defendant. The public authorities accepted the plaintiff's bid on December thirtieth, the defendant having meanwhile written a letter of confirmation of its withdrawal, received on the thirty-first. The plaintiff formally accepted the offer on January second, and, as the defendant persisted in declining to recognize the existence of a contract, sued it for damages on a breach.

Unless there are circumstances to take it out of the ordinary doctrine, since the offer was withdrawn before it was accepted, the acceptance was too late. Restatement of Contracts, § 35. To meet this the plaintiff argues as follows: It was a reasonable implication from the defendant's offer that it should be irrevocable in case the plaintiff acted upon it, that is to say, used the prices quoted in making its bid, thus putting itself in a position from which it could not withdraw without great loss. While it might have withdrawn its bid after receiving the revocation, the time had passed to submit another, and as the item of linoleum was a very trifling part of the cost of the whole building, it would have been an unreasonable hardship to expect it to lose the contract on that account, and probably forfeit its deposit. While it is true that the plaintiff might in advance have secured a contract conditional upon the success of its bid, this was not what the defendant suggested. It understood that the contractors would use its offer in their bids, and would thus in fact commit themselves to supplying the linoleum at the proposed prices. The inevitable implication from all this was that when the contractors acted upon it, they accepted the offer and promised to pay for the linoleum, in case their bids were accepted.

It was of course possible for the parties to make such a contract, and the question is merely as to what they meant; that is, what is to be imputed to the words they used. Whatever plausibility there is in the argument is in the fact that the defendant must have known the predicament in which the contractors would be put if it withdrew its offer after the bids went in. However, it seems entirely clear that the contractors did not suppose that they accepted the offer merely by putting in their bids. If, for example, the successful one had repudiated the contract with the public authorities after it had been awarded to him, certainly the defendant could not have sued him for a breach. If he had become bankrupt, the defendant could not prove against his estate. It seems plain therefore that there was no contract between them. And if there be any doubt as to this, the language of the offer sets it at rest. The phrase, "if successful in being awarded this contract," is scarcely met by the mere use of the prices in the bids. Surely such a use was not an "award" of the contract to the defendant. Again, the phrase, "we are offering these prices for . . . prompt acceptance after the general contract has been awarded," looks to the usual communication of an acceptance, and precludes the idea that the use of the offer in the bidding shall be the equivalent. It may indeed be argued that this last language contemplated no more than an early notice that the offer had been accepted, the actual acceptance being the bid, but that would wrench its natural meaning too far, especially in the light of the preceding phrase. The contractors had a ready escape from their difficulty by insisting upon a contract before they used the figures; and in commercial transactions it does not in the end promote justice to seek strained interpretations in aid of those who do not protect themselves.

But the plaintiff says that even though no bilateral contract was made, the defendant should be held under the doctrine of "promissory estoppel." This is to be chiefly found in those cases where persons subscribe to a venture, usually charitable, and are held to their promises after it has been completed. It has been applied much more broadly, however, and has now been generalized in section 90, of the Restatement of Contracts. We may arguendo accept it as it there reads, for it does not apply to the case at bar. Offers are ordinarily made in exchange for a consideration, either a counter-promise or some other act which the promisor wishes to secure. In such cases they propose bargains; they presuppose that each promise or performance is an inducement to the other. . . . But a man may make a promise without expecting an equivalent; a donative promise, conditional or absolute. The common law provided for such by sealed instruments, and it is unfortunate that these are no longer generally available. The doctrine of "promissory estoppel" is to avoid the harsh results of allowing the promisor in such a case to repudiate, when the promisee has acted in reliance upon the promise. . . . But an offer for an exchange is not meant to become a promise until a consideration has been received, either a counter-promise or whatever else is stipulated. To extend it would be to hold the offeror regardless of the stipulated condition of his offer. In the case at bar the defendant offered to deliver the linoleum in exchange for the plaintiff's acceptance, not for its bid, which was a matter of indifference to it. That offer could become a promise to deliver only when the equivalent was received; that is, when the plaintiff promised to take and pay for it. There is no room in such a situation for the doctrine of "promissory estoppel."

Nor can the offer be regarded as of an option, giving the plaintiff the right seasonably to accept the linoleum at the quoted prices if its bid was accepted, but not binding it to take and pay, if it could get a better bargain elsewhere. There is not the least reason to suppose that the defendant meant to subject itself to such a one-sided obligaion. True, if so construed, the doctrine of "promissory estoppel" might apply, the plaintiff having acted in reliance upon it, though, so far as we have found, the decisions are otherwise. Ganss v. Guffey Petroleum Co., 125 App.Div. 760, 110 N.Y.S. 176; Comstock v. North, 88 Miss. 754, 41 So. 374. As to that, however, we need not declare ourselves.

Judgment affirmed.

NOTE

Problem. Suppose that Gimbel's bid had included the following language instead of that quoted by the court: "If successful in being awarded this contract, it will be absolutely guaranteed. If our bid is used, wire us collect no later than the twenty-eighth or else our bid is withdrawn." And suppose that before Gimbel wired Baird of its mistake, it had already received a telegram from Baird reading, "We used your bid on the Pennsylvania job." Same result? See Williams v. Favret, 161 F.2d 822 (5th Cir. 1947).

Suppose that Gimbel had not made a mistake, but had withdrawn its bid because it had changed its mind. Same result? See Tatsch v. Hamilton-Erickson Mfg. Co., 76 N.M. 729, 418 P.2d 187 (1966).

DRENNAN v. STAR PAVING CO.

Supreme Court of California, In Bank, 1958.
51 Cal.2d 409, 333 P.2d 757.

General contractor brought action against paving subcontractor to recover damages because of refusal of subcontractor to perform paving according to bid which subcontractor submitted to general contractor. The Superior Court, Kern County, William L. Bradshaw, J., entered judgment adverse to the subcontractor, and the subcontractor appealed.

TRAYNOR, Justice. Defendant appeals from a judgment for plaintiff in an action to recover damages caused by defendant's refusal to perform certain paving work according to a bid it submitted to plaintiff.

On July 28, 1955, plaintiff, a licensed general contractor, was preparing a bid on the "Monte Vista School Job" in the Lancaster school district. Bids had to be submitted before 8:00 p. m. Plaintiff testified that it was customary in that area for general contractors to receive the bids of subcontractors by telephone on the day set for bidding and to rely on them in computing their own bids. Thus on that day plaintiff's secretary, Mrs. Johnson, received by telephone between fifty and seventy-five subcontractors' bids for various parts of the school job. As each bid came in, she wrote it on a special form, which she brought into plaintiff's office. He then posted it on a master cost sheet setting forth the names and bids of all subcontractors. His own bid had to include the names of subcontractors who were to perform one-half of one per cent or more of the construction work, and he had also to provide a bidder's bond of ten per cent of his total bid of $317,385 as a guarantee that he would enter the contract if awarded the work.

Late in the afternoon, Mrs. Johnson had a telephonce conversation with Kenneth R. Hoon, an estimator for defendant. He gave his name and telephone number and stated that he was bidding for defendant for the paving work at the Monte Vista School according to plans and specifications and that his bid was $7,131.60. At Mrs. Johnson's request he repeated his bid. Plaintiff listened to the bid over an extension telephone in his office and posted it on the master sheet after receiving the bid form from Mrs. Johnson. Defendant's was the lowest bid for the paving. Plaintiff computed his own bid accordingly and submitted it with the name of defendant as the subcontractor for the paving. When the bids were opened on July 28th, plaintiff's proved to be the lowest, and he was awarded the contract.

On his way to Los Angeles the next morning plaintiff stopped at defendant's office. The first person he met was defendant's construction engineer, Mr. Oppenheimer. Plaintiff testified: "I introduced myself and he immediately told me that they had made a mistake in their bid to me the night before, they couldn't do it for the price they had bid, and I told him I would expect him to carry through with their original bid because I had used it in compiling my bid and the job was being awarded them. And I would have to go and do the job according to my bid and I would expect them to do the same."

Defendant refused to do the paving work for less than $15,000. Plaintiff testified that he "got figures from other people" and after trying for several months to get as low a bid as possible engaged L & H Paving Company, a firm in Lancaster, to do the work for $10,948.-60.

The trial court found on substantial evidence that defendant made a definite offer to do the paving on the Monte Vista job according to the plans and specifications for $7,131.60, and that plaintiff relied on defendant's bid in computing his own bid for the school job and naming defendant therein as the subcontractor for the paving work. Accordingly, it entered judgment for plaintiff in the amount of $3,817.00 (the difference between defendant's bid and the cost of the paving to plaintiff) plus costs.

Defendant contends that there was no enforceable contract between the parties on the ground that it made a revocable offer and revoked it before plaintiff communicated his acceptance to defendant.

There is no evidence that defendant offered to make its bid irrevocable in exchange for plaintiff's use of its figures in computing his bid. Nor is there evidence that would warrant interpreting plaintiff's use of defendant's bid as the acceptance thereof, binding plaintiff, on condition he received the main contract, to award the subcontract to defendant. In sum, there was neither an option supported by consideration nor a bilateral contract binding on both parties.

Plaintiff contends, however, that he relied to his detriment on defendant's offer and that defendant must therefore answer in damages for its refusal to perform. Thus the question is squarely presented: Did plaintiff's reliance make defendant's offer irrevocable?

Section 90 of the Restatement of Contracts states: "A promise which the promisor should reasonably expect to induce action or forbearance of a definite and substantial character on the part of the promisee and which does induce such action or forbearance is binding if injustice can be avoided only by enforcement of the promise." This rule applies in this state. . . .

Defendant's offer constituted a promise to perform on such conditions as were stated expressly or by implication therein or annexed thereto by operation of law. (See 1 Williston, Contracts [3rd ed.], § 24A, p. 56, § 61, p. 196.) Defendant had reason to expect that if its bid proved the lowest it would be used by plaintiff. It induced "action . . . of a definite and substantial character on the part of the promisee."

Had defendant's bid expressly stated or clearly implied that it was revocable at any time before acceptance we would treat it accordingly. It was silent on revocation, however, and we must therefore determine whether there are conditions to the right of revocation imposed by law or reasonably inferable in fact. In the analogous problem of an offer for a unilateral contract, the theory is now obsolete that the offer is revocable at any time before complete performance. Thus section 45 of the Restatement of Contracts provides: "If an offer for a unilateral contract is made, and part of the consideration requested in the offer is given or tendered by the offeree in response thereto, the offeror is bound by a contract, the duty of immediate performance of which is conditional on the full consideration being given or tendered within the time stated in the offer, or, if no time is stated therein, within a reasonable time." In explanation, comment *b* states that the "main offer includes as a subsidiary promise, necessarily implied, that if part of the requested performance is given, the offeror will not revoke his offer, and that if tender is made it will be accepted. Part performance or tender may thus furnish consideration for the subsidiary promise. Moreover, merely acting in justifiable reliance on an offer may in some cases serve as sufficient reason for making a promise binding (see § 90)."

Whether implied in fact or law, the subsidiary promise serves to preclude the injustice that would result if the offer could be revoked after the offeree had acted in detrimental reliance thereon. Reasonable reliance resulting in a foreseeable prejudicial change in position affords a compelling basis also for implying a subsidiary promise not to revoke an offer for a bilateral contract.

The absence of consideration is not fatal to the enforcement of such a promise. It is true that in the case of unilateral contracts the Restatement finds consideration for the implied subsidiary promise in the part performance of the bargained-for exchange, but its reference to section 90 makes clear that consideration for such a promise is not always necessary. The very purpose of section 90 is to make a promise binding even though there was no consideration "in the sense of something that is bargained for and given in exchange." (See 1 Corbin, Contracts 634 et seq.) Reasonable reliance serves to hold the offeror in lieu of the consideration ordinarily required to make the offer binding. In a case involving similar facts the Supreme Court of South Dakota stated that "we believe that reason and justice demand that the doctrine [of section 90] be applied to the present facts. We cannot believe that by accepting this doctrine as controlling in the state of facts before us we will abolish the requirement of a consideration in contract cases, in any different sense than an ordinary estoppel abolishes some legal requirement in its application. We are of the opinion, therefore, that the defendants in executing the agreement [which was not supported by consideration] made a promise which they should have reasonably expected would induce the plaintiff to submit a bid based thereon to the Government, that such promise did induce this action, and that injustice can be avoided only by enforcement of the promise." Northwestern Engineering Co. v. Ellerman, 69 S.D. 397, 408, 10 N.W.2d 879, 884; see also, Robert Gordon, Inc., v. Ingersoll-Rand Co., 7 Cir., 117 F.2d 654, 661; cf. James Baird Co. v. Gimbel Bros., 2 Cir., 64 F.2d 344.

When plaintiff used defendant's offer in computing his own bid, he bound himself to perform in reliance on defendant's terms. Though defendant did not bargain for this use of its bid neither did defendant make it idly, indifferent to whether it would be used or not. On the contrary it is reasonable to suppose that defendant submitted its bid to obtain the subcontract. It was bound to realize the substantial possibility that its bid would be the lowest, and that it would be included by plaintiff in his bid. It was to its own interest that the contractor be awarded the general contract; the lower the subcontract bid, the lower the general contractor's bid was likely to be and the greater its chance of acceptance and hence the greater defendant's chance of getting the paving subcontract. Defendant had reason not only to expect plaintiff to rely on its bid but to want him to. Clearly defendant had a stake in plaintiff's reliance on its bid. Given this interest and the fact that plaintiff is bound by his own bid, it is only fair that plaintiff should have at least an opportunity to accept defendant's bid after the general contract has been awarded to him.

It bears noting that a general contractor is not free to delay acceptance after he has been awarded the general contract in the hope of getting a better price. Nor can he reopen bargaining with the subcontractor and at the same time claim a continuing right to accept the original offer. See, R. J. Daum Const. Co. v. Child, Utah, 247 P. 2d 817, 823. In the present case plaintiff promptly informed defendant that plaintiff was being awarded the job and that the subcontract was being awarded to defendant.

Defendant contends, however, that its bid was the result of mistake and that it was therefore entitled to revoke it. It relies on the rescission cases of M. F. Kemper Const. Co. v. City of Los Angeles, 37 Cal.2d 696, 235 P.2d 7, and Brunzell Const. Co. v. G. J. Weisbrod, Inc., 134 Cal.App.2d 278, 285 P.2d 989. See also, Lemoge Electric v. San Mateo County, 46 Cal.2d 659, 662, 297 P.2d 638. In those cases, however, the bidder's mistake was known or should have been known to the offeree, and the offeree could be placed in status quo. Of course, if plaintiff had reason to believe that defendant's bid was in error, he could not justifiably rely on it, and section 90 would afford no basis for enforcing it. Robert Gordon, Inc., v. Ingersoll-Rand, Inc., 7 Cir., 117 F.2d 654, 660. Plaintiff, however, had no reason to know that defendant had made a mistake in submitting its bid, since there was usually a variance of 160 per cent between the highest and lowest bids for paving in the desert around Lancaster. He committed himself to performing the main contract in reliance on defendant's figures. Under these circumstances defendant's mistake, far from relieving it of its obligation, constitutes an additional reason for enforcing it, for it misled plaintiff as to the cost of doing the paving. Even had it been clearly understood that defendant's offer was revocable until accepted, it would not necessarily follow that defendant had no duty to exercise reasonable care in preparing its bid. It presented its bid with knowledge of the substantial possibility that it would be used by plaintiff; it could foresee the harm that would ensue from an erroneous underestimate of the cost. Moreover, it was motivated by its own business interest. Whether or not these considerations alone would justify recovery for negligence had the case been tried on that theory (see Biakanja v. Irving, 49 Cal.2d 647, 650, 320 P.2d 16), they are persuasive that defendant's mistake should not defeat recovery under the rule of section 90 of the Restatement of Contracts. As between the subcontractor who made the bid and the general contractor who reasonably relied on it, the loss resulting from the mistake should fall on the party who caused it.

Leo F. Piazza Paving Co. v. Bebek & Brkich, 141 Cal.App.2d 226, 296 P.2d 368, 371, and Bard v. Kent, 19 Cal.2d 449, 122 P.2d 8, 139 A.L.R. 1032, are not to the contrary. In the Piazza case the court sustained a finding that defendants intended, not to make a firm bid, but only to give the plaintiff "some kind of an idea to use" in making its bid; there was evidence that the defendants had told plaintiff they were unsure of the significance of the specifications. There was thus no offer, promise, or representation on which the defendants should reasonably have expected the plaintiff to rely. The Bard case held that an option not supported by consideration was revoked by the death of the optionor. The issue of recovery under the rule of section 90 was not pleaded at the trial, and it does not appear that the offeree's reliance was "of a definite and substantial character" so that injustice could be avoided "only by the enforcement of the promise."

There is no merit in defendant's contention that plaintiff failed to state a cause of action, on the ground that the complaint failed to allege that plaintiff attempted to mitigate the damages or that they could not have been mitigated. Plaintiff alleged that after defendant's default, "plaintiff had to procure the services of the L & H Co. to perform said asphaltic paving for the sum of $10,948.60." Plaintiff's uncontradicted evidence showed that he spent several months trying to get bids from other subcontractors and that he took the lowest bid. Clearly he acted reasonably to mitigate damages. In any event any uncertainty in plaintiff's allegation as to damages could have been raised by special demurrer. Code Civ.Proc. § 430, subd. 9. It was not so raised and was therefore waived. Code Civ.Proc. § 434.

The judgment is affirmed.

NOTES

(1) *Preparing to Cross the Brooklyn Bridge.* Can the two preceding cases be distinguished on their facts? The rationale of the Drennan case is reflected in Restatement Second, § 87(2). Would this rule protect B in the Brooklyn Bridge hypothetical, p. 305 supra, if he had spent time and money in preparing to cross the bridge but had not begun to cross it when A revoked? Would you advise B, in such a situation, to cross the bridge in spite of the revocation? Would this rule protect the broker in Note 1, p. 309 supra, who has done no more than advertise the property? Would it affect the result in the case in Note 4, p. 307 supra?

(2) *Problem.* Suppose that after receiving Star Paving's bid on July 28, Drennan had telephoned Star Paving and asked if it "could shave it a little," Star Paving had said it would "have to think it over," and that Star Paving's bid had then been used without further inquiry. Same result? Compare Jaybe Constr. Co. v. Beco, 3 Conn.Cir. 406, 216 A.2d 208 (1965) with State ex rel. Sorenson v. Wisner State Bank, 125 Neb. 345, 250 N.W. 89 (1933). Suppose that this telephone conversation had taken place after the award to Drennan but before Star Paving had discovered its mistake and that before any further discussion could be had it had discovered its mistake and told Drennan of its unwillingness to perform. Same result? See N. Litterio & Co. v. Glassman Constr. Co., 319 F.2d 736 (D.C.Cir. 1963); Note 3, p. 282 supra.

(3) *Questions.* Under the rule in the Drennan case, would it make a difference if the bid in question were much lower than the bids of other subcontractors? (Would the fact that the general contractor had asked the subcontractor to check its bid affect your answer?) Would it make a difference if the subcontractor could show that "bid shopping" and "bid chopping" were widespread in the industry? If the subcontractor could show that the general contractor had, after receiving the award, been successful in making contracts with most of its other subcontractors and suppliers at prices lower than the bids on which the general contractor had based its own bid? If the subcontractor could show that the general contractor had, after receiving the award, used the subcontractor's bid in an unsuccessful attempt at "bid shopping"? See Saliba-Kringlen Corp. v. Allen Engineering Co., 15 Cal.App.3d 95, 92 Cal.Rptr. 799 (1971); Constructors Supply Co. v. Bostrom Sheet Metal Works, Inc., 291 Minn. 113, 190 N.W.2d 71 (1971).

SOUTHERN CALIFORNIA ACOUSTICS CO. v. C. V. HOLDER, 71 Cal.2d 719, 456 P.2d 975 (1969). [Acoustics, a subcontractor, telephoned to Holder, a general contractor, an $83,400 bid on the acoustical tile work for a construction job for the Los Angeles Unified School District. Later that day, Holder submitted its bid to the school district, listing subcontractors, including Acoustics. California Government Code, § 4104, a part of the 1963 Subletting and Subcontracting Fair Practices Act, required listing of subcontractors whose work made up more than one-half of one per cent of the bid.

Holder was awarded the prime contract and a local trade paper reported the award, along with the names of the subcontractors listed in its bid. When Acoustics read this, it refrained from bidding on other construction jobs in order to remain within its bonding limits. Holder then obtained the consent of the school district to substitute another subcontractor for Acoustics on the ground that the latter had been inadvertently listed in place of the former. Acoustics sought a writ of mandamus to compel the school district to rescind its consent and, when that proceeding was dismissed, sued Holder and the school district for damages. From dismissal of its complaint against both defendants, plaintiff appealed.]

TRAYNOR, Chief Justice. . . . There was no contract between plaintiff and Holder, for Holder did not accept plaintiff's offer. . . . The listing by the general contractor of the subcontractors he intends to retain is in response to a statutory command (Gov.Code, § 4104) and cannot reasonably be construed as an expression of acceptance. . . . Plaintiff contends, however, that its reliance on Holder's use of its bid and Holder's failure to reject its offer promptly after Holder's bid was accepted constitute acceptance of plaintiff's bid by operation of law under the doctrine of promissory estoppel. . . . Plaintiff urges us to find an analogous subsidiary promise [to that found in Drennan] not to reject its bid in this case, but it fails to allege facts showing the existence of any promise by Holder to it upon which it detrimentally relied. Plaintiff did not rely on any promise by Holder, but only on the listing of subcontractors required by section 4104 of the Government Code and on the statutory restrictions on Holder's right to change its listed subcontractors without the consent of the school district. (Gov.Code, § 4701.) [a] . . .

[The court then reviewed the 1963 Subletting and Subcontracting Fair Practice Act and concluded that, in contrast to the earlier statute in effect at the time of the Drennan case, its purpose was not only to allow the awarding authority to investigate and approve subcontractors, but] also to protect the public and subcontractors from the evils attendant upon the practices of bid shopping and bid peddling subsequent to the award of the prime contract for a public facility. . . . [W]e hold that it confers the right on the listed subcontractor to perform the subcontract unless statutory grounds for a valid substitution exist. Moreover, that right may be enforced by an action for damages against the prime contractor to recover the benefit of the bargain the listed subcontractor would have realized had he not wrongfully been deprived of the subcontract. [The court

a. This section forbids a prime contractor whose bid has been accepted to substitute another subcontractor for a listed subcontractor without the consent of the awarding authority, and then only in situations involving the unwillingness or inability of the listed subcontractor.

concluded that the statute did not, however, confer on the subcontractor a right of action against the school district.]

[Affirmed as to the school district. Reversed and remanded as to Holder.]

NOTES

(1) *Rejected Low Bid (Reprise).* In Swinerton & Walberg Co. v. City of Inglewood-Los Angeles County Civic Center Authority, 40 Cal.App.3d 98, 114 Cal.Rptr. 834 (1974), Argo, a general contractor that had submitted the lowest bid on a public works contract to be awarded by the City of Inglewood-Los Angeles County Civic Center Authority, sued the Authority for having awarded the contract to the second lowest bidder. The court held that Argo had failed to state a claim based on statutory right like that in the Southern California Acoustics case because, in contrast to the statutory requirements involved in that case, there was nothing in the competitive bidding requirements involved here "to lead one to infer reasonably that competitive bidding requirements were imposed for the benefit of the bidders as well as for the benefit of the public." The court held, however, that Argo had stated a "cause of action in promissory estoppel . . . . Clearly, the Authority promised in its solicitation of bids to award the contract to the lowest responsible bidder and Argo's reasonable and detrimental reliance upon this promise brings [Restatement Second] section 90 into play unless the final clause [of paragraph 1] of the section prevents this result. . . . It would seem, however, that the damages that Argo may recover in promissory estoppel might well be limited to those it sustained directly by reason of its justifiable reliance upon the Authority's promise—in other words, to the expenses it incurred in its fruitless participation in the competitive bidding process . . . . What recovery Argo may attain on such cause of action will have to await . . . the trial court's consideration of what is just under all of the circumstances . . . ."

Was the Authority's promise an offer? See Note 2, p. 194 supra. Compare the Heyer case, p. 347 infra.

(2) *The Case of the Detonation Detection Team.* AT wrote to a number of companies, including GE, which were planning to bid on an Air Force contract to establish nuclear detonation detection stations, indicating its interest in being a subcontractor to provide the electromagnetic sensors. Representatives of AT and GE then met several times to discuss terms and how "AT would be a team member, subject to Air Force approval." As the result of the success of these meetings, GE submitted a proposal contemplating a cost-plus-fixed-fee contract and listed itself, AT, and three other companies on the cover of its proposal to the Air Force. Two AT scientists participated in an oral presentation of GE's proposal to the Air Force. GE was selected as prime contractor, subject to negotiation of a suitable contract, but when that contract was concluded on a cost-plus-incentive-fee basis, giving GE a strong interest in cutting costs below its target, GE refused to deal exclusively with AT and sought other bids on the sensors. AT brought suit in equity to restrain GE from using information supplied to it by AT, for a declaration that GE had breached a fiduciary relation to AT, and for damages. AT was denied injunctive relief, but awarded $128,734. Both parties appealed. *Held:* Reversed and remanded for redetermination of damages. The master who heard the case below had con-

cluded that since AT had furnished similar information to GE's competitors, it was not a trade secret and GE owed no duty to AT based on its appropriation alone. But the court held that the situation was distinguishable from that in the Cronin case, p. 313 supra, because GE had agreed that AT would be a "team member," which suggested "some form of joint undertaking." Although it was not technically a "joint venture," GE "may be held to its contractual responsibility to AT as a team member," which was that if GE was awarded the contract, AT would receive, subject to Air Force approval, a subcontract for the sensors that would give AT a "reasonable opportunity to recover its costs plus a fair profit." The uncertainties about the subcontract, such as those created by the prospect of bargaining with GE and the requirement of Air Force approval, do not preclude recovery by AT for its lost opportunity, but were not properly taken into account by the master in calculating damages. In no event may the damages be less than the higher of "(a) the value reasonably expended by AT in the performance of the joint arrangement, and (b) the fair value of AT's contribution to that arrangement." Air Technology Corp. v. General Elec. Co., 347 Mass. 613, 199 N.E.2d 538 (1964). What rationale lies behind this limitation on damages?

(3) *The Case of the Contractor Caught in the Act.* Page & Wirtz, a general contractor, was preparing a bid for construction on the Western Plaza Shopping Center, and already had a subcontractor's bid of about $214,000 on the masonry from Southwestern Bricklaying. At 11:00 a. m., a few hours before the 2:00 p. m. deadline for general contractors' bids, Van Doran, another subcontractor, left his bid of $204,395 with Walter Wirtz after discussing it. Van Doran was still in the building talking to Wirtz' son Jack, when Wirtz came out of his office and told Page to get Southwestern on the telephone immediately. When Wirtz turned around and saw that Van Doran had overheard him, there was "an atmosphere of embarrassment," particularly because Van Doran had accused other general contractors of bid shopping in the past. At 1:00 p. m. Southwestern submitted a second bid, $1,595 under the Van Doran bid. Page & Wirtz submitted its own bid based on Van Doran's figures by 2:00 p. m. At 4:00 p. m. Van Doran telephoned Walter Wirtz, who said "this morning I made the biggest bust I ever made in my life" and "under existing conditions, I can do nothing but give you the job." Van Doran replied, "Well, Walter, now, as I understand it, if you get this job, I've got a job," and Wirtz said "Yes." Page & Wirtz was awarded the contract and awarded the masonry contract to Southwestern. Van Doran sued Page & Wirtz for breach of contract, claiming loss of prospective profits. From a judgment for $25,000, defendant appealed. *Held:* Reversed. "Van Doran admitted throughout his testimony to numerous conditions of the contract between it and Wirtz which would have to be later negotiated." These related to lien rights, a two-year guarantee, an escalator clause, and arrangements that would have to be made if the owners refused to use the standard contract conditions of the American Institute of Architects. "It is clear in the record that before Van Doran's bid was submitted the [owners] were insisting on the conditions just related and Van Doran and Wirtz had discussed the fact that efforts would be made by Wirtz to secure modifications thereof to conform to Van Doran's bid. . . . In view of the several essential conditions Van Doran testified would have to be negotiated between his company and Wirtz

we do not believe [that Air Technology Corp. v. General Electric Co., discussed in Note 1, supra] is decisive to make a binding contract between them. . . . There is not even a contention of any species of joint venture in our case." Page & Wirtz Const. Co. v. Van Doran Bri-Tico Co., 432 S.W.2d 731 (Tex.Civ.App.1968). See also Plumbing Shop Inc. v. Pitts, 67 Wash.2d 514, 408 P.2d 382 (1965).

POSSIBLE SOLUTIONS

Which of the following three solutions, suggested in the Baird and Drennan opinions, do you favor?

First, treat the subcontractor's bid as an offer revocable at any time until the general contractor has accepted it by his return promise following the award. This leaves the general contractor with only the practical sanction of refusing to do further business with a subcontractor who withdraws a bid on which the general contractor has relied.

Second, treat the subcontractor's bid as an offer irrevocable until the general contractor has had a reasonable time to accept it by his return promise following the award. This binds the subcontractor but not the general contractor, and the subcontractor who is already vulnerable to bid shopping during this period can be expected to regard it as aggravating an existing imbalance. (Market changes during this period may also cause the subcontractor concern, but these he can avoid by using an "escalator" clause.)

Third, treat the subcontractor's bid as an offer revocable until the general contractor has accepted it by his return promise before the award, the resulting contract being subject to the condition that the general contractor receive the award. This, of course, would bind both parties and prevent bid shopping. How practical is this solution? Consider the delay of subcontractors in submitting their bids and the haste in which the general contractor's bid is often submitted. Consider also the fact that subcontractors' bids are often stated in different ways (e. g., lumping various items together) so that comparison is difficult on the basis of the bids alone. Should a return promise by the general contractor be implied from his use of the subcontractor's bid? How practical is this solution if there is no requirement of listing? What if the general contractor has discounted the bid in anticipation of bid shopping? What if he has "doctored" subcontractors' bids by combining figures from several of them?

To what extent should the solution depend on whether the subcontractor stated that his bid was irrevocable? On whether the bid was in writing? Does UCC 2–205 provide a useful analogy? [a]

a. For a decision following the Drennan case, even though the contract may have come within Article 2 of the Code and the subcontractor's of-

NOTE

Industry Attitudes and Practices. Would your answer be affected by any of the following industry attitudes and practices, suggested by Professor Schultz' study in Indiana, cited at p. 252 supra? A substantial majority of subcontractors' bids are, by their terms, firm offers, and in most cases this is required by the general contractor. Where the subcontractor has made a firm offer, the great majority of general contractors feel bound to give him the job if they have used his bid and been awarded the contract, and the great majority of subcontractors feel bound by their bid, even if there is an unexpected rise in the price of materials. But the overwhelming majority of subcontractors who feel bound base their feeling on moral or ethical rather than legal grounds, and only a tiny minority of general contractors would even threaten a lawsuit if a subcontractor withdrew. Only a distinct minority of general contractors ever consider legal devices such as an option contract, a contract conditional on award, or a bid bond to bind the subcontractor before the award, and in most of the cases consideration is given to a bid bond. An even smaller minority of subcontractors consider legal devices, since most feel that their bargaining position does not make them practical. See also Note, 53 Va.L.Rev. 1720 (1967).

Professor Schultz' own conclusion was that the second of the three solutions in the preceding note would add further to the existing imbalance in favor of the general contractor, and that it would be better to accept the first solution and leave the matter to be worked out by the parties without the aid of legal sanctions. Do you agree?

C. R. FEDRICK, INC. v. BORG-WARNER CORP.

United States Court of Appeals, Ninth Circuit, 1977.
552 F.2d 852.

EAST, District Judge: The appellant (Fedrick) appeals from a summary judgment in favor of the appellee (Borg) entered by the District Court on the several grounds that the provision of the Statute of Frauds, California Commercial Code (C.C.C.) § 2201(1) and (2), barred Fedrick's action against Borg for the breach of an alleged oral bid or contract to supply and sell certain motor driven pumping units (pumps), and relief could not be granted under any theory of equitable estoppel. We affirm.

Fedrick raises two issues on review. Did the District Court err in determining that:

(1) The Statute of Frauds, C.C.C. § 2201, was applicable to Borg's oral offer to sell the pumps? and

(2) Borg was not estopped from raising the defense of the Statute of Frauds in the action for damages?

fer was not irrevocable under UCC 2–205, see E. A. Coronis Associates v. M. Gordon Construction Co., 90 N.J. Super. 69, 216 A.2d 246 (1966).

Fedrick originally instituted the proceedings in the Superior Court of California for the County of Marin. Borg timely removed the action to the District Court pursuant to 28 U.S.C.A. § 1446 and moved for summary judgment. Jurisdiction in the District Court and in this court is established.

The undisputed facts pertinent to review are:

> Fedrick had prepared a bid as the prime contractor on a construction project under the auspices of the United States Bureau of Reclamation (Bureau). At 9:50 a. m. on May 30, 1974, approximately ten minutes before the time fixed for the submission of bids on the project and after Fedrick had fixed the amount of its intended bid, Borg was asked and did submit a telephonic offer to supply and sell Fedrick the pumps required by the specifications of the prime contract for the price of $826,550, with an increased cost escalation. Borg's telephonic figure was $450,000, plus, lower than the next lowest bid which Fedrick had received for the pumps. Whereupon Fedrick reduced its intended prime contract bid figure of $15,766,693 by an even $200,000.
>
> On the following day, Fedrick in turn orally indicated to Borg that in the likely event it was awarded the prime contract, Fedrick intended to purchase the pumps from Borg.
>
> Some three weeks later, on June 20, representatives of Fedrick and Borg met to discuss the contemplated transaction. During the meeting, Borg expressed concern that its proposed exceptions might not be acceptable to the Bureau. To avoid potential problems, Borg, as an alternative proposal, suggested certain modifications to bring the pumps more in accordance with the Bureau's published specifications. Thereafter on the same day Borg wrote Fedrick detailing the proposed modifications and fixing a revised price of $1,114,572 for the pumps.

Fedrick's counsel responded by letter dated June 25 denying that Borg's original telephonic offer was subject to the additional exceptions as claimed by Borg and further stating in its pertinent parts:

"Your bid was the lowest bid received by our client for the subject matter thereof and our client relied upon your bid and used the amount thereof in compiling its bid to the Bureau of Reclamation. On May 31, 1974, Mr. Ohman advised your Mr. Amaral that your bid was low and that our client had so used your bid. You are aware, of course, that our client's bid for the captioned contract was the lowest bid submitted.

"Promptly after the captioned contract is awarded, our client intends to send to you its standard form of Purchase Order Agreement which will incorporate the price and terms of the bid you submitted. If you do not promptly execute and return that Purchase Order Agreement to our client, I have been instructed to file suit against you for the damages which our client will sustain as a consequence of your refusal to honor your bid. . . . "

Borg replied by letter dated July 15 that it was prepared to abide by the original telephonic offer as Borg claimed it was made or the June 20th modified offer.

The prime contract was awarded to Fedrick on July 11 next, and on July 19 Fedrick's counsel wrote Borg a letter stating in its pertinent parts:

"This will confirm my telephone conversation of this morning with your Mr. Christensen on the subject of my letters to you . . . I stated [Fedrick] is willing to issue a purchase order to you for the price and on the terms of your bid to Fedrick, as stated in my letter to you, dated June 25, 1974. Mr. Christensen stated that you would not accept such a purchase order and denied that the terms of your bid were as stated in my letter to you, dated June 25, 1974. Accordingly, Fedrick intends to purchase the pumps in question from another supplier and immediately will commence an action against you for all damages which it sustains as a consequence of your refusal to honor your bid."

Thereafter Fedrick purchased the pumps from another supplier for the price of $1,162,200, incurring thereby the alleged damage of $95,903 sued for in the proceedings.

Issue 1:

We are, as was the District Court, bound to look to the substantive law of California for the resolution of the issues. Erie Railway Co. v. Tompkins, 304 U.S. 64, 58 S.Ct. 817, 82 L.Ed. 1188 (1938).

We believe that throughout their dealings concerning the pumps, Fedrick and Borg were "merchants" within the meaning of that term as used in C.C.C. § 2201(2). *See* C.C.C. § 2104; 1 Anderson, Uniform Commercial Code, 283, § 2–201:50, and 219–22, §§ 2–104:4–2–104:7 (2d Ed. 1970). So it follows from the undisputed facts that Borg's telephonic bid of May 30 in and of itself was subject to revocation by Borg during and awaiting "a reasonable time [for Fedrick's] writing in confirmation of the contract and sufficient against [Fedrick was] received and [Borg after receipt has] reason to know its contents, ..." [sic] C.C.C. § 2201(2).

The dispute over the actual terms and exceptions in Borg's telephonic bid raised by Borg at the June 20th conference, and especially Borg's letter of June 20 proposing modifications of the telephonic bid, constituted a clear and decisive communicated revocation of the telephonic bid prior to any "writing" from Fedrick as permitted under C.C.C. § 2201(2). However, in order to deal with Fedrick's letters to Borg of June 25 and July 19, we will assume *arguendo* that Borg's telephonic bid or offer in and of itself remained outstanding.

We are satisfied that at most Fedrick's letters were self-serving statements of actions taken by Fedrick in reliance upon Borg's telephonic bid.

We then deem Fedrick's "writing" of June 25, as well as the subsequent letter of July 19, each to be far short of constituting a "confirmation of the contract." The express language of the second paragraph of the quotation from Fedrick's letter of June 25 speaks of a future intended executed agreement incorporating "the price and terms of the bid you submitted." Again, Fedrick's letter of July 19 speaks of future action and acknowledges that Borg would not accept a purchase order with the specifications required by Fedrick. None of Fedrick's writings were sufficient to bind Fedrick to the terms of Borg's telephonic bid. 1 Anderson, *supra,* 283, § 2–201:51, n. 8. See Doral Hosiery Corp. v. Sav-A-Stop, Inc., 377 F.Supp. 387, 389 (E.D. Pa.1974).

Accordingly we conclude that by virtue of C.C.C. § 2201(1), Borg's telephonic bid of May 30 in and of itself is not enforceable by Fedrick as a contract for the sale and delivery of the pumps.

The District Court did not commit error on this issue.

Issue 2:

Fedrick would avoid the barring effect of C.C.C. § 2201 through the application of the doctrine of estoppel. Fedrick claims that its cause of action is not actually for a breach of contract but rather in substance a cause for Borg's unlawful revocation of its telephonic bid or offer after reliance thereon by Fedrick to its detriment.

Fedrick first relies upon the rationale of Drennan v. Star Paving Co., 51 Cal.2d 409, 414–15, 333 P.2d 757 (1958); H. W. Stanfield Constr. Corp. v. Robert McMullan & Son, Inc., 14 Cal.App.3d 848, 852, 92 Cal.Rptr. 669 (1971); and Saliba-Kringlen Corp. v. Allen Engineering Co., 15 Cal.App.3d 95, 111, 92 Cal.Rptr. 799 (1971). The District Court with reference to those authorities succinctly stated the rationale of those authorities as being "clear . . . in the context of competitive bidding, an offer once relied upon is irrevocable even though it lacks consideration." However, the District Court quickly pointed out that *Drennan* and its progeny involved contractors bidding for construction *work and materials* subcontracts as opposed to vendors of specific goods such as Borg. Consequently C.C.C. § 2201 was not applicable nor considered in those authorities.

We find those California authorities lacking of definitive adjudication of this issue. Also our independent search for controlling California authority is wanting. Accordingly we are, as was the District Court, directed under *Erie* to reach the resolution of this issue as the Supreme Court of California would probably reach under the same facts. Furthermore, for us the "[a]nalysis by a district judge of the law of the state in which he sits . . . is entitled to great weight . . . That determination 'will be accepted on review *unless shown to be clearly wrong.*'" United States v. Pollard, 524 F.2d 808 (9th Cir. 1975) . . . .

The District Court laid considerable stress upon the Arizona authority in Tiffany Inc. v. W. M. K. Transit Mix, Inc., 16 Ariz.App. 415, 493 P.2d 1220, 1225–26 (1972), and stated: "In that case, as in the instant proceeding, plaintiff-contractor sued a seller of construction materials for refusing to honor a previously submitted bid upon which plaintiff had relied. The court there considered the question of whether a contractor could 'avoid the defense of the Statute of Frauds by claiming damages on the theory of promissory estoppel.' *Tiffany*, supra, 493 P.2d at 1225. Relying on Restatement of Contracts § 178 and the law of other jurisdictions, as well as on various policy arguments, the court held that ' "the defense of the Statute of Frauds is only precluded when there has been (1) a *misrepresentation* that the Statute's requirements have been complied with, or (2) a promise to make a memorandum." (21 Turtle Creek Sq., Ltd. v. New York St. Teach. Retire. Sys., 432 F.2d 64, 65 (5th Cir. 1970).' *Tiffany*, supra, 493 P.2d at 1226 (emphasis in original). . . ."

We conclude that the Supreme Court of California in considering this issue would probably adopt the rationale, or a variation thereof, in *Tiffany* rather than render C.C.C. § 2201(1) and (2) a nullity by extending to vendor's oral bids for sale and delivery of specific goods the doctrine of estoppel as applied in *Drennan* and its progeny to subcontractors' *work and materials* oral bids.

Next Fedrick relies upon the rationale of estoppel as enunciated in Monarco v. Lo Greco, 35 Cal.2d 621, 623–24, 220 P.2d 737 (1950). In *Monarco*, a decedent failed to devise real property honoring his oral promise which had been relied upon to the prejudice of the promisee. The Supreme Court of California applied the following sound equitable doctrine of estoppel: "In those cases . . . where either an unconscionable injury or unjust enrichment would result from refusal to enforce the contract, the doctrine of estoppel has been applied whether or not plaintiff relied upon representations going to the requirements of the statute itself. . . . In reality it is not the representation that the contract will be put in writing or that the statute will not be invoked, but the promise that the contract will be performed that a party relies upon when he changes his position because of it." *Monarco*, supra at 625–26, 220 P.2d at 741."

The following authorities, Irving Tier Co. v. Griffin, 244 Cal. App.2d 852, 863, 53 Cal.Rptr. 469 (1966); Sloan v. Hiatt, 245 Cal. App.2d 926, 54 Cal.Rptr. 351 (1966); Mintz v. Rowitz, 13 Cal.App.3d

216, 224–25, 91 Cal.Rptr. 435 (1970); and others have interpreted *Monarco* as requiring a showing of either unconscionable injury or unjust enrichment to preclude the Statute of Frauds defense.

Rather than indulging in a detailed analysis and discussion as to why those authorities are distinguishable, we reach directly for the Achilles heel of Fedrick's equitable stance. Fedrick candidly concedes that Borg was not unjustly enriched in the situation, but does strenuously contend it has suffered an "unconscionable injury" at Borg's hands.

The "unconscionable injury" claimed by Fedrick is the amount of $95,903 incurred when Fedrick was forced under its prime contract to purchase the required pumps from another supplier at a higher price following Borg's revocation of its telephonic bid. The precise issue and contention of a resulting unconscionable injury from such a predicament was met and decided adversely to Fedrick by this court in Caplan v. Roberts, 506 F.2d 1039 (9th Cir. 1974).

In *Caplan*, a supplier of heavy construction equipment was sued for breach of an oral sales contract when it refused to deliver the goods to plaintiff and instead conveyed to plaintiff's customers. This court, based upon California authorities, affirmed the District Court's summary judgment for the defendant with this statement: ". . . the only injury appellant, as the buyer under the oral contract, might have suffered from the seller's refusal to deliver, is the loss of the profit he was to make on the resale of the equipment. And, as Carlson v. Richardson, 267 Cal.App.2d 204, 208, 72 Cal.Rptr. 769 (1968) noted, the mere 'loss of bargain, and damage resulting therefrom, do not themselves estop a seller from relying upon the Statute of Frauds.' " *Caplan*, supra at 1041. See also In re Estate of Baglione, 65 Cal.2d 192, 198, 53 Cal.Rptr. 139, 417 P.2d 683 (1966).

Caplan controls here, and we are satisfied that the only injury Fedrick might have suffered from Borg's refusal to supply the pumps under the telephonic bid amount was "the loss of the profit [Fedrick] was to make on . . ." its prime contract with the Bureau.

We conclude that Borg was not estopped from relying upon C.C. C. § 2201(1) in the course of action taken, and the District Court did not err on this issue.

The summary judgment in favor of Borg entered by the District Court on January 24, 1975 is affirmed.

Affirmed.

DUNIWAY, Circuit Judge (concurring): I concur because I believe that, when the California Legislature adopted California Commercial Code § 2201, it was providing a special statutory method of alleviating at least to some extent, the hardship that can be caused by the Statute of Frauds in cases to which § 2201 applies. Therefore, the decisions of the Supreme Court of California and the California

Courts of Appeal which have established judicial rules mitigating the hardships caused by the Statute of Frauds should not be applied in a case in which § 2201 applies. I know of no reason why the California Legislature cannot provide a substitute for the judicially created mitigating rules, and think that that is what the California Legislature has done. I think that this is the essence of what Judge Renfrew was holding when he concluded that the California courts would probably apply the decision of the Arizona court in the *Tiffany* case, which deals with the comparable Arizona statute.

WALLACE, Circuit Judge, dissenting: As a general proposition, California courts have applied the doctrine of equitable estoppel to bar a Statute of Frauds defense in those cases where the defense would lead either to an unjust enrichment or to an unconscionable injury. Monarco v. Lo Greco, 35 Cal.2d 621, 220 P.2d 737 (1950); Goldstein v. McNeil, 122 Cal.App.2d 608, 265 P.2d 113 (1954). In my opinion, both the district court and the majority incorrectly relied upon Caplan v. Roberts, 506 F.2d 1039 (9th Cir. 1974), to support their positions that the injury to Fedrick was not unconscionable. *Caplan* and the California case upon which it relies, Little v. Union Oil Co., 73 Cal.App. 612, 238 P. 1066 (1925), were cases where the plaintiff attempted to recover an expectancy, i. e., the profit he would have made on the resale of goods had the defendant performed.[1] This case, however, does not involve an attempt to recover lost profits. Here Fedrick seeks to recover the out-of-pocket losses which it incurred when, in order to meet its contractual responsibilities, it purchased pumps at a price significantly higher than that offered by Borg.

The majority contends that even if Fedrick incurred a loss on the pumps, there was still no unconscionable injury inasmuch as Fedrick made a profit on the prime contract. In essence, the majority would offset the $95,903 loss on the Borg transaction with any profit derived from Fedrick's independent transactions with other suppliers and subcontractors. I can see no reasonable justification for such a principle, and *Caplan* certainly does not require it. Accordingly, the district court's opinion should be reversed and the case remanded for trial.

NOTES

(1) *Promises Enforceable Because of Reliance.* Is it arguable that the statute of frauds simply does not apply to promises that are enforceable because of reliance rather than because of consideration? A few courts have thought so. "The statute of frauds relates to the enforceability of *contracts*; promissory estoppel relates to *promises* which have no contractual basis and are enforced only when necessary to avoid injustices." Janke

1. Whereas the plaintiffs in *Caplan* and *Little* were absolved of their obligations to the third parties, Fedrick was bound—at the original bid price—to its contract with the government.

Constr. Co. v. Vulcan Materials Co., 386 F.Supp. 687, 697 (W.D.Wis.1974), aff'd, 527 F.2d 772 (7th Cir. 1976). On the Fedrick case, see Comment, 66 Calif.L.Rev. 1219 (1978).

In R. S. Bennett & Co. v. Economy Mechanical Industries, 606 F.2d 182 (7th Cir. 1979), the court, applying Illinois law, held that the statute of frauds was not a bar to "recovery on a theory of promissory estoppel" in spite of the decision in Ozier v. Haines, p. 169 supra. The court suggested that the enactment of the Code—and in particular of UCC 2–201(3)(b) dealing with admissions—made the possibility that the statute would be rendered "nugatory" as feared in Ozier "so much more remote that we do not think that court would consider a universal bar to recovery on promissory estoppel necessary to preserve the purpose of the statute."

(2) *The Case of the Subcontractor's Burden.* Dave Hall submitted a bid to the Alfred I. duPont School District that incorporated an oral bid from the Glover School and Office Equipment Co. to supply and install chalkboards, tackboards and lockers in a school. These were standard items that did not have to be specially manufactured by Glover, but Glover's bid did not separate the cost of the supplying and the installation. After Hall's bid had been accepted, Glover refused to perform at the price orally agreed upon. Hall sued Glover and recovered damages. Glover appealed on the ground that the agreement was unenforceable under UCC 2–201. *Held:* Affirmed. The court quoted from UCC 2–106(1) and 2–105(1) and (2). "It is clear that some work at the job site is involved. Whether this is a major or minor part of the contract is not shown . . . . In approaching the defense of statute of frauds, the beginning premise is that an oral contract is valid and enforceable unless prohibited or restricted by some statutory provision. . . . Where a party asserts the statute of frauds defense to a claim, the applicability of the statute of frauds to the transaction must clearly appear from the claim or else that party must carry the burden of establishing that the transaction is controlled by the statute of frauds. . . . After a review of the evidence, I conclude that defendant has not sustained its burden of proving that the primary purpose of this contract was for the sale and delivery of goods and that the service aspect of the contract was merely incidental to the sale of goods. The trial Court held that this is a contract for services and not for sale of goods. While I do not find sufficient evidence in the record to support the finding that the contract was primarily a service contract, it does not support a contrary finding." Glover School & Office Equipment Co. v. Dave Hall, Inc., 372 A.2d 221 (Del.Super.1977).

FRANCHISES

The next cases deal with franchised dealers, who have been described by Professor Kessler as occupying a position intermediate between "the independent retailer, exemplified by the general store or the corner grocery store" and the "agent who may be a branch or subsidiary of the manufacturer." [a] An exerpt from his article follows.

a. As to the applicability of Article 2 of the Uniform Commercial Code to franchises, compare Di Filippo v. Ford Motor Co., 516 F.2d 1313 (3d

KESSLER, AUTOMOBILE DEALER FRANCHISES: VERTICAL INTEGRATION BY CONTRACT, 66 Yale L.J. 1135, 1136–41 (1957).[a] The unique advantage of franchising for the manufacturer lies in the considerable control over the process of distribution he may exercise without exposure to the burdens and responsibilities of an agency relationship. Ideally, the dealers are carefully chosen from among those of proven ability. Selected dealers, experience has shown, tend to be more aggressive in cultivating a market and servicing the product. They are generally "co-operative" in carrying out the manufacturer's suggested program of selling. And the franchises of dealers who do not prove their worth may be eliminated by cancellation or non-renewal.

In return, the franchised dealer receives from the manufacturer added capacity to build and maintain a strong retail organization. Restriction of outlets tends to protect the dealer's inventory and plant investment. Moreover, the nature of the relationship fosters mutual dependence, and the dealer can expect the manufacturer to assist him in effective merchandising. The dealer also gains increased prestige through affiliation with a large organization, frequently of national extension.

Finally, the consumer, we are told, gets better service under the franchise system and is assured that the retailer carries a complete stock of the manufacturer's products.

However great these advantages, the franchise system is not free from shortcomings and frictions. The manufacturer may suffer because the dealer, sheltered by the restriction of outlets, does not exert his "best efforts." The "un-co-operative" dealer may lose his franchise and, to the extent it is built around exclusive representation, his business. Again, due to lack of outlet competition the consumer may suffer from a high price level or be at the mercy of a dealer whose services are inadequate.

Retail distribution through franchise arrangements has grown significantly during the last forty years. It has become the principal market channel for such products as automobiles, electrical appliances, farm implements, radios, television, tires and wall paper. Because of the nature of the commodity involved, the franchise system has had its most spectacular development in the automobile industry. As the system exists today, the manufactured product is channelled through the manufacturer's own sales organization directly to selected retailers. With the industry's development of its own decentralized assembly plants, the independent distributor-wholesaler, once important in the distribution process, has largely disappeared, except in

Cir. 1975), cert. denied, 423 U.S. 912 (1975), with Buttorff v. United Electronic Laboratories, 459 S.W.2d 581 (Ky.1970).

a. Reprinted by permission of The Yale Law Journal Company and Fred B. Rothman & Company.

low-volume lines. Large manufacturers usually regard the distributor as an economic luxury. And direct sales by manufacturers to the consumer, always small in number, are limited to fleet vehicles or those that require special design or finish. . . .

Although the [automobile] franchise system had many staunch supporters among dealers even before recent modifications, it has been a source of conflicts and tensions. . . . Its actual operation, the dealers complained, precluded them from attaining an independence as full as that of most merchants. In reality, the argument runs, automobile dealers have been in large measure the manufacturers' agents. Through their dominant economic position, the manufacturers have employed the franchise, a "one-sided document which is neither contract, license or agreement," to gain maximum control over the management of the dealers' business without corresponding "legal" responsibility. Under the terms of the franchise, the factories "give the orders while the dealer takes the losses."

The modern franchise indeed enables the manufacturer to wield great "vertical power" in the form of supervisory control over retail operations. The franchise is embodied in a detailed standardized contract presented by the manufacturer to the dealer. The master contract is frequently accompanied by printed addenda concerning such matters as capital requirements and succession. Modern franchise contracts show great similarity; the absence of complete uniformity may be ascribed to the competition for dealers among the . . . remaining manufacturers. This high degree of standardization is best illustrated by the "entire agreement" clauses. Patterned after provisions frequently found in insurance policies, the modern franchise states that it supersedes all prior agreements, that it constitutes the "entire agreement of the parties" and that only certain executives of the manufacturer, usually the Vice-President or Sales Manager, have authority to alter the written contract.

The terms of the franchise contract, however elaborate, do not give a complete picture of the dealership as an institution. "[They] do not show [that] 'priceless ingredient' of prime importance—namely, the manner in which the contract is administered." The policies and practices of the manufacturer may be made relevant with the help of skillfully drafted clauses in the franchise agreement. But often the dealer must comply simply because of the economic power of the manufacturer. A prospective dealer, to be sure, is free to accept or reject a dealer franchise. Once he has committed his capital and entered the business, however, the power of the manufacturer comes into operation. The dealer must, on pain of cancellation or non-renewal, accede to the demands which the manufacturer, in the interest of market penetration, deems necessary and reasonable. Thus the manufacturer has an assured market in his dealers. Of course, his power to terminate or not to renew is tempered by considerations of enlightened self-interest. The manufacturer gains nothing by destroying a valuable member of a sales organization developed over the years with his own assistance and financial contribution. On the other hand, cancellation or non-renewal are valuable means of replacing inefficient dealers with new ones, selected from the waiting list prepared by field representatives. . . .

With the gradual development of the terms of the franchise, several unique features have become apparent. Today the dealer is required to develop his territory to the satisfaction of the manufacturer, a requirement buttressed by a host of ancillary provisions. Termination clauses are designed to assure adequate performance and attempt to insulate the manufacturer from liability. But franchises do not compensate the franchised dealer by giving him "territorial security," a protected sales area. Small wonder dealers complained that the modern franchise is "one-sided," "neither contract, license or agreement." In response to dealer complaints, adverse public opinion and new federal legislation, the terms of franchises have recently been considerably changed in the dealers' favor.

GOODMAN v. DICKER

United States Court of Appeals, District of Columbia, 1948.
83 U.S.App.D.C. 353, 169 F.2d 684.

PROCTOR, Associate Justice. This appeal is from a judgment of the District Court in a suit by appellees for breach of contract.

Appellants are local distributors for Emerson Radio and Phonograph Corporation in the District of Columbia. Appellees, with the knowledge and encouragement of appellants, applied for a "dealer franchise" to sell Emerson's products. The trial court found that appellants by their representations and conduct induced appellees to incur expenses in preparing to do business under the franchise, including employment of salesmen and solicitation of orders for radios. Among other things, appellants represented that the application had been accepted; that the franchise would be granted, and that appellees would receive an initial delivery of thirty to forty radios. Yet, no radios were delivered, and notice was finally given that the franchise would not be granted.

The case was tried without a jury. The court held that a contract had not been proven but that appellants were estopped from denying the same by reason of their statements and conduct upon which appellees relied to their detriment. Judgment was entered for $1,500, covering cash outlays of $1,150 and loss of $350, anticipated profits on sale of thirty radios.

The main contention of appellants is that no liability would have arisen under the dealer franchise had it been granted because, as understood by appellees, it would have been terminable at will and would have imposed no duty upon the manufacturer to sell or appellees to buy any fixed number of radios. From this it is argued that the franchise agreement would not have been enforceable (except as to acts performed thereunder) and cancellation by the manufacturer would have created no liability for expenses incurred by the dealer in preparing to do business. Further, it is argued that as the dealer franchise would have been unenforceable for failure of the manufacturer to supply radios appellants would not be liable to fulfill their assurance that radios would be supplied.

We think these contentions miss the real point of this case. We are not concerned directly with the terms of the franchise. We are dealing with a promise by appellants that a franchise would be granted and radios supplied, on the faith of which appellees with the knowledge and encouragement of appellants incurred expenses in making preparations to do business. Under these circumstances we think that appellants cannot now advance any defense inconsistent with their assurance that the franchise would be granted. Justice and fair dealing require that one who acts to his detriment on the faith of conduct of the kind revealed here should be protected by estopping the party who has brought about the situation from alleging anything in opposition to the natural consequences of his own course of conduct. Dair v. United States, 1872, 16 Wall. 1, 4, 21 L.Ed. 491. In Dickerson v. Colgrove, 100 U.S. 578, 580, 25 L.Ed. 618, the Supreme Court, in speaking of equitable estoppel, said: "The law upon the subject is well settled. The vital principle is that he who by his language or conduct leads another to do what he would not otherwise have done, shall not subject such person to loss or injury by disappointing the expectations upon which he acted. Such a change of position is sternly forbidden. . . . This remedy is always so applied as to promote the ends of justice." See also Casey v. Galli, 94 U.S. 673, 680, 24 L.Ed. 168; Arizona v. Copper Queen Mining Co., 233 U.S. 87, 95, 34 S.Ct. 546, 58 L.Ed. 863.

In our opinion the trial court was correct in holding defendants liable for moneys which appellees expended in preparing to do business under the promised dealer franchise. These items aggregated $1,150. We think, though, the court erred in adding the item of $350 for loss of profits on radios promised under an initial order. The true measure of damage is the loss sustained by expenditures made in reliance upon the assurance of a dealer franchise. As thus modified, the judgment is

Affirmed.

NOTES

(1) *Amount of Recovery.* Why did the court in Goodman v. Dicker deny recovery for the lost profits on the thirty radios? Would it have been possible to have calculated that profit so that it did not give double recovery

for some of the expenditures included in the $1,150? How? Cf. Chrysler Corporation v. Quimby, 51 Del. 264, 144 A.2d 123, 885 (1958). Similar problems will be encountered in connection with remedies in Chapter 6.

(2) *Culpa in Contrahendo.* The German scholar Jhering, writing in 1861, formulated a doctrine of *culpa in contrahendo* (fault in negotiating), under which "damages should be recoverable against the party whose blameworthy conduct during negotiations for a contract brought about its invalidity or prevented its perfection. . . . Of course, the party who has relied on the validity of the contract to his injury will not be able to recover the value of the promised performance, the expectation interest. But, he suggested, the law can ill afford to deny the innocent party recovery altogether; it has to provide for the restoration of the *status quo* by giving the injured party his 'negative interest' or reliance damages. The careless promisor has only himself to blame when he has created for the other party the false appearance of a binding obligation. This is the meaning of *culpa in contrahendo.*"[a] Kessler and Fine, *Culpa in Contrahendo,* Bargaining in Good Faith, and Freedom of Contract: A Comparative Study, 77 Harv. L.Rev. 401, 401–02 (1964). On developments in this country, including the cases in this subsection, see Henderson, Promissory Estoppel and Traditional Contract Doctrine, 78 Yale L.J. 343 (1969); R. Summers, "Good Faith" in General Contract Law and the Sales Provisions of the Uniform Commercial Code, 54 Va.L.Rev. 195, 220–32 (1968); Note, 37 U.Chi.L.Rev. 559 (1970).

HOFFMAN v. RED OWL STORES

Supreme Court of Wisconsin, 1965.
26 Wis.2d 683, 133 N.W.2d 267.

[Hoffman and his wife owned and operated a bakery in Wautoma, Wisconsin. In November, 1959, he contacted Red Owl, which operated a supermarket chain, seeking to obtain a franchise for a Red Owl store in Wautoma. He mentioned that he had only $18,000 to invest and was assured that this would be sufficient. In February, 1961, on the advice of Red Owl's representative, Lukowitz, he acquired a small grocery store as a means of gaining experience. After three months, the store was operating at a profit, and Lukowitz advised him to sell it, assuring him that Red Owl would find him a larger store elsewhere. Hoffman did so in June, 1961, although he was reluctant to lose the summer tourist business. He was again assured that $18,000 would suffice to obtain a franchise. In September, on Lukowitz' advice, Hoffman put $1,000 down on a lot in Chilton selected by Red Owl. Later in September, after meeting with Hoffman to prepare a financial statement, Lukowitz told him, "[E]verything is

a. The impact of the doctrine in contemporary German law has shifted to problems that we would characterize as problems of tort rather than of contract. Might it be instructive to view the following case, Hoffman v. Red Owl, through the optic of tort? Does the statute of frauds protect such a "careless promisor"?

ready to go. Get your money together and we are set." Lukowitz then told Hoffman to sell his bakery, which Hoffman did in November for $10,000, a loss of $2,000. He paid a month's rent of $125 on a house in Chilton, and they spent $140 in moving his family to Neenah where Red Owl suggested that he get experience by working at their store near there. When that job did not materialize, he went to work on the night shift at an Appleton bakery.

[By this time, Lukowitz and Hoffman had considered a variety of arrangements under which Red Owl would get some third party to acquire the Chilton lot, build the building, and lease it to Hoffman, and had agreed on some of the terms of a ten-year lease, with an option in Hoffman to renew the lease or purchase the property. Late in November they met with Red Owl's credit manager and drew up a proposed financing statement showing Hoffman contributing $24,100 of which $4,600 was an actual cash contribution, and another $7,500 was to be borrowed from his father-in-law. A week or two later, Lukowitz said that according to the home office, if Hoffman could get another $2,000 for promotion, the deal could go through for $26,000. Hoffman got his father-in-law to agree to put up $13,000 if he could come in as a partner. The home office, however, insisted that the father-in-law sign an agreement that the $13,000 was either a gift or a loan subordinate to all general creditors. Early in February, 1962, the negotiations collapsed when Hoffman refused to accede to a proposed financial statement that showed his contribution as $34,000, including $13,000 from his father-in-law as an outright gift. The Hoffmans sued Red Owl and the jury gave a special verdict, assessing damages as $16,735 for the sale of the Wautoma store, $2,000 for the sale of the bakery, $1,000 for taking up the option on the Chilton lot, $140 for moving expenses to Neenah, and $125 for house rental in Chilton. The trial court confirmed the verdict, except for the figure of $16,735 for the sale of the Wautoma store, as to which it ordered a new trial.]

CURRIE, Chief Justice. . . . The record here discloses a number of promises and assurances given to Hoffman by Lukowitz in behalf of Red Owl upon which plaintiffs relied and acted upon to their detriment. . . . There remains for consideration the question of law raised by defendants that agreement was never reached on essential factors necessary to establish a contract between Hoffman and Red Owl. Among these were the size, cost, design, and layout of the store building; and the terms of the lease with respect to rent, maintenance, renewal, and purchase options. This poses the question of whether the promise necessary to sustain a cause of action for promissory estoppel must embrace all essential details of a proposed transaction between promisor and promisee so as to be the equivalent of an offer that would result in a binding contract between the parties if the promisee were to accept the same.

Originally the doctrine of promissory estoppel was invoked as a substitute for consideration rendering a gratuitous promise enforceable as a contract. See Williston, Contracts (1st ed.), p. 307, sec. 139. In other words, the acts of reliance by the promisee to his detriment provided a substitute for consideration. If promissory estoppel were to be limited to only those situations where the promise giving rise to the cause of action must be so definite with respect to all details that a contract would result were the promise supported by consideration, then the defendants' instant promises to Hoffman would not meet this test. However, sec. 90 of Restatement, 1 Contracts, does not impose the requirement that the promise giving rise to the cause of action must be so comprehensive in scope as to meet the requirements of an offer that would ripen into a contract if accepted by the promisee. Rather the conditions imposed are:

> (1) Was the promise one which the promisor should reasonably expect to induce action or forbearance of a definite and substantial character on the part of the promisee?
>
> (2) Did the promise induce such action or forbearance?
>
> (3) Can injustice be avoided only by enforcement of the promise? [1]

We deem it would be a mistake to regard an action grounded on promissory estoppel as the equivalent of a breach of contract action. As Dean Boyer points out, it is desirable that fluidity in the application of the concept be maintained. 98 University of Pennsylvania Law Review (1950), 459, at page 497. While the first two of the above listed three requirements of promissory estoppel present issues of fact which ordinarily will be resolved by a jury, the third requirement, that the remedy can only be invoked where necessary to avoid injustice, is one that involves a policy decision by the court. Such a policy decision necessarily embraces an element of discretion.

We conclude that injustice would result here if plaintiffs were not granted some relief because of the failure of defendants to keep their promises which induced plaintiffs to act to their detriment. . . .

[With regard to damages, all of the items properly represented losses that he had reasonably sustained in reliance on Red Owl's promises except for the $16,735 for the sale of the Wautoma store. This should have been] limited to the difference between the sales price received and the fair market value of the assets sold, giving consideration to any goodwill attaching thereto by reason of the transfer of a going business. There was no direct evidence presented

1. See Boyer, 98 University of Pennsylvania Law Review (1950), 459, 460. "Enforcement" of the promise embraces an award of damages for breach as well as decreeing specific performance.

as to what this fair market value was on June 6, 1961. The evidence did disclose that Hoffman paid $9,000 for the inventory, added $1,500 to it and sold it for $10,000 or a loss of $500. His 1961 federal income tax return showed that the grocery equipment had been purchased for $7,000 and sold for $7,955.96. Plaintiffs introduced evidence of the buyer that during the first eleven weeks of operation of the grocery store his gross sales were $44,000 and his profit was $6,000 or roughly 15 percent. On cross-examination he admitted that this was gross and not net profit. Plaintiffs contend that in a breach of contract action damages may include loss of profits. However, this is not a breach of contract action.

The only relevancy of evidence relating to profits would be with respect to proving the element of goodwill in establishing the fair market value of the grocery inventory and fixtures sold. Therefore, evidence of profits would be admissible to afford a foundation for expert opinion as to fair market value.

Where damages are awarded in promissory estoppel instead of specifically enforcing the promisor's promise, they should be only such as in the opinion of the court are necessary to prevent injustice. Mechanical or rule of thumb approaches to the damage problem should be avoided. . . .

At the time Hoffman bought the equipment and inventory of the small grocery store at Wautoma he did so in order to gain experience in the grocery store business. At that time discussion had already been had with Red Owl representatives that Wautoma might be too small for a Red Owl operation and that a larger city might be more desirable. Thus Hoffman made this purchase more or less as a temporary experiment. Justice does not require that the damages awarded him, because of selling these assets at the behest of defendants, should exceed any actual loss sustained measured by the difference between the sales price and the fair market value.

Since the evidence does not sustain the large award of damages arising from the sale of the Wautoma grocery business, the trial court properly ordered a new trial on this issue.

Order affirmed. . . .

NOTES

(1) *The Case of the Uncertain Loan.* Wheeler owned a tract of land in Port Arthur, Texas, on which he wanted to build a commercial structure. He made a written agreement with White, under which White was to either make or obtain a loan of $70,000, payable in monthly installments over 15 years at not more than 6%, to finance the project and to receive a $5,000 fee for obtaining the loan and a 5% commission on all rentals from tenants that he procured. Later White assured Wheeler that he would make the loan himself if the money was unobtainable elsewhere, and urged him to proceed with the demolition of the existing buildings, which had a value of $58,500 and a rental value of $400 a month. After Wheeler had razed the

old buildings and begun to prepare the site, White refused to perform. When Wheeler was unable to obtain a loan himself, he sued White. From judgment dismissing Wheeler's complaint, Wheeler appealed. *Held:* Reversed. "[T]he pleaded contract did not contain essential elements to its enforceability in that it failed to provide the amount of monthly installments, the amount of interest due upon the obligation, how much interest would be computed, [and] when such interest would be paid. . . ." The court then discussed Goodman v. Dicker. "We agree with the reasoning announced in those jurisdictions that, in cases such as we have before us, where there is actually no contract the promissory estoppel theory may be invoked, thereby supplying a remedy which will enable the injured party to be compensated for his foreseeable, definite and substantial reliance. Where the promisee has failed to bind the promisor to a legally sufficient contract, but where the promisee has acted in reliance upon a promise to his detriment, the promisee is to be allowed to recover no more than reliance damages measured by the detriment sustained." Wheeler v. White, 398 S.W.2d 93 (Tex.1965). How should those damages be calculated when the case goes back for trial? Does this case go beyond Goodman v. Dicker? Beyond Hoffman v. Red Owl?

(2) *The Case of Miller High Life.* In October, 1963, Prince, an established beer distributor, undertook the Miller High Life distributorship in East Harris County, Texas, although he knew that the area had been poorly serviced in the past and that it would be two or three years before he would realize a profit. The contract provided, "Either of us can terminate this relationship at any time without incurring liability to the other." Miller terminated in June, 1965 because it had become involved in a lawsuit with a corporation that Prince controlled. Prince had just begun to make a profit, after having sustained losses of over $20,000, not including his own time and effort and that of his wife. Miller then appointed another distributor, whose operation showed a continued and substantial increase in sales volume. Prince sued Miller for the money he had spent in preparation for and operation of the distributorship and for reasonable compensation for his services. The trial court directed a verdict for the defendant and the plaintiff appealed. *Held:* Affirmed. "It is appellant's contention that where a manufacturer and a distributor enter into an arrangement whereby the distributor is to develop a market for and sell the manufacturer's products, and it is contemplated by both parties that expenditures of time and money by the distributor are necessary to build up his distributorship, though the relationship be one terminable at will, the law will not allow the manufacturer to exercise its rights of cancellation with impunity, but will imply an obligation on its part to respond in damages sufficient to compensate the distributor for his expenditures made and losses incurred in reliance upon the agreement if the manufacturer terminates the distributorship before the distributor is afforded a reasonable time to recoup his losses. . . . This statement of the law is supported by respectable authority. . . . [However], each of these cases presented situations where the contract was oral, of indefinite duration, or void, and were considered cancellable at will as a matter of law. There was no specific written agreement authorizing cancellation without liability. . . . In Wheeler v. White [Note 1, supra], the Supreme Court recognized the case of Goodman v. Dicker. . . . In this case, however, there is a legally sufficient contract.

. . . Appellant cannot disregard the contract and sue for his reliance damage. Because of the valid contract the theory of promissory estoppel is not applicable." Prince v. Miller Brewing Co., 434 S.W.2d 232 (Tex.Civ. App.1968).

What result if Prince had been able to show that Miller had terminated the contract in order to let a close personal friend of one of its officers have a profitable franchise? In Goodman v. Dicker, would Dicker have had any recourse if Emerson had granted him a franchise and then terminated it immediately? Would the wording of the termination clause affect your answer? What answer if it read, "Either of us can terminate this relationship at any time"? See Lockewill v. United States Shoe, p. 741 infra; Gellhorn, Limitations on Contract Termination Rights—Franchise Cancellations, 1967 Duke L.J. 465 (1967).

REFUSAL TO DEAL OR TO BARGAIN IN GOOD FAITH

Refusal to Deal. In a few narrow fields of economic activity a doctrine of "compulsory contract" is recognized. Businesses described generally as "public utilities," such as telephone companies, gas and electric companies and railroads, are considered to be under "a duty to serve without discrimination and on proper terms all who request [their] service." Restatement of Torts, § 763. Their duty arises without regard to whether any negotiations have taken place of not. "The duty to serve without discrimination is the result partly of historical development, partly of the nature of the services which they render and partly of their less competitive and more monopolistic character." Id., Comment a. The term "compulsory contract" is somewhat misleading because the liability for refusal to deal is not in contract, but in tort. The circumstance that the terms of the contract that should have been made are standard terms is, however, a significant factor in facilitating the assessment of damages.

Although insurance companies have not been brought within the ambit of "compulsory contract," a related sort of liability has been imposed on life insurers. When an aspiring policyholder applies for a policy insuring his life, and the insurer takes an unreasonable length of time to act on his application, the insurer has been held liable if the applicant dies during the period of delay. See, e. g., Rosin v. Peninsular Life Ins. Co., 116 So.2d 798 (Fla.App.1960); R. Keeton, Basic Text on Insurance Law 45–50 (1971).

Refusal to Bargain in Good Faith. Instead of attaching legal consequences to refusal to deal, the law may require a party to bargain according to acceptable standards, in the hope that the usual, although not the necessary, result of such bargaining will be a contract. The standard adopted, where such a requirement has been imposed, has been that of good faith. Thus the National Labor Relations Act, § 8 imposes a duty on both employer and labor union to bargain collectively—"to meet at reasonable times and confer in good faith

. . . , but such obligation does not compel either party to agree to a proposal or require the making of a concession." The collective bargaining agreement is admittedly a special sort of agreement, in good part because of what has been called the "compulsory character of the bargaining relationship," in which the employer is required to bargain with the union that represents a majority of employees, to the exclusion of all other unions. See C. Summers, Collective Agreements and the Law of Contracts, 78 Yale L.J. 525, 530–33 (1969). Its study is best left for another course.[a]

Nevertheless, there have been suggestions that the notion might be more generally applied. An example is Heyer Products Co. v. United States, 140 F.Supp. 409 (Ct.Cl.1956), in which Heyer, a disappointed bidder on a contract with the Army Ordnance Corps, sued the government alleging that, although its bid had been the lowest, the government had awarded the contract to another bidder in order to retaliate against Heyer for having testified against the Ordnance Corps at a Senate hearing. The court held that while the government "could accept or reject an offer as it pleased, and no contract resulted until an offer was accepted," it was "an implied condition of the request for offers that each of them would be honestly considered," and the government was under an "obligation to honestly consider [the bid] and not to wantonly disregard it." It would therefore be liable to Heyer for its expense in preparing its bid if "bids were not invited in good faith." [b] The rule must be regarded with caution, since it was framed in the particular circumstances of an invitation to bid on a government contract where, it will be remembered, the bidder's power to revoke his bid is restricted. See Note 1, p. 264 supra. Nevertheless, one writer has hailed the decision as a unique one "in which a court has recognized, in the absence of a statutory or contractual duty to negotiate, that a cause of action exists against a party who negotiates without serious intent to contract." R. Summers, "Good Faith" in General Contract Law and the Sales Provisions of the Uniform Commercial Code, 54 Va.L.Rev. 195, 221 (1968).

NOTES

(1) *Refusal to Deal for Improper Motive.* In addition to the rare examples involving public utilities and insurers (where there is a general liability for refusal to deal), there are other important instances in which a refusal to deal may have legal consequences if it is improperly motivated. Where, for example, its purpose is to restrain trade or gain a monopoly, a

a. An analogous problem arises in communist countries where, as a result of state planning, the bargaining relationship between a producing enterprise and a consuming enterprise also takes on a "compulsory" character. As a consequence, in the Soviet Union, for example, a system of economic courts (*Arbitrazh*) resolves pre-contractual disputes by determining the terms of agreements. See H. Berman, Justice in the U.S.S.R. 131–34 (1963).

b. But cf. Rapp v. Salt Lake City, 527 P.2d 651 (Utah 1974).

refusal to deal may be wrongful under either the common law relating to business torts or statutes in the fields of antitrust and trade regulation. And where it is motivated by racial or religious discrimination, it may be wrongful under one of the anti-discrimination laws. Although these topics must be left to special courses in their respective fields, it is worth noting that to the extent that civil liability is imposed for refusal to deal, here too it generally is on a theory of tort rather than of contract.

(2) *Agreement to Negotiate in Good Faith.* Could the parties impose upon themselves a duty to negotiate in good faith? Consider Itek Corp. v. Chicago Aerial Industries, 248 A.2d 625 (Del.1968). On January 15, after negotiations looking to the purchase by Itek of all CAI's assets, the parties executed a "letter of intent" confirming the terms of the sale and providing that, "Itek and CAI shall make every reasonable effort to agree upon and have prepared as quickly as possible a contract providing for the foregoing purchase by Itek and sale by CAI, . . . embodying the above terms and such other terms and conditions as the parties shall agree upon. If the parties fail to agree upon and execute such a contract they shall be under no further obligation to one another." On February 23, CAI insisted on three new conditions, to which Itek agreed. On March 2, CAI, evidently having received a more favorable offer from Bourns, telegraphed Itek that it was not going ahead with the transaction as a result of unforeseen circumstances and the failure of the parties to reach agreement. Itek sued CAI for breach of contract, but the trial court granted summary judgment for CAI, relying on the second sentence quoted above. The Supreme Court of Delaware reversed, reasoning that "it is apparent that the parties obligated themselves to 'make every reasonable effort' to agree upon a formal contract, and only if such effort failed were they absolved from 'further obligation' for having 'failed' to agree upon and execute a formal contract. We think these provisions of the January 15 letter obligated each side to attempt in good faith to reach final and formal agreement." Since there was evidence that in order to accept a more favorable offer from Bourns, "CAI willfully failed to negotiate in good faith and to make 'every reasonable effort' to agree upon a formal contract, as it was required to do," it was error to grant summary judgment. What sorts of facts might CAI show at the trial to establish its "good faith"? If Itek proves its case at trial, how should damages be measured? In support of the somewhat unconventional result in the Itek case, see Knapp, Enforcing the Contract to Bargain, 44 N.Y.U.L.Rev. 673 (1969). See the discussion of "agreements to agree" in Note, p. 243 supra.

Chapter 5

POLICING THE BARGAIN

In some exchanges, the assent of a party is more apparent than real. That is evidently so when the offer takes the form, "Your money or your life." When a promise is exacted through lawless threat or through fraud, one would expect the courts not to enforce it. Naturally, many offenses committed in bargaining processes are somewhat less egregious than these. Bargaining abuses take many subtle forms in commercial societies, and the means of abating them are correspondingly varied, some curative, some prophylactic. We treat these means under the title, "policing the bargain."

One sort of policing measure attends chiefly to the *status* of the parties. In its strongest form, this method disqualifies certain classes of persons from committing themselves by contract: minors and married women are among the historic classes. (See Section 1.) Another attends chiefly to the *behavior* of the parties—how they bargained in fact. The treatment of fraud and duress illustrates this method. A third sort of policing measure attends to the *substance* of the bargain in question. As we have seen, exchanges of highly unequal advantage are commonly enforced. Yet the courts have found ways to discountenance them. This is the mainspring, more or less overt, of certain applications of the doctrine of consideration.

A great chancellor of the 18th century expressed concern for inequality "apparent from the intrinsic nature and subject of the bargain itself; such as no man in his senses . . . would make." [a] For such a bargain Lord Hardwicke's opprobrium was "fraud"—a name for bad behavior. But his concern (only modestly veiled) was about substance. The policing of bargains by the courts still proceeds both in ancient forms, such as rescission for fraud, and in veiled forms, such as the strict construction of harsh terms. (Sections 2 and 3 depict the background of conventional controls over unequal bargains and misconduct in bargaining.) Yet in this century the rapid production of new means of policing (illustrated in Section 4) has somewhat eclipsed the old, and has perhaps reduced the dependence of courts on "covert tools" for attacking abuses.

One reading of the courts' performance in policing bargains is that they are moved by moral conviction, including a "rights theory" of contract.[b] Another, now strongly influenced by economic thought,

a. Earl of Chesterfield v. Janssen, 28 Eng.Rep. 82, 100 (1751).

b. "Contract theory either does not recognize, or characterizes as void-is that they are deterred by certain social inutilities from investing in the enforcement of bargains that have special anomalies—such as mistaken premises. However that may be, no one now believes that the courts can go it alone. The discriminating powers of legislatures and administrative agencies have increasingly come to bear in setting the proper conditions for effective bargaining. Much of their effort is directed to consumer protection. In this matter it is a special challenge to disentangle concerns about behavior, about status, and about substance: the shifts of focus in the courts and elsewhere are sometimes obtrusive, sometimes not.

In a final section, the chapter deals with illegal bargains, which threaten interests of the public at large. Here again the direction is partly set by legislation and hard questions arise about coordinating the judicial and the legislative functions.

SECTION 1. CAPACITY

What classes of persons are considered by the law to have less than full power to contract? Since the materials in this section are confined to the two important classes of infants and insane persons, some words may here be in order concerning others.

As to intoxicated persons, a common standard of capacity is stated in Lucy v. Zehmer, p. 173 supra: "Zehmer was not intoxicated to the extent of being unable to comprehend the nature or consequences of the instrument he executed." An older case puts the test this way: "To render a transaction voidable on account of the drunkenness of a party to it, the drunkenness must have been such as to have drowned reason, memory, and judgment, and to have impaired the mental facilities to such an extent as to render the party non compos mentis for the time being." Martin v. Harsh, 231 Ill. 384, 83 N.E. 164 (1907).[c]

The common-law incapacities of married women have also been alluded to. They were largely removed, in this country, by statutes during the nineteenth century—long before women were given the vote.

Another important class consists of corporations, on which limited powers are conferred by charter. The extent to which ultra vires

able, arrangements between parties who lack adequate bargaining power. . . . Contract obligations are enforceable as a matter of 'right,' and contract theory is based on the intention of parties who possess the freedom to agree or disagree." Boggs v. Blue Diamond Coal Co., 590 F.2d 655 (6th Cir. 1979).

c. As to a transaction effected by a drunkard in a sober interval, see Olsen v. Hawkins, 90 Idaho 28, 408 P.2d 462 (1965) (change of insurance beneficiary).

acts of a corporation—acts beyond its powers—may be effective is best left to a course in corporations.

KESER v. CHAGNON

Supreme Court of Colorado, 1966.
159 Colo. 209, 410 P.2d 637.

McWILLIAMS, Justice. This writ of error concerns the purchase of an automobile by a minor and his efforts to thereafter avoid the contract of purchase. The salient facts are as follows:

1. on June 11, 1964 Chagnon bought a 1959 Edsel from Keser for the sum of $1025, payment therefor being in cash which Chagnon obtained by borrowing a portion of the purchase price from the Cash Credit Company on a signature note, with the balance of the money being obtained from the Public Finance Corporation, the latter loan being secured by a chattel mortgage upon the automobile;
2. as of June 11, 1964 Chagnon was a minor of the age of twenty years, ten months and twenty days, although despite this fact Chagnon nonetheless falsely advised Keser that he was then over the age of twenty-one; and
3. on about September 25, 1964, when Chagnon was then of the age of twenty-one years, two months and four days, Chagnon formally advised Keser of his desire to disaffirm the contract theretofore entered into by the parties, and thereafter on October 5, 1964 Chagnon returned the Edsel to Keser.

Based on this sequence of events Chagnon brought an action against Keser wherein he sought to recover the $1025 which he had allegedly theretofore paid Keser for the Edsel. By answer Keser alleged, among other things, that he had suffered damage as the direct result of Chagnon's false representation as to his age.

A trial was had to the court, sitting without a jury, all of which culminated in a judgment in favor of Chagnon against Keser in the sum of $655.78. This particular sum was arrived at by the trial court in the following manner: the trial court found that Chagnon initially purchased the Edsel for the sum of $995 (not $1025) and that he was entitled to the return of his $995; and then by way of set-off the trial court subtracted from the $995 the sum of $339.22, this latter sum apparently representing the difference between the purchase price paid for the vehicle and the reasonable value of the Edsel on October 5, 1964, which was the date when the Edsel was returned to Keser. By writ of error Keser now seeks reversal of this judgment.

In this court Keser summarizes his argument as follows:

1. Chagnon's attempted disaffirmance was ineffective because though he returned the automobile, he nonetheless failed to also return the certificate of title thereto which was then and there in the possession of the Public Finance Corporation;
2. Chagnon in reality ratified the contract because he failed to disaffirm within a reasonable time after reaching his majority and for such length of time retained possession of the Edsel; and
3. in connection with Keser's set-off the trial court erred in its determination of Keser's damages resulting from Chagnon's false representation as to his age.

Before considering each of these several matters, it is deemed helpful to allude briefly to some of the general principles pertaining to the longstanding policy of the law to protect a minor from at least some of his childish foibles by affording him the right, under certain circumstances, to avoid his contract, not only during his minority but also within a reasonable time after reaching his majority. In Mosko v. Forsythe, 102 Colo. 115, 76 P.2d 1106 we held that when a minor elects to disaffirm and avoid his contract, the "contract" becomes invalid ab initio and that the parties thereto then revert to the same position as if the contract had never been made. In that case we went on to declare that when a minor thus sought to avoid his contract and had in his possession the specific property received by him in the transaction, he was in such circumstance required to return the same as a prerequisite to any avoidance.

In C.J.S. Infants § 75 at page 171 it is said that a minor failing to disaffirm within a "reasonable time" after reaching his majority loses the right to do so and that just what constitutes a "reasonable time" is ordinarily a question of fact. As regards the necessity for restoration of consideration, in C.J.S. Infants at page 174 it is stated that the minor after disaffirming is "usually required . . . to return the consideration, if he can, or the part remaining in his possession or control."

Finally, we believe that Doenges-Long Motors, Inc. v. Gillen, 138 Colo. 31, 328 P.2d 1077 answers most of the matters sought to be raised here by Keser. In that case it was held that the right of an infant to disaffirm his contract is absolute and is not lost by reason of the fact that the infant induced the making of the contract by a deliberate misrepresentation of his age. However, in that case it was also held that even though an infant has the right to disaffirm his contract, if he falsely represents his age and as a result thereof obtains an automobile, he is at the same time answerable to the seller for his tort. In other words, though the seller is required to return to the infant that which he, the seller, received in exchange for the automobile, the seller is entitled to set-off against such sum any damage sustained by him as a result of the infant's false representation as to his age. And in this regard the measure of damage was declared to be the difference between the reasonable value of the automobile at the time of its sale and delivery and its reasonable value at the time of its return.

Proceeding, then, to a consideration of those matters which Keser now contends require a reversal of this case, it is first urged that Chagnon's attempted disaffirmance is ineffective because, although Chagnon did return the Edsel to Keser, he did not at the same time return the certificate of ownership thereto, which certificate was then in possession of the Public Finance Corporation. And needless to say, Public Finance Corporation was not about to voluntarily give up the certificate of title! This contention, however, is without merit. It is true that Mosko v. Forsythe, supra, holds that a prerequisite to the avoidance of an executed contract by a minor is that if he then has in his possession the property which he received in the transaction, he must return the same. All that is required in this regard, however, is that the disaffirming party return only those fruits of his contract which are then in his possession and if for any reason he cannot thus place the other party in status quo, he does not because of such inability lose his right to disaffirm. To hold otherwise would strike at the very root of the well-settled principle that with certain exceptions which are not applicable to the instant controversy, he who deals with a minor does so at his own peril and with the attendant risk that the minor may at his election disaffirm the transaction because of his minority. Weathers v. Owen, 78 Ga.App. 505, 51 S.E. 2d 584 presents a factual situation most analogous to the instant one. See also Dawson v. Fox, 64 A.2d 162 (D.C.Mun.App.); and Freiburghaus v. Herman, 102 S.W.2d 743 (Mo.App.). In the instant case Chagnon returned to Keser all of the fruits of the transaction which were then in his possession or under his control, i. e., the Edsel. The fact that the Public Finance Corporation held the certificate of title and would not deliver it over to either Chagnon or Keser does not defeat Chagnon's right to disaffirm.

Keser's next contention that Chagnon upon attaining his majority ratified the contract by his failure to disaffirm within a reasonable time after becoming twenty-one and by his retention and use of the Edsel prior to its return to the seller is equally untenable. In this connection it is pointed out that Chagnon did not notify Keser of his desire to disaffirm until 66 days after he became twenty-one and that he did not return the Edsel until 10 days after his notice to disaffirm, during all of which time Chagnon had the possession and use of the vehicle in question. As already noted, when an infant attains his majority he has a reasonable time within which he may thereafter disaffirm, a contract entered into during his minority. And this rule is not as strict where, as here, we are dealing with an executed contract. There is no hard and fast rule as to just what constitutes a "reasonable" time within which the infant may disaffirm. In Fellows v. Cantrell, 143 Colo. 126, 352 P.2d 289 we held that the failure to disaffirm for a period of five years after a minor reached his majority, together with other acts recognizing the validity of the contract, constituted ratification. In Merchants' Credit Union v. Ariyama, 64 Utah 364, 230 P. 1017 disaffirmance four months after reaching majority was held to be within a reasonable time. Similarly, in Haines v. Fitzgerald, 108 Pa.Super. 290, 165 A. 52, three months was held to be a reasonable time within which to disaffirm; and in Adamroski v. Curtis-Wright, 300 Mass. 281, 15 N.E.2d 467 "nearly a year" was also held to be "reasonable." Suffice it to say, that under the circumstances disclosed by the record we are not prepared to hold that as a matter of law Chagnon ratified the contract either by his actions or by his alleged failure to disaffirm within a reasonable time after reaching his majority. In other words, there is competent evidence to support the conclusion of the trial court that Chagnon disaffirmed the contract within a reasonable time after reaching his majority and such finding of fact cannot be disturbed by us on review.

Finally, error is predicated upon the trial court's finding in connection with Keser's set-off for the damage occasioned him by Chagnon's admitted false representation of his age. In this regard the trial court apparently found that the reasonable value of the Edsel when it was returned to Keser by Chagnon was $655.78, and accordingly went on to allow Keser a set-off in the amount of $339.22, this latter sum representing the difference between the purchase price, $995, and the value of the vehicle on the date it was returned. Finding, then, that Chagnon was entitled to the return of the $995 which he had theretofore paid Keser for the Edsel, the trial court then subtracted therefrom Keser's set-off in the amount of $339.22, and accordingly entered judgment for Chagnon against Keser in the sum of $655.78. Whether it was by accident or design we know not, but $655.78 is apparently the exact amount which Chagnon "owed" the Public Finance Corporation on his note with that company.

In this regard as concerns his set-off Keser complains that the trial court did not follow the rule regarding the measure of damages as laid down in Doenges-Long v. Gillen, supra. More particularly, Keser claims that there is no evidence which supports the trial court's finding that the value of the automobile on the date it was returned to Keser was $655.78. The evidence as to the value of the Edsel on the date Chagnon returned it to Keser was as follows:

1. Chagnon said the car was worth more when he returned it than when be bought it;

2. An expert called by Keser opined that the car was worth $245 and
3. Keser testified that if he had a clear title to the vehicle it had a reasonable value of $395.

Based on this evidence the trial court found that the reasonable value of the automobile on the date of its return to Keser was $655.-78, which determination from the arithmetical standpoint, at least, permitted the trial court to then enter judgment in favor of Chagnon in an amount equal to the balance then due and owing the Public Finance Corporation. Without belaboring the point, it is apparent that on its determination of the reasonable value of the Edsel on the date of its return to Keser, the trial court was influenced by factors other than the evidence before it as to such value.

The judgment is reversed and the cause remanded with direction that the trial court determine Keser's set-off in accord with the rule in Doenges-Long v. Gillen, supra, and once this set-off has been thus determined, to then enter judgment for Chagnon in an amount equal to the difference between $995 and the amount of such set-off.

NOTES

(1) *Should Appearances Count?* If Keser reasonably believed Chagnon when he lied about his age, why should Chagnon be allowed to rely upon his infancy? Does not this clash with the objective standard advanced in Lucy v. Zehmer, p. 173 supra? Why was not Chagnon estopped to deny his representation of age? Can it be argued that every agreement a minor makes, otherwise effective as a contract, ought to be taken as implying a representation that he is competent to contract? Are there differences among infancy, mental incapacity and intoxication in this regard?

(2) *Voidable Not Void.* In many statutes and cases the promise of a person without capacity is said to be "void." As the discussion of disaffirmance in the Keser case suggests, it is more accurate to regard it as "voidable." In Holt v. Ward Clarencieux, 2 Strange 937, 93 Eng.Rep. 954 (K.B.1732), the court sustained an action for a breach of promise of marriage brought on behalf of a young woman, who had been a girl of 15 at the time of the agreement. "[W]e are all of opinion that this contract is not void, but only voidable at the option of the infant. . . . And no dangerous consequences can follow from this determination, because our opinion protects the infant even more than if we rule the contract to be absolutely void."

KIEFER v. FRED HOWE MOTORS, INC., 39 Wis.2d 20, 158 N.W.2d 288 (1968). [Steven Kiefer bought a five-year-old Willys station wagon from Fred Howe Motors when he was married, the father of a child, working, and a few months short of 21 years. The contract that he signed stated: "I represent that I am 21 years of age or over and recognize that the dealer sells the above vehicle upon this representation." He had difficulty with the car which he claimed had a cracked block, and after becoming of age, he sought to return it, and later sued to recover the price. From judgment for plaintiff, defendant appealed.]

WILKIE, J. . . . The law governing agreements made during infancy reaches back over many centuries. The general rule is that ". . . the contract of a minor, other than for necessaries, is either void or voidable at his option." The only other exceptions to the rule permitting disaffirmance are statutory or involve contracts which deal with duties imposed by law such as a contract of marriage or an agreement to support an illegitimate child. The general rule is not affected by the minor's status as emancipated or unemancipated.

Appellant does not advance any argument that would put this case within one of the exceptions to the general rule, but rather urges that this court, as a matter of public policy, adopt a rule that an emancipated minor over eighteen years of age be made legally responsible for his contracts.

The underpinnings of the general rule allowing the minor to disaffirm his contracts were undoubtedly the protection of the minor. It was thought that the minor was immature in both mind and experience and that, therefore, he should be protected from his own bad judgments as well as from adults who would take advantage of him. The doctrine of the voidability of minors' contracts often seems commendable and just. If the beans that the young naive Jack purchased from the crafty old man in the fairy tale "Jack and the Bean Stalk" had been worthless rather than magical, it would have been only fair to allow Jack to disaffirm the bargain and reclaim his cow. However, in today's modern and sophisticated society the "infancy doctrine" seems to lose some of its gloss.

Paradoxically, we declare the infant mature enough to shoulder arms in the military, but not mature enough to vote; mature enough to marry and be responsible for his torts and crimes, but not mature enough to assume the burden of his own contractual indiscretions. In Wisconsin, the infant is deemed mature enough to use a dangerous instrumentality—a motor vehicle—at sixteen, but not mature enough to purchase it without protection until he is twenty-one.

No one really questions that a line as to age must be drawn somewhere below which a legally defined minor must be able to disaffirm his contracts for nonnecessities. The law over the centuries has considered this age to be twenty-one. Legislatures in other states have lowered the age. We suggest that the appellant might better seek the change it proposes in the legislative halls rather than this court. A recent law review article in the Indiana Law Journal explores the problem of contractual disabilities of minors and points to three different legislative solutions leading to greater freedom to contract. The first approach is one gleaned from the statutes of California and New York, which would allow parties to submit a proposed contract to a court which would remove the infant's right of disaffirmance upon a finding that the particular contract is fair. This suggested approach appears to be extremely impractical in light of the expense and delay that would necessarily accompany the procedure. A second approach would be to establish a rebuttable presumption of incapacity to replace the strict rule. This alternative would be an open invitation to litigation. The third suggestion is a statutory procedure that would allow a minor to petition a court for the removal of disabilities. Under this procedure a minor would only have to go to court once, rather than once for each contract as in the first suggestion.

Undoubtedly, the infancy doctrine is an obstacle when a major purchase is involved. However, we believe that the reasons for allowing that obstacle to remain viable at this point outweigh those for casting it aside. Minors require some protection from the pitfalls of the market place. Reasonable minds will always differ on the extent of the protection that should be afforded. For this court to adopt a rule that the appellant suggests and remove the contractual disabilities from a minor simply because he becomes emancipated, which in most cases would be the result of marriage, would be to suggest that the married minor is somehow vested with more wisdom and maturity than his single counterpart. However, logic would not seem to dictate this result especially when today a youthful marriage is oftentimes indicative of a lack of wisdom and maturity.

[The court went on to rule that the dealer had not established deceit. The recital in the contract should have been supplemented by evidence of intent to defraud on the part of Kiefer, and of justifiable reliance on the part of the dealer.]

[Affirmed.]

HALLOWS, Chief Justice (dissenting) . . . The magical age limit of 21 years as an indication of contractual maturity no longer has a basis in fact or in public policy. [Furthermore,] an automobile to this respondent was a necessity and therefore the contract could not be disaffirmed. . . . Automobiles for parents under 21 years of age to go to and from work in our current society may well be a necessity, and I think in this case the record shows it is. . . .

NOTES

(1) *Change in the Age.* In most states the age of capacity to contract has been reduced to 18 years, and other statutory changes in the common-law rules on infancy are widespread. Should a change in the voting age affect the common-law rule?

(2) *Benefit or Burden.* Some of those whose capacity was limited under the common law, such as infants and married women, were described as "favorites" of the law. Is lack of capacity a benefit or a burden to the

"favorite"? Would married women applaud revival of the old rules that made them "favorites"? Would they refuse to take advantage of analogous rules if they were made generally applicable to all "consumers"?

Lack of capacity can obviously be a serious burden to the person who is underage and who seeks to buy a substantial item, such as an automobile, on credit. For some items the burden is avoided by the exception that makes an infant liable for "necessaries." What sort of assurances might satisfy a prospective creditor where "necessaries" are not involved?

But lack of capacity was obviously a significant benefit to Kiefer when he became dissatisfied with the performance of his Willys station wagon. What would his situation have been if he had not had his infancy as an ace up his sleeve? It has been suggested that the refuge of nonage may no longer be needed, as laws are progressively developed to protect *all* the public from unscrupulous dealings.[a]

(3) *Problem.* An employer lends money to a youthful employee for the purpose of paying his tuition while training for greater responsibilities. The employee got the job through the services of an employment agency, for which he promised it a fee. He completes the course and attains majority at the same time, and promptly repudiates his undertakings both to the employer and the agency. Is he liable to either of them? See Gastonia Personnel Corp. v. Rogers, 276 N.C. 279, 172 S.E.2d 19 (1970).

ORTELERE v. TEACHERS' RETIREMENT BD.

New York Court of Appeals, 1969.
25 N.Y.2d 196, 303 N.Y.S.2d 362, 250 N.E.2d 460.

[Grace Ortelere was a 60-year-old New York City schoolteacher, who had suffered a nervous breakdown diagnosed as involving "involutional psychosis, melancholia type," and was on leave for mental illness. Her psychiatrist also suspected that she suffered from cerebral arteriosclerosis. Her husband of 38 years had quit his job as an electrician to stay home and care for her. She had a reserve of $70,925 in the public retirement system in which she had participated for over 40 years. In 1965, without telling her husband she borrowed from the system the maximum possible, $8,760, and made an irrevocable election to take maximum retirement benefits of $450 a month during her lifetime. This revoked an earlier election under which she would have received only $375 a month but her husband would have taken the unexhausted reserve on her death, and it left him and their

a. See Navin, The Contracts of Minors Viewed from the Perspective of Fair Exchange, 50 N.C.L.Rev. 517 (1972), and the student note cited by the court in footnote 2.

That note also invites speculation that the age of capacity should be increased because of the academic seclusion of modern young people and the growing complexity of commercial affairs. It is thought that early English law may have responded to technological advances by increasing the age of maturity from 15 to 21 when the introduction of chain mail armor made military service unduly burdensome for older boys.

two grown children with no benefits in the event of her death. Two months later she died of cerebral arteriosclerosis. Her husband sued to set aside her 1965 election on the ground of mental incompetence. Her psychiatrist testified that she was incapable of making a decision of any kind and that victims of involutional melancholia "can't think rationally. . . . They will even tell you . . . 'I don't know whether I should get up or whether I should stay in bed.' . . . Everything is impossible to decide." From a judgment for the plaintiff, the defendant appealed to the Appellate Division, which reversed and dismissed the complaint. The plaintiff appealed.]

BREITEL, Judge.[a] . . . Traditionally, in this State and elsewhere, contractual mental capacity has been measured by what is largely a cognitive test . . . . Under this standard the "inquiry" is whether the mind was "so affected as to render him wholly and absolutely incompetent to comprehend and understand the nature of the transaction" . . . . A requirement that the party also be able to make a rational judgment concerning the particular transaction qualified the cognitive test . . . . Conversely, it is also well recognized that contractual ability would be affected by insane delusions intimately related to the particular transaction . . . .

These traditional standards governing competency to contract were formulated when psychiatric knowledge was quite primitive. They fail to account for one who by reason of mental illness is unable to control his conduct even though his cognitive ability seems unimpaired. When these standards were evolving it was thought that all the mental faculties were simultaneously affected by mental illness. . . . This is no longer the prevailing view . . . .

Of course the greatest movement in revamping legal notions of mental responsibility has occurred in the criminal law. The nineteenth century cognitive test embraced in the *M'Naghten* rules has long been criticized and changed by statute and decision in many jurisdictions (see *M'Naghten's Case*, 10 Clark & Fin. 200; 8 Eng.Rep. 718 [House of Lords, 1843]; Weihofen, Mental Disorder as a Criminal Defense [1954], pp. 65–68; British Royal Comm. on Capital Punishment [1953], ch. 4; A.L.I. Model Penal Code, § 4.01, supra; cf. Penal Law, § 30.05).

It is quite significant that Restatement, 2d, Contracts, states the modern rule on competency to contract. . . . Thus, the new Restatement section reads: "(1) A person incurs only voidable contrac-

a. Charles D. Breitel (1908–) was appointed to the New York Supreme Court in 1950 after law practice in New York City and service with Thomas E. Dewey, first on his staff when Dewey was district attorney and later as his counsel when Dewey was governor. He was elevated to the Appellate Division in 1952 and to the Court of Appeals in 1967, serving as Chief Judge from 1974 to 1978. He also taught jurisprudence as an adjunct professor at Columbia.

tual duties by entering into a transaction if by reason of mental illness or defect . . . (b) he is unable to act in a reasonable manner in relation to the transaction and the other party has reason to know of his condition." (Restatement, 2d, Contracts [T.D. No. 1, April 13, 1964], § 18C.) [renumbered 15] . . . .[b]

The system was, or should have been, fully aware of Mrs. Ortelere's condition. They, or the Board of Education, knew of her leave of absence for medical reasons and the resort to staff psychiatrists by the Board of Education. Hence, the other of the conditions for avoidance is satisfied.

Lastly, there are no significant changes of position by the system other than those that flow from the barest actuarial consequences of benefit selection.

Nor should one ignore that in the relationship between retirement system and member, and especially in a public system, there is not involved a commercial, let alone an ordinary commercial, transaction. It is not a sound scheme which would permit 40 years of contribution and participation in the system to be nullified by a one-instant act committed by one known to be mentally ill. This is especially true if there would be no substantial harm to the system if the act were avoided. Of course, nothing less serious than medically classified psychosis should suffice or else few contracts would be invulnerable to some kind of psychological attack. As noted earlier, the trial court's finding and perhaps some of the testimony attempted to fit into the rubrics of the traditional rules. For that reason rather than reinstatement of the judgment at Trial Term there should be a new trial under the proper standards frankly considered and applied.

[Reversed (5–2).]

JASEN, Judge (dissenting). [The dissent set out the full text of a letter from Grace to the Retirement System prior to her election, in which she put eight questions typified by the following (No. 6): "If I take a loan of $5,000 before retiring and select option four-a on both the pension and annuity, what would my allowance be?"] It seems clear that this detailed, explicit and extremely pertinent list of queries reveals a mind fully in command of the salient features of the Teachers' Retirement System. Certainly, it cannot be said the decedent could possess sufficient capacity to compose a letter indicating such a comprehensive understanding of the retirement system, and yet lack the capacity to understand the answers.

As I read the record, the evidence establishes that the decedent's election to receive maximum payments was predicated on the need for

b. The section was approved in Krasner v. Berk, 366 Mass. 464, 319 N.E.2d 897 (1974), in an opinion by Mr. Justice Braucher. As Professor Braucher he was the Reporter for this portion of the Restatement, Second.

a higher income to support two retired persons—her husband and herself. Since the only source of income available to decedent and her husband was decedent's retirement pay, the additional payment of $75 per month which she would receive by electing the maximal payment was a necessity. . . . Under these circumstances, an election of maximal income during decedent's lifetime was not only a rational, but a necessary decision. . . . Moreover, there is nothing in the record to indicate that the decedent had any warning, premonition, knowledge or indication at the time of retirement that her life expectancy was, in any way, reduced by her condition.

The generally accepted test of mental competency to contract which has thus evolved . . . represents a balance struck between policies to protect the security of transactions between individuals and freedom of contract on the one hand, and protection of those mentally handicapped on the other hand. In my opinion, this rule has proven workable in practice and fair in result. . . . As in every situation where the law must draw a line between liability and nonliability, between responsibility and nonresponsibility, there will be borderline cases, and injustices may occur by deciding erroneously that an individual belongs on one side of the line or the other. To minimize the chances of such injustices occurring, the line should be drawn as clearly as possible. . . .

NOTES

(1) *Question.* Can you envisage any adverse consequences for a pension plan offering a choice among various modes of benefit, if the choice made by a large number of participants proved to be revocable after death? See Kennedy v. Retirement System, 51 A.D.2d 296, 301, 381 N.Y.S.2d 79, 82–83 (1st Dept.1976), aff'd, 41 N.Y.2d 854, 393 N.Y.S.2d 708, 362 N.E.2d 259 (1977).

(2) *Scope of the Precedent.* How expansible is the Ortelere decision? Soon after it was announced the principle was naturally invoked in an ordinary business setting. In Fingerhut v. Kralyn Enterprises, 71 Misc.2d 846, 337 N.Y.S.2d 394 (Sup.Ct.N.Y.Co.1971), the seller of a golf course met resistance from the buyer who, he claimed, had been in the manic phase of a psychosis when he agreed to pay $3 million for it.[c]

Is the Ortelere rule limited to cases in which the employee has had psychiatric or similar consultation before making an election? How significant was it that "the system was, or should have been, fully aware of Mrs. Ortelere's condition"? Many employers fund their pension plans through professional insurers, who are not likely to know of an employee's psychosis. Should the knowledge of such an employer be attributed to the insurer? Why should it matter whether or not *either* was aware of the employee's

c. What degree of competence is required for a patient to consent to psychiatric treatment? For a view of *Ortelere* taken by a psychiatrist, see G. Alexander & T. Szasz, From Contract to Status Via Psychiatry, 13 Santa Clara Law. 537 (1973).

condition? Does it matter under Restatement Second, § 15? See Pentinen v. Retirement System, 60 A.D.2d 366, 401 N.Y.S.2d 587 (3d Dept.1978).

(3) *Testamentary Capacity.* "The test of mental capacity [to make a will] is whether one possesses sufficient mental capacity to retain in the memory, without prompting, the extent and condition of one's property and to comprehend how one is disposing of it and to whom." Taylor v. Edoe, Inc., 264 Ark. 746, 574 S.W.2d 894 (1978). But more is required for making a contract. See Krasner v. Berk, n. b, p. 360 supra, and In re Estate of Faris, 159 N.W.2d 417 (Iowa 1968). Is this because death is compulsory, whereas contracting is not? What other reason can you think of?

What degree of competence should be required for contracting to dispose of property by will? When the question arose in Simmons First Nat. Bank v. Luzader, 246 Ark. 302, 438 S.W.2d 25 (1969), where the decedent promised a bequest in return for lifetime care, the court observed: "this is not a case where a man is depriving his wife or children of needed monies . . . . To the contrary, all heirs are collateral . . . ." Was that a proper consideration?

CUNDICK v. BROADBENT

United States Court of Appeals, Tenth Circuit, 1967.
383 F.2d 157.

[Darwin Cundick was a 59-year-old sheep rancher who had sometimes sold his lamb crop to J. R. Broadbent. At a meeting between the two men in September, 1963, they signed a one-page contract in longhand by which Cundick agreed to sell all of his ranching properties to Broadbent. Mr. and Mrs. Cundick then took the contract to their lawyer, who refined and amplified it into an eleven-page document, which the parties signed in his office. In October, 1963, the agreement was amended, again with a lawyer's aid, so as to increase the price to Cundick and in another respect favorable to him. Under the amended agreement, more than 2,000 acres of range land went for about $40,000. (An expert later valued it at $89,000.) Also included was Cundick's interest in a development company of which Broadbent was a director, at a price of $46,750. (A witness for Cundick later valued this at $184,000, and one for Broadbent at $73,743.) As late as February, 1964, he was executing documents to carry out the sale. In March, 1964, when the price had been paid and the sale was almost completed, Cundick sought to rescind. His wife, who had been appointed his guardian ad litem, for the purpose of suing, brought an action against Broadbent to set aside the agreement. She asserted that her husband had been mentally incompetent to contract, and that in any event he was mentally infirm and that Broadbent had knowingly overreached him. The evidence showed that Cundick had psychiatric treatment in 1961. Thereafter his family doctor saw him many times about various ailments, but nothing was said or done about a mental condition until suit was commenced. The court ordered examinations in 1964, which disclosed premature arteriosclerosis. Two neurosurgeons and a psychologist testified that he had been incapable, the previous September, of transacting important business affairs, that he was a "confused and befuddled man with very poor judgment." There was no medical evidence to the contrary. The trial court nevertheless found: "The acts and conduct of Cundick between September 2, 1963, and the middle of February, 1964, were the acts, conduct and behavior of a person competent to manage his affairs and cognizant of the effect of his actions." It also found that the contract was not unconscionable, unfair or inequitable. From a dismissal of the action, the plaintiff appealed.]

MURRAH, Chief Judge. . . . At one time, in this country and in England, it was the law that since a lunatic or non compos mentis had no mind with which to make an agreement, his contract was wholly void and incapable of ratification. But, if his mind was merely confused or weak so that he knew what he was doing yet was incapable of fully understanding the terms and effect of his agreement, he could indeed contract, but such contract would be voidable at his option. . . . But in recent times courts have tended away from the concept of absolutely void contracts toward the notion that even though a contract be said to be void for lack of capacity to make it, it is nevertheless ratifiable at the instance of the incompetent party. The modern rule, and the weight of authority, seems to be [that] ". . . the contractual act by one claiming to be mentally deficient, but not under guardianship, absent fraud, or knowledge of such asserted incapacity by the other contracting party, is not a void act but at most only voidable at the instance of the deficient party; and then only in accordance with certain equitable principles." Rubenstein v. Dr. Pepper Co., 8 Cir., 228 F.2d 528. . . .

In recognition of different degrees of mental competency the weight of authority seems to hold that mental capacity to contract depends upon whether the allegedly disabled person possessed sufficient reason to enable him to understand the nature and effect of the act in issue. Even average intelligence is not essential to a valid bargain. . . . "Mere weakness of body or mind, or of both, do not constitute what the law regards as mental incompetency sufficient to render a contract voidable. . . . A condition which may be described by a physician as senile dementia may not be insanity in a legal sense." Kaleb v. Modern Woodmen of America, 51 Wyo. 116, 64 P.2d 605, 607. Weakmindedness is, however, highly relevant in determining whether the deficient party was overreached and defrauded. . . .

There was, to be sure, evidence of a change in his personality and attitude toward his business affairs during [the period between his mental examinations in 1961 and 1964]. But the record is conspicuously silent concerning any discussion of his mental condition among his family and friends in the community where he lived and operated his ranch. Certainly, the record is barren of any discussion or comment in Broadbent's presence. It seems incredible that Cundick could have been utterly incapable of transacting his business affairs, yet such condition be unknown on this record to his family and friends, especially his wife who lived and worked with him and participated in the months-long transaction which she now contends was fraudulently conceived and perpetrated. . . .

The narrated facts of this case amply support the trial court's finding to the effect that Broadbent did not deceive or overreach Cundick. . . . [Although] there is positive evidence that the property was worth very much more than what Broadbent paid for it, . . . there was evidence to the effect that after the original contract was signed and some complaint made about the purchase price, the parties agreed to raise the price and the contract was so modified.

[Affirmed.]

HILL, Circuit Judge (dissenting): . . . . The evidence relied upon by the majority is actually trivial and inconsequential as compared with the undisputed medical testimony. . . . It is inconceivable to me that any mentally competent person, with a lifetime of experience as a successful rancher and stockman, would dispose of his ranch interests at a price equal to less than one-half of the actual value. . . .[a]

NOTES

(1) *Orientation.* Are the Ortelere and Cundick cases distinguishable? At p. 349 supra mention was made of status, behavior and substance orientation. To what extent do the differences among the majority and dissenting opinions in those cases reflect different orientations? For a discussion of mental illness and contracts, see Note 57 Mich.L.Rev. 1020 (1959).

(2) *Supervision.* Guardians and conservators may be appointed for persons of mental debility, as authorized by statutes. In California there is a procedure for the judicial appointment of conservators for persons who, for specified reasons, are "likely to be deceived or imposed upon by artful or designing persons." See Board of Regents of State University, State of Wisconsin v. Davis, 14 Cal.3d 33, 120 Cal.Rptr. 407, 533 P.2d 1047 (1975). What virtues and hazards do you see in the process?

(3) *Of Minors Again.* Professor Navin has noted some elements that figure in rulings about mental competence to contract—the degree of impairment, the claimant's means of knowing of it, and the fairness of the exchange—and has compared them favorably with the less flexible rules about

a. Compare Bliss v. Rhodes, 66 Ill. App.3d 895, 23 Ill.Dec. 718, 384 N.E. 2d 512 (1978), concerning a comparable contract, in which the evidence was that the seller's life was disordered before and after the sale, that he was then depressed and sometimes intoxicated, and that the fair market value of his farm was greater than the contract price.

minors' contracts. (Some undertakings by "older minors," he believes, should be enforced.) Should the rules about minors' contracts be made more amenable to assessments of individual circumstances? Or are they adaptable enough by reason of looseness in the notions of "necessaries" and "ratification"? See Navin, The Contracts of Minors Viewed from the Perspective of Fair Exchange, 50 N.C.L.Rev. 517 (1972).

In Swarb v. Lennox, 314 F.Supp. 1091 (E.D.Pa.1970), aff'd, 405 U.S. 191 (1972),[b] the court entered a decree prohibiting the routine enforcement of a provision common in standardized credit contracts, relying on constitutional grounds. (This was the cognovit, or confession-of-judgment clause.) The decree was framed so as to apply only in consumer transactions—as defined—and to protect only "natural persons . . . having incomes . . . of less than $10,000. per year."[c] The contours of this decree obviously resemble the rules about minors' contracts more than the broad standards for determining mental capacity to contract. Should status-oriented rules be a last resort for the courts in policing bargains?[d] For legislatures? How can one identify a problem in bargaining processes that calls for such a rule?

SECTION 2. UNFAIRNESS: CONVENTIONAL CONTROLS

In this section we turn attention to inequality of exchange, as manifested in the terms of a bargain. Is it the proper business of a court to calculate the advantages of a contract for each party, and see to it that neither of them suffers a disproportionate loss, or enjoys a disproportionate gain? Put in that form the question has an obvious answer, supported by a powerful tradition. "Parties of sufficient mental capacity for the management of their own business," it is said, "have the right to make their own bargains."[a] We have seen that the core idea of consideration is the fact of a bargain, and the law on that subject contains an implicit judgment that a promise should be enforced whether or not something of equal value was given for it. "If the requirement of a consideration is met, there is no additional requirement of . . . equivalence in the values exchanged." [b] As the materials to follow will show, that judgment is supported by substantial reasons of policy.

Nevertheless, a number of limiting principles serve to prevent the routine enforcement of unequal bargains. Some of them have

b. The decision was appealed to the Supreme Court by the *complainants.* They were represented by a legal services organization. The Attorney General of Pennsylvania did not seek to sustain the validity of the state statutes. In affirming, the Court declined to delineate the issues "in the one-sided appeal in this case."

c. "or conjugal incomes where both spouses have signed the documents."

d. See P. S., In re: Social Science in the Eastern District of Pennsylvania, 32 U.Pitt.L.Rev. 463 (1971).

a. Hardesty v. Smith, 3 Ind. 39 (1851).

b. Restatement Second, § 79(b).

long been fixed in the law. They are the subject of this section. The less traditional means that courts have developed in recent years to police against unfairness in the substance of an exchange are explored in Section 4, infra.

The function of policing has always been something of a specialty of equity courts. Relying on the element of discretion, or grace, associated with granting specific performance, they have refused that remedy in cases where the exchange appeared highly disproportionate. In cases "at law," by contrast, the means of policing have had to be either more direct, or more devious, depending on the circumstances. A direct measure is to pronounce a public policy by which a particularly overbearing provision of a contract may be disregarded. That course is exceptional. More commonly, the courts have manipulated the doctrine of consideration to serve the ideal of fairness. It will be seen in this section that that ideal plays a part in determining whether or not any "bargain" at all has been effected.

NOTE

Good Faith. According to the Restatement Second, "Every contract imposes upon each party a duty of good faith and fair dealing in its performance and its enforcement." Section 205. This "rule" has no predecessor in the original Restatement; but see UCC 1–203. According to a comment, neither § 205 nor the Code provision deals with good faith in the formation of a contract.

Is it useful to draw a sharp distinction between the formation and performance stages of contracting? Why is there no recognition of a generalized duty of good faith in negotiation in the Code or the Restatement? In going through the chapter, you should consider how many of the problems could helpfully be approached in terms of such a duty. See p. 348 supra.

McKINNON v. BENEDICT

Supreme Court of Wisconsin, 1968.
38 Wis.2d 607, 157 N.W.2d 665.

[In 1960 Roderick McKinnon, the owner of a home on Mamie Lake, Wisconsin, amid more than a thousand acres, gave help to Mr. and Mrs. Roy Benedict in buying a resort known as Bent's Camp. It consisted of a lodge and some cabins on about 80 acres that were enclosed by the lake and McKinnon's property. McKinnon promised some help in getting business and in other minor respects, but his principal contribution was in making a loan of $5,000. The Benedicts used the advance as part of a down payment on a land purchase contract with the previous owners of the camp. The Benedicts promised McKinnon to cut no trees between the camp and his property, and to make no improvements "closer to [his] property than the present buildings." The term of these restrictions was 25 years.

They did not affect all the resort tract, but did affect all the most desireable portion.

The resort business did not prosper, after the Benedicts bought it, although they repaid the loan in about seven months. In 1964 they decided to add a trailer park and tent camp. In the fall and following spring they invested some $9,000 in bulldozing and installing utilities. The summer of 1965 brought McKinnon from Arizona, where he spent the winters, and brought also a suit against the Benedicts. The trial court enjoined them from continuing with their projected improvements, and they appealed.]

HEFFERNAN, Justice. . . . No action at law has been commenced for damages by virtue of the breach of the restrictions; and, in fact, the plaintiffs in their complaint claim that they have no adequate remedy at law. [The court expounded some "ancient principles of equity," and quoted the Restatement of Contracts, § 367.[c]]

Coupled with the general equitable principle that contracts that are oppressive will not be enforced in equity is the principle of public policy that restrictions on the use of land "are not favored in the law" (Mueller v. Schier (1926), 189 Wis. 70, 82, 205 N.W. 912, 916), and that restrictions and prohibitions as to the use of real estate should be resolved, if a doubt exists, in favor of the free use of the property. Stein v. Endres Home Builders, Inc. (1938) 228 Wis. 620, 629, 280 N.W. 316. . . .

The great hardship sought to be imposed upon the Benedicts is apparent. What was the consideration in exchange for this deprivation of use? The only monetary consideration was the granting of a $5,000 loan, interest free, for a period of seven months. The value of this money for that period of time, if taken at the same interest rate as the 5 percent used on the balance of the land contract, is approximately $145; and it should be noted that this was not an unsecured loan, since McKinnon took a mortgage on the cottage property of the Benedicts in Michigan. In addition, McKinnon stated that he would "help you try" to reach a solution of the problem posed by Mrs. Vair's occupancy of one of the cottages on a fifty-year lease at $5 per year. His one attempt, as stated above, was a failure; and McKinnon's promise to generate business resulted in an occupancy by only one group for less than a week. For this pittance and these feeble attempts to help with the operational problems of the camp, the

c. Specific enforcement of a contract may be refused if

(a) the consideration for it is grossly inadequate or its terms are otherwise unfair, or

(b) its enforcement will cause unreasonable or disproportionate hardship or loss to the defendant or to third persons, or

(c) it was induced by some sharp practice, misrepresentation, or mistake.

Benedicts have sacrificed their right to make lawful and reasonable use of their property.

In oral argument it was pointed out that the value of the $5,000 loan could not be measured in terms of the interest value of the money, since, without this advance, Benedict would have been unable to purchase the camp at all. To our mind, this is evidence of the fact that Benedict was not able to deal at arm's length with McKinnon, for his need for these funds was obviously so great that he was willing to enter into a contract that results in gross inequities. Lord Chancellor Northington said "necessitous men are not, truly speaking, free men." Vernon v. Bethell (1762), 2 Eden 110, 113.

We find that the inadequacy of consideration is so gross as to be unconscionable and a bar to the plaintiffs' invocation of the extraordinary equitable powers of the court.

While there is no doubt that there are benefits from this agreement to McKinnon, they are more than outweighed by the oppressive terms that would be imposed upon the Benedicts. McKinnon testified that he and his wife spend only the summer months on their property. Undoubtedly, these are the months when it is most important that there be no disruption of the natural beauty or the quiet and pleasant enjoyment of the property, nevertheless, there was testimony that the trailer camp could not be seen from the McKinnon home, nor could the campsite be seen during the summer months of the year, when the leaves were on the trees. Thus, the detriment of which the McKinnons complain, that would be cognizable in an equity action, is minimal,[1] while the damage done to the Benedicts is severe.

Considering all the factors—the inadequacy of the consideration, the small benefit that would be accorded the McKinnons, and the oppressive conditions imposed upon the Benedicts—we conclude that this contract failed to meet the test of reasonableness that is the *sine qua non* of the enforcement of rights in an action in equity.

5A Corbin, Contracts, sec. 1164, p. 219, points out that, although a contract is harsh, oppressive, and unconscionable, it may nevertheless be enforceable at law; but, in the discretion of the court, equitable remedies will not be enforced against one who suffers from such harshness and oppression.

A fair reading of the transcript indicates no sharp practice, dishonesty, or overreaching on the part of McKinnon. However, there was a wide disparity between the business experience of the parties. McKinnon was a man of stature in the legal field, an investment counsellor, a former officer of a major corporation, and had held

1. McKinnon testified that the value of his property had depreciated in the amount of $50,000. That testimony was properly admissible, but its probative value was slight, especially since plaintiff's expert real estate witness stated that he was unable to testify to the amount of the depreciated value.

posts of responsibility with the United States government, while, insofar as the record shows, Benedict was a retail jeweler and a man of limited financial ability. He no doubt overvalued the promises of McKinnon to assist in getting the operation "well organized" and to solve the lease problem and to "generate business." These factors, in view of Benedict's financial inability to enter into an arms-length transaction, may be explanatory of the reason for the agreement, but the agreement viewed even as of the time of its execution was unfair and based upon inadequate consideration. We, therefore, have no hesitancy in denying the plaintiffs the equitable remedy of injunction. . . .

[Reversed.[d]]

NOTES

(1) *Questions.* Has it been decided that the Benedicts may bulldoze on their property and make improvements wherever they please? If the Benedicts had begun their new business immediately after making the agreement of 1960, would the court have given McKinnon the relief then that he is now denied?

(2) *Specific Performance and Damages.* In a sense it is extraordinary for a contract claimant to be entitled to specific performance, in English and American law. The "normal" remedy is conceived to be a judgment for damages resulting from the breach, or for other relief at law. Exceptionally, when such a remedy is inadequate, specific performance may be had in a "court of equity." The power to grant this remedy was historically exercised by the English Court of Chancery, centuries ago, and is today administered in courts succeeding to the powers and traditions of that court. Owing to modern procedural reforms both legal and equitable remedies are now generally provided in the same court, but some distinctions remain.

By tradition, a decree of specific performance is not a matter of right in the same sense as damages are, but may be withheld in the court's discretion. Specific performance is often denied because the bargain was procured by sharp practice or was affected by a mistake. If the remedy seems oppressive simply because the exchange is grossly unequal, the result may be the same; but the issue has been debated.[e]

d. Except insofar as the trial court had given relief on a separate cause of action for trespass.

e. As to inadequacy of price, Lord Eldon said that unless it is "such as shocks the conscience, and amounts in itself to conclusive and decisive evidence of fraud in the transaction it is not in itself a sufficient ground for refusing a specific performance." Coles v. Trecothick, 9 Ves. 234, 32 Eng.Rep. 592 (1804). But this is a proposition on which very great men have differed, it has been said. Savage, C. J., in Seymour v. Delancey, 3 Cowen 445 (N.Y.1824). This was said, by the way, in a dissent. The majority overturned a decree of Chancellor Kent, who disputed Eldon's view.

See also Community Sports, Inc. v. Denver Ringsby Rockets, 429 Pa. 565, 240 A.2d 832 (1968), an action to enjoin breach of contract, in which the court said: "Although the rule in Pennsylvania is that lack of consideration will not preclude enforcement of a contract under seal, this rule does not apply in a court of equity where extraordinary relief such as this is sought."

In principle, when specific performance is denied on such a ground it may be possible for the claimant to obtain damages in a suit at law. The thought that courts of law are less sensitive than courts of equity to issues of fairness is repulsive to some. It has been described as a "moral curtain that, heavy with the mold of centuries, still hangs across our law." Newman, The Rennaissance of Good Faith in Contracting in Anglo-American Law, 54 Corn.L.Rev. 553, 554 (1969). This writer observes that the dual standard may have ceased to exist in practice, though it continues to be repeated. Only two cases have been found, it seems, in which specific performance was denied and damages awarded (and in one of these the judgment was set aside for an error in calculating it).[f]

One way to eliminate the "dual standard" would be for equity courts to rescind or cancel contracts for unfairness, using the same standards as they apply in specific performance cases. In McKinnon v. Benedict, if the Benedicts had sought to have the restrictions on their use of the property cancelled, does it appear that they would have been successful? The power to cancel has not been freely exercised. This fact may mean that damage claims are more readily available to parties who fail to get specific performance than the reported cases happen to show. "One suspects that the Chancellors thought there was a real remedy at law, and that the litigants did too; else the actions for cancellation and the judges' agonizing over them make little sense." [g]

In denying specific performance to a claimant, the courts sometimes take comfort in the thought, as many opinions show, that the decision does not deprive him of all remedy, but only remits him to the more perfunctory one of damages. But that may be an empty justification in a case like McKinnon v. Benedict. Perhaps there was no effective remedy available to the McKinnons other than specific performance: notice their allegation that they had no adequate remedy at law. This might be so because of the rule that no damages will be awarded unless the amount of loss can be calculated with some degree of certainty. Or it might be so because damages are a poor substitute for the performance agreed upon. Remedies for breach of contract are dealt with in more detail in the following chapter.

(3) *Certainty.* In going through the cases in this chapter, you should consider whether or not certainty in commercial affairs has been overvalued or undervalued. "There does come a point where the additional costs of having personalized transactions may be too great; a little injustice may be a social good."[h]

f. See also Frank and Endicott, Defenses in Equity and "Legal Rights," 14 La.L.Rev. 380 (1954).

g. Leff, Unconscionability and the Code—The Emperor's New Clause, 115 U.Pa.L.Rev. 485, 541 n. 237 (1967).

h. Leff, Injury, Ignorance and Spite—The Dynamics of Coercive Collection, 80 Yale L.J. 1, 42 (1970).

TUCKWILLER v. TUCKWILLER

Supreme Court of Missouri, 1967.
413 S.W.2d 274.

[John and Ruby Tuckwiller lived on the Hudson family farm in Missouri, and John farmed it as a renter. Almost half of the property—160 acres—was owned by Mrs. Metta Hudson Morrison. When she was about 70 years of age, Mrs. Morrison contracted Parkinson's disease, and at about the same time she gave up her residence in New York. She had been educated at Columbia and other schools, had been a teacher for many years, and had held other jobs. After leaving New York she travelled extensively, but early in 1963 she returned to the Hudson farm, where some rooms were reserved for her use. In April she was hospitalized for about a week, as a result of dizziness and falling. She was thought then to have had a "stroke," and showed some mental confusion. But at the first of May her doctor and a friend found her mentally clear—"clear as a bell." She knew, the doctor said, that Parkinsonism is a progressive disease, leaving the victim ultimately dependent entirely on outside care.

[Before the April incident, Mrs. Tuckwiller had been urged by Mrs. Morrison to quit a job she held and care for her for the rest of her life, and the subject was discussed again after Mrs. Morrison's release from the hospital. The two were quite congenial. On May 3, a Saturday, when she was with the Tuckwillers, Mrs. Morrison signed the following paper, written by Mrs. Tuckwiller:

> My offer to Aunt Metta is as follows
>
> I will take care of her for her lifetime; by that I mean provide her 3 meals per day—a good bed—do any possible act of nursing and provide her every pleasure possible.
>
> In exchange she will will me her (Corum) farm at her death keeping all money made from it during her life. She will maintain expense of her medicine.

On May 6 Mrs. Tuckwiller resigned her job, and Mrs. Morrison made an appointment with a lawyer to change her will. Later that day, however, she fainted and fell. She was taken to the hospital, where, except for four days, she remained until her death on June 14. She was 73 at that time. Mrs. Tuckwiller spent much time at the hospital during Mrs. Morrison's final illness, assisting as she could, but Mrs. Morrison was attended by special nurses.

[Before leaving for the hospital on May 6, Mrs. Morrison had the date put on the paper set out above, and obtained the signatures of the two ambulance attendants as witnesses. Her will, dated in 1961, was never changed. It provided for the sale of the farm, the proceeds to be used for a student loan fund at Davidson College. The farm had an "inventory value" of $34,400.

[Mrs. Tuckwiller brought a bill for specific performance of the contract, which was resisted by the College and Mrs. Morrison's executor. The trial court granted the relief, and the defendants appealed.]

WELBORN, Commissioner. . . . [I]n determining whether or not a contract is so unfair or inequitable or is unconscionable so as to deny its specific performance, the transaction must be viewed prospectively, not retrospectively. The same rule applies with respect to sufficiency of consideration. . . . Viewed in this light, we find that plaintiff gave up her employment with which she was well satisfied and undertook what was at the time of the contract an obligation of unknown and uncertain duration, involving duties which, in the usual course of the disease from which Mrs. Morrison suffered, would have become increasingly onerous. . . . Viewed from the standpoint of Mrs. Morrison, the contract cannot be considered unfair. She was appreciative of the care and attention which plaintiff had given her prior to the agreement. Although, as defendants suggest, such prior services cannot provide the consideration essential to a binding contract, such prior services and the past relation of the parties may properly be considered in connection with the fairness of the contract and adequacy of the consideration. 5A Corbin on Contracts, § 1165, p. 227. Aware of her future outlook and having no immediate family to care for her, Mrs. Morrison was understandably appreciative of the personal care and attention of plaintiff and concerned with the possibility of routine impersonal care over a long period of time in a nursing home or similar institution. Having no immediate family which might be the object of her bounty, she undoubtedly felt more free to agree to dispose of the farm without insisting upon an exact quid pro quo. Her insistence that the contract be witnessed prior to her hospitalization is clear evidence of her satisfaction with the bargain as was her unsuccessful effort to change her will to carry out her agreement. . . .

Properly viewed from the standpoint of the parties at the time of the agreement, we find that the contract was fair, not unconscionable, and supported by an adequate consideration. Although not conceding that such conclusion is correct, defendants argue, in effect, that in view of the obviously brief duration of plaintiff's services and their value in comparison with the value of the farm, plaintiff should be obliged to accept the offered payment of the reasonable value of her services and denied the relief of specific performance. Defendants point out that the trial court found that valuing the services which plaintiff rendered might be "possible." That conclusion is undoubtedly correct and unquestionably the monetary value of plaintiff's services would have been a quite small proportion (perhaps one percent) of the value of the farm. Once, however, the essential fairness of the contract and the adequacy of the consideration are found, the fact that the subject of the contract is real estate answers any question of adequacy of the legal remedy of monetary damages. "Whenever a contract concerning real property is in its nature and incidents entirely unobjectionable—that is, when it possesses none of those features which . . . appeal to the discretion of the court —it is as much a matter of course for a court of equity to decree a specific performance of it, as it is for a court of law to give damages for the breach of it." Pomeroy's Specific Performance of Contracts (3d ed.), § 10, p. 23.[a]

[Affirmed.]

NOTES

(1) *Question.* Part of the plaintiff's evidence was that the life expectancy of a 73-year-old person is about nine years. Do you see any reason to discount this evidence?

(2) *Professional Services.* In Gladding v. Langrall, Muir & Noppinger, 285 Md. 210, 401 A.2d 662 (1979),[b] the court rejected a claim of "unconscionability" in reliance on the principle that a bargain is to be evaluated by reference to the situation existing at the time it was struck. Is this principle of special importance to lawyers who contract for contingent fees? Would you expect it to be equally reliable for an attorney and for an accountant, working for such a fee? The court spoke of "the broader judicial interest in attorney-client contracts, which exists only because of the attorney's status as an officer of the court." The claimant was an accounting firm. It recovered a fee of more than $30,000 (in addition to a retainer of $10,000) for seventeen hours of professional services. The fee was a percentage of tax savings effected for the firm's clients through a settlement with the Internal Revenue Service. Compare Brobeck, Phleger & Harrison v. Telex Corp., 602 F.2d 866 (9th Cir. 1979), in which a law firm recovered a million dollars for filing a petition for certiorari.

(3) *Equitable Discretion.* "Within the ambit of those factors of contract-producing behavior which would result in a denial of specific performance, a bewildering number of permutations work to inform the chancellor's discretion. In these cases one runs continually into the old, the young, the ignorant, the necessitous, the illiterate, the improvident, the drunken, the naive and the sick, all on one side of the transaction, with the sharp and hard on the other. Language of quasi-fraud and quasi-duress abounds. Certain whole classes of presumptive sillies like sailors and heirs and farmers and women continually wander on and off stage. Those not certifiably crazy, but nonetheless pretty peculiar, are often to be found. And in most of the cases, of course, several of these factors appear in combination.

a. The court rejected the defendants' "hint that the contract was unfair because of evidence of mental confusion of Mrs. Morrison at her hospitalization in April and again on May 6." At the time of agreement, it said, it appeared from the evidence that she was "mentally alert and fully aware of what she was doing."

b. Citing Mortgage Investors v. Citizens Bank & Trust Co., 278 Md. 505, 511–14, 366 A.2d 47, 50–52 (1976), for a discussion of the role of the court in regulating attorneys and their fees.

. . . Amost without exception, actions for specific performance were (and are) brought with respect to transactions involving real property." Leff, Unconscionability and the Code—the Emperor's New Clause, 115 U. Pa.L.Rev. 485, 531–34 (1967).

(4) *Problem.* George A. Shea contracted to sell twenty acres of land, worth $24,000, and a badly used Cadillac, to Dr. Joseph Hodge for $4,000 and a "new $6600 Coupe DeVille Cadillac." Shea was a man of means, but badly in need of cash to pay taxes. After accepting the car, he refused to convey. On these facts alone, should specific performance be granted, at the instance of the doctor? Which of the following circumstances, if any, should tip the scales against the plaintiff? (a) Shea was 75 years old at the time. (b) He was fatuously fond of new Cadillacs. (c) He was an inebriate of long standing, and afflicted with grievous chronic illnesses. (d) He had been the plaintiff's patient for many years. See Hodge v. Shea, 252 S.C. 601, 168 S.E.2d 82 (1969).

BLACK INDUSTRIES, INC. v. BUSH

United States District Court, D. New Jersey, 1953.
110 F.Supp. 801.

FORMAN, Chief Judge. The plaintiff, Black Industries, Inc., a citizen of Ohio, is suing the defendant, George F. Bush, a citizen of New Jersey doing business as G. F. Bush Associates, for breach of a contract. The defendant has moved for a summary judgment in its favor.

The complaint alleges as a first cause of action that the plaintiff, a manufacturer of drills, machine parts and components thereof and a purchaser of subcontract work from other suppliers, obtained an invitation to bid upon certain contracts with The Hoover Company upon three parts known as anvils, holder primers and plunger supports. The plaintiff assumed the task of obtaining a supplier of these parts and on about March 22, 1951, the defendant reached an agreement with the plaintiff to manufacture 1,300,000 anvils at a price of $4.40 per thousand; 750,000 holder primers at $11.50 per thousand and 700,000 plunger supports at a price of $12 per thousand, all of which were to be made in accordance with government specifications and in conformity with certain drawings. The plaintiff agreed to "service the contract", be responsible for all dealings with The Hoover Company and would be entitled to the difference between the defendant's quotations and the ultimate price. The Hoover Company agreed to purchase the parts from the plaintiff at a rate of $8.10 per thousand anvils, $16 per thousand holder primers and $21.20 per thousand plunger supports.

The complaint further alleges that after undertaking performance of this contract, the defendant failed to complete the order, which caused a loss of $14,625 to the plaintiff, for which sum, together with interest, the plaintiff demands judgment.

[As a second cause of action the plaintiff alleges "understandings" between these parties whereby the defendant agreed to manufacture other quantities of plunger supports and anvils, for which plaintiff made a re-sale contract with Standby Products Company; and that defendant's failure to comply with this undertaking caused plaintiff a loss of $4,460.95, for which plaintiff seeks judgment. To each cause of action defendant pleads various defenses not here relevant, and then alleges that the contract set forth in the complaint is void as against public policy. The defendant, on this last ground, now moves for summary judgment.

[The contract alleged in the first count was evidenced by a letter of April 13, 1951, from plaintiff's Gepfert to defendant Bush, and signed as "agreed to" by the latter. In this letter Gepfert stated that he had "spent considerable time, effort and money in developing the contract" to the point where The Hoover Company issued a purchase order. The letter continued as follows: "The purchase order, when received, will run directly to George F. Bush and Associates . . . Your company is to ship the material directly to The Hoover Co. . . . Your company, however, is not to bill The Hoover Co. All shipping invoices, documents of transfer and title are to be forwarded to me, and I shall have the exclusive right to bill, upon (your) billing forms and receive payment therefor in your behalf . . . It is understood that I shall have the right to receive payment, cash checks made payable to your company under The Hoover Co. contract; and to remit to you (retaining sums) as compensation due me." The compensation stipulated by Gepfert "for my services" was to be the difference between Bush's price to Black and Black's price to Hoover. The products to be purchased both by Hoover and by Standby Products were to be used by them to fulfill United States government contracts in aid of "the defense effort," i. e., the Korean War of 1950–53. Defendant then alleges that plaintiff was to receive a "profit" of 84.09% on anvils, 39.13% on holder primers and 68.33% on plunger supports under the Hoover contract, and similar percentages under the Standby contract. Defendant further alleges that these contracts are void as against public policy because these "profits" of Black were passed on to the government and the public in the form of increased prices; and cites two Federal laws intended to prevent excessive profits on war contracts: Renegotiation Act, 50 U.S.C.A. Appendix, § 1211, and 41 U.S.C.A. § 51.]

In order to declare a contract, entered by the parties freely and without evidence of fraud, void as against public policy, the contract must be invalid on the basis of recognized legal principles. [In an omitted passage, the court quotes from Muschany v. United States, 324 U.S. 49, 66–67 (1945), as follows: "It is a matter of public importance that good faith contracts of the United States should not be lightly invalidated." Then it discusses three types of illegal contracts, as indicated in the following paragraph.]

The contract in the present case, however, does not fall in any of these categories. It is not a contract by the defendant to pay the plaintiff for inducing a public official to act in a certain manner; it is not a contract to do an illegal act; and it is not a contract which contemplates collusive bidding on a public contract. It should be noted that the first and third categories of cases, upon which the defendant relies most heavily, involve agreements which directly impinge upon government activities. In the case at hand, the contract's only effect on the government was that ultimately the government was to buy the product of which defendant's goods were to be a component. Neither the defendant nor the plaintiff had any dealings with the United States on account of this contract, and therefore the profit accruing to the plaintiff was not to have been earned as a result of either inducing government action or interfering with the system of competitive bidding. This contract cannot, therefore, be declared void as against public policy on the basis of the precedents cited by the defendant.

It is quite possible that the plaintiff was to have received a very high profit on the sale of the parts, either because The Hoover Company agreed to pay too high a price or because the defendant quoted too low a price. Further proof would be required to establish this as a fact. Even if it were proved that the plaintiff was to have received a far greater profit than the defendants for a much smaller contribution, the defendant would nevertheless be bound by his agreement by the familiar rule that relative values of the consideration in a contract between business men dealing at arm's length without fraud will not affect the validity of the contract. The Coast National Bank v. Bloom, 113 N.J.L. 597, 174 A. 576, 95 A.L.R. 528 (E. & A. 1934); Restatement of the Law of Contracts § 81 (1932).

The fact that the government is the ultimate purchaser of the product in which defendant's parts are used is cited by the defendant as a reason to hold that this contract is void as against public policy. To so hold would necessitate either ruling that all contracts are void if they provide for compensation for middlemen, such as Black Industries, between producer and purchaser of goods which ultimately are incorporated in products sold to the government, a result which is not supported by precedent and which would defy the realities of our economic life, or deciding in every case involving such a contract whether the compensation paid a middleman such as the plaintiff here who locates purchasers and assists the producer in other ways, is reasonable. This latter course would, in effect, impose price regulatory functions on the court. There are other and more effective methods of insuring that the government does not pay an unreasonable price for its supplies. The manufacturer selling directly to the United States must conform to procedures such as bidding designed to protect the government, and which should, in conjunction with the ordinary considerations of profits and loss, insure that prime contractors do not pay outlandish prices for the products they buy in order to fulfill a government contract. The contract may be subject to renegotiation. 50 U.S.C.A. Appendix, § 1211 et seq. I do not believe that it is the function of the court to interfere by determining the validity of a contract between ordinary business men on the basis of its beliefs as to the adequacy of the consideration. Consequently, I hold that, assuming the facts to be as stated by the defendant, the contract sued on in this case is not void as against public policy and the defendant's motion for a summary judgment will, therefore, be denied.

Let an order be submitted in accordance with this opinion.

NOTES

(1) *"Adequacy" of Consideration.* The arguments against courts' inquiring into the "relative value of the consideration in a contract between business men dealing at arm's length without fraud" have been summarized as follows: "(1) The efficient administration of the law of contracts requires that courts shall not be required to prescribe prices. (2) The test of enforceability should be certain and should not be beclouded by such vague terms as 'fair' or 'reasonable' as tests of validity. (3) There is still the somewhat old-fashioned theory that persons of maturity and sound mind should be free to contract imprudently as well as prudently." Patterson, An Apology for Consideration, 58 Colum.L.Rev. 929 (1958).

Does it appear that courts of equity, in specific performance actions, have undertaken price regulatory functions? Does the dispensing power exercised in McKinnon v. Benedict invite litigation in a large proportion of contracts about land? If so, it may tend to impair the value of such contracts as the Tuckwillers made with Mrs. Morrison, in Tuckwiller v. Tuckwiller. Should the courts be cautious, on that account, in attempting supervision over the values exchanged?

(2) *Middlemen.* The court acknowledges the possibility that Black might have stood to receive a "far greater profit" than Bush "for a much smaller contribution." What is the nature of the "contribution" of a middleman such as Black?

He may perform an "informational" function, by bringing together buyers and sellers who would otherwise be ignorant of each other's needs. (See Note 3, infra.) He may also perform a "risk-shifting" function, by taking on himself risks of market fluctuations that would otherwise have to be borne by buyers or sellers. Both of these functions are highly developed in well organized markets, such as commodities exchanges, where brokers clearly perform both an "informational" function by facilitating transactions between buyers and sellers and a "risk-shifting" function through stabilizing foreseeable market fluctuations. See Samuelson, Economics, Appendix to Chap. 21 (8th ed. 1970).

Does it appear that Black's "contribution" involved either an "informational" or a "risk-shifting" function? If it involved the former, did Black supply Hoover with enough information about available suppliers to merit the compensation he received? Why did not Hoover contact Bush directly? Why did not Bush contact Hoover directly? Would Bush have been able to charge Black more if he had known how much Hoover was paying Black?

We have already spent some time on an important type of middleman, the general contractor in the construction industry. At one extreme, he may be little more than a broker between owner and subcontractors, maintaining only a small office with supervisory personnel and contracting out substantially all the work. It has been suggested that the evils of bid shopping can be avoided if the owner bypasses the general contractor and makes separate contracts directly with the subcontractors, leaving their supervision to his architect. Can you see any disadvantages to this? See Note, 39 N.Y.U.L.Rev. 816, 828–29 (1964).

(3) *An Economist's View.* George Stigler, an economist, has written of the phenomenon of "search," by which, in a market economy, buyers (or sellers) canvass various sellers (or buyers). If the dispersion of prices quoted "is at all large (relative to the cost of search), it will pay, on average, to canvass several sellers." Thus the optimal amount of search varies directly with the dispersion of prices in a market and inversely with the cost of search. In markets with search the low-price sellers will attract more buyers than the high-price sellers, which will tend to force the latter out of business and decrease the dispersion. Once the dispersion is known to be low, the system becomes stable. Stigler, The Economics of Information, 69 J. Political Economy 213 (1961). See also Stigler, Information in the Labor Market, 70 J. Political Economy (Supp.) 94 (1962).

What does this have to say about the merits of the decision in Black v. Bush?

(4) *Excessive Profits in Contracts with the Government.* Should the courts, as a matter of public policy, deny enforcement to a military procurement contract or other contract with the United States, when it is demonstrable that the contractor's profits have been or will be exorbitant? The leading case is U. S. v. Bethlehem Steel Corporation, 315 U.S. 289 (1952), in which counsel for the government contended that a contract for building war vessels during World War I had yielded such great profits that it should be treated as having been induced by "duress" on the United States. But the Court, over strenuous dissenting opinions, held that the contract had not been induced by duress. In World War II, a number of legislative and administrative devices were used to limit profits on war contracts. These devices included: (1) compulsory renegotiation of procurement contracts so as to reduce the contractor's profits to reasonable margins; (2) administrative price regulation and priority control of scarce materials; (3) a sharply graduated "excess profits" tax; and (4) elimination of the cost-plus-percentage-of-cost contract in government procurement.

One of Bush's arguments was that Black's profits were passed on to the government and the public in the form of excessive prices, contrary to "public policy." If Bush had been granted the relief that he sought, what would have been the probable impact on prices paid by the government in similar transactions?

SECTION 3. OVERREACHING: CONVENTIONAL CONTROLS

Under the leadership, again, of equity, the courts have traditionally been insistent that no advantage should be gained through gross unfairness in the process of bargaining. The means reprobated in classical equity are fraud, mistake, and duress. The ordinary remedy, when a contract is found to be subject to one of these infirmities, is to rescind or avoid it, at the instance of the victim. Not only fraud, in the more shameful sense, but an innocent misrepresentation made in the bargaining process may be a ground for avoiding a contract. Indeed, it is sometimes required that a party possessed of information material to the exchange either disclose it or refrain from imposing on the ignorance of the other. What privilege of exploiting superior knowledge for a bargaining advantage should be recognized? How should the risks of inaccuracy in statements and of errors of fact be allocated between the parties? What pressures may conscientiously be exerted by one party on another to gain his assent to a bargain or the settlement of a dispute? These are questions examined here.

Some further aspects of the doctrine of consideration are also presented. The doctrine has sometimes been extended to prevent overreaching in bargaining. Is it too blunt an instrument for that purpose? If so, how should it be reshaped?

The subject of this section has a complex relation to the problems of capacity and of unfairness in the substance of bargains, presented above. If the parties are fully competent to contract, and the bargaining process is cleansed of overreaching, is there any need for the courts to concern themselves with possible imbalances in the resulting exchange? Should all of these elements be considered together, from case to case? Or is it important, for purposes of predictability, that when a court declines to enforce a contract it specify a single deficiency of the bargain, or in the capacity of a party? Do you find instances of each method?

NOTE

Law and Equity. As the successors to equity powers, virtually all courts in which contract litigation is conducted are now competent to avoid a contract without requiring an independent proceeding for rescission. (The procedure of the court may reflect the origin in equity of these defenses, however; notably, it may not be necessary to submit them to juries. Courses in civil procedure examine this difference.) Quite apart from equity "jurisdiction," there are instances of fraud, mistake and duress that serve as invalidating causes in contract law: the contract affected is said to be "void."

(a) Pressure in Bargaining

When a person has used compulsion on another to obtain a benefit, he may sometimes be required to give it up. Money paid and property transferred under duress may be recovered; if assent to a contract is obtained by duress it may not be enforced against the victim. At p. 400 infra an example is given of duress in a contemporary form. In early English cases from which the current doctrine stems, relief was confined to situations in which imprisonment and threats of confinement or bodily harm were the instruments of coercion. Threats of purely economic injury became a ground for relief when "duress of goods" was recognized. In comparatively recent times, duress has been recognized in a greatly enlarged range of situations, and the general conception of "economic coercion" has won a place as a sort of junior partner of duress in redressing oppression.[a]

These developments have not yet made duress a commonplace defense in contract actions. Freehanded applications of the doctrine are still prevented by a number of policy considerations, as well as some surviving technical obstacles. A mention of these will be useful as a prelude to the materials that follow.

In some courts a reasonable degree of temerity in the face of a threat is insisted on. This requirement serves to restrict relief for duress by denying it to persons who yield to pressure too readily. As one court puts it, duress consists of "restraint or danger, either actually inflicted or impending, which is sufficient in severity or apprehension to overcome the mind of a person of ordinary firmness."[b] Some expressions of the courts imply an even stricter test: it is duress, as they describe it, to deprive a person of free choice,[c] or to destroy his volition,[d] or to obtain his consent only in form.[e] Such expressions, often somewhat metaphorical, appear largely in cases where relief was *granted*, and it has often been granted where no such total mastery existed. A classical passage rejecting the "no will" conception of duress is this from Holmes:

a. See McCubbin v. Buss, 180 Neb. 624, 144 N.W.2d 175 (1966).

b. Carrier v. William Penn Broadcasting Co., 426 Pa. 427, 233 A.2d 519 (1967).

c. Joannin v. Ogilvie, 49 Minn. 564, 52 N.W. 217 (1892); State ex rel. State Highway Comm. v. City of St. Louis, 575 S.W.2d 712 (Mo.App.1978) ("bereft of the free exercise of his will power").

d. See Konsuvo v. Nitzke, 91 N.J.Super. 353, 220 A.2d 424 (1966); cf. Kaplan v. Kaplan, 25 Ill.2d 181, 182 N.E.2d 706 (1962).

e. See United States v. Huckabee, 16 Wall. (83 U.S.) 414 (1873) (alleged duress by a rebel government); Gerber v. First Nat. Bank, 30 Ill.App.3d 776, 332 N.E.2d 615, 79 A.L.R.3d 592 (1975) ("bereft of the quality of mind essential to the making of a contract").

> It always is for the interest of a party under duress to choose the lesser of two evils. But the fact that a choice was made according to interest does not exclude duress. It is the characteristic of duress properly so called.[f]

On the other hand, it is regularly acknowledged that a perfectly honorable agreement may be made with a person who must either accede to it or face some repugnant alternative.[g] "The question is one of degree." [h]

Duress is sometimes associated with unlawful conduct. In a recent case the court detected a "marked shift in emphasis from the subjective effect of a threat to the nature of the threat itself." [i] One who yields to a threat of criminal or tortious injury may be given relief on this ground. On cognate reasoning, it has been held that a threat of lawful action cannot be wrongful. "It is not duress to threaten to do what there is a legal right to do." [j]

Such reasoning has particular application to cases in which a dispute is compromised under a threat of suit.[k] As it is not unlawful to institute legal proceedings, a person threatened with suit may not buy his way out and thereafter complain of the bargain: such is a usual argument in support of settlements. Yet it is not now accepted as a general proposition that one may rightfully threaten what he may rightfully do. "An unjust and inequitable threat is wrongful, although the threatened act would not be a violation of duty in the sense of an independent actionable wrong in the law of crimes, torts, or contracts." [l] This view is illustrated in cases of benefit that an

f. Union Pacific R. Co. v. Public Service Comm., 248 U.S. 67 (1918) (duress by a state agency).

g. See Sheraton Hawaii Corp. v. Poston, 51 Hawaii 142, 172, 454 P.2d 369 (1969).

h. Hellenic Lines, Ltd. v. Louis Dreyfus Corp., 372 F.2d 753 (2d Cir. 1967) (valuable discussion).

i. Food Fair Stores, Inc. v. Joy, 283 Md. 205, 389 A.2d 874 (1978) (claim for slander et al.; release given by accused shoplifter in consideration of offer by state's attorney to enter a nolle prosequi; divided court). Traditionally, the court said, emphasis has been placed on "the effect of wrongful act or threat upon the person claiming thereby to have been coerced." The court relied on Restatement Second, § 175, Comment b. But see State ex rel. State, Etc. v. City of St. Louis, n. c supra. See further as to threat of criminal prosecution Buhrman v. International Harvester Co., 181 Neb. 633, 150 N.W.2d 220 (1967).

j. This proposition, in one form or another, is relied on in a mass of American cases. In Chouinard v. Chouinard, 568 F.2d 430 (5th Cir. 1978), the court said that a lawful demand, or insistence on a legal right, even as against a necessitous person, is not duress.

k. See Dunbar v. Dunbar, 102 Ariz. 352, 429 P.2d 949 (1967): "It is not duress to declare an intention to resort to the courts for the purpose of insisting on what one believes are one's legal rights." See also Helena Chemical Co. v. Rivenbark, 263 S.E. 2d 305 (N.C.App.1980).

l. McCubbin v. Buss, footnote a, supra. See also Silsbee v. Webber, 171 Mass. 378, 50 N.E. 555 (1898): "When it comes to the question of obtaining contracts by threats, it does not fol-

employer exacts from an employee, under threat to discharge him, where the employment contract is terminable at will.[m]

Professor Dawson has pointed out that preventing unjust enrichment is a principal function of the doctrines of duress, and that the limitations on relief mentioned above tend to obscure that function.[n] These limitations have been considerably relaxed, at least in some situations.[o] Instances are given at a later point in this chapter, following materials on related topics. Sections 174 through 177 of the Restatement Second treat of duress and undue influence.

NOTES

(1) *Duress by Threat of Suit.* When a person seeks relief from a contract on the ground of coercion, it is not uncommon to find that he is himself adept at coercive practices. An example is Undersea Eng. & Const. Co. v. International Tel. & Tel. Corp., 429 F.2d 548 (9th Cir. 1970).[p] In that case the plaintiff, Undersea, had been a subcontractor on a job for which the defendant, ITT, was the general contractor. Disputes between them led to extended negotiations, and to a settlement which the plaintiff later sought to void. The defendant was depicted as a billion-dollar corporation having elephantine power over the plaintiff. The court observed, however, that before the settlement "Undersea was using every threat of economic and moral pressure to coerce and force ITT to settle rather than face a law suit with threatened world-wide publicity."

If a settlement of a disputed claim does not put a period to the dispute, the claimant may usually begin second-round negotiations with the valuable advantage that he has already been paid a portion of his claim. If it were the rule that a settlement *never* puts an end to a dispute, the rule might put an end to settlements. The courts are quite alive to the demerit of prolonging controversy indefinitely. They do not, for instance, regard a threat of civil suit as coercive, in ordinary circumstances. Nevertheless, it is generally recognized that a threat to bring a civil action is sometimes an instrument of duress.[q]

(2) *Restitution.* Duress is a ground not only for avoiding an agreement or settlement, but also for recovering a payment exacted by lawless

low that, because you cannot be made to answer for the act, you may use the threat."

m. See Laemmar v. J. Walter Thompson Company, 435 F.2d 680 (7th Cir. 1970); Gerber v. First Nat. Bank, 30 Ill.App.3d 776, 332 N.E.2d 615, 79 A.L.R.3d 592 (1975).

n. Dawson, Economic Duress—An Essay in Perspective, 45 Mich.L.Rev. 253, 282 ff. (1947). See also Patterson, Compulsory Contracts in the Crystal Ball, 43 Colum.L.Rev. 731, 741 (1943).

o. See Hellenic Lines, Ltd. v. Louis Dreyfus Corp., footnote h, supra.

p. See also Grad v. Roberts, 14 N.Y.2d 70, 198 N.E.2d 26 (1964); Hellenic Lines Ltd. v. Louis Dreyfus Corp., footnote h, supra.

q. E. g., Link v. Link, 278 N.C. 181, 179 S.E.2d 697 (1971): "corrupt intent to coerce a transaction grossly unfair to the victim and not related to the subject of such proceedings." On the topic of this note, see especially Dawson, Duress Through Civil Litigation, 45 Mich.L.Rev. 571(I) and 679(II) (1947).

compulsion. The fountainhead case on the law of restitution, Moses v. Macferlan,[r] speaks to the point. In that case Lord Mansfield said that an action for money had and received lies "for money got through imposition (express or implied); or extortion; or oppression; or an undue advantage taken of the plaintiff's situation, contrary to laws made for the protection of persons under those circumstances."

(3) *Leading from Weakness.* Something like an arm's-length relation developed in the home of Donald and Theresa Stauffer, when she learned that he had committed adultery with her married sister. She consulted a lawyer; Donald ceased to be the dominant party in the relationship. Many gripping scenes apparently ensued between them, but "the prevailing mood was that they would continue to live together." At length, Donald conveyed the family home to Theresa; he had previously shared its ownership with her, and it was his principal asset. Three days later the family atmosphere changed altogether: Theresa ceased sexual relations with Donald, ceased discussing a threat of suit by her brother-in-law, and ceased to suffer from hysterical outbursts—so Donald testified. He brought an action in equity against Theresa to compel reconveyance, and she appealed from an adverse decree. *Held:* Affirmed. Stauffer v. Stauffer, 465 Pa. 558, 351 A.2d 236 (1976).

Theresa was unjustly enriched by the transfer. The court did not quite say that a "confidential relationship" existed between the parties, in the traditional sense; but it did not regard the transaction as one at arm's-length either. "Human relationships are frequently too complex to be classified simply," either way. The court conceded that Theresa's conduct might be thought evidence of weakness, not dominance. But this, it said, "would be to ignore the extent to which weakness, whether real or apparent, can be a source of power over one who feels a sense of guilt . . . ."

THE PRE-EXISTING DUTY RULE

"Performance of a legal duty owed to a promisor which is neither doubtful nor the subject of honest dispute is not consideration . . . ." Restatement Second, § 73. This is a recent version of an old rule that has given rise to some dissatisfaction. Professor Edwin W. Patterson[a] observed that it is, "on the whole, that adjunct of the doctrine of consideration which has done most to give it a bad name." Patterson, An Apology for Consideration, 58 Colum.L.Rev. 929, 936 (1958). On the other hand, some decisions that can be referred to the rule are generally applauded. In such cases there is commonly an element of coercion, as illustrated in the following well-known case.

r. 2 Burr. 1005, 97 Eng.Rep. 676 (K.B. 1760).

a. Edwin W. Patterson (1889–1965) practiced for four years in Kansas City and then taught at Texas, Colorado, Iowa and Columbia. Among his writings are books on contracts, insurance and jurisprudence, including four editions of the predecessor of this casebook. He was one of the Advisers for the Restatement of Restitution.

A group of workmen had individually signed a contract to work on Alaska Packers' ship during the salmon canning season, from San Francisco to Pyramid Harbor, Alaska, and return, for a specified compensation. Upon arrival at the canning factory in Alaska, they presented a demand to Alaska Packers' superintendent for a very substantial increase in compensation, and they refused to work any further unless this demand was agreed to. Since it was impossible to get other men to replace them, the superintendent signed an agreement to pay the larger amount. Upon the return of the men to San Francisco at the end of the season, Alaska Packers paid them in accordance with the first agreement, and the employees sued in admiralty to recover the additional compensation. From judgment for the libelants, the defendant appealed. *Held*: Reversed. The agreement to pay the increased compensation was without consideration and was induced by the coercion of libelants' unjustified refusal to perform their contracts. Alaska Packers Ass'n v. Domenico, 117 Fed. 99 (9th Cir. 1902).

In some states the pre-existing duty rule has been largely rejected by judicial decision. In Alabama, for example, the rule is that "an executory contract may be modified by the parties without any new consideration other than mutual consent." [b] Yet in Rosellini v. Banchere, 83 Wash.2d 268, 517 P.2d 955 (1974), the court examined statements of like effect that it had made in opinions running over half a century and rejected them. Sometimes a decision seems to depend on the singular facts presented, as in a suit brought by Christian Busse against Albro Bishop. Following the great Chicago fire, Busse undertook to rebuild a structure for its owner at fixed rates, such as $15 per thousand for bricks laid. It seems that while the work was under way the prices of labor and materials increased rapidly, by as much as 50%. The builder said he "could not and would not go on under the contract;" but the owner persuaded him to continue with a promise to pay "what was right." In the litigation that ensued, Busse won a judgment on that promise and it was affirmed on appeal. The court did not look seriously for a technical consideration in the abandonment of a fixed-price contract. (Might it have been found?) But it did consider the owner's business calculations. With the rise in prices, the court said, rents must have risen proportionately. Moreover, the owner might have had a damage claim against the builder—"But this he may have considered of less advantage to him than the completion of the building . . . ." Bishop v. Busse, 69 Ill. 403 (1873).[c] *Questions*: How would the Alaska Packers case

b. Winegardner v. Burns, 361 So.2d 1054 (Ala.1978). For an extensive recital of cases see Brody, Performance of a Pre-Existing Contractual Duty as Consideration, 52 Denver L.J. 433 (1975).

c. See also Okemah Constr., Inc. v. Barkley-Farmer, Inc., 583 S.W.2d 458 (Tex.Civ.App.1979) (contractor demanded pay at increased rate because he "wasn't making any money").

have been decided under Alabama law? How would Bishop v. Busse have been decided under Washington law?

For a statutory modification of the rule, see UCC 2–209(1).

NOTES

(1) *Problem.* Construction company proposed to advise Hospital about an addition, supervise its selection of contractors, and coordinate their work. Hospital accepted this proposal, which provided also that the parties might modify it from time to time by mutual agreement in writing. Thereafter Hospital asked Construction for a commitment that the work would not cost it more than a given amount, and Construction agreed to a "guaranteed maximum cost." What consideration may be found for the new term? Is it enforceable without consideration? Would the problem be different if, in the original proposal, Construction had agreed to guarantee a maximum cost as soon as "meaningful" bids from contractors were in hand? See City of Parkersburg, West Virginia v. Turner Constr. Co., 442 F.Supp. 673 (N.D.W.Va.1977).

(2) *New York Statute.* How would the Alaska Packers case have been decided under the following provision of New York law?[d]

Written agreement for modification or discharge. An agreement, promise or undertaking to change or modify, or to discharge in whole or in part, any contract, obligation, or lease, or any mortgage or other security interest in personal or real property, shall not be invalid because of the absence of consideration, provided that the agreement, promise or undertaking changing, modifying, or discharging such contract, obligation, lease, mortgage or security interest, shall be in writing and signed by the party against whom it is sought to enforce the change, modification or discharge, or by his agent.

(3) *Duress?* Might a modifying agreement that is within UCC 2–209 (1) or the New York statute quoted above still be voidable for duress where it was induced by one party's threat to break his contract? Comment 2 to UCC 2–209 states, in part, that "modifications made thereunder must meet the test of good faith imposed by this Act . . . and the extortion of a 'modification' without legitimate commercial reason is ineffective as a violation of the duty of good faith." See Farnsworth, Good Faith Purchase and Commercial Reasonableness Under the Uniform Commercial Code, 30 U. Chi.L.Rev. 666, 675–76 (1963).

A thoughtul review of the pre-existing duty rule by Professor Hillsman concludes that it has been dismissed too summarily in the Code provision. He recommends that the person relying on a concession under certain modifying agreements be put to proof that it was not unfairly coerced. Does the rule of Restatement Second § 89, make a satisfying balance of the opposing considerations? See Hillsman, Policing Contract Modifications under the UCC: Good Faith and the Doctrine of Economic Duress, 64 Iowa L.Rev. 849 (1979). *Question*: Would you expect the definition of "good faith" in

d. New York General Obligations Law, § 5–1103. See also Mich.C.L.A. § 566.1.

UCC 1–201(19) or that in UCC 2–103(1)(b) to be the more decisive in this connection?

(4) *Problem.* Refer again to Ever-Tite Roofing Corp. v. Green, p. 204 supra. Suppose the following situation: Ever-Tite's workmen arrived at the Green's residence and found no other roofer engaged. They advised the Greens that, though new gutters were called for in the signed agreement, Ever-Tite had discontinued gutter work. They then persuaded the Greens to initial an amendment to the agreement, "gutter installation eliminated." Would it be possible for the Greens, on changing their minds, to repudiate the amendment? See Engle v. Shapert Constr. Co., 443 F.Supp. 1383 (M.D.Pa.1978). Would it matter whether or not the court considers that Article 2 of the Code applies to a sale and installation of roofing materials?

SCHWARTZREICH v. BAUMAN-BASCH, INC.

Court of Appeals of New York, 1921.
231 N.Y. 196, 131 N.E. 887.

[On August 31, 1917, the plaintiff contracted in writing to work for the defendant as a designer of coats and wraps at $90 per week, the employment to continue for one year from November 22, 1917. The plaintiff was later offered similar employment by another at $115 per week. Upon plaintiff's informing the defendant of the offer, the defendant suggested that he would pay the plaintiff $100 per week if he would stay. The plaintiff agreed. Whereupon, on October 17, 1917, a new agreement, exactly like the first except as to the amount of pay, was drawn up and signed by the parties. Simultaneously with the signing of the new contract, the signatures were torn off the old one by the plaintiff and his copy surrendered to the defendant. The plaintiff was discharged in the following December and brought this action on the contract of October 17th, in the City Court of the city of New York. A verdict was rendered for the plaintiff for the amount due on the contract of October 17th, the court instructing that if the old contract was canceled "prior to or at the time of the execution" of the new there was consideration for the new. The trial court set aside the verdict and dismissed the complaint. The Appellate Term reversed and reinstated the verdict. The defendant appealed unsuccessfully to the Appellate Division First Department, and appealed again.]

CRANE, J. . . . . The question remains, therefore, whether the charge of the court as above given, was a correct statement of the law, or whether on all the evidence in the plaintiff's favor a cause of action was made out.

Can a contract of employment be set aside or terminated by the parties to it and a new one made or substituted in its place? If so, is it competent to end the one and make the other at the same time?

It has been repeatedly held that a promise made to induce a party to do that which he is already bound by contract to perform is without consideration. But the cases in this state, while enforcing this rule, also recognize that a contract may be canceled by mutual consent and a new one made. Thus Vanderbilt v. Schreyer, 91 N.Y. 392, 402, held that it was no consideration for a guaranty that a party promise to do only that which he was before legally bound to perform. This court stated, however:

"It would doubtless be competent for parties to cancel an existing contract and make a new one to complete the same work at a different rate of compensation, but it seems that it would be essential to its validity that there should be a valid cancellation of the original contract. Such was the case of Lattimore v. Harsen, 14 Johns. 330."

In Cosgray v. New England Piano Co., 10 App.Div. 351, 353, 41 N.Y.S. 886, it was decided that where the plaintiff had bound himself to work for a year at $30 a week, there was no consideration for a promise thereafter made by the defendant that he should notwithstanding receive $1,800 a year. Here it will be noticed that there was no termination of the first agreement which gave occasion for Bartlett, J., to say in the opinion:

"The case might be different if the parties had, by word of mouth, agreed wholly to abrogate and do away with a pre-existing written contract in regard to service and compensation, and had substituted for it another agreement."

Any change in an existing contract, such as a modification of the rate of compensation, or a supplemental agreement, must have a new consideration to support it. In such a case the contract is continued, not ended. Where, however, an existing contract is terminated by consent of both parties and a new one executed in its place and stead, we have a different situation and the mutual promises are again a consideration. Very little difference may appear in a mere change of compensation in an existing and continuing contract and a termination of one contract and the making of a new one for the same time and work, but at an increased compensation. There is, however, a marked difference in principle. Where the new contract gives any new privilege or advantage to the promisee, a consideration has been recognized, though in the main it is the same contract. Triangle Waist Co., Inc. v. Todd, 223 N.Y. 27, 119 N.E. 85.

If this which we are now holding were not the rule, parties having once made a contract would be prevented from changing it no matter how willing and desirous they might be to do so, unless the terms conferred an additional benefit to the promisee.

All concede that an agreement may be rescinded by mutual consent and a new agreement made thereafter on any terms to which the parties may assent. Prof. Williston in his work on Contracts says (Vol. 1, sec. 130a): "A rescission followed shortly afterwards by a new agreement in regard to the same subject-matter would create the legal obligations provided in the subsequent agreement."

The same effect follows in our judgment from a new contract entered into at the same time the old one is destroyed and rescinded by mutual consent. The determining factor is the rescission by consent. Provided this is the expressed and acted upon intention, the time of the rescission, whether a moment before or at the same time as the making of the new contract, is unimportant.

The decisions are numerous and divergent where one of the parties to a contract refuses to perform unless paid an additional amount. Some states hold the new promise to pay the demand binding though there be no rescission. It is said that the new promise is given to secure performance in place of an action for damages for not performing (Parrot v. Mexican Central Railway Co., 207 Mass. 184, 93 N.E. 90, 34 L.R.A.,N.S., 261), or that the new contract is evidence of the rescission of the old one and it is the same as if no previous contract had been made (Coyner v. Lynde, 10 Ind. 282; Connelly v. Devoe, 37 Conn. 570; Goebel v. Linn, 47 Mich. 489, 11 N.W. 284, 41 Am.Rep. 723), or that unforeseen difficulties and hardships modify the rule (King v. Duluth, M. & N. Ry. Co., 61 Minn. 482, 63 N.W. 1105), or that the new contract is an attempt to mitigate the damages which may flow from the breach of the first. Endriss v. Belle Isle Ice Co., 49 Mich. 279, 13 N.W. 590. . . .

The contrary has been held . . . . In none of these cases, however, was there a full and complete rescission of the old contract and it is this with which we are dealing in this case. Rescission is not presumed; it is expressed; the old contract is not continued with modifications; it is ended and a new one made.

The efforts of the courts to give a legal reason for holding good a promise to pay an additional compensation for the fulfillment of a pre-existing contract is commented upon in note upon Abbott v. Doane, 163 Mass. 433, 40 N.E. 197, in 34 L.R.A. 33, 39, 47 Am.St. Rep. 465, and the result reached is stated as follows: "The almost universal rule is that without any express rescission of the old contract, the promise is made simply for additional compensation, making the new promise a mere nudum pactum." As before stated, in this case we have an express rescission and a new contract.

There is no reason that we can see why the parties to a contract may not come together and agree to cancel and rescind an existing contract, making a new one in its place. We are also of the opinion that reason and authority support the conclusion that both transactions can take place at the same time.

For the reasons here stated, the charge of the trial court was correct, and the judgments of the Appellate Division and the Appellate Term should be affirmed, with costs.

CHASE, J., dissents.

NOTES

(1) *Case Analysis.* Does the court in the principal case find that the parties made two contracts or three? What was the legal significance, if any, of the ceremony in which the signatures were torn off the original employment contract? Would the decision have been different if the signatures had not been torn off the old contract until after the parties had signed the new one?

In a study of agreements modifying contracts, the New York Law Revision Commission was critical of the Schwartzreich case: "Whether the evidence shows an intention by both parties to rescind the old contract will in most cases be a question for the jury. Thus, until the jury decides, the contractual rights of the parties can only be described by a prediction of what a jury will do, always an uncertain process." Second Annual L.R.C. Report 255 (Leg.Doc.No.65, 1936).

The Commission proposed the statute that has become N.Y.Gen.Obl.L. § 5–1103, Note 2, p. 385 supra.

(2) *Question.* Consult Restatement Second, § 89(a). Should the job offer at $115 a week be regarded as a circumstance not anticipated when the contract was made, such that a $10 raise was "fair and equitable"?

(3) *Problem.* The foreman for a contracting firm sued it for a promised bonus, and recovered: half the difference between the actual cost of the work he had directed and its projected cost. The firm appealed. The trial court had charged the jury that the modification of an employment contract (as by including a bonus) is supported by consideration if the employee is free to terminate the contract at will. Should the judgment be reversed? See Leone v. Precision Plumbing & Heating of Southern Arizona, Inc., 121 Ariz. 514, 591 P.2d 1002 (1979).

(4) *The Fighting Farmer's Case.* A resurgence of the pre-existing duty rule has occurred in Iowa. Reviewing some of its earlier opinions, the Iowa court concluded that they "digressed" from the rule without sound reasoning, and caused confusion by blurring the distinction between the modification and the rescission of a contract. The case concerned the sale of a farm and an increase in the agreed price. The buyers agreed to the increase when the seller's attorney told them that his clients were willing to go to court to get out of the initial agreement, and that litigation was expensive. The court directed specific performance of that agreement, overcoming difficulties about definiteness and the statute of frauds. Taking note of the Restatement position—§ 89(a)—the court called it interesting but inapplicable; in other circumstances, the court said, it would not "discount" its application. Recker v. Gustafson, 279 N.W.2d 744 (Iowa, 1979). *Questions:* Are there circumstances in which you, as attorney for the sellers, would have declined to negotiate for them in the manner stated? If so, would your decision turn on whether or not the buyers also had a legal adviser? If an attorney for the buyers has advised them to agree to the price increase, is he at liberty later to question the consideration for it? See Rickett v. Doze, 603 P.2d 679 (Mont.1979).

ARZANI v. PEOPLE, 149 N.Y.S.2d 38 (Sup.Ct., Onondaga County, 1956). [The State of New York let a contract for the reconstruction of a highway to Kranz and Martin, as general contractors. They entered into a written subcontract with Victor Arzani, by which he agreed to do part of the work, including contract paving. After doing it, and being paid $106,000, Arzani brought suit against Kranz and Martin (including the State as a defendant) for an unpaid balance. After adjusting for various charges and credits, the court gave judgment for Arzani, in the amount of $19,520.62. It rejected Arzani's claim for an additional amount of some $1,500, based on an oral promise made to him by Kranz.]

GORMAN, Justice. . . . The proposal issued by the State listed the minimum wage for laborers as $1.95 per hour, which amount was in effect when the plaintiff commenced work on his subcontract. A few days later, the union representative demanded an increase of twenty cents per hour or he would call a strike and shut down the job. The plaintiff says that he then told the defendant Kranz that he, himself, would pull off the job if Kranz did not agree to pay one-half of the additional labor cost, and that Kranz agreed. This testimony is uncontradicted. The plaintiff further stated on cross-examination that it constituted the entire conversation with Kranz and was not reduced to writing. The proof showed that the plaintiff thereafter paid his laborers the sum of $3,003.40 over the amount he would have paid at the lesser rate, and that the work proceeded to a satisfactory conclusion.

It is the contention of the defendant contractors that there is no enforceable contract between the interested parties as to this item because of failure of consideration. It is competent for the parties to a contract to abandon it or to substitute another in its place. Merger of the rescission and promise into one transaction does not destroy them as elements composing the transaction. See Schwartzreich v. Bauman-Basch, Inc., 231 N.Y. 196, 131 N.E. 887. But there must be a new consideration, and there is general acceptance in this state that where A is under a contract with B, a promise made by one to the other to induce performance is void. Consideration is not necessary to an act of rescission, waiver, release or discharge, but rather to the enforceability of executory promises. But it is necessary that there be a valid abrogation of the existing contract, and this by mutual agreement. This fact has not been established, whether the test be factual or legal.

It is true that this is not a situation where coercion or expediency has been utilized by the plaintiff in a mere attempt to exact more money. The conceded circumstances might spell out factually a mutual acceptance of immediate danger to the completion of one of interrelated contracts. But termination is not shown. The most that the plaintiff shows beyond the promise is his reliance upon his capacity to breach the contract, and his statement that he would do so if the excess labor cost was not shared. See McGowan & Connolly Co., Inc., v. Kenny-Moran Co., Inc., 207 App.Div. 617, 202 N.Y.S. 513. Judged from the standpoint of ordinary business morality, the situation of the promisor contractor may well be less defensible than that of the plaintiff. But termination is not presumed. It must be proved and upon this record the plaintiff has failed to sustain his burden.

NOTES

(1) *Question.* Would this decision have been different under the rule of Restatement Second, § 89?

(2) *The Sheep and the Goats.* It has been urged that the courts should endeavor "to separate the sheep from the goats" by enforcing the new promise in favor of the honest contractor and refusing to enforce it in favor of the dishonest or extortionate contractor. Corbin, Does a Preexisting Duty Defeat Consideration?, 27 Yale L.J. 362, 373 (1918). What facts, provable in court, can provide the basis for separating "the sheep from the goats"? How would the plaintiff in the present case be characterized, as "sheep" or "goat"? Is it clear that he used no coercion to secure the agreement about labor costs? (Part of the court's opinion in Arzani—"Judged from the standpoint of ordinary business morality . . ."—is an unacknowledged excerpt from Corbin's writing.)

(3) *Avoiding the Rule.* Speaking of the preexisting duty rule, one court has said: "any consideration for the new undertaking, however insignificant, satisfies this rule. For instance, an undertaking to pay part of the debt before maturity, or at a place other than that where the obligor was legally bound to pay, or to pay in property, regardless of its value, or to effect a composition with creditors by the payment of less than the sum due, has been held to constitute a consideration sufficient in law."[a] The same thought was expressed by Lord Coke, in Pinnel's Case: "by no possibility, a lesser sum can be satisfaction to the plaintiff for a greater sum: but the gift of a horse, hawk or robe, etc. in satisfaction is good."[b]

What modern equivalent of a "horse, hawk or robe" might suitably be used to make a creditor's concession to his debtor irreversible? In Restatement Second, § 73 it is said that a performance "similar" to that owing "is consideration if it differs from what was required . . . in a way which reflects more than a pretense of a bargain." Does the concluding phrase encourage lawyers to make a pioneering search for trivial new objects of bargaining?

Reach of the Rule

Consideration is only a test of the enforceability of an executory promise, it has been said. Angel v. Murray, 113 R.I. 482, 322 A.2d 630 (1974). At the least this seems to mean that when a payment

a. Levine v. Blumenthal, 117 N.J.L. 23, 186 A. 457 (1936), aff'd on opinion of Supreme Court, 117 N.J.L. 426, 189 A. 54 (Ct. of Err. & App.1937).

b. See n. d infra.

has been made, or some other performance given, the recipient cannot be required to make restitution on the simple ground that he gave nothing in exchange. (Recovery for payment made under mistake or under duress is another matter.) There is little reason to doubt this proposition.[c]

A more debatable issue arises when a promisee, having supplied the agreed exchange in full, agrees to be satisfied with part performance of the promise. May he (or she) retract that concession? The two cases mentioned next answer "yes"; but there is substantial dissent.

Foakes v. Beer. Mrs. Beer had a judgment against Dr. Foakes for £2,000. In order to induce him to pay it, she agreed to accept part payment at once, and stated installments in the future, foregoing her right to interest. After Foakes paid the principal in full, Mrs. Beer sued for the interest. The House of Lords found a controlling precedent in Pinnel's Case, decided by Lord Coke in 1602.[d] There it was said that "payment of a lesser sum on the day, i. e., on or after the due date of a money debt cannot be any satisfaction for the whole." In agreeing to pay the judgment, Dr. Foakes did no more than he was obliged to do in any event. Hence Mrs. Beer was not bound by the agreement. Foakes v. Beer, 1884 L.R. 9 A.C. 605 (H. L.)[e]

Kennedy v. Kennedy. Linda Kennedy was entitled, under a divorce decree, to payments for child support of $42 a week from her former husband, Thomas. Falling far behind in paying, he was prosecuted, but was acquitted because of his poor financial condition. Linda and Thomas then discussed the matter, and she agreed (as Thomas later testified) to "forget all sums that I had owed her up to date, if I would pay her $30 every two weeks until I got back on my feet." Later, Linda brought garnishment proceedings to have the arrears, calculated at $42 a week, paid out of Thomas's wages. The garnishments were quashed, and Linda appealed. *Held*: Reversed. Kennedy v. Kennedy, 575 S.W.2d 833 (Mo.App.1978). As to the payments accrued at the time of the agreement, the court said, Linda received no consideration for releasing Thomas.

The doctrine applied in these cases has often been doubted or denounced. One eminent judge called it a relic of antique law, and "evidence of the former capacity of lawyers and judges to make the re-

c. A curious fact about the case last cited is that it appears to resist the logic of its own premise.

d. Cited as 5 Coke's Rep. 117a (in Vol. 3, Part V), 77 Eng.Rep. 237 (Common Pleas).

e. Some of the law lords doubted that the operative document purported to foreclose Mrs. Beer's interest claim. Others did not acquiesce in the authority of Pinnel's Case. But there was a majority ruling as stated in the text.

For an assault on the rule of Foakes v. Beer see Comment, 11 Ariz.L.Rev. 344 (1969).

quirement of consideration an overworked shibboleth rather than a logical and just standard of actionability." [f] Do you agree?

NOTES

(1) *Promises to Thomas.* In Kennedy v. Kennedy, Thomas argued his case partly on the ground of reliance. But for Linda's forbearance, he said, he would have applied to the divorce court to modify his child-support obligation. The court distinguished between payments overdue at the time of the agreement and those to be made thereafter. As to the latter, the court said, Linda could not lawfully contract to excuse Thomas. As to the former she could not reasonably have expected her promise to induce Thomas not to seek modification.[g] *Question*: Does the court's reasoning treat the agreement as if Linda made *two* promises to Thomas—one as to payments overdue, and one as to future payments? Do you suppose the parties understood their agreement this way? What result in the case under Restatement Second, § 89(c)?

(2) *Bird in the Hand.* A creditor is most likely to be content with a "lesser sum," it seems, when he knows that payment in full is beyond the debtor's means. If that is a fair observation, how does it connect with the rule in Texas?—that if the debtor is a "known insolvent" his part payment of a debt already due will discharge it; otherwise not. See Prather v. Citizens Nat. Bank of Dallas, 582 S.W.2d 903 (Tex.Civ.App.1979).

(3) *Assignment.* In Foakes v. Beer (p. 392 supra) if Dr. Foakes had anticipated Mrs. Beer's change of heart, and the result of her suit, it might have occurred to him to set up the agreement differently. Consider this arrangement: Foakes agrees to pay the principal amount of the judgment, in installments, and Beer assigns to him her right to interest on the judgment. An assignment of a contract (or judgment) claim, having the character of a present transfer, is generally effective without regard to consideration. Given certain formalities, at least, a gift assignment is irrevocable. However, it is arguable that an assignment of a claim by its holder *to the obligor* is a distinct species, less favored than an assignment to a third party. Given the rule of Foakes v. Beer, is it a logical corollary that a gift assignment of this species is impossible?

In the following case the court justified its decision, in part, by reference to the law of gifts. (That part of the opinion is omitted.) However, the facts did not lend themselves to an assignment analysis, for the agreement in question was oral. The rule as to an *oral* gift assignment, acknowledged by the court, is that it may be revoked. The court refused, therefore, to peg its decision on the law of assignments: "when a creditor releases his debtor, without full payment of the debt, no assignment is involved." (Chapter 11 presents assignment law in some detail.)

f. Stone, J., in Rye v. Phillips, 203 Minn. 567, 282 N.W. 459 (1938).

Taking broader ground, some scholars have challenged the general rule about pre-existing duty, as it affects the modification of contracts. One thoughtful appraisal is that of Patterson, in An Apology for Consideration, 58 Col.L.Rev. 929, 936–38 (1958), concluding: "The nineteenth century, striving to bring unity out of diversity, included too many different ideas under the general heading of consideration."

g. Compare Rhoades v. Rhoades, 40 Ohio App.2d 559, 321 N.E.2d 242, 69 O.O.2d 22 (1974).

WATKINS & SON v. CARRIG

Supreme Court of New Hampshire, 1941.
91 N.H. 459, 21 A.2d 591, 138 A.L.R. 131.

Assumpsit for work done. By a written contract between the parties the plaintiff agreed to excavate a cellar for the defendant for a stated price. Soon after the work was commenced solid rock was encountered. The plaintiff's manager notified the defendant, a meeting between them was held, and it was orally agreed that the plaintiff should remove the rock at a stipulated unit price about nine times greater than the unit price for excavating upon which the gross amount to be paid according to the written contract was calculated. The rock proved to constitute about two-thirds of the space to be excavated.

A referee found that the oral agreement "superseded" the written contract, and reported a verdict for the plaintiff based on the finding. To the acceptance of the report and an order of judgment thereon the defendant excepted. Further facts appear in the opinion. Transferred by Burque, C. J.

ALLEN, Chief Justice. When the written contract was entered into, no understanding existed between the parties that no rock would be found in the excavating. The plaintiff's manager made no inquiry or investigation to find out the character of the ground below the surface, no claim is made that the defendant misled him, and the contract contains no reservations for unexpected conditions. It provides that "all material" shall be removed from the site, and its term that the plaintiff is "to excavate" is unqualified. In this situation a defence of mutual mistake is not available. A space of ground to be excavated, whatever its character, was the subject matter of the contract, and the offer of price on that basis was accepted. Leavitt v. Dover, 67 N.H. 94, 32 A. 156, 68 Am.St.Rep. 640. If the plaintiff was unwise in taking chances, it is not relieved, on the ground of mistake, from the burden incurred in being faced with them. The case differs from that of King Co. v. Aldrich, 81 N.H. 42, 121 A. 434, in which the parties did not contract for the property delivered in purported performance of the contract actually made.

The referee's finding that the written contract was "superseded" by an oral contract when the rock was discovered is construed to mean that the parties agreed to rescind the written contract as though it had not been made and entered into an oral one as though it were the sole and original one. The defendant either thought that the contract did not require the excavation of rock on the basis of the contract price or was willing to forego his rights under the contract in respect to rock. It was important to him that the work should not be delayed, and other reasons may have contributed to induce him to the concession he made. In any event, he consented to a special price for excavating rock, whatever his rights under the contract. The plaintiff on the strength of the promise proceeded with the work.

But the defendant contends that the facts do not support a claim of two independent and separate transactions, one in rescission of the written contract as though it were nugatory, and one in full substitution of it. All that is shown, as he urges, is one transaction by which he was to pay more for the excavating than the written contract provided, with that contract otherwise to remain in force. And upon the basis of this position he relies upon the principle of contract law that his promise to pay more was without consideration, as being a promise to pay the plaintiff for performance of its obligation already in force and outstanding. Whether the contract was rescinded with a new one to take its place or whether it remained in force with a modification of its terms, is not important. In the view of a modification, the claim of a promise unsupported by consideration is as tenable as under the view of a rescission. A modification involves a partial rescission.

In the situation presented the plaintiff entered into a contractual obligation. Facts subsequently learned showed the obligation to be burdensome and the contract improvident. On insistent request by the plaintiff, the defendant granted relief from the burden by a promise to pay a special price which overcame the burden. The promise was not an assumption of the burden; the special price was fair and the defendant received reasonable value for it.

The issue whether the grant of relief constituted a valid contract is one of difficulty. The basic rule that a promise without consideration for it is invalid leads to its logical application that a promise to pay for what the promisor already has a right to receive from the promisee is invalid. The promisee's performance of an existing duty is no detriment to him, and hence nothing is given by him beyond what is already due the promisor. But the claim is here made that the original contract was rescinded, either in full or in respect to some of its terms, by mutual consent, and since any rescission mutually agreed upon is in itself a contract, the claim of a promise to pay for performance of a subsisting duty is unfounded. The terms of the contract of rescission are of course valid if the rescission is valid. The defendant's answer to this claim is well stated in this quotation from Williston, Contr., 2d Ed., § 130a: "But calling an agreement an agreement for rescission does not do away with the necessity of consideration, and when the agreement for rescission is coupled with a further agreement that the work provided for in the earlier agreement shall be completed and that the other party shall give more than he originally promised, the total effect of the second agreement is that one party promises to do exactly what he had previously bound himself to do, and the other party promises to give an additional compensation therefor."

With due respect for this eminent authority, the argument appears to clothe consideration with insistence of control beyond its proper demands. With full recognition of the legal worthlessness of a bare promise and of performance of a subsisting duty as a void consideration, a result accomplished by proper means is not necessarily bad because it would be bad if the means were improper or were not employed.

It is not perceived that the requirement of consideration is necessarily disregarded in spite of the net result of a promise to pay more for less, without additional obligation of the promisee. If the process in reaching such a result is inoffensive to the doctrine of consideration, the result does not become a naked promise. If in analysis of the transaction compliance with the elements of a valid contract may be found, it is hardly a perversion of principle to give the steps taken recognition. The result being reasonable, the means taken to reach it may be examined to determine their propriety.

In common understanding there is, importantly, a wide divergence between a bare promise and a promise in adjustment of a contractual promise already outstanding. A promise with no supporting consideration would upset well and long-established human interrelations if the law did not treat it as a vain thing. But parties to a valid contract generally understand that it is subject to any mutual action they may take in its performance. Changes to meet changes in circumstances and conditions should be valid if the law is to carry out its function and service by rules conformable with reasonable practices and understandings in matters of business and commerce.

Rescission in full or in modification being intended, it should be effective although the result benefits only one party and places a burden only on the other. It is the fact of rescission rather than the effect of it that determines its legal quality. The difference between a rescission unrelated to a new contract and one interdependent with a new contract, with the result the same in each case, signifies no failure of consideration in the latter case. The result, whatever it may be, is indecisive of the contractual character of the transaction. The steps taken being pointed out by the law, the result should not be held an idle one. Merger of the rescission and promise into one transaction does not destroy them as elements composing the transaction. . . .

Whether the gift to a debtor of an intangible right be termed a waiver, a surrender, an abandonment, or a release, seems broadly immaterial. Its nature, in yielding the right, or in forgiving the obligation, is determinative, rather than its appellation. There may be distinctions and discriminations in the required manner of their metaphysical delivery, but here . . . no symbolism or particular form of evidence is an essential of proof. The case is one of a simple relinquishment of a right pertaining to intangible personalty. The defendant intentionally and voluntarily yielded to a demand for a special price for excavating rock. In doing this he yielded his contract right to the price it provided. Whether or not he thought he had the right, he intended, and executed his intent, to make no claim of the right. The promise of a special price for excavating rock necessarily imported a release or waiver of any right by the contract to hold the plaintiff to the lower price the contract stipulated. In mutual understanding the parties agreed that the contract price was not to control. The contract right being freely surrendered, the issue of contract law whether the new promise is valid is not doubtful. If the totality of the transaction was a promise to pay more for less, there was in its inherent makeup a valid discharge of an obligation. Although the transaction was single, the element of discharge was distinct in precedence of the new promise.

The foregoing views are considered to meet the reasonable needs of standard and ethical practices of men in their business dealings with each other. Conceding that the plaintiff threatened to break its contract because it found the contract to be improvident, yet the defendant yielded to the threat without protest, excusing the plaintiff, and making a new arrangement. Not insisting on his rights but relinquishing them, fairly he should be held to the new arrangement. The law is a means to the end. It is not the law because it is the law, but because it is adapted and adaptable to establish and maintain reasonable order. If the phrase justice according to law were transposed into law according to justice, it would perhaps be more accurately expressive. In a case like this, of conflicting rules and authority, a result which is considered better to establish "fundamental justice and reasonableness" (Cavanaugh v. Boston & M. Railroad, 76 N. H. 68, 72, 79 A. 694, 696), should be attained. It is not practical that the law should adopt all precepts of moral conduct, but it is desirable that its rules and principles should not run counter to them in the important conduct and transactions of life.

Exceptions overruled.[a]

NOTES

(1) *Presumption of Duress.* Professor Hillsman urges the courts to apply a presumption against a modifying agreement—that it was "a product of unlawful means"—if the effect of it is a material net loss in the value of the contract to the party making the concession. Op. cit. supra Note 3, p. 385, at 883. Do you find a case on the topic pre-existing duty in which this presumption would not apply?

(2) *The Hawaiian Housing Case.* Richards contracted to build housing in Hawaii for the Marine Air Corps, using a subcontractor's bid for the metal work, by the Air Conditioning Company (AC). By error, AC had

a. For a very similar case relying on Restatement Second, § 89, see Brian Constr. & Development Co., Inc. v. Brighenti, 176 Conn. 162, 405 A.2d 72 (1978).

calculated its bid on the assumption that galvanized sheet metal would be used, rather than zinc alloy. When AC informed Richards that it would not do the work for the bid price, Richards "blew up." Over the next two months, hard bargaining ensued, during which Richards insisted that AC was bound by its bid price. At length, Richards and AC executed a contract for the metal work at $62,000. (The AC bid had been less than $49,000). After paying some $50,000 as the work progressed, Richards refused to pay more. In fact, Richards never intended to pay the agreed price. When sued for the remainder, Richards relied on the pre-existing duty rule, and cited Alaska Packers Ass'n v. Domenico. (See brief of the case at p. 384 supra.) From judgment for the plaintiff, the defendant appealed. *Held*: Affirmed. Richards Constr. Co. v. Air Conditioning Co. of Hawaii, 318 F.2d 410 (9th Cir. 1963).

Was the Alaska Packers case easily distinguishable? Was Richards in a good position to assert the rule, having retreated from the position that AC was bound by its bid?

An additional fact in the case was that AC did not inform Richards of its error for about a month after it had learned of the award of the main contract, and after it had discovered the error. What conclusion does this suggest? Another fact was that the second lowest bid was $83,000.[b] What conclusion does this suggest?

A Judicial Tour De Force

De Cicco v. Schweizer [c] is a well-known New York case in which Cardozo wrote for the court on the subject of consideration. Its chief interest is not the decision itself, but the dazzling ingenuity he displayed in reaching it.

On the merits, the plaintiff's claim had a strong intrinsic appeal, but the pre-existing duty rule presented an obstacle. Blanche Schweizer and Count Oberto Gulinelli were engaged to be married. Four days before the wedding occurred the Count and the bride's parents executed "articles of agreement" in which the father, Joseph Schweizer, promised to make an annual payment to Blanche of $2,500 as long as he (Joseph) and Blanche should both live.[d] The sentence containing this promise began as follows:[e] "Whereas, Miss Blanche Josephine Schweizer . . . is now affianced to and is to be married to the above said Count Oberto Giacomo Giovanni Francesco Maria Gulinelli: Now in consideration of all that is herein set forth the said Mr. Joseph Schweizer promises," etc. The first payment was made on the wedding day. After the tenth payment, no more

b. Richards' architect had estimated the cost of the metal work at $16,000. One of the bids it received was for more than $173,000.

c. 221 N.Y. 431, 117 N.E. 807 (1917).

d. Mrs. Schweizer covenanted to continue the payments after her husband's death, and there were testamentary provisions as well.

e. Translated; the agreement was in Italian.

were made. The couple assigned their rights in the contract to Attilio De Cicco, and he sued Schweizer.[f]

Cardozo first stated the defendant's contention: "that Count Gulinelli was already affianced to Miss Schweizer, and that the marriage was merely the fulfillment of an existing legal duty." Turning to the law, he accepted the premise of the defendant's argument: "The courts of this state are committed to the view that a promise by A. to B. to induce him not to break his contract with C. is void." He then developed at length a distinction, showing that Schweizer's promise was not of that character. Instead, he reasoned, it was a promise to induce the Count not to join with Blanche in a voluntary rescission of their engagement. Although neither could rightfully withdraw without the other's consent, *together* they were free to terminate the engagement or postpone the marriage. The consideration, then, for Schweizer's promise was that they did not do so.[g]

In some beautifully articulated paragraphs the opinion seeks to make this reading plausible: "It does not seem a far-fetched assumption [in relation to contracts to marry] that one will release where the other has repented . . . one does not commonly apply pressure to coerce the will and action of those who are anxious to proceed. The attempt to sway their conduct by new inducements is an implied admission that both may waver . . . . The springs of conduct are subtle and varied. One who meddles with them must not insist upon too nice a measure of proof that the spring which he released was effective to the exclusion of all others." And in a final paragraph, Cardozo takes higher ground, appealing to "those considerations of public policy which cluster about contracts that touch the marriage relation." [h]

NOTES

(1) *Questions.* Is the principle of this case usable in any situation that does not involve a marriage? In Arzani v. People, p. 390 supra, would it have been plausible for the plaintiff to cite De Cicco v. Schweizer? If not, what change in the facts would make the two cases comparable?

In a later opinion, Cardozo cited De Cicco v. Schweizer as a "signpost on the road" toward general acceptance of the doctrine of promissory estoppel. See Allegheny College v. National Chautauqua County Bank, referred to at p. 90 supra. Do you see a connection between the case and that doctrine? See also Restatement Second, § 90, Illustration 8.

f. The court assumed, properly, that Attilio's right to enforce the contract was as good as that of either Blanche or the Count. It did not indicate which of them might have enforced it, or when the assignment was given, or for what consideration, if any.

g. Along the way, Cardozo rejected the contention that Schweizer had only made a promise of a gift: "One does not commonly pledge one's self to generosity in the language of a covenant."

h. One judge concurred in a separate opinion.

(2) *The Case of the Cotton-Picking Lawyer.* As charged by a grievance committee, attorney James H. Dodd violated the Code of Professional Responsibility. He undertook to press a personal-injury claim for a minor of 18, by an agreement with her mother. The fee was to be some fraction of any recovery, and was, in some eventualities, to be less than half. After he filed suit, the young person asked him to have her "declared 21." He proceeded to have her nonage removed, and then contracted with her to represent her for 50% "in the event that suit is filed." (In testimony before the committee, Dodd explained, "This is a new client, and I got the best cotton picking contract I could get.") Reviewing the evidence, the state supreme court was inclined to believe that Dodd had forgotten the terms of his contract with the mother. The mother—who was at odds with her daughter—complained to the committee. The court approved a finding of guilt and a six-month suspension from practice. *Questions*: What consideration did Dodd give in making an agreement with the young person for a larger fee? If she had not been "declared 21," would it nevertheless have been possible for her to bind herself to pay his fee? What precept of professional responsibility did Dodd violate? See Dodd v. Board of Comm'rs of Alabama State Bar, 350 So.2d 700 (Ala.1977).

(3) *The Jockey's Case.* Mike McDevitt was a jockey who had accepted employment from Shaw to drive a mare named Grace in the Kentucky Futurity. Stokes owned "relatives" of the mare, and stood to gain if she should win. Stokes promised McDevitt a bonus of $1,000 for riding in and winning the race. McDevitt won, but Stokes refused to pay, and McDevitt sued him. From judgment for the defendant on a demurrer to the plaintiff's complaint, the plaintiff appealed. *Held*: Affirmed. "To hold that [plaintiff] would not have won the race with Grace but for the agreement of [defendant] to pay him the $1,000 . . . would be to say that he would have been recreant to the obligation arising out of his employment by Shaw . . ." McDevitt v. Stokes, 174 Ky. 515, 192 S.W. 681 (1917). Does this case illustrate (to use Cardozo's words) "a promise by A. to B. to induce him not to break his contract with C."?

AUSTIN INSTRUMENT, INC. v. LORAL CORPORATION

Court of Appeals of New York, 1971.
29 N.Y.2d 124, 272 N.E.2d 533.

FULD, Chief Judge.[a] The defendant, Loral Corporation, seeks to recover payment for goods delivered under a contract which it had with the plaintiff Austin Instrument, Inc., on the ground that the evidence establishes, as a matter of law, that it was forced to agree to an increase in price on the items in question under circumstances amounting to economic duress.

a. Stanley H. Fuld (1903–) practiced law in New York City from 1926 to 1935 when he became assistant district attorney. In 1946 he was appointed to the New York Court of Appeals. He became chief judge in 1967 and served until 1974.

In July of 1965, Loral was awarded a $6,000,000 contract by the Navy for the production of radar sets. The contract contained a schedule of deliveries, a liquidated damages clause applying to late deliveries and a cancellation clause in case of default by Loral. The latter thereupon solicited bids for some 40 precision gear components needed to produce the radar sets, and awarded Austin a subcontract to supply 23 such parts. That party commenced delivery in early 1966.

In May, 1966, Loral was awarded a second Navy contract for the production of more radar sets and again went about soliciting bids. Austin bid on all 40 gear components but, on July 15, a representative from Loral informed Austin's president, Mr. Krauss, that his company would be awarded the subcontract only for those items on which it was low bidder. The Austin officer refused to accept an order for less than all 40 of the gear parts and on the next day he told Loral that Austin would cease deliveries of the parts due under the existing subcontract unless Loral consented to substantial increases in the prices provided for by that agreement—both retroactively for parts already delivered and prospectively on those not yet shipped—and placed with Austin the order for all 40 parts needed under Loral's second Navy contract. Shortly thereafter, Austin did, indeed, stop delivery. After contacting 10 manufacturers of precision gears and finding none who could produce the parts in time to meet its commitments to the Navy,[1] Loral acceded to Austin's demands; in a letter dated July 22, Loral wrote to Austin that "We have feverishly surveyed other sources of supply and find that because of the prevailing military exigencies, were they to start from scratch as would have to be the case, they could not even remotely begin to deliver on time to meet the delivery requirements established by the Government. . . . Accordingly, we are left with no choice or alternative but to meet your conditions."

Loral thereupon consented to the price increases insisted upon by Austin under the first subcontract and the latter was awarded a second subcontract making it the supplier of all 40 gear parts for Loral's second contract with the Navy.[2] Although Austin was granted until September to resume deliveries, Loral did, in fact, receive parts in August and was able to produce the radar sets in time to meet its commitments to the Navy on both contracts. After Austin's last delivery under the second subcontract in July, 1967, Loral notified it of its intention to seek recovery of the price increases.

On September 15, 1967, Austin instituted this action against Loral to recover an amount in excess of $17,750 which was still due on

1. The best reply Loral received was from a vendor who stated he could commence deliveries sometime in October.

2. Loral makes no claim in this action on the second subcontract.

the second subcontract. On the same day, Loral commenced an action against Austin claiming damages of some $22,250—the aggregate of the price increases under the first subcontract—on the ground of economic duress. The two actions were consolidated and, following a trial, Austin was awarded the sum it requested and Loral's complaint against Austin was dismissed on the ground that it was not shown that "it could not have obtained the items in question from other sources in time to meet its commitment to the Navy under the first contract." A closely divided Appellate Division affirmed (35 A.D.2d 387, 316 N.Y.S.2d 528, 532). There was no material disagreement concerning the facts; as Justice Steuer stated in the course of his dissent below, "[t]he facts are virtually undisputed, nor is there any serious question of law. The difficulty lies in the application of the law to these facts." (35 A.D.2d 392, 316 N.Y.S.2d 534.)

The applicable law is clear and, indeed, is not disputed by the parties. A contract is voidable on the ground of duress when it is established that the party making the claim was forced to agree to it by means of a wrongful threat precluding the exercise of his free will. . . . The existence of economic duress or business compulsion is demonstrated by proof that "immediate possession of needful goods is threatened" . . . or, more particularly, in cases such as the one before us, by proof that one party to a contract has threatened to breach the agreement by withholding goods unless the other party agrees to some further demand. . . . However, a mere threat by one party to breach the contract by not delivering the required items, though wrongful, does not in itself constitute economic duress. It must also appear that the threatened party could not obtain the goods from another source of supply [3] and that the ordinary remedy of an action for breach of contract would not be adequate.[4]

We find without any support in the record the conclusion reached by the courts below that Loral failed to establish that it was the victim of economic duress. On the contrary, the evidence makes out a classic case, as a matter of law, of such duress.[5]

3. See, e. g., Du Pont de Nemours & Co. v. J. I. Hass Co., 303 N.Y. 785, 103 N.E.2d 896, supra; Gallagher Switchboard Corp. v. Heckler Elec. Co., 36 Misc.2d 225, 226, 232 N.Y.S. 2d 590, 591, supra; 30 East End v. World Steel Prods. Corp., Sup., 110 N.Y.S.2d 754, 757.

4. See, e. g., Kohn v. Kenton Assoc., 27 A.D.2d 709, 280 N.Y.S.2d 520; Colonie Constr. Corp. v. De Lollo, 25 A.D.2d 464, 465, 266 N.Y.S.2d 283, 285; Halperin v. Wolosoff, 282 App. Div. 876, 124 N.Y.S.2d 572; J. R. Constr. Corp. v. Berkeley Apts., 259 App.Div. 830, 19 N.Y.S.2d 500; Boss v. Hutchinson, 182 App.Div. 88, 92, 169 N.Y.S. 513, 516.

5. The suggestion advanced that we are precluded from reaching this determination because the trial court's findings of fact have been affirmed by the Appellate Division ignores the question to be decided. That question, undoubtedly one of law (see Cohen and Karger, Powers of the New York Court of Appeals [1952], § 115, p. 492), is, accepting the facts found, did the courts below properly apply the law to them.

It is manifest that Austin's threat—to stop deliveries unless the prices were increased—deprived Loral of its free will. As bearing on this, Loral's relationship with the Government is most significant. As mentioned above, its contract called for staggered monthly deliveries of the radar sets, with clauses calling for liquidated damages and possible cancellation on default. Because of its production schedule, Loral was, in July, 1966, concerned with meeting its delivery requirements in September, October and November, and it was for the sets to be delivered in those months that the withheld gears were needed. Loral had to plan ahead and the substantial liquidated damages for which it would be liable, plus the threat of default, were genuine possibilities. Moreover, Loral did a substantial portion of its business with the Government, and it feared that a failure to deliver as agreed upon would jeopardize its chances for future contracts. These genuine concerns do not merit the label " 'self-imposed, undisclosed and subjective' " which the Appellate Division majority placed upon them. It was perfectly reasonable for Loral, or any other party similarly placed, to consider itself in an emergency, duress situation.

. . . [T]he parts needed for the October schedule were delivered in late August and early September. Even so, Loral had to "work . . . around the clock" to meet its commitments. Considering that the best offer Loral received from the other vendors it contacted was commencement of delivery sometime in October, which, as the record shows, would have made it late in its deliveries to the Navy in both September and October, Loral's claim that it had no choice but to accede to Austin's demands is conclusively demonstrated.

We find unconvincing Austin's contention that Loral, in order to meet its burden, should have contacted the Government and asked for an extension of its delivery dates so as to enable it to purchase the parts from another vendor. Aside from the consideration that Loral was anxious to perform well in the Government's eyes, it could not be sure when it would obtain enough parts from a substitute vendor to meet its commitments. The only promise which it received from the companies it contacted was for *commencement* of deliveries, not full supply, and, with vendor delay common in this field, it would have been nearly impossible to know the length of the extension it should request. It must be remembered that Loral was producing a needed item of military hardware. Moreover, there is authority for Loral's position that nonperformance by a subcontractor is not an excuse for default in the main contract. (See, e. g., McBride & Wachtel, Government Contracts, § 35.10, [11].) In light of all this, Loral's claim should not be held insufficiently supported because it did not request an extension from the Government.

Loral, as indicated above, also had the burden of demonstrating that it could not obtain the parts elsewhere within a reasonable time, and there can be no doubt that it met this burden. The 10 manufacturers whom Loral contacted comprised its entire list of "approved vendors" for precision gears and none was able to commence delivery soon enough.[6] As Loral was producing a highly sophisticated item of military machinery requiring parts made to the strictest engineering standards, it would be unreasonable to hold that Loral should have gone to other vendors, with whom it was either unfamiliar or dissatisfied, to procure the needed parts. As Justice Steuer noted in his dissent, Loral "contacted all the manufacturers whom it believed capable of making these parts" (35 A.D.2d at p. 393, 316 N.Y.S.2d at p. 534), and this was all the law requires.

It is hardly necessary to add that Loral's normal legal remedy of accepting Austin's breach of the contract and then suing for damages would have been inadequate under the circumstances, as Loral would still have had to obtain the gears elsewhere with all the concomitant consequences mentioned above. In other words, Loral actually had no choice, when the prices were raised by Austin, except to take the gears at the "coerced" prices and then sue to get the excess back.

Austin's final argument is that Loral, even if it did enter into the contract under duress, lost any rights it had to a refund of money by waiting, until July, 1967, long after the termination date of the contract, to disaffirm it. It is true that one who would recover moneys allegedly paid under duress must act promptly to make his claim known. . . . In this case, Loral delayed making its demand for a refund until three days after Austin's last delivery on the second subcontract. Loral's reason—for waiting until that time—is that it feared another stoppage of deliveries which would again put it in an untenable situation. Considering Austin's conduct in the past, this was perfectly reasonable, as the possibility of an application by Austin of further business compulsion still existed until all of the parts were delivered.

In sum, the record before us demonstrates that Loral agreed to the price increases in consequence of the economic duress employed by Austin. Accordingly, the matter should be remanded to the trial court for a computation of its damages.

The order appealed from should be modified, with costs, by reversing so much thereof as affirms the dismissal of defendant Loral Corporation's claim and, except as so modified, affirmed.

BERGAN, Judge (dissenting).

Whether acts charged as constituting economic duress produce or do not produce the damaging effect attributed to them is normally a routine type of factual issue.

6. Loral, as do many manufacturers, maintains a list of "approved vendors," that is, vendors whose products, facilities, techniques and performance have been inspected and found satisfactory.

Here the fact question was resolved against Loral both by the Special Term and by the affirmance at the Appellate Division. It should not be open for different resolution here. . . .

When the testimony of the witnesses who actually took part in the negotiations for the two disputing parties is examined, sharp conflicts of fact emerge. Under Austin's version the request for a renegotiation of the existing contract was based on Austin's contention that Loral had failed to carry out an understanding as to the items to be furnished under that contract and this was the source of dissatisfaction which led both to a revision of the existing agreement and to entering into a new one.

This is not necessarily and as a matter of law to be held economic duress. On this appeal it is needful to look at the facts resolved in favor of Austin most favorably to that party. Austin's version of events was that a threat was not made but rather a request to accommodate the closing of its plant for a customary vacation period in accordance with the general understanding of the parties.

Moreover, critical to the issue of economic duress was the availability of alternative suppliers to the purchaser Loral. . . .

Austin asserted and Loral admitted on cross-examination that there were many suppliers listed in a trade registry but that Loral chose to rely only on those who had in the past come to them for orders and with whom they were familiar. It was, therefore, at least a fair issue of fact whether under the circumstances such conduct was reasonable and made what might otherwise have been a commercially understandable renegotiation an exercise of duress.

The order should be affirmed.

BURKE, SCILEPPI and GIBSON, JJ., concur with FULD, C.J.

BERGAN, J., dissents and votes to affirm in a separate opinion in which BREITEL and JASEN, JJ., concur.

NOTES

(1) *Questions.* Suppose that Loral had renounced its agreement with Austin a year before it did, shortly after acceding to Austin's demands. Laying aside the problem of duress, would it have been justified in renouncing the price increases? Would it have been justified in renouncing the purchase order under the second Navy contract? What is the answer to these questions under the New York Gen.Obl.L. § 5–1103, p. 385 supra? What is the answer apart from such a statute?

(2) *Objective Standard?* Does the court apply the test for duress that the danger must have been sufficient to "overcome the mind of a person of ordinary firmness"? See Note, p. 380 supra. Holmes once remarked that to apply a requirement of ordinary courage in duress cases is "an attempt to apply an external standard of conduct in the wrong place." Silsbee v.

Webber, 171 Mass. 378, 50 N.E. 555 (1898).[a] And Holmes was usually insistent on objective criteria in the law.

(3) *Opposing Reflections.* There is a duty, it has been said, "to exercise superior bargaining power reasonably in a superior bargain situation." Wurtz v. Fleischman, 89 Wis.2d 291, 278 N.W.2d 266 (1979). And on the other hand: "it has been said wisely that contracts made under stress are a daily occurrence, and that if such urgency is to affect their validity, no one could safely negotiate with a party who finds himself in difficulty by virtue of financial adversities." Barker v. Walter Hogan Enterprises, Inc., 23 Wash.App. 450, 596 P.2d 1359 (1979). Does the main case mediate successfully between these observations? What cases do you find earlier in this chapter that might have been decided differently on the strength of one of them? What cases that were not reasoned in such terms, but might have been explained by reference to the law of duress?

(4) *The Government's Bargaining Power.* Simmonds Precision Products, Inc. was in default on several contracts to supply the government with aircraft parts and equipment. Concerned about the delays, the government sent an armed-services procurement officer to the Simmonds plant to investigate and negotiate new delivery dates. Simmonds' manager and general counsel resisted giving firm delivery dates as to the items already overdue, but yielded when the officer said he might have to put Simmonds' name on the so-called "Contractor Experience List," i. e., a list of those contractors whose capability must be evaluated prior to the award of any contract by the services.

Some of Simmonds' contracts provided for liquidated damages in the event of delays in delivery; others did not. One upshot of the negotiations was that all the contracts so provided. Ultimately the government withheld part of its payments on the strength of the new liquidated-damages terms.

Suing the government, Simmonds complained of duress—though not in relation to the damages clauses—and want of consideration in relation to them. The trial judge (whose recommended decision was adopted) observed that "the inclusion of a liquidated damages clause involves in its very nature an exchange of consideration since each party sacrifices an otherwise existing right to prove actual damages . . . and, in effect, settles in advance a potential future dispute." As to duress, he said: "Mere aggressiveness of a Government representative in pursuing his duties can hardly rise to the status of coercion."[b] Simmonds Precision Products, Inc. v. United States, 546 F.2d 886 (Ct.Cl.1976). *Question*: Which of these observations—taken out of context—is the more open to question?

(5) *Problem.* In wartime, when the national interest requires a program of rapid production of ships for the government, a large shipbuilding firm drives a hard bargain for its services, yielding immense profits. The government seeks later to reclaim part of its cost, charging the firm with duress. Is there a common-law remedy? Apart from making a one-sided bargain, what responses to the pressure might the government have made?

a. See also Rubenstein v. Rubenstein, 20 N.J. 359, 120 A.2d 11 (1956).

b. For a review of cases in which an official of the government has exerted sharp pressure on one of its contractors, see Urban Plumbing & Heating Co. v. United States, 408 F.2d 382 (Ct.Cl.1969).

Should the courts pass judgment on its choice of responses? When it seeks a judicial remedy for duress, is there any way for the courts to avoid passing such a judgment? See United States v. Bethlehem Steel Corp., 315 U.S. 289 (1952).

VICTIM'S OPTIONS

Some threats are so empty ("last opportunity to buy at this low price") that they cannot well amount to duress in a legal sense. In most cases where an issue of duress is fairly arguable, it has to be asked whether the victim of the threat was opportunistic in yielding to it, or might have resisted it and found a reasonably satisfactory remedy for any resulting injury. In the leading case on duress of goods, the defendant, a pawnbroker, argued that the plaintiff borrower might have gone to law to regain the property being wrongfully withheld from him. (Instead, he overpaid his debt to get it.) But the court said, "plaintiff might have had such an immediate want of his goods that an action of trover would not do his business." [a] Since then, allowance has regularly been made for the delay attendant on legal proceedings.[b]

If the threat is one to sue for a money judgment, the obvious mode of resistance is to make a defense. Some legal proceedings, however, such as mortgage foreclosure and body seizure, commonly put the debtor in a situation of greater urgency. Even so, he may have recourse to injunctive relief, or to damages for abuse of legal process. To forego such a remedy, in favor of a settlement, is naturally prejudicial to the debtor when he later complains of duress. Should the law insist on its preference that wrongful threats be met by resort to the courts? Professor Dawson observes that if the "freedom to litigate" is prized, to control abuses of it by injunction or tort recoveries impairs that freedom more directly than to do so through relief for duress. "The most that is sought," in the latter form, "is judicial review of a settlement, after surrender to the pressure. The object is neither to transfer nor to prevent losses but to cancel out the gain."[c]

a. Astley v. Reynolds, 2 Str. 915, 93 Eng.Rep. 939 (K.B.1732). See Goff and Jones, The Law of Restitution 148 ff. (1966).

b. E. g., Pecos Constr. Co. v. Mortgage Invest. Co. of El Paso, 80 N.M. 680, 459 P.2d 842 (1960); Ross Systems v. Linden Dari-Delite, 35 N.J. 329, 173 A.2d 258 (1961) ("no immediate and adequate remedy in the courts"). See also Silsbee v. Webber, 171 Mass. 378, 50 N.E. 555 (1898), as to the shortfall in the law of its own aspirations.

In a somewhat related connection, it has been said that "the notion of the arms' length transaction still requires that the 'arm' hold a boxing glove, rather than a mace." Roberts, J., dissenting in Fratto v. New Amsterdam Cas. Co., 434 Pa. 136, 252 A.2d 606, 609, 610 (1969).

c. Dawson, Duress Through Civil Litigation: I, 45 Mich.L.Rev. 571, 577 (1947).

NOTE

Problem. The company building the Alyeska pipeline let a contract to a newly-formed corporation to barge pipe from Houston to Alaska. Impediments were met in loading and sailing, which caused long delays, wrangling between the parties, and finally termination of the contract. The goods were offloaded at Long Beach. The carrier has presented bills for services of several hundreds of thousands of dollars. Prompt payment is required; the carrier's president believes that its creditors' demands will otherwise cause bankruptcy. Officials of Alyeska have negotiated with the carrier's attorney, and are prepared to offer it $100,000 in full settlement. If you were counsel to Alyeska, would you advise it that the carrier may not accept such a settlement and thereafter make a triable claim for further payment? See Totem Marine Tug & Barge v. Alyeska Pipeline Service Co., 584 P.2d 15 (Alaska, 1978) (summary judgment for Alyeska reversed). What distinctions are there between this case and Austin Instrument. Inc. v. Loral Corp? Compare National American Corp. v. Federal Republic of Nigeria, 448 F.Supp. 622, 644–45 (S.D.N.Y.1978), aff'd, 597 F.2d 314 (2d Cir. 1979).

"PAYMENT IN FULL"

Some of the law affecting claim settlements has been illustrated above (e. g., Fiege v. Boehm, p. 52 supra) and more is said on the subject in a Note at p. 412 infra. At this point we examine an aspect of the subject closely related to the materials of this section: the tender by a debtor of a payment that he designates as conclusive settlement of the account between him and the creditor. As will be seen, an important issue exists about the effect of the Uniform Commercial Code on this situation. The first step, however, is to appreciate the pre-Code law.

The primary line of argument about the situation was stated by Cardozo as follows, in Hudson v. Yonkers Fruit Co:[a] "A debtor paying his own money may couple the payment with such conditions as he pleases. . . . From this the rule has grown up in connection with the satisfaction of unliquidated demands that one who sends a check to another upon a condition explicitly declared, that the demand shall be extinguished or the check sent back unused, may hold the creditor to the condition, however embarrassing the choice." For a declaration of the condition it is usual for the debtor to inscribe a legend on the check. An example is given in the next main case: the debtor issued a check inscribed with appropriate words as follows: "this check when paid is accepted in full payment of the following account [designating the account for which the check was meant]." Whether it appears on the check or in a cover letter, the "condition explicitly declared" produces a settlement of the payee's claim when

a. 258 N.Y. 168, 179 N.E. 373, 80 A.L.R. 1052 (1932).

he accepts payment, if the case is otherwise within the rule stated by Cardozo. The procedure is widely used to deal with claims considered questionable. An insurance company, for example, might offer a "payment in settlement" when faced with what it regards as an inflated claim.[b] Or a tenant disputing a rent claim might deal with the landlord in that way.

NOTES

(1) *Pre-existing Duty.* If the sum offered is no more than what is concededly due, some courts would give the creditor leave to accept it without prejudice. Note that the rule as set out above supposes some uncertainty about the fact or the amount of the debtor's obligation: it is an "unliquidated demand" that creates an opportunity for him. In Hudson v. Yonkers Fruit Company, the case last cited, Cardozo said: "the condition is unlawful when what is paid is no more than must certainly be due. . . . The doctrine of accord and satisfaction by force of an assent that is merely constructive or imputed assumes as its foundation stone the existence of a condition lawfully imposed." *Questions*: What is the relation between this principle and the doctrine of Foakes v. Beer (p. 392 supra)? Does either of them necessarily entail the other?

(2) *Payment by Fiduciary.* Suppose this case: A lawyer has agreed to attempt collection of a client's claim, for a "reasonable" fee. Having collected the claim, the lawyer forwards a check to his client for 75% of the amount collected. In a cover letter he states that 25% is his usual charge and directs the client not to deposit the check if he considers the fee unreasonable. May the client deposit the check and call the attorney to account for any additional amount?

In Hudson v. Yonkers Fruit Company the defendant company had effected a sale of apples owned by Hudson, at his request. The company sent Hudson a check for 90% of the price along with a statement indicating a deduction of 10% as a commission. Hudson sued for the balance, contending that the company had agreed to find a buyer without charge, as a friendly accommodation. In affirming a judgment for Hudson the court said: "The defendant was not merely a debtor, paying its own money, which it would have been free to retain or to disburse according to its pleasure. It was an agent, a fiduciary, accounting for money belonging to its principal. . . . The law will not suffer an agent to withhold moneys collected for a principal's account by the pressure of a threat that no part of the moneys will be remitted to the owner without the approval of

b. An insurance company seeking to make a final settlement with an insured or a beneficiary under its insurance contract has frequently been held to owe a duty to act in good faith and to give the other party full information as to the effects of cashing the check. Kellogg v. Iowa State Traveling Men's Ass'n, 239 Iowa 196, 29 N.W.2d 559 (1947) ("the relationship between the parties is closely akin to a fiduciary one"). Compare Connell v. Provident Life & Acc. Ins. Co., 148 Tex. 311, 224 S.W.2d 194, 196 (1949) (insurer took exceptional care to inform the insured that the final draft, written on paper of a different color from the previous ones, was in final settlement, and check-cashing was deemed a final discharge) with Metropolitan Life Ins. Co. v. Richter, 173 Okl. 489, 49 P.2d 94 (1935) (routine "payment-in-full" endorsement on check was insufficient notice of finality).

deductions beneficial to the agent. Such conduct is a flagrant abuse of the opportunities and powers of a fiduciary position."[c]

(3) *Evading the Choice.* In cases where the debtor is free to condition his payment, and he makes the condition explicit enough, the rule of settlement has been exigently applied. In Toledo Edison Co. v. Roberts, 50 Ohio App. 74, 197 N.E. 500 (1934), the payee of a check tried to evade the choice, deposit or settle, by erasing a statement on the instrument; he failed.[d] But see Pederson v. First Nat. Bank of Nevada, 93 Nev. 388, 566 P.2d 89 (1977).

KIBLER v. FRANK L. GARRETT & SONS, INC.

Supreme Court of Washington, 1968.
73 Wash.2d 523, 439 P.2d 416.

[William Kibler harvested the wheat on 37 acres owned by Frank L. Garrett & Sons, Inc., under an agreement that he would be paid 18¢ a bushel, "and perhaps more, depending on the circumstances." He sent Garrett a bill for $826.20, calculated at 20¢ a bushel. He justified the price by reference to obstructions encountered in the fields. Garrett responded with a check for $444 ($12 an acre), and a covering letter explaining the basis for this figure ("50% more than we paid last year," etc.). The letter concluded: "Billing on this acreage for approximately $30 an acre is ridiculous." Kibler called his lawyer to ask if he could safely deposit the check. The lawyer asked him to read the notations on it. He read the typing on the check, including the notation, "Harvesting Wheat Washington Ranch." He did not read or notice a line of fine print as follows: "By endorsement this check when paid is accepted in full payment of the following account." On the lawyer's advice, Kibler deposited the check. Then he brought an action against Garrett for the difference between his bill and the amount of the check. The trial court dismissed the action, and the plaintiff appealed.]

c. As an alternate ground of decision the court ruled that the statement of account sent by the defendant with its check was insufficient to inform the plaintiff that he was being offered the check in full settlement of a disputed account.

d. Compare Palladi Realty Co. v. Ohlinger, 190 Md. 303, 58 A.2d 125 (1948). In that case the payee of a check, discontented with the terms on which it was offered, brought an action against the issuer. With the court's permission, the plaintiff negotiated the check to the court clerk, to be held "to the credit of the cause." The issuer contended that this maneuver amounted to an acceptance of his terms. From an adverse judgment he appealed. *Held:* Affirmed. Three of the appellate judges agreed with him. "The other three [were] equally firm in their view that the deposit of the check in court . . . was not a tortious exercise of dominion over the appellant's money. In view of this situation, the ruling of the chancellor on this point will be affirmed without discussion."

For another strategem for evading the choice see Roylex, Inc. v. S & B Engineers, Inc., 592 S.W.2d 59 (Tex. Civ.App.1979).

ROSELLINI, Judge. [The court first concluded that the letter did not contain an unequivocal statement that the check was to be payment in full.] Since there were no conditions attached to the acceptance of the check in this case, the letter was not an offer of an accord.

Was the condition sufficiently expressed on the check itself? It is unquestioned that the plaintiff did not see the fine print, and his attorney did not see it. The defendant's attorney did not notice it, apparently, until it was called to his attention at the trial. This was a form check, presumably used in the payment of all of the defendant's accounts, whether the payments made were payments in full or partial payments. There was nothing on the check to indicate that the language was particularly applicable to the plaintiff's claim. The trial court felt that the tone of the letter cast upon the plaintiff the duty to examine the check minutely or cash it at his peril. We do not agree. The burden is upon the party alleging an accord and satisfaction to show that there was indeed a meeting of the minds. See Brear v. Klinker Sand & Gravel Co., 60 Wash.2d 443, 374 P.2d 370 (1962). If the language contained in the fine print on the check was of significance in forming an accord, it must appear that the fact of its significance was brought to the plaintiff's attention. The evidence is to the contrary.

In the case of Washington Fish & Oyster Co. v. G. P. Halferty & Co., 44 Wash.2d 646, 269 P.2d 806 (1954), the respondent sued to recover the balance due on a contract. A partial payment had been made by a check with a voucher attached bearing a similar notation, accompanied by a detailed statement showing the "balance" as that amount which was contained in the check. This court held that the language on the check was of no significance, inasmuch as it was a form voucher apparently attached to all checks of the company. It is true that in that case the respondent had received checks previously from the company, presumably with the same form of voucher attached, and that in this case there was no evidence that the parties had had previous dealings, but we do not think that fact is determinative. It is the fact that the notation is obviously formal and applies to all payments made by check, whether or not they are intended as full payment, that renders the language ineffective, and also the fact that it is in print so small that no recipient can be presumed to have read it.

We hold that the proof in this case did not show an accord and satisfaction, since while the claim was disputed, there was no showing that the defendant manifested to the plaintiff his intention to pay no more than the amount which he remitted. To sustain the trial court would necessitate a holding that payment of an amount less than that claimed by the creditor operates as an accord and satisfaction if the amount paid is all that the debtor admits that he owes. This . . . would place a creditor at a disadvantage in accepting partial payments from a reluctant debtor, since by doing so he would be jeopardizing his right to receive the balance, even though in law that balance was in fact due him. It is true that the courts look with favor on compromise, but this means genuine compromise, arrived at through mutual agreement, and not compromise fallen into inadvertently.

The plaintiff's witnesses testified that the reasonable value of his services was close to the amount which he claimed was due him. The defendant did not present evidence on this question, since the court dismissed the action at the close of the plaintiff's case. As the record now stands, there is no evidence of overreaching on the part of the plaintiff.

The judgment is reversed and the cause remanded for a new trial.

[Three judges dissented, relying on the terms and circumstances of the letter alone.]

NOTE

Problem. A landlord cashed his tenant's monthly rent check, bearing the notation "Final and termination payment under the lease." The tenant had asserted the right to terminate the lease for inadequacy in the heat supply. Was the lease terminated by the landlord's conduct? See Kramas v. Beattie, 107 N.H. 321, 221 A.2d 236 (1966). Cf. Gottlieb v. Charles Scribner's Sons, 232 Ala. 33, 166 So. 685 (1936).

CODE EFFECT

As we have seen it appeared reasonably certain in pre-Code law that a person against whom an ordinary debt claim was asserted might put the claimant to a clear choice when the two of them had a well-founded dispute over the existence or the amount of the claim. On this clear scene UCC 1–207 cast a considerable cloud. When a check is marked, "payment in full of [specified] claim," the section suggests that the payee may escape the dilemma by adding a suitable rubric before cashing it. Some courts have given the section that effect. But the draftsmen did not signal a purpose to overthrow the settled rule and other purposes have been ascribed to the section.[a] The pre-Code rule may seem harsh; but persuasive arguments have been made that it is serviceable in the process of claim-adjustment.[b]

a. See Fritz v. Marantette, 404 Mich. 329, 273 N.W.2d 425 (1978)—a case in which the court avoided resolution of the issue, however. See also Hannah v. James A. Ryder Corp., 380 So.2d 507 (Fla.App.1980).

b. "Offering a check for less than the contract amount, but 'in full settlement' inflicts an exquisite form of commercial torture on the payee." R. Summers & J. White, The Uniform Commercial Code § 13–21 (1972).

NOTES

(1) *Scope of Section.* Whatever force UCC 1–207 has, there is doubt whether it (and some other Article 1 provisions) extend beyond situations otherwise governed by the Code. See Jahn v. Burns, 593 P.2d 828 (Wyo. 1979); Restatement Second, § 281, Reporter's Note to Comment d; Rosenthal, op. cit. supra n. b (comprehensive review of this and other problems associated with the section).

(2) *Question.* A credit-card issuer provides, in the agreement it exacts from cardholders: "We can accept . . . partial payments or checks . . . marked 'paid in full' without losing any of our rights under this Agreement." Effective?

(b) Concealment, Misrepresentation and Mistake

According to Chancellor Kent: "*Cicero de Officiis,* lib. 3. sec. 12–17, states the case of a corn merchant of Alexandria arriving at Rhodes in a time of great scarcity, with a cargo of grain, and with knowledge that a number of other vessels, with similar cargoes, had already sailed from Alexandria for Rhodes, and whom he had passed on the voyage. He then puts the question, whether the Alexandrine merchant was bound in conscience to inform the buyers of that fact, or to keep silence, and sell his wheat for an extravagant price; and he answers it by saying, that, in his opinion, good faith would require of a just and candid man, a frank disclosure of the fact."[a]

What is the requirement that the law makes, as opposed to the demand of conscience, for disclosing facts in a bargaining context? Many courts have said that they will not insist on the degree of disclosure that a person of exceptional scruple might make. On the other hand, in allowing bargaining advantages to be secured by persons of little scruple, the law may attach a competitive disadvantage to conscientious conduct.

"Perhaps one should balance against [that] the exquisite pleasure that the rule of the conditioned check has afforded to many aggrieved consumers." Rosenthal, Discord and Dissatisfaction, 78 Colum.L.Rev. 48, 56 (1978) [recommended reading—Wright, P. J., in Bivins v. White Dairy, 378 So.2d 1122, 1124 (Ala.App.1979), cert. denied, 378 So.2d 1125 (1980)].

a. 2 Kent's Commentaries 491 * n. c (3d ed. 1836). Kent cited Grotius, Puffendorf, and Pothier for the contrary opinion, but he added, "It is a little singular, however, that some of the best ethical writers under the Christian dispensation, should complain of the moral lessons of Cicero, as being too austere in their texture, and too sublime in speculation, for actual use."

Comparable problems continue to arise in the maritime trades. See United States v. Waterman S. S. Corp., 471 F.Supp. 87 (D.C.1979), concerning a vessel loading goods destined for Saigon in the closing days before its "fall" on April 29, 1975. The Government, which was responsible for paying the freight even if the vessel had to turn back, thought it had been imposed upon.

NOTES

(1) *Expert Knowledge.* Should there be special rules about information derived from research, training, and experience? It is generally understood that dealers in certain types of merchandise, such as antiques and rare coins, for example, trade on their expertness, and they are not expected to disclose to their customers all the elements that enter into their evaluations. The expense of acquiring such expertness would not be justified if it did not yield bargaining advantages. To some extent the same consideration affects the degree of disclosure required in most commercial exchanges. Compare the market expertness of middlemen, mentioned in Note 2, p. 377 supra.

The next main case is a suit in tort, for deceit, rather than in contract. It demonstrates, however, the wide extent of the privilege commonly allowed to keep silent about material facts in the bargaining process.

(2) *The Kidd Creek Strike.* The discovery of an extremely valuable ore deposit near Timmins, Ontario, touched off an immense number of trades. The finder, Texas Gulf Sulphur Company, detected the deposit through aerial searches for electromagnetic "anomalies." Having found one, it purchased mineral rights and options from landlowners in the vicinity. When the deposit was verified, but not publicly announced, officers of the firm made purchases of its stock. Some of the officers were successfully charged with violations of the securities laws, for wrongful use of "inside" information.[b] One of the landlowners sued the firm for wrongful use of its information in dealing with him: it had failed to disclose "an unusually promising indication of economic mineralization on [his] property." A justification for enforcing the option is given in Kronman, Mistake, Disclosure, Information, and the Law of Contracts, 7 J.Leg.Studies 1 (1978).[c]

Certain information, Professor Kronan argues, is "in essence a property right," at least when produced by a "deliberate search for socially useful information." The law tends (he says) to recognize such a right, and "not to recognize it where the information has been casually acquired"—so enhancing efficiency in resource allocation. Id. at 33.

SWINTON v. WHITINSVILLE SAV. BANK

Supreme Judicial Court of Massachusetts, 1942.
311 Mass. 677, 42 N.E.2d 808, 141 A.L.R. 965.

QUA, Justice. The declaration alleges that on or about September 12, 1938, the defendant sold the plaintiff a house in Newton to be

b. See S. E. C. v. Texas Gulf Sulphur Co., 446 F.2d 1301 (2d Cir. 1971), cert. denied, 404 U.S. 1005, reh. denied, 404 U.S. 1064. And the company itself was held accountable to former stockholders for its mismanagement of the news. Mitchell v. Texas Gulf Sulphur Co., 446 F.2d 90 (10th Cir. 1971), cert. denied, 404 U.S. 1004, reh. denied, 404 U.S. 1064.

c. The "landowner" was actually the corporate representative of a trust. For an account of the suit see M. Shulman, The Billion Dollar Windfall, Ch. 7 (1969). The case was settled, Professor Kronman reports.

occupied by the plaintiff and his family as a dwelling; that at the time of the sale the house "was infested with termites, an insect that is most dangerous and destructive to buildings"; that the defendant knew the house was so infested; that the plaintiff could not readily observe this condition upon inspection; that "knowing the internal destruction that these insects were creating in said house", the defendant falsely and fraudulently concealed from the plaintiff its true condition; that the plaintiff at the time of his purchase had no knowledge of the termites, exercised due care thereafter, and learned of them about August 30, 1940; and that, because of the destruction that was being done and the dangerous condition that was being created by the termites the plaintiff was put to great expense for repairs and for the installation of termite control in order to prevent the loss and destruction of said house.

There is no allegation of any false statement or representation, or of the uttering of a half truth which may be tantamount to a falsehood. There is no intimation that the defendant by any means prevented the plaintiff from acquiring information as to the condition of the house. There is nothing to show any fiduciary relation between the parties, or that the plaintiff stood in a position of confidence toward or dependence upon the defendant. So far as appears the parties made a business deal at arm's length. The charge is concealment and nothing more; and it is concealment in the simple sense of mere failure to reveal, with nothing to show any peculiar duty to speak. The characterization of the concealment as false and fraudulent of course adds nothing in the absence of further allegations of fact. Province Securities Corp. v. Maryland Casualty Co., 269 Mass. 75, 92, 168 S.E. 252.

If this defendant is liable on this declaration every seller is liable who fails to disclose any nonapparent defect known to him in the subject of the sale which materially reduces its value and which the buyer fails to discover. Similarly it would seem that every buyer would be liable who fails to disclose any nonapparent virtue known to him in the subject of the purchase which materially enhances its value and of which the seller is ignorant. See Goodwin v. Agassiz, 283 Mass. 358, 186 N.E. 659. The law has not yet, we believe, reached the point of imposing upon the frailties of human nature a standard so idealistic as this. That the particular case here stated by the plaintiff possesses a certain appeal to the moral sense is scarcely to be denied. Probably the reason is to be found in the facts that the infestation of buildings by termites has not been common in Massachusetts and constitutes a concealed risk against which buyers are off their guard. But the law cannot provide special rules for termites and can hardly attempt to determine liability according to the varying probabilities of the existence and discovery of different possible defects in the subjects of trade. The rule of nonliability for bare nondisclosure has been stated and followed by this court in [seven cases cited]. It is adopted in the American Law Institute's Restatement of Torts, § 551. See Williston on Contracts, Rev.Ed., §§ 1497, 1498, 1499.

The order sustaining the demurrer is affirmed, and judgment is to be entered for the defendant. Keljikian v. Star Brewing Co., 303 Mass. 53, 55–63, 20 N.E.2d 465.

So ordered.

NOTES

(1) *Questions.* Does it follow from this holding that the plaintiff could not have rescinded the sale, on establishing the facts he alleged? If the decision had been to the contrary, overruling the demurrer, would it follow that the plaintiff *could* have rescinded the sale? (An answer to this question is suggested by the next main case.) If the sale had not been executed, and the seller had brought an action against the buyer for specific performance, would it have succeeded?

(2) *Authorities.* Although the Swinton holding has been approved in several courts, there are some contrary decisions. For a twenty-page Annotation on the duty of a vendor to give information to a purchaser as to termite infestation, see 22 A.L.R.3d 972 (1968).

In Weintraub v. Krobatsch, 64 N.J. 445, 317 A.2d 68 (1974), concerning roach infestation of a home, the court said: "we are far from certain that [Swinton] represents views held by the current members of the Massachusetts court. See Kannavos v. Annino . . . [the case that follows]. In any event we are certain that it does not represent our sense of justice or fair dealing and it has understandably been rejected by persuasive opinions elsewhere."

For an extensive discussion of concealment problems see Ollerman v. O'Rourke Co., Inc., 288 N.W.2d 95 (Wis.1980).

(3) *Concealment and Stocks.* With respect to transactions in securities, Congress has committed a major role in protecting investors from deceptive "devices" to the Securities and Exchange Commission. In turn, the S. E. C. has formulated rules for identifying fraud, including omissions to disclose material facts. The effects of these rules must be studied in another course, but it may be observed here that corporate officials are expected to strike a nice balance between optimism and pessimism in preparing press releases. For a thoughtful set of opinions on this problem, see S. E. C. v. Great American Industries, Inc., 407 F.2d 453 (2d Cir. 1968), cert. denied 395 U.S. 920 (1969). One of the judges, referring to the main case, remarked: "The Securities and Exchange Commission, seeking to enjoin manipulation of such 'intricate merchandise' as securities . . ., should not be fettered by such a wholehearted embrace of the doctrine of caveat emptor." (Irving R. Kaufman, J., concurring, at 462, 463)

(4) *A Change of Career.* A religious congregation employed a man of the cloth to provide spiritual and educational leadership on the strength of two services he conducted, some conversations, and a sparse resume ("references on request"). Thereafter it transpired that he had been convicted for scheming to defraud an insurance company and had been disbarred as an attorney for bribing a police officer. In an action by the employer for re-

scission of the contract, summary judgment was granted for the plaintiff. See Jewish Center of Sussex County v. Whale, 165 N.J.Super. 84, 397 A.2d 712 (1978) (Concealment), aff'd 86 N.J. 619, 432 A.2d 52 (1981) (Misrepresentation).

KANNAVOS v. ANNINO

Supreme Judicial Court of Massachusetts, 1969.
356 Mass. 42, 247 N.E.2d 708.

[In 1961 or 1962, Mrs. Carrie Annino bought a one-family dwelling in Springfield: No. 11, Ingersoll Grove.[b] She converted it into a multi-family building with eight apartments, without obtaining a building permit, and in knowing violation of the city zoning ordinance. The house was in a "Residence A" district, where multi-family uses were prohibited. In 1965 a real-estate broker was employed to try to sell the property. He placed newspaper ads, of which the following is an example: "Income gross $9,600 yr in lg. single house, converted to 8 lovely, completely furn. (includ. TV and china) apts. 8 baths, ideal for couple to live free with excellent income. By apt. only. Foote Realty."

[Apostolos Kannavos read one of the ads, and got in touch with the broker, Foote. Foote showed him the house, and gave him income and expense figures supplied by Mrs. Annino. Without the aid of a lawyer, Kannavos contracted to buy the property, and did so, borrowing money from a bank for the purpose, and giving it a mortgage. At the closing, attorneys for the seller and for the mortgagee were present, and the latter prepared the papers. Mrs. Annino and Foote knew that Kannavos' reason for buying was to rent the apartments. He was unaware of any zoning or building permit violation, and would not have purchased the property if he had known of any such violation. It was worth substantially less if operated only as a single-family dwelling than it was as an apartment building.

[Soon after the sale, the city started legal proceedings to abate the non-conforming use of the building.[c] Kannavos brought a bill in

---

a. Asserting his competence as a rabbi, the defendant argued that his concealment had caused no damage; but the court said that "where fraud is found damage may be presumed." But in somewhat comparable cases that proposition is not entirely reliable. See N.Y.Ins.L. § 149(2): "No misrepresentation shall avoid any contract of insurance or defeat recovery thereunder unless such misrepresentation was material." See also Earl v. Saks & Co., 36 Cal.2d 602, 226 P.2d 340 (1951) for a fascinating problem in business morality, and a comment on the case in E. Cahn, The Moral Decision 123 ff. (1959 paperback edition).

b. Throughout the transactions described, Mrs. Annino acted as the authorized agent for the Annino Realty Trust. Her co-defendants, not mentioned hereafter, were Samuel Annino and Joseph Santospirito.

c. As to other, similar properties that Kannavos (and an associate) also bought from Mrs. Annino, the city also asserted violations of the building code, but the opinion does not make it clear whether or not No. 11 was in question on this score.

equity against Mrs. Annino to rescind the purchase. The trial court overruled a demurrer, and granted rescission on the basis of findings by a master. Mrs. Annino appealed.

[It appeared that Kannavos had immigrated from Greece in 1957, when he was about thirty years old. In this country he had learned English, and become a self-employed hairdresser. It was found that he made no inquiry of anyone about zoning or building permits before or during the closing, and that no statements were made to him on these subjects. Everything that was said to him by or on behalf of the seller was substantially true.]

CUTTER, Justice. . . . We assume that, if the vendors had been wholly silent and had made no references whatsoever to the use of the Ingersoll Grove houses, they could not have been found to have made any misrepresentation. See Swinton v. Whitinsville Sav. Bank, 311 Mass. 677, 678–679, 42 N.E.2d 808, 141 A.L.R. 965,[1] where this court affirmed an order sustaining a demurrer to a declaration in an action of tort brought by a purchaser of a house. . . . The court (p. 679) indicated that it was applying a long standing "rule of nonliability for *bare nondisclosure*" (emphasis supplied).

As in the *Swinton* case, the parties here were dealing at arm's length, the vendees were in no way prevented from acquiring information, and the vendors stood in no fiduciary relationship to the vendees. In two aspects, however, the present cases differ from the *Swinton* case: viz. (a) The vendees themselves could have found out about the zoning violations by inquiry through public records, whereas in the *Swinton* case the purchaser would have probably discovered the presence of termites only by retaining expert investigators; and (b) there was something more here than the "bare nondisclosure" of the seller in the *Swinton* case.

(a) We deal first with the affirmative actions by the vendors, their conduct, advertising, and statements. Was enough said and done by the vendors so that they were bound to disclose more to avoid deception of the vendees and reliance by them upon a half truth? In other words, did the statements made by the vendors in their advertising and otherwise take the cases out of the "rule of nonliability for bare nondisclosure" applied in the *Swinton* case?

Although there may be "no duty imposed upon one party to a transaction to speak for the information of the other . . . if he

1. The *Swinton* case may not represent the law elsewhere. See Restatement 2d: Torts, § 551 (Tent. Draft No. 11, April 15, 1965), p. 43; Prosser, Torts (3d ed.), § 101, p. 711. Cf. discussions of situations in landlord and tenant cases like Cutter v. Hamlen, 147 Mass. 471, 474, 18 N.E. 397, 1 L.R.A. 429; Stumpf v. Leland, 242 Mass. 168, 172–174, 136 N.E. 399; Cooper v. Boston Housing Authy., 342 Mass. 38, 40, 172 N.E.2d 117. For general consideration of silence as misrepresentation, see Restatement: Restitution, § 8; Williston, Contracts (2d ed.) § 1497.

does speak with reference to a given point of information, voluntarily or at the other's request, he is bound to speak honestly and to divulge all the material facts bearing upon the point that lie within his knowledge. Fragmentary information may be as misleading . . . as active misrepresentation, and half-truths may be as actionable as whole lies . . . ." See Harper & James, Torts, § 7.14. See also Restatement: Torts, § 529; Williston, Contracts (2d ed.) §§ 1497–1499. The existence of substantially this principle was assumed in the *Swinton* case, 311 Mass. 677, 678, 42 N.E.2d 808, 141 A.L.R. 965, in the first sentence of the passage from that case quoted above. Massachusetts decisions have applied this principle. See Kidney v. Stoddard, 7 Metc. 252, 254–255 (a father represented that his son was entitled to credit but failed to disclose that the son was a minor; statement treated as a fraudulent representation); Burns v. Dockray, 156 Mass. 135, 137, 30 N.E. 551 (assertion that title was good [see Lyman v. Romboli, 293 Mass. 373, 374, 199 N.E. 916] but omitting to refer to the possible insanity of one whose incompetence might cloud title); Van Houten v. Morse, 162 Mass. 414, 417–419, 38 N.E. 705, 26 L.R.A. 430 (partial disclosure by a woman to her financé about a prior divorce). See also . . . Boston Five Cents Sav. Bank v. Brooks, 309 Mass. 52, 55–56, 34 N.E.2d 435, 437 ("Deception need not be direct . . .. Declarations and conduct calculated to mislead . . . which . . . do mislead one . . . acting reasonably are enough to constitute fraud"). Cf. Wade v. Ford Motor Co., 341 Mass. 596, 597–598, 171 N.E.2d 282.

The master's report provides ample basis for treating the present cases as within the decisions just cited. The original advertisements in effect offered the houses as investment properties and referred to them as single houses converted to apartments. The investment aspect of the houses was emphasized by Foote's action in furnishing income and expense figures. There was an express assertion that 11 Ingersoll Grove was "being rented to the public for multi-family purposes" and that Kannavos and Bellas "could continue to operate . . . [the other properties] as multi-dwelling property." The master's conclusions indicate that this statement applied to all the properties.[2] The buildings were divided into apartments. The sales included refrigerators, stoves, and other furnishings appropriate for apartment use as well as real estate. The vendors knew that the vendees were planning to continue to use the buildings for apartments, and yet the vendors still failed to disclose the zoning and building violations. We conclude that enough was done affirmatively to make the disclosure inadequate and partial, and, in the circumstances, intentionally deceptive and fraudulent.

2. In any event some discussions with respect to all these properties in the same neighborhood were going on about the same time and the later transaction appears to have been commenced either before or about the time the earlier one was completed.

(b) The second difference between these cases and the *Swinton* case is the character of the defect not disclosed.

In the *Swinton* case, the presence of predatory insects threatened the structure sold. In the absence of any seller's representations whatosever, there was no duty to disclose this circumstance, even though doubtless it would have been difficult to discover. In the present cases, the defect in the premises related to a matter of public regulation, the zoning and building ordinances. Its applicability to these premises could have been discovered by these vendees or by the vendees' counsel if, acting with prudence, they had retained counsel, which they did not. The bank mortgagee's counsel presumably was looking only to the protection of the bank's security position. Nevertheless, where there is reliance on fraudulent representations or upon statements and action treated as fraudulent, our cases have not barred plaintiffs from recovery merely because they "did not use due diligence . . . [when they] could readily have ascertained from . . . records" what the true facts were. See Yorke v. Taylor, 332 Mass. 368, 373, 124 N.E.2d 912. There this court allowed rescission because of the negligent misrepresentation, innocent but false, of the current assessed value of the property being sold. Here the representations made by the advertising and the vendors' conduct and statements in effect were that the property was multi-family housing suitable for investment and that the housing could continue to be used for that purpose. Because the vendors did as much as they did do, they were bound to do more. Failing to do so, they were responsible for misrepresentation. We think the situation is comparable to that in Yorke v. Taylor, 332 Mass. 368, 374, 124 N.E.2d 912, even though there the misrepresentation was "not consciously false" and here it was by half truth.

We hold that the vendors' conduct entitled the vendees to rescind. See Yorke v. Taylor, 332 Mass. 368, 371–372, 374, 124 N.E.2d 912; Restatement: Contracts, §§ 472, 489; Restatement: Restitution, § 28; Williston, Contracts (2d ed.) §§ 1497–1500. There was, in our opinion, much more than "bare nondisclosure" as in the *Swinton* case. Cf. Spencer v. Gabriel, 328 Mass. 1, 2, 101 N.E.2d 369; Donahue v. Stephens, 342 Mass. 89, 92, 172 N.E.2d 101.

[The court affirmed the decree below overruling the demurrer. However, it reversed the final decree so that there might be further consideration of the relief, in view of a fire that had occurred at No. 11 after that decree.][a]

a. For covering odors in a home caused by animal urine it seems that scented candles and other deodorizers may be helpful. Should a prospective buyer, making an inspection, be on guard against these devices? See Campbell v. Booth, 526 S.W.2d 167 (Tex.Civ.App.1975), writ ref. n. r. e. An amusing way to represent a home as having a fireplace is to construct one of newspaper and paint it black. Lantner v. Carson, 374 Mass. 606, 373 N.E.2d 973 (1978). See also Nordstrom v. Miller, 605 P.2d 545 (Kan. 1980).

NOTES

(1) *Question.* Does it follow from this decision that Kannavos could have maintained an action in deceit against Mrs. Annino? The requisites of that action, and the remedy it affords, are dealt with in detail in courses on torts. It should be noted, however, that contract remedies are not the only guarantees of minimum decencies in the bargaining process.

(2) *Sales Talk.* Consider the following cases, briefly sketched, as problems in assigning responsibility for a buyer's disappointment to the seller. What variables do they present? How would the Massachusetts court have decided them? (In two of them damages—not rescission—was sought.)

(a) X contracted to buy property from A, but avoided the contract by suit when he found that a "well" on the property was dry. A then put the property in the hands of a broker, who arranged a contract with B. When B first looked at the property the broker told him, on inquiry, that "he didn't know much about" the well. The A-to-B sale contract recited that the well was not guaranteed and that B did not rely on any representations of A concerning the property. Contract voidable at B's instance for disappointment over the well? See Bodenhamer v. Patterson, 278 Or. 367, 563 P.2d 1212 (1977).

(b) Answering a dealer's ad, C bought a used car after a test drive. The salesman had told him it was air-conditioned (repeating a statement in the ad), "and that Chrysler was a nice car and all that jazz." Contract voidable by C when he learns that the knobs marked "air" are for ventilation only? See Williams v. Rank & Son Buick, Inc., 44 Wis.2d 239, 170 N.W.2d 807 (1969) (fraud action; 4–3 decision).

(c) Having inherited a residence, S showed it for sale to P who lived nearby. S said, "these are good, sound buildings and they will make you a good investment." P bought the property without taking other advice. He later found there was serious damage, owing to general termite infestation. Whether or not S knew of the fault was disputed in evidence presented to a jury; P testifed that he had never heard of a termite. Contract voidable by P, if the jury believes his evidence? See Maser v. Lind, 181 Neb. 365, 148 N.W.2d 831, 22 A.L.R.3d 965 (1967).

MISREPRESENTATION

Misrepresentation is a ground for rescinding a contract, closely related to concealment. As a predicate for a tort action, it may be necessary for the plaintiff to establish that the defendant made the misrepresentation knowing it to be false, or at least with reckless disregard for its truth. This element in deceit actions is known as *scienter*. The requirement was insisted on in 19th century English cases, and remains influential in many courts.[a] In contract law it

a. See Jo Ann Homes at Bellmore, Inc. v. Dworetz, 25 N.Y.2d 112, 250 N.E. 2d 214 (1969).

generally has never had the same force, owing partly to the equitable character of rescission. See Halpert v. Rosenthal, 107 R.I. 406, 267 A.2d 730 (1970), a "termite case" making the distinction. As a rule, a party to a contract may avoid it if the other party obtained his assent by an innocent misrepresentation, i. e., one that the party making it believed to be true. What difference between the functions of tort and contract law might explain this difference in sensitivity to the nature of a falsehood?

In both tort and contract law relief for misrepresentation is restricted in some ways that merit at least a mention. (To the extent that they are distinctive, the principles of tort law will not be pursued here.)

It has sometimes been held that a misrepresentation of law is innocuous. The same thought underlies the view that *mistake* of law is not a ground for relief: everyone should know the law. Apart from the general discredit that has fallen on such reasoning, its influence on misrepresentation cases has been limited in practice. One reason is that the author of a misrepresentation of law is frequently one better placed to know the law than the victim of it is: a lawyer speaking to his client, an insurance agent to a customer, and so on. In such cases the inequality of competence is perceived as a reason for giving relief.

A misrepresentation of opinion, as opposed to one of fact, is not a ground for relief, by tradition.[b] Doubtless the distinction retains considerable force as it affects ordinary "puffing" of the style, "This property is worth every cent I am asking for it." Yet the distinction has lost much of its clarity, as witness the foregoing note case in which the seller's statement was: "these are good, sound buildings and they will make you a good investment." Again, the relative positions of the parties may influence the decision more than the form of words that was used.

The misrepresentation must be a material one. This requirement is prominent in insurance litigation, where a misrepresentation by a policy buyer relating to his health is a commonplace ground for rejecting a claim. A policy of medical expense insurance, for example, was voidable because the application for it omitted reference to various prior occasions of hospital treatment, including one for angina pectoris. As to the applicant's prior treatment for an infected toenail, however, the judges thought that the misrepresentation was immaterial.[c] Various standards of materiality have been expressed, and

b. See Fifty Associates v. Prudential Insurance Co. of America, 450 F.2d 1007 (9th Cir. 1971) (appraisal of property value).

In George Backer Management v. Acme Quilting Co., 46 N.Y.2d 211, 413 N.Y. S.2d 135, 385 N.E.2d 1062 (1978), it was said that an expression not relating to "a concrete fact or a past or existing event" cannot form the basis for a claim of misrepresentation.

c. Delaney v. Prudential Ins. Co., 29 Wis.2d 345, 139 N.W.2d 48 (1966).

none of them is applied uniformly. They serve the common function, however, of justifying a certain control by judges over the more volatile behavior of juries.

When a contract is enforced in favor of a party who made a misrepresentation, a reason sometimes given is that the other party was negligent in relying on it.[d] Naturally, the degree of diligence required of a party in detecting a falsehood is a function partly of his capacities, partly of the nature of the transaction, and partly of the plausibility of the representation. The question of diligence should be distinguished from the question whether any credence was placed in the representation at all. If it was not relied upon in that sense, no legal consequences follow from a misrepresentation. There can be no complaint about a statement by one who heard it and proceeded to satisfy himself about its accuracy: "reliance and verification are incompatible."[e] There is a necessary dimension in a complaint about misrepresentation, however, that goes beyond the fact of reliance. In the currently preferred formulation, the complainant must show *justifiable* reliance.

Other limitations on relief for misrepresentation mentioned above, notably those having to do with statements of law and statements of opinion, have been considerably relaxed, if not subsumed entirely under the issue last mentioned. There is a plain tendency to consider the character of the statement in question as only one aspect of the broader issue whether or not the complainant justifiably relied upon it.

NOTES

(1) *The Olds Man's Case.* James Gour was an "Oldsmobile man" for 20 years. The seventh Olds he bought proved to have an engine manufactured by the Chevrolet division of General Motors—a fact that Gour learned only after driving it for 17,000 miles. He then sued GM and the dealer for annulment of the sale and for damages. On appeal, a judgment in his favor was affirmed, as amended. Gour v. Daray Motor Co., Inc., 373 So.2d 571 (La.App.1979). The judgment was based on the state's "baby F.T.C. act"; it included an attorney's fee of $2,000 and a price recovery, offset by a credit for Gour's use of the car at the rate of 8¢ a mile. The statute provides for class actions to redress violations, brought by the state attorney

d. Or that he simply did not believe it. See Williams v. Van Hersh, 578 S.W. 2d 373 (Tenn.App.1978), cert. denied (1979), "wherein the plaintiff testified that he contracted to purchase real property for $1,100,000 in reliance on the verbal assurance of a real estate agent that a named insurance company would lend to some unnamed party $6,000,000 for the development of the property, at some unknown time, due at some unknown date, at an unknown rate of interest and under unknown conditions that any such lender might attach to the development. The claim of the plaintiff that he relied upon such false assurance is incredible."

e. Hayat Carpet Cleaning Co., Inc. v. Northern Assur. Co., 69 F.2d 805 (2d Cir. 1934) (L. Hand).

general, in which "actual damages" may be recovered, but not restitution.[f] *Question*: Is there a special reason for permitting restitutionary relief for an individual claimant?

In dictum, the court said that Gour had made out a rescission claim apart from the statute. The engine bore an eye-catching decal marked "Oldsmobile." The trial court credited evidence that the car salesman had said to Gour, "we have, in here, a Chevrolet engine"; but it found also that Gour did not hear, or get the message, being busy checking options on the car. On these findings was the case one of misrepresentation or of concealment? Is the answer the same for Daray Motor Company and for GM?

(2) *The Case of the Low Dive.* In June, 1976, Robert Gardner took possession of the Punjab Tavern under a contract to purchase it from Jon Meiling. He soon learned that it had a reputation for being rowdy, and was not a place to take a female companion. Moreover, he learned that the gross income for a recent three-month period had been less than half the amount stated to him in May. On May 20 Gardner had been present when Meiling reported inflated figures to an investigator for the state liquor control commission, with a view to transferring the liquor license. Gardner's payments for the business had been arranged as follows: $1,000 paid in February as earnest money, $7,000 paid on change of possession, and $32,000 in installments. The written agreement of sale had been executed on March 15. Gardner's discoveries in June led him to sue Meiling for rescission of the sale and recovery of his $8,000 payments. Meiling counterclaimed for unpaid installments of the purchase price: $4,000. From a decree of rescission, Meiling appealed. *Held:* Reversed. Gardner v. Meiling, 280 Or. 665, 572 P.2d 1012 (1977). The court found no evidence of assertions by Meiling or his selling agent about the tavern's reputation, good or bad. There was evidence that ¾ths of the purchase price was allocated to "good will"; but it appeared that Gardner had based his offering price on matters such as inspections and "keggage reports." As for any misrepresentation about income, the court ruled that it came after the formation of a binding contract—too late to count. There was, to be sure, a "contingency" clause in the March contract. It provided for nullifying the sale if Gardner should fail to obtain all the licenses he needed to conduct the business. (Otherwise agreement to be null and void, and unexpended earnest money returned.) As to this the court said: "[It] was not a condition precedent to the agreement of sale being made but was a condition upon which performance of the agreed terms was contingent."

Gardner's claim of misrepresentation failed for want of reliance. His claim of mistake failed because Meiling had no reason to suppose Gardner was mistaken, on the date of contracting, about the income or reputation of the business. (The court distinguished the case of a bid on a public contract, so low that it would "put the public body on notice" of a mistake in calculation.)

Question: Taking this decision as sound, do you consider that the law attaches too little importance to the morality of candor, and too much to the moment of contracting?[g] (In dictum the court said that the earnest-money

f. The opinion describes proceedings of the Federal Trade Commission with respect to alleged deceptive practices by GM.

g. For a somewhat different balancing see Bursey v. Clement, 118 N.H. 412, 387 A.2d 346 (1978), and Lockard v. Carson, 287 N.W.2d 871 (Iowa 1980).

agreement of February released Meiling from duties of disclosure.) Gardner had been a school teacher who approached Meiling through a business broker, and the broker had explained to him some of the pitfalls of tavern operations. Should that matter?

(3) *Insurance Law.* The doctrines of concealment and misrepresentation have somewhat specialized application to insurance cases. When an applicant for life insurance is asked whether or not he uses alcohol to excess, the response is likely to be treated as a "matter of opinion," so that all the insurer is entitled to is an honest expression of the applicant's view. In this fashion, and in others more or less direct, it is often made a requirement that the insurer show scienter in order to avoid the contract. See, for instance, Metropolitan Life Ins. Co. v. Fugate, 313 F.2d 788 (5th Cir. 1963): "In his own mind, the decedent may have thought that he was not suffering from alcoholism." But in this case the policy, a contract of life insurance, was avoided because the applicant had actively concealed medical treatments for his affliction. The court said: "There is no room for opinion about the hospital visits."

As to concealment it has been said, in an influential case: "[I]f a man, about to fight a duel, should obtain life insurance without disclosing his intention, it would seem that no argument or additional evidence would be needed to show the fraudulent character of the non-disclosure. On the other hand, where men may reasonably differ as to the materiality of a fact concerning which the insurer might have elicited full information, and did not do so, the insurer occupies no such position of disadvantage in judging of the risk as to make it unjust to require that before the policy is avoided it shall appear, not only that the undisclosed fact was material, but also that it was withheld in bad faith."[h]

CONFIDENTIAL RELATIONS

In attempting to avoid contracts on the ground of overreaching, the key to success often lies in establishing that a relation of trust and confidence existed between the parties, so that the bargain was not an arm's length transaction. In the absence of such a relation, it is said, fraud must be affirmatively shown, and will not be presumed. Furthermore, it is the tradition derived from equity practice that the evidence required to establish fraud must be "clear and convincing"—meeting a more exacting standard than that applied to most issues in civil litigation.

By contrast, when a confidential relation existed, and the party asserting rights under the contract is the one in whom confidence was reposed, he is required to show that the bargain was "fair, conscientious, and beyond the reach of suspicion." Young v. Kaye, 443

Compare Hauben v. Harmon, 605 F.2d 920 (5th Cir. 1979) (concealment; divided court).

h. Taft, Cir. J., in Penn Mutual Life Ins. Co. v. Mechanics Savings Bank & Trust Co., 72 F. 413 (6th Cir. 1896); on rehearing, 73 F. 653 (1896).

Pa. 335, 279 A.2d 759 (1971). In this case, representative of many like it, an elderly man was imposed upon by an ex-convict who provided him services and won his confidence as a "tax consultant." As examples of confidential relations, the court mentioned guardian and ward, principal and agent, attorney and client. Beyond such routine entries, however, the list is not pre-determined. A "confidential relation" does not necessarily attend a friendship, or even a marriage; [a] yet an automobile dealer and his customer have been found to be in that relation, with respect to an arcane feature of their dealings.[b] "It is not restricted to any specific association . . . but is deemed to exist whenever the relative position of the parties is such that one has power and means to take advantage of or exert undue influence over the other." [c]

NOTES

(1) *The Case of the Confiding Clerk.* Some factors of particular relevance in identifying a confidential relationship are said to be "disparity of age, education and business experience between the parties." These were found to exist when Peter Roberts, a minor, assigned to Sears, Roebuck & Company all rights in an invention of his for a royalty not to exceed $10,000. Roberts relied on Sears' advice about the value of the invention, and on the advice of an attorney who (without informing Roberts) also accepted employment from Sears. There was evidence that in less than two years Sears made "an incremental profit of $44,032,082 from the sales of its wrenches with Roberts' quick release feature." When negotiating with him, Sears "downgraded" the value of the invention, though it had formed a high opinion of its merit.[d]

In a suit by Roberts, jury verdicts were held to justify relief against Sears. (What relief seems suitable)? Both parties appealed from a judgment for a million dollars. *Held*: Reversed in part, and remanded. Roberts v. Sears, Roebuck & Co., 573 F.2d 976 (7th Cir. 1978), cert. denied, 439 U.S. 860. In approving the jury's finding of a confidential relationship, the court thought it significant that Roberts had submitted his idea to Sears while working for it as a sales clerk. (Sears' negotiating attorney, it seems, may not have been aware of that).

What changes in Sears' procedure with ideas would you suggest? Should it have disclosed to Roberts that it anticipated sales which would more than recapture its royalty costs in one year?

a. Eaton v. Sontag, 387 A.2d 33 (Me. 1978); Francois v. Francois, 599 F.2d 1286 (3d Cir. 1979).

b. Browder v. Hanley Dawson Cadillac, 62 Ill.App.3d 623, 20 Ill.Dec. 138, 379 N.E.2d 1206 (1978).

c. Young v. Kaye, supra. See also Ruggieri v. West Forum Corp., 444 Pa. 175, 282 A.2d 304 (1971), as to trust reposed in a son by his parents, and Gordon v. Bialystoker Center & Bikur Cholim, Inc., 45 N.Y.2d 692, 412 N.Y.S.2d 593, 385 N.E.2d 285 (1978), as to nursing home and patient (gift case).

d. Some of the facts recited here are drawn from an opinion in the case on remand: Roberts v. Sears, Roebuck and Co., 471 F.Supp. 372 (N.D.Ill. 1979). Further proceedings are reported at: 473 F.Supp. 372 (1979), remanded 617 F.2d 460 (1980), cert. denied 449 U.S. 975 (1980), reh. denied 449 U.S. 1105 (1981).

(2) *The Case of the Confiding Cook.* In Wolf v. Brungardt, 215 Kan. 272, 524 P.2d 726 (1974), the owner of a business in bad financial condition found an investor and business partner in a 19-year-old employee of a Pizza Hut. In failing to disclose a major bank obligation of the business, the owner was found to have violated a fiduciary responsibility to the young man. In such a relationship, the court said, "the duty of due diligence to discover the true facts is reduced." *Questions*: Did the ordinary requirement of prudence apply *before* the partnership was formed? If so, how could the court's observation help sustain any remedy for the junior partner?

MISTAKE

Like concealment and misrepresentation, mistake is sometimes a ground for rescinding a contract. Mistakes in the computation and communication of prices have been explored in Chapter 2. A kind of mistake that may be described as misunderstanding is to be examined in Chapter 7. At this point, by contrast, we consider mistakes having to do with the relative advantages of the bargain as between the parties. The configuration of the law on this subject somewhat resembles that of the law relating to concealment and misrepresentation, the most notable difference being that the element of fault is less prominent in mistake cases.[a]

One limitation commonly placed on relief for mistake, when the relief sought is avoidance of a contract, is that the mistake must be "mutual", i. e., common to the parties. Examples may be found of relief for unilateral mistake, but they are somewhat exceptional. In a concealment case, there is invariably a unilateral mistake. However, in the usual case of that type the party charged with concealment is aware, or should be, that the other party is less well informed than he is. By contrast, the assumption in a "pure" mistake case is that each party supposed the other to be equally informed about the material facts.

A second limitation on relief has to do with the character of the mistake, in relation to the transaction. The operative word, in some formulations of the rule, is "basic".[b] Or it is said that the parties must have been mistaken in an essential point, or that the mistake

a. "The legal concept of 'mistake' is similar to the legal concept of 'misrepresentation' in that, under each, a party to a contract may be relieved from his obligations if he was unaware of certain material facts. 'Mistake', however, is only such error as is made without representation or deception by the other party to the transactions." Leasco Corp. v. Taussig, 473 F.2d 777 (2d Cir. 1972) (no case for relief on either ground).

b. See Restatement Second, § 152: "mistake . . . as to a basic assumption on which the contract was made"; Raddue v. Le Sage, 138 Cal. App.2d 852, 292 P.2d 522 (1956); Reliance Finance Corp. v. Miller, 557 F. 2d 674, 678–81 (9th Cir. 1977).

The Restatement Second formulation was relied on in Covich v. Chambers, 397 N.E.2d 1115 (Mass.App.1979).

must go to the root of the contract. Something more than materiality is implied. If it is concluded that the parties to a contract entered into it under a mistake about a fact so basic as to justify rescission, it would therefore follow that if one party had misrepresented that fact to the other the victim would have had no difficulty, on the score of materiality, in obtaining relief. The converse is not entailed: the subject of a mistake may not be regarded as fundamental to the bargain resulting from it, although it would be characterized as deceit for either party to *induce* a mistake on the point in the mind of the other party.

Identifying basic mistake is sometimes a nice problem of judgment: "In the vital areas the answer will depend upon the magnitude of the mistake, the degree of certainty in the minds of the parties, and the attitude towards the type of transaction involved."[c] A celebrated case of avoidance is Sherwood v. Walker, 66 Mich. 568, 33 N.W. 919 (1887), in which the parties were a cattle breeder, Walker, and a banker, Sherwood. Walker sold Sherwood a cow of distinguished ancestry named Rose 2d of Aberlone. Rose went for $80 because both parties believed that she was sterile. When Walker discovered that Rose was pregnant and therefore worth between $750 and $1000, he refused to deliver her and Sherwood sued in replevin. Judgment for plaintiff was reversed on appeal. "If there is a difference or misapprehension as to the substance of the thing bargained for . . . and intended to be sold, then there is no contract; but if it be only a difference in some quality or accident, even though the mistake may have been the actuating motive to the purchaser or seller, or both of them, yet the contract remains binding. . . . A barren cow is substantially a different creature than a breeding one. . . . She was not in fact the animal, or the kind of animal, the defendants had intended to sell or the plaintiff to buy."[d]

Referring to Sherwood v. Walker and cases like it, Professor Seavey observed: "Through these cases, where the older common-law rules of contracts would demand the pound of flesh, the rules of resti-

c. W. Seavey, Problems in Restitution, 7 Okla.L.Rev. 257, 267 (1954).

d. There was a vigorous dissent.

Literati will want to consult Professor Brainerd Currie's ballad about Rose of Aberlone in Student Law., April 1956, 1965, p. 4, Harv.L.S.Record, March 4, 1954, p. 3. The final lines of this epic read:

She rules the cases, she stalks the page
Even in this atomic age.
In radioactive tracts of land,
In hardly collectible notes of hand,
In fiddles of dubious pedigree,
In releases of liability,
In zoning rules unknown to lessors,
In weird conceipts of law professors,
In printers' bids and ailing kings,
In all mutations and sorts of things,
In many a hypothetical
With characters alphabetical,
In many a subtle and sly disguise
There lurks the ghost of her sad brown eyes.
That she will turn up in some set of facts is
Almost as certain as death and taxes:
For students of law must still atone
For the shame of Rose of Aberlone.

tution help to create a limit beyond which the customs of the horse trader will not be permitted to control the rules of normal bargaining."[e]

NOTES

(1) *References.* For analyses of mistake cases (including situations of unilateral mistake) see Kronman, Mistake, Disclosures, Information, and the Law of Contract, 7 J.Leg.Studies 1 (1978); G. Palmer, 2 Law of Restitution, Ch. 12 (1978); and Rabin, A Proposed Black-Letter Rule Concerning Mistaken Assumptions in Bargain Transactions, 45 Tex.L.Rev. 1273 (1967). See also Chapter 12 of the Restatement Second.

(2) *The Bargain-Hunter's Case.* Professor Warren Seavey put the case of a second-hand book dealer who places a valuable first edition on a shelf of $5 books. He considered that a sale at that price should not be rescinded, at least if the customer was bargain hunting, and had no reason to suppose the book was misplaced. The case is one, he said, where the book dealer "matches his judgment against that of a purchaser."[f]

(3) *Economic Analysis.* Reconsider the "property right" argument made in Note 2, p. 414 supra. How might this analysis help in dealing with information about termite infestations? See Kronman, op. cit. supra at 25–27. How might it help in the case of a bargain-hunting shopper? See id. at 30–32.

BEACHCOMBER COINS, INC. v. BOSKETT

New Jersey Superior Court, 1979.
166 N.J.Super. 442, 400 A.2d 78.

CONFORD, P. J. A. D. (retired and temporarily assigned).

Plaintiff, a retail dealer in coins, brought an action for rescission of a purchase by it from defendant for $500 of a dime purportedly minted in 1916 at Denver. Defendant is a part-time coin dealer. Plaintiff asserts a mutual mistake of fact as to the genuineness of the coin as Denver-minted, such a coin being a rarity and therefore having a market value greatly in excess of its normal monetary worth. Plaintiff's evidence at trial that the "D" on the coin signifying Denver mintage was counterfeited is not disputed by defendant. Although at trial defendant disputed that the coin tendered back to him by plaintiff was the one he sold, the implicit trial finding is to the contrary, and that issue is not raised on appeal.

The trial judge, sitting without a jury, held for defendant on the ground that the customary "coin dealing procedures" were for a dealer purchasing a coin to make his own investigation of the genuineness of the coin and to "assume the risk" of his purchase if his inves-

e. Seavey, op. cit. supra n. c at 268.

f. But he added: "I would suppose that if a valuable first edition, by mistake of the bookseller's clerk, got mixed with a current cheap edition, the $5 purchaser would have to return it." Id. at 267–68 (1954).

tigation is faulty. The judge conceded that the evidence demonstrated satisfaction of the ordinary requisites of the rule of rescission for mutual mistake of fact that both parties act under a mistake of fact and that the fact be "central" [material] to the making of the contract. The proofs were that the seller had himself acquired this coin and two others of minor value for a total of $450 and that his representative had told the purchaser that he would not sell the dime for less than $500. The principal of plaintiff firm spent from 15 to 45 minutes in close examination of the coin before purchasing it. Soon thereafter he received an offer of $700 for the coin subject to certification of its genuineness by the American Numismatic Society. That organization labelled it a counterfeit, and as a result plaintiff instituted the present action.

The evidence and trial judge's findings establish this as a classic case of rescission for mutual mistake of fact. As a general rule,

> . . . where parties on entering into a transaction that affects their contractual relations are both under a mistake regarding a fact assumed by them as the basis on which they entered into the transaction, it is voidable by either party if enforcement of it would be materially more onerous to him than it would have been had the fact been as the parties believed it to be. [Restatement, Contracts, § 502 at 961 (1932);[1] 13 Williston on Contracts (3 ed. 1970), § 1543, 74–75]

By way of example, the Restatement posits the following:

> A contracts to sell to B a specific bar of silver before them. The parties supposed that the bar is sterling. It has, however, a much larger admixture of base metal. The contract is voidable by B. [Op. cit. at 964].

Moreover, "negligent failure of a party to know or to discover the facts as to which both parties are under a mistake does not preclude rescission or reformation on account thereof." Restatement, op. cit., § 502 at 977. The law of New Jersey is in accord. See Riviere v. Berla, 89 N.J.Eq. 596, 597, 106 A. 455 (E. & A. 1918); Dencer v. Erb, 142 N.J.Eq. 422, 429, 60 A.2d 282 (Ch.1948). In the *Ri-*

1. No substantial change in the rule was effected by Restatement, Contracts 2d, § 294(1), Tent. Dr. No. 10 (1975) at 10. This provides:

> (1) Where a mistake of both parties at the time a contract was made as to a basic assumption on which the contract was made has a material effect on the agreed exchange of performances, the contract is voidable by the adversely affected party unless he bears the risk of the mistake under the rule stated in § 296.

The exceptions in § 296 are not here applicable.

[See Restatement Second, §§ 152, 154.—eds.]

viere case relief was denied only because the parties could not be restored to the *status quo ante.* In the present case they can be. It is undisputed that both parties believed that the coin was a genuine Denver-minted one. The mistake was mutual in that both parties were laboring under the same misapprehension as to this particular, essential fact. The price asked and paid was directly based on that assumption. That plaintiff may have been negligent in his inspection of the coin (a point not expressly found but implied by the trial judge) does not, as noted above, bar its claim for rescission. Cf. Smith v. Zimbalist, 2 Cal.App.2d 324, 38 P.2d 170 (D.Ct.App.1934).

Defendant's contention that plaintiff assumed the risk that the coin might be of greater or lesser value than that paid is not supported by the evidence. It is well established that a party to a contract can assume the risk of being mistaken as to the value of the thing sold. 13 Williston, Contracts, op. cit., § 1543A at 85. The Restatement states the rule this way:

> Where the parties know that there is doubt in regard to a certain matter and contract on that assumption, the contract is not rendered voidable because one is disappointed in the hope that the facts accord with his wishes. The risk of the existence of the doubtful fact is then assumed as one of the elements of the bargain. [Restatement, op. cit., § 502, Comment f at 964. See also Restatement, Contracts 2d, op. cit., § 296(b), Comment c at 4.]

However, for the stated rule to apply, the parties must be conscious that the pertinent fact may not be true and make their agreement at the risk of that possibility. 17 Am.Jur.2d, Contracts, § 145 at 492. In this case both parties were certain that the coin was genuine. They so testified. Plaintiff's principal thought so after his inspection, and defendant would not have paid nearly $450 for it otherwise. A different case would be presented if the seller were uncertain either of the genuineness of the coin or of its value if genuine, and had accepted the expert buyer's judgment on these matters.

The trial judge's rationale of custom of the trade is not supported by the evidence. It depended upon the testimony of plaintiff's expert witness who on cross-examination as to the "procedure" on the purchase by a dealer of a rare coin, stated that the dealer would check it with magnification and then "normally send it to the American Numismatic Certification Service for certification." This testimony does not in our opinion establish that practice as a usage of trade "having such regularity of observance in a . . . trade as to justify an expectation that it will be observed with respect to the transaction in question," within the intent of the Uniform Commercial Code, N.J.S.A. 12A:1–205(2).

Reversed.

NOTES

(1) *The Case of the One-Dollar Diamond.* A girl found a pretty stone, about the size of a canary bird's egg. She did not know what it was. She showed it to a jeweler, who bought it from her for a dollar, although he too did not know what it was. The stone turned out to be an uncut diamond worth an estimated $700. The girl tendered the price back and sued the jeweler for rescission. Judgment for the defendant was affirmed on appeal. "There is no pretense of any mistake as to the identity of the thing sold. . . . When this sale was made the value of the thing sold was open to the investigation of both parties, neither knew its intrinsic value, and, so far as the evidence in this case shows, both supposed that the price paid was adequate." Wood v. Boynton, 64 Wis. 265, 25 N.W. 42 (1885).

In the Restatement Second, the "basic rule" for mistake of both parties "allows avoidance by the adversely affected party if the mistake was one as to a basic assumption on which the contract was made, if it had a material effect on the agreed exchange of performance, and if he does not bear the risk of the mistake." Chapter 16, Introductory Note. What element was missing in the diamond case? Is it possible that a *mistake* was missing? Compare Matter of Estates of Thompson, 226 Kan. 437, 601 P.2d 1105 (1979).

(2) *Case Comparisons.* Sherwood v. Walker—the case of Rose, the pregnant cow, described at p. 428 supra—might be distinguished from the case of the one-dollar diamond on the ground that the diamond had been delivered, whereas Rose had not. But that would not square with the main case, would it? (In Sherwood v. Walker the court assumed that if an enforceable contract had been made the buyer could have had a remedy, replevin, based on his ownership of Rose.)

In each of these cases and in the main case a dealer was the victor—either in claiming or in resisting relief. What reason might there be for favoring, in general, the person who is not a dealer in goods of the type concerned? That the dealer is a better risk-bearer? That he has better access to information about the goods? Did any of the dealers seem to act as a *conscious* risk-taker? Any of the other parties?

Which of the cases mentioned above does most to open opportunities for fraud? Which does least?

(3) *Unilateral Mistake.* Is either the diamond case or the cow case difficult to square with the rule in Elsinore Union Elementary School District v. Kastorff, p. 258 supra? If the jeweler had known that the stone was a diamond, and Sherwood had known that Rose was pregnant, the cases would have presented problems of unilateral mistake. Assuming those facts, would it be possible to justify a different result in either case? *Both* cases? What if there had been a unilateral mistake in the main case (the seller of the "Denver" dime knew it was a counterfeit)? On avoiding a contract for unilateral mistake see Restatement Second, § 153.

WARRANTY COMPARED

Many problems arising in sales of goods that might otherwise be solved in terms of concealment, mistake, or the like, are dealt with instead by reference to warranties given by a seller, and particularly "implied" warranties. The following section of this chapter touches on some of the means used to qualify a seller's warranty, or to limit a buyer's remedy for breach of warranty, but the content and scope of warranties must be examined in a course on commercial transactions. A series of Code provisions on the subject begins with UCC 2–312, which states a warranty by the seller that "the title conveyed shall be good, and its transfer rightful." In this manner the risk of mistake about ownership of the article sold is placed largely on the seller, unless the warranty is excluded or modified as permitted by the section.

When a warranty on a given subject is disclaimed, obviously the buyer may have difficulty establishing a right to relief for mistake on that subject. If he can establish a misrepresentation by the seller he is more likely to find a remedy, owing to the grounding that fraud claims have in tort law. Sometimes a recovery for "fraud" is permitted when it seems to be only a surrogate for the seller's liability on a warranty, which is foreclosed by a provision of the sale contract. This is the case especially when the seller's expression characterized as fraudulent is in the form of a promise, and he is held accountable without a showing that he intended any deception. For a notable case of this character, see Clements Auto Co. v. Service Bureau Corp., 444 F.2d 169 (8th Cir. 1971).

Implied warranties are traditionally associated with sales of goods, but transactions of other types have been subjected to warranty analysis with increasing frequency in recent years. Buyers of newly-built houses have recently found an expanded remedy on this basis in some courts. Developments along this line tend to narrow the range in which principles of mistake and misrepresentation operate. In large part, however, the extension of implied warranties to non-sale transactions has occurred in relation to personal injury claims. Problems such as termite infestation in old houses are not, as yet, within the purview of the law of implied warranties.

NOTE

Promissory Fraud. For a promise made in bargaining with the intent not to keep it, it is clear in most courts that the promisee is entitled at least to rescission. It may be said that the fact misrepresented is the promisor's intention—a state of mind. A claim for damages is more questionable, especially in the face of disclaimer clauses such as appeared in the Clements Auto case. As against oral assurances in the bargaining process, the provisions of a written contract are commonly reinforced by the parol evidence rule. Cases concerning this doctrine are presented in Chapter 7.

CLAIM SETTLEMENTS

Settlements are favored in the law. Some evidence of this truth appears in Fiege v. Boehm, p. 52 supra. In that case the person resisting enforcement of the settlement agreement (Fiege) was the one charged with liability in the first instance. Here we consider challenges to settlement agreements launched from the other side—by a person who asserted a claim at the outset. His object, of course, will usually be to revive that claim by undermining the supposed settlement.

The bases available for such a challenge are plentiful. One is that "the party making the claim was forced to agree to [the settlement] by means of a wrongful threat," as in Austin Instrument, Inc. v. Loral Corp., p. 400 supra. Like other supposed contracts, one of settlement may also be contested on the ground that consideration or effective assent was wanting. The doctrine of Foakes v. Beer (p. 392 supra) is the principal basis on which a creditor may use the requirement of consideration to circumvent a settlement. Often the question of consideration goes hand-in-hand with a question about the character of assent that a creditor has exhibited in moderating his claim. One reason is that, in a situation where the consideration for his concession is not apparent, it is easy to suppose that the debtor has used subterfuge, or something nearly like it, to create the appearance of agreement. See the Note, "Payment in Full," p. 408 supra, and the materials that follow it.

Another basis for challenge by a plaintiff-creditor is that the defendant imposed on him by misrepresenting the facts in such a way that the settling plaintiff was led to undervalue his claim.

Another is mistake. An example is the release given by Willie Lee of "all my claims and causes of action I now have and hereafter may have" against the Seaboard Ice Co. on account of a collision between its truck and one he was driving. About a month after the collision an attorney for Seaboard's adjuster offered him $6 for a release, the cost of two visits to a doctor. Lee offered to sign for $100, and did so, after estimating an amount for his lost earnings while the truck was out of operation. Unknown to either party, Lee had been seriously injured: he suffered nerve injury and muscle atrophy requiring hospitalization and extended treatment. (One of the doctors who examined him testified, "we missed it cold.") A judgment avoiding the release was affirmed. Seaboard Ice Co. v. Lee, 199 Va. 243, 99 S.E.2d 721 (1957).[a] A more difficult issue of settlement-mistake is presented in the main case that follows.

a. This case did not, when it was decided, appear so clearly to be one of mutual mistake as it now does. The court said that the minds of the parties did not meet. Twenty years later the same court considered a comparable case in which the trial court had avoided a settlement which in terms released claims of one Mrs. Muncy for both damage to her automobile and her personal injuries. "It was in [her] mind," the trial court said, "to release only as to the automobile . . . ." On an appeal by a beneficiary of the release, *held*: Reversed. Nationwide Mut. Ins. Co. v. Muncy, 217 Va. 916, 234 S.E.2d 70 (1977). The trial court may have been misled by the meeting-of-minds observation in Lee's case. Mrs. Muncy's case was different from his in that the parties were aware of her injury.

NOTES

(1) *Settling Personal-Injury Claims.* Several factors combine to make settlements of such claims especially fragile. Some statutes permit the person injured to avoid a settlement made in defined circumstances, notably when little time has elapsed between injury and release. (What is the principle of such a measure?) In Finch v. Carlton, 84 Wash.2d 140, 524 P.2d 898 (1974), the court candidly avowed that for releases embracing personal-injury claims it applied standards of validity more demanding than for releases in commercial transactions. (The observation may have been uncalled-for there; a general release of claims connected with an automobile collision had been purchased for the exact amount of the car-repair bill.) In cases of serious injury and ill-advised settlements, some courts try to distinguish between an injury unknown at the time of release and the unknown consequence of a known injury. See Myers v. Fecker Co., 312 Minn. 469, 252 N.W.2d 595 (1977). It is characteristic of personal-injury settlements that the payor is represented by a careerist in negotiation—an attorney or insurance adjuster—a fact of which the courts sometimes take note.

(2) *Mistake of Law.* Releases based on imperfect perceptions of the law produce results that may appear erratic. In Bradbury v. Aetna Cas. & Surety Co., 91 Wash.2d 504, 589 P.2d 785 (1979), an insurance claim was "settled" at the highest figure that seemed to be warranted by decisions construing similar policies. When a later decision doubled the potential liability under such a policy, the settlement was reopened. The court pitched its decision on a rule occasionally applied: retroactive application of decisional law. Compare Browning v. Johnson, 70 Wash.2d 145, 422 P.2d 314 (1967). In that case a medical man, having agreed to sell his practice, changed his mind and promised to pay the buyer $40,000 for rescinding the sale agreement. He was held bound by that promise although he was able to satisfy the court that the rules of contract law—those requiring definiteness and mutuality—would not have permitted the sale agreement to be enforced against him. *Questions*: What is the best way to reconcile these cases? Should they be analyzed in terms of mistake or of consideration? Or in other terms altogether?

(3) *Questions.* When mistake is asserted as a reason for avoiding the compromise of a dispute, is the problem different in kind from that of rescinding a sale of goods? If a difference of approach is required at all, how would you express it? Refer to Fiege v. Boehm, p. 52 supra, and the cases cited in the notes after it. Was any of these a case where the court could properly have ruled that the agreement was voidable for mistake? The second agreement in Browning v. Johnson (foregoing note) for instance? Do you see distinctions among the cases in this respect?

(4) *The Accord.* Sometimes a settlement is ineffective because of the form it takes. At common law an agreement in the form of an "executory accord" was unenforceable. That is an agreement by which a supposed liability is to be terminated upon a performance in the future by the obligor. The accord as such is wholly ineffective, either to foreclose assertion of the old liability, or to create a new one upon the promise. Only after full performance of the promise is the attempted settlement effective; it is then known as an "accord and satisfaction." The common-law rule has been

modified by statute in some states,[b] and limited by a number of refined distinctions.[c] It retains a certain force, however, possibly because promissory settlements do not ameliorate discord and uncertainty very well.

SEARS, ROEBUCK AND CO. v. JARDEL CO.

United States Court of Appeals, Third Circuit, 1970.
421 F.2d 1048.

VAN DUSEN, Circuit Judge. This is an appeal from a District Court order entering summary judgment for the third-party defendant, Hirsch, Arkin, Pinehurst, Inc.

John A. Robbins Co., Inc. (Robbins, Inc.) is a Pennsylvania general construction corporation, wholly owned by John A. Robbins (Robbins) and his wife. In 1958 Robbins, Inc. formed Jardel Co., Inc. (Jardel), the appellant in this action, as a wholly owned Delaware subsidiary with principal offices in Pennsylvania. Robbins has at all times been the president and controlling figure in both corporations.

In 1962 Jardel began the development of Price's Corner Shopping Center on land it owned in Delaware. Jardel hired Robbins, Inc. as general contractor under a contract that prevented Robbins, Inc., and apparently its subcontractors, from securing a lien against Jardel's property, thus protecting the mortgagee's interest. Robbins, Inc. in turn subcontracted the plumbing, heating and air-conditioning work to Hirsch, Arkin, Pinehurst, Inc. (Hirsch), a Pennsylvania corporation and appellee in this action. Hirsch agreed to payment on a time and material basis, plus fixed fee.

When Hirsch completed its portion of the construction in the fall of 1963, it was still owed approximately $70,000. by Robbins, Inc. Robbins, Inc. refused to pay, demanding that Hirsch rectify certain errors in the construction. Hirsch made several attempts to correct the problems, but, feeling that it could not satisfy Robbins, finally instituted negotiations for a settlement. As a result of these negotiations, on January 7, 1964, Hirsch agreed to accept $36,000. in full payment of Robbins, Inc.'s obligation to it, in return for which Robbins, Inc. released Hirsch of all liability arising or to arise out of its Price's Corner contract. Jardel was not a party to the release, nor did it participate as a corporation in the negotiations.

On July 9, 1965, a substantial portion of one of the buildings in Price's Corner Shopping Center collapsed. The tenant, Sears, Roebuck and Co., demanded that Jardel rebuild the destroyed portion of the building, which Jardel did as required by the lease. In addition,

b. E. g., N.Y.Gen.Obl.L. § 15–501.

c. See Goldbard v. Empire State Mutual Life Ins. Co., 5 A.D.2d 230, 171 N.Y.S.2d 194 (1st Dept.1958).

Sears sued Jardel for $150,000., alleging that its loss of supplies, payroll and other expenses, equipment and profits was due to Jardel's breach of the construction provisions of the contract under which Sears had agreed to rent the building, as well as to Jardel's breach of its duty of maintenance and to negligence.[1] Jardel then sued Hirsch in a third-party action, alleging that "Hirsch breached its agreement with the contractor and was negligent" in failing to meet the Sears' specifications which had been incorporated into Hirsch's contract with Robbins, Inc. Judgment was asked against Hirsch to cover any judgment that Sears might recover against Jardel.[2]

Hirsch filed an answer generally denying the allegations of the third-party complaint. After interrogatories were answered, it amended its answer to plead the release between it and Robbins, Inc. as an affirmative defense against Jardel's claim "because of the relationship between [Jardel] and [Robbins, Inc.]".[3] After depositions were taken, Hirsch moved for summary judgment.

The District Court granted the motion, holding [4] that (a) the general release was valid to bar Jardel's claim if the release bound Jardel as well as Robbins, Inc., and (b) the release bound Jardel because "justice" required the disregard of the corporate distinction between Jardel and its parent, Robbins, Inc. The appellant, Jardel, challenges both these findings.

It is undisputed that the parties negotiating the release did not specifically mention or consider the leaking pipe causing the collapse of the Sears' building, nor can it be disputed, for the purposes of a motion for summary judgment, that the pipe was not installed in accordance with the contract or that this breach was the cause of the building's collapse.[5] Because of these facts, Jardel argues that the release would not be binding even against Robbins, Inc.; it argues that there can never be an enforceable accord and satisfaction to claims that neither party discussed or knew existed at the time of settlement.

1. Sears alleged that the collapse was caused by the breaking of a water pipe leading from the building to an outside service island. Specifically, Sears claimed that Jardel, in constructing the building, failed to use thick pipe, soft rather than hard pipe, and "sleeving" where the pipe passed through the building's foundation, all of which were required by contract. Another allegation of breach is not relevant here.

2. Jardel later moved to amend its complaint to include a prayer for $73,000., the cost to Jardel of repairing the building. After ruling that judgment would be entered for Hirsch, the District Court said, ". . . the Court need not consider Jardel's motion . . . ."

3. In support of its motion to amend, Hirsch declared that it had learned that Jardel was a wholly-owned subsidiary of Robbins, Inc. only after Jardel's answers to the interrogatories.

4. The District Court opinion is not reported.

5. Hirsch, in its answer, denied that the pipe was not in conformity with the contract specifications and that any fault on its part caused the collapse.

We do not believe that the law of Pennsylvania[6] goes this far. A general release by its terms discharging a party of "all manner of actions and causes of action, suits, debts, dues, accounts, bonds, covenants, contracts, agreements, judgments, claims and demands whatsoever in law or equity arising or to arise from a contract between the parties,"[7] will ordinarily be enforced absent a showing that the parties did not intend what they wrote:

> "It is well settled that where the terms of a release and the facts and circumstances existing at the time of its execution indicate the parties had in mind a general settlement of accounts, the release will be given effect according to its terms. . . ."

Brill's Estate, 337 Pa. 525, 528, 12 A.2d 50, 52 (1940); see Cockcroft v. Metropolitan Life Ins. Co., 125 Pa.Super. 293, 299, 189 A. 687, 689 (1937) (dictum).

The facts leading to the release were related in depositions by two of the three principals of Hirsch, and their statements have not been refuted by Jardel. After completing the plumbing, heating and air-conditioning work at the Price's Corner project, Hirsch demanded payment from Robbins, Inc. It was met with a series of alleged defects that Hirsch corrected, while denying that the defects were its responsibility. Hirsch again demanded payment, and again it was met with a different list of defects that, once again, it corrected. Finally, upon once again demanding payment and once again being met with a different list of defects, Hirsch asked to negotiate a settlement. Hirsch's purpose in these negotiations was clear—it wished to terminate its relationship with the Robbins organization

6. Under Klaxon Co. v. Stentor Electric Mfg. Co., 313 U.S. 487, 61 S.Ct. 1020, 85 L.Ed. 1477 (1941), the conflict of laws principles of the forum state, Delaware, must be applied to this action. Delaware follows a strict jurisdiction selection test looking to the law of the place of contracting to determine the validity and construction of a contract. . . . ; Restatement of Conflict of Laws, § 332(f) (1934). In the instant case, the Jardel-Robbins, Inc. contract, the Robbins, Inc.-Hirsch contract, and the release were all executed in Pennsylvania. The Robbins, Inc.-Hirsch contract specifically provided that Pennsylvania law would govern its interpretation. The release made no provision as to applicable law.

7. The release, in pertinent part, provided:

"JOHN A. ROBBINS CO., INC. . . . does hereby remise, release and forever discharge HIRSCH, ARKIN, PINEHURST, INC., its successors and assigns of and from all, and all manner of, actions and causes of action, suits, debts, dues, accounts, bonds, covenants, contracts, agreements, judgments, claims and demands whatsoever in law or equity arising or to arise from a contract between the parties . . . for the performance of plumbing, heating, air-conditioning and ventilation work, in connection with a project known as Price's Corner . . . or arising out of any addendum or oral or written modification or extension of these contracts, which against the said HIRSCH . . . , JOHN A. ROBBINS CO., INC. ever had, now has, or which its successors or assigns, or any of them, hereafter can, shall or may have, for, or by reason of any cause, matter or thing whatsoever, from the beginning of the world to the date of these presents."

completely.[8] The negotiations took place at the office of Robbins, Inc.'s (and Jardel's) attorney in Philadelphia; both parties were represented by counsel. Although it does not appear that the principals of Hirsch were directly involved, both Robbins and Mr. Anglin [9] were present for Robbins, Inc. The principals of Hirsch deposed that it was told to their attorney that if Hirsch signed the release, "at no future time would we even hear the name John A. Robbins." And it was on this basis that they accepted:

"We wanted to make sure we would not be responsible for anything else when we signed this and accepted the final payment; that we would not be responsible for anything else.

. . . .

"[O]ur attorney came out and said, 'Will you accept this? This is what they offer.'

"We said, 'We will accept it on the condition that we are released of all possible claims that come out of it [the Price's Corner project],' and he went back in and apparently, obviously they agreed on it and this is what came out of it."

The release, as signed by Robbins and attested to by the secretary of Robbins, Inc., stated that Robbins, Inc. released all its claims against Hirsch in exchange for $34,000.[10]

Jardel now seeks to challenge the release by the allegation that Hirsch "failed to disclose" the defects of the piping.[11] Even if it were

8. Abraham Hirsch's testimony was as follows:

"Q. What was the purpose which your organization had in mind in obtaining a release from the Robbins organization?

"A. Just to get our money and get away from this nut.

"Q. Did you intend that after the release was executed that there would be any further negotiations or further claims?

"A. It was definitely told to our lawyers that if we signed any release it was on the basis that at no future time were we to even hear the name John A. Robbins, if I can say it that way. We wanted nothing further to do with that man."

David Hershman's testimony was to the same effect:

"[W]e wanted to make sure that we weren't going to be pinned against the wall for something we had no responsibility for or anything on the job if he was going to negotiate us out of something like $35,000, which he ended up doing."

9. Mr. Anglin was executive vice president of Robbins, Inc. at the time of the negotiations. Although he was an employee also of Jardel, it is not clear whether he was an officer.

10. Robbins, Inc. owed $70,000. on the contract. It paid Hirsch, under the terms of the release, $36,000.

11. In its brief before this court, Jardel also argued that it was the intention of the parties to release Hirsch only of those claims specifically enumerated in the list presented by Robbins to Hirsch immediately before the negotiations. We find nothing in the record to support this contention. In fact, the only mention of the list came from Hirsch's principals, who asserted that at no time did they consider the list a relevant factor:

"Q. Was it your intention that this release would release you only from those claims [contained in the list] or from all claims in contact with the job?

"A. [by Hershman] At the moment I couldn't tell you what the

true that Hirsch knew of the alleged defects,[12] this fact would not defeat the validity of the general release. Under Pennsylvania law, the only question open to challenge is whether the parties intended the release to be honored according to its terms.[13] There is ample evidence in the record supporting the conclusion that the parties intended so to honor the release, and there is no evidence to the contrary. Since it was Jardel's burden to refute the explicit language of the instrument and the corroborating testimony of the Hirsch principals, and since it made no attempt to do so, summary judgment on this issue, against Jardel, was proper.

[The court proceeded to consider whether or not the release given by Robbins to Hirsch was binding on Jardel. This portion of the opinion appears at p. 1062 infra.]

[Affirmed.]

NOTE

Questions. Note the testimony for Hirsch (footnote 11) that the defects listed by Robbins were "very unimportant as far as we were concerned." If Hirsch had known that the plumbing was improperly installed, should it be deemed to have known that Robbins was dealing under a material mistake of fact? What would justify its failure to correct that mistake, under the rule in Kannavos v. Annino, p. 417 supra? Suppose that a principal of Hirsch had said to Robbins during the negotiations, "We believe there are no significant defects in our work." Different result? Note that Hirsch apparently conducted the negotiations through its attorney as a go-between. Do you see an advantage for Hirsch in this procedure?

claims were. They were very unimportant as far as we were concerned. As I say, we considered them a smoke screen to stop us from what was directly due us. The release was to get us out of the job completely one hundred per cent. It had nothing to do with the claim as far as we were concerned because the claims were unjust to start off with."

12. Hirsch argues that the mere "averment" by Robbins in his affidavit of these facts does not create a "genuine" issue of fact as contemplated by Rule 56(e) of the Federal Rules of Civil Procedure. Because of our disposition of the underlying dispute, we need not reach this issue.

13. Jardel has cited many cases to support the general proposition that a mistake by one of the parties to a release, such as "to amount to a complete difference between what he supposed he was receiving or giving up and what was in fact received or given up." C.J.S. Accord and Satisfaction § 3(c), at p. 471 (1936), makes the release unenforceable. In this case, however, the only evidence is that the parties bargained for and received a general release, covering all claims having arisen or "to arise," which Robbins, Inc. "ever had, now has, or which . . . [it] hereafter can, shall or may have." By its own terms, therefore, the release covered claims unknown to the parties at the time of execution.

SECTION 4. UNCONSCIONABILITY AND PROBLEMS OF ADHESION CONTRACTS

In the preceding sections of this chapter a number of familiar principles aimed at preserving the decencies of bargaining have been seen at work, both limiting and supplementing the process. In this section some newly established or newly expanded ones are presented. The notion of unconscionability in contracts is by no means new, but it has taken on new life since it was embodied as a test of enforceability in the Uniform Commercial Code; a substantially new body of case law has formed about it, and there has been an explosion of literature on the subject. Also, the "contract of adhesion" has emerged in this century as a type of agreement requiring distinctive treatment. The principles mentioned thus far have been developed largely through judicial decisions. In this section it will be seen that legislative and administrative measures have an important and developing role in policing bargains. The question arises whether or not these are better means for dealing with overreaching by contract than any remedies the courts can devise.

In the policing rules to be illustrated, elements of status, behavior, and substance are often combined. That being so, it is perhaps inevitable that the rules are largely undefined. The notions of unconscionability and adhesion have not yet become fixed quantities in the law. Is it desirable that they should be? Would they cease to be useful as agents for the law's renewal if they were rigorously defined? Or do they cause needless uncertainty and confusion?

NOTE

Strict Construction. It is often objected that courts introduce uncertainty and confusion by interpreting and construing agreements in accordance with their predispositions. The opinion that follows speaks of "strict construction" of provisions in leases whereby landlords attempt to immunize themselves from liability for negligence to their tenants. In reading the case, it will be well to have in mind the fact that a court's idea of fairness between the parties can sometimes be imposed on them by a purposive reading of their agreement. Many examples might be given, but one must suffice here: Galligan v. Arovitch, 421 Pa. 301, 219 A.2d 463 (1966). The plaintiff was a tenant in an apartment building who suffered injury in a fall on the lawn. She sued the owner, charging that he was accountable for negligence in maintenance. Judgment was given for the defendant on the pleadings. The plaintiff's lease excluded liability of the owner for injury arising from her use of the hallways and six other common areas, including sidewalks. On appeal, the judgment was reversed. One judge declared the provision violative of public policy, and another expressed serious doubt on that score. The opinion of the court, however, was based on the location of the injury—the lawn was not mentioned in the lease. "A lawn and a sidewalk are clearly different locations." Two judges dissented. Might the decision have been based on a better ground?[a] Consider the view of Professor Llewellyn:

"A court can 'construe' language into patently not meaning what the language is patently trying to say. It can find inconsistencies between clauses and throw out the troublesome one. It can even reject a clause as counter to the whole purpose of the transaction. . . . Indeed, the law of agreeing can be subjected to divers modes of employment, to make the whole bargain or a clause stick or not stick according to the status of the party claiming under it. . . . The difficulty with these techniques of ours is threefold. First, since they all rest on the admission that the clauses in question are permissible in purpose and content, they invite the draftsman to recur to the attack. Give him time, and he will make the grade. Second, since they do not face the issue, they fail to accumulate either experience or authority in the needed direction: that of marking out for any given type of transaction what the *minimum decencies* are which a court will insist upon as essential to an enforceable bargain of a given type, or as being inherent in a bargain of that type. Third, since they purport to construe, and do not really construe, nor are intended to, but are instead tools of intentional and creative misconstruction, they seriously embarrass later efforts at true construction, later efforts to get at the true meaning of those wholly legitimate contracts and clauses which call for their meaning to be got at instead of avoided. The net effect is unnecessary confusion and unpredictability, together with inadequate remedy, and evil persisting that calls for remedy. Covert tools are never reliable tools." Llewellyn, Book Review, 52 Harv.L.Rev. 700, 702 (1939).[b] See also Kessler, Contracts of Adhesion—Some Thoughts About Freedom of Contract, 43 Colum.L.Rev. 629, 631 (1943).

O'CALLAGHAN v. WALLER & BECKWITH REALTY CO.

Supreme Court of Illinois, 1958.
15 Ill.2d 436, 155 N.E.2d 545.

SCHAEFER, Justice.[c] This is an action to recover for injuries allegedly caused by the defendant's negligence in maintaining and op-

a. In Spallone v. Siegel, 239 Pa.Super. 586, 362 A.2d 263 (1976), five of seven judges concluded that an exculpatory clause in an apartment lease failed of effect because it did not apply, on the doctrine of strict construction, to the place of injury. One of these, Judge Spaeth, developed another ground for the decision: "We do not wish to base our holding solely on [that] doctrine . . . . The courts of this state have too long used this circuitous route to avoid the harsh result of exculpatory clauses in leases . . . . [W]here such clauses appear in standard form leases they are presumptively invalid." None of his colleagues cared to join in these remarks; some of them observed that the legislature had the issue before it.

Problems of interpreting agreements are dealt with in detail in Chapter 7 infra.

b. Copyright (1939) by the Harvard Law Review Association.

c. Walter V. Schaefer (1904–) practiced law and served in a variety of governmental posts in Chicago between 1928 and 1940, when he became a professor of law at Northwestern University. From 1951 to

erating a large apartment building. Mrs. Ella O'Callaghan, a tenant in the building, was injured when she fell while crossing the paved courtyard on her way from the garage to her apartment. She instituted this action to recover for her injuries, alleging that they were caused by defective pavement in the courtyard. Before the case was tried, Mrs. O'Callaghan died and her administrator was substituted as plaintiff. The jury returned a verdict for the plaintiff in the sum of $14,000, and judgment was entered on the verdict. Defendant appealed. The Appellate Court held that the action was barred by an exculpatory clause in the lease that Mrs. O'Callaghan had signed, and that a verdict should have been directed for the defendant. 15 Ill. App.2d 349, 146 N.E.2d 198. It therefore reversed the judgment and remanded the cause with directions to enter judgment for the defendant. We granted leave to appeal.

In reaching its conclusion the Appellate Court relied upon our recent decision in Jackson v. First National Bank, 415 Ill. 453, 114 N.E.2d 721. There we considered the validity of such an exculpatory clause in a lease of property for business purposes. We pointed out that contracts by which one seeks to relieve himself from the consequences of his own negligence are generally enforced "unless (1) it would be against the settled public policy of the State to do so, or (2) there is something in the social relationship of the parties militating against upholding the agreement." 415 Ill. at page 460, 114 N.E.2d at page 725. And we held that there was nothing in the public policy of the State or in the social relationship of the parties to forbid enforcement of the exculpatory clause there involved.

The exculpatory clause in the lease now before us clearly purports to relieve the lessor and its agents from any liability to the lessee for personal injuries or property damage caused by any act or neglect of the lessor or its agents. It does not appear to be amenable to the strict construction to which such clauses are frequently subjected. See 175 A.L.R. 8, 89. The plaintiff does not question its applicability, and she concedes that if it is valid it bars her recovery. She argues vigorously, however, that such a clause is contrary to public policy, and so invalid, in a lease of residential property.

Freedom of contract is basic to our law. But when that freedom expresses itself in a provision designed to absolve one of the parties from the consequences of his own negligence, there is danger that the standards of conduct which the law has developed for the protection of others may be diluted. These competing considerations have produced results that are not completely consistent. This court has refused to enforce contracts exculpating or limiting liability for negligence between common carriers and shippers of freight or paying passengers (Chicago and Northwestern Railway Co. v. Chapman, 133

1976 he was a member of the Illinois Supreme Court. He is one of the Advisers for the Restatement Second of Contracts.

Ill. 96, 24 N.E. 417, 8 L.R.A. 508), between telegraph companies and those sending messages (Tyler, Ullman & Co. v. Western Union Telegraph Co., 60 Ill. 421), and between masters and servants (Campbell v. Chicago, Rock Island and Pacific Railway Co., 243 Ill. 620, 90 N.E. 1106). The obvious public interest in these relationships, coupled with the dominant position of those seeking exculpation, were compelling considerations in these decisions, which are in accord with similar results in other jurisdictions. See 175 A.L.R. 8.

On the other hand, as pointed out in the *Jackson* case, the relation of lessor and lessee has been considered a matter of private concern. Clauses that exculpate the landlord from the consequences of his negligence have been sustained in residential as well as commercial leases. . . . There are intimations in other jurisdictions that run counter to the current authority. See Kuzmiak v. Brookchester, Inc., 1955, 33 N.J.Super. 575, 111 A.2d 425; Kay v. Cain, 1946, 81 U.S.App.D.C. 24, 154 F.2d 305. The New Hampshire court applies to exculpatory clauses in all leases its uniform rule that any attempt to contract against liability for negligence is contrary to public policy. Papakalos v. Shaka, 1941, 91 N.H. 265, 18 A.2d 377. But apart from the Papakalos case we know of no court of last resort that has held such clauses invalid in the absence of a statute so requiring.

A contract shifting the risk of liability for negligence may benefit a tenant as well as a landlord. See Cerny-Pickas & Co. v. C. R. Jahn Co., 7 Ill.2d 393, 131 N.E.2d 100. Such an agreement transfers the risk of a possible financial burden and so lessens the impact of the sanctions that induce adherence to the required standard of care. But this consideration is applicable as well to contracts for insurance that indemnify against liability for one's own negligence. Such contracts are accepted, and even encouraged. See Ill.Rev.Stat.1957, chap. 95½, pars. 7–202(1) and 7–315.

The plaintiff contends that due to a shortage of housing there is a disparity of bargaining power between lessors of residential property and their lessees that gives landlords an unconscionable advantage over tenants. And upon this ground it is said that exculpatory clauses in residential leases must be held to be contrary to public policy. No attempt was made upon the trial to show that Mrs. O'Callaghan was at all concerned about the exculpatory clause, that she tried to negotiate with the defendant about its modification or elimination, or that she made any effort to rent an apartment elsewhere. To establish the existence of a widespread housing shortage the plaintiff points to numerous statutes designed to alleviate the shortage (see Ill.Rev.Stat.1957, chap. 67½, *passim*) and to the existence of rent control during the period of the lease. 65 Stat. 145 (1947), 50 U.S.C.A.Appendix, § 1894.

Unquestionably there has been a housing shortage. That shortage has produced an active and varied legislative response. Since legislative attention has been so sharply focused upon housing problems in recent years, it might be assumed that the legislature has taken all of the remedial action that it thought necessary or desirable. One of the major legislative responses was the adoption of rent controls which placed ceilings upon the amount of rent that landlords could charge. But the very existence of that control made it impossible for a lessor to negotiate for an increased rental in exchange for the elimination of an exculpatory clause. We are asked to assume, however, that the legislative response to the housing shortage has been inadequate and incomplete, and to augment it judicially.

The relationship of landlord and tenant does not have the monopolistic characteristics that have characterized some other relations with respect to which exculpatory clauses have been held invalid. There are literally thousands of landlords who are in competition with one another. The rental market affords a variety of competing types of housing accommodations, from simple farm house to luxurious apartment. The use of a form contract does not of itself establish disparity of bargaining power. That there is a shortage of housing at one particular time or place does not indicate that such shortages have always and everywhere existed, or that there will be shortages in the future. Judicial determinations of public policy cannot readily take account of sporadic and transitory circumstances. They should rather, we think, rest upon a durable moral basis. Other jurisdictions have dealt with this problem by legislation. McKinney's Consol.Laws of N.Y.Ann., Real Property Laws, sec. 234, Vol. 49, Part I; Ann.Laws of Mass., Vol. 6, c. 186, sec. 15. In our opinion the subject is one that is appropriate for legislative rather than judicial action.

The judgment of the Appellate Court is affirmed.

BRISTOW, Justice, and DAILY, Chief Justice (dissenting). We cannot accept the conclusions and analysis of the majority opinion, which in our judgment not only arbitrarily eliminates the concept of negligence in the landlord and tenant relationship, but creates anomalies in the law, and will produce grievous social consequences for hundreds of thousands of persons in this State.

According to the undisputed facts in the instant case, this form lease with its exculpatory clause, was executed in a metropolitan area in 1947, when housing shortages were so acute that "waiting lists" were the order of the day, and gratuities to landlords to procure shelter were common. (U.S.Sen.Rep.1780, Committee on Banking & Currency, vol. II, 81st Cong., 2nd Sess. (1950), p. 2565 et seq.; Cremer v. Peoria Housing Authority, 399 Ill. 579, 589, 78 N.E.2d 276.) While plaintiff admittedly did not negotiate about the exculpatory clause, as the majority opinion notes, the record shows unequivocally that the apartment would not have been rented to her if she had quibbled about any clause in the form lease. According to the uncontroverted testimony, "If a person refused to sign a [form] lease in the form it was in, the apartment would not be rented to him."

Apparently, the majority opinion has chosen to ignore those facts and prevailing circumstances, and finds instead that there were thousands of landlords competing with each other with a variety of rental units. Not only was the element of competition purely theoretical—and judges need not be more naive than other men—but there wasn't even theoretical competition, as far as the exculpatory clauses were concerned, since these clauses were included in all form leases used by practically all landlords in urban areas. Simmons v. Columbus Venetian Stevens Building, Inc., Ill.App., 155 N.E.2d 372; 1952 Ill.L.Forum, 321, 328. This meant that even if a prospective tenant were to "take his business elsewhere," he would still be confronted by the same exculpatory clause in a form lease offered by another landlord.

Thus, we are *not* construing merely an isolated provision of a contract specifically bargained for by one landlord and one tenant, "a matter of private concern," as the majority opinion myoptically [sic] views the issue in order to sustain its conclusion. We are construing, instead, a provision affecting thousands of tenants now bound by such provisions, which were foisted upon them at a time when it would be pure fiction to state that they had anything but a Hobson's choice in the matter. Can landlords, by that technique, immunize themselves from liability for negligence, and have the blessings of this court as they destroy the concept of negligence and standards of law painstakingly evolved in the case law? That is the issue in this case, and the majority opinion at no time realistically faces it.

In resolving this issue, it is evident that despite the assertion in the majority opinion, there is no such thing as absolute "freedom of contract" in the law. West Coast Hotel Co. v. Parrish, 300 U.S. 379, 392, 57 S.Ct. 578, 582, 81 L.Ed. 703. As Mr. Justice Holmes stated, "pretty much all law consists in forbidding men to do some things that they want to do, and contract is no more exempt from law than other acts." Dissent, Adkins v. Children's Hospital of District of Columbia, 261 U.S. 525, 568, 43 S.Ct. 394, 405, 67 L.Ed. 785. Thus, there is no freedom to contract to commit a crime; or to contract to give a reward for the commission of a crime; or to contract to violate essential morality; or to contract to accomplish an unlawful purpose, or to contract in violation of public policy. 12 I.L.P. Contracts §§ 151, 154.

In the instant case we must determine whether the exculpatory clause in the lease offends the public policy of this State. We realize that there is no precise definition of "public policy" or rule to test whether a contract is contrary to public policy, so that each case must be judged according to its own peculiar circumstances. First Trust & Savings Bank of Kankakee v. Powers, 393 Ill. 97, 102, 65 N.E.2d

377. None would dispute, however, that there is a recognized policy of discouraging negligence and protecting those in need of goods or services from being overreached by those with power to drive unconscionable bargains.

Even the majority opinion recognizes this policy as a possible limitation on the concept of "freedom of contract" in its statement, "when that freedom expresses itself in a provision designed to absolve one of the parties from the consequences of his own negligence, there is danger that the standards of conduct which the law has developed for the protection of others may be diluted." Diluted? As applied in the instant case, the word is "destroyed." When landlords are no longer liable for failure to observe standards of care, or for conduct amounting to negligence by virtue of an exculpatory clause in a lease, then such standards cease to exist. They are not merely "diluted." Negligence cannot exist in abstraction. The exculpatory clause destroys the concept of negligence in the landlord-tenant relationship, and the majority opinion, in sustaining the validity of that clause, has given the concept of negligence in this relationship a "judicial burial."

This court, however, has refused to countenance such a destruction of standards of conduct and of the concept of negligence in other relationships. We have invalidated such exculpatory clauses as contrary to our public policy in contracts between common carriers and shippers or paying passengers . . .; between telegraph companies and those sending messages . . ., and between employers and employees . . ..

By what logic and reasoning can you hold that such clauses are void and contrary to public policy in an employer-employee contract, but valid in contracts between landlords and tenants, as the majority opinion does? If the criterion for invalidating exculpatory clauses is the presence of "monopolistic characteristics" in the relationship, as the majority opinion suggests, then do employers have a greater monopoly on the labor market than landlords have on the tenant market? Is there less competition among employers for employees than among landlords for tenants? The facts defy any such reasoning. Nor are there any other cogent grounds for distinguishing between these categories. . . .

The basis of voiding exculpatory clauses is that they are contrary to the public policy of discouraging negligence and protecting those in need of goods or services from being overreached by those with power to drive unconscionable bargains. Bisso v. Inland Waterways Corp., 349 U.S. 85, 91, 75 S.Ct. 629, 99 L.Ed. 911. In determining whether such clauses should be deemed void, the courts have weighed such factors as the importance which the subject has for the physical and economic well-being of the group agreeing to the release; their bargaining power; the amount of free choice actually exercised in agreeing to the exemption; and the existence of competition among the group to be exempted. (Williston, Contracts, vol. 6, p. 4968; "The Significance of Bargaining Power in the Law of Exculpation," 37 Col.L.Rev. 248; 175 A.L.R. 8, 48; 15 Univ.Pitt.L.Rev. 493.) Adjudged by such criteria, it is evident that the subject matter of the exculpatory clause herein—shelter—is indispensable for the physical well being of tenants; that they have nothing even approaching equality of bargaining power with landlords and no free choice whatever in agreeing to the exemption, since they will be confronted with the same clause in other form leases if they seek shelter elsewhere. Although the majority opinion claims that such clauses may also benefit tenants, it is hard for us to envisage a tenant on a waiting list for an apartment, insisting that the lease include a provision relieving him from liability for his negligence in the maintenance of the premises. Consequently, in our judgment, every material ground for voiding the exculpatory clause exists in the lease involved in the instant case. . . .

NOTES

(1) *Public Policy Revisited.* In 1959 the Illinois legislature enacted a statute similar to those of Massachusetts and New York, cited in Judge Schaefer's opinion. It condemned agreements in connection with real property leases, exempting a lessor from liability for his negligence in operating or maintaining the property, as "void as against public policy." Certain business leases were excepted, however, including leases granted by "regulated" corporations.

In 1969 the Illinois Supreme Court had to consider a lease in the excepted class, when a freight train was derailed and damaged an adjacent bulk oil station. The oil company brought a negligence action against the railroad. The oil station was on ground leased by the railroad, and a provision in the lease was held to preclude recovery. The oil company asserted a disparity of bargaining power, saying that by common knowledge a firm in its position is required either to accept the railroad's terms or to forego essential rail services. But the court found no support in the evidence for this contention. Sweney Gasoline & Oil Co. v. Toledo, P. & W. R. Co., 42 Ill.2d 265, 247 N.E.2d 603 (1969). The rule of O'Callaghan, the court said, "accords to the individual the dignity of being considered capable of making and standing by his own agreements." The court also ruled that the statute violated the state constitution, in that it made a "discriminatory classification without any reasonable basis" and unlawfully granted a special privilege and immunity to "regulated" corporations.

Justice Schaefer dissented from the result, although he agreed that the statute was invalid. Remembering that he wrote the opinion of the court in O'Callaghan, what do you suppose his reasoning was?

The Illinois legislature then passed a bill voiding exculpation clauses in leases generally, dropping the exception that created the constitutional problem. The Governor vetoed it on the ground that the public policy of Illinois favors freedom of contract. But in 1971 a similar measure was approved. Ill.Ann.Stat. ch. 80, § 91.

(2) *Public Policy Revised.* In 1953 a California court said that "the relationship of landlord and tenant does not affect the public interest." Twenty five years later the state Supreme Court said that "this is not true today," if it was so earlier. Henrioulle v. Marin Ventures, Inc., 20 Cal.3d 512, 143 Cal.Rptr. 247, 573 P.2d 465 (1978). The court reasoned as follows on facts fairly comparable to those in *O'Callaghan*:

> (a) The marks identifying an agreement in which exculpation is invalid include this (No. 4): "As a result of the essential nature of the service, in the economic setting of the transaction, the party invoking exculpation possesses a decisive advantage of bargaining strength against any member of the public who seeks his services."
>
> (b) Criterion No. 4 is present: "In a state and local market characterized by a severe shortage of low-cost housing, tenants are likely to be in a poor position to bargain with landlords."
>
> (c) "[E]xculpatory clauses in residential leases violate public policy . . . ."

Do you have any fault to find with the reasoning? At another point the court said that "the exculpatory clause in *this* lease is unenforceable under the common law . . ." (emphasis supplied). It also observed that the injured plaintiff was an unemployed widower with two children, receiving a county rent subsidy, and that he gave evidence of a shortage of housing for low-income persons in the county. The court referred to the widespread enactment of housing codes as evidence that residence leasing is "a business of a type generally thought suitable for public regulation" (Criterion No. 1).

Between the trial of the case and its final disposition the state legislature acted to override exculpation clauses in dwelling leases thereafter executed. Civ.Code, § 1953.

For a comparable but perhaps more limited ruling, see McCutcheon v. United Homes Corp., 79 Wash.2d 443, 486 P.2d 1093 (1971), suggesting a distinction between apartment rentals and some others.

(3) *Abusive Drafting?* A landlord asks you, his attorney, to prepare for his use a waiver of tenants' rights that you know to be unenforceable. What procedure would you follow in dealing with the situation? It is said that "many tenants give credence to lease provisions even if they are unenforceable." Note, 64 Corn.L.Q. 522, 526 (1979). To the extent that they do, whatever public policy supports their rights is naturally thwarted. In responding to your client, would it matter to you what that policy is? What if you did not know, but only suspected, the suggested provision to be unenforceable? The Note cited suggests some legislative and administrative means for dealing with the problem of credulous and unadvised tenants. If effective means were in place, would that affect your conduct? For a partial answer to these questions see Opinions on Professional Ethics, No. 435, Committee, Association of the Bar of the City of New York (1956).

STANDARD FORM CONTRACTS

Standard form contracts have become a commonplace aspect of daily life. Their use in business affairs is so prevalent that they provide a vehicle for every move in the dealings of consumers with merchants and others.[a] Take, for example, a man who buys a car "on time." The contract of sale will be on a standard form prepared by a finance company. The car will be insured under a standard form prepared by an insurance company. The check with which he makes his down payment will be drawn on an account governed by a standard form prepared by a bank. When he parks the car in a parking lot he will receive a ticket on a standard form prepared by a parking lot operator. And so it goes. Sometimes such items as quantity, quality and price will be open to actual bargain; sometimes they will not.

Mass production of contracts, like mass production of goods, may serve the interests of all parties. Among the advantages claimed for the use of standard form contracts are these: it takes advantage of the lessons of experience and enables a judicial interpretation of one contract to serve as an interpretation of all contracts; it reduces uncertainty and saves time and trouble; it simplifies planning and administration and makes the skill of the draftsman available to all personnel; it makes risks calculable and "increases that real security which is the necessary basis of initiative and the assumption of foreseeable risks." Cohen, The Basis of Contract, 46 Harv.L.Rev. 553, 558 (1933). See also Llewellyn, Book Review, 52 Harv.L.Rev. 700, 701 (1939). Professor Kessler has discussed some of these advantages more fully:

"The development of large scale enterprise with its mass production and mass distribution made a new type of contract inevitable—the standardized mass contract. A standardized contract, once its contents have been formulated by a business firm, is used in every bargain dealing with the same product or service. The individuality of the parties which so frequently gave color to the old type of contract has disappeared. The stereotyped contract of today reflects the

a. A study of 500 contracts cases reported in 1951 revealed that written contracts were involved in 341, and that of these 187 seemed to have been the product of bargaining and negotiation, 123 to have been printed form contracts, with the remainder uncertain. Shepherd, Contracts in a Prosperity Year, 6 Stan.L.Rev. 208, 212 (1954). In another study, "Requests for copies of business documents used in buying and selling were sent to approximately 6,000 manufacturing firms which do business in Wisconsin. Approximately 1,200 replies were received and 850 companies used some type of standardized planning. With only a few exceptions, the firms that did not reply and the 350 that indicated they did not use standardized planning were very small manufacturers such as local bakeries, soft drink bottlers and sausage makers." Macaulay, Non-Contractual Relations in Business: A Preliminary Study, 28 Am. Sociological Rev. 55, 58 (1963).

impersonality of the market. It has reached its greatest perfection in the different types of contracts used on the various exchanges. Once the usefulness of these contracts was discovered and perfected in the transportation, insurance, and banking business, their use spread into all other fields of large scale enterprise, into international as well as national trade, and into labor relations. It is to be noted that uniformity of terms of contracts typically recurring in a business enterprise is an important factor in the exact calculation of risks. Risks which are difficult to calculate can be excluded altogether. Unforeseeable contingencies affecting performance, such as strikes, fire, and transportation difficulties can be taken care of. The standard clauses in insurance policies are the most striking illustrations of successful attempts on the part of business enterprises to select and control risks assumed under a contract. The insurance business probably deserves credit also for having first realized the full importance of the so-called 'juridical risk', the danger that a court or jury may be swayed by 'irrational factors' to decide against a powerful defendant. Ingenious clauses have been the result. Once their practical utility was proven, they were made use of in other lines of business. It is highly probable that the desire to avoid juridical risks has been a motivating factor in the widespread use of warranty clauses in the machine industry limiting the common law remedies of the buyer to breach of an implied warranty of quality and particularly excluding his right to claim damages. The same is true for arbitration clauses in international trade. Standardized contracts have thus become an important means of excluding or controlling the 'irrational factor' in litigation. In this respect they are a true reflection of the spirit of our time with its hostility to irrational factors in the judicial process, and they belong in the same category as codifications and restatements." Kessler, Contracts of Adhesion—Some Thoughts About Freedom of Contract, 43 Colum.L.Rev. 629, 631–32 (1943).

But there are dangers inherent in standardized contract as well, for it may be the means by which one party imposes his will upon another unwilling or even unwitting party. Such contracts have come to be known generally as "contracts of adhesion" [b] but courts and

b. The term "contract of adhesion" was first used in the United States by Patterson, The Delivery of a Life-Insurance Policy, 33 Harv.L.Rev. 198, 222 (1919). It was coined by Raymond Saleilles as "contrat d'adhésion" to describe contracts "in which one predominant unilateral will dictates its law to an undetermined multitude rather than to an individual . . . as in all employment contracts of big industry, transportation contracts of big railroad companies and all those contracts which, as the Romans said, resemble a law much more than a meeting of the minds." Saleilles, De la Declaration de Volonté 229 (1901). It has been popularized in the United States by scholars who were educated on the continent of Europe and who later taught in this country. See Kessler, Contracts of Adhesion—Some Thoughts About Freedom of Contract, 43 Colum.L.Rev. 629 (1943); Ehrenzweig, Adhesion Contracts in the Conflict of Laws, 53 Colum.L.Rev. 1072 (1953). Both articles were cited by the court in the Henningsen case, infra.

writers have not always been careful to articulate precisely the means of the imposition. There are at least three distinct possibilities, which often appear in combination. First, bargaining over terms may not be between equals. The standardized contract may be used by an enterprise with such disproportionately strong economic power that it can dictate its terms to the weaker party. Second, there may be no opportunity to bargain over terms at all. The standardized contract may be a take-it-or-leave-it proposition in which the only alternatives are adherence or outright rejection. Third, one party may be completely, or at least relatively, unfamiliar with the terms. The standardized contract may be used by a party who has had the advantage of time and expert advice in preparing it while the other party may have no real opportunity to scrutinize it. This may be compounded by the use of fine print and convoluted clauses.

NOTE

Status to Contract, and Back. One of the great generalizations about social history is the thesis of Sir Henry Maine that the history of progressive societies may be described as a movement from status to contract. His influential book, Ancient Law, developing this thesis, was published in 1864. More recently, some writers have detected a reverse tendency in the law. Curiously, a high regard for freedom of contract may be seen as providing a climate for the reverse movement. The prevalence of standard form contracts is conducive to a regime of status, as the argument goes, and they are implemented in the name of freedom to contract. The following excerpts represent these views:

(a) Maine, Ancient Law 163–65: "The movement of the progressive societies has been uniform in one respect. Through all its course it has been distinguished by the gradual dissolution of family dependency and the growth of individual obligation in its place. The individual is steadily substituted for the Family, as the unit of which civil laws take account. . . . Nor is it difficult to see what is the tie between man and man which replaces by degrees those forms of reciprocity in rights and duties which have their origin in the Family. It is Contract. Starting, as from one terminus of history, from a condition of society in which all the relations of Persons are summed up in the relations of Family, we seem to have steadily moved towards a phase of social order in which all these relations arise from the free agreement of individuals. . . . All the forms of Status taken notice of in the Law of Persons were derived from, and to some extent are still coloured by, the powers and privileges anciently residing in the Family. If then we employ Status, agreeably with the usage of the best writers, to signify these personal conditions only, and avoid applying the term to such conditions as are the immediate or remote result of agreement, we may say that the movement of the progressive societies has hitherto been a movement *from Status to Contract.*"

(b) Kessler, op. cit. supra, 640: "With the decline of the free enterprise system due to the innate trend of competitive capitalism towards monopoly, the meaning of contract has changed radically. Society, when granting freedom of contract, does not guarantee that all members of the community will be able to make use of it to the same extent. On the contrary, the law, by protecting the unequal distribution of property, does nothing to prevent freedom of contract from becoming a one-sided privilege. Society, by proclaiming freedom of contract, guarantees that it will not interfere with the exercise of power by contract. Freedom of contract enables enterprisers to legislate by contract and, what is even more important, to legislate in a substantially authoritarian manner without using the appearance of authoritarian forms. Standard contracts in particular could thus become effective instruments in the hands of powerful industrial and commercial overlords enabling them to impose a new feudal order of their own making upon a vast host of vassals. . . . Thus the return back from contract to status which we experience today was greatly facilitated by the fact that the belief in freedom of contract has remained one of the firmest axioms in the whole fabric of the social philosophy of our culture."

TICKETS, PASSES AND STUBS

Printed slips and tickets are issued to their customers by firms offering services of many kinds: laundries, parking lot operators, and firms storing and carrying baggage, for examples. It is common to find a provision on such a ticket that purports to limit the liability of the issuer for injury or loss. To what extent are these provisions effective?

Consider this case: visitors are admitted by ticket to an ocean liner when it is about to set sail. A person wishing to attend a *bon voyage* party for a friend, held on board, is required to pay 50 cents for the privilege of boarding. He is issued a ticket at the foot of the gangway, to be turned in at the top. A sign over the counter where the money is paid indicates that it is a "contribution" to the seamen's welfare fund. The ticket contains the legend: "The steamship line is not responsible for any injury suffered by a visitor while on board." The print is not distinguished in size or color from other material on the ticket. The visitor's attention is not called to the printing on the ticket, and he does not read it. On these facts it can be said with assurance that the legend has no effect on any claim that he may thereafter make against the line. The reasoning might be that the visitor has not manifested assent to any contract with the steamship line. In contrast, the traveller who has purchased a steamship ticket is likely to be held bound by a limitation of liability appearing in it whether or not it is conspicuous, and whether or not he reads it.[a] What is the difference? Imagine an apartment lease having signatures on the front of a sheet and printed terms continued on the back. Could it be held, on the authority of a ruling about a boarding pass, that the terms on the back do not affect the tenant's rights?

a. See Secoulsky v. Oceanic Steam Nav. Co., 223 Mass. 465, 112 N.E. 151 (1916) (loss of baggage; plaintiff not literate in language of ticket).

In one well-known case the ticket reproduced was issued by a firm offering a checking service to the public.

H. & M. PARCEL ROOM, INC.
BROADWAY & 33rd ST., HUDSON TUNNELS
OPEN 7:00 A. M. - CLOSE 1:00 A. M.
(E. S. Time Except When Another Time Is In Effect)

■ CONTRACT ■

THIS CONTRACT IS MADE ON THE FOLLOWING CONDITIONS AND IN CONSIDERATION OF THE LOW RATE AT WHICH THE SERVICE IS PERFORMED, AND ITS ACCEPTANCE BY THE DEPOSITOR, EXPRESSLY BINDS BOTH PARTIES TO THE CONTRACT.
CHARGE—10 CENTS FOR EVERY 24 HOURS OR FRACTION THEREOF. FOR EACH PIECE COVERED BY THIS CONTRACT
LOSS OR DAMAGE—NO CLAIM SHALL BE MADE IN EXCESS OF $25.00 FOR LOSS OR DAMAGE TO ANY PIECE.
UNCLAIMED ARTICLES REMAINING AFTER 90 DAYS MAY BE SOLD AT PUBLIC OR PRIVATE SALE TO SATISFY ACCRUED CHARGES.
PHONE PEnnsylvania 6-2467 H. & M. PARCEL ROOM, INC.

34--971

[C1224]

One Ellis, acting for a patron, left a package for storage at the parcel room and received the ticket but did not read it. Two days later, when the patron went to reclaim the package, he was told that it had been delivered to someone else by mistake. He sued the storage firm for the alleged value of the contents: $1,000. The trial court gave judgment for nearly that amount. On successive appeals, the judges were in disagreement, some believing that the recovery should be limited to $25. One judge holding that view wrote as follows: "The parcel check . . . had conspicuously printed the word "Contract" on the face thereof near the top in bold face type, clearly legible in red ink. . . . The whole form was exceptionally brief. . . . Plaintiffs . . . had ample opportunity to read the notice on the check stub . . . . The package, alleged to contain valuable furs, was tied up with a piece of cord in a brown paper parcel. The charge for checking was the trivial sum of ten cents."[b]

The court affirmed the trial court's judgment, however. An excerpt from the opinion is as follows: " 'The coupon was presumptive-

b. The relation between Ellis and the plaintiff is not known.

A conceivable one is suggested by the following report: "Public lockers in Penn Station. Locked trunks in parked cars. This is where the contraband is hidden, deposited there surreptitiously by one party and picked up quietly by another. Is it narcotics, jewels, gold bullion? No, it is furs, or, more accurately, parts of fur garments, awaiting sewing so that the complete garment can be made available for sale. The lined skins are placed in lockers or car-trunks by fur-garment producers willing to use nonunion contractors, usually a one-man sewing shop or a shop with a few workers. After picking up the garments at their convenience, the contractors sew them for 50 per cent less than a unionized shop would. They then return the garments via the same conduits to their unionized clients. Although outlawed in labor-management contracts, the increasing use of such contractors has produced consternation in an already-troubled industry." —The New York Times, March 26, 1972, Business Section, p. 1.

ly intended as between the parties to serve the special purpose of affording a means of identifying the parcel left by the bailor. In the mind of the bailor the little piece of cardboard . . . did not arise to the dignity of a contract by which he agreed that in the event of the loss of the parcel, even through the negligence of the bailee itself, he would accept therefor a sum which, perhaps, would be but a small fraction of its actual value.' . . . While the defendant bailee should be protected in its legal right to limit its responsibility, the public should also be safeguarded against imposition. If the bailee wishes to limit its liability for negligence, it must at least show that it has given adequate notice of the special contract and that it has received the assent thereto of those with whom it transacts business." Klar v. H. & M. Parcel Room, Inc., 270 App.Div. 538, 61 N.Y.S.2d 285, aff'd mem. 296 N.Y. 1044, 73 N.E.2d 912 (1947).

Compare the case of the steamship boarding pass. Even if the parcel room's liability had been limited to $25, what distinguishing reasons could be given for disregarding the legend on the boarding pass?

Would the parcel-room case have been decided differently if the defendant had posted a placard, plainly visible to customers, stating the limitation on its liability? Would it have been decided differently if the customer had read the ticket when he deposited the package? If he had not read the ticket, but had previously read this note?

The Restatement Second deals with the problem in § 211. What distinction does it make between persons who read the tickets handed to them and those who do not? Does it satisfactorily explain why a limitation of liability on a travel ticket is given effect, whereas one on a checking stub is not? (The comments after the section are more helpful in making the distinction, and are generally valuable on the subject of standard form contracts.)

NOTES

(1) *Bargaining Process.* In Klar v. Parcel Room and similar cases, it may be said that the courts have policed against overreaching in contracts by manipulating the principles of contract formation. What are the limits of this method? Specialized conceptions of offer and acceptance doubtless have something to contribute to substantive fairness in enforcing contracts, as these cases show. See also the note on knowledge of mistake, p. 257 supra. Are the ticket cases based on the principle stated there?

(2) *Sport Cases.* Releases of anticipated claims for personal injury permeate the world of sports, from sky- to scuba-diving. The release forms are sometimes amateurishly made, and in the nature of the case the signers are often youthful and eager for the day's diversion. Yet injured sportsmen of every description turn up as plaintiffs: neophyte aeronauts, skiers well-versed in college tournament rules, and gasoline-propelled golfers. In a characteristic case the defendant is an instructor, sponsor, or supplier of equipment connected with the sport. Being sued for negligence, he pro-

duces the plaintiff's "release" and moves for summary judgment. The variety of other particulars may be illustrated by two cases as follows.[c] Should summary judgment be granted for either defendant? What arguments one way or the other come to mind?

(a) William Jones, 17 years old, contracted with a sport aviation company (Free Flight, Inc.) for facilities for parachute jumping. He would not have been allowed to engage in the activity if he had not signed its standard form contract. It purported to exempt Free Flight from liability arising out of injury to Jones while so engaged. He was injured in the crash of a plane furnished by Free Flight, caused (he alleges) by its negligence. At that time he was 18 years and 10 months of age. See Jones v. Dressel, 40 Colo.App. 459, 582 P.2d 1057 (1978).

(b) Robert Baker executed the document set out below when he went to play golf and rented a cart from Westweld Metal Works. As he was returning the cart the brakes failed and it overturned, causing him personal injury; so he alleged in suing Westweld. See Baker v. City of Seattle, 79 Wash. 198, 484 P.2d 405 (1971).

GOLF CART RENTAL AGREEMENT

LESSOR - Westweld Metal Works

GOLF COURSE JA DATE 7/7 1967

LESSEE - CUSTOMER ROBERT R. BAKER

ADDRESS 20723 54th Ave W.

CITY - STATE LYNNWOOD, WASH

CART NO. 0 NO. OF HOLES 18 AMOUNT 3.66

The above numbered MODEL TEE Golf Cart is hereby leased to the lessee for the number of holes of play on the date and on the golf course indicated above. If Lessee retains said cart after expiration thereof, such retention shall be construed as a new rental at the same rate of rental, and under the same terms and conditions as contained in this agreement. Said cart is not to be removed from the above named golf course and is to be returned promptly to the Lessor after use. Lessee represents that he is familiar with the use and operation of said cart. Lessee agrees to keep said cart in the Lessee's custody and not to sub-lease or re-rent same. Lessee agrees to keep and return said cart in the same condition as when received. Lessee agrees that in using said cart, he does so at his own risk. It is expressly understood and agreed that the Lessor shall not be liable for any damages whatsoever arising from injuries to the person and/or property damage or loss, of the Lessee arising from the use of, operation of, or in any way connected with said cart or any part thereof, from whatever cause arising. All provisions contained herein constitute the entire and exclusive agreement between the parties. Any promises, representations, understanding and/or agreement per-

c. Other instances: Zimmer v. Mitchell & Ness, 253 Pa.Super. 474, 385 A.2d 437 (1978) (ski rental; bindings did not release on fall); Hewitt v. Miller, 11 Wash.App. 72, 521 P.2d 244 (1974) (death during scuba-diving instruction); Garretson v. United States, 456 F.2d 1017 (9th Cir. 1972) (college student signed tournament entry blank at top of slope); Gross v. Sweet, 49 N.Y.2d 102, 400 N.E.2d 306 (1979) (parachuting; release not specific as to negligence).

taining directly or indirectly to the agreement which are not contained herein, are hereby waived. The receipt of the above described cart, in good order and repair, is hereby acknowledged by Lessee.

THIS CART SHALL BE USED SOLELY FOR THE PURPOSES DESIGNED AND NO MORE THAN ONE PERSON AND TWO GOLF BAGS SHALL BE ON SAID CART AT ANY ONE TIME.

3448 (CUSTOMER) - LESSEE

Flatpakit ● Moore Business Forms, Inc.

[A3994]

(3) *Declared Values.* Stipulated valuations of goods stored and shipped are somewhat uncertain in effect. The common-law liabilities of storers and carriers have generally been codified, and in some respects reshaped by statute. A shipper of goods, for example, has rights against an interstate common carrier as stated by the Interstate Commerce Act, which may not be disclaimed by agreement. However, carriers are permitted under the Act to file tariffs, or rate schedules "dependent upon the value declared in writing by the shipper or agreed upon in writing as the released value of the property," and with the approval of the Interstate Commerce Commission a limitation is effective as a "released value." According to the Act, a carrier "may establish rates varying with the value so declared and agreed upon." [d]

The objections usually made to standard form contracts are naturally blunted in this context. In Foremost Ins. Co. v. National Trailer Convoy, 370 So.2d 258 (La.App.1979), the contents of a home, destroyed in transit by fire, yielded a claim of $250 under the bill of lading ("shipper hereby releases such property to a value not exceeding . . ."). Judge Lemmon, dissenting, said: "A casualty insurer would be laughed out of court if it tried to obtain a limitation of liability with such language." Id. at 1260, 1261. (Note who was suing the carrier: a casualty insurer subrogated to the shipper's claim.) See also Shirazi v. Greyhound Corp., 145 Mont. 421, 401 P.2d 559 (1965) ($25 for baggage lost by immigrant, whose English was limited to 400 words). For variations in facts and decisions see Chandler v. Aero Mayflower Transit Co., 374 F.2d 129 (4th Cir. 1967), and Lerner v. Brettschneider, 123 Ariz. 152, 598 P.2d 515 (1979) (construing UCC 7–204 and collecting cases).

HENNINGSEN v. BLOOMFIELD MOTORS, INC.

Supreme Court of New Jersey, 1960.
32 N.J. 358, 161 A.2d 69, 75 A.L.R.2d 1.

[Claus Henningsen purchased a new Plymouth automobile from Bloomfield Motors. His wife Helen was injured when the steering mechanism failed while she was driving it ten days after it had been delivered. They both sued Bloomfield Motors and the manufacturer, Chrysler Corporation, for breach of an implied warranty of merchantability imposed by the Uniform Sales Act. The defendants con-

d. 49 U.S.C.A. § 20(11).

tended that the warranty had been disclaimed, as permitted by the Act, and relied upon a provision contained on the back of the purchase contract, among eight and a half inches of fine print, which purported to limit liability for breach of warranty to replacement of defective parts for the period of 90 days after delivery or 4,000 miles of driving, whichever was shorter.[a] The provisions on the back of the purchase contract were referred to on the front, above the signature elements, in language printed in six point type, as follows, although most of the language on the front was in twelve point type:[b]

"The front and back of this Order comprise the entire agreement affecting this purchase and no other agreement or understanding of any nature concerning same has been made or entered into, or will be recognized. I hereby certify that no credit has been extended to me for the purchase of this motor vehicle except as appears in writing on the face of this agreement.

"I have read the matter printed on the back hereof and agree to it as a part of this order the same as if it were printed above my signature. I certify that I am 21 years of age, or older, and hereby acknowledge receipt of a copy of this order."

From judgment for the plaintiffs the defendant appealed.]

FRANCIS, J.[c] . . . In assessing [the disclaimer's] significance we must keep in mind the general principle that, in the absence of fraud, one who does not choose to read a contract before signing it, cannot later relieve himself of his burdens. . . . And in applying that principle, the basic tenet of freedom of competent parties to contract is a factor of importance. But in the framework of modern

a. It is expressly agreed that there are no warranties, express or implied, made by either the dealer or the manufacturer on the motor vehicle, chassis, or parts furnished hereunder except as follows:

"The manufacturer warrants each new motor vehicle (including original equipment placed thereon by the manufacturer except tires), chassis or parts manufactured by it to be free from defects in material or workmanship under normal use and service. Its obligation under this warranty being limited to making good at its factory any part or parts thereof which shall, within ninety (90) days after delivery of such vehicle to the original purchaser or before such vehicle has been driven 4,000 miles, whichever event shall first occur, be returned to it with transportation charges prepaid and which its examination shall disclose to its satisfaction to have been thus defective; this warranty being expressly in lieu of all other warranties expressed or implied, and all other obligations or liabilities on its part, and it neither assumes nor authorizes any other person to assume for it any other liability in connection with the sale of its vehicles. . . . ."

b. The cases in this book are set in 10 point type, the notes in 9 point type, and the footnotes in 8 point type. To a considerable extent, however, the readability of type depends not only on its size but also upon the width of the column, a point that is humorously made in "A Contract with Cunard," The New Yorker magazine, February 4, 1961, p. 36.

c. The official report of this case fills sixty pages. It has been severely edited here to save space.

commercial life and business practices, such rules cannot be applied on a strict, doctrinal basis. . . . The traditional contract is the result of free bargaining of parties who are brought together by the play of the market, and who meet each other on a footing of approximate economic equality. In such a society there is no danger that freedom of contract will be a threat to the social order as a whole. But in present-day commercial life the standardized mass contract has appeared. It is used primarily by enterprises with strong bargaining power and position. "The weaker party, in need of the goods or services, is frequently not in a position to shop around for better terms, either because the author of the standard contract has a monopoly (natural or artificial) or because all competitors use the same clauses. His contractual intention is but a subjection more or less voluntary to terms dictated by the stronger party, terms whose consequences are often understood in a vague way, if at all." Kessler, "Contracts of Adhesion—Some Thoughts About Freedom of Contract," 43 Colum. L.Rev. 639, 632 (1943); Ehrenzweig, "Adhesion Contracts in the Conflict of Laws," 53 Colum.L.Rev. 1072, 1075, 1089 (1953). Such standardized contracts have been described as those in which one predominant party will dictate its law to an undetermined multiple rather than to an individual. They are said to resemble a law rather than a meeting of the minds. Siegelman v. Cunard White Star, 221 F.2d 189, 206 (2 Cir. 1955). . . .

The warranty before us is a standardized form designed for mass use. It is imposed upon the automobile consumer. He takes it or leaves it, and he must take it to buy an automobile. No bargaining is engaged in with respect to it. In fact, the dealer through whom it comes to the buyer is without authority to alter it; his function is ministerial—simply to deliver it. The form warranty is not only standard with Chrysler but, as mentioned above, it is the uniform warranty of the Automobile Manufacturers Association. Members of the Association are: General Motors, Inc., Ford, Chrysler, Studebaker-Packard, American Motors (Rambler), Willys Motors, Checker Motors Corp., and International Harvester Company. Automobile Facts and Figures (1958 Ed., Automobile Manufacturers Association) 69. Of these companies, the "Big Three" (General Motors, Ford, and Chrysler) represented 93.5% of the passenger-car production for 1958 and the independents 6.5%. Standard & Poor (Industrial Surveys, Autos, Basic Analysis, June 25, 1959) 4109. And for the same year the "Big Three" had 86.72% of the total passenger vehicle registrations. Automotive News, 1959 Almanac (Slocum Publishing Co., Inc.) p. 25.

The gross inequality of bargaining position occupied by the consumer in the automobile industry is thus apparent. There is no competition among the car makers in the area of the express warranty. Where can the buyer go to negotiate for better protection? Such control and limitation of his remedies are inimical to the public welfare and, at the very least, call for great care by the courts to avoid injustice through application of strict common-law principles of freedom of contract. Because there is no competition among the motor vehicle manufacturers with respect to the scope of protection guaranteed to the buyer, there is no incentive on their part to stimulate good will in that field of public relations. Thus, there is lacking a factor existing in more competitive fields, one which tends to guarantee the safe construction of the article sold. Since all competitors operate in the same way, the urge to be careful is not so pressing. See "Warranties of Kind and Quality," 57 Yale L.J. 1389, 1400 (1948).

Although the courts, with few exceptions, have been most sensitive to problems presented by contracts resulting from gross disparity in buyer-seller bargaining positions, they have not articulated a general principle condemning, as opposed to public policy, the imposition on the buyer of a skeleton warranty as a means of limiting the responsibility of the manufacturer. They have endeavored thus far to avoid a drastic departure from age-old tenets of freedom of contract by adopting doctrines of strict construction, and notice and knowledgeable assent by the buyer to the attempted exculpation of the seller. 1 Corbin, supra, 337; 2 Harper & James [Law of Torts], 1590; Prosser, "Warranty of Merchantable Quality," 27 Minn.L.Rev. 117, 159 (1932). Accordingly to be found in the cases are statements that disclaimers and the consequent limitation of liability will not be given effect if "unfairly procured," . . . International Harvester Co. of America v. Bean, 159 Ky. 842, 169 S.W. 549 (Ct.App.1914); if not brought to the buyer's attention and he was not made understandingly aware of it . . . or if not clear and explicit. . . .

The rigid scrutiny which the courts give to attempted limitations of warranties and of the liability that would normally flow from a transaction is not limited to the field of sales of goods. Clauses on baggage checks restricting the liability of common carriers for loss or damage in transit are not enforceable unless the limitation is fairly and honestly negotiated and understandingly entered into. If not called specifically to the patron's attention, it is not binding. It is not enough merely to show the form of a contract; it must appear also that the agreement was understandingly made. . . . The same holds true in cases of such limitations on parcel check room tickets . . . and on storage warehouse receipts . . .; on automobile parking lot or garage tickets or claim checks . . . ; as to exculpatory clauses in leases releasing a landlord of apartments in a multiple dwelling house from all liability for negligence where inequality of bargaining exists, see Annotation, 175 A.L.R. 8 (1948). And the validity of release clauses in orders signed by a depositor directing a bank to stop payment of his check, exonerating the bank from liability for negligent payment, has been seriously questioned on public policy grounds in this State. . . . Elsewhere they have been declared void as opposed to public policy. . . .

It is true that the rule governing the limitation of liability cases last referred to is generally applied in situations said to involve services of a public or semi-public nature. Typical, of course, are the public carrier or storage or parking lot cases. Kuzmiak v. Brookchester, 33 N.J.Super. 575, 111 A.2d 425 (App.Div.1954); Annotation, supra, 175 A.L.R. at pp. 14–17. But in recent times the books have not been barren of instances of its application in private contract controversies. . . .

Basically, the reason a contracting party offering services of a public or *quasi*-public nature has been held to the requirements of fair dealing, and, when it attempts to limit its liability, of securing the understanding consent of the patron or consumer, is because members of the public generally have no other means of fulfilling the specific need represented by the contract. Having in mind the situation in the automobile industry as detailed above, and particularly the fact that the limited warranty extended by the manufacturers is a uniform one, there would appear to be no just reason why the principles of all of the cases set forth should not chart the course to be taken here.

It is undisputed that the president of the dealer with whom Henningsen dealt did not specifically call attention to the warranty on the back of the purchase order. The form and the arrangement of its face, as described above, certainly would cause the minds of reasonable men to differ as to whether notice of a yielding of basic rights stemming from the relationship with the manufacturer was adequately given. The words "warranty" or "limited warranty" did not even appear in the fine print above the place for signature, and a jury might well find that the type of print itself was such as to promote lack of attention rather than sharp scrutiny. The inference from the facts is that Chrysler placed the method of communicating its warranty to the purchaser in the hands of the dealer. If either one or both of them wished to make certain that Henningsen became aware of that agreement and its purported implications, neither the form of the document nor the method of expressing the precise nature of the obligation intended to be assumed would have presented any difficulty.

But there is more than this. Assuming that a jury might find that the fine print referred to reasonably served the objective of directing a buyer's attention to the warranty on the reverse side, and, therefore, that he should be charged with awareness of its language, can it be said that an ordinary layman would realize what he was relinquishing in return for what he was being granted? Under the law, breach of warranty against defective parts or workmanship which caused personal injuries would entitle a buyer to damages even if due care were used in the manufacturing process. Because of the great potential for harm if the vehicle was defective, that right is the most important and fundamental one arising from the relationship. Difficulties so frequently encountered in establishing negligence in manufacture in the ordinary case make this manifest. 2 Harper & James, supra, §§ 28.14, 28.15; Prosser, supra, 506. Any ordinary layman of reasonable intelligence, looking at the phraseology, might well conclude that Chrysler was agreeing to replace defective parts and perhaps replace anything that went wrong because of defective workmanship during the first 90 days or 4,000 miles of operation, but that he would not be entitled to a new car. It is not unreasonable to believe that the entire scheme being conveyed was a proposed remedy for physical deficiencies in the car. *In the context* of this warranty, only the abandonment of all sense of justice would permit us to hold that, as a matter of law, the phrase "its obligation under this warranty being limited to making good at its factory any part or parts thereof" signifies to an ordinary reasonable person that he is relinquishing any personal injury claim that might flow from the use of a defective automobile. Such claims are nowhere mentioned. The draftsmanship is reflective of the care and skill of the Automobile Manufacturers Association in undertaking to avoid warranty obligations without drawing too much attention to its effort in that regard. No one can doubt that if the will to do so were present, the ability to inform the buying public of the intention to disclaim liability for injury claims arising from breach of warranty would present no problem. . . .

The task of the judiciary is to administer the spirit as well as the letter of the law. On issues such as the present one, part of that burden is to protect the ordinary man against the loss of important rights through what, in effect, is the unilateral act of the manufacturer. The status of the automobile industry is unique. Manufacturers are few in number and strong in bargaining position. In the matter of warranties on the sale of their products, the Automobile Manufacturers Association has enabled them to present a united front. From the standpoint of the purchaser, there can be no arms length negotiating on the subject. Because his capacity for bargaining is so grossly unequal, the inexorable conclusion which follows is that he is not permitted to bargain at all. He must take or leave the automobile on the warranty terms dictated by the maker. He cannot turn to a competitor for better security.

Public policy is a term not easily defined. Its significance varies as the habits and needs of a people may vary. It is not static and the field of application is an ever increasing one. A contract, or a particular provision therein, valid in one era may be wholly opposed to the public policy of another. . . . Courts keep in mind the principle that the best interests of society demand that persons should not be unnecessarily restricted in their freedom to contract. But they do not hesitate to declare void as against public policy contractual provisions which clearly tend to the injury of the public in some way. . . .

[Affirmed.]

NOTES

(1) *Principles and Positivism.* Professor Ronald Dworkin makes use of the Henningsen case in his attack on positivism as a theory of law. Positivism has been probably the dominant strain in English and American legal philosophy over the past century and a half. As worked out by Professor H. L. A. Hart, for example, the theory purports to account for the rules that are authoritative in law.[a] Dworkin argues against it on the ground, among others, that it does not account for authoritative legal *principles.* "Rules" are illustrated from baseball: if the batter has had three strikes, he is out. Principles are (logically) different. Dworkin illustrates them with a set of six standards found in the Henningsen opinion. Two of them form the opening sentences of the foregoing excerpt. Another, not quoted above is: "In a society such as ours, where the automobile is a common and necessary adjunct of daily life, and where its use is so fraught with danger to the driver, passengers and the public, the manufacturer is under a special obligation in connection with the construction, promotion and sale of his cars. Consequently, the courts must examine purchase agreements closely to see if consumer and public interests are treated fairly." [b] If this passage expresses a consideration that a court *ought* to take into account (weighing it with and against others of the same sort), then it is wrong to characterize a legal system as one of rules or norms, after the fashion of positivism. Of course this is only one point in Dworkin's argument, which is highly complex and highly controversial.[c]

(2) *Questions.* If the accident in Henningsen had occurred four months after the car had been delivered, would the disclaimer have been effective to bar recovery? Is there any indication that the Henningsens were concerned about their warranty protection? Was there an agreement among the American automobile manufacturers, at the time of the case, to follow the language proposed by the Association?

Within a few years after the decision they began to jockey for competitive advantage by extending and advertising their warranties. More recently car buyers have been offered still further protection against defects, in the form of term contracts for repair, sold for a separate price. Do these developments seriously undercut the court's reasoning? [d]

a. The Concept of Law (1961).

b. R. Dworkin, Taking Rights Seriously 22 ff. (1977). Further to the view that unconscionability is best understood as a "principle" (and not as a policy, or a rule), see Fort, Understanding Unconscionability: Defining the Principle, 9 Loy.U.L.J. 765 (1978).

c. For critical observations on it, see Weinreb, Law as Order, 91 Harv.L. Rev. 909 (1978) (also referring to *Henningsen*).

d. "The experience proved beyond doubt that consumers do care enough about warranties to make their selections felt competitively *if they are sufficiently informed to do so.*" Slawson, Standard Form Contracts, 84 Harv.L.Rev. 529, 548 (1971).

(3) *Legal Developments.* In New Jersey the Code was adopted in 1961 (effective in 1963). Mr. Henningsen bought his Plymouth in 1955. If the Code had been in effect then, would it have been sufficient for the court's purposes to cite UCC 2–719(3)? Compare UCC 2–316(2). See Matthews v. Ford Motor Co., 479 F.2d 399 (4th Cir. 1973).

The *Henningsen* case, which has become a landmark in the field of warranty disclaimers, will be discussed further in a course on sales or commercial law.

(4) *Contracts Compared.* What factors distinguish the Henningsen case from *O'Callaghan*, p. 442 supra? Is a standard-form apartment lease any less a contract of adhesion than a new-car purchase contract?[e] If not, is it unconscionable for a landlord to stipulate with apartment tenants that they shall have no compensation or abatement of rent for the breakdown (say) of an air-conditioning system? Does it matter where the building is? See Harwood v. Lincoln Square Apartments Section 5, 78 Misc.2d 1097, 359 N.Y.S.2d 387 (N.Y.City Civ.Ct. 1974). Compare a landlord's seizure of the belongings of a Mexican migrant worker, without notice, as authorized by the lease. Gonzalez v. County of Hidalgo, Texas, 489 F.2d 1043 (5th Cir. 1973) (not a private-contract case).

How do the contracts in these cases compare with an appliance-dealership contract? (See Corenswet, Inc. v. Amana Refrigeration, Inc., p. 521 infra.) Which is most like a gasoline service-station lease? See Jordan, Unconscionability at the Gas Station, 62 Minn.L.Rev. 813 (1978). Or a community-home and lifetime care contract? See Onderdonk v. Presbyterian Homes of New Jersey, 171 N.J.Super. 529, 410 A.2d 252 (1979).

(5) *Problem.* In Royal Indemnity Co. v. Westinghouse Electric Corp., 385 F.Supp. 520 (S.D.N.Y.1974), a complaint was made against the manufacturer of a ten-million-dollar generator in that it had limited its liability for breakdown—unconscionably, the plaintiff charged. Which of the following circumstances is most significant in such a case?—(a) the buyer had insured itself against the mishap; (b) it was a utility, having some power to pass through its costs to customers; (c) only two manufacturers were capable of supplying the item; (d) other.

GENERAL PROBLEMS OF POLICING

Recognizing that serious problems attend the use of standard form contracts, the decision what to do about them remains a difficult one. What combination of judicial, legislative, and administrative remedies promises the best result? There are deep divisions among legal observers about both the appropriate agencies and the

e. The opinion in *Henningsen* refers to a decision of a New Jersey intermediate court (Kuzmiak v. Brookchester, Inc.) on facts similar to those in *O'Callaghan.* In that case the court reversed a summary judgment for the defendant landlord, emphasizing the presumed inequality of bargaining power between the parties. On the uses—and limitations—of unconscionability in relation to landlord-tenant relations, see Berger, Hard Leases Make Bad Law, 74 Colum. L.Rev. 791 (1974).

most effective measures for reform. These differences correspond, in some degree, with opposing judgments about what the courts may be able to accomplish, and especially about the procedure they should adopt in dealing with problems of unconscionability. The differences extend even to the question whether or not freedom of contract can long be maintained in an increasingly structured society.[a]

Professor Llewellyn thought that the courts had the solution to problems of standard form contracts ready at hand. Essentially it is to recognize a distinction between "dickered" terms and boiler-plate clauses, to the specifics of which no assent is asked or given. Building on that distinction, he wrote, "the true answer to the whole problem seems, amusingly, to be one which could occur to any court or any lawyer, at any time . . . ." He was not sanguine about an approach through legislation, "which seems to be dubious, uncertain, and likely to be both awkward in manner and deficient or spotty in scope." [b]

Some of the disadvantages associated with legislation, such as inflexibility, can be avoided if control over contract terms is given by the legislature to an administrative agency. For some, that step portends a decay of liberty; they are likely to espouse measures to reinvigorate bargaining processes, such as requirements of disclosure in connection with standard form contracts. Others have little confidence in efforts to deal that way with market imperfections, as manifested in standard forms.[c] Some advocates of broader substantive regulation of consumer trades are inspired by recent developments abroad, chiefly in Common Market countries. (See Note 2, p. 474 infra.)

Legislation is, of course, the traditional means of curbing abuses of economic power. As we have seen, the courts sometimes join in that endeavor: the very idea of "adhesion contracts" makes a claim

a. See Gilmore, Introduction, 1979 Ariz.St.L.J. 165: "It is unlikely that the nineteenth century idea of freedom of contract will have any role to play in the twenty-first century." This prediction, even as applied to twentieth-century ideas, is not unwelcome to everyone: "courts have demonstrated unjustifiably strong ties to the doctrine of freedom of contract and corresponding reluctance to deny enforcement of harsh terms in standard forms unless such terms are truly egregious." Rotkin, Standard Forms: Legal Documents in Search of an Appropriate Body of Law, 1977 Ariz.St.L.J. 599, 615.

b. The Common Law Tradition: Deciding Appeals 370 (1960). For a ringing endorsement of Professor Llewellyn's analysis, see Dawson, Unconscionable Coercion: The German Version, 89 Harv.L.Rev. 1011, 1117–18 (1976).

c. Mr. Arnold Rotkin is one of these, classifying himself as an "imperfectionist." See n. a. He disassociates himself from the "disclosurists" and the "adhesionists" (those who favor increased judicial supervision over standard form contracts). Commentators of his persuasion, he says, are marked by a clear grasp of the market's imperfections and their importance in relation to standard forms. His prescription is for (a) substantive regulation, (b) fashioned on a market-by-market basis, (c) directed by a legislative/administrative mechanism.

on their attention to inequality of bargaining power. Yet there is sharp debate over their capacity in this matter. According to Professor Dawson, "the courts have neither the equipment nor the materials for resolving the basic conflicts of modern society over . . . the limits to be set to the use, or misuse, of economic power."[d] In like vein, the doctrine of unconscionability, at least in some formulations, is criticized as a cover for smuggling notions of distributive justice into the judicial process. That is an improper use of it: "The unequal bargaining power concept should be abandoned."[e] Some scholars, whether or not they profess that view, have urged the courts to take wide liberties with the terms of standard form contracts and have proposed models of judicial activity more elaborate than anything Llewellyn suggested. One is to construct a hypothetical bargaining process between the parties and to implement only the terms that would survive, the judge acting as "impartial arbiter." [f] (So acting, what weight should he assign to inequality of bargaining power?) Another proposal derives from judicial review of administrative regulations, as an analogy. Recognizing that disseminating standard form contracts is a species of lawmaking, the courts would develop a "set of legal principles" for dealing with them, "so as to reconcile the interests of issuers in setting such terms as they wish . . . and of the consumer in having his reasonable expectations fulfilled."[g] (Would it be one of those principles that consumers not suffer from feeble bargaining positions?)

So go the debates. Sometimes they draw on explicit economic premises, sometimes on a particular slice of experience, and always on perceptions of what is ideal in law.[h]

d. Economic Duress—An Essay in Perspective, 45 Mich.L.Rev. 253, 289 (1947).

e. Schwartz, Seller Unequal Bargaining Power and the Judicial Process, 49 Ind.L.J. 367, 396 (1974).

f. Oldfather, Toward a Usable Method of Judicial Review of the Adhesion Contractor's Lawmaking, 16 U.Kan. L.Rev. 303 (1968).

g. Slawson, Standard Form Contracts and Democratic Control of Lawmaking Power, 84 Harv.L.Rev. 529 (1971). Automobile manufacturers, Professor Slawson observes, "make more warranty law in a day than most legislatures or courts make in a year." Id. at 530.

Compare Ellinghaus, In Defense of Unconscionability, 78 Yale L.J. 757, 773 (1969), on UCC 2–302: "Comment 1 goes to some lengths to establish a climate in which courts will feel emboldened to strike directly at contracts or contractual terms which appear too heavily weighted in favor of one of the parties; that is to act, in some measure at least, as a tribunal of constitutional review applying 'bill-of-rights' prescriptions to the parties' private legislation."

h. For additional references on unconscionability see Fort, Understanding Unconscionability: Defining the Principle, 9 Loyola U. of Chi.L.J. 765 (1978); Kornhauser, Unconscionability in Standard Forms, 64 Calif.L. Rev. 1151 (1978); Murray, Unconscionability, Unconscionability, 31 U. Pitt.L.Rev. 1 (1969); Schwartz, A Reexamination of Nonsubstantive Unconscionability, 63 Va.L.Rev. 1053 (1977); Spanogle, Analyzing Unconscionability Problems, 117 U.Pa.L. Rev. 931 (1969); Speidel, Unconscionability, Assent and Consumer Protection, 31 U.Pitt.L.Rev. 359 (1970).

NOTE

Llewellyn on Boiler-Plate. Professor Llewellyn repeatedly addressed problems of standard form contracts. One statement of his influential views is as follows:

"The answer, I suggest, is this: Instead of thinking about 'assent' to boiler-plate clauses, we can recognize that so far as concerns the specific, there is no assent at all. What has in fact been assented to, specifically, are the few dickered terms, and the broad type of the transaction, and but one thing more. That one thing more is a blanket assent (not a specific assent) to any not unreasonable or indecent terms the seller may have on his form, which do not alter or eviscerate the reasonable meaning of the dickered terms. The fine print which has not been read has no business to cut under the reasonable meaning of those dickered terms which constitute the dominant and only real expression of agreement, but much of it commonly belongs in. . . .

" . . . There has been an arm's-length deal, with dickered terms. There has been accompanying that basic deal another which, if not on any fiduciary basis, at least involves a plain expression of confidence, asked and accepted, with a corresponding limit on the powers granted: the boiler-plate is assented to en bloc, 'unsight, unseen,' on the implicit assumption and to the full extent that (1) it does not alter or impair the fair meaning of the dickered terms when read alone, and (2) that its terms are neither in the particular nor in the net manifestly unreasonable and unfair. Such is the reality, and I see nothing in the way of a court's operating on that basis, to truly effectuate the only intention which can in reason be worked out as common to the two parties, granted good faith. And if the boiler-plate party is not playing in good faith, there is law enough to bar that fact from benefiting it. . . . [A]ny contract with boiler-plate results in *two* several contracts: the *dickered* deal, and the collateral one of *supplementary* boiler-plate. Rooted in sense, history, and simplicity, it is an answer which could occur to anyone." Llewellyn, The Common Law Tradition: Deciding Appeals 370–71 (1960).

Judicial Control

For the courts to be concerned about standard form contracts is no new thing. In 1873 Chief Justice Doe of New Hampshire described with passion and irony the difficulty an insurance buyer would face in appreciating the terms of an elaborate insurance policy. "The compound, if read by him, would, unless he were an extraordinary man, be an inexplicable riddle, a mere flood of darkness and confusion. . . . [I]t was printed in such small type, and in lines so long and so crowded, that the perusal of it was made physically difficult, painful, and injurious. Seldom has the art of typography been so successfully diverted from the diffusion of knowledge to the suppression of it. There was ground for the premium payer to argue that the print alone was evidence, competent to be submitted to a jury, of a fraudulent plot." Delancey v. Insurance Co., 52 N.H. 581.

As a main counterpoise to such "plots," the courts have developed the principle that ambiguities in an insurance contract are to be resolved against the draftsman. In some cases the principle has been pressed beyond the limits of common sense. "The conclusion is inescapable that courts have sometimes invented ambiguity where none existed, then resolving the invented ambiguity contrary to the plainly expressed terms of the contract document." Keeton, Insurance Law (Basic Text) 356 (1971). To some degree the same technique is evident in cases concerning standard form contracts of many other types as well. In particular, some courts have shown a perverse inability to understand the terms of contracts that purport to exculpate a party from the consequences of his own negligence.

Decisions of this character have been regarded by some judges, and others, as discreditable. In one case of strained interpretation of an insurance form, for example, Judge Charles E. Clark [a] concurred on the ground that the insurer's conduct was "unpardonable." He wrote: "I do not think we can properly or should rest upon an ambiguity of the company's forms. . . . [A] result placed not squarely upon inequity, but upon interpretation, seems sure to produce continuing uncertainty in the law of insurance contracts."[b] In like vein, Judge Frank dissented from a decision which denied a steamship passenger recovery for personal injuries because of clauses printed on her ticket:

"The ticket is what has been called a 'contract of adhesion' or a 'take-it-or-leave-it' contract. In such a standardized or mass-production agreement, with one-sided control of its terms, when the one party has no real bargaining power, the usual contract rules, based on the idea of 'freedom of contract,' cannot be applied rationally. For such a contract is 'sold not bought.' The one party dictates its provisions; the other has no more choice in fixing those terms than he has about the weather. The insurance policy cases are outstanding examples, but there are many others. Our courts, in particular contexts, have, in effect, nullified many provisions of such agreements, if unfair to the weaker party who must take-or-leave. Often our courts have done so by rather strained constructions of seemingly unambiguous language or by other indirect or 'back-door' methods. Referring to such decisions, several brilliant commentators [including Kessler, Llewellyn and Patterson] have suggested that the courts forthrightly adopt a general doctrine which calls for refusal to enforce directly—i. e., without recourse to such indirect devices—highly

a. Charles Edward Clark (1889–1963) practiced in New York City for six years, joined the faculty of the Yale Law School in 1919, and became its dean in 1929. In 1939 he was appointed to the United States Court of Appeals for the Second Circuit, and he served as its chief judge from 1954–1959. As a scholar, he was particularly active in the field of civil procedure.

b. Gaunt v. John Hancock Mut. Life Ins. Co., 160 F.2d 599 (2d Cir. 1947), cert. denied, 331 U.S. 849.

unfair provisions of all so-called 'contracts of adhesion' where there was no possibility of real bargaining. These writers urge that some decisions, in cases where this point of view was not presented to, or considered by, the courts should not now be deemed controlling. Their position is that of Holmes and Corbin, i. e., that the courts will do justice better by forthrightly, not obliquely, articulating important doctrines of public policy. The commentators on 'adhesion' contracts do not at all suggest that all standardized contracts be stricken down, for they recognize that such contracts often serve a highly useful purpose when the parties are not markedly unequal in bargaining power (as in many 'commercial' contracts)." Siegelman v. Cunard White Star, 221 F.2d 189, 204–05 (2d Cir. 1955).

NOTE

Problem. The Rev. Elmer Russell took his wife, Bertha, to the Kansas City airport, from which she flew to attend a brother's funeral in Texas. They stopped at a booth for air-trip insurance. The attendant asked about the duration of the trip, and Russell said that four days should be allowed. The policy was written for that period, at a premium of $2.25. Mrs. Russell died in a crash on the return flight, about twelve hours after the policy expired. (The brother's funeral had been delayed.) Russell brought an action against the insurer for reformation of the policy, extending it to the return flight. The trial court found that the Russells intended to buy insurance for the round trip, which they thought would occur within four days. He found also that the attendant did not warn them of the expiration time, or explain the policy, or mention any other available policies. For a lesser premium, they could have purchased straight flight insurance in the same amount for the round trip (limited to 12 months), either at the booth or at a nearby vending machine. (It would not have afforded coverage, however, for risks unrelated to air travel, as the policy in question did.)

The trial court reformed the policy, and gave judgment for its face amount: $20,000. Both parties appealed, Russell contending that the judgment should have been for the amount of the straight flight insurance his premium would have bought: $90,000. The appellate opinion begins as follows: "Does the speed of the modern jet age and the restless, irrepressible, increased tempo of all who are in its vortex impose on a flight insurer the obligation toward prospective policy buyers of explaining the distinctive differences of the several available coverages? Does the insurer's attractive sales booth, neon signs heralding the need for and availability of 'flight insurance', and the other catchy advertising come-ons carry the inevitable message to scurrying people on the move the notion that the coverage is for the traveler's intended round trip rather than for a definitive period of time? And to avoid this misreading by people in a hurry of printed contracts plain enough that even those who run may read, must the insurer affirmatively take steps by extra-contract informational statements to overcome such misapprehension?"

What is your answer to these questions? See Mutual of Omaha Ins. Co. v. Russell, 402 F.2d 339, 29 A.L.R.3d 753, cert. denied, 394 U.S. 973 (1969).

Legislative Control

Much legislation is addressed to a problem associated with standard form contracts: imbalances of bargaining power. An example is the massing of employees' bargaining power, as fostered by the federal statutes governing labor relations. The anti-trust laws may also have an incidental effect by helping to preserve a party's opportunity to choose among those with whom he may deal; but they have no immediate concern with ensuring that his choice is among parties whose bargaining power approximates his own. More direct intervention in the "standard form" problem is now to be described.

Statutes asserting *control* over the *terms* of contracts may be contrasted with those designed to enhance freedom of choice by requiring *disclosures* in connection with the terms offered, or disclosure in an intelligible form. The choice between these techniques sometimes requires a choice between uncertain expectations. Loosely speaking, one is that consumers can best improve their position through well-informed shopping, and the other is that prescribed and standardized benefits will alleviate their worst misfortunes. Naturally it is possible to hold both these expectations, even if they sometimes collide. Some legislative initiatives reflect efforts, more or less ingenious, to capitalize on both expectations at once. An example is the Magnuson-Moss Warranty Act, described at p. 480 infra. In the following paragraphs, more single-minded legislation is illustrated. In the main the method of imposing contract terms has been confined to contracts offered to the public by some well-organized segment of business or industry, such as insurance policies and installment-sale contracts with consumers. (Why should this be so?)

Control of Terms. The classic example of statutes controlling the terms of agreements is usury legislation. Statutes that restrict charges for credit (not only usury laws, but also many specialized provisions for consumer credit) are characterized by precise limits. A very different example of statutory intervention in agreements is UCC 2–302, directing courts to refuse enforcement of a contract or term found to be "unconscionable". (Materials on this topic appear below.) Considered as approaches to the problems of standard form contracts, rules about usury and about unconscionability show that legislative and judicial methods do not confront one another along a simple line.

Statutes about exculpation clauses in leases, mentioned in the O'Callaghan case and the notes after it, illustrate legislative *prohibitions* on the use of particular terms. A Code illustration is UCC 2–318, forbidding a provision by which a buyer's family or guests might be deprived of the benefit of the seller's warranties. More generally, the Code prohibits disclaimer of "the obligations of good faith, diligence, reasonableness and care prescribed by this Act." UCC 1–

102(3). Many other state statutes, again concentrated in fields such as insurance and consumer sales, also deny effect to proscribed terms.

Another legislative technique for controlling the terms of an agreement is to *require the inclusion* of a term. In some instances a complete contract is prescribed. A standard form of fire insurance policies is generally set out in state statutes or departmental regulations, and the terms of ocean bills of lading are set out in the federal Carriage of Goods by Sea Act. A more usual form of statute is one that prescribes one or more standard provisions for a given type of contract, leaving the remainder to be created by the parties. This is a common method of control in the fields of life, accident and health, and liability insurance. Whether the entire contract or only some of its provisions are prescribed, the statute may provide that the dominant party may use language different from that set out in the statute as long as this does not result in a "lessening" of his liability, or as long as it is "not less favorable" to the other party. But the risks involved in tampering with the statutory formulations are obvious.

The sanctions provided for violation of legislative controls over the contract vary widely. Among the most common are invalidation of the offending provision or of so much of it as is offensive, revocation of a license to engage in the business involved, and the criminal penalties of fine and imprisonment.

Disclosure. Numberless statutory provisions are aimed at increasing the awareness and appreciation of contract terms in one segment or another of the public that they affect. For example, merchants who sell to consumers on credit and firms providing consumer loans are the object of both federal and state regulation. They are directed to disclose credit terms in ways supposed to permit ready comparison. In 1968 the Congress moved forcefully on this subject with the Truth-in-Lending Act.[a] Since then it has addressed disclosure requirements to a variety of other markets and practices.[b] The

a. Part of the Consumer Credit Protection Act, 15 U.S.C.A. § 1601 et seq. As to its purposes and effects see White and Munger, Consumer Sensitivity to Interest Rates, 69 Mich.L. Rev. 1209 (1971).

b. Another example is an elaborate statute designed to require (and enable) the seller of an automobile to give the buyer an accurate, written statement about the reliability of the odometer reading. Seventeen sections of the United States Code, together with implementing rules prescribed by the Secretary of Transportation, are devoted to the subject of odometer readings. A dealer providing an inaccurate OM statement to a customer through clerical error, it has been held, is accountable to him for rescission: a careful record-keeping system is "a clear, implicit requirement of the Motor Vehicle Information and Cost Savings Act," the court said. Jones v. Fenton Ford, Inc., 427 F.Supp. 1328 (D.Conn.1977); cf. Carroll Motors, Inc. v. Purcell, — S.C. —, 259 S.E.2d 604 (1979) (common-law action). For violating the act with intent to defraud, a seller is liable for treble damages or $1,500, whichever is greater; a knowing and willful violation exposes him to imprisonment and a heavy fine; and there are other sanctions. A motorist whose odometer is faulty may also collide with the act. 15 U.S.C.A. § 1984.

same general purpose is manifested in many state and local enactments: merchants in many lines are required to give their customers ready access to certain information thought essential to the making of intelligent choices among goods and services. The Truth-in-Lending Act is notable for having engendered an immense body of case law. Moreover, it set something of a pattern by committing the particulars of disclosure regulation to an administrative agency.[c] But the means of implementing statutory disclosure requirement are quite diverse: witness the Uniform Commercial Code, some provisions of which can be counted as disclosure requirements. Some other variations are described below.

NOTE

Judicial vs. Legislative Action. The following excerpts suggest some arguments about the relative merits of efforts in the courts and in legislatures to deal with standard form contracts.

"Attempts to revise the more basic unequal distribution of coercive power among individuals which is registered in normal market prices themselves, would require remedies which courts alone would be incapable of furnishing, and inquiries for which they are not fitted. . . . But because courts can do nothing to revise the underlying pattern of market relationships, it does not follow that other organs of government should make no attempt to accord greater freedom to the economically weak from the restrictions which stronger individuals place upon them by means of the coercive bargaining power which the law now permits or enables them to assert." Hale, Bargaining, Duress, and Economic Liberty, 43 Colum.L.Rev. 603, 625 (1943).

"It is hard to prove the factual justification of laissez faire capitalism; it is also hard to disprove it. In practical politics, in disputes about the wisdom of particular legislation, the issue is framed differently. The immediate effects of restrictive legislation, in mitigating or removing certain evils, can often be measured with as much precision as the value of the conclusions requires. On the contrary, the effects of such a restriction in diminishing the beneficent effects of freedom of enterprise often cannot be measured at all. The economic evaluation of compulsory contract vs. freedom of enterprise is thus a weighing of ponderables against imponderables." Patterson, Compulsory Contracts in the Crystal Ball, 43 Colum.L.Rev. 731, 746 (1943).

"[Legislation] has a serious disadvantage. It does away with the flexibility without which only very few trades can do. It enlarges the business man's risk and does not allow him to take measures against its increase, measures which only he can devise and which must be applied rapidly. Legislative compulsion works best where a trade has grown into a quasi-governmental function, as, e. g., insurance or traffic; it is almost impossi-

c. In this instance the chief instrument of control is Regulation Z of the Federal Reserve Board; but the Federal Trade Commission is usually the agency of congressional choice for rulemaking about disclosure to consumers.

ble in all other branches." Prausnitz, The Standardization of Commercial Contracts in English and Continental Law 145 (1937).

Administrative Control

Agencies on the federal, state and local levels play a significant role in controlling contract terms in many areas. In some instances they act in a quasi-judicial way, as when the Federal Trade Commission charges a merchant with deceptive practices. Some agencies have a policing function with respect to statutory controls over contract terms. This is notably true of insurance departments. For example, in New York a life insurer may employ a suicide clause as stated by statute, or one which is in the opinion of the superintendent of insurance "substantially the same or more favorable to policyholders." [a] As to certain policies, he has the larger function of disapproving a form "if it contains provisions which encourage misrepresentation or are unjust, unfair, unequitable, misleading, deceptive, contrary to law or to the public policy of this state." [b]

The charge given to many administrative agencies has to do more with controlling the charges made within a given business or industry than with the language of agreements employed in it. That is so with respect to the regulation of common carriers and public utilities. Yet agencies engaged in such regulation have on occasion used their powers so as to exert control over contract language as well as rates.

NOTES

(1) *The Red-Letter Auto Policy.* An insurer doing business in Maine proposed to issue an automobile liability policy containing this warning, in red letters, on its cover: "This is not a Standard Automobile Policy . . [and] in general does not cover operation of the insureds' automobiles by others." The Insurance Commissioner disapproved the form, one of his findings being (in summary) as follows: "it is so limited as to be beyond the reasonable comprehension of the average policyholder, who through the years, has been educated to a broadening of coverages under liability policies insuring his automobile."

The insurer appealed against the Commissioner's action, and observed that the charge for the policy would be less than that for more conventional coverages. The action was based on a statute prohibiting the use of forms

a. Ins.L. § 155.

b. Ins.L. § 141.

In 1971 the New York department was directed to regulate accident and health insurance policies so as to achieve, among other objectives, "reasonable standardization and simplification of coverages to facilitate understanding and comparisons," and the elimination of provisions which "may be contrary to the health care needs of the public," and of "coverages which are so limited in scope as to be of no substantial economic value to the holders thereof." N.Y.Ins. L. § 174–2(2).

found to be illegal, misleading, or "capable of a construction which is unfair to the assured or the public."

The appeal was allowed in part. Most of the Commissioner's specific objections were unwarranted, except in the opinion of one justice. The court observed that affording the coverage might induce more motorists to insure themselves, particularly those in the "less endowed financial group." American Fidelity Co. v. Mahoney, 157 Me. 507, 174 A.2d 446 (1961).

(2) *Consumer Protection Overseas.* In several Western countries new strategies have been devised for the protection of consumers. They feature new standards or new agencies, or both, for the evaluation of standard-contract terms. As to British legislation see R. Lawson, Exclusion Clauses After the Unfair Contract Terms Act (1978). Earlier, in Israel, an administrative board was empowered to act on applications to approve "restrictive" terms that suppliers propose to use in standard contracts. Upon approval, a term was not to be questioned judicially for a period set by the board. Standard Contracts Law of 1958. See Comment, 66 Colum.L.Rev. 1430 (1966). In some countries industrial associations have been given substantial warrant for evaluating terms of interest to them. Probably the Swedish experiments have attracted more attention than others, in this country. They include the institution of a consumer ombudsman and a "market court" on which both merchants and consumers are represented. For rather mixed notices see Sheldon, Consumer Protection and Standard Contracts: The Swedish Experiment in Administrative Control, 22 Am.J. Comp.L. 17 (1974), and Rotkin, Standard Forms, etc., 1977 Ariz.St.L.J. 599.

FAIRNESS IN INSURING

In relation to insurance contracts some special adaptations have occurred in the cluster of principles that are used to promote fairness in contract relations, such as unconscionability. The doctrines of waiver and estoppel are applied with special force in favor of claims made on insurance contracts. The enforcement of such claims has also produced many of the most notable examples of the purposeful interpretation of contract language. In a case reported above, a rule about competence to contract was recast so as to favor an insurance claimant (Ortelere v. Teachers' Retirement Bd., p. 358). These various adaptations rest in part on concern about the way in which insurance contracts are prepared and marketed. For the popular lines of insurance coverage, certainly, the buyer has little if any opportunity to vary the clauses of the agreement. The terms may be prescribed by the insurer, or by a drafting committee of an industry association, or by statute. The "sale" of a policy may be arranged by an agent who is compensated by a commission, but has no authority to negotiate over the terms; in group insurance cases the beneficial holder of the policy may never have any dealing with its issuer; and for some activities (such as motoring) it is simply mandatory to pay for prescribed benefits. In addition to concern over such circumstances, the courts and legislatures are moved by the special characteristics of insurance contracts. For the public, one of the incentives in buying is to have a sense of security. Yet relatively few buyers are able to make an informed judgment about the balance between cost (premium) and the benefits promised. That is so for a reason intrinsic to insurance: the contract is *aleatory*; which is to say that the payout depends heavily on the contingency of loss. Most buyers are quite ignorant of the estimations of chance that are properly used to determine a (net) premium. All these considerations have led to many an indulgence for claimants in the courts, sometimes running to extremes that appear to be simple raids on insurance reserves.[a]

NOTES

(1) *Morbidity Conditions.* Cases of long-drawn-out suffering have presented some gruesome choices in insurance law. Until 1973 it was generally supposed that an insurer against injury or death by accident could insist on a condition that there be no long interval between the accident and the consequence. In that year the Supreme Court of Pennsylvania ruled on an accidental-death benefit which the policy, as expressed, would have withheld if the death occurred more than 90 days after the date of the accident. The person insured, being struck by an automobile, had lived for more than four years in a vegetative state. The purpose of the limitation can best be seen, perhaps, by considering how many of the persons dying each year might be shown to have suffered an accident within the preceding three or four years—or even four months. (In the insurance lexicon, "accident" has a very wide signification.) In this instance, of course, the death was traceable quite directly to the accident. The court condemned the 90-day limitation for this case and for death benefits generally.[b] The case has won a certain following. It was relied on, for example, by the Supreme Court of Georgia when considering coverage of "dismemberment by severance" within 90 days of an injury.[c] In that case, when the policyholder's leg was injured, medical efforts were made to save it, lasting nearly four months; it was then amputated. The Georgia court was less sure of itself in this case than the Pennsylvania court had been.[d] As usual in such cases, it noticed the possibility that the policy as limited might affect the decision whether or not to sustain treatment. But its conclusion was only that "an insurance limitation forcing such a gruesome choice *may* be unreasonable and thus *may* be void as against public policy." (emphasis supplied). In reversing a

a. E. g., Neumann v. State Farm Fire & Cas. Co., 369 So.2d 803 (Ala.1979).

See Kimball & Pfennigstorf, Legislative and Judicial Control of the Terms of Insurance Contracts: A Comparative Study of American and European Practice, 39 Ind.L.J. 675 (1964).

b. Burne v. Franklin Life Ins. Co., 451 Pa. 218, 301 A.2d 799 (1973). Thereafter a Pennsylvania court sustained a ruling of the State Insurance Commissioner that all similar time limitations in accident policies are unreasonable. INA Life Ins. Co. v. Commonwealth Ins. Department, 31 Pa. Cmwlth. 416, 376 A.2d 670 (1977).

c. Strickland v. Gulf Life Ins. Co., 240 Ga. 723, 242 S.E.2d 148 (1978).

d. The Pennsylvania ruling was rejected in Kirk v. Financial Security Life Ins. Co., 75 Ill.2d 367, 27 Ill.Dec. 332, 389 N.E.2d 144 (1978). The court placed great weight on the approval of the policy form by the insurance department.

summary judgment for the insurer, the court directed that evidence be taken on the public policy issue, and listed some questions on which it hoped for enlightenment. What fact issues seem most worth exploring? [e]

(2) *Burglary.* The C & J Fertilizer Co. suffered a $10,000 loss from a weekend burglary. Almost all the loss was of chemicals taken from an inside room that had been broken into. When the burglary insurer for the firm disclaimed liability, its agent expressed astonishment. The reason for its rejecting the claim was that the exterior of the plant showed no "visible marks" of forcible entry (though the door to the chemicals room did). The definition of "burglary" in the policies concerned required such evidence of force applied to the exterior of the premises. It appeared that the outside door through which entry was made could have been forced without leaving visible marks. In an action against the insurer the trial court ruled for it on the ground that no burglary (as defined) was proved; the insured appealed. *Held:* Reversed. C & J Fertilizer, Inc. v. Allied Mut. Ins. Co., 227 N.W.2d 169 (Iowa, 1975) (5–4 decision).

The case produced a four-part opinion, concluding that the definition was, in the circumstances, unconscionable. The opinion also deals comprehensively with problems of adhesion contracts and the principle of protecting a policyholder's reasonable expectations. One part of the opinion charged the insurer with breach of an implied warranty to provide the plaintiff with a policy reasonably fit for its intended purpose. However, only a minority of the court joined in this part.

A comparable result had been reached earlier in a neighboring state, as reported in Note 1, p. 777 infra. In that case the court said: "We hold that where a rule of evidence is imposed by a provision in an insurance policy, as here, the assertion of such rule by the insurance carrier, beyond the reasonable requirements necessary to prevent fraudulent claims against it in proof of the substantive conditions imposed by the policy, contravenes the public policy of this state." Ferguson v. Phoenix Assur. Co., 189 Kan. 459, 370 P.2d 379, 99 A.L.R.2d 118 (1962). *Question:* In your judgment, which leaves the law in healthier condition—the rather brusque assertion of the Kansas court or the refined rationale of the Iowa court?

(3) *Overservice by the Profession.* "The lawyer who serves his client without regard to the public welfare, though he succeed in getting the decision in a particular case, in the long run does his client no real service, and, if you want an illustration, let me briefly refer to the extraordinary service which insurance lawyers rendered the insurance business in years gone by, in exaggerating warranties to the point where they were almost one hundred per cent protection against claims, only to develop a public atmosphere resulting in judicial decision and legislation which puts the insurer under his contract in a worse position today than is any other contracting party. That is overservice by the profession." Parkinson, Are the Law Schools Adequately Training for the Public Service?, 8 Am.Law School Rev. 291, 294 (1935).

e. On the problem of giving meaning to "good faith," with special reference to insurance contracts, see Holmes, A Contextual Study of Commercial Good Faith: Good-Faith Disclosure in Contract Formation, 39 U. Pitt.L.Rev. 381 (1978).

(4) *An Industry Agreement.* Holders of British property and casualty policies may take some comfort in a "Statement of Insurance Practice" to which their insurers have subscribed. Among other things, it provides that, where the circumstances of a loss are "unconnected" with a breach of condition or warranty that might afford a defense to a loss claim, the insurer will not, on that ground, "unreasonably repudiate liability to indemnify" the policyholder. In the United States, most underwriters and insurance scholars would probably regard this settlement policy as unwise. A British critic has complained of the Statement on another ground: it represents a tendency of British insurers to reform their conduct by agreement among themselves. Birds, The Statement, etc., 40 Mod.L.Rev. 677 (1977). What unfortunate effect can you imagine?

The Duty to Read and the Right to Understand

One who signs a contract document without reading it runs a risk. It has been said (with some exaggeration): "The whole panoply of contract law rests on the principle that one is bound by the contract which he voluntarily and knowingly signs."[a] The rule may be thought of as an aspect of the objective theory of contract law (see Note p. 171 supra). However, it is older than that general theory and it has limitations based on duress, mistake and the like, also very old. The rule is also subject to some new qualifications created both by courts and by legislatures. A statutory example already noted is the rule that an "assurance" creating a firm offer under the Code, which is on a form supplied by the offeree, is ineffective unless it is "separately signed" by the offeror. UCC 2–205. This rule will usually—not always—operate on a document designed to produce a standard form contract.

Presenting a standard form contract to a consumer for his assent entails a certain obligation to make it intelligible. This general proposition, though not yet fully defined, is exemplified by widespread decisions, statutes, and regulations, quite various in detail. Under one statute or another, one who neglects the obligation may find that the consumer has a monetary claim against him (sometimes designated a "penalty") or that official action will be taken against him. At least three general types of provision may be discerned. First, for certain classes of contracts there are detailed prescriptions about how they must be expressed, in whole or in part. Examples at the state level are statutes affecting retail installment sales, insurance, and so on; at the federal level an example is the Truth-in-Lending Act. In many such statutes there are points where general standards of clarity (e. g., "meaningful sequence") are stated; but

a. National Bank of Washington v. Equity Investors, 81 Wash.2d 886, 912–13, 506 P.2d 20, 36 (1973). See also Washington v. Claasen, 218 Kan. 577, 545 P.2d 387 (1976); Evans v. State Farm Auto Ins. Co., 269 S.C. 584, 239 S.E.2d 76 (1977).

they rely largely on rules of high definition about such matters as the content, sequence and type-size of disclosures. A second type of statute depends chiefly, or entirely, on imprecise standards of clarity. For example, the matter concerning warranties required to be disclosed by the Magnuson-Moss Warranty Act must be expressed "clearly and conspicuously" and "in simple and readily understood language."[b] Finally, there are formulary prescriptions of plain language, such as that in a Connecticut statute described below.

The courts' efforts for clarity are also diverse. As already indicated, they include "ameliorating" interpretations of standard form contracts. One judicial remedy for a person who—excusably—accedes to a form without understanding it is to deny any enforcement of the agreement as written. If the difficulty lies in part of the writing only, a court may deny enforcement of that part. The Restatement Second provides that where a party effectively manifests assent to a standardized expression of agreement, and the other party has reason to believe he would not have done so if he had known that it contained a particular term, "the term is not part of the agreement."[c] Still another available procedure is to treat the agreement as if it contained a different term on the same subject.

In Fraass Surgical Mfg. Co., Inc. v. United States, 571 F.2d 34 (Ct.Cl.1978), an Air Force procurement contract assigned a risk to the supplier which, in previous contracts between the same parties, had been assigned to the government. If the government had known that the supplier was unaware of the change, an appropriate remedy would have been to reform the document so as to assign the risks as before.[d] That knowledge was not proved, however. The testimony of the supplier's president was that he did not read the contract "because contracts that he had signed in 1963 and 1960 had contained the other clause." The court found this testimony unacceptable: "He is an experienced businessman and should know better." The Restatement rule for that case is that "he adopts the writing as an integrated agreement with respect to the terms included in the writing."[e]

The failure of a signer to appreciate the effect of a writing is not such a mistake as will ordinarily excuse him. (One who cannot read may bind himself to a written agreement.[f]) Yet the require-

b. 15 U.S.C.A. § 2302(a) ("to the extent required by rules of the [Federal Trade] Commission"); 16 C.F.R. § 701.3 (1979). Further as to the Act, see p. 480 infra.

c. Section 211(3).

d. See Restatement Second, § 166, Comment a.

e. Restatement Second, § 211(1).

f. "The general rule is that, in the absence of fraud, one who signs a written agreement is bound by its terms whether he read and understood it or not, or whether he can read or not." Cohen v. Santoianni, 330 Mass. 187, 192, 112 N.E. 267, 271 (1953).

As for protecting "the non-English speaker" see Comment, 30 Baylor L. Rev. 765 (1978).

ments of a relievable mistake have been loosened; and to that may now be added an even looser exception for unconscionability. Certainly in situations where other marks of unconscionability may appear, one who devises a standard form contract without troubling to make it intelligible has weakened the claim he might otherwise have on a signer's duty to read. See Calamari, Duty to Read—A Changing Concept, 43 Fordham L.Rev. 341 (1974).[g]

In the materials to follow you will find instances of both the duty to read and the right to understand.

NOTES

(1) *Problem.* On Restatement Second § 211(3), see Dawson, Unconscionable Coercion: The German Version, 89 Harv.L.Rev. 1041, 1120–21 (1976). Can you state a case to which the rule plainly and precisely applies? For suggestive situations see the following cases concerning dealership contracts with more or less unlettered gas-station operators: Weaver v. American Oil Co., 257 Ind. 458, 276 N.E.2d 144 (1971) (risk of personal injury), and Johnson v. Mobil Oil Corp., 415 F.Supp. 264 (E.D.Mich.1976) (risk of property damage).

(2) *Disclosure: Form and Substance.* A recent venture in state legislation is to require that certain contracts be expressed in "plain language." The bellwether New York statute prohibits the use of "technical" language and requires the use of "words with common every day meanings." Gen. Obl.L. § 5–702. The plain-language enterprise has antecedents in the Uniform Commercial Code, and in earlier statutes. It is a common adjunct of such legislation to require that the information be disclosed in a particular form. The use of red ink for certain terms is required; more commonly requirements about captions and size of type are imposed. The Code is free of such provisions, but it occasionally demands that a provision be "conspicuous," and other legislation has followed suit. For some purposes it is required in the Code that the recipient of a writing have "reason to know its contents." See, e. g., UCC 2–201(2). The Code also requires in a few instances that terms be "separately signed" as a protection against inadvertent signing. See, e. g., UCC 2–209(2); UCC 1–201(39) (definition of "signed" includes initials). On a simpler level, there is the requirement in a New York statute on retail installment sale contracts that they include this admonition to buyers: "Do not sign this agreement until you read it." Pers. Prop.L. § 402.

Requirements of red ink and conspicuous terms cannot assure that the "ordinary layman would realize what he was relinquishing in return for what he was being granted"—to quote from the *Henningsen* case. In the

g. For an analysis of the duty to read in relation to a structured set of legal policies, see Macaulay, Private Legislation and the Duty to Read, 19 Vand.L.Rev. 1051 (1966). For an amusing discussion of methods employed to prevent the written word from conveying any message, see Mellinkoff, How to Make Contracts Illegible, 5 Stan.L.Rev. 418 (1953).

On the difficulty in determining, in this connection, what makes for a (roughly) equal bargaining position, see Brokers Title Co. v. St. Paul F. & M. Ins. Co., 610 F.2d 1174 (3d Cir. 1979).

Code some attempts are made to deal with this aspect of the problem, notably in relation to warranties. The few plain-language statutes that have so far been enacted address the problem more comprehensively. (Materials on both these efforts are presented below.)

The utility of disclosure requirements is intrinsically limited, and especially so as to groups who suffer most from an imbalance of bargaining power. The following comment makes the point in relation to low-income consumers: "In sum, the new wave of informational legislation will be of little help to the poor because it presupposes values, motivation and knowledge which do not generally exist among them. The actual problem is not just a shortage of a narrowly defined sort of information—such as the price per pound of prepackaged food—but a total breakdown in the function the consumer is supposed to play in the market. 'Bad buys' are the rule and price and quality competition the exception. As one merchant in New York put it: "People do not *shop* in this area . . . . It is just up to who catches him.' " Note, Consumer Legislation and the Poor, 76 Yale L.J. 745, 754 (1967).

(3) *UCC 2–316: Conspicuous.* Curtailment of the implied fitness warranty must, according to subsection (2), be "conspicuous". Is an exception to that requirement to be found in subsection (3)? See Smith v. Sharperstein, 521 P.2d 394, 73 A.L.R.3d 244 (Okl.1974).

The Code defines "conspicuous" with reference to what "a reasonable person against whom it is to operate ought to have noticed." UCC 1–201(10). In Avenell v. Westinghouse Electric Corp., 41 Ohio App.2d 150, 324 N.E.2d 583 (1974), a finding of conspicuousness was made—and approved on appeal—for the reason, among others, that the buyer was a "prominent, sophisticated entity": the Toledo Edison Company. Is there a difference between this case and one in which the buyer is an "average Joe," but happens to know of the disclaimer? See Anno., 73 A.L.R.3d at 273, 299–300 (1976). What reason might there be for refusing to recognize a distinction?

THE MAGNUSON–MOSS WARRANTY ACT

The legislation known by this name [a] is a bravura effort by the Congress to improve marketing practices in consumer products and to make the rights and remedies of consumers under warranties more effectual. The most striking technique of the Act is that it builds on the impulse of manufacturers and dealers to provide warranties in writing for promoting consumer sales. Any "supplier" who yields to that impulse incurs elaborate obligations, some of them substantive and others relating to disclosure and remedies. One may resist simply by failing to provide a "written warranty"; and in that event neither the Act nor the rules of the Federal Trade Commission that supplement it [b] have any application. Given a written warranty, the Act

a. Title I of the Magnuson-Moss Warranty-FTC Improvement Act of January 5, 1975: 15 U.S.S.C. §§ 2301–2312.

b. 16 C.F.R. §§ 700.1–703.8 (1979).

requires that it carry a conspicuous designation, as either a FULL or a LIMITED warranty. The idea of this invidious distinction is evidently twofold. One object is to alert consumers to the limitations that commonly attend warranty protection; the other is to spur merchants to compete by enlarging their warranty undertakings.

The Act establishes minimum standards of accountability in connection with a full warranty. The warrantor, for example, must remedy a defect without charge. ("Without charge" is defined, however, so as to permit consumers to be charged with incidental expenses.) Probably this requirement does not deter many merchants from providing full warranties. A more important specification is this: one who offers a "full" warranty may not limit the duration of any implied warranty on the product. The Act does not set uniform content for implied warranties; it allows for state-to-state variation in this matter. However, even in connection with a limited (written) warranty, it suppresses some restrictions on implied warranties, most notably in this provision:[c]

> [I]mplied warranties may be limited in duration to the duration of a written warranty of reasonable duration, if such limitation is conscionable and is set forth in clear and unmistakable language and prominently displayed on the face of the warranty.

The Act contemplates an evasive tactic: withholding written warranties altogether, and tendering service contracts to customers in lieu thereof. In effect, such a contract is treated as a limited warranty, so far as concerns restrictions on implied warranties, unless it is entered into well after the sale.

The Commission is given an especially prominent role in specifying the disclosures that must attend all written warranties. However, the Act both suggests a long menu of items appropriate for disclosure and puts some compulsions on the Commission. It may not prescribe any warranty period, for example. On the other hand, it is directed to adopt rules for making the terms of a written warranty "available" to the consumer *prior to the sale* to him. (The Commission's rules do not require *display* of the text, even in relation to in-store sales. In varying detail, they provide for references to texts in notebooks, in catalogs, and in the briefcases of door-to-door salesmen.) Some of the information that must be made available is remarkably uninformative. The reasons are that the Act aims at disclosure of consumers' rights as well as the terms of their contracts, and that in some states their rights are extended in distinctive ways. Hence the following statements, required by rule: "This warranty gives you specific legal rights, and you may also have other rights which vary from state to state." "Some states do not allow the exclusion or limi-

c. Section 2803(b).

tation of incidental or consequential damages . . . ." "Some states do not allow limitations on how long an implied warranty lasts . . . ." There are indications that consumer comprehension might be enhanced by deleting such advices.[d]

(Federalism is at its worst in requiring disclosures of finance charges to consumers. In some states it seems necessary to state such a charge as computed on federal principles, and to continue: "The following statements are inconsistent with the requirements of the federal statute—Truth in Lending—under which the statements above are made." [e])

Attorneys of the Commission, and the Attorney General, have authority to restrain violations of the Act, and the making of "deceptive" warranties. (The definition of this expression builds upon the notion of misleading of a reasonable individual.) Other means of enforcement are individual and class suits. Though these are permitted in both federal and state courts, the conditions of litigation are largely federal. A winning consumer may recover his reasonable suit costs. Remarkably, that is so even though he asserts only an implied-warranty claim (none under a written warranty, and none under the Act), and even in a state-court action. Not many non-class suits are eligible for federal adjudication because few meet the jurisdictional amount requirement of $50,000.

For many a merchant liability for suit costs may be the most pressing part of the Act. Many suppliers pass on written warranties that manufacturers offer to consumers without further involving themselves. As sellers, however, making implied warranties, they are affected by the remedy provisions of the Act. Many merchants undertake, as manufacturers' reps, to make good on warranties. In itself, that adds nothing under the Act to their responsibilities to consumers (except consumers as plaintiffs). Indeed, the Act requires in this situation that the warrantor make reasonable arrangements for compensation of designated representatives. (What protection for consumers in this?) Whatever the Act does for private suitors, it qualifies, by permitting a warrantor to put a barrier in the way of consumers' legal proceedings. The barrier must include an "informal dispute settlement procedure." In the Act the Congress cast not only an encouraging but also a wary eye on such procedures: while fostering their use, it assigned to the Commission special duties of surveillance over their fairness and quality. Of course, if a supplier gives a written warranty and requires out-of-court settlement efforts by a purchaser as a condition to suit, he must disclose that fact, in addi-

d. See Davis, Protecting Consumers from Overdisclosure and Gobbledygook, 63 Va.L.Rev. 841 (1977).

e. See Mason v. General Finance Corp. of Virginia, 542 F.2d 1226 (4th Cir. 1976); Anderson v. Southern Discount Co., 582 F.2d 883 (4th Cir. 1978).

tion to giving a "brief, general description of the legal remedies available to the consumer."[f]

Some limitations of scope on the requirements of the Act may be illustrated by the sale of a smoke ball (see Carlill v. Carbolic Smoke Ball Co., p. 303 supra).[g] If the consumer's cost is not more than $15, a written warranty given with the ball need not call itself "full" or "limited." If Carlill bought the smoke ball from a local apothecary, and not the Smoke Ball Company, though both sellers would probably be within the statutory definitions of "supplier" and "warrantor," nothing in the Act enlarges the substantive undertakings of the retailer. If Carlill herself were to become a (casual) seller, she would be incapable of giving a written warranty, for only a "supplier" is eligible to do that, and the definition of that word requires a business of making a consumer product available to consumers. (However, one who received the ball from her, even as a gift, during the warranty period, would be a "consumer." Where the Act refers to consumer purposes—personal, family, household—it does so in connection with the normal use of a product, not the wants of a buyer.[h]) In Carlill's case, the company argued that she should have sat down—before catching flu—and communicated to it her acceptance of the offer. Makers of written warranties often show favor for this procedure, and (for various reasons) provide consumers with warranty registration cards to be filled out and mailed. The Commission has indicated that warranty protection may not be conditioned on the mailing.

Finally, there is the question what advertisements and the like count as "written warranties" under the Act. The automobile ad "A-1 condition" fails to bring the Act into play surely; but "air-conditioned" is different, if that becomes part of the basis of a bargain. (And note: bargain between *a* supplier and *a* buyer.) The smoke ball ad that Carlill saw would qualify as a written warranty in the form of a promise, subject only to the doubt that it related to material or workmanship.

The assertions made in most ads (other than catalogs) probably do not satisfy the Act's standards of intelligibility for the required disclosures. One standard of diction is "words or phrases which would not mislead a reasonable, average consumer as to the nature or scope of the warranty."[i] More generally, the terms and conditions of a warranty should be "fully and conspicuously disclose[d] in simple and readily understood language."[j] However, the Act does some-

f. Section 2802(a)(9).

g. For the suggestion, appreciation is due C. Reitz, Consumer Protection Under the Magnuson-Moss Warranty Act (1978), a thoughtful exposition.

h. But note that one who buys for the purpose of resale is not, by force of anything said by his seller, the recipient of a "written warranty."

i. Section 2802(a)(13).

j. Section 2802(a).

thing to protect draftsmen from cheap shots. First, both these standards are insisted on only "to the extent required by rules of the Commission." [k] Moreover: "The Commission may by rule devise detailed substantive warranty provisions which warrantors may incorporate by reference in their warranties." [l]

In a written (Sears) warranty set out below, the form is largely dictated by the Act. Note that the supplier provides both a full and a limited warranty on a single item, as the Act permits. It does not purport to limit consequential damages, as the Act would allow. What effect does it have on implied warranties, if any? In extending the "full" warranty, Sears did not exploit the opportunity permitted by the Act of offering replacement or a refund in lieu of repair, "whichever . . . the warrantor elects." [m] Consider what situation would impel a supplier to choose refunding the price over repair or replacement. The Act permits a consumer to rule out refund if one of the other remedies is fairly feasible. In a certain case, the consumer's preference becomes more compelling: after the failure of a reasonable number of attempts at repair, he may elect either replacement or refund.[n] The remedies for the limited warranty are not specified by the Act.

NOTES

(1) *Illustrative Warranty.*

FULL ONE YEAR WARRANTY

For one year from the date of purchase, Sears will repair this typewriter, free of charge, if defective in material or workmanship.

LIMITED WARRANTY

After one year and until five years from the date of purchase, Sears will furnish, free of charge, a replacement part for any defective part of the typewriter (except the motor on an electric model). You pay for labor.

Warranty service is available by simply returning the typewriter to the nearest Sears store throughout the United States.

This warranty gives you specific legal rights, and you may also have other rights which vary from state to state.

Sears, Roebuck and Co.
BSC 41–3
Sears Tower
Chicago, IL 60684

(2) *Economic Analysis.* What is the rationale for giving to the supplier the choice between repair, replacement and refund? Some influential stu-

k. Ibid. For the Commission's action see 16 C.F.R. § 701.3.

l. Section 2802(d).

m. Section 2801(10).

n. Section 2804(a)(4).

dents of sales law reached the conclusion in the first half of this century that, with respect to goods sold to a *merchant* which do not conform to the requirements of the contract, economic efficiency does not require that he be given the privilege of rejecting them. Professors Llewellyn and Honnold, it is said, "viewed the typical merchant buyer as a commodity broker —one who frequently sells various grades of goods and therefore is able to resell defective or subgrade goods more cheaply than the typical consumer buyer, and often at a cost equal to that of the seller. For such buyers, the remedy of damages—or its equivalent, a price allowance—is more likely to minimize costs." Priest, Breach and Remedy for the Tender of Nonconforming Goods Under the Uniform Commercial Code: An Economic Approach, 91 Harv.L.Rev. 960, 971 (1978).

Professor Priest surveyed the cases in which disappointed buyers sought to reject goods (or to "revoke acceptance" of them) with a view to comparing the success rates for merchants and for consumers. His hypothesis was that a high rate for consumers—which he found—is probable, owing to the courts' perception that the "joint costs" of breach are the more likely to be greater when a consumer obtains damages. In most of his cases where the seller was required to retake goods from a consumer, the item was a new car; "it is plausible [he says] that a dealer will be able to resell a defective automobile more cheaply than the initial purchaser." Id. at 996.

(3) *Significance.* "Considering the potential benefits of implied warranties of quality to buyers of consumer durable goods, the reintroduction of such warranties from behind the cover of prevailing disclaimer clauses may fairly be said to represent the most profound effect of the Magnuson-Moss Warranty Act. While predictions about any new statute may be fallible, it now seems that the Act's regulatory scheme for written warranties or service contracts will be overshadowed by its prohibition of disclaimers of implied warranties. The practical significance of the Act to sellers and buyers alike will be seen primarily in the implementation of the warranties of merchantability and fitness for purpose." C. Reitz, Consumer Protection Under the Magnuson-Moss Warranty Act 75–76 (1978). However, it does appear from an inspection of old and new texts of warranties that the Act accomplished some increase in intelligibility. Note, 31 Stan.L.Rev. 1117 (1979).

A PLAIN-LANGUAGE STATUTE

New York was the first state to enact a broadly applicable requirement that consumer contracts be written in "plain language" (see p. 479 supra). Some features of that statute are indicated here. But this Note directs attention in the main to a comparable statute in Connecticut for the reason that, while it is closely analogous to the New York act in its proscription of technical language, it goes beyond that act in providing a set of precise standards for compliance. The two statutes provide competing models for other legislation on the subject. Their similarities and differences, now to be noticed, are instructive.[a]

a. The New York statute (the so-called Sullivan Law) is set out in the Supplement. It is said to have signalled "the beginning of a new era of gov-

Unlike the New York statute, the Connecticut one provides mechanical tests of "plainness", in section 2(c). One of the eleven requirements stated there is that the average number of syllables per word be less than 1.55. Of course, in such a statute it is necessary to indicate what counts as a word, and what as a sentence, and to explain the procedure for relating the elements.[b] ("Count the . . . syllables and words . . . . . Then divide . . . . . The result is the average number of syllables per word.") Comparable procedures lead to the average number of words per sentence and per paragraph —two other calculations that figure in the tests. The statute features a choice for the draftsman, however, between meeting the objective tests of section 2(c) or a shorter set of tests, rather more vague, set out in section 2(b). These may be illustrated by an excerpt: "(1) [The contract] uses short sentences . . . (2) . . . everyday words; and . . . (4) . . . simple and active verb forms . . . ." What merit is there in providing two means of satisfying the statute? [c]

The statute provides that a consumer party is entitled to $100 (plus a modest attorney's fee, at the discretion of the court) as statutory damages for a violation by the other party. "No class action may be brought under this act." [d] Whereas the New York statute authorizes recovery for "any actual damages sustained" through a violation, the Connecticut statute is silent on that point. The latter provides: "A consumer contract shall remain enforceable, even though it violates this act." [e] (The New York statute contains an analogous provision.) A party who has "attempted in good faith to com-

ernment regulation of business;" comparable legislation has been introduced in about half the states and in the Congress. Semegen, Plain Language Legislation, 33 Pers.Fin.L.Q. Rev. 26 (1979).

The Connecticut statute—Public Act No. 79–532—was enacted in 1979, for effect in 1980.

The New York statute—Gen.Obl.L. § 5–702—became effective in 1978.

b. Section 8(i).

c. Actually there are three. Consider Section 5(e): "No consumer may bring an action under this act on a contract, if

(1) The consumer was represented at the signing of the contract by an attorney; and

(2) This fact is shown by the attorney's signed and dated statement on the contract." (If it were shown that the attorney providing this statement was nominated, or compensated, by the nonconsumer party, should that vitiate the statement? Would the service be unprofessional in that case?)

For adverse comment on the "safe harbor provided by the scientific test" see Semegen, op.cit. supra n. a: "for the most part illusory."

d. Section 5(c). The New York statute allows $50, and a "class action penalty" of as much as $10,000. It also provides for enforcement by the attorney general.

The statute took effect on November 1, 1978. A year later the State Consumer Protection Board issued a report on lease forms then in use, as showing "how resistant landlords and lawyers are to plain language and to tenants' rights." Consumer News, Nov. 1, 1979.

e. Section 7(a).

ply" with section 2(b) is exonerated of the stated sanctions.[f] (An attempt to comply with the objective tests counts for nothing, apparently, unless it succeeds.)

The scope of the statute is large. Important exclusions are made for insurance policies, mortgages, and real-estate deeds. In general, a party is exempt from liability under the statute (unless he is a landlord) if he does not act in the transaction "in the ordinary course of business"; and those entitled to claim under it are persons entering into written agreements primarily for personal, family or household purposes.

If the Connecticut statute had been applicable to the situation in the Henningsen case, could it have been used as the basis for the decision? As a contributing justification for it? Suppose not only that the statute applied in *Henningsen* but also that the contract complied with the objective tests of plainness. Would that have required the court to modify its opinion in any way? The statute provides that nothing in it precludes a consumer from making a claim (or raising a defense) that would have been available to him if the act were not in effect. Is it possible that the enactment had no effect on the law that preceded it, except to create many small claims when an error occurs in a matter such as miscounting the syllables in a standard form contract?

NOTES

(1) *An Insurance Experiment.* A Massachusetts statute sets objective tests of readability, in the manner of the Connecticut plain-language law, and requires that certain insurance policies meet them.[g] Before it was enacted the insurance law of that state, like that of all others, required that certain statutory language, or its substantial equivalent, be used to express various benefits. The new statute dispenses with mandated language. On the other hand, it provides that the benefits provided by a complying (plain-language) policy shall be both (a) those expressed in it and (b) those that the previously mandated language would have afforded. Do you see a potential of disadvantage for policyholders in this arrangement?

The Connecticut plain-language statute provides: "The use of specific language expressly required or authorized by court decision, statute, regulation or governmental agency shall not be a violation of this act." Section 6(a). It does not explain how to count the syllables, words, and paragraphs in such language.

(2) *A Bureaucratic Solution.* In Maine a consumer loan agreement (as defined) must be written "in a clear and coherent manner" and meet other

f. Section 5(b).

From the viewpoint of suppliers, this is said to be the single concession most to be desired in the course of legislation. Semegen, op.cit. supra n. a.

g. Mass.Ann.Stat. c. 175, § 2B (Supp. 1979).

The statute draws on the work of Dr. Rudolf Flesch, who is well known for testing the "readability" of texts and advising writers how to score well. For musings on his advice by a stylist see E. B. White, The Second Tree From the Corner 166 (1954).

tests (requirement effective July 4, 1981). The proponent of a form affected may submit it to the Bureau of Consumer Protection; its failure to act within a prescribed period has the effect of a certificate of compliance; and the Bureau may issue such a certificate. Me.Rev.Civ.Stat. Tit. 10, §§ 1121–26.

(3) *Test Market.* A study of the understandability of consumer-credit contracts appears to show that simplification helps, at least in seizing the gross ideas. Davis, Protecting Consumers from Overdisclosure and Gobbledygook, 63 Va.L.Rev. 841 (1977). Professor Davis administered reading-comprehension tests to some shoppers and to some students, using contracts in various forms. One aid to understanding was the removal of certain disclosures required by law in such contracts; but other measures proved more helpful. Classifying the test-takers, as by education, race, and so on, Professor Davis concluded that his re-drafting was comparatively most useful to low-income respondents.

(4) *Test Case.* A critic of the New York statute has suggested that it may generate an "entirely new rule" of liability in contract litigation—one that the legislature must not have intended: "[I]f a 'consumer' has damages following the execution of a contract which violates the plain English law, he may recover such damages from the creditor, seller or lessor even though (1) the damages did not flow from the violation, (2) the consumer understood the contract, and (3) there is language in the contract which, taken by itself, complies with the plain English law and which would bar the suit." [h] Can you think of a situation in which the Connecticut statute might produce that result?

One provision of the statute (paralleled in New York) is that "No consumer may bring an action under this act after the contract has been fully performed." [i] Does that dispose of the problem?

(5) *Meaning of "Consumer".* The Uniform Commercial Code, true to its name, was meant to leave consumer-protection laws in place, for the most part.[j] It does not give special treatment to consumers, and so has no definition for the class. It does, however, embody special rules about "consumer goods" [k] as defined in section 9–109(1): "used or bought for use primarily for personal, family or household purposes." Some form of this expression is regularly used (often with qualifiers) to identify the beneficiaries of reform legislation. More artful definitions of "consumer" can readily be thought of; [l] but it has been rightly observed that "no legal defi-

h. Letter of September 28, 1978, to an editor, from Wilbur H. Friedman, Esq., of the New York Bar. See also New York L.J., June 28, 1978, for Mr. Friedman's views. For further criticism see Goldstein, The Plain Language Law, 1 Communications and the Law 69 (1979). For a defense of the statute see Givens, Practice Commentary, McKinney's Consol.L. of N. Y., § 5–702 (Supp.), and for a panegyric see Note, 8 Ford.Urb.L.J. 451 (1980).

i. Section 5(f).

j. See UCC 9–201 and Comment.

k. For examples of special rules about transactions in consumer goods see UCC 9–204(2), 9–206(1), and 9–505.

l. Consider such a "business" transaction as the purchase of a car by a doctor.

Because we are all consumers, it has been said, it is somewhat crass to classify any of us as such. Skilton & Helstad, Protection of the Installment Buyer of Goods Under the UCC, 65 Mich.L.Rev. 1465 (1967).

nition, however sophisticated, could adequately cater for all borderline cases." [m]

UNCONSCIONABLE CONTRACTS UNDER THE UNIFORM COMMERCIAL CODE

One of the most controversial sections of the Uniform Commercial Code is UCC 2–302, which authorizes a court to refuse enforcement or to limit the application of a contract or clause that it determines to have been "unconscionable." The comment to that section reads in part:

"This section is intended to make it possible for the courts to police explicitly against the contracts or clauses which they find to be unconscionable. In the past such policing has been accomplished by adverse construction of language, by manipulation of the rules of offer and acceptance or by determinations that the clause is contrary to public policy or to the dominant purpose of the contract. . . . The principle is one of the prevention of oppression and unfair surprise (Cf. Campbell Soup Co. v. Wentz, 172 F.2d 80, 3d Cir. 1948) and not of disturbance of allocation of risks because of superior bargaining power." [a]

Professor Llewellyn, the Chief Reporter of the Code, defended the section at the hearings of the New York Law Revision Commission in 1954 in these words:

"Business lawyers tend to draft to the edge of the possible. Any engineer makes his construction within a margin of safety, and a wide margin of safety, so that he knows for sure that he is getting what he is gunning for. The practice of business lawyers has been, however—it has grown to be so in the course of time—to draft, as I said before, to the edge of the possible.

"Let me rapidly state that I do not find that this is desired by the business lawyers' clients. In all the time that I have been working on this Code, and before, one of the more striking phenomena has been to me that the lawyers insist on having all kinds of things that their clients don't want at all. If I get together with a gang of business lawyers in regard to a portion of the Code, I have a perfectly terrible time trying to make them see any sense at all. If, on the other hand, I can get some of their clients into the same room, when the lawyer insists, 'Under no circumstances!' the client says, 'why not?' He is apparently satisfied in the main with reasonable business judgment, and that kind of drafting is going to be very easy under the unconscionable clause, because that kind of drafting in which

m. Exemption Clauses in Contracts, First Report of the [English] Law Commission, etc., 30–32 (1969).

a. The comment is reprinted in full in the Supplement. The section itself appears there and in Jones v. Star Credit Co., p. 511 infra.

you get for your client or ask for your client things only within the margin of safety and don't try to take more than 80 per cent of the pie, is never going to be regarded as unconscionable. The only doubt that comes up in regard to unconscionability is, if you start drafting to the absolute limit of what the law can conceivably bear. At that point you run into what they run into now, and what you run into now is, the court kicks it over.

"We have all of us seen this kind of series of cases, haven't we? Case No. 1 comes up. The clause is perfectly clear and the court said, 'Had it been desired to provide such an unbelievable thing, surely language could have been made clearer.' Then counsel redrafts, and they not only say it twice as well, but they wind up saying, 'And we mean it,' and the court looks at it a second time and says, 'Had this been the kind of thing really intended to go into an agreement, surely language could have been found,' and so on down the line.

"This kind of thing does not make for good business, it does not make for good counseling, and it does not make for certainty. It means that you never know where you are, and it does a very bad thing to the law indeed. The bad thing that it does to the law is to lead to precedent after precedent in which language is held not to mean what it says and indeed what its plain purpose was, and that upsets everything for everybody in all future litigation.

"We believe that if you take this and bring it out into the open, if you say, 'When it gets too stiff to make sense, then the court may knock it out,' you are going to get a body of principles of construction instead of principles of misconstruction, and the precedents are going to build up so that the language will be relied upon and will be construed to mean what it says." Report of the New York State Law Revision Commission for 1954, N.Y.Leg.Doc. (1954) No. 65, pp. 177–78.

The Campbell Soup case, cited in the comment to the Code, involved a standard grower-canner contract for the sale to the canner of the growers' entire harvest of Chantenay carrots during the coming season for up to $30 per ton. Because of a scarcity of Chantenay carrots, they were virtually unobtainable at the time for delivery and their price had risen to at least $90 per ton. The growers began to sell some of the carrots to others in violation of the contract, and the canners brought suit against the growers to enjoin further sales and to compel specific performance. The court of appeals refused to grant equitable relief, saying that the "form has quite obviously been drawn by skilful draftsmen with the buyer's interests in mind," and "it is too hard a bargain to entitle the plaintiff to relief in a court of conscience." Of the several clauses that the court found objectionable, the "hardest of all" was a provision that excused the canner from performance if production was curtailed due to circumstances beyond its control, but prohibited the grower, even though he could no longer require the canner to take the carrots, from selling them elsewhere without the canner's written consent. But the court added, "we are not suggesting that the contract is illegal. Nor are we suggesting any excuse for the grower in this case who has deliberately broken an agreement. . . ." Presumably the canner could have recovered damages from the grower, but these would have been limited by a liquidated damage clause in the contract. Does this case support the rule of UCC 2–302? [b]

NOTES

(1) *Code Drafting.* For an illuminating and amusing account of the development, in successive Code drafts, of what became UCC 2–302, see Leff, Unconscionability and the Code—The Emperor's New Clause, 115 U. Pa.L.Rev. 485 (1967). Early drafts focussed on improprieties in bargaining, or the absence of it. Then the focus shifted: at one stage there was a comment condemning a "lopsided bargain," though deliberately entered into, with full knowledge and awareness. By Professor's Leff's account, the element of "naughty bargaining conduct" proved impossible to formulate, and a prohibition on lopsided terms proved unacceptable to important backers of the Code. "Thus faced with a dilemma, the difficulty of the first alternative and the unpopularity of the second, the draftsmen opted for a third solution. They fudged." Id., 501.

(2) *Restatement Second.* Section 208 of the Restatement Second states a rule in virtually the same terms as UCC 2–302(1). It is without parallel in the original Restatement. The comments and Reporter's Note cite some twenty cases, running back to 1750. More than half of them, however, were decided in the 1960's. Illustration 1 is based on the Campbell Soup case. Is the subject ripe for restatement? What weight might the Restatement section carry in California, where the legislature omitted UCC 2–302 in enacting the Code?

(3) *Equal Treatment.* Professor Robert Keeton has pıoposed the following generalization as a mode of striking down or modifying overly restrictive provisions in insurance policies:

> If the enforcement of a policy provision would defeat the reasonable expectations of the great majority of policyholders to whose claims it is relevant, it will not be enforced even against those who know of its restrictive terms.[c]

Many of the precedents he relies on purport to be interpretations of policy terms, rather than "policing of the bargain." As to these he says: "A better explanation of these precedents is that the language of the policy provision unambiguously provides so little coverage that it would be unconscionable to permit the insurer to enforce it . . . ." [d] Professor Keeton maintains that it would be unconscionable to enforce a harsh term, appearing in many similar policies, only against the few policyholders who are aware of

b. The case is discussed in 58 Yale L. J. 1161 (1949).

c. R. Keeton, Insurance Law (Basic Text) 358 (1971).

d. Id. at 360.

its existence and purport. Is "unconscionability" the same in Professor (now Judge) Keeton's lexicon as it is in the Code?

(4) *Trade-Association Terms.* In Northwest Lumber Sales v. Continental Forest Products, the Oregon Supreme Court had to deal with a trade-association term incorporated by reference in a contract for the sale of a carload of studs. The court denied effect to the term as written, on the ground that it diverged too far from a Code provision on the same subject. An alternative way of dealing with the term would be to refer it to section 2–302. In that way the court's attention would be directed to the "commercial setting, purpose and effect" of the term as it was not in the case cited. Giving attention to such matters in relation to a trade-association term might be especially rewarding because disinterested evidence of the drafter's purpose can be had. On the other hand, the procedure for decision chosen by the court has this happy effect: in a single decision the validity or invalidity of the term is determined for *all* contracts incorporating it (though only so far as *stare decisis* can be depended upon, of course). This advantage has to be balanced against the possibility that a trade-association term might be approved *in vacuo* as a permissible variation of the relevant Code provision (see UCC 1–102(3)), and yet be condemned as unconscionable for the particular instance of its use. How serious a prospect is that?

(The Northwest Lumber Sales case is reproduced at p. 806 infra.)

CONSUMER MARKET REMEDIES

In Vasquez v. Superior Court of San Joaquin County, 4 Cal.3d 800, 94 Cal.Rptr. 796, 484 P.2d 964 (1971), the court considered the merit of a complaint that a firm selling food freezers had defrauded customers in two counties; an action had been brought on behalf of all of them. Approving, the court said: "Individual actions by each of the defrauded consumers is often impracticable . . . . A class action by consumers produces several salutary by-products . . . ." What examples occur to you? Would the by-products be better if an action were brought by the state attorney general for restitution, an injunction, or another remedy as appropriate? Might it be better still to withhold any "collective" remedy and to assist individual victims of consumer fraud, as litigants, with recoveries of the costs of suing, treble damages, a "penalty", or some combination? Some offenses against consumers are subject to sanction without a showing that anyone was misled or injured. For what sorts of offense does that seem right? Is it equally right for private and for official claimants? If the initiative may be taken either by an official or by an individual (for himself or for a class) and preferences differ about the remedy, which action should have priority over the other? Firms doing business with consumers generally object to the cumulation of remedies, especially when the statutory offense may be committed by inadvertence. A fair and effective system of enforcement is an elusive goal in consumer-protection legislation.

In some states consumer-protection measures have been gathered into fairly comprehensive statutes with much detail.[a] Some of these were built more or less explicitly on the provisions of the Uniform Consumer Credit Code.[b] In other states, while particular older regulations remain in force, new offenses have been defined in general terms and remedies provided for them. The meaning of the general terms—whether "consumer fraud" or "unfair trade practice"—appears remarkably like that of "unconscionability".[c] *Questions*: Might an injunction, class action, or claim for damages (actual or penal) be predicated on UCC 2–302 alone?[d] What reason do you see to doubt it?

NOTES

(1) *Settlement Statutes*. Some legislatures have taken a hand in complaint-settlement procedures. Congress has encouraged firms extending warranties to consumers to establish "informal mechanisms" for settling disputes over them "fairly and expeditiously," and has entrusted some surveillance over procedures to the F.T.C.[e] This measure (part of the Magnuson-Moss Warranty Act) makes for interesting comparison with a state experiment pressing the disputants to make offers and counteroffers and calling on the courts to evaluate their terms.[f]

a. E. g., Vernon's Tex.Civ.Stat. Title 79, especially Subtitles 2 and 3; Wis. Stat.Ann. Chapters 421–28.

b. Not more than a dozen general enactments are traceable to the Code, including the Wisconsin statutes last cited.

c. See Kugler v. Romain, 58 N.J. 522, 279 A.2d 640 (1971); Ford Motor Co. v. Mayes, 575 S.W.2d 480 (Ky.App. 1979) (described below at p. 501).

d. In Kugler v. Romain, cited in the preceding footnote, the court left the question open whether or not the attorney general can maintain an action based solely on the section. It said that such an action is not maintainable "if the right of each individual claimant to relief depended upon a separate set of facts applicable only to him." As to damages see W. L. May Co., Inc. v. Philco-Ford Corp., 273 Or. 701, 543 P.2d 283 (1975) (issue not decided); Vom Lehn v. Astor Art Galleries, Ltd., 86 Misc.2d 1, 380 N.Y.S.2d 532 (Sup.Ct.1976); Pearson v. National Budgeting Systems, Inc., 31 A.D.2d 792, 297 N.Y.S.2d 59 (1969) (punitive damages).

e. 15 U.S.C.A. § 2310(a)(1).

f. Section 9 of the Massachusetts "Regulation of Business Practice and Consumer Protection Act" (Ann.L. c. 93A) provides special consumer protection, including punitive recoveries, for consumers injured by "unfair or deceptive acts or practices" in trade or commerce. An interesting prerequisite is a written demand for relief mailed or delivered to "any prospective respondent." If the recipient makes a timely "written tender of settlement," he is permitted, in any subsequent action, to represent it to the court as "reasonable in relation to the injury actually suffered by the petitioner." So finding, the court must "limit any recovery to the relief tendered." Subsection (3).

The special consumer remedies have been denied application against a nonprofessional home seller. Lantner v. Carson, 374 Mass. 596, 373 N.E.2d 973 (1978). In an action by Ralph Nader against a speakers' booking agency another section of the act was applied, under which the respondent has a more generous settlement opportunity. Nader v. Citron, 372 Mass. 96, 360 N.E.2d 870 (1977). In the former case the court said that the positions of the parties did not require statutory equalization. Does Nader's bargaining position require it, vis-a-vis a speakers' bureau?

(2) *Relief Against Deceptive Practices.* Unfair and deceptive trade practices are condemned by the Federal Trade Commission Act,[g] and many state legislatures have enacted parallel prohibitions—so-called little FTC acts.[h] Some of the latter authorize private rights of action,[i] although for the most part only a state official, such as the attorney general, may bring enforcement proceedings. For such an official, or for the Commission, to take preventive action against deception there would usually be no need to show conscious wrongdoing or even that anyone had suffered injury. But the statutes are less free-handed with private remedies. For example, in Bartner v. Carter, 405 A.2d 194 (Me.1979), the buyers of real property failed in a claim against the brokers, who had overstated the acreage in advertising the property. Though the state attorney general might have sought injunctive relief or issued regulations about such advertising, the court thought, the plaintiffs had not shown the requisite right of restitution, in the technical sense of the word. (They had gone forward with the purchase after the owner offered rescission.)

WILSON TRADING CORPORATION v. DAVID FERGUSON, LTD.

Court of Appeals of New York, 1968.
23 N.Y.2d 398, 244 N.E.2d 685.

JASEN, Judge. The plaintiff, Wilson Trading Corporation, entered into a contract with the defendant, David Ferguson, Ltd., for the sale of a specified quantity of yarn. After the yarn was delivered, cut and knitted into sweaters, the finished product was washed. It was during this washing that it was discovered that the color of the yarn had "shaded"—that is, "there was a variation in color from piece to piece and within the pieces." This defect, the defendant claims, rendered the sweaters "unmarketable".

This action for the contract price of the yarn was commenced after the defendant refused payment. As a defense to the action and as a counterclaim for damages, the defendant alleges that "[p]laintiff has failed to perform all of the conditions of the contract on its part required to be performed, and has delivered . . . defective and unworkmanlike goods".

The sales contract provides in pertinent part:

"2. No claims relating to excessive moisture content, short weight, count variations, twist, quality or shade shall be allowed *if made after weaving, knitting, or processing*, or more than 10 days

g. "Unfair methods of competition in or affecting commerce, and unfair or deceptive acts or practices in or affecting commerce, are declared unlawful." 15 U.S.C.A. § 45(a)(1).

h. E. g., Me.Rev.Stat.Ann. § 213 (1979). A Uniform Consumer Sales Practices Act has been proposed and in a few states enacted. See 7A Uniform Laws Ann. 1 et seq.

i. For a collection see Note, 64 Corn. L.Q. 522 (1979).

after receipt of shipment. . . . The buyer shall within 10 days of the receipt of the merchandise by himself or agent examine the merchandise for any and all defects." (Emphasis supplied.)

"4. This instrument constitutes the entire agreement between the parties, superseding all previous communications, oral or written, and no changes, amendments or additions hereto will be recognized unless in writing signed by both seller and buyer or buyer's agent. It is expressly agreed that no representations or warranties, express or implied, have been or are made by the seller except as stated herein, and the seller makes no warranty, express or implied, as to the fitness for buyer's purposes of yarn purchased hereunder, seller's obligations, except as expressly stated herein, being limited to the *delivery of good merchantable yarn of the description stated herein*". (Emphasis supplied.)

Special Term granted plaintiff summary judgment for the contract price of the yarn sold on the ground that "notice of the alleged breach of warranty for defect in shading was not given within the time expressly limited and is not now available by way of defense or counterclaim." The Appellate Division affirmed, without opinion.

The defendant on this appeal urges that the time limitation provision on claims in the contract was unreasonable since the defect in the color of the yarn was latent and could not be discovered until after the yarn was processed and the finished product washed.

Defendant's affidavits allege that its sweaters were rendered unsaleable because of latent defects in the yarn which caused "variation in color from piece to piece and within the pieces." This allegation is sufficient to create a question of fact concerning the merchantability of the yarn (Uniform Commercial Code, § 2–314, subd. [2]). Indeed, the plaintiff does not seriously dispute the fact that its yarn was unmerchantable, but instead, like Special Term, relies upon the failure of defendant to give notice of the breach of warranty within the time limits prescribed by paragraph 2 of the contract.

Subdivision (3) (par. [a]) of section 2–607 of the Uniform Commercial Code expressly provides that a buyer who accepts goods has a reasonable time after he discovers or should have discovered a breach to notify the seller of such breach. (Cf. 5 Williston, Contracts [3d ed.], § 713.) Defendant's affidavits allege that a claim was made immediately upon discovery of the breach of warranty after the yarn was knitted and washed, and that this was the earliest possible moment at which the defects could reasonably be discovered in the normal manufacturing process. Defendant's affidavits are, therefore, sufficient to create a question of fact concerning whether notice of the latent defects alleged was given within a reasonable time. (Cf. Ann., 17 A.L.R.3d 1010, 1112–1115 [1968].)

However, the Uniform Commercial Code allows the parties, within limits established by the code, to modify or exclude warranties and to limit remedies for breach of warranty. The courts below have found that the sales contract bars all claims not made before knitting and processing. Concededly, defendant discovered and gave notice of the alleged breach of warranty after knitting and washing.

We are, therefore, confronted with the effect to be given the time limitation provision in paragraph 2 of the contract. Analytically, paragraph 2 presents separate and distinct issues concerning its effect as a valid limitation on remedies for breach of warranty (Uniform Commercial Code, § 2–316, subd. [4]; § 2–719) and its effect as a modification of the express warranty of merchantability (Uniform Commercial Code, § 2–316, subd. [1]) established by paragraph 4 of the contract.

Parties to a contract are given broad latitude within which to fashion their own remedies for breach of contract (Uniform Commercial Code, § 2–316, subd. [4]; §§ 2–718–2–719). Nevertheless, it is clear from the official comments to section 2–719 of the Uniform Commercial Code that it is the very essence of a sales contract that at least minimum adequate remedies be available for its breach. "If the parties intend to conclude a contract for sale within this Article they must accept the legal consequence that there be at least a fair quantum of remedy for breach of the obligations or duties outlined in the contract. Thus any clause purporting to modify or limit the remedial provisions of this Article in an *unconscionable manner* is subject to deletion and in that event the remedies made available by this Article are applicable as if the stricken clause had never existed." (Uniform Commercial Code, § 2–719, official comment 1; emphasis supplied.)

It follows that contractual limitations upon remedies are generally to be enforced unless unconscionable. This analysis is buttressed by the fact that the official comments to section 2–302 of the Uniform Commercial Code, the code provision pertaining to unconscionable contracts or clauses, cites Kansas City Wholesale Grocery Co. v. Weber Packing Corp. (93 Utah 414, 73 P.2d 1272 [1937]), a case invalidating a time limitation provision as applied to latent defects, as illustrating the underlying basis for section 2–302.[1]

1. We recognize that the Superior Court of Pennsylvania in Vandenberg & Sons, N. V. v. Siter (204 Pa. Sup. 392, 204 A.2d 494 [1964]) held that the manifest unreasonableness of a time limitation clause presented a question of fact for trial (citing Uniform Commercial Code, § 1–204 and two pre-Uniform Commercial Code cases). However, the Pennsylvania Superior Court did not consider the sections of the code pertaining to limitation of remedies for breach of warranty. (Uniform Commercial Code, § 2–316, subd. [4]; §§ 2–718, 2–719.) When these interrelated sections are considered in light of the official comments to section 2–719 of the Uniform Commercial Code it is clear that the issue of the reasonability of limitations upon contractual remedies presents a question of unconscionability for the court. For this reason we decline to follow Vandenberg & Sons, N. V. v. Siter (supra).

Whether a contract or any clause of the contract is unconscionable is a matter for the court to decide against the background of the contract's commercial setting, purpose, and effect, and the existence of this issue would not therefore bar summary judgment.[2]

However, it is unnecessary to decide the issue of whether the time limitation is unconscionable on this appeal for section 2–719 (subd. [2]) of the Uniform Commercial Code provides that the general remedy provisions of the code apply when "circumstances cause an exclusive or limited remedy to fail of its essential purpose". As explained by the official comments to this section: "where an apparently fair and reasonable clause because of circumstances fails in its purpose or operates to deprive either party of the substantial value of the bargain, it must give way to the general remedy provisions of this Article." (Uniform Commercial Code, § 2–719, official comment 1.) Here, paragraph 2 of the contract bars all claims for shade and other specified defects made after knitting and processing. Its effect is to eliminate any remedy for shade defects not reasonably discoverable within the time limitation period. It is true that parties may set by agreement any time not manifestly unreasonable whenever the code "requires any action to be taken within a reasonable time" (Uniform Commercial Code, § 1–204, subd. [1]), but here the time provision eliminates all remedy for defects not discoverable before knitting and processing and section 2–719 (subd. [2]) of the Uniform Commercial Code therefore applies.

Defendant's affidavits allege that sweaters manufactured from the yarn were rendered unmarketable because of latent shading defects not reasonably discoverable before knitting and processing of the yarn into sweaters. If these factual allegations are established at trial, the limited remedy established by paragraph 2 has failed its "essential purpose" and the buyer is, in effect, without remedy. The time limitation clause of the contract, therefore, insofar as it applies to defects not reasonably discoverable within the time limits established by the contract, must give way to the general code rule that a buyer has a reasonable time to notify the seller of breach of contract after he discovers or should have discovered the defect. (Uniform Commercial Code, § 2–607, subd. [3], par. [a].) As indicated above, defendant's affidavits are sufficient to create a question of fact concerning whether notice was given within a reasonable time after the shading defect should have been discovered.

2. In construing section 2–302 (subd. [2]) as a matter of first impression, Sinkoff Beverage Co. v. Schlitz Brewing Co. (51 Misc.2d 446, 273 N.Y.S.2d 364) acknowledges that the issue of unconscionability is a matter of law for the court, but holds that a hearing to determine the commercial setting, purpose, and effect of a contract is mandatory rather than discretionary when the court accepts the possibility of unconscionability. Neither party argues that Special Term should have held an evidentiary hearing on the issue of unconscionability, and accordingly we express no opinion on this issue. (Cf. Cohen and Karger, Powers of the New York Court of Appeals [Rev. ed., 1952], §§ 161, 162.)

It can be argued that paragraph 2 of the contract, insofar as it bars all claims for enumerated defects not reasonably discoverable within the time period established, purports to exclude these defects from the coverage of the express warranty of merchantability. By this analysis, the contract not only limits remedies for its breach, but also purports to modify the warranty of merchantability. An attempt to both warrant and refuse to warrant goods creates an ambiguity which can only be resolved by making one term yield to the other (cf. Hawkland, Limitation of Warranty under the Uniform Commercial Code, 11 How.L.J. 28 [1965]). Section 2–316 (subd. [1]) of the Uniform Commercial Code provides that warranty language prevails over the disclaimer if the two cannot be reasonably reconciled.

Here, the contract expressly creates an unlimited express warranty of merchantability while in a separate clause purports to indirectly modify the warranty without expressly mentioning the word merchantability. Under these circumstances, the language creating the unlimited express warranty must prevail over the time limitation insofar as the latter modifies the warranty. It follows that the express warranty of merchantability includes latent shading defects and defendant may claim for such defects not reasonably discoverable within the time limits established by the contract if plaintiff was notified of these defects within a reasonable time after they were or should have been discovered.

The result reached under the Uniform Commercial Code is, therefore, similar to the pre-code case law holding unreasonable contractual provisions expressly limiting the time for inspection, trial or testing of goods inapplicable or invalid with respect to latent defects. (Randy Knitwear Inc. v. American Cyanamid Co., 7 N.Y.2d 791, 194 N.Y.S.2d 530, 163 N.E.2d 349 . . .) In fact, in Randy Knitwear (supra) this court held a contractual provision remarkably similar to the time limitation clause in the instant case to present a factual question for trial concerning the reasonableness of the time limitation.

In sum, there are factual issues for trial concerning whether the shading defects alleged were discoverable before knitting and processing, and, if not, whether notice of the defects was given within a reasonable time after the defects were or should have been discovered. If the shading defects were not reasonably discoverable before knitting and processing and notice was given within a reasonable time after the defects were or should have been discovered, a further factual issue of whether the sweaters were rendered unsaleable because of the defect is presented for trial.

The order of the Appellate Division should be reversed, with costs, and plaintiff's motion for summary judgment should be denied.

FULD, Chief Judge (concurring). I agree that there should be a reversal—but on the sole ground that a substantial question of fact has been raised as to whether the clause limiting the time in which to make a claim is "manifestly unreasonable" (Uniform Commercial Code, § 1–204) as applied to the type of defect here complained of. In this view, it is not necessary to consider the relevancy, if any, of other provisions of the Uniform Commercial Code (e. g., §§ 2–302, 2–316, 2–719), dealing with "unconscionable" contracts or clauses, exclusion of implied warranties or limitations on damages.[a]

NOTES

(1) *Case Criticism.* The court's reliance on UCC 2–719(2) has not been well-received. One objection is that the court drew "an unanalyzed distinction between 'discoverable' and 'undiscoverable' defects." Eddy, On the "Essential" Purpose of Limited Remedies: The Metaphysics of UCC Section 2–719(2), 65 Calif.L.Rev. 23, 50 (1977). See also Comment, Article Two Warranties in Commercial Transactions, 64 Corn.L.Rev. 30 (1978), making the following observations: (a) In effect, the clause disclaimed was [an express warranty] against defects not discoverable until processing; (b) A clause that allocates to the buyer all risk of damage from certain deficiencies accomplishes precisely what the parties intended; (c) It cannot fail of its purpose; (d) Absent procedural deficiencies, a remedy limitation cannot both be unconscionable and fail of its essential purpose.[b] Which of these propositions would you accept?

Assuming the purport of the Code to be that a disclaimer of warranty is subject to one set of standards (e. g., mention merchantability) and a limitation of remedies to another (e. g., failure of essential purpose), *Wilson Trading* has been cited as one of a number of instances in which courts have disregarded the distinction. Such a ruling may favor buyers unduly, some would say. But the procedure of the court in this case is said to afford the buyer the *least* protection: the term in the form there in question would be effective if it were to pass muster under *either* UCC 2–316 or 2–719. Is this fair criticism? See Note, Warranty Liability Limitation, 63 Va.L.Rev. 791 (1977) (advocating cumulative application of controls).

(2) *Disclaimer and Unconscionability.* Can you envisage an exclusion or modification of warranty that is effective under UCC 2–316, but may be found to be unconscionable under UCC 2–302? Professor Leff considers it incredible that a term passing muster under the former section should fail under the latter. Notice that unconscionability is employed as a limitation

a. For a comparable case see Neville Chemical Corp. v. Union Carbide Corp., 422 F.2d 1205 (3d Cir. 1970), cert. denied, 400 U.S. 826, in which the trial court said: "Like tulip bulbs shipped in the fall which did not bloom in the spring, a time limitation of a few days after receipt of shipment renders any warranties ineffective as to defects not discoverable on ordinary inspection," and cited Vandenberg & Sons N. V. v. Siter, footnote 1 supra (a bulb case). The appellate court construed the seller's disclaimers of warranties as inapplicable to the buyer's claim of negligence.

For an indication of the international character of the problem of disclaimers and exculpation clauses, and a comparative study, see Hippel, The Control of Exemption Clauses, 16 Int. & Comp.L.Q. 591 (1967).

b. Id. at 232–34. All but (c) are direct quotations.

in section 2–719, which is in turn referred to in section 2–316(4). Does this fact support or impair Professor Leff's argument?

Comment 1 after UCC 2–302 illustrates the "underlying basis" of the section with a series of ten cases. It has often been observed that about half of these concern unsuccessful attempts to disclaim warranties, and that all of them are in the range of topics dealt with in UCC 2–316, 2–718, 2–719. It seems curious that the comment writer could not find instances of unconscionability that are not curable by the Code's more explicit proscriptions.

The careful comment-reader may be further mystified by Comment 3 after section 2–719, which seems to revive Professor Leff's argument after other comments have done it in. One sentence in the comment is: "The seller in all cases is free to disclaim warranties in the manner provided in Section 2–316." See Leff, Unconscionability and the Code—The Emperor's New Clause, 115 U.Pa.L.Rev. 485, 520–32 (1967). But see Ellinghaus, In Defense of Unconscionability, 78 Yale L.J. 757, 793–97, 800–802 (1969).

Alter the facts in *Wilson Trading* so that they provide a test of the proposition, "seller in all cases is free to disclaim warranties." How would your hypothetical case be decided by the New York court? By Chief Judge Fuld?

(3) *Cross-Reference.* How much concordance can be found between the general dispositions of standardized-agreement law and the specific Code directives about the so-called battle of the forms (UCC 2–207)? Consider a "seller" whose standardized confirmation of a purchase order expresses an acceptance "predicated on the following clarifications, additions or modifications to the order"—listing them. (See Construction Aggregates Corp. v. Hewitt-Robins, p. 298 supra.) In interpreting the expression quoted, should a court consult the principle of Restatement Second, § 211(2)?—"treating alike all those similarly situated," so far as is reasonable? For this purpose, is every prospective buyer from this seller similarly situated? Or only those roughly equal in perspicacity? Or only those whose purchase orders bear some resemblance or other? If these are hard questions, perhaps it is because the Restatement principle addresses problems of a different order. Do you find more concordance between section 2–207 and other controls over standardized agreements? See Murray, Section 2–207 of the UCC: Another Word About Incipient Warranty, 39 U.Pitts.L.Rev. 597 (1978).

THE "REPAIR OR REPLACE" WARRANTY

Buyers of cars, appliances, equipment, and other "hard goods" regularly receive express warranties against defects. In a common form, the warranty commits the manufacturer, dealer, or both, to repair or replace the item, or parts or it, in certain circumstances. The Code gives its blessing to agreements making this the limit of the buyer's remedies: UCC 2–719(1)(a). However, beginning in the late 60's it became a flourishing industry to break through the limitation in the courts. Owing to post-Code legislation it is now virtually impossible to preclude a consumer buyer from all remedies other than repair or replacement, when he buys from a dealer. Moreover, the Code itself provides for overriding the limitation in certain cases; note the opening phrase of section 2–719(1): "Subject to the provisions [cited]."

An illustrative case concerned the warranty provided by the Ford Motor Company to buyers of its 1976 cars. It provided for repair or replacement "free" for a limited period, and continued with a disclaimer, as follows:

> Neither Ford nor any of its dealers shall have any responsibility for loss of use of the vehicle, loss of time, inconvenience, commercial loss or consequential damages.

Notwithstanding these restrictive provisions, in Ford Motor Co. v. Mayes, 575 S.W.2d 480 (Ky.App.1978), the buyers of a warranted truck obtained a verdict for such items as (1) the difference between the cost of the truck and its market value when they returned it to the dealer, (2) taxes, fees and finance charges they had paid, (3) gas and mileage expenses, (4) time lost from work, (5) an attorney's fee, and (6) punitive damages. In an appeal by Ford, not all of these recoveries survived; but most of them did. The judgment was based on the Kentucky Consumer Protection Act of 1972 (KRS 367.110–.300). The truck was seriously defective. "As required by Ford's warranty, Mr. and Mrs. Mayes returned the truck to the selling dealer, North City, seven or eight times for major repairs. The problems were never corrected. When the trouble was finally diagnosed as a twisted and diamonded frame, Ford would not extend the duration of the warranty . . . ." Some of the court's observations on the case are as follows:

> Although the limitation of the buyer's remedies was not unconscionable on its face, Ford's warranty policy was unconscionable as applied to Mr. and Mrs. Mayes. . . . After breach of its duty under the express warranty to repair or replace defective parts within a reasonable time, Ford could not, in good conscience, attempt to hide behind any provision making the express warranty the sole remedy of the buyer. . . .
>
> Because the truck could not be repaired within a reasonable time, Ford acted "unconscionably" when it insisted that Mr. and Mrs. Mayes had no remedy other than to allow Ford and its dealer to continue indefinitely in their efforts to correct the problem.

Many courts have reached a like conclusion on comparable facts. What is usually at stake is "consequential" damages. These are to be distinguished from "direct" damages, such as the difference between the price and the value of the defective item (see Chapter 6 for elaboration). Some courts would have awarded consequential damages to the truck buyers on the ground that the remedy as limited in the contract failed of its essential purpose.[a] Alternatively, it might be said that the failure to keep a warranty amounts to a repudiation of it and that the repudiator may not assert provisions of the warranty beneficial to it.[b]

For a contrasting case see S. M. Wilson & Co. v. Smith Int'l, Inc., 587 F.2d 1363 (9th Cir. 1978). The court said: "[W]e are influenced heavily by the characteristics of the contract . . . . Parties of relatively equal bargaining power negotiated an allocation of their risks of loss."

Owing to decisions like these, limited to the facts at hand, and to some avowed differences of opinion, the law on the point is unsettled.[c] Many decisions can be reconciled by distinguishing between commercial and consumer goods. (The case just quoted concerned a tunnel-boring machine, designed and built by the seller for more than half a million dollars.[d]) However, one court has refused to distinguish between the purchase of an automobile and the purchase of a commercial laser: "not that different."[e] Does UCC 2–719(2) admit of the distinction?[f] What others might be made? Should anything turn on the conscientiousness of the seller's

a. E. g., Murray v. Holiday Rambler, Inc., 83 Wis.2d 406, 265 N.W.2d 513 (1978). But see Polycon Industries, Inc. v. Hercules Inc., 471 F.Supp. 1316 (E.D.Wis.1979) ("not . . . all of the remedies available under the Code are appropriate in this case").

b. See Adams v. J. I. Case Co., 125 Ill.App.2d 388, 261 N.E.2d 1 (1970).

c. Erie County Water Authority v. Hen-Gar Constr. Corp., 473 F.Supp. 1310 (W.D.N.Y.1979).

d. As the seller knew, the buyer meant to use it to drive a coal-mine shaft. Owing to poor performance of the machine, there was a long delay in the project. In suing the seller, the buyer alleged damages of more than $1.8 million, all related to its use of the machine. The contract purported to limit the seller's obligation to the repair and replacement of certain parts and to exclude liability for the losses claimed. After delivery, the seller made repeated efforts to put the machine in good working order, but never succeeded. (Late in the day it was discovered that important elements of the machine had been installed backward, through the seller's fault.) The trial court gave summary judgment for the seller, and it was affirmed on appeal. No issue of unconscionability was presented; but the buyer invoked UCC 2–719(2).

The court noted that the seller "did not ignore his obligation to repair; he simply was unable to perform it. This is not enough to require that the seller absorb losses the buyer plainly agreed to bear. Risk shifting is socially expensive and should not be undertaken in the absence of a good reason . . . . The default of the seller is not so total and fundamental as to require that its consequential damage limitation be expunged from the contract.

"Each case must stand on its own facts." For a contrasting decision see Soo Line Railroad Co. v. Fruehauf Corp., 547 F.2d 1365 (8th Cir. 1977).

e. AES Technology Systems, Inc. v. Coherent Radiation, 583 F.2d 933 (7th Cir. 1978).

f. See Comment, 64 Corn.L.Rev. 30, 235–39 (1978).

efforts at repair? On whether the loss in question occurred before or after a reasonable time for making repairs had elapsed? [g]

NOTES

(1) *A Blow-Out Case.* A tire manufacturer warrants its products against defects. In addition, it wishes to provide a buyer with a replacement or refund if its tire fails during the first two years of normal use. (In that event he is to be charged with a fraction of the price of a new tire, determined with reference to the unexpired portion of that period.) The manufacturer does *not* wish to pay for other physical damage or for personal injury that a blow-out may cause. How would you draft a provision about warranties to achieve these purposes?

In Collins v. Uniroyal, Inc., 64 N.J. 260, 315 A.2d 16 (1974), a tire manufacturer was adjudged liable for death and other injuries, resulting from the blow-out of a tire, on a jury verdict. For purposes of the appeal the jury findings were understood to mean that there was no defect in the tire, and no liability in tort. The tire had been sold with a guarantee of repair or replacement and the liability was pitched on that. In light of this ruling, would you give up the effort to draft an express warranty and limit the remedy to refund and the like? If so, would that be a disservice to consumers? Justice Clifford, dissenting in *Collins,* argued that manufacturers would be discouraged by the decision from offering "extra" protection (i. e., more than buyers are entitled to under implied warranties and the like). The court said: "We deem this position not consonant with the commercial and human realities."

The contract in *Collins* recited: "This Guarantee does not cover consequential damages." Was this clearly unconscionable? Another court has said: "to give what looks like relief in the form of an express warranty, but is not, is unconscionable as a surprise limitation and therefore against public policy." [c] Does that beg the question? The same court observed that under the Code it is "very difficult" to create an express warranty and limit the remedy: and it remarked on the anomaly that UCC 2–316 permits warranties to be disclaimed altogether. Do you find the anomaly in the Code or in the decisions?

For a discriminating criticism of the Collins case—and of UCC 2–713(3)—see Note, 50 N.Y.U.L.Rev. 146 (1975). It suggests that importing unconscionability into the section is to state a "principle distorted by a rule."

(2) *Problem.* A manufacturer of commercial aircraft has had this experience: Two days after delivering a craft to a customer, the nose wheel malfunctioned, causing damage to the hull. The manufacturer was compelled to pay for that damage. For the future, is it possible for the manufacturer to restrict its liability in such a case by agreeing to replace the wheel only? See Delta Air Lines, Inc. v. Douglas Aircraft Co., 238 Cal. App.2d 95, 47 Cal.Rptr. 518 (1965). (In that case the head of the manufac-

g. One judgment is that the "courts are utilizing unfortunate distinctions that appeal more to our sense of moral outrage than our understanding of commercial life." Eddy, On the "Essential" Purposes of Limited Remedies: The Metaphysics of UCC Section 2–719(2), 65 Calif.L.Rev. 28 (1977).

c. Tuttle v. Kelly-Springfield Tire Co., 585 P.2d 1116 (Okla.1978).

turer's legal department testified that customers frequently asked that a remedy-limitation clause be removed, to which the normal reply was, "We will take it out only at an increase in price.")

(3) *A Lost Life.* A couple named Mieske kept a home-movie record of their wedding and their family life over many years thereafter. Wishing to have the films spliced into four reels, Mrs. Mieske delivered them to the Bartell Drug Co. for transmittal to a processor. She said, "Don't lose these. They are my life." At the same time she was handed a receipt (which she did not read) containing the language, "We assume no responsibility beyond retail cost of film unless otherwise agreed to in writing." The films being lost, the Mieskes sued Bartell Drug and the processor for $7,500. Each of them admitted negligence.

Assume that the plaintiffs' recovery depends upon establishing unconscionability in the receipt. (What else might it depend upon?) If the court finds the facts only as stated above, may it direct the jury that the limitation of liability is not binding? Or must it consider further evidence if offered by the defendant? If the court may not take judicial notice of the "commercial setting, purpose, and effect" of the agreement, what sort of evidence might the defendant suitably offer?

The trial court entered judgment for the plaintiff in the amount claimed, and Bartell Drug appealed. For the appellate disposition see Mieske v. Bartell Drug Co., 92 Wash.2d 40, 593 P.2d 1308 (1979).

WILLIAMS v. WALKER-THOMAS FURNITURE CO.

United States Court of Appeals, District of Columbia Circuit, 1965.
350 F.2d 445, 18 A.L.R.3d 1297.

J. SKELLY WRIGHT, Circuit Judge. Appellee, Walker-Thomas Furniture Company, operates a retail furniture store in the District of Columbia. During the period from 1957 to 1962 each appellant in these cases purchased a number of household items from Walker-Thomas, for which payment was to be made in installments. The terms of each purchase were contained in a printed form contract which set forth the value of the purchased item and purported to lease the item to appellant for a stipulated monthly rent payment. The contract then provided, in substance, that title would remain in Walker-Thomas until the total of all the monthly payments made equaled the stated value of the item, at which time appellants could take title. In the event of a default in the payment of any monthly installment, Walker-Thomas could repossess the item.

The contract further provided that "the amount of each periodical installment payment to be made by (purchaser) to the Company under this present lease shall be inclusive of and not in addition to the amount of each installment payment to be made by (purchaser) under such prior leases, bills or accounts; *and all payments now and hereafter made by (purchaser) shall be credited pro rata on all outstanding leases, bills and accounts* due the Company by (purchaser) at the time each such payment is made." (Emphasis added.) The effect of this rather obscure provision was to keep a balance due on every item purchased until the balance due on all items, whenever purchased, was liquidated. As a result, the debt incurred at the time of purchase of each item was secured by the right to repossess all the items previously purchased by the same purchaser, and each new item purchased automatically became subject to a security interest arising out of the previous dealings.

On May 12, 1962, appellant Thorne purchased an item described as a Daveno, three tables, and two lamps, having total stated value of $391.10. Shortly thereafter, he defaulted on his monthly payments and appellee sought to replevy all the items purchased since the first transaction in 1958. Similarly, on April 17, 1962, appellant Williams bought a stereo set of stated value of $514.95.[1] She too defaulted shortly thereafter, and appellee sought to replevy all the items purchased since December, 1957. The Court of General Sessions granted judgment for appellee. The District of Columbia Court of Appeals affirmed, and we granted appellants' motion for leave to appeal to this court.

Appellants' principal contention, rejected by both the trial and the appellate courts below, is that these contracts, or at least some of them, are unconscionable and, hence, not enforceable. In its opinion in Williams v. Walker-Thomas Furniture Company, 198 A.2d 914, 916 (1964), the District of Columbia Court of Appeals explained its rejection of this contention as follows:

"Appellant's second argument presents a more serious question. The record reveals that prior to the last purchase appellant had reduced the balance in her account to $164. The last purchase, a stereo set, raised the balance due to $678. Significantly, at the time of this and the preceding purchases, appellee was aware of appellant's financial position. The reverse side of the stereo contract listed the name of appellant's social worker and her $218 monthly stipend from the government. Nevertheless, with full knowledge that appellant had to feed, clothe and support both herself and seven children on this amount, appellee sold her a $514 stereo set.

"We cannot condemn too strongly appellee's conduct. It raises serious questions of sharp practice and irresponsible business dealings. A review of the legislation in the District of Columbia affecting retail sales and the pertinent decisions of the highest court in this jurisdiction disclose, however, no ground upon which this court can declare the contracts in question contrary to public policy. We note that were the Maryland Retail Installment Sales Act, Art. 83 Sections 128–153, or its equivalent, in force in the District of Columbia, we

1. At the time of this purchase her account showed a balance of $164 still owing from her prior purchases. The total of all the purchases made over the years in question came to $1,800. The total payments amounted to $1,400.

could grant appellant appropriate relief. We think Congress should consider corrective legislation to protect the public from such exploitive contracts as were utilized in the case at bar."

We do not agree that the court lacked the power to refuse enforcement to contracts found to be unconscionable. In other jurisdictions, it has been held as a matter of common law that unconscionable contracts are not enforceable.[2] While no decision of this court so holding has been found, the notion that an unconscionable bargain should not be given full enforcement is by no means novel. In Scott v. United States, 79 U.S. (12 Wall.) 443, 445, 20 L.Ed. 438 (1870), the Supreme Court stated:

". . . If a contract be unreasonable and unconscionable, but not void for fraud, a court of law will give to the party who sues for its breach damages, not according to its letter, but only such as he is equitably entitled to. . . ."

Since we have never adopted or rejected such a rule, the question here presented is actually one of first impression.

Congress has recently enacted the Uniform Commercial Code, which specifically provides that the court may refuse to enforce a contract which it finds to be unconscionable at the time it was made. (Section 2–302) The enactment of this section, which occurred subsequent to the contracts here in suit, does not mean that the common law of the District of Columbia was otherwise at the time of enactment, nor does it preclude the court from adopting a similar rule in the exercise of its powers to develop the common law for the District of Columbia. In fact, in view of the absence of prior authority on the point, we consider the congressional adopting of Section 2–302 persuasive authority for following the rationale of the cases, from which the section is explicitly derived.[3] Accordingly, we hold that where the element of unconscionability is present at the time a contract is made, the contract should not be enforced.

Unconscionability has generally been recognized to include an absence of meaningful choice on the part of one of the parties together with contract terms which are unreasonably favorable to the other party. Whether a meaningful choice is present in a particular case can only be determined by consideration of all the circumstances surrounding the transaction. In many cases the meaningfulness of the

2. Campbell Soup Co. v. Wentz, 172 F.2d 80 (3d Cir. 1948); Indianapolis Morris Plan Corp. v. Sparks, 132 Ind.App. 145, 172 N.E.2d 899 (1961); Henningsen v. Bloomfield Motors, Inc., 32 N.J. 358, 161 A.2d 69, 84–96, 75 A.L.R.2d 1 (1960). Cf. 1 Corbin, Contracts Section 128 (1963).

3. See Comment, Sec. 2–302, Uniform Commercial Code (1962). Compare Note, 45 Va.L.Rev. 583, 590 (1959), where it is predicted that the rule of Sec. 2–302 will be followed by analogy in cases which involve contracts not specifically covered by the section. Cf. 1 State of New York Law Revision Commission, Report and Record of Hearings on the Uniform Commercial Code 108–110 (1954) (remarks of Professor Llewellyn).

choice is negated by a gross inequality of bargaining power.[4] The manner in which the contract was entered is also relevant to this consideration. Did each party to the contract, considering his obvious education or lack of it, have a reasonable opportunity to understand the terms of the contract, or were the important terms hidden in a maze of fine print and minimized by deceptive sales practices? Ordinarily, one who signs an agreement without full knowledge of its terms might be held to assume the risk that he has entered a one-sided bargain.[5] But when a party of little bargaining power, and hence little real choice, signs a commercially unreasonable contract with little or no knowledge of its terms, it is hardly likely that his consent, or even an objective manifestation of his consent, was ever given to all the terms. In such a case the usual rule that the terms of the agreement are not to be questioned [6] should be abandoned and the court should consider whether the terms of the contract are so unfair that enforcement should be withheld.[7]

In determining reasonableness or fairness, the primary concern must be with the terms of the contract considered in light of the circumstances existing when the contract was made. The test is not simple, nor can it be mechanically applied. The terms are to be considered "in the light of the general commercial background and the commercial needs of the particular trade or case." [8] Corbin suggests the test as being whether the terms are "so extreme as to ap-

4. See Henningsen v. Bloomfield Motors, Inc., supra Note 2, 161 A.2d 69 at 86, and authorities there cited. Inquiry into the relative bargaining power of the two parties is not an inquiry wholly divorced from the general question of unconscionability, since a one-sided bargain is itself evidence of the inequality of the bargaining parties. This fact was vaguely recognized in the common law doctrine of intrinsic fraud, that is, fraud which can be presumed from the grossly unfair nature of the terms of the contract. See the oft-quoted statement of Lord Hardwicke in Earl of Chesterfield v. Janssen, 28 Eng. Rep. 82, 100 (1751):

> ". . . (Fraud) may be apparent from the intrinsic nature and subject of the bargain itself; such as no man in his senses and not under delusion would make . . ."

5. See Restatement, Contracts Sec. 70 (1932); Note, 63 Harv.L.Rev. 494 (1950). See also Daley v. People's Building, Loan & Savings Ass'n, 178 Mass. 13, 59 N.E. 452, 453 (1901), in which Mr. Justice Holmes, while sitting on the Supreme Judicial Court of Massachusetts, made this observation:

> ". . . Courts are less and less disposed to interfere with parties making such contracts as they choose, so long as they interfere with no one's welfare but their own. . . . It will be understood that we are speaking of parties standing in an equal position where neither has any oppressive advantage or power. . . ."

6. This rule has never been without exception. In cases involving merely the transfer of unequal amounts of the same commodity, the courts have held the bargain unenforceable for the reason that "in such a case, it is clear, that the law cannot indulge in the presumption of equivalence between the consideration and the promise." 1 Williston, Contracts Sec. 115 (3d ed. 1957).

7. See the general discussion of "Boiler-Plate Agreements" in Llewellyn The Common Law Tradition 362–371 (1960).

8. Comment, Uniform Commercial Code Sec. 2–307.

pear unconscionable according to the mores and business practices of the time and place." 1 Corbin, op. cit. supra Note 2.[9] We think this formulation correctly states the test to be applied in those cases where no meaningful choice was exercised upon entering the contract.

Because the trial court and the appellate court did not feel that enforcement could be refused, no findings were made on the possible unconscionability of the contracts in these cases. Since the record is not sufficient for our deciding the issue as a matter of law, the cases must be remanded to the trial court for further proceedings.

So ordered.

DANAHER, Circuit Judge (dissenting):

The District of Columbia Court of Appeals obviously was as unhappy about the situation here presented as any of us can possibly be. Its opinion in the *Williams* case, quoted in the majority text, concludes: "We think Congress should consider corrective legislation to protect the public from such exploitive contracts as were utilized in the case at bar."

My view is thus summed up by an able court which made no finding that there had actually been sharp practice. Rather the appellant seems to have known precisely where she stood.

There are many aspects of public policy here involved. What is a luxury to some may seem an outright necessity to others. Is public oversight to be required of the expenditures of relief funds? A washing machine, e. g., in the hands of a relief client might become a fruitful source of income. Many relief clients may well need credit, and certain business establishments will take long chances on the sale of items, expecting their pricing policies will afford a degree of protection commensurate with the risk. Perhaps a remedy when necessary will be found within the provisions of the "Loan Shark" law, D. C.Code Sections 26–601 et seq. (1961).

I mention such matters only to emphasize the desirability of a cautious approach to any such problem, particularly since the law for so long has allowed parties such great latitude in making their own contracts. I dare say there must annually be thousands upon thousands of installment credit transactions in this jurisdiction, and one can only speculate as to the effect the decision in these cases will have.[10]

9. See Henningsen v. Bloomfield Motors, Inc., supra Note 2; Mandel v. Liebman, 303 N.Y. 88, 100 N.E.2d 149 (1951). The traditional test as stated in Greer v. Tweed . . ., 13 Abb.Pr., N.S. (N.Y.1872), at 429, is "such as no man in his senses and not under delusion would make on the one hand, and as no honest or fair man would accept, on the other."

10. However the provision ultimately may be applied or in what circumstances, D.C.Code Sec. 28–2–302 (Supp.IV, 1965) did not become effective until January 1, 1965.

I join the District of Columbia Court of Appeals in its disposition of the issues.[a]

NOTES

(1) *Effect of Repossession.* The contract provision authorizing the seller to repossess one item for the buyer's failure to pay for another is known as a cross-collateral, or "dragnet" provision. Is it clear that the furniture company would be overpaid by the enforcement of this provision? If the repossessed items are resold for less than the buyer's indebtedness, the seller is entitled to a deficiency judgment for the difference, plus certain expenses. (The right to such a judgment is curtailed, however, in some consumer credit legislation, such as section 5.103 of the Uniform Consumer Credit Code.) If they are resold for more than is due, the seller must account to the buyer for the surplus. What is the likelihood of a surplus, on a resale of second-hand consumer goods? On the subject of enforcing security interests, Article 9, Part 5, of the Uniform Commercial Code may be consulted, but the subject must be pursued in a course concerning security interests in personal property.

(2) *Questions.* If the furniture company's contracts had not contained a cross-collateral provision, would there have been anything offensive about them? Should Mrs. Williams have been permitted to keep the stereo set without paying for it? To keep it on paying part of the price? To return it and keep the other furniture she had bought? Do your answers depend in part on what you know of her financial position? Note the remarks of the lower court on the subject. Do they contain a patronizing implication that storekeepers may decide who can and who cannot afford their merchandise?

(3) *Pro-Rata Payments.* Mrs. Williams was represented by the legal assistance office of the bar association.[b] "The Legal Assistance Office was willing to concede that the store could repossess the stereo record player for nonpayment, but what stirred them to action was that the seller sought to scoop up all that it had ever sold to Ora. . . . The store's records showed that of a combined total claim of $444 as of December 26, 1962, Ora still owed 25¢ on item 1, purchased December 23, 1957 (price $45.65); 3¢ on item 2, purchased December 31, 1957 (price $13.21); . . . and similarly for subsequent purchases . . . ." Skilton and Helstad, Protection of the Installment Buyer of Goods under the UCC, 65 Mich.L.Rev. 1465 (1967).[c] Mrs. Williams had made payments of more than $1,000. Apparently the store applied each payment in the proportion that the outstanding balances on the several items bore to one another at the time of the payment.

Another way to apportion a payment is in relation to the *original* debt for each item. If the store had applied Mrs. Williams' payments that way,

a. The case is the basis for illustration 5 after Restatement Second, § 208, referring especially to the clause, "all payments . . . shall be credited pro rata on all outstanding . . . accounts." The Illustration concludes: "It may be determined that either the quoted clause or the contract as a whole was unconscionable when made."

b. In addition, the court of appeals appointed amicus curiae.

c. Of many comments on the Williams case, this is an outstanding one.

she would evidently have paid in full for about a dozen of the 16 items she bought from the store. Could the store have been compelled to reallocate her payments in that manner, as a plausible reading of the contract?

The manner of apportioning payments is widely prescribed by legislation on retail installment sales. For a case like that of Mrs. Williams the Uniform Consumer Credit Code states this rule: "payments received by the seller . . . are deemed, for the purpose of determining the amount of the debt secured by the various security interests, to have been applied first to the payment of the debts arising from the sales first made. To the extent debts are paid according to this section, security interests in items of property terminate as the debt originally incurred with respect to each item is paid." UCCC 3.303(1).[d]

The specific legislation germane to the Williams case, and many concrete prohibitions on particular practices, suggest some questions: Is a court less likely to declare a contract unconscionable by reason of the fact that the legislature has placed contracts of its type in a straitjacket of exact proscriptions designed to protect one of the parties? That is, does statutory control of contract terms, as it grows, limit the range of unconscionability doctrine? If so, is this a good thing?

(4) *The Lawyer's Role.* As a legal precedent, the court's ruling on unconscionability is more significant for consumers generally than any victory Mrs. Williams could have won on the basis of interpretation of her contract. Sometimes a client's interest is better served by seeking relief on a narrow basis than by treating his problem as a test case on a broader principle, such as unconscionability. In this situation, what is the duty of the lawyer? If he is dedicated to the interests of consumers at large, should he seek to advance them by risking the interest of an individual client? Legal-aid lawyers report that they can commonly settle complaints of consumer debtors on favorable terms, with little effort. Should they urge such a client to forego settlement in the hope of obtaining a landmark ruling? What are the ethical considerations? For a legal-aid lawyer, who is not compensated by individual clients, is it necessary to enlist himself in general causes more than for a lawyer charging fees? Permissible?

(5) *Problem.* High-pressure selling by the agent of a fuel utility, who speaks no Spanish, produces the sale of a furnace to the owner of an apartment building whose native language is Spanish and who has a limited knowledge of English. What more is required to show that the contract is unconscionable? See Brooklyn Union Gas Co. v. Jimeniz, 82 Misc.2d 948, 371 N.Y.S.2d 289 (N.Y.Civ.Ct.1978).

d. As for sales pursuant to a revolving charge account, see subsection (2). The Uniform Commercial Code affords a modest measure of protection for buyers of successive consumer items in UCC 9–204(2).

JONES v. STAR CREDIT CORP.

Supreme Court of New York, Nassau County, 1969.
59 Misc.2d 189, 298 N.Y.S.2d 264.

WACHTLER, J. On August 31, 1965 the plaintiffs, who are welfare recipients, agreed to purchase a home freezer unit for $900 as the result of a visit from a salesman representing Your Shop At Home Service, Inc. With the addition of the time credit charges, credit life insurance, credit property insurance, and sales tax, the purchase price totalled $1,234.80. Thus far the plaintiffs have paid $619.88 toward their purchase. The defendant claims that with various added credit charges paid for an extension of time there is a balance of $819.81 still due from the plaintiffs. The uncontroverted proof at the trial established that the freezer unit, when purchased, had a maximum retail value of approximately $300. The question is whether this transaction and the resulting contract could be considered unconscionable within the meaning of Section 2–302 of the Uniform Commercial Code which provides in part:

> (1) If the court as a matter of law finds the contract or any clause of the contract to have been unconscionable at the time it was made the court may refuse to enforce the contract, or it may enforce the remainder of the contract without the unconscionable clause, or it may so limit the application of any unconscionable clause as to avoid any unconscionable result.
>
> (2) When it is claimed or appears to the court that the contract or any clause thereof may be unconscionable the parties shall be afforded a reasonable opportunity to present evidence as to its commercial setting, purpose and effect to aid the court in making the determination. L.1962, c. 553, eff. Sept. 27, 1964.

There was a time when the shield of "caveat emptor" would protect the most unscrupulous in the marketplace—a time when the law, in granting parties unbridled latitude to make their own contracts, allowed exploitive and callous practices which shocked the conscience of both legislative bodies and the courts.

The effort to eliminate these practices has continued to pose a difficult problem. On the one hand it is necessary to recognize the importance of preserving the integrity of agreements and the fundamental right of parties to deal, trade, bargain, and contract. On the other hand there is the concern for the uneducated and often illiterate individual who is the victim of gross inequality of bargaining power, usually the poorest members of the community.

Concern for the protection of these consumers against overreaching by the small but hardy breed of merchants who would prey on them is not novel. The dangers of inequality of bargaining power were vaguely recognized in the early English common law when Lord Hardwicke wrote of a fraud, "which may be apparent from the intrinsic nature and subject of the bargain itself; such as no man in his senses and not under delusion would make." The English authorities on this subject were discussed in Hume v. United States, 132 U.S. 406, 10 S.Ct. 134, 33 L.Ed. 393 (1889) where the United States Supreme Court characterized these as "cases in which one party took advantage of the other's ignorance of arithmetic to impose upon him, and the fraud was apparent from the face of the contracts."

The law is beginning to fight back against those who once took advantage of the poor and illiterate without risk of either exposure or interference. From the common law doctrine of intrinsic fraud we have over the years, developed common and statutory law which tells not only the buyer but also the seller to beware. This body of laws recognizes the importance of a free enterprise system but at the same time will provide the legal armor to protect and safeguard the prospective victim from the harshness of an unconscionable contract.

Section 2–302 of the Uniform Commercial Code enacts the moral sense of the community into the law of commercial transactions. It authorizes the court to find, as a matter of law, that a contract or a clause of a contract was "unconscionable at the time it was made", and upon so finding the court may refuse to enforce the contract, excise the objectionable clause or limit the application of the clause to avoid an unconscionable result. "The principle", states the Official Comment to this section, "is one of the prevention of oppression and unfair surprise". It permits a court to accomplish directly what heretofore was often accomplished by construction of language, manipulations of fluid rules of contract law and determinations based upon a presumed public policy.

There is no reason to doubt, moreover, that this section is intended to encompass the price term of an agreement. In addition to the fact that it has already been so applied (State by Lefkowitz v. ITM, Inc., 52 Misc.2d 39, 275 N.Y.S.2d 303; Frostifresh Corp. v. Reynoso, 52 Misc.2d 26, 274 N.Y.S.2d 757, affd. 54 Misc.2d 119, 281 N.Y.S.2d 964; American Home Improvement, Inc. v. MacIver, 105 N.H. 435, 201 A.2d 886, 14 A.L.R.3d 324), the statutory language itself makes it clear that not only a clause of the contract, but the contract in toto, may be found unconscionable as a matter of law. Indeed, no other provision of an agreement more intimately touches upon the question of unconscionability than does the term regarding price.

Fraud, in the instant case, is not present; nor is it necessary under the statute. The question which presents itself is whether or not, under the circumstances of this case, the sale of a freezer unit having a retail value of $300 for $900 ($1,439.69 including credit charges and $18 sales tax) is unconscionable as a matter of law. The court believes it is.

Concededly, deciding the issue is substantially easier than explaining it. No doubt, the mathematical disparity between $300, which presumably includes a reasonable profit margin, and $900, which is exorbitant on its face, carries the greatest weight. Credit charges alone exceed by more than $100 the retail value of the freezer. These alone, may be sufficient to sustain the decision. Yet, a caveat is warranted lest we reduce the import of Section 2–302 solely to a mathematical ratio formula. It may, at times, be that; yet it may also be much more. The very limited financial resources of the purchaser, known to the sellers at the time of the sale, is entitled to weight in the balance. Indeed, the value disparity itself leads inevitably to the felt conclusion that knowing advantage was taken of the plaintiffs. In addition, the meaningfulness of choice essential to the making of a contract, can be negated by a gross inequality of bargaining power. (Williams v. Walker-Thomas Furniture Co., 121 U.S.App.D.C. 315, 350 F.2d 445.)

There is no question about the necessity and even the desirability of instalment sales and the extension of credit. Indeed, there are many, including welfare recipients, who would be deprived of even the most basic conveniences without the use of these devices. Similarly, the retail merchant selling on instalment or extending credit is expected to establish a pricing factor which will afford a degree of protection commensurate with the risk of selling to those who might be default prone. However, neither of these accepted premises can clothe the sale of this freezer with respectability.

Support for the court's conclusion will be found in a number of other cases already decided. In American Home Improvement, Inc. v. MacIver, supra, the Supreme Court of New Hampshire held that a contract to install windows, a door and paint, for the price of $2,568.60, of which $809.60 constituted interest and carrying charges and $800. was a salesman's commission was unconscionable as a matter of law. In State by Lefkowitz v. ITM, Inc., supra, a deceptive and fraudulent scheme was involved, but standing alone, the court held that the sale of a vacuum cleaner, among other things, costing the defendant $140 and sold by it for $749 cash or $920.52 on time purchase was unconscionable as a matter of law. Finally, in Frostifresh Corp. v. Reynoso, supra, the sale of a refrigerator costing the seller $348 for $900 plus credit charges of $245.88 was unconscionable as a matter of law. . . .

Having already paid more than $600 toward the purchase of this $300 freezer unit, it is apparent that the defendant has already been amply compensated. In accordance with the statute, the application of the payment provision should be limited to amounts already paid by the plaintiffs and the contract be reformed and amended by changing the payments called for therein to equal the amount of payment actually so paid by the plaintiffs.

NOTES

(1) *The Question of Remedies.* If Mr. and Mrs. Jones had paid $1,000 before complaining of the contract, would the court have permitted them to recover a part of it? If they had paid only $300, would the court have required them to pay more? What is the rationale of stopping the payments at $619.88?

One of the cases cited by the court, Frostifresh Corp. v. Reynoso, is a well-known action by the seller of a freezer for the unpaid balance of the price. The Reynosos had made only one payment, of $32. The plaintiff had paid $348 for the appliance. The trial court made a simple deduction, and gave judgment for $316. On appeal, the judgment was reversed, and the trial court was directed to give judgment for the "net cost for the refrigerator-freezer, plus a reasonable profit, in addition to trucking and service charges necessarily incurred and reasonable finance charges." Two comments on the case are as follows:

"This case means that sellers can charge the most exorbitant rates, secure in the knowledge that at the worst they will be able to recover a reasonable profit plus all their expenses." Narral, interview, in The Law and the Low Income Consumer 330 ff. (Katz, ed., 1968).

"It must be recognized that even in the poverty situations, putting aside the cases of fraud and high pressure in home sales, the buyers do want the goods. Even in the famous *Frostifresh* case, the question of remedies was complicated by the fact that the Spanish-speaking people deceived into buying a home freezer at a high price *chose to keep the freezer.* Thus we cannot adopt restrictions on remedies so punitive as to put the credit sellers in the poverty areas, and their financers, out of business. Despite the present high social cost, they serve a social purpose." Kripke, Consumer Credit Regulation: A Creditor-Oriented Viewpoint, 68 Colum.L.Rev. 455, 478 ff. (1968).

(2) *Unconscionability Unconfined.* Appeals have been made against price unconscionability, with success, not only by buyers of food freezers and of home improvements (as the foregoing opinion shows) but also by buyers of Oriental jade carvings for a price of some $67,000. Vom Lehn v. Astor Art Galleries, Ltd., 86 Misc.2d 1, 380 N.Y.S.2d 532 (1976). What divers things might the doctrine mean, in relation to such differing consumers?

(3) *Unconscionability: Two Varieties.* The unconscionability provision of the Code is criticized in Leff, Unconscionability and the Code—The Emperor's New Clause, 115 U.Pa.L.Rev. 485 (1967), and defended in Ellinghaus, In Defense of Unconscionability, 78 Yale L.J. 757 (1969). That debate draws a helpful distinction between unfairness in the content of the agreement (which is termed "substantive unconscionability") and unfairness in the bargaining process by which agreement is reached (which is termed "procedural unconscionability"). Among the questions that the authors raise are the following:

To what extent are substantive and procedural unconscionability either necessary or sufficient? For example, when, if ever, will a showing of procedural unconscionability be enough, without regard to whether or not there is substantive unconscionability? Or, when, if ever, will a showing of *fairness* in the bargaining process "insulate" an otherwise objectionable agreement from a claim of substantive unconscionability? And what is the significance of potential as opposed to actual, unfairness in the form of inequality of bargaining power? What account is to be taken of the peculiar social and economic status of the weaker party in such a situation? To what extent are unfairness in the entire contract (which has been termed "overall imbalance") and unfairness in a particular part of the contract either necessary or sufficient? To the extent that unfairness in a particular part is sufficient, what is the impact of an excessive price, a disclaimer of warranties, a limitation of remedies, and so on? And which sorts of cases justify a refusal to enforce the entire contract and which sorts call for a more limited response?

Is it helpful to regard the problem of unconscionability as one of allocating risks? See Murray, Unconscionability: Unconscionability, 31 U. Pitt.L.Rev. 1 (1969), and comments beginning at id., 333 (1970).

For further exploration of questions of unconscionability see the discussions cited in connection with the text at p. 466 supra.

PRICE UNCONSCIONABILITY

How may a court determine that the price charged for goods is so high that the contract is unconscionable, if there is no other element of overreaching? Must the court be prepared to say what the "intrinsic" value of the goods is? Must it be prepared to say what costs of doing business the seller may reasonably incur? What would be a reasonable profit for him? Can it be maintained that a price is unconscionable if it yields the seller "a greater profit than similarly situated sellers ordinarily receive"? See Note, 67 Mich.L.Rev. 1248, 1259 (1969).

The Uniform Consumer Credit Code (not widely adopted) puts the focus on what is too much for the buyer to pay, rather than on what is too much for the seller to charge. It directs that a comparison be made between the for-credit price agreed to by the buyer (of property or services) and the value "measured by the price at which similar property or services are readily obtainable in credit transactions by like consumers . . . ." If gross disparity exists, that is one of several stated factors to be considered in determining whether or not an agreement is unconscionable.[a]

To some observers the conceptions "like buyers" and "similarly situated sellers" appear to be fatally undefined. As we have seen, however, there is authority for condemning prices as unconscionable. Another example is Kugler v. Romain, 58 N.J. 522, 279 A.2d 640 (1971), which concerned sales of an "educational package" of books

a. Section 5.108. The Code authorizes injunctive relief at the behest of a consumer and also of a public official. See also the Uniform Consumer Sales Practices Act § 4(c).

and related materials. The court ruled that the price charged was "unconscionable in relation to [the seller's] cost and the value to the consumers." The action was brought by the state's attorney general under its Consumer Fraud Act. He "pointed out that . . . the books had very little and in some cases no value for the purpose for which the consumers were persuaded to buy them." Also, the court accepted testimony that the price "was about two and a half times a reasonable price in the relevant market."

If sales are made through home solicitations, is the relevant market the universe of such sales or the universe of sales (of like merchandise) both in-store and door-to-door? As will be seen, the judgment has been made that door-to-door selling is so distinctive as to warrant special legislative treatment. One of the premises is that selling costs are exceptionally high, yet the statutes on the subject do *not* preclude pricing to cover those costs.[b] In Jones v. Star Credit Corp., p. 511 supra, is it implicit that exceptional selling costs ought not to be countenanced? In that case reference is made to taking advantage of "the poor and illiterate." In a comparable case the court noted that the buyer had to claim welfare benefits while paying for the goods.[c] Do these observations suggest any appropriate basis for classifying buyers?

A classification of sellers was attempted in an F.T.C. survey of retailing in the District of Columbia. Two groups were identified: those catering primarily to low-income customers and those catering to a more general market. The former used comparatively high markups and prices, it was found; but their costs appeared to be correspondingly high: their "net profit on sales . . . was only slightly higher and net profit return on net worth was considerably lower when compared to general market retailers." [d] For low-income market retailers, what elements of cost would you expect to be above average? Presumably the residents of low-income neighborhoods are relatively poor credit risks, as a class. If that fact imposes a special cost on such a resident who would otherwise qualify for favorable credit terms (why should it?), and the cost takes the form of a high markup, does it follow that the price is unconscionable as to him? Would it be well to require that a retailer offering credit in that neighborhood—at high prices—disclose to his customers that merchandise like his is available elsewhere at a lower price? [e]

b. On the significance of high costs, see Note, 20 Me.L.Rev. 159 (1968).

c. Toker v. Westerman, 8 UCC Rep. 789 (N.J.Dist.Ct.1970). The court reasoned, in part, that a dealer using door-to-door salesmen "would have less overhead expense than a dealer maintaining a store or showroom."

d. Federal Trade Commission, Economic Report on Installment Credit and Retail Sales Practices of District of Columbia Retailers (1968).

e. See H. Kripke, Consumer Credit 228–29 (1970).

NOTES

(1) *Trial Tactics.* On the difficulties of procedure, and delaying tactics, in maintaining an action for consumer relief on grounds of fraud and unconscionability, see Schrag, Bleak House 1968: A Report on Consumer Test Litigation, 44 N.Y.U.L.Rev. 115 (1969). A bare allegation of price unconscionability is not enough, it has been held, to require the seller to respond to disclosure proceedings aimed at ascertaining his costs.[f] If he insists that his prices, though relatively high, are warranted by his exceptional costs, what reply can be made? It has been suggested that a price exceeding the "average" by 100% be deemed prima facie unconscionable. Speidel, Unconscionability, Assent and Consumer Protection, 31 U.Pitt.L. Rev. 359, 372–73 (1970). Would it be better to focus attention on the mark-up of an item than on its price?[g]

Under UCC 2–302 the issue of unconscionability is not to be submitted to a jury.[h] Why this reservation?

(2) *F.T.C. Action.* The Federal Trade Commission has taken action, particularly in the District of Columbia, against deceptive credit practices by some merchants. A seminal instance is the case, Leon A. Tashoff, No. 8714 (F.T.C.1968), CCH Trade Reg.Rep. ¶ 18,606. The case resulted in a cease-and-desist order against a seller of eyeglasses and jewelry. The following quotations will suggest the tenor of the lengthy, thoughtful opinion:

"We conclude, therefore, that respondent has deceived his customers and dealt unfairly with them, through its use of 'easy credit' advertising and its markup and other promotion practices. When the entire format of respondent's business is considered, it is clear that it is attracting customers who cannot obtain credit elsewhere by the two pronged, doubly deceptive gimmick of 'discount' prices and 'easy' credit. As utilized by this respondent, both practices are deceptive and are in violation of Section 5 of the Federal Trade Commission Act. . . . [I]t is manifestly unfair to adopt a marketing policy which has the effect of luring unsophisticated customers into entering contractual obligations which in all likelihood they have little understanding of, convincing them that the credit is 'easy' and prices are low and at the same time following a rigid collection policy resulting in default judgments and garnishments being levied against their meager wages."

(3) *Ghetto Market Improvement.* The "Riot Commission" report of 1968—Report of the National Advisory Commission on Civil Disorders—contained a section on Exploitation of Disadvantaged Consumers By Retail

f. Patterson v. Walker-Thomas Furniture Co., 277 A.2d 111 (D.C.App. 1971).

g. See Capitol Furniture & Appliance Co., Inc. v. Morris, 8 UCC Rep. 321 (D.C.Gen.Sess.1970) ("It is a fact of common knowledge that mark-up on furniture frequently exceeds 100%."), aff'd, Morris v. Capitol Furniture & Appliance Co., 9 UCC Rep. 577 (D.C. App.1971).

h. On that matter, and on the necessity of a separate hearing, see County Asphalt, Inc. v. Lewis Welding & Engineering Corp., 444 F.2d 372 (2d Cir. 1971), cert. denied, 404 U.S. 939. For an excellent use of commercial "setting, purpose and effect" in support of a seeming-harsh provision, see Geldermann & Co., Inc. v. Lane Processing, Inc., 527 F.2d 571 (8th Cir. 1975).

Merchants, including these remarks: "Forced to use credit, [ghetto residents] have little understanding of the pitfalls of credit buying. But because they have unstable incomes and frequently fail to make payments, the cost to the merchants of serving them is significantly above that of serving middle-income consumers. Consequently, a special kind of merchant appears to sell them goods on terms designed to cover the high cost of doing business in ghetto neighborhoods. . . . While higher prices are not necessarily exploitative in themselves, many merchants in ghetto neighborhoods take advantage of their superior knowledge of credit buying by engaging in various exploitative tactics—high-pressure salesmanship, bait advertising, misrepresentation of prices, substitution of used goods for promised new ones, failure to notify consumers of legal actions against them, refusal to repair or replace substandard goods, exorbitant prices or credit charges, and use of shoddy merchandise. Such tactics affect a great many low-income consumers." [i]

Various remedial measures for improving the quality of the marketing process described here have been attempted or proposed, including buyers' strikes and consumer education programs. One of the most elaborate is designed to make property insurance available to slum-area merchants. Cooperative efforts to this end by Congress, state legislatures, administrators, and the insurance industry have resulted in FAIR plans in many states—Fair Access to Insurance Requirements.[j]

(4) *Question.* Have you seen a definition of "unconscionable" that would lend itself to use in a statute by which the sale of (say) fuel for home use, at an unconscionable price, is made a crime? Cf. N.Y.Gen.Bus.L. § 396–r.

HOME SOLICITATION SALES AND "COOLING OFF" PERIODS

Since 1963, following the lead of Parliament, a number of American legislatures have enacted statutes directed at door-to-door selling, and providing what is known as a cooling-off period. A representative one, embodied in the Uniform Consumer Credit Code, is quoted below. There is a federal provision of this character, in the Consumer Credit Protection Act of 1968. It applies to most home-improvement loan contracts.[a] There are significant variances in the state statutes, both as to scope and as to the mechanics of cancellation.

i. Report, 274–76 (Bantam ed. 1968).

j. The workings of such a plan are described in Pohorily v. Kennedy, 269 A.2d 240 (Del.Super.1970). For an appraisal by the Federal Insurance Administrator, see Bernstein, Critical Evaluation of FAIR Plans, 38 J. Risk & Ins. 269 (1971).

a. But only when a security interest is granted "in any real property which is used or is expected to be used as a residence of the person to whom credit is extended." In explaining why "uncommon emphasis" on disclosure of the borrower's entitlement under this statute is warranted, one court observed that it is "an important and novel right in the history of contract law, for under the Act a customer may rescind for no more reason than a 'change of heart.'" Reed v. Washington Trailer Sales, Inc., 393 F.Supp. 886 (M.D.Tenn.1974). For problems under the statute see Turner v. West Memphis Federal S. & L. Ass'n, 266 Ark. 530, 588 S.W.2d 691 (1979).

The basic rule of the UCCC is stated in section 3.502:

> (1) Except as provided in subsection (5),[b] in addition to any right otherwise to revoke an offer, the buyer may cancel a home solicitation sale until midnight of the third business day after the day on which the buyer signs an agreement or offer to purchase which complies with this Part.

The definition of "home solicitation sale" embraces most consumer credit sales "in which the seller or a person acting for him personally solicits the sale, and the buyer's agreement or offer to purchase is given to the seller or a person acting for him, at a residence." [c]

The power to cancel cannot be terminated until the end of the statutory period *following* the time when the buyer signs a document containing this statement:

> BUYER'S RIGHT TO CANCEL [d]
>
> If you decide you do not want the goods or services, you may cancel this agreement by mailing a notice to the seller. The notice must say that you do not want the goods or services and must be mailed before midnight of the third business day after you sign this agreement. The notice must be mailed to: ________________________.
>
> (insert name and mailing address of seller)

NOTES

(1) *Questions.* Would it be well to extend the principle of this legislation to in-store sales? What arguments might be made for and against such an extension? It is a well-known practice in some stores to let customers take merchandise out of stock "on approval," or virtually so. If it could be shown that this practice is least prevalent among merchants catering to poor persons, would the distinction seem invidious?

(2) *Unconscionability and Incapacity.* Should the principle of unconscionability be regarded as defining a new class of persons lacking the capacity to contract? An analogy between unconscionability cases and those on capacity has been drawn by Professor Leff. As he sees it, the notion of Williams v. Walker-Thomas Furniture Company, p. 504 supra, is that the poor should be discouraged from frill-buying, and is comparable to the premise in infancy cases ("all persons under twenty-one lack sufficient

b. According to subsection (5), the buyer may not cancel in certain circumstances, if he "requests the seller to provide goods or services without delay" in an emergency.

c. Section 3.501.

d. This caption must be conspicuous. The Code definition of "conspicuous" follows that of the Truth-in-Lending Act: "A term or clause is conspicuous when it is so written that a reasonable person against whom it is to operate ought to have noticed it. Whether a term or clause is conspicuous or not is for decision by the court." Section 1.301(10). It is derived in part from UCC 1–201(10). Section 3.503(2)(b). An alternative—(a)—is compliance with an applicable F.T.C. rule.

probity"). Both of them illustrate a tendency toward stereotyping of parties. He writes: "One can see it enshrined in the old English equity courts' jolly treatment of English seamen as members of a happy, fun-loving race (with, one supposes, a fine sense of rhythm), but certainly not to be trusted to take care of themselves. What effect, if any, this had upon the sailors is hidden behind the judicial chuckles as they protected their loyal sailor boys, but one cannot help wondering how many sailors managed to get credit at any reasonable price. In other words, the benevolent have a tendency to colonize, whether geographically or legally." [e]

Is this fair criticism of the *Williams* case? Should new conceptions of capacity to contract be framed as a solution to consumer credit problems, or should the focus remain on the characteristics of the credit *transactions*?

(3) *Review Problems*. The buyer of a large tract of timber, representing to the owners that he was a knowledgeable timber buyer, told them it was worth 18–20 thousand dollars. After obtaining the contract, he was shocked to find that he could resell it for as much as $50,000. Upon the owners' refusal to perform, should the court assess damages? If not, is that because of UCC 2–302? See Davis v. Kolb, 263 Ark. 158, 563 S.W.2d 438 (1978). The price agreed on was $10,500 plus half of all the proceeds of the buyer's receipts on resale above $12,500, net of the expense of removal. Does that affect your answers?

What distinction might be drawn between this case and one in which a farmer sells his cotton crop in March and shortly witnesses a meteoric rise in the market price of cotton? In that case, would it matter that the buyer, a cotton dealer, told the farmer that prices would be lower in the fall? Or (what was not true) that the dealer had not offered higher prices to other farmers? See R. L. Kimsey Cotton Co., Inc. v. Ferguson, 233 Ga. 962, 214 S.E.2d 360 (1975).

In another cotton case the trial court looked with favor on a growers' argument that their contracts were unconscionable, observing that the prices set in the contracts before him were less than half the market value of the cotton at delivery time. If you were to represent the buyer on appeal, what counter-arguments would you make? See Bradford v. Plains Cotton Cooperative Ass'n, 539 F.2d 1249, 1255 (10th Cir. 1976), cert. denied, 429 U.S. 1042. In that case it appeared that periodically during the season the buyer, Plains, would estimate its promised supply of cotton and make forward contracts of its own, to textile mills, for 75% of the total.[f]

e. Leff, Unconscionability and the Code—The Emperor's New Clause, 115 U.Pa.L.Rev. 485, 556–58 (1967). Professor Leff regards the Williams case as an example of certain decisions which have relied on UCC 2–302 as a way of escape from difficult policy judgments. (He regards the opinion in *Henningsen* with favor: "it is most significant that the court did *not* have § 2–302 to work with."). See also Schwartz, A Reexamination of Nonsubstantive Unconscionability, 63 Va.L.Rev. 1053 (1977).

With these views compare Ellinghaus, In Defense of Unconscionability, 78 Yale L.J. 757, 766–67, 773 (1969): "nothing could be more misconceived"; "Just because the contract I signed was proffered to me by Almighty Monopoly Incorporated does not mean that I may subsequently argue exemption from any or all obligation: at the very least, some element of deception or substantive unfairness must presumably be shown."

f. Fearful of a shortfall, it would not commit 100% of its expectations. However, for 25% it made hedging contracts.

Should that fact count against the growers? If so, why? If it appeared that Plains made a tremendous profit on the year's crop, should that fact count in favor of the growers? If not, why not? (Would you call a million dollars tremendous? The right answer is, "In relation to what?").

In framing your argument, can you make anything of Comment 1 after UCC 2–302?

CORENSWET, INC. v. AMANA REFRIGERATION, INC.

United States Court of Appeals, Fifth Circuit, 1979.
594 F.2d 129.

WISDOM, Circuit Judge.

Consolidated appeals in this diversity litigation [1] arise from the termination of a distributorship. Corenswet, Inc.[2], headquartered in New Orleans, has been an authorized, exclusive distributor of certain home appliances manufactured by Amana Refrigeration, Inc. ("Amana"). Corenswet sued to prevent Amana from terminating the relationship, on the ground that Amana's attempted termination was arbitrary and capricious. The district court found that the termination was arbitrary and was therefore in breach of the distributorship agreement as well as of the Uniform Commercial Code's general "good faith" principle. Amana challenges the district court's finding that the termination was arbitrary and without cause. We hold that the finding is not clearly erroneous. That is far from settling the dispute. The court issued a preliminary injunction forbidding the termination. No. 77–1538 is Amana's appeal from that ruling.

While that appeal was pending, Amana drew up a new standard form distributorship agreement, which limited the term of distributorships to one year. Corenswet, alone among Amana's distributors, refused to execute the new agreement, which it viewed as an attempt to circumvent the injunction. Amana responded with the contention that Corenswet's refusal to sign constituted just cause for terminating the distributorship. The district court agreed with Amana that Corenswet's refusal to sign the new contract would constitute cause for termination, but ruled that if Corenswet signed Amana could not refuse to renew the agreement at the end of any one-year term without good reason. Amana's appeal from that ruling is No. 77–3474.

The basic question at the heart of these appeals is whether Amana was entitled to terminate the distributorship arbitrarily. Amana assails the district court's interpretation of the contract to forbid an arbitrary termination, as well as the court's alternative rationale that the attempted termination is barred by the Iowa U.C.C.'s

1. Under the contract and by stipulation of the parties the substantive law of Iowa controls.

2. In 1972 Select Brands Industries, Inc., a Missouri corporation, acquired Corenswet. Sam Corenswet remained as president and chief executive officer.

"good faith" principle. We hold that an arbitrary termination is permissible under both the contract and the law of Iowa. We reverse the district court's judgments.

I.

The primary facts are not disputed.

The plaintiff, Corenswet, Inc., is an independent wholesale distributor of appliances, dishware, and similar products. Since 1969 Corenswet has been the exclusive distributor of Amana refrigerators, freezers, room air conditioners, and other merchandise in southern Louisiana. Amana is a Delaware corporation domiciled in Iowa. Under the Amana system, products manufactured by Amana are sold to wholesale distributors such as Corenswet and to Amana's factory wholesale branches. The independent distributors and the factory branches then resell the merchandise to retail dealers who, in turn, sell to the public. The first distributorship agreement executed between Amana and Corenswet was of indefinite duration, but terminable by either party at any time "with or without cause" on ten days' notice to the other party. According to the record, the agreement was modified twice, in 1971 and again in July 1975, before the institution of this lawsuit. The 1975 agreement modified the termination provision to allow termination by either party "at any time for any reason" on ten days' notice.

As is so often the case with franchise and distributorship relationships, the termination clause in the standard form contract was of little interest or concern to the parties so long as things were going well between them. At the hearing before the district court, Corenswet introduced testimony that it understood, in the early 1970's, that the relationship would be a lasting one, a relationship that would continue so long as Corenswet performed satisfactorily. According to Corenswet, it developed an organization for wholesale distribution of Amana merchandise: it hired a manager and salesmen for the line, as well as specially trained repairmen. Corenswet also expanded its physical plant. In all, Corenswet contended, it invested over $1.5 million over the period of 1969 to 1976 in developing the market for Amana products in the southern Louisiana area. The parties stipulated in district court that the annual sales of Amana products in the distributorship area increased from $200,000 in 1969 to over $2.5 million in 1976. The number of retail outlets selling Amana products in the area increased from six in 1969 to seventy-two in 1976. Corenswet, in short, developed an important new market for Amana products. And Amana became as important to Corenswet as Corenswet became to Amana: sales of Amana products as a percentage of Corenswet's total sales of all products swelled from six percent in 1969 to nearly twenty-six percent in 1976. Over the seven and one-half-year period, Amana representatives repeatedly praised Corenswet for its performance.

At the 1976 mid-year meeting of Amana distributors, however, George Foerstner, Amana's president, informed Corenswet that Amana would soon terminate its relationship with Corenswet because Corenswet was underfinanced. The parties agree that in early 1976 Corenswet had exceeded its credit limit with Amana, and that Amana at that time indicated that it might have to take a security interest in Corenswet's Amana inventory. According to a January communication from Amana, however, the "problem" was viewed by Amana as "a good kind of problem", reflecting, as it did, the growth of Corenswet's sales and hence purchases of Amana products. It is Corenswet's contention that the problem was not a serious one. Amana executives, the record reflects, assured Corenswet at the 1976 mid-year meeting that "satisfactory arrangements would be made" and that, Foerstner's statement notwithstanding, Corenswet would retain its distributorship.

There followed a complicated sequence of negotiations concerning Amana's security for credit extended. Amana sought a security interest in Corenswet's Amana inventory, to which Corenswet agreed. Amana asked also that Corenswet obtain more working capital from its parent corporation, Select Brands, Inc., as well as a bank letter of credit or line of credit. There is ample evidence in the record that Corenswet responded adequately to each Amana request, but that Amana persisted in changing its requirements as quickly as Corenswet could respond to its requests. . . . [In September the plaintiff's president, Sam Corenswet, told an Amana representative that the plaintiff was ready and able to meet the latest request; but the plaintiff was notified of termination within a week.

[In its first action against Amana, the plaintiff obtained a preliminary injunction barring termination. In 1977, the plaintiff brought another action, this time for a declaratory judgment. In a hearing leading to the injunction it appeared that as far back as 1972 the president of Corenswet's parent corporation (Select Brands, Inc.) had incurred the animosity of Amana's president by intervening with Amana's parent (the Raytheon Corporation) against replacing Corenswet with an official of Amana. This animosity, the trial court found, was the "real factor" in the termination. At the time of the appeal, the injunction required Corenswet to execute the revised distributorship agreement (or suffer termination), and required Amana to renew that agreement if it was "without reason" to refuse. As to the "for any reason" provision of the 1975 agreement, the trial court rejected the interpretation suggested by each party, and ruled that it meant "for some reason, . . . for something that appeals to the reason, to the mind, to the judgment," and not "for no reason (or) something that is arbitrary, capricious or wanton."]

II.

[The Court of Appeals approved the district court's action in part: "Following the entry of the original injunction, the district court, faced with what could justifiably be viewed as an attempt by Amana to circumvent the court's command that it not terminate Corenswet without cause, did Amana a good turn, it seems to us, by permitting Amana, subject to a good cause limitation on its non-renewal rights, to put Corenswet, like all its other distributors, under the new distributorship agreement." But the Court of Appeals expressed a reservation about a decree "forcing these antagonistic parties to maintain their relationship indefinitely and requiring the continuous supervision of the district court.[3]" Then the court turned to the district court's interpretation of the contract, observing that Amana "has the burden of persuading us that the court's interpretation was clearly erroneous."]

In assessing [this matter] we must look to the appropriate rules of construction found in applicable state law—in this case, as the parties have stipulated, the law of Iowa. Although most distributorship agreements, like franchise agreements, are more than sales contracts, the courts have not hesitated to apply the Uniform Commercial Code to cases involving such agreements. . . . We therefore look to the constructional rules of the Code, as adopted by Iowa, chapter 554 of the Iowa Code.

The starting point under the Code is the express terms of the agreement. UCC 1–205, 2–208(2); Iowa Code Ann. §§ 554.1205, 554.2208(2). Under the contract, Amana was free to terminate the relationship "at any time and for any reason". [A dictionary definition of "reason" is] "a ground or a cause; that in the reality which makes any fact intelligible". Id. We consider that this is the usual sense of the word when used in the phrase "for any reason".[4]

3. [D]ifficulty of enforcement is, in itself, often a sufficient reason for denying injunctive relief. [citations omitted]. The Court should not be called upon to weld together two business entities which have shown a propensity for disagreement, friction, and even adverse litigation. Refrigeration Engineering Corp. v. Frick Co., 1974, W.D.Tex., 370 F.Supp. 702, 715.

4. Indeed, Corenswet uses the word in this sense in its brief when it urges that "the real reason [for the termination] was because Mr. Foerstner wanted it."

Corenswet cites, in support of the district court's construction, the case of Dubois v. Gentry, 1945, 182 Tenn. 103, 184 S.W.2d 369, in which the Tennessee Supreme Court ruled that the term "for any reason" in a termination clause "should be construed to mean 'any good reason or just reason'." Id. 184 S.W.2d at 371. The court, however, was not making a factual determination. Rather, it was ruling that the law of the state implies a "just reason" limitation. The question that we are addressing at this point in the opinion is a question of fact. If judicial authority is of aid on this point, we note that the Iowa Supreme Court has used the term "for any reason" to mean the same thing as "at will". Harper v. Cedar Rapids Television Co., Inc., Iowa, 1976, 244 N.W.2d 782, 791. ("The contract being terminable at will, plaintiff could have been discharged for virtually any reason.").

. . . Even if it is assumed that Amana needed "some reason" to terminate the contract, that reason is supplied by its evident desire to give the New Orleans distributorship to the Lehleitner company, just as we think that Corenswet would, under the contract, be entitled to terminate the relationship by reason, to take an example, of its wish to handle Kelvinator, rather than Amana, products.

There is no evidence in the record that the parties understood the phrase otherwise. . . .

We take Corenswet to be arguing that the contractual language must be interpreted in light of Amana's historical treatment of Corenswet and its other distributors. Although Amana's past dealing with Corenswet does not fit the Code categories of sources relevant to contract interpretation—usage of trade, course of dealing, and course of performance [5]—we may assume that it is a source sufficiently similar to the Code categories to be relevant in construing the contract. Courses of commercial conduct "may not only supplement or qualify express [contract] terms, but in appropriate circumstances may even override express terms". J. White & R. Summers, Handbook of the Law under the Uniform Commercial Code § 3–3 at 84 (1972). The Code commands that express contract terms and "an applicable course of dealing or usage of trade shall be construed wherever reasonable as consistent with each other". UCC 1–205, Iowa Code Ann. § 554.1205; see also UCC 2–208(2), Iowa Code Ann. § 554.2208(2). In this case, however, no reasonable construction can reconcile the contract's express terms with the interpretation Corenswet seeks to glean from the conduct of the parties. The conflict could not be more complete: Amana's past conduct, with regard both to Corenswet and to its other distributors, may have created a reasonable expectation that Amana would not terminate a distributor arbitrarily, yet the contract expressly gives Amana the right to do so. We can find no justification, except in cases of conduct of the sort giving rise to promissory estoppel, for holding that a contractually reserved power, however distasteful, may be lost through nonuse. The express contract term cannot be construed as Corenswet would constitute it, and it therefore controls over any allegedly conflicting usage or course of dealing. UCC 1–205, 2–208(2), Iowa Code Ann. §§ 554.1205, 554.2208 (2).[6]

5. See UCC 1–205(2) (defining usage of trade); § 1–205(1) (defining course of dealing), § 2–208(2) (defining course of performance).

6. Corenswet's complaint also alleged the existence of an oral agreement or an oral modification of the existing agreement. The district court did not address this point in the preliminary injunction opinion. The injunction cannot be sustained on the ground that Corenswet is likely to prevail on the merits of this claim. The hearing produced little evidence to support this allegation and produced no proof of the validating "writing" evidencing such an agreement that is required by sections 2–201 and 2–209 of the Code for maintaining a claim or defense based on an oral contract or modification.

The district court's alternative rationale was that arbitrary termination of a distributorship agreement contravenes the Code's general obligation of good faith dealing. Section 1–203 states: "Every contract or duty within this Act imposes an obligation of good faith in its performance or enforcement". Iowa Code Ann. § 554.1203. The good faith obligation is one of those obligations that section 1–102 of the Code says "may not be disclaimed by agreement". Iowa Code Ann. § 554.1102(3). As courts and scholars have become increasingly aware of the special problems faced by distributors and franchisees, and of the inadequacy of traditional contract and sales law doctrines to the task of protecting the reasonable expectations of distributors and franchisees, commentators have debated the utility of the Code's general good faith obligation as a tool for curbing abuse of the termination power. See, e. g., E. Gellhorn, Limitations on Contract Termination Rights—Franchise Cancellations, 1967 Duke L.J. 465; Hewitt, Good Faith or Unconscionability—Franchise Remedies for Termination, 29 Bus.Law 227 (1973).

The courts of late have begun to read a good faith limitation into termination clauses of distributorship contracts that permit termination without cause. E. g., . . . Baker v. Ratzlaff, 1976, 1 Kan. App.2d 285, 564 P.2d 153. Of the cited cases, however, only the Baker case relies squarely on the Code. . . . [7]

In similar cases other courts have held that agency or distributorship contracts of indefinite duration are terminable by either party with or without cause. . . . Those courts have relied on section 2–309(2) of the Code, which states:

> Where the contract provides for successive performances but is indefinite in duration it is valid for a reasonable time but unless otherwise agreed may be terminated at any time by either party.

Iowa Code Ann. § 554.2309(2). The division in the authorities, then, is between those courts that hold that the Code's general good faith obligation overrides the specific rule of section 2–309(2) as applied to distributorship or franchise agreements, and those that give precedence to section 2–309.

The parties have not cited and we have not found Iowa cases on the issue decided under the Uniform Commercial Code. The Iowa case law on this question is pre-Code and follows the common law rule, which is essentially the rule of section 2–309 as applied to dis-

7. The Pennsylvania Supreme Court has recently held that the Code's good faith provision bars termination without cause of a gasoline dealership even after the dealer service station lease has expired. Atlantic Richfield Co. v. Razumic, 1978, 480 Pa. 366, 390 A.2d 736; Kowatch v. Atlantic Richfield Co., 1978, 480 Pa. 388, 390 A.2d 747. The court emphasized, however, that Arco's contract with the dealers contained no provision giving Arco the right to terminate the relationship at will. Atlantic Richfield Co. v. Razumic, 390 A.2d at 741.

tributorship contracts. In Des Moines Blue Ribbon Distributors, Inc. v. Drewrys Limited, U.S.A., Inc., 1964, 256 Iowa 899, 129 N.W.2d 731, the Iowa Supreme Court held that an exclusive distributorship contract of indefinite duration may be terminated without cause only upon reasonable notice. Although the plaintiff in that case did not, so far as appears from the opinion, claim the right not to be terminated without cause, the court's treatment of the issues raised makes it clear that the requirement of reasonable notice was thought by the court to be the only restriction on the manufacturer's right to cancel the agreement.[8]

. . .

We are not persuaded that the adoption of the Code has effected any change in Iowa law with regard to distributorship terminations. We do not agree with Corenswet that the section 1–203 good faith obligation, like the Code's unconscionability provision, can properly be used to override or strike express contract terms. According to Professor Farnsworth, "[T]he chief utility of the concept of good faith performance has always been as a rationale in a process . . . of implying contract terms . . . ." Farnsworth, Good Faith Performance and Commercial Reasonableness under the Uniform Commercial Code, 30 U.Chi.L.Rev. 666, 672 (1963). He defines the Code's good faith obligation as "an implied term of the contract requiring cooperation on the part of one party to the contract so that another party will not be deprived of his reasonable expectations". Id. at 666. When a contract contains a provision expressly sanctioning termination without cause there is no room for implying a term that bars such a termination. In the face of such a term there can be, at best, an expectation that a party will decline to exercise his rights.[9]

8. At one point in its opinion the *Drewrys* court seemed to add another limitation: that the agreement must continue in force for a reasonable time. 129 N.W.2d at 736. This is the so-called "Missouri doctrine", a hardship rule of agency law designed to give an agent a reasonable time in which to recoup his original investment in the agency. See generally E. Gellhorn, supra, at 479–483. The *Drewrys* court did not face a claim based on insufficient duration, so its "adoption" of the Missouri doctrine is dictum. Even assuming that the doctrine is indeed law in Iowa, it has no application to this case. The reasonable duration envisioned by the doctrine is quite short, see E. Gellhorn, supra, at 482; Bushwick-Decatur Motors, Inc. v. Ford Motor Co., 2 Cir. 1940, 116 F.2d 675; and the minimum duration requirement may be eliminated contractually. E. Gellhorn, supra, at 482, and authorities cited in 482 nn. 62 & 63. [But see Lichnovsky v. Ziebart Intern. Corp., 285 N.W.2d 795 (Mich.App.1979)–eds.]

9. Furthermore, the proposition that the Code's good faith obligation cannot be disclaimed must be qualified. Section 1–102(3) of the Code, which provides that the obligation of good faith is not disclaimable, goes on to state that "the parties may by agreement determine the standards by which the performance of such obligation is to be measured if such standards are not manifestly unreasonable." It could be argued that even if arbitrary termination of a distributorship under an agreement silent as to grounds for termination would be in "bad faith", section 1–102(3) nevertheless permits the parties to the contract to stipulate that termination "without cause" or "for any reason" is not in bad faith.

As a tool for policing distributorship terminations, moreover, the good faith test is erratic at best. It has been observed that the good faith approach

> is analytically unsound because there is no necessary correlation between bad motives and unfair terminations . . . . The terminated dealer seeks relief against the harsh effects of termination which may be unfairly placed on him, not against the manufacturer's ill will.

E. Gellhorn, supra, at 521. The better approach, endorsed by Professor Gellhorn, is to test the disputed contract clause for unconscionability under section 2–302 of the Code. The question these cases present is whether public policy forbids enforcement of a contract clause permitting unilateral termination without cause. Since a termination without cause will almost always be characterizable as a "bad faith" termination, focus on the terminating party's state of mind will always result in the invalidation of unrestricted termination clauses. We seriously doubt, however, that public policy frowns on any and all contract clauses permitting termination without cause. Such clauses can have the salutary effect of permitting parties to end a soured relationship without consequent litigation. Indeed when, as here, the power of unilateral termination without cause is granted to both parties, the clause gives the distributor an easy way to cut the knot should he be presented with an opportunity to secure a better distributorship from another manufacturer. What public policy does abhor is economic overreaching—the use of superior bargaining power to secure grossly unfair advantage. That is the precise focus of the Code's unconscionability doctrine; it is not at all the concern of the Code's good faith performance provision. It is the office of the unconscionability concept, and not of the good faith concept, to strike down "unfair" contract terms.[10]

. . .

III.

It follows from what we have said that the preliminary injunction was erroneously entered. . . . Although Corenswet alleged in its complaint that the contract term was unconscionable, it never pressed that issue, and the district court made no finding in that regard, as indeed it could not on the state of the record.[11]

10. The leading case applying the unconscionability doctrine to bar arbitrary termination of a dealership is Shell Oil Co. v. Marinello, 1973, 63 N.J. 402, 307 A.2d 598.

11. Sometime between Corenswet's filing of the lawsuit and the hearing on whether to issue a preliminary injunction the unconscionability issue dropped from the case. The issues for the hearing were narrowed to include only the meaning of the contract and the reasons for Amana's termination of Corenswet. To prevail on a theory of unconscionability Corenswet would have to demonstrate (1) that it had no "meaningful choice" but to deal with Amana and accept the contract as offered, and

Corenswet's rights with respect to termination extend only to a right to notice. The Amana contract permits termination on ten days' notice. Under the Code, section 2–309(3), and under the *Drewrys* case, however, a distributor is entitled to reasonable notice. Section 2–309(3) of the Code states that "an agreement dispensing with notification is invalid if its operation would be unconscionable." But any claim that Corenswet might have based on inadequate notice would not entitle Corenswet to injunctive relief, for it appears from the *Drewrys* case and from C. C. Hauff Hardware, Inc. v. Long Mfg. Co., 1965, 257 Iowa 1127, 136 N.W.2d 276, that the manufacturer's failure to give proper notice is adequately remediable at law.

The district court's decisions are reversed, and the preliminary injunction is vacated.

NOTES

(1) *Good Cause Required.* So far as the common law is concerned, Shell Oil Co. v. Marinello, 63 N.J. 402, 307 A.2d 598 (1973), cert. denied, 415 U.S. 920 (1974), is perhaps the most notable setback suffered recently by franchisors seeking termination. A curiosity about the case is that it was decided after the legislature had acted to curb powers of termination—though not with respect to franchise agreements already in place.[a] A brief statement of the case is as follows:

"Shell involved a lease and dealership agreement between a major oil company and a service station operator who sought to avoid enforcement of one of the terms of the lease. The lease could be terminated by Shell upon 30 days' notice, and the dealership agreement upon 10 days' notice. Shell gave the dealer six weeks' notice of termination of both the lease and the dealership agreements, without stating any reasons for its action. The dealer was granted equitable relief upon the trial court's holding that 'there was an implied covenant in said lease and agreement on the part of Shell not to terminate the relationship without good cause, and these instruments must be reformed to include such covenant; . . . .' Id. at 406, 307 A.2d at 600. Citing 'the public policy of this State affecting such [a] relationship,' the Supreme Court of New Jersey indicated

(2) that the termination clause was "unreasonably favorable" to Amana. Williams v. Walker-Thomas Furniture Co., 1965, 121 U.S.App.D.C. 315, 319, 350 F.2d 445, 449; see also E. Gellhorn, supra, at 510–513. The record evidence relevant to these questions is scanty. Sam Corenswet testified that Amana in 1969 aggressively sought Corenswet as a distributor and that he only reluctantly decided to commit his company to Amana. Another Corenswet witness, at one point in his testimony, said of the 1975 amended contract that, in view of Corenswet's heavy investment in the Amana line, "we had to take it." The court interrupted that testimony and expressed its view that it was irrelevant to the hearing issues. There was no other evidence regarding the parties' relative bargaining power at the time the relationship began, nor any evidence as to the relative usefulness of the termination clause to the two sides.

a. The position became even more curious when a federal judge ruled that the Lanham Act gives immunity to an oil company's power to terminate a franchise, as against the public policy of New Jersey. Mariniello v. Shell Oil Co., 368 F.Supp. 1401 (D. N.J.1974), rev'd, 511 F.2d 853 (3d Cir.).

> full agreement with the basic determination of the trial court that Shell had no legal right to terminate its relationship with Marinello except for good cause, i. e., the failure of Marinello to substantially comply with his obligations under the lease and dealer agreement.

Id.

"Facts deemed significant by the Shell court in reaching its decision included the gross disparity in bargaining power between Shell and Marinello, resulting in Shell's ability to dictate the terms of the agreements; the grossly unfair contractual provisions at issue; and the clear tendency to injure the public." [b]

(2) *New Wine.* In Henningsen v. Bloomfield Motors, Inc., p. 457 supra, as indicating the "illusory character" of a car buyer's warranty protection, the court observed that "dealers' franchises are precarious." Do the later developments in franchise law undercut this part of the court's reasoning?

FRANCHISE REGULATION

"The franchise system is a method of selling products and services identified by a particular trade name which may be associated with a patent, a trade secret, a particular product design or management expertise. The franchisee usually purchases some products from the franchisor . . . and makes royalty payments on the basis of units sold, in exchange for the right to offer products for sale under the trademark. The franchise agreement establishes the relationship between the parties and usually regulates the quality of the product, sales territory, the advertising and other details; and it usually requires that certain supplies be purchased from the franchisor." [a]

Several branches of law intersect in the regulation of franchise relations. The subject is increasingly dominated by statutes and regulations. These include the federal Lanham Act [b] (trademark protection), the various bodies of antitrust law, federal and state, and the mandate of the Federal Trade Commission (FTC) Act that the Commission prevent "unfair methods of competition and unfair or deceptive acts or practices." "Baby" FTC Acts—analogous state legislation—exist almost everywhere. A number of state fair-practices acts are directed particularly to franchising, either in general or in specified lines of business. In a number of states it is required that a franchisor make extensive disclosures before or in the process of soliciting franchisees.[c] In 1979, by rule, the FTC established a mini-

b. Schultze v. Chevron Oil Co., 579 F. 2d 776 (3d Cir. 1978), cert. denied, 439 U.S. 985 (1978).

a. Kosters v. Seven-Up Co., 595 F.2d 347 (6th Cir. 1979).

b. 15 U.S.C.A. § 1055 et seq.

c. For meeting these requirements a Uniform Franchise Offering Circular has been devised. An excerpt from one of its 20-odd items is as follows:

"State the number of franchises in each of the following categories which within the three-year period immedi-

mum federal standard of disclosure applicable to all "franchise and business opportunity offerings." [d]

A federal statute of 1956, the Automobile Dealers' Day in Court Act,[e] proved to be a bellwether for comparable state legislation. It imposed on the automobile manufacturers a duty of good faith "in performing or complying with any of the terms or provisions of [a dealer's] franchise, or in terminating, canceling, or not renewing the franchise." [f] Note that the statute does not purport to restrict the grounds on which a franchise may be terminated. The definition of the critical term "good faith" is

> the duty of each party to any franchise, and all officers, employees, or agents thereof to act in a fair and equitable manner toward each other so as to guarantee the one party freedom from coercion, intimidation, or threats of coercion or intimidation from the other party: Provided, That recommendation, endorsement, exposition, persuasion, urging or argument shall not be deemed to constitute a lack of good faith.[g]

The failure of a *dealer* to act in good faith may serve as a defense when he charges the manufacturer with a violation of the statute.[h]

ately preceding the close of franchisor's most recent fiscal year have:

(1) been cancelled or terminated by the franchisor for:

(a) failure to comply with quality control standards; and

(b) other reasons;

(2) not been renewed by the franchisor; . . . ."

d. See Disclosure Requirements and Prohibitions Concerning Franchising and Business Opportunity Ventures, 16 C.F.R. § 436; Comment, 40 Ohio St.L.J. 387 (1979).

The rule does not preempt "substantive regulation of the franchisor-franchisee relationship, such as termination practices nor disclosure laws and regulations requiring more extensive disclosures than those provided by the rule." Indeed, the Commission will permit use of the UFOC format to satisfy the federal requirements. Interpretative Guides, ¶ D, CCH Trade Reg.Rep.No.396 (1979).

e. 15 U.S.C.A. § 1221 et seq.

f. Id. at § 1222.

g. Id. at § 1221(e).

h. Id. at § 1222.

Claims of dealers under the act have foundered in a number of cases by reason of its restricted definition of "good faith." The statute "does not mean 'good faith' in a hazy or general way, nor does it mean unfairness. The existence or nonexistence of 'good faith' must be determined in the context of actual or threatened coercion or intimidation." Autohaus Brugger, Inc. v. SAAB Motors, Inc., 567 F.2d 901 (9th Cir. 1978), cert. denied, 436 U.S. 946. "In applying the definition . . . it is necessary to consider not only whether the manufacturer brought pressure on the dealer, but also his reason for doing so." Overseas Motors, Inc. v. Import Motors Limited, Inc., 519 F.2d 119 (6th Cir. 1975), cert. denied, 423 U.S. 987. A poor sales record may be an adequate reason, it seems; but Chrysler Motors Corporation has been held accountable for the way it administered its dealers' Minimum Sales Responsibility (MSR), a system for assigning to a dealer an expectable volume of sales in his business. Marquis v. Chrysler Corp., 577 F.2d 624 (9th Cir. 1978).

For an extensive discussion of the act see S. Macaulay, Law and the Balance of Power (1966).

Statutes which restrict the grounds for termination by a franchisor have come to be known as "good cause" legislation. In this matter the states have led the way; beginning in the mid-70's the Congress gave sustained consideration to good-cause bills, but has not yet acted in favor of franchisees generally. "The fundamental thrust of good cause legislation is to confirm the franchisee's ownership of the business of his own which was granted by the franchisor." [i] Whether the interest of a franchise-holder is dependent on the law of agreements or deserves some other form of recognition—as a status or an ownership interest, say—is a question of at least rhetorical importance, and perhaps much more. The good will attached to a trade name is largely attributable to the energies and investments of all who operate under it. By the same token a franchisor has an imposing interest in high-quality service to the public by franchise holders. (See Kessler, op. cit. supra p. 337.) One means of maintaining discipline over them, naturally, is the threat of termination.

Question: Would any of the statutes affect Goodman v. Dicker, p. 339 supra?

In 1978 the Congress extended "franchise protection" to service-station operators (and others) by the Petroleum Marketing Practices Act.[j] Periods of notice and knowledge figure prominently in the statute. It includes an open-ended list of events justifying termination: events "relevant to the franchise relationship and as a result of which termination of the franchise or nonrenewal of the franchise relationship is reasonable." [k] Item 12 on the list, for an example, is "conviction of the franchisee of any felony involving moral turpitude." [l]

i. H. Brown, Franchising: Realities and Remedies 201 (1978).

j. 15 U.S.C.A. § 2801 et seq.

k. Id. at § 2802(c).

l. When good-cause legislation is enacted, it does not usually purport to affect existing relationships until they are renegotiated or extended. (In part, constitutional considerations have restrained legislatures from acting "retroactively." See Fornaris v. Ridge Tool Co., 400 U.S. 41 (1970).) Hence it is possible for a franchisor to defer for a time the application to it of the statutory constraints. "In Massachusetts, shortly after enactment of a motor vehicle dealers statute, automobile manufacturers made a broad scale grant of five-year dealerships one or two months before the prescribed effective date of the new legislation." Brown & Cohen, Constitutional Considerations for "Good Cause" State Legislation, 16 Houston L.Rev. 21, 51 (1978). That is, the franchisor may gain time *unless* the courts determine that the enactment is only the "articulate recognition of pre-existing policy," and apply it retrospectively. The New Jersey court did that, in effect, divining principles of common law, older than the pertinent statute, which embodied the very terms of the act. See Note 1, p. 529 supra. In contrast, though the New York Court of Appeals thought that a similar statute may not have generated new policy, it ruled that "the legislative determination was that legal sanction to support such policy should be prospective only." Mobil Oil Corp. v. Rubenfeld, 40 N.Y. 2d 936, 937, 390 N.Y.S.2d 57, 58, 358 N.E.2d 882, 883 (1976).

In answering an attack on the New Jersey decision, based on the Obligation of Contracts Clause, the Court of Appeals for the Third Circuit said: "There is no basis for concluding that

May a court properly infer, from the "recent surge" of franchise legislation, that a franchisor owes fiduciary obligations to the franchise holders? See Arnott v. American Oil Co., 609 F.2d 873 (8th Cir. 1979).

NOTES

(1) *Grounds for Termination.* Some of the justifications offered by franchisors in suits over terminations are sketched in this note and the next. They should be examined with the following questions in mind:

(a) Would the franchisor's termination violate a duty of good faith and fair dealing? Would it satisfy a requirement in the agreement of "just cause" for termination?

(b) Would the termination, if otherwise objectionable, be justified by a provision in the agreement for the franchisor to pay the franchisee fair compensation in the circumstances? [m]

(c) Would the termination measure up to a statutory requirement that some delinquency of the franchisee be shown, such as a substantial failure to comply with his contract? To a requirement that the franchisor have a "legitimate business reason" for termination?

A wine importer terminates a dealer's contract because the two of them develop irreconcilable "business philosophies." See Excello Wine Co. v. Monsieur Henri Wines, Ltd., 474 F.Supp. 203 (S.D.Ohio 1979).

A major corporation having several divisions needs to improve its cash position and arranges to sell the assets of its profitable forest-products division. For that purpose it terminates the contract of a distributor of its prefabricated homes under which he has exclusive rights of sale in his state. See J & S Home Realty, Inc. v. Anaconda Co., 172 Mont. 236, 563 P. 2d 566 (1977).

Federal regulations make it desirable for an oil company to reduce its marketing costs. Having evaluated a dealer's operation and prospects, it terminates his franchise as part of a program to reduce station density. See Westfield Centre Service v. Cities Service Oil, 158 N.J.Super. 455, 386 A.2d 448 (1978).

(2) *Fat Years, Lean Years.* A difference of business judgment arose between an oil company and one of its station operators which apparently led the company to notify him of termination of his dealership. The issue was whether or not the operator could maintain his volume of gasoline sales through modest price cuts. The reason given for termination, as permitted by the agreement, was a decline in volume after a period of quite successful marketing by the operator. He sued to enjoin the termination. The court considered the Petroleum Marketing Practices Act, under which a franchise may be terminated for the holder's failure to make good-faith efforts to carry out the provisions of the franchise. *Held*: Injunction denied. By

the New Jersey Supreme Court . . in fact retroactively applied the Franchise Practices Act." Mariniello v. Shell Oil Co., 511 F.2d 853, 854 (3d Cir. 1975).

m. See Mason v. Farmers Ins. Companies, 281 N.W.2d 344 (Minn.1979).

decision day, however, it appeared that the company might have to ration gas to its dealers, and the court observed that the company "may one day discover that it has sacrificed one of its best retailers for nothing." Malone v. Crown Central Petroleum Corp., 474 F.Supp. 306 (D.Md.1979).

SECTION 5. ILLEGALITY

In the preceding sections our concern was with protecting one party to an agreement against imposition by the other party. In this section our concern is with protecting the public at large against imposition by both parties. When will a court refuse to enforce an agreement, fairly and freely entered into by both parties, on the ground that to enforce it would contravene "public policy"?

To begin with, where do courts get their notions of public policy? In some cases they formulate them for themselves, or rely on prior formulations by other courts. Examples, from the following pages, include the common law policies against improper restraint of competition and against improper influence in public affairs. In other cases they derive them from legislation. Rarely, however, do statutes proscribing conduct speak to the enforceability of contracts involving such conduct. (The main exceptions are the usury and gambling statutes which characteristically state that contracts in violation of them are "void.") But courts often look to statutes as sources of public policy, even when they are silent on enforceability itself. This phenomenon is not, of course, peculiar to the law of contracts, but is merely one aspect of the broader problem of adjusting the body of existing law to take account of statutory directions. A comparable phenomenon can be seen in the law of torts when conduct in violation of a criminal statute is held to constitute negligence per se.

It may at first seem strange that the impact of public policy upon the enforceability of agreements is relegated to a single section at the end of this chapter. The explanation lies in the fact that most of the conduct that society finds objectionable (e. g., pollution, discrimination, crime in the streets) involves private agreement only peripherally or not at all. In discouraging such conduct, the threat of the conventional criminal sanctions of fine and imprisonment is far more likely to be effective than is the threat of the unenforceability of private agreement. Even where the conduct (e. g., usury, gambling, restraint of competition) is more intimately connected with private agreement, the relative efficacy of the threat of unenforceability may be questionable. In short, policing the bargain in the interests of society is not likely to be a very effective way of furthering those interests.

The illegality of an agreement often precludes not only enforcement of it but also restitutionary claims associated with it. When public policy forecloses all remedies, it can produce what appear to be striking injustices in individual cases.

NOTE

Non-Connubial Rights. "Who should pay for what in a live-in type relationship?"—letter to Dear Abby. When one of the partners in a supposed marriage finds belatedly that the ceremony was a nullity (the other was a bigamist, say) he or she is quite likely to have a quasi-contract claim against the other. When one of the partners in a genuine marriage is cast off (as by divorce) generous compensation for the other's enrichment can often be arranged, or compelled. But what of a "home worker" who is cast off by a "marketplace laborer" after years of cohabitation without marriage? As a rule he or she will not be compensated for benefits conferred in the relationship, even—or especially—if sexual services were expressly bartered for compensation. But "as the number of cohabitants increases, pressure mounts to ascribe to their relationships certain marriage-like incidents to protect cohabitants from hardship and injustice when death or renunciation separates them." [a] Lee Marvin, the actor, was the most celebrated marketplace laborer to feel the pressure.[b] He was neither the first nor the last, but his liability was perhaps unique. It was for a sum—$104,000—intended to permit his ex-companion to "have the economic means to educate herself and to learn new, employable skills." The court did not acknowledge that the award represented either a restitutionary interest or an expectancy interest of the plaintiff. However, it had already said that an agreement by the partners to "combine their efforts and earnings and . . . share equally any and all property accumulated as a result of their efforts" would be enforceable and observed that most sharers in a live-in type relationship probably mean "to deal fairly with each other."

In Green v. Richmond, 369 Mass. 47, 337 N.E.2d 691 (1975), the plaintiff had rendered services for a decedent in reliance on his oral promise of a bequest, which was not kept. Reviewing a judgment for the value of the services, the court noted evidence of many instances of sexual intercourse between the promisor and the promisee, and conceded that one might be naive to think that it was not "central in the arrangement." Yet the court approved a recovery: the jury was justified in finding that "the sexual aspect" was only incidental to the relationship. Compare Hewitt v. Hewitt, 76 Ill.3d 459, 31 Ill.Dec. 827, 394 N.E.2d 1204 (1979), condemning naiveté and finding in Illinois statutes "a strong continuing interest in the institution of marriage." [c]

a. Casad, Unmarried Couples and Unjust Enrichment: From Status to Contract and Back Again? 77 Mich. L.Rev. 47, 48 (1978). See G. Douthwaite, Unmarried Couples and the Law, Ch. 4 (1979); also Kay & Amyx, Marvin v. Marvin: Preserving the Options, 65 Calif.L.Rev. 937 (1977). As for developments in courts of England and the Commonwealth, see Dwyer, Immoral Contracts, 93 Law Q.Rev. 386 (1977).

b. Marvin v. Marvin, 18 Cal.3d 660, 134 Cal.Rptr. 815, 557 P.2d 106 (1976) (dissent by Clark, J.).

c. As to the possible sexual aspects of a loan contract see Taylor v. Frost, 202 Neb. 652, 276 N.W.2d 656 (1979). On agreements affecting the marriage relation see Reynolds v. Reynolds' Estate, 238 Ga. 1, 230 S.E.2d 842 (1976).

KARPINSKI v. INGRASCI

Court of Appeals of New York, 1971.
28 N.Y.2d 45, 268 N.E.2d 751.

FULD, Chief Judge. This appeal requires us to determine whether a covenant by a professional man not to compete with his employer is enforceable and, if it is, to what extent.

The plaintiff, Dr. Karpinski, an oral surgeon, had been carrying on his practice alone in Auburn—in Cayuga County—for many years. In 1953, he decided to expand and, since nearly all of an oral surgeon's business stems from referrals, he embarked upon a plan to "cultivate connections" among dentists in the four nearby Counties of Tompkins, Seneca, Cortland and Ontario. The plan was successful, and by 1962 twenty per cent of his practice consisted of treating patients referred to him by dentists located in those counties. In that year, after a number of those dentists had told him that some of their patients found it difficult to travel from their homes to Auburn, the plaintiff decided to open a second office in centrally-located Ithaca. He began looking for an assistant and, in the course of his search, met the defendant, Dr. Ingrasci, who was just completing his training in oral surgery at the Buffalo General Hospital and was desirous of entering private practice. Dr. Ingrasci manifested an interest in becoming associated with Dr. Karpinski and, after a number of discussions, they reached an understanding; the defendant was to live in Ithaca, a locale with which he had no prior familiarity, and there work as an employee of the plaintiff.

A contract, reflecting the agreement, was signed by the defendant in June, 1962. It was for three years and, shortly after its execution, the defendant started working in the office which the plaintiff rented and fully equipped at his own expense. The provision of the contract with which we are concerned is a covenant by the defendant not to compete with the plaintiff. More particularly, it recited that the defendant

"promises and covenants that while this agreement is in effect and forever thereafter, he will never practice dentistry and/or Oral Surgery in Cayuga, Cortland, Seneca, Tompkins or Ontario counties except: (a) In association with the [plaintiff] or (b) If the [plaintiff] terminates the agreement and employs another oral surgeon".

In addition, the defendant agreed, "in consideration of the . . . terms of employment, and of the experience gained while working with" the plaintiff, to execute a $40,000 promissory note to the plaintiff, to become payable if the defendant left the plaintiff and practiced "dentistry and/or Oral Surgery" in the five enumerated counties.[1]

When the contract expired, the two men engaged in extended discussions as to the nature of their continued association—as employer and employee or as partners. Unable to reach an accord, the defendant, in February, 1968, left the plaintiff's employ and opened his own office for the practice of oral surgery in Ithaca a week later. The dentists in the area thereupon began referring their patients to the defendant rather than to the plaintiff, and in two months the latter's practice from the Ithaca area dwindled to almost nothing and he closed the office in that city. In point of fact, the record discloses that about 90% of the defendant's present practice comes from referrals from dentists in the counties specified in the restrictive covenant, the very same dentists who had been referring patients to the plaintiff's Ithaca office when the defendant was working there.[2]

The plaintiff, alleging a breach of the restrictive covenant, seeks not only an injunction to enforce it but also a judgment of $40,000 on the note. The Supreme Court, after a nonjury trial, decided in favor of the plaintiff and granted him both an injunction and damages as requested. On appeal, however, the Appellate Division reversed the resulting judgment and dismissed the complaint; it was that court's view that the covenant was void and unenforceable on the ground that its restriction against the practice of both dentistry *and* oral surgery was impermissibly broad.

There can be no doubt that the defendant violated the terms of the covenant when he opened his own office in Ithaca. But the mere fact of breach does not, in and of itself, resolve the case. Since there are "powerful considerations of public policy which militate against sanctioning the loss of a man's livelihood," the courts will subject a covenant by an employee not to compete with his former employer to an "overriding limitation of 'reasonableness' ". (Purchasing Assoc. v. Weitz, 13 N.Y.2d 267, 272, 246 N.Y.S.2d 600, 603, 196 N.E.2d 245, see Millet v. Slocum, 5 N.Y.2d 734, 177 N.Y.S.2d 716, 152 N.E.2d 672, affg. 4 A.D.2d 528, 167 N.Y.S.2d 136; Lynch v. Bailey, 300 N.Y. 615, 90 N.E.2d 484, affg. 275 App.Div. 527, 90 N.Y.S.2d 359; Interstate Tea Co. v. Alt, 271 N.Y. 76, 80, 2 N.E.2d 51, 53; see, also, Note, An Employer's Competitive Restraints on Former Employees, 17 Drake L.Rev. 69; Blake, Employee Agreements Not to Compete, 73 Harv.L. Rev. 625; Wetzel, Employment Contracts and Noncompetition Agreements, 1969 U.Ill.L.F. 61.) Such covenants by physicians are, if reasonable in scope, generally given effect. (See Millet v. Slocum, 5 N.

1. Either party was privileged to terminate the agreement on 60 days' notice within the three-year period and, if the plaintiff were to do so, the contract recited, the defendant was released from the restrictive covenant and the note.

2. There are two other oral surgeons, in addition to the plaintiff and the defendant, serving the Ithaca area.

Y.2d 734, 177 N.Y.S.2d 716, 152 N.E.2d 672, affg. 4 A.D.2d 528, 167 N.Y.S.2d 136, supra; Foster v. White, 273 N.Y. 596, 7 N.E.2d 710, affg. 248 App.Div. 451, 290 N.Y.S. 394; see, also, Ann., Restriction on Practice of Physician, 58 A.L.R. 156; 6A Corbin, Contracts [1962], § 1393.) "It is a firmly established doctrine", it has been noted, "that a member of one of the learned professions, upon becoming assistant to another member thereof, may, upon a sufficient consideration, bind himself not to engage in the practice of his profession upon the termination of his contract of employment, within a reasonable territorial extent, as such an agreement is not in restraint of trade or against public policy" (Ann., Restriction on Practice of Physician, 58 A.L.R. 156, 162).

Each case must, of course, depend, to a great extent, upon its own facts. It may well be that, in some instances, a restriction not to conduct a profession or a business in two counties or even in one, may exceed permissible limits. But, in the case before us, having in mind the character and size of the counties involved, the area restriction imposed is manifestly reasonable. The five small rural counties which it encompasses comprise the very area from which the plaintiff obtained his patients and in which the defendant would be in direct competition with him. Thus, the covenant's coverage coincides precisely with "the territory over which the practice extends", and this is proper and permissible. (6A Corbin, Contracts [1962], § 1393, p. 87; see Interstate Tea Co. v. Alt, 271 N.Y. 76, 80, 2 N.E.2d 51, 53, supra; see, also, Ann., Employees—Restrictive Covenant—Area, 43 A.L.R.2d 94, 162.) In brief, the plaintiff made no attempt to extend his influence beyond the area from which he drew his patients, the defendant being perfectly free to practice as he chooses outside the five specified counties.

Nor may the covenant be declared invalid because it is unlimited as to time, forever restricting the defendant from competing with the plaintiff. It is settled that such a covenant will not be stricken merely because it "contains no time limit or is expressly made unlimited as to time". (37 N.Y.Jur., Master and Servant, § 179, p. 60; see Diamond Match Co. v. Roeber, 106 N.Y. 473, 484, 13 N.E. 419, 422; Goos v. Pennisi, 10 A.D.2d 643, 644, 197 N.Y.S.2d 253, 254; Foster v. White, 248 App.Div. 451, 456, 290 N.Y.S. 394, 399, affd. 273 N.Y. 596, 7 N.E.2d 710, supra; see, also, Ann.—Employee—Restrictive Covenant—Time, 41 A.L.R.2d 15, 35.) "According to the weight of authority as applied to contracts by physicians, surgeons and others of kindred profession," the court wrote in *Foster* (248 App.Div., at p. 456, 290 N.Y.S. at p. 399), "relief for violation of these contracts will not be denied merely because the agreement is unlimited as to time, where as to area the restraint is limited and reasonable." In the present case, the defendant opened an office in Ithaca, in competition with the plaintiff, just one week after his employment had come to an end. Under the circumstances presented, we thoroughly agree with the trial judge that it is clear that nearly all of the defendant's practice was, and would be, directly attributable to his association with his former employer.

This brings us to the most troublesome part of the restriction imposed upon the defendant. By the terms of the contract, he agreed not to practice "dentistry and/or Oral Surgery" in competition with the plaintiff. Since the plaintiff practices only "oral surgery," and it was for the practice of that limited type of "dentistry" that he had employed the defendant, the Appellate Division concluded that the plaintiff went beyond permissible limits when he obtained from the defendant the covenant that he would not engage in any "dentistry" whatsoever.[3] The restriction, *as formulated*, is, as the Appellate Division concluded, too broad; it is not reasonable for a man to be excluded from a profession for which he has been trained when he does not compete with his former employer by practicing it.

The plaintiff seeks to justify the breadth of the covenant by urging that, if it had restricted only the defendant's practice of oral surgery and permitted him to practice "dentistry"—that is, to hold himself out as a dentist generally—the defendant would have been permitted, under the Education Law (§ 6601, subd. 3), to do all the work which an oral surgeon could. We have no sympathy with this argument; the plaintiff was not privileged to prevent the defendant from working in an area of dentistry in which he would not be in competition with him. The plaintiff would have all the protection he needs if the restriction were to be limited to the practice of oral surgery, and this poses the question as to the court's power to "sever" the impermissible from the valid and uphold the covenant to the extent that it is reasonable.

Although we have found no decision in New York directly in point, cases in this court support the existence of such a power. (See, e. g., Purchasing Assoc. v. Weitz, 13 N.Y.2d 267, 272, 246 N.Y.S.2d 600, 603, supra; Carpenter & Hughes v. De Joseph, 10 N.Y.2d 925, 224 N.Y.S.2d 9, 179 N.E.2d 854, affg., 13 A.D.2d 611, 213 N.Y.S.2d 860; Interstate Tea Co. v. Alt, 271 N.Y. 76, 80, 2 N.E.2d 51, 53, supra.) Moreover, a number of out-of-state decisions, and they are supported by authoritative texts and commentators, explicitly recognize the court's power of severance and divisibility in order to sustain the covenant insofar as it is reasonable.[4] As Professor Blake put it (73 Harv.L.Rev., at pp. 674–675), "If in balancing the equities the

3. Some of the things a dentist may do, which a practitioner who limits himself to oral surgery is ethically prevented from doing include the filling of teeth, placing crowns on teeth, doing reconstruction work of the mouth, dentures, prophylaxis or straightening of the teeth.

4. [Citations omitted.] Some of these authorities would only sever by applying the so-called "blue pencil" rule—that is, dividing the contract only when it is grammatically severable. Even this limited approach, however, would be sufficient in the case before us.

court decides that his [the employee's] activity would fit within the scope of a reasonable prohibition, it is apt to make use of the tool of severance, paring an unreasonable restraint down to appropriate size and enforcing it." In short, to cull from the Washington Supreme Court's opinion in Wood v. May, 73 Wash.2d 307, 314, 438 P.2d 587, 591, "we find it just and equitable to protect appellant [employer] by injunction to the extent necessary to accomplish the basic purpose of the contract insofar as such contract is reasonable." Accordingly, since his practice is solely as an oral surgeon, the plaintiff gains all the injunctive protection to which he is entitled if effect be given only to that part of the covenant which prohibits the defendant from practicing oral surgery.

The question arises, however, whether injunctive relief is precluded by the fact that the defendant's promissory note for $40,000 was to become payable if he breached the agreement not to compete. We believe not. The mere inclusion in a covenant of a liquidated damages provision does not automatically bar the grant of an injunction. (See Rubinstein v. Rubinstein, 23 N.Y.2d 293, 298, 296 N.Y.S. 2d 354, 358, 244 N.E.2d 49, 51; Wirth & Hamid Fair Booking v. Wirth, 265 N.Y. 214, 224, 192 N.E. 297, 301; Diamond Match Co. v. Roeber, 106 N.Y. 473, 486, 13 N.E. 419, 423, supra; Foster v. White, 248 App.Div. 451, 457, 290 N.Y.S. 394, 400, affd., 273 N.Y. 596, 7 N. E.2d 710, supra; see, also, 5 Corbin, Contracts [1964], § 1071; Ann. —Restriction on Practice of Physician, 58 A.L.R. 156, 172–174.) As this court wrote in the *Diamond Match Co.* case (106 N.Y. at p. 486, 13 N.E., at p. 424.), "It is a question of intention, to be deduced from the whole instrument and the circumstances; and if it appear that the performance of the covenant was intended, and not merely the payment of damages in case of a breach, the covenant will be enforced." The covenant under consideration in this case may not reasonably be read to render "the liquidated damages provision . . . the sole remedy." (Rubinstein v. Rubinstein, 23 N.Y.2d 293, 298, 296 N.Y.S.2d 354, 358, 244 N.E.2d 49, 51, supra.) On the other hand, it would be grossly unfair to grant the plaintiff, in addition to an injunction, the full amount of damages ($40,000) which the parties apparently contemplated for a total breach of the covenant, since the injunction will halt any further violation. The proper approach is that taken in *Wirth* (265 N.Y. 214, 192 N.E. 297, supra). The court, there faced with a similar situation, granted the injunction sought and, instead of awarding the amount of liquidated damages specified, remitted the matter for determination of the *actual* damages suffered during the period of the breach.

The hardship necessarily imposed on the defendant must be borne by him in view of the plaintiff's rightful interest in protecting the valuable practice of oral surgery which he built up over the course of many years. The defendant is, of course, privileged to practice "dentistry" generally in Ithaca or continue to practice "oral surgery" anywhere in the United States outside of the five small rural counties enumerated. The covenant, part of a contract carefully negotiated with no indication of fraud or overbearing on either side, must be enforced, insofar as it reasonably and validly may, according to its terms. In sum, then, the plaintiff is entitled to an injunction barring the defendant from practicing oral surgery in the five specified counties and to damages actually suffered by him in the period during which the defendant conducted such a practice in Ithaca after leaving the plaintiff's employ.

The order appealed from should be reversed, with costs, and the case remitted to Supreme Court, Cayuga County, for further proceedings in accordance with this opinion.

NOTES

(1) *Agreements Not to Compete.* How does the court's concern in this case differ from that in the cases in the preceding section? From what source did the court derive the "powerful considerations of public policy" that it mentioned? Do they—like freedom to contract—seem to have a non-statutory base? On the general subject, see Blake, Employee Agreements Not to Compete, 73 Harv.L.Rev. 625 (1960). Contracts in restraint of trade are dealt with in more detail in courses on trade regulation and antitrust law.[a]

Restrictive covenants between attorneys threaten the interests of clients, and are therefore "unreasonable *per se,*" it has been said. (How do they threaten clients' interests?) If that is so, how can it be that comparable covenants among physicians are compatible with the interests of patients? On these matters see Karlin v. Weinberg, 77 N.J. 408, 390 A.2d 1161 (1978), and the ABA Code of Professional Responsibility, DR 2–108(A). Detroit Bank & Trust Co. v. Coopes, 287 N.W.2d 266 (Mich.App.1980).

(2) *Problem.* An orthopedic surgeon accepted employment in a "clinic" in Elko, Nevada, and contracted that, upon the termination of his employment, he would not practice medicine within five miles of Elko for a period of two years. From a decree enforcing the covenant against the surgeon, when he decided to open his own office, he appealed. *Held:* Injunction modified. Ellis v. McDaniel, 95 Nev. —, 596 P.2d 222 (1979). What modification, if any, is indicated, given the following facts? (a) no other doctor at the Elko Clinic was an orthopedic surgeon, and (b) outside of Elko, the nearest hospital available for major surgery is 200 miles distant.

(3) *Consideration Revisited.* "Whether a covenant not to compete entered into after employment has commenced is supported by independent consideration is a question that has evoked considerable disagreement in the courts . . . [Some] courts require something in addition to the mere continuance of employment."[b] Modern Controls, Inc. v. Andreakis, 578 F.

a. See Goldschmid, Antitrust's Neglected Stepchild: A Proposal for Dealing With Restrictive Covenants Under Federal Law, 73 Colum.L.Rev. 1193 (1973). "Thousands, perhaps hundreds of thousands, of employees are being needlessly immobilized by unreasonable post-employment restraints." Id. at 1201.

b. One that does is the Pennsylvania court: George W. Kistler, Inc. v. O'Brien, 464 Pa. 475, 347 A.2d 311 (1975). Contra: Smith, Batchelder & Rugg v. Foster, — N.H. —, 406 A. 2d 1310 (1979). See also Jenkins v. Jenkins Irrigation, Inc., 244 Ga. 94, 259 S.E.2d 47 (1979), and Note 4, p. 49 supra.

2d 1264 (8th Cir. 1978). In this case Modern Controls employed a research scientist without getting his signature on a confidentiality agreement. Nine weeks later, when the company insisted that he sign, he did so. According to the agreement, if he resigned he was not to accept work in any division of a firm concerned with a product in competition with one he might work on for Modern Controls.[c] It also provided that Modern Controls would continue his base salary for as long as two years if (a) he was unable to find suitable employment by reason of the restraint, and (b) Modern Controls did not release him from the restraint. In signing the agreement, what consideration did the employee receive?

Suppose the agreement had prohibited the employee only from disclosing inventions that he made for Modern Controls to a competitor. Would there have been consideration *to the firm* for its salary-continuation promise?

(4) *Severance.* The Georgia court will not curtail a covenant against competition "staking out more territory than is reasonable" in conjunction with an employment contract. T. V. Tempo, Inc. v. T. V. Venture, Inc., 262 S.E.2d 54 (1979). The court is prepared to curtail such a covenant made by a seller in conjunction with the sale of a business. But it is concerned that covenant writers may claim vast territories—"e. g., America"—secure in the expectation that the courts will allow whatever proscription of area the parties could validly have negotiated. Against that possibility the court has stated the novel rule that when the judges' curative efforts are called on they should usually draw the line closer than the parties might have done. Jenkins v. Jenkins Irrigation, Inc., 244 Ga. 94, 259 S.E.2d 47 (1979). In some other courts an overbroad covenant will simply not be enforced.[d]

In Wisconsin a statute forbids the enforcement of an employee's covenant not to compete with his employer unless the restrictions are "reasonably necessary." One that imposes an unreasonable restraint is unenforceable, the statute continues, "even as to so much of the covenant or performance as would be a reasonable restraint." Wis.Stat.Ann. § 103.465 (1974).[e] Compare footnote 4 in the main case.

c. Is it an essential feature of a fully effective covenant that it distinguish between the case of an employee's resignation and that of his being fired? See Orion Broadcasting, Inc. v. Forsythe, 477 F.Supp. 198 (W.D. Ky.1979) (TV anchorperson); Foti v. Cook, 263 S.E.2d 430 (Va.1980).

d. For an overbroad covenant that the New York court refused to pare down, see Columbia Ribbon & Carbon Mfg. Co. v. A–I–A Corp., 42 N.Y.2d 496, 398 N.Y.S.2d 1004, 369 N.E.2d 4 (1977). But in Triggs v. Triggs, 46 N.Y.2d 305, 413 N.Y.S.2d 325, 385 N.E.2d 1254 (1978), the court approved severance of an illegal provision of a contract and enforcement of the remainder. An arbitrator's award of specific performance may be confirmed though it is not one that the court itself would have enforced. Sprinzen v. Nomberg, 46 N.Y.2d 623, 415 N.Y.S.2d 974, 389 N.E.2d 456 (1979).

e. This provision returned Wisconsin law to a position its courts had earlier espoused. The statute was a response to the decision in Fullerton Lumber Co. v. Torborg, 270 Wis. 133, 70 N.W.2d 585 (1955), granting partial enforcement to an over-broad covenant. Professor Macaulay has traced out the engrossing misadventures of the parties to this case: see R. Danzig, The Capability Problem in Contract Law (1978). He reports that although Torborg, the defendant,

What is to be said for the policy of the Wisconsin statute? Does it make the draftsman's work needlessly hard? Might he deal with the statute by inserting several covenants in the same contract, imposing restraints in concentric circles? Given the blue-pencil rule, how may the draftsman go to the limit of what the law allows?

Section 184 of the Restatement Second, according to the Reporter's Note, "rejects the so-called 'blue-pencil rule' of former § 518."[f] But it rejects also the principle of the Wisconsin statute: see Illustration 3. It resembles the position taken by the Iowa court: if an employee's agreement results from the employer's "taking unconscionable advantage" of him, it will not be enforced even in part. What circumstances would indicate that undue advantage was taken? See Tasco, Inc. v. Winkel, 281 N.W.2d 280 (Iowa, 1979); Smith, Batchelder & Rugg v. Foster, n. b. supra. How useful can drafting be in this connection?

(5) *Pruning a Wild Claim?* "A man who wildly claims that he owns all the cherry trees in the country cannot be denied protection of the orchard in his back yard." This judicial gem was quoted in Peripheral Dynamics, Inc. v. Holdsworth, 254 Pa.Super. 310, 385 A.2d 1354 (1978)—but it did not determine the result. The plaintiff in that case was a firm seeking to prevent its former sales manager from working for a competitor. The firm's president testified that Tibet and the North Pole were the only places where he would be content to let the defendant pursue his career. This evidence cannot have been helpful to the plaintiff. What would be an effective and ethical way for a lawyer to deal with a client's damaging emotions?

(6) *Problem.* Consult Note 4, p. 49 supra, and draft a covenant about competition for Marine Contractors to submit for Hurley's signature in connection with their negotiations. What facts that your client might supply do you need for the assignment?

Ex-employee Benefits

Employee benefits commonly include entitlements to a disbursement after the employment is terminated: pension payments, insurance costs, distributions under profit-sharing plans, and the like. One way for an employer to forestall competitive activity by an ex-employee is to place a condition about other employment in the plan, such that disbursements may be terminated or suspended unless he complies with it. The validity of such a plan was tested in Bradford v. New York Times Co., 501 F.2d 51 (2d Cir. 1974). Bradford had

was subjected to damages and an injunction for competing with his former employer, he had the damages judgment discharged in bankruptcy and that his new venture continued without interruption. It seems that Mrs. Torborg substituted for him as an officer of the firm. (As to that circumstance compare Brown v. Fraley, 222 Md. 480, 161 A.2d 128 (1960).) For a compilation of statutes on the subject see Krendl & Krendl, Noncompetition Covenants in Colorado, 52 Denver L.J. 499, 521–22 (1975).

f. The section was relied on in Cullman Broadcasting Co., Inc. v. Bosley, 373 So.2d 830 (Ala.1979).

been a participant in the Incentive Compensation Plan of the New York Times Company; as General Manager he had helped draft the plan and as a Director he had voted for it. Upon resigning, he received "Times" stock worth about $7,000 under the plan, and much more was reserved for later distribution to him. But the plan provided for "discontinuing" distributions if he should take employment in competition with the company. Owing to other newspaper work he did, no further installments were paid. After giving up that work, Bradford demanded resumption of the stock distributions (at that time the stock entitlement he claimed was worth about $230,000), and later sued for it. On appeal from a judgment for the company, *held*: Affirmed.

Some courts draw an analogy between such a "forfeiture" provision and a covenant not to compete and apply requirements of reasonableness to both. That was done in Bradford's case. Others have perceived a "clear and obvious distinction." [a] What grounds for distinction do you see? [b]

In the mid-70's the Congress entered the field with ERISA—the Employee Retirement Income Security Act. For certain employment arrangements, know as "qualified retirement plans" there are minimum vesting requirements such that the permissible grounds for forfeiture are limited. "The public policy declared by Congress in ERISA," it has been said, "is unequivocal: forfeitures of pension benefits because of post-employment competitive activity are no longer permissible." Ellis v. Lionikis, 152 N.J.Super. 321, 377 A.2d 1208 (1977). See also CCH(1) Pension Plan Guide ¶ 3201.

NOTE

A Post-Christmas Present. Though enacted in 1974, ERISA does not in terms deal with forfeitures declared prior to 1976. In the case last cited, the trustees of a firm's profit-sharing plan sought to take timely action. The firm was owned by Lionikis, and the plan was administered by him and his wife as trustees. In 1975 Lionikis learned that Ellis, a salesman he had earlier fired, was working for a competitor. On December 29 Mr. and Mrs. Lionikis held a hearing (Ellis chose not to attend), at which they resolved to deny plan benefits to Ellis. Until then the trust fund was charged with a credit for Ellis of nearly $30,000; the effect of the trustees' decision was to divert more than 70% of this to Lionikis, as the best-paid employee. Ellis brought the action for a declaration that his interest in the fund had not been divested. What grounds do you see for a ruling in his favor, in the

a. See Almers v. South Carolina Nat. Bank of Charleston, 265 S.C. 48, 217 S.E.2d 135 (1975)—refusing to draw one. See also Post v. Merrill Lynch, Etc., 48 N.Y.2d 84, 397 N.E.2d 358 (1979).

b. See Shandor v. Wells Nat. Service Corp., 478 F.Supp. 12 (N.D.Ga.1979) (deferred commissions for sales manager). In the *Almers* case, cited in the foregoing footnote, Littlejohn, J., dissenting, compared the plan in question with an employer's policy of raising salaries so as to prevent employees from being hired away. In his view the word "forfeiture" was misapplied by the court: "one cannot forfeit that to which he was never entitled."

face of a plan provision authorizing the trustees' action? (For several reasons the plan as described would not now comport with ERISA.)

INDUCING OFFICIAL ACTION

Influence peddling is a common subject of judicial denunciation, but lawyers above all should be aware that services in procuring favorable official action are worthy of a price.[a] Contracts to pay lobbyists are by no means condemned as such. The proper line has been stated as follows: "The authorities very generally hold that a contract to pay for services to be performed in the endeavor to obtain or defeat legislation by other means than the use of argument addressed to the reason of the legislators, such as, for example, for the exertion of personal or political influence apart from the appeal to reason as applied to the consideration of the merits or demerits of the legislation in question, is an illegal contract." Campbell County v. Howard & Lee, 133 Va. 19, 112 S.E. 876 (1922). The consequence of stepping over the line is illustrated in Ewing v. National Airport Corporation, 115 F.2d 859 (4th Cir. 1940), cert. denied, 312 U.S. 705 (1941).

In the latter case the court said: "Contingent fees for services in securing the passage of legislation are especially regarded with disfavor by the courts." Why should this be? Tort litigation in this country is customarily conducted by lawyers for claimants under contracts for contingent fees. It has been said that in such cases, "Because of the very fact that [the contingent fee] does insure the most humble citizen equal justice under law, while at the same time preserving the lawyer's independence of judgment and action, it serves the highest public interest." Cohen, Book Review, 24 Vand.L.Rev. 433, 441 (1971). Is it significant that in some courts there are disclosure requirements and regulations designed to control immoderate contingent fees for lawyers, and there are schedules and ceilings for the compensation of lawyers pressing certain types of claims?

NOTES

(1) *Chutzpah Illustrated.* Being offered a bribe, a judge consulted the state's attorney and was advised to accept the money. It became evidence in criminal proceedings against the payor, who was imprisoned. He then moved for the return of the money by the state, and that was ordered (by another judge). The state appealed. The court considered the case under

a. Agreements that have been questioned range from an agreement supposedly made by a justice of the peace to collect a doctor's bills "under color of his office" (In re Robertson, 7 N.C.App. 186, 171 S.E.2d 801 (1970)) to an agreement made by a lawyer with good political connections to present to President Kennedy, on behalf of a railroad, the case for the intervention of the Department of Justice in a proceeding involving the I.C.C. (Troutman v. Southern Railway Co., 441 F.2d 586 (5th Cir. 1971) (the presentation was successful)).

the aspect of failure of consideration, or breach by the "bribed" judge. *Held*: Reversed. The court opened its opinion with a definition of "chutzpah". It went on to say that the courts will not order damages for breach of a contract to commit a crime. "Parties of that ilk are left where they are found, to stew in their own juice." State v. Strickland, 42 Md.App. 357, 400 A.2d 451 (1979).

(2) *Multiple Choice.* Construction Company let a subcontract for work on a section of state highway to Bridge Company. The firms executed two contracts for the same work (contract A and contract B), the difference being that the materials required were to be furnished by Construction Company under A and by Bridge Company under B. The parties exhibited A to the state highway department for approval, but they operated under B. The department would not have approved B, for it delegated to Bridge Company more than half the total job of construction, determined by cost. If Construction Company refuses to pay anything to Bridge Company for its work and materials, and Bridge Company sues on contract B, should the court (a) grant recovery for both, or (b) deny recovery for both, or (c) grant recovery for its work only? See Holloway & Son Constr. Co., Inc. v. Mattingly Bridge Co., 581 S.W.2d 568 (Ky.1979). Compare Apex Contracting, Inc. v. William Robinson Constr. Co., Inc., 581 S.W.2d 573 (Ky.1979).

(3) *Problem.* An electrical contractor (S–1) gave a bid to a general contractor (G) who was in competition for a sizeable government contract. G's chief estimator said it was "very interesting," and S–1 asked, "Do we have a job if you have one?" The answer was that G would like some "protection". This was understood to mean that S–1 would submit higher bids to G's competitors so that G would have the lowest electrical costs. S–1 told G he would give what was asked: "we are banking on you getting the job and we are willing to gamble on you and you only." G's estimator made a commitment to S–1, including the promise, "I am not going to tell anybody else what your number is." In spite of that, he telephoned another electrical contractor with whom G had often done business (S–2) and asked if it could beat S–1's bid. At the last moment before the general contractors' bids were opened G recast its bid on the basis of a figure supplied by S–2. G won the contract and sublet the electrical work to S–2. Does S–1 have a claim against G? See Premier Electrical Constr. Co. v. Miller-Davis Co., 291 F.Supp. 295 (N.D.Ill.1968), aff'd, 422 F.2d 1132 (7th Cir.), cert. denied, 400 U.S. 828.

SIRKIN v. FOURTEENTH ST. STORE

New York Supreme Court, Appellate Division (2d Dept.), 1908.
124 App.Div. 384, 108 N.Y.S. 830.

[Sirkin sued the Fourteenth Street Store for $1,555, the purchase price of hosiery and wrappers that he had sold and delivered to the store. The store alleged as a defense that Sirkin had bribed McGuiness, its purchasing agent, by promising him 5% on all orders he placed with it, and that he had paid the purchasing agent $75 for the transaction sued on. The New York Penal Code made it a misdemeanor, punishable by a fine of up to $500 and imprisonment of up to one year, for a seller to offer an agent "authorized to procure materials, supplies or other articles either by purchase or contract for his principal . . . a commission, discount or bonus," or for an agent to receive it. The trial court directed a verdict for the plaintiff, without allowing the defendant to prove the defense alleged, reasoning that since the goods had been delivered, the defendant could not retain them and decline to pay. The defendant appealed.]

LAUGHLIN, J. . . . There can be no doubt that the act of the plaintiff in bribing the purchasing agent of the defendant was a violation of . . . the Penal Code. . . . The Legislature has not expressly declared either that the contract to pay the bribe or the contract induced by the bribe is void or unenforceable. A contract, however, made in violation of a penal statute, although not expressly prohibited or declared to be void, is prohibited, void, and unenforceable, whether executory or executed . . . . A contract to do an illegal act or to aid another in violating the law is likewise void and unenforceable, whether executory or executed. . . . Upon the same principle one who is required by law to procure a license to conduct any trade, calling, or profession may not recover for services rendered or property sold, without first obtaining such license, regardless of whether or not it was known by the person for whom the services were rendered or to whom the property was sold that the license had not been obtained. . . . It is therefore quite clear that the purchasing agent could not enforce the contract to recover the consideration agreed to be paid to him; and it may be here observed that this would have been so under the common law, if the statute had not been enacted, for the contract contravened public policy. The question appears to be presented now for the first time as to whether this is the limitation of the disability for violating the penal statute, or whether the court may refuse its aid to the party obtaining the contract for the purchase or sale of property, or for work, in violation of the statute, upon the same ground that it leaves a party to a contract which is void as against public policy, or offends against good morals, where it finds him. It is manifest that the Legislature in enacting this penal statute intended to emphasize and extend the public policy of the common law, which rendered such contracts by agents for their own benefit void. It being the province of the Legislature to declare the public policy of the state, it is the duty of the court to be guided thereby in administering the law. The acts of the plaintiff not only offended against good morals and public policy at common law, but constituted a crime under the statutory law of this state; and he is here seeking the aid of the court to enforce a contract which he procured by violating our penal statute. Nothing could be more corrupting, nor have a greater tendency to lead to disloyalty and dishonesty on the part of servants, agents, and employés, and to a betrayal of the confidence and trust reposed in them, than these practices which the Legislature has endeavored to stamp out;

and I think nothing will be more effective in stopping the growth and spread of this corrupting and now criminal custom than a decision that the courts will refuse their aid to a guilty vendor or vendee, or to any one who has obtained a contract by secretly bribing the servant, agent, or employé of another to purchase or sell property, or to place the contract with him. . . .

The servant would be accountable to his master or employer for any moneys thus received, but that affords no adequate remedy, for the reason that such contracts are made secretly, and it would be difficult to discover or prove the facts. The vice lies in making the agreement without the knowledge of the master. Of course, it is perfectly competent for a master to employ a servant as a purchasing or selling agent, and to give him a commission upon the purchase price or allow a commission to be paid by the vendee upon the selling price and it may well be, as was recently held in Ballin v. Fourteenth Street Store, 54 Misc. 359, 105 N.Y.S. 1028, affirmed (Sup.) 108 N.Y.S. 26, that, where the bribe is received with the knowledge of the master, the statute does not apply, and the contract of sale will be enforced. It is perfectly plain that, if the contract had not been performed by the plaintiff, the defendant, upon discovering the fact that its agent had been bribed to place the contract, would have had the right to rescind. . . . It is contended that its only remedies upon discovering the facts were to rescind the contract, or, if that were impracticable, to counterclaim for any damages it has sustained by reason of the plaintiff's fraud in inducing the contract, and that by a failure to rescind or thus counterclaim it is deemed to have ratified and affirmed the contract. I am of opinion that this is not a case in which the rule of ratification, applicable to ordinary contracts induced by fraud, should be applied. The public policy of our state forbids the ratification, as well as the making, of such a contract. Usually private contracts concern only the parties thereto, and it is optional with a person who has discovered that he has been defrauded whether to ratify the contract or to rescind it. There is ordinarily, at least, no general public policy involved in such cases. . . .

[Reversed (3–2).]

SCOTT, J. (dissenting) . . . . Undoubtedly the secret agreement to pay a commission to plaintiff [McGuiness?] was a fraud on defendant, and rendered the contract voidable at its option. It might, if it had discovered the fraud in time, have refused to receive the goods, or, having received them, might have tendered them back, or might even now counterclaim for the damages it suffered from the fraud, if, in fact and law, it could show that it had suffered damage. The statute which has made that a crime, which heretofore was merely immoral, has affixed to that crime an appropriate penalty. It is no part of our duty to assume legislative power and prescribe an additional punishment, nor are we to assume, in the absence of allegations to that effect, that the defendant did, in fact, suffer damage as a result of plaintiff's unlawful agreement with McGuiness. . . .

NOTES

(1) *Recovery of the Bribe.* Could the Fourteenth Street Store have kept the goods, refused to pay for them, and recovered the bribe from McGuiness? Consider McDevitt v. Stokes, p. 400 supra, as to which the Restatement Second proposes as a solution that the jockey's driving in the race is consideration for the promise of a bonus, but the employer may be entitled to it. Restatement Second § 73, Illustration 12.

(2) *Unjust Enrichment.* Does not the decision in the Sirkin case result in the unjust enrichment of the Fourteenth Street Store? Recovery in restitution is not generally allowed a party for benefits conferred under a contract unenforceable because of illegality. (See p. 562 infra.) Is it possible to avoid such enrichment in some other way?

Rush v. Curtiss-Wright Export Corp., 175 Misc. 873, 25 N.Y.S.2d 597 (1941), suggests a possible approach. An ex-naval officer was employed by the Republic of Colombia as its full-time military aircraft procurement advisor for $21,000 a year. He took this job at the urging of Export Co., an aircraft manufacturer, which promised to supplement his Colombia salary by paying him commissions and bonuses on its sales of aircraft to Colombia. In an action by his assignee against Export Co. to recover $41,000 in commissions and bonuses, the trial court refused to dismiss the complaint and directed entry of judgment for the plaintiff "as trustee for the Republic of Colombia." On appeal, however, the judgment was reversed, the Appellate Division concluding that the agreement was "corrupt and illegal," but ordering that the complaint be dismissed for that reason. Rush v. Curtiss-Wright Export Co., 263 App.Div. 69, 31 N.Y.S.2d 550 (1942), aff'd, 289 N.Y. 562, 43 N.E.2d 712 (1943). Do you agree? See Seavey, Problems in Restitution, 7 Okla.L.Rev. 257, 259 (1954).[a]

Under Soviet law, "in the event a contract is invalid [because of illegality], neither of the parties shall have the right to demand from the other the return of whatever has been performed under the contract; instead it may be treated as unjust enrichment to be forfeit to the state." H. Berman, Justice in the U.S.S.R. 141 (1963). Compare the "chutzpah" case, p. 545 supra.

(3) *Fighting Fire with a Committee.* A leading manufacturer of handbags, Jaclyn, Inc., developed a line of bags so popular that retailers were under irresistible pressure to stock them. Nevertheless, Jaclyn promoted sales through payments to buyers, including substantial sums paid to the senior buyer for Edison Brothers Stores. When reports of the payments reached Edison's highest officers, in January, 1975, they formed a committee of investigation and took legal advice. Three months passed before the disloyal agent was confronted, during which he ordered merchandise from Jaclyn worth hundreds of thousands of dollars. Edison refused to pay for it and when sued for the price raised the defense of commercial bribery. Edison also counterclaimed for actual and punitive damages. The court censured Jaclyn severely for a "corrosive pattern of covert payments

a. Commenting on Reading v. Attorney General, [1951] A.C. 507 (P.C.).

to the agents of its vendees," contravening the penal code and "desecrating the sanctity of the fiduciary bond." On the counterclaim the court awarded a modest amount as actual damages and $75,000 as punitive damages. On the main claim it awarded Jaclyn nearly all it sought: $436,000. Jaclyn, Inc. v. Edison Brothers Stores, Inc., 170 N.J.Super. 334, 406 A.2d 474 (1979).

The court distinguished a Seventh Circuit case [b] on several grounds, one of them being that the commercial bribery statute applicable to Jaclyn's conduct described the miscreant mildly as a "disorderly person." *Question:* Is the statutory name of the offense a suitable guide to decision? [c]

(4) *Two Views.* In 1692 Lord Holt expressed the following influential view: "Every contract made for or about any matter or thing which is prohibited and made unlawful by any statute is a void contract though the statute itself doth not mention that it shall be so, but only inflicts a penalty on the offender, because a penalty implies a prohibition, though there are no prohibitory words in the statute." Bartlett v. Vinor, Carth, 251, 252, 90 Eng.Rep. 750. In 1936 Professor Gellhorn wrote: "The judges are not bound to regard as void every contract which seems in some way to fall within the general aura of the criminal law, but only those whose enforcement, they are persuaded, after respectfully studying the 'public policy' involved, will disserve the general interest as it has been indicated by the legislature." Contracts and Public Policy, 35 Colum.L.Rev. 679, 686 (1936).

LICENSING

The court went too far in the *Sirkin* case when it said that "one who is required by law to procure a license to conduct any trade, calling, or profession may not recover for services rendered or property sold, without first obtaining such license." When the purpose of a licensing requirement is ascertained to be raising public revenue, and not the protection of public "welfare"—health, morals or the like—a claimant's want of the license is generally not a bar. In Cope v. Rowlands, 2 M. & W. 149, 150 Eng.Rep. 707 (Exch.1836), a London stockbroker sued for a commission and was met by a plea that he was not licensed by the Mayor and Aldermen as required by statute. According to the court, the question is, "whether the enactment of the statute is meant merely to secure a revenue to the city . . . or whether one of its objects be the protection of the public, and the prevention of improper persons acting as brokers." The court concluded that since the statute provided for licensing of brokers "under such restrictions and limitations for their honest and good behavior as the [Mayor and Aldermen] should think fit and reasonable" it was of the latter sort; and the court denied recovery.

b. Nathan v. Tenna Corp., 560 F.2d 761 (7th Cir. 1977).

c. The Model Penal Code provision on the subject (since enacted in New Jersey) is entitled "commercial bribery." Section 224.8(c), 10 U.L.A. 561–62 (1974). For a compilation of statutes see Perrin v. United States, 100 S.Ct. 311 (1979).

What is the justification for the distinction between "regulation" and "revenue" measures? How can they be distinguished?

Recently the judgments in some (non)license cases have become more complex than they once appeared to be. See for example Town Planning & Engineering Associates, Inc. v. Amesbury Specialty Co., Inc., 369 Mass. 737, 342 N.E.2d 706 (1976). There the court said that the certification requirement for a professional engineer could be taken "as aimed in part at least at enhancing public safety." Yet the court approved a recovery for services assumed to have been rendered in violation of the statute. It arrived at its decision by proceeding along the "vector" of various considerations, including the strength of the public policy in question, and "how serious or deserved would be the forfeiture suffered by the plaintiff,[a] how gross and undeserved the defendant's windfall." *Question:* Is it germane in such a case that the observance of building codes is enforced by public officials?

NOTES

(1) *Second Thoughts.* In 1897 the Maine Supreme Judicial Court held that a hotel keeper was barred from recovering the price ($28) of board and lodging he had furnished to a lady because he did not hold a "victualer's" license. Many years later the owner of a Maine resort sued a California corporation, in the federal court for Maine, and obtained a verdict for some $65,000 as part of the price for lodgings and meals he had furnished in a summer month. The defendant counterclaimed for $185,000 that it had paid under the contract. The defendant appealed from an adverse judgment on both claims. The court of appeals agreed with the defendant that for the period in question the plaintiff had been without a required victualer's license, and that sanitation licenses for his buildings were wanting. It found the best indication of Maine law to be the hotel-keeper's case mentioned above. However, evidently finding the precedent repugnant, the court directed that inquiry be made of the Maine Supreme Judicial Court—through certified question—about its view of the case. The federal court pointed to decisions in other states permitting restitutionary recoveries, or simply making an "equitable exception," in like cases. Hiram Ricker & Sons v. Students Int'l Meditation Society, 501 F.2d 550 (1st Cir. 1974). The Maine court accepted the invitation to overrule its 1897 decision. Id., 342 A.2d 262 (Me.1975).

(2) *Liquor Distinguished from Milk.* In John E. Rosasco Creameries, Inc. v. Cohen, 276 N.Y. 274, 11 N.E.2d 908, 118 A.L.R. 641 (1937), an agreement for a dealer-to-dealer sale of milk was enforced although the seller who sued for the price of approximately $11,000 was unlicensed. The statutory provision read: "No milk dealer shall buy milk . . . or deal in . . . milk unless such dealer be duly licensed. . . . It shall be unlawful for a milk dealer to buy milk from . . . a milk dealer who is unlicensed, or in any way deal in or handle milk which he has reason to be-

a. For an elaboration on this point see Valley Stream Teachers Federal Credit Union v. Commissioner of Banks, — Mass. —, 384 N.E.2d 200 (1978). As to licensing of contractors, see Stucki v. Mailander, 589 P.2d 778 (Utah 1979), making a comparable analysis.

lieve has previously been dealt in or handled in violation of the provisions of this chapter." Violations were made punishable, as misdemeanors, by fine of up to $200 and imprisonment for up to six months. The purpose of the statute was economic regulation, as shown by the fact that exemptions were authorized for dealers in a small way, and in small communities. The court said: "If the contract is declared unenforceable, the effect will be to punish the plaintiff to the extent of a loss of approximately $11,000 and permit the defendants to evade the payment of a legitimate debt." Was this decision consistent with the reasoning in the case of the London stockbroker?

Four years later, however, the same court refused to allow an unlicensed liquor dealer to recover $6,400, the price of liquor sold and delivered by him. The Alcoholic Beverage Control Law of New York makes it a criminal offense to sell liquor without a permit from the proper state authority but does not expressly provide that contracts made by unlicensed dealers are unenforceable. In Carmine v. Murphy, 261 App.Div. 17, 23 N.Y.S.2d 723 (1940), the court held that an unlicensed liquor dealer could recover: "The reasoning in that [Rosasco] case should apply with equal force to the controversy here under consideration." But the Court of Appeals reversed in a cryptic opinion which said merely: "The present case is not excepted from the general rule of law that no right of action can spring out of an illegal contract." 285 N.Y. 413, 35 N.E.2d 19 (1941).

Are the cases distinguishable?

REMITTERS' LIABILITY

"If a party to an illegal transaction turns over money or property to a third person for the use of the other party to the transaction, the latter can enforce the express or implied promise or trust of the third party to turn over the money or property, notwithstanding the fact that he could not have enforced payment or delivery by the party who voluntarily made the payment or deposit. A mere agent or depository of the proceeds of an illegal transaction will not be permitted to assert the defense of illegality in an action to recover the proceeds by a party to the illegal transaction." Southwestern Shipping Corp. v. National City Bank, 6 N.Y.2d 454, 160 N.E.2d 836 (1959). For a possible application of this rule consider the fanciful case, Solon v. Lexis. The Casino Company agreed with Solon, a legislator, to pay him $10,000 if he procured the passage of a bill reducing its taxes. Upon enactment of the bill the company paid that amount to Lexis, a legislative assistant to Solon, who knew the money was meant for Solon. Lexis gambled it away at the casino. Is he liable to Solon for the amount of the bribe?

In the case quoted above an Italian firm had established an account in a New York bank "in favor of" a United States citizen, Anlyan. The object was to pay lire to the Southwestern Shipping Corporation for goods to be shipped to a buyer in Italy. Anlyan was lending his privilege to receive the funds as a cover for a payment in violation of international exchange controls. He had transferred the bank credit to Southwestern and so advised the bank. Yet he seized the opportunity of a bank error to misappropriate the credit and abscond with the proceeds. Southwestern sued the bank for refusing its demand for the funds. What weaknesses do you see in the plaintiff's claim, as compared with the claim of Solon against Lexis?

The bank was held accountable. Judge Desmond dissented. Note that in the opinion to follow he distinguishes the Southwestern Shipping case.

NOTE

Problem. Suppose that two friends, in a state where gambling is illegal, make a $1,000 bet on the outcome of a prize fight. Each deposits $1,000 with a third friend, who agrees to act as stakeholder pending the event. After the fight, the successful better demands the money from the stakeholder. The stakeholder, who has become financially embarrassed, refuses to turn the money over and the successful better sues to recover the $2,000 from the stakeholder. Decision? Is the case distinguishable from Southwestern Shipping Corp. v. National City Bank, and, if so, on what ground?

McCONNELL v. COMMONWEALTH PICTURES CORP.

Court of Appeals of New York, 1960.
7 N.Y.2d 465, 166 N.E.2d 494.

DESMOND, Chief Judge. The appeal is by defendant from so much of an Appellate Division, First Department, order as affirmed that part of a Special Term order which struck out two defenses in the answer.

Plaintiff sues for an accounting. Defendant had agreed in writing that, if plaintiff should succeed in negotiating a contract with a motion-picture producer whereby defendant would get the distribution rights for certain motion pictures, defendant would pay plaintiff $10,000 on execution of the contract between defendant and the producer, and would thereafter pay plaintiff a stated percentage of defendant's gross receipts from distribution of the pictures. Plaintiff negotiated the distribution rights for defendant and defendant paid plaintiff the promised $10,000 but later refused to pay him the commissions or to give him an accounting of profits.

Defendant's answer contains, besides certain denials and counterclaims not now before us, two affirmative defenses the sufficiency of which we must decide. In these defenses it is asserted that plaintiff, without the knowledge of defendant or of the producer, procured the distribution rights by bribing a representative of the producer and that plaintiff agreed to pay and did pay to that representative as a bribe the $10,000 which defendant paid plaintiff. The courts below (despite a strong dissent in the Appellate Division) held that the defenses were insufficient to defeat plaintiff's suit. Special Term's opinion said that, since the agreement sued upon—between plaintiff and defendant—was not in itself illegal, plaintiff's right to be paid for performing it could not be defeated by a showing that he had misconducted himself in carrying it out. The court found a substantial difference between this and the performance of an illegal contract. We take a different view. Proper and consistent application of a prime and long-settled public policy closes the doors of our courts to those who sue to collect the rewards of corruption.

New York's policy has been frequently and emphatically announced in the decisions. " 'It is the settled law of this State (and probably of every other State) that a party to an illegal contract cannot ask a court of law to help him carry out his illegal object, nor can such a person plead or prove in any court a case in which he, as a basis for his claim, must show forth his illegal purpose', Stone v. Freeman, 298 N.Y. 268, 271, 82 N.E.2d 571, 572, 8 A.L.R.2d 304, citing the leading cases. The money plaintiff sues for was the fruit of an admitted crime and 'no court should be required to serve as paymaster of the wages of crime'. Stone v. Freeman, supra, 298 N.Y. at page 271, 82 N.E.2d at page 572. And it makes no difference that defendant has no title to the money since the court's concern 'is not with the position of the defendant' but with the question of whether 'a recovery by the plaintiff should be denied for the sake of public interests', a question which is one 'of public policy in the administration of the law'. Flegenheimer v. Brogan, 284 N.Y. 268, 272, 30 N.E.2d 591, 592, 132 A.L.R. 613. That public policy is the one described in Riggs v. Palmer, 115 N.Y. 506, 511–512, 22 N.E. 188, 190, 5 L.R.A. 340: 'No one shall be permitted to profit by his own fraud, or to take advantage of his own wrong, or to found any claim upon his own iniquity, or to acquire property by his own crime. These maxims are dictated by public policy, have their foundation in universal law administered in all civilized countries, and have nowhere been superseded by statutes' " (Carr v. Hoy, 2 N.Y.2d 185, 187, 158 N.Y.S.2d 572, 574–575, 139 N.E.2d 531, 533).

We must either repudiate those statements of public policy or uphold these challenged defenses. It is true that some of the leading decisions (Oscanyan v. Arms Co., 103 U.S. 261, 26 L.Ed. 539; Stone v. Freeman, 298 N.Y. 268, 82 N.E.2d 571, 8 A.L.R.2d 304) were in suits on intrinsically illegal contracts but the rule fails of its purpose unless it covers a case like the one at bar. Here, as in Stone v. Freeman and Carr v. Hoy (supra), the money sued for was (assuming the truth of the defenses) "the fruit of an admitted crime." To allow this plaintiff to collect his commissions would be to let him "profit by his own fraud, or to take advantage of his own wrong, or to found [a] claim upon his own iniquity, or to acquire property by his own crime" (Riggs v. Palmer, 115 N.Y. 506, 511, 22 N.E. 188, 190, 5 L.R.

A. 340). The issue is not whether the acts alleged in the defenses would constitute the crime of commercial bribery under section 439 of the Penal Law, Consol.Laws, c. 40, although it appears that they would. "A seller cannot recover the price of goods sold where he has paid a commission to an agent of the purchaser (Sirkin v. Fourteenth Street Store, 124 App.Div. 384, 108 N.Y.S. 830); neither could the agent recover the commission, even at common law and before the enactment of section 384–r of the Penal Law (now section 439)" (Judge Crane in Reiner v. North American Newspaper Alliance, 259 N.Y. 250, 261, 181 N.E. 561, 565, 83 A.L.R. 23). The Sirkin opinion (124 App.Div. 384, 108 N.Y.S. 830) has been cited with approval by this court in Merchants' Line v. Baltimore & Ohio R. Co., 222 N.Y. 344, 347, 118 N.E. 788, and Morgan Munitions Supply Co. v. Studebaker Corp., 226 N.Y. 94, 99, 123 N.E. 146. In unmistakable terms it forbids the courts to honor claims founded on commercial bribery.

We are not working here with narrow questions of technical law. We are applying fundamental concepts of morality and fair dealing not to be weakened by exceptions. So far as precedent is necessary, we can rely on Sirkin v. Fourteenth Street Store, 124 App.Div. 384, 108 N.Y.S. 830, supra, and Reiner v. North American Newspaper Alliance, 259 N.Y. 250, 181 N.E. 564, 83 A.L.R. 23, supra. Sirkin is the case closest to ours and shows that, whatever be the law in other jurisdictions, we in New York deny awards for the corrupt performance of contracts even though in essence the contracts are not illegal. Sirkin had sued for the price of goods sold and delivered to defendant. Held to be good was a defense which charged that plaintiff seller had paid a secret commission to an agent of defendant purchaser. There cannot be any difference in principle between that situation and the present one where plaintiff (it is alleged) contracted to buy motion-picture rights for defendant but performed his covenant only by bribing the seller's agent. In the Reiner case (supra), likewise, the plaintiff had fully performed the services required by his agreement with the defendant but was denied a recovery because his performance had involved and included "fraud and deception" practiced not on defendant but on a third party. It is beside the point that the present plaintiff on the trial might be able to prove a prima facie case without the bribery being exposed. On the whole case (again assuming that the defenses speak the truth) the disclosed situation would be within the rule of our precedents forbidding court assistance to bribers.

It is argued that a reversal here means that the doing of any small illegality in the performance of an otherwise lawful contract will deprive the doer of all rights, with the result that the other party will get a windfall and there will be great injustice. Our ruling does not go as far as that. It is not every minor wrongdoing in the course of contract performance that will insulate the other party from liability for work done or goods furnished. There must at least be a direct connection between the illegal transaction and the obligation sued upon. Connection is a matter of degree. Some illegalities are merely incidental to the contract sued on (see Messersmith v. American Fidelity Co., 187 App.Div. 35, 175 N.Y.S. 169, affirmed 232 N.Y. 161, 133 N.E. 432, 19 A.L.R. 876; De Persia v. Merchants Mut. Cas. Co., 268 App.Div. 176, 49 N.Y.S.2d 324, affirmed 294 N.Y. 708, 61 N.E.2d 449; Ferkin v. Board of Education, 278 N.Y. 263, 268, 15 N.E.2d 799, 800). We cannot now, any more than in our past decisions, announce what will be the results of all the kinds of corruption, minor and major, essential and peripheral. All we are doing here is labeling the conduct described in these defenses as gross corruption depriving plaintiff of all right of access to the courts of New York State. Consistent with public morality and settled public policy, we hold that a party will be denied recovery even on a contract valid on its face, if it appears that he has resorted to gravely immoral and illegal conduct in accomplishing its performance.[a]

Perhaps this application of the principle represents a distinct step beyond Sirkin and Reiner (supra) in the sense that we are here barring recovery under a contract which in itself is entirely legal. But if this be an extension, public policy supports it. We point out that our holding is limited to cases in which the illegal performance of a contract originally valid takes the form of commercial bribery or similar conduct and in which the illegality is central to or a dominant part of the plaintiff's whole course of conduct in performance of the contract.

There is no pertinence here of the rule which makes such defenses unavailable to one who is a mere depository or escrowee—that is, one who is holding money or goods for one of the parties without himself being a party to the transaction sued upon (see Southwestern Shipping Corp. v. National City Bank of New York, 6 N.Y.2d 454, 190 N.Y.S.2d 352, 160 N.E.2d 836) [p. 552 supra]. That exception is used when, in execution or satisfaction of an illegal transaction, one of the parties thereto turns over money or property to a third person (not a party to the illegal deal) for the use of one who is a party. In our case there were two parties only—plaintiff and defendant. There is no third person holding money or property.

The sufficiency of defendant's counterclaim (for the return of its $10,000) was litigated below but it is not before us on this appeal.

The order appealed from should be reversed, with costs, the certified question answered in the negative, and plaintiff's motion, inso-

a. In Jaclyn, Inc. v. Edison Bros. Stores, Inc., Note 3, p. 549 supra, the court observed: "Prior to *McConnell* courts probed the record in search of an independent legal consideration which would sustain the contract notwithstanding a peripheral element of wrongdoing. By contrast, courts in recent years have focused upon 'the extent and seriousness of the illegal conduct and its relationship to the contract at issue' before denying recovery."

far as it attacks the sufficiency of the two separate defenses, should be denied.

FROESSEL, Judge (dissenting). . . .

This is not a case where the contract *sued upon* is intrinsically illegal (cf. Stone v. Freeman, 298 N.Y. 268, 82 N.E.2d 571, 8 A.L.R.2d 304; Reiner v. North American Newspaper Alliance, 259 N.Y. 250, 181 N.E. 561, 83 A.L.R. 23); or was *procured* by the commission of a crime (Sirkin v. Fourteenth Street Store, 124 App.Div. 384, 108 N. Y.S. 830); or where a beneficiary under a will murdered his ancestor in order to obtain the speedy enjoyment of his property (Riggs v. Palmer, 115 N.Y. 506, 22 N.E. 188, 5 L.R.A. 340). In the Sirkin case, so heavily relied upon by the majority, the plaintiff obtained the very contract he was seeking to enforce by paying secret commissions to defendant's own purchasing agent. In Merchants' Line v. Baltimore & Ohio R. Co., 222 N.Y. 344, 347, 118 N.E. 788, we pointed out that in Sirkin "the plaintiff reached and bribed the man who made *the contract under which he was seeking to recover*" (emphasis supplied). In Morgan Munitions Supply Co. v. Studebaker Corp., 226 N.Y. 94, 99, 123 N.E. 146, 147, we likewise cited the Sirkin case for the proposition that "a contract *procured by* the commission of a crime is unenforceable even if executed" (emphasis supplied).

In the instant case, the contract which plaintiff is seeking to enforce is perfectly valid, and it was not intended or even contemplated that plaintiff would perform the contract by illegal or corrupt means. Having received and retained the full benefits of plaintiff's performance, defendant now seeks to "inject into" its contract with plaintiff, "which was fair and legal in itself, the illegal feature of the other independent transaction" Messersmith v. American Fidelity Co., 187 App.Div. 35, 37, 175 N.Y.S. 169, 170, affirmed 232 N.Y. 161, 133 N. E. 432, 19 A.L.R. 876. This court is now adopting a rule that a party may retain the benefits of, but escape his obligations under, a wholly lawful contract if the other party commits some illegal act not contemplated nor necessary under the contract. By way of a single illustration an owner may thus avoid paying his contractor for the cost of erecting a building because the contractor gave an inspector a sum of money to expedite an inspection.

The majority opinion seeks to distinguish between "major" and "minor" illegality and "direct" and "peripheral" corruption. It decides this case on the ground that the manner in which plaintiff performed his admittedly valid contract with defendant was "gravely immoral and illegal". Such distinctions are neither workable nor sanctioned by authority. If a contract was lawfully made, and did not contemplate wrongdoing, it is enforcible; if, on the other hand, it was *procured* by the commission of a crime, or was in fact for the performance of illegal services, it is not enforcible. These are the criteria distinguishing enforcible from unenforcible contracts—not "nice" distinctions between degrees of illegality and immorality in the performance of lawful contracts, or whether the illegal act of performance was "directly" or "peripherally" related to the main contract.

Moreover, a reversal here would be contrary to the spirit, if not the letter, of our holding in Southwestern Shipping Corp. v. National City Bank, 6 N.Y.2d 454, 190 N.Y.S.2d 352, 160 N.E.2d 836. The broad proposition for which that case stands is that a party unconnected with an illegal agreement should not be permitted to reap a windfall by pleading the illegality of that agreement, to which he was a stranger. There, the contract between the plaintiff and the bank was entirely lawful, and the bank attempted to avoid the consequences of its breach of contract and negligence by asserting the illegality of a different contract between plaintiff and a third party. Here, the contract between plaintiff and defendant was perfectly legal, and defendant is seeking to avoid its obligations under the contract—of which it has reaped the benefits for some 12 years—by asserting the illegality of a *different* and subsequent agreement between plaintiff and a third party. This it should not be permitted to do.

The order appealed from should be affirmed, with costs, and the question certified answered in the affirmative.

VAN VOORHIS, Judge (dissenting). Public morals and fair dealing are likely to be advanced by limiting rather than by enlarging the rule that is being extended to the facts of this case. This rule is grounded on considerations of public policy. Courts will not intervene between thieves to compel them to divide the spoils. But in a situation like the present, it seems to me that the effect of this decision will not be to restrain the corrupt influencing of agents, employees or servants but to encourage misappropriation of funds and breaches of faith between persons who do not stand in corrupt relationships with one another. The public interest is not served best by decisions which put a premium on taking unconscionable advantage of such situations, or which drive the enforcement of obligations of this kind underground. I concur in the dissenting opinion by Judge FROESSEL.

DYE, FULD, BURKE and FOSTER, JJ., concur with DESMOND, C. J. FROESSEL, J., dissents in an opinion in which VAN VOORHIS, J., concurs in a separate memorandum.

Order reversed, with costs in all courts, and matter remitted to the Appellate Division for further proceedings in accordance with the opinion herein. Question certified answered in the negative.

NOTE

Question. The dissent gives the illustration of "an owner [who] may thus avoid paying his contractor for the cost of erecting a building because the contractor gave an inspector a sum of money to expedite an inspection." How would the majority have decided that case? See Tocci v. Lembo, 325 Mass. 707, 92 N.E.2d 254 (1950), in which the contractor used materials then, in 1946, in short supply and under federal priorities control, without securing or applying for the required authorization from the Civilian Production Administration.

DEGREE OF INVOLVEMENT

The court in the McConnell case says, "There must at least be a direct connection between the illegal transaction and the obligation sued upon." For a contrasting conclusion as to "connection," consider Graves v. Johnson, 179 Mass. 58, 60 N.E. 383 (1901). A buyer defaulted on an agreement to buy liquor in Massachusetts, where such a sale was lawful. When sued by the seller for the price, his defense was that he had intended to resell the liquor in Maine, in violation of a statute of that state, and that the seller was aware of his purpose. Rejecting the defense, Holmes wrote: "All that is necessary for us to say now is that in our opinion a sale otherwise lawful is not connected with subsequent unlawful conduct by the mere fact that the seller correctly divines the buyer's unlawful intent, closely enough to make the sale unlawful. It will be observed that the finding puts the plaintiffs' knowledge of the defendant's intent no higher than an uncommunicated inference as to what the defendant was likely to do. Of course the defendant was free to change his mind, and there was no communicated desire of the plaintiffs to co-operate with the defendant's present intent . . . but on the contrary an understood indifference to everything beyond an ordinary sale in Massachusetts. It may be that, as in the case of attempts, . . . the line of proximity will vary somewhat according to the gravity of the evil apprehended, . . . and in different courts with regard to the same or similar matters. . . . But the decisions tend more and more to agree that the connection with the unlawful act in cases like the present is too remote."

Hull v. Ruggles, 56 N.Y. 424 (1874), shows that the seller may not fare as well if he exhibits more than an "understood indifference" to the buyer's unlawful purpose. The goods sold were 300 packages of candy and 60 pieces of silverware. Packed inside 60 of the candy boxes were tickets, each identifying a piece of silverware. The buyer intended to induce his customers to buy the candy at an inflated price in the hope of getting a piece of silverware "free," in violation of the statute against lotteries. In denying the seller recovery of the price, the court relied on "the not unfamiliar English cases, in which it is held, that if goods be bought with the purpose of smuggling them into England, though the vendor have knowledge of the purpose, he may recover the price of the goods, if he do nothing to aid in carrying out the design . . .; but if he has so packed the goods as to facilitate the smuggling, he is regarded as particeps criminis and cannot recover." [a]

Do you agree with the distinction drawn in these cases?

PROBLEMS

(1) Fineman sold an Edison phonograph to Mamie Faulkner, on credit, for use in her home. Fineman "knew by general reputation that she was a prostitute carrying on her trade at her home." Can Fineman recover the price of the phonograph? See Fineman v. Faulkner, 174 N.C. 13, 93 S.E. 384 (1917). Compare Pearce v. Brooks, L.R. 1 Exch. 213 (1866).

(2) When a person is wrongfully discharged from his employment to design electronic amusement devices, and the employer has been convicted of "Promoting Gambling in the First Degree" for the way he deployed slot machines, what more proof is needed to preclude a recovery by the ex-employee on the employment contract? See Hendrix v. McKee, 281 Or. 123, 575 P.2d 134 (1978).

(3) *R* and *M* had a joint arrangement for selling Irish sweepstakes tickets and for their efforts received two tickets for every twenty they sold. On each bonus ticket one or the other put his name, but only on the agreement that they would share any winnings. A penal statute in their state makes it unlawful to promote a lottery (although the state conducts one). *R* has collected a "super prize" on a bonus ticket bearing his name. Does *M* have a claim against *R*? See Miller v. Radikopf, 394 Mich. 83, 228 N.W. 2d 386 (1975).[b]

WAGERS

Though at the common law gambling was not illegal, it came to be generally condemned in this country. Recently a powerful movement has been noted toward "the *de facto* decriminalization of various forms of illicit gambling along with the socialization [i. e., licensing or state sponsorship] of selected games." [c] But marked regional differences of attitude prevail. Moreover, in jurisdictions where law-

a. For a case growing out of the smuggling of electronic equipment into Mexico, in violation of its laws, see International Aircraft Sales v. Betancourt, 582 S.W.2d 632 (Tex.Civ. App.1979), error ref. n.r.e. A firm supplying the smugglers with goods assisted by packing them deceptively and by making sales on credit. In suing for the unpaid price, the firm argued that the buyers were morally obligated to pay. How would you reply to this argument?

b. In Williams v. Weber Mesa Ditch Extension Co., Inc., 572 P.2d 412 (Wyo.1977), the conductor of a raffle, when sued for the prize, took advantage of the rule that a court may raise an issue of legality sua sponte: its pleadings called attention to the character of the agreement without describing it as unlawful.

c. National Institute for Law Enforcement, etc., The Development of the Law of Gambling: 1776–1976, xx (1977).

ful casinos flourish there may be opposing rules about the enforceability of gambling debts—e. g., Nevada (unenforceable) and Puerto Rico (generally enforceable).

One by-product is the phenomenon of migrant gamblers. Touring patrons of casinos are tempted, it seems, to stop payment on their loss checks on returning home. But such a check is apt to prove collectible if it would be so where the bet was made and the home state authorizes gambling in some form. See, for example, Intercontinental Hotels Corp. (P.R.) v. Golden, 15 N.Y.2d 9, 254 N.Y.S.2d 527, 203 N.E.2d 210 (1964), where the court said: "Informed public sentiment in New York is only against unlicensed gambling." [d]

For contrast, consider an action local to New York. It was brought by Watts, an amateur gambler, against Malatesta, a professional bookmaker, for sums that he had won from the plaintiff over a two-year period. Malatesta counterclaimed for much larger sums that he had lost to Watts. Judgment was given for Watts on both claims. On appeal, *held*: Affirmed. The decision rested on a statute making the winner of a prohibited bet accountable to the loser for his receipts. As the court construed the statute, its benefit was not available to Malatesta. "Curb the professional with his constant offer of temptation coupled with ready opportunity, and you have to a large extent controlled the evil. It is clear that in the eyes of the law the professional gambler and his customer do not stand in the same place. They are not in pari delicto." Watts v. Malatesta, 262 N.Y. 80, 186 N.E. 210 (1933).

NOTE

Problem. Some "Onassis' companies," ship operators, were persuaded to switch their purchases of paint to the Red Hand Compositions Company by the efforts of Costa Colyvas, who then sued Red Hand for a 5% commission that it had promised him on the sales. He gave evidence that his main contact in the Onassis companies was a department head named Paizis, with whom he had agreed to divide the commission evenly. The agreement was not disclosed to Paizis' employer for, according to Colyvas, "if anything of this would leak out, it would not be very nice for this person mentioning the five percent." Red Hand moved for summary judgment, citing the *McConnell* case, p. 553 supra. Colyvas countered with the *Intercontinental Hotels* case cited in the Note above (apparently the transactions in question had occurred in Monte Carlo). On these facts alone, what decision? See Colyvas v. Red Hand Compositions Co., 318 F.Supp. 1376 (S.D.N.Y.1970).

d. As the court stated the law of Puerto Rico, it permits the enforcement of gambling debts, except to the extent that they represent losses that "exceed the customs of a good father of a family." On the problem of migratory suits the court referred to Paulsen and Sovern, "Public Policy" in the Conflict of Laws, 56 Colum.L. Rev. 969 (1956).

Other like cases are Caribe Hilton Hotel v. Toland, 63 N.J. 301, 307 A.2d 85 (1973), and Hilton Int'l Co. v. Arace, 35 Conn.Sup. 522, 394 A.2d 739 (1977) (Full Faith and Credit Clause applied).

RESTITUTION

Courts, in cases of illegal bargains, are fond of citing the maxim: *In pari delicto potior est conditio defendentis* (In a case of equal fault, the condition of the party defending is the stronger). It is applied not only to deny enforcement of the bargain, but to bar restitution as well. There are, however, two mitigating doctrines that may be invoked to allow restitution.

First, the party seeking restitution may not be considered to be *in pari delicto* with the other. He may be allowed restitution if, for example, he has been the victim of fraud or duress, or of overreaching based on a superior bargaining position. (It has, however, been urged that the doctrine not be extended to cases in which the only fraud consists of representations as to the profitability, as opposed to the legality, of the transaction. Williston, § 1791.) Second, even though the party seeking restitution is *in pari delicto* with the other, he may have decided to withdraw from the bargain before the attainment of the illegal purpose. He is ordinarily given a *locus poenitentiae* and allowed restitution if his withdrawal comes in time to prevent its attainment. On the limits of the theory of restitution in actions to recover for benefits conferred on another pursuant to an illegal bargain, see G. Palmer, 2 Law of Restitution, ch. 8 (1978); and Wade, Benefits Obtained Under Illegal Transactions, 25 Texas L.Rev. 31 (1946); Restitution of Benefits Acquired Through Illegal Transactions, 95 U.Pa.L.Rev. 261 (1947).

Much of the discussion of these two mitigating doctrines has come in the context of gambling agreements.

NOTES

(1) *The Case of the Penitent Pledgor.* Gehres lost $225 to Ater in a social crap game, giving rise to an unenforceable gambling debt. Lacking the cash to pay Gehres pledged a municipal bond to Ater as security for the claim. Some months later Gehres tendered $225 to Ater and asked for his bond back. Ater could not comply because he had sold it. Gehres sued for $540, the market value of the bond. From judgment for the defendant on his demurrer to the plaintiff's petition, the plaintiff appealed. *Held:* Reversed. The court saw two competing principles. One is the broad principle that courts will leave parties who are in pari delicto where they find them. The other is that repentance should be encouraged. "At common law one who makes a wager with another may always withdraw from the wager and retain or recover his property or money before it goes into the hands of the winner, even after the result of the wager is known. So long as the title to the property or money has not passed to the winner, the loser may repudiate the wager and retain his money or property or recover it in a common-law action. . . . One who places money or property in the hands of a stakeholder may, while such money or property remains in the stakeholder's hands, withdraw his wager or repudiate the illegal contract, under which the money or property was deposited, and demand the return

of such money or property, and if the stakeholder refuses to return the money or property the loser may bring an action against him for its recovery." The bond was not given in payment, but merely as security. "Title to the bond did not pass to the defendant but remained in the plaintiff." Gehres v. Ater, 148 Ohio St. 89, 73 N.E.2d 513 (1947). *Question:* Does the rule of this case provide comfort for one who is regretful of wrongdoing or for one who is regretful of the other party's failure to perform as agreed? For a case drawing the distinction see Bigos v. Bousted, 1951, 1 All E.R. 92 (K.B.).

(2) *The Law of Nature Case.* In Liebman v. Rosenthal, Justice Hooley denied a motion by the defendant for summary judgment on a claim alleged as follows: Fleeing the German armies through France in 1941, Liebman met Rosenthal and turned over to him jewelry worth $28,000. Rosenthal had represented that by bribing a Portuguese consul, his friend, he could get visas for Liebman and his family. Rosenthal absconded with the jewelry. The two next met in New York City. Liebman brought this action for the value of the jewelry, having demanded its return without success.

On Rosenthal's appeal, *held:* Affirmed. Liebman v. Rosenthal, 269 App.Div. 1062, 59 N.Y.S.2d 148 (2d Dept. 1945) (cryptic opinion). Justice Adel, dissenting, wrote: "There is no authority for the holding that urgency of motive provides an excuse for entering into an illegal engagement." The trial court's opinion [185 Misc. 837, 57 N.Y.S.2d 875 (1945)] made reference to the executory character of the contract and denied that the parties were in pari delicto. Further: "There is no question of public policy involved in a case like this where a man is attempting to save himself from an enemy who has violated all the laws of civilization. Protection of one's self and one's family is among the first laws of nature . . . . Rather it may be said that public policy should not permit the defendant to profit by what plaintiff maintains happened here."

CLEAN HANDS

Courts of equity exhibit a special sense of delicacy when confronted with unsavory claims and claimants. Suits for equitable remedies such as specific performance and rescission are sometimes disposed of on the colorful maxim, "He who comes into equity must come with clean hands." For example the professional football player Charles Flowers obtained the benefit of the maxim when he signed to play with the Los Angeles Chargers, in violation of his contract with the New York Giants. As described in Note 1, p. 36 supra, the Giants had sullied their hands by permitting Flowers, then a college student, to play in the Sugar Bowl by keeping their contract with him a secret. Hence when the Giants sought an injunction against his playing with the Chargers it was denied.

Is there a difference between the thought of the maxim and the thought that a court of equity should avoid sullying *its* hands? In

North Pacific Lumber Co. v. Oliver, 286 Or. 639, 596 P.2d 931 (1979), the court said that the clean-hands doctrine "is designed to protect the court's integrity by permitting it to avoid sullying its hands with the enforcement of a corrupt bargain"—not to punish or reward a party. (If that is the import of the doctrine, why was Flowers permitted to play for the Chargers?) The court also said: "Even equity does not require saintliness. Perhaps more importantly, the misconduct must bear a certain kind of relationship to the subject matter of the suit before a court will consider it."

All that being said, the court approved the dismissal of an action by a firm to enforce a covenant against competition against a former employee, for the plaintiff came to court with unclean hands.

NOTES

(1) *The Traders' Rakeoff.* In the case last cited the plaintiff company was a lumber wholesaler. The defendant, Les A. Oliver, had worked for it as a trader. It appeared that when the company's customers complained of shipments it had arranged they sought settlement through the company's traders. On occasion a trader would obtain substantial compensation from the supplier in question (stressing the seriousness of the complaint) and settle with the customer for a smaller sum (minimizing the complaint). The plaintiff pocketed the difference. The incidence of this practice was not insignificant: management personnel encouraged it at meetings of traders and in a manual. This was one improper practice of the plaintiff. Another, in which Oliver engaged a few times, was illegal spying on fellow-employees by monitoring their telephone calls.

After becoming assistant manager of the plaintiff's hardwood division, Oliver resigned to work for a competitor; and his former employer sued for enforcement of a covenant he had made not to compete with it. The enforcement of the covenant would be improper, the court concluded, because his position with the firm involved his participation in the illicit settlement practices. He had gained substantially through sharing in the hardwood division's profits—and had not resigned, by the way, for reasons of conscience. As for the telephone monitoring, the court found nothing venal in it, and discounted the practice on the ground that it was not connected with Oliver's employment.

(2) *Shades of Cleanliness.* The sellers of a business committed a "serious offense" through attempting to conceal a feature of the sale from the tax authorities. Agents of the buyer, purporting to have expertness in taxation, advised the sellers that a full statement of the transaction would jeopardize certain lawful tax advantages. The chairman of the buyer's board assured the sellers that the board members—"honorable men"—would agree to rescission if the tax advantages did not materialize. When this assurance was not honored, the sellers sued to recover the property they had sold. On an appeal from a judgment in their favor, *held:* Affirmed. West Los Angeles Institute for Cancer Research v. Mayer, 366 F.2d 220 (9th Cir. 1966), cert. denied, 385 U.S. 1010. The plaintiffs' motive, the court said, was not to circumvent the tax laws, but to exclude "an extraneous fact

which might improperly influence the [Internal Revenue Service]. The parties were not in pari delicto. The agents [of the buyer] stood in a superior position. They were the active parties. . . . And the forfeiture . . . if relief were denied would be extreme."

(3) *Question:* Does it appear from the foregoing cases that the clean-hands maxim is shaped by the same factors that affect courts of "law" in dealing with illegal agreements? (As to the relevance of the maxim in a law action, see Gratreak v. North Pacific Lumber Co., — Or.App. —, 609 P.2d 375 (1980).)

Chapter 6

REMEDIES FOR BREACH

SECTION 1. MEASURING EXPECTATION

We have already seen that the usual goal of the law of contract remedies is to give the injured party relief based on his expectation interest, as measured by the net gain that he would have enjoyed had the contract been performed. This is commonly done by awarding a sum of damages that will, to the extent that money can, put the injured party in the position in which he would have been had the promise been performed.

In principle, the expectation interest is that of the injured party himself, quite without regard to that of a hypothetical reasonable person, and depends on his own particular circumstances or those of his enterprise. Where the injured party's expected advantage consists largely or exclusively of the realization of profit, as is the case for most commercially significant exchanges, it can be expressed in money with some assurance. Its calculation depends on two ingredients.

The first is his *loss on the bargain*, which he suffers by the frustration of the exchange for which he bargained. It may have two components. One is the *loss in value* to the injured party of the other party's performance, and represents the difference in the value to the injured party of what the other party was to have done and of what he did. This component is always present, whether the breach is partial or total. Where the breach is total, and the injured party has been relieved of the balance of his own performance, a second component enters into the calculation. This is the cost that he avoided as a result of being excused. His *loss on the bargain* is then the difference between *loss in value* and *cost avoided.*

The second ingredient is *other loss,* such as physical harm to the injured party's person or property and expenses incurred by him in an attempt to salvage the transaction after breach. The general measure, then, is the sum of these two ingredients, which gives Formula A.

(A) *Damages* = *loss in value* − *cost avoided* + *other loss.*

Since, in most agreements, one of the parties (here called the "recipient") is required to pay money, the estimation of *loss in value* and *cost avoided* usually poses problems only in connection with the performance of the other party (here called the "supplier"), who may be required, for example, to furnish goods, land, or services in return. Where the supplier is the injured party, and the breach consists of the recipient's promise to pay, the difficulty lies in the determination of the supplier's *cost avoided,* since his *loss in value* is simply the amount of money that the recipient has failed to pay. Where the recipient is the injured party, and the supplier is in breach, the difficulty lies in the determination of the recipient's *loss in value,* since his *cost avoided* is simply the amount of money that he has not yet paid.

The building contract cases afford a simple illustration. Suppose that Builder contracts with Owner to construct a factory on Owner's land for $1,000,000 payable on completion. If the recipient (Owner) is the party in breach and the supplier (Builder) has used the breach to excuse his further performance, the controversy will center on the *cost avoided* by Builder in his not having to complete construction of the factory. The *loss in value* to Builder will be simply the amount remaining unpaid. If, for example, Builder can show that it would have cost him $400,000 more to complete the job, his recovery under Formula A (ignoring *other loss*) would be $1,000,000 less $400,000 or $600,000. Builder will often calculate his *cost avoided* by determining the cost already incurred in reliance on the contract. Assuming that this sum is $500,000, the *cost of complete performance* would be the total of the *cost of reliance* and the *cost avoided,* that is $500,000 plus $400,000, or $900,000. In other words:

Cost avoided = *cost of complete performance* – *cost of reliance.*

Substituting the right hand side of this equation for *cost avoided* in Formula A, and remembering that the difference between *loss in value* and *cost of complete performance* is Builder's expected *profit,* we get Formula B as the equivalent of Formula A.[a]

(B) *Damages* = *cost of reliance* + *profit* + *other loss.*

In the illustration given, Builder's recovery under Formula B (ignoring *other loss*) would be $500,000 plus $100,000 or $600,000, just as under Formula A. How should items of overhead be treated under either Formula A or Formula B?

NOTE

More on the Lost Life. In the case described in Note 3, p. 504 supra, the court affirmed a judgment for $7,500 with this explanation. "The fact that damages are difficult to ascertain and measure does not diminish the loss to the person whose property has been destroyed. Indeed, the very statement of the rule suggests the opposite. If one's destroyed property has a market value, presumably its equivalent is available on the market and the owner can acquire that equivalent property. However, if the owner

a. For the sake of simplicity, it is assumed that Builder has not received any payment from Owner. If he has, the amount of the payment must be subtracted in applying Formula B.

cannot acquire the property in the market or by replacement or reproduction, then he simply cannot be made whole.

"The problem is to establish the value to the owner. Market and replacement values are relatively ascertainable by appropriate proof. Recognizing that value to the owner encompasses a subjective element, the rule has been established that compensation for sentimental or fanciful values will not be allowed. . . . That restriction was placed upon the jury in this case by the court's damages instruction.

"What is sentimental value? The broad dictionary definition is that sentimental refers to being 'governed by feeling, sensibility or emotional idealism. . . . ' Webster's Third New International Dictionary (1963). Obviously that is not the exclusion contemplated by the statement that sentimental value is not to be compensated. If it were, no one would recover for the wrongful death of a spouse or a child. Rather, the type of sentiment which is not compensable is that which relates to 'indulging in feeling to an unwarranted extent' or being 'affectedly or mawkishly emotional . . . .' Webster's Third New International Dictionary (1963).

"Under these rules, the court's damages instruction was correct. In essence it allowed recovery for the actual or intrinsic value to the plaintiffs but denied recovery for any unusual sentimental value of the film to the plaintiffs or a fanciful price which plaintiffs, for their own special reasons, might place thereon." [b]

VITEX MANUFACTURING CORP. v. CARIBTEX CORP.

United States Court of Appeals, Third Circuit, 1967.
377 F.2d 795.

STALEY, Chief Judge. This is an appeal by Caribtex Corporation from a judgment of the District Court of the Virgin Islands finding Caribtex in breach of a contract entered into with Vitex Manufacturing Company, Ltd., and awarding $21,114 plus interest to Vitex for loss of profits. The only substantial question raised by Caribtex is whether it was error for the district court, sitting without a jury, not to consider overhead as part of Vitex's costs in determining the amount of profits lost. We conclude that under the facts presented, the district court was not compelled to consider Vitex's overhead costs, and we will affirm the judgment.

Before discussing the details of the controversy between the parties, it will be helpful to briefly describe the peculiar legal setting in which this suit arose. At the time of the events in question, there were high tariff barriers to the importation of foreign wool products. However, under § 301 of the Tariff Act of 1930, 19 U.S.C.A. § 1301a, repealed but the provision continued under Revised Tariff Schedules, 19 U.S.C.A. § 1202, note 3(a)(i)(ii) (1965), if such goods were im-

b. Oenophiles will want to consult Bowes v. Fox-Stanley Photo Products, 379 So.2d 844 (La.App.1980).

ported into the Virgin Islands and were processed in some manner so that their finished value exceeded their importation value by at least 50%, then the high tariffs to importation into the continental United States would be avoided. Even after the processing, the foreign wool enjoyed a price advantage over domestic products so that the business flourished. However, to keep the volume of this business at such levels that Congress would not be stirred to change the law, the Virgin Islands Legislature imposed "quotas" on persons engaging in processing, limiting their output. 33 V.I.C. § 504 (Supp.1966).

Vitex was engaged in the business of chemically shower-proofing imported cloth so that it could be imported duty-free into the United States. For this purpose, Vitex maintained a plant in the Virgin Islands and was entitled to process a specific quantity of material under the Virgin Islands quota system. Caribtex was in the business of importing cloth into the islands, securing its processing, and exporting it to the United States.

In the fall of 1963, Vitex found itself with an unused portion of its quota but no customers, and Vitex closed its plant. Caribtex acquired some Italian wool and subsequently negotiations for a processing contract were conducted between the principals of the respective companies in New York City. Though the record below is clouded with differing versions of the negotiations and the alleged final terms, the trial court found upon substantial evidence in the record that the parties did enter into a contract in which Vitex agreed to process 125,000 yards of Caribtex's woolen material at a price of 26 cents per yard.

Vitex proceeded to re-open its Virgin Islands plant, ordered the necessary chemicals, recalled its work force and made all the necessary preparations to perform its end of the bargain. However, no goods were forthcoming from Caribtex, despite repeated demands by Vitex, apparently because Caribtex was unsure that the processed wool would be entitled to duty-free treatment by the customs officials. Vitex subsequently brought this suit to recover the profits lost through Caribtex's breach.

Vitex alleged, and the trial court found, that its gross profits for processing said material under the contract would have been $31,250 and that its costs would have been $10,136, leaving Vitex's damages for loss of profits at $21,114. On appeal, Caribtex asserted numerous objections to the detailed computation of lost profits. While the record below is sometimes confusing, we conclude that the trial court had substantial evidence to support its findings on damages. It must be remembered that the difficulty in exactly ascertaining Vitex's costs is due to Caribtex's wrongful conduct in repudiating the contract before performance by Vitex. Caribtex will not be permitted to benefit by the uncertainty it has caused. Thus, since there was a sufficient basis in the record to support the trial court's determination of substantial damages, we will not set aside its judgment. Stentor Elec. Mfg. Co. v. Klaxon Co., 115 F.2d 268 (C.A.3, 1940), rev'd other grounds 313 U.S. 487, 61 S.Ct. 1020, 85 L.Ed. 1477 (1941); 5 Williston, Contracts § 1345 (rev. ed. 1937).

Caribtex first raised the issue at the oral argument of this appeal that the trial court erred by disregarding Vitex's overhead expenses in determining lost profits. In general, overhead ". . . may be said to include broadly the continuous expenses of the business, irrespective of the outlay on a particular contract." Grand Trunk W.R.R. Co. v. H. W. Nelson Co., 116 F.2d 823, 839 (C.A.6, 1941). Such expenses would include executive and clerical salaries, property taxes, general administration expenses, etc.[1] Although Vitex did not expressly seek recovery for overhead, if a portion of these fixed expenses should be allocated as costs to the Caribtex contract, then under the judgment of the district court Vitex tacitly recovered these expenses as part of its damages for lost profits, and the damages should be reduced accordingly. Presumably, the portion to be allocated to costs would be a pro rata share of Vitex's annual overhead according to the volume of business Vitex would have done over the year if Caribtex had not breached the contract.

Although there is authority to the contrary, we feel that the better view is that normally, in a claim for lost profits, overhead should be treated as a part of gross profits and recoverable as damages, and should not be considered as part of the seller's costs. A number of cases hold that since overhead expenses are not affected by the performance of the particular contract, there should be no need to deduct them in computing lost profits. E. g., Oakland California Towel Co. v. Sivils, 52 Cal.App.2d 517, 520, 126 P.2d 651, 652 (1942); Jessup & Moore Paper Co. v. Bryant Paper Co., 297 Pa. 483, 147 A. 519, 524 (1929); Annot., 3 A.L.R.3d 689 (1965) (collecting cases on both sides of the controversy). The theory of these cases is that the seller is entitled to recover losses incurred and gains prevented in excess of savings made possible, Restatement, Contracts § 329 (made part of the law of the Virgin Islands, 1 V.I.C. § 4); since overhead is fixed and nonperformance of the contract produced no overhead cost savings, no deduction from profits should result.

The soundness of the rule is exemplified by this case. Before negotiations began between Vitex and Caribtex, Vitex had reached a lull in business activity and had closed its plant. If Vitex had entered into no other contracts for the rest of the year, the profitability of its operations would have been determined by deducting its production costs and overhead from gross receipts yielded in previous

1. Caribtex could not be referring to overhead expenses as including labor costs and the like, because the trial judge did charge as costs all the expenses directly associated with the reactivation of Vitex's plant, and the actual processing of Caribtex's goods according to the terms of the contract.

transactions. When this opportunity arose to process Caribtex's wool, the only additional expenses Vitex would incur would be those of re-opening its plant and the direct costs of processing, such as labor, chemicals and fuel oil. Overhead would have remained the same whether or not Vitex and Caribtex entered their contract and whether or not Vitex actually processed Caribtex's goods. Since this overhead remained constant, in no way attributable-to or affected-by the Caribtex contract, it would be improper to consider it as a cost of Vitex's performance to be deducted from the gross proceeds of the Caribtex contract.

However, Caribtex may argue that this view ignores modern accounting principles, and that overhead is as much a cost of production as other expenses. It is true that successful businessmen must set their prices at sufficient levels to recoup all their expenses, including overhead, and to gain profits. Thus, the price the businessman should charge on each transaction could be thought of as that price necessary to yield a pro rata portion of the company's fixed overhead, the direct costs associated with production, and a "clear" profit. Doubtless this type of calculation is used by businessmen and their accountants. Pacific Portland Cement Co. v. Food Mach. & Chem. Corp., 178 F.2d 541 (C.A.9, 1949). However, because it is useful for planning purposes to allocate a portion of overhead to each transaction, it does not follow that this allocate share of fixed overhead should be considered a cost factor in the computation of lost profits on individual transactions.

First, it must be recognized that the pro rata allocation of overhead costs is only an analytical construct. In a similar manner one could allocate a pro rata share of the company's advertising cost, taxes and/or charitable gifts. The point is that while these items all are paid from the proceeds of the business, they do not normally bear such a direct relationship to any individual transaction to be considered a cost in ascertaining lost profits.

Secondly, even were we to recognize the allocation of overhead as proper in this case, we should uphold the tacit award of overhead expense to Vitex as a "loss incurred." Conditioned Air Corp. v. Rock Island Motor Transit Co., 253 Iowa 961, 114 N.W.2d 304, 3 A.L.R.3d 679, cert. denied, 371 U.S. 825, 83 S.Ct. 46, 9 L.Ed.2d 64 (1962). By the very nature of this allocation process, as the number of transactions over which overhead can be spread becomes smaller, each transaction must bear a greater portion or allocate share of the fixed overhead cost. Suppose a company has fixed overhead of $10,000 and engages in five similar transactions; then the receipts of each transaction would bear $2000 of overhead expense. If the company is now forced to spread this $10,000 over only four transactions, then the overhead expense per transaction will rise to $2500, significantly reducing the profitability of the four remaining transactions. Thus, where the contract is between businessmen familiar with commercial practices, as here, the breaching party should reasonably foresee that his breach will not only cause a loss of "clear" profit, but also a loss in that the profitability of other transactions will be reduced. Resolute Ins. Co. v. Percy Jones, Inc., 198 F.2d 309 (C.A.10, 1952); Cf. In re Kellett Aircraft Corp., 191 F.2d 231 (C.A.3, 1951). Therefore, this loss is within the contemplation of "losses caused and gains prevented," and overhead should be considered to a compensable item of damage.

Significantly, the Uniform Commercial Code, adopted in the Virgin Islands, 11A V.I.C. § 1–101 et seq., and in virtually every state today, provides for the recovery of overhead in circumstances similar to those presented here. Under 11A V.I.C. § 2–708, the seller's measure of damage for non-acceptance or repudiation is the difference between the contract price and the market price, but if this relief is inadequate to put the seller in as good position as if the contract had been fully performed, ". . . then the measure of damages is the *profit (including reasonable overhead)* which the seller would have made from full performance by the buyer . . . ." 11A V.I.C. § 2–708(2). (Emphasis added.) While this contract is not controlled by the Code, the Code is persuasive here because it embodies the foremost modern legal thought concerning commercial transactions. Indeed, it may overrule some of the cases denying recovery for overhead. E. g., Wilhelm Lubrication Co. v. Brattrud, 197 Minn. 626, 632, 268 N.W. 634, 636, 106 A.L.R. 1279 (1936).

Caribtex also argued that the contract should not be enforced because it was unconscionable. While Vitex was to make a large profit on the processing and Caribtex did bear the risk of failure to meet customs standards, the contract was freely entered-into, after much negotiation, between parties of apparently equal bargaining strength. This was not a contract of adhesion—Vitex was not the only processor in the Virgin Islands and Caribtex's bargaining strength was evidenced by the successive and substantial price reductions it wrested from Vitex during the negotiations. Compare, Campbell Soup Co. v. Wentz, 172 F.2d 80 (C.A.3, 1948); Henningsen v. Bloomfield Motors, Inc., 32 N.J. 358, 161 A.2d 69, 75 A.L.R.2d 1 (1960).

The judgment of the district court will be affirmed.

NOTE

Overhead. Vitex's *loss on the bargain* was the difference between *loss in value* and *cost avoided* (see Formula A, supra). Did the trial court include overhead costs in *cost avoided*? Should it have? Or, from a different perspective, Vitex's *loss on the bargain* was the sum of *cost of reliance* and *profit* (see Formula B, supra). Did the trial court include overhead costs in *cost of reliance* and in *profit*? Should it have? On the computation of *cost avoided,* see Harris, A General Theory for Measuring Seller's Damages for Total Breach of Contract, 60 Mich.L.Rev. 577 (1962).

LAREDO HIDES CO. v. H & H MEAT PRODUCTS CO.

[For the report of this case, see p. 2 supra.]

NOTES

(1) *Substitute Transaction.* Often, following breach, the injured party arranges a substitute transaction and claims damages based on that transaction rather than on one of the damage formulas set out earlier. Laredo Hides did just this by arranging substitute purchases of hides and basing its damages on the cover price in those transactions under UCC 2–712. If the seller is the injured party, the Code accords him a similar remedy of reselling the goods and basing his damages on the resale price in that transaction under UCC 2–706.

(2) *Substitute Employment.* The use of a substitute transaction as the basis of a claim for damages is not, however, confined to the sale of goods. If an employee is fired in breach of a contract and does other work as a result of being freed from that contract, the employee's damages are based on the salary that would have been earned under the broken contract less that earned by doing the other work. In State ex rel. Schilling v. Baird, 65 Wis.2d 394, 222 N.W.2d 666 (1974), Schilling, a deputy sheriff who was wrongfully suspended, argued that he was not required to deduct his earnings from other work because they were not made between midnight and eight in the morning, the shift to which he was assigned as a deputy. "With this conclusion the Court cannot agree. It lends itself to an almost absurd result. Under this interpretation all Schilling had to do was to refrain from getting a third shift job and could then earn as much as he wanted or was fortunate enough to earn and would not be required to deduct any of it."

Courts have divided over whether an employee must deduct sums received from a "collateral source," such as unemployment compensation and similar benefits. For a thorough discussion, see Sporn v. Celebrity, Inc., 129 N.J.Super. 449, 324 A.2d 71 (1974). The court there took note of "the majority rule in the United States today, that receipt of benefits from a source collateral to the defendant, while lessening the effect of the financial losses of plaintiff, will not diminish damages otherwise recoverable from the wrongdoer in tort cases." It concluded that "the rationale applied in a case involving the breach of an employment contract, which also may have fault elements, should be the same as applied in a tort action." For a contrary view, see Dehnart v. Waukeshaw Brewing Co., 21 Wis.2d 583, 124 N.W.2d 664 (1963). See also Note, 48 B.U.L.Rev. 271 (1968).

(3) *What is a Substitute?* It is sometimes no simple matter to decide whether another comparable opportunity accepted by the injured party after breach should be treated as a "substitute" for this purpose. Where the injured party is the supplier of personal services under a contract of full-time employment, another comparable opportunity may be viewed as a substitute transaction since "No man can serve two masters" and the employee could not have taken advantage of the second opportunity had not the first contract been broken. Where, however, the injured party is a supplier of services that are not personal, under a contract for construction of a build-

ing for example, another comparable opportunity is not ordinarily viewed as a substitute. Rather, it is assumed that the contractor could have expanded his business to undertake additional jobs so that the breach of the original contract resulted in "lost volume" that could not be recaptured by a second similar contract. On this assumption, the second contract is not a substitute for the first and the amount earned on the second contract should not be subtracted in calculating the damages for breach of the first. The materials that follow explore the borderlines of this distinction.

OLDS v. MAPES-REEVE CONSTRUCTION CO., 177 Mass. 41, 58 N.E. 478 (1900). [Mapes-Reeve, a general contractor, engaged Olds, a subcontractor, to do the marble work on a building for $3,000. Mapes-Reeve wrongfully ordered Olds to stop work, at a time when it would have cost $717 to complete it. Olds at once made a contract with the owner to complete it at a price of $1,053. Olds sued for $2,283 ($3,000 minus $717). The trial court allowed $1,947 ($3,000 minus $1,053). Plaintiff appealed.]

KNOWLTON, J. . . . The rule which is applicable to one who is under a contract to render personal services, and who, being discharged without cause before the end of his term, sues for damages, requires him, in estimating the damages, to allow for his services, during the unexpired term whatever he is able to obtain for them, or if damages are assessed before the end of the term, whatever he reasonably can be expected to obtain for them during the time covered by the contract. . . . But there is this difference between the case of one who is discharged while under a contract to render personal services, and a case like the present. In the former case, the person discharged, whose personal services come back to him, is bound to dispose of them in a reasonable way, so as to make the damages to the other party not unreasonably large, while, in a case like the present, one deprived of his contract is under no obligation to enter into new contracts with a view to make profits for the other party. In a contract of the kind before the court, personal services are not necessarily included. The labor or supervision may be personally performed by the contractor or may be furnished through agents or employees. In either case the value of it is all included for the benefit of the other party when the contractor is charged with the whole cost of completing the work, as an amount to be deducted from the contract price in estimating his damages. Since the damages properly are assessable in this way immediately after the breach of the contract, can it make any difference that the contractor afterwards makes a new contract with the owner which includes the unfinished work? . . . The plaintiffs were at liberty to leave this work entirely to the care of hired servants, and to take as many other contracts as they chose elsewhere, and to give their personal time and attention to any occupation that they might choose. The question is, whether the profits from the new contract with the landowner were a direct result of the defendant's breach of contract, or whether they came from an independent intervening cause. It does not appear, and it is not to be assumed that the plaintiffs were not competent to carry on several contracts at one time, and the making of profits on a new contract does not appear to be because of relief from the obligations of the old one. There is usually plenty of work to be contracted for, and the addition of one more possible job for which contractors may bid does not make the subsequent contract to do the work a direct result of the increase of opportunities for work. The addition of a new piece of work is merely a condition of the subsequent contract to do the work, and not a direct or proximate cause of it. Moreover, the making of such a contract involves many considerations besides the existence of the work to be done. There must be calculations and estimates. In making a contract of this kind there is always a risk of loss as well as a possibility of gain. To say nothing of the fact that the plaintiffs' new contract included work which was not included in the old one, the cost of which could be fixed only as matter of estimate, this contract with the landowner was a new undertaking, in which the plaintiffs were under no obligation to engage, and which involved risks that they could assume for themselves alone. If the contract had resulted in a loss to them, they could not have charged the defendant with the loss, to the increase of their damages. As the contract resulted in a gain to them, there is no reason why the defendant should receive this gain in diminution of the damages for which it was liable. . . . If another person had taken this contract and made profits on it, as the plaintiffs did, it would hardly have been contended that the plaintiffs' damages were to be diminished on that account; or if the plaintiffs, instead of taking this contract after the breach of the former one, had gone elsewhere and taken another contract which afforded them similar profits, there would be no ground for a claim of the defendant to be allowed these profits in diminution of the damages.

[Reversed.]

NOTE

Contract for Same Performance. Most of the few cases that have dealt with this problem are in accord. See e. g., Grinnell Co. v. Voorhees, 1 F.2d 693 (3d Cir. 1924), cert. denied, 266 U.S. 629 (1924). This decision was criticized in Note, 34 Yale L.J. 553 (1925), and the rule proposed that "the repudiator should not be entitled to the benefit of any contract of the injured party except such as the injured party could not have made but for the repudiation." But suppose the other contract turned out to be a losing one?

What would have been the subcontractor's recovery if he had refused the owner's offer of a new contract? Suppose that when the contractor had repudiated his agreement with the subcontractor no offer from the owner had been forthcoming, but the contractor himself had offered the subcontractor $2,800 instead of $3,000 for the completed job, with no surrender of any rights the subcontractor might have on the original contract. What would have been the subcontractor's recovery if he had refused the contractor's offer of a new contract? What if he had accepted it?

NERI v. RETAIL MARINE CORP.

Court of Appeals of New York, 1972.
30 N.Y.2d 393, 334 N.Y.S.2d 165, 285 N.E.2d 311.

GIBSON, Judge. The appeal concerns the right of a retail dealer to recover loss of profits and incidental damages upon the buyer's repudiation of a contract governed by the Uniform Commercial Code. This is, indeed, the correct measure of damage in an appropriate case and to this extent the code (§ 2–708, subsection [2]) effected a substantial change from prior law, whereby damages were ordinarily limited to "the difference between the contract price and the market or current price".[1] Upon the record before us, the courts below erred in declining to give effect to the new statute and so the order appealed from must be reversed.

The plaintiffs contracted to purchase from defendant a new boat of a specified model for the price of $12,587.40, against which they made a deposit of $40. They shortly increased the deposit to $4,250 in consideration of the defendant dealer's agreement to arrange with the manufacturer for immediate delivery on the basis of "a firm sale", instead of the delivery within approximately four to six weeks originally specified. Some six days after the date of the contract plaintiffs' lawyer sent to defendant a letter rescinding the sales contract for the reason that plaintiff Neri was about to undergo hospitalization and surgery, in consequence of which, according to the letter, it would be "impossible for Mr. Neri to make any payments". The boat had already been ordered from the manufacturer and was delivered to defendant at or before the time the attorney's letter was received. Defendant declined to refund plaintiffs' deposit and this action to recover it was commenced. Defendant counterclaimed, alleging plaintiffs' breach of the contract and defendant's resultant damage in the amount of $4,250, for which sum defendant demanded judgment. Upon motion, defendant had summary judgment on the issue of liability tendered by its counterclaim; and Special Term directed an assessment of damages, upon which it would be determined whether plaintiffs were entitled to the return of any portion of their down payment.

Upon the trial so directed, it was shown that the boat ordered and received by defendant in accordance with plaintiffs' contract of

1. Personal Property Law, Consol. Laws, c. 41, § 145, repealed by Uniform Commercial Code, § 10–102 (L. 1962, ch. 553, eff. Sept. 27, 1964); Lenobel, Inc. v. Senif, 252 App.Div. 533, 300 N.Y.S. 226.

purchase was sold some four months later to another buyer for the same price as that negotiated with plaintiffs. From this proof the plaintiffs argue that defendant's loss on its contract was recouped, while defendant argues that but for plaintiffs' default, it would have sold two boats and have earned two profits instead of one. Defendant proved, without contradiction, that its profit on the sale under the contract in suit would have been $2,579 and that during the period the boat remained unsold incidental expenses aggregating $674 for storage, upkeep, finance charges and insurance were incurred. Additionally, defendant proved and sought to recover attorneys' fees of $1,250.

The trial court found "untenable" defendant's claim for loss of profit, inasmuch as the boat was later sold for the same price that plaintiffs had contracted to pay; found, too, that defendant had failed to prove any incidental damages; further found "that the terms of section 2–718, subsection 2(b), of the Uniform Commercial Code are applicable and same make adequate and fair provision to place the sellers in as good a position as performance would have done" and, in accordance with paragraph (b) of subsection (2) thus relied upon, awarded defendant $500 upon its counterclaim and directed that plaintiffs recover the balance of their deposit, amounting to $3,750. The ensuing judgment was affirmed, without opinion, at the Appellate Division, 37 A.D.2d 917, 326 N.Y.S.2d 984, and defendant's appeal to this court was taken by our leave.

The issue is governed in the first instance by section 2–718 of the Uniform Commercial Code which provides, among other things, that the buyer, despite his breach, may have restitution of the amount by which his payment exceeds: (a) reasonable liquidated damages stipulated by the contract or (b) absent such stipulation, 20% of the value of the buyer's total performance or $500, whichever is smaller (§ 2–718, subsection [2], pars. [a], [b]). As above noted, the trial court awarded defendant an offset in the amount of $500 under paragraph (b) and directed restitution to plaintiffs of the balance. Section 2–718, however, establishes, in paragraph (a) of subsection (3), an alternative right of offset in favor of the seller, as follows: "(3) The buyer's right to restitution under subsection (2) is subject to offset to the extent that the seller establishes (a) a right to recover damages under the provisions of this Article other than subsection (1)".

Among "the provisions of this Article other than subsection (1)" are those to be found in section 2–708, which the courts below did not apply. Subsection (1) of that section provides that "the measure of damages for non-acceptance or repudiation by the buyer is the difference between the market price at the time and place for tender and the unpaid contract price together with any incidental damages provided in this Article (Section 2–710), but less expenses saved in consequence of the buyer's breach." However, this provision is made ex-

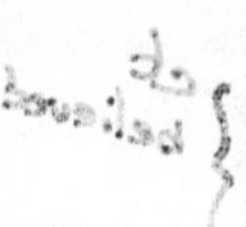

pressly subject to subsection (2), providing: "(2) If the measure of damages provided in subsection (1) is inadequate to put the seller in as good a position as performance would have done then the measure of damages is the profit (including reasonable overhead) which the seller would have made from full performance by the buyer, together with any incidental damages provided in this Article (Section 2–710), due allowance for costs reasonably incurred and due credit for payments or proceeds of resale."

The provision of the code upon which the decision at Trial Term rested (§ 2–718, subsection [2], par. [b]) does not differ greatly from the corresponding provisions of the prior statute (Personal Property Law, § 145–a, subd. 1, par. [b]), except as the new act includes the alternative remedy of a lump sum award of $500. Neither does the present reference (in § 2–718, subsection [3], par. [a]) to the recovery of damages pursuant to other provisions of the article differ from a like reference in the prior statute (Personal Property Law, § 145–a, subd. 2, par. [a]) to an alternative measure of damages under section 145 of that act; but section 145 made no provision for recovery of lost profits as does section 2–708 (subsection [2]) of the code. The new statute is thus innovative and significant and its analysis is necessary to the determination of the issues here presented.

Prior to the code, the New York cases "applied the 'profit' test, contract price less cost of manufacture, only in cases where the seller [was] a manufacturer or an agent for a manufacturer" (1955 Report of N.Y.Law Rev.Comm., vol. 1, p. 693). Its extension to retail sales was "designed to eliminate the unfair and economically wasteful results arising under the older law when fixed price articles were involved. This section permits the recovery of lost profits in all appropriate cases, which would include all standard priced goods." (Official Comment 2, McKinney's Cons.Laws of N.Y., Book 62½, Part 1, p. 605, under Uniform Commercial Code, § 2–708.) Additionally, and "[i]n all cases the seller may recover incidental damages" (id., Comment 3). The buyer's right to restitution was established at Special Term upon the motion for summary judgment, as was the seller's right to proper offsets, in each case pursuant to section 2–718; and, as the parties concede, the only question before us, following the assessment of damages at Special Term, is that as to the proper measure of damage to be applied. The conclusion is clear from the record—indeed with mathematical certainty—that "the measure of damages provided in subsection (1) is inadequate to put the seller in as good a position as performance would have done" (Uniform Commercial Code, § 2–708, subsection [2]) and hence—again under subsection (2)—that the seller is entitled to its "profit (including reasonable overhead) . . . together with any incidental damages . . ., due allowance for costs reasonably incurred and due credit for payments or proceeds of resale."

It is evident, first, that this retail seller is entitled to its profit and, second, that the last sentence of subsection (2), hereinbefore quoted, referring to "due credit for payments or proceeds of resale" is inapplicable to this retail sales contract.[2] Closely parallel to the factual situation now before us is that hypothesized by Dean Hawkland as illustrative of the operation of the rules: "Thus, if a private party agrees to sell his automobile to a buyer for $2,000, a breach by the buyer would cause the seller no loss (except incidental damages, i. e., expense of a new sale) if the seller was able to sell the automobile to another buyer for $2000. But the situation is different with dealers having an unlimited supply of standard-priced goods. Thus, if an automobile dealer agrees to sell a car to a buyer at the standard price of $2000, a breach by the buyer injures the dealer, even though he is able to sell the automobile to another for $2000. If the dealer has an inexhaustible supply of cars, the resale to replace the breaching buyer costs the dealer a sale, because, had the breaching buyer performed, the dealer would have made two sales instead of one. The buyer's breach, in such a case, depletes the dealer's sales to the extent of one, and the measure of damages should be the dealer's profit on one sale. Section 2–708 recognizes this, and it rejects the rule developed under the Uniform Sales Act by many courts that the profit cannot be recovered in this case." (Hawkland, Sales and Bulk Sales [1958 ed.], pp. 153–154; and see Comment, 31 Fordham L.Rev. 749, 755–756.)

The record which in this case establishes defendant's entitlement to damages in the amount of its prospective profit, at the same time confirms defendant's cognate right to "any incidental damages provided in this Article (Section 2–710)" [3] (Uniform Commercial Code, § 2–708, subsection [2]). From the language employed it is too clear to require discussion that the seller's right to recover loss of profits is

2. The concluding clause, "due credit for payments or proceeds of resale", is intended to refer to "the privilege of the seller to realize junk value when it is manifestly useless to complete the operation of manufacture" (Supp. No. 1 to the 1952 Official Draft of Text and Comments of the Uniform Commercial Code, as Amended by the Action of the American Law Institute of the National Conference of Commissioners on Uniform Laws [1954], p. 14). The commentators who have considered the language have uniformly concluded that "the reference is to a resale as scrap under . . . Section 2–704" (1956 Report of N.Y.Law Rev. Comm., p. 397; 1955 Report of N.Y. Law Rev.Comm., vol. 1, p. 761; New York Annotations, McKinney's Cons. Laws of N. Y. Book 62½, Part 1, p. 606, under Uniform Commercial Code, § 2–708; 1 Willier and Hart, Bender's Uniform Commercial Code Service, § 2–708, pp. 1–180—1–181). Another writer, reaching the same conclusion, after detailing the history of the clause, says that " 'proceeds of resale' previously meant the resale value of the goods in finished form; now it means the resale value of the components on hand at the time plaintiff learns of breach" (Harris, Seller's Damages, 18 Stanf.L.Rev. 66, 104).

3. "Incidental damages to an aggrieved seller include any commercially reasonable charges, expenses or commissions incurred in stopping delivery, in the transportation, care and custody of goods after the buyer's breach, in connection with return or resale of the goods or otherwise resulting from the breach" (Uniform Commercial Code 2–710).

not exclusive and that he may recoup his "incidental" expenses as well (Procter & Gamble Distr. Co. v. Lawrence Amer. Field Warehousing Corp., 16 N.Y.2d 344, 354, 266 N.Y.S.2d 785, 792, 213 N.E.2d 873, 878). Although the trial court's denial of incidental damages in the uncontroverted amount of $674 was made in the context of its erroneous conclusion that paragraph (b) of subsection (2) of section 2–718 was applicable and was "adequate . . . to place the sellers in as good a position as performance would have done", the denial seems not to have rested entirely on the court's mistaken application of the law, as there was an explicit finding "that defendant completely failed to show that it suffered any incidental damages." We find no basis for the court's conclusion with respect to a deficiency of proof inasmuch as the proper items of the $674 expenses (being for storage, upkeep, finance charges and insurance for the period between the date performance was due and the time of the resale) were proven without objection and were in no way controverted, impeached or otherwise challenged, at the trial or on appeal. Thus the court's finding of a failure of proof cannot be supported upon the record and, therefore, and contrary to plaintiffs' contention, the affirmance at the Appellate Division was ineffective to save it.

The trial court correctly denied defendant's claim for recovery of attorney's fees incurred by it in this action. Attorney's fees incurred in an action such as this are not in the nature of the protective expenses contemplated by the statute (Uniform Commercial Code, § 1–106, subd. [1]; § 2–710; § 2–708, subsection [2]) and by our reference to "legal expense" in Procter & Gamble Distr. Co. v. Lawrence Amer. Field Warehousing Corp. (16 N.Y.2d 344, 354–355, 266 N.Y.S.2d 785, 792–793, 213 N.E.2d 873, 878–879, supra), upon which defendant's reliance is in this respect misplaced.

It follows that plaintiffs are entitled to restitution of the sum of $4,250 paid by them on account of the contract price less an offset to defendant in the amount of $3,253 on account of its lost profit of $2,579 and its incidental damages of $674.

The order of the Appellate Division should be modified, with costs in all courts, in accordance with this opinion, and, as so modified, affirmed.

NOTES

(1) *Lost Volume.* An extensive literature has developed on the subject of the seller's claim of lost volume resulting from the buyer's breach. Two early articles are Harris, A General Theory for Measuring Seller's Damages for Total Breach of Contract, 60 Mich.L.Rev. 577, 599–605 (1962); Harris, A Radical Restatement of the Law of Seller's Damages: Sales Act and Commercial Code Results Compared, 18 Stan.L.Rev. 66 (1965). The latter article, at 97–99, discusses the drafting history of UCC 2–708(2). Articles using economic analysis include Childres & Burgess, Seller's Remedies: The Primacy of UCC 2–708(2), 48 N.Y.U.L.Rev. 833 (1973); Goetz & Scott,

Measuring Seller's Damages: The Lost-Profits Puzzle, 31 Stan.L.Rev. 323 (1979); Speidel & Clay, Seller's Recovery of Overhead under UCC Section 2–708(2): Economic Cost Theory and Contract Remedial Policy, 57 Cornell L.Rev. 681 (1972); Comment, 24 Case W.Res.L.Rev. 686 (1973). One of the recurring themes in these discussions is that "even if the . . . seller was somehow forced to lose a sale because of the breach, it is doubtful that the lost sale would create an appreciable reduction in the seller's lost profits [because] for any profit-maximizing firm . . . the marginal sales, which are the ones that will be 'lost,' will probably either produce only insignificant amounts of profit or be unprofitable." Comment, supra, at 728.[a]

(2) *Burden as to Lost Volume.* Who has the burden of proof on the issue of lost volume? Goetz and Scott argue that "the concern for reducing measurement errors which prompted the increase in lost-profits recoveries is misguided" and that "an initial presumption of replacement efficiently minimizes total enforcement costs whenever sellers have access to a market." Goetz & Scott, supra Note 1, at 373.

In Famous Knitwear Corp. v. Drug Fair, 493 F.2d 251 (4th Cir. 1974), the court remanded for a determination of the issue on the facts. "It may well be that Famous Knitwear, a 'middleman' between manufacturer and retailer (Drug Fair), was a lost volume seller as was the retailer in Neri v. Retail Marine Corp. . . . Because there are no findings of fact by the district judge as to the conflicting assertions, we are unable to determine if Famous Knitwear is a lost volume seller and, as such, entitled to lost profits under UCC 2–708(2)."

In Snyder v. Herbert Greenbaum & Associates, 38 Md.App. 144, 380 A. 2d 618 (1977), the court also remanded for a determination of the issue on the facts, adding that the seller was to prevail only if he "carried his burden of proving that he is a lost volume seller."

SECTION 2. ALTERNATIVES TO EXPECTATION

SULLIVAN v. O'CONNOR

Supreme Judicial Court of Massachusetts, 1973.
363 Mass. 579, 296 N.E.2d 183.

[For the report of this case, see p. 6 supra.]

FARNSWORTH, LEGAL REMEDIES FOR BREACH OF CONTRACT, 70 Colum.L.Rev. 1145, 1175–78 (1970).[b] Ordinarily the injured party will be content to base his recovery on his expectation interest, since this will be more favorable to him than recovery based

a. As to whether a seller can insist on damages based on market price if they are greater, see Nobs Chemical v. Koppers Co., 616 F.2d 212 (5th Cir. 1980).

b. Reprinted and slightly adapted by permission of the Columbia Law Review.

on either his restitution interest or his reliance interest. There are, however, some exceptions.

One instance in which restitution may appear an attractive alternative occurs when the party in breach has committed a total breach in spite of the fact that the bargain has turned out to favor him—that is, when the value to the party in breach of the benefit conferred upon him would exceed the value of his promised performance to the injured party. Needless to say, this sort of situation is not common since there is usually no reason for the more favored party to refuse to perform his part of a bargain that is favorable to him. Nevertheless, when this situation does arise, restitution is allowed if the benefit conferred on the party in breach consists simply of the payment of money.[1]

> *Illustration 1.* Builder contracts with Owner to construct a factory on Owner's land for $1,000,000 payable in advance. Owner pays the $1,000,000 and Builder breaches by failing to construct the factory. Owner sues Builder for return of the full $1,000,000, although the value of the factory to Owner would in fact have been only $700,000.

Owner will be allowed restitution of the full $1,000,000, with no deduction for the $300,000 loss he would have suffered had Builder constructed the factory. Owner's position after the breach is consequently better than it would have been had Builder performed.

Restitution is not, however, generally allowed where the benefit conferred on the party in breach consists of something other than the payment of money.[2]

> *Illustration 2.* Builder contracts with Owner to construct a factory on Owner's land for $1,000,000 payable on completion. Builder constructs the factory and Owner breaches by failing to pay the price. Builder sues Owner for $2,000,000, the actual value of the factory to Owner, rather than for the $1,000,000 that Owner promised to pay.

Here Builder's recovery will be limited to the $1,000,000 promised, which was the limit of his expectation. The results in Illustrations 1 and 2 both of which favor the party who has agreed to pay money, can be reconciled on the ground that in each case the court chooses the measure of recovery that permits it to avoid the problem of determining loss in value due to nonperformance of the promise to do

1. Bush v. Canfield, 2 Conn. 485 (1818), discussed in G. Palmer, Law of Restitution § 4.3 (1978); Palmer, The Contract Price as a Limit on Restitution for Defendant's Breach, 20 Ohio St.L.J. 264–65 (1959); Restatement Second, § 373(1).

2. E. g., Oliver v. Campbell, 43 Cal.2d 298, 273 P.2d 15 (1954); Restatement Second, § 373(2).

something other than pay money.[3] If, however, the benefit conferred on the party in breach consists of other than the payment of money, and if the injured party has performed only in part, as where Owner breaches by repudiating when Builder is in the process of constructing the factory, the problem of valuation cannot be avoided. Here courts have generally allowed recovery based on the restitution interest, a point that will be illustrated shortly in connection with the protection of the reliance interest in this situation.[4]

Dawson points out a second instance in which recovery based on the restitution interest, broadly conceived, might exceed the expectation.[5] This occurs where one party refuses to perform so that he may take advantage of another, more attractive, opportunity.

> *Illustration 3.* Builder contracts with Owner to construct a factory on Owner's land for $1,000,000 payable on completion. Builder would have made a profit of $100,000 on this contract. Immediately after making the contract, he receives from another owner an offer of a contract under which he can make a profit of $300,000. He accepts it, although he cannot do both jobs, and repudiates his contract with Owner. Owner sues Builder for restitution of the $200,000 additional profit that Builder made as a result of his breach, although it appears that Owner would not have made a profit had the factory been built.

Dawson concludes, however, that Owner would be denied recovery of the $200,000:

> This kind of recovery could not be explained as restitution under present day tests; there would be a fatal break in the chain of causation, for the asset or conduct that was merely promised would not have come *from* the promisee [Owner]. Perhaps another way to express the idea is that the prevention of profit through mere breach of contract is not yet an approved aim of our legal order, as it is with breach of "fiduciary" duties.[6]

3. For this reason Restatement Second, § 373(2) allows restitution where, for example, the injured party has parted with goods in return for a promise to perform services.

4. Restatement Second, § 373(1). See United States v. Algernon Blair, p. 585 infra. The formulas for recovery based on the expectation interest and the restitution interest, respectively, have a discontinuity at the line between part and full performance. An example is Oliver v. Campbell, 43 Cal.2d 298, 273 P.2d 15 (1954), in which a five-judge majority held that a lawyer had fully performed his services for his client and was limited to the $750 fee that they had fixed, while two dissenting judges contended that the services were not fully performed so that he was entitled to their reasonable value, $5,000.

5. Dawson, Restitution or Damages?, 20 Ohio St.L.J. 175, 186–87 (1959).

6. Dawson, supra note 5, at 187. He cites Acme Mills & Elevator Co. v. Johnson, 141 Ky. 718, 133 S.W. 784 (1911), in which a seller failed to deliver wheat which he had contracted to sell for $1.03 a bushel, sold it before the delivery date to another buy-

The limits on the restitution interest as a basis of recovery, therefore, usually make it unattractive to the injured party as an alternative to the expectation interest. The reliance interest, however, is more promising.

One instance in which the injured party might prefer recovery based on his reliance interest occurs when his expectations under the the contract were less than his expectations under some other bargain that he declined in reliance on the contract.

Illustration 4. The facts being otherwise as stated in Illustration 3, Builder would have made a profit of $100,000 on this contract. Builder rejects the other offer because he cannot do both jobs. Owner then breaches by repudiating the contract after it is too late for Builder to accept the other offer. Builder sues Owner for $300,000 in damages, based on what he lost in reliance on his contract with Owner, rather than for $100,000 based on what he lost in disappointed expectations upon its breach.

Although $300,000 would be required to put Builder in the position in which he would have been had he not made the contract with Owner,[7] no court would allow him this larger sum. A court will not, as Fuller and Perdue stated it, "knowingly put the plaintiff in a better position than he would have occupied had the contract been fully performed." [8] Expectation here operates as an upper limit on recovery, a defensible limit since one of the justifications for the protection of the expectation interest in the first place is that it yields rules that are superior, because of their certainty and ease of application, to those derived from the reliance interest.[9] Businessmen regularly rely on con-

er for $1.16 a bushel, and was held liable for nominal damages only when the market dropped below the contract price by the delivery date. See also Restatement, Second, of Agency § 404 (1957), Illustration 2. But in Timko v. Useful Homes Corp., 114 N.J.Eq. 433, 168 A. 824 (1933), it was held that a vendor of lots, for which the purchaser had partly paid, held them in trust for the purchaser and was liable to him for damages based on the price at which he wrongfully sold them to a third party.

7. To eliminate the possibility that Builder might have repudiated the contract with Owner and accepted the more profitable offer, remaining liable to Owner for damages, assume that those damages would be at least $200,000, so that this course of action would have been less desirable for Builder.

8. Fuller & Perdue, The Reliance Interest in Contract Damages 1, 46 Yale L.J. 52, 79. See also their discussion of the compensability of gains prevented through reliance at 417–18.

9. Id. at 61–62. They also suggest that in a hypothetical society in which all values were available on the market and where all markets were "perfect" in the economic sense . . . there would be no difference between the reliance interest and the expectation interest. The plaintiff's loss in foregoing to enter another contract would be identical with the expectation value of the contract he did make.

Id. at 62. They give the illustration of a "physician who by making one appointment deprives himself of the opportunity of making a precisely similar appointment with another patient . . . ." Id. at 74.

tracts by foregoing other opportunities and adjusting their business to the expected performance, and basing recovery on such reliance would pose grave problems of measurement.

A second exceptional case, in which the injured party may prefer damages based on reliance to those based on expectation, arises when the breach has relieved him from finishing performance of what has turned out to be a losing contract.[10]

> *Illustration 5.* Builder contracts with Owner to construct a factory on Owner's land for $1,000,000 payable on completion. Owner breaches by repudiating the contract after Builder has begun performance. Builder has already spent $500,000 and would have to spend $600,000 more to finish performance, which would result in a $100,000 loss on the contract. Builder sues Owner for $500,000 in damages, based on his expenditures in reliance on the contract and ignoring the $100,000 loss, rather than for the $400,000 to which he would otherwise be entitled.

NOTES

(1) *Losing Contracts.* What result in Illustration 5 under Formula A? Under Formula B? For a case applying Formula A, see Millen v. Gulesian, 229 Mass. 27, 118 N.E. 267 (1918).

(2) *Problem.* Buyer made a $5,000 payment on a contract for the sale of flour for a total price of $14,000. Seller broke the contract by failing to deliver the flour, although the market price of the flour had dropped to $11,000 by the time of delivery. Is Buyer entitled to restitution of $5,000 from Seller? See Bush v. Canfield, 2 Conn. 485 (1818).

UNITED STATES v. ALGERNON BLAIR, INC.

United States Court of Appeals, Fourth Circuit, 1973.
479 F.2d 638.

CRAVEN, Circuit Judge. May a subcontractor, who justifiably ceases work under a contract because of the prime contractor's breach, recover in quantum meruit the value of labor and equipment already furnished pursuant to the contract irrespective of whether he would have been entitled to recover in a suit on the contract? We think so, and, for reasons to be stated, the decision of the district court will be reversed.

The subcontractor, Coastal Steel Erectors, Inc., brought this action under the provisions of the Miller Act, 40 U.S.C.A. § 270a et

10. It may be that the injured party entered into the contract because of some special advantage, such as the enhancement of his experience or reputation or good will, with respect to which his proof fails to meet the standard of certainty, discussed in Subsection 3(c) infra. What he then regarded as an advantageous contract may thus appear as a "losing" contract.

seq., in the name of the United States against Algernon Blair, Inc., and its surety, United States Fidelity and Guaranty Company. Blair had entered a contract with the United States for the contruction of a naval hospital in Charleston County, South Carolina. Blair had then contracted with Coastal to perform certain steel erection and supply certain equipment in conjunction with Blair's contract with the United States. Coastal commenced performance of its obligations, supplying its own cranes for handling and placing steel. Blair refused to pay for crane rental, maintaining that it was not obligated to do so under the subcontract. Because of Blair's failure to make payments for crane rental, and after completion of approximately 28 percent of the subcontract, Coastal terminated its performance. Blair then proceeded to complete the job with a new subcontractor. Coastal brought this action to recover for labor and equipment furnished.

The district court found that the subcontract required Blair to pay for crane use and that Blair's refusal to do so was such a material breach as to justify Coastal's terminating performance. This finding is not questioned on appeal. The court then found that under the contract the amount due Coastal, less what had already been paid, totaled approximately $37,000. Additionally, the court found Coastal would have lost more than $37,000 if it had completed performance. Holding that any amount due Coastal must be reduced by any loss it would have incurred by complete performance of the contract, the court denied recovery to Coastal. While the district court correctly stated the " 'normal' rule of contract damages," we think Coastal is entitled to recover in quantum meruit.

In United States for Use of Susi Contracting Co. v. Zara Contracting Co., 146 F.2d 606 (2d Cir. 1944), a Miller Act action, the court was faced with a situation similar to that involved here—the prime contractor had unjustifiably breached a subcontract after partial performance by the subcontractor. The court stated:

> For it is an accepted principle of contract law, often applied in the case of construction contracts, that the promisee upon breach has the option to forego any suit on the contract and claim only the reasonable value of his performance.

146 F.2d at 610. . . . Quantum meruit recovery is not limited to an action against the prime contractor but may also be brought against the Miller Act surety, as in this case. Further, that the complaint is not clear in regard to the theory of a plaintiff's recovery does not preclude recovery under quantum meruit. Narragansett Improvement Co. v. United States, 290 F.2d 577 (1st Cir. 1961). A plaintiff may join a claim for quantum meruit with a claim for damages from breach of contract.

In the present case, Coastal has, at its own expense, provided Blair with labor and the use of equipment. Blair, who breached the subcontract, has retained these benefits without having fully paid for them. On these facts, Coastal is entitled to restitution in quantum meruit.

> The "restitution interest," involving a combination of unjust impoverishment with unjust gain, presents the strongest case for relief. If, following Aristotle, we regard the purpose of justice as the maintenance of an equilibrium of goods among members of society, the restitution interest presents twice as strong a claim to judicial intervention as the reliance interest, since if A not only causes B to lose one unit but appropriates that unit to himself, the resulting discrepancy between A and B is not one unit but two.

Fuller & Perdue, The Reliance Interest in Contract Damages, 46 Yale L.J. 52, 56 (1936).

The impact of quantum meruit is to allow a promisee to recover the value of services he gave to the defendant irrespective of whether he would have lost money on the contract and been unable to recover in a suit on the contract. Scaduto v. Orlando, 381 F.2d 587, 595 (2d Cir. 1967). The measure of recovery for quantum meruit is the reasonable value of the performance, Restatement of Contracts § 347 (1932); and recovery is undiminished by any loss which would have been incurred by complete performance. 12 Williston on Contracts § 1485, at 312 (3d ed. 1970). While the contract price may be evidence of reasonable value of the services, it does not measure the value of the performance or limit recovery. Rather, the standard for measuring the reasonable value of the services rendered is the amount for which such services could have been purchased from one in the plaintiff's position at the time and place the services were rendered.

Since the district court has not yet accurately determined the reasonable value of the labor and equipment use furnished by Coastal to Blair, the case must be remanded for those findings.[1] When the amount has been determined, judgment will be entered in favor of Coastal, less payments already made under the contract. Accordingly, for the reasons stated above, the decision of the district court is

Reversed and remanded with instructions.

NOTES

(1) *Measure of Restitution Interest.* What result in Illustration 5, p. 585 supra, under the Algernon Blair case? What is the court's justification for measuring Coastal's restitution interest by "the reasonable value of

1. Under the view of the case taken by the district court it was unnecessary to precisely appraise the value of services and materials rendered; an approximation was thought to suffice because the hypothetical loss had the contract been fully performed was greater in amount.

the performance"? Is this a proper measure of the "benefits" that Blair "retained without having fully paid for"? How does it differ from Coastal's reliance interest? See Restatement Second § 371. The conclusion that "the property owner is enriched by each stroke of the hammer or the paint brush" is characterized as "Pickwickian" in Patterson, The Scope of Restitution and Unjust Enrichment, 1 Mo.L.Rev. 223, 230 (1936); see also Fuller & Perdue, The Reliance Interest in Contract Damages 1: 46 Yale L.J. 52, 77 (1936); Perillo, Restitution in a Contractual Context, 73 Colum.L. Rev. 1208 (1973).

A particularly generous measure of the injured party's restitution interest was suggested in Acme Process Equipment Co. v. United States, 347 F.2d 509 (Ct.Cl.1965), rev'd on other grounds, 385 U.S. 138 (1966). The United States, interested in obtaining a new arms supplier, awarded a contract to Acme, which had never before had a defense contract, to manufacture recoilless rifles for $385 each. The government terminated after it had received and paid for about one-third of the rifles. Acme claimed that the termination was wrongful and sued to recover its costs, which were $1,179 each at first and dropped to $690 each by the time of the termination. The trial commissioner allowed recovery based on the amount by which Acme could have reduced its loss if it had been allowed to complete performance. On appeal, the Court of Claims remanded, quoting Comment a to Restatement, § 348, to the effect that the value of the service may be recovered "even though there never was any product created by the service that added to the wealth of the defendant." But it concluded that only reasonable costs can be recovered and sent the case back for a determination of whether Acme's costs were excessive. The case is discussed in 1 G. Palmer, Law of Restitution § 4.2 (1978); Childres & Garamella, The Law of Restitution and the Reliance Interest in Contract, 64 Nw.U.L.Rev. 433, 444–51 (1969).

(2) *Contract Price as a Ceiling.* Should the injured party be allowed to recover "the reasonable value of the performance" even if it exceeds the contract price? Using the contract price as a ceiling on recovery in such a case will not entirely avoid problems of measurement of the benefit conferred on the party in breach, since that benefit must, at least in principle, be measured before it can be known whether the ceiling has been reached. On the other hand, not using the contract price as a ceiling on recovery may result in a more generous recovery for part performance than would have been allowed for full performance.

For authority that the contract price is a ceiling, see Johnson v. Bovee, 40 Colo.App. 317, 574 P.2d 513 (1978). For authority that it is not, see Southern Painting Co. v. United States, 222 F.2d 431 (10th Cir. 1955). The latter view is taken in 1 G. Palmer, Restitution § 4.4 (1978); Palmer, The Contract Price as a Limit on Restitution for Defendant's Breach, 20 Ohio St.L.J. 264 (1959). This view is criticized in Childres & Garamella, The Law of Restitution and the Reliance Interest in Contract, 64 Nw.U.L.Rev. 433 (1969), an article that is itself criticized in Sullivan, The Concept of Benefit in the Law of Quasi-Contract, 64 Geo.L.J. 1 (1975).

KEHOE v. RUTHERFORD, 56 N.J.Law 23, 27 A. 912 (1893). [Kehoe contracted to grade Montrose Avenue in the borough of Rutherford, New Jersey, for 65 cents per running foot. After he had done part of the work and had been paid $1,850, the borough defaulted. He sued for breach of contract and for quantum meruit. He proved that the length of the whole work was 4,220 feet, giving a price of $2,743. He also proved that the fair cost of the work done was $3,153 and that the fair cost of the work remaining to be done was $1,891, giving a total cost of $5,044. Kehoe was nonsuited and appealed.]

DIXON, J. . . . The non-suit was ordered upon the theory that a plaintiff could recover, for the work done, only such a proportion of the contract price as the fair cost of that work bore to the fair cost of the whole work required, and, in respect of the work not done, only such profit (if any) as he might have made by doing it, for the unpaid balance of the contract price. Under this theory, his recovery for the work done was to be limited to such a proportion of $2,743 as three thousand one hundred and fifty-three bears to five thousand and forty-four, viz., $1,715; and as to the work not done, since it would cost him $1,891 to do it, while the unpaid balance of the price was only $893, no profit could be earned by doing it. Hence it was considered that he had been overpaid to the extent of the difference between $1,850 and $1,715.

But the contention of the plaintiff was and is that, as he was prevented from completing the contract without fault on his part, he is entitled to the reasonable value of the work done, without reference to the contract price; and if this be the correct rule, undoubtedly the case should have gone to the jury. But at the very threshold we are confronted with this possible result of the application of the rule contended for, that the plaintiff might recover $3,153 for doing about three-fifths of the work, while if he had done it all he could have recovered only $2,743. The absurdity of the result condemns the application of such a rule. . . .

[Affirmed.]

NOTES

(1) ***Possible Solutions.*** What result in Illustration 5, p. 585 supra, under Kehoe v. Rutherford?[a] What solution do you prefer? What position does the Restatement take? See Restatement Second, §§ 349, 373.

a. The percentage-of-completion method is one commonly used in accounting practice. See Herwitz, Accounting for Long-Term Construction Contracts: A Lawyer's Approach, 70 Harv.L.Rev. 449, 452, n. 11 (1952).

However, various factors may have influenced Builder to name a smaller price, in proportion, for a large performance than he would have named for a small performance, and that he may have suffered various inconveniences from owner's breach, which are not compensated for by giving him only a pro rata part of the total contract price. For further discussion, see Patterson, Builder's Measure of Recovery for Breach of Contract, 31 Colum.L.Rev. 1286, 1299–1303 (1931.)

(2) *Burden of Proof.* Consider the following as a possible solution. "In cases where the venture would have proved profitable to the promisee, there is no reason why he should not recover his expenses. On the other hand, on those occasions in which the performance would not have covered the promisee's outlay, such a result imposes the risk of the promisee's contract upon the promisor. We cannot agree that the promisor's default in performance should under this guise make him an insurer of the promisee's venture; yet it does not follow that the breach should not throw upon him the duty of showing that the value of the performance would in fact have been less than the promisee's outlay. It is often very hard to learn what the value of the performance would have been; and it is a common expedient, and a just one, in such situations to put the peril of the answer upon that party who by his wrong has made the issue relevant to the rights of the other. On principle therefore the proper solution would seem to be that the promisee may recover his outlay in preparation for the performance, subject to the privilege of the promisor to reduce it by as much as he can show that the promisee would have lost, if the contract had been performed." Learned Hand in L. Albert & Son v. Armstrong Rubber Co., 178 F.2d 182, 189 (2d Cir. 1949).

The case just quoted from involved material delay by a seller of machines to be used by the buyer to reclaim old rubber during World War II. The buyer did not ask for loss of profits when the delay caused this speculative venture to fall through, but did claim expenses in reliance on the seller's promise to deliver on time, including the cost of laying foundations for the machines. It was this claim to which Hand spoke. Note that in the preceding cases in this section the profit in question was profit to be made from the transaction between the parties, while here the profit in question was profit to be made from *other* transactions which were to be made possible by the one between the parties. Similarly, in the preceding cases the reliance in question was reliance in performing or at least in preparing to perform in the transaction between the parties, while here the reliance was in preparing to perform in *other* transactions which were to be made possible by this transaction. Should this make a difference?

(3) *The Case of the Severable Subdivision.* Day contracted to pay Shapiro Engineering $43,000 for constructing storm sewers in Oakwood Knolls Subdivision, Bethesda, Maryland. The subdivision was laid out in two sections. Lots had been sold and some homes were under construction on Section I, but not on Section II. An addendum to the contract read, "Section I . . . shall amount to $23,000, and Section II will amount to $20,000, for purposes of paying on account of this contract only." Day defaulted after Shapiro Engineering had completed Section I. Shapiro Engineering sued for $23,000. At the trial Day offered an estimate that it would have cost Shapiro Engineering $27,347 to have completed Section II. From a judgment for the plaintiff for $23,000, the defendant appealed, contending that the trial court erred in making no finding on the cost to complete Section II. *Held:* Affirmed. "The contract itself made an apportionment for purposes of payment, and upon the facts stated the two parts of the work were separate and distinct. [Moreover, in its correspondence] the defendant itself recognized that the payments on account would completely pay for the first section, without regard to the completion of Section II. A clearer acknowledgement of the severability of the contract in relation to

payment can hardly be imagined." Shapiro Engineering Corp. v. Francis O. Day Co., 215 Md. 373, 137 A.2d 695 (1958).

Is this decision simply an application of the principle laid down in Kehoe v. Rutherford? Is the contract there "severable" in this sense? Is the contract in Illustration 5, p. 585 supra, "severable" in this sense?

(4) *Problem.* Security Stove in Kansas City had developed a furnace which it was anxious to exhibit at a trade association convention in Atlantic City, although it was not yet on the market. Since it was too late to ship it by freight, Security Stove made a contract for its shipment with Express Company, explaining its need, asking that it be shipped to arrive by October 8, and reminding Express Company of the urgency shortly before the date for shipment. Express Company picked up the shipment of 21 numbered packages, but the package containing the gas manifold, the most important part of the exhibit, was mislaid and did not arrive until the convention closed. Security Stove sues to recover from Express Company for express charges to Atlantic City, freight charges back to Kansas City, travel and hotel expenses and salaries for its employees who went to the convention to exhibit the furnace, and rental for the booth. What decision? See Security Stove & Mfg. Co. v. American Ry. Express Co., 227 Mo.App. 175, 51 S.W.2d 572 (1932).

SECTION 3. LIMITATIONS ON DAMAGES

(a) Avoidability

In Virtue v. Bird, 3 Keble 766, 84 Eng.Rep. 1000, (same case) 1 Ventris 310, 86 Eng.Rep. 200 (1678), a quaint case from three centuries ago, the plaintiff contracted to carry goods to Ipswich and to deliver it to a place to be appointed by the defendant. When the plaintiff arrived in Ipswich, however, "the defendant delayed by the space of six hours the appointment of the place; insomuch that his horses being so hot . . . and standing in aperto aere, they died soon after." The court denied him recovery of this loss on the ground that "it was the plaintiff's folly to let the horses stand," for he "might have taken his horses out of the cart, or have laid down the [goods] any where in Ipswich." Although it is sometimes said that in such cases the injured party is under a "duty" to mitigate damages, he incurs no liability to the party in breach for his failure to mitigate. His recovery is the same regardless of whether he takes steps in mitigation or not. He is simply precluded from recovering for loss that he could reasonably have avoided. See Restatement Second, § 350.

ROCKINGHAM COUNTY v. LUTEN BRIDGE CO.

United States Circuit Court of Appeals, Fourth Circuit, 1929.
35 F.2d 301, 66 A.L.R. 735.

[Action at law, instituted in the district court, to recover an amount alleged to be due under a contract for the construction of a bridge in North Carolina. The contract was entered into, by the Board of County Commissioners, on January 7, 1924; but there was considerable public opposition to the building of the bridge, and on February 21, 1924, the board notified the plaintiff not to proceed any further under the contract, which it refused (unjustifiably, as the court found) to recognize as valid.[a] At that time plaintiff had expended about $1900 for labor done and material on the ground. Despite this notice from the county commissioners, plaintiff continued to build the bridge in accordance with the terms of the contract. The present action is brought to recover $18,301.07, the amount alleged to be due plaintiff for work done before November 3, 1924. The trial court directed a verdict for plaintiff for this sum. Defendant appealed.]

PARKER, Circuit Judge. . . . Coming, then, to the third question—i. e., as to the measure of plaintiff's recovery—we do not think that, after the county had given notice, while the contract was still executory, that it did not desire the bridge built and would not pay for it, plaintiff could proceed to build it and recover the contract price. It is true that the county had no right to rescind the contract, and the notice given plaintiff amounted to a breach on its part; but, after plaintiff had received notice of the breach, it was its duty to do nothing to increase the damages flowing therefrom. If A enters into a binding contract to build a house for B, B, of course, has no right to rescind the contract without A's consent. But if, before the house is built, he decides that he does not want it, and notifies A to that effect, A has no right to proceed with the building and thus pile up damages. His remedy is to treat the contract as broken when he receives the notice, and sue for the recovery of such damages as he may

a. The vote of the commissioners had been three to two in favor of the contract, but on February 11 one of the commissioners who had voted in favor sent his resignation to the clerk, who immediately accepted it. Later the same day this commissioner attempted to withdraw his resignation, but the clerk ignored this and appointed another person to succeed him. The three commissioners who had voted in favor attended no further meetings, but the new commissioner together with the two who had voted against met frequently and, on February 21, unanimously adopted a resolution asserting that the contract was not valid and directing the clerk to so notify Luten, which he did. On April 7, the board passed a resolution reciting that it had been informed that one of its members was privately insisting that the bridge be built and repudiating this action by the member. In September it passed a resolution stating that it would pay no bills for the bridge.

have sustained from the breach, including any profit which he would have realized upon performance, as well as any other losses which may have resulted to him. In the case at bar, the county decided not to build the road of which the bridge was to be a part, and did not build it. The bridge, built in the midst of the forest, is of no value to the county because of this change of circumstances. When, therefore, the county gave notice to the plaintiff that it would not proceed with the project, plaintiff should have desisted from further work. It had no right thus to pile up damages by proceeding with the erection of a useless bridge.

The contrary view was expressed by Lord Cockburn in Frost v. Knight, L.R. 7 Ex. 111, but, as pointed out by Prof. Williston (Williston on Contracts, vol. 3, p. 2347), it is not in harmony with the decisions in this country. The American rule and the reasons supporting it are well stated by Prof. Williston as follows:

"There is a line of cases running back to 1845 which holds that, after an absolute repudiation or refusal to perform by one party to a contract, the other party cannot continue to perform and recover damages based on full performance. This rule is only a particular application of the general rule of damages that a plaintiff cannot hold a defendant liable for damages which need not have been incurred; or, as it is often stated, the plaintiff must, so far as he can without loss to himself, mitigate the damages caused by the defendant's wrongful act. The application of this rule to the matter in question is obvious. If a man engages to have work done, and afterwards repudiates his contract before the work has been begun or when it has been only partially done, it is inflicting damage on the defendant without benefit to the plaintiff to allow the latter to insist on proceeding with the contract. The work may be useless to the defendant, and yet he would be forced to pay the full contract price. On the other hand, the plaintiff is interested only in the profit he will make out of the contract. If he receives this it is equally advantageous for him to use his time otherwise." . . .

Judgment reversed.

NOTE

The Code. Under UCC 2–704(2), a seller who is to manufacture goods may proceed to complete their manufacture upon the buyer's repudiation, instead of halting manufacture and salvaging them while in process, "in the exercise of reasonable commercial judgment for the purposes of avoiding loss and of effective realization." If he does so he may then base his recovery on the goods as completed, even if his "reasonable commercial judgment" turned out to be wrong. Is the manufacturer's situation in any way distinguishable from that of the Luten Bridge Co.?

"CONSTRUCTIVE SERVICE"

It is one thing to say that the injured party cannot recover for cost that he could have avoided by simply stopping performance. It is another to say that he cannot recover for loss that he could have avoided by taking affirmative steps to arrange a substitute transaction. In Gandell v. Pontigny, 4 Camp. 375, 171 Eng.Rep. 119 (1816), the court refused to take this second step. A merchant was sued by his clerk, whom he had wrongfully discharged in the middle of a quarter. The clerk was allowed to recover the agreed compensation for the entire quarter, including the part when he had not worked, on Lord Ellenborough's reasoning that:

> Having served a part of the quarter and being willing to serve the residue, in contemplation of law he may be considered to have served the whole.

In Howard v. Daly, 61 N.Y. 362 (1875), a leading American case, Dwight [a] rejected this doctrine of "constructive service" as

> so wholly irreconcilable to that great and beneficent rule of law, that a person discharged from service must not remain idle, but must accept employment elsewhere if offered, that we cannot accept it . . . . The doctrine of "constructive service" is not only at war with principle but with the rules of political economy, as it encourages idleness and gives compensation to men who fold their arms and decline service, equal to those who perform with willing hands their stipulated amount of labor.

PARKER v. TWENTIETH CENTURY-FOX FILM CORP.

Supreme Court of California, 1970.
3 Cal.3d 176, 474 P.2d 689.

BURKE, Justice. Defendant Twentieth Century-Fox Film Corporation appeals from a summary judgment granting to plaintiff the recovery of agreed compensation under a written contract for her services as an actress in a motion picture. As will appear, we have concluded that the trial court correctly ruled in plaintiff's favor and that the judgment should be affirmed.

a. Theodore William Dwight (1822–1892) served as a professor of law at Hamilton College, and then as a professor of law and later as warden of the law school at Columbia from 1858 to 1891. His principal field was contracts. His method of teaching involved interrogation of his students on an assigned text, and it is reported that, "He could so cross-examine a dunce that the dunce would come off amazed at his own unconscious cerebration." From 1873 to 1875 he was a member of the New York Commission of Appeals, which had been created to help the Court of Appeals dispose of its backlog of undecided cases. It was said that his sixty-eight opinions were "monographs, exhausting the particular subject," and it was doubted "whether in any reports a greater amount of learning is anywhere condensed into an equal number of pages."

Plaintiff is well known as an actress[a], and in the contract between plaintiff and defendant is sometimes referred to as the "Artist." Under the contract, dated August 6, 1965, plaintiff was to play the female lead in defendant's contemplated production of a motion picture entitled "Bloomer Girl." The contract provided that defendant would pay plaintiff a minimum "guaranteed compensation" of $53,571.42 per week for 14 weeks commencing May 23, 1966, for a total of $750,000. Prior to May 1966 defendant decided not to produce the picture and by a letter dated April 4, 1966, it notified plaintiff of that decision and that it would not "comply with our obligations to you under" the written contract.

By the same letter and with the professed purpose "to avoid any damage to you," defendant instead offered to employ plaintiff as the leading actress in another film tentatively entitled "Big Country, Big Man" (hereinafter, "Big Country"). The compensation offered was identical, as were 31 of the 34 numbered provisions or articles of the original contract.[1] Unlike "Bloomer Girl," however, which was to have been a musical production, "Big Country" was a dramatic "western type" movie. "Bloomer Girl" was to have been filmed in California; "Big Country" was to be produced in Australia. Also, certain terms in the proffered contract varied from those of the original.[2] Plaintiff was given one week within which to accept; she

a. Mrs. Parker may be better known to the reader under her professional name, Shirley MacLaine. The following listing from Who's Who in America (1970–1971) may be of interest in connection with the case. "Broadway plays include Me and Juliet, 1953, Pajama Game, 1954; actress movies The Trouble With Henry, 1954, Artists and Models, 1954, Around the World in 80 Days, 1955–56, Hot Spell, 1957, The Matchmaker, 1957, The Sheepman, 1957, Some Came Running, 1958 (Fgn. Press award 1959), Ask Any Girl, 1959 (Silver Bear award as best actress Internat. Berlin Film Festival 1959), Career, 1959, Can-Can, 1959, The Apartment, 1959 (best actress prize Venice Film Festival 1960); Two for the Seesaw, 1962; Irma La Douce, 1963; What A Way to Go! 1964; The Yellow Rolls Royce, 1964; John Goldfarb Please Come Home, 1965; Gambit [1966]; Woman Times Seven [1967]."

1. Among the identical provisions was the following found in the last paragraph of Article 2 of the original contract: "We [defendant] shall not be obligated to utilize your [plaintiff's] services in or in connection with the Photoplay hereunder, our sole obligation, subject to the terms and conditions of this Agreement, being to pay you the guaranteed compensation herein provided for."

2. Article 29 of the original contract specified that plaintiff approved the director already chosen for "Bloomer Girl" and that in case he failed to act as director plaintiff was to have approval rights of any substitute director. Article 31 provided that plaintiff was to have the right of approval of the "Bloomer Girl" dance director, and Article 32 gave her the right of approval of the screenplay.

Defendant's letter of April 4 to plaintiff, which contained both defendant's notice of breach of the "Bloomer Girl" contract and offer of the lead in "Big Country," eliminated or impaired each of those rights. It read in part as follows: "The terms and conditions of our offer of employment are identical to those set forth in the 'BLOOMER GIRL' Agreement, Articles 1 through 34 and Exhibit A to the Agreement, except as follows:

"1. Article 31 of said Agreement will not be included in any contract of employment regarding

did not and the offer lapsed. Plaintiff then commenced this action seeking recovery of the agreed guaranteed compensation.

The complaint sets forth two causes of action. The first is for money due under the contract; the second, based upon the same allegations as the first, is for damages resulting from defendant's breach of contract. Defendant in its answer admits the existence and validity of the contract, that plaintiff complied with all the conditions, covenants and promises and stood ready to complete the performance, and that defendant breached and "anticipatorily repudiated" the contract. It denies, however, that any money is due to plaintiff either under the contract or as a result of its breach, and pleads as an affirmative defense to both causes of action plaintiff's allegedly deliberate failure to mitigate damages, asserting that she unreasonably refused to accept its offer of the leading role in "Big Country."

Plaintiff moved for summary judgment under Code of Civil Procedure section 437c, the motion was granted, and summary judgment for $750,000 plus interest was entered in plaintiff's favor. This appeal by defendant followed. . . .

The general rule is that the measure of recovery by a wrongfully discharged employee is the amount of salary agreed upon for the period of service, less the amount which the employer affirmatively proves the employee has earned or with reasonable effort might have earned from other employment. . . . However, before projected earnings from other employment opportunities not sought or accepted by the discharged employee can be applied in mitigation, the employer must show that the other employment was comparable, or substantially similar, to that of which the employee has been deprived; the employee's rejection of or failure to seek other available employment of a different or inferior kind may not be resorted to in order to mitigate damages. . . .

In the present case defendant has raised no issue of *reasonableness of efforts* by plaintiff to obtain other employment; the sole issue is whether plaintiff's refusal of defendant's substitute offer of "Big

'BIG COUNTRY, BIG MAN' as it is not a musical and it thus will not need a dance director.

"2. In the 'BLOOMER GIRL' agreement, in Articles 29 and 32, you were given certain director and screenplay approvals and you had preapproved certain matters. Since there simply is insufficient time to negotiate with you regarding your choice of director and regarding the screenplay and since you already expressed an interest in performing the role in 'BIG COUNTRY, BIG MAN,' we must exclude from our offer of employment in 'BIG COUNTRY, BIG MAN' any approval rights as are contained in said Articles 29 and 32; however, we shall consult with you respecting the director to be selected to direct the photoplay and will further consult with you with respect to the screenplay and any revisions or changes therein, provided, however, that if we fail to agree . . . the decision of . . . [defendant] with respect to the selection of a director and to revisions and changes in the said screenplay shall be binding upon the parties to said agreement."

Country" may be used in mitigation. Nor, if the "Big Country" offer was of employment different or inferior when compared with the original "Bloomer Girl" employment, is there an issue as to whether or not plaintiff acted reasonably in refusing the substitute offer. Despite defendant's arguments to the contrary, no case cited or which our research has discovered holds or suggests that reasonableness is an element of a wrongfully discharged employee's option to reject, or fail to seek different or inferior employment lest the possible earnings therefrom be charged against him in mitigation of damages.[3]

Applying the foregoing rules to the record in the present case, with all intendments in favor of the party opposing the summary judgment motion—here, defendant—it is clear that the trial court correctly ruled that plaintiff's failure to accept defendant's tendered substitute employment could not be applied in mitigation of damages because the offer of the "Big Country" lead was of employment both different and inferior, and that no factual dispute was presented on that issue. The mere circumstance that "Bloomer Girl" was to be a musical review calling upon plaintiff's talents as a dancer as well as an actress, and was to be produced in the City of Los Angeles, whereas "Big Country" was a straight dramatic role in a "Western Type" story taking place in an opal mine in Australia, demonstrates the difference in kind between the two employments; the female lead as a dramatic actress in a western style motion picture can by no stretch of imagination be considered the equivalent of or substantially similar to the lead in a song-and-dance production. Additionally, the substitute "Big Country" offer proposed to eliminate or impair the director and screenplay approvals accorded to plaintiff under the original "Bloomer Girl" contract (see fn. 2, ante), and thus constituted an offer of inferior employment. No expertise or judicial notice is required in order to hold that the deprivation or infringement of an

3. Instead, in each case the reasonableness referred to was that of the *efforts* of the employee to obtain other employment that was not different or inferior; his right to reject the latter was declared as an unqualified rule of law. Thus, Gonzales v. Internat. Assn. of Machinists, supra, 213 Cal.App.2d 817, 823–824, 29 Cal.Rptr. 190, 194, holds that the trial court correctly instructed the jury that plaintiff union member, a machinist, was required to make "such *efforts* as the average [member of his union] desiring employment would make at that particular time and place" (italics added); but, further, that the court *properly rejected* defendant's *offer of proof of* the *availability of other kinds of employment* at the same or higher pay than plaintiff usually received and all outside the jurisdiction of his union, as plaintiff could not be required to accept different employment or a nonunion job.

In Harris v. Nat. Union, etc., Cooks and Stewards, supra, 116 Cal.App.2d 759, 761, 254 P.2d 673, 676, the issues were stated to be, inter alia, whether comparable employment was open to each plaintiff employee, and if so whether each plaintiff made a *reasonable effort* to secure such employment. It was held that the trial court *properly sustained an objection to an offer to prove a custom of accepting a job in a lower rank* when work in the higher rank was not available, as "The duty of mitigation of damages . . . does not require the plaintiff 'to seek or to accept other employment of a different or inferior kind.' " (p. 764[5], 254 P.2d p. 676.)

employee's rights held under an original employment contract converts the available "other employment" relied upon by the employer to mitigate damages, into inferior employment which the employee need not seek or accept. (See Gonzales v. Internat. Assn. of Machinists, supra, 213 Cal.App.2d 817, 823–824, 29 Cal.Rptr. 190; and fn. 3, ante.) . . .

In view of the determination that defendant failed to present any facts showing the existence of a factual issue with respect to its sole defense—plaintiff's rejection of its substitute employment offer in mitigation of damages—we need not consider plaintiff's further contention that for various reasons, including the provisions of the original contract set forth in footnote 1, ante, plaintiff was excused from attempting to mitigate damages.

The judgment is affirmed.

SULLIVAN, Acting Chief Justice (dissenting). . . . Over the years the courts have employed various phrases to define the type of employment which the employee, upon his wrongful discharge, is under an obligation to accept. Thus in California alone it has been held that he must accept employment which is "substantially similar" (Lewis v. Protective Security Life Ins. Co. (1962) 208 Cal.App.2d 582, 584, 25 Cal.Rptr. 213; De La Falaise v. Gaumont-British P. Corp. (1940) 39 Cal.App.2d 461, 469, 103 P.2d 447); "comparable employment" (Erler v. Five Points Motors, Inc. (1967) 249 Cal.App. 2d 560, 562, 57 Cal.Rptr. 516; Harris v. Nat. Union, etc., Cooks and Stewards (1953) 116 Cal.App.2d 759, 761, 254 P.2d 673); employment "in the same general line of the first employment" (Rotter v. Stationers Corporation (1960) 186 Cal.App.2d 170, 172, 8 Cal.Rptr. 690, 691); "equivalent to his prior position" (De Angeles v. Roos Bros., Inc. (1966) 244 Cal.App.2d 434, 443, 52 Cal.Rptr. 783); "employment in a similar capacity" (Silva v. McCoy (1968) 259 Cal. App.2d 256, 260, 66 Cal.Rptr. 364); employment which is "not . . . of a different or inferior kind. . . ." (Gonzales v. Internat. Assn. of Machinists (1963) 213 Cal.App.2d 817, 822, 29 Cal. Rptr. 190, 193.)

For reasons which are unexplained, the majority cite several of these cases yet select from among the various judicial formulations which contain one particular phrase, "Not of a different or inferior kind," with which to analyze this case. I have discovered no historical or theoretical reason to adopt this phrase, which is simply a negative restatement of the affirmative standards set out in the above cases, as the exclusive standard. Indeed, its emergence is an example of the dubious phenomenon of the law responding not to rational judicial choice or changing social conditions, but to unrecognized changes in the language of opinions or legal treatises. However, the phrase is a serviceable one and my concern is not with its use as the standard but rather with what I consider its distortion.

The relevant language excuses acceptance only of employment which is of a *different kind.* . . . It has never been the law that the mere existence of *differences between two jobs in the same field* is sufficient, as a matter of law, to excuse an employee wrongfully discharged from one from accepting the other in order to mitigate damages. Such an approach would effectively eliminate any obligation of an employee to attempt to minimize damage arising from a wrongful discharge. The only alternative job offer an employee would be required to accept would be an offer of his former job by his former employer.

Although the majority appear to hold that there was a difference "in kind" between the employment offered plaintiff in "Bloomer Girl" and that offered in "Big Country", an examination of the opinion makes crystal clear that the majority merely point out differences between the two *films* (an obvious circumstance) and then apodictically assert that these constitute a difference in the *kind* of *employment.* The entire rationale of the majority boils down to this: that the "*mere circumstances*" that "Bloomer Girl" was to be a musical review while "Big Country" was a straight drama "demonstrates the difference in kind" since a female lead in a western is not "the equivalent of or substantially similar to" a lead in a musical. This is merely attempting to prove the proposition by repeating it. It shows that the vehicles for the display of the star's talents are different but it does not prove that her employment as a star in such vehicles is of necessity different *in kind* and either inferior or superior.

I believe that the approach taken by the majority (a superficial listing of differences with no attempt to assess their significance) may subvert a valuable legal doctrine.[1] The inquiry in cases such as this should not be whether differences between the two jobs exist (there will always be differences) but whether the differences which are present are substantial enough to constitute differences in the *kind* of employment or, alternatively, whether they render the substitute work employment of an *inferior kind.* . . .

I remain convinced that the relevant question in such cases is whether or not a particular contract provision is so significant that its omission create employment of an inferior kind. This question is, of course, intimately bound up in what I consider the ultimate issue: whether or not the employee acted reasonably. This will generally involve a factual inquiry to ascertain the importance of the particular contract term and a process of weighing the absence of that term

1. The values of the doctrine of mitigation of damages in this context are that it minimizes the unnecessary personal and social (e. g., nonproductive use of labor, litigation) costs of contractual failure. If a wrongfully discharged employee can, through his own action and without suffering financial or psychological loss in the process, reduce the damages accruing from the breach of contract, the most sensible policy is to require him to do so. I fear the majority opinion will encourage precisely opposite conduct.

against the countervailing advantages of the alternate employment. In the typical case, this will mean that summary judgment must be withheld. . . .

NOTES

(1) *Same Employer.* The court lays no stress on the fact that the offer of substitute employment came from the employer who had broken the contract in suit. Might this fact ever be significant? Would this be affected by the circumstances of the breach? Would it make a difference if the offer of substitute employment were conditioned on the injured party's surrender of rights under the old contract? See Gilson v. F. S. Royster Guano Co., 1 F.2d 82 (3d Cir. 1924).

(2) *Problem.* Seller agreed to deliver lumber to Buyer in installments, payment for each installment to be made 90 days after delivery. After the delivery of the first installment, Seller wrongfully refused to deliver the remainder of the lumber on credit, but offered to supply it for cash at the same price less a discount sufficient to offset the interest for 90 days. Although the market for lumber had risen substantially, Buyer insisted upon his rights under the contract and refused to buy for cash from Seller. Can Buyer recover damages for Seller's breach based upon the difference between contract and market value? See Lawrence v. Porter, 63 F. 62 (6th Cir. 1894).

(3) *Problem.* The Public Utilities Commission of Hibbing advertised for bids for a propane-air gas plant. Minnesota Limited bid $137,560 and was awarded the contract. The Commission then asked Minnesota Limited if it would agree to cancellation of the contract and, when the response was in the negative, the Commission informed Minnesota Limited that it "revoked" its award and intended to call for new bids under altered specifications. Does Minnesota Limited run any risk if it bids in response to a second invitation? Does the effect of a second bid on Minnesota Limited's rights depend on whether that bid is the lowest? See Minnesota Ltd., Inc. v. Public Utilities Comm. of Hibbing, 296 Minn. 316, 208 N.W.2d 284 (1973).

CONTRACTS FOR THE SALE OF GOODS

The limitation of avoidability is of particular importance in connection with contracts for the sale of goods since, in a free enterprise economy, it is assumed that the injured party generally has available to him a market on which he can arrange a substitute transaction. If the seller fails to deliver goods, the assumption is that the buyer can go into the market and "cover" by obtaining substitute goods, so that his damages should be based on the difference between a presumably greater price that he will have to pay on the market and the lesser contract price. See UCC 2–712. If the buyer fails to take and pay for goods, the assumption is that the seller can go into the market and resell to a substitute buyer, so that his damages should be based on the difference between the presumably greater contract price and a lesser price he will receive on the market. See UCC 2–706.

For the injured party who fails to take advantage of the availability of a substitute transaction on the market, the limitation of avoidability results in a formula based on the difference between the contract price and the market price at which he could have arranged a hypothetical substitute transaction. If, when the seller fails to deliver goods, the buyer fails to go into the market and "cover," his damages are based on "the difference between the market price . . . and the contract price." UCC 2–713. If, when the buyer fails to take and pay for goods, the seller fails to go into the market and resell, his damages are based on "the difference between the market price . . . and the unpaid contract price." UCC 2–708. On proof of market price, see UCC 2–723, 2–724.

In Orester v. Dayton Rubber Co., 228 N.Y. 134, 126 N.E. 510 (1920), the court discussed these and related principles of sales law in the context of the Dayton Rubber Co.'s breach of a contract to supply the "Dayton pneumatic tire" to its distributor in Syracuse. "In the case of sales, where the articles may be purchased in the market, the value of the contract to the purchaser is the difference between the price at which in like quantities they may be bought at the time and place of delivery and the price which he would have had to pay under the contract. This rule assumes, however, the possibility of such a purchase in the market. Then the injured party may obtain the articles, but at a greater price. If this is made good, he is compensated. But it may be none can be bought. Then the rule is inapplicable. Some other method by which his loss may be fixed must be used. . . . Such is the case before us. The plaintiff could not purchase the tires from others in Syracuse. He himself was the sole source of supply. . . . If there was a market elsewhere at which tires in the quantity desired by the plaintiff could be freely purchased the damages would be the difference between the contract price and the price at that market plus the transportation charges to Syracuse. . . . Possibly there was such a market, although, if other buyers from the defendant were limited as was he to sales in specified localities, this may be doubtful. In the absence of such a foreign market, if the plaintiff might purchase a substitute tire, equally available for his reasonable purposes, then his damages would be the difference between the market price of such substitute and the contract price. . . . It should be remarked, however, that this contract contemplated building up a business for the sale of the 'Dayton pneumatic tire' and creating a demand for that particular tire. Whether another tire, even equally as good, but sold under another trade-name, would be a satisfactory substitute to a dealer in Dayton tires, may be at least doubtful. . . . Finally, if none of these tests are practicable, another must be adopted. . . . Here the tires were purchased to be resold at a profit. This profit, if reasonably certain, may be said to measure the value of the contract to the plaintiff. It was this that he lost by the default of the defendant. Not the gross profit, however, which is what the jury was permitted to allow. What the plaintiff might have made had the contract been carried out was this gross profit less the expenses of the business properly chargeable to the sale of Dayton tire."

The details of the Code rules in this area have occasioned confusion and criticism. Consideration of these rules as they apply to a repudiation before the time for performance will be postponed until the material on anticipatory repudiation is reached in Chapter 8, Section 4. The following materials consider them as they apply to a breach by nonperformance.

NOTES

(1) *Symmetry.* As has just been suggested, there is a certain symmetry between the remedies of the seller and those of the buyer. Compare UCC 2–706(1) with 2–712 and UCC 2–708(1) with 2–713. There are, however, some significant differences. Note, for example, that in dealing with the seller's damages, UCC 2–708 speaks of "the market price at the time and the place for tender." However, in dealing with the buyer's damages, UCC 2–713 picks "the market price at the time when the buyer learned of the breach" and "as of the place for tender or, in cases of rejection after arrival or revocation of acceptance, as of the place of arrival."

Suppose that the seller is to tender the goods in Sellersville by putting them in the hands of a carrier, such as a railroad, that will receive them on the buyer's behalf and transport them to Buyersville, where the buyer will then receive and inspect them. If the goods conform to the contract, but the buyer wrongfully rejects them, how is market price to be determined for the purpose of calculating the seller's damages? On what hypothetical substitute transaction is this rule based? Does the rule make sense? If goods do not conform to the contract, and the buyer rightfully rejects them, how is market price to be determined for the purpose of calculating the buyer's damages? On what hypothetical substitute transaction is this rule based? Does this rule make more sense? On remedies under the Code in general and on these questions in particular, see J. White & R. Summers, Law Under the Uniform Commercial Code § 6–4 (2d ed. 1980); Peters, Remedies for Breach of Contracts Relating to the Sale of Goods Under the Uniform Commercial Code: A Roadmap for Article Two, 73 Yale L.J. 199, 270–71 (1963).

(2) *Lost Volume (Reprise).* A seller who could have arranged a substitute transaction to dispose of the goods elsewhere but does not do so, may still argue that he should not be limited to damages based on market price but should have his lost profit on the ground that such a sale would have resulted in lost volume. See UCC 2–708(2). The issues raised by such a contention have already been discussed in connection with the Neri case, p. 576 supra, in the context of the seller who actually makes such a sale and then claims his lost profit on the ground that that sale resulted in lost volume. See Note 1, p. 580 supra.

(3) *Specific Relief.* The possibility of specific relief for the buyer in the form of a decree of specific performance under UCC 2–716(1) has already been discussed. See Chapter 1, Section 1. In some circumstances the buyer may also obtain specific relief through an action to replevy the goods

under UCC 2–716(3). Can he do so if he can cover? What would you advise an aggrieved buyer to do following breach in order to lay the foundation for a possible action for replevin under this section? Would Dunlop's distributor have been able to replevy the tires that Dunlop had contracted to deliver? (Does it appear that they were "identified" under UCC 2–501(1)?)

In some circumstances the seller may also obtain what amounts to specific relief through an action for the price under UCC 2–709(1)(b). Can he do so if he can resell? What would you advise an aggrieved seller to do following breach in order to lay the foundation for a possible action for the price under this section?

ILLINOIS CENTRAL RAILROAD CO. v. CRAIL, 281 U.S. 57 (1930). [A coal dealer in Minneapolis purchased, while in transit, a carload of coal weighing at shipment 88,700 pounds. On delivery there was a shortage of 5,500 pounds, for which the carrier was liable under a federal statute to the extent of "the full actual loss, damage or injury." The coal was added to the dealer's stock for resale, but the shortage did not interfere with the maintenance of his usual stock. He lost no sales by reason of it and purchased no coal to replace the shortage, except in carload lots. He regularly purchased similar coal in carload lots of 60,000 pounds or more for $5.50 per ton plus freight. The market price in Minneapolis for like coal sold at retail in less than carload lots was $13.00 per ton, including $3.30 freight. The coal dealer sued the carrier.[a] From a judgment awarding him damages based on the retail price, the carrier appealed.]

Mr. Justice STONE.[b] . . . [R]espondent contends, as was held below, that the established measure of damage for non-delivery of a shipment of merchandise is the sum required to replace the exact amount of the shortage at the stipulated time and place of delivery,

a. From these figures, it is evident that the difference in damages based on the two markets was less than twelve dollars. See Crail v. Illinois Central R. Co., 21 F.2d 836, 842 (D.C.Minn.1927). The railroad's petition for writ of certiorari explained: "While the amount involved is small the effect of the judgment is far reaching and the case most important, not alone to your petitioner but to all carriers and shippers. . . . The decision of this case by this court will settle the troublesome, important, and constantly arising question as to what is the proper measure of damages in a case where a part of a carload of coal is lost in transit. . . . This has been an ever present source of dispute and controversy between the carriers and shippers. . . . In fact the carriers and shippers all over the country are awaiting the decision of this case by this court. Hundreds of cases have been built up and will not be disposed of until your Honors pass on and decide this case." Petition of Illinois Central Railroad Co., pp. 2–4 (1929).

b. Harlan Fiske Stone (1872–1946) both taught and practiced law after his graduation from law school. He served as dean of the Columbia School of Law from 1910 to 1923. His writing up to this time was largely in the field of equity. In 1924 he was appointed Attorney General of the United States. In 1925 he was appointed to the Supreme Court of the United States and in 1941 he succeeded Charles Evans Hughes as Chief Justice.

which, in this case, would be its retail value, and that convenience and the necessity for a uniform rule require its application here. This contention ignores the basic principle underlying common law remedies that they shall afford only compensation for the injury suffered . . ., and leaves out of account the language of the amendment, which likewise gives only a right of recovery for "actual loss." The rule urged by respondents was applied below in literal accordance with its conventional statement. As so stated, when applied to cases as they usually arise, it is a convenient and accurate method of arriving at an amount of recovery which is compensatory. As so stated, it would have been applicable here if there had been a failure to deliver the entire carload of coal, since the wholesale price, at which a full carload could have been procured at point of destination, would have afforded full compensation . . ., or, in some circumstances, if respondent had been under any constraint to purchase less than a carload lot to repair his loss or carry on his business, for in that event the measure of his loss would have been the retail market cost of the necessary replacement. Haskell v. Hunter, 23 Mich. 305, 309. But in the actual circumstances the cost of replacing the exact shortage at retail price was not the measure of the loss, since it was capable of replacement and was, in fact, replaced in the course of respondent's business from purchases made in carload lots at wholesale market price without added expense. There is no greater inconvenience in the application of the one standard of value than the other and we perceive no advantage to be gained from an adherence to a rigid uniformity, which would justify sacrificing the reason of the rule, to its letter. The test of market value is at best but a convenient means of getting at the loss suffered. It may be discarded and other more accurate means resorted to if, for special reasons, it is not exact or otherwise not applicable. . . .

Reversed.

NOTES

(1) *Actual or Hypothetical Substitution?* If the injured party has arranged an actual substitute transaction for a price *less* favorable than the market price, he may nevertheless recover damages under the Code based on the price in that actual transaction and is not limited to damages based on market price.[a] The seller can do this if his substitute transaction comes within the requirements for resale under UCC 2–706. The buyer can do this if his substitute transaction comes within the requirements for cover under UCC 2–712.[b]

a. His right to do this before the Code was less than clear. See King v. D. E. Ryan Co., 179 Minn. 385, 229 N.W. 348 (1930). The right of an injured party under a contract for the sale of real property to do this is, at most, doubtful. See Aboud v. Adams, 84 N.M. 683, 507 P.2d 430 (1973). Restatement Second, § 350 (2), however, states the right as generally applicable to all contracts.

b. Where the buyer makes frequent purchases, as in the Crail case, and the price fluctuates, how is a court to determine which goods are "in substitution for those due from the seller"?

Whether the reverse is true is less clear. What if, as in the Crail case, the injured party has arranged an actual substitute transaction for a price *more* favorable than the market price? Can he still recover damages based on the market price? Or is he limited to damages based on the actual substitute transaction? There seems to be merit in Chief Justice Stone's assertion in the Crail case that it is a "basic principle underlying common law remedies that they shall afford only compensation for the injury suffered," and that the "test of market value is at best but a convenient means of getting the loss suffered." Furthermore, Comment 5 to UCC 2–713 says that that section "provides a remedy which is completely alternative to cover . . . and applies only when and to the extent that the buyer has not covered." See also UCC 2–711.

Nevertheless, a contrary view has been advanced on the grounds that the Code imposes no such restriction on the seller and that "a non-restrictive reading of the various remedies sections to preserve full options to use or ignore substitute transactions as a measure of damages makes more sense." Peters, Remedies for Breach of Contracts Relating to the Sale of Goods Under the Uniform Commercial Code: A Roadmap for Article Two, 73 Yale L.J. 199, 260 (1963). For a contrary view, see J. White & R. Summers, Law Under the Uniform Commercial Code § 6–4 (2d ed. 1980).

(2) *Problem.* Seller contracts with Buyer to deliver goods on a specified date for $100,000. Buyer makes a contract to resell the goods to another purchaser at $125,000. Seller fails to deliver. The market price of similar goods at and immediately after the delivery date is $110,000. Since Buyer's resale contract does not require him to deliver for six months, Buyer waits and does not go into the market for six months, by which time the market price has dropped to $90,000. How much should Buyer recover? Suppose that the market price had risen to $120,000 during Buyer's delay. How much should Buyer recover? See Farnsworth, Legal Remedies for Breach of Contract, 70 Colum.L.Rev. 1145, 1190 n. 190 (1970).

(3) *Problem.* Seller contracts with Buyer to deliver goods on a specified date for $100,000. Buyer then makes a contract to resell the goods to another purchaser for $125,000. Seller fails to deliver. The market price of similar goods at and immediately after the delivery date is $130,000. How much should Buyer recover? Would your answer be different if Buyer, in making his resale contract had protected himself by reserving the power to cancel on breach by Seller? (Would the circumstances of Seller's breach be relevant in that case?) Would your answer be different if Buyer had not so protected himself but his purchaser had released him from his obligation on the resale contract? Would your answer be different if Buyer had made no resale contract? See Farnsworth, Legal Remedies for Breach of Contract, 70 Colum.L.Rev. 1145, 1190 n. 189 (1970); Simon & Novak, Limiting the Buyer's Market Damages to Lost Profits: A Challenge to the Enforceability of Market Contracts, 92 Harv.L.Rev. 1395 (1979); Iron Trade Products Co. v. Wilkoff, p. 798 infra.

AVOIDABILITY AND COST TO REMEDY DEFECT

Cases of defective, as distinguished from merely incomplete, performance may raise difficult problems of avoidability. If the breach consists merely of incomplete performance, the injured party can usually arrange to have someone else complete the work at less than the loss in value to him. The limitation of avoidability then has the effect of restricting him to damages based on that lesser cost to complete the work rather than on the loss in value. Suppose, for example, that a builder breaks a contract to construct a factory by failing to finish the roof, making the factory unusable. The owner cannot recover the relatively enormous loss resulting from his inability to use the factory but is relegated to the relatively small amount that it will cost him to get another builder to finish the roof.

Trouble may arise, however, if the performance is defective rather than merely incomplete. In that case, part of the cost to remedy the defect and complete performance as agreed will probably be the cost of undoing some of the work already done. The total cost to remedy the defect may then exceed the loss in value to the injured party so that an award based on that cost would to that extent be a windfall. The following case involves this situation.

NOTE

The Case of the Inapposite Analogy. Freund made a contract with Washington Square Press under which the Press was to publish his book on modern drama on a royalty basis. Freund was paid a nonreturnable $2,000 "advance." After Freund delivered his manuscript, the Press merged with another publisher and refused to publish his book. Freund sued the Press and recovered $10,000 as the amount that publication would have cost Freund. *Held:* Damages reduced from $10,000 to six cents, with costs to the plaintiff. "[T]he analogy . . . to the construction contract situation was inapposite. In the typical construction contract, the owner agrees to pay money or other consideration to a builder and expects, under the contract, to receive a completed building in return. The value of the promised performance to the owner is the properly constructed building. In this case, unlike the typical construction contract, the value to plaintiff of the promised performance—publication—was a percentage of sales of the books published and not the books themselves. Had the plaintiff contracted for the printing, binding and delivery of a number of hardbound copies of his manuscript, to be sold or disposed of as he wished, then perhaps the construction analogy, and measurement of damages by the cost of replacement or completion, would have some application. Here, however, the specific value to plaintiff of the promised publication was the royalties he stood to receive from defendant's sales of the published book." Since the amount of royalties was not proved with sufficient certainty, the plaintiff could recover only nominal damages. Freund v. Washington Square Press, 34 N.Y. 2d 379, 357 N.Y.S.2d 857, 314 N.E.2d 419 (1974).

JACOB & YOUNGS v. KENT

Court of Appeals of New York, 1921.
230 N.Y. 239, 129 N.E. 889, 23 A.L.R. 1429.

CARDOZO, J. The plaintiff built a country residence for the defendant at a cost of upwards of $77,000, and now sues to recover a balance of $3,483.46, remaining unpaid. The work of construction ceased in June, 1914, and the defendant then began to occupy the dwelling. There was no complaint of defective performance until March, 1915. One of the specifications for the plumbing work provides that "all wrought iron pipe must be well galvanized, lap welded pipe of the grade known as 'standard pipe' of Reading manufacture." The defendant learned in March, 1915, that some of the pipe, instead of being made in Reading, was the product of other factories. The plaintiff was accordingly directed by the architect to do the work anew. The plumbing was then encased within the walls except in a few places where it had to be exposed. Obedience to the order meant more than the substitution of other pipe. It meant the demolition at great expense of substantial parts of the completed structure. The plaintiff left the work untouched, and asked for a certificate that the final payment was due. Refusal of the certificate was followed by this suit.[a]

The evidence sustains a finding that the omission of the prescribed brand of pipe was neither fraudulent nor willful. It was the result of the oversight and inattention of the plaintiff's sub-contractor. Reading pipe is distinguished from Cohoes pipe and other brands only by the name of the manufacturer stamped upon it at intervals of between six and seven feet. Even the defendant's architect, though he inspected the pipe upon arrival, failed to notice the discrepancy. The plaintiff tried to show that the brands installed, though made by other manufacturers, were the same in quality, in appearance, in market value and in cost as the brand stated in the contract—that they were, indeed, the same thing, though manufactured in another place. The evidence was excluded, and a verdict directed for the defendant. The Appellate Division reversed, and granted a new trial.[b]

We think the evidence, if admitted, would have supplied some basis for the inference that the defect was insignificant in its relation

a. The record on appeal indicates that, under the contract, payments were to be made monthly as the work progressed, on the certificate of the architect in an amount which "in his judgment" represented the amount due less 15% to be withheld. The specifications attached to the contract made the architect's decision "as to the character of any material or labor furnished by the Contractor . . . final and conclusive." Furthermore, "Any work furnished by the Contractor, the material or workmanship of which is defective or which is not fully in accordance with the drawings and specifications, in every respect, will be rejected and is to be immediately torn down, removed and remade or replaced in accordance with the drawings and specifications, whenever discovered. . . . The Owner will have the option at all times to allow the defective or improper work to stand and to receive from the Contractor a sum of money equivalent to the difference in value of the work as performed and as herein specified." Record pp. 98–108.

b. The two paragraphs that follow discuss an issue that will not be reached until later in this book. The same is true of the dissent. It is the last major paragraph of Cardozo's opinion that is of interest at present. See Note 1 following the opinion.

to the project. The courts never say that one who makes a contract fills the measure of his duty by less than full performance. They do say, however, that an omission, both trivial and innocent, will sometimes be atoned for by allowance of the resulting damage, and will not always be the breach of a condition to be followed by a forfeiture (Spence v. Ham, 163 N.Y. 220, 57 N.E. 412; Woodward v. Fuller, 80 N.Y. 312; Glacius v. Black, 67 N.Y. 563, 566; Bowen v. Kimbell, 203 Mass. 364, 370, 89 N.E. 542.) The distinction is akin to that between dependent and independent promises, or between promises and conditions (Anson on Contracts, Corbin's Ed., sec. 367: 2 Williston on Contracts, sec. 842). Some promises are so plainly independent that they can never by fair construction be conditions of one another. (Rosenthal Paper Co. v. Nat. Folding Box & Paper Co., 226 N.Y. 313, 123 N.E. 766; Bogardus v. N. Y. Life Ins. Co., 101 N.Y. 328, 4 N.E. 522.) Others are so plainly dependent that they must always be conditions. Others, though dependent and thus conditions when there is departure in point of substance, will be viewed as independent and collateral when the departure is insignificant (2 Williston on Contracts, secs. 841, 842; Eastern Forge Co. v. Corbin, 182 Mass. 590, 592, 66 N.E. 419; Robinson v. Mollett, L.R., 7 Eng. & Ir.App. 802, 814; Miller v. Benjamin, 142 N.Y. 613, 37 N.E. 631). Considerations partly of justice and partly of presumable intention are to tell us whether this or that promise shall be placed in one class or another. The simple and the uniform will call for different remedies from the multifarious and the intricate. The margin of departure within the range of normal expectation upon a sale of common chattels will vary from the margin to be expected upon a contract for the construction of a mansion or a "skyscraper." There will be harshness sometimes and oppression in the implication of a condition when the thing upon which labor has been expended is incapable of surrender because united to the land, and equity and reason in the implication of a like condition when the subject-matter, if defective, is in shape to be returned. From the conclusions that promises may not be treated as dependent to the extent of their uttermost minutiae without a sacrifice of justice, the progress is a short one to the conclusion that they may not be so treated without a perversion of intention. Intention not otherwise revealed may be presumed to hold in contemplation the reasonable and probable. If something else is in view, it must not be left to implication. There will be no assumption of a purpose to visit venial faults with oppressive retribution.

Those who think more of symmetry and logic in the development of legal rules than of practical adaptation to the attainment of a just result will be troubled by a classification where the lines of division are so wavering and blurred. Something, doubtless, may be said on the score of consistency and certainty in favor of a stricter standard. The courts have balanced such considerations against those of equity and fairness, and found the latter to be the weightier. The decisions in this state commit us to the liberal view, which is making its way, nowadays, in jurisdictions slow to welcome it (Dakin & Co. v. Lee, 1916, 1 K.B. 566, 579). Where the line is to be drawn between the important and the trivial cannot be settled by a formula. "In the nature of the case precise boundaries are impossible" (2 Williston on Contracts, sec. 841). The same omission may take on one aspect or another according to its setting. Substitution of equivalents may not have the same significance in fields of art on the one side and in those of mere utility on the other. Nowhere will change be tolerated, however, if it is so dominant or pervasive as in any real or substantial measure to frustrate the purpose of the contract (Crouch v. Gutmann, 134 N.Y. 45, 51, 31 N.E. 271). There is no general license to install whatever, in the builder's judgment, may be regarded as "just as good" (Easthampton L. & C., Ltd. v. Worthington, 186 N.Y. 407, 412, 79 N.E. 323). The question is one of degree, to be answered, if there is doubt, by the triers of the facts (Crouch v. Gutmann; Woodward v. Fuller, supra), and, if the inferences are certain, by the judges of the law (Easthampton L. & C. Co., Ltd. v. Worthington, supra). We must weigh the purpose to be served, the desire to be gratified, the excuse for deviation from the letter, the cruelty of enforced adherence. Then only can we tell whether literal fulfillment is to be implied by law as a condition. This is not to say that the parties are not free by apt and certain words to effectuate a purpose that performance of every term shall be a condition of recovery. That question is not here. This is merely to say that the law will be slow to impute the purpose, in the silence of the parties, where the significance of the default is grievously out of proportion to the oppression of the forfeiture. The willful transgressor must accept the penalty of his transgression (Schultze v. Goodstein, 180 N.Y. 248, 251, 73 N.E. 21; Desmond-Dunne Co. v. Friedman-Doscher Co., 162 N.Y. 486, 490, 56 N.E. 995). For him there is no occasion to mitigate the rigor of implied conditions. The transgressor whose default is unintentional and trivial may hope for mercy if he will offer atonement for his wrong (Spence v. Ham, supra).

In the circumstances of this case, we think the measure of the allowance is not the cost of replacement, which would be great, but the difference in value, which would be either nominal or nothing. Some of the exposed sections might perhaps have been replaced at moderate expense. The defendant did not limit his demand to them, but treated the plumbing as a unit to be corrected from cellar to roof. In point of fact, the plaintiff never reached the stage at which evidence of the extent of the allowance became necessary. The trial court had excluded evidence that the defect was unsubstantial, and in view of that ruling there was no occasion for the plaintiff to go farther with an offer of proof. We think, however, that the offer, if it had been made, would not of necessity have been defective because directed to difference in value. It is true that in most cases the cost of replacement is the measure (Spence v. Ham, supra). The owner is entitled to the money which will permit him to complete, unless the cost of completion is grossly and unfairly out of proportion to the good to be attained. When that is true, the measure is the difference in value. Specifications call, let us say, for a foundation built of granite quarried in Vermont. On the completion of the building, the owner learns that through the blunder of a subcontractor part of the foundation has been built of granite of the same quality quarried in New Hampshire. The measure of allowance is not the cost of reconstruction. "There may be omissions of that which could not afterwards be supplied exactly as called for by the contract without taking down the building to its foundations and at the same time the omission may not affect the value of the building for use or otherwise, except so slightly as to be hardly appreciable" (Handy v. Bliss, 204 Mass. 513, 519, 90 N.E. 864. Cf. Foeller v. Heintz, 137 Wis. 169, 178, 118 N.W. 543; Oberlies v. Bullinger, 132 N.Y. 598, 601, 30 N.E. 999; 2 Williston on Contracts, sec. 805, p. 1541). The rule that gives a remedy in cases of substantial performance with compensation for defects of trivial or inappreciable importance, has been developed by the courts as an instrument of justice. The measure of the allowance must be shaped to the same end.

The order should be affirmed, and judgment absolute directed in favor of the plaintiff upon the stipulation, with costs in all courts.

McLAUGHLIN, J. (dissenting). I dissent. The plaintiff did not perform its contract. Its failure to do so was either intentional or due to gross neglect which, under the uncontradicted facts, amounted to the same thing, nor did it make any proof of the cost of compliance, where compliance was possible. . . .

I am of the opinion the trial court was right in directing a verdict for the defendant. The plaintiff agreed that all the pipe used should be of the Reading Manufacturing Company. Only about two-fifths of it, so far as appears, was of that kind. If more were used, then the burden of proving that fact was upon the plaintiff, which it could easily have done, since it knew where the pipe was obtained. The question of substantial performance of a contract of the character of the one under consideration depends in no small degree upon the good faith of the contractor. If the plaintiff had intended to, and had complied with the terms of the contract except as to minor omissions, due to inadvertence, then he might be allowed to recover the contract price, less the amount necessary to fully compensate the defendant for damages caused by such omissions. Woodward v. Fuller, 80 N.Y. 312; Nolan v. Whitney, 88 N.Y. 648. But that is not this case. It installed between 2,000 and 2,500 feet of pipe, of which only 1,000 feet at most complied with the contract. No explanation was given why pipe called for by the contract was not used, nor was any effort made to show what it would cost to remove the pipe of other manufacturers and install that of the Reading Manufacturing Company. The defendant had a right to contract for what he wanted. He had a right before making payment to get what the contract called for. It is no answer to this suggestion to say that the pipe put in was just as good as that made by the Reading Manufacturing Company, or that the difference in value between such pipe and the pipe made by the Reading Manufacturing Company would be either "nominal or nothing." Defendant contracted for pipe made by the Reading Manufacturing Company. What his reason was for requiring this kind of pipe is of no importance. He wanted that and was entitled to it. . . . The rule, therefore, of substantial performance, with damages for unsubstantial omissions, has no application. (Crouch v. Gutmann, 134 N.Y. 45, 31 N.E. 271; Spence v. Ham, 163 N.Y. 220, 57 N.E. 412.) . . .

HISCOCK, CH. J., HOGAN and CRANE, JJ., concur with CARDOZO, J.; POUND and ANDREWS, JJ., concur with McLAUGHLIN, J.

Order affirmed, etc.

NOTES

(1) *Substantial Performance.* Kent promised to pay Jacob & Youngs if it built him a house as specified. Building the house as specified was therefore a condition of Jacob & Youngs' right to recover from Kent on that promise. In the first part of the opinion, Cardozo explains why Jacob & Youngs can recover from Kent on that promise in spite of the fact that it did not strictly fulfill that requirement. As to this, three judges dissent. This notion of substantial, as opposed to strict, performance and the law of conditions in general are taken up in Chapter 8, Performance and Breach. For present purposes, we are concerned only with the second part of Cardozo's opinion, in which he considers how much, if anything, should be deducted from that recovery as Kent's damages. (To remove the problem of substantial performance from the picture, assume that Kent had paid Jacob & Youngs in full and was suing them for damages.)

(2) *Determining Diminution in Value.* Do you agree that the "difference in value" *to Kent* "would be either nominal or nothing"? It may be that the difference between the *market price* of a house with Reading pipe and one with Cohoes pipe is zero, because buyers of houses consider the two kinds of pipe to be of equal value *to them.* But why should *Kent's* recovery be limited by this? [c]

Diminution in market price is, however, useful in fixing a lower limit for recovery, since the value of property to its owner is usually no less than the net price at which he could sell it. Similarly, cost to remedy the defect

c. "If a proud householder, who plans to live out his days in the home of his dreams, orders a new roof of red barrel tile and the roofer instead installs a purple one, money damages for the reduced value of his house may not be enough to offset the strident offense to aesthetic sensibilities, continuing over the life of the roof." Gory Associated Industries v. Jupiter Roofing & Sheet Metal, 358 So.2d 93, 95 (Fla.App.1978).

is useful in fixing an upper limit for recovery since, even if that cost is less than the loss in value to him, the lesser sum will enable him to complete and avoid any loss in value.

The problem of determining loss in value is most acute when, as in the principal case, there is great disparity between the minimum of diminution in market price and the maximum of cost to remedy the defect. Which better approximates loss in value? Although the opinion gives us no insight into why Kent might have specified Reading rather than some other brand of pipe, it does suggest one reason for the disparity between the maximum and minimum. Does that reason suggest which better approximates loss in value? (If a very large fraction of the disparity represents the cost of undoing and redoing the work, how large a fraction represents the loss in value to Kent?)

GROVES v. JOHN WUNDER CO.

Supreme Court of Minnesota, 1939.
205 Minn. 163, 286 N.W. 235.

STONE, J. Action for breach of contract. Plaintiff got judgment for a little over $15,000. Sorely disappointed by that sum, he appeals.

In August, 1927 S. J. Groves & Sons Company, a corporation (hereinafter mentioned simply as Groves), owned a tract of 24 acres of Minneapolis suburban real estate. It was served or easily could be reached by railroad trackage. It is zoned as heavy industrial property. But for lack of development of the neighborhood its principal value thus far may have been in the deposit of sand and gravel which it carried. The Groves company had a plant on the premises for excavating and screening the gravel. Nearby defendant owned and was operating a similar plant.

In August, 1927, Groves and defendant made the involved contract. For the most part it was a lease from Groves, as lessor, to defendant, as lessee; its term seven years. Defendant agreed to remove the sand and gravel and to leave the property "at a uniform grade, substantially the same as the grade now existing at the roadway . . . on said premises, and that in stripping the overburden . . . it will use said overburden for the purpose of maintaining and establishing said grade."

Under the contract defendant got the Groves screening plant. The transfer thereof and the right to remove the sand and gravel made the consideration moving from Groves to defendant, except that defendant incidentally got rid of Groves as a competitor. On defendant's part it paid Groves $105,000. So that from the outset, on Groves' part the contract was executed except for defendant's right to continue using the property for the stated term. (Defendant had a right to renewal which it did not exercise.)

Defendant breached the contract deliberately. It removed from the premises only "the richest and best of the gravel" and wholly failed, according to the findings, "to perform and comply with the terms, conditions, and provisions of said lease . . . with respect to the condition in which the surface of the demised premises was required to be left." Defendant surrendered the premises, not substantially at the grade required by the contract "nor at any uniform grade." Instead, the ground was "broken, rugged and uneven." Plaintiff sues as assignee and successor in right of Groves.

As the contract was construed below, the finding is that to complete its performance 288,495 cubic yards of overburden would need to be excavated, taken from the premises, and deposited elsewhere. The reasonable cost of doing that was found to be upwards of $60,000. But, if defendant had left the premises at the uniform grade required by the lease, the reasonable value of the property on the determinative date would have been only $12,160. The judgment was for that sum,[a] including interest, thereby nullifying plaintiff's claim that cost of completing the contract rather than difference in value of the land was the measure of damages. The gauge of damage adopted by the decision was the difference between the market value of plaintiff's land in the condition it was [in] when the contract was made and what it would have been if defendant had performed. The one question for us arises upon plaintiff's assertion that he was entitled, not to that difference in value, but to the reasonable cost to him of doing the work called for by the contract which defendant left undone.

1. Defendant's breach of contract was wilful. There was nothing of good faith about it. Hence, that the decision below handsomely rewards bad faith and deliberate breach of contract is obvious. That is not allowable. Here the rule is well settled, and has been since Elliott v. Caldwell, 43 Minn. 357, 45 N.W. 845, 9 L.R.A. 52, that, where the contractor wilfully and fraudulently varies from the terms of a construction contract, he cannot sue thereon and have the benefit of the equitable doctrine of substantial performance. That is the rule generally. See Annotation, "Wilful or intentional variation by contractor from terms of contract in regard to material or work as affecting measure of damages," 6 A.L.R. 137.

Jacob & Youngs, Inc. v. Kent, 230 N.Y. 239, 243, 244, 129 N.E. 889, 891, 23 A.L.R. 1429, is typical. It was a case of substantial performance of a building contract. (This case is distinctly the opposite.) Mr. Justice Cardozo, in the course of his opinion, stressed the distinguishing features. "Nowhere," he said, "will change be tolerated, however, if it is so dominant or pervasive as in any real or sub-

a. This was on the assumption that the land as it was left could not have been sold on the market.

stantial measure to frustrate the purpose of the contract." Again, "the willful transgressor must accept the penalty of his transgression."

2. In reckoning damages for breach of a building or construction contract, the law aims to give the disappointed promisee, so far as money will do it, what he was promised. 9 Am.Jur. Building and Construction Contracts, sec. 152. It is so ruled by a long line of decisions in this state beginning with Carli v. Seymour, Sabin & Co., 26 Minn. 276, 3 N.W. 348, where the contract was for building a road. There was a breach. Plaintiff was held entitled to recover what it would cost to complete the grading as contemplated by the contract. For our other similar cases, see 2 Dunnell, Minn.Dig., 2 Ed. & Supp., secs. 2561, 2565.

Never before, so far as our decisions show, has it even been suggested that lack of value in the land furnished to the contractor who had bound himself to improve it [gave] any escape from the ordinary consequences of a breach of the contract. . . .

Even in case of substantial performance in good faith, the resulting defects being remediable, it is error to instruct that the measure of damage is "the difference in value between the house as it was and as it would have been if constructed according to contract." The "correct doctrine" is that the cost of remedying the defect is the "proper" measure of damages. Snider v. Peters Home Building Co., 139 Minn. 413, 414, 416, 167 N.W. 108.

Value of the land (as distinguished from the value of the intended product of the contract, which ordinarily will be equivalent to its reasonable cost) is no proper part of any measure of damages for wilful breach of a building contract. The reason is plain.

The summit from which to reckon damages from trespass to real estate is its actual value at the moment. The owner's only right is to be compensated for the deterioration in value caused by the tort. That is all he has lost.[1] But not so if a contract to improve the same land has been breached by the contractor who refuses to do the work, especially where, as here, he has been paid in advance. The summit from which to reckon damages for that wrong is the hypothetical peak of accomplishment (not value) which would have been reached had the work been done as demanded by the contract.

The owner's right to improve his property is not trammeled by its small value. It is his right to erect thereon structures which will reduce its value. If that be the result, it can be of no aid to any contractor who declines performance. As said long ago in Chamberlain v. Parker, 45 N.Y. 569, 572: "A man may do what he will with his own, . . . and if he chooses to erect a monument to his caprice

1. So also in condemnation cases, where the owner loses nothing of promised contractual performance.

or folly on his premises, and employs and pays another to do it, it does not lie with a defendant who has been so employed and paid for building it, to say that his own performance would not be beneficial to the plaintiff." To the same effect is Restatement, Contracts, sec. 346, p. 576, Illustrations of Subsection (1), par. 4.

Suppose a contractor were suing the owner for breach of a grading contract such as this. Would any element of value, or lack of it, in the land have any relevance in reckoning damages? Of course not. The contractor would be compensated for what he had lost, i. e., his profit. Conversely, in such a case as this, the owner is entitled to compensation for what he has lost, that is, the work or structure which he has been promised, for which he has paid, and of which he has been deprived by the contractor's breach.

To diminish damages recoverable against him in proportion as there is presently small value in the land would favor the faithless contractor. It would also ignore and so defeat plaintiff's right to contract and build for the future. To justify such a course would require more of the prophetic vision than judges possess. This factor is important when the subject matter is trackage property in the margin of such an area of population and industry as that of the Twin Cities. . . .

The genealogy of the error pervading the argument contra is easy to trace. It begins with Seely v. Alden, 61 Pa. 302, 100 Am.Dec. 642, a tort case for pollution of a stream. Resulting depreciation in value of plaintiff's premises, of course, was the measure of damages. About 40 years later, in Bigham v. Wabash-Pittsburg T. Ry., 223 Pa. 106, 72 A. 318, the measure of damages of the earlier tort case was used in one for breach of contract, without comment or explanation to show why. . . .

It is at least interesting to note Morgan v. Gamble, 230 Pa. 165, 79 A. 410, decided two years after the Bigham case. The doctrine of substantial performance is there correctly stated, but plaintiff was denied its benefit because he had deliberately breached his building contract. It was held that: "Where a building contractor agrees to lay an extra strong lead water pipe, and he substitutes therefor an iron pipe, he will be required to allow to the owners in a suit upon the contract, not the difference [in value] between the iron and lead pipes, but the cost of laying a lead pipe as provided in the agreement."

To show how remote any factors of value were considered, it was also held that: "Where a contractor of a building agrees to construct two gas lines, one for natural gas, and one for artificial gas, he will not be relieved from constructing both lines, because artificial gas was not in use in the town in which the building was being constructed."

The objective of this contract of present importance was the improvement of real estate. That makes irrelevant the rules peculiar to damages to chattels, arising from tort or breach of contract. . . . In tort, the thing lost is money value, nothing more. But under a construction contract, the thing lost by a breach such as we have here is a physical structure or accomplishment, a promised and paid for alteration in land. That is the "injury" for which the law gives him compensation. Its only appropriate measure is the cost of performance.

It is suggested that because of little or no value in his land the owner may be unconscionably enriched by such a reckoning. The answer is that there can be no unconscionable enrichment, no advantage upon which the law will frown, when the result is but to give one party to a contract only what the other has promised; particularly where, as here, the delinquent has had full payment for the promised performance.

3. It is said by the Restatement, Contracts, sec. 346, comment b: "Sometimes defects in a completed structure cannot be physically remedied without tearing down and rebuilding, at a cost that would be imprudent and unreasonable. The law does not require damages to be measured by a method requiring such economic waste. If no such waste is involved, the cost of remedying the defect is the amount awarded as compensation for failure to render the promised performance."

The "economic waste" declaimed against by the decisions applying that rule has nothing to do with the value in money of the real estate, or even with the product of the contract. The waste avoided is only that which would come from wrecking a physical structure, completed, or nearly so, under the contract. The cases applying that rule go no further. Illustrative are Buchholz v. Rosenberg, 163 Wis. 312, 156 N.W. 946; Burmeister v. Wolfgram, 175 Wis. 506, 185 N.W. 517. Absent such waste, as it is in this case, the rule of the Restatement, Contracts, sec. 346, is that "the cost of remedying the defect is the amount awarded as compensation for failure to render the promised performance." That means that defendants here are liable to plaintiff for the reasonable cost of doing what defendants promised to do and have wilfully declined to do.

It follows that there must be a new trial. The initial question will be as to the proper construction of the contract. Thus far the case has been considered from the standpoint of the construction adopted by plaintiff and acquiesced in, very likely for strategic reasons, by defendants. The question has not been argued here, so we intimate no opinion concerning it, but we put the question whether the contract required removal from the premises of any overburden. The requirement in that respect was that the overburden should be used for the purpose of "establishing and maintaining" the grade. A uniform slope and grade were doubtless required. But whether, if it could not be accomplished without removal and deposit elsewhere of large amounts of overburden, the contract required as a condition that the grade everywhere should be as low as the one recited as "now existing at the roadway" is a question for initial consideration below.

The judgment must be reversed with a new trial to follow.

So ordered.

[JULIUS J. OLSON, J., dissenting in an opinion in which HOLT, J. concurred, urged that the diminished value rule be applied in the absence of evidence to show that the completed product was to satisfy the personal taste of the promisee, and denied that the wilfulness of the breach should affect the measure of damages. HILTON and LORING, JJ., took no part.]

NOTES

(1) *Explanation.* In 1927, when the parties were bargaining over the terms of their contract, they would surely not knowingly have agreed to have Wunder assume such a burdensome task if it would have been of so slight a benefit to Groves. What is the explanation for the circumstance that, after seven years, Wunder's task was so burdensome and Groves' benefit was apparently so slight? That Wunder had underestimated the burden? That Groves had overestimated the benefit? That the cost of Wunder's performance had risen? That the amount of the benefit to Groves had fallen? That Wunder's performance would not have been so burdensome if it had done the restoration as the work progressed? That the actual benefit to Groves would have been greater than that reflected in the market price of the land? Some combination of these? Which of these possible explanations would justify the court's decision?

According to one critic, "The court never alluded to the real economic issue in the case, which was how the contract allocated the risk of a fall in the market for real estate, the Depression of the 1930's having occurred after the contract was signed. . . . The effect of the court's judgment was to give the plaintiff a cushion, for which he had not contracted, against the impact of the Depression on land values." R. Posner, Economic Analysis of Law 91 (2d ed. 1977).

After the decision in Groves, the Wunder paid Groves $55,000 to settle the claim. The land was left until 1951, when some grading was done on a portion at a cost of $6,000, and in 1953 this portion was sold for $45,000 to a buyer who planned to use it for a factory. J. Dawson and W. Harvey, Cases on Contracts 12 (3d ed. 1977). Does this suggest anything about the proper measure of recovery?

(2) *Economics of Breach (Reprise).* If you had been counsel for Wunder and had been asked by your client whether it should perform its promise to do the grading at a cost of $60,000 if the benefit to Groves would be under $13,000, what advice would you have given?

(3) *"Wilfulness."* The court says that Wunder's "breach of contract was wilful." [a] What does "wilful" mean in this connection? If Wunder had refused to perform as a result of your advice (see Note 2 supra), would its breach have been "wilful"?

Holmes said, "If a contract is broken the measure of damages generally is the same, whatever the cause of the breach." Globe Refining Co. v. Landa Cotton Oil Co., 190 U.S. 540, 544 (1903). Is the Groves case an exception? If Wunder must pay over $47,000 more in damages if its breach is "wilful," is this not a penalty for "wilfulness"? Is that consistent with the goals of contract remedies?

PEEVYHOUSE v. GARLAND COAL & MINING CO., 382 P.2d 109 (Okla.1962)[a] [In 1954 Willie and Lucille Peevyhouse leased their farm for five years to Garland Coal & Mining Co. to strip mine coal. In addition to the usual covenants, Garland agreed to perform specified restorative and remedial work at the end of the lease. It failed to do this work, which would have involved the moving of many thousands of cubic yards of dirt at a cost of about $29,000. Had the work been done, the market price of the farm would have been increased by only $300. The Peevyhouses sued for $25,000 in damages. The trial court gave judgment on a verdict for $5,000. Both parties appealed.]

JACKSON, Justice. . . . On appeal, the issue is sharply drawn. Plaintiffs contend that the true measure of damages in this case is what it will cost plaintiffs to obtain performance of the work that was not done because of defendant's default. Defendant argues that the measure of damages is the cost of performance "limited, however, to the total difference in the market value before and after the work was performed". It appears that this precise question has not heretofore been presented to this court. . . .

Plaintiffs rely on Groves v. John Wunder Co., 205 Minn. 163, 286 N.W. 235, 123 A.L.R. 502. In that case, the Minnesota court, in a substantially similar situation, adopted the "cost of performance" rule as opposed to the "value" rule. The result was to authorize a jury to give plaintiff damages in the amount of $60,000, where the real estate concerned would have been worth only $12,160, even if the work contracted for had been done.

It may be observed that Groves v. John Wunder Co., supra, is the only case which has come to our attention in which the cost of performance rule has been followed under circumstances where the cost of performance greatly exceeded the diminution in value result-

a. In H. P. Droher & Sons v. Toushin, 250 Minn. 490, 85 N.W.2d 273 (1957), the court distinguished Groves on the ground that, "The majority opinion is based, at least in part, on the fact that the breach of the contract was wilful and in bad faith".

a. Cert. denied, 375 U.S. 906 (1963).

ing from the breach of contract. Incidentally, it appears that this case was decided by a plurality rather than a majority of the members of the court. . . .

We do not think [that] either [the] analogy [of a "building and construction" or a "grading and excavation" contract] is strictly applicable to the case now before us. The primary purpose of the lease contract between plaintiffs and defendant was neither "building and construction" nor "grading and excavation". It was merely to accomplish the economical recovery and marketing of coal from the premises, to the profit of all parties. The special provisions of the lease contract pertaining to remedial work were incidental to the main object involved.

Even in the case of contracts that are unquestionably building and construction contracts, the authorities are not in agreement as to the factors to be considered in determining whether the cost of performance rule or the value rule should be applied. The American Law Institute's Restatement of the Law, Contracts, Volume 1, Sections 346(1)(a)(i) and (ii) submits the proposition that the cost of performance is the proper measure of damages "if this is possible and does not involve *unreasonable economic waste*"; and that the diminution in value caused by the breach is the proper measure "if construction and completion in accordance with the contract would involve *unreasonable economic waste*". (Emphasis supplied.) In an explanatory comment immediately following the text, the Restatement makes it clear that the "economic waste" referred to consists of the destruction of a substantially completed building or other structure. Of course no such destruction is involved in the case now before us.

On the other hand, in McCormick, Damages, Section 168, it is said with regard to building and construction contracts that ". . . in cases where the defect is one that can be repaired or cured without *undue expense*" the cost of performance is the proper measure of damages, but where ". . . the defect in material or construction is one that cannot be remedied without *an expenditure for reconstruction disproportionate to the end to be attained*" (emphasis supplied) the value rule should be followed. The same idea was expressed in Jacob & Youngs, Inc. v. Kent, 230 N.Y. 239, 129 N.E. 889, 23 A.L.R. 1429, as follows: "The owner is entitled to the money which will permit him to complete, unless the cost of completion is grossly and unfairly out of proportion to the good to be attained. When that is true, the measure is the difference in value."

It thus appears that the prime consideration in the Restatement was "economic waste"; and that the prime consideration in McCormick, Damages, and in Jacob & Youngs, Inc. v. Kent, supra, was the relationship between the expense involved and the "end to be attained"—in other words, the "relative economic benefit". . . .

We . . . hold that where, in a coal mining lease, lessee agrees to perform certain remedial work on the premises concerned at the end of the lease period, and thereafter the contract is fully performed by both parties except that the remedial work is not done, the measure of damages in an action by lessor against lessee for damages for breach of contract is ordinarily the reasonable cost of performance of the work; however, where the contract provision breached was merely incidental to the main purpose in view, and where the economic benefit which would result to lessor by full performance of the work is grossly disproportionate to the cost of performance, the damages which lessor may recover are limited to the diminution in value resulting to the premises because of the non-performance. . . .

[Judgment reduced to $300 and affirmed (4–3).]

IRWIN, Justice (dissenting). . . . Although the contract speaks for itself, there were several negotiations between the plaintiffs and defendant before the contract was executed. Defendant admitted in the trial of the action, that plaintiffs insisted that the above provisions be included in the contract and that they would not agree to the coal mining lease unless the above provisions were included. . . .

[I]n my opinion, the plaintiffs were entitled to specific performance of the contract and since defendant has failed to perform, the proper measure of damages should be the cost of performance. Any other measure of damage would be holding for naught the express provisions of the contract; would be taking from the plaintiffs the benefits of the contract and placing those benefits in defendant which has failed to perform its obligations; would be granting benefits to defendant without a resulting obligation; and would be completely rescinding the solemn obligation of the contract for the benefit of the defendant to the detriment of the plaintiffs by making an entirely new contract for the parties. . . .

NOTES

(1) *Groves and Peevyhouse.* Are Groves and Peevyhouse distinguishable? Is it clear that the loss in value to the Peevyhouses was not $5,000? See Farnsworth, Legal Remedies for Breach of Contract, 70 Colum.L.Rev. 1145, 1167–75 (1970). What result in these cases under Restatement Second, § 348(2).

(2) *"Economic Waste."* The first Restatement, we are told by the court in Peevyhouse, speaks of "economic waste" in the sense of destruction of a substantially completed structure. If Kent had been awarded damages measured by the cost to replace the pipe with Reading pipe, would he then have been required to replace it? Does it seem likely that he would have done so? In what sense is there "economic waste" if he is awarded damages measured by the cost to complete? See Comment *c* to Restatement Second, § 348.

(b) Foreseeability

Until the nineteenth century, judges left the assessment of damages for breach of contract largely to the discretion of the jury. It was no accident that the development of rules to curb this discretion and the "outrageous and excessive" verdicts that resulted coincided with the end of the industrial revolution and with a consequent solicitude for burgeoning enterprise.[a] Hadley v. Baxendale is the leading case in this development.

HADLEY v. BAXENDALE

Court of Exchequer, 1854.
9 Ex. 341, 156 Eng.Rep. 145.

[Plaintiffs, who operated a mill at Gloucester, sued defendants, who were common carriers, for damages for breach of a contract of carriage. The declaration contained two counts but prior to the trial plaintiffs entered a *nolle prosequi* as to the first. In the second count plaintiffs alleged that they were forced to shut their mill down because the crank shaft of the steam engine, by which their mill was operated, became broken; that they arranged with W. Joyce & Co., of Greenwich, the manufacturers of the engine, to make a new shaft from the pattern of the old one; that they delivered the broken shaft to defendants who, in consideration of the payment of their charges, promised to use due care to deliver it to W. Joyce & Co. within a reasonable time but that defendants failed to do so; that by reason of defendants' negligence the completion of the new shaft and the reopening of plaintiffs' mill were delayed five days longer than would otherwise have been the case; and that during that period plaintiffs were compelled to pay wages and lost profits aggregating 300£ for which amount plaintiffs sought judgment. Defendants pleaded that they had paid 25£ into court in satisfaction of plaintiffs' claim; plaintiffs replied that this sum was insufficient for that purpose; and issue was joined upon this replication.]

At the trial before Crompton, J., at the last Gloucester Assizes, it appeared that the plaintiffs carried on an extensive business as millers at Gloucester; and that, on the 11th of May, their mill was stopped by a breakage of the crank shaft by which the mill was worked. The steam-engine was manufactured by Messrs. Joyce & Co., the engineers at Greenwich, and it became necessary to send the shaft as a pattern for a new one to Greenwich. The fracture was discovered

a. An analogy may be drawn from these restrictions on the extent of liability in terms of the amount for which a promisor may be held liable to restrictions on the extent of liability in terms of the persons to whom a promisor may be held liable. The latter will be explored in Chapter 10, Third Party Beneficiaries.

on the 12th, and on the 13th the plaintiffs sent one of their servants to the office of the defendants, who are the well known carriers trading under the name of Pickford & Co., for the purpose of having the shaft carried to Greenwich. The plaintiffs' servant told the clerk that the mill was stopped, and that the shaft must be sent immediately; and in answer to the inquiry when the shaft would be taken, the answer was, that if it was sent up by twelve o'clock any day, it would be delivered at Greenwich on the following day. On the following day the shaft was taken by the defendants, before noon, for the purpose of being conveyed to Greenwich, and the sum of 2£ 4*s*. was paid for its carriage for the whole distance; at the same time the defendants' clerk was told that a special entry, if required, should be made to hasten its delivery. The delivery of the shaft at Greenwich was delayed by some neglect; and the consequence was, that the plaintiffs did not receive the new shaft for several days after they would otherwise have done, and the working of their mill was thereby delayed, and they thereby lost the profits they would otherwise have received.

On the part of the defendants, it was objected that these damages were too remote, and that the defendants were not liable with respect to them. The learned Judge left the case generally to the jury, who found a verdict with 25£ damages beyond the amount paid into Court.

Whateley, [for defendants], in last Michaelmas Term, obtained a rule nisi for a new trial, on the ground of misdirection.

[The arguments of counsel are omitted. After they were completed the court took the case under consideration until the next term.]

The judgment of the Court was now delivered by

ALDERSON, B. We think that there ought to be a new trial in this case; but, in so doing, we deem it to be expedient and necessary to state explicitly the rule which the Judge, at the next trial, ought, in our opinion, to direct the jury to be governed by when they estimate the damages.

It is, indeed, of the last importance that we should do this; for, if the jury are left without any definite rule to guide them, it will, in such cases as these, manifestly lead to the greatest injustice. The Courts have done this on several occasions; and, in Blake v. Midland Railway Company, 21 L.J., Q.B. 237, the Court granted a new trial on this very ground, that the rule had not been definitely laid down to the jury by the learned judge at Nisi Prius.

"There are certain established rules," this Court says, in Alder v. Keighley, 15 M. & W. 117, "according to which the jury ought to find." And the Court, in that case, adds: "and here there is a clear rule, that the amount which would have been received if the contract had been kept is the measure of damages if the contract is broken."

Now we think the proper rule in such a case as the present is this: Where two parties have made a contract which one of them has broken, the damages which the other party ought to receive in respect of such breach of contract should be such as may fairly and reasonably be considered either arising naturally, i. e., according to the usual course of things, from such breach of contract itself, or such as may reasonably be supposed to have been in the contemplation of both parties, at the time they made the contract, as the probable result of the breach of it. Now, if the special circumstances under which the contract was actually made were communicated by the plaintiffs to the defendants, and thus known to both parties, the damages resulting from the breach of such a contract, which they would reasonably contemplate, would be the amount of injury which would ordinarily follow from a breach of contract under these special circumstances so known and communicated. But, on the other hand, if these special circumstances were wholly unknown to the party breaking the contract, he, at the most, could only be supposed to have had in his contemplation the amount of injury which would arise generally, and in the great multitude of cases not affected by any special circumstances, from such a breach of contract. For, had the special circumstances been known, the parties might have specially provided for the breach of contract by special terms as to the damages in that case; and of this advantage it would be very unjust to deprive them. Now the above principles are those by which we think the jury ought to be guided in estimating the damages arising out of any breach of contract. It is said, that other cases, such as breaches of contract in the nonpayment of money, or in the not making a good title to land, are to be treated as exceptions from this, and as governed by a conventional rule. But as, in such cases, both parties must be supposed to be cognizant of that well-known rule, these cases may, we think, be more properly classed under the rule above enunciated as to cases under known special circumstances, because there both parties may reasonably be presumed to contemplate the estimation of the amount of damages according to the conventional rule. Now, in the present case if we are to apply the principles above laid down, we find that the only circumstances here communicated by the plaintiffs to the defendants at the time the contract was made, were, that the article to be carried was the broken shaft of a mill, and that the plaintiffs were the millers of that mill. But how do these circumstances show reasonably that the profits of the mill must be stopped by an unreasonable delay in the delivery of the broken shaft by the carrier to the third person? Suppose the plaintiffs had another shaft in their possession put up or putting up at the time, and that they only wished to send back the broken shaft to the engineer who made it; it is clear that this would be quite consistent with the above circumstances, and yet the unreasonable delay in the delivery would have no effect upon the intermediate profits of the mill. Or, again, suppose that, at the time of the delivery to the carrier, the machinery of the mill had been in other respects defective, then, also, the same results would follow. Here it is true that the shaft was actually sent back to serve as a model for a new one, and that the want of a new one was the only cause of the stoppage of the mill, and that the loss of profits really arose from not sending down the new shaft in proper time, and that this arose from the delay in delivering the broken one to serve as a model. But it is obvious that, in the great multitude of cases of millers sending off broken shafts to third persons by a carrier under ordinary circumstances, such consequences would not, in all probability, have occurred; and these special circumstances were here never communicated by the plaintiffs to the defendants. It follows, therefore, that the loss of profits here cannot reasonably be considered such a consequence of the breach of contract as could have been fairly and reasonably contemplated by both the parties when they made this contract. For such loss would neither have flowed naturally from the breach of this contract in the great multitude of such cases occurring under ordinary circumstances, nor were the special circumstances, which, perhaps, would have made it a reasonable and natural consequence of such breach of contract, communicated to or known by the defendants. The Judge ought, therefore, to have told the jury that, upon the facts then before him, they ought not to take the loss of profits into consideration at all in estimating the damages. There must therefore be a new trial in this case.

Rule absolute.

NOTES

(1) *Rule of Hadley v. Baxendale.* Do you think that in Hadley v. Baxendale the court applied the rule which it formulated correctly or incorrectly? Cf. Victoria Laundry (Windsor) Ltd. v. Newman Industries Ltd., 2 K.B. 528, 537 (1949): "In considering the meaning and application of these rules, it is essential to bear clearly in mind the facts on which Hadley v. Baxendale proceeded. The head-note is definitely misleading in so far as it says that the defendant's clerk, who attended at the office, was told that the mill was stopped and that the shaft must be delivered immediately. The same allegation figures in the statement of facts which are said on page 344 to have 'appeared' at the trial before Crompton J. If the Court of Exchequer had accepted these facts as established, the court must, one would suppose, have decided the case the other way round. . . . But it is reasonably plain from Alderson B.'s judgment that the court rejected this evidence, for on page 355 he says: 'We find that the only circumstances here communicated by the plaintiffs to the defendants at the time when the contract was made were that the article to be carried was the broken shaft of a mill and that the plaintiffs were the millers of that mill.' . . . ." Compare the rule laid down in Hadley v. Baxendale with the formulations of Restatement Second, § 351 and UCC 2–715(2)(a).

(2) *Meaning of "Contemplation."* In British Columbia Saw Mill Co. v. Nettleship, L.R. 3 C.P. 499 (1868), plaintiff delivered to defendant's ship at

Glasgow machinery needed for construction of a mill at Vancouver, British Columbia, as defendant knew. As a result of the loss of one box of machinery somewhere in transit the mill could not be put into operation for almost a year, the time required to replace the missing machinery. The court awarded damages for the cost of replacing the machinery, including the cost of procuring new machinery from England, plus interest at 5% for the time plaintiffs were delayed, but denied recovery for the loss incurred due to stoppage of the mill. "Bovill, C. J. . . . [A defendant] is not to be made liable for damages beyond what may fairly be presumed to have been contemplated by the parties at the time of entering into the contract. It must be something which could have been foreseen and reasonably expected, and to which he has assented expressly or impliedly by entering into the contract. . . . Willes, J. . . . If that had been presented to the mind of the shipowner at the time of making the contract, as the basis upon which he was contracting, he would at once have rejected it. And, though he knew from the shippers the use they intended to make of the articles, it could not be contended that the mere fact of knowledge without more, would be a reason for imposing upon him a greater degree of liability than would otherwise have been cast upon him." In this case Willes, J. rejected the result reached in an old case "said to have been decided two centuries ago where a man going to be married to an heiress, his horse having cast a shoe on the journey, employed a blacksmith to replace it, who did the work so unskilfully that the horse was lamed, and the rider not arriving in time, the lady married another; and the blacksmith was held liable for the loss of the marriage." [a] What would have been the result under the test laid down by Restatement Second, § 351? What *should* have been the result?

(3) *"Tacit Agreement Test."* In Globe Refining Co. v. Landa Cotton Oil Co., 190 U.S. 540 (1903), Justice Holmes declared that "the extent of liability . . . should be worked out on terms which it fairly may be presumed he would have assented to if they had been presented to his mind. . . . [It] depends on what liability the defendant fairly may be supposed to have assumed consciously, or to have warranted the plaintiff reasonably to suppose that it assumed, when the contract was made. . . . [M]ere notice to a seller of some interest or probable action of the buyer is not enough."

This "tacit agreement" test has not, however, found favor. According to Comment 2 to UCC 2–715, "The 'tacit agreement' test for the recovery of consequential damages is rejected." For an exceptional recent case applying the test, see Morrow v. First Nat. Bank, 261 Ark. 568, 550 S.W.2d 429 (1977).

a. But cf. Coppola v. Kraushaar, 102 App.Div. 306, 92 N.Y.S. 436 (1905), in which a disappointed suitor whose betrothed broke their engagement after their wedding was delayed, sued to recover five hundred dollars, expended uselessly on the wedding, from the defendant, whose failure to deliver two gowns, ordered for the bride, had caused the postponement of the wedding. The court said: "Before the defendant can be held to these alleged damages . . . I think that the parties must have had in contemplation that the wedding would never occur if the defendant failed to furnish the 'two dresses' on the day before the appointed time. . . . While such a disappointment would naturally be keen to any prospective bride, it was hardly to be contemplated, in the absence of specific warning, that she would forever refuse to wed if those 'two dresses' were not forthcoming before the day set for the ceremony. The damages are too remote. (Hadley v. Baxendale, 9 Exch. 341. . . .)"

(4) *Limitation of Risk.* "The rule of Hadley v. Baxendale is an attempt to restrict the promisor's liability for breach of promise to those consequences, the risk of which he knew about, or must be taken to have known about, when he made the contract. The scope of damage for breach of contract is much narrower than the 'proximate consequence' rule which prevails in actions to recover for a tort. If we may assume that the defaulting promisor is usually an *entrepreneur,* a business man who has undertaken a risky enterprise, the law here manifests a policy to encourage the *entrepreneur* by reducing the extent of his risk below that amount of damage which, it might be plausibly argued, the promisee has actually been caused to suffer." Patterson, The Apportionment of Business Risks Through Legal Devices, 24 Colum.L.Rev. 335, 342 (1924); but see Schiro, Prospecting for Lost Profits in the Uniform Commercial Code—The Buyer's Dilemmas, 52 So.Cal. L.Rev. 1727 (1979). For a thorough discussion of the background of Hadley v. Baxendale, see Danzig, *Hadley* v. *Baxendale*: A Study in the Industrialization of the Law, 4 J.Legal Stud. 249 (1975). For an unorthodox suggestion that Hadley v. Baxendale actually expanded liability in contract by making some lost profits and other consequential damages recoverable where none had been before, see G. Gilmore, The Death of Contract 51–52 (1974). Compare Restatement Second, § 351 with Restatement, Second, of Torts, § 435; compare UCC 2–715(2)(a) with (2)(b).

SPANG INDUSTRIES, INC. v. AETNA CAS. & SURETY CO.

United States Court of Appeals, Second Circuit, 1975.
512 F.2d 365.

MULLIGAN, Circuit Judge. Torrington Construction Co., Inc. (Torrington), a Connecticut corporation, was the successful bidder with the New York State Department of Transportation for a highway reconstruction contract covering 4.47 miles of road in Washington County, New York. Before submitting its bid, Torrington received an oral quotation from Spang Industries, Inc., Fort Pitt Bridge Division (Fort Pitt), a Pennsylvania corporation, for the fabrication, furnishing and erection of some 240 tons of structural steel at a unit price of 27.5 cents per pound; the steel was to be utilized to construct a 270 foot long, double span bridge over the Battenkill River as part of the highway reconstruction. The quotation was confirmed in a letter from Fort Pitt to Torrington dated September 5, 1969, which stated in part: "Delivery to be mutually agreed upon." On November 3, 1969, Torrington, in response to a request from Fort Pitt, advised that its requirements for delivery and erection of the steel would be late June, 1970. On November 12, 1969, Fort Pitt notified Torrington that it was tentatively scheduling delivery in accordance with these requirements. On January 7, 1970, Fort Pitt wrote to Torrington asking if the June, 1970 erection date was still valid; Torrington responded affirmatively on January 13, 1970. However, on January 29, 1970, Fort Pitt advised that it was engaged in an extensive expansion program and that "[d]ue to unforeseen delays caused by weather, deliveries from suppliers, etc., it is our opinion that the June date cannot be met." On February 2, 1970, Torrington sent a letter requesting that Fort Pitt give a delivery date and, receiving no response, wrote again on May 12, 1970 requesting a written confirmation of the date of delivery and threatening to cancel out if the date was not reasonably close to the originally scheduled date. On May 20, 1970, Fort Pitt responded and promised that the structural steel would be shipped early in August, 1970.

Although some 25 tons of small steel parts were shipped on August 21, 1970, the first girders and other heavy structural steel were not shipped until August 24, 26, 27, 31 and September 2 and 4, 1970. Fort Pitt had subcontracted the unloading and erection of the steel to Syracuse Rigging Co. but neglected to advise it of the August 21st shipment. The steel began to arrive at the railhead in Shushan, New York about September 1st and the railroad demanded immediate unloading. Torrington was therefore compelled to do the unloading itself until Syracuse Rigging arrived on September 8, 1970. Not until September 16 was there enough steel delivered to the job site to permit Syracuse to commence erection. The work was completed on October 8, 1970 and the bridge was ready to receive its concrete deck on October 28, 1970. Because of contract specifications set by the State requiring that concrete be poured at temperatures of 40° Fahrenheit and above, Torrington had to get special permission from the State's supervising engineer to pour the concrete on October 28, 1970, when the temperature was at 32°.

Since the job site was in northern New York near the Vermont border and the danger of freezing temperatures was imminent, the pouring of the concrete was performed on a crash basis in one day, until 1 a. m. the following morning, which entailed extra costs for Torrington in the form of overtime pay, extra equipment and the protection of the concrete during the pouring process.

In July, 1971, Fort Pitt instituted an action against Aetna Casualty and Surety Co., which had posted a general contractor's labor and material bond, in the United States District Court for the Western District of Pennsylvania, seeking to recover the balance due on the subcontract, which at that point was $72,247.37 with interest. Thereafter in 1972 Torrington made two further payments totalling $48,983.92. That action was transferred pursuant to 28 U.S.C.A. § 1406(a) to the United States District Court for the Northern District of New York by order dated December 9, 1971. In the interim, Torrington had commenced suit in New York Supreme Court, Washington County, seeking damages in the sum of $23,290.81 alleged to be caused by Fort Pitt's delay in furnishing the steel. Fort Pitt then removed the case to the United States District Court for the Northern District of New York (where the two cases were consolidated), and counterclaimed for the balance due on the contract. From May 29 to

31, 1973, the cases were tried without a jury before Hon. James S. Holden, Chief Judge of the United States District Court for the District of Vermont, who was sitting by designation. On September 12, 1973, Judge Holden filed his findings of fact and conclusions of law in which he held that Fort Pitt had breached its contract by its delayed delivery and that Torrington was entitled to damages in the amount of $7,653.57. He further held that Fort Pitt was entitled to recover from Torrington on the counterclaim the sum of $23,290.12, which was the balance due on its contract price plus interest, less the $7,653.57 damages sustained by Torrington. He directed that judgment be entered for Fort Pitt against Torrington and Aetna on their joint and several liability for $15,636.55 with interest from November 12, 1970.

Fort Pitt on this appeal does not take issue with any of the findings of fact of the court below but contends that the recovery by Torrington of its increased expenses constitutes special damages which were not reasonably within the contemplation of the parties when they entered into the contract.

I

While the damages awarded Torrington are relatively modest ($7,653.57) in comparison with the subcontract price ($132,274.37), Fort Pitt urges that an affirmance of the award will do violence to the rule of Hadley v. Baxendale, 156 Eng.Rep. 145 (Ex. 1854), and create a precedent which will have a severe impact on the business of all subcontractors and suppliers.

While it is evident that the function of the award of damages for a breach of contract is to put the plaintiff in the same position he would have been in had there been no breach, Hadley v. Baxendale limits the recovery to those injuries which the parties could reasonably have anticipated at the time the contract was entered into. If the damages suffered do not usually flow from the breach, then it must be established that the special circumstances giving rise to them should reasonably have been anticipated at the time the contract was made.

There can be no question but that Hadley v. Baxendale represents the law in New York and in the United States generally. E. g., Hughes Tool Co. v. United Artists Corp., 279 App.Div. 417, 110 N.Y. S.2d 383 (1st Dep't 1952), aff'd, 304 N.Y. 942, 110 N.E.2d 884 (1953); J. Calamari & J. Perillo, Contracts 329 (1970); C. McCormick, Damages § 138 (1935); 11 S. Williston, Contracts § 1356 (3d ed (W. Jaeger) 1968); Restatement of Contracts § 330 (1932). There is no dispute between the parties on this appeal as to the continuing viability of Hadley v. Baxendale and its formulation of the rule respecting special damages, and this court has no intention of challenging or questioning its principles, which Chief Judge Cardozo characterized to be, at least in some applications, "tantamount to a rule of property," Kerr S. S. Co. v. Radio Corporation of America, 245 N.Y. 284, 291, 157 N.E. 140, 142 (1927).

The gist of Fort Pitt's argument is that, when it entered into the subcontract to fabricate, furnish and erect the steel in September, 1969, it had received a copy of the specifications which indicated that the total work was to be completed by December 15, 1971. It could not reasonably have anticipated that Torrington would so expedite the work (which was accepted by the State on January 21, 1971) that steel delivery would be called for in 1970 rather than in 1971. Whatever knowledge Fort Pitt received after the contract was entered into, it argues, cannot expand its liability, since it is essential under Hadley v. Baxendale and its Yankee progeny that the notice of the facts which would give rise to special damages in case of breach be given at or before the time the contract was made. The principle urged cannot be disputed. Czarnikow-Rionda Co. v. Federal Sugar Refining Co., 255 N.Y. 33, 41, 173 N.E. 913, 915 (1930); 11 S. Williston, supra, § 1357; Restatement, supra, § 330. We do not, however, agree that any violence to the doctrine was done here.

Fort Pitt also knew from the same specifications that Torrington was to commence the work on October 1, 1969. The Fort Pitt letter of September 5, 1969, which constitutes the agreement between the parties, specifically provides: "Delivery to be mutually agreed upon." On November 3, 1969, Torrington, responding to Fort Pitt's inquiry, gave "late June 1970" as its required delivery date and, on November 12, 1969, Fort Pitt stated that it was tentatively scheduling delivery for that time. Thus, at the time when the parties, pursuant to their initial agreement, fixed the date for performance which is crucial here, Fort Pitt knew that a June, 1970 delivery was required. It would be a strained and unpalatable interpretation of Hadley v. Baxendale to now hold that, although the parties left to further agreement the time for delivery, the supplier could reasonably rely upon a 1971 delivery date rather than one the parties later fixed. The behavior of Fort Pitt was totally inconsistent with the posture it now assumes. In November, 1969, it did not quarrel with the date set or seek to avoid the contract. It was not until late January, 1970 that Fort Pitt advised Torrington that, due to unforeseen delays and its expansion program, it could not meet the June date. None of its reasons for late delivery was deemed excusable according to the findings below, and this conclusion is not challenged here. It was not until five months later, on May 20, 1970, after Torrington had threatened to cancel, that Fort Pitt set another date for delivery (early August, 1970) which it again failed to meet, as was found below and not disputed on this appeal.

We conclude that, when the parties enter into a contract which, by its terms, provides that the time of performance is to be fixed at a later date, the knowledge of the consequences of a failure to perform is to be imputed to the defaulting party as of the time the parties agreed upon the date of performance. This comports, in our view, with both the logic and the spirit of Hadley v. Baxendale. Whether the agreement was initially valid despite its indefiniteness or only became valid when a material term was agreed upon is not relevant. At the time Fort Pitt did become committed to a delivery date, it was aware that a June, 1970 performance was required by virtue of its own acceptance. There was no unilateral distortion of the agreement rendering Fort Pitt liable to an extent not theretofore contemplated.

Having proceeded thus far, we do not think it follows automatically that Torrington is entitled to recover the damages it seeks here; further consideration of the facts before us is warranted. Fort Pitt maintains that, under the Hadley v. Baxendale rubric, the damages flowing from its conceded breach are "special" or "consequential" and were not reasonably to be contemplated by the parties. Since Torrington has not proved any "general" or "direct" damages, Fort Pitt urges that the contractor is entitled to nothing. We cannot agree. It is commonplace that parties to a contract normally address themselves to its performance and not to its breach or the consequences that will ensue if there is a default. See J. Calamari & J. Perillo, *supra*, at 331; C. McCormick, *supra*, at 580; 11 S. Williston, *supra*, at 295. As the New York Court of Appeals long ago stated:

> [A] more precise statement of this rule is, that a party is liable for all the direct damages which both parties to the contract would have contemplated as flowing from its breach, if at the time they entered into it they had bestowed proper attention upon the subject, and had been fully informed of the facts. [This] may properly be called the fiction of law . . .

Leonard v. New York, Albany & Buffalo Electro-Magnetic Telegraph Co., 41 N.Y. 544, 567 (1870). It is also pertinent to note that the rule does not require that the direct damages must necessarily follow, but only that they are likely to follow; as Lord Justice Asquith commented in Victoria Laundry, Ltd. v. Newman Industries, Ltd., [1949] 2 K.B. 528, 540, are they "on the cards"? We believe here that the damages sought to be recovered were also "in the cards." [a]

It must be taken as a reasonable assumption that, when the delivery date of June, 1970 was set, Torrington planned the bridge erection within a reasonable time thereafter. It is normal construction procedure that the erection of the steel girders would be followed by the installation of a poured concrete platform and whatever railings

a. "On the cards" was, however, severely disapproved as excessively liberal, and other tests, such as "a real danger" and "a serious possibility," were suggested by the noble lords in The Heron II, [1967] 3 All E.R. 686 (H.L.).

or superstructure the platform would require. Fort Pitt was an experienced bridge fabricator supplying contractors and the sequence of the work is hardly arcane. Moreover, any delay beyond June or August would assuredly have jeopardized the pouring of the concrete and have forced the postponement of the work until the spring. The work here, as was well known to Fort Pitt, was to be performed in northern New York near the Vermont border. The court below found that continuing freezing weather would have forced the pouring to be delayed until June, 1971. Had Torrington refused delivery or had it been compelled to delay the completion of the work until the spring of 1971, the potential damage claim would have been substantial. Instead, in a good faith effort to mitigate damages, Torrington embarked upon the crash program we have described. It appears to us that this eventuality should have reasonably been anticipated by Fort Pitt as it was experienced in the trade and was supplying bridge steel in northern climes on a project requiring a concrete roadway.

Torrington's recovery under the circumstances is not substantial or cataclysmic from Fort Pitt's point of view. It represents the expenses of unloading steel from the gondola due to Fort Pitt's admitted failure to notify its erection subcontractor, Syracuse Rigging, that the steel had been shipped, plus the costs of premium time, extra equipment and the cost of protecting the work, all occasioned by the realities Torrington faced in the wake of Fort Pitt's breach. In fact, Torrington's original claim of $23,290.81 was whittled down by the court below because of Torrington's failure to establish that its supervisory costs, overhead and certain equipment costs were directly attributable to the delay in delivery of the steel.

Professor Williston has commented:

> The true reason why notice to the defendant of the plaintiff's special circumstances is important is because, just as a court of equity under circumstances of hardship arising after the formation of a contract may deny specific performance, so a court of law may deny damages for unusual consequences where the defendant was not aware when he entered into the contract *how serious an injury would result from its breach.*

11 S. Williston, supra, at 295 (footnote omitted) (emphasis added).

In this case, serious or catastrophic injury was avoided by prompt, effective and reasonable mitigation at modest cost. Had Torrington not acted, had it been forced to wait until the following spring to complete the entire job and then sued to recover the profits it would have made had there been performance by Fort Pitt according to the terms of its agreement, then we might well have an appropriate setting for a classical Hadley v. Baxendale controversy. As this case comes to us, it hardly presents that situation. We therefore affirm the judgment below permitting Torrington to offset its damages against the contract price. . . .

NOTES

(1) *Availability of Cover.* Courts have often assumed that in our market economy there is ordinarily a market on which an injured buyer can cover. They have therefore concluded that losses resulting from the buyer's inability to cover do not follow from the breach in the ordinary course and are foreseeable by the seller only if he was aware of facts making the buyer's inability to cover foreseeable. See Marcus & Co. v. K. L. G. Baking Co., 122 N.J.Law 202, 3 A.2d 627 (1939). Does UCC 2–715(2)(a) dispense with the requirement that the buyer's inability to cover be foreseeable?

In Southern Idaho Pipe & Steel Co. v. Cal-Cut Pipe & Supply, p. 291 supra, the court (in an omitted part of the opinion, 98 Idaho at 504, 567 P. 2d at 1255) concluded that the trial court had properly awarded Southern Idaho, the injured buyer, damages for its loss of profits. "Cal-Cut knew that Southern Idaho was purchasing its used pipe for resale . . . . The trial court found . . . that because of a shortage of a steel pipe at the time of the breach plaintiff was unable to minimize its losses by purchasing steel pipe elsewhere." There was no mention of a finding that such a shortage was foreseeable by Cal-Cut when it made the contract. Should such a finding have been required?

(2) *Problem.* Federal contracted to sell 75,000 tons of sugar to Czarnikow, to be delivered directly to Czarnikow's customers. In the contracts that Czarnikow then made in turn with its customers, it described the sugar as "Federal" brand, but this was not known to Federal. When the sugar delivered by Federal turned out to be defective, Czarnikow spent $340,000 in the settlement of claims and the defense of law suits brought by its customers, an amount that was inflated because Czarnikow's obligations to them could not be met by delivery of sugar from other suppliers, which it might have obtained on the market. Is Federal liable for $340,000? Czarnikow-Rionda Co. v. Federal Sugar Refining Co., 255 N.Y. 33, 173 N.E. 913 (1930).

Assuming that Federal is liable for $340,000, could Czarnikow recover an additional $100,000 by showing that it had lost this much in profits when its volume dropped because it was deprived of $340,000 in capital? See Lewis v. Mobil Oil Corp., 438 F.2d 500 (8th Cir. 1971).

EMOTIONAL DISTURBANCE

Another limitation on contract damages results from the traditional reluctance of courts to allow damages for emotional disturbance. "Life in the competitive commercial world has at least equal capacity to bestow ruin as benefit, and it is presumed that those who enter this world do so willingly, accepting the risk of encountering the former as part of the cost of achieving the latter." Hatfield v.

Max Rouse & Sons Northwest, —— Idaho ——, 606 P.2d 944 (1980).[a] Recovery of damages for emotional disturbance has, however, long been allowed against defendants who occupy a special position toward the public—telegraph companies, innkeepers, common carriers and the like. Because the obligations of these persons are to a large extent imposed by law, without regard to contract, it is often difficult to tell whether recovery is on a theory of contract or of tort. (Should the rules as to recovery for emotional disturbance be different in contract and in tort?) According to Restatement Second, § 353, recovery may also be allowed where "the breach also caused bodily harm or the contract or the breach is of such a kind that serious emotional disturbance was a particularly likely result."

NOTES

(1) *The Case of the "Whole Damned Business."* Mrs. Lamm employed the Shingletons, undertakers, to inter her first husband, Mr. Waddell, in a vault guaranteed to be watertight. About three months later, during a heavy rain, the vault rose above the ground, and the Shingletons undertook to reinter the body. In her presence, they raised the vault and found that the casket was wet. The sight "caused her considerable shock and made her extremely nervous as a result of which she became a nervous wreck." One of the Shingletons said he would not get the mud out of the vault and "to hell with the whole damned business, it's no concern of mine." This made her "so nervous she could hardly stand up." She sued for breach of contract and, from judgment that she take nothing, she appealed. ***Held:*** Reversed. Although "as a general rule," damages for mental anguish are not recoverable in a contract action, the law is "in a state of flux . . . . Where the contract is personal in nature and the contractual duty or obligation is so coupled with matters of mental concern or solicitude, or with the sensibilities of the party to whom the duty is owed, that a breach of that duty will necessarily or reasonably result in mental anguish or suffering, and it should be known to the parties from the nature of the contract that such suffering will result from its breach, compensatory damages therefor may be recovered. . . . The tenderest feelings of the human heart center around the remains of the dead. . . . The contract was predominantly personal in nature and no substantial pecuniary loss would follow its breach. Her mental concern, her sensibilities, and her solicitude were the prime considerations for the contract, and the contract itself was such as to put the defendants on notice that a failure on their part to inter the body properly would probably produce mental suffering on her part." Lamm v. Shingleton, 231 N.C. 10, 55 S.E.2d 810 (1949).[b]

a. In that case the court denied an owner of logging equipment recovery for emotional disturbance occasioned by an auctioneer's sale of it for less than the minimum price specified.

b. For an unusual case granting recovery for "mental anguish" resulting from the defective construction of a new home, see B & M Homes v. Hogan, 376 So.2d 667 (1979). The court noted that the "largest single investment the average American family will make is the purchase of a home" and concluded that "any reasonable builder could easily foresee that an individual would undergo extreme mental anguish if their newly constructed house contained defects as severe as those shown to exist in this case." For a contrary and more traditional view, see Ostrowe v. Darensbourg, 377 So.2d 1201 (La.1979).

(2) *The Case of the Designer Dress.* The purchaser of a custom-made wedding dress sued "the high fashion designer . . . known to the cognoscenti simply as Halston" for "mental anguish" caused because the dress was allegedly improperly made and could not be worn by the purchaser's daughter at her wedding. *Held:* Cause of action dismissed. Levin v. Halston Ltd., 91 Misc.2d 601, 398 N.Y.S.2d 339 (1977).

(c) Certainty

According to the opinion in a leading New York case decided in 1858, damages for breach of contract must "be shown, by clear and satisfactory evidence, to have been actually sustained" and "be shown with certainty, and not left to speculation or conjecture." Griffin v. Colver, 16 N.Y. 489, 491 (1858). Contemporary formulations, however, insist only on "reasonable certainty" rather than on "certainty" itself. Restatement Second, § 352, for example, precludes recovery "for loss beyond an amount that the evidence permits to be established with reasonable certainty." Comment 1 to UCC 1–106 explains that damages need not "be calculable with mathematical accuracy," are "at best approximate," and "have to be proved with whatever definiteness and accuracy the facts permit, but no more." Nevertheless, it is clear that in this regard the injured party has a more onerous burden than that imposed by the ordinary requirement that he make out his case by the "preponderance of evidence." What does this mean in practice? Are there similarities between the operation of this requirement and that of foreseeability?

EVERGREEN AMUSEMENT CORP. v. MILSTEAD

Court of Appeals of Maryland, 1955.
206 Md. 610, 112 A.2d 901.

HAMMOND, Judge. The Evergreen Amusement Corporation, the appellant, operator of a drive-in movie theater, was held liable by the court, sitting without a jury, to Harold D. Milstead, the appellee, a contractor, for the balance due on a written contract for the clearing and grading of the site of the theater and certain extras, less the cost of completing a part of the work and damages for delay in completion, based on rental value of the theater property during the period of delay and out-of-pocket costs for that time.

The appellant, by counterclaim, sought recovery of lost profits for the period of delay. The court held the amount claimed to have been so lost to be too uncertain and speculative, and refused evidence proffered to support appellant's theory. . . .

. . .

The real reliance of the Evergreen Amusement Corporation is on the slowness of the contractor in completing the work. It says that the resulting delay in the opening of the theater from June first to the middle of August cost it twelve thousand five hundred dollars in profits. It proffered a witness to testify that he had built and operated a majority of the drive-in theaters in the area, that he is in the theater equipment business and familiar with the profits that drive-in theaters make in the area, that a market survey was made in the area before the site of the theater was selected, and that it had shown the need for such a theater in the neighborhood. It was said he would testify as to the reasonably anticipated profits during the months in question by comparing the months in its second year of operation with those in which it could not operate the year before, and would say that the profits would have been the same. His further testimony would be, it was claimed, that weather conditions, the population, and competition were all approximately the same in the year the theater opened and the following year.

We think the court did not err in refusing the proffered evidence. Under the great weight of authority, the general rule clearly is that loss of profit is a definite element of damages in an action for breach of contract or in an action for harming an established business which has been operating for a sufficient length of time to afford a basis of estimation with some degree of certainty as to the probable loss of profits, but that, on the other hand, loss of profits from a business which has not gone into operation may not be recovered because they are merely speculative and incapable of being ascertained with the requisite degree of certainty. Restatement, Contracts, § 331, states the law to be that damages are recoverable for profits prevented by breach of contract "only to the extent that the evidence affords a sufficient basis for estimating their amount in money with reasonable certainty", and that where the evidence does not afford a sufficient basis, "damages may be measured by the rental value of the property." Comment "d" says this: "If the defendant's breach has prevented the plaintiff from carrying on *a well-established business*, the amount of profits thereby prevented is often capable of proof with reasonable certainty. On the basis of its past history, a reasonable prediction can be made as to its future." (Italics supplied.) That damages for profits anticipated from a business which has not started may not be recovered, is laid down in C.J.S., Damages § 42, and 15 Am.Jur., Damages, § 157; 5 Corbin, Contracts, §§ 1022, 1023; Cramer v. Grand Rapids Show Case Co., 223 N.Y. 63, 119 N.E. 227, 1 A.L.R. 156; Sinclair Ref. Co. v. Hamilton & Dotson, 164 Va. 203, 178 S.E. 777, 99 A.L.R. 938. See also The Requirement of Certainty for Proof of Lost Profits, 64 Harvard Law 317. The article discusses the difficulties of proving with sufficient certainty the profits which were lost, and then says: "These difficulties have given rise to a rule in some states that no new business can recover for its lost profits." While this Court has not laid down a flat rule (and does not hereby do so), nevertheless, no case has permitted recovery of lost profits under comparable circumstances. In Abbott v. Gatch, 13 Md. 314, the claim for loss of profits arose because of delay in completion of a flour mill. The Court held that the mill owner's loss was to be established by fair rental value for the time of the delay resulting from failure to complete it according to contract, that he could not recover estimated profits, because it was dependent, as they were, upon the quality of flour available, the fluctuation of prices of flour, continuance of the mill in running order and other variants. The Court labelled the damages claimed speculative and refused to follow a Vermont case which had allowed them to be shown. The rule laid down in this case has been followed in a number of others. . . .

. . .

Judgment affirmed, with costs.

NOTES

(1) *New Businesses.* In Ferrell v. Elrod, 63 Tenn.App. 129, 469 S.W. 2d 678 (1971), the court had this to say of the principal case: "Acknowledging the practical difficulty of proving with reasonable certainty the amount of anticipated profits of a new enterprise, this Court is unable to agree with the holding of Evergreen, which would effectively exonerate a defaulting contractor from damages suffered by a new business." It sustained an award of damages for breach of an agreement to lease premises to a new "school of cosmetology" based on the school's record of profits after it opened nine months later at another location.

A similar view was expressed in Handi Caddy, Inc. v. American Home Products Corp., 557 F.2d 136 (8th Cir. 1977): "We recognize that a distinction is to be made between claims for profits derived from a new business venture and those derived from a going concern. A new business labors under a greater burden of proof in overcoming the general rule that evidence of expected profits is too speculative, uncertain, and remote to be considered and does not meet the legal standard of reasonable certainty. . . . It does not follow, however, that a so-called 'new' business can never recover lost profits as an item of damages for breach of contract. In the final analysis, the question is primarily a problem of proof. Each case must rest upon the evidence adduced and it is for the trial judge in the first instance to determine whether the complaining party has produced the quantum and quality of evidence sufficient to submit the issue to a jury."

(2) *Royalties from Artistic Creations.* The requirement of reasonable certainty has plagued plaintiffs whose claims are based on lost royalties on artistic creations. In Freund v. Washington Square Press, Inc., 34 N.Y.2d 379, 357 N.Y.S.2d 857, 314 N.E.2d 419 (1974), for example, the author of a book on modern drama sued his publisher for breach of its contract to publish and pay royalties on the book. The court held that he was properly denied recovery for his lost royalties. "His expectancy interest in the royalties—the profit he stood to gain from the sale of the published book—while theoretically compensable, was speculative. Although this work is not

plaintiff's first, at trial he provided no stable foundation for a reasonable estimate of royalties he would have earned had defendant not breached its promise to publish."

The plaintiff fared somewhat better, however, in Contemporary Mission, Inc. v. Famous Music Corp., 557 F.2d 918 (2d Cir. 1977), in which New York law was applied. There a group of Roman Catholic priests who wrote musical compositions and recordings sued Famous Music for breach of its contract to make and sell records on a royalty basis from the master tape recording of their rock opera "Virgin." It was held that the trial court erred in excluding a statistical analysis, together with expert testimony, in order to prove how successful the most successful of the opera's single recordings, "Fear No Evil," would have been. The court acknowledged, citing the Freund case, that the requirement of certainty "operates with particular severity in cases involving artistic creations such as books, . . . movies, . . . and, by analogy, records." Nevertheless, at the time of the breach, "the record was real, the price was fixed, the market was buying and the record's success, while modest, was increasing. Even after the promotional efforts ended, the record was withdrawn from the marketplace, it was carried, as a result of its own momentum, to an additional 10,000 sales and to a rise from approximately number 80 on the "Hot Soul Singles' chart of Billboard magazine to number 61." The court, however, rejected the plaintiff's "domino theory" of projected damages under which, if "Fear No Evil" had become a "hit," it would have generated opportunities for concert and theatrical tours and similar benefits on the ground that "these additional benefits are too dependent upon taste or fancy to be considered anything other than speculative and uncertain."

(3) *Good Will.* In Harry Rubin & Sons v. Consolidated Pipe Co., p. 152 supra, the case of the failure to deliver "hula hoops," the Supreme Court of Pennsylvania (in an omitted part of the opinion, 396 Pa. at 512–13, 153 A.2d at 476) rejected the buyer's claim for loss of his customers' good will. "Our research fails to reveal any judicial authority in Pennsylvania which sustains, under the [prior Uniform] Sales Act, a recovery for a loss of good will occasioned either by nondelivery or by the delivery of defective goods. . . . There is no indication that the Uniform Commercial Code was intended to enlarge the scope of a buyer's damages to include a loss of good will. In the absence of a specific declaration in this respect, we believe that damages of this nature would be entirely too speculative . . . ." For a different view on recovery for loss of good will, see Stott v. Johnston, 36 Cal.2d 864, 229 P.2d 348 (1951); Sol-O-Lite Laminating Corp. v. Allen, 223 Or. 80, 353 P.2d 843 (1960).

LEE v. JOSEPH E. SEAGRAM & SONS, INC.

United States Court of Appeals, Second Circuit, 1977.
552 F.2d 447.

[The facts and another part of the opinion in this case are at p. 235 supra and another part of the opinion is at p. 669 infra.]

GURFEIN, Circuit Judge: . . .

III

The jury awarded the two sons and the estate of the father damages in the amount of $407,850. The essence of the court's charge on the subject was that in a contract action the basic principle of damages "is to indemnify a plaintiff for the gains prevented and the losses sustained by a defendant's breach, to leave him no worse but in no better position than he would have been had the breach not occurred." The court charged that the jury was to determine the reasonable value of the injury, if any. It charged further that "from the sum thus arrived at, you will then deduct such amount, if any, as from the evidence you find fairly measures the benefit to plaintiffs resulting from the fact that plaintiffs were freed to engage their services and capital in other situations during the time they would otherwise have been engaged in the management of an investment in the alleged promised distributorship."

Plaintiffs introduced testimony by Ernest L. Sommers, a certified public accountant, whom the District Court found to be qualified as an expert. Sommers compared one-half of the profits of Capitol City in its *last* fiscal year ending June 1, 1970 on the theory that profits for the past five years showed an upward trend, with the amount earned on investments in bonds by the plaintiffs in the year succeeding the sale. He found that one-half of the Capitol City pre-tax profits, based on one-half the sales price, amounted to 14.508%. The return on the bond investment was 7.977%. He then subtracted the percentage return on the investment bonds from the percentage return of the Capitol City operation, which gave him a percentage figure for the loss occasioned by the breach, of 6.531%. This figure, applied to one-half the sales price, came to $83,800 per annum before taxes. Multiplying this figure by only ten years—an assumed minimum measure for the life of the "new" distributorship—would make an $838,000 total loss. Discounting to present value, the witness reduced the figure to $549,000. The jury returned a verdict, as we have seen, for a lesser amount, $407,850. There is, therefore, no element of damage in the verdict amount for which no evidence was submitted to the jury. *See* Locke v. United States, 283 F.2d 521, 151 Ct.Cl. 262 (1960). Appellant contends, however, that plaintiffs' proof of damages was speculative and incompetent.

Appellant's position is based in large measure on some confusion about the precise nature of the agreement found by the jury, *see* notes 2 and 7 supra.[a] Plaintiffs' evidence bore directly on the damages sustained by breach of a contract to provide a distributorship of one-half the cost and worth of Capitol City, and on the "fair measure" of the sums properly deducted. Appellant's contention that plaintiffs should have been required to prove, as a *sine qua non* to

a. Note 2 is at p. 237 supra, and 7 is at p. 238 supra.

any damage award, that there was a Seagram distributor actually willing to sell his distributorship to them, is without merit. The oral agreement, as the jury was permitted to find, was for Seagram to *provide* a distributorship for the Lees. The jury was permitted to find that Seagram could have fulfilled this obligation by steering a voluntary sale of a distributorship to the plaintiffs or could have financed an intermediate transaction, warehousing the acquired distributorship for the plaintiffs, *see* note 2 supra.

Seagram contends that lost profits are not the proper measure of damages for breach of contract, and that cases allowing damages for destruction of injury to an ongoing business are not controlling. Lost profits can, however, be a proper measure of damages for breach of contract. As the Court of Appeals for the First Circuit said in Standard Machinery Co. v. Duncan Shaw Corp., 208 F.2d 61, 64:

"Certainly no authority need be cited for the broad proposition that prospective profits, if proved, are an element of a plaintiff's damages for breach of contract, or for the further proposition that evidence of past profits from an established business provides a reasonable basis for estimating future profits from the business."

. . . This is so even if the prospective business has not yet begun operation. . . .

Seagram objects to the fact that plaintiffs' proof concerned the profit experience of Capitol City. It suggests that the best way of determining profits would be to consider the profits of an existing distributorship. But it came forward with no such proof, presumably for tactical reasons. We hold that the method of proof used by the plaintiffs was adequate in the circumstances. Since Seagram's breach has made difficult a more precise proof of damages, it must bear the risk of uncertainty created by its conduct. Bigelow v. RKO Radio Pictures, 327 U.S. 251, 264–65, 66 S.Ct. 574, 90 L.Ed. 652 (1946) . . . .[b] New York law is in accord. Spitz v. Lesser, 302 N.Y. 490, 99 N.E.2d 540 (1951). As the court said in Wakeman v. Wheeler Mfg. Co., 101 N.Y. 205, 209, 4 N.E. 264, 266 (1886):

"When it is certain that damages have been caused by a breach of contract, and the only uncertainty is as to their amount, there can rarely be good reason for refusing, on account of such uncertainty, any damages whatever for the breach. A person violating his contract should not be permitted entirely to escape liability because the amount of damages which he has caused is uncertain."

. . .

Mere dispute on the validity of some of the figures cannot wipe out the evidence but merely emphasizes that the jury was presented

b. The Bigelow case involved a private action for treble damages under the antitrust laws, not a suit for breach of contract. The more liberal rule laid down under the antitrust laws has had, as the Lee case indicates, a liberalizing effect in contract actions too.

with a factual question whose determination we should not change. . . . "The trial court has a large amount of discretion in determining whether to submit the question of profits to the jury; and when it is so submitted, the jury will also have a large amount of discretion in determining the amount of its verdict." 5 Corbin on Contracts § 1022, at 145–46. . . .

Affirmed.

NOTES

(1) *The Fact of Loss.* Some courts have taken the extreme position that as long as "a reasonable probability of damage can be clearly established, uncertainty as to the amount will not preclude recovery." Locke v. United States, 283 F.2d 521, 524 (Ct.Cl.1960). What does this leave of the requirement of certainty?

(2) *The Value of a Chance.* In Collatz v. Fox Wisconsin Amusement Corp., 239 Wis. 156, 300 N.W. 162 (1941), the plaintiff, one of two finalists in a quiz contest held at the defendant's theater, claimed a half interest in the automobile offered as a prize, on the ground that it had been arbitrarily awarded to the other finalist before completion of the contest. The court held for the defendant. The plaintiff "suffered no damage because of the defendant's breach of the contract, for it cannot be assumed nor is it susceptible of proof that had the contest proceeded to a proper finish he would have become the winner." The classic case to the contrary is Chaplin v. Hicks, [1911] 2 K.B. 786, in which the winner of a preliminary round in a beauty contest prevailed. Accord: Wachtel v. National Alfalfa Journal Co., 190 Iowa 1293, 176 N.W. 801 (1920). See Restatement Second, § 348(3); Note, 18 Rutgers L.Rev. 875 (1964); see also Schaefer, Uncertainty and the Law of Damages, 19 Wm. & Mary L.Rev. 719 (1978).

(3) *The Case of the Predictable Percentage.* Rombola agreed to train, maintain and race Cosindas' horse Margy Sampson, for a period of about a year, Rombola to receive seventy-five percent and Cosindas twenty-five percent of all gross purses. Cosindas broke the contract by taking the horse at Suffolk Downs, thereby depriving Rombola of his right to race the horse at six stake races at the end of the period. (In such a race the purse is shared in diminishing percentages by the first five finishers out of eight or nine starters, and the horse had already raced against several of the horses that were entered in these races.) Rombola sued and the judge directed a verdict against him after his opening statement to the jury. Rombola appealed. *Held:* Reversed. "It appears that Margy Sampson had already been accepted as a participant in the stake races and transported to the site of the meet. She had already proved her ability both prior to and while under Rombola's management and training, over an extended period of time, against many competitors and under varying track conditions. Her consistent performance in the year subsequent to the breach negates any basis for an inference of a diminution in ability or in earning capacity at the time of the Suffolk Downs meet. While it is possible that no profits would have been realized if Margy Sampson had participated in the scheduled stake races, that possibility is inherent in any business venture. It is not sufficient to foreclose Rombola's right to prove prospective profits. . . . Her earnings record, while not conclusive, is admissible as evidence of the extent of damages caused by the breach." Rombola v. Cosindas, 351 Mass. 382, 220 N.E.2d 919 (1966).

(4) ***The Right to Work.*** In Shirley MacLaine Parker's case, p. 594 supra, could she have recovered more than $750,000? Was not the right to star in "Bloomer Girl" a valuable right that would have enhanced her reputation as an actress? A few courts have recognized such a right in cases like Mrs. Parker's. See e. g., Herbert Clayton & Jack Waller, Ltd. v. Oliver [1930] A.C. 209, in which the court said: "Here both parties knew that as flowing from the contract the plaintiff would be billed and advertised as appearing at the Hippodrome, and in the theatrical profession this is a valuable right." For a different view, see Quinn v. Strauss Broadcasting Group, 309 F.Supp. 1208 (S.D.N.Y.1970). Can the value of such a right be established with sufficient certainty? What advice would you have given Mrs. Parker concerning her chances of recovery of damages based on such a right?

(5) *Nominal Damages.* The plaintiff who proves a breach of contract but fails to prove damages is traditionally awarded nominal damages (six cents or one dollar). Such an award may serve as a declaration of the plaintiff's rights and may also carry with it an award of court costs.

SECTION 4. "LIQUIDATED DAMAGES" AND "PENALTIES"

At the beginning of this book, it was pointed out that our law's concern is directed at relief of promisees to redress breach rather than at punishment of promisors to compel performance, and that for this reason punitive damages are not ordinarily awarded for breach of contract. See White v. Benkowski, p. 14 supra. The *promisee,* however, may be concerned with compulsion of the promisor. Consider the following explanation given by a bridge engineer for the California Division of Highways of the completion assessment, the per-day assessment against a contractor for each day he overruns the specified contract time. "The sole purpose of a completion assessment is to assure that the contract work will be done within the time specified, . . . to threaten the Contractor with sufficient monetary loss so that he will find it advantageous to apply sufficient men and equipment to the work to get it done on time. Whereas moderate liquidated damages such as $100 per day may well be used to insure the completion of a normal project having no special urgency, higher amounts are used to force faster work on jobs which must be finished in less than a normal construction time. High assessments may be used to emphasize the need for haste and should be of sufficient size to make it economically desirable that the contractor expedite his work by the use of multiple shifts or additional equipment." Elliott, A Study of Liquidated Damages on Highway Contracts 5 (1956). Should courts lend their aid to the enforcement of such penalties where the parties have bargained for and agreed to them?

The attitude of common law courts toward penalties has been strongly influenced by the development of equitable relief in cases arising under penal bonds. A penal bond, originally a sealed instrument, takes the form of a promise to pay a stated sum, coupled with a condition of defeasance. Here is an example:

> Know All Men By These Presents that A. B. is held and firmly bound to C. D. in the sum of $10,000 for the payment of which the said A. B. binds himself, his executors, administrators and assigns. The condition of the foregoing obligation is such that if A. B. shall well and truly pay unto C. D. the sum of $5,000 on . . . , the above obligation to be void; otherwise to be in full force and effect. A. B. (Seal).

The persistence of legal forms can be seen in the A.I.A.'s standard performance bond which, after setting out the amount of the bond, goes on to provide:

> Now, therefore, the condition of this obligation is such that, if Contractor shall promptly and faithfully perform said Contract, then this obligation shall be null and void; otherwise it shall remain in full force and effect.

At common law, unless the obligor had strictly performed the condition of the bond, a court would give judgment in debt against him for the penal sum, regardless of the amount of loss caused the obligee by the non-performance of the condition. By the time of the Restoration it had become settled that equity would enjoin the collection of the penal sum by the obligee and send the case to trial at law for ascertainment of the amount of damage caused by the breach of condition.[a] Upon this equity practice were based statutes under which the obligee was required at common law to state the breach of condition, and (although he was at first given a judgment for the entire penal sum) was allowed to have execution only for the amount of damages actually proved. American courts, usually by virtue of similar statutes, took over the notion that the obligee under a penal bond must plead and prove the damages caused by the breach of condition. See Loyd, Penalties and Forfeitures, 29 Harv.L.Rev. 117 (1915).

The principles developed first for penal bonds were later extended to apply to penalties in contracts of all kinds. They have also been invoked where a sum has actually been paid as a deposit, if that sum is so unreasonably large as to appear to be a penalty. On the effect of a deposit on the revocability of an offer, see Note 3, p. 264 supra.

However, not every stipulation of damages is a penalty. Such stipulations are often sustained as valid provisions for liquidated

a. This development was analogous to that of the mortgagor's "equity of redemption." See p. 775 infra.

damages. Once it is conceded that a line is to be drawn between "penalties" and "liquidated damages," there remains the not inconsiderable task of drawing it.

A typical case is Dave Gustafson & Co. v. State, 83 S.D. 160, 156 N.W.2d 185 (1968). Gustafson surfaced a new state highway that paralleled an older road that remained open during and after the construction. From the $530,724.14 due for the work, the state withheld $14,070 that it claimed as liquidated damages for a delay of 67 days. The contract provided a graduated scale of "liquidated damages per day" under which damages of $210 per day were fixed for a contract in an amount of over $500,000 but not more than $1,000,000. This daily damage multiplied by 67 gave $14,070. The Supreme Court of South Dakota held that this was a valid provision for liquidated damages. It affirmed its earlier statement that, "A provision for payment of a stipulated sum as a liquidation of damages will ordinarily be sustained if it appears that at the time the contract was made the damages in the event of a breach will be incapable or very difficult of accurate estimation, that there was a reasonable endeavor by the parties as stated to fix fair compensation, and that the amount stipulated bears a reasonable relation to probable damages and not disproportionate to any damages reasonably to be anticipated." Observing that there is a "modern tendency not to look with disfavor upon 'liquidated damages' provisions in contracts," it concluded that the provision in question met those tests. "I. Damages for delay in constructing a new highway are impossible of measurement. II. The amount stated in the contract as liquidated damages indicates an endeavor to fix fair compensation for the loss, inconvenience, added costs, and deprivation of use caused by delay. Daily damage is graduated according to total amount of work to be performed. It may be assumed that a large project involves more loss than a small one and each day of delay adds to the loss, inconvenience, cost and deprivation of use. . . . III. For the same reasons we must conclude the amount stipulated in the contract bears a reasonable relation to probable damages and is not, as a matter of law, disproportionate to any and all damage reasonably to be anticipated from the unexcused delay in performance."

Compare the rule in UCC 2–718(1). See, generally, Macneil, Power of Contract and Agreed Remedies, 47 Cornell L.Q. 495 (1962); Sweet, Liquidated Damages in California, 60 Calif.L.Rev. 84 (1972); Comments, 45 Fordham L.Rev. 1349 (1977); 72 Nw.U.L.Rev. 1055 (1978). As to the economic justification for the distinction between penalties and liquidated damages, compare Clarkson, Miller & Muris, Liquidated Damages v. Penalties: Sense or Nonsense?, 1978 Wis.L. Rev. 351, with Goetz & Scott, Liquidated Damages, Penalties and the Just Compensation Principle . . ., 77 Colum.L.Rev. 554 (1977).

NOTES

(1) *Penalties in Other Legal Systems.* Are there reasons of public policy that justify the limitation on freedom of contract with respect to penalties? Are terms providing for penalties more onerous than other terms? Some insights may be gained from a look at other legal systems.

According to article 1152 of the French Civil Code: "When the agreement provides that the party who fails to carry it out shall pay a certain sum as damages, no larger or smaller amount can be awarded to the other party." In 1975, however, following a recommendation that there be judicial control over penal clauses in leases, this article was amended by adding: "However, the judge may reduce or increase the penalty that has been agreed upon if it is plainly excessive or ridiculously low. No effect will be given to an agreement to the contrary." What might have prompted these changes? On these and related changes, see A. von Mehren & J. Gordley, The Civil Law System 818 (2d ed. 1977); Beardsley, Compelling Contract Performance in France, Hastings Int. & Comp.L.Rev. 93–102 (Inaug. Issue 1977).

In the communist countries, where the contracts of state enterprises are designed to carry out an economic plan and the injured party ordinarily does not have alternative sources of supply or demand, penalties for breach of contract are common and are paid to the injured party rather than to the state. It has been suggested that this has the advantage of giving "the other party an incentive to sue and thus to expose defects in planning, violations of contract discipline, and the like." Berman, Protection of Rights Arising out of Economic Contracts under Socialist Legal Systems: A Comparative Approach, 14 Osteuropa-Recht 213, 217 (1968); see also Loeber, Plan and Contract Performance in Soviet Society in W. La Fave (ed.), Law in the Soviet Society 128, 169–72 (1965).

(2) *What the Traffic Will Bear.* How much should the draftsman ask for in preparing a liquidated damage clause? As much as the traffic will bear, consistent with the cases? Or are there practical limitations as well? Consider the following analysis. "High liquidated damages have a tendency to make the contractors jittery. A fear of the high cost of delay will cause an involuntary rise in bid prices. All of the bidders' thinking on prices must inevitably be colored by the specter of the high damages lurking in the background. This only emphasizes the need to use this specialized treatment and high liquidated damages only on those projects where the urgency really exists. Otherwise the State will be paying extra for expediting jobs which do not need the hurry and will not justify the higher cost. High liquidated damages make a contractor susceptible to considerable labor pressure. When a contractor is working under high liquidated damages, it gives the unions a powerful lever to force compliance with demands which may or may not be justified. The contractor is forced to give in because he cannot afford a delaying argument or strike. This pressure also may have a widespread effect. When labor unions make an advance by this sort of a squeeze play against the contractor working under high liquidated damages, other contractors in the area find that they too must give the same benefits or face considerable trouble." Elliott, A Study of Liquidated Damages on Highway Contracts 21–22 (1956).

(3) *Equitable Relief.* Should a valid liquidated damage clause bar equitable relief that would otherwise be available? See Karpinski v. Ingrasci, p. 536 supra; Bauer v. Sawyer, 8 Ill.2d 351, 134 N.E.2d 329 (1956).

(4) *Problem.* Seller contracts to deliver to Buyer a machine that is readily available on the market for $1,000 more than the contract price. If Seller fails to deliver, what are the rights of the parties under each of the following provisions?

(a) "In the event of Seller's failure to deliver, he shall pay Buyer a penalty of $10,000."

(b) "In the event of Seller's failure to deliver, he shall be liable to Buyer for $10,000 in liquidated damages."

(c) "Seller hereby agrees, at his option, to either deliver the machine to Buyer or to pay Buyer $10,000."

(d) "In the event of Seller's failure to deliver, Buyer shall be entitled to keep the $10,000 deposit that Seller has made to secure performance of this contract."

SEEMAN v. BIEMANN, 108 Wis. 365, 84 N.W. 490 (1900). [A contractor agreed with the owner of a building to do carpenter and joiner work by a specified date. The contract provided that if the work was not completed by this date, the contractor "should forfeit the sum of $10 as liquidated damages for each day's delay." The same provision was contained in six other contracts made by the owner for work on the building. The total amount of all the contracts was $5,000 and the value of the building and land was less than $6,000. The work was completed with a delay of fifty-three days, and the owner claimed liquidated damages under the clause.]

MARSHALL, J. . . . This court, in harmony with the weight of authority, early adopted the rule that where damages may be readily computed and the stipulated damages, so called, are largely in excess of actual damages, the court will disregard what the parties say they intended, and presume that they intended what is fair and reasonable under the circumstances, however much that may violate their language. . . . Applying [this rule] to the case before us, the stipulation of $10 per day for delay must be held to be a penalty merely, and not necessarily recoverable to the whole amount. The rental value of the property as found by the court was $38 per month. This is the true measure of actual damages, since there were no special circumstances shown by the evidence, brought home to the knowledge of the contractor at the time of the making of the contract, from which we can say the damages which the parties then had in contemplation as the probable result of a breach of contract as to time of completing the building were other than loss of use for the period of delay. . . .

The rental value of the building is trifling in amount as compared with the stipulated damages, so called, of $10 per day. There was, in the nature of the case, at the time the contract was made, no difficulty to be apprehended in arriving at the actual damages that might arise from mere delay in completing the building. So we have the two elements recognized as controlling the language of parties respecting stipulated damages, first, the amount the parties say they agreed upon is grossly in excess of the actual damages sustained or that could have been reasonably apprehended at the time of making the contract; second, the damages actually sustained are readily ascertainable. It follows that we must hold that the parties intended the $10 per day as a mere penalty to secure the performance of the contract, and limit the recoverable damages to such as were actually sustained, to wit $38 per month for fifty-three days, or $67.12, with six per cent interest thereon from the date the breach of the contract was complete. . . .

NOTES

(1) *Bonus.* Would the court have refused to enforce a provision calling for a bonus of $10 a day if the contractor finished the work earlier than the specified date?

(2) *"Blunderbuss" Clauses.* A clause in which a single sum is provided for any breach, regardless of its nature, is sometimes characterized as a "shotgun" or "blunderbuss" clause. Such clauses have usually been held to be invalid. See, e. g., Seidlitz v. Auerbach, 230 N.Y. 167, 129 N.E. 461 (1920), in which a lease containing many covenants of varying importance provided for a deposit by the tenant of $7,500 "as security for the faithful performance by the tenant of all the covenants and agreements herein contained" and that as damages for any default by the tenant the landlord could retain the full amount of the deposit. Occasionally, however, a court may so interpret the clause as to limit its application to substantial breaches and then hold it valid. See, e. g., Hackenheimer v. Kurtzmann, 235 N.Y. 57, 138 N.E. 735 (1923), in which the same court as in the case just cited interpreted a provision for $50,000 damages "in case of breach" to apply only to important breaches and held it valid. Cf. Karpinski v. Ingrasci, p. 536 supra. Why should such a clause be stricken as long as it was a reasonable forecast as to the breach that actually occurred?

(3) *Arbitration and Liquidated Damages.* Suppose that in Seeman v. Biemann, the contract had included the arbitration clause recommended by the American Arbitration Association. See Note 1, p. 40 supra. Would the court have enforced an arbitration award granting damages under the clause that it held unenforceable in the actual case? See Associated General Contractors v. Savin Brothers, 36 N.Y.2d 957, 373 N.Y.S.2d 555, 335 N.E.2d 859 (1975). How does the question differ from that in Note 3, p. 40 supra?

(4) *Problem.* Buyer contracted to purchase land from Seller for $60,000. Buyer paid $100 when the contract was signed, the balance to be paid at the time of settlement. The contract contained the following provision:

> Should the buyer fail to make settlement as herein provided, sum or sums paid on account are to be retained by the seller either on

account of the purchase money, or as compensation for the damages and expenses he has been put to in this behalf, as the seller shall elect and in the latter case this contract shall become null and void and all copies to be returned to the seller for cancellation.

Buyer broke the contract by refusing to take a deed and pay the balance of the price. Although Seller had a legal right to recover the balance of the price from Buyer, it chose instead to sell the land to another purchaser for $54,000. What are Seller's rights against Buyer? See Harris v. Dawson, 479 Pa. 463, 388 A.2d 748 (1978).

SOUTHWEST ENGINEERING CO. v. UNITED STATES

United States Court of Appeals, Eighth Circuit, 1965.
341 F.2d 998.

VAN OOSTERHOUT, Circuit Judge. Plaintiff Southwest Engineering Company, hereinafter called Southwest, has appealed from summary judgment dismissing its complaint against the United States for recovery of $8,300 withheld as liquidated damages for delay in performance on four construction contracts entered into between Southwest and the United States.

This appeal is before us upon an agreed statement of the record. Four contracts entered into between Southwest and the Government called for the construction by Southwest of three V. O. R. radio facilities at Readsville, Blackwater, and Maryland Heights, Missouri, and for a high intensity approach light lane at Lambert Field, Missouri. Each of the contracts fixed a completion date and provided for liquidated damages on a per diem basis for each day's delay beyond the agreed completion date. The agreed liquidated damage on the Lambert Field project was $100 per day, and $50 per day on each of the other projects. Each contract contained the general provisions set forth in Standard Form 23–A (March 1953) prescribed by the General Services Administration, including, among others, a provision that plaintiff was not to be charged with delays "due to unforeseeable causes beyond the control and without the fault or negligence of the Contractor, including, but not restricted to, acts of God, or of the public enemy, acts of the Government, in either its sovereign or contractual capacity, acts of another contractor in the performance of a contract with the Government, fires, floods, epidemics, quarantine restrictions, strikes, freight embargoes, and unusually severe weather, or delays of subcontractors or suppliers due to such causes." Within ten days from the beginning of any such delay, plaintiff was to notify the contracting officer in writing of the causes of delay. The contracting officer was to ascertain the facts and extent of the delay, and extend the time for completing the work when "in his judgment the findings of fact justify such an extension." His findings of fact were to be final, subject only to appeal to the "head of the department."

The Blackwater project was completed 97 days late. Plaintiff requested time extensions, alleging the delay resulted from causes for which it was not responsible, including acts and omissions of defendant. Administrative appeals resulted in extensions by the C.A.A. because of delays by the Government, and, later on, a remission of an additional $4,200 liquidated damages by the Comptroller General under the authority of 41 U.S.C.A. § 256a, because of late delivery of Government-furnished material. This left $550 (11 days) withheld as liquidated damages on the Blackwater project.

The Readsville project was completed 84 days late. Administrative appeals resulted in a three-days extension, leaving liquidated damages for 81 days totalling $4,050.

The Maryland Heights project was completed 48 days late. On administrative appeal, a fourteen-days extension was allowed resulting in liquidated damages of $1,700 for 34 days delay.

The Lambert Field project was completed 54 days late, 34 days extension was granted, leaving $2,000 as liquidated damages for 20 days delay.

The parties stipulated "although each project was not completed until after the date prescribed in its contract, defendant suffered no actual damage on any project." The Government withheld the liquidated damages for delays provided in the contracts after giving credit for the extensions of time administratively allowed. This suit by Southwest is for recovery of the $8,300 so withheld as liquidated damages. The Government counterclaimed for the liquidated damages here involved. Plaintiff by reply admitted the projects were not completed within the time limits as administratively extended but denied the Government was entitled to liquidated damages because the Government caused and contributed to the delays and because the Government suffered no actual damages.

The trial court determined that the Government was entitled to liquidated damages in the amount claimed, offset such damages which equaled the amount of payments withheld, sustained the motion for summary judgment, and dismissed the complaint.

Southwest as a basis for reversal urges the trial court's decision was induced by two erroneous views of the law, either of which requires reversal. The points relied upon for reversal are thus stated:

1. "The court erred in awarding the Government liquidated damages because the Government, in order to enforce a contract provision for liquidated damages for delay, must not cause or contribute to such delay, and if the Government does cause or contribute to such delay, it cannot assess liquidated damages."

2. "The court erred in awarding the Government liquidated damages because a contract provision for liquidated damages is clearly a penalty and not enforceable where the party seeking to enforce it formally admits he sustained no actual damage."

At the outset, we observe that the contracts here involved were entered into pursuant to federal law by an authorized federal agency. Federal law controls in the construction and determination of rights under federal contracts. Priebe & Sons, Inc. v. United States, 332 U.S. 407, 411, 68 S.Ct. 123, 92 L.Ed. 32; Clearfield Trust Co. v. United States, 318 U.S. 363, 63 S.Ct. 573, 87 L.Ed. 838; United States v. Le Roy Dyal Co., 3 Cir., 186 F.2d 460, 461.

In the Priebe case, the Supreme Court states: "It is customary, where Congress has not adopted a different standard, to apply to the construction of government contracts the principles of general contract law. United States v. Standard Rice Co., 323 U.S. 106, 111, [65 S.Ct. 145, 147, 89 L.Ed. 104] and cases cited. That has been done in other cases where the Court has considered the enforceability of 'liquidated damages' provisions in government contracts." 332 U.S. 407, 411, 68 S.Ct. 123, 125.

Southwest's first point, to the effect that the Government is not entitled to liquidated damages because it caused or contributed to the delay, is without merit. It is true that in the administrative appeals a finding was made that some of the delay was caused by the Government and that some other delays were excusable. No damages were withheld for excusable delays as administratively determined. . . .

Southwest's second point in substance is that the parties' stipulation that the Government suffered no actual damage bars any recovery of liquidated damages. Such stipulation was made. It relates to the situation as it existed at the time of the completion of the work. The stipulation does not go to the extent of agreeing that the parties at the time of contracting did not reasonably contemplate that damages would flow from a delay in performance.

The contracts prescribe the payments to be made for delays as liquidated damages. Southwest urges that such provision is a penalty provision. The agreed record is highly condensed and does not show the contract price for the various projects, but such projects appear to be substantial. There is no showing that the liquidated damages for delay provided for are beyond damages reasonably contemplated by the parties at the time of the contract.

Two requirements must be considered to determine whether the provision included in the contract fixing the amount of damages payable on breach will be interpreted as an enforceable liquidated damage clause rather than an unforceable penalty clause: First, the amount so fixed must be a reasonable forecast of just compensation for the harm that is caused by the breach, and second, the harm that is caused by the breach must be one that is incapable or very difficult of accurate estimation. See J. D. Street & Co. v. United States, 8 Cir., 256 F.2d 557, 559; United States v. Le Roy Ryal Co., supra; Restatement, Contracts § 339.

Whether these requirements have been complied with must be viewed as of the time the contract was executed rather than when the contract was breached or at some other subsequent time. Courts presently look with candor upon provisions that are deliberately entered into between parties and therefore do not look with disfavor upon liquidated damage stipulations. Rex Trailer Co. v. United States, 350 U.S. 148, 151, 76 S.Ct. 219, 100 L.Ed. 149; Priebe & Sons, Inc. v. United States supra; United States v. Bethlehem Steel Co., 205 U.S. 105, 119, 27 S.Ct. 450, 51 L.Ed. 731; Sun Printing & Publishing Ass'n v. Moore, 183 U.S. 642, 660, 22 S.Ct. 240, 46 L.Ed. 366.

In the *Bethlehem Steel* case, the Court sets out the standard to be applied for determining whether a liquidated damage provision can be upheld as follows: "The question always is, What did the parties intend by the language used? When such intention is ascertained it is ordinarily the duty of the court to carry it out." 205 U.S. 105, 119, 27 S.Ct. 450, 455.

Here Southwest has failed to establish that the intention of the parties was to do anything other than execute a valid liquidated damage provision.

Priebe & Sons, Inc. v. United States, supra, involved a Government contract for purchase of dried eggs for foreign shipment. The Court observes the contract contains two provisions for liquidated damages. The one involved in the case related to failure to have eggs inspected and ready for delivery for the date specified in the order. The court construed the contract to mean that performance was not due until demand for delivery and held that since inspection was made before such demand, the provision for liquidated damages could not possibly be a reasonable forecast of just compensation for breach of contract. The Court further observes that the contract contains a provision for liquidated damages for delay in delivery upon demand and with respect to such provision, breach of which was not involved, states: "It likewise is apparent that the only thing which could possibly injure the Government would be failure to get prompt performance when delivery was due. We have no doubt of the validity of the provision for 'liquidated damages' when applied under those circumstances." 332 U.S. 407, 412, 68 S.Ct. 123, 126.

The Court also speaks of standards applicable to allowance of liquidated damages, stating: "Today the law does not look with disfavor upon 'liquidated damages' provisions in contracts. When they are fair and reasonable attempts to fix just compensation for anticipated loss caused by breach of contract, they are enforced. . . . . They serve a particularly useful function when damages are uncertain in nature or amount or are unmeasurable, as is the case in many government contracts. . . . . And the fact that the damages suffered are shown to be less than the damages contracted for is not fatal. These provisions are to be judged as of the time of making the contract." 332 U.S. 407, 411–412, 68 S.Ct. 123, 126.

In Rex Trailer Co. v. United States, supra, recovery was allowed upon the statutory penalty imposed for fraud in obtaining a Government contract. The Court states: "Liquidated-damage provisions, when reasonable, are not to be regarded as penalties, ..." 350 U.S. 148, 151, 76 S.Ct. 219, 221. And then says: "The Government's recovery here is comparable to the recovery under liquidated-damage provisions which fix compensation for anticipated loss. As this Court recognized in Priebe & Sons v. United States, 332 U.S. 407, 411–412, [68 S.Ct. 123, 126, 92 L.Ed. 32] liquidated damages 'serve a particularly useful function when damages are uncertain in nature or amount or are unmeasurable, as is the case in many government contracts. . . . ' And the fact that no damages are shown is not fatal." 350 U.S. 148, 153, 76 S.Ct. 219, 222.

In United States v. J. D. Streett & Co., E.D.Mo., 151 F.Supp. 469, 472, Judge Harper, in upholding a claim for liquidated damages, states: "Although it is clear that a finding that a provision is one for liquidated damages requires that damages could be anticipated at the time of execution of the contract, whether actual damage did or did not occur or was not proved to have occurred does not prevent recovery."
We affirmed upon appeal. J. D. Streett & Co. v. United States, 8 Cir., 256 F.2d 557.

The late Judge Goodrich in United States v. Le Roy Dyal Co., supra, in a well-considered opinion dealing with numerous aspects of the liquidated damage issue, states: "If a provision for liquidated damages is upheld the fact that actual damage did nor did not occur or was not proved to have occurred does not prevent the recovery of the stipulated sum. There is some dissent on this point, but the statement just made represents the great weight of decided cases." 186 F.2d 460, 462.

In Frick Co. v. Rubel Corp., 2 Cir., 62 F.2d 765, 768, the late Judge Learned Hand allowed liquidated damages, stating inter alia: "My brothers think, though I do not, that evidence as to the *actual* loss was not material to the issue of the losses in *contemplation*, though we all agree that it is the comparison of the liquidated damages with the last, not the first, which can raise the point at all."

C.J.S. Damages § 115d; 15 Am.Jur., Damages, § 263, and 34 A.L.R. 1336, 1341, and supporting cases cited in such authorities, indicate that the majority view is that proof of actual damages is not required to sustain an action for liquidated damages, unless the contracts so provide, at least in situations where damages could reasonably be anticipated at the time of contracting.

We recognize that there are cases, including Massman Const. Co. v. City Council of Greenville, 5 Cir., 147 F.2d 925, Rispin v. Midnight Oil Co., 9 Cir., 291 F. 481, 34 A.L.R. 1331, and Northwest Fixture Co. v. Kilbourne & Clark Co., 9 Cir., 128 F. 256, cited by Southwest, which reach a contrary result.

We believe that the cases holding that the situation existing at the time of the contract is controlling in determining the reasonableness of liquidated damages are based upon sound reasoning and represent the weight of authority. Where parties have by their contract agreed upon a liquidated damage provision as a reasonable forecast of just compensation for breach of contract and damages are difficult to estimate accurately, such provision should be enforced. If in the course of subsequent developments, damages prove to be greater than those stipulated, the party entitled to damages is bound by the liquidated damage agreement. It is not unfair to hold the contractor performing the work to such agreement if by reason of later developments damages prove to be less or nonexistent. Each party by entering into such contractual provision took a calculated risk and is bound by reasonable contractual provisions pertaining to liquidated damages.

Southwest has completely failed to demonstrate that the court committed an error of law in determining that absence of actual damages at the time of breach of the contract or thereafter does not bar recovery of liquidated damages. The court at least impliedly found that the liquidated damage provisions of the contracts here involved were reasonable when viewed in the light of circumstances existing at the time the contract was entered into. We find nothing in the record which would compel a contrary conclusion. The court committed no error in allowing liquidated damages.

The judgment appealed from is affirmed.

NOTES

(1) *A Different View.* In Massman Constr. Co. v. City Council of Greenville, 147 F.2d 925 (5th Cir. 1945), cited in the principal case, the court took a different view. There a city withheld $250 per day as liquidated damages for a delay of 96½ days in building four piers for a toll bridge over the Mississippi River. In spite of the delay, however, the bridge was finished at least 30 days before the road on the other side of the river was opened, during which time it was "All dressed up and nowhere to go." The court held that enforcement of the damage provision "would be inequitable and unreasonable, would amount to the infliction of a penalty." It noted that the contract recited that the $250 per day was to represent the "actual damages" that would be "caused by a delay in completion." It concluded that the contract "presupposed" that actual damages would be caused by delay "but if the contingency upon which the presupposition is based never happens, the presupposition must vanish." Might the result have been different absent such a recital?

(2) *"Anticipated or Actual Harm."* UCC 2–718(1) speaks of "the anticipated or actual" loss caused by the breach. Do the words "or actual" make it easier or harder to sustain a clause?

In Equitable Lumber Corp. v. IPA Land Development Corp., 38 N.Y.2d 516, 521, 381 N.Y.S.2d 459, 462, 344 N.E.2d 391, 395 (1975), the court concluded that it was enough under the Code if the provision was "reasonable with respect to *either* (1) the harm which the parties anticipate will result from the breach at the time of contracting or (2) the actual damages suffered . . . at the time of the breach." The court suggested, however, that the provision might "nonetheless be invalidated under the last sentence of [UCC 2–718(1)] if it is so large that it serves as a penalty rather than a good faith attempt to pre-estimate damages."

Must the "actual" loss be reasonably foreseeable under the rule in Hadley v. Baxendale?

(3) *"Difficulty of Proof of Loss."* UCC 2–718(1) speaks of the "difficulties of proof of loss." Does this refer to difficulties as of the time the contract is made or as of the time it is broken? Why should there be such a requirement as long as the estimate is "reasonable in the light of the anticipated or actual" loss? See Hutchison v. Tompkins, 259 So.2d 129 (Fla. 1972).

(4) *Other Bases of Recovery.* Granting that the parties cannot shift the basis of recovery from relief to compulsion, can they make other fundamental shifts? From expectation to restitution or reliance? From substitutional to specific relief? From diminution in value to cost to complete? Could they do away with the requirements of unavoidability, foreseeability and certainty? In the Problem in Note 2, p. 632 supra, what sort of clause would you have advised Czarnikow to include in its contract with Federal?

(5) *Injunctive Relief.* What is the effect of the following provision of the NFL Player Contract, used in the National Football League?

> Player represents that he has special, exceptional and unique knowledge, skill, ability, and experience as a football player, the loss of which cannot be estimated with any certainty and cannot be fairly or adequately compensated by damages. Player therefore agrees that Club will have the right, in addition to any other right which Club may possess, to enjoin Player by appropriate proceedings from playing football or engaging in football-related activities other than for Club or from engaging in any activity other than football which may involve a significant risk of personal injury.

(6) *Problem.* Give your opinion on the suitability of the following clause for inclusion by a lessor of trucks in its printed leases:

> Upon termination as a result of breach of this agreement by Lessee, Lessor shall be entitled to liquidated damages in the amount of fifty per cent of the sum of all rents that would have been due during the balance of the term of this lease after the date of termination.

See Truck Rent-A-Center v. Puritan Farms 2nd, Inc., 41 N.Y.2d 420, 393 N.Y.S.2d 365, 361 N.E.2d 1015 (1977); cf. Knutton v. Cofield, 273 N.C. 355, 160 S.E.2d 29 (1968).

EPILOGUE

By this time it will probably have occurred to the reader that in providing for relief through damages, the law by and large assumes a frictionless system and ignores the cost to the claimant of obtaining that relief. It is, of course, true that the successful party may ordinarily recover the rather modest court costs that he has incurred as well as damages and interest, and it is also true that both parties can avail themselves of machinery of justice that is largely paid for by others. But in contrast to the situation in many countries, including Great Britain, an award of costs does not traditionally include attorney's fees, and even the winner is left to pay his own lawyer, not to mention the many other costs, some monetary and some not, of litigation.

This helps to explain why, as we have already seen, businessmen often put little stock in the legal enforceability of agreements (see pp. 276–79 supra), and why so many disputes are settled out of court. Where the transaction is a substantial one between businessmen, the cost of litigation may not seem overwhelming in relation to the amount in dispute. But what of the typical consumer transaction in which the amount in dispute is likely to be much smaller, whether the aggrieved party is the merchant or the consumer?

The merchant is clearly in the better position to cope with this problem. He has enough disputes to have them handled in bulk by specialists in collection. He can provide for liquidated damages and for attorney's fees. He engages the professionals who write the contract. He may also be able to secure himself in some way, e. g., by taking a deposit where he has not yet delivered goods or by preserving the right to repossess goods where he has delivered them. Indeed, our concern in Chapter 5, Policing the Bargain, was not that he could do too little but that he could do too much.

That leaves the consumer. He may not know a lawyer. He adhered to the contract. He could not have changed its terms even if he had known what changes he had wanted. He may, depending on how trusting the merchant has been, be able to stop payment on a check or to refuse to pay for goods delivered on credit, but even here he risks the onslaught of the merchant's specialists in collection. It is not that "The customer is always right." He is often wrong and sometimes a "deadbeat." The problem is that he and the merchant stand on an unequal footing in attempting to show who is right.

A wide variety of solutions has been suggested and attempted in limited areas. One sort of solution is to "sweeten the pot" by increasing the successful consumer's recovery: by allowing him a civil penalty, multiple (e. g., treble) damages, or attorney's fees. Another sort of solution is to give him support by having others subsidize his representation: by providing free or inexpensive legal services, by allowing him to join with claimants similarly situated in a class action, or by having a public agency handle the claim and distribute any recovery to the aggrieved consumers. Another sort of solution is to reduce the cost of litigation through special tribunals: by expanding the use of small claims courts or by instituting a system of arbitration.

Since most of these solutions are essentially procedural, this is not the place to explore them in detail. For an elaborate discussion of the problem in general, see Leff, Injury, Ignorance and Spite—The Dynamics of Coercive Collection, 80 Yale L.J. 1 (1970).

NOTES

(1) *Attorney's Fees.* Because the party who wins a lawsuit is usually not allowed to recover his attorney's fees from the losing party, contracts often provide for recovery by the winning party of his fees. A simple provision for attorney's fees will be sustained as the basis for an award of such fees as may be reasonable. If, however, the parties attempt to fix a particular sum as fees or set out a formula for their calculation, the provision must meet the same test as a liquidated damage clause. See Equitable Lumber Corp. v. IPA Land Development Corp., 38 N.Y.2d 516, 381 N.Y.S.2d 459, 344 N.E.2d 391 (1976).

(2) *The "Work of the Law Machine at the Margin."* Llewellyn concluded "that the real major effect of law will be found not so much in the cases in which law officials actually intervene, nor yet in those in which such intervention is consciously contemplated as a possibility, but rather in contributing to, strengthening, stiffening attitudes toward performance as what is to be expected and what 'is done'. If the contract-dodger *cannot* be bothered, if all he needs is a rhinoceros hide to thumb his nose at his creditor with impunity, more and more men will become contract-dodgers. Only saps will work, in an economy of indirect, non-face-to-face contacts. And as between individual enterprises, the competition of the contract-dodger will drive the contract-keeper into lowering his own standards of performance, on pain of destruction. This work of the law machine at the margin, in helping keep the level of social practice and expectation up to where it is, as against slow canker, is probably the most vital single aspect of contract law. For in this aspect each hospital case is a case with significance for the hundreds of thousands of normal cases." Llewellyn, What Price Contract?—An Essay in Perspective, 40 Yale L.J. 704, 725 n. 47 (1931).

Chapter 7

FINDING THE LAW OF THE CONTRACT

Much of what we think of as "contract law" consists of the legal framework within which parties may create their own rights and duties. Thus far this book has been largely concerned with this framework—with enforceability and enforcement. And yet in many contract disputes the disagreement relates not to such matters but rather to the nature and extent of the rights and duties that have been created. These disputes, over what are commonly called the "interpretation" and "construction" of contracts, are representative of a hefty and growing fraction of contract disputes. They are referred to here as disputes over the "law of the contract," to distinguish them from disputes over "contract law."

The purpose of this chapter is to introduce some of the problems encountered and the techniques used by the courts in finding the law of the contract. At the same time it would be well to remember that many potential disputes of this kind do not arise at all because the language of the contract is clear, and that many actual disputes would not have arisen had the language of the contract been clearer. It would not, therefore, be amiss to ask yourself how the parties, or their lawyers, in each case might have drafted a contract which would have avoided litigation.

SECTION 1. DETERMINING THE SUBJECT MATTER TO BE INTERPRETED

A threshold problem goes to the limitations on the sources that a court may consider in finding the law of the contract. Our initial concern is with a rule, or complex of rules, that goes under the name of "the parol evidence rule." Typically it is called into play where a contract has been reduced to writing after oral or written negotiations during which the parties have given assurances, made promises, or reached understandings. In the event of litigation, one of them may seek to introduce evidence of the negotiations in order to establish that the terms of the contract are other than as shown in the writing. Here he will be met with the parol evidence rule which, where the parties have embodied their agreement in writing, may preclude reliance on such extrinsic evidence as negotiations.

Professor Thayer said of the parol evidence rule that, "Few things are darker than this, or fuller of subtle difficulties," and it is not purposed to explore it fully here.[a] Certain it is that, in spite of its name, it is not limited to oral agreements; it also operates to exclude writings, such as letters or telegrams. There is also a general consensus that it is not, strictly speaking, a rule of evidence (such as the hearsay rule), which bars the use of some types of evidence to prove an ultimate matter of fact but which permits that fact to be established in a different way; rather it is a rule of "substantive" law, which precludes any showing of the ultimate matter of fact itself, that is, that the terms of the contract are other than as expressed in the writing. So much for what the rule is not. It is more difficult to state what it is.

NOTE

Rule of Substantive Law. Characterization of the parol evidence rule as "substantive" has some important practical consequences. For example, in our adversary trial system it is traditionally incumbent upon the aggrieved party to make timely objection to the admission of evidence in order to give the trial judge an opportunity to rule on its admissibility. Under an exclusionary rule of evidence, failure to object at trial is ordinarily a waiver of any ground of complaint against admission, and the evidence becomes part of the proof in the case. That this is not the case under the parol evidence rule, see Tahoe Nat. Bank v. Phillips, 4 Cal.3d 11, 92 Cal.Rptr. 704, 480 P.2d 320 (1971); Gajewski v. Bratcher, 221 N.W.2d 614 (N.D. 1974). But for a contrary view, see Higgs v. DeMaziroff, 263 N.Y. 473, 189 N.E. 555 (1934).

To take another example, in our federal court system, under the Erie doctrine, federal courts sitting in diversity cases are bound to apply state rather than federal law to matters that are "substantive." That a federal court sitting in a diversity case is bound to apply the parol evidence rule of the state in question, see Long v. Morris, 128 F.2d 653 (3d Cir. 1942).

GIANNI v. R. RUSSELL & CO., INC.

Supreme Court of Pennsylvania, 1924.
281 Pa. 320, 126 A. 791.

Action by Frank Gianni against R. Russell & Co., Inc. From judgment for plaintiff, defendant appeals.

Reversed, and judgment entered for defendant.

SCHAFFER, J. Plaintiff had been a tenant of a room in an office building in Pittsburgh wherein he conducted a store, selling tobacco, fruit, candy and soft drinks. Defendant acquired the entire

a. In England, the Law Commission was even less kind to the rule. "It is a technical rule of uncertain ambit which, at best, adds to the complications of litigation without affecting the outcome and, at worst, prevents the courts from getting at the truth. We accordingly make the provisional recommendation that it should be abolished. The [English] Law Commission, Law of Contract, The Parol Evidence Rule 25, Working Paper No. 70 (1976).

property in which the storeroom was located, and its agent negotiated with plaintiff for a further leasing of the room. A lease for three years was signed. It contained a provision that the lessee should "use the premises only for the sale of fruit, candy, soda water," etc., with the further stipulation that "it is expressly understood that the tenant is not allowed to sell tobacco in any form, under penalty of instant forfeiture of this lease." The document was prepared following a discussion about renting the room between the parties and after an agreement to lease had been reached. It was signed after it had been left in plaintiff's hands and admittedly had been read over to him by two persons, one of whom was his daughter.

Plaintiff sets up that in the course of his dealings with defendant's agent it was agreed that, in consideration of his promises not to sell tobacco and to pay an increased rent, and for entering into the agreement as a whole, he should have the exclusive right to sell soft drinks in the building. No such stipulation is contained in the written lease. Shortly after it was signed defendant demised the adjoining room in the building to a drug company without restricting the latter's right to sell soda water and soft drinks. Alleging that this was in violation of the contract which defendant had made with him, and that the sale of these beverages by the drug company had greatly reduced his receipts and profits, plaintiff brought this action for damages for breach of the alleged oral contract, and was permitted to recover. Defendant has appealed.

Plaintiff's evidence was to the effect that the oral agreement had been made at least two days, possibly longer, before the signing of the instrument, and that it was repeated at the time he signed; that, relying upon it, he executed the lease. Plaintiff called one witness who said he heard defendant's agent say to plaintiff at a time admittedly several days before the execution of the lease that he would have the exclusive right to sell soda water and soft drinks, to which the latter replied if that was the case he accepted the tenancy. Plaintiff produced no witness who was present when the contract was executed to corroborate his statement as to what then occurred. Defendant's agent denied that any such agreement was made, either preliminary to or at the time of the execution of the lease.

Appellee's counsel argues this is not a case in which an endeavor is being made to reform a written instrument because of something omitted as a result of fraud, accident, or mistake, but is one involving the breach of an independent oral agreement which does not belong in the writing at all and is not germane to its provisions. We are unable to reach this conclusion.

"Where parties, without any fraud or mistake, have deliberately put their engagements in writing, the law declares the writing to be not only the best, but the only evidence of their agreement." Martin v. Berens, 67 Pa. 459, 463; Irvin v. Irvin, 142 Pa. 271, 287, 21 A. 816.

"All preliminary negotiations, conversations and verbal agreements are merged in and superseded by the subsequent written contract, . . . and 'unless fraud, accident, or mistake be averred, the writing constitutes the agreement between the parties, and its terms cannot be added to nor subtracted from by parol evidence.'" Union Storage Co. v. Speck, 194 Pa. 126, 133, 45 A. 48, 49; Vito v. Birkel, 209 Pa. 206, 208, 58 A. 127.

The writing must be the entire contract between the parties if parol evidence is to be excluded, and to determine whether it is or not the writing will be looked at, and if it appears to be a contract complete within itself, "couched in such terms as import a complete legal obligation without any uncertainty as to the object or extent of the engagement, it is conclusively presumed that the whole engagement of the parties, and the extent and manner of their undertaking, were reduced to writing." Seitz v. Brewers' Refrigerating Machine Co., 141 U.S. 510, 517, 12 S.Ct. 46, 48, 35 L.Ed. 837.

When does the oral agreement come within the field embraced by the written one? This can be answered by comparing the two, and determining whether parties, situated as were the ones to the contract, would naturally and normally include the one in the other if it were made. If they relate to the same subject-matter, and are so interrelated that both would be executed at the same time and in the same contract, the scope of the subsidiary agreement must be taken to be covered by the writing. This question must be determined by the court.

In the case at bar the written contract stipulated for the very sort of thing which plaintiff claims has no place in it. It covers the use to which the storeroom was to be put by plaintiff and what he was and what he was not to sell therein. He was "to use the premises only for the sale of fruit, candy, soda water," etc., and was not "allowed to sell tobacco in any form." Plaintiff claims his agreement not to sell tobacco was part of the consideration for the exclusive right to sell soft drinks. Since his promise to refrain was included in the writing, it would be the natural thing to have included the promise of exclusive rights. Nothing can be imagined more pertinent to these provisions which were included than the one appellee avers.

In cases of this kind, where the cause of action rests entirely on an alleged oral understanding concerning a subject which is dealt with in a written contract it is assumed that the writing was intended to set forth the entire agreement as to that particular subject.

"In deciding upon this intent [as to whether a certain subject was intended to be embodied by the writing], the chief and most satisfactory index . . . is found in the circumstance whether or not the particular element of the alleged extrinsic negotiation is dealt with at all in the writing. If it is mentioned, covered, or dealt with in the writing, then presumably the writing was meant to represent all of the transaction on that element, if it is not, then probably the writing was not intended to embody that element of the negotiation." Wigmore on Evidence, 2d Ed., vol. 5, p. 309.

As the written lease is the complete contract of the parties, and since it embraces the field of the alleged oral contract, evidence of the latter is inadmissible under the parol evidence rule.

"The [parol evidence] rule also denies validity to a subsidiary agreement within [the] scope [of the written contract] if sued on as a separate contract, although except for [that rule], the agreement fulfills all the requisites of a valid contract." 2 Williston, Contracts, 1222; Penn Iron Co. v. Diller, 1 Sad., Pa., 82, 1 A. 924; Krueger v. Nicola, 205 Pa. 38, 54 A. 494; Wodock v. Robinson, 148 Pa. 503, 24 A. 73.

There are, of course, certain exceptions to the parol evidence rule, but this case does not fall within any of them. Plaintiff expressly rejects any idea of fraud, accident, or mistake, and they are the foundation upon which any basis for admitting parol evidence to set up an entirely separate agreement within the scope of a written contract must be built. The evidence must be such as would cause a chancellor to reform the instrument, and that would be done only for these reasons (Pioso v. Bitzer, 209 Pa. 503, 58 A. 891) and this holds true where this essentially equitable relief is being given, in our Pennsylvania fashion, through common-law forms.

We have stated on several occasions recently that we propose to stand for the integrity of written contracts. . . . We reiterate our position in this regard.

The judgment of the court below is reversed, and is here entered for defendant.

NOTE

Rationale. What is the reason behind the parol evidence rule? According to Corbin: "Any contract . . . can be discharged or modified by subsequent agreement of the parties . . . . If the foregoing is true of antecedent contracts that were once legally operative and enforceable, it is equally true of preliminary negotiations that were not themselves mutually agreed upon or enforceable at law. The new agreement is not a discharging contract, since there were no legal relations to be discharged; but the legal relations of the parties are now governed by the terms of the new agreement." 3 Corbin § 574. See Restatement Second, § 213 for a reflection of this view.

Many of the older cases, however, suggested a different rationale. Over three centuries ago, an English judge warned that, "It would be inconvenient, that matters in writing made by advice and on consideration, and which finally import the certain truth of the agreement of the parties should be controlled by averment of the parties to be proved by the uncertain testimony of slippery memory." Countess of Rutland's Case, 5 Co. 25b, 77 Eng.Rep. 89 (1604). Although this view has waned, a recent reflection of it appears in the explanation of Professor McCormick, an expert on the law of evidence, that "usually the one who sets up the spoken against the written word is economically the under-dog," and jurors would tend to favor him in spite of the unreliability of evidence of spoken words when given months or years later, even by a disinterested witness and particularly by a party himself. C. McCormick, Handbook of the Law of Evidence § 210 (1954). Does this explain why the rule bars prior *written* negotiations and does not bar *subsequent* oral ones?

MASTERSON v. SINE

Supreme Court of California, 1968.
68 Cal.2d 222, 436 P.2d 561.

TRAYNOR, Chief Justice. Dallas Masterson and his wife Rebecca owned a ranch as tenants in common. On February 25, 1958, they conveyed it to Medora and Lu Sine by a grant deed "Reserving unto the Grantors herein an option to purchase the above described property on or before February 25, 1968" for the "same consideration as being paid heretofore plus their depreciation value of any improvements Grantees may add to the property from and after two and a half years from this date." Medora is Dallas' sister and Lu's wife. Since the conveyance Dallas has been adjudged bankrupt. His trustee in bankruptcy and Rebecca brought this declaratory relief action to establish their right to enforce the option.

The case was tried without a jury. Over defendants' objection the trial court admitted extrinsic evidence that by "the same consideration as being paid heretofore" both the grantors and the grantees meant the sum of $50,000 and by "depreciation value of any improvements" they meant the depreciation value of improvements to be computed by deducting from the total amount of any capital expenditures made by defendants grantees the amount of depreciation allowable to them under United States income tax regulations as of the time of the exercise of the option.

The court also determined that the parol evidence rule precluded admission of extrinsic evidence offered by defendants to show that the parties wanted the property kept in the Masterson family and that the option was therefore personal to the grantors and could not be exercised by the trustee in bankruptcy.

The court entered judgment for plaintiffs, declaring their right to exercise the option, specifying in some detail how it could be exercised, and reserving jurisdiction to supervise the manner of its exercise and to determine the amount that plaintiffs will be required to pay defendants for their capital expenditures if plaintiffs decide to exercise the option.

Defendants appeal. They contend that the option provision is too uncertain to be enforced and that extrinsic evidence as to its meaning should not have been admitted. The trial court properly refused to frustrate the obviously declared intention of the grantors to reserve an option to repurchase by an overly meticulous insistence on completeness and clarity of written expression. . . . It properly admitted extrinsic evidence to explain the language of the deed . . . to the end that the consideration for the option would appear with sufficient certainty to permit specific enforcement . . . . The trial court erred, however, in excluding the extrinsic evidence that the option was personal to the grantors and therefore nonassignable.

When the parties to a written contract have agreed to it as an "integration"—a complete and final embodiment of the terms of an agreement—parol evidence cannot be used to add to or vary its terms. . . . When only part of the agreement is integrated, the same rule applies to that part, but parol evidence may be used to prove elements of the agreement not reduced to writing. . . .

The crucial issue in determining whether there has been an integration is whether the parties intended their writing to serve as the exclusive embodiment of their agreement. The instrument itself may help to resolve that issue. It may state, for example, that "there are no previous understandings or agreements not contained in the writing," and thus express the parties' "intention to nullify antecedent understandings or agreements." (See 3 Corbin, Contracts (1960) § 578, p. 411.) Any such collateral agreement itself must be examined, however, to determine whether the parties intended the subjects of negotiation it deals with to be included in, excluded from, or otherwise affected by the writing. Circumstances at the time of the writing may also aid in the determination of such integration. . . .

California cases have stated that whether there was an integration is to be determined solely from the face of the instrument and that the question for the court is whether it "appears to be a complete . . . agreement . . . ." (See Ferguson v. Koch (1928) 204 Cal. 342, 346, 268 P. 342, 344, 58 A.L.R. 1176; . . .) Neither of these strict formulations of the rule, however, has been consistently applied. The requirement that the writing must appear incomplete on its face has been repudiated in many cases where parol evidence was admitted "to prove the existence of a separate oral agreement as to any matter on which the document is silent and which is not inconsistent with its terms"—even though the instrument appeared to state a complete agreement. . . . Even under the rule that the writing alone is to be consulted, it was found necessary to examine the alleged collateral agreement before concluding that proof of it was precluded by the writing alone. (See 3 Corbin, Contracts (1960) § 582, pp. 444–446.) It is therefore evident that "The conception of a writing as wholly and intrinsically self-determinative of the parties' intent to make it a sole memorial of one or seven or twenty-seven subjects of negotiation is an impossible one." (9 Wigmore, Evidence (3d ed. 1940) § 2431, p. 103.) For example, a promissory note given by a debtor to his creditor may integrate all their present contractual rights and obligations, or it may be only a minor part of an underlying executory contract that would never be discovered by examining the face of the note.

In formulating the rule governing parol evidence, several policies must be accommodated. One policy is based on the assumption that written evidence is more accurate than human memory. . . . This policy, however, can be adequately served by excluding parol evidence of agreements that directly contradict the writing. Another policy is based on the fear that fraud or unintentional invention by witnesses interested in the outcome of the litigation will mislead the finder of facts. (. . . Mitchill v. Lath (1928) 247 N.Y. 377, 388, 160 N.E. 646, 68 A.L.R. 239. . . .) . . . McCormick has suggested that the party urging the spoken as against the written word is most often the economic underdog, threatened by severe hardship if the writing is enforced. In his view the parol evidence rule arose to allow the court to control the tendency of the jury to find through sympathy and without a dispassionate assessment of the probability of fraud or faulty memory that the parties made an oral agreement collateral to the written contract, or that preliminary tentative agreements were not abandoned when omitted from the writing. (See McCormick, Evidence (1954) § 210.) He recognizes, however, that if this theory were adopted in disregard of all other considerations, it would lead to the exclusion of testimony concerning oral agreements whenever there is a writing and thereby often defeat the true intent of the parties. (See McCormick, op. cit. supra, § 216, p. 441.)

Evidence of oral collateral agreements should be excluded only when the fact finder is likely to be misled. The rule must therefore be based on the credibility of the evidence. One such standard, adopted by section 240(1)(b) of the Restatement of Contracts, permits proof of a collateral agreement if it "is such an agreement as might *naturally* be made as a separate agreement by parties situated as were the parties to the written contract." (Italics added; see McCormick, Evidence (1954) § 216, p. 441; see also 3 Corbin, Contracts (1960) § 583, p. 475, § 594, pp. 568–569; 4 Williston, Contracts (3d ed. 1961) § 638, pp. 1039–1045.) The draftsmen of the Uniform Commercial Code would exclude the evidence in still fewer instances: "If the additional terms are such that, if agreed upon, they would *certainly* have been included in the document in the view of the court, then evidence of their alleged making must be kept from the trier of fact." (Com. 3, § 2–202, italics added.)[1]

1. Corbin suggests that, even in situations where the court concludes that it would not have been natural for the parties to make the alleged collateral oral agreement, parol evidence of such an agreement should nevertheless be permitted if the court is convinced that the unnatural actually happened in the case being adjudicated. (3 Corbin, Contracts, § 485, pp.

The option clause in the deed in the present case does not explicitly provide that it contains the complete agreement, and the deed is silent on the question of assignability. Moreover, the difficulty of accommodating the formalized structure of a deed to the insertion of collateral agreements makes it less likely that all the terms of such an agreement were included. . . . The statement of the reservation of the option might well have been placed in the recorded deed solely to preserve the grantors' rights against any possible future purchasers and this function could well be served without any mention of the parties' agreement that the option was personal. There is nothing in the record to indicate that the parties to this family transaction, through experience in land transactions or otherwise, had any warning of the disadvantages of failing to put the whole agreement in the deed. This case is one, therefore, in which it can be said that a collateral agreement such as that alleged "might naturally be made as a separate agreement." *A fortiori,* the case is not one in which the parties "would certainly" have included the collateral agreement in the deed.

It is contended, however, that an option agreement is ordinarily presumed to be assignable if it contains no provisions forbidding its transfer or indicating that its performance involves elements personal to the parties. . . . The fact that there is a written memorandum, however, does not necessarily preclude parol evidence rebutting a term that the law would otherwise presume. . . .

In the present case defendants offered evidence that the parties agreed that the option was not assignable in order to keep the property in the Masterson family. The trial court erred in excluding that evidence.

The judgment is reversed.

PETERS, TOBRINER, MOSK, and SULLIVAN, JJ., concur.

BURKE, Justice (dissenting). I dissent. The majority opinion:

(1) Undermines the parol evidence rule as we have known it in this state since at least 1872 by declaring that parol evidence should have been admitted by the trial court to show that a written option, absolute and unrestricted in form, was intended to be limited and nonassignable;

(2) Renders suspect instruments of conveyance absolute on their face;

(3) Materially lessens the reliance which may be placed upon written instruments affecting the title to real estate; and

478, 480; cf. Murray, The Parol Evidence Rule: A Clarification (1966) 4 Duquesne L.Rev. 337, 341–342.) This suggestion may be based on a belief that judges are not likely to be misled by their sympathies. If the court believes that the parties intended a collateral agreement to be effective, there is no reason to keep the evidence from the jury.

(4) Opens the door, albeit unintentionally to a new technique for the defrauding of creditors.

The opinion permits defendants to establish by parol testimony that their grant to their brother (and brother-in-law) of a written option, absolute in terms, was nevertheless agreed to be nonassignable by the grantee (now a bankrupt), and that therefore the right to exercise it did not pass, by operation of the bankruptcy laws, to the trustee for the benefit of the grantee's creditors.

And how was this to be shown? By the proffered testimony of the bankrupt optionee himself! Thereby one of his assets (the option to purchase defendants' California ranch) would be withheld from the trustee in bankruptcy and from the bankrupt's creditors. Understandably the trial court, as required by the parol evidence rule, did not allow the bankrupt by parol to so contradict the unqualified language of the written option.

The court properly admitted parol evidence to explain the intended meaning of the "same consideration" and "depreciation value" phrases of the written option to purchase defendants' land, as the intended meaning of those phrases was not clear. However, there was nothing ambiguous about the *granting* language of the option and not the slightest suggestion in the document that the option was to be nonassignable. Thus, to permit such words of limitation to be added by parol is to *contradict* the absolute nature of the grant, and to directly violate the parol evidence rule.

Just as it is unnecessary to state in a deed to "lot X" that the house located thereon goes with the land, it is likewise unnecessary to add to "I grant an option to Jones" the words "*and his assigns*" for the option to be assignable. As hereinafter emphasized in more detail, California statutes expressly declare that it *is* assignable, and only if I add language in writing showing my intent to withhold or restrict the right of assignment may the grant be so limited. Thus, to seek to restrict the grant by parol is to *contradict* the written document in violation of the parol evidence rule.

The majority opinion arrives at its holding via a series of false premises which are not supported either in the record of this case or in such California authorities as are offered. . . .

At the outset the majority in the present case reiterate that the rule against contradicting or varying the terms of a writing remains applicable when only part of the agreement is contained in the writing, and parol evidence is used to prove elements of the agreement not reduced to writing. But having restated this established rule, the majority opinion inexplicably proceeds to subvert it. . . .

Options are property, and are widely used in the sale and purchase of real and personal property. One of the basic incidents of property ownership is the right of the owner to sell or transfer it. . . . These rights of the owner of property to transfer it, are elementary rules of substantive law and not the mere disputable presumptions which the majority opinion in the present case would make of them. Moreover, the right of transferability applies to an option to purchase, unless there are words of limitation in the option forbidding its assignment or showing that it was given because of a peculiar trust or confidence reposed in the optionee. . . .

The right of an optionee to transfer his option to purchase property is accordingly one of the basic rights which accompanies the option unless limited under the language of the option itself. To allow an optionor to resort to parol evidence to support his assertion that the written option is not transferable is to authorize him to limit the option by attempting to restrict and reclaim rights with which he has already parted. A clearer violation of two substantive and basic rules of law—the parol evidence rule and the right of free transferability of property—would be difficult to conceive. . . .

[D]espite the law which until the advent of the present majority opinion has been firmly and clearly established in California and relied upon by attorneys and courts alike, that parol evidence may *not* be employed to vary or contradict the terms of a written instrument, the majority now announce that such evidence "should be excluded only when the fact finder is *likely to be misled,*" and that "The rule must therefore be based on the *credibility of the evidence.*" (Italics added.) But was it not, inter alia, to avoid misleading the fact finder, and to further the introduction of only the evidence which is most likely to *be* credible (the written document), that the Legislature adopted the parol evidence rule as a part of the substantive law of this state?

Next, in an effort to implement this newly promulgated "credibility" test, the majority opinion offers a choice of two "standards": one, a "certainty" standard, quoted from the Uniform Commercial Code, and the other a "natural" standard found in the Restatement of Contracts, and concludes that at least for purposes of the present case the "natural" viewpoint should prevail.

This new rule, not hitherto recognized in California, provides that proof of a claimed collateral oral agreement is admissible if it is such an agreement as might *naturally* have been made a separate agreement by the parties under the particular circumstances. I submit that this approach opens the door to uncertainty and confusion. Who can know what its limits are? Certainly I do not. For example, in its application to this case who could be expected to divine as "natural" a separate oral agreement between the parties that the assignment, absolute and unrestricted on its face, was intended by the parties to be limited to the Masterson family?

Or, assume that one gives to his relative a promissory note and that the payee of the note goes bankrupt. By operation of law the note becomes an asset of the bankruptcy. The trustee attempts to enforce it. Would the relatives be permitted to testify that by a separate oral agreement made at the time of the execution of the note it was understood that should the payee fail in his business the maker would be excused from payment of the note, or that, as here, it was intended that the benefits of the note would be *personal* to the payee? I doubt that trial judges should be burdened with the task of conjuring whether it would have been "natural" under those circumstances for such a separate agreement to have been made by the parties. Yet, under the application of the proposed rule, this is the task the trial judge would have, and in essence the situation presented in the instant case is no different.

Under the application of the codes and the present case law, proof of the existence of such an agreement would not be permitted, "natural" or "unnatural." But conceivably, as loose as the new rule is, one judge might deem it natural and another judge unnatural. And in each instance the ultimate decision would have to be made ("naturally") on a case-by-case basis by the appellate courts.

In an effort to provide justification for applying the newly pronounced "natural" rule to the circumstances of the present case, the majority opinion next attempts to account for the silence of the writing in this case concerning assignability of the option, by asserting that "the difficulty of accommodating the formalized structure of a deed to the insertion of collateral agreements makes it less likely that all the terms of such an agreement were included." What difficulty would have been involved here, to add the words "this option is nonassignable"? The asserted "formalized structure of a deed" is no formidable barrier. . . .

Comment hardly seems necessary on the convenience to a bankrupt of such a device to defeat his creditors. He need only produce parol testimony that any options (or other property, for that matter) which he holds are subject to an oral "collateral agreement" with family members (or with friends) that the property is nontransferable "in order to keep the property in the family" or in the friendly group. In the present case the value of the ranch which the bankrupt and his wife held an option to purchase has doubtless increased substantially during the years since they acquired the option. The initiation of this litigation by the trustee in bankruptcy to establish his right to enforce the option indicates his belief that there is substantial value to be gained for the creditors from this asset of the bankrupt. Yet the majority opinion permits defeat of the trustee and of the creditors through the device of an asserted collateral oral agreement that the option was "personal" to the bankrupt and nonassignable "in order to keep the property in the family"! . . .

I would hold that the trial court ruled correctly on the proffered parol evidence, and would affirm the judgment.

McCOMB, J., concurs.

NOTES

(1) *"Integrated" Agreements and the Restatement.* According to the Restatement Second, where a writing has been adopted by the parties as "a final expression of one or more terms of an agreement" that writing is known as an "integrated agreement," and "evidence of prior agreements or negotiations is not admissible in evidence to contradict a term of the writing." Restatement Second, §§ 209, 215. Where the writing has been "adopted by the parties as a complete and exclusive statement of the terms of the agreement," it is known as a "completely integrated agreement," and not even evidence of "a consistent additional term is admissible to explain or supplement" it. Restatement Second, §§ 210, 216. Such evidence is, however, admissible if the writing is only a "partially integrated agreement."

Are Gianni v. Russel and Masterson v. Sine distinguishable? How would the writings in those cases be characterized in Restatement Second terms? Who characterized them? See Restatement Second, § 209(2). On the basis of what evidence were they characterized? See Restatement Second, § 214. For what purpose did Gianni and the Sines seek to introduce extrinsic evidence? What rationale for the parol evidence rule was relied on in reaching each decision?

The Code's version of the parol evidence rule is found in UCC 2–202. It does not, of course, apply to transactions like those in the preceding two cases. Are its provisions consistent with the results in those cases?

For discussion of the parol evidence rule, see Calamari and Perillo, A Plea for a Uniform Parol Evidence Rule and Principles of Contract Interpretation, 42 Ind.L.J. 333 (1967); Murray, The Parol Evidence Process and Standardized Agreements under the Restatement (Second) of Contracts, 123 U.Pa.L.Rev. 1342 (1975); Sweet, Contract Making and Parol Evidence: Diagnosis and Treatment of a Sick Rule, 53 Cornell L.Rev. 1036 (1968); Notes, 41 Fordham L.Rev. 945 (1973); 44 N.Y.U.L.Rev. 972 (1969).

(2) *Test of Complete Integration.* Chief Justice Traynor refers to the "strict formulations of the rule" under which "whether there was an integration is to be determined solely from the face of the instrument and . . . the question for the court is whether it 'appears to be a complete . . . agreement.'" This was Williston's view, and many courts, particularly in cases like Gianni, decided in the first half of this century, agreed. See 4 Williston § 633.

Corbin led the opponents of this view, arguing that "The writing cannot prove its own completeness and accuracy." Corbin, The Parol Evidence Rule, 53 Yale L.J. 603, 630 (1944), reprinted in 3 Corbin § 582. The trend clearly favors Corbin. As Comment *b* to Restatement Second, § 210 phrases it, "a writing cannot of itself prove its own completeness, and wide latitude must be allowed for inquiry into circumstances bearing on the intention of the parties."

(3) *Merger Clauses.* Chief Justice Traynor observed that the "instrument may help to resolve" the issue of whether the agreement is completely integrated. It is a common practice to include in written contracts a clause known as a "merger clause," which may read somewhat as follows: "There are no promises, verbal understandings, or agreements of any kind, pertain-

ing to this contract other than specified herein." Since integration is a matter of the parties' intention, such clauses have usually been given effect, in situations like those in the two preceding cases, to show complete integration. Tapper Chevrolet Co. v. Hansen, 95 Idaho 436, 510 P.2d 1091 (1973); Jordan v. Doonan Truck & Equipment, Inc., 220 Kan. 431, 552 P. 2d 881 (1976).[a] Compare the function of a merger clause with that of a home-office-approval clause in the control of representatives. See Note 1, p. 200 supra.

(4) *"Collateral Agreements."* The fact that the parties have adopted a writing as an integration of one agreement has, of course, no effect on another entirely separate agreement. Note that Chief Justice Traynor speaks of a "collateral agreement" in Masterson v. Sine. What was that agreement? What was its consideration? Does the notion of a "collateral agreement," as he uses it, differ from that of "partial integration"?

He cites Mitchill v. Lath, 247 N.Y. 377, 160 N.E. 646 (1928). In that case the buyer of land under a written contract attempted to show a prior agreement by the seller to remove an unsightly ice house from a nearby tract. The court held that the parol evidence rule precluded such a showing. For evidence of a contemporaneous oral agreement to be admissible: "(1) The agreement must in form be a collateral one; (2) it must not contradict express or implied provisions of the written contract; (3) it must be one that parties would not ordinarily be expected to embody in the writing." The court thought that "an inspection of this contract shows a full and complete agreement, setting forth in detail the obligations of each party. On reading it, one would conclude that the reciprocal obligations of the parties were fully detailed." Judge Lehman dissenting says: "[T]he question we must decide is whether or not, *assuming* an agreement was made for the removal of an unsightly icehouse from one parcel of land as an inducement for the purchase of another parcel, the parties would ordinarily or naturally be expected to embody the agreement for the removal of the icehouse from one parcel in the written agreement to convey the other parcel." He thought they would not and that therefore the oral agreement was valid.

LEE v. JOSEPH E. SEAGRAM & SONS, INC.

United States Court of Appeals, Second Circuit, 1977.
552 F.2d 447.

[The facts and another part of the opinion in this case are at p. 235 supra.]

GURFEIN, Circuit Judge: . . .

I

Judge Tenney, in a careful analysis of the application of the parol evidence rule, decided that the rule did not bar proof of the oral agreement. We agree.

a. Comment *b* to Restatement Second, § 209 cautions that "such a declaration may not be conclusive." See also Comment *e* to § 216. Cases to support this are few. Matthews v. Drew Chem. Corp., 475 F.2d 146 (5th

The District Court, in its denial of the defendant's motion for summary judgment, treated the issue as whether the written agreement for the sale of assets was an "integrated" agreement not only of all the mutual agreements concerning the sale of Capitol City assets, but also of *all* the mutual agreements of the parties. Finding the language of the sales agreement "somewhat ambiguous," the court decided that the determination of whether the parol evidence rule applies must await the taking of evidence on the issue of whether the sales agreement was intended to be a complete and accurate integration of all of the mutual promises of the parties.

Seagram did not avail itself of this invitation. It failed to call as witnesses any of the three persons who negotiated the sales agreement on behalf of Seagram regarding the intention of the parties to integrate all mutual promises or regarding the failure of the written agreement to contain an integration clause.

Appellant contends that, as a matter of law, the oral agreement was "part and parcel" of the subject-matter of the sales contract and that failure to include it in the written contract barred proof of its existence. Mitchill v. Lath, 247 N.Y. 377, 380, 160 N.E. 646 (1928). The position of appellant, fairly stated, is that the oral agreement was either an inducing cause for the sale or was a part of the consideration for the sale, and in either case, should have been contained in the written contract. In either case, it argues that the parol evidence rule bars its admission.

Appellees maintain, on the other hand, that the oral agreement was a collateral agreement and that, since it is not contradictory of any of the terms of the sales agreement, proof of it is not barred by the parol evidence rule. Because the case comes to us after a jury verdict we must assume that there actually was an oral contract, such as the court instructed the jury it could find. The question is whether the strong policy for avoiding fraudulent claims through application of the parol evidence rule nevertheless mandates reversal on the ground that the jury should not have been permitted to hear the evidence. See Fogelson v. Rackfay Constr. Co., 300 N.Y. 334 at 337–38, 90 N.E.2d 881 (1950).

The District Court stated the cardinal issue to be whether the parties "intended" the written agreement for the sale of assets to be the complete and accurate integration of all the mutual promises of the parties. If the written contract was not a complete integration,

Cir. 1973) (dictum: in spite of a merger clause it was not "improper for the judge below to have heard parol evidence regarding the intent of the parties as to whether this document was to be a total integration"); cf. Hull-Dobbs, Inc. v. Mallicoat, 57 Tenn. App. 100, 415 S.W.2d 344 (1966) (court avoided application of merger clause by strained interpretation). See Broude, The Consumer and the Parol Evidence Rule: Section 2–202 of the Uniform Commercial Code, 1970 Duke L.J. 881; Comment, 27 Tex.L.Rev. 361 (1949).

the court held, then the parol evidence rule has no application.[3] We assume that the District Court determined intention by objective standards. See 3 Corbin on Contracts §§ 573–574. The parol evidence rule is a rule of substantive law. Fogelson v. Rackfay Constr. Co., supra; Higgs v. De Maziroff, 263 N.Y. 473, 477, 189 N.E. 555 (1934); Smith v. Bear, 237 F.2d 79, 83 (2d Cir. 1956).

The law of New York is not rigid or categorical, but is in harmony with this approach. As Judge Fuld said in Fogelson: "Decision in each case must, of course, turn upon the type of transaction involved, the scope of the written contract and the content of the oral agreement asserted." 300 N.Y. at 338, 90 N.E.2d at 883. And the Court of Appeals wrote in Ball v. Grady, 267 N.Y. 470, 472, 196 N.E. 402, 403 (1935): "In the end, the court must find the limits of the integration as best it may by reading the writing in the light of surrounding circumstances." Accord, Fogelson, supra, 300 N.Y. at 338, 90 N.E.2d 881. Thus, certain oral collateral agreements, even though made contemporaneously, are not within the prohibition of the parol evidence rule "because [if] they are separate, independent, and complete contracts, although relating to the same subject. . . . [t]hey are allowed to be proved by parol, because they were made by parol, and no part thereof committed to writing." Thomas v. Scutt, 127 N.Y. 133, 140–41, 27 N.E. 961, 963 (1891).

Although there is New York authority which in general terms supports defendant's thesis that an oral contract inducing a written one or varying the consideration may be barred, see e. g., Fogelson v. Rackfay Constr. Co., supra, 300 N.Y. at 340, 90 N.E.2d 881, the overarching question is whether, in the context of the particular setting, the oral agreement was one which the parties would ordinarily be expected to embody in the writing. Ball v. Grady, supra, 267 N.Y. at 470, 196 N.E. 402; *accord,* Fogelson v. Rackfay Constr. Co., supra, 300 N.Y. at 338, 90 N.E.2d 881. See Restatement on Contracts § 240. For example, integration is most easily inferred in the case of real estate contracts for the sale of land, e. g., Mitchill v. Lath, supra, 247 N.Y. 377, 160 N.E. 646, or leases, Fogelson, supra; Plum Tree, Inc. v. N. K. Winston Corp., 351 F.Supp. 80, 83 (S.D.N.Y.1972). In more complex situations, in which customary business practice may be more varied, an oral agreement can be treated as separate and independent of the written agreement even though the written contract contains a strong integration clause. See Gem Corrugated Box Corp. v. National Kraft Container Corp., 427 F.2d 499, 503 (2d Cir. 1970).

Thus, as we see it, the issue is whether the oral promise to the plaintiffs, as individuals, would be an expectable term of the contract

3. Though the parties have not urged the particular choice of law applicable, both parties appear to assume that New York law governs. We note that in cases of this type, which depend so much on their particular facts and for which direct precedent is therefore so sparse, virtually all jurisdictions would be expected to follow general common law principles.

for the sale of assets by a corporation in which plaintiffs have only a 50% interest, considering as well the history of their relationship to Seagram.

Here, there are several reasons why it would *not* be expected that the oral agreement to give Harold Lee's sons another distributorship would be integrated into the sales contract. In the usual case, there is an identity of parties in both the claimed integrated instrument and in the oral agreement asserted. Here, although it would have been physically possible to insert a provision dealing with only the shareholders of a 50% interest, the transaction itself was a *corporate* sale of assets. Collateral agreements which survive the closing of a corporate deal, such as employment agreements for particular shareholders of the seller or consulting agreements, are often set forth in separate agreements. See Gem Corrugated Box Corp. v. National Kraft Container Corp., supra, 427 F.2d at 503 ("it is . . . plain that the parties ordinarily would not embody the stock purchase agreement in a writing concerned only with box materials purchase terms"). It was expectable that such an agreement as one to obtain a new distributorship for certain persons, some of whom were not even parties to the contract, would not necessarily be integrated into an instrument for the sale of *corporate* assets. As with an oral condition precedent to the legal effectiveness of an otherwise integrated written contract, which is not barred by the parol evidence rule if it is not directly contradictory of its terms, Hicks v. Bush, 10 N.Y.2d 488, 225 N.Y.S.2d 34, 180 N.E.2d 425 (1962); cf. 3 Corbin on Contracts § 589, "it is certainly not improbable that parties contracting in these circumstances would make the asserted oral agreement . . . ." 10 N.Y.2d at 493, 225 N.Y.S.2d at 39, 180 N.E.2d at 428.

Similarly, it is significant that there was a close relationship of confidence and friendship over many years between two old men, Harold Lee and Yogman, whose authority to bind Seagram has not been questioned. It would not be surprising that a handshake for the benefit of Harold's sons would have been thought sufficient. In point, as well, is the circumstance that the negotiations concerning the provisions of the sales agreement were not conducted by Yogman but by three other Seagram representatives, headed by John Barth. The two transactions may not have been integrated in their minds when the contract was drafted.[4]

Finally, the written agreement does not contain the customary integration clause, even though a good part of it (relating to warranties and negative covenants) is boilerplate. The omission may, of

4. Barth in a confidential memorandum dated June 12, 1970 to Yogman and Edgar Bronfman stated that "he [Harold Lee] would very much like to have another distributorship in another area for his two sons." Apparently Barth, who was not present at Harold Lee's meeting with Yogman, assumed that this was a desire on the part of Lee rather than a promise made by Yogman for Seagram.

course, have been caused by mutual trust and confidence, but in any event, there is no such strong presumption of exclusion because of the existence of a detailed integration clause, as was relied upon by the Court of Appeals in Fogelson, supra, 300 N.Y. at 340, 90 N.E. 881.

Nor do we see any contradiction of the terms of the sales agreement. Mitchill v. Lath, supra, 247 N.Y. at 381, 160 N.E. 646; 3 Corbin on Contracts § 573, at 357. The written agreement dealt with the sale of corporate assets, the oral agreement with the relocation of the Lees. Thus, the oral agreement does not vary or contradict the money consideration recited in the contract as flowing to the selling corporation. That is the only consideration recited, and it is still the only consideration to the corporation.[5]

We affirm Judge Tenney's reception in evidence of the oral agreement and his denial of the motion under Rule 50(b) with respect to the parol evidence rule. . . .

NOTES

(1) *Questions.* How does the argument that the oral agreement was a collateral agreement differ from the argument that the writing is only a partial integration? Would it make a difference if the writing contained a merger clause?

(2) *Problem.* A number of jobbers of corrugated boxes consulted Kipnis, who knew the field, for ways to improve their financial condition. As a result, he organized a new corporation, National Kraft, which was to make long term contracts for the purchase of materials from St. Regis Paper Company. Under an oral agreement with National Kraft, jobbers could become stockholders in National Kraft and buy as many shares as they wished if they would make contracts to buy their corrugated paper products requirements from it. Gem, one of the jobbers, made a written contract with National Kraft to purchase its requirements for five years. The contract contained a merger clause. The price was not attractive, since consummation of the stock purchase agreement was the real inducement to make the requirements contract. However, at the urging of Kipnis, the consummation of that agreement was postponed. Several months later Gem asked for 7,000 shares, but they were never delivered. Gem sues National Kraft for damages for breach of the oral agreement. Formulate an argument for Gem that evidence of the oral agreement is admissible in spite of the parol evidence rule. Gem Corrugated Box Corp. v. National Kraft Container Corp., 427 F.2d 499 (2d Cir. 1970).

BOLLINGER v. CENTRAL PENNSYLVANIA QUARRY STRIPPING AND CONSTRUCTION CO.

Supreme Court of Pennsylvania, 1967.
425 Pa. 430, 229 A.2d 741.

MUSMANNO, Justice. Mahlon Bollinger and his wife, Vinetta C. Bollinger, filed an action in equity against the Central Pennsylvan-

5. Cf. Mitchill v. Lath, 247 N.Y. 377, 380–81, 160 N.E. 646, 647 (1928) (to escape the parol evidence rule, the oral agreement "must not contradict express or implied provisions of the written contract."). The parties do not contend, and we would be unwilling to hold, that the oral agreement was not "in form a collateral one." Id.

ia Quarry Stripping Construction Company asking that a contract entered into between them be reformed so as to include therein a paragraph alleged to have been omitted by mutual mistake and that the agreement, as reformed, be enforced.

The agreement, as executed, provided that the defendant was to be permitted to deposit on the property of the plaintiffs, construction waste as it engaged in work on the Pennsylvania Turnpike in the immediate vicinity of the plaintiffs' property. The Bollingers claimed that there had been a mutual understanding between them and the defendant that, prior to depositing such waste on the plaintiffs' property, the defendant would remove the topsoil of the plaintiffs' property, pile on it the waste material and then restore the topsoil in a way to cover the deposited waste. The Bollingers averred that they had signed the written agreement without reading it because they assumed that the condition just stated had been incorporated into the writing.

When the defendant first began working in the vicinity of the plaintiffs' property, it did first remove the topsoil, deposited the waste on the bare land, and then replaced the topsoil. After a certain period of time, the defendant ceased doing this and the plaintiffs remonstrated. The defendant answered there was nothing in the written contract which required it to make a sandwich of its refuse between the bare earth and the topsoil. It was at this point that the plaintiffs discovered that that feature of the oral understanding had been omitted from the written contract. The plaintiff husband renewed his protest and the defendant's superintendent replied he could not remove the topsoil because his equipment for that operation had been taken away. When he was reminded of the original understanding, the superintendent said, in effect, he couldn't help that.

The plaintiffs then filed their action for reformation of the contract, the Court granted the requested relief, and the defendant firm appealed. We said in Bugen v. New York Life Insurance Co., 408 Pa. 472, 184 A.2d 499: "A court of equity has the power to reform the written evidence of a contract and make it correspond to the understanding of the parties. . . . However, the mistake must be mutual to the parties to the contract." The fact, however, that one of the parties denies that a mistake was made does not prevent a finding of mutual mistake. Kutsenkow v. Kutsenkow, 414 Pa. 610, 612, 202 A.2d 68.

Once a person enters into a written agreement he builds around himself a stone wall, from which he cannot escape by merely asserting he had not understood what he was signing. However, equity would completely fail in its objectives if it refused to break a hole through the wall when it finds, after proper evidence, that there was a mistake between the parties, that it was real and not feigned, actual and not hypothetical.

The Chancellor, after taking testimony, properly concluded: "We are satisfied that plaintiffs have sustained the heavy burden placed upon them. Their understanding of the agreement is corroborated by the undisputed evidence. The defendant did remove and set aside the topsoil on part of the area before depositing its waste and did replace the topsoil over such waste after such depositing. It follows it would not have done so had it not so agreed. Further corroboration is found in the testimony that it acted similarly in the case of plaintiffs' neighbor Beltzner."

After the Court handed down its Decree Nisi, the defendant petitioned for a rehearing on the ground of after-discovered evidence. Even assuming, without so deciding, that the so-called after-discovered evidence qualified as such, it is not clear that it was sufficiently material or relevant to bring about a change in the result reached by the Chancellor, and he so stated in his Opinion. We are satisfied that the proffered evidence would not be inconsistent with the Chancellor's findings.

Decree affirmed, costs on the appellant.

NOTES

(1) *Reformation for Mistake.* How did the situation of the Bollingers differ from that of Gianni? What would he have had to show in order to bring himself within the rule of the Bollinger case? See Palmer, Reformation and the Parol Evidence Rule, 65 Mich.L.Rev. 833 (1967), reprinted in 3 G. Palmer, The Law of Restitution §§ 13.10, 13.11 (1978).

(2) *Validity of Written Agreement.* It is generally held that, since the parol evidence rule proceeds on the assumption that there is a written agreement, it does not bar extrinsic evidence to show that the written agreement is not valid. It does not, for example, preclude the use of such evidence to show that the writing was a sham not intended to be enforced (see Note 1, p. 176 supra) or that a recital of a performance as consideration (e. g., "in consideration of the payment of $10, receipt of which is hereby acknowledged") is false (see Note 1, p. 224 supra). See Restatement Second, § 214(d). (However, the rule does apply if the consideration is a promise rather than a performance.)

(3) *Fraud.* For the reason suggested in the preceding note, it is also generally held that the parol evidence rule does not preclude the use of extrinsic evidence to show fraud.[a] Is the rule the same under UCC 2–202? For an affirmative answer, see Associated Hardware Supply Co. v. Big Wheel Distributing Co., 355 F.2d 114 (3d Cir. 1965). What language of UCC 2–202 supports such a result? Is UCC 1–103 relevant?

Might a carefully drafted merger clause preclude the use of extrinsic evidence to show fraud? Consider the following language, which was incorporated in a contract of sale of a lease of a building:

a. For a curious Pennsylvania case to the contrary, see Bardwell v. Willis Co., 375 Pa. 503, 100 A.2d 102 (1953) (not enough that "oral representations were *fraudulently made*" if they were not "*fraudulently* or by accident or mistake *omitted* from the subsequent complete written contract").

> Purchaser hereby expressly acknowledges that no such representations have been made, and the Purchaser further acknowledges that it has inspected the premises and agrees to take the premises 'as is' . . . and that [this contract] is entered into after full investigation, neither party relying upon any statement, not embodied in this contract, made by the other.

See Danann Realty Corp. v. Harris, 5 N.Y.2d 317, 184 N.Y.S.2d 599, 157 N.E.2d 597 (1959). But cf. Central Constr. Co. v. Osbahr, 186 Neb. 1, 180 N.W.2d 139 (1970). That such a clause is effective in the case of a non-fraudulent representation, see Wilkinson v. Carpenter, 276 Or. 311, 554 P.2d 512 (1976).

NO-ORAL-MODIFICATION CLAUSES

Suppose that one of the parties seeks to prove that the provisions of a carefully drafted written contract were varied by a conversation between the parties *after* the contract was made. The parol evidence rule does not speak to this problem. Yet to the party who seeks to exclude such proof it is not dissimilar from the problems to which the rule does speak. If one wants to do business on the basis of the written word (preferably one's own), to the exclusion of oral agreements, one has as much interest in excluding subsequent as in excluding prior oral agreements. The owner under a construction contract has a particularly strong interest in preventing claims by the builder for extra work allegedly done under oral modifications by the owner's representative on the site. A typical clause reads:

> No extra work or changes from plans and specifications under this contract will be recognized or paid for, unless agreed to in writing before the extra work is started or the changes made.[a]

The following case deals with this problem.

UNIVERSAL BUILDERS, INC. v. MOON MOTOR LODGE, INC.

Supreme Court of Pennsylvania, 1968.
430 Pa. 550, 244 A.2d 10.

[Universal Builders made a written contract with Moon Motor Lodge to build a motel and restaurant. The contract provided that all change orders had to be in writing and signed by Moon or the architect. Universal performed and sued Moon to recover $127,760, the balance due on the contract price together with extras. From a judgment for the plaintiff, the defendant appealed.]

a. This clause is taken from Wagner v. Graziano Constr. Co., 390 Pa. 445, 136 A.2d 82 (1957), where it appeared in a contract between a general contractor and a subcontractor. As to the desirability of extra work from the builder's point of view, see Note 2, p. 257 supra.

EAGEN, Justice. . . . Moon submits that the chancellor erred in not enforcing the contract provision that extras would not be paid for unless done pursuant to a written, signed change order.

Unless a contract is for the sale of goods, see the Uniform Commercial Code-Sales, the Act of April 6, 1953, P.L. 3, § 2–209(3), as amended, 12A P.S. § 2–209(2), it appears undisputed that the contract can be modified orally although it provides that it can be modified only in writing. E. g., Wagner v. Graziano Construction Co., 390 Pa. 445, 136 A.2d 82 (1957); 4 Williston on Contracts § 591 (3rd ed. 1961); 6 Corbin on Contracts, § 1295 (1962); Restatement of Contracts § 407 (1932). Construction contracts typically provide that the builder will not be paid for extra work unless it is done pursuant to a written change order, yet courts frequently hold that owners must pay for extra work done at their oral direction. See generally Annot., 2 A.L.R.3rd 620, 648–82 (1965). This liability can be based on several theories. For example, the extra work may be said to have been done under an oral agreement separate from the written contract and not containing the requirement of a written authorization. 3A Corbin on Contracts, § 756 at p. 505 (1960). The requirement of a written authorization may also be considered a condition which has been waived. 5 Williston on Contracts § 689 (3rd ed. 1961).

On either of the above theories, the chancellor correctly held Moon liable to pay for the extras in spite of the lack of written change orders. The evidence indicates that William Berger, the agent of Moon, requested many changes, was informed that they would involve extra cost, and promised to pay for them. In addition, Berger frequently was on the construction site and saw at least some of the extra work in progress. The record demonstrates that he was a keen observer with an extraordinary knowledge of the project in general and the contract requirements in particular. Thus it is not unreasonable to infer that he was aware that extra work was being done without proper authorization, yet he stood by without protesting while the extras were incorporated into the project. Under these circumstances there also was an implied promise to pay for the extras.

C.I.T. Corp. v. Jonnet, 419 Pa. 435, 214 A.2d 620 (1965), does suggest that such non-written modifications are ineffective unless the contract provision requiring modifications to be in writing was first waived. That case, however, is misleading. Although it involved a contract for the sale of movable bar and restaurant equipment, which is a contract for the sale of "goods" controlled by the Uniform Commercial Code-Sales, supra, § 2–101 et seq., as amended, 12A P.S. § 2–101 et seq., it overlooks that legislation, in particular § 2–209. [The court quoted UCC 2–209.] From subsection (5) it can be inferred that a provision in a contract for the sale of goods that the contract can be modified only in writing is waived, just as such a provision in a construction contract is waived, under the circumstances described by Restatement of Contracts § 224 (1932), which provides: "The performance of a condition qualifying a promise in a contract within the Statute [of Frauds or in a contract containing a provision requiring modifications to be in writing (§ 407)] may be excused by an oral agreement or permission of the promisor that the condition need not be performed, if the agreement or permission is given while the performance of the condition is possible, and in reliance on the agreement or permission, while it is unrevoked, the promisee materially changes his position." Obviously a condition is considered waived when its enforcement would result in something approaching fraud. 5 Williston on Contracts § 689 at pp. 306–07 (3rd ed. 1961). Thus the effectiveness of a non-written modification in spite of a contract condition that modifications must be written depends upon whether enforcement of the condition is or is not barred by equitable considerations, not upon the technicality of whether the condition was or was not expressly and separately waived before the non-written modification.

In view of these equitable considerations underlying waiver, it should be obvious that when an owner requests a builder to do extra work, promises to pay for it and watches it performed knowing that it is not authorized in writing, he cannot refuse to pay on the ground that there was no written change order. Focht v. Rosenbaum, 176 Pa. 14, 34 A. 1001 (1876). When Moon directed Universal to "go ahead" and promised to pay for the extras, performance of the condition requiring change orders to be in writing was excused by implication. It would be manifestly unjust to allow Moon, which misled Universal into doing extra work without a written authorization, to benefit from non-performance of that condition. . . .

The decree of the lower court therefore was correct, except [on a point omitted here].

MUSMANNO, Justice (Dissenting). . . . Even the plaintiff did not contend that the requirement in writing was waived by agreement of the parties, as in Wagner v. Graziano Construction Co., 390 Pa. 445, 136 A.2d 82, relied upon by the Majority. The most that the plaintiff has shown are oral modifications of the work called for under the contract, which is exactly what is prohibited by the solemn agreement entered into between the parties. The oral modification certainly cannot be used as evidence of a waiver, for otherwise, a requirement of writing would become meaningless. This Court clearly pointed out this fundamental proposition of law in C.I.T. Corp. v. Jonnet, 419 Pa. 435, 438, 214 A.2d 620, 622. . . .

NOTES

(1) *Earlier Pennsylvania Cases.* As the preceding opinion of the Supreme Court of Pennsylvania suggests, this was not its first encounter with a no-oral-modification clause.

In Wagner v. Graziano Constr. Co., 390 Pa. 445, 136 A.2d 82 (1957), the court had allowed recovery for extra work. In Justice Musmanno's florid prose: "The most ironclad written contract can always be cut into by the acetylene torch of parol modification supported by adequate proof . . . . The hand that pens a writing may not gag the mouths of the assenting parties." The opinion in that case, however, assumes that before the oral modification, "the defendant's authorized agent informed [the plaintiff] that the requirement for written orders for extra work was being waived."

Eight years later Justice Musmanno again spoke for the Supreme Court of Pennsylvania in a case involving a contract for the sale of goods in which it was urged that a written contract may be modified by subsequent oral agreement even though the written contract prohibits oral modification. "This is true but there must first be a waiver of the requirement which has been spelled out in the contract. Otherwise, written documents would have no more permanence than writings penned in disappearing ink . . . ., contractual obligations would become phantoms, solemn obligations would run like pressed quicksilver, and the whole edifice of business would rest on sand dunes supporting pillars of rubber and floors of turf. Chaos would envelop the commercial world." C.I.T. Corp. v. Jonnet, 419 Pa. 435, 214 A.2d 620 (1965).

It was the lack of such a separate step preceding the oral modification that prompted Musmanno's dissent in the Universal Builders case.[a]

(2) *Restatement Second and Code.* According to the Restatement Second, a no-oral-modification clause does not limit the power of the parties subsequently to contract. See Comment *b* to § 148 and Comment *b* to § 283. Is it clear the Supreme Court of Pennsylvania would go this far? (What if Moon had repudiated the agreements made by Berger before Universal Builders had done the work?)

The Code takes a radical departure from the common law position in UCC 2–209(2).[b] Does the fact that the Code (see UCC 2–209(1)) has gone further than has the common law (see Restatement Second, § 89) in abolishing the requirement of consideration for a modification make it more desirable for the Code to give effect to a no-oral-modification clause?[c] As

a. Particularly in view of the majority's unkind remark in Universal Builders about Musmanno's failure to cite UCC 2–209(2) in the Jonnet case, the reader may be interested in a brief account of one of Musmanno's more dramatic skirmishes with his brethren, in which he demanded that the entire supreme court disqualify itself and argued before that court *in propria persona.* See Note, 73 Harv.L.Rev. 1358, 1366 n. 51 (1960).

b. Comment 3 to UCC 2–209 states: "Subsections (2) and (3) are intended to protect against false allegations of oral modifications. . . . Subsection (2) permits the parties in effect to make their own Statute of Frauds as regards any future modification of the contract by giving effect to a clause in a signed agreement which expressly requires any modification to be by signed writing."

c. Consider Comment 7 to UCC 2–313: "The precise time when words of description or affirmation are made . . . is not material. The sole question is whether the language . . . [is] fairly to be regarded as part of the contract. If language is used after the closing of the deal (as when the buyer when taking delivery asks and receives an additional assurance), the warranty becomes a modification, and need not be supported by consideration if it is other-to the provisions of UCC 2–209(4) and (5) on waiver, see p. 858 infra and Note, 5 Ga.L.Rev. 783 (1971).

(3) *Drafting.* What circumstances might make it desirable or undesirable to limit the terms of the contract to those contained in a writing and to exclude prior, contemporaneous and subsequent oral agreements? Draft a clause to accomplish this result for a contract for the sale of water filters that will be serviced by the seller after installation.[d] (To what extent is the clause analogous to a home-office-approval clause? See Note 1, p. 200 supra.)[e]

SECTION 2. INTERPRETATION OF CONTRACT LANGUAGE

" 'When *I* use a word,' Humpty Dumpty said, in rather a scornful tone, 'it means just what I choose it to mean—neither more nor less.'

" 'The question is,' said Alice, 'whether you *can* make words mean so many different things.'

" 'The question is,' said Humpty Dumpty, 'which is to be master—that's all.' " Lewis Carroll, Through the Looking Glass, Chapter VI.

As this familiar excerpt suggests, the problem of interpretation of language is not peculiar to the law. However, language is commonly involved in social control through law, and the interpretation of this language may have consequences of great practical moment. The critical language may come from one of a variety of sources, such as a constitution, a statute, an administrative regulation, a will, a deed, or a contract. We are concerned with contracts.

Scholars less boastful than Humpty Dumpty have cautioned us on what Professor Chafee has called "the disorderly conduct of words." There is no "lawyers Paradise" where, in Professor Thayer's language, "all words have a fixed, precisely ascertained meaning, . . . and where, if the writer has been careful, a lawyer, having a document referred to him may sit in his chair, inspect the text, and answer all questions without raising his eyes." As Justice Holmes put it, "A word is not a crystal, transparent and unchanged, it is the skin of a living thought and may vary greatly in color and content according to the circumstances and the time in which it is used."

wise reasonable and in order (Section 2–209)." Would the same be true of language used to placate a buyer who complains about the goods after delivery?

d. New York has a statute similar to UCC 2–209(2) that applies to contracts generally. N.Y.General Obligations L. § 15–301.

e. Here, too, a clause limiting the power of the seller's representatives in the field to bind him might be considered, but this raises questions of the law of agency that are beyond the scope of this course. See footnote b, p. 200 supra.

Towne v. Eisner, 245 U.S. 418 (1918). One of the most perceptive of these scholars, Professor Willard van Orman Quine, has emphasized a distinction between *vagueness* and *ambiguity*. See Quine, Word and Object (1960).

According to Quine, "stimulations eliciting a verbal response, say 'red', are best depicted as forming not a neatly bounded class but a distribution about a central *norm*." A word is vague to the extent that its applicability in marginal situations is uncertain. The parties, for example, contract for the removal of "all the dirt" on a given tract. May sand from a stratum of subsoil be taken?[a]

Ambiguity, as Quine defines it, is an entirely distinct concept from that of vagueness. A word that may or may not apply in marginal situations is vague. But a word may also have two entirely different connotations so that it may be at the same time both appropriate and inappropriate, as the word "light" may be when applied to dark feathers. Such a word is ambiguous.[b] Ambiguities may be classified into those of term and those of syntax.

Ambiguities of term are relatively rare in contract cases. A contract specifies "tons." Are they to be long or short tons?[c] Ambiguity of syntax is, in the strictest sense, an ambiguity of grammatical structure, of what is syntactically connected to what. It is more common a cause of contract disputes than is ambiguity of term. A health insurance policy excludes any "disease of organs of the body not common to both sexes." Does the policy cover a fibroid tumor (which can occur in any organ) of the uterus?[d]

Consideration of whether such distinctions as these, between vagueness and ambiguity, play a meaningful role in the interpretation of contracts can be deferred until later. It is plain that they are useful in describing disputes about language. Here are two simple techniques to the same end.

The first is to state the issue in terms of the contract language, much as an issue arising under a statute is stated in terms of the statutory language. It should be framed so that it can be answered "yes" or "no," as a court ordinarily must do. It should be framed so that it contains the controlling language of the contract, with such emphasis as is helpful. And it should be framed so that it recognizes that different meanings are attached to words in different contexts. For example:

a. See Highley v. Phillips, 176 Md. 463, 5 A.2d 824 (1939) (held: yes).

b. Since "ambiguous" is often used to comprehend vague, as well as ambiguous in the narrow sense, some writers prefer to use "equivocal" for this purpose.

c. Compare Chemung Iron & Steel Co. v. Mersereau Metal Bed Co., 179 N.Y.S. 577 (1920) (short tons), with Higgins v. California Petroleum & Asphalt Co., 120 Cal. 629, 52 P. 1080 (1898) (long tons).

d. Business Men's Assur. Ass'n v. Read, 48 S.W.2d 678 (Tex.Civ.App. 1932) (held: yes).

Is a fibroid tumor of the uterus a "*disease* of *organs* of the body *not common to both sexes*" within the insured's contract of insurance?

The second technique is to redraft the language twice, staying as faithful to the original as possible, so that it would clearly require a decision, first for one party, then for the other. (See Note 1, p. 183 supra.) For example:

(For insured) "disease of organs of the body that is not common to both sexes"
(For insurer) "disease of organs of the body that are not common to both sexes"

Try, in each of the following problems: (1) to describe the problem in Quine's terms; (2) to state the issue in terms of the contract language; and (3) to redraft the contract language, first for one party and then for the other. (Consider, also, what additional information would be useful in answering the problems.)

(a) A contract for the sale of a photography studio provides that the seller will not compete with the buyer "for the school photography work in any school in Grant County, with the exception of Marion High School and Bennett High School." May the seller compete with the buyer for the photography of Marion College students? See Lawrence v. Cain, 144 Ind.App. 210, 245 N.E.2d 663 (1969).

(b) A contract for the sale of a grocery store provides that the seller will not engage in a similar business "within a radius of five city blocks from the above mentioned premises." May the seller establish a grocery four blocks north and two blocks east of his old store before the five years are up? See Kunin v. Weller, 296 Pa. 161, 145 A. 719 (1929).

(c) A construction contract provides that "All domestic water piping and rainwater piping installed above finished ceilings under this specification shall be insulated." Must the contractor insulate domestic water piping installed below finished ceilings? See Paul W. Abbott v. Axel Newman Heating & Plumbing, 282 Minn. 493, 166 N.W.2d 323 (1969).

The cases that follow are concerned with how to answer questions like those raised in these problems. A threshold problem is posed by the fact that unlike a will, which expresses the intention of a single testator, or even a statute, which expresses the collective intention of a single legislature, a contract involves *two* parties who may attach very different meanings to language and have very different expectations. The next cases deal with this problem.

On interpretation in general, see Farnsworth, "Meaning" in the Law of Contracts, 76 Yale L.J. 939 (1967); Farnsworth, Some Considerations in the Drafting of Agreements: Problems in Interpretation and Gap-Filling, 23 Record of N.Y.C.B. Ass'n 105 (1968); Patterson, The Interpretation and Construction of Contracts, 64 Colum. L.Rev. 833 (1964); Williams, Language and the Law, 61 L.Q.Rev. 71, 179, 293, 384 (1945), 62 L.Q.Rev. 387 (1946); Friedman, Law, Rules, and the Interpretation of Written Documents, 59 Nw.U.L.Rev. 751 (1965).

NOTES

(1) *Care in Drafting.* "It is a popular belief, especially prevalent amongst lawyers, that the efficient business man requires that obligations incurred in business should be expressed in writing in simple, intelligible and unambiguous language. It is a belief encouraged by the sayings of business men themselves. But in practice nothing appears to be further from the truth. Business men habitually adventure large sums of money on contracts which, for the purpose of defining legal obligations, are a mere jumble of words. They trust to luck or the good faith of the opposite party, with the comfortable assurance that any adverse result of litigation may be attributed to the hairsplitting of lawyers and the uncertainty of the law." Lord Atkin in Phoenix Insurance Co. of Hartford v. DeMonchy, 141 L.T. 439, 445 (H.L.1929).

One of the most common results of carelessness in drafting is a conflict between different parts of the contract. For an example, see Robinhorne Construction Corp. v. Snyder, 47 Ill.2d 349, 265 N.E.2d 670 (1970), in which Justice Schaefer wrote: "This is the kind of case that has been described as 'one where no principle of law is involved, but only the meaning of careless and slovenly documents.' . . . The parties used a standard cost-plus contract form. They modified it to specify a maximum contract price, but they failed to modify the termination provision. The conditions that they attached had been prepared for use with a lump-sum contract." For another example, see Schauerman v. Haag, 68 Wash.2d 868, 416 P.2d 88 (1966) ("Glaziers should glaze and lawyers should scriven, and neither ought do the other; for, when glaziers write and lawyers glaze, they are apt to make porous contracts and drafty windows.").

(2) *Interpretation in the Agreement Process.* We have already encountered problems of interpretation in the agreement process. See, for example, Owen v. Tunison, p. 181 supra, and Harvey v. Facey, p. 183 supra. Consider in this connection the remarks of Judge Medina in United States v. Braunstein, 73 F.Supp. 137 (S.D.N.Y.1947): "It is true that there is much room for interpretation once the parties are inside the framework of a contract, but it seems that there is less in the field of offer and acceptance. Greater precision of expression may be required, and less help from the court given, when the parties are merely at the threshold of a contract." This view was echoed in Henry Simons Lumber Co. v. Simons, 232 Minn. 187, 44 N.W.2d 726 (1950): "Because of strict rules governing offer and acceptance, which require that an acceptance be in terms of the offer, we are reluctant to follow by analogy rules laid down with respect to contracts already formed. In passing upon questions of offer and acceptance, courts may wisely require greater exactitude than when they are trying to salvage an existing contract. Where no contract has been completed and neither party has acted to his detriment, there is no compulsion on a court to guess at what the parties intended."

(3) *Intentional Vagueness.* Are there reasons why a draftsman may intentionally leave language vague? Consider such Code terms as "good faith," "best efforts" and "reasonable time." Are there contract analogues?

(4) *Drafting Problem.* Tomayne, Inc., furnishes cafeteria service to business firms. It is about to employ your client Claiborne Craig as manager of its cafeteria operation at the Kent Data Processing plant under a two-year contract. The draft contains the following restrictive covenant:

> For one year after my employment with you ends, I will not participate in the management of any cafeteria operated by any firm who shall have been your client within the period of one year prior to the termination of my employment or with whom you may have been negotiating during my employment with you if I have participated in such negotiations or had contact with that firm in the course of my employment with you.

Do you see any important ambiguity in this clause? How can it be corrected? (Suppose that Craig leaves Tomayne at the end of two years and takes a job managing a cafeteria for a firm with which he has had no previous connection but which had been Tomayne's client three months earlier, before deciding to operate its own cafeteria?) See Servomation Mathias, Inc. v. Englert, 333 F.Supp. 9 (M.D.Pa.1971).

(5) *Drafting Problem.* Your client is about to lease property that he owns under a two-year lease. The draft contains the following provision relating to the lessee's right of "first refusal" in the event that your client sells the property:

> If Lessor sells the property during the term of the lease, he shall have the right to cancel the lease on six months' written notice. In the event the Lessor receives an offer to buy the leased property, the Lessee shall be given the first opportunity to purchase at the same terms and conditions as the offer.

Do you see any important ambiguity in this clause? How can it be corrected? (Suppose that your client receives an offer to sell the property during the last six months of the lease?) See Zephyr Cove Lodge, Inc. v. First Nat. Bank, 478 F.2d 1121 (9th Cir. 1973).

FRIGALIMENT IMPORTING CO. v. B. N. S. INTERNATIONAL SALES CORP.

United States District Court, S.D.N.Y., 1960.
190 F.Supp. 116.

FRIENDLY, Circuit Judge. The issue is, what is chicken?[a] Plaintiff says "chicken" means a young chicken, suitable for broiling

a. In the 1940's, American chicken producers began to differentiate chickens raised for meat from those raised for eggs, and started using "assembly-line" techniques for the former, giving rise to a new consumer product, the "broiler chicken." Production grew phenomenally, prices dropped correspondingly, and exports to Europe increased sharply. Between 1956 and 1962, German chicken consumption went from 136 million pounds (of which 2.5 million or 1% was exported from the United States)

and frying. Defendant says "chicken" means any bird of that genus that meets contract specifications on weight and quality, including what it calls "stewing chicken" and plaintiff pejoratively terms "fowl". Dictionaries give both meanings, as well as some others not relevant here. To support its, plaintiff sends a number of volleys over the net; defendant essays to return them and adds a few serves of its own. Assuming that both parties were acting in good faith, the case nicely illustrates Holmes' remark "that the making of a contract depends not on the agreement of two minds in one intention, but on the agreement of two sets of external signs—not on the parties' having *meant* the same thing but on their having *said* the same thing." The Path of the Law, in Collected Legal Papers, p. 178. I have concluded that plaintiff has not sustained its burden of persuasion that the contract used "chicken" in the narrower sense.

The action is for breach of the warranty that goods sold shall correspond to the description, New York Personal Property Law, McKinney's Consol.Laws, c. 41, § 95. Two contracts are in suit. In the first, dated May 2, 1957, defendant, a New York sales corporation, confirmed the sale to plaintiff, a Swiss corporation, of

> "US Fresh Frozen Chicken, Grade A, Government Inspected, Eviscerated
> 2½–3 lbs. and 1½–2 lbs. each
> all chicken individually wrapped in cryovac, packed in secured fiber cartons or wooden boxes, suitable for export
> 75,000 lbs. 2½–3 lbs. .... @$33.00
> 25,000 lbs. 1½–2 lbs. .... @$36.50
> per 100 lbs. FAS New York
> scheduled May 10, 1957 pursuant to instructions from Penson & Co., New York."

The second contract, also dated May 2, 1957, was identical save that only 50,000 lbs. of the heavier "chicken" were called for, the price of the smaller birds was $37 per 100 lbs., and shipment was scheduled for May 30. The initial shipment under the first contract was short but the balance was shipped on May 17. When the initial shipment arrived in Switzerland, plaintiff found, on May 28, that the 2½–3 lbs. birds were not young chicken suitable for broiling and frying but stewing chicken or "fowl"; indeed, many of the cartons and bags plainly so indicated. Protests ensued. Nevertheless, shipment under the second contract was made on May 29, the 2½–3 lbs. birds again being stewing chicken. Defendant stopped the transportation of these at Rotterdam.

to 716 million pounds (of which 169.6 million or 26% was exported from the United States). For more on chickens in international trade and the resulting "chicken war," see 1 Chayes, Ehrlich and Lowenfeld, International Legal Process 249–306 (1968).

This action followed. Plaintiff says that, notwithstanding that its acceptance was in Switzerland, New York law controls under the principle of Rubin v. Irving Trust Co., 1953, 305 N.Y. 288, 305, 113 N.E.2d 424, 431; defendant does not dispute this, and relies on New York decisions. I shall follow the apparent agreement of the parties as to the applicable law.

Since the word "chicken" standing alone is ambiguous, I turn first to see whether the contract itself offers any aid to its interpretation. Plaintiff says the 1½–2 lbs. birds necessarily had to be young chicken since the older birds do not come in that size, hence the 2½–3 lbs. birds must likewise be young. This is unpersuasive—a contract for "apples" of two different sizes could be filled with different kinds of apples even though only one species came in both sizes. Defendant notes that the contract called not simply for chicken but for "US Fresh Frozen Chicken, Grade A, Government Inspected." It says the contract thereby incorporated by reference the Department of Agriculture's regulations, which favor its interpretation; I shall return to this after reviewing plaintiff's other contentions.

The first hinges on an exchange of cablegrams which preceded execution of the formal contracts. The negotiations leading up to the contracts were conducted in New York between defendant's secretary, Ernest R. Bauer, and a Mr. Stovicek, who was in New York for the Czechoslovak government at the World Trade Fair. A few days after meeting Bauer at the fair, Stovicek telephoned and inquired whether defendant would be interested in exporting poultry to Switzerland. Bauer then met with Stovicek, who showed him a cable from plaintiff dated April 26, 1957, announcing that they "are buyer" of 25,000 lbs. of chicken 2½–3 lbs. weight, Cryovac packed, grade A Government inspected, at a price up to 33¢ per pound, for shipment on May 10, to be confirmed by the following morning, and were interested in further offerings. After testing the market for price, Bauer accepted, and Stovicek sent a confirmation that evening. Plaintiff stresses that, although these and subsequent cables between plaintiff and defendant, which laid the basis for the additional quantities under the first and for all of the second contract, were predominantly in German, they used the English word "chicken"; it claims this was done because it understood "chicken" meant young chicken whereas the German word, "Huhn," included both "Brathuhn" (broilers) and "Suppenhuhn" (stewing chicken), and that defendant, whose officers were thoroughly conversant with German, should have realized this. Whatever force this argument might otherwise have is largely drained away by Bauer's testimony that he asked Stovicek what kind of chickens were wanted, received the answer "any kind of chickens," and then, in German, asked whether the cable meant "Huhn" and received an affirmative response. . . .

Plaintiff's next contention is that there was a definite trade usage that "chicken" meant "young chicken." Defendant showed that it was only beginning in the poultry trade in 1957, thereby bringing itself within the principle that "when one of the parties is not a member of the trade or other circle, his acceptance of the standard must be made to appear" by proving either that he had actual knowledge of the usage or that the usage is "so generally known in the community that his actual individual knowledge of it may be inferred." 9 Wigmore, Evidence (3d ed. 1940) § 2464. Here there was no proof of actual knowledge of the alleged usage; indeed, it is quite plain that defendant's belief was to the contrary. In order to meet the alternative requirement, the law of New York demands a showing that "the usage is of so long continuance, so well established, so notorious, so universal and so reasonable in itself, as that the presumption is violent that the parties contracted with reference to it, and made it a part of their agreement." Walls v. Bailey, 1872, 49 N.Y. 464, 472–473.

Plaintiff endeavored to establish such a usage by the testimony of three witnesses and certain other evidence. Strasser, resident buyer in New York for a large chain of Swiss cooperatives, testified that "on chicken I would definitely understand a broiler." However, the force of this testimony was considerably weakened by the fact that in his own transactions the witness, a careful businessman, protected himself by using "broiler" when that was what he wanted and "fowl" when he wished older birds. Indeed, there are some indications, dating back to a remark of Lord Mansfield, Edie v. East India Co., 2 Burr. 1216, 1222 (1761), that no credit should be given "witnesses to usage, who could not adduce instances in verification." 7 Wigmore, Evidence (3d ed. 1940) § 1954; see McDonald v. Acker, Merrall & Condit Co., 2d Dept. 1920, 192 App.Div. 123, 126, 182 N.Y.S. 607. While Wigmore thinks this goes too far, a witness' consistent failure to rely on the alleged usage deprives his opinion testimony of much of its effect. Niesielowski, an officer of one of the companies that had furnished the stewing chicken to defendant, testified that "chicken" meant "the male species of the poultry industry. That could be a broiler, a fryer or a roaster," but not a stewing chicken; however, he also testified that upon receiving defendant's inquiry for "chickens," he asked whether the desire was for "fowl or frying chickens" and, in fact, supplied fowl, although taking the precaution of asking defendant, a day or two after plaintiff's acceptance of the contracts in suit, to change its confirmation of its order from "chickens," as defendant had originally prepared it, to "stewing chickens." Dates, an employee of Urner-Barry Company, which publishes a daily market report on the poultry trade, gave it as his view that the trade meaning of "chicken" was "broilers and fryers." In addition to this opinion testimony, plaintiff relied on the fact that the Urner-Barry service, the Journal of Commerce, and Weinberg Bros. & Co. of Chicago, a large supplier of poultry, published quotations in a manner which, in one way or another, distinguish between "chicken," comprising broilers, fryers and certain other categories, and "fowl," which, Bauer acknowledged, included stewing chickens. This material would be impressive if there were nothing to the contrary. However, there was, as will now be seen.

Defendant's witness Weininger, who operates a chicken eviscerating plant in New Jersey, testified "Chicken is everything except a goose, a duck, and a turkey. Everything is a chicken, but then you have to say, you have to specify which category you want or that you are talking about." Its witness Fox said that in the trade "chicken" would encompass all the various classifications. Sadina, who conducts a food inspection service, testified that he would consider any bird coming within the classes of "chicken" in the Department of Agriculture's regulations to be a chicken. The specifications approved by the General Services Administration include fowl as well as broilers and fryers under the classification "chickens." Statistics of the Institute of American Poultry Industries use the phrases "Young chickens" and "Mature chickens," under the general heading "Total chickens." and the Department of Agriculture's daily and weekly price reports avoid use of the word "chicken" without specification.

Defendant advances several other points which it claims affirmatively support its construction. Primary among these is the regulation of the Department of Agriculture, 7 C.F.R. §§ 70.300–70.370, entitled, "Grading and Inspection of Poultry and Edible Products Thereof." and in particular § 70.301 which recited:

"*Chickens.* The following are the various classes of chickens:

(a) Broiler or fryer . . .

(b) Roaster . . .

(c) Capon . . .

(d) Stag . . .

(e) Hen or stewing chicken or fowl . . .

(f) Cock or old rooster . . ."

Defendant argues, as previously noted, that the contract incorporated these regulations by reference. Plaintiff answers that the contract provision related simply to grade and Government inspection and did not incorporate the Government definition of "chicken," and also that the definition in the Regulations is ignored in the trade. However, the latter contention was contradicted by Weininger and Sadina; and there is force in defendant's argument that the contract made the regulations a dictionary, particularly since the reference to Government grading was already in plaintiff's initial cable to Stovicek.

Defendant makes a further argument based on the impossibility of its obtaining broilers and fryers at the 33¢ price offered by plaintiff for the 2½–3 lbs. birds. There is no substantial dispute that, in late April, 1957, the price for 2½–3 lbs. broilers was between 35 and

37¢ per pound, and that when defendant entered into the contracts, it was well aware of this and intended to fill them by supplying fowl in these weights. It claims that plaintiff must likewise have known the market since plaintiff had reserved shipping space on April 23, three days before plaintiff's cable to Stovicek, or, at least, that Stovicek was chargeable with such knowledge. It is scarcely an answer to say, as plaintiff does in its brief, that the 33¢ price offered by the 2½–3 lbs. "chickens" was closer to the prevailing 35¢ price for broilers than to the 30¢ at which defendant procured fowl. Plaintiff must have expected defendant to make some profit—certainly it could not have expected defendant deliberately to incur a loss.

Finally, defendant relies on conduct by the plaintiff after the first shipment had been received. On May 28 plaintiff sent two cables complaining that the larger birds in the first shipment constituted "fowl." Defendant answered with a cable refusing to recognize plaintiff's objection and announcing "We have today ready for shipment 50,000 lbs. chicken 2½–3 lbs. 25,000 lbs. broilers 1½–2 lbs.," these being the goods procured for shipment under the second contract, and asked immediate answer "whether we are to ship this merchandise to you and whether you will accept the merchandise." After several other cable exchanges, plaintiff replied on May 29 "Confirm again that merchandise is to be shipped since resold by us if not enough pursuant to contract chickens are shipped the missing quantity is to be shipped within ten days stop we resold to our customers pursuant to your contract chickens grade A you have to deliver us said merchandise we again state that we shall make you fully responsible for all resulting costs." Defendant argues that if plaintiff was sincere in thinking it was entitled to young chickens, plaintiff would not have allowed the shipment under the second contract to go forward, since the distinction between broilers and chickens drawn in defendant's cablegram must have made it clear that the larger birds would not be broilers. However, plaintiff answers that the cables show plaintiff was insisting on delivery of young chickens and that defendant shipped old ones at its peril. Defendant's point would be highly relevant on another disputed issue—whether if liability were established, the measure of damages should be the difference in market value of broilers and stewing chicken in New York or the larger difference in Europe, but I cannot give it weight on the issue of interpretation. Defendant points out also that plaintiff proceeded to deliver some of the larger birds in Europe, describing them as "poulets"; defendant argues that it was only when plaintiff's customers complained about this that plaintiff developed the idea that "chicken" meant "young chicken." There is little force in this in view of plaintiff's immediate and consistent protests.

When all the evidence is reviewed, it is clear that defendant believed it could comply with the contracts by delivering stewing chicken in the 2½–3 lbs. size. Defendant's subjective intent would not be significant if this did not coincide with an objective meaning of "chicken." Here it did coincide with one of the dictionary meanings, with the definition in the Department of Agriculture Regulations to which the contract made at least oblique reference, with at least some usage in the trade, with the realities of the market, and with what plaintiff's spokesman had said. Plaintiff asserts it to be equally plain that plaintiff's own subjective intent was to obtain broilers and fryers; the only evidence against this is the material as to market prices and this may not have been sufficiently brought home. In any event it is unnecessary to determine that issue. For plaintiff has the burden of showing that "chicken" was used in the narrower rather than in the broader sense, and this it has not sustained.

This opinion constitutes the Court's findings of fact and conclusions of law. Judgment shall be entered dismissing the complaint with costs.

NOTES

(1) *"What is Chicken"?* Judge Friendly says that "The issue is, what is chicken?" Is this the issue that the court had to decide? He also says that the case "nicely illustrates Holmes' remark 'that the making of a contract depends . . . not on the parties' having *meant* the same thing but on their having *said* the same thing.'" Does it? Would the result have been the same if *both* parties had *meant* broilers although they had *said* "chicken?"[a] Is there any reason to hold the parties to a meaning that *neither* attached to their language? The Frigaliment case is discussed in Corbin, The Interpretation of Words and the Parol Evidence Rule, 50 Cornell L.Q. 161, 164–70 (1965).[b]

(2) *Incorporation by Reference.* Are there any special problems that arise in the interpretation of terms, such as the regulations of the Department of Agriculture, that have been incorporated in a contract by reference? Cf. Wilcox v. Wilcox, 406 S.W.2d 152 (Ky.1966), involving a divorce settlement in which the husband agreed to make maintenance payments until his daughter reached "the age of majority." The court held that the husband's obligation continued until the child reached 21, the statutory age of majority at the time of the agreement, even though the statutory age had subsequently been lowered to 18.

a. Since both parties were corporations, the notion that either "meant" anything or had any "intention" may seem somewhat strained. It would seem even more strained if other persons, including lawyers, had participated in the negotiations along with Bauer and Stovicek. Courts have not been greatly troubled by the problems of finding a collective "intention" in such cases. (For example, Judge Friendly states that B.N.S. "was only beginning in the poultry trade." Would it have been significant if Bauer had been hired by B.N.S. because of his long experience in that trade?) For a rare instance where such a problem was raised, see Franklin Life Insurance Co. v. Mast, 435 F.2d 1038 (9th Cir. 1970), where the court said, "Whatever may have been the secret intent of Mast, it is clear that the intent of his attorney in fact, Attorney Lohse, was to enter into a bona fide agreement."

b. For an afterthought by Judge Friendly, see Dadourian Export Corp. v. United States, 291 F.2d 178, 187 n. 4 (2d Cir. 1961).

(3) *The Case of the Contractor with Experience.* The National Park Service, a Division of the Department of the Interior, engaged Perry and Wallis, a contractor, to construct guard houses, fences and sidewalks at the White House. Later, when a change order was issued, Perry and Wallis engaged a subcontractor to make the changes. Perry and Wallis' contract with the Park Service allowed it the "actual necessary cost" of changes plus a fixed fee of 15 percent, the cost "in no case" to include "general expense not directly attributable to the extra work." Perry and Wallis claimed that "actual necessary cost" meant cost to it, the contractor, and therefore included the subcontractor's overhead and profits. The Park Service rejected this claim on the ground that "actual necessary cost" meant cost to the subcontractor only. After an unsuccessful appeal to the Interior Board of Contract Appeals, Perry and Wallis sued the United States in the Court of Claims, and both parties moved for summary judgment. *Held:* United States' motion granted and petition dismissed. The court relied on three prior decisions of the Interior Board of Contract Appeals, which had reached the same conclusion. In one of those cases, "the Department of Interior was, as here, the agency of the government involved and our present plaintiff was the subcontractor of the complaining contractor in the case. . . . [P]laintiff, as subcontractor, was aware of the ruling and of defendant's interpretation of the clause involved. Therefore, when he signed the instant contract, he did so with knowledge of the defendant's past interpretation of this phase of the contract. A party who willingly and without protest enters into a contract with knowledge of the other party's interpretation of it is bound by such interpretation and cannot later claim that it thought something else was meant." Perry and Wallis, Inc. v. United States, 427 F.2d 722 (Ct.Cl.1970). What does this suggest as to the point in the Lefkowitz case discussed in footnote a, p. 194 supra?

(4) *Problem.* Fredrick Hamann, who taught at the Garden City Community Junior College, wanted a year's leave to take a teacher training course. The college regulations incorporated by reference in his contract of employment provided:

> Professional employees granted leaves will, if possible, be reinstated in positions that are similar to the position held when granted the leave.

When he was offered a leave, he knew that the college interpreted this to mean that they would not be required to re-hire him unless there was a similar position open when he re-applied. However, he consulted a lawyer, who advised that in his judgment the provision should be interpreted to mean that the college was required to re-hire him even though a similar position might not be open. Secure in this knowledge, Hamann said nothing and accepted the leave. When he sought to return, the college told him that he could not do so because there was no similar position available. What do you think of the lawyer's advice? See **Hamann v. Crouch, 211 Kan. 852, 508 P.2d 968 (1973).**

OBJECTIVE AND SUBJECTIVE THEORIES OF CONTRACT INTERPRETATION

Just as the objective and subjective theories have influenced the law of contract formation (see p. 171 supra), they have also influenced the law of contract interpretation. There would be little disagreement with the proposition that, where the parties have in fact attached different meanings to their language, an objective standard should determine which meaning will prevail. But the objectivists argue that, even where the parties have in fact attached the same meaning to their language, an objective standard should determine the meaning, which might be different from their shared meaning. Hand, for example, said: "It is quite true that we commonly speak of a contract as a question of intent, and for most purposes it is a convenient paraphrase, accurate enough, but, strictly speaking, untrue. It makes not the least difference whether a promisor actually intends that meaning which the law will impose upon his words. The whole House of Bishops might satisfy us that he had intended something else, and it would make not a particle of difference in his obligation. That obligation the law attaches to his act of using certain words, provided, of course, the actor be under no disability. The scope of those words will, in the absence of some convention to the contrary, be settled, it is true, by what the law supposes men would generally mean when they used them; but the promisor's conformity to type is not a factor in his obligation. Hence it follows that no declaration of the promisor as to his meaning when he used the words is of the slightest relevancy, however formally competent it may be as an admission. Indeed, if both parties severally declared that their meaning had been other than the natural meaning, and each declaration was similar, it would be irrelevant, saving some mutual agreement between them to that effect. When the court came to assign the meaning to their words, it would disregard such declarations, because they related only to their state of mind when the contract was made, and that has nothing to do with their obligations." Eustis Mining Co. v. Beer, Sondheimer & Co., 239 F. 976 (S.D.N.Y.1917). The currency of this view can be judged from the following cases. See Restatement Second, § 201.

NOTE

The Case of John's Other Wife. In 1921, Ira Soper penned several suicide notes to Adeline, his wife of ten years, parked his car containing his hat and some clothing by a canal, and left Louisville, Kentucky, without a trace, for Minneapolis, Minnesota, where he began a new life under the name of John W. Young. There he married Gertrude Whitby, took out a $5,000 insurance policy on his own life, payable to a trust company, and made an "escrow" agreement with his partner Karstens and the trust company by which the company would pay the proceeds to "the wife" of the insured. In 1932 he actually did commit suicide, and the trustee paid the proceeds to Gertrude as his surviving wife. Several months later Adeline appeared and brought suit against Gertrude for the proceeds. From a judgment for defendant, plaintiff appealed. *Held:* Affirmed. Although Gertrude was not the legal wife of the deceased, evidence was admissible to show that she was intended as beneficiary. "Were we to award the insurance fund to plaintiff Adeline, it is obvious that we would thereby be doing violence to the contract . . . . That agreement points to no one else than Gertrude as Young's 'wife'. To hold otherwise is to give the word 'wife' 'a fixed symbol,' as 'something inherent and objective, not subjective and personal'. . . . . The trust agreement has become 'susceptible of construction' because 'ambiguity appears when attempt is made to operate the contract.'" One judge dissented, arguing: "A man can have only one wife. . . . The contract in this case designates the 'wife' as the one to whom the money was to be paid. I am unable to construe this word to mean anyone else than the only wife of Soper then living." In re Soper's Estate (Cochran v. Whitby), 196 Minn. 60, 264 N.W. 427 (1935). But cf. State Farm Mutual Automobile Ins. Co. v. Thompson, 372 F.2d 256 (9th Cir. 1967).

RAFFLES v. WICHELHAUS

Court of Exchequer, 1864.
2 H. & C. 906, 159 Eng.Rep. 375.

Declaration. For that it was agreed between the plaintiff and the defendants, to wit, at Liverpool, that the plaintiff should sell to the defendants, and the defendants buy of the plaintiff, certain goods, to wit, 125 bales of Surat cotton, guaranteed middling fair merchant's Dhollorah, to arrive ex Peerless from Bombay; and that the cotton should be taken from the quay, and that the defendants would pay the plaintiff for the same at a certain rate, to wit, at the rate of 17¼*d.* per pound, within a certain time then agreed upon after the arrival of the said goods in England. Averments: that the said goods did arrive by the said ship from Bombay in England, to wit, at Liverpool, and the plaintiff was then and there ready and willing and offered to deliver the said goods to the defendants, etc. Breach: that the defendants refused to accept the said goods or pay the plaintiff for them.

Plea. That the said ship mentioned in the said agreement was meant and intended by the defendants to be the ship called the Peerless, which sailed from Bombay, to wit, in October; and that the plaintiff was not ready and willing, and did not offer, to deliver to the defendants any bales of cotton which arrived by the last-mentioned ship, but instead thereof was only ready and willing, and offered to deliver to the defendants 125 bales of Surat cotton which arrived by another and different ship, which was also called the Peerless, and which sailed from Bombay, to wit, in December.

Demurrer, and joinder therein.

MILWARD in support of the demurrer. The contract was for the sale of a number of bales of cotton of a particular description, which the plaintiff was ready to deliver. It is immaterial by what ship the cotton was to arrive, so that it was a ship called the Peerless. The words "to arrive ex Peerless," only mean that if the vessel is lost on the voyage, the contract is to be at an end. [Pollock, C.B. It would be a question for the jury whether both parties meant the same ship called the Peerless.] That would be so if the contract was for the sale of a ship called the Peerless; but it is for the sale of cotton on board a ship of that name. [Pollock, C.B. The defendant only bought that cotton which was to arrive by a particular ship. It may as well be said that if there is a contract for the purchase of certain goods in warehouse A that is satisfied by the delivery of goods of the same description in warehouse B.] In that case there would be goods in both warehouses; here it does not appear that the plaintiff had any goods on board the other Peerless. [Martin, B. It is imposing on the defendant a contract different from that which he entered into. Pollock, C.B. It is like a contract for the purchase of wine coming from a particular estate in France or Spain, where there are two estates of that name.] The defendant has no right to contradict by parol evidence a written contract good upon the face of it. He does not impute misrepresentation or fraud, but only says that he fancied the ship was a different one. Intention is of no avail, unless stated at the time of the contract. [Pollock, C.B. One vessel sailed in October and the other in December.] The time of sailing is no part of the contract.

MELLISH (Cohen with him) in support of the plea. There is nothing on the face of the contract to show that any particular ship called the Peerless was meant; but the moment it appears that two ships called the Peerless were about to sail from Bombay there is a latent ambiguity, and parol evidence may be given for the purpose of showing that the defendant meant one Peerless and the plaintiff another. That being so, there was no consensus ad idem, and therefore no binding contract. He was then stopped by the court.

PER CURIAM. There must be judgment for the defendants.

Judgment for the defendants.

NOTE

The Meaning of "Peerless." Can the result be explained only on the subjective theory? Holmes thought not: "By the theory of our language, while other words may mean different things, a proper name means one person or thing and no other. . . . In theory of speech your name means you and my name means me, and the two names are different. They are different words. . . . In the use of common names and words a plea of different meaning from that adopted by the court would be bad, but here the parties have said different things and never have expressed a contract." Holmes, The Theory of Legal Interpretation, 12 Harv.L.Rev. 417, 418 (1899).

OSWALD v. ALLEN, 417 F.2d 43 (2d Cir. 1969). [Dr. Oswald, a coin collector from Switzerland, arranged to see Mrs. Allen's collection of Swiss coins in Newburgh, New York, where two of her collections, referred to as the Swiss Coin Collection and the Rarity Coin Collection, were located in separate bank vaults. After examining the coins in the Swiss Coin Collection, he was shown several valuable Swiss coins from the Rarity Coin Collection, although he later testified that he did not know that they were in a separate "collection." During the drive back to New York City, Dr. Oswald, who spoke very little English, arranged with the help of his brother to buy for $50,000 what Mrs. Allen thought was her Swiss coin collection and what Dr. Oswald thought were all her Swiss coins. He later wrote her to "confirm my purchase of all your Swiss coins (gold, silver and copper) at the price of $50,000" and she wrote back that she had arranged to go to Newburgh with Dr. Oswald's agent. When Dr. Oswald was informed that she would not go through with the sale because of her children's wishes, he sued for specific performance. From a judgment dismissing his complaint after trial, he appealed.]

MOORE, Circuit Judge . . . . . In such a factual situation the law is settled that no contract exists. The Restatement of Contracts in section 71(a) adopts the rule of Raffles v. Wichelhaus, 2 Hurl. & C. 906, 159 Eng.Rep. 375 (Ex. 1864). Professor Young states that rule as follows: "when any of the terms used to express an agreement is ambivalent, and the parties understand it in different ways, there cannot be a contract unless one of them should have been aware of the other's understanding." Young, Equivocation in Agreements, 64 Colum.L.Rev. 619, 621 (1964). Even though the mental assent of the parties is not requisite for the formation of a contract (see Comment to Restatement of Contracts § 71 (1932)), the facts found by the trial judge clearly place this case within the small group of exceptional cases in which there is "no sensible basis for choosing between conflicting understandings." Young, at 647. The rule of Raffles v. Wichelhaus is applicable here.

[The court also held that the exchange of letters did not satisfy the Statute of Frauds.]

Affirmed.

NOTE

Another View. In the article quoted by Judge Moore, Professor Young writes: "Roughly speaking, the rule is restricted to differences of understanding which have their source in the ambivalence or 'double meaning' of an expression. Neither the courts nor the logicians have succeeded, so far as I am aware, in establishing a criterion by which we can readily decide whether or not a particular expression has a 'double meaning.' Holmes's formulation [in Note, p. 694 supra] would have limited the application of the Peerless rule too narrowly. The Restatement test [now stated in Restatement Second, § 20] is too broad." Young, Equivocation in the Making of Agreements, 64 Colum.L.Rev. 619, 646–47 (1964).

See also Palmer, The Effect of Misunderstanding on Contract Formation and Reformation under the Restatement of Contracts Second, 65 Mich. L. Rev. 33 (1966), adapted and reprinted in 3 G. Palmer, Law of Restitution § 15.2 (1978). For a recent case, see Flower City Painting Contractors, Inc. v. Gumina Constr. Co., 591 F.2d 162 (2d Cir. 1979).

FUNCTION OF JUDGE AND JURY

A detailed consideration of the respective roles of judge and jury, where trial is had by jury, in matters of contract interpretation is best left to a course in evidence or procedure. Nevertheless, a few elementary generalizations may be in order. It is clear that the meaning of language is, strictly speaking, a question of fact. Yet the interpretation of written agreements, as to which there is no dispute over the words used by the parties, has often been withdrawn from the jury by calling it a question of "law" for the judge, rather than a question of "fact" for the jury. This has been done for a variety of reasons, including a distrust of unsophisticated, uneducated, and—at least at one time—illiterate jurors, and a desire for consistency in interpretation of some kinds of contracts, such as standard insurance policies.

The difficulty in drawing a line between the province of the judge and that of the jury is suggested by this dictum of Justice Story:[a] "It is certainly true, as a general rule, that the interpretation of written instruments properly belongs to the court, and not to the jury. But there certainly are cases in which, from the different senses of the words used, or their obscure and indeterminate reference to unexplained circumstances, the true interpretation of the language may be left to the consideration of the jury for the purpose of carrying into effect the real intention of the parties." Brown & Company v. M'Gran, 39 U.S. (14 Pet.) 479, 493 (1840). A similar view has been more recently expressed by Chief Justice Traynor, who wrote, "It is . . . solely a judicial function to interpret a written instrument unless the interpretation turns upon the credibility of extrinsic evidence." Parsons v. Bristol Development Co., 62 Cal.2d 861, 865, 44 Cal.Rptr. 767, 770, 402 P.2d 839, 842 (1965).

But Judge Friendly has pointed out: "With the courts' growing appreciation of Professor Corbin's lesson that words are seldom so 'plain and clear' as to exclude proof of surrounding circumstances and other extrinsic aids to interpretation, . . . the exception

a. Joseph Story (1779–1845) was appointed to the United States Supreme Court in 1811. In 1829, while retaining his seat on the Court, he became a professor of law at the Harvard Law School, where he reorganized the curriculum and revitalized the school. From his lectures developed his nine commentaries on subjects ranging from the Constitution to conflict of laws, which played an important role in promoting uniformity in the development of American law during the first half of the nineteenth century.

bids fair largely to swallow the supposed general rule. . . . Whether determination of meaning be regarded as a question of fact, a question of law, or just itself, reliance on the jury to resolve ambiguities in the light of extrinsic evidence seems quite as it should be, save where the form or subject-matter of a particular contract outruns a jury's competence . . . ." Meyers v. Selznick Co., 373 F. 2d 218, 222 (2d Cir. 1966).

NOTE

"What is Chicken"? (Reprise). At the end of the *Frigaliment* case, Judge Friendly said that "the burden of showing that 'chicken' was used in the narrower rather than in the broader sense" was on the buyer. Its action for breach of warranty therefore failed. See UCC 2–607(4). Suppose, however, that immediately after the contracts were made, the buyer had told the seller that it would accept nothing but broilers, and the seller had treated this as a repudiation and sued for damages. Would not the burden of showing that "chicken" was used in the broader sense have then been on the seller? Is it possible that the seller might have failed to sustain this burden?

In a case like Raffles v. Wichelhaus, is it possible that the seller might fail to meet the burden of showing that "Peerless" was used in the sense of the ship sailing in December and that the buyer might also fail to meet the burden of showing that "Peerless" was used in the sense of the ship sailing in October? Do the preceding excerpts on the function of judge and jury suggest that interpretation is a question of "fact" as to which a party can be said to have a "burden"?

PACIFIC GAS & ELECTRIC CO. v. G. W. THOMAS DRAYAGE & RIGGING CO.

Supreme Court of California, 1968.
69 Cal.2d 33, 69 Cal.Rptr. 561, 442 P.2d 641.

TRAYNOR, Chief Justice. Defendant appeals from a judgment for plaintiff in an action for damages for injury to property under an indemnity clause of a contract.

In 1960 defendant entered into a contract with plaintiff to furnish the labor and equipment necessary to remove and replace the upper metal cover of plaintiff's steam turbine. Defendant agreed to perform the work "at [its] own risk and expense" and to "indemnify" plaintiff "against all loss, damage, expense and liability resulting from . . . injury to property, arising out of or in any way connected with the performance of this contract." Defendant also agreed to procure not less than $50,000 insurance to cover liability for injury to property. Plaintiff was to be an additional named insured, but the policy was to contain a cross-liability clause extending the coverage to plaintiff's property.

During the work the cover fell and injured the exposed rotor of the turbine. Plaintiff brought this action to recover $25,144.51, the amount it subsequently spent on repairs. During the trial it dismissed a count based on negligence and thereafter secured judgment on the theory that the indemnity provision covered injury to all property regardless of ownership.

Defendant offered to prove by admissions of plaintiff's agents, by defendant's conduct under similar contracts entered into with plaintiff, and by other proof that in the indemnity clause the parties meant to cover injury to property of third parties only and not to plaintiff's property. Although the trial court observed that the language used was "the classic language for a third party indemnity provision" and that "one could very easily conclude that . . . its whole intendment is to indemnify third parties," it nevertheless held that the "plain language" of the agreement also required defendant to indemnify plaintiff for injuries to plaintiff's property. Having determined that the contract had a plain meaning, the court refused to admit any extrinsic evidence that would contradict its interpretation.

When a court interprets a contract on this basis, it determines the meaning of the instrument in accordance with the ". . . extrinsic evidence of the judge's own linguistic education and experience." (3 Corbin on Contracts (1960 ed.) [1964 Supp. § 579, p. 225, fn. 56].) The exclusion of testimony that might contradict the linguistic background of the judge reflects a judicial belief in the possibility of perfect verbal expression. (9 Wigmore on Evidence (3d ed. 1940) § 2461, p. 187.) This belief is a remnant of a primitive faith in the inherent potency [1] and inherent meaning of words.[2]

The test of admissibility of extrinsic evidence to explain the meaning of a written instrument is not whether it appears to the court to be plain and unambiguous on its face, but whether the offered evidence is relevant to prove a meaning to which the language of the instrument is reasonably susceptible. . . .

A rule that would limit the determination of the meaning of a written instrument to its four-corners merely because it seems to the

1. E. g., "The elaborate system of taboo and verbal prohibitions in primitive groups; the ancient Egyptian myth of Khern, the apotheosis of the word, and of Thoth, the Scribe of Truth, the Giver of Words and Script, the Master of Incantations; the avoidance of the name of God in Brahmanism, Judaism and Islam; totemistic and protective names in mediaeval Turkish and Finno-Ugrian languages; the misplaced verbal scruples of the 'Précieuses'; the Swedish peasant custom of curing sick cattle smitten by witchcraft, by making them swallow a page torn out of the psalter and put in dough. . . ." from Ullman, The Principles of Semantics (1963 ed.) 43. (See also Ogden and Richards, The Meaning of Meaning (rev. ed. 1956) pp. 24–47.)

2. " 'Rerum enim vocabula immutabilia sunt, homines mutabilia,' " (Words are unchangeable, men changeable) from Dig. XXXIII, 10, 7 § 2, de sup. leg. as quoted in 9 Wigmore on Evidence, op. cit. supra, § 2461, p. 187.

court to be clear and unambiguous, would either deny the relevance of the intention of the parties or presuppose a degree of verbal precision and stability our language has not attained.

Some courts have expressed the opinion that contractual obligations are created by the mere use of certain words, whether or not there was any intention to incur such obligations.[3] Under this view, contractual obligations flow, not from the intention of the parties but from the fact that they used certain magic words. Evidence of the parties' intention therefore becomes irrelevant.

In this state, however, the intention of the parties as expressed in the contract is the source of contractual rights and duties. A court must ascertain and give effect to this intention by determining what the parties meant by the words they used. Accordingly, the exclusion of relevant, extrinsic evidence to explain the meaning of a written instrument could be justified only if it were feasible to determine the meaning the parties gave to the words from the instrument alone.

If words had absolute and constant referents, it might be possible to discover contractual intention in the words themselves and in the manner in which they were arranged. Words, however, do not have absolute and constant referents. "A word is a symbol of thought but has no arbitrary and fixed meaning like a symbol of algebra or chemistry, ..." (Pearson v. State Social Welfare Board (1960) 54 Cal.2d 184, 195, 5 Cal.Rptr. 553, 559, 353 P.2d 33, 39.) The meaning of particular words or groups of words varies with the ". . . verbal context and surrounding circumstances and purposes in view of the linguistic education and experience of their users and their hearers or readers (not excluding judges). . . . A word has no meaning apart from these factors; much less does it have an objective meaning, one true meaning." (Corbin, The Interpretation of Words and the Parol Evidence Rule (1965) 50 Cornell L.Q. 161, 187.) Accordingly, the meaning of a writing ". . . can only be found by interpretation in the light of all the circumstances that reveal the sense in which the writer used the words. The exclusion of parol evidence regarding such circumstances merely because the words do not appear ambiguous to the reader can easily lead to the attribution to a written instrument of a meaning that was never intended. [Citations omitted.]" (Universal Sales Corp. v. Cal. Press Mfg. Co., supra, 20 Cal.2d 751, 776, 128 P.2d 665, 679 (concurring opinion); . . ..)

3. "A contract has, strictly speaking, nothing to do with the personal, or individual, intent of the parties. A contract is an obligation attached by the mere force of law to certain acts of the parties, usually words, which ordinarily accompany and represent a known intent." (Hotchkiss v. National City Bank of New York (S.D.N.Y. 1911) 200 F. 287, 293. . . .)

Although extrinsic evidence is not admissible to add to, detract from, or vary the terms of a written contract, these terms must first be determined before it can be decided whether or not extrinsic evidence is being offered for a prohibited purpose. The fact that the terms of an instrument appear clear to a judge does not preclude the possibility that the parties chose the language of the instrument to express different terms. That possibility is not limited to contracts whose terms have acquired a particular meaning by trade usage, but exists whenever the parties' understanding of the words used may have differed from the judge's understanding.

Accordingly, rational interpretation requires at least a preliminary consideration of all credible evidence offered to prove the intention of the parties.[4] (Civ.Code, § 1647; Code Civ.Proc., § 1860; see also 9 Wigmore on Evidence, op. cit. supra, § 2470, fn. 11, p. 227.) Such evidence includes testimony as to the "circumstances surrounding the making of the agreement . . . including the object, nature and subject matter of the writing . . ." so that the court can "place itself in the same situation in which the parties found themselves at the time of contracting." (Universal Sales Corp. v. Cal. Press Mfg. Co., supra, 20 Cal.2d 751, 761, 128 P.2d 665, 671.) If the court decides, after considering this evidence, that the language of a contract, in the light of all the circumstances, is "fairly susceptible of either one of the two interpretations contended for . . .." (Balfour v. Fresno C. & I. Co. (1895) 109 Cal. 221, 225, 44 P. 876, 877; . . .) extrinsic evidence relevant to prove either of such meanings is admissible.[5]

In the present case the court erroneously refused to consider extrinsic evidence offered to show that the indemnity clause in the contract was not intended to cover injuries to plaintiff's property. Although that evidence was not necessary to show that the indemnity clause was reasonably susceptible of the meaning contended for by defendant, it was nevertheless relevant and admissible on that issue. Moreover, since that clause was reasonably susceptible of that meaning, the offered evidence was also admissible to prove that the clause

4. When objection is made to any particular item of evidence offered to prove the intention of the parties, the trial court may not yet be in a position to determine whether in the light of all of the offered evidence, the item objected to will turn out to be admissible as tending to prove a meaning of which the language of the instrument is reasonably susceptible or inadmissible as tending to prove a meaning of which the language is not reasonably susceptible. In such case the court may admit the evidence conditionally by either reserving its ruling on the objection or by admitting the evidence subject to a motion to strike. (See Evid.Code, § 403.)

5. Extrinsic evidence has often been admitted in such cases on the stated ground that the contract was ambiguous (e. g., Universal Sales Corp. v. Cal. Press Mfg. Co., supra, 20 Cal.2d 751, 761, 128 P.2d 665). This statement of the rule is harmless if it is kept in mind that the ambiguity may be exposed by extrinsic evidence that reveals more than one possible meaning.

had that meaning and did not cover injuries to plaintiff's property.[6] Accordingly, the judgment must be reversed. . . .

The judgment is reversed.

NOTE

Extrinsic Evidence in California. The preceding opinion followed by only four months that in Masterson v. Sine, p. 661 supra. Six months later the California Supreme Court decided the following case.

DELTA DYNAMICS, INC. v. ARIOTO, 69 Cal.2d 525, 72 Cal. Rptr. 785, 446 P.2d 785 (1968). [Delta Dynamics made a contract with Pixey Distributing Co., running for five years and renewable by Pixey for another five, under which Delta was to supply trigger locks for firearms to Pixey as its exclusive distributor. Pixey agreed to pay specified prices and promised to promote the locks diligently and "to sell not less than 50,000 units within one year from the date of delivery of the initial order" and not less than 100,000 units in each of the succeeding four years. "Should Pixey fail to distribute in any one year the minimum number of devices to be distributed by it . . . this agreement shall be subject to termination" by Delta on 30 days' notice. The contract also provided that "In the event of breach of this agreement by either party, the party prevailing in any action for damages or enforcement of the terms of this Agreement shall be entitled to reasonable attorneys' fees." After taking delivery of only 10,000 locks, Pixey failed to request further deliveries and, at the end of the first year, Delta terminated the agreement and sued Pixey for damages for failure to purchase the first year's quota. Pixey argued that Delta's exclusive remedy for Pixey's failure to meet the quota was to terminate the contract. From a judgment for Delta, Pixey appealed.]

TRAYNOR, Chief Justice. . . . [T]he parties may have included the termination clause to spell out with specificity the condition on which Delta would be excused from further performance under the contract, or to set forth the exclusive remedy for a failure to meet the quota in any year, or for both such purposes. That clause is

6. The court's exclusion of extrinsic evidence in this case would be error even under a rule that excluded such evidence when the instrument appeared to the court to be clear and unambiguous on its face. The controversy centers on the meaning of the word "indemnify" and the phrase "all loss, damage, expense and liability." The trial court's recognition of the language as typical of a third party indemnity clause and the double sense in which the word "indemnify" is used in statutes and defined in dictionaries demonstrate the existence of an ambiguity. (Compare Civ.Code, § 2772, "Indemnity is a contract by which one engages to save another from a legal consequence of the conduct of one of the parties, or of some other person," with Civ. Code, § 2527, "Insurance is a contract whereby one undertakes to indemnify another against loss, damage, or liability, arising from an unknown or contingent event."

therefore reasonably susceptible of the meaning contended for by Pixey, namely, that it expresses the parties' determination that Delta's sole remedy for Pixey's failure to meet a quota was to terminate the contract. There is nothing in the rest of the contract to preclude that interpretation. It does not render meaningless the provision for the recovery of attorneys' fees in the event of an action for damages for breach of the contract, for the attorneys' fees provision would still have full effect with respect to other breaches of the contract.[1] Accordingly, the trial court committed prejudicial error by excluding extrinsic evidence offered to prove the meaning of the termination clause contended for by Pixey. The judgment must therefore be reversed. . . .

PETERS, TOBRINER, and SULLIVAN, JJ., concur.

MOSK, Justice (dissenting). . . . Once again this court adopts a course leading toward emasculation of the parol evidence rule. During this very year Masterson v. Sine (1968) 68 A.C. 223, 65 Cal.Rptr. 545, 436 P.2d 561, and Pacific Gas & Elec. Co. v. G. W. Thomas Drayage & Rigging Co. (1968) 69 A.C. 28, 69 Cal.Rptr. 561, 442 P.2d 641, have contributed toward that result. Although I had misgivings at the time, I must confess to joining the majority in both of those cases. Now, however, that the majority deem negotiations leading to execution of contracts admissible, the trend has become so unmistakably ominous that I must urge a halt.

It can be contended that there may be no evil per se in considering testimony about every discussion and conversation prior to and contemporaneous with the signing of a written instrument and that social utility may result in some circumstances. The problem, however, is that which devolves upon members of the bar who are commissioned by clients to prepare a written instrument able to withstand future assaults. Given two experienced businessmen dealing at arm's length, both represented by competent counsel, it has become virtually impossible under recently evolving rules of evidence to draft a written contract that will produce predictable results in court. The written word, heretofore deemed immutable, is now at all times subject to alteration by self-serving recitals based upon fading memories of antecedent events. This, I submit, is a serious impediment to the certainty required in commercial transactions.

I would affirm the judgment.

McCOMB and BURKE, JJ., concur.

NOTES

(1) *Variation by Contract.* Could the parties, by a provision in their contract, prevent the court from admitting extrinsic evidence that it would

1. For example, Pixey might have breached the contract by failing diligently to promote the locks or by not paying for locks that had been delivered. Delta might also have breached the contract in various ways.

otherwise admit as an aid to interpretation? In Garden State Plaza Corp. v. S. S. Kresge Co., 78 N.J.Super. 485, 189 A.2d 448 (1963), certif. denied, 40 N.J. 226, 191 A.2d 63 (1963), the court held void as against public policy a clause providing that no "previous negotiations, arrangements, agreements and understandings . . . shall be used to interpret or construe this lease." The clause would, the court said, have it construe the contract "wearing judicial blinders. We are requested to conform to a private agreement mandating our performance of a judicial function in a manner which, under our precedents, is not the path to justice in arriving at the binding meaning of a contract." Do you agree? See also United States v. Waterman Steamship Corp., 397 F.2d 577 (5th Cir. 1968).

(2) *Private Conventions or Codes.* Even the objectivists disagreed on the admissibility of private conventions or codes. Note that Learned Hand, in the excerpt quoted on p. 692 supra, made a distinction between the case where "both parties severally declared that their meaning had been other than the natural meaning, and each declaration was similar," and that where there was "some mutual agreement between them to that effect." Holmes, on the contrary did "not suppose that you could prove, for purposes of construction . . . for instance, that the parties to a contract orally agreed that when they wrote five hundred feet it should mean one hundred inches, or that Bunker Hill Monument should signify Old South Church."[a] Holmes, The Theory of Legal Interpretation, 12 Harv.L.Rev. 417, 420 (1899).

Ward contracted in writing to furnish crushed stone at $2.75 per cubic yard to Smith, the general contractor for the construction of a state highway. Shortly thereafter they orally agreed that each of Ward's trucks fully loaded, contained four cubic yards of crushed stone. Ward was paid for 12,955 cubic yards, figured on this basis. He sued Smith for $24,432, claiming that the quantity actually delivered was 21,538 cubic yards, and introduced, over objection, the testimony of a civil engineer that by a more accurate method of measurement Ward had delivered the larger amount. From judgment for plaintiff, defendant appealed. *Held:* Reversed. "When a contract specifies the mode of measurement to be adopted such mode should be followed." Ward v. Smith, 140 W.Va. 791, 86 S.E.2d 539 (1955). Was the case rightly decided? Under Holmes' view? Under Hand's? Is Hand's distinction justifiable?

(3) *Reformation and Interpretation.* As the Bollinger case, p. 673 supra, indicates, if by mistake the parties have omitted an agreed term from a writing, a court, exercising its equity powers, will decree reformation to include it. It is sometimes assumed that where the parties have used words in an unclear way, reformation is also appropriate to clarify their meaning for the purpose of enforcement. Is not there an adequate remedy "at law" in such cases, through interpretation? See 3 Corbin § 540.

General Discount Corp. v. Sadowski, 183 F.2d 542 (6th Cir. 1950), is illustrative. Sadowski and General Discount entered into a two-year contract under which he was to create and sell mortgages through General Discount on a commission basis. On mortgages where General Discount received an

a. " 'That's a great deal to make one word mean,' Alice said in a thoughtful tone. 'When I make a word do a lot of work like that,' said Humpty Dumpty, 'I always pay it extra.' " Lewis Carroll, Through the Looking-Glass, Chapter VI.

additional service fee over the life of the mortgage, it was to "pay such excess to second party [Sadowski] monthly." When the contract term expired after two years, Sadowski contended that he was still entitled to receive the payments on each such mortgage monthly for the life of the *mortgage*, while General Discount contended that he had been entitled to them only monthly for the life of the *contract*. The court held that Sadowski was entitled to reformation to have the writing reflect his interpretation and to a judgment for the amount due under that interpretation. Was reformation necessary? [b]

RULES IN AID OF INTERPRETATION

The Statutory Analogy. There is an obvious similarity between the interpretation of contracts and that of statutes. To what extent is the analogy a valid one? For example, are the policies for or against the use of legislative history as an aid to statutory interpretation similar to those for or against the use of negotiations ("transactional history") as an aid to contract interpretation?

Purpose Interpretation. Is there an analogy to what is known as "purpose interpretation" in the field of statutory interpretation? According to the formulation in Heydon's Case, 3 Coke 7a, 76 Eng. Rep. 637 (Ex. 1584), it involves these steps: examination of the law before enactment of the statute; ascertainment of the "mischief or defect" for which the law did not provide; analysis of the remedy provided by the legislature to "cure the disease"; determination of the "true reason of the remedy"; and then application of the statute so as to "suppress the mischief, and advance the remedy." Can you formulate an analogous technique for contract interpretation?

In the case of a statute, purpose interpretation does not depend on the availability of legislative history, and the court may even find a helpful statement of the purpose of enactment set forth in the preamble or purpose clause of the statute itself. Similarly, it is not uncommon for written contracts to begin with a series of recitals of the surrounding circumstances and of the objectives of the parties. Usually prefixed by the word "whereas," contract recitals are not ordinarily drafted as promises or conditions, and their proper rule in the interpretation of the main body of the contract has been a source

b. Sadowski had already brought an action in a state court to recover his compensation and had lost, the Supreme Court of Michigan deciding (5–2) in favor of General Discount on the ground that the contract "is not ambiguous and the definite contract period of two years controls . . . and, in the absence of fraud or mistake, excludes prior, contemporaneous and subsequent talks as to its scope and purport." Sadowski v. General Discount Corp., 295 Mich. 340, 294 N.W. 703 (1940). He then sought reformation in the federal courts. The decision in his favor was based in part on the testimony of General Discount's lawyer, that the understanding of the parties was monthly for the life of the mortgage. (In spite of the decision of the Supreme Court of Michigan, he still considered that the language reflected that understanding.)

of bafflement to many a judge and lawyer. Courts in this country have frequently repeated with approval Lord Esher's "three rules": "If the recitals are clear and the operative part is ambiguous, the recitals govern the construction. If the recitals are ambiguous, and the operative part is clear, the operative part must prevail. If both the recitals and the operative part are clear, but they are inconsistent with each other, the operative part is to be preferred." Ex parte Dawes, 17 Q.B.D. 275, 286 (1886). But these, like many rules of interpretation, are easier of statement than of application.

Maxims. Many of the same rules of thumb that are used in the interpretation of statutes are also used in the interpretation of contracts. Maxims such as "ejusdem generis" and "expressio unius est exclusio alterius" are as popular here as they are there. See J. E. Faltin Motor Transportation, Inc. v. Eazor Express, Inc., 273 F.2d 444 (3d Cir. 1960). Their reliability is also as questionable here as it is there. A classic discussion of maxims appears in Llewellyn, The Common Law Tradition—Deciding Appeals 521–35 (1960), a later version of Llewellyn, Remarks on the Theory of Appellate Decision and the Rules or Canons about How Statutes are to be Construed, 3 Vand.L.Rev. 395 (1950).

Some of the maxims of contract interpretation are not shared by statutory interpretation. One of the most time-honored maxims of contract interpretation is that a contract is to be interpreted *contra proferentem*—against its author ("profferer"). In North Gate Corp. v. National Food Stores, Inc., 30 Wis.2d 317, 140 N.W.2d 744 (1966), the court applied this to a clause in a printed shopping center lease prepared by the lessee for use by its retail food stores throughout the country. "Where various meanings can be given a term, the term is to be strictly construed against the draftsman of the contract." Why? To carry out the intention of the parties? To penalize sloppy draftsmen? To encourage careful draftsmen? Has this maxim no statutory analogue? In many of the instances where the rule has been applied, the party who chose the contract language also had superior bargaining power. Consider in this connection the problems raised in Chapter 5, Policing the Bargain, supra.[c]

c. For an application of this maxim in connection with real estate brokerage listings, discussed at p. 308 supra, see Foltz v. Begnoche, 222 Kan. 383, 388–89, 565 P.2d 592, 597 (1977), in which the court said: "we are persuaded that an 'exclusive right to sell,' by its very nature, should be created only by clear and unambiguous language. The owner of property, frequently unfamiliar with the terminology of brokerage transactions, should not be held to give up his right to sell his own property, unless the broker's contract in some way or other imposes liability upon the owner for payment of a commission in the event of a sale by the owner, either expressly or by the grant to the broker of such exclusive right as the court may deem necessarily implies such liability. . . . Therefore, a real estate broker seeking to create an 'exclusive right to sell' in which the owner may not sell his property without paying the broker a commission, whether or not the broker procured the buyer, must do so in clear and unambiguous language within the four corners of the written brokerage contract."

The United States Court of Claims, in applying the rule to government contracts, has explained: "This rule is fair both to the drafters and to those who are required to accept or reject the contract as proffered, without haggling. Although the potential contractor may have some duty to inquire about a major patent discrepancy, or obvious omission, or a drastic conflict in provisions, . . . he is not normally required (absent a clear warning in the contract) to seek clarification of any and all ambiguities, doubts, or possible differences in interpretation. The Government, as the author, has to shoulder the major task of seeing that within the zone of reasonableness the words of the agreement communicate the proper notions—as well as the main risk of a failure to carry that responsibility. If the defendant chafes under the continued application of this check, it can obtain a looser rein by a more meticulous writing of its contracts and especially of the specifications. Or it can shift the burden of ambiguity (to some extent) by inserting provisions in the contract clearly calling upon possible contractors aware of a problem-in-interpretation to seek an explanation before bidding." WPC Enterprises v. United States, 323 F.2d 874, 877 (Ct.Cl.1963).[d]

Should it make a difference if the party who proffered the contract invited suggestions for change from the other party? See Acme Markets v. Dawson Enterprises, 253 Md. 76, 251 A.2d 839 (1969), in which the court noted that the other party had kept the contract for sixty days before signing it, that its president was a member of the bar, and that it had, at least earlier in the negotiations, been represented by "a member of a prominent Washington law firm." The court quoted with approval its suggestion in an earlier case that "perhaps [the *contra proferentem* rule] should have but slight force in a situation where both parties are represented by counsel."

Public Interest. In the North Gate case, supra, the court pointed out that "the intent of the provision in question"—which prohibited the owner of the shopping center from leasing to other retail food stores—was "to restrict trade and the use of land. Such provisions are to be strictly construed." In Chapter 5, Policing the Bargain, we saw that contracts involving performance that would be in violation of some strongly rooted public interest, often expressed in a statute, may be held to be unenforceable. As the North Gate case shows, public interest may also affect interpretation and construction of contracts.

d. But see Shedd, Resolving Ambiguities in Interpretation of Government Contracts, 36 Geo.Wash.L.Rev. 1, 21 (1967), where the author concludes, "The rule of interpreting against the drafter, if not discarded entirely, should be relegated to a rule of last resort in contract interpretation . . . ." For dispute in the Supreme Court of the United States over the application of the rule, see United States v. Seckinger, 397 U.S. 203 (1970).

In State ex rel. Youngman v. Calhoun, 231 S.W. 647 (Mo.App. 1921), a physician sold his practice, agreeing not to "establish [himself] as a practicing physician and surgeon within a radius of five miles" of his former office. The court held that he was not precluded from making calls within this area or treating patients from this area who might call at his office outside the area. "The contract in question is clearly one in restraint of trade and personal liberty, and as such should not be construed to extend beyond its fair import." Why? Because of the intention of the parties?

See also Sun Oil Co. v. Vickers Refining Co., 414 F.2d 383 (8th Cir. 1969), in which the court remarked, in rejecting Sunray's interpretation under which the contract would have been void because of a violation of the antitrust laws: "Sunray's attorneys, experienced in antitrust work, approved the contract without any question of antitrust consequences."

NOTES

(1) *"Woe Unto You, Lawyers."* Should it make a difference, in interpreting a contract, whether the parties were represented by lawyers? In Gulf Oil Corporation v. American Louisiana Pipe Line Co., 282 F.2d 401 (6th Cir. 1960), the court relied on a difference in language between two sections of a contract in interpreting the contract. "We cannot believe that the difference in language in the two sections of the contract was inadvertent, particularly in view of the extended negotiations of the parties who were represented by lawyers presumably skilled in this field of the law, and observed great care in drafting and redrafting various provisions of the contract."

In Weiland Tool & Mfg. Co. v. Whitney, 44 Ill.2d 105, 251 N.E.2d 242 (1969), the court wrote: "In interpreting the letter . . . we have taken into consideration not only that inferences from ambiguous language must be resolved against its author . . ., but also that he is a lawyer with a number of years of trial experience and experience as a legal adviser in commercial transactions. He must have had the ability to express [his intention] in concise and clear English . . . if that were his intention. Since he did not do so, we are further persuaded that this was not his intention."

(2) *Problem.* Following a dispute between a general contractor and a subcontractor, in which each claims damages for breach of contract by the other, they sign a writing in which the subcontract "is hereby cancelled without prejudice by mutual agreement." Do the words "without prejudice" mean that claims to damages arising out of the subcontract survive or that they do not? Might it make a difference whether the parties were represented by lawyers when they signed the writing? See Copeland Process Corp. v. Nalews, Inc., 113 N.H. 612, 312 A.2d 576 (1973).

HURST v. W. J. LAKE & CO.

Supreme Court of Oregon, 1932.
141 Or. 306, 16 P.2d 627.

Action by Roscoe P. Hurst against W. J. Lake & Co., Inc., in the nature of assumpsit to recover an alleged balance of $5 per ton on 140 tons of horse meat scraps purchased by defendant from plaintiff pursuant to a written contract. From a judgment for defendant allowing defendant's motion for judgment on the pleadings after the complaint, answer, and reply had been filed, plaintiff appeals.

ROSMAN, J. From the portion of the pleadings which we are required to deem true, it appears that March 20, 1930, the plaintiff and the defendant entered into an agreement in writing, a copy of which follows:

"March 20, 1930.

"Messrs. Roscoe P. Hurst, Yeon Building, Portland, Oregon.

Dear Sirs: We confirm our purchase from you today as follows:

Buyer:	W. J. Lake & Co., Inc. Seattle, Washington.
Commodity:	Horse meat scraps.
Quantity:	350 tons of 2000 lbs. each.
Price:	$50.00 per ton f.o.b. cars Portland.
Terms of Payment:	Net cash in Portland on delivery with analysis certificate.
Time of Shipment:	Prior to April 20th, 1930.
Route:	As directed by buyer.
Specifications:	Minimum 50% protein, ground and sacked in 100 lb. net each.
	Additional specifications on supplementary page.

Yours truly,
W. J. Lake & Company, Inc.,
By L. E. Branchflower.

Accepted by:
"Roscoe P. Hurst."

"March 20, 1930.

"Mr. Roscoe P. Hurst, Yeon Building, Portland, Oregon.

Dear Sir: In case any of the Horse Meat Scraps, covered by our purchase order No. 1352 analyzes less than 50% of protein, it is understood that W. J. Lake & Company, Inc., the buyers, are to receive a discount of $5.00 per ton.

"It is further understood that in case the buyer does not take delivery of the entire lot by April 20th, 1930, the seller agrees to carry the stock one (1) month more for 50¢ per ton additional.

"The Northwest Testing Laboratories are to instruct the warehouse in the loading and are to furnish analysis certificates, at the buyer's expense. In case of an analysis dispute findings of a refree (sic) chemist, who shall be mutually agreed upon, shall be final.

Yours very truly,
W. J. Lake & Co., Inc.,
[Signed] L. E. Branchflower.
L. E. Branchflower.

LEB:G
Accepted by:
[Signed] Roscoe P. Hurst."

Pursuant to the contract, the plaintiff delivered to the defendant 349.25 tons of horse meat scraps which contained the following percentages of protein, and for which the defendant paid the following sums of money: 180 tons contained an excess of 50 per cent. protein, and the defendant paid for it $50 per ton; 29.25 tons contained 48.66 per cent. protein, and the defendant paid therefor $45 per ton; 140 tons contained protein varying from 49.53 per cent. to 49.96 per cent., for which the defendant paid $45 per ton.

[It appears from the pleadings, which we are required to deem true,] (1) that there is a group of dealers who trade in the commodity known as horse meat scraps; (2) that both plaintiff and defendant are members of that group; (3) that the terms "minimum 50% protein" and "less than 50% protein" are trade terms to which the group has attached meanings different from their common ones; (4) that this usage, prevalent among this group, demanded that, whenever those terms appeared in a contract for the sale of horse meat scraps, it became the duty of the buyer to accept all scraps containing 49.5 per cent. protein or more, and to pay for them at the rate provided for scraps containing full 50 per cent. protein; and (5) that the defendant was aware of all of the foregoing when it attached its signature to the aforementioned contract.

The flexibility of or multiplicity in the meaning of words is the principal source of difficulty in the interpretation of language. Words are the conduits by which thoughts are communicated, yet scarcely any of them have such a fixed and single meaning that they are incapable of denoting more than one thought. In addition to the multiplicity in meaning of words set forth in the dictionaries, there are the meanings imparted to them by trade customs, local uses, dialects, telegraphic codes, etc. One meaning crowds a word full of significance, while another almost empties the utterance of any import. The various groups above indicated are constantly amplifying our language; in fact, they are developing what may be called languages of their own. Thus one is justified in saying that the language of the dictionaries is not the only language spoken in America. For instance, the word "thousand" as commonly used has a very specific meaning; it denotes ten hundreds or fifty scores, but the language of the various trades and localities has assigned to it meanings quite different from that just mentioned. Thus in the bricklaying trade a contract which fixes the bricklayer's compensation at "$5.25 a thousand" does not contemplate that he need lay actually 1,000 bricks in order to earn $5.25, but that he should build a wall of a certain size. Brunold v. Glasser, 25 Misc. 285, 52 N.Y.S. 1021; Walker v. Syms, 118 Mich. 183, 76 N.W. 320. In the lumber industry a contract requiring the delivery of 4,000 shingles will be fulfilled by the delivery of only 2,500 when it appears that by trade custom two packs of a certain size are regarded as 1,000 shingles, and that hence the delivery of eight packs fulfills the contract, even though they contain only 2,500 shingles by actual count. Soutier v. Kellerman, 18 Mo. 509. And, where the custom of a locality considers 100 dozen as constituting a thousand, one who has 19,200 rabbits upon a warren under an agreement for their sale at the price of 60 pounds for each thousand rabbits will be paid for only 16,000 rabbits. Smith v. Wilson, 3 Barn. & Adol. 728. Numerous other instances could readily be cited showing the manner in which the meaning of words has been contracted, expanded, or otherwise altered by local usage, trade custom, dialect influence, code agreement, etc. In fact, it is no novelty to find legislative enactments preceded by glossaries or brief dictionaries defining the meaning of the words employed in the act. Technical treatises dealing with aeronautics, the radio, engineering, etc., generally contain similar glossaries defining the meaning of many of the words employed by the craft. A glance at these glossaries readily shows that the different sciences and trades, in addition to coining words of their own, appropriate common words and assign to them new meanings. Thus it must be evident that one cannot understand accurately the language of such sciences and trades without knowing the peculiar meaning attached to the words which they use. It is said that a court in construing the language of the parties must put itself into the shoes of the parties. That alone would not suffice; it must also adopt their vernacular.

Wigmore on Evidence (2d) § 2460, points out that the interpretation of language may be thus approached: "The standard of the community, or popular standard, meaning the common and normal sense of words; the local standard including the special usages of a religious sect, a body of traders, an alien population or a local dialect; the mutual standard covering those meanings which are peculiar to both or all the parties to a transaction but shared in common by them; and the individual standard of one party to an act, as differing from that of the other party or parties, if any."

After Dean Wigmore has reviewed at length the overthrow of what he calls the traditional rule which insists that the meaning of all words is rigid and inflexible, and the development of what he terms the liberal rule which recognizes, to some extent at least, the four aforementioned standards of interpretation, he continues (section 2463): "The liberal rule, on the other hand, is today conceded practically everywhere, to permit resort in any case to the usage of a trade or locality, no matter how plain the apparent sense of the word to the ordinary reader; and some of the extreme instances are persuasive to demonstrate the fallacy of ignoring the purely relative meaning of words and the injustice of attempting to enforce a supposed rigid standard."

From Williston on Contracts, § 650, we quote: "Though Professor Thayer has said that 'In contracts it was always recognized that familiar words may have different meanings in different places, so that "every bargain as to such a thing shall have relation to the custom of the country where it is made," ' it may be doubted how far it was allowable under early law to show that a word in a written contract (or perhaps in an oral agreement) having a clear and fixed ordinary meaning bore a meaning contrary to its usual significance, if nothing in the context showed that a particular meaning was intended. But there are now numerous decisions (not all of them of recent date) where words with a clear, normal meaning have been shown by usage to bear a meaning which nothing in the context would suggest. This is not only true of technical terms, but of language which, at least on its face, has no peculiar or technical significance; though even today it is still occasionally said by courts that usage cannot control words having 'a definite legal meaning'; or cannot be used to interpret a contract unless there is an uncertainty on the face of the instrument."

The defendant cites numerous cases in many of which the courts held that, when a contract is expressed in language which is not ambiguous upon its face the court will receive no evidence of usage, but will place upon the words of the parties their common meaning; in other words, in those decisions the courts ran the words of the parties through a judicial sieve whose meshes were incapable of retaining anything but the common meaning of the words, and which permitted the meaning which the parties had placed upon them to run away as waste material. Surely those courts did not believe that words are always used in their orthodox sense. The rulings must have been persuaded by other considerations. The rule which rejects evidence of custom has the advantage of simplicity; it protects the writing from attack by some occasional individual who will seek to employ perjured testimony in proof of alleged custom; and, if one can believe that the parol evidence rule is violated when common meaning is rejected in favor of special meaning, then the above rule serves the purpose of the parol evidence rule. Without setting forth the manner in which we came to our conclusion, we state that none of these reasons appeals to us as sufficient to exclude evidence of custom and assign to the words their common meaning only, even though the instrument is nonambiguous upon its face. The defendant argues that this court has held that custom or usage cannot be resorted to in the interpretation of the meaning of an instrument where no ambiguity appears upon its face, and cites in support of his contention Williams v. Ledbetter, 132 Or. 145, 285 P. 214; Darling-Singer Lbr. Co. v. Oriental Navigation Co., 127 Or. 655, 259 P. 420, 272 P. 275; Interior Warehouse Co. v. Dunn, 80 Or. 528, 157 P. 806; Oregon Fisheries Co. v. Elmore Packing Co., 69 Or. 340, 138 P. 862; Barnard & Bunker v. Houser, 68 Or. 240, 137 P. 227; Savage v. Salem Mills Co., 48 Or. 1, 85 P. 69, 10 Ann.Cas. 1065; Abraham v. Oregon & California R. R. Co., 37 Or. 495, 60 P. 899, 64 L.R.A. 391, 82 Am.St.Rep. 779; and Holmes v. Whitaker, 23 Or. 319, 31 P. 705. It must be admitted that language can be found in some of these decisions which lends weight to his argument. But a reading of these cases will disclose that in all of them, with the exception of Abraham v. Oregon & California R. R. Co., the party was not resorting to custom for the purpose of interpreting the language of the instrument, but for the purpose of annexing or engrafting on to the contract an additional term; in other words, he sought to prove that the written instrument did not embody the entire agreement. Such a contention invoked a principle quite different from the one with which we are now concerned. For comment see Wigmore on Evidence (2d) § 2440. In Abraham v. Oregon & California R. R. Co., the decision does not mention custom. The appellant in that case sought to prove that he and the party with whom he dealt had placed upon one of the terms of the instrument a mutual meaning distinct from its normal one. . . .

Without setting forth herein our review of the many authorities cited in the briefs, all of which we have read with care, we state our conclusion that members of a trade or business group who have employed in their contracts trade terms are entitled to prove that fact in their litigation, and show the meaning of those terms to assist the court in the interpretation of their language.

Finally, it is suggested that the employment of the terms "minimum 50% protein" and "less than 50% of protein" indicates that the parties rejected the mercantile custom in effecting their contract. It will be recalled that under the state of the record we are compelled to regard these two terms as trade terms possessed of a special significance. We believe that it is safe to assume, in the absence of evidence to the contrary, that, when tradesmen employ trade terms, they attach to them their trade significance. If, when they write their trade terms into their contracts, they mean to strip the terms of their special significance and demote them to their common import, it would seem reasonable to believe that they would so state in their agreement. Otherwise they would refrain from using the trade term and express themselves in other language. We quote from Nicoll v. Pittsvein Coal Co. (C.C.A.) 269 F. 968, 971: "Indeed when tradesmen say or write anything, they are perhaps without present thought on the subject, writing on top of a mass of habits or usages which they take as matter of course. So (with Prof. Williston) we think that any one contracting with knowledge of a usage will naturally say nothing about the matter unless desirous of excluding its operation; if he does wish to exclude, he will say so in express terms. Williston, Contracts, § 653." Nothing in the contract repels the meaning assigned by the trade to the two above terms unless the terms themselves reject it. But if these terms repel the meaning which usage has attached to them, then every trade term would deny its own meaning. We reject this contention as being without merit. We have considered all other contentions presented by the respondent, but have found no merit in them.

It follows that, in our opinion, the circuit court erred when it sustained the defendant's motion for judgment on the pleadings.

Reversed.

NOTES

(1) *Proof of Usage.*[a] State the issue in Hurst v. Lake in terms of the contract language. How will usage help resolve that issue at the trial? How can Hurst prove usage? Why did the buyer fail in his attempt to prove usage in the Frigaliment case, p. 684 supra?[b] Would he have succeeded under the Code? See UCC 1–205. Under the Code, what is the difference between a usage and a course of dealing? How would a party like Hurst prove a course of dealing?

(2) *Role of Usage.* Professor Lawrence Friedman has criticized what he calls "pure" contract law, which is "blind to details of subject matter and person," and "does not ask who buys and who sells, and what is bought and sold." Friedman, Contract Law in America: A Social and Economic Case Study 20 (1965). May acceptance of usage help to meet this criticism? Professor Hurst, in his study of the lumber industry in Wisconsin,

a. The terms "usage" and "custom" are often used interchangeably. "Custom" has the more ancient tradition, and the Uniform Commercial Code adopts "usage of trade" to reject some of the restrictions that had been traditionally placed upon the use of "custom." Comments 4 and 5 to UCC 1–205 say: "By adopting . . . the term 'usage of trade' this Act expresses its intent to reject those cases which see evidence of 'custom' as representing an effort to displace or negate 'established rules of law.' . . . The ancient English tests for 'custom' are abandoned . . . . Therefore, it is not required that a usage of trade be 'ancient or immemorial,' 'universal' or the like." Williston, however, attaches different meanings to the two terms. "Usage derives its efficacy from the assent thereto of parties to the transaction; custom derives its efficacy from its adoption into the law, and when once established is binding irrespective of any manifestation of assent by the parties concerned. Usage is, therefore, of importance only in consensual agreements since it is the assent of the parties which gives it its force." 5 Williston, § 649.

b. For a case in which a party failed to prove a course of dealing to arbitrate disputes, see Schubtex, Inc. v. Allen Snyder, Inc., 49 N.Y.2d 1, 399 N.E.2d 1154 (1979).

found this "generality in contract concepts . . . a source of strength, so far as it meant that the legal order could efficiently and smoothly adapt itself to varied circumstances. But there was weakness, so far as contract law achieved this generality by intense devotion to a quite limited range of policies, abstracted from the living context in which they arose." He went on to suggest that "lumber-contract case law made its most distinctive adaptation to the peculiarities of the industry" by allowing proof of usage. Hurst, Law and Economic Growth: The Legal History of the Lumber Industry in Wisconsin 1836–1915 290 (1964).

On usage and custom generally, see Note, 55 Colum.L.Rev. 1192 (1955); Restatement Second, §§ 219–223. Hibernians may be interested in Ermolieff v. R.K.O. Radio Pictures, Inc., 19 Cal.2d 543, 122 P.2d 3 (1942), in which a usage of the motion picture industry was admitted to establish that the term "The United Kingdom," as used in an agreement granting movie rights, included Eire, the Irish Free State.[c] Devotees of detective stories in general and of Sam Spade in particular may be interested in an entertaining case in which the court, in construing a contract, took judicial notice that, "It has long been common practice among detective-fiction writers to make use of the same central and supporting characters in subsequent works." Warner Bros. Pictures v. Columbia Broadcasting System, 102 F.Supp. 141 (S.D.Cal.1951), affirmed as to this point but reversed in part in 216 F.2d 945 (9th Cir. 1954).

(3) *Course of Performance.* UCC 2–208 is concerned with the use in interpretation of a course of performance by one party, acquiesced in by the other party. Courts have often resorted to "course of performance" or, as it is also called, "practical interpretation." Why? Because the conduct indicates what the intention of the parties was at the time of original agreement? Because the parties are free to modify their contract by subsequent conduct? What would be the effect of a merger clause on this rule? Of a no-oral-modification clause? Course of performance should be considered again in connection with waiver at p. 856 infra.

(4) *Problem.* Black telegraphed Cage, a dealer in rice, asking him to "name price of carload Honduras rice." Cage answered, "Have 200 sacks left, second year, highly graded, $5.75, f. o. b. here. Wire quick. Very scarce." Black replied, "Ship one hundred and seventy sacks rice. Instructions in letter." Cage who had meant $5.75 a barrel, according to an understanding in the rice trade, wrote Black, "In accordance with telegrams exchanged between us, we confirm sale to you 170 sacks Honduras seed rice, highly graded, at $5.75 per barrel." Black had understood the offer to mean $5.75 a sack. There are 195 barrels in 170 sacks. Advise Black. Would additional facts be helpful? What facts? See Cage v. Black, 97 Ark. 613, 134 S.W. 942 (1911).

c. Even Holmes endorsed usage, as distinguished from private codes or conventions. After the passage quoted in Note 2, p. 703 supra, he continued: "On the other hand, when you have the security of a local or class custom or habit of speech, it may be presumed that the writer conforms to the usage of his place or class when that is what a normal person in his situation would do." Does this give some insight into Holmes' reasons for espousing the objective theory?

SECTION 3. DECIDING "OMITTED CASES"

Thus far we have concerned ourselves with finding the law of the contract by interpreting its language. But what is the law of the contract if the language, when interpreted, does not cover the case at hand—what if it is an "omitted case"? As we have already seen as far back as in Wood v. Lucy, p. 81, supra, and again in the Southwest Engineering case, p. 245, supra, a term may be implied in such a situation.

The French sociologist Emile Durkheim pointed out that "we can neither foresee the variety of possible circumstances in which our contract will involve itself, nor fix in advance with the aid of simple mental calculus what will be in each case the rights and duties of each, save in matters in which we have a very definite experience." If, at the time of contracting "it were necessary each time to begin the struggles anew, to again go through the conferences necessary to establish firmly all the conditions of agreement for the present and the future, we would be put to rout." Implied terms, the handwork of society and tradition, provide for "what we cannot foresee individually" and regulate "what we cannot regulate." Contract imposes on us duties "that we did not desire," which we can, but rarely do, change. "In principle, the rule applies; innovations are exceptional." Durkheim, On the Division of Labor in Society 213–15 (Simpson's tr. 1933). See also Restatement Second, § 204 (a section that has no counterpart in the earlier Restatement); Farnsworth, Disputes Over Omissions in Contracts, 68 Colum.L.Rev. 860 (1968). But when will a court imply a term in a contract? Justice Holmes wrote: "Behind the logical form lies a judgment as to the relative worth and importance of competing legislative grounds, often an inarticulate and unconscious judgment, it is true, and yet the very root and nerve of the whole proceeding. You can give any conclusion a logical form. You can always imply a condition in a contract. But why do you imply it? It is because of some belief as to the practice of the community or of a class, or because of some opinion as to policy, or, in short, because of some attitude of yours upon a matter not capable of exact quantitative measurement, and therefore not capable of founding exact logical conclusions. Such matters really are battle grounds where the means do not exist for determinations that shall be good for all time, and where the decision can do no more than embody the preference of a given body in a given time and place." Holmes, The Path of the Law, 10 Harv.L.Rev. 457, 466 (1897); also in Holmes, Collected Legal Papers 167, 181 (1920).

Some of the most significant applications of this process of dealing with omitted cases arise in connection with the next two chapters. In Chapter 8 we shall consider how the process is used to secure the expectations of the parties during performance. In Chapter 9 we shall consider how it is used in coping with extraordinary events that render performance impossible or frustrate the purpose of the contract. As an introduction to the process itself, however, we shall focus on applications that are both more familiar and less complex—the obligations to use "good faith" and "best efforts" that, as we have already seen, are often implied in contracts.

NOTES

(1) *Implied Terms.* We are speaking here of terms that are "implied in law" rather than "implied in fact." Corbin explains that difference in this way: "When a promise is said to be 'implied in fact' we are describing one that is found by interpretation of a promisor's words or conduct. When a promise is said to be 'implied in law,' we are declaring the existence of legal duty created otherwise than by assent and without any words or conduct that are interpreted as promissory." 3 Corbin, § 561. Corbin's distinction found its way into the Uniform Commercial Code, which defines "agreement" as "the bargain of the parties in fact" and "contract" as "the total legal obligation which results." Compare UCC 1–201(3) with (11).

(2) *"Interpretation" and "Construction."* Although the words "interpretation" and "construction" are often used interchangeably, attempts have been made to give them distinct meanings. Professor Corbin proposed the following distinction: "By 'interpretation of language' we determine what ideas that language induces in other persons. By 'construction of the contract,' as that term will be used here, we determine its legal operation—its effect upon the action of courts and administrative officials. If we make this distinction, then the construction of a contract starts with the interpretation of its language but does not end with it; while the process of interpretation stops wholly short of a determination of the legal relations of the parties. . . . When a court is filling gaps in the terms of an agreement, with respect to matters that the parties did not have in contemplation and as to which they had no intention to be expressed, the judicial process should not be called interpretation."[a] 3 Corbin, § 534.

(3) *Implied Warranties.* Perhaps the most noted of the many terms that courts have supplied for omitted cases are the warranties implied in contracts for the sale of goods. See UCC 2–314, 2–315 and p. 433 supra. They have, however, been creatures of statute for so long that it is easy to

a. Corbin succeeded in popularizing the term "constructive condition," to refer to conditions implied *in law*, in order to distinguish them from conditions implied *in fact*. 3A Corbin, §§ 632, 653: Corbin, Conditions in the Law of Contract, 28 Yale L.J. 739, 743–44 (1919), Selected Readings 871, 876. Its analogue, "constructive promise," is not used, however, and lawyers speak, somewhat inconsistently, of "*implied* promises" and "*constructive* conditions." For more on conditions, see Chapter 8, infra.

Lawyers from civil law systems tend not to think of specific terms "implied" in the particular case but of generalized rules which apply to all such cases unless the parties provide otherwise. In France these rules are called *facultative, interprétative* or *suppletive,* in contrast to those that are *impérative* and which the parties are powerless to alter. Perhaps the happiest English equivalents are "suppletive" and "mandatory." Since civil law lawyers are accustomed to finding such rules spelled out in a code in advance of controversy, they are less tempted to attribute them to the supposed "intentions" of the parties.

lose sight of their judicial origins. Of greater current interest is the question of the extent to which similar implied warranties will be imposed in other fields. The Supreme Court of New Jersey has provided some striking examples. In just over five years, it handed down leading decisions imposing implied warranties, by analogy to those in the sale of goods, in the lease of personal property (a truck), the sale of real property (a development house), the lease of real property (both commercial and residential), and the furnishing of goods in connection with a contract for services (a permanent wave).[b] For an interesting opinion, relying on such cases, holding that "a warranty of habitability, measured by the standards set out in the Housing Regulations for the District of Columbia, [is] implied by operation of law into leases of urban dwelling units covered by those Regulations," see Javins v. First National Realty Corp., 428 F.2d 1071 (D.C.Cir. 1970). See also Farnsworth, Implied Warranties of Quality in Non-Sales Cases, 57 Colum.L.Rev. 653 (1957).

WOOD v. LUCY, LADY DUFF-GORDON

Court of Appeals of New York, 1917.
222 N.Y. 88, 118 N.E. 214.

[For the report of this case, see p. 81 supra.]

NOTES

(1) *Cardozo on Holmes.* What answer would Cardozo give to Holmes' question, "why do you imply it?" Cardozo says that "implication of a promise here finds support in many circumstances." What circumstances? What support? Comment 5 to UCC 2–306, which lays down a similar rule, has this to say: "Subsection (2), on exclusive dealing, makes explicit the commercial rule embodied in this Act under which the parties to such contracts are held to have impliedly, even when not expressly, bound themselves to use reasonable diligence as well as good faith in their performance of the contract. . . . An exclusive dealing agreement brings into play all of the good faith aspects of the output and requirement problems of subsection (1)." Why?

(2) *Showing Implied Terms and the Parol Evidence Rule.* What is the impact of the parol evidence rule on an attempt to show an implied term? Assuming, as seems likely, that the agreement in Wood v. Lucy was completely integrated, why did not the parol evidence rule prevent Wood from showing his "promise to use reasonable efforts"? What evidence did he need to show his promise?

In some situations, in contrast to the situation in Wood v. Lucy, the implication of a term may turn on a showing of facts that are not estab-

b. Cintrone v. Hertz Truck Leasing & Rental Service, 45 N.J. 434, 212 A.2d 769 (1965) (lease of truck); Schipper v. Levitt & Sons, 44 N.J. 70, 207 A.2d 314 (1965) (sale of development house); Reste Realty Corp. v. Cooper, 53 N.J. 444, 251 A.2d 268 (1969) (lease of offices); Marini v. Ireland, 56 N.J. 130, 265 A.2d 526 (1970) (lease of apartment); Newmark v. Gimbel's Inc., 54 N.J. 585, 258 A.2d 697 (1969) (furnishing of permanent wave solution). For a more recent discussion of the implied warranty of habitability in the construction and sale of a new home, see McDonald v. Mianecki, 79 N.J. 275, 398 A.2d 1283 (1979).

lished by the writing itself. For example, under UCC 2–315, in order to show an implied warranty of fitness for a particular purpose, a buyer must show that the seller "has reason to know [the] particular purpose . . . and that the buyer is relying on the seller's skill and judgment." Could the buyer establish this by showing conversations that he had with the salesman prior to signing an integrated agreement? Note that under UCC 2–202, an integrated agreement excludes even "consistent additional terms." But is an implied warranty of fitness a "term"? See UCC 1–201(42). Compare the definition of "agreement" in UCC 1–201(3) with that of "contract" in UCC 1–201(11).

(3) *Derogating from Implied Terms and the Parol Evidence Rule.* What is the impact of the parol evidence rule on an attempt to derogate from a term that would otherwise be implied? In Hayden v. Hoadley, 94 Vt. 345, 111 A. 343 (1920), the parties signed a written "memorandum of agreement" reciting the exchange of their properties and a promise on one side to make stated repairs. The agreement was signed on May 2, and no time was fixed for the repairs. When suit was brought for failure to make the repairs, the defendant sought to show that it had been orally agreed at the time the writing was signed that they should have until October 1 to make them. The court decided that this evidence was properly excluded. "The legal effect of the contract before us—it being silent as to the time of performance—was to require the repairs specified to be completed within a reasonable time . . . . To admit the testimony offered by the defendants to the effect that the parties agreed upon October 1 as the limit of time given for the repairs would be to allow the plain legal effect of the written contract to be controlled by oral evidence. That is not permissible."

Corbin disagrees with the decision on the ground that if the parties have orally agreed to such matters as price, place of payment, and time of performance, but have omitted these items from the writing, it is probable that the parties did not intend the agreement to be integrated. Oral testimony, therefore, should be admissible to "rebut the usual presumptions and inferences." 3 Corbin, § 593. See the penultimate paragraph of the majority opinion in Masterson v. Sine, p. 661 supra.

The court in Hayden v. Hoadley noted that the evidence "was not offered on the ground that it was admissible on the question of what was a reasonable time under the circumstances, so we give that question no attention." If, before offering the evidence, the attorney for the defendant had stated that it was being offered to show what was a reasonable time for performance, would the evidence have been admissible? In support of an affirmative answer, see American Bridge Co. v. American Dist. Steam Co., 107 Minn 140, 119 N.W. 783 (1909). Should the admissibility of the evidence turn upon the inference it is to support?

BLOOR v. FALSTAFF BREWING CORP.

United States Court of Appeals, Second Circuit, 1979.
601 F.2d 609.

FRIENDLY, Circuit Judge: This action, wherein federal jurisdiction is predicated on diversity of citizenship, 28 U.S.C. § 1332, was brought in the District Court for the Southern District of New York, by James Bloor, Reorganization Trustee of Balco Properties Corporation, formerly named P. Ballantine & Sons (Ballantine), a venerable and once successful brewery based in Newark, N.J. He sought to recover from Falstaff Brewing Corporation (Falstaff) for breach of a contract dated March 31, 1972, wherein Falstaff bought the Ballantine brewing labels, trademarks, accounts receivable, distribution systems and other property except the brewery. The price was $4,000,000 plus a royalty of fifty cents on each barrel of the Ballantine brands sold between April 1, 1972 and March 31, 1978. Although other issues were tried, the appeals concern only two provisions of the contract. These are:

> 8. *Certain Other Covenants of Buyer.*
>
> (a) After the Closing Date the [Buyer] will use its best efforts to promote and maintain a high volume of sales under the Proprietary Rights.
>
> 2(a)(v) [The Buyer will pay a royalty of $.50 per barrel for a period of 6 years], provided, however, that if during the Royalty Period the Buyer substantially discontinues the distribution of beer under the brand name "Ballantine" (except as the result of a restraining order in effect for 30 days issued by a court of competent jurisdiction at the request of a governmental authority), it will pay to the Seller a cash sum equal to the years and fraction thereof remaining in the Royalty Period times $1,100,000, payable in equal monthly installments on the first day of each month commencing with the first month following the month in which such discontinuation occurs . . . .

Bloor claimed that Falstaff had breached the best efforts clause, 8(a), and indeed that its default amounted to the substantial discontinuance that would trigger the liquidated damage clause, 2(a)(v). In an opinion that interestingly traces the history of beer back to Domesday Book and beyond, Judge Brieant upheld the first claim and awarded damages but dismissed the second. Falstaff appeals from the former ruling, Bloor from the latter. Both sides also dispute the court's measurement of damages for breach of the best efforts clause.

We shall assume familiarity with Judge Brieant's excellent opinion, 454 F.Supp. 258 (S.D.N.Y.1978), from which we have drawn heavily, and will state only the essentials. Ballantine had been a family owned business, producing low-priced beers primarily for the northeast market, particularly New York, New Jersey, Connecticut and Pennsylvania. Its sales began to decline in 1961, and it lost money from 1965 on. On June 1, 1969, Investors Funding Corporation (IFC), a real estate conglomerate with no experience in brewing, acquired substantially all the stock of Ballantine for $16,290,000. IFC increased advertising expenditures, levelling off in 1971 at $1 million a year. This and other promotional practices, some of dubious legality, led to steady growth in Ballantine's sales despite the increased activities in the northeast of the "nationals" [1] which have greatly augmented their market shares at the expense of smaller brewers. However, this was a profitless prosperity; there was no month in which Ballantine had earnings and the total loss was $15,500,000 for the 33 months of IFC ownership.

After its acquisition of Ballantine, Falstaff continued the $1 million a year advertising program, IFC's pricing policies, and also its policy of serving smaller accounts not solely through sales to independent distributors, the usual practice in the industry, but by use of its own warehouses and trucks—the only change being a shift of the retail distribution system from Newark to North Bergen, N.J., when brewing was concentrated at Falstaff's Rhode Island brewery. However, sales declined and Falstaff claims to have lost $22 million in its Ballantine brand operations from March 31, 1972 to June 1975. Its other activities were also performing indifferently, although with no such losses as were being incurred in the sale of Ballantine products, and it was facing inability to meet payrolls and other debts. In March and April 1975 control of Falstaff passed to Paul Kalmanovitz, a businessman with 40 years experience in the brewing industry. After having first advanced $3 million to enable Falstaff to meet its payrolls and other pressing debts, he later supplied an additional $10 million and made loan guarantees, in return for which he received convertible preferred shares in an amount that endowed him with 35% of the voting power and became the beneficiary of a voting trust that gave him control of the board of directors.

Mr. Kalmanovitz determined to concentrate on making beer and cutting sales costs. He decreased advertising, with the result that the Ballantine advertising budget shrank from $1 million to $115,000 a year.[2] In late 1975 he closed four of Falstaff's six retail distribution centers, including the North Bergen, N.J. depot, which was ultimately replaced by two distributors servicing substantially fewer accounts. He also discontinued various illegal practices that had been used in selling Ballantine products.[3] What happened in terms of sales volume is shown in plaintiff's exhibit 114 J, a chart which we

1. Miller's, Schlitz, Anheuser-Busch, Coors and Pabst.

2. This was for cooperative advertising with purchasers.

3. There were two kinds of illegal practices, the testimony on both of which is, unsurprisingly, rather vague. Certain "national accounts", i. e. large draught beer buyers, were gotten or retained by "black bagging", the trade term for commercial bribery. On a smaller scale, sales to taverns were facilitated by the salesman's offering a free round for the house of Ballantine if it was available ("retention"), or the customer's choice ("solicitation"). Both practices seem to have been indulged in by many brewers, including Falstaff before Kalmanovitz took control.

reproduce in the margin.[4] With 1974 as a base, Ballantine declined, 29.72% in 1975 and 45.81% in 1976 as compared with a 1975 gain of 2.24% and a 1976 loss of 13.08% for all brewers excluding the top 15. Other comparisons are similarly devastating, at least for 1976.[5] Despite the decline in the sale of its own labels as well as Ballantine's, Falstaff, however, made a substantial financial recovery. In 1976 it had net income of $8.7 million and its year-end working capital had increased from $8.6 million to $20.2 million and its cash and certificates of deposit from $2.2 million to $12.1 million.

Seizing upon remarks made by the judge during the trial that Falstaff's financial standing in 1975 and thereafter "is probably not relevant" and a footnote in the opinion, 454 F.Supp. at 267 n. 7,[6] appellate counsel for Falstaff contend that the judge read the best efforts clause as requiring Falstaff to maintain Ballantine's volume by any sales methods having a good prospect of increasing or maintaining sales or, at least, to continue lawful methods in use at the time of purchase, no matter what losses they would cause. Starting from this premise, counsel reason that the judge's conclusion was at odds with New York law, stipulated by the contract to be controlling, as last expressed by the Court of Appeals in Feld v. Henry S. Levy & Sons, Inc., 37 N.Y.2d 466, 373 N.Y.S.2d 102, 335 N.E.2d 320 (1975). The court was there dealing with a contract whereby defendant agreed to sell and plaintiff to purchase all bread crumbs produced by defendant at a certain factory. During the term of the agreement defendant ceased producing bread crumbs because production with existing facilities was "very uneconomical", and the plaintiff sued for

4. Percentage Increase or Decline in Sales Volume of Ballantine Beer, Falstaff Beer and Comparable Brewers for Years Ending December 31, 1972-1976

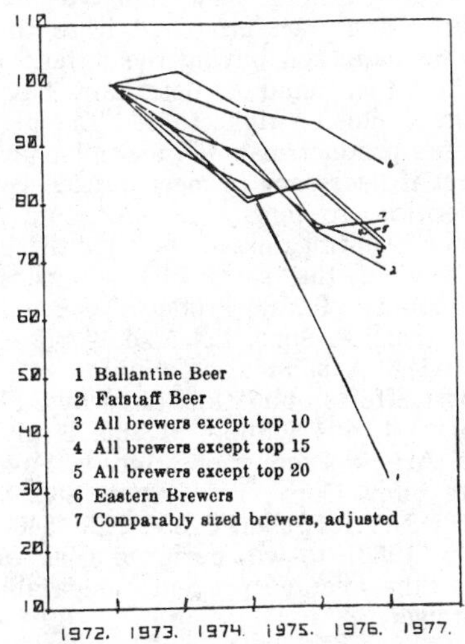

5. Falstaff argues that a trend line projecting the declining volume of Ballantine's sales since 1966, before IFC's purchase, would show an even worse picture. We agree with plaintiff that the percentage figures since 1974 are more significant; at least the judge was entitled to think so.

6. "Even if Falstaff's financial position had been worse in mid-1975 than it actually was, and even if Falstaff had continued in that state of impecuniosity during the term of the contract, performance of the contract is not excused where the difficulty of performance arises from financial difficulty or economic hardship. As the New York Court of Appeals stated in 407 E. 61st Garage, Inc. v. Savoy Corp., 23 N.Y.2d 275, 281, 296 N.Y.S. 2d 338, 344, 244 N.E.2d 37, 41 (1968):

> '[W]here impossibility or difficulty of performance is occasioned only by financial difficulty or economic hardship, even to the extent of insolvency or bankruptcy, performance of a contract is not excused.' (Citations omitted.)"

breach. This case was governed by § 2–306 of the Uniform Commercial Code [which the opinion quoted].

Affirming the denial of cross-motions for summary judgment, the court said that, absent a cancellation on six months' notice for which the contract provided:

> defendant was expected to continue to perform in good faith and could cease production of the bread crumbs, a single facet of its operation, only in good faith. Obviously, a bankruptcy or genuine imperiling of the very existence of its entire business caused by the production of the crumbs would warrant cessation of production of that item; the yield of less profit from its sale than expected would not. Since bread crumbs were but a part of defendant's enterprise and since there was a contractual right of cancellation, good faith required continued production until cancellation, even if there be no profit. In circumstances such as these and without more, defendant would be justified, in good faith, in ceasing production of the single item prior to cancellation only if its losses from continuance would be more than trivial, which, overall, is a question of fact.

37 N.Y.2d 471–72, 373 N.Y.S.2d 106, 335 N.E.2d 323.[7] Falstaff argues from this that it was not bound to do anything to market Ballantine products that would cause "more than trivial" losses.

7. The text of the Feld opinion did not refer to the case cited by Judge Brieant in the preceding footnote, 407 East 61st Garage, Inc. v. Savoy Fifth Avenue Corporation, 23 N.Y.2d 275, 296 N.Y.S.2d 338, 244 N.E.2d 37 (1968), which might suggest a more onerous obligation here. The Court of Appeals there reversed a summary judgment in favor of the defendant, which had discontinued operating the Savoy Hilton Hotel because of substantial financial losses, in alleged breach of a five-year contract with plaintiff wherein the defendant had agreed to use all reasonable efforts to provide the garage with exclusive opportunity for storage of the motor vehicles of hotel guests. Although the court did use the language quoted by Judge Brieant, the actual holding was simply that "an issue of fact is presented whether the agreement did import an implied promise by Savoy to fulfill its obligations for an entire five-year period." 23 N.Y.2d at 281, 296 N.Y.S.2d at 343, 244 N.E.2d at 41.

Other cases suggest that under New York law a "best efforts" clause imposes an obligation to act with good faith in light of one's own capabilities. In Van Valkenburgh v. Hayden Publishing Co., 30 N.Y.2d 34, 330 N.Y.S.2d 329, 281 N.E.2d 142 (1972), the court held a publisher liable to an author when, in clear bad faith after a contract dispute, he hired another to produce a book very similar to plaintiff's and then promoted it to those who had been buying the latter. On the other hand, a defendant having the exclusive right to sell the plaintiff's product may sell a similar product if necessary to meet outside competition, so long as he accounts for any resulting losses the plaintiff can show in the sales of the licensed product. Parev Products Co. v. I. Rokeach & Sons, 124 F.2d 147 (2 Cir. 1941). A summary definition of the best efforts obligation, cited by Judge Brieant, 454 F.Supp. at 266, is given in Arnold Productions, Inc. v. Favorite Films Corp., 176 F.Supp. 862, 866 (S.D.N.Y.1959), aff'd 298 F.2d 540 (2 Cir. 1962), to wit, performing as well as "the average prudent comparable" brewer.

The net of all this is that the New York law is far from clear and it is unfortunate that a federal court must have to apply it.

We do not think the judge imposed on Falstaff a standard as demanding as its appellate counsel argues that he did. Despite his footnote 7, see note 6 supra, he did not in fact proceed on the basis that the best efforts clause required Falstaff to bankrupt itself in promoting Ballantine products or even to sell those products at a substantial loss. He relied rather on the fact that Falstaff's obligation to "use its best efforts to promote and maintain a high volume of sales" of Ballantine products was not fulfilled by a policy summarized by Mr. Kalmanovitz as being:

> We sell beer and you pay for it . . . .
>
> We sell beer, F.O.B. the brewery. You come and get it.

—however sensible such a policy may have been with respect to Falstaff's other products. Once the peril of insolvency had been averted, the drastic percentage reductions in Ballantine sales as related to any possible basis of comparison, see fn. 5, required Falstaff at least to explore whether steps not involving substantial losses could have been taken to stop or at least lessen the rate of decline. The judge found that, instead of doing this, Falstaff had engaged in a number of misfeasances and nonfeasances which could have accounted in substantial measure for the catastrophic drop in Ballantine sales shown in the chart, see 454 F.Supp. at 267–72. These included the closing of the North Bergen depot which had serviced "Mom and Pop" stores and bars in the New York metropolitan area; Falstaff's choices of distributors for Ballantine products in the New Jersey and particularly the New York areas, where the chosen distributor was the owner of a competing brand; its failure to take advantage of a proffer from Guinness-Harp Corporation to distribute Ballantine products in New York City through its Metrobeer Division; Falstaff's incentive to put more effort into sales of its own brands which sold at higher prices despite identity of the ingredients and were free from the $.50 a barrel royalty burden; its failure to treat Ballantine products evenhandedly with Falstaff's; its discontinuing the practice of setting goals for salesmen; and the general Kalmanovitz policy of stressing profit at the expense of volume. In the court's judgment, these misfeasances and nonfeasances warranted a conclusion that, even taking account of Falstaff's right to give reasonable consideration to its own interests, Falstaff had breached its duty to use best efforts as stated in the Van Valkenburgh decision, supra, 30 N.Y.2d at 46, 330 N.Y.S.2d at 334, 281 N.E.2d at 145.

Falstaff levels a barrage on these findings. The only attack which merits discussion is its criticism of the judge's conclusion that Falstaff did not treat its Ballantine brands evenhandedly with those under the Falstaff name. We agree that the subsidiary findings "that Falstaff but not Ballantine had been advertised extensively in Texas and Missouri" and that "[i]n these same areas Falstaff, although a 'premium' beer, was sold for extended periods below the price of Ballantine," while literally true, did not warrant the inference drawn from them. Texas was Falstaff territory and, with advertising on a cooperative basis, it was natural that advertising expenditures on Falstaff would exceed those on Ballantine. The lower price for Falstaff was a particular promotion of a bicentennial can in Texas, intended to meet a particular competitor.

However, we do not regard this error as undermining the judge's ultimate conclusion of breach of the best efforts clause. While that clause clearly required Falstaff to treat the Ballantine brands as well as its own, it does not follow that it required no more. With respect to its own brands, management was entirely free to exercise its business judgment as to how to maximize profit even if this meant serious loss in volume. Because of the obligation it had assumed under the sales contract, its situation with respect to the Ballantine brands was quite different. The royalty of $.50 a barrel on sales was an essential part of the purchase price. Even without the best efforts clause Falstaff would have been bound to make a good faith effort to see that substantial sales of Ballantine products were made, unless it discontinued under clause 2(a)(v) with consequent liability for liquidated damages. Cf. Wood v. Duff-Gordon, 222 N.Y. 88, 118 N.E. 214 (1917) (Cardozo, J.). Clause 8 imposed an added obligation to use "best efforts to promote and maintain a *high* volume of sales . . . ." (emphasis supplied). Although we agree that even this did not require Falstaff to spend itself into bankruptcy to promote the sales of Ballantine products, it did prevent the application to them of Kalmanovitz' philosophy of emphasizing profit *über alles* without fair consideration of the effect on Ballantine volume. Plaintiff was not obliged to show just what steps Falstaff could reasonably have taken to maintain a high volume for Ballantine products. It was sufficient to show that Falstaff simply didn't care about Ballantine's volume and was content to allow this to plummet so long as that course was best for Falstaff's overall profit picture, an inference which the judge permissibly drew. The burden then shifted to Falstaff to prove there was nothing significant it could have done to promote Ballantine sales that would not have been financially disastrous.

Having correctly concluded that Falstaff had breached its best efforts covenant, the judge was faced with a difficult problem in computing what the royalties on the lost sales would have been. There is no need to rehearse the many decisions that, in a situation like this, certainty is not required; "[t]he plaintiff need only show a 'stable foundation for a reasonable estimate of royalties he would have earned had defendant not breached' ". Contemporary Mission, Inc. v. Famous Music Corp., 557 F.2d 918, 926 (2 Cir. 1977), quoting Freund v. Washington Square Press, Inc., 34 N.Y.2d 379, 383, 357 N.Y.S.2d 857, 861, 314 N.E.2d 419, 421 (1974). After carefully considering other possible bases, the court arrived at the seemingly sensible conclusion that the most nearly accurate comparison was with the combined sales of Rheingold and Schaefer beers, both, like Ballantine, being "price" beers sold primarily in the northeast, and computed what Ballantine sales would have been if its brands had suffered only the same decline as a composite of Rheingold and Schaefer. . . .

We also reject plaintiff's complaint on his cross-appeal that the court erred in not taking as its standard for comparison the grouping of all but the top 15 brewers, Ballantine having ranked 16th in 1971. The judge was entirely warranted in believing that the Rheingold-Schaefer combination afforded a better standard of comparison. [Finally, the court rejected plaintiff's contention that Falstaff's actions triggered the liquidated damage clause.]

The judgment is affirmed. Plaintiff may recover two-thirds of his costs.

NOTE

Questions. Would the result have been different if the contract had not contained the best efforts clause, 8(a)? Is Feld v. Henry S. Levy & Sons, the output contract case discussed by the court, apposite to a dispute over the meaning of "best efforts"?

PAREV PRODUCTS CO. v. I. ROKEACH & SONS, 124 F.2d 147 (2d Cir. 1941). [In 1924, Parev Products made a contract with I. Rokeach & Sons under which Parev gave Rokeach the exclusive rights to Parev Schmaltz, a liquid kosher cooking oil made by a secret process. Parev was, in return, to receive royalties on all sales. The contract was to run for 25 years, with an option in Rokeach to renew for another 25 years. Rokeach marketed the oil under the name Nyafat and paid royalties of about $135,000 over the first 15 years. In 1940, Rokeach began distributing Kea, a semisolid kosher cooking oil, in competition with Spry and Crisco, new products that were cutting into the Nyafat market. Parev sued to enjoin Rokeach from further sales of Kea. From a dismissal of its complaint, Parev appealed.]

CLARK, Circuit Judge . . . . Certainly we cannot say that defendant must market Nyafat, come what may, down to the sale of a mere can a year, while the vegetable oil business goes to outsiders. . . . [But it would state the rule too narrowly to say] that so long as defendant acts in good faith in judging the extent to which Kea must be sold to meet the competition of Crisco and Spry, no cause of action lies. . . . The really equitable solution is to permit defendant to sell Kea so long as it does not invade Nyafat's market if that point is susceptible of proof, as we think it is. . . . Hence, all the plaintiff is entitled to is the market Nyafat has created and will retain, regardless of outside competition.

An injunction to reach such a conclusion would be so vague as to be meaningless under present circumstances. Its practical effect would be to restrain defendant from any sales of Kea—which we have held to be unfair. Only by inserting "good faith" in the restraining order could defendant be protected; and this would be equivalent to the rule we have found too narrow. It follows, then, that on the present record plaintiff cannot obtain an injunction. A broad one would be unfair to defendant; a narrow one would be an empty gesture.

But plaintiff could not be denied the opportunity to show a loss of the Nyafat market as we have thus defined it. Plaintiff may be protected if it can be determined what sales of Kea represent loss to outside products, what sales represent loss to Nyafat. Expert appraisal of market conditions would, it seems to us, answer this. If loss were established, the measure of damages would be the amount of royalties on the displaced jars of Nyafat. On this record, the evidence is too fragmentary to be conclusive. Since an injunction was sought, the action was brought too soon to reflect the nature of the competition among the various cooking oils. If the plaintiff has further evidence of the inroads of Kea, it should be entitled to present it, either hereinafter in this case or in a later action.

Judgment affirmed, with costs to defendant and with leave to plaintiff either to move to reopen the action, or to bring a subsequent action, for relief not inconsistent with this opinion.

NOTES

(1) *The Case of the "Fritos" and "Fandangos."* Frito-Lay and So Good Potato Chip Company agreed that So Good was to be licensed to manufacture and distribute corn chips made by Frito-Lay's secret process within a prescribed area under the trademark "Fritos." The contract provided that Frito-Lay "will neither authorize nor permit the use of its trademark 'FRITOS' on corn chips by anyone other than Licensee." It also prohibited So Good from engaging "directly or indirectly . . . in the manufacture and/or sale of corn chips or similar products" other than "Fritos." When Frito-Lay introduced "Doritos," "Fandangos" and "Intermission" corn chips in the licensed territory, So Good sought an injunction. From an adverse judgment, So Good appealed. *Held:* Affirmed. "Unlike Parev Products, the parties here have expressly touched on the point in controversy. . . . A covenant cannot be implied if the parties have either expressly dealt with the matter in the contract or have left the agreement intentionally silent on the point. . . . [T]he franchise agreement expressly deals with the sale of products by Frito-Lay in the franchised territory, and thus precludes any implied covenant." Furthermore, even if a negative covenant were to be implied, under which Frito-Lay was prohibited from distributing "competitive" corn chips, that covenant was not broken because "the sales of 'Doritos,' 'Fandangos,' and 'Intermission' corn chips were no more 'competitive' . . . than the sales of the other products, such as cheese flavored corn puffs ('Chee-tos'), onion flavored corn snacks ('Funyums'), etc., introduced by either party. . . ." So Good Potato Chip Co. v. Frito-Lay, Inc., 462 F.2d 239 (8th Cir. 1972).

(2) *Technological Breakthroughs.* Troublesome problems are posed when an unanticipated technological breakthrough drastically changes the

situation, in which the contracting parties find themselves, from that which they had expected. The development of "talkie" moving pictures in the 1920's gave rise to some particularly interesting cases, of which a leading example is Kirke La Shelle Co. v. Paul Armstrong Co., 263 N.Y. 79, 188 N. E. 163 (1933).

In 1921, when "talkies" were unknown commercially, the Paul Armstrong Co., in settlement of a lawsuit, agreed to pay to Kirke La Shelle Co. half of the receipts from revivals of Armstrong's plays "Alias Jimmy Valentine" and "Salomy Jane." The contract provided that "all contracts . . . affecting the title to the dramatic rights (exclusive of motion picture rights) to the above two plays" would be subject to the approval of the Kirke La Shelle Co. In 1928, the Paul Armstrong Co. sold the exclusive "talkie" rights to "Salomy Jane" to Metro-Goldwyn Mayer, receiving $13,500 and the Kirke La Shelle Co. claimed the right to half of that sum, and prevailed in the New York Court of Appeals. The court concluded that since talkies were unknown when the contract was made, they were not "within the contemplation of the parties either as a subject for the transfer of an interest . . . or as included in the motion picture rights specifically excepted." Nevertheless, "[b]y entering into the contract and accepting and retaining the consideration therefor, [Armstrong] assumed a fiduciary relationship which had its origin in the contract and which imposed on them the duty of utmost good faith. . . . From the inclusion in the contract of the express agreement . . . not to enter into any contract affecting the title to the dramatic rights . . . without . . . approval, may be implied the obligation to hold the profits resulting from such breach for the benefit of the parties to the agreement in accordance with their rights under the contract." Why did Judge Clark limit Parev to damages based on the sales of Kea that "represent loss to Nyafat"? Why should not Parev have damages based on *all* the sales of Kea?

Further problems posed by technological breakthroughs will be considered in connection with impossibility and frustration in Chapter 9.

PERCENTAGE LEASES

An example of flexible pricing (see p. 243 supra) that is especially favored by retailers is the percentage lease, which fixes the rent as a stated percentage of the lessee's receipts or profits. Under such a lease the lessor has a useful hedge against inflation and also shares to some extent the lessee's risk of success or failure. Although a wide variety of formulas is possible, the most common is based, for obvious reasons of accounting convenience, on the lessee's gross receipts.

Use of gross receipts may, however, bring the parties' interests into sharp conflict. Under such a formula, it is in the lessor's interest that the lessee maximize his gross receipts, while it is in the lessee's own interest that he maximize his net profit. When these goals become markedly inconsistent, as may happen if the profit margin dwindles, trouble is the likely result. The extreme case arises when the lessee finds that he is operating at a loss and wants to go out of business.

If the situation is viewed through the optic of Wood v. Lucy, it would appear that, since the lessor has given the lessee the exclusive use of his land in return for a percentage of gross receipts, the lessee would be under a duty to use best efforts. Although the law in this field has developed with surprisingly little regard to cases such as Wood v. Lucy, it has nevertheless reached results that are in harmony with those cases.

A representative statement of the law was occasioned by a percentage lease to a physical therapist who, when the business of physical therapy turned out to be unprofitable, abandoned it and paid no rent. In holding that this was a breach, the court said: "The lessee obligated herself to pay rent at the rate of 5% of the gross receipts of the business. No minimum rent was reserved. Under these circumstances we are of the opinion that the lease must be construed as including an implied covenant to continue the business. . . . Any other construction would excuse the plaintiff from the obligation to pay any rent to the defendants and would, therefore, defeat the defendants' purpose in entering into the lease." Prins v. Van Der Vlugt, 215 Or. 682, 701–02, 337 P.2d 787, 796 (1959). Accord: Lippman v. Sears, Roebuck & Co., 44 Cal.2d 136, 280 P.2d 775 (1955).

The court's observation that there was no minimum rental suggests a simple way of dealing with the problem. By inserting a provision for a minimum rental in a percentage lease the lessor can eliminate some of the risk that he would otherwise face. If the lessor chooses this kind of protection is the lessee still under a duty to use best efforts? The next cases address this problem.

For discussion of percentage leases, see Notes, 51 Minn.L.Rev. 1139 (1967); 60 Nw.U.L.Rev. 677 (1965).

NOTE

Maximum Rental. Just as the lessor may want to fix a minimum rental, the lessee may want to fix a maximum rental. The final result is, of course, the result of the negotiations between the parties.

DICKEY v. PHILADELPHIA MINIT–MAN CORP.

Supreme Court of Pennsylvania, 1954.
377 Pa. 549, 105 A.2d 580.

HORACE STERN, Chief Justice. . . . Plaintiff, Samuel Dickey, in 1947 leased to defendant, Philadelphia Minit-Man Corporation, a vacant piece of land in Millbourne, Delaware County, for a term of ten years with an option to the lessee of an additional ten-year term. The lease provided that the premises were to be occupied by the lessee "in the business of washing and cleaning automobiles within the scope of the business of the Philadelphia Minit-Man Corporation, . . . and for no other purpose." As rent the lessee was to pay a sum equal to 12½% on the amount of the annual gross sales but a minimum of $1,800 per year; the term "gross sales" was to include the sales price of all merchandise sold and also all charges for services performed by the lessee in the course of the business conducted on the premises. The lessee agreed to erect and place on the premises the buildings and equipment needed to carry on the business; all buildings and fixtures erected by the lessee were to become the property of the lessor as and when the lease agreement should expire for any reason whatever. If default were made in the observance or performance of any of the conditions or agreements the lessor was to have the right to terminate the lease and reenter the premises.

Defendant erected the buildings, installed the necessary equipment, and washed and cleaned cars until August, 1952, when it discontinued that feature of its business except as incidental to simonizing and polishing, and it so notified the public. Defendant never failed to pay at least the minimum rental, but in September, 1953, plaintiff filed the present action in ejectment seeking recovery of possession of the property on the ground that defendant had defaulted by discontinuing the business specified in the lease. Defendant filed preliminary objections in the nature of a demurrer to the complaint; the court below sustained the objections and dismissed the action. Plaintiff appeals.

The question involved is whether there was any implied obligation on the part of the lessee to continue to conduct the business on the premises of washing and cleaning cars if its failure to do so resulted in a diminution of rental payable to the lessor.

Generally speaking, a provision in a lease that the premises are to be used only for a certain prescribed purpose imports no obligation on the part of the lessee to use or continue to use the premises for that purpose; such a provision is a covenant against a noncomplying use, not a covenant to use. Plaintiff urges, however, that in a lease such as that here involved, in which the amount of rental to be paid is based upon the lessee's gross sales, there arises an implied obligation on his part to continue the business on the premises to the fullest extent reasonably possible. Defendant, on the other hand, contends that, where such an obligation is intended, it must be expressly inserted in the lease, and that the raising of an implied covenant is never justified except where obviously necessary to effectuate the intention of the parties and so clearly within their contemplation that they deemed it unnecessary to express it, and that this is especially true where a substantial minimum rental is provided the obvious purpose of which is to protect the lessor from any unfavorable circumstances that might subsequently arise whether caused by voluntary conduct of the lessee or by events beyond his control. . . .

If an implied covenant, as claimed by plaintiff, should be held to arise in such cases what would be the extent of the restriction thereby imposed upon the lessee? Would it extend to each and every act on his part that might serve to reduce the extent of his business and thereby the percentage rental based thereon? Would it forbid him, for example, if operating a retail store, from keeping it open for a fewer number of hours each day than formerly? Would it forbid him from dismissing salesmen whereby his business might be reduced in volume? Would it forbid him from discontinuing any department of his business even though he found it to be operating at a loss? It would obviously be quite unreasonable and wholly undesirable to imply an obligation that would necessarily be vague, uncertain and generally impracticable.

. . . Defendant has not moved any part of its business to another location nor deliberately sought to decrease the percentage of rent payable in order to induce plaintiff to declare a termination of the lease; on the contrary, it is seeking to maintain the lease. Nor is there anything in the present case to indicate that defendant's action in discontinuing the washing and cleaning of cars except as incidental to simonizing and polishing was taken other than in good faith and in the exercise of legitimate business judgment. In our opinion it was not forbidden by any implied obligation in the lease.

The decree is affirmed and judgment is here entered for defendant.[a]

NOTES

(1) *Meaning of "Good Faith."* Chief Justice Stern pointed out that there was no indication that the lessee had acted "other than in good faith and in the exercise of legitimate business judgment." What did he mean by "good faith"? How could Dickey have shown "bad faith"? What result if Minit-Man had moved part of its business to another location?

UCC 1–203 provides that "Every contract or duty within this Act imposes an obligation of good faith in its performance or enforcement." "Good faith" is generally defined in the Code to mean only "honesty in fact in the conduct or transaction concerned," a purely subjective test. UCC 1–201(19). But the Sales Article, Article 2, contains a special definition of "good faith" which "in the case of a merchant means honesty in fact and the observance of reasonable commercial standards of fair dealing in the trade." UCC 2–103(1)(b). What sort of evidence might parties adduce to define "good faith"?

The notion of an obligation of good faith in the performance of contract duties is a familiar one to civil law systems, most notably the German. Article 242 of the German Civil Code imposes an obligation of "performance according to the requirements of good faith [*Treu und Glauben*], common habits being duly taken into consideration." It is a novel one to the common law and the Code provisions have already occasioned considerable

a. The dissenting opinion of Musmanno, J., has been omitted.

discussion. See Farnsworth, Good Faith Performance and Commercial Reasonableness under the Uniform Commercial Code, 30 U.Chi.L.Rev. 666 (1963); Summers, "Good Faith" in General Contract Law and the Sales Provisions of the Uniform Commercial Code, 54 Va.L.Rev. 195 (1968).

(2) *Substantial Minimum Rental.* In deciding whether there is "any implied obligation on the part of the lessee to continue to conduct the business on the premises," many courts have, like that in the principal case, taken account of whether "a substantial minimum rental is provided." Why should this be influential? How can a court determine whether a minimum rental is "substantial" or not? Was it significant that Minit-Man was to build the necessary buildings? Might the result have been different if the lease had required Dickey to build the buildings? The opinion does not disclose the extent, if any, by which the rental during the first five years of operation exceeded the minimum. Would it be interesting to know? To what extent could the parties have avoided the dispute by careful drafting?

(3) *The Case of the Tailored Woman's Furs.* The Tailored Woman, a retail store, had a percentage lease on the lower floors of a Fifth Avenue building. Later it acquired from the same landlord a fixed rental lease on the fifth floor, where it opened a custom-made dress department. When this venture failed, it moved its fur department from the second to the fifth floor. The landlord sued for additional rental based on a percentage of sales of furs on the fifth floor. From an adverse judgment, the landlord appealed. *Held:* Affirmed. "In deciding this case as we do, we are not moving away from the good old rule that there is in every contract an implied covenant of fair dealing. Kirke La Shelle Co. v. Paul Armstrong Co. [Note 2, p. 726 supra]. Defendant, as we see it, was merely exercising its rights." There was no "unconscionable diversion of business from percentage-lease premises to others." Two judges dissented. "[I]n every contract there is an implied covenant that neither party shall do anything which shall have the effect of injuring or destroying the right of the other party to receive the fruits of the contract." Mutual Life Ins. Co. v. Tailored Woman, 309 N.Y. 248, 128 N.E.2d 401 (1955).

HML CORP. v. GENERAL FOODS CORP.

United States Court of Appeals, Third Circuit, 1966.
365 F.2d 77.

FREEDMAN, Circuit Judge. In this suit for breach of a contract, plaintiff HML Corporation (formerly Cream Wipt Foods, Inc.), appeals from a judgment of dismissal entered at the conclusion of its case by the district judge sitting without a jury.

The following facts are uncontested. Beginning in 1934 plaintiff had been manufacturing and distributing a salad dressing under the trademarked name "Cream Wipt". In 1956 defendant began to distribute a dessert topping mix under the name "Dream Whip", and applied for trademark protection. Plaintiff successfully opposed the application on the ground that "Dream Whip" should be barred because of its "Cream Wipt" registration. Cream Wipt Foods, Inc. v.

General Foods Corp., 278 F.2d 521 (C.C.P.A.1960). This decision, announced on May 24, 1960, seriously imperiled defendant's four year investment in the name "Dream Whip".

On September 14, 1960 the parties executed two contracts, which they arrived at after negotiations in which they were represented by counsel. In the so-called "Main Agreement" defendant agreed to purchase from plaintiff and its president and principal shareholder, Harry M. Levin, the "Cream Wipt" trademark, the process, and a patent, for a total price of $250,000 in cash. The agreement contained the usual covenants and representations, and in addition provided that defendant's obligation to close, which was set for October 31, 1960, was contingent on the simultaneous execution of a "Supply Agreement", which both parties would execute in good faith. The "Main Agreement" also provided that plaintiff would change its name from "Cream Wipt Foods, Inc.", and that neither plaintiff nor Mr. Levin would compete with General Foods for ten years in the manufacture of salad dressing.

In the "Supply Agreement" plaintiff agreed to sell and defendant agreed to buy for thirty-two months in monthly orders at least 85% of its "requirements" of salad dressing in a designated geographic area. The price was carefully spelled out in a formula which provided reimbursement to plaintiff of its cost of ingredients and processing and a fixed profit, plus one-half of defendant's profits in excess of 28%. Defendant reserved the right to buy from others what plaintiff could not produce, or to terminate the contract if plaintiff consistently failed to meet quality controls or to supply 85% of defendant's requirements. No minimum quantity was fixed, but a maximum requirement was set at 5,000 gallons per day. The agreement gave to the defendant extensive rights to supervise, inspect and reject and to instruct plaintiff in the manufacture of the salad dressing, but at defendant's expense except in so far as plaintiff failed to meet quality standards. Plaintiff had the right to terminate the contract if its profits should fall below 5% of its costs.

After the closing, defendant, acting under a provision in the agreements, directed plaintiff to terminate its brokerage and advertising and promotion contracts and reimbursed it for the costs of cancellation. Both parties gave notice to the trade that defendant had assumed the sales and distribution of the salad dressing. Defendant undertook certain market tests, while continuing to distribute the salad dressing through brokers designated by it. During this period, defendant's requirements amounted to about 5,000 gallons monthly. Although plaintiff had anticipated such a period of cautious study and evaluation by defendant, it continued to take an active interest in the progress of the product and frequently volunteered to defendant suggestions and requests, of which a few minor ones were acted upon.

On February 17, 1961, after four months had run under the agreement, defendant notified plaintiff that it had determined that it could not profitably market the salad dressing and therefore would not require any further production. Plaintiff's efforts to persuade defendant to alter this decision were unavailing, although defendant agreed to permit plaintiff to manufacture and distribute the product to one customer on its own account under a different name without royalty or other liability. Two years later, on January 1, 1963, plaintiff's plant was destroyed by fire and defendant terminated the contract on the ground that plaintiff could no longer produce any requirements it might have. Plaintiff responded that it was still prepared to fill defendant's orders, notwithstanding the destruction of its plant and equipment.

In addition to these facts, plaintiff introduced testimony of Mr. Levin and his wife that plaintiff had demanded $750,000 to settle the trademark dispute, and had agreed to the offer of $250,000 because it expected to realize the difference through the "Supply Contract", as a result of oral assurances given by defendant's representatives during the negotiations that defendant would exert its best efforts to promote the salad dressing and that a great success was likely "if it clicked". Mrs. Levin also testified to subsequent oral statements by defendant's representatives which bore on the good faith of its decision to cease distribution.

As the case was tried in the court below, the issue was whether defendant had a duty to promote the salad dressing and if so, whether it had acted in good faith in deciding to cease distribution. Plaintiff specifically acknowledged that it made no claim that defendant had misrepresented its intentions during the negotiations leading to the contracts. At the close of plaintiff's case the court dismissed the action. It held that the parole evidence of Mr. and Mrs. Levin was legally inadmissible to prove an undertaking by defendant to promote the sale of salad dressing and found that plaintiff had not proven the factual existence of a duty to promote and that none was to be implied in law in the circumstances. The court also found that plaintiff had not established by any evidence of probative value that defendant's decision to cease distribution had been made in bad faith.

Plaintiff now contends that either as a matter of construction of the intention of the parties, or by implication of law, defendant assumed a duty to promote the product or at least to maintain requirements by continuing to distribute it. It argues that a good faith determination to cease promotion or distribution, if exculpatory at all, would constitute a justification or excuse for a breach, and that defendant therefore was required to prove it.

We apply the law of New York, which the parties by their contract agreed should govern. Although New York has adopted the Uniform Commercial Code, it applies only to transactions entered into after September 27, 1964, when it went into effect and therefore is inapplicable here. Uniform Commercial Code (New York) § 10–

105, 62½ McKinney's Consolidated Laws of New York Annot. (1964) § 10–105, p. 654.

Where an owner of a product gives an exclusive agency, solely in return for royalties, but no promise is expressed on the part of the agent to use his best efforts to promote it, the courts have implied such a promise. In the leading case of Wood v. Lucy, Lady Duff-Gordon, 222 N.Y. 88, 91, 118 N.E. 214 (1917) Judge Cardozo said: "The law has outgrown its primitive stage of formalism when the precise word was the sovereign talisman, and every slip was fatal. . . . The defendant gave an *exclusive* privilege. She was to have no right for at least a year to place her own indorsements or market her own designs except through the agency of the plaintiff. The acceptance of the exclusive agency was an assumption of its duties. . . . We are not to suppose that one party was to be placed at the mercy of the other. . . . Many other terms of the agreement point the same way. . . . [T]he terms of the defendant's compensation are even more significant. Her sole compensation for the grant of an exclusive agency is to be one-half of all the profits resulting from the plaintiff's efforts. Unless he gave his efforts, she could never get anything."

That rule is inapplicable here. While plaintiff originally was the owner of the product, this was not the simple grant of an exclusive distributorship in return for a share of the profits. Defendant bought from the plaintiff its interest and good will in the product, as well as the name, in return for a substantial cash payment. The court below found that the primary purpose of the "Supply Agreement" was for the benefit of the defendant so that it would have a ready source of supply of the product in accordance with its requirements. We cannot say from an examination of the agreements and the record that this conclusion is erroneous. Nor need we definitively determine the precise limits of the defendant's obligation in the peculiar circumstances of this case. Cases such as percentage leases and the distinctions which have been drawn regarding an implied obligation of the lessee to use and occupy the premises where a substantial minimum rental is provided and those where there is no minimum rental may be looked to for some analogy.[1] In these and similar circumstances the seller or lessor is not at the mercy of the buyer or lessee and the terms of the contract which provide a substantial minimum payment therefore negative an implication of a duty to promote, drawn from equitable considerations. The choice lies between implying a promise to correct an apparent injustice in the contract, as against holding the parties to the bargain which they have made. The latter alternative has especial force where the bargain is the result of elaborate negotiations in which the

1. See . . . Dickey v. Philadelphia Minit-Man Corp., 377 Pa. 549, 105 A. 2d 580 (1954). . . .

parties are aided by counsel, and in such circumstances it is easier to assume that a failure to make provision in the agreement resulted not from ignorance of the problem, but from an agreement not to require it. In this case the plaintiff argues that in a requirements contract the buyer impliedly promises to maintain his requirements. Here, as in percentage lease cases, the decisions are not all uniform in the strength assigned to the effort to equalize the agreement on the one hand and the reliance on the parties' bargain on the other. The better view, however, is that generally the buyer in a requirements contract is required merely to exercise good faith in determining his requirements and the seller assumes the risk of all good faith variations in the buyer's requirements even to the extent of a determination to liquidate or discontinue the business. The rule is based on a reliance on the self-interest of the buyer, who ordinarily will seek to have the largest possible requirements. Protection against abuse is afforded by penetrating through any device by which the requirement is siphoned off in some other form to the detriment of the seller. The requirement of good faith is the means by which this is enforced and self-interest in its undistorted form is maintained as the standard. New York accepts this view.[2]

Professor Corbin gives us an excellent analysis of the problem: "As to these matters there is certainly a gap in the express words of agreement. Shall it be filled by process of implication, thereby increasing the burden of performance by the buyer, the extent of his contractual duty. . . . If it were necessary in order that the contract should not be unreasonable or unfair to one of the parties (the seller) according to prevailing standards and usage, the implication should be made; but it is not necessary for that purpose. If such agreements, in spite of the unfilled gap, were commonly so understood and performed by business men, the additional unstated duty and burden should be put upon the buyer by implication; but no such understanding or performance can as yet be shown.

"Here, then, is a gap that should not be filled by the court. The implication suggested might not be unreasonable—at least the added promise is one that men sometimes make in words; but refusal to make the implication does not make the contract unenforceable, unreasonable or one-sided. The seller may be quite willing to trust to the self-interest of the buyer, to his desire to continue a profitable business, and to his promise to buy exclusively of the seller, without any further promise on the buyer's part. The risk of there being no needs or requirements the seller may be quite willing to carry; and he can adjust his prices in proportion to the risk.

2. . . . Although the Uniform Commercial Code, § 2–306(1), is not applicable to this case, the text and the official comment show that it does not intend to establish any new doctrine. . . .

"Only the least thought is necessary to realize that a 'gap' in an agreement should not be filled merely because a gap exists. . . . The subject matter and content of any contract is limited, all the rest of the world being excluded. . . . A promise that is not there in language, or an unexpressed condition of an express promise, should be put in by process of implication only when the conduct of the parties reasonably interpreted already has expressed it. It should be put in by construction of law, in the absence of justified implication, only when justice imperiously demands it under the circumstances that have arisen." (3 Corbin, Contracts (1960) § 569, pp. 339–341).

The parties were well aware that the contract arose out of the defendant's desire to use the trademarked name. And in the circumstances if defendant after acquiring it and having the plaintiff's obligation to supply the product needed was to be bound by any specific obligations of performance the usual desirability of providing for it in the agreement was here even more pronounced. The absence of such a provision in the agreement therefore has greater significance in this case than in the ordinary requirements contract.

The normal interpretation of the agreement cannot be altered by the plaintiff's effort to show a parol representation that defendant would exert additional effort to promote the product. The parties reduced their bargain to writing and plaintiff formally disavowed at the trial any claim of fraud. Indeed, each contract contained the explicit statement that it incorporated the entire agreement of the parties, and the "Supply Agreement" provided in addition that "as an inducement to us [defendant] to enter into this agreement you [plaintiff] represent that no representations or statements have been made to you by us or our officers, agents, employees, or representatives, which would in any way tend to add to, modify, or change any one or more of the provisions of this agreement". The agreement, therefore, "was complete in itself". Edison Electric Illuminating Co. v. Thacher, supra, at 229 N.Y. 178, 128 N.E. 124.

Moreover, the result reached by the court below would not be altered even if the parol evidence were to be considered. Indeed, the claim that plaintiff was greatly concerned over a guarantee that defendant would expend effort and energy on the product shows that it was sufficiently in mind to have been embodied in the agreement if both parties intended it to be binding. Certainly the silence of the agreement on this subject, although it specified a maximum quantity, justifies the conclusion that no such obligation existed. In any event, the trial judge refused to credit Mr. Levin's testimony on which this claim is largely based; and this, of course, was an issue which was peculiarly for his judgment.

There remains then the question whether defendant acted in good faith in deciding that it had no need for the product. There is not much dispute on whether this was shown. On the contrary, it is argued by plaintiff that the burden was upon the defendant to establish the good faith of its decision. Since the contract made no provision for a minimum requirement by defendant, its notice to plaintiff that it had no requirement did not of itself constitute a breach of the agreement. It follows that since plaintiff claimed a breach it was its duty to prove it, and the burden, therefore, rested upon it to show that defendant had acted in bad faith. See New York Central Iron Works Co. v. United States Radiator Co., supra, 174 N.Y. at 335–336, 66 N.E. 967. The court below found that this burden was not met and we cannot say that its finding was so clearly erroneous that it must be set aside.

The judgment of the court below therefore will be affirmed.

NOTES

(1) *Questions.* What was General Food's duty under the "Main Agreement"? Was there a breach of that duty? (Is the court's reasoning in this regard reflected in the language of UCC 2–306(2)?) What was its duty under the "Supply Agreement"? Was there a breach of that duty?

(2) *The Case of the Bad Faith Order.* Massachusetts Gas & Electric Light Supply, a distributor of appliances, had a distributorship agreement with V–M, a manufacturer, cancellable by V–M on 30 days' notice. In June, Massachusetts learned that V–M was about to cancel and on June 28 it ordered 892 units, its estimated need for the rest of the year, although its normal inventory was about 100 units. V–M cancelled and refused to fill the order, but offered to fill a part of it. Massachusetts took the position that it wanted the whole order or nothing, and sued. From judgment for the defendant, the plaintiff appealed. *Held:* Affirmed. "The agreement was a distributorship and not a mere sales agreement, and it was the disclosed intention that when plaintiff ceased to be a distributor it should, at least shortly, cease to carry defendant's goods. . . . [T]he maximum June 28 order which defendant should have had to respect was to maintain an appropriate inventory through July. Plaintiff's order was not a good faith attempt to accomplish this, see U.C.C. §§ 1–203, 2–103(1)(b), 2–306, but an effort to nullify the termination clause." Massachusetts Gas & Electric Light Supply Corp. v. V–M Corp., 387 F.2d 605 (1st Cir. 1967).

(3) *Problem.* Levy & Sons, bakers of bread, made a contract with the Crushed Toast Company for the sale of "all bread crumbs produced" by Levy's Brooklyn factory at a fixed price for a period of one year with provision for periodic renewals. The process of producing crumbs involved running stale or imperfect loaves through grinders, toasting them in an oven and bagging them. After some crumbs had been delivered, Levy considered that the process was uneconomical, refused to deliver at the contract price, dismantled the crumb making machinery and sold its stale and imperfect loaves to animal food manufacturers. Advise Crushed Toast of its rights under the contract. See Feld v. Henry S. Levy & Sons, Inc., 37 N.Y.2d 466, 373 N.Y.S.2d 102, 335 N.E.2d 320 (1975).

(4) *Problem.* The 61st Street Garage made a written contract with the Savoy Hilton Hotel to furnish garage service to the hotel's guests for a period of five years and to pay Savoy 10% of its gross receipts. Savoy

agreed to use reasonable efforts to give the garage the exclusive opportunity to serve its guests. After less than two years, Savoy decided to stop operating the hotel for financial reasons, the hotel building was demolished, and an office building was built on the site. Advise the garage of its rights under the contract. (Is it helpful to regard the contract as a requirements contract? An output contract? One for exclusive dealing? Would it make a difference if the only provision of the contract concerning termination gave Savoy the right to terminate on the garage's default? That the garage had made substantial commitments for additional insurance, supplies and employees for the lifetime of the contract? That Savoy knew that the garage would have to make these commitments when it made the contract?) See 407 E. 61st Garage, Inc. v. Savoy Fifth Avenue Corp., 23 N.Y.2d 275, 296 N.Y.S.2d 338, 244 N.E.2d 37 (1968).

BAK–A–LUM CORP. OF AMERICA v. ALCOA BLDG. PRODUCTS, INC.

Supreme Court of New Jersey, 1976.
69 N.J. 123, 351 A.2d 349.

CONFORD, P. J. A. D., Temporarily Assigned. Plaintiff corporation ("BAL" hereinafter) sued defendant ("ALCOA" hereinafter) for an injunction and damages for alleged breach of an exclusive distributorship of aluminum siding and related products manufactured by ALCOA. It was denied an injunction but awarded damages for breach of contract; at the same time the trial court granted defendant judgment on a counterclaim for merchandise sold to plaintiff, together with interest thereon. Plaintiff appealed on the ground the damages awarded were inadequate; the defendant cross-appealed, asserting its conduct was not actionable. The Appellate Division affirmed. We granted plaintiff's petition for certification and defendant's cross-petition. . . .

We find the record to support the trial court's finding of fact that in or about 1962 or 1963 BAL entered into a verbal agreement with ALCOA whereby BAL would be exclusive distributor in Northern New Jersey for ALCOA's aluminum siding and certain related products. Although the agreement did not preclude BAL handling other lines of siding, the understanding was that it would maintain an adequate organization and exert its best efforts to promote the sales of the ALCOA products, and the evidence and trial findings were that BAL produced to the satisfaction of ALCOA, even meeting fixed quotas of sales set by ALCOA during the latter phase of the relationship.

ALCOA terminated the "exclusive" in January 1970 by appointing four additional distributors to share the North Jersey territory with plaintiff, thereby precipitating the controversy that gave rise to this action. The trial court, although refusing a request for a preliminary injunction against the termination of the exclusive distributorship, held after trial that there was a binding agreement between the parties terminable only after a reasonable period of time and on reasonable notice. It found that a reasonable period of time had passed before termination but that a reasonable period of notice of termination would be seven months. It established plaintiff's damages at $5,000 per month and entered judgment in plaintiff's favor for $35,000 together with interest from September 1, 1970.

In addition to a complaint that it established losses in sales profits as a result of the termination of the exclusive at a rate of $10,000 per month rather than at the $5,000 rate determined by the court, plaintiff's major grievance is that in the Spring of 1969, at a time when defendant had already decided upon the termination of the distributorship but was secreting that plan from plaintiff, the latter undertook a major expansion of its warehouse facilities at substantial added operating expense. Plaintiff asserts that defendant knew of and encouraged this step, leading plaintiff to believe it was well warranted in view of the expected enlargement of the business of both of the contracting parties. On the basis of defendant's concealment of its intentions in the face of plaintiff's incurrence of a five year lease obligation for the new space, plaintiff asserts it is entitled to additional damages from defendant for the excess of its expense for the period of the lease over its operating expenses in its former headquarters—a loss allegedly attributable directly to defendant's breach of contract.

The trial court found that if ALCOA's decision, made in January or February of 1969, to enlarge the number of North Jersey distributors, had been promptly communicated to BAL's president, "it is unlikely that he would have signed the lease [for the new quarters] in April [1969] without first getting from [ALCOA] the assurance of continuance of the distributorship which he sought to get after the lease was signed". The court further found that all the circumstances surrounding the defendant's attitude to and treatment of plaintiff preceding and attending the disruption of the contractual arrangement "bespeak a certain hypocrisy as well as ruthlessness on the part of [ALCOA] toward its distributor of many years". The court further "surmised" that the reason defendant had concealed during the year 1969 its intention to terminate plaintiff's exclusive even though it had arrived at that intent before plaintiff entered into the new lease in 1969 was "that the men at [ALCOA] in charge of sales thought a period of secrecy ending with a sudden announcement to Mr. Diamond [plaintiff's president] of the accomplished fact of new distributors would avoid any risk of cooling plaintiff's interest in selling ALCOA products during the several months before the new distributors were named and made ready to go". Indeed, defendant's salesman induced plaintiff in January 1970, just before the announcement of the termination of the exclusive, to order $150,000 worth of merchandise—a very heavy order for that time of year.

In fixing seven months as a reasonable period of notice of termination of the exclusive agreement the trial court stated that the criterion for such a period of notice is the amount of time the notified party needs to make adjustments and to plan and arrange for business activities to replace those which are to be eliminated. However, the court apparently placed little if any weight on the circumstances of the new lease as an element going to the reasonableness of the period for notice of termination, although it stated that the lease was a "factor" for consideration. It pointed out that the decision to undertake the lease was plaintiff's and that plaintiff was able to use the space to store merchandise other than that purchased from defendant as well as defendant's lines.

Our review of the record leads us to concur in the trial court's holding that there was a valid distributorship agreement terminable only on reasonable notice. . . . Plaintiff's contention that the agreement was not terminable at all without "cause" based on the recent holding of this court in Shell Oil Co. v. Marinello, 63 N.J. 402, 307 A.2d 598 (1973), is without merit. The "franchise" agreement here is in no sense comparable with that which produced the holding of non-terminability in *Shell.*

However, we are constrained to differ with the trial court's assessment of seven months as an adequate period for notice of termination of this agreement. It may be true that defendant ordinarily would be under no strictly legal obligation to inform plaintiff that it was about to terminate its exclusive distributorship although it knew that in all probability plaintiff was enlarging its plant upon an assumption of the continuation of the business arrangement for the indefinite future. However, we have been at pains recently to point out that "[i]n every contract there is an implied covenant that 'neither party shall do anything which will have the effect of destroying or injuring the right of the other party to receive the fruits of the contract; in other words, in every contract there exists an implied covenant of good faith and fair dealing.'" Association Group Life, Inc. v. Catholic War Vets. of U. S., 61 N.J. 150, 153, 293 A.2d 382, 384 (1972). . . .

While the contractual relation of manufacturer and exclusive territorial distributor continued between the parties an obligation of reciprocal good-faith dealing similarly persisted between them. In such circumstances defendant's selfish withholding from plaintiff of its intention seriously to impair its distributorship although knowing plaintiff was embarking on an investment substantially predicated upon its continuation constituted a breach of the implied covenant of dealing in good faith of which we have spoken. As such it must be given substantial weight in determining the reasonableness of a period of notice of termination of the distributorship.

We cannot, however, agree with plaintiff that the period should encompass the remaining 4½ years of the lease as of the date of breach. The evidence justifies the conclusion that the prospects were fair for ultimate utilization to a substantial extent of the expanded warehouse space for new business plaintiff was able to obtain after defendant's breach or for other means of mitigating that phase of the damage attributable to defendant's conduct.

Exercising our original fact finding jurisdiction in order to bring this litigation to a close, it is our determination that a reasonable period of notice of termination of the distributorship, under all the circumstances, would have been 20 months.

Moreover, we find unwarranted the trial court's determination of plaintiff's monthly losses of profits of sales at $5,000 in the face of apparently unchallenged proofs by plaintiff, accepted by the court, that the damage figures were about $10,000 monthly. . . .

On defendant's appeal the judgment is affirmed, with costs. On plaintiff's appeal the judgment is modified in accordance with this opinion, with costs to plaintiff.

NOTE

Questions. How does the problem raised in this case differ from that in the Corenswet case, p. 521 supra? Could Alcoa have protected itself by providing for termination on 30-days notice? For termination at will?

LOCKEWILL, INC. v. UNITED STATES SHOE CORP., 547 F. 2d 1024 (8th Cir. 1976), cert. denied, 431 U.S. 956 (1977). [In 1965, Grant Williams, a man experienced in the shoe business, made an oral agreement with Pappagallo, Inc., a distributor of fashionable women's shoes that then sold only through small stores, each known as "The Shop for Pappagallo." Under the agreement, Williams was to open such a shop in the St. Louis area and purchase shoes in reasonable volume, in return for the exclusive right to market Pappagallo products in that area. Nothing was said about duration or termination. When Williams asked about the propriety of a written contract, Maurice Bandler, the sole owner of Pappagallo and a lawyer, said that none was necessary and that their handclasp was sufficient. Williams organized a corporation to run the shop, invested about $100,000 in the venture and sold Pappagallo products for years. During this time, however, United States Shoe Corp. bought out Bandler's interest in Pappagallo, and in the summer of 1973 an arrangement was made under which Stix, Baer & Fuller, a large St. Louis department store would be allowed to sell Pappagallo shoes in competition with Williams' shop. In September, 1973, Williams' lawyer wrote a letter to Pappagallo protesting this and, when, in February 1974, Stix, Baer & Fuller began selling Pappagallo shoes, suit was brought against Pappagallo and United States Shoe for breach of the exclusivity provision of the 1965 distributorship agreement. From a judgment awarding the plaintiff $150,000 in damages, the defendants appealed.

HENLEY, Circuit Judge. . . . The law of Missouri, which we are undertaking to apply in this case, appears to be that where the parties to a franchise or exclusive agency or distributorship agreement which is silent as to duration and which does not deal specifically with termination begin to perform thereunder, the agreement is construed to be terminable at the will of either party. See . . . Beebe v. Columbia Axle Co., 233 Mo.App. 212, 117 S.W.2d 624 (1938).

That general rule, however, is subject to an important limitation which was expressed in *Beebe*, supra, in the following language (117 S.W.2d at 629): "The limitation is that, in any case of an indefinite agency where it is revoked by the principal, if it appears that the agent, induced by his appointment, has in good faith incurred expense and devoted time and labor in the matter of the agency without having had a sufficient opportunity to recoup such from the undertaking, the principal will be required to compensate him in that behalf; for the law will not permit one thus to deprive another of value without awarding just compensation. The just principle acted upon by the courts in the circumstances suggested requires no more than that, in every instance, the agent shall be afforded a reasonable opportunity to avail himself of the primary expenditures and efforts put forth to the end of executing the authority conferred upon him and that, if such opportunity is denied him, the principal shall compensate him accordingly. (Citations omitted.)" In a case to which the limitation of the general rule is applicable, the agent is entitled to recoupment or to compensation on a quantum meruit basis rather than by way of ordinary damages for breach of contract. . . . Applying to this case the principles of Missouri law that have been mentioned, we hold that apart from any question of the statute of frauds, which was pleaded by the defendants, the agreement between plaintiff and Pappagallo was binding, at least quasi-contractually, on Pappagallo and later on U. S. Shoe for a reasonable time after plaintiff had opened its shop in May, 1965, to the end that plaintiff might have a reasonable opportunity to recover its initial investment and expenses. During that period of time Pappagallo and U. S. Shoe were required to supply goods to the plaintiff and to refrain from interfering with his exclusive distributorship in the St. Louis area.

However, we are convinced that reasonable men could not differ on the proposition that by late 1973 and early 1974 such a reasonable time or period had expired, and that U. S. Shoe and Pappagallo had the right to terminate their contractual relations with plaintiff entirely, which they did not do, or to cancel the exclusivity feature of plaintiff's distributorship, which they did do when they permitted SBF to open Shops for Pappagallo in its stores.

And, we are convinced that plaintiff suffered no legal wrong when U. S. Shoe and Pappagallo finally implemented a change in marketing policy which had evidently been in contemplation for some years.

It is true that plaintiff was not given any formal or written notice of what the defendants intended to do. However, it is evident that at least by late September, 1973 plaintiff had received actual notice of what was in the wind, and there is nothing to indicate that plaintiff sustained any loss or damage by the fact that it was not given formal notice. It will be remembered that the contract said nothing about termination and naturally there was no requirement of formal notice of cancellation. . . .

[Reversed.]

NOTES

(1) *Agreements without End.* Agreements that involve continuing performance sometimes fail to provide for the period over which that performance is to take place. In the case of employment agreements, the traditional response has been to regard both the employer and the employee as having the power to terminate at will. In the case of other agreements, the response has been different. Here are two classic cases.

In 1881, Dr. J. J. Lawrence granted J. W. Lambert the exclusive commercial use of the secret formula for an antiseptic known as Listerine for which Lambert bound himself and his successors "to pay monthly to the said Dr. J. J. Lawrence his heirs, executors or assigns, the sum of twenty dollars for each and every gross of said Listerine hereafter sold by myself, my heirs, executors or assigns." There was no termination date. Although the amount of the royalties was later reduced, royalties rose to a million and a half dollars a year. Gradually the formula unavoidably became a matter of public knowledge, so that by the middle of the twentieth century the same antiseptic could be produced by anyone. Warner-Lambert sought a declaratory judgment that it was no longer required to pay royalties, but the court refused "gratuitously to rewrite the contract" and held that Warner-Lambert "is obligated to make the periodic payments called for . . . as long as it continues to sell the preparation described . . . as Listerine." Warner-Lambert Pharmaceutical v. John J. Reynolds, Inc., 178 F.Supp. 655 (S.D.N.Y.1959), aff'd, 280 F.2d 197 (2d Cir. 1960); 74 Harv.L.Rev. 409 (1960). But cf. April Productions, Inc. v. G. Schirmer, Inc., 308 N.Y. 366, 126 N.E.2d 283 (1955).

In 1892, the town of Readsboro and the Deerfield River Railroad Company agreed that the expense of maintaining a bridge, which was then used for both a narrow gauge railroad and a highway, "shall be borne equally" by the two parties. There was no termination date. The bridge became too weak for standard gauge equipment, and in 1915 its use was discontinued by the railroad company. When the railroad refused to bear half the expenses of renovation and improvement, the town did the work in 1919 and sued the railroad for half the sum that it spent. The court held that although the railroad was not liable to this extent, it was liable for "one-half of that sum which in 1915 would have sufficed to put the bridge in the same condition in which it was in 1888, not including such permanent repairs as the plaintiff made in 1919." Town of Readsboro v. Hoosac Tunnel & W. R. Co., 6 F.2d 733 (2d Cir. 1925).

(2) *The Case of the Schoharie Sewage.* In 1924, the City of New York and two upstate communities made an agreement prompted by the city's desire to prevent the discharge of untreated sewage into Gooseberry Creek, which fed a reservoir of the city's water supply system in the Schoharie watershed. The city agreed to construct and maintain a sewage system and to extend the sewer lines when "necessitated by future growth and building constructions of the respective communities." The communities were to obtain the necessary easements. The plant began operation in 1928. After fifty years, the demand exceeded the plant's capacity so that it would have to be enlarged or a new one built, and the city refused to do this. At the instance of a developer, an action was brought against the city for injunctive and declaratory relief. The lower court ruled that, while the contract did not call for perpetual performance, the city was bound to construct additional facilities until the communities were legally obligated to maintain a sewage system. *Held:* Order modified. "We conclude that the city is presently obligated to maintain the existing plant but is not required to expand that plant or construct any new facilities to accommodate plaintiff's substantial, or any other, increased demands on the sewage system. . . . In the absence of an express term fixing the duration of a contract, the courts may inquire into the intent of the parties and supply the missing term if a duration may be fairly and reasonably fixed by the surrounding circumstances and the parties' intent. . . . [I]t is reasonable to infer from the circumstances of the 1924 agreement that the parties intended the city to maintain the sewage disposal facility until such time as the city no longer needed or desired the water, the purity of which the plant was designed to insure. The city argues that it is no longer obligated to maintain the plant because State law now prohibits persons from discharging raw sewage into streams such as Gooseberry Creek. However, the parties did not contemplate the passage of environmental control laws which would prohibit individuals or municipalities from discharging raw, untreated sewage into certain streams. Thus, the city agreed to assume the obligation of assuring that its water supply remained unpolluted and it may not now avoid that obligation for reasons not contemplated by the parties when the agreement was executed, and not within the purview of their intent, expressed or implied. . . . [However the] city should not be required to extend the lines to plaintiffs' property if to do so would overload the system and result in its inability to properly treat sewage. In providing for the extension of sewer lines, the contract does not obligate the city to provide sewage disposal services for properties in areas of the municipalities not presently served or even to new properties in areas which are presently served where to do so could reasonably be expected to significantly increase the demand on present plant facilities." Haines v. City of New York, 41 N.Y. 769, 396 N.Y.S.2d 155, 364 N.E.2d 820 (1977).

In its opinion, the court also mentioned that the "compelling policy reasons" that applied to employment contracts "do not obtain here." What are those reasons?

(3) *The Case of "New Unprecedented Law."* Monge, was employed as a factory worker by Beebe Rubber Company under an agreement that spec-

ified no period of time. When she was fired, she sued Beebe, claiming "that she was harassed by her foreman because she refused to go out with him and that his hostility, condoned if not shared by defendant's personnel manager, ultimately resulted in her being fired." After a verdict in her favor for $2,500, defendant's objections were reserved and transferred to the Supreme Court. *Held:* Remanded unless plaintiff consents to a reduction in the amount of $1,083.80. "The employer has long ruled the workplace with an iron hand by reason of the prevailing common-law rule that such a hiring is presumed to be at will and terminable at any time by either party. . . . When asked to reexamine the long-standing common-law rule of property based on an ancient feudal system which fostered in a tenancy at will a relationship heavily weighted in favor of the landlord, this court did not hesitate to modify that rule to conform to modern circumstances. . . . The law governing the relations between employer and employee has similarly evolved over the years to reflect changing legal, social and economic conditions. . . . In all employment contracts, whether at will or for a definite term, the employer's interest in running his business as he sees fit must be balanced against the interest of the employee in maintaining his employment, and the public's interest in maintaining a proper balance between the two. . . . We hold that a termination by the employer of a contract of employment at will which is motivated by bad faith or malice or based on retaliation is not the best interest of the economic system or the public good and constitutes a breach of the employment contract." However, $1,083.80 of the verdict appeared to be "attributable to mental suffering. Such damages are not generally recoverable in a contract action." One judge dissented, unable to "subscribe to the broad new unprecedented law laid down in this case." Monge v. Beebe Rubber Co., 114 N.H. 130, 316 A.2d 549 (1974).

COLLECTIVE BARGAINING AGREEMENTS AND TREATIES

Problems similar to those just considered are encountered in the interpretation of other kinds of legal writings, such as wills. In the case of a will, however, there is only one testator, while in the case of a contract there are two parties. More interesting analogies can be found by turning to two types of agreements that are often considered to be distinct from "ordinary" contracts: collective bargaining agreements and treaties. Here are some comments on these analogies by two experts in the respective fields.

Speaking of collective bargaining agreements and contracts, Professor Archibald Cox explains that, in the case of the former, "neither the employer nor the employees collectively have the freedom to disagree which characterizes typical contracts between business firms and individuals. . . . The compulsion . . . partially explains the gaps and deliberate ambiguities in collective bargaining agreements which create distinctive problems of interpretation. The pressure to reach an agreement is so great that the parties are willing to contract although each knows that the other places a different meaning on the words and they share only the common intent to postpone the issue and take a gamble upon an arbitrator's ruling if decision is required. . . . These consequences of the practical compulsion to sign . . . mean that interpretation must assume a more creative role than in most commercial or property litigation." Professor Cox also stresses the "governmental nature of a collective bargaining agreement [which] results partly from the number of people affected and the diversity of their interests," as well as from the fact that, "since it also operates prospectively over a long period, a labor agreement must provide for countless unforeseeable contingencies. One consequence is that many provisions of the labor agreement must be expressed in general and flexible terms. . . . One simply cannot spell out every detail of life in an industrial establishment, or even of that portion which both management and labor agree is a matter of mutual concern. . . . The governmental nature of a collective bargaining agreement should have predominant influence in its interpretation. The generalities, the deliberate ambiguities, the gaps, the unforeseen contingencies, the need for a rule although the agreement is silent—all require a creativeness quite unlike the attitude of one construing a deed or a promissory note or a three-hundred page corporate trust indenture." Professor Cox goes on to urge that, as in the case of a statute, so too with a collective bargaining agreement, "the best guide to . . . meaning is its policy or purpose." Cox, The Legal Nature of Collective Bargaining Agreements, 57 Mich.L.Rev. 1, 3–26 (1958).[a] For more on collective bargaining agreements and contracts, see Feller, A General Theory of the Collective Bargaining Agreement, 61 Calif.L.Rev. 663 (1973); Summers, Collective Agreements and the Law of Contracts, 78 Yale L.J. 525 (1969); Wellington, Labor and the Legal Process, ch. 3 (1968). See also the discussion of "good faith" bargaining at p. 346 supra.

How different is the compulsion on management and labor from, say, that on landlord and tenant negotiating a renewal of a lease? Do any of the preceding cases in this chapter involve "gaps and deliberate ambiguities" that might be explained by such compulsion? Have you encountered in this course any agreements that partake of the "governmental nature" ascribed by Professor Cox to collective bargaining agreements?

a. Professor Cox, however, also says: "The ease with which one can show that collective bargaining agreements have characteristics which preclude the application of some of the familiar principles of contracts . . . creates the danger that those who are knowledgeable about collective bargaining will demand that we discard all the precepts of contract law and create a new law of collective bargaining agreements. I have already expressed the view that courts would ignore the plea but surely it is unwise even if they would sustain it. Many legal rules have hardened into conceptual doctrines which lawyers invoke with little thought for the underlying reasons, but the doctrines themselves represent an accumulation of tested wisdom, they are bottomed upon notions of fairness and sound policy, and it would be a foolish waste to climb the ladder all over again just because the suggested principles were developed in other contexts and some of them are demonstrably inapposite." Id. at 14.

Speaking of treaties and contracts, Sir Hersch Lauterpacht found "the influence of private law on the subject of treaties" to be "considerable." He wrote, "In elucidating the intention of the parties as a matter of interpretation of treaties, the practice of States and tribunals is increasingly reverting to broad principles of private law which, in its determination to disclose the real intention of the contracting parties, refuses to be bound by rigid rules of interpretation." H. Lauterpacht, 1 International Law—Collected Papers 202–03 (1970).

Professor Abram Chayes, however, argued that "contracts analogies lead treaty lawyers astray [not only] in the orientation to judicial remedies . . ., but in positing the discrete purchase and sale as the architypal contract." The analogy afforded by the contract of sale is imperfect because the "functional setting was the impersonal market relationship of perfect competition," a setting that is not analogous to that of agreements among nations, and because the typical contract of sale is "a one-shot proposition," while a treaty is only one event in "an ongoing relationship." Chayes, "Consent and Coercion: Reflections from International Law" (Sherril Lecture at Yale Law School, 1970).

To what extent is the contract analogy misleading "in the orientation to judicial remedies"? See the excerpt at p. 276 supra, which suggests that businessmen pay little attention to those remedies. What types of contracts would you choose as more apt analogies if you were to write the rest of Professor Chayes' piece?

NOTE

The Case of the Discharged Driver. Lucas Flour and Local 174 of the Teamsters union were parties to a collective bargaining agreement which provided: "The Employer reserves the right to discharge any man in his employ if his work is not satisfactory." There was one arbitration clause which provided that "any difference . . . between the employer and the employee . . . shall be submitted to arbitration," and that the arbitrators' decision "shall be final and binding." There was also a second arbitration clause which provided for arbitration of "any difference as to the true interpretation of this agreement." In contrast to the first arbitration clause, it contained a "no-strike" clause, which provided that "during such arbitration, there shall be no suspension of work." Welsh, an employee, was discharged for unsatisfactory work after he had run a new forklift truck off a loading platform onto some railroad tracks. In an attempt to force Lucas to rehire Welsh, the union struck Lucas for eight days, until Lucas obtained an injunction and the issue of Welsh's discharge was submitted to arbitration. The arbitrator upheld Lucas, with both parties agreeing that the dispute came within the first of the two arbitration clauses quoted above. In the meantime, Lucas had sued the union for damages caused by the strike. A judgment for Lucas was affirmed by the Supreme Court of Washington, and the Supreme Court of the United States granted certiorari. *Held:* Affirmed. Justice Stewart wrote that "a strike to settle a dispute which a collective bargaining agreement provides shall be settled exclusively and finally by compulsory arbitration constitutes a violation of the agreement. . . . To hold otherwise would obviously do violence to accepted principles of traditional contract law [and] would be completely at odds with the basic policy of national labor legislation to promote the arbitral process as a substitute for economic warfare." Local 174, Teamsters, Chauffeurs, Warehousemen & Helpers of America v. Lucas Flour Co., 369 U.S. 95 (1962).

Justice Black dissented, calling attention to the difference in language in the two arbitration provisions. "[I]t seems to me plain that the parties to this contract, knowing how to write a provision binding a union not to strike, deliberately included a no-strike clause with regard to disputes over broad questions of contractual interpretation and deliberately excluded such a clause with regard to the essentially factual disputes arising out of the application of the contract in particular instances. . . . I had supposed . . . that the job of courts enforcing contracts was to give legal effect to what the contracting parties actually agreed to do, not to what courts think they ought to do. In any case, I have been unable to find any accepted principle of contract law—traditional or otherwise—that permits courts to change completely the nature of a contract by adding new promises that the parties themselves refused to make in order that the new court-made contract might better fit into whatever social, economic, or legal policies the courts believe to be so important that they should have been taken out of the realm of voluntary contract by the legislative body and furthered by compulsory legislation. . . . Both parties to collective bargaining discussions have much at stake as to whether there will be a no-strike clause in any resulting agreement. It is difficult to believe that the desire of employers to get such a promise and the desire of the union to avoid giving it are matters which are not constantly in the minds of those who negotiate these contracts. In such a setting, to hold—on the basis of no evidence whatever—that a union, without knowing it, impliedly surrendered the right to strike by virtue of 'traditional contract law' or anything else is to me just fiction."

In support of Justice Black, see Wellington, Freedom of Contract and the Collective Bargaining Agreement, 112 U.Pa.L.Rev. 467, 484–87 (1964). Which result would Professor Cox favor? Do "accepted principles of traditional contract law" compel a decision in favor of Lucas?

COLUMBIA NITROGEN CORP. v. ROYSTER CO.

United States Court of Appeals, Fourth Circuit, 1971.
451 F.2d 3.

BUTZNER, Circuit Judge. Columbia Nitrogen Corp. appeals a judgment in the amount of $750,000 in favor of F. S. Royster Guano Co. for breach of a contract for the sale of phosphate to Columbia by Royster. Columbia defended on the grounds that the contract, construed in light of the usage of the trade and course of dealing, imposed no duty to accept at the quoted prices the minimum quantities stated in the contract. . . . The district court excluded the evidence about course of dealing and usage of the trade. . . . The jury found for Royster . . . . . We hold that Columbia's proffered evidence was improperly excluded and Columbia is entitled to a new trial. . . .

I.

Royster manufactures and markets mixed fertilizers, the principal components of which are nitrogen, phosphate and potash. Columbia is primarily a producer of nitrogen, although it manufactures some mixed fertilizer. For several years Royster had been a major purchaser of Columbia's products, but Columbia had never been a significant customer of Royster. In the fall of 1966, Royster constructed a facility which enabled it to produce more phosphate than it needed in its own operations. After extensive negotiations, the companies executed a contract for Royster's sale of a minimum of 31,000 tons of phosphate each year for three years to Columbia, with an option to extend the term. The contract stated the price per ton, subject to an escalation clause dependent on production costs.[1]

1. In pertinent part, the contract provides:

"Contract made as of this 8th day of May between COLUMBIA NITROGEN CORPORATION, a Delaware corporation, (hereinafter called the Buyer) hereby agrees to purchase and accept from F. S. ROYSTER GUANO COMPANY, a Virginia corporation, (hereinafter called the Seller) agrees to furnish quantities of Diammonium Phosphate 18–46–0, Granular Triple Superphosphate 0–46–0, and Run-of-Pile Triple Superphosphate 0–46–0 on the following terms and conditions.

"*Period Covered by Contract*—This contract to begin July 1, 1967, and continue through June 30, 1970, with renewal privileges for an additional three year period based upon notification by Buyer and acceptance by Seller on or before June 30, 1969. Failure of notification by either party on or before June 30, 1969, constitutes an automatic renewal for an additional one-year period beyond June 30, 1970, and on a year-to-year basis thereafter unless notification of cancellation is given by either party 90 days prior to June 30 of each year.

"*Products Supplied Under Contract*

	Minimum Tonnage Per Year
"Diammonium Phosphate 18–46–0	15,000
Granular Triple Superphosphate 0–46–0	15,000
Run-of-Pile Triple Superphosphate 0–46–0	1,000

"Seller agrees to provide additional quantities beyond the minimum specified tonnage for products listed above provided Seller has the capacity and ability to provide such additional quantities.

. . .

"*Price*—In Bulk F.O.B. Cars, Royster, Florida.

Diammonium Phosphate 18–46–0	$61.25 Per Ton
Granular Triple Superphosphate 0–46–0	$40.90 Per Ton
Run-of-Pile Triple Superphosphate 0–46–0	$0.86 Per Unit

. . .

"*Default*—If Buyer fails to pay for any delivery under this contract within 30 days after Seller's invoice to Buyer and then if such invoice is not paid within an additional 30 days after the Seller notifies the Buyer of such default, then after that time the Seller may at his option defer further deliveries hereunder or take such action as in their judgment they may decide including cancellation of this contract. Any balances carried beyond 30 days will carry a service fee of ¾ of 1% per month.

. . .

"*Escalation*—The escalation factor up or down shall be based upon the effects of changing raw material cost of sulphur, rock phos-

Phosphate prices soon plunged precipitously. Unable to resell the phosphate at a competitive price, Columbia ordered only part of the scheduled tonnage. At Columbia's request, Royster lowered its price for diammonium phosphate on shipments for three months in 1967, but specified that subsequent shipments would be at the original contract price. Even with this concession, Royster's price was still substantially above the market. As a result, Columbia ordered less than a tenth of the phosphate Royster was to ship in the first contract year. When pressed by Royster, Columbia offered to take the phosphate at the current market price and resell it without brokerage fee. Royster, however, insisted on the contract price. When Columbia refused delivery, Royster sold the unaccepted phosphate for Columbia's account at a price substantially below the contract price.

II.

Columbia assigns error to the pretrial ruling of the district court excluding all evidence on usage of the trade and course of dealing between the parties. It offered the testimony of witnesses with long experience in the trade that because of uncertain crop and weather conditions, farming practices, and government agricultural programs, express price and quantity terms in contracts for materials in the mixed fertilizer industry are mere projections to be adjusted according to market forces.[2]

phate, and labor as follows. These escalations up or down to become effective against shipments of products covered by this contract 30 days after notification by Seller to Buyer.

. . . .

"No verbal understanding will be recognized by either party hereto; this contract expresses all the terms and conditions of the agreement, shall be signed in duplicate and shall not become operative until approved in writing by the Seller."

2. Typical of the proffered testimony are the following excerpts:

¶ "The contracts generally entered into between buyer and seller of materials has always been, in my opinion, construed to be the buyer's best estimate of his anticipated requirements for a given period of time. It is well known in our industry that weather conditions, farming practices, government farm control programs, change requirements from time to time. And therefore allowances were always made to meet these circumstances as they arose."

¶ "Tonnage requirements fluctuate greatly, and that is one reason that the contracts are not considered as binding as most contracts are, because the buyer normally would buy on historical basis, but his normal average use would be per annum of any given material. Now that can be affected very decidedly by adverse weather conditions such as a drought, or a flood, or maybe governmental programs which we have been faced with for many, many years, seed grain programs. They pay the farmer not to plant. If he doesn't plant, he doesn't use the fertilizer. When the contracts are made, we do not know of all these contingencies and what they are going to be. So the contract is made for what is considered a fair estimate of his requirements. And, the contract is considered binding to the extent, on him morally, that if he uses the tonnage that he will execute the contract in good faith as the buyer. . . . "

¶ "I have never heard of a contract of this type being enforced legally. . . . Well, it undoubtedly sounds ridiculous to people from other industries, but there is a very definite, several very definite

Columbia also offered proof of its business dealings with Royster over the six-year period preceding the phosphate contract. Since Columbia had not been a significant purchaser of Royster's products, these dealings were almost exclusively nitrogen sales to Royster or exchanges of stock carried in inventory. The pattern which emerges, Columbia claimed, is one of repeated and substantial deviation from the stated amount or price, including four instances where Royster took none of the goods for which it had contracted. Columbia offered proof that the total variance amounted to more than $500,000 in reduced sales. This experience, a Columbia officer offered to testify, formed the basis of an understanding on which he depended in conducting negotiations with Royster.

The district court held that the evidence should be excluded. It ruled that "custom and usage or course of dealing are not admissible to contradict the express, plain, unambiguous language of a valid written contract, which by virtue of its detail negates the proposition that the contract is open to variances in its terms. . . . ."

A number of Virginia cases have held that extrinsic evidence may not be received to explain or supplement a written contract unless the court finds the writing is ambiguous. E. g., Mathieson Alkali Works v. Virginia Banner Coal Corp., 147 Va. 125, 136 S.E. 673 (1927). This rule, however, has been changed by the Uniform Commercial Code which Virginia has adopted. The Code expressly states that it "shall be liberally construed and applied to promote its underlying purposes and policies," which include "the continued expansion of commercial practices through custom, usage and agreement of the parties . . . ." Va.Code Ann. § 8.1–102 (1965). The importance of usage of trade and course of dealing between the parties is shown by § 8.2–202, which authorizes their use to explain or supplement a contract. The official comment states this section rejects the old rule that evidence of course of dealing or usage of trade can be introduced only when the contract is ambiguous.[3] And the Virginia commentators, noting that "[t]his section reflects a more liberal approach to the introduction of parol evidence . . . . than has been followed in Virginia," express the opinion that *Mathieson*, supra, and

reasons why the fertilizer business is always operated under what we call gentlemen's agreements. . . ."

¶ "The custom in the fertilizer industry is that the seller either meets the competitive situation or releases the buyer from it upon proof that he can buy it at that price. . . . [T]hey will either have the option of meeting it or releasing him from taking additional tonnage or holding him to that price. . . ."

¶ And this custom exists "regardless of the contractual provisions."

¶ "[T]he custom was that [these contracts] were not worth the cost of the paper they were printed on."

3. Va.Code Ann, § 8.2–202, Comment 1 states:

"This section definitely rejects:

. . . .

"(c) The requirement that a condition precedent to the admissibility of the type of evidence specified in paragraph (a) is an original determination by the court that the language used is ambiguous."

similar Virginia cases no longer should be followed. Va. Code Ann. § 8.2–202, Va. Comment. See also Portsmouth Gas Co. v. Shebar, 209 Va. 250, 253 n. 1, 163 S.E.2d 205, 208 n. 1 (1968) (dictum). We hold, therefore, that a finding of ambiguity is not necessary for the admission of extrinsic evidence about the usage of the trade and the parties' course of dealing.

We turn next to Royster's claim that Columbia's evidence was properly excluded because it was inconsistent with the express terms of their agreement. There can be no doubt that the Uniform Commercial Code restates the well established rule that evidence of usage of trade and course of dealing should be excluded whenever it cannot be reasonably construed as consistent with the terms of the contract. Division of Triple T Service, Inc. v. Mobil Oil Corp., 60 Misc.2d 720, 304 N.Y.S.2d 191, 203 (1969), aff'd mem., 311 N.Y.S.2d 961 (1970). Royster argues that the evidence should be excluded as inconsistent because the contract contains detailed provisions regarding the base price, escalation, minimum tonnage, and delivery schedules. The argument is based on the premise that because a contract appears on its face to be complete, evidence of course of dealing and usage of trade should be excluded. We believe, however, that neither the language nor the policy of the Code supports such a broad exclusionary rule. Section 8.2–202 expressly allows evidence of course of dealing or usage of trade to explain or supplement terms intended by the parties as a final expression of their agreement. When this section is read in light of Va. Code Ann. § 8.1–205(4), it is clear that the test of admissibility is not whether the contract appears on its face to be complete in every detail, but whether the proffered evidence of course of dealing and trade usage reasonably can be construed as consistent with the express terms of the agreement.

The proffered testimony sought to establish that because of changing weather conditions, farming practices, and government agricultural programs, dealers adjusted prices, quantities, and delivery schedules to reflect declining market conditions. For the following reasons it is reasonable to construe this evidence as consistent with the express terms of the contract:

The contract does not expressly state that course of dealing and usage of trade cannot be used to explain or supplement the written contract.

The contract is silent about adjusting prices and quantities to reflect a declining market. It neither permits nor prohibits adjustment, and this neutrality provides a fitting occasion for recourse to usage of trade and prior dealing to supplement the contract and explain its terms.

Minimum tonnages and additional quantities are expressed in terms of "Products Supplied Under Contract." Significantly, they are not expressed as just "Products" or as "Products Purchased Under Contract." The description used by the parties is consistent with the proffered testimony.

Finally, the default clause of the contract refers only to the failure of the buyer to pay for delivered phosphate.[4] During the contract negotiations, Columbia rejected a Royster proposal for liquidated damages of $10 for each ton Columbia declined to accept. On the other hand, Royster rejected a Columbia proposal for a clause that tied the price to the market by obligating Royster to conform its price to offers Columbia received from other phosphate producers. The parties, having rejected both proposals, failed to state any consequences of Columbia's refusal to take delivery—the kind of default Royster alleges in this case. Royster insists that we span this hiatus by applying the general law of contracts permitting recovery of damages upon the buyer's refusal to take delivery according to the written provisions of the contract. This solution is not what the Uniform Commercial Code prescribes. Before allowing damages, a court must first determine whether the buyer has in fact defaulted. It must do this by supplementing and explaining the agreement with evidence of trade usage and course of dealing that is consistent with the contract's express terms. Va.Code Ann. §§ 8.1–205(4), 8.2–202. Faithful adherence to this mandate reflects the reality of the marketplace and avoids the overly legalistic interpretations which the Code seeks to abolish.

Royster also contends that Columbia's proffered testimony was properly rejected because it dealt with mutual willingness of buyer and seller to adjust contract terms to the market. Columbia, Royster protests, seeks unilateral adjustment. This argument misses the point. What Columbia seeks to show is a practice of mutual adjustments so prevalent in the industry and in prior dealings between the parties that it formed a part of the agreement governing this transaction. It is not insisting on a unilateral right to modify the contract.

Nor can we accept Royster's contention that the testimony should be excluded under the contract clause: "No verbal understanding will be recognized by either party hereto; this contract expresses all the terms and conditions of the agreement, shall be signed in duplicate, and shall not become operative until approved in writing by the Seller." Course of dealing and trade usage are not synonymous with verbal understandings, terms and conditions. Section 8.2–202 draws a distinction between supplementing a written contract by consistent additional terms and supplementing it by course of dealing or usage of trade. Evidence of additional terms must be excluded when "the court finds the writing to have been intended also as a complete and exclusive statement of the terms of the agreement." Significantly, no similar limitation is placed on the introduction of evidence of course of dealing or usage of trade. Indeed the official comment notes that course of dealing and usage of trade, unless carefully ne-

4. The default clause is set forth at note 1, supra.

gated, are admissible to supplement the terms of any writing, and that contracts are to be read on the assumption that these elements were taken for granted when the document was phrased.[5] Since the Code assigns course of dealing and trade usage unique and important roles, they should not be conclusively rejected by reading them into stereotyped language that makes no specific reference to them. Cf. Provident Tradesmens Bank & Trust Co. v. Pemberton, 196 Pa.Super. 180, 173 A.2d 780 (1961). Indeed, the Code's official commentators urge that overly simplistic and overly legalistic interpretation of a contract should be shunned.[6]

We conclude, therefore, that Columbia's evidence about course of dealing and usage of trade should have been admitted. Its exclusion requires that the judgment against Columbia must be set aside and the case retried. . . .

The judgment for Royster on the contract is vacated, and the case is remanded for further proceedings consistent with this opinion. . . .

NOTES

(1) *Questions.* Is this a case, like Hurst v. Lake, p. 708 supra, in which usage is used, in the words of UCC 1–205(3) to "give particular meaning to . . . terms of an agreement"? To "supplement" those terms? To "qualify" them? (If the purpose is interpretation, what language is being interpreted?)

(2) *Usage and Omitted Cases.* Look back at the Baird and Drennan cases, pp. 315, 318 supra. Could a general contractor use usage of trade to show that a subcontractor's bid, which was silent as to revocability, was irrevocable? What facts would be sufficient to establish such a usage?

5. Va.Code Ann. § 8.2–202, Comment 2 states:

"Paragraph (a) [of § 8.202] makes admissible evidence of course of dealing, usage of trade and course of performance to explain or supplement the terms of any writing stating the agreement of the parties in order that the true understanding of the parties as to the agreement may be reached. Such writings are to be read on the assumption that the course of prior dealings between the parties and the usages of trade were taken for granted when the document was phrased. Unless carefully negated they have become an element of the meaning of the words used. Similarly, the course of actual performance by the parties is considered the best indication of what they intended the writing to mean."

See also Levie, Trade Usage and Custom under the Common Law and the Uniform Commercial Code, 40 N.Y.U.L.Rev. 1101, 1111 (1965).

6. Referring to the general provisions about course of dealing and trade usage, Va.Code Ann. § 8.1–205, Comment 1 states:

"This Act rejects both the 'lay dictionary' and the 'conveyancer's' reading of a commercial agreement. Instead the meaning of the agreement of the parties is to be determined by the language used by them and by their action, read and interpreted in the light of commercial practices and other surrounding circumstances. The measure and background for interpretation are set by the commercial context, which may explain and supplement even the language of a formal or final writing."

See Albert v. R. P. Farnsworth & Co., 176 F.2d 198 (5th Cir. 1949); cf. Industrial Electric-Seattle v. Bosko, 67 Wash.2d 783, 410 P.2d 10 (1966).

For a suggestion of the role that usages might play in consumer claims, see Carroll, Harpooning Whales . . ., 12 B.C.Ind. & Com.L.Rev. 139, 166 (1970).

(3) *The Case of the Cantor Who Wouldn't.* Fisher, an orthodox Jewish rabbi-cantor, contracted in writing with an orthodox Jewish congregation to officiate as cantor at its snyagogue at the time when the congregation conducted its services in accordance with orthodox practices, including the separate seating of men and women. The contract, however, was silent as to the orthodox character of the congregation and its seating practices. Shortly thereafter, on the eve of moving into a new synagogue, the congregation determined to modify its practice of separate seating by setting aside the first four rows for men, the next four rows for women, and the remainder for mixed seating. When Fisher was informed of this, he notified the congregation that he would be unable to officiate during the coming season because to do so would be a violation of his beliefs. When the congregation refused to change its decision, he sued for breach of contract. Three rabbis testified on his behalf that orthodox Judaism required the separation of the sexes in the synagogue and that an orthodox rabbi-cantor could not conscientiously officiate in a synagogue that violated this law. From judgment for the plaintiff, the defendant appealed. *Held:* Affirmed. "[T]he ancient provision of the Hebrew law relating to separate seating is read into the contract only because implicit in the writing as to the basis—according to the evidence—upon which the parties dealt. . . . In our law the provision became a part of the written contract under a principle analogous to the rule applicable to the construction of contracts in the light of custom or immemorial and invariable usage. . . . From the findings of the trial judge supported by the evidence it is clear that the parties contracted on the common understanding that the defendant was an orthodox synagogue which observed the mandate of the Jewish law as to separate seating. That intention was implicit in this contract though not referred to in the writing, and therefore must be read into it." Fisher v. Congregation B'Nai Yitzhok, 177 Pa.Super. 359, 110 A.2d 881 (1955).[a]

(4) *The Case of the Cantor Who Couldn't.* Richard Tucker, the renowned opera singer and cantor, was engaged to conduct the 1964 Passover Seder at the Eden Roc Hotel in Miami Beach under a standard American Guild of Variety Artists form for the first Seder Service, with the typewritten provision: "If second Seder service to be held, same price as first night." He performed the first service but, although the second service had been advertised nationally and he had hired a choir and turned down other engagements, he was told by a waiter at the end of the first service and without further explanation that there would be no second service. He sued for breach of contract, and was denied recovery for the second night. He

a. In Congregation B'Nai Sholom v. Martin, 382 Mich. 659, 173 N.W.2d 504 (1969), the court held that persons who had signed pledge cards in connection with a fund-raising drive to build a new synagogue "should have been permitted to assert, as a defense, their claim as to the custom of their religion which requires disputes between the synagogue and its members over religious matters to be resolved according to Jewish law," including a prohibition on a law suit in a nonreligious court before resort is had to a religious court.

appealed. *Held:* Affirmed. The court quoted "the Passover Haggadah itself—'Wherein is this night different from all other nights?' For purposes of our legal analysis, this may be paraphrased to be: Wherein is a contract for the performance of a Passover Seder different from all other contracts? . . . We first consider whether a different result might have been reached had the controversy been resolved by construing the agreement in light of prevailing religious custom. Although Tucker testified that in the Orthodox Jewish religion two Sedarim are always held, the period of observance is, for us at least, a problematical one. Owing to the unsettled state of the Jewish calendar in olden times, Passover was celebrated for seven days in Palestine and eight days elsewhere. This meant that those outside of Palestine (now Israel) conducted two Sedarim, while those in Palestine conducted only one. The Reform Jews in America today have adopted the latter procedure and observe but one Seder. It appears that while Tucker may have been Orthodox in his observance, the Eden Roc had traditionally followed the Reform view and had only one Seder in each year prior to 1964. We cannot therefore treat the instant agreement as different from any other agreement, and must look to the common, every day principles of law to resolve the dispute." The court decided that the trial court had not erred in concluding that there was no legally binding contract for the second Seder. Tucker v. Forty-Five Twenty-Five, 199 So. 2d 522 (Fla.App.1967).

Chapter 8

PERFORMANCE AND BREACH

An exchange of promises will lead to an exchange of performances, in the ordinary course of affairs. One who has committed himself in exchange for a return performance is entitled, as stated in a Code comment, to "a continuing sense of reliance and security that the promised performance will be forthcoming when due."[a] In the Restatement Second a close connection is noticed between this principle and the duty of good faith and fair dealing in the performance of a contract.[b] Much detail in the law of contract is understandable only with reference to the principle that a party's fair expectation of performance deserves protection. One means of protection is to afford him an immediate remedy as for breach when that expectation is impaired in a certain way. Hence in this chapter we pursue further the matter of damages, building on a preceding chapter. But there are other means of at least equal importance for assuring a party's expectations, such as permitting him to defer or withhold his own performance when a threat of a certain order arises that he will not receive what he was promised in exchange. Protection in this form is generally described in the language of condition.

Section 1 considers what a party may do to establish a condition, basing himself on an expression used or to be used in his agreement. It will be seen that the parties have wide liberties both to shape their commitments and to protect their expectations through suitable use of the language of conditions. Section 2 offers a conspectus of means the law provides for these purposes. It features the idea of an implied or "constructive" condition as a natural inference from an exchange of promises. It treats also of a party's right to be assured that due performance will be forthcoming and of the effects of the wrongful action known as repudiation. Various types of breach are illustrated, together with the responses permissible to the injured party.

A different sort of expectation arises when a contracting party has invested substantially in his performance, expending labor, materials, or the like. If he fails after all to meet his commitment, does he lose all under the doctrine of constructive conditions? The answer is compounded of many elements. Section 3 considers the possibility of restitutionary relief. Section 4, focussing on construction contracts, develops the doctrine of substantial performance. Problems of performance and breach associated with sale contracts, some concerning goods and others concerning land, are grouped in Section 5.

a. UCC 2–609, Comment 1.

b. Section 251, Comment *a*.

SECTION 1. CONDITIONS

Thus far, this book has been largely concerned with the imposition and enforcement of *duties*. What follows deals mainly with how duties are qualified by being subjected to the occurrence of *conditions*. According to Restatement Second, § 224, "A condition is an event, not certain to occur, which must occur, unless its nonoccurrence is excused, before performance under a contract becomes due." [a]

Our present interest is with the interpretation of language relating to such events.[b] Two sorts of questions arise. First, does the language make the occurrence of an event a condition? And second, if it does make the occurrence of an event a condition, what is the nature of that event? We turn to the first of these questions.

In most doubtful cases the alternative interpretation is that the language is that of promise, used to impose a duty. The first question therefore usually takes the form: Does the language impose a duty that the event occur or does it make the occurrence of the event a condition?

The significance of this question derives from the fact that the two most common contractual devices by which an obligor may attempt to induce an obligee to do an act are, first, by having the obligee undertake a duty to do it and, second, by making the obligee's doing of the act a condition of the obligor's duty.[c] Here is an example based on the venerable case of Constable v. Cloberie, Palmer 397, 81 Eng.Rep. 1141 (K.B.1626).

A cargo owner desires a ship owner to sail from England to Cadiz and back carrying his cargo. This the ship owner agrees to do in return for the cargo owner's promise to pay freight. In addition, the cargo owner wants the ship owner to sail with the next wind. To in-

a. Comment *a* to § 224 adds that sometimes the word "is used to refer to a term . . . in an agreement that makes an event a condition, or more broadly to refer to any term in an agreement (e. g., 'standard conditions of sale')."

b. If the event is fortuitous, i. e., not within the power of the parties, the promise is sometimes said to be "aleatory."

c. They are not the only devices used for this purpose. Another is the "unilateral" offer in which, for example, A attempts to induce B to walk across the Brooklyn Bridge by saying, "I will give you $100 if you walk across the Brooklyn Bridge." See p. 305 supra. It would, to be sure, be possible to call walking across the bridge a "condition" of A's promise, even though it is also the acceptance of A's offer, but the term is not ordinarily used in this broad sense. According to Comment c to Restatement Second, § 224: "Events which must occur before there is a contract, such as offer and acceptance, are . . . excluded under the definition in this section. It is not customary to call such events conditions. . . . For the most part, they are required by law and may not be dispensed with by the parties, while conditions are the result of, or at least subject to, agreement."

duce the ship owner to do this, he can have the ship owner undertake a duty to sail with the next wind, or can make sailing with the next wind a condition of his own duty to pay the freight, or can do both. The consequences will, however, be different in each case.

Suppose that he has the ship owner undertake a duty to sail with the next wind. If the ship owner delays in sailing, the cargo owner can recover any damages caused by the ship owner's breach of duty, but will not be excused from his own duty to pay the freight.[d]

Suppose that he makes sailing with the next wind a condition of his own duty to pay the freight. If the ship owner delays in sailing, the cargo owner can not recover damages but will be excused from his own duty to pay the freight.

Suppose that he does both.[e] If the ship owner delays in sailing, the cargo owner can recover damages caused by the ship owner's breach of duty *and* will be excused from his own duty to pay the freight. (In calculating damages, however, the court will have to take account of the fact that the cargo owner will not have to pay the freight. See p. 567 supra.)

What are the relative advantages to the cargo owner of these three solutions? Plainly the third, which gives him the advantages of both the first two, would be the best. But how much better is it, assuming that freight rates vary according to the relative disadvantage to the ship owner? As between the first two solutions, what are the relative advantages to the cargo owner?

NOTES

(1) *Drafting.* Assume that the contract begins: "In consideration of Ship Owner's promise to sail to Cadiz and return with cargo, Cargo Owner promises to pay freight at [a specified rate]." Draft clauses to follow which would make sailing with the next wind: (1) a duty of Ship Owner; (2) a condition of Cargo Owner's duty; (3) both a duty of Ship Owner and a condition of Cargo Owner's duty.[f]

(2) *Conditions "Precedent" and "Subsequent".* "Parties sometimes provide that the occurrence of an event, such as the failure of one of them to commence an action within a prescribed time, will extinguish a duty after performance has become due, along with any claim for breach. Such an

d. This ignores the impact of the doctrine of "constructive conditions of exchange," which is taken up in the next section.

e. Corbin uses the term "promissory condition" to describe this case. 3A Corbin, § 633.

f. Those with a penchant for law French may find assistance in the facts of the actual case. The cargo owner covenanted to pay freight "si le niefe [ship] va le intended voyage [to Cadiz], & retorn." The ship owner covenanted that his ship would go with "le prochien vent," and the cargo owner denied that it did so, and refused to pay the freight. The ship owner sued, and the cargo owner's plea was held bad on demurrer, "car le substance del covenant . . . est que le niefe vaera le voyage, & ceo fuit primary intention del parties." Sailing with the next wind was not a condition to the plaintiff's right to the freight. The case is discussed in 3A Corbin, § 633.

event has often been called a 'condition subsequent' while an event of the kind defined in this section has been called a 'condition precedent.'" Comment *e* to Restatement Second, § 224. The Restatement Second abandons the term "condition subsequent" and deals with such events in § 230, Event That Terminates a Duty. It calls a "condition precedent" simply a "condition."

(3) *Significance for Procedure.* The terms "conditions precedent" and "conditions subsequent" have a significance in the law of procedure that is independent of their significance, or lack of it, in the law of contracts. "The elements of a cause of action or claim for breach of contract are these: (1) a contract or agreement involving a quid pro quo (or the presence of some other factor which under substantive law makes an agreement binding); (2) performance by plaintiff of all conditions precedent to be performed by him; and (3) breach of the contract by defendant." F. James and G. Hazard, Civil Procedure § 3.12 (2d ed. 1977). See also Cleary, Presuming and Pleading, 12 Stan.L.Rev. 5 (1959).

With respect to the second of these, the plaintiff's burden of pleading is commonly eased by statutes and rules of court which permit him to allege generally that all conditions have occurred. For example, Rule 9(c) of the Federal Rules of Civil Procedure provides: "In pleading the performance or occurrence of conditions precedent, it is sufficient to aver generally that all conditions precedent have been performed or have occurred." The defendant may prove that the allegation is not true only if he pleads facts showing the failure to perform. For example, Rule 9(c) continues: "A denial of performance or occurrence shall be made specifically and with particularity."

It is commonly said that although the burden of proof as well as of pleading is on the plaintiff as to "conditions precedent," these burdens are on the defendant as to "conditions subsequent." The distinction between conditions "precedent" and "subsequent" for this purpose is not, however, a matter of substantive contract law but of civil procedure and is best left to a course in that field. See F. James and G. Hazard, Civil Procedure § 7.8 (2d ed. 1977).

PEACOCK CONSTR. CO. v. MODERN AIR CONDITIONING, INC.

Supreme Court of Florida, 1977.
353 So.2d 840.

BOYD, Acting Chief Justice. We issued an order allowing certiorari in these two causes because the decisions in them of the District Court of Appeal, Second District, conflict with the decision in Edward J. Gerrits, Inc. v. Astor Electric Service, Inc., 328 So.2d 522 (Fla.3d DCA 1976). The two causes have been consolidated for all appellate purposes is this Court because they involve the same issue. That issue is whether the plaintiffs, Modern Air Conditioning and Overly Manufacturing, were entitled to summary judgments against Peacock Construction Company in actions for breaches of identical contractual provisions.

Peacock Construction was the builder of a condominium project. Modern Air Conditioning subcontracted with Peacock to do the heating and air conditioning work and Overly Manufacturing subcontracted with Peacock to do the "rooftop swimming pool" work. Both written subcontracts provided that Peacock would make final payment to the subcontractors,

"within 30 days after the completion of the work included in this sub-contract, written acceptance by the Architect and full payment therefor by the Owner."

Modern Air Conditioning and Overly Manufacturing completed the work specified in their contracts and requested final payment. When Peacock refused to make the final payments the two subcontractors separately brought actions in the Lee County Circuit Court for breach of contract. In both actions it was established that no deficiencies had been found in the completed work. But Peacock established that it had not received from the owner [1] full payment for the subcontractors' work. And it defended on the basis that such payment was a condition which, by express term of the final payment provision, had to be fulfilled before it was obligated to perform under the contract. On motions by the plaintiffs, the trial judges granted summary judgments in their favor. The orders of judgment implicitly interpreted the contract not to require payment by the owner as a condition precedent to Peacock's duty to perform.

The Second District Court of Appeal affirmed the lower court's judgment in the appeal brought by Modern Air Conditioning. In so doing it adopted the view of the majority of jurisdictions in this country that provisions of the kind disputed here do not set conditions precedent but rather constitute absolute promises to pay, fixing payment by the owner as a reasonable time for when payment to the subcontractor is to be made. When the judgment in the *Overly Manufacturing* case reached the Second District Court, *Modern Air Conditioning* had been decided and the judgment, therefore was affirmed on the authority of the latter decision. These two decisions plainly conflict with *Gerrits,* supra.

In *Gerrits,* the Court had summarily ordered judgment for the plaintiff/subcontractor against the defendant/general contractor on a contractual provision for payment to the subcontractor which read,

> The money to be paid in current funds and at such times as the General Contractor receives it from the Owner. Id. at 523.

In its review of the judgment, the Third District Court of Appeal referred to the fundamental rule of interpretation of contracts that it be done in accordance with the intention of the parties. Since the defendant had introduced below the issue of intention, a material issue, and since the issue was one that could be resolved through a factual

1. The owner, a corporation, had entered proceedings in bankruptcy.

determination by the jury, the Third District reversed the summary judgment and remanded for trial.

Peacock urges us to adopt *Gerrits* as the controlling law in this State. It concedes that the Second District's decisions are backed by the weight of authority. But it argues that they are incorrect because the issue of intention is a factual one which should be resolved after the parties have had an opportunity to present evidence on it. *Peacock* urges, therefore, that the causes be remanded for trial. If there is produced no evidence that the parties intended there be condition precedents, only then, says *Peacock*, should the judge, by way of a directed verdict for the subcontractors, be allowed to take the issue of intention from the jury.

The contractual provisions in dispute here are susceptible to two interpretations. They may be interpreted as setting a condition precedent or as fixing a reasonable time for payment. The provision disputed in *Gerrits* is susceptible to the same two interpretations. The questions presented by the conflict between these decisions, then, are whether ambiguous contractual provisions of the kind disputed here may be interpreted only by the factfinder, usually the jury, or if they should be interpreted as a matter of law by the court, and if so what interpretation they should be given.

Although it must be admitted that the meaning of language is a factual question, the general rule is that interpretation of a document is a question of law rather than of fact. 4 Williston on Contracts, 3rd Ed., § 616. If an issue of contract interpretation concerns the intention of parties, that intention may be determined from the written contract, as a matter of law, when the nature of the transaction lends itself to judicial interpretation. A number of courts, with whom we agree, have recognized that contracts between small subcontractors and general contractors on large construction projects are such transactions. Cf. Thos. J. Dyer Co. v. Bishop International Engineering Co., 6 Cir., 303 F.2d 655 (1965). The reason is that the relationship between the parties is a common one and usually their intent will not differ from transaction to transaction, although it may be differently expressed.

That intent in most cases is that payment by the owner to the general contractor is not a condition precedent to the general contractor's duty to pay the subcontractors. This is because small subcontractors, who must have payment for their work in order to remain in business, will not ordinarily assume the risk of the owner's failure to pay the general contractor. And this is the reason for the majority view in this country, which we now join.

Our decision to require judicial interpretation of ambiguous provisions for final payment in subcontracts in favor of subcontractors should not be regarded as anti-general contractor. It is simply a recognition that this is the fairest way to deal with the problem. There is nothing in this opinion, however, to prevent parties to these contracts from shifting the risk of payment failure by the owner to the subcontractor. But in order to make such a shift the contract must unambiguously express that intention. And the burden of clear expression is on the general contractor.

The decisions of the Second District Court of Appeal to affirm the summary judgments were correct. We adopt, therefore, these two decisions as the controlling law in Florida and we overrule *Gerrits*, to the extent it is inconsistent with this opinion.

The orders allowing certiorari in these two causes are discharged. It is so ordered.

NOTES

(1) *Condition or Not?* Can you draft a clause that would "unambiguously" shift to the subcontractor the risk of the owner's failure to pay? Was this a controversy over whether the occurrence of an event was made a condition or over the nature of such an event? Can you explain the exclusion in Restatement Second, § 224 of events "not certain to occur"?

(2) *Brokers and Conditions.* In Amies v. Wesnofske, 255 N.Y. 156, 174 N.E. 436 (1931), a seller of land made a contract with the brokers who had arranged its sale. Under this contract the seller agreed "to pay for their services in bringing about such sale the sum of Five Thousand ($5,000) Dollars, one-half of which is paid this date and the balance to be paid on the closing of title." When the buyers failed to go through with the sale because of lack of funds, the seller kept $10,000 that the buyer had already paid on the total price of $124,000, but refused to pay the brokers the remaining $2,500. In holding that the seller was not obligated to do so, the court stated: "The employment of such words 'when,' 'after,' or 'as soon as,' clearly indicate that a promise is not to be performed except upon a condition . . . . We think that reason and authority compel the conclusion that we have here a promise to pay a broker upon a condition which has not been fulfilled."

Is the situation of the broker distinguishable from that of the subcontractor?

(3) *Problem.* A printed form of a contract for sale supplied by a real estate broker provided that the seller would pay the broker a stated commission "which commission is earned by agent when this agreement is signed by both parties [seller and buyer]." A typewritten sentence was added at the bottom: "Seller agrees to pay the agent at the consummation of sale the amount of the commission in cash." The agreement was signed by seller and buyer, but the sale was never consummated because the buyer refused to take title. Must the seller pay the broker the commission? See Kuhn v. Stan A. Plauche Real Estate Co., 249 La. 85, 185 So.2d 210 (1966).

MASCIONI v. I. B. MILLER, INC., 261 N.Y. 1, 184 N.E. 473 (1933). [Mascioni, a subcontractor, made a contract with Miller, a general contractor, for the erection of concrete walls as required by

Miller's contract with Village Apartments. The contract between Mascioni and Miller provided, "Payments to be made as received from Owner." When Village Apartments failed to pay Miller, Miller refused to pay Mascioni, and Mascioni sued Miller. Miller appealed from a judgment of the Appellate Division reversing a judgment of the trial court in his favor.]

LEHMAN, J. . . . The problem presented on this appeal is whether the defendant assumed an absolute obligation to pay, though for convenience payment might be postponed till moneys were received from the Owner, or whether the defendant's obligation to pay arose only if and when the Owner made payment to the defendant. At the trial the plaintiffs, claiming that the contract was ambiguous, were permitted to introduce testimony to show that before the written contract was signed, much of the work had been performed under an oral contract by which the defendant assumed an absolute obligation to pay; and the defendant, though claiming that the written contract, in unambiguous terms, annexed a contingency to the defendant's obligation to pay, produced parol testimony to show that the plaintiffs expressly assumed the risk that they might never be paid.[a] A judgment in favor of the defendant was reversed by the Appellate Division on the ground that the contract is unambiguous and that the provision with respect to payment "merely fixed the time of payment and did not create a condition precedent." . . .

Here on its face the contract provides for a promise to perform in exchange for a promise to pay as payments are "received from the Owner." Performance by the plaintiff would enure directly to the benefit of the Owner and indirectly to the benefit of the defendant, because the defendant had a contract with the Owner to perform the work for a stipulated price. The defendant would not profit by the plaintiffs' performance unless the Owner paid the stipulated price. That was the defendant's risk, but the defendant's promise to pay the plaintiffs for stipulated work on condition that payment was received by the defendant shifted that risk to the plaintiffs, if the condition was a material part of the exchange of plaintiffs' promise to perform for defendant's promise to pay. . . .

Here we are not called upon to decide whether the language of the contract, read in the light of the situation of the parties and the

a. Additional facts appear from the record on appeal. The contract was made on December 18, 1930. Samuel J. Winterberg, secretary of Miller, Inc., testified that in a conversation about payments "previous to the drawing up of the written contract, I explained to Mr. Mascioni that his contract would be made out contingent upon our contract with the owners. . . . Mr. Mascioni at that time said he wanted to check into the worth of the owner before he entered into such a contract with us." He testified that the disputed provision "is used in the business because during these times, which are not normal, we receive contracts from other contractors in that manner and we give contracts out in that manner." (Record, p. 47.) Did Mascioni make a tactical error in "claiming that the contract was ambiguous?

subject-matter of the contract, shows clearly and unambiguously that the condition attached to the debt or obligation to pay, and did not merely fix the time of payment. Certainly on its face it is open to the construction that the plaintiffs accepted the condition as a material part of the exchange for their own promise or performance. The trial judge, after receiving parol evidence of the actual intention of the parties, gave it this construction, and that construction was not erroneous as matter of law.

[Judgment of the Appellate Division reversed and that of the trial court affirmed.]

NOTE

Reconciliation. Can the preceding two cases be reconciled? On the basis of differences in contract language? On procedural grounds?

LUTTINGER v. ROSEN

Supreme Court of Connecticut, 1972.
164 Conn. 45, 316 A.2d 757.

LOISELLE, Associate Justice. The plaintiffs contracted to purchase for $85,000 premises in the city of Stamford owned by the defendants and paid a deposit of $8500. The contract was "subject to and conditional upon the buyers obtaining first mortgage financing on said premises from a bank or other lending institution in an amount of $45,000 for a term of not less than twenty (20) years and at an interest rate which does not exceed 8½ per cent per annum." The plaintiffs agreed to use due diligence in attempting to obtain such financing. The parties further agreed that if the plaintiffs were unsuccessful in obtaining financing as provided in the contract, and notified the seller within a specific time, all sums paid on the contract would be refunded and the contract terminated without further obligation of either party.

In applying for a mortgage which would satisfy the contingency clause in the contract, the plaintiffs relied on their attorney who applied at a New Haven lending institution for a $45,000 loan at 8¼ percent per annum interest over a period of twenty-five years. The plaintiffs' attorney knew that this lending institution was the only one which at that time would lend as much as $45,000 on a mortgage for a single-family dwelling. A mortgage commitment was obtained for $45,000 with "interest at the prevailing rate at the time of closing but not less than 8¾%." Since this commitment failed to meet the contract requirement, timely notice was given to the defendants and demand was made for the return of the down payment. The defendants' counsel thereafter offered to make up the difference between the interest rate offered by the bank and the 8½ percent rate provided in the contract for the entire twenty-five years by a funding arrangement, the exact terms of which were not defined. The plaintiffs did not accept this offer and on the defendants' refusal to return the deposit an action was brought. From a judgment rendered in favor of the plaintiffs the defendants have appealed.

The defendants claim that the plaintiffs did not use due diligence in seeking a mortgage within the terms specified in the contract. The unattacked findings by the court establish that the plaintiffs' attorney was fully informed as to the conditions and terms of mortgages being granted by various banks and lending institutions in and out of the area and that the application was made to the only bank which might satisfy the mortgage conditions of the contingency clause at that time. These findings adequately support the court's conclusion that due diligence was used in seeking mortgage financing in accordance with the contract provisions. Brauer v. Freccia, 159 Conn. 289, 293, 268 A.2d 645. The defendants assert that notwithstanding the plaintiffs' reliance on their counsel's knowledge of lending practices, applications should have been made to other lending institutions. This claim is not well taken. The law does not require the performance of a futile act. Vachon v. Tomascak, 155 Conn. 52, 57, 230 A.2d 5; Tracy v. O'Neill, 103 Conn. 693, 699, 131 A. 417; Janulewycz v. Quagliano, 88 Conn. 60, 64, 89 A. 897.

The remaining assignment of error briefed by the defendants is that the court erred in concluding that the mortgage contingency clause of the contract, a condition precedent, was not met and, therefore, the plaintiffs were entitled to recover their deposit. "A condition precedent is a fact or event which the parties intend must exist or take place before there is a right to performance." Lach v. Cahill, 138 Conn. 418, 421, 85 A.2d 481, 482. If the condition precedent is not fulfilled the contract is not enforceable. Lach v. Cahill, supra; Bialeck v. Hartford, 135 Conn. 551, 556, 66 A.2d 610. In this case the language of the contract is unambiguous and clearly indicates that the parties intended that the purchase of the defendants' premises be conditioned on the obtaining by the plaintiffs of a mortgage as specified in the contract. From the subordinate facts found the court could reasonably conclude that since the plaintiffs were unable to obtain a $45,000 mortgage at no more than 8½ percent per annum interest "from a bank or other lending institution" the condition precedent to performance of the contract was not met and the plaintiffs were entitled to the refund of their deposit. Any additional offer by the defendants to fund the difference in interest payments could be rejected by the plaintiffs. See Lach v. Cahill, supra, 138 Conn. 420, 85 A.2d 481. There was no error in the court's exclusion of testimony relating to the additional offer since the offer was obviously irrelevant.

There is no error.

NOTES

(1) *Questions.* Why was the buyer's promise made conditional? What was the event on which it was conditioned? Why did not the mortgage commitment at $8\frac{3}{4}\%$ together with the seller's offer to make up the difference in interest rates amount to occurrence of that event? [a]

(2) *Financing Conditions.* Note the specificity of the clause in Luttinger v. Rosen. A poll of Wisconsin lawyers and brokers on such clauses is reported in Raushenbush, Problems and Practices with Financing Conditions in Real Estate Purchase Contracts, 1963 Wis.L.Rev. 566. According to the responses: such clauses are in widespread use, general language like "subject to financing" was not favored by most of the respondents, and a majority of them felt unable to say what would be a "reasonable loan" for a buyer. Would an agreement "contingent upon the purchaser's obtaining the proper amount of financing" have been enforceable? See Gerruth Realty Co. v. Pire, 17 Wis.2d 89, 115 N.W.2d 557 (1962).

GIBSON v. CRANAGE

Supreme Court of Michigan, 1878.
39 Mich. 49.

MARSTON, J. Plaintiff in error brought assumpsit to recover the contract price for the making and execution of a portrait of the deceased daughter of defendant. It appeared from the testimony of the plaintiff that he at a certain time called upon the defendant and solicited the privilege of making an enlarged picture of his deceased daughter. He says "I was to make an enlarged picture that he would like, a large one from a small one, and one that he would like and recognize as a good picture of his little girl, and he was to pay me."

The defendant testified that the plaintiff was to take the small photograph and send it away to be finished, "and when returned if it was not perfectly satisfactory to me in every particular, I need not take it or pay for it. I still objected and he urged me to do so. There was no risk about it; if it was not perfectly satisfactory to me I need not take it or pay for it."

There was little if any dispute as to what the agreement was. After the picture was finished it was shown to defendant who was dissatisfied with it and refused to accept it. Plaintiff endeavored to ascertain what the objections were, but says he was unable to ascertain clearly, and he then sent the picture away to the artist to have it changed.

On the next day he received a letter from defendant reciting the original agreement, stating that the picture shown him the previous day was not satisfactory and that he declined to take it or any other

a. As to the effect of an offer of a purchase money mortgage by the seller himself, compare Simms Co. v. Wolverton, 232 Ore. 291, 375 P.2d 87 (1962), with Kovarick v. Vesely, 3 Wis.2d 573, 89 N.W.2d 279 (1958).

similar picture, and countermanded the order. A further correspondence was had, but it was not very material and did not change the aspect of the case. When the picture was afterwards received by the plaintiff from the artist, he went to see defendant and to have him examine it. This defendant declined to do, or to look at it, and did not until during the trial, when he examined and found the same objections still existing.

We do not consider it necessary to examine the charge in detail, as we are satisfied it was as favorable to plaintiff as the agreement would warrant.

The contract (if it can be considered such) was an express one. The plaintiff agreed that the picture when finished should be satisfactory to the defendant, and his own evidence showed that the contract in this important particular had not been performed. It may be that the picture was an excellent one and that the defendant ought to have been satisfied with it and accepted it, but under the agreement the defendant was the only person who had the right to decide this question. Where parties thus deliberately enter into an agreement which violates no rule of public policy, and which is free from all taint of fraud or mistake, there is no hardship whatever in holding them bound by it.

Artists or third parties might consider a portrait an excellent one, and yet it prove very unsatisfactory to the person who had ordered it and who might be unable to point out with clearness or certainty the defects or objections. And if the person giving the order stipulates that the portrait when finished must be satisfactory to him or else he will not accept or pay for it, and this is agreed to, he may insist upon his right as given him by the contract. McCarren v. McNulty, 7 Gray, 141; Brown v. Foster, 113 Mass., 136; 18 Amer., 465.

The judgment must be affirmed with costs.

NOTES

(1) *Satisfaction.* Would the result have been the same if Gibson's promise had been to paint Cranage's barn? In Mattei v. Hopper, 51 Cal.2d 119, 330 P.2d 625 (1958), the court noted that "satisfaction" clauses have been divided into two categories. "First, in those contracts where the condition calls for satisfaction as to commercial value or quality, operative fitness, or mechanical utility, dissatisfaction cannot be claimed arbitrarily, unreasonably, or capriciously, . . . and the standard of a reasonable person is used in determining whether satisfaction has been received. [Second, in those contracts] involving fancy, taste, or judgment. . . . the promisor's determination that he is not satisfied, when made in good faith, has been held to be a defense to an action on the contract. . . . Although these decisions do not expressly discuss the issues of mutuality of obligation or illusory promises, they necessarily imply that the promisor's duty to exercise his judgment in good faith is an adequate consideration to support the contract. None of these cases voided the contracts on the

ground that they were illusory or lacking in mutuality of obligation." Would the result have been the same if Cranage had refused to look at the portrait at all?

Can you draft language that would make an objective test applicable to the painting of a portrait? That would make a subjective test applicable to the painting of a barn?

(2) *Conditions and Promises of Satisfaction.* Note that the court said that Gibson "agreed that the picture when finished should be satisfactory" to Cranage. Did the court hold that Gibson was under a duty to furnish a picture satisfactory to Cranage? Could Cranage have recovered damages from Gibson for his failure to do so?

Fursmidt v. Hotel Abbey Holding Corp., 10 A.D.2d 447, 200 N.Y.S.2d 256 (1960), sheds some light on this last question. Fursmidt had a three-year contract with the Hotel Abbey to supply its patrons with valet and laundry services. It was "distinctly understood and agreed that the services . . . shall meet with the approval of the [Hotel], who shall be the sole judge of the sufficiency and propriety of the services." After six months, the Hotel put Fursmidt out of his space in the basement and brought in someone else to render the services. He sued and the Hotel counterclaimed for his failure to render proper services. The jury was instructed to find for Fursmidt if it believed that the Hotel's dissatisfaction was unreasonable, even if honest. From a judgment entered on a verdict in Fursmidt's favor, the Hotel appealed. *Held:* Reversed. "[A] literal construction of the 'satisfaction' provisions is made where the agreements provide for performance involving 'fancy, taste, sensibility, or judgment,'" and this contract was sufficiently of this character to make the test of "dissatisfaction honestly arrived at" appropriate under the quoted clause. The court went on to say, however, that the trial court's charge may be "correct for the purpose of determining whether the plaintiff breached the agreement so as to entitle the defendant to damages on its counterclaim as distinguished from its right to terminate the contract. Honest dissatisfaction . . . will not, in and of itself, entitle it to recover damages on its counterclaim. . . . [W]e do not pass on that phase of the case at this time."

DEVOINE CO. v. INTERNATIONAL CO., 151 Md. 690, 136 A. 37 (1927). [By written contract, International sold Devoine, a manufacturer of candies, 400 50-gallon barrels of cherries in syrup, "quality satisfactory." After accepting 97 barrels, Devoine refused to take more, claiming that the quality was not satisfactory. International sued Devoine for damages. From a judgment for the plaintiff, the defendant appealed.]

BOND, C. J. . . . Taking up the . . . question . . . of the construction and effect of the provision, "quality satisfactory," we assume there can be no doubt that this means of a quality satisfactory to the buyer. . . . When parties to a valid contract refer any question of performance to the decision of the other party, or of a third person, the decision contracted for is final. . . . But it is only the decision contracted for that is final.

. . . And in those cases in which there may be a question open to decision, if the person to whom it is referred decides, not on the question submitted, but on some question of interest or advantage not made the basis of rights or obligations by the contract, the decision is outside of the contract and is given no effect by it.[a] Apart from any possible difficulty in proof, and assuming it to be made clear in any case, as, for instance, by a clear admission to that effect, that the tendered performance did meet the test stipulated for, that it was satisfactory or sufficient, as the case might be, a rejection on the ground of dissatisfaction or insufficiency would be beyond the right of the party who is to approve, in bad faith, and ineffectual. . . .

It is furthermore settled by our decisions that, on the issue of good faith in rejection of performance, the evidence may take a wide range, and facts such as the appellee sought to elicit in this case against objections of the appellant should be admitted. . . . [T]he seller was at liberty to prove if he could that his goods were rejected not because the quality was unsatisfactory, but because the buyer had found a cheaper source of supply. . . . He accordingly introduced testimony that of the 97 barrels of cherries delivered on the contract before refusal of further deliveries, none were rejected, and there was no complaint. Testimony was given of careful selection and putting up of the cherries in the seller's factory, and of a quality up to the highest grade known to the trade. A letter written by the buyer during the progress of deliveries, and expressing satisfaction, was read in evidence. It had been used by the seller as an advertisement. Further testimony was given to the effect that calls from this buyer for deliveries slackened to such an extent as to cause the seller some inconvenience, and that when the president of the seller company called on the buyer, the president of the latter explained, first, that his own sales had slackened, and, later, that he had an arrangement for putting up his own supply of cherries and therefore could not use the undelivered portion of the International Company's cherries, but would try to dispose of them to other consumers. Two letters followed from the International Company to the Devoine Company on a suggestion for deliveries in small installments, and these were answered by the final letter from the Devoine Company, stating that, as the International Company's president had previously been informed, the Devoine Company found the cherries unsatisfactory and would take no more. This evidence was met by contradictory testimony on behalf of the Devoine Company, but no exception brings that up for review. Our conclusion is that the evidence of the International Company just outlined was relevant to prove a rejection for reasons other than dissatisfaction with the cherries . . ., and

a. "The promisor may in fact be satisfied with the performance, but not with the bargain." Learned Hand, J., in Thompson-Starrett Co. v. La Belle Iron Works, 17 F.2d 536 (2d Cir. 1927).

that it was sufficient, no matter how strong the evidence of the Devoine Company may have been to the contrary, to require submission to the jury of the question of good faith in making the rejection. . . .

[Affirmed.]

NOTE

Good Faith. Compare the court's discussion of good faith with UCC 1–203. Cf. UCC 1–208. Is the test of good faith subjective (honesty) or objective (reasonableness)? Compare UCC 1–201(19) with 2–103(1)(b). Would Devoine have been entitled to reject the cherries if it had both been dissatisfied with International's cherries and found a cheaper source of supply? See Columbia Christian College v. Commonwealth Properties, Inc., 286 Or. 321, 594 P.2d 401 (1979).

ARCHITECTS' CERTIFICATES

Some of the problems inherent in making a party's duty conditional on his own satisfaction can be eliminated by making his duty conditional instead on the satisfaction of an independent third party, usually an expert of some kind. Widespread use is made of such terms in construction contracts, where the owner's duty to pay the contractor is often conditional on satisfaction of the architect.[a] The next two cases arise in this setting.

SECOND NAT. BANK v. PAN-AMERICAN BRIDGE CO.

United States Circuit Court of Appeals, Sixth Circuit, 1910.
183 F. 391.

[Pan-American Bridge furnished structural steel for Second National's bank building under a contract providing for payments as the work progressed "upon a certificate of the architect," 15% to be retained from the amount of each certificate and paid within 30 days of completion of the work "and the acceptance of the same by the architects." According to the specifications, Pan-American was to furnish the architect with detail drawings for approval and to do the work "in strict accordance with such approved drawings," but the architect, in approving them, "approves them in a general manner as being in or out of conformance with the general requirements of his drawings and specifications and does not relieve the contractor of responsibility for the correctness of the work shown by them." Pan-American's drawings, approved in writing by the architect, plainly showed 8 holes for the connections of beams and columns. After the steel had reached the sixth story, however, the architect insisted that

a. It is also possible to make the architect's approval conclusive on the owner, that is, to make his approval the *sole* condition of the owner's duty. Such provisions are discussed in Note 2, p. 890 infra.

Pan-American replace the 8-rivet connections with 10-rivet connections. On its refusal, Second National made the changes at a cost of $2,370 and withheld this sum. Pan-American sued. The trial judge instructed the jury that if Pan-American's work conformed to the contract, it could recover, although the architect refused to accept or certify it, if it was withheld "unreasonably and unfairly." Second National insisted that relief from the refusal could be had only in equity. From judgment for the plaintiff, the defendant appealed.]

KNAPPEN, Circuit Judge. . . . We cannot accede to the proposition that resort to equity is necessary in order to avoid the effect of failure to obtain the architect's certificate. The contention most strongly urged seems to be that the plaintiff must, as condition precedent to recovery on the contract, procure the setting aside of the contract provisions requiring such certificate, although the suggestion is also made that the architect's action needs reforming. Neither of those contentions is, in our opinion, maintainable. The plaintiff does not attack the validity of the contract provision requiring the architect's certificate as a condition precedent to recovery. Nor is there any certificate of the architect standing in the way and requiring reformation. The plaintiff's complaint in this respect is not that the contract is wrong, nor that any certificate of the architect is wrong. Its grievance is that the architect has improperly refused, as alleged, to accept the work and to certify accordingly. . . .

The right of a party to a building contract to show in an action at law thereon that the certificate required by the contract as a condition precedent to action was fraudulently withheld has been at least impliedly recognized in numerous cases, . . . and has never, so far as we have seen, been denied. But in our opinion the trial judge erred in holding that the architect's certificate could be dispensed with if the jury were satisfied that it was "unreasonably and unfairly" withheld. It is true that this instruction finds apparent support in several decisions of state courts cited in plaintiff's brief. But the rule is well settled in the federal courts that under contract provisions such as those existing here the certificate of acceptance is a condition precedent to recovery upon the contract in the absence of fraud or of mistake so gross as to imply bad faith; in other words, that the withholding of the certificate must have been in bad faith. . . .

In other words, the actual conformity of the work and materials to the plans and specifications was made the test of the bad faith which the law requires for setting aside the action of the architect. It is strongly insisted that the bad faith of the architect is clearly shown by his refusal to accept the plaintiff's work on account of defects apparent in the detail drawings approved by the architect. While the record was such as to justify submitting to the jury the question whether the architect acted in bad faith in refusing the certificate, and while it is possible that the defendant and the architect as well, in requiring the substituted connections, were influenced by a fear of criticism upon the sufficiency of the building, we cannot say, as a matter of law, that the admitted facts lead only to a conclusion of bad faith on the architect's part. . . .

The conclusion we have reached makes it unnecessary to consider the propriety of the instruction that a "capricious and arbitrary" refusal to accept avoided the effect of the failure to obtain the certificate; and perhaps the record should not be construed as sufficiently raising that question. We content ourselves with the suggestion that, if the words referred to are to be used, it should be made clear that they involve either bad faith or a refusal or failure to exercise honest judgment.

Judgment reversed, and new trial ordered.

NOTES

(1) *A. I. A. Provisions.* An American Institute of Architects form of General Conditions for an owner-contractor agreement (AIA Document A107, 8th ed. 1978) contains elaborate provisions on the role of the architect. He "will provide administration of the Contract and will be the Owner's representative during construction and until final payment is due [and] will be the interpreter of the requirements of the Contract Documents." His "decisions in matters relating to artistic effect will be final if consistent with the intent of the Contract Documents." (Other decisions of his shall be subject to arbitration.) Article 8. "The Contractor shall promptly correct any Work rejected by the Architect as defective or as failing to conform to the Contract Documents . . . ." Article 19. As provided in the Contract Documents, the Owner shall make progress payments "Based upon Applications for Payment submitted to the Architect by the Contractor and Certificates for Payment issued by the Architect." Article 4. "Based on the Architect's observations and an evaluation of the Contractor's Applications for Payment, the Architect will determine the amounts owning to the Contractor and will issue Certificates for Payment . . . ." Article 8. "When the Architect agrees that the Work is substantially complete, he will issue a Certificate of Substantial Completion." Article 15. Final payment by the owner is made contingent on certain conditions, including the issuance of "a final Certificate for Payment . . . by the Architect." Article 5.[a]

What would have been the results in the preceding cases if these provisions had been applicable?

(2) *Satisfaction in New York.* New York courts have tended to read "satisfaction" to mean "reasonable satisfaction." An early example is Duplex Safety Boiler Co. v. Garden, 101 N.Y. 387, 4 N.E. 749 (1886), in which an owner of boilers agreed to pay for repairs only if "satisfied that the boilers, as changed, were a success." The Court of Appeals concluded that it "cannot be presumed" that the parties supposed that the owner was "to be sole judge in [his] own cause." This tendency carries over into cases involving architects' certificates.

a. The form is reproduced in full in the Supplement.

In the leading case of Nolan v. Whitney, 88 N.Y. 648 (1882), a contractor, who had agreed to do masonry work to the satisfaction of the architect, sued for a $2,700 final payment on the total price of $11,700, although the architect had refused to give a certificate for that payment. The Court of Appeals affirmed a judgment for the contractor for the $2,700 less a $200 deduction for trivial defects in the plastering. "[W]hen he had substantially performed his contract, the architect was bound to give him the certificate, and his refusal to give it was unreasonable, and it is held that an unreasonable refusal on the part of an architect in such a case to give the certificate dispenses with its necessity." [b]

In Van Iderstine Co. v. Barnet Leather Co., 242 N.Y. 425, 152 N.E. 250 (1926), a seller of vealskins sued the buyer for failure to take and pay for some of the skins. The contract made the buyer's obligation subject to the approval of the skins by an expert broker. The trial judge charged the jury that the plaintiff could recover if approval was unreasonably withheld. On appeal this instruction was disapproved. The court explained the rule applied in Nolan v. Whitney on the ground that "enforcement of the contract according to its strict terms would cause forfeiture of compensation for work done and materials furnished.[c] The rule should not be extended by analogy where the reason for the rule fails." If the avoidance of forfeiture lies behind the decision in Nolan v. Whitney, why is not recovery in restitution the solution?

RIZZOLO v. POYSHER, 89 N.J.L. 618, 99 A. 390 (1916). [Rizzolo, a contractor, brought a mechanics' lien suit against Stahl, the owner, whose defenses included Rizzolo's failure to procure the architect's certificate required for payment under the contract. Rizzolo's complaint alleged "fraud on the part of the architect." A judgment of the trial court for Rizzolo was reversed on appeal, and he appeals from the reversal.]

PARKER, J. . . . It is inferable from the architect's own testimony that he was ready to issue the certificate, but that the defendants wished to cut down the final payment by several hundred dollars on account of a counterclaim which the architect refused to recognize or support except for a much smaller sum; that he advised the plaintiff to "get after them and get his money;" and that when plaintiff asked for the certificate, it was on the day before suit was begun, after plaintiff had retained counsel, and that he then refused it because he "did not want it to appear that he was issuing a certificate for a case." Such a reason was, of course, no reason at all, and led the judge very naturally to inquire of the witness whether he did

b. Does this help to explain why the failure of Jacob & Youngs to obtain the architect's certificate troubled neither Cardozo for the majority nor MacLaughlin for the dissenters in Jacob & Youngs v. Kent, p. 606 supra.

c. Does this line of reasoning assume that the builder would have no right to recover from the owner on a theory of unjust enrichment if he were barred from suit on the contract by his failure to get a certificate? This question will be deferred until Section 3 infra.

not think that he had assumed responsibilities not belonging to his duties as architect. If the witness' statement was true, and there was no reason to believe the contrary, his refusal under such circumstances was fraudulent in the sense in which the court understood it in Chism v. Schipper, [51 N.J.L. 1, 16 A. 316], and Bradner v. Roffsell, [57 N.J.L. 412]. It is claimed that, to constitute such fraud, the owner must be a participant. If this were the rule, a corrupt architect would be greatly aided in extorting money from the contractor as a condition of awarding a certificate that was fully earned. . . .

[Reversed and judgment of trial court affirmed.]

NOTE

The Case of Constructive Fraud. A contract for the construction of low rent housing required the Wilmington Housing Authority to extend the time for completing the work "when in its judgment the findings of fact of the [Authority's] Contracting Officer justify such an extension, and his findings of fact thereon shall be final and conclusive upon the parties." The contractor gave notice of a delay resulting from a shortage of plumbers, and the officer found that a delay of 15 days was justifiable on this account. In an action against the Authority, the contractor complained that the officer had arrived at the figure of 15 days by taking 8% of the actual delay of 182 days because the plumbing cost was only that percentage of the cost of the entire contract. The Authority moved for summary judgment. *Held:* Summary judgment denied. The officer's finding may be set aside, and the issue of allowable delay presented to a jury. "It is unfortunate that a finding of constructive fraud must be made in so many words when, in fact, we are actually dealing with serious errors in calculations. However, the decisions refer to such miscalculations as constructive fraud and I find it necessary to pin that label upon the contracting officer's erroneous findings here although, actually, there is no hint of bad faith, dishonesty or deliberate wrongful conduct upon the part of the contracting officer or the Authority. I am sure that these errors were the product of inexperience and mistaken judgment." Anthony P. Miller, Inc. v. Wilmington Housing Authority, 179 F.Supp. 199 (D.Del.1959). See Illustration 8 to Restatement Second, § 227. Is a contacting officer the same sort of third party as an architect?

CONDITIONS, FORFEITURE, AND MORTGAGES

It should be apparent by now that the law of conditions is more tolerant of the Draconian draftsman than is the law of liquidated damages. Courts have shown more tolerance for the forfeiture that results from the nonoccurrence of an event that the draftsman has made a condition than for the penalty that he has provided as the consequence of breach. But there are limits even to the former, and they can be usefully considered against the background of the history of the mortgage.

A mortgage is a conveyance by a debtor, the mortgagor, to his creditor, the mortgagee, of an interest in property, whose purpose is to secure the payment of the debt. The advantages to the creditor of having this kind of security interest (which is usually called a lien) are of two sorts. First, a secured creditor has an array of remedies in case of nonpayment in addition to those available to an unsecured creditor. Second, in the event of the distribution of the debtor's assets in insolvency proceedings, an effective security interest preempts the claims of unsecured creditors against the property subject to the interest. Details may be left to courses on land transactions, commercial transactions, creditors' rights, and the like. Our immediate concern is with the first of these sorts of advantages.

Although contemporary mortgage forms simply recite that the mortgagor "mortgages" the property to the mortgagee, the mortgage formerly took the form of a conveyance subject to a condition. Littleton, writing in the fifteenth century, explained it in this way. "If a feoffment be made upon such condition, that if the feoffor pay to the feoffee at a certain day, etc., 40*l.* of money, that then the feoffor may re-enter, etc., in this case the feoffee is called tenant in mortgage . . . and if he doth not pay, then the land which is put in pledge upon condition for the payment of the money, is taken from him for ever, and so dead to him upon condition, etc." Littleton's Tenures § 332.

Here is a description of the historical development that followed. "In [this] earlier era, the mortgagee obtained title to the mortgagor's property subject to divestment if the debt were paid on the due or law day. Often this arrangement meant hardship for the mortgagor, for a late tender of payment, late even by so little as one day, would not bring a return of title unless the mortgagee volunteered to give it. In time, chancery intervened in behalf of defaulting mortgagors by letting them 'redeem' the property from the mortgagee if they tendered payment within a reasonable period after the law day. This equitable right of redemption grew into an implied term of every mortgage bargain.

"Now the mortgagee faced hardship—the hardship of uncertainty—for he could not be sure, after default, when his title would indefeasibly vest. A late tendering mortgagor might yet persuade chancery that the tender was not unreasonably delayed. Taking the initiative, mortgagees began to petition the courts to cut off, or foreclose, the mortgagor's equity of redemption. In this way, the procedural remedy of foreclosure was born. The decree of foreclosure, which was issued some months after the law date and upon notice to the defaulting mortgagor, vested the mortgagee's title to the real estate security; prior to the decree redemption was possible, but after the decree, it was not.

"If, when foreclosure occurred, the real estate was worth more than the mortgage debt, still another source of hardship remained for the mortgagor. Since foreclosure vested title in the mortgagee, he stood to benefit, while the mortgagor stood to lose, from any surplus in property value. No restitution was necessary. By the early 1800s, state legislatures began to respond to the evident harshness of this situation; mortgagees who applied for a foreclosure decree were ordered to sell the property at a public sale and to pay over to the mortgagor (and to any junior lienors) the surplus moneys from the sale, i. e., the moneys not needed to satisfy the claims of the foreclosing mortgagee. (Sometimes, of course, the sales price fails to satisfy the debt, and this may give rise to further claim for a deficiency judgment.) In a substantial majority of states, *foreclosure by judicial sale* has become the exclusive or generally used process, and it is available everywhere. The process it supplanted, which for obvious reasons became known as *strict foreclosure,* survives in only a few states as a permitted remedy.

"One other form of foreclosure deserves mention, for it does not depend upon judicial decree. Where the mortgage instrument gives the mortgagee the power, and state law does not prevent its exercise, a sale arranged for by the mortgagee may be held to transfer the interest of the defaulted mortgagor. . . . In the United States the sale is invariably public and statutes carefully regulate the conduct of the sale and the method of giving notice."[a] Axelrod, Berger, and Johnstone, Land Transfer and Finance 138–40 (1971).

NOTES

(1) *The Case of the Evidentiary Condition.* Ferguson, who ran a drugstore, had an insurance policy under which Phoenix Assurance promised to pay $1,000 for loss by safe burglary, which was defined, under the heading "CONDITIONS," so as to require "felonious entry . . . provided such entry shall be made by actual force and violence, of which force and violence there are visible marks made by tools, explosives, electricity or chemicals upon the exterior of . . . all of said doors of such vault or such safe and any vault containing the safe, if entry is made through such doors." Ferguson's safe was opened by a thief who took $400 after opening the outer locked door by manipulating its combination lock and the inner locked door by punching out the lock. When Phoenix denied liability Ferguson sued and recovered. Phoenix appealed. *Held:* Affirmed. "The reason for such restrictions, quite obviously, is to protect the companies from what are commonly known as "inside jobs," and from frauds that would inevitably result, but for such protection . . . . The recital that there be visible marks upon the exterior of all of the doors to the safe has reference only to evidence of the force and violence used in making the felonious entry into the safe. In other words, the substantive condition of the proviso is that entry into the safe be made by actual force and violence. The further condition that there be visible marks upon the exterior of all doors to the safe, if entry is made through such doors is merely evidentiary to show an entry into the safe by actual force and violence. . . .

We hold that where a rule of evidence is imposed by a provision in an insurance policy, as here, the assertion of such rule by the insurance car-

a. Reproduced by permission of Little, Brown and Company.

rier, beyond the reasonable requirements necessary to prevent fraudulent claims against it in proof of the substantive conditions imposed by the policy, contravenes the public policy of the state." Ferguson v. Phoenix Assur. Co., 189 Kan. 459, 370 P.2d 379, 99 A.L.R.2d 118 (1962).

(2) *Problem.* Bostick's was an International Harvester dealer. Under their contract, "to qualify for the annual volume discount a dealer must pay in full, within thirty days after the end of the period, all obligations to the company." At the end of the period in question, Bostick's was credited provisionally with an annual volume discount of $5,068.56, but had obligations to International Harvester of $24,000. Bostick's did not pay these obligations by November 30. On November 6, however, the parties agreed to terminate the dealership. On termination, International Harvester became obligated under the contract to repurchase $40,000 in returnable inventory from Bostick's. Is Bostick's entitled to the $5,068.56? See International Harvester Co. v. Bostick's Int'l, 365 So.2d 84 (Ala.Civ.App.1978).

HOLIDAY INNS OF AMERICA, INC. v. KNIGHT

Supreme Court of California, 1969.
70 Cal.2d 327, 74 Cal.Rptr. 722, 450 P.2d 42.

TRAYNOR, Chief Justice. Plaintiffs appeal from a judgment for defendants in an action seeking a declaration that a contract was still effective. The judgment was entered after plaintiffs' motion for summary judgment was denied and defendants' motion for summary judgment was granted.

The pleadings and affidavits of the parties establish the following undisputed facts.

Plaintiffs are the successors in interest to the optionee under a written option contract between the optionee and the owners of the option property, defendant D. Manley Knight and his mother, Mary Knight. Mary Knight is now deceased and D. Manley Knight is the sole owner of the property. Although his wife is also named a defendant herein, she has no interest in the contract or the option property. We will therefore refer to D. Manley Knight as defendant.

The contract, executed on September 30, 1963, granted an option to purchase real property in Orange County for $198,633, the price to be subject, however, to prescribed adjustments for changes in the cost of living. Unless cancelled as provided in the agreement, the option could be exercised by giving written notice thereof no later than April 1, 1968. The contract provided for an initial payment of $10,000 and for four additional payments of $10,000 to be made directly to the optionors on July 1 of each year, commencing in 1964, unless the option was exercised or cancelled before the next such payment became due. These payments were not to be applied to the purchase price. The cancellation provision provided that "it is mutually understood that failure to make payment on or before the prescribed date will automatically cancel this option without further notice."

On December 9, 1963, the parties amended the contract by executing escrow instructions that provided that the annual payments were to be deposited in escrow with the Security Title Insurance Company, and that, in "the event you [Security Title] do not receive the $10,000 annual payments [by July 1] and upon receiving notice from Optionors to cancel the option, without further instructions from Optionee you are to terminate the escrow."

The initial payment of $10,000 and the annual installments for 1964 and 1965 were paid. After the execution of the contract, plaintiffs expended "great amounts of money" to develop a major residential and commercial center on the land adjacent to the option property. These expenditures have caused the option property to increase substantially in value since the contract was executed. Plaintiffs' purpose in entering into the contract was to put themselves in a position to secure the advantage of this increase in value resulting from their development efforts.

In 1966 plaintiffs mailed a check for $10,000 to defendant. It was made out to D. Manley Knight and his wife, Lavinia Knight, and dated June 30, 1966. Defendant received the check on July 2, 1966 and returned it to plaintiffs on July 8, stating that the option contract was cancelled. On July 8 plaintiffs tendered another check directly to defendant, and he again refused it. On July 15 plaintiffs deposited a $10,000 check with Security Title payable to defendant. Security Title tendered the check to defendant, but his attorney returned it to plaintiffs on July 27 and advised them that the agreement was terminated pursuant to the cancellation provision.

Plaintiffs contend that payment of the annual installment was timely on the ground that the check became the property of defendant when mailed; that even if the payment was late, the trial court should have relieved them from forfeiture and declared the option in force under section 3275 of the Civil Code; and that, in any event, the trial court erred in excluding extrinsic evidence offered to prove that the escrow instructions modified the contract to permit payment at any time before defendant notified the title company that the option was cancelled. Since the undisputed facts establish that plaintiffs are entitled to relief from forfeiture pursuant to section 3275, it is unnecessary to consider plaintiffs' other contentions.

Section 3275 provides: "Whenever, by the terms of an obligation, a party thereto incurs a forfeiture, or a loss in the nature of a forfeiture, by reason of his failure to comply with its provisions, he may be relieved therefrom, upon making full compensation to the other party, except in case of a grossly negligent, willful, or fraudulent breach of duty." The tumultuous history of this section has been recorded in a lengthy series of major decisions in the area of property and contract law.

Although most of the cases considering section 3275 have involved land sale contracts, its proscriptions against forfeiture apply in any case in which the party seeking relief from default has brought himself within the terms of the section by pleading and proving facts that justify its application. (Barkis v. Scott, supra, 34 Cal.2d at pp. 118, 120, 208 P.2d 367.) In determining whether a given case falls within section 3275, however, it is necessary to consider the nature of the contract and the specific clause in question. Although the contract in the instant case is an option contract, the question is not whether the exercise of the option was timely, but whether the right to exercise the option in the future was forfeited by a failure to pay the consideration for that right precisely on time. Defendant's reliance on Cummings v. Bullock (9th Cir. 1966) 367 F. 2d 182, and Wilson v. Ward (1957) 155 Cal.App.2d 390, 317 P.2d 1018, is therefore misplaced. Both those cases dealt with the time within which an option must be exercised and correctly held that such time cannot be extended beyond that provided in the contract. To hold otherwise would give the optionee, not the option he bargained for, but a longer and therefore more extensive option. In the present case, however, plaintiffs are not seeking to extend the period during which the option can be exercised but only to secure relief from the provision making time of the essence in tendering the annual payments. (See Scarbery v. Bill Patch Land & Water Co. (1960) 184 Cal.App.2d 87, 102, 103, 7 Cal.Rptr. 408.) In a proper case, relief will be granted under section 3275 from such a provision. (Barkis v. Scott, supra, 34 Cal.2d at p. 122, 208 P.2d 367.)

The sole issue in this case is whether the plaintiffs have brought themselves within section 3275; whether there would be a loss in the nature of a forfeiture suffered by plaintiffs if the option contract were terminated. Essentially, the position of defendant is that there is no forfeiture since plaintiffs got precisely what they bargained for, namely, the exclusive right to buy the property for the three years during which they made payments. Cancellation because of the late 1966 payment amounts to nothing more than terminating a contract providing for that exclusive right during 1966. As viewed by defendant, this contract is in effect wholly executory and therefore its termination would not result in a forfeiture to either party. (Martin v. Morgan (1890) 87 Cal. 203, 25 P. 350.)

To sustain defendant's argument, the contract would have to be viewed as a series of independent contracts, each for a one-year option. Only if this were true, could it be said that plaintiffs received their bargained for equivalent of the $30,000 payments. (Sheveland v. Reed (1958) 159 Cal.App.2d 820, 822, 324 P.2d 633.) The economic realities of the transaction, however, do not support this analysis. First, the language of the agreement states that the "Optioners hereby grant to Optionee the exclusive right and option for a five year period . . . ." The parties agreed to bind themselves to a period of five years with the price payable in five installments. On the basis of risk allocation, it is clear that each payment of the $10,000 installment was partially for an option to buy the land during that year and partially for a renewal of the option for another year up to a total of five years. With the passage of time, plaintiffs have paid more and more for the right to renew, and it is this right that would be forfeited by requiring payment strictly on time. At the time the forfeiture was declared, plaintiffs had paid a substantial part of the $30,000 for the right to exercise the option during the last two years. Thus, they have not received what they bargained for and they have lost more than the benefit of their bargain. In short, they will suffer a forfeiture of that part of the $30,000 attributable to the right to exercise the option during the last two years.[1]

Plaintiffs have at all times remained willing and able to continue with the performance of the contract and have acted in good faith to accomplish this end. Defendant has not suffered any injury justifying termination of the contract, and none of his reasonable expectations have been defeated.[2] Moreover, he will receive the benefit of his bargain, namely, the full price of the option granted plaintiffs. As we stated in *Barkis*, "when the default has not been serious and the vendee is willing and able to continue with his performance of the contract, the vendor suffers no damage by allowing the vendee to do so." (Barkis v. Scott, supra, 34 Cal.2d at p. 122, 208 P.2d at p. 371.)

The judgment is reversed and the trial court is directed to enter a summary judgment for plaintiffs in accord with the views herein expressed.

NOTES

(1) *Rule of the Case.* Consider again the few lines of legal history on p. 776 above, with special reference to the development of the mortgagor's equity of redemption: "In time, chancery intervened in behalf of defaulting mortgagors by letting them 'redeem' the property from the mortgagee if they tendered payment within a reasonable period after the law day." This development was complete by the middle of the 17th century, it should be added.[a] Do you consider the main case a ruling peculiar to "installment op-

1. Plaintiffs also allege forfeiture of "great amounts of money" expended for the development of surrounding land. Evidently none of the investment was made in the option property. Since there is nothing to indicate that the development was not highly profitable in its own right or that inclusion of defendant's property was necessary to make the development a success, it would not seem that any part of these expenditures can be considered forfeited by a termination of the contract. (Cf. Scarbery v. Bill Patch Land & Water Co., supra, where the plaintiff offered evidence justifying the allocation of collateral development expenditures to the amounts forfeited by cancellation.)

2. Although the initial tender was made to defendant and his wife and not to the Security Title Insurance Company as the escrow instructions specified, it gave defendant notice within one day of the due date that plaintiffs sought to keep the contract in force.

a. See Turner, The Equity of Redemption, Chapter 2 (Cambridge Studies in English Legal History 1931).

tion" contracts, or as a twentieth century extension of an ancient principle about land financing? Is it significant that it does not appear that Holiday Inns had a duty to make the payment in question? See Restatement Second, § 229.

(2) *Mailing or Receipt?* On the face of it, an attractive basis for the foregoing decision is the plaintiffs' contention that their check became the property of defendant when mailed. How strong is the analogy to the "mailbox rule" (see Note 2, p. 275 supra)?

(3) *Land Pricing.* Holiday Inns was not the original optionholder, be it noted. But it may have been his undisclosed principal. A developer beginning a program of land acquisition will often employ a "front" or "straw" man to conceal its identity, fearing that a disclosure would drive up local land values prematurely. The possible effect of such a program is dramatically shown in Banner v. Elm, 251 Md. 694, 248 A.2d 452 (1969). There the buyer contracted to buy nearby parcels from A at 30 cents per square foot in October, from B at 75 cents in November and from C at $1 in December.[b] Subsequently A reneged on his contract, and the question in the case was whether or not the buyer should be granted specific performance. On the facts given here, can you formulate any principle for granting specific enforcement of the Holiday Inns option, while denying similar enforcement against A?

HICKS v. BUSH

Court of Appeals of New York, 1962.
10 N.Y.2d 488, 225 N.Y.S.2d 34, 180 N.E.2d 425.

FULD, Judge. In this action for specific performance of a written agreement, we granted the plaintiff leave to appeal to consider whether the parol evidence rule was violated by the receipt of testimony tending to establish that the parties had orally agreed that the legal effectiveness of the written agreement should be subject to a stated condition precedent.

On July 10, 1956, the plaintiff Frederick Hicks, together with defendant Michael Congero and one Jack McGee, executed a written agreement with the individual defendants, members of defendant Clinton G. Bush Company, whereby the parties were to merge their various corporate interests into a single "holding" company in order to achieve more efficient operation and greater financial strength. The document recited, among other things, that the plaintiff would subscribe for some 425,000 shares of stock in the new holding corporation, known as Bush-Hicks Enterprises, Inc., and that the defendants comprising the Bush Company would subscribe for more than a million shares. The other parties to the agreement were to subscribe for a total of less than 50,000 shares. The principal consideration for the subscription was the transfer to the holding company of stock in the operating corporations which the several parties owned.

b. A's property may, unlike that of the others, have been unimproved.

The written agreement provided expressly that the subscriptions for the stock in Bush-Hicks Enterprises were to be made "within five days after the date of this Agreement" and that, "If within twenty-five days after the date hereof Bush-Hicks shall have failed to accept any of said subscriptions delivered to it . . . then and in any such event the obligations of all of the parties hereto shall be terminated and cancelled." The subscriptions were promptly made and accepted and, although the plaintiff turned over the stock of his corporations, the defendants did not transfer the stock of their companies to Bush-Hicks Enterprises. In consequence, the plaintiff never received the Bush-Hicks stock as provided in the agreement and the merger never eventuated.

Alleging a breach of contract, the plaintiff brought this suit for specific performance and for an accounting. In their answer, the defendants urged, as an affirmative defense, that the written agreement was executed "upon a parol condition" that it "was not to operate" as a contract and that the contemplated merger was not "to become effective" until so-called "equity expansion funds", amounting to $672,500, were first procured. And to support that allegation, the defendants upon the trial offered evidence of such an oral understanding. The court admitted the evidence, over the plaintiff's objection that it varied and contradicted the terms of the writing, and finding that the oral condition asserted had actually been agreed on by the parties, rendered judgment in favor of the defendants.

A reading of the record unquestionably supports the decision of the courts below, that the parties, have concluded that $672,500 was essential to successful operation of the proposed merger, agreed that the entire merger deal was to be subject to the condition precedent that that sum be raised. Thus, one witness, the president of the defendant Bush Company, declared that everyone "understood" that the writing was not to become operative as a binding contract until the specified equity expansion funds were obtained. Indeed, his expressive and colorful testimony leaves no doubt as to the nature of the agreement arrived at: "I used the Chinese slang phrase of 'No tickie, no shirtie.' Let's get signed so we would be ready. I said, 'You all know what that means, that if we do not get the funds, this document [the written agreement] does not become operative . . ..' . . . There is only one understanding, verbal understanding that we have had. That speaks of 'Get the money or no deal.' "

The expansion capital of $672,500, which the parties hoped would be procured by December 31, 1956, was never raised.

The applicable law is clear, the relevant principles settled. Parol testimony is admissible to prove a condition precedent to the legal effectiveness of a written agreement (see Saltzman v. Barson, 239 N.Y. 332, 337, 146 N.E. 618, 619; Grannis v. Stevens, 216 N.Y. 583, 587, 111 N.E. 263, 265; Reynolds v. Robinson, 110 N.Y. 654, 18 N.E.

127; see, also, 4 Williston, Contracts [3d ed., 1961], § 634, p. 1021; 3 Corbin, Contracts [1960 ed.], § 589, p. 530 et seq.),[a] if the condition does not contradict the express terms of such written agreement. (See Fadex Foreign Trading Corp. v. Crown Steel Corp., 297 N.Y. 903, 79 N.E.2d 739, affg. 272 App.Div. 273, 274–276, 70 N.Y.S.2d 892, 893–894; see, also, Restatement, Contracts, § 241.) A certain disparity is inevitable, of course, whenever a written promise is, by oral agreement of the parties, made conditional upon an event not expressed in the writing. Quite obviously, though, the parol evidence rule does not bar proof of every orally established condition precedent, but only of those which in a real sense contradict the terms of the written agreement. (See, e. g., Illustration to Restatement, Contracts, § 241.) Upon the present appeal, our problem is to determine whether there is such a contradiction.

The Fadex case (297 N.Y. 903, 79 N.E.2d 739, supra) is illustrative. The plaintiff, seeking damages for nondelivery of certain goods, relied upon written agreements which specifically provided that the goods were "Ready now" and that the time of delivery was to be "Prompt" and "Within 4 to 6 weeks, if possible earlier". Despite these express recitals, plus the further explicit notation that no oral arrangement or modification was to be binding upon the parties, the defendant sought to show a contemporaneous oral agreement that the sales were conditioned upon its ability to obtain the goods within a month. In connection with a motion for partial summary judgment, this court decided that an oral condition precedent to the formation of a contract could be established when not contradictory of the written agreement itself, but concluded that the condition attempted to be proved by the defendant Crown Steel Corporation would, if ruled operative, actually annul the express terms of the writing.

The present case differs materially from Fadex. There is here no direct or explicit contradiction between the oral condition and the writing; in fact, the parol agreement deals with a matter on which the written agreement, as in some of the cases cited (10 N.Y.2d p. 491, 225 N.Y.S.2d 36, 180 N.E.2d 427, supra), is silent. The plaintiff, however, contends that, since the written agreement provides in

a. The classic case is Pym v. Campbell, 6 El. & Bl. 370, 119 Eng.Rep. 903 (Q.B.1856). Pym, an inventor, was negotiating with Campbell and his associates for the sale to them of Pym's invention. The parties prepared a written agreement containing the terms of the proposed sale and were awaiting an opinion from Abernathie, an engineer. In order to avoid having to meet again, they signed the agreement on the oral understanding that it would be an agreement only if Abernathie approved of the invention. When Pym sued on the agreement, Campbell and his associates prevailed at the trial by proving that Abernathie had not approved. The reasoning of the court in upholding this decision is suggested by Earle, J.: "The distinction in point of law is that evidence to vary the terms of an agreement in writing is not admissible, but evidence to show that there is not an agreement at all is admissible."

terms that the obligations of the parties were to be terminated if the merged corporation failed to accept any of their stock subscriptions within 25 days, the additional oral condition—that the writing "was [not] to become operative" and that the merger was "not to become effective" until the expansion funds had been raised—is irreconcilable with the written agreement.

As already indicated, and analysis confirms it, the two conditions may stand side by side. The oral requirement that the writing was not to take effect as a contract until the equity expansion funds were obtained is simply a further condition—a condition added to that requiring the acceptance of stock subscriptions within 25 days—and not one which is contradictory. If both provisions had been contained in the written agreement, it is clear that the defendants would not have been under immediate legal duty to transfer the stock in their companies to Bush-Hicks Enterprises until both conditions had been fulfilled and satisfied. And it is equally clear that evidence of an oral condition is not to be excluded as contradictory or "inconsistent" merely because the written agreement contains other conditions precedent. . . .

In short, the parties in the case before us intended that their respective rights and duties with respect to the contemplated transfers of stock in the operating companies to the holding company be subject to two conditions, each independent of the other—the acceptance of the stock subscription within a specified period and the procuring of expansion funds of $672,500. As the courts below found, the parties did not contemplate performance of the written agreement until such funds were first received. In other words, it was their desire and understanding that the merger was to be one of proposal only and that, even though the formal preliminary steps were to be taken, the writing was not to become operative as a contract or the merger effective until $672,500 was raised. It is certainly not improbable that parties contracting in these circumstances would make the asserted oral agreement; the condition precedent at hand is the sort of condition which parties would not be inclined to incorporate into a written agreement intended for public consumption. The challenged evidence was, therefore, admissible and, since there was ample proof attesting to the making of the oral agreement, the trial court was fully warranted in holding that no operative or binding contract ever came into existence.

The judgment appealed from should be affirmed, with costs.

NOTES

(1) *Conditions and the Parol Evidence Rule.* Were the defendants attempting to show that the writing was not to have any effect until the funds were procured or that the obligations of the parties under the instrument were conditional on the procurement of the funds? If the former, was there an integrated agreement? If the latter, does the case stand for

the proposition that the parol evidence rule does not apply to conditions precedent? That it does not apply to a condition like that in the Peacock Construction case, p. 760 supra? Like that in Luttinger v. Rosen, p. 765 supra? See Luria Bros. & Co. v. Pielet Bros. Scrap Iron & Metal, Inc., 600 F.2d 103 (7th Cir. 1979).

For a later opinion by the New York Court of Appeals on when there is a "contradiction" between an oral condition and a writing, see Long Island Trust Co. v. International Institute for Packaging Educ., 38 N.Y.2d 493, 381 N.Y.S.2d 445, 344 N.E.2d 377 (1976).

(2) *The Code.* What would have been the result in Hicks v. Bush if UCC 2–202 had been applicable? See Hunt Foods & Industries v. Doliner, 26 A.D.2d 41, 270 N.Y.S.2d 937 (1st Dept.1966).

(3) *Merger Clauses and Conditions.* In Kryl v. Mechalson, 259 Wis. 204, 47 N.W.2d 899 (1951), the court held that an oral condition to the contract could be established in spite of the following language: "It is understood that this contract is complete in itself, and that the party of the first part is not bound by any other terms or agreements other than are herein contained." Can you draft a clause which would be more likely to be effective? See Edward T. Kelly Co. v. Von Zakobiel, 168 Wis. 579, 171 N.W. 75 (1919).

Review the clause that you drafted in response to Note 3, p. 680 supra. Can you improve it in the light of Hicks v. Bush?

SECTION 2. SECURING EXPECTATIONS

The conceptions presented in this section call for comparisons with much of the material in earlier sections, especially with that on conditions. Much may be done to secure the fair expectations of a contracting party by the use of appropriate express conditions, as the foregoing section shows. In addition, however, expectations are secured by a number of settled doctrines about performance and breach. Substantial performance, material breach, and anticipatory breach are among the doctrines now to be illustrated. Like the principles of contract interpretation, they prevail chiefly by force of judicial authority. Also these doctrines address some of the same problems as interpretation does; but they are less dependent on the facts of an individual case and more authoritative for contracts cases at large. The doctrine of divisibility of contract, as will be seen, relates to the prevention of forfeitures. The manner in which a party responds to a breach, or to the threat of one, may substantially alter the undertakings initially exchanged by the parties. The ideas of waiver, estoppel, and election are instrumental in transformations of this sort and so have something in common with the process of agreement. Still other reminders of the preceding sections of the book should be watched for in this one.

NOTE

Constructive Conditions. In the remainder of this chapter instances of "constructive condition" appear in some variety. The expression is preferred—at least by commentators such as Corbin and Patterson—as being more precise than "implied condition." [a]

The opinion in the case to follow does not use the word "condition" at all. After reading it consider how the ruling might have been expressed in terms of a condition. If the decision does rest on an unfulfilled condition, is the court's process of reasoning one of implication or of construction?

WASSERBURGER v. AMERICAN SCIENTIFIC CHEM., INC.

Supreme Court of Oregon, 1973.
267 Or. 77, 514 P.2d 1097.

TONGUE, Justice.

In November 1968, plaintiff [Wasserburger] and defendant entered into an oral contract under which plaintiff was to be paid by defendant 50 per cent of the net profits earned by defendant from sales of certain medical laboratory supplies sold by it to United Medical Laboratories, which plaintiff had obtained as a customer for the purchase of such goods.

[The present action was brought on that contract. The plaintiff appeals from a judgment for defendant, entered after a bench trial. "We affirm."]

The findings of fact by the trial court included the following:

"2. The contract was terminated by the plaintiff's attempt to sell goods for a competitor of the defendant American Scientific Chemical, Inc.

"3. That the defendant American Scientific Chemical, Inc. performed its contract in all respects until the plaintiff acted in a manner which defeated further performance of the contract by attempting to represent a competitor of the defendant; . . . ."

The question to be decided is whether these findings are supported by substantial evidence and, if so, whether it follows that plaintiff is barred from recovery of commissions allegedly earned by him prior to such a termination of the contract.

One of plaintiff's two assignments of error is that:

"The trial court erred in holding that plaintiff's right to commissions under the contract ceased the moment plaintiff discussed with United the possibility of United buying their medical laboratory supplies from a different supplier."

a. The first Restatement employed the term in black-letter rules; see § 253. The Restatement Second incorporates the idea, but not in such rules; see §§ 204 and 237 (especially Comment a).

[The court determined to consider this "attempted assignment"—though it failed to comply with a rule of the court—"because the question raised controls the disposition of this case on its merits."][b]

The first order placed by United with defendant was shipped in December 1968. Payment was received by defendant in January 1969, from which defendant then paid the commission due to plaintiff. According to plaintiff, the payment of his commission on the next order should have been paid at the time of shipment, but was late. Plaintiff admitted, however, that it was then agreed that commission payments would be made to plaintiff as and when defendant received payments from United, even though such payments were not received for from 60 to 90 days after shipments were made.

The next commission payment to plaintiff was made in April 1969, the reason for the delay being the "pay period lapse" in receiving payment by defendant from United. No further payment was made until July, both because of United's "paying practices" and also because of a disagreement between the parties during that period over plaintiff's responsibility to contact and develop further accounts in Oregon, Washington and Northern California.

It appears that plaintiff had not made such an effort to develop further accounts and that even later he secured only one such order —an order from a hospital in July 1969. Plaintiff denied that there had been any agreement that he would make any such effort. There was substantial evidence, however, that plaintiff had originally agreed to do so. In addition, there was testimony that defendant had not previously handled these items; that it was not profitable for defendant to sell these items to United alone, and that defendant offered to pay the "back commissions" to plaintiff if he would get out and try to sell these laboratory supplies to other purchasers, as originally agreed.

Plaintiff admitted this matter had been originally "discussed." He also admitted that he was told by defendant that the reason for withholding further commission payments was his failure to make an effort to develop further accounts.

In May 1969, plaintiff went to work as a salesman for another employer. He then called on the United purchasing agent and made an effort to persuade him to purchase from his new employer the same laboratory supplies that United had been purchasing from defendant.

In May 1969, the United purchasing agent reported this to defendant, which then wrote a letter to plaintiff terminating the agreement. In August, however, at the request of the United purchasing agent, defendant paid commissions owing to plaintiff through May

b. These excerpts from the opening of the opinion have been somewhat rearranged.

1969, but refused to pay him any further commissions. United continued, however, to purchase laboratory supplies from defendant for some time before it finally terminated such purchases.

Plaintiff then filed this action. Plaintiff's complaint alleges that the parties made an "oral contract" under which plaintiff was to "procure purchasers for merchandise sold by the defendants" and be paid as "a sales commission, an amount equal to fifty percent (50%) of the gross profit realized on the sales made by the plaintiff"; that plaintiff sold certain laboratory supplies to United on which there was an unpaid balance of such commissions due and owing to plaintiff in the sum of $6,100.02, "which defendants refuse to pay or any part thereof."

It is well established, at least as a general rule, that a plaintiff who seeks to recover under the terms of an express contract for defendant's failure to perform its terms must plead and prove his own substantial performance or a valid excuse for his failure to perform. . . . .

It is also well established, at least as a general rule, that a breach or nonperformance of a promise by one party to a bilateral contract so material as to justify a refusal of the other party to perform a contractual duty, discharges that duty. 2 Restatement, Contracts 750, § 397. . . . Whether a breach is so material as to have such a result is ordinarily a question of fact. See 1 Restatement, Contracts 402, § 275.

Plaintiff contends that "there was a full performance on his part under the terms of the agreement and that he was justified in discussing with United the possibility of buying from a source other than [defendant] because [defendant] was not paying him in a timely manner."

In this case, however, and wholly aside from the sufficiency of plaintiff's complaint, the evidence was overwhelming to the effect that there was not a substantial performance of this contract by the plaintiff, but that, on the contrary, there was a material breach, if not a willful breach, of the contract by him. Plaintiff not only failed to substantially perform that part of the agreement under which he was required to contact and develop accounts elsewhere in Oregon, Washington and Northern California, but his attempt to persuade United to purchase from his new employer the same kinds of laboratory supplies which were the subject of his oral agreement with defendant was clearly a material, if not also a willful breach of the contract. There was no evidence sufficient to constitute a valid excuse for such flagrant misconduct.[1]

1. Plaintiff does not contend that any agreement to solicit additional accounts were [was?] severable or independent from the agreement to pay commissions on sales to United, but denies that there was any agreement to solicit additional accounts. We hold, however, that there was substantial evidence that there was such an agreement and that it was not a severable agreement or one involving independent covenants.

In Perkins v. Standard Oil Co., 235 Or. 7, 16, 383 P.2d 107, 383 P.2d 1002 (1963), this court quoted with approval from 3 Corbin, Contracts 278 n. 2, § 561, as follows:

> " 'In every contract there is an implied covenant that neither party shall do anything that will have the effect of destroying or injuring the right of the other party to receive the fruits of the contract, which means that in every contract there exists a covenant of good faith and fair dealing.' "

It follows that there was substantial evidence to support the finding that "plaintiff acted in a manner which defeated further performance" of the contract, thus constituting a breach so material as to justify a refusal by defendant to continue performance. It also follows that plaintiff failed by his proof to establish either substantial performance by him or a valid excuse for his failure to perform.

Plaintiff also contends, however, that defendant "cannot rely on such nonperformance to excuse its own nonperformance of nonpayment"; that defendant "continued to reap the benefits from its dealings with United which were . . . an outgrowth of plaintiff's efforts," in excess of any injury suffered by them, with the result that defendant was "under a quasi-contractual duty to pay that excess" citing 2 Restatement, Contracts 623, § 357, and 3A Corbin, Contracts 308–11, § 700. See also 3A Corbin, Contracts 334, § 709.

It is true that in a long line of cases arising under personal service and construction contracts, beginning in Steeples v. Newton, 7 Or. 110, 113–114 (1879), we have held that a plaintiff who has failed to complete the performance of a contract may nevertheless recover in quasi-contract or quantum meruit for the reasonable value of the work performed or material furnished, provided that his breach or abandonment of the contract was not willful. See Trachsel v. Barney, 96 Or.Adv.Sh. 32, 35–36, 503 P.2d 696 (1972). . . .

In this case there was substantial evidence to support a finding of fact that the breach by plaintiff was willful. The trial court, however, did not make such a finding, apparently because plaintiff made no contention in the trial court that he was entitled to recover on a theory of quasi-contract or quantum meruit, but relied solely upon a theory of express contract, as pleaded in his complaint. Also, no evidence was offered from which the trial court could find the amount of any benefit accruing to defendant in excess of any damages suffered by it as a result of plaintiff's breach of contract, as now contended for by plaintiff.

Under these circumstances and this new theory of recovery having been raised for the first time on appeal, it would be improper for us to either consider that theory on appeal or to remand this case to the trial court for further proceedings and further findings.

For these reasons we affirm the holding by the trial court that plaintiff did not establish his right to recovery in that court. It thus becomes unnecessary to consider plaintiff's second assignment of error in which he contends that the trial court erred in finding, as an alternative basis for its decision, that the oral agreement in this case was invalid under the Statute of Frauds (ORS 41.580).

Affirmed.[c]

NOTES

(1) *Some Themes Announced.* Wasserburger's case touches on a number of the major themes presented in the remainder of this chapter. Consider the following propositions, all of which the court seems to accept in one form or another:

(a) A party may lose his rights under a contract by behavior that impairs the other party's expectations of gain under it and may indeed commit a breach of an "implied covenant" in this manner. (Note the excerpt from Corbin: ". . . injuring the right of the other party to receive the fruits of the contract.") This matter is developed below, beginning at p. 803.

(b) Nonperformance of a certain seriousness disqualifies one from enforcing the reciprocal promise of the other party. (Note the court's references to "material breach.") And by inference it appears that there is a category of "immaterial breach," which does *not* discharge the duty of the other promisor although it gives rise to a claim for damages. This distinction is developed below beginning at p. 816.

(c) An agreement may be severable, or divisible, into parts, such that even a serious default as to one part of it may not preclude enforcement of another part. (See the court's ruling in footnote 2.) The divisibility of contracts, for this purpose, is considered below at p. 826. (The same footnote mentions "independent covenants." What that may signify is indicated in the materials beginning at p. 812.)

(d) Substantial performance of a contract—the converse of an immaterial breach—is required of a party to qualify him to enforce a reciprocal promise of the other. This conception is featured in the materials below beginning at p. 890.

(e) A defaulting party, ineligible to recover "on the contract," may nevertheless have restitution for benefit conferred on the other party. (Note the court's reference to quasi-contract.) Such recoveries are illustrated below, beginning at p. 865.

(f) The "willfulness" of a breach by the claimant is an obstacle to his recovery on any basis: on the contract through substantial performance, or in restitution. (Note the court's repeated allusions to evidence of Wasserburger's willfulness.) For further discussion of his attitude, see pp. 876 and 893, below.

(2) *An Unannounced Theme.* Some of the topics to follow are not foreshadowed in the main case. One that is not—not plainly at least—is forfeiture. Would it be accurate to say that the decision caused a forfeiture of the plaintiff's commissions on sales that American Scientific made

c. McAllister, J., concurred in the result.

to United Medical after May, 1969? If so, of course the court might not find it expedient to say so. However, in somewhat similiar cases the law's resistance to forfeitures is often spoken of.

GODBURN v. MESERVE

Supreme Court of Errors of Connecticut, 1944.
130 Conn. 723, 37 A.2d 235.

Action by Lulu Godburn and another against George Meserve and another, executors of the estate of Carrie J. Wells, deceased, to recover damages for breach of a contract by defendants' decedent and for value of services rendered to her, which action was tried to a jury.

BROWN, Judge. In this action based on an agreement by the plaintiffs to provide and care for the defendants' decedent in her house in Stratford in consideration of her promise to leave the property to them by will, the jury rendered a verdict for the plaintiffs which, it was undisputed, was predicated upon the decedent's breach of an express agreement alleged in the first count. There was a second count based on quantum meruit. The defendants have appealed from the court's denial of their motion to set aside the verdict and from the judgment, assigning error in the court's charge to the jury. In the view which we take of the case it is necessary to consider only the claimed error in the court's denial of the motion.

For more than three years prior to February 21, 1936, the plaintiffs had lived as tenants of the decedent in a house owned by her in Stratford. As of the above date, the decedent, seventy-six years of age, was living alone in the house next door, which she also owned. On that date, the parties entered into an express written agreement which provided that for the remainder of the decedent's life they were to live together in her homestead, she occupying the front upstairs room and they furnishing her with board, heat, light and laundry, providing care for her in case of any minor ailments or sickness not requiring a nurse or hospital service, and paying ten dollars per month rent. It further provided that the plaintiffs' family was to be limited to themselves and daughter, and that the decedent was to leave the property to them by will at her death. The decedent made a will in accordance with the agreement and the plaintiffs occupied the house with the decedent and provided for her as stipulated until on or about August 5, 1941, when the plaintiffs moved out and did nothing further in performance of the contract. Thereupon the decedent revoked her will. She died May 21, 1942, at the age of eighty-three. During the first two years that the parties lived together their relations were generally harmonious and mutually agreeable, but thereafter increasing friction developed. Just before the plaintiffs moved out Mr. Godburn proposed a modification of the agreement whereby the decedent would have two rooms, get her own meals and do her own laundry, and the plaintiffs would make an increased cash payment monthly. The decedent refused to modify the agreement. These facts are undisputed.

The jury could reasonably have further found that the plaintiffs faithfully and fully performed their part of the contract up to the time they left; that the decedent objected to the plaintiffs' having their grandchildren and others stay in the home as their guests; that she objected to being left alone in the house at night and thus prevented the plaintiffs from going out or away on vacation; that she constantly found fault with many minor things around the house; that she, without reason, objected to the amount of water used by the plaintiffs which she had to pay for; that she, likewise without reason, demanded food other than that which the plaintiffs provided; constantly objected to the manner in which Mrs. Godburn cooked food and at times refused to eat it, developed a habit of tapping her foot on the floor while eating, and once when Mr. Godburn was seriously ill made a disturbance because her meal was not served on time; and that this course of conduct so disturbed the plaintiffs' home life that they became very nervous, and rendered it very disagreeable and difficult for them to continue to reside with her.

The contract was bilateral containing mutual and dependent covenants demanding of each of the parties readiness and willingness to perform. It therefore required, "as a condition of judicial enforcement or redress for breach at the complaint of either such readiness and willingness on his part or a showing of sufficient excuse for their absence. Phillips v. Sturm, 91 Conn. 331, 335, 99 A. 689; Smith v. Lewis, 24 Conn. 624, 625, 63 Am.Dec. 180." Stierle v. Rayner, 92 Conn. 180, 183, 102 A. 581, 582; Lunde v. Minch, 105 Conn. 657, 659, 136 A. 552. Therefore here, if the plaintiffs on their part were prevented by the decedent from completing the contract, they were entitled to bring their action for damages for her breach of it. Valente v. Weinberg, 80 Conn. 134, 135, 67 A. 369, 13 L.R.A.,N.S., 448; Dadio v. Dadio, 123 Conn. 88, 92, 192 A. 557; Restatement, 1 Contracts, § 295, Conn.Annot., § 295. However, "In order to amount to a prevention of performance by the adversary party, the conduct on the part of the party who is alleged to have prevented performance must be wrongful, and, accordingly, in excess of his legal rights." 5 Page, Contracts, § 2919, p. 5145; Lansdowne v. Reihmann, Ky., 124 S.W. 353. Although " 'where a party stipulates that another shall do a certain thing, he thereby impliedly promises that he will himself do nothing which will hinder or obstruct that other in doing that thing' " (3 Williston, Contracts, Rev.Ed., § 677, p. 1956), manifestly this principle has no application where the hindrance is due to some action of the promisor which he was permitted to take under either the express or implied terms of the contract. See Restatement, 1 Contracts, § 295. The mere fact that permitted conduct of this nature by one promisor renders unpleasant or inconvenient performance by the other of his agreement effects no discharge of that obligation. See 5 Page, Contracts, § 2919, p. 5146; Smoot's Case, 15 Wall. 36, 46, 82 U.S. 36, 46, 21 L.Ed. 107; Thompson & Son v. Brown, 106 Iowa 367, 372, 76 N.W. 819.

Accordingly, the question for determination is whether the decedent's conduct complained of was wrongful in the sense of being violative of her obligations under the contract. In other words was it or was it not conduct which must be said to have been fairly within the contemplation of the parties when the agreement was entered into? See Huminsky v. Gary Nat. Bank, 107 W.Va. 658, 150 S.E. 9. In addition to the facts already mentioned, the undisputed testimony was that for twenty years prior to the agreement Mr. Godburn had known the decedent as a customer in the grocery store where he was employed, that during the last three and one-half years of this period, while he and his family were living next door as her tenants, the plaintiffs came to know the decedent very well, that she was regularly and frequently in their home as a guest and ate meals there, and that they knew she was an elderly lady apparently about seventy-six or seven years of age. It is a matter of common knowledge that a gradually increasing impairment of powers and a not unusual tendency to more or less eccentricity naturally are to be expected as incident to the advancing years of one of that age, and under the circumstances the only reasonable conclusion upon the record before us is that the decedent's conduct was fairly within the contemplation of the parties under their contract as made. The gist of the situation is apparently well summarized by Mr. Godburn's testimony that "the only thing she complained about was the eats," which everybody else thought were all right, that her conduct was upsetting and disturbing to the plaintiffs and that they "didn't have to take it" and they "wouldn't." It follows from what we have said that not only is there no evidence that the decedent "forced the plaintiffs to leave said premises in violation of the terms of the contract," as alleged in the complaint, but furthermore there is none that what she did was "wrongful, and, accordingly, in excess of [her] legal rights" within the principle quoted above. The defendants' motion to set aside the verdict should therefore have been granted.

There is error, the judgment is set aside, and a new trial is ordered.

In this opinion, the other Judges concurred.

NOTES

(1) *Early Cases.* "The older common law did not uniformly require the promisor to refrain from actively preventing the promisee from performing the condition of the promise. In one early case the defendant had given his penal bond to pay the plaintiff eighty pounds unless the defendant should procure a marriage to take place between the plaintiff and one Bridget Pal-

mer, before a certain day. The defendant pleaded that before that day the plaintiff addressed Bridget in such vile and insulting language that the defendant could not bring about the marriage. The plea was adjudged bad on the ground that the defendant should show that he used due diligence to bring about the marriage. [Blandford v. Andrews, Cro.Eliz. 694, 78 Eng. Rep. 930 (K.B.1599)] . . . These decisions show that the implication of a condition of non-prevention was by no means inevitable." Patterson, Constructive Conditions in Contracts, 42 Colum.L.Rev. 903, 931–2 (1942).

(2) *The Case of the School Board's Lesson.* The New York City Board of Education let a contract for work on a school building, containing a condition that the agreement should be binding only if "the comptroller shall indorse hereon his certificate" that appropriated and unexpended funds were on hand to meet the estimated expense. After the contractor had done some preliminary work, the Board "rescinded" the contract. Although it did not question that the required funds were available, it justified its action by the comptroller's failure to certify the contract. He had withheld certification at the Board's request. The contractor sued the Board. From a judgment for the defendant, the plaintiff appealed. *Held*: Reversed. The Board's action could not be justified by the comptroller's failure to certify the contract. "The general rule is, as it has been frequently stated, that a party to a contract cannot rely on the failure of another to perform a condition precedent where he has frustrated or prevented the occurrence of the condition." Kooleraire Serv. & Inst. Corp. v. Board of Ed., 28 N.Y.2d 101, 268 N.E.2d 782 (1971).[a]

Is there any difference, in legal effect, between wrongful prevention of the fulfillment of a constructive condition and similar action with respect to an express condition?

(3) *Prevention as Excuse and as Breach.* Compare the quotation in the foregoing note with this: "It is a general rule of contract law that each party impliedly covenants not to hinder, prevent or make more burdensome the other party's performance. . . . A breach of this covenant may . . . be construed as an actual breach of the contract." State of California v. United States, 151 F.Supp. 570, 573 (N.D.Cal.1957).[b]

Does it matter, in substance, whether the act of prevention is regarded as being itself a breach, or as maturing a further duty of the defendant? In a somewhat comparable case, Justice Holmes said: "The sole difference would be in the form of the declaration." St. Louis Dressed Beef & Prov. Co. v. Maryland Cas. Co., 201 U.S. 173 (1906). After the defendant's first breach in that case, he said, "we think that the plaintiff was entitled to

a. Compare Nodland v. Chirpich, 307 Minn. 360, 240 N.W.2d 513 (1976): Johanna Paschal, one of nine heirs to a farm, was expected to be the last to sign a contract to sell it. She would have done so except that some who had already signed (having changed their minds) telephoned her long-distance and put "pressure" on her not to sign. Having qualms of conscience, Johanna asked one of the callers to "tell her directly not to sign"; and she followed this order. In an action by the prospective purchaser against that signer (and the other heirs), is the defendant precluded from showing that Johanna's signing was a condition precedent to the duty to transfer the farm?

b. And may also, "in some cases, be construed as a failure of a condition precedent, thereby relieving the other party from the duty of counterperformance under the terms of the contract, and providing him with a defense to an action on the contract . . . ."

treat the contract as on foot, notwithstanding the defendant's act, and go on with it *cy-près*." But that was a singular case in some ways; it is sometimes risky for the victim of a breach of contract to disregard it, and "go on" with the contract. In the Case of the School Board's Lesson, would the plaintiff have been well advised to proceed with the work, notwithstanding the comptroller's failure to certify the contract? What risks would it run?

What is the most illuminating way to express the ruling in Godburn v. Meserve?—(a) that though Carrie Wells contributed to the non-occurrence of performance by the plaintiffs that did not excuse their performance as a condition because her conduct was not a breach; (b) that Carrie did not fail of good faith and fair dealing in her "performance" of the contract; or (c) that a proper interpretation of the contract permitted her a large measure of idiosyncratic behavior. Can the issue in the case usefully be stated in terms of Restatement Second, § 205?

(5) *Questions.* If it had been found that some of Carrie Wells' behavior was designed to irritate the Godburns, should the trial court's judgment have been affirmed? What result if she had been given to drink and had abused the plaintiffs under its influence? If she had caused them to leave by assaulting them with a deadly weapon? For allegations of drunkenness and assault, in a comparable case, see Barron v. Cain, 216 N.C. 282, 4 S.E. 2d 618 (1939).

In contracts concerning real property one party is sometimes required, as a matter of good faith, to cooperate with the other in procuring official approval for a particular use of the property. If the party owing cooperation does not provide it, should he be excused if it appears that the approval would not have been granted in any event?

PREVENTION AND BROKERS' COMMISSIONS

It has been said that the issue of prevention most frequently arises in cases involving real-estate brokers. Shear v. National Rifle Ass'n of America, 606 F.2d 1251 (D.C.Cir. 1979). When a broker has brought a seller and a buyer to the point of executing a sale contract—if not sooner—he will naturally expect that he will be paid a commission. But the expectation may be dashed if the sale is not consummated. That is especially so if the agreement for a commission makes it payable "on the closing of title," "at the consummation of sale," or the like. See Notes 2 and 3, p. 763 supra. In the case last cited, the National Rife Association (NRA) contracted to pay Shear $150,000 for having found a purchaser for its Washington headquarters, "contingent on settlement." Though no settlement occurred, Shear sued for the commission. His theory was that the NRA had excused the condition by acts of prevention. (Particulars of the case are given in Note 2 infra.) The court discussed what it called the "assumption of risk" rule, to the effect that the prevention doctrine does not apply when the contract authorizes prevention. By making settlement a condition of his duty to pay a commission, the seller may protect himself from expense when the buyer refuses to perform. The court gave this as an instance of assumption of risk by the broker.[a]

In the case supposed, where the buyer has refused to perform, it may occur to the broker to sue *him* for the loss of a commission. In such a case would it be proper to say that the broker assumed the risk?

NOTES

(1) *Broker v. Buyer.* Consult again Note 3, p. 763 supra. If the decision is that the broker may not claim the commission from the seller, what are his chances of collecting it from the buyer? In Professional Realty Corp. v. Bender, 216 Va. 737, 222 S.E.2d 810 (1976), there was a sale contract executed by the brokerage firm as well as the sellers and the buyers. In it the sellers, who had employed the broker, promised it a commission. The sale was not consummated. In an action by the broker against the buyers, the court gave summary judgment for the defendants. On appeal, the broker urged the court to adopt the rule that, in these circumstances, "the buyer's promise to purchase implies a promise to pay the commission if he defaults on his contract with the seller." *Held*: Affirmed. "We decline to adopt such a rule," the court said.[b]

(2) *A Coup at the NRA.* At the annual meeting of the National Rifle Association in May 1977 the organization was "taken over" by dissident members. Earlier, the decision had been taken to move its headquarters to Colorado and sell its site in the District of Columbia. Indeed, the president had signed a contract of sale to a purchaser procured by Shear, as broker, "subject to the approval of the Board." His commission was confirmed early in May, before the takeover, under an agreement making it "contingent on settlement." After the takeover, the Management Committee, which had earlier selected the purchaser, declined to recommend the sale to the Board. Moreover, the Association by-laws were amended to prohibit changing the headquarters and to strip the Board of Directors of power to approve the sale.

All the foregoing "facts" were alleged by Shear in suing the Association for breach of contract. From a dismissal of his complaint, he appealed.

a. In Ellsworth Dobbs, Inc. v. Johnson, 50 N.J. 528, 236 A.2d 843 (1967), the commission agreement was not so conditioned, and the court addressed the question whether or not a broker may earn a commission from a seller by producing a responsible buyer and effecting a contract, whatever happens thereafter. In ordinary circumstances, the court ruled, he may not, even under an explicit agreement in his favor. Apparently the court concluded that in all his usual employment the broker enjoys such bargaining power that that agreement is contrary to public policy. The court discussed unconscionability at length, citing Henningsen v. Bloomfield Motors (p. 457 supra) and UCC 2–302. It described brokers as fiduciaries. The court also adverted to the standardization of brokers' contracts and the statutory schemes for licensing them.

b. A dictum in the case cited in the foregoing footnote was a main basis for the broker's argument.

For other commercial issues of prevention, see Rosenquist v. Harding, — Mont. —, 587 P.2d 416 (1978), Canyon Land Park, Inc. v. Riley, 575 F.2d 550 (5th Cir. 1978), and Instrumentation Services, Inc. v. General Resource Corp., 283 N.W.2d 902 (Minn. 1979).

Held: Reversed. The court ruled that the doctrine of prevention applied, and not the exception, assumption of risk. "Actually," the court said, "it is somewhat inaccurate to call the assumption of risk rule . . . an 'exception' to the prevention doctrine." Prevention, as defined, is a breach of contract. "A corollary of this definition is that there is no prevention when the contract authorizes a party to prevent a condition from occurring. . . . Shear did not assume the risk that the Management Committee would refuse to recommend the contract, or that the Board would be deprived . . . of authority to approve the contract." Shear v. National Rifle Association, p. 796 supra.

The court also rejected the Association's contention that "nothing but abject speculation could show that 'the condition [settlement] would have occurred'." [c]

IRON TRADE PRODUCTS CO. v. WILKOFF CO.

Supreme Court of Pennsylvania, 1922.
272 Pa. 172, 116 A. 150.

WALLING, J. In July, 1919, plaintiff entered into a written contract with defendant for the purchase of 2,600 tons of section relaying rails, to be delivered in New York harbor at times therein specified for $41 a ton. Defendant failed to deliver any of the rails, and plaintiff brought this suit, averring, by reason of such default, it had been compelled to purchase the rails elsewhere (2,000 tons thereof at $49.20 per ton and 600 tons at $49 per ton), also that the market or current price of the rails at the time and place of delivery was approximately $50 per ton, and claiming as damages the difference between what it had been compelled to pay and the contract price. Defendant filed an affidavit of defense and a supplement thereto, both of which the court below held insufficient and entered judgment for plaintiff, from which defendant brought this appeal.

In effect, the affidavit of defense avers the supply of such rails was very limited, there being only two places in the United States (one in Georgia and one in West Virginia) where they could be obtained in quantities to fill the contract, and that pending the time for delivery defendant was negotiating for the required rails when plaintiff announced to the trade its urgent desire to purchase a similar quantity of like rails, and in fact bought 887 tons and agreed to purchase a much larger quantity from the parties with whom defendant had been negotiating, further averring this conduct on behalf of plaintiff reduced the available supply of relaying rails and enhanced the price to an exorbitant sum, rendering performance by defendant

c. Shear also alleged that when he signed his contingent-on-settlement agreement the NRA official who signed for it knew of the impending coup, and that he (Shear) would not have signed if he had known of it. What sort of claim does this allegation support?

impossible. The affidavit, however, fails to aver knowledge on part of plaintiff that the supply of rails was limited or any intent on its part to prevent, interfere with, or embarrass defendant in the performance of the contract; and there is no suggestion of any understanding, express or implied, that defendant was to secure the rails from any particular source, or that plaintiff was to refrain from purchasing other rails; hence it was not required to do so. The true rule is stated in Williston on Contracts, p. 1308, as quoted by the trial court, viz.:

"If a party seeking to secure all the merchandise of a certain character which he could entered into a contract for a quantity of the required goods, and subsequently made performance of the contract by the seller more difficult by making other purchases which increased the scarcity of the available supply, his conduct would furnish no excuse for refusal to perform the prior contract."

Mere difficulty of performance will not excuse a breach of contract. Corona C. & C. Co. v. Dickinson, 261 Pa. 589, 104 A. 741; Janes v. Scott, 59 Pa. 178, 98 Am.Dec. 328; 35 Cyc. 245. Defendant relies upon the rule stated in United States v. Peck, 102 U.S. 64, 26 L.Ed. 46, that—

"The conduct of one party to a contract which prevents the other from performing his part is an excuse for nonperformance."

The cases are not parallel. Here plaintiff's conduct did not prevent performance by defendant, although it may have added to the difficulty and expense thereof. There is no averment that plaintiff's purchases exhausted the supply of rails, and the advance in price caused thereby is no excuse. The Peck Case stands on different ground. There Peck contracted to sell the government a certain quantity of hay for the Tongue River station, and the trial court found it was mutually understood the hay was to be cut on government lands called "the Big Meadows," in the Yellowstone valley, which was the only available source of supply, also that thereafter the government caused all of that hay to be cut for it by other parties, in view of which Peck was relieved from his contract.

The affidavit "denies that there was any market or market price or current price for such relaying rails" at any time from the date of the contract to the beginning of this suit, but other statements therein amount to an admission of a market price. For example, it speaks of "the trade in Pittsburgh, New York, and other centers of such trade"; also of "the very small quantity of such rails in the market." The affidavit further states that—

"After making the said contract with the plaintiff the defendant began negotiations with the persons from whom the said rails in Georgia and West Virginia might be purchased; and in each of the two cases referred to such negotiations had proceeded so far that defendant could have purchased 2,600 tons of such rails either in Georgia or West Virginia at some such price as that contracted to the plaintiff, or less, or not greatly in excess thereof.

"In fact, the plaintiff bought a quantity of such rails, to wit, 887 tons, and at one time had contracted for the purchase of a much larger quantity thereof, from the same persons with whom the defendant had been negotiating for the same, and at higher prices than had been offered to the defendant by the same persons within the terms of the said contract.

"And affiant, while denying, as aforesaid, that the plaintiff was compelled to purchase the said rails or any of them, avers that, if the plaintiff was so compelled, it was only as the result of plaintiff's own interference with the defendant's performance of the said contract, and avers that but for the said interference the defendant would have made full performance of its said contract."

The above and the admitted facts that plaintiff actually bought the 2,600 tons and had previously resold the same indicate a market value, and the specific averment thereof, in the statement of claim is not sufficiently denied in the affidavit. An affidavit of defense must be considered as a whole, and therein a general denial is of no avail against an admission of the same fact. An affidavit that is contradictory or equivocal is insufficient. See Noll v. Royal Exchange Assurance Corp., 76 Pa.Super.Ct. 510.

The supplemental affidavit avers that when the contract in suit was made plaintiff, to the knowledge of defendant, had resold the 2,600 tons of rails at $42.25 per ton, and, furthermore, that the purchaser at such resale released plaintiff from all claim for damages under the contract. . . . The fact that a vendee has resold the goods contracted for is of no moment unless made a part of the contract; for, if not, he is entitled to the benefit of his bargain, regardless of the disposition he may intend to make of the property involved. To hold otherwise would inject collateral issues in trials for breaches of such contracts.

The assignments of error are overruled, and the judgment is affirmed.

NOTES

(1) *Middlemen's Expectations.* Iron Trade Products might have obtained some protection against competition from the Wilkoff Company by contracting with one of the major rail suppliers to act as its exclusive sales agent in the line or area concerned—perhaps through a franchise arrangement. Why is it that the movement to protect franchise holders has not touched sporadic contracts of sale?

Some evidence that it has not is provided by Alice v. Robett Mfg. Co., 328 F.Supp. 1377 (N.D.Ga.1970), aff'd 445 F.2d 316 (5th Cir. 1971). In that case John Alice had been invited by the General Services Administration to bid for a contract to supply uniforms to the Government. He then made a contract to purchase shirts and trousers for the uniforms from the Robett Company: 3500 shirts at $4 each and the trousers at $3 each. Alice told Robett that its price would be the basis for his bid to GSA. About ten days later Robett made its own bid, offering to supply the uniforms to the Government for $7.78 each; and the Government accepted. Alice sued Robett for breach. On defendant's motion for summary judgment, *held*: granted. The court rejected the plaintiff's contention that "an offer from a manufacturer, to a supplier who is bidding for resale over to a third party contains an implied term prohibiting the manufacturer from submitting its own bid directly to the third party, in competition with the supplier."

Still another defeat for a middleman occurred in Kaiser Trading Co. v. Associated Metals & Minerals Corp., 321 F.Supp 923 (N.D.Cal.1970), appeal dismissed, 443 F.2d 1364 (9th Cir. 1971). The plaintiff in that case, Kaiser, was the purchasing agent for a major aluminum producer. For several years the producer had relied on supplies of cryolite from an Italian firm, contracting annually with a dealer, Associated, for supplies of the mineral. The litigation arose over the 1969 contract, when Associated withheld deliveries due in 1970. The dealer had learned that "surreptitious" negotiations had occurred between Kaiser and the Italian firm for a direct supply relationship beginning in 1971. In an action brought by Kaiser the court ruled that this discovery did not justify Associated in renouncing its contract.

(2) *Distinctions*. Comparing the main case with those in the foregoing note, is Alice's case distinctive because the dealing that offended the middleman (Robett's bid to the GSA) was apparently prompted by information that the middleman supplied? (On the market value of information see Black Industries, Inc. v. Bush, p. 374 supra, and the notes following.) Or is *Iron Trade Products* the more distinctive case because there the plaintiff's rail purchases might have forced the middleman into a breach of contract?

An additional feature of Alice's case was that its contract for shirts and trousers was unenforceable. Robett had made a written offer to sell these items, and Alice had given an acceptance by telephone. Hence at the time of Robett's bid to supply uniforms its dealings with Alice had produced a revocable offer, at most. (See UCC 2–201.) *Question*: Would the decision have been the same if Robett had made a "firm offer" of shirts and trousers to Alice, under UCC 2–205?

(3) *The Case of the Overbidding Buyer*. Some houses in Brooklyn were about to be offered for sale in a foreclosure proceeding. Patterson was in a favorable position to buy them at the public sale, and Mrs. Meyerhofer was interested in owning them. Therefore they entered into an ordinary sale contract whereby Mrs. Meyerhofer agreed to pay Patterson $23,000 for the property. No mention was made of the fact that he did not own it. When Patterson attended the foreclosure sale Mrs. Meyerhofer was also there, and whenever he made a bid she bid higher. The four houses in question were struck down to her for $22,380. Patterson sued for damages, and it was said that on these facts he was entitled to $620. "In the case of every contract there is an implied undertaking on the part of each party that he will not intentionally and purposely do anything to prevent the other party from carrying out the agreement on his part." Patterson v. Meyerhofer, 204 N.Y. 96, 97 N.E. 472 (1912). *Question*: What differentiates this case from the ones presented above?

COOPERATION

In a quotation from Professor Corbin, the court in Wasserburger's case (p. 787 supra) made reference to the right of a party "to receive the fruits of the contract". The other party is proscribed, Corbin said, from doing anything the effect of which will be to destroy or injure that right. To this it may be added that in many situations the "other party" is responsible for taking affirmative steps to bring the fruits of the contract to harvest. That is so even when the parties have not troubled to express the duty in their agreement. (See Chapter 7, Section 3, supra; Restatement Second, § 205. See also § 245, Comment a.) One way of putting the matter is to say that a person entering a contract comes under a "constructive condition of cooperation." Patterson, Constructive Conditions in Contracts, 42 Colum.L.Rev. 903 (1942). That is especially apt when he complains of the non-performance of a promise on the other side, and it can be shown that cooperative effort on his part was essential to performance of the promise. The principle is frequently applied in construction cases: under building contracts it is understood that a contractor, or subcontractor, cannot proceed effectively until he is provided with a site, prepared in a way appropriate for the work.[a] In the Restatement Second, an illustration from sales law is given:

> A contracts with B to manufacture and deliver 100,000 plastic containers for a price of $100,000. The colors of the containers are to be selected by B from among those specified in the contract. B delays in making his selection for an unreasonable time, holding up their manufacture and causing A loss. B's delay is a breach. His duty of good faith and fair dealing (§ 205) includes a duty to make his selection within a reasonable time. [Section 235, Illus. 3].

This illustration is based on Kehm Corp. v. United States, 93 F.Supp. 620 (Ct.Cl.1950), in which the Government was held accountable for a supplier's delays in producing concrete bombs for practice in the Navy. Owing to delays by the Government in providing tail assemblies, Kehm's casting work was extended, sporadic, and costly. (In truth, the Navy had lost interest in the concrete bomb program.) Speaking of Kehm as the promisor, the court said: "The promisor's undertaking normally gives rise to an implied complementary obligation on the part of the promisee: he must not only not hinder his promisor's performance, he must do whatever is necessary to enable

a. See R. G. Pope Constr. Co., Inc. v. Guard Rail of Roanoke, Inc., 219 Va. 111, 244 S.E.2d 774 (1978) (contractor vs. subcontractor, with counterclaim: "the defendant's performance of the duty to install guardrail was subject to certain conditions, the most important of which was the implied condition that a site would be available for such installation").

See also Shea-S & M Ball v. Massman-Kiewit-Early, 606 F.2d 1245 (D.C.Cir. 1979); Goldberg, The Owner's Duty to Coordinate Multi-Prime Construction Contractors, 28 Emory L.J. 377 (1979).

him to perform. . . . The implied obligation is as binding as if it were spelled out. Wood v. Lucy [p. 81 supra]."

Naturally there are contracting parties who, in a spirit of self-pity or worse, demand more than their fair share of cooperation. There is a countervailing principle that "enthusiasm is not required in performing contractual obligations." Esmieu v. Hzieh, 20 Wash.App. 455, 580 P.2d 1105 (1978).

NOTES

(1) *Influences in Cooperation Cases.* Patterson, Constructive Conditions in Contracts, 42 Colum.L.Rev. 903 (1942), gives an historical and critical survey of the requirement of cooperation at pp. 928–42. "While not every act or omission by the obligor which may expedite performance by the obligee (of his promise or of a condition) is required, the acts or omissions which are clearly within the obligor's control and which are the normal or obvious means of the obligee's performance, are presumably required of the obligor, or he assumes the risk of their non-occurrence. The justifiable reliance by the obligee, the usages of the trade or activity, the mores of the community, are obviously influential in determining what co-operation is required in a particular transaction. Judicial opinions reveal these influences. The moral notions of carelessness or diligence, malice or inadvertence, have sporadic influence. The avoidance of unjust enrichment seems also influential." Id., pp. 937–8. How many of these "influences" would be relevant in applying Restatement Second, § 205? Is the phrase "terms of the contract" unduly restrictive, as Patterson suggests?

(2) *Express Requirements.* Sometimes an express provision is made in a contract for one party to cooperate with the other in bringing about a common objective. When a man engaged an artist to paint portraits of himself and the members of his family he agreed to make himself and them available for sittings. Brockhurst v. Ryan, 2 Misc.2d 747, 146 N.Y.S.2d 386 (Sup.Ct.1955). Also, in standard policies of liability insurance there is a requirement that the policyholder cooperate with the insurer in the defense of suits. Would such requirements be implicit in the contracts if not expressed? See Keeton, Ancillary Rights of the Insured, 13 Vand.L.Rev. 837, 847 (1960).

THE RIGHT TO ASSURANCE OF PERFORMANCE

"Ordinarily an obligee has no right to demand reassurance by the obligor that the latter will perform when his performance is due. However, a contract 'imposes an obligation on each party that the other's expectation of receiving due performance will not be impaired.' Uniform Commercial Code § 2–609(1). When, therefore, an obligee reasonably believes that the obligor will commit a breach by non-performance that would of itself give him a claim for damages for total breach (§ 243), he may, under the rule stated in this Section, be entitled to demand assurance of performance." Restatement Second, § 251, Comment a.

Section 251 had no counterpart in the first Restatement. It is a generalization from UCC 2–609, which was itself something of a legislative innovation. It remains to be seen whether or not the courts will accede to the Restatement position in cases not governed by Article 2 of the Code.

The sort of case that chiefly inspired the Code section was one in which a seller committed himself to supply goods for payment thereafter, and received signals before making delivery that the buyer was in financial distress.[a] In an extreme case of this type a supplier named Gestetner was sued by Turntables, Inc. for his failure to deliver goods on credit, as promised. It seems that Gestetner had demanded assurance of payment under 2–609 after learning these facts: Turntables was in arrears in payment for goods already delivered; it had a bad credit reputation; its "Fifth Avenue Showroom" turned out to be a telephone answering service; and its "factory" turned out to be someone else's premises, to which Turntables did not have a key. (The court said that Gestetner "obviously" had reasonable grounds for insecurity.) Turntables' response to the demand for assurance was to cancel the contract and sue. Gestetner made a counterclaim for damages and obtained a judgment from which Turntables appealed. *Held*: Affirmed. Turntables, Inc. v. Gestetner, 52 A.D.2d 776, 382 N.Y.S.2d 799 (1st Dept. 1976).

It will help in understanding UCC 2–609 to make an inventory of the principal differences between this case and that described in Comment 4 after the section (reproduced in the Supplement).[b]

Questions

Some of the questions relating to insecurity that are to be addressed are these:

(1) Suppose that a demand for assurance is made on reasonable grounds, but not expressed in writing. Under the Code section 2–609 or the Restatement § 251, is the demand effective? Hazardous?

(2) Suppose a demand made for "assurance" in general terms. Is the recipient justified in demanding to know from the sender what specific form of assurance would or might satisfy him?

(3) Suppose a demand made for a specific form of assurance (e. g., a bank guarantee of payment) which is in-

a. The principal cases are cited in the Reporter's Note to Restatement Second, § 252. See also United States for Use and Benefit of Industrial Instrument Corp. v. Paul Hardeman, Inc., 202 F.Supp. 124 (N.D.Tex.1962), aff'd, 320 F.2d 115 (5th Cir. 1963).

b. Actually, the facts presented in Corn Products Refining Co. v. Fasola bear almost no resemblance to the case as stated in the comment.

convenient or impossible for the recipient to give. If another form would serve the purpose equally well, is the demand effective? Hazardous?

(4) Suppose a demand made on insufficient grounds. Is the recipient entitled to treat that as a breach?

On some of these matters judgment should be reserved until the material on anticipatory breach, to follow, has been examined. Even then some of the answers may appear problematical.

NOTES

(1) *Problem.* A buyer of iron rails to be delivered in installments complained that the first two shipments were short, and expressed the wish to be absolved from the contract. The seller answered by letter asking "to know definitely what is your intention." The buyer answered: "You ask us to determine whether we will or will not object to receive further shipments because of past defaults. We tell you we will if we are entitled to do so, and will not if we are not entitled to do so. We do not think you have the right to compel us to decide a disputed question of law to relieve you from the risk of deciding it yourself. You know quite as well as we do what is the rule and its uncertainty of application." On receiving this letter, how should the seller act? See Norrington v. Wright, 115 U.S. 188 (1885). Would he be justified in demanding assurance of due performance under UCC 2–609?

(2) *The Case of the Joyless Credit Manager.* At the request of the Brookhaven Manor Water Company, Pittsburgh-Des Moines Steel Company (PDM) submitted a revised proposal to build an elevated tank for $175,000. The original proposal called for progress payments to PDM; the revised offer called for no payment until the tank had been built and tested. After Brookhaven's acceptance, PDM heard something about a loan that Brookhaven was negotiating for. The credit manager for PDM wrote the prospective lender (copy to PDM) asking for a notice that $175,000 had been put in escrow for the job, and adding: "As a matter of good business we are holding this matter in abeyance until receipt of such notification." The loan did not go through. Then the credit manager wrote the president of Brookhaven asking for his personal guarantee of payment, "to protect us between now and the time your loan is completed." The letter mentioned the escrow again, this time as a requirement. The president sent a statement of his personal worth. PDM stopped fabricating parts, and the tank was never built. In a suit by PDM, each party claimed damages for breach by the other. The trial court gave judgment n. o. v. for Brookhaven covering its costs of building and demolishing a foundation for the tank. On appeal by PDM, *held:* Affirmed. Pittsburgh-Des Moines Steel Co. v. Brookhaven Manor Water Co., 532 F.2d 572 (7th Cir. 1976).

Question: Was PDM unwarranted in demanding *any* assurance from Brookhaven, or only in the form of assurance it sought? The court divided on this point. Judge Cummings, concurring, indicated that whether reasonable grounds for insecurity existed or not was an issue for the jury. Judge Pell, writing for himself and Justice Tom C. Clark, hinted that only a change in Brookhaven's financial condition, after the contract was made, would have justified a demand. The opinion refers to the "not entirely unfamiliar situation of a corporate credit department not viewing a contract of sale with the same *joie de vivre* as did the sales department." [a]

NORTHWEST LUMBER SALES, INC. v. CONTINENTAL FOREST PRODUCTS, INC.

Supreme Court of Oregon, 1972.
261 Or. 480, 495 P.2d 744.

McALLISTER, Justice.

This is a dispute between two wholesale lumber dealers involving three carloads of forest products. Northwest Lumber Sales, Inc., is a Washington corporation, with its office in Spokane, and the defendant Continental Forest Products, Inc., is an Oregon corporation with its office in Lake Oswego. Neither party was satisfied with the decree of the trial court and the defendant has appealed and the plaintiff cross-appealed. Since the case is tried de novo in this court we will relate the controlling facts.

The controversy centers on a car of plywood which defendant's employee Jack Cutsforth, referred to as a lumber trader, ordered from plaintiff on December 19, 1968. Defendant's purchase order called for shipment in two weeks and stated that defendant would advise plaintiff later of the destination and routing of the car. On December 20 plaintiff acknowledged the order on those terms. On January 3, 1969, defendant sold the car of plywood to a customer in Illinois.

For reasons which will later appear, plaintiff did not ship the plywood to defendant's customer and defendant had to buy a car of plywood from another source at a substantially increased price and sustained a loss on the transaction of $4,387.97. After the dispute arose over the plaintiff's liability for failing to deliver the plywood,

a. On Judge Cummings' view, what might PDM have been justified in demanding by way of an assurance of payment?

Part of the opinion is devoted to the question whether or not Article 2 of the Code was applicable to the contract. In Schenectady Steel Co., Inc. v. Bruno Trimpoli General Constr. Co., Inc., 34 N.Y.2d 939, 359 N.Y.S.2d 560, 316 N.E.2d 875 (1974), the trial court concluded that a contractor was justified in terminating its contract with a steel fabricator for failure to respond adequately to a demand under UCC 2–609. The Appellate Division affirmed (except as to damages), but not on that ground. It reasoned that the contract was one for work, labor and materials to which Article 2 did not apply, and said: "Of course, at common law no such duty to provide adequate assurances existed." On further appeal, the Court of Appeals also affirmed, but without approving either opinion below: "We would further indicate that on the facts of this case it is immaterial whether article 2 . . . applies."

To the effect that UCC 2–609 is inapplicable to a plumbing contract see Cork Plumbing Co., Inc. v. Martin Bloom Associates, Inc., 573 S.W.2d 947 (Mo.App.1978). See also Note 3, p. 833 infra.

defendant declined to pay plaintiff for a carload of select pine lumber which it had bought from plaintiff. Plaintiff then, in turn, refused to ship defendant a carload of 2 x 4 dimension lumber referred to as "studs," which it had sold to defendant. Defendant had to buy a replacement car of studs on a rising market at a loss of $2,096.60.

We next describe the legal posture of this suit. [The plaintiff brought proceedings to recover the purchase price of the pine lumber. By stipulation the defendant acceded to this liability in the amount of $7,999.06 (and interest) but asserted two claims as setoffs, one for the plywood and one for the studs. The trial court allowed setoff only as to the latter.

[Next the court took up the plywood claim, and concluded that the trial court had erred. The evidence presented an issue of fact: whether or not the defendant had assented to a cancellation of the plywood order in a crucial telephone conversation. Reviewing the evidence, the court concluded that the order was never cancelled. The court observed that the plywood market was rising sharply about this time, and said: "We find Cutsforth's testimony more credible for several reasons. First, we think if the order had been cancelled on December 30, 1968, plaintiff would have sent a written memorandum of the cancellation to defendant. We have taken note of the testimony that much of the business transacted between plaintiff and defendant was on an informal word-of-mouth basis. However, defendant's written order for a car of plywood was immediately acknowledged in writing by plaintiff. In view of the admittedly unstable market we think it is significant that plaintiff did not send a memorandum of the cancellation to defendant. . . . We attach some importance to the fact that it was not until February 27, 1969, that plaintiff first made a claim in writing that the plywood order had been cancelled on December 30th and, as we have pointed out, the first such claim was not unequivocal."]

. . .

We consider next the issues raised by plaintiff's cross-appeal from the trial court's allowance of the setoff involving the studs. Defendant ordered the studs in November, 1968. There was a delay in shipment by plaintiff's supplier, and the order was still pending when, because of the dispute over the plywood, defendant withheld payment for the order of pine lumber.

On March 4, 1969, defendant's attorneys wrote to plaintiff stating that if the studs were not shipped by March 10, defendant would buy the studs elsewhere and deduct any loss from the amount due on the pine lumber order. Plaintiff's attorneys, on March 7, answered by letter in which they stated that payment for the pine lumber was then approximately thirty days past due:

" . . . In view of this circumstance, and under the terms and conditions of quotation and sale of the Association to which these parties belong and subject to which the orders written are made, my client declines to ship by reason of the failure of yours to pay. . . ." The issues on appeal concern the effect of the "terms and conditions" referred to in that letter.

Plaintiff's written acknowledgment of the stud order provides:

" . . . These goods will be shipped under the terms and conditions of sale of the Western Pine Association unless otherwise specified, ..."

The Western Pine Association was no longer in existence at the time the order was placed. Witnesses for both parties testified that a new organization, the Western Wood Products Association, had taken its place. The "Terms and Conditions of Quotation and Sale" of the Western Wood Products Association provide, in paragraph VI b:

"*The seller shall have the right to cancel* on account of any arbitrary deductions made by the buyer with respect to, or failure to comply with, contract terms in respect to any prior shipment, or *on account of* any transfer of or change in the buyer's business, his insolvency, suit by other creditors, *failure of buyer to meet financial obligations to seller,* impairment of buyer's credit information, or for unfavorable credit reports made to seller through usual channels of credit information unless the buyer shall promptly furnish to the seller's satisfaction guaranty of full payment for any shipment made or to be made. Notice of such cancellation shall be given in writing." (Emphasis added.)

Plaintiff contends that under the italicized portion of this paragraph it had the right to cancel the stud order when defendant failed to pay for the pine lumber, and that its attorneys' letter of March 7 gave the required notice of cancellation. Defendant contends that under a proper construction of paragraph VI b, plaintiff was not entitled to cancel the order. We have concluded that defendant is correct. We therefore find it unnecessary to reach the question, which the trial court found determinative, whether there was sufficient evidence that the parties understood the reference to the Western Pine Association to apply to the Western Wood Products Association.

We may assume that paragraph VI b of the Association's terms and conditions was incorporated into the contract between the parties. We also assume for purposes of this decision, although defendant contends otherwise, that defendant's action in withholding payment for the pine lumber order was not legally justified and that defendant had failed to meet a financial obligation to plaintiff. The question is whether this failure justified plaintiff in cancelling the stud order.

Neither the Uniform Commercial Code nor general contract law gives either party to a contract the right to refuse performance because the other has breached a separate contract between them. See ORS 72.7030, 72.7170; 3A Corbin on Contracts 290–291, § 696; 6

Williston on Contracts (3d ed. 1962) 535, § 887D; 27 A.L.R. 1157. Plaintiff's right of cancellation depends solely on the provisions of paragraph VI b of the Association's terms and conditions. That right of cancellation exists only "unless the buyer shall promptly furnish to the seller's satisfaction guaranty of full payment for any shipment made or to be made." Plaintiff never requested such a guarantee; although the terms and conditions do not specifically state that the seller must make such a request, we construe them to include that requirement. The seller's right of cancellation may also be exercised for a number of reasons under paragraph VI b, among them being unfavorable credit information. A buyer might be totally unaware of such matters unless the seller called them to his attention. The provision for furnishing a guarantee of payment would at times be meaningless unless the provision is construed to require the seller to request such a guarantee before exercising his right of cancellation.

The alternative construction, requiring the buyer to take the initiative without notice or request by the seller, would be of doubtful validity under the Uniform Commercial Code. ORS 72.6090 provides for the right of either party to suspend performance if there are reasonable grounds for insecurity as to the other's performance; assurance of performance may then be demanded in writing, and a failure to provide adequate assurance within a reasonable time after demand may be treated as a repudiation of the contract. ORS 71.1020(3) provides:

"The effect of provisions of the Uniform Commercial Code may be varied by agreement, except as otherwise provided in the Uniform Commercial Code and except that the obligations of good faith, diligence, reasonableness and care prescribed by the Uniform Commercial Code may not be disclaimed by agreement but the parties may by agreement determine the standards by which the performance of such obligations is to be measured if such standards are not manifestly unreasonable."

Paragraph VI b is a variation of the terms of ORS 72.6090 by agreement of the parties, and should be construed with reference to that provision. The Official Comments to UCC 2–609 (ORS 72.6090) state:

"6. Clauses seeking to give the protected party exceedingly wide powers to cancel or readjust the contract when ground for insecurity arises must be read against the fact that good faith is a part of the obligation of the contract and not subject to modification by agreement and includes, in the case of a merchant, the reasonable observance of commercial standards of fair dealing in the trade. Such clauses can thus be effective to enlarge the protection given by the present section to a certain extent, to fix the reasonable time within which requested assurance must be given, or to define adequacy of the assurance in any commercially reasonable fashion. But any clause seeking to set up arbitrary standards for action is ineffective under this Article."

The mere fact that payment under one contract is not made when due is not necessarily a reasonable ground for insecurity as to payment under another contract. In the present case there was no question of defendant's financial ability to pay its bills; plaintiff knew that defendant was withholding payment in order to cover possible losses when it replaced the plywood order, and the amount withheld was clearly more than enough for that purpose.

But even if plaintiff had reason to suppose that defendant might also refuse to pay for the stud order if it was shipped, cancellation of the stud order without a prior request for guarantee of payment was not justified. A construction of paragraph VI b which would permit such cancellation without prior notice and opportunity to furnish a guarantee would permit sellers to act in an arbitrary fashion.

We cannot say that a request for guarantee would have been futile in this case. There is no apparent reason why defendant would not have been willing to guarantee payment of the stud order, and it might well have offered a conditional guarantee or escrow arrangement as to the amount due for the pine lumber which would have protected both parties. Defendant should at least have been offered the opportunity to suggest a reasonable method of assurance of performance.

We hold, therefore, that plaintiff's cancellation of the stud order was unjustified and that the trial court correctly held plaintiff liable for defendant's losses in covering that order in the market.

The trial court's decree is modified to provide that the defendant is entitled, in addition to the setoff allowed by the trial court against plaintiff's judgment, to a further setoff in the amount of $4,387.97 plus interest at six per cent from February 25, 1969. As so modified, the decree of the trial court is affirmed.

Defendant is entitled to recover costs in this court.

NOTES

(1) *The Rationale.* In a description of this case given above (Note 4, p. 492) it is said that the court denied effect to the cancellation term as written. Would it be more accurate to say that the term was construed in light of the purposes of the Uniform Commercial Code? Or to say that it was held to be preempted by UCC 2–609? What difference does it make whether the opinion means the one thing or the other?

(2) *Consolidation of Contracts.* The opinion does not disclose when the carload of pine lumber was contracted for. Suppose that the defendant had ordered it in January, and that the following actions had ensued. The plaintiff replied with an "acceptance" expressly conditioned on the defendant's assent to rescission and re-writing of the stud-sale contract. The defendant acceded to the condition, so that the deliveries of lumber and of studs were to be made on the terms of defendant's orders, but all the terms

were consolidated in a single set of contract documents. These facts are designed to make inapplicable the court's statement that the law does not give one party to a contract "the right to refuse performance because the other has breached a separate contract between them." It seems that the plaintiff's justification for canceling as to the studs would not depend on Paragraph VI b, but on the defendant's breach of the very contract—or a part of it—requiring delivery of the studs.

The means just suggested for strengthening the seller's hand might seem fanciful except that contract law has generated a potent instrument for dealing with just such arrangements. By the doctrine of divisibility (or "severability"), when discrete undertakings within a single agreement are more or less unrelated in substance they can be disassociated for various purposes. (Divisibility has been described in Chapter 5 as a means of dealing with illegality; and other uses are described below.)

Does Paragraph VI b of the trade-association terms signify that all dealings between one member and another are to be regarded as parts of a single agreement? Does UCC 2–609 itself—within limits—call for such treatment of a series of separate sale contracts between the same parties?

(3) *A Closer Case.* On December 1, 1972, Bartlett & Company (buyer) had thirteen contracts for the delivery of grain thereafter by the National Farmers Organization (seller). Four of these called for December deliveries. On another contract, calling for wheat in September, seller had not completed deliveries. Eight contracts permitted deliveries after January. Some deliveries that should have been made in December were delayed until January, and even then were not complete. During most of these two months buyer "retained" part of the price of the grain delivered then, as protection against seller's delay or default. After making some demands for current payment, seller advised buyer orally, on January 26, that it was not going to deliver more grain on any of the fourteen contracts unless and until it was paid a substantial part of the amount owing for deliveries under the four December contracts. The next day seller suspended deliveries and on January 30 seller sent buyer a telegram of cancellation. Buyer calculated its losses on all the undelivered grain (market price less contract price) and paid for the grain it had received, less its losses. Seller conceded responsibility for some of the losses, but sued for an additional sum. Its position was that buyer had no compensable loss on the eight post-January contracts. From a judgment for buyer, seller appealed. *Held:* Affirmed. National Farmers Organization v. Bartlett & Co., Grain, 560 F.2d 1350 (8th Cir. 1977).

The court was troubled by two points. First, the buyer's withholding of payments was wrongful, under the "separate contract" rule. Second, the January 26 communication from the seller, "unlike the communication in *Northwest Lumber Sales*, did not purport to be an outright cancellation or renouncement of any obligation under any of the contracts." The facts in that case presented an easier question, the court observed. "On the other hand," several points favored the buyer. One was that "Time was not of the essence under the contracts." Another was that the seller could plainly have availed itself of a section 2–609 remedy on January 26, and "plainly" did not do so. (In a footnote, the court observed that the buyer did not pursue that remedy either.) *Questions:* What is the difference, precisely, between a seller's demand that the buyer give him adequate assurance of due performance and a threat to withhold deliveries unless the buyer pays some arrears on prior deliveries? Is it that the latter is an *overdemand* for assurance?

(4) *Unwritten Demand.* In the foregoing case the court said that the seller's communication of January 26 was not a demand under 2–609 because it was not in writing. But it has been held that a written demand is not required by the Code, at least when the failure to use a writing is excusable. See AMF, Inc. v. McDonald's Corp., 536 F.2d 1167 (7th Cir. 1976) (first party had a clear understanding that "other" was awaiting assurance before proceeding). In Kunian v. Development Corp. of America, 165 Conn. 300, 334 A.2d 427 (1973), a supplier of building materials, conferring with the buyer, insisted that payment be made for goods delivered as a condition to continuing deliveries. "Under the circumstances," the court said, "this was equivalent to a written demand for assurances." See also Toppert v. Bunge Corp., p. 832 infra. Is there any reason for requiring a writing, as the Code seems to do?

DEPENDENT AND INDEPENDENT PROMISES

Kingston v. Preston, the case that follows, was regarded in its own time as a notable advance in the doctrine of dependency of covenants, and has been so referred to ever since. To speak in current terms, it is regarded as the chief inspiration for constructive conditions. The views expressed by Lord Mansfield have been commonly seen as modifying an attitude of the common law that was centuries old. One source is a case in which a seller of an interest in land sued the buyer for a sum stipulated to be paid if either party failed to perform. The issue presented by the pleadings was whether or not the plaintiff might recover without having made any move to convey the property. According to Lord Kenyon (who succeeded Mansfield as Chief Justice), the claim would be good under "the old cases"; but he said that they "outrage common sense."[a] Some hypothetical cases supposed to express the law were stated in 1500.[b] One of them concerned a father who covenants to transfer an estate to his daughter and her husband-to-be, as part of a marriage settlement between the two men. According to the old text, if the latter is faithless—"if I marry another woman"—nevertheless the father can be compelled to convey. That result represents in an extreme degree the principle that mutual covenants are *independent* unless expressed to be otherwise; in current terms we might say that the marriage is not a constructive condition of the father's undertaking. (The result is otherwise, says the note, if the father's covenant refers to the marriage promise in a certain way, being made "for the same cause.")[c]

a. Goodisson v. Nunn, 4 T.R. 761, 100 Eng.Rep. 1288 (K.B.1792).

b. Y.B.Trin. 15 Hen. 7, f. 10, pl. 17 (1500).

c. The law French is as follows—as amalgamated from two prints of the yearbook and with some translation and transliteration, all by the editors—:

Students of legal history have shown that Kingston v. Preston was not a simple turnabout in the law as it has sometimes been depicted. The dependency of promises was neither invented nor finally resolved in that case, though it is the most celebrated of a long series on the subject.[d] However that may be, Kingston v. Preston was surely influential in shaping the principle of dependency of covenants in English law, and the historical facts may well prove to be less important than the way they have been perceived.

The defendant in the case was in business as a silk mercer, and the plaintiff had entered his business as a "covenant servant," or apprentice. The articles of indenture provided that after a year and a quarter the defendant would retire from the business. Thereafter it was to be carried on by the plaintiff and a partner—either a nephew of the defendant or someone else nominated by the defendant. The plaintiff was to pay for his share of the business in monthly installments of 250 £. (The payments were to represent the value of the inventory, or stock in trade, which was to be fixed at a fair valuation.) For assuring these payments, the plaintiff agreed to give the defendant "good and sufficient security," approved of by him, "at and before the sealing and delivery of the deeds" conveying the business.

All this was alleged by the plaintiff, and further that he had performed and been ready to perform his covenants, but that the defendant had refused to surrender the business at the appointed time. The defendant pleaded that the plaintiff did not give sufficient security for the payments. To this the plaintiff demurred, and arguments ensued as reported below.

KINGSTON v. PRESTON

King's Bench, 1773.
Lofft 194, 2 Doug. 689, 99 Eng.Rep. 437.

On the part of the plaintiff, the case was argued by Mr. Buller, who contended that the covenants were mutual and independent, and therefore a plea of the breach of one of the covenants to be performed by the plaintiff was no bar to an action for a breach by the defendant of one which he had bound himself to perform, but that the

Nota, p(er) Fineux Chief Justice Issint (Ainsi) si jeo covenant ave(c) un home que jeo marierai sa fille, et il covenant ave(c) moy qu' il fera estat a moy et a sa fille, et a les h(ei)rs de n(otre) 2 corps ingendrez, si jeo puis mary autr(e) fem, ou la fille mary autre home; unc (unques; yet) jeo aurai act de Covenant vers luy, de compellat luy de faire cett(e) estat. Mes (mais) si le covenant fuit, que il ferra estat a nous deux *p(o)ur me[s]me le cause*, donq (donc) il no fera estate tancR (tanque) nous sumus (sommes) mariez. Et issint Opinio Curiae.

Rede Justice disoit, que issint est sanz doubte.

(emphasis supplied).

d. See Stoljar, Dependent and Independent Promises, 2 Syd.L.Rev. 217 (1957); McGovern, Dependent Promises in the History of Leases and Other Contracts, 52 Tul.L.Rev. 659 (1978).

defendant might have his remedy for the breach by the plaintiff in a separate action. On the other side, Mr. Gross insisted that the covenants were dependent in their nature, and therefore performance must be alleged: the security to be given for the money was manifestly the chief object of the transaction, and it would be highly unreasonable to construe the agreement so as to oblige the defendant to give up a beneficial business, and valuable stock-in-trade, and trust to the plaintiff's personal security (who might, and, indeed was admitted to be worth nothing), for the performance of his part.

In delivering the judgment of the Court, Lord Mansfield expressed himself to the following effect: There are three kinds of covenants: 1. Such as are called mutual and independent, where either party may recover damages from the other for the injury he may have received by a breach of the covenants in his favor, and where it is no excuse for the defendant to allege a breach of the covenants on the part of the plaintiff. 2. There are covenants which are conditions and dependent, in which the performance of one depends on the prior performance of another, and, therefore, till this prior condition is performed, the other party is not liable to an action on his covenant. 3. There is also a third sort of covenants, which are mutual conditions to be performed at the same time; and in these, if one party was ready and offered to perform his part, and the other neglected or refused to perform his, he who was ready and offered has fulfilled his engagement, and may maintain an action for the default of the other; though it is not certain that either is obliged to do the first act. His Lordship then proceeded to say, that the dependence or independence of covenants was to be collected from the evident sense and meaning of the parties, and that, however transposed they might be in the deed, their precedency must depend on the order of time in which the intent of the transaction requires their performance. That, in the case before the Court, it would be the greatest injustice if the plaintiff should prevail: the essence of the agreement was, that the defendant should not trust to the personal security of the plaintiff, but, before he delivered up his stock and business, should have good security for the payment of the money. The giving such security, therefore, must necessarily be a condition precedent. Judgment was accordingly given for the defendant, because the part to be performed by the plaintiff was clearly a condition precedent.

NOTE

Serjeant Williams' Rules. In 1798 Serjeant John Williams sought to rationalize the law of dependency of covenants by stating five rules on the subject, which maintained a certain influence into the present century. According to one rule, if a payment is to be made *after* the day appointed for the thing to be done as consideration for it, the duty to pay is conditional, or "dependent". By another rule, the duty to pay is dependent if the *same day* is appointed for the two performances. Not all of the rules are consistent with present understanding, however.

Of these rules Professor Corbin says: "They tended to crystallize the law, when perhaps it should have been flexible. At the same time, they have themselves suffered at the hands of later courts and writers. They show that a Restatement works; but also that even an influential Restatement will require Restating. An attempt to crystallize fails; and the law remains flexible." § 662. See also Williston, §§ 819–23.

TENDER

"A formal tender is seldom made in business transactions," it is said, "except to lay the foundation for subsequent assertion in a court of justice of rights which spring from refusal of the tender." [a] Courts are not often called on to say what is or is not a formal tender of performance under a contract. Partly for that reason, perhaps, as the word "tender" is commonly used it suggests a degree of punctilio in conduct that is seldom achieved. Paradoxically, the strict sense of the word is supported by a set of rules dispensing with the necessity of tender in ordinary contract litigation.

The Code states the requisites, under contracts for the sale of goods, for a seller's tender of delivery (UCC 2–507) and for a buyer's tender of payment (UCC 2–511). A comment after the former section identifies two senses of the word "tender." In the stricter sense, it "contemplates an offer coupled with a present ability to fulfill all the conditions resting on the tendering party and must be followed by actual performance if the other party shows himself ready to proceed." But the comment indicates that something less than this will suffice to put the other party in default, "if he fails to proceed in some manner."

If a buyer has not made an arrangement with the seller for credit, must he proffer payment in money—i. e., "legal tender"? The Code recognizes that it is commercially normal to accept a check from a "seemingly solvent party," and states a rule designed to avoid "commercial surprise." Tendering a check is commonly sufficient under this rule, "unless the seller demands payment in legal tender and gives any extension of time reasonably necessary to procure it." UCC 2–511(2); and see Comments 2–4.

In Lawrence v. Miller, 86 N.Y. 131 (1881), a contract for the sale of land had fallen through, and the buyer sought to recover an initial payment of $2,000. The buyer contended that the seller could retain the money only if he had put the buyer in default by making tender of a deed, and that he had not done so. The court said: "it may be taken that by the term tender is generally meant the actual physical production of the deed, and the reaching it out, with words

a. Lehman, J., dissenting, in Petterson v. Pattberg, 248 N.Y. 86, 161 N.E. 428 (1928). For a longer excerpt see Note 4, p. 307 supra. See also Dunham v. Dangeles, 67 Ill. App.3d 252, 23 Ill.Dec. 929, 384 N.E. 2d 836 (1978).

of offer of it, to the vendee." But the court ruled that the buyer had been put in default without such a ceremony; "the requirement of the law is not cast in a rigid mould. . . ." It appeared that the parties had met twice "with a view to perform." Each time the seller had laid the deed on the table, and the buyer had asked for more time. On the second occasion the seller refused to allow another day. The court's opinion can be understood as saying either that the seller's conduct was a sufficient tender, or that a perfect tender was excused by the buyer's conduct. An exact definition of the word, if it could be achieved, would not be decisive in many cases.

NOTE

The Case of the Cool Customer. On November 16 Pelletier contracted to pay Dwyer $83,000 for a tract of land and made a $5,000 down payment. Dwyer did not own the property at the time, but had a contract to buy it. His agreement with Pelletier provided for refund of the $5,000 if his title was not made good within seven months. "But if the title . . . is made good in [Dwyer on or before June 16] and the purchaser refuses to accept the same, said sum of $5,000 shall be forfeited." On June 15 an agent for Dwyer wrote to Pelletier warning him of the midnight expiration on the following day. On the morning of the 16th Dwyer received a deed to the property. Nothing more passed between the parties until Pelletier sued Dwyer for $5,000. From judgment for the defendant, plaintiff appealed. *Held*: Reversed. The defendant failed to establish a tender of his performance such as was necessary to entitle him to the money. "It may appear that the plaintiff evinced a degree of coolness that approached diffidence by not getting in touch with Mr. Dwyer as the time for performance neared and passed. Still, to put the plaintiff in default, Dwyer could not bank on plaintiff's apathy or passively and hopefully watch the clock tick toward midnight." Pelletier v. Dwyer, 334 A.2d 867 (Me.1975).[b] *Question:* What result would you expect if, changing the facts, Dwyer had called on Pelletier on the evening of the 16th, by appointment, with deed in hand, and found that Pelletier had gone for a circuit of the local night clubs? See O'Toole & Nedeau Co. v. Boelkins, 254 Mich. 44, 235 N.W. 820 (1931).

WALKER & CO. v. HARRISON

Supreme Court of Michigan, 1957.
347 Mich. 630, 81 N.W.2d 352.

SMITH, Justice. This is a suit on a written contract. The defendants are in the dry-cleaning business. Walker & Company, plaintiff, sells, rents, and services advertising signs and billboards.

b. The decision is clearly compatible with Restatement Second, §§ 237 and 238. Is it also compatible with § 242(c)?

Suppose that Dwyer had been unable to "make his title good" notwithstanding his best efforts to do so, which cost him $78,000. It seems apparent that he would not be in a position to claim that sum from Pelletier.

These parties entered into an agreement pertaining to a sign. The agreement is in writing and is termed a "rental agreement." It specifies in part that:

"The lessor agrees to construct and install, at its own cost, one 18′ 9″ high x 8′ 8″ wide pylon type d. f. neon sign with electric clock and flashing lamps . . . . The lessor agrees to and does hereby lease or rent unto the said lessee the said SIGN for the term, use and rental and under the conditions, hereinafter set out, and the lessee agrees to pay said rental . . . .

"(a) The term of this lease shall be 36 months . . . .

"(b) The rental to be paid by lessee shall be $148.50 per month for each and every calendar month during the term of this lease; . . . .

"(d) Maintenance. Lessor at its expense agrees to maintain and service the sign together with such equipment as supplied and installed by the lessor to operate in conjunction with said sign under the terms of this lease; this service is to include cleaning and repainting of sign in original color scheme as often as deemed necessary by lessor to keep sign in first class advertising condition and make all necessary repairs to sign and equipment installed by lessor. . . ."

At the "expiration of this agreement," it was also provided, "title to this sign reverts to lessee." This clause is in addition to the printed form of agreement and was apparently added as a result of defendants' concern over title, they having expressed a desire "to buy for cash" and the salesman, at one time, having "quoted a cash price."

The sign was completed and installed in the latter part of July, 1953. The first billing of the monthly payment of $148.50 was made August 1, 1953, with payment thereof by defendants on September 3, 1953. This first payment was also the last. Shortly after the sign was installed, someone hit it with a tomato. Rust, also, was visible on the chrome, complained defendants, and in its corners were "little spider cobwebs." In addition, there were "some children's sayings written down in here." Defendant Herbert Harrison called Walker for the maintenance he believed himself entitled to under subparagraph (d) above. It was not forthcoming. He called again and again. "I was getting, you might say, sorer and sorer. . . . Occasionally, when I started calling up, I would walk around where the tomato was and get mad again. Then I would call up on the phone again." Finally, on October 8, 1953, plaintiff not having responded to his repeated calls, he telegraphed Walker that:

"You Have Continually Voided Our Rental Contract By Not Maintaining Signs As Agreed As We No Longer Have A Contract With You Do Not Expect Any Further Remuneration."

[Walker answered by letter, pointing out that the telegram did not "make any specific allegations as to what the failure of maintenance comprises," and concluding:]

"We would like to call your attention to paragraph G in our rental contract, which covers procedures in the event of a Breach of Agreement. In the event that you carry out your threat to make no future monthly payments in accordance with the agreement, it is our intention to enforce the conditions outlined under paragraph G[1] . . . Unless we receive both the September and October payments by October 25th, this entire matter will be placed in the hands of our attorney for collection in accordance with paragraph G which stipulates that the entire amount is forthwith due and payable."

No additional payments were made and Walker sued in assumpsit for the entire balance due under the contract, $5,197.50, invoking paragraph (g) of the agreement. Defendants filed answer and claim of recoupment, asserting that plaintiff's failure to perform certain maintenance services constituted a prior material breach of the agreement, thus justifying their repudiation of the contract and grounding their claim for damages. The case was tried to the court without a jury and resulted in a judgment for the plaintiff. The case is before us on a general appeal.

Defendants urge upon us again and again, in various forms, the proposition that Walker's failure to service the sign, in response to

1. (g) Breach of Agreement. Lessee shall be deemed to have breached this agreement by default in payment of any installment of the rental herein provided for; abandonment of the sign or vacating premises where the sign is located; termination or transfer of lessee's interest in the premises by insolvency, appointment of a receiver for lessee's business; filing of a voluntary or involuntary petition in bankruptcy with respect to lessee or the violation of any of the other terms or conditions hereof. In the event of such default, the lessor may, upon notice to the lessee, which notice shall conclusively be deemed sufficient if mailed or delivered to the premises where the sign was or is located, take possession of the sign and declare the balance of the rental herein provided for to be forthwith due and payable, and lessee hereby agrees to pay such balance upon any such contingencies. Lessor may terminate this lease and without notice, remove and repossess said sign and recover from the lessee such amounts as may be unpaid for the remaining unexpired term of this agreement. Time is of the essence of this lease with respect to the payment of rentals herein provided for. Should lessee after lessor has declared the balance of rentals due and payable, pay the full amount of rental herein provided, he shall then be entitled to the use of the sign, under all the terms and provisions hereof, for the balance of the term of this lease. No waiver by either party hereto of the nonperformance of any term, condition or obligation hereof shall be a waiver of any subsequent breach of, or failure to perform the same, or any other term, condition or obligation hereof. It is understood and agreed that the sign is especially constructed for the lessee and for use at the premises now occupied by the lessee for the term herein provided; that it is of no value unless so used and that it is a material consideration to the lessor in entering into this agreement that the lessee shall continue to use the sign for the period of time provided herein and for the payment of the full rental for such term."

repeated requests, constituted a material breach of the contract and justified repudiation by them. The legal proposition is undoubtedly correct. Repudiation is one of the weapons available to an injured party in event the other contractor has committed a material breach. But the injured party's determination that there has been a material breach, justifying his own repudiation, is fraught with peril, for should such determination, as viewed by a later court in the calm of its contemplation, be unwarranted, the repudiator himself will have been guilty of material breach and himself have become the aggressor, not an innocent victim.

What is our criterion for determining whether or not a breach of contract is so fatal to the undertaking of the parties that it is to be classed as "material"? There is no single touchstone. Many factors are involved. They are well stated in section 275 of Restatement [first] of Contracts in the following terms:

"In determining the materiality of a failure fully to perform a promise the following circumstances are influential:

"(a) The extent to which the injured party will obtain the substantial benefit which he could have reasonably anticipated;

"(b) The extent to which the injured party may be adequately compensated in damages for lack of complete performance;

"(c) The extent to which the party failing to perform has already partly performed or made preparations for performance;

"(d) The greater or less hardship on the party failing to perform in terminating the contract;

"(e) The wilful, negligent or innocent behavior of the party failing to perform;

"(f) The greater or less uncertainty that the party failing to perform will perform the remainder of the contract."

We will not set forth in detail the testimony offered concerning the need for servicing. Granting that Walker's delay (about a week after defendant Herbert Harrison sent his telegram of repudiation Walker sent out a crew and took care of things) in rendering the service requested was irritating, we are constrained to agree with the trial court that it was not of such materiality as to justify repudiation of the contract, and we are particularly mindful of the lack of preponderant evidence contrary to his determination. Jones v. Eastern Michigan Motorbuses, 287 Mich. 619, 283 N.W. 710. The trial court, on this phase of the case, held as follows:

"Now Mr. Harrison phoned in, so he testified, a number of times. He isn't sure of the dates but he sets the first call at about the 7th of August and he complained then of the tomato and of some rust and some cobwebs. The tomato, according to the testimony, was up on the clock; that would be outside of his reach, without a stepladder or something. The cobwebs are within easy reach of Mr. Harrison and so would the rust be. I think that Mr. Bueche's argument that these were not materially a breach would clearly be true as to the cobwebs and I really can't believe in the face of all the testimony that there was a great deal of rust seven days after the installation of this sign. And that really brings it down to the tomato. And, of course, when a tomato has been splashed all other (sic) your clock, you don't like it. But he says he kept calling their attention to it, although the rain probably washed some of the tomato off. But the stain remained, and they didn't come. I really can't find that that was such a material breach of the contract as to justify rescission. I really don't think so."

Nor, we conclude, do we. There was no valid ground for defendants' repudiation and their failure thereafter to comply with the terms of the contract was itself a material breach, entitling Walker, upon this record, to judgment.

The question of damages remains. [The court's discussion of this question is omitted.] Judgment was, therefore, rendered for the cash price of the sign, for such services and maintenance as were extended and accepted, and interest upon the amount in default. There was no error.

Affirmed. Costs to appellee.[a]

NOTES

(1) *Counselling Problems.* What might the telegram have said in order to put pressure on Walker without risking liability for the price of the sign?

Suppose that on Harrison's second or third call about the sign Walker had said: "You might try wiping the sign with ammonia or look for a cleaning service in the Yellow Pages." Would that have justified Harrison in telegraphing as he did? See Central Garment Co., Inc. v. United Refrigerator Co., 369 Mass. 633, 341 N.E.2d 669 (1976).

(2) *Condition v. Promise.* Maintenance of the sign by the plaintiff with some diligence, and in some degree of respectability, was of course a constructive condition of the defendant's duty to keep up the rental payments. The plaintiff's duty of maintenance, as stated in paragraph (d), would not be met by anything less than punctilious performance. But the condition resting on the plaintiff need not be so stringent. Obviously there is some softening effect, or "play", in the process of deriving a condition from a promise. (See also the cases on substantial performance, in Section 4 infra.) Compare the effect the paragraph might have had if it had been written in terms of an express condition. At the extreme, it might have been written so as to excuse the lessee from all further duties upon any shortcoming in the maintenance services.

Does this difference between express and constructive conditions suggest a preference in interpreting agreements? According to the Restate-

a. As for the "penal" aspect of a provision such as that in footnote 1, see Young Electric Sign Co. v. Vetas, 564 P.2d 758 (Utah, 1977).

ment Second, § 227(3), in case of doubt, "an interpretation under which an event is a condition of an obligor's duty is preferred over an interpretation under which the non-occurrence of the event is a ground for discharge of that duty after it has become a duty to perform." Is there a notion of fairness behind this rule?

Refer again to the drafting problem in Note 1, p. 759 supra, especially the direction to draft a clause making "sailing with the next wind" the subject of a duty alone. Do you now see a difficulty in doing this, not apparent till now?

(3) *Question of Law or Fact?* Does the court make its own judgment whether or not Walker's conduct amounted to a material breach? Or does it accept the trial judge's determination as a permissible finding on the evidence? Should the issue of materiality of a breach ever be submitted to a jury? And if so, should they be directed to balance the factors mentioned in Restatement Second, § 241, or in some similar list? What merit or demerit do you find in treating the issue as a "question of law"? [b]

(4) *Restatement Second.* The most serious consequences of non-performance of a contract promise are that (a) it "discharges the injured party's remaining duties" and (b) it "gives rise to a claim for damages for total breach." In general the second of these consequences cannot occur unless the breach entails the first, in a case like Walker & Co. v. Harrison. Restatement Second, § 243(1).[c] In that case, be it noted, there remained performances to be exchanged when the parties reached an impasse. Several interconnected sections of the Restatement Second relate the idea of discharge by non-performance to the time when a performance is due, to the possibility of cure, and to the materiality of the breach. See §§ 225, 237, and 241. The latter offers guidance about when a failure to perform is material. Section 242 uses the considerations listed there—and others—to determine when an "uncured material failure to perform" results in a discharge of the other party's remaining duties. That section is the one directed immediately to the question whether or not the behavior of Walker & Company, plaintiff, excused Harrison from further performance under the contract. As to the question whether or not its behavior exposed it to a "total breach" claim by Harrison, section 243(1)—quoted above—is controlling. Hence the two issues are apparently congruent in that case.

In some other situations the comparable pairs of issues would not be congruent. For example, a repudiation by Walker & Company would have brought subsection (2) of 243 into play. Subsection (4) might have application if Harrison had pre-paid in full for the sign and the services associated with it—an exceptional situation. According to Comment e this subsection "states a general rule for residual cases." In applying the rule, some of the considerations listed in the two preceding sections are rele-

b. For complex attitudes toward a trial court's findings, in opposing opinions, see Baith v. Knapp-Stiles, Inc., 380 Mich. 119, 156 N.W.2d 575 (1968). For a case in which a jury's opinion was taken on the issue of materiality of breach by a pro football player, who had flirted with a club in competition with the one entitled to his services, see McLean v. Buffalo Bills Football Club, Inc., 32 A.D.2d 881, 301 N.Y.S.2d 872 (4th Dept. 1969).

c. The exception stated in the concluding phrase relates to the "divisibility" of contracts, as to which see p. 826 infra.

vant, according to the comment—although they are "intended for use in determining whether the injured party is discharged."

The reciprocal of discharge under section 242 is timely "cure" of a failure to perform. "The term 'cure' is used in a broader sense than in Uniform Commercial Code § 2–508, to include performance by one party before the other party's remaining duties of performance have been discharged, even though the other party has a claim for damages for partial breach because of the delay." Reporter's Note to § 237. *Question:* As a matter of litigation tactics, would it be better to present the case for Harrison as one of a partial but material failure to perform by the plaintiff, or one of total failure to attempt cure?

A less serious consequence of non-performance is that the injured party may *suspend* his own performance: see Restatement Second, § 225(1). But Harrison was not indulgent enough to rest on that remedy—and lived to regret it.

(5) *The Case of the Jack of All Trades.* At the end of 1968 the B & B Equipment Company had a net worth of about $45,000. One of its working shareholders wished to retire and withdraw his investment. The company brought in a new man, John Bowen, promising ultimately to issue him enough stock (100 shares) to make him a one-third owner. In the meanwhile he and the two continuing owners were to receive equal salaries. On Bowen's side, he paid $2,500 in advance for the stock and agreed with the company to apply any dividends paid on the stock to retiring the remainder of the purchase price. The total purchase price to him was fixed at $15,000 plus an interest charge. Moreover, Bowen was to devote himself to the business, with special responsibility for bookkeeping.

For three years or more all went smoothly. But then Bowen began to scant his services to B & B. In 1976, after a period of warnings, he was fired. He had taken long lunch breaks and absented himself for personal dealings in real estate and farm machinery. When at the firm's premises he sometimes used its equipment to make ornamental rings. At times he delegated the bookkeeping, and at others he neglected it: records of the company's cash and inventory, the reconciliation of its bank accounts, and its monthly balance sheets were not kept up. Bowen's discharge precipitated a suit in which B & B sought a declaratory judgment that its duty to convey the stock was terminated, and he sought a contrary ruling.

The trial court declared that B & B was entitled to rescind the sale contract upon paying Bowen $2,500 plus dividends on the hundred shares. On appeal, *held:* Affirmed (with an adjustment for income taxes paid by Bowen on the company's retained earnings). B & B Equipment Co., Inc. v. Bowen, 581 S.W.2d 80 (Mo.App.1979).

As an exercise, analyze this case with reference to each "guideline" in section 275 of the (first) Restatement, and compare your assessments with those of the court. Is anything different required by Restatement Second, § 241? What do these sections require in Wasserburger's case, p. 787 supra?

"SOFT" RESPONSES TO BREACH

The victim of a breach who is too complaisant in dealing with the contract breaker runs a sizeable set of risks. One possibility is that by delay he will be precluded from asserting *any* remedy. See UCC 2–607(3)(a) as to delay in giving notice of a seller's breach. Short of that, a delay in asserting a particular remedy may preclude the victim from invoking it. Under some authorities a party who continues performance, or accepts further performance by the other, for a substantial period after being subjected to a material breach may not thereafter base a termination of the contract on that breach. This is said to be a "strict formulation" of the doctrine of election. Cities Service Helex, Inc. v. United States, 543 F.2d 1306 (Ct.Cl. 1976). Do you see another hazard in continuing performance after the other party has repudiated the contract? See Rockingham County v. Luten Bridge Co., p. 592 supra. The victim may be placed in a particularly poignant situation when the breach is in the form of a repudiation and the repudiating party offers to complete performance on terms more favorable to him. See p. 600 supra, n. 2.

If the breach is a less-than-material one, what liberty should the victim have in deciding what to do about it?[a] Assuming that the breach would entitle him to "assurance of due performance," should he be under any compulsion to demand it? Compare UCC 2–609 with Restatement Second, § 251. Does your answer depend on which rule governs the case? The Northwest Lumber Sales case (p. 806 supra) has been read as making it "mandatory" for the victim to invoke the Code remedy.[b] Do you understand the case that way?

One basis for dealing with a victim of breach who reacts with tolerance is to adjust his rights and duties with reference only to any detrimental reliance that his attitude produces on the other side. The principle is that of equitable estoppel (see p. 88 supra).[c] The Cities Service case cited above names authorities for relaxing the doctrine of election.

NOTES

(1) *Drafting.* How effective would you expect the following provision to be?—

> In the event of a breach of this agreement, the aggrieved party may take any and all of the following actions without foreclosing

a. For a case in which the national interest in conserving a natural resource helped to justify continued performance see Northern Helex Co. v. United States, 455 F.2d 546 (Ct.Cl. 1972).

b. Hillman, Keeping the Deal Together after Material Breach—Common Law Mitigation Rules, the UCC, and the Restatement (Second) of Contracts, 47 U.Colo.L.Rev. 553, 589–93 (1976).

c. A note on waiver, estoppel, and election appears at p. 856 infra.

any remedy that would be available to him if the breach were determined to be a material one:

(a) continue with his own performance;

(b) retain indefinitely a performance rendered by the other party;

(c) accede to continued performance by the other party;

(d) assert a claim against the other party for partial breach, in judicial proceedings or otherwise.

For another drafting suggestion see S. S. Steiner, Inc. v. Hill, 191 Or. 391, 230 P.2d 537 (1951).

(2) *Problem.* B consults you with this bittersweet story: About three months ago he bought a small business, for which he is making monthly payments to S. He has found it quite profitable, especially in the receipts of a coin-operated dry-cleaning machine in the basement. But he has just made the dismal discovery that that operation violates the municipal fire code. You write the following letter to S's lawyer:

> On behalf of my client B, I am writing to suggest that circumstances have arisen which I believe justify a complete rescission of the agreement between my client and yours. The business is being operated in violation of the fire code, which raises a situation of commercial frustration. Under the circumstances perhaps the best manner of handling the case would be for the parties to agree to a rescission, cancellation of B's indebtedness and return of his funds. Perhaps a meeting should be set up to discuss these matters.

The letter gets no response. After making three more payments to S, B withholds further payments. That gets a response: S sues B for the remainder of the purchase price. Answering for B, you assert a right of rescission. Having lost, do you see in hindsight ways you might have served B better? See Lazorcak v. Feuerstein, 273 Md. 69, 327 A.2d 477 (1974).

THE FIRST–BREACH RULE

When performance under a contract has ceased, short of completion, and damages are claimed, the courts are driven to determine which of the contestants is guilty of the first material breach. "He who commits the first substantial breach of a contract cannot maintain an action against the other contracting party for failure to perform." [a] That is the point of the court's observation, in Walker & Co. v. Harrison, that one who uses repudiation to express a grievance "will . . . himself have become the aggressor" if it is later determined that the other party had committed no material breach.

In VanVelsor v. Dzewaltowski, 136 Vt. 103, 385 A.2d 1102 (1978), a house builder sued the owner upon being commanded to cease operations. The owner met the builder's claim for damages

a. Ehlinger v. Bodi Lake Lumber Co., 324 Mich. 77, 36 N.W.2d 311 (1949).

with a counterclaim for his expense in completing the job; he had been dissatisfied with the plaintiff's work. The trial court awarded damages on both claims, and the builder appealed. Reversing, the appellate court declared it "inexplicable" that the trial court had made no finding whether or not the owner was justified in terminating the contract.[b] (For a less usual procedure see Admiral Plastics Corp. v. Trueblood, Inc., 436 F.2d 1335 (6th Cir. 1971), in which the court found evidence to support a "mutual breaching of the contract." One of the parties was left with a prepayment of almost $30,000 for design work of an undetermined cost.[c])

Are there remedies for breach of contract which do not force a decision about who committed the first material breach? See Restatement Second, § 236(2). Should a court refuse to enforce an assessment of damages against a party by an arbitrator, if the arbitrator made a finding that, so far as the evidence went, that party may have been "an innocent victim," or that the other party repudiated the contract without justification? As for the rule in specific performance actions, see McMillan v. Smith, p. 949 infra.

PROBLEMS

(1) *Lucy v. Wood.* Lucy charges Wood with gross dereliction in failing to market her fashion designs, as he has contracted to do. In fact, Wood has carelessly neglected to report the results of his exceptional efforts for a brief period. When she sues for a declaration that the contract is at an end, he suspends all further effort on her behalf. Is it possible that he has now committed a material breach? Certain? See Riess v. Murchison, 503 F.2d 999 (9th Cir. 1974).

Wood has been derelict in marketing Lucy's designs, but whether or not his breach is a material one is problematical. When she sues him, as above, he amplifies his efforts on her behalf, and attempts a defense on the ground that he has complied with his duty in full. Is it possible that he has now committed a material breach? Certain?

b. The agreed price (including "extras" ordered by the owner) was $22,382.43. The builder had been paid $15,400. The trial court gave judgments as follows:

(1) For the builder:
$6,982.43—unpaid balance, less
1,303.80—builder's estimated cost to complete
$5,678.63

(2) For the owner:
$3,869.92—paid to others to complete work

The appellate court concluded that the trial court committed error, no matter which party committed the first breach. It remanded, giving the builder the election to try his claim anew or to accept a corrected judgment. The (net) judgment appealed from was $1,808.71. What should be the amount of the "corrected judgment"?

c. See also Westinghouse Electric Corp. v. Garrett Corp., 601 F.2d 155 (4th Cir. 1979).

(2) *The Flawless Fabric Case.* In October the sales manager for a manufacturer of knitted fabrics called on a retailer to show its line for the forthcoming spring season, and obtained an order for 12,000 yards of "first quality" goods. Within weeks the price of yarn began a precipitous decline. In November the retailer sent a cancellation of the order, but withdrew it in December under threat of suit. At the same time, the retailer declared that it would return the entire shipment if it contained one flaw. The manufacturer decided not to ship (though it had substantially completed production of the goods), believing it was impossible to produce so large an order without a single flaw. The Knitted Textile Association subscribes to standards by which certain types and amounts of flaws are permissible in first-quality knitted goods. The manufacturer sued the retailer for its loss on the transaction.

If the decision turns on the question which party committed the first material and unexcused breach of the contract, who will prevail? If other facts are needed for deciding that question, what are they? See Foxco Industries, Ltd. v. Fabric World, Inc., 595 F.2d 976 (5th Cir. 1979).

Could you have counselled a course of action for either party which would have reduced its risk of loss?

(3) *The Salesman's Slip.* Until September 1975 John Prince was an employee of ADP, a firm supplying and installing materials for Arkansas construction projects. Then Prince "made a mistake" (to use his words): he divulged to a competing firm the amount bid by ADP on a job in Hot Springs. For that he was fired. He had previously worked as a sales agent for ADP, receiving as a commission for each job he arranged a fraction of the net profit on completion. ("This necessarily caused payments to [Prince] to be paid at a date much later than the actual sale.") At first "ADP" was simply a trade name for Jerry Baldwin. He and Prince had contracted that the business would be incorporated, and the ownership divided between them. Now ADP has been incorporated. All of the shares belong to Baldwin, and Prince has received nothing for some jobs, now completed, that he arranged. Does Baldwin or ADP owe Prince anything? See Baldwin v. Prince, 265 Ark. 384, 578 S.W.2d 240 (1979). If this case can be readily distinguished from Wasserburger's case, p. 787 supra, is it because Prince's claim relates to parts of his job performance that stand apart from his breach? Is that a reason to deviate from the first-breach rule?

GILL v. JOHNSTOWN LUMBER CO.

Supreme Court of Pennsylvania, 1892.
151 Pa. 534, 25 A. 120.

[Assumpsit for driving logs under a written contract, the terms of which are set forth in the opinion. Plaintiff agreed to drive some four million feet of logs, and to begin driving at once, "if sufficient natural water, or by the use of splash dams." The trial court directed a verdict for defendant on the ground that the contract was "entire" and that plaintiff had defaulted in that a flood had carried a considerable proportion of the logs past defendant's boom.[a] Plaintiff appeals.]

Opinion by Mr. Justice HEYDRICK, October 31, 1892. The single question in this case is whether the contract upon which the plaintiff sued is entire or severable. If it is entire it is conceded that the learned court below properly directed a verdict for the defendant; if severable, it is not denied that the cause ought to have been submitted to the jury. The criterion by which it is to be determined to which class any particular contract shall be assigned is thus stated in 1 Parsons on Contracts, 29–31: "If the part to be performed by one party consists of several and distinct items, and the price to be paid by the other is (1) apportioned to each item to be performed, or (2) is left to be implied by law, such a contract will generally be held to be severable. . . . But if the consideration to be paid is single and entire the contract must be held to be entire, although the subject of the contract may consist of several distinct and wholly independent items." The rule thus laid down was quoted with approval and applied in Lucesco Oil Co. v. Brewer, 66 Pa. 351, and followed in Rugg & Bryan v. Moore, 110 Pa. 236, 1 A. 320. It was also applied in Ritchie v. Atkinson, 10 East, 295, a case not unlike the present. There the master and freighter of a vessel of four hundred tons mutually agreed that the ship should proceed to St. Petersburg, and there load from the freighter's factors a complete cargo of hemp and iron and deliver the same to the freighter at London on being paid freight for hemp £5 per ton, for iron 5*s*. per ton, and certain other charges, one half to be paid on delivery and the other at three months. The vessel proceeded to St. Petersburg, and when about half loaded was compelled by the imminence of a Russian embargo upon British vessels to leave, and returning to London deliver to the freighter so much of the stipulated cargo as had been taken on board. The freighter, conceiving that the contract was entire and the delivery of a complete cargo a condition precedent to a recovery of any compensation, refused to pay at the stipulated rate for so much as was delivered. Lord Ellenborough said: "The delivery of the cargo is in its nature, divisible, and therefore I think it is not a condition precedent; but the plaintiff is entitled to recover freight in proportion to the extent of such delivery; leaving the defendant to his remedy in damages for the short delivery."

Applying the test of an apportionable or apportioned consideration to the contract in question, it will be seen at once that it is severable. The work undertaken to be done by the plaintiff consisted of several items, viz., driving logs, first, of oak, and second of various

a. On May 31, 1889, ten days after the date of the contract, the then-largest earthen dam, above Johnstown, broke. More than 2,000 lives were lost. That and other flooding in the area, caused by a great rain, carried log booms estimated at many millions of feet of timber into the Potomac River and the Chesapeake Bay. R. O'Connor, Johnstown—The Day the Dam Broke (1957).

other kinds of timber, from points upon Stony creek and its tributaries above Johnstown to the defendant's boom at Johnstown, and also driving cross-ties from some undesignated point or points, presumably understood by the parties, to Bethel in Somerset county, and to some other point or points below Bethel. For this work the consideration to be paid was not an entire sum, but was apportioned among the several items at the rate of one dollar per thousand feet for the oak logs; seventy-five cents per thousand feet for all other logs; three cents each for cross-ties driven to Bethel, and five cents each for cross-ties driven to points below Bethel. But while the contract is severable, and the plaintiff entitled to compensation at the stipulated rate for all logs and ties delivered at the specified points, there is neither reason nor authority for the claim for compensation in respect to logs that were swept by the flood to and through the defendant's boom, whether they had been driven part of the way by the plaintiff or remained untouched by him at the coming of the flood. In respect to each particular log the contract in this case is like a contract of common carriage, which is dependent upon the delivery of the goods at the designated place, and if by casus the delivery is prevented the carrier cannot recover pro tanto for freight for part of the route over which the goods were taken: Wharton, Law of Contracts, sec. 714. Indeed this is but an application of the rule already stated. The consideration tò be paid for driving each log is an entire sum per thousand feet for the whole distance and is not apportioned or apportionable to parts of the drive.

The judgment is reversed and a venire facias de novo is awarded.

NOTES

(1) *Question.* Into how many parts was the contract divisible? Two parts: one for logs and one for cross-ties? Four parts? One part for each log and cross-tie properly delivered? If some of the oak logs had been driven half way, might the plaintiff have recovered at the rate of 50¢ per thousand feet for them? Why was the contract not divisible by distances?

(2) *The Lowy Case.* A contractor bids for work in developing a tract of land, to consist chiefly of cleaning, grading and compaction, and laying down streets. For the street work (paving, curbs, and gutters) he bids unit prices; e. g., $4 a foot. For the remainder he bids a lump-sum price. The street work cannot be done until the other work is completed. Is there any way to write the contract such that it will not be found "divisible" into two parts?

In Lowy v. United Pacific Insurance Co., 67 Cal.2d 87, 429 P.2d 577 (1967), a contract of this character stated the price for grading, etc., as $73,500 in "Exhibit A." It stated unit prices for paving, etc., in "Exhibit B." The court said: "since the consideration was apportioned, the contract was a severable or divisible one. . . . Under the circumstances, the fact that [the contractor] did not perform the second phase of the contract does not prevent his recovering for work done under the first phase."

Suppose the contract had provided that a material default by the contractor in phase two would bar his recovery for work in phase one. Would you expect the courts to implement this provision? Can you improve on it, as a sanction against default by the contractor?

The agreement for street work in the *Lowy* case was probably not divisible into a paving part, a gutter part, and a curb part, even though a separate price was named for each. A contract for several performances may be "entire," even though the consideration is apportioned among them. The holding in Lowy is not to the contrary, for there were other indications of divisibility not mentioned here. Indeed, the apportionment test does not support the Lowy result very well, inasmuch as the lump price of $73,500 included the "*labor and material* necessary for street improvements" (emphasis supplied).

(3) *Pay Periods.* Work done under a contract of employment for a term may go uncompensated if the employee abandons the job, or is justifiably discharged, before the end of the term. (Quasi-contractual recovery is granted by some courts: see Section 3, infra.) The doctrine of divisibility, liberally applied, would tend to alleviate such losses by permitting the employee to enforce partial payments for units of his work—so much per week, for instance—prior to the end of the term. But findings of divisibility were not readily obtained, in the early cases: a reference in the agreement to weekly or monthly pay periods might not count. The problem rarely arises in contemporary litigation. Several reasons have been suggested; one is "the passage in many jurisdictions of wage statutes which inexorably clamp divisibility down upon large classes of employment contracts . . ." McGowan, The Divisibility of Employment Contracts, 21 Iowa L.Rev. 50, 67 (1935).

(4) *Question.* In the Case of Jack of All Trades (Note 5, p. 822 supra) why shouldn't Bowen have prevailed on the ground that the stock-sale part of his contract with B & B was severable from the services part? Compare Rudd v. Parks, 588 P.2d 709 (Utah 1978).

(5) *Problem.* Paul agreed to erect and maintain six signs for Pete. Four of them were to read "4 miles to Pete's Place," "3 miles to Pete's Place," and so on. One large one was to read, "You are at Pete's Place," and the sixth, "Turn around for Pete's Place." Pete agreed to pay $35 a month for the large sign, and $10 a month for each of the others. Is the contract divisible into six parts? Or divisible at all? How would you write the agreement so as to make it clearly so? How write it to make it clearly entire? See John v. United Advertising, Inc., 165 Colo. 193, 439 P.2d 53 (1968).

PENNSYLVANIA EXCHANGE BANK v. UNITED STATES, 170 F.Supp. 629 (Ct.Cl.1959). [The United States Army Signal Corps contracted to pay certain sums to Joseph Lerner & Son, Inc., under an "Industrial Preparedness Contract." Lerner's obligation was to equip itself for the production, in volume, of an item called a microwave magic tee. The work was to be done in four steps. Steps I and II entailed acquiring information about and making plans for production, subject to approval, making a pilot run, and going through "all production processes short of procuring tooling and materials and short of actual volume manufacture." Step III required Lerner to acquire certain equipment for which it spent about $38,000.

These steps were substantially completed by October 1, 1953, and the Government had paid Lerner about $128,000. Step IV, which was to be taken only in case of a national emergency, and after receipt of an order from the Government, required "volume production in accordance with previously planned schedules." Lerner was obligated to maintain a status of readiness for this over a six-year period in anticipation of a national emergency. On October 1 Lerner transferred all its assets to assignees for the benefit of creditors, as an alternative to bankruptcy. The assignees sued the Government for about $45,000, the sum owed for completing steps I–III, and the Government counterclaimed for damages.]

WHITAKER, Judge. [The court considered the purpose of the contract, as stated in a Signal Corps procurement specification, and said that Steps I, II, and III were] merely incidental to Step IV, which was the ultimate objective. . . . The duty to stand by and be ready to perform Step IV was the essential element of the bargain. The contract was not divisible. . . .

The assignment for the benefit of creditors operates as a present and total breach of the contract, for it is an implied condition in every contract that the promisor will not permit itself, through insolvency or acts of bankruptcy, to be disabled from making performance. Central Trust Co. of Illinois v. Chicago Auditorium Ass'n, 240 U.S. 581, 591, 36 S.Ct. 412, 60 L.Ed. 811; Roehm v. Horst, 178 U.S. 1, 20 S.Ct. 780, 44 L.Ed. 953; Pennsylvania Steel Co. v. New York City R. Co., 2 Cir., 198 F. 721, 743.

[The Government's motion for summary judgment was granted.]

NOTES

(1) *Insolvency Proceedings.* Assignments for the benefit of creditors, and ordinary ("straight") bankruptcy proceedings, are arrangements for the expeditious liquidation of a debtor's business and other assets, and the distribution of the proceeds among his creditors. Therefore the assignees for Joseph Lerner & Son could not well have undertaken complete performance of its "industrial preparedness" contract. However, the Bankruptcy Code (title 11, U.S.C.A.) makes provision for preserving the going-concern value of an enterprise, through reorganization. When that is undertaken, usually under Chapter 11, the bankruptcy trustee or a manager having like powers may well wish to keep the firm's gainful contracts in force. (With some important exceptions, he may reject its executory contracts that are burdensome, subject to the court's approval. Rejection will usually give rise to a claim against the bankruptcy estate.) The Bankruptcy Code contains elaborate provisions both to protect and to restrict the trustee's right to "assume" a contract: 11 U.S.C.A. § 365. If the debtor has already committed a default, the trustee may yet assume the contract, but only if he is

able at the same time to give certain assurances, including "adequate assurance of future performance." Some trustees, pushing the law to its limit or beyond, have sought to resume operations under contracts that have been terminated for the debtor's default before the inception of bankruptcy proceedings.

(2) *More on Assurance of Performance.* The source of the bankruptcy phrase just quoted should be readily recognized: it is UCC 2–609. As noted above, the Restatement Second embodies the same style of expression when dealing with a party's "apparent inability to perform": see § 251. The succeeding section deals particularly with insolvency. Part of Comment a is as follows: "An obligor's insolvency is not a repudiation (Comment e to § 250) and may not even give the obligee reasonable grounds for insecurity (Comment c to § 251). It does, however, have this latter effect when the obligee is to pay for goods on credit, and Uniform Commercial Code § 2–702(1) states a statutory rule for that situation. This Section [252] states an analogous rule for other situations in which insolvency gives reasonable grounds for insecurity." [a]

SEPARATE CONTRACTS

Rudman v. Cowles Communications, Inc., 30 N.Y.2d 1, 330 N.Y.S.2d 33, 280 N.E.2d 867 (1972), describes a characteristic buy-out arrangement. Cowles, a large publishing enterprise, bought all the stock of a small company (Old College Publishing) whose principal assets were a line of test-preparation books and the skill of Jack Rudman in devising them. Rudman had been a teacher who started publishing test manuals as a sideline; he and his wife owned 99% of the Old College stock. Cowles paid for that company with its own stock. It also contracted to employ the couple; Mr. Rudman was promised five years in a supervisory role, at a fixed salary with a sales incentive. Within a few months serious differences emerged between him and other officers of Cowles' educational division. After six months Rudman was discharged, ostensibly for insubordination; but in the ensuing litigation the breach was charged to Cowles. (It had placed the Rudmans in isolated offices, without staff, and largely ignored them.)

Part of the remedy claimed by Rudman, as plaintiff, was rescission of the stock sale, but the trial court determined that that was an independent transaction. The employment contract was executed on a different day—though in the same month—and the parties were formally different. In reviewing the case the Court of Appeals noted these facts and said: "Although form is not conclusive, . . .

a. Whatever the shape of state law may be, a variant federal rule overrides it. Hence it seems that a party to an executory contract has, in effect, reasonable grounds for insecurity when the other party—whether or not insolvent in any sense—has defaulted and is a debtor in bankruptcy. That is hardly a remarkable proposition. Yet it bears noting that the bankruptcy courts may determine for themselves what counts as "adequate assurance of performance" and when it must be given.

the conclusion of separateness becomes all but inescapable." Also: "Whether the parties intended to treat both agreements as mutually dependent contracts, the breach of one undoing the obligations under the other, is a question of fact."

Questions: Would any of the parties have said, when contracting, that the two transactions were "independent"? Could the draftsman of the stock-sale contract have compelled a contrary result by inserting appropriate recitals? (The opinion observes that the trial court had discretion, even if the contracts were mutually dependent, to confine Rudman to his remedy at law, damages.) Was there *any* way for the draftsman to overcome the finality of the stock sale?

In Toppert v. Bunge Corp., 60 Ill.App.3d 607, 18 Ill.Dec. 171, 377 N.E.2d 324 (1978), four contracts were made, on different days, for deliveries of corn by Toppert to the Bunge Corporation. Toppert's father and brother made similar contracts with Bunge. (The three men sometimes exchanged work among themselves.) None of the parties was punctual in performance: deliveries were delayed and Bunge withheld payment under one of Toppert's contracts. After conferences among all the parties concerned failed to resolve their differences, Bunge cancelled two of Toppert's contracts. He sued it for the price of corn delivered and Bunge made a counterclaim for damages. The trial court gave judgment for Toppert on both claims, finding that Bunge had held up payment "to insure the continuing performance by plaintiff's brother and father under their contracts [and] to use leverage on plaintiff for continuing performance." On appeal, *held:* Affirmed. The trial court had found that the dealings between the parties were not separate and distinct contracts, but were ongoing arrangements between them. Passing over that issue, the appellate court relied on UCC 2–609. It observed that default on one contract may create reasonable ground for insecurity with respect to another and said that Toppert's demands for payment under one contract were demands for assurance as to others.

NOTES

(1) *Doubts.* Is the reasoning of the court in the corn-sale case invalidated by the fact that Toppert did not characterize his demand as one *for assurance*? Or that he did not make any demand of Bunge *in writing*?

(2) *Tactics.* Is there any way Bunge might have expressed its contracts with Toppert so that UCC 2–609 could not serve to link them? So that, for example, no delay in paying under contract No. 3 would threaten it with loss of corn under contract No. 4?

Is there any way in which Bunge might have written to Toppert in terms justifying (say) the following conclusion?—"All things considered, we must demand a written undertaking from you to complete deliveries under No. 4 before we pay on No. 3." As possible justification for the demand consider the following recitals in the letter: (a) You have not yet

signed our confirmation of contract No. 4; (b) The price of corn has run up rapidly in the last few weeks; and (c) You seemed 'sore' when you left yesterday's meeting. Would the letter itself give Toppert ground for insecurity assuming the assertions were true? And if not?

(3) *A Dixieland Case.* The Dixie Floor Company contracted to install flooring in two buildings to be erected by the Ranger Construction Company, one in North Carolina and one in South Carolina. The contracts were separately negotiated. In April, 1975, Ranger requested Dixie to begin work in South Carolina. At that time the North Carolina work had been completed for nearly a year, and Ranger had refused to pay for it, without apparent justification. (In 1976 the price was at last paid, but only after Dixie brought a successful lawsuit.) Dixie refused to install the South Carolina floor and Ranger sued it for the additional cost of using another subcontractor. On plaintiff's motion for a summary judgment, *held:* Denied. Ranger Constr. Co. v. Dixie Floor Co., Inc., 433 F.Supp. 442 (D.S.C. 1977). "Under the theory of anticipatory repudiation," the court said, "there is a question of fact for the jury . . . ."

Before refusing to do the South Carolina work, Dixie had requested that Ranger provide it with assurance of due performance, and professed to be dissatisfied with the response. Most of the court's discussion concerned UCC 2–609 as the source of a repudiation. The court ruled that it was not, inasmuch as the contract was predominantly one for services and not for a sale.

Questions: Does the decision support Restatement Second, § 251, or confute it? Apart from the "request" for assurance, what conduct by Ranger could be called a repudiation of the South Carolina contract?

K & G CONSTRUCTION CO. v. HARRIS

Court of Appeals of Maryland, 1960.
223 Md. 305, 164 A.2d 451.

[A case was stated for appeal in an action by a Contractor against a Subcontractor, and the following facts were given. K & G Construction Company was the owner and general contractor for a housing subdivision project. Harris and Brooks contracted with it to do excavating and earth-moving work on the project. Certain provisions of the agreement were as follows:

"Section 4. (b) Progress payments will be made each month during the performance of the work. Subcontractor will submit to Contractor, by the 25th of each month, a requisition for work performed during the preceding month. Contractor will pay these requisitions, less a retainer equal to ten per cent (10%), by the 10th of the months in which such requisitions are received.[1]

"(c) No payments will be made under this contract until the insurance requirements of Sec. 9 hereof have been complied with.

. . .

1. This section is not a model for clarity.

"Section 8. . . . All work shall be performed in a workmanlike manner, and in accordance with the best practices.

"Section 9. Subcontractor agrees to carry, during the progress of the work, . . . liability insurance against . . . property damage, in such amounts and with such companies as may be satisfactory to Contractor and shall provide Contractor with certificates showing the same to be in force."

While in the course of his employment by the Subcontractor on the project, a bulldozer operator drove his machine too close to Contractor's house while grading the yard, causing the immediate collapse of a wall and other damage to the house. Contractor was generally satisfied with Subcontractor's work and progress as required by the contract until September 12, 1958, with the exception of the bulldozer accident which occurred on August 9. The Subcontractor and its insurance carrier refused to repair damage or compensate Contractor for damage to the house, claiming that there was no liability on the part of the Subcontractor.

For work done prior to July 25, the Subcontractor submitted a requisition payable under the terms of the contract on or before August 10. Contractor refused to pay it because the bulldozer damage had not been repaired or paid for. Subcontractor continued to work on the project until September 12, when it discontinued work because of Contractor's refusal to pay the said requisition, but notified Contractor by registered letter of its willingness to return to the job upon payment. Contractor later requested it to return and complete work, which Subcontractor refused to do because of nonpayment of work requisitions of July 25 and thereafter. Contractor had another excavating concern complete the work, for which it paid $450 above the contract price.

Contractor's suit against Subcontractor contained two counts: (1) for the bulldozer damage, alleging negligence, and (2) for $450 as damages for breach of contract. Subcontractor filed a counterclaim for work done and not paid for and for profit it lost by not being permitted to finish the job, totalling $2,824.50. The bulldozer damage claim was submitted to a jury, who found in favor of Contractor in the amount of $3,400, and that judgment has been paid. The other claims were submitted to the trial judge, who allowed the Subcontractor's claim in full. Contractor appealed from this determination.]

PRESCOTT, Judge. . . . The vital question, more tersely stated, remains: Did the contractor have a right, under the circumstances, to refuse to make the progress payment due on August 10, 1958?

The answer involves interesting and important principles of contract law. Promises and counter-promises made by the respective parties to a contract have certain relations to one another, which determine many of the rights and liabilities of the parties. Broadly speaking, they are (1) independent of each other, or (2) mutually dependent, one upon the other. They are independent of each other if the parties intend that *performance* by each of them is in no way conditioned upon *performance* by the other. 5 Page, The Law of Contracts, ¶ 2971. In other words, the parties exchange promises for promises, not the *performance* of promises for the *performance* of promises. 3 Williston, Contracts (Rev.Ed.), ¶ 813, n. 6. A failure to perform an independent promise does not excuse non-performance on the part of the adversary party, but each is required to perform his promise, and, if one does not perform, he is liable to the adversary party for such non-performance. (Of course, if litigation ensues questions of set-off or recoupment frequently arise.) Promises are mutually dependent if the parties intend *performance* by one to be conditioned upon *performance* by the other, and, if they be mutually dependent, they may be (a) precedent, i. e., a promise that is to be performed before a corresponding promise on the part of the adversary party is to be performed, (b) subsequent, i. e., a corresponding promise that is not to be performed until the other party to the contract has performed a precedent covenant, or (c) concurrent, i. e., promises that are to be performed at the same time by each of the parties, who are respectively bound to perform each. Page, op. cit., ¶¶ 2941, 2951, 2961. . . .

In the early days, it was settled law that covenants and mutual promises in a contract were *prima facie* independent, and that they were to be so construed in the absence of language in the contract clearly showing that they were intended to be dependent. Williston, op. cit., ¶ 816; Page, op. cit., ¶¶ 2944, 2945. In the case of Kingston v. Preston, 2 Doug. 689, decided in 1774, Lord Mansfield, contrary to three centuries of opposing precedents, changed the rule, and decided that performance of one covenant might be dependent on prior performance of another, although the contract contained no express condition to that effect. Page, op. cit., ¶ 2946; Williston, op. cit., ¶ 817. The modern rule, which seems to be of almost universal application, is that there is a presumption that mutual promises in a contract are dependent and are to be so regarded, whenever possible. Page, op. cit., ¶ 2946; Restatement, Contracts, ¶ 266. Cf. Williston, op. cit., ¶ 812. . . .

. . . It would, indeed present an unusual situation if we were to hold that a building contractor, who has obtained someone to do work for him and has agreed to pay each month for the work performed in the previous month, has to continue the monthly payments, irrespective of the degree of skill and care displayed in the performance of work, and his only recourse is by way of suit for ill-performance. If this were the law, it is conceivable, in fact, probable, that many contractors would become insolvent before they were able to complete their contracts. As was stated by the Court in Measures

Brothers Ltd. v. Measures, 2 Ch. 248: "Covenants are to be construed as dependent or independent according to the intention of the parties and the good sense of the case."

We hold that when the subcontractor's employee negligently damaged the contractor's wall, this constituted a breach of the subcontractor's promise to perform his work in a "workmanlike manner, and in accordance with the best practices." Gaybis v. Palm, 201 Md. 78, 85, 93 A.2d 269; Johnson v. Metcalfe, 209 Md. 537, 544, 121 A.2d 825; 17 C.J.S. Contracts § 515; Weiss v. Sheet Metal Fabricators, 206 Md. 195, 203, 110 A.2d 671. And there can be little doubt that the breach was material: the damage to the wall amounted to more than double the payment due on August 10. Speed v. Bailey, 153 Md. 655, 661, 662, 139 A. 534. 3A Corbin, Contracts, § 708, says: "The failure of a contractor's [in our case, the subcontractor's] performance to constitute 'substantial' performance may justify the owner [in our case, the contractor] in refusing to make a progress payment . . . If the refusal to pay an installment is justified on the owner's [contractor's] part, the contractor [subcontractor] is not justified in abandoning work by reason of that refusal. His abandonment of the work will itself be a wrongful repudiation that goes to the essence, even if the defects in performance did not." See also Restatement, Contracts, § 274; . . . and compare Williston, op. cit., §§ 805, 841 and 842. Professor Corbin, in § 954, states further: "The unexcused failure of a contractor to render a promised performance when it is due is always a breach of contract . . .. Such failure may be of such great importance as to constitute what has been called herein a 'total' breach. . . .. For a failure of performance constituting such a 'total' breach, an action for remedies that are appropriate thereto is at once maintainable. Yet the injured party is not required to bring such action. He has the option of treating the nonperformance as a 'partial' breach only . . .." In permitting the subcontractor to proceed with work on the project after August 9, the contractor, obviously, treated the breach by the subcontractor as a partial one. As the promises were mutually dependent and the subcontractor had made a material breach in his performance, this justified the contractor in refusing to make the August 10 payment; hence, as the contractor was not in default, the subcontractor again breached the contract when he, on September 12, discontinued work on the project, which rendered him liable (by the express terms of the contract) to the contractor for his increased cost in having the excavating done—a stipulated amount of $450. Cf. Keystone Engineering Corp. v. Sutter, 196 Md. 620, 628, 78 A.2d 191. . . .

[Defendant also contended] that the contractor had no right to refuse the August 10 payment, because the subcontractor had furnished the insurance against property damage, as called for in the contract. There is little, or no, merit in this suggestion. The subcontractor and his insurance company denied liability. The furnishing of the insurance by him did not constitute a license to perform his work in a careless, negligent, or unworkmanlike manner; and its acceptance by the contractor did not preclude his assertion of a claim for unworkmanlike performance directly against the subcontractor.

Judgment against the appellant reversed; and judgment entered in favor of the appellant against the appellees for $450, the appellees to pay the costs.

NOTES

(1) *Questions.* Did the contractor withhold the payment due on August 10 because the subcontractor "did his work in a careless, negligent or unworkmanlike manner"? Or because the insurer denied liability? (It is a customary condition in liability insurance policies that the insured shall not assume any obligation in connection with an accident, except at his own cost.) If the subcontractor and his insurer had conceded liability at once, reserving only the question how much damage was done, would the contractor have been justified in withholding the August payment? Or if the subcontractor had promised at once to repair the damage?

Did the court overlook a clear implication in the contract (§§ 4c and 9) that the contractor's duty to pay was *independent* of isolated acts of carelessness by the subcontractor?[a] What may the subcontractor include in his next contract that would alter the foregoing result?

Would the court's reasoning have been simpler if it had said that the contractor was entitled to set off the bulldozer damage against the requisition payable August 10th? Sound?

(2) *Wrongful Refusal to Make Progress Payments.* If the jury had found that the bulldozer damage was not due to the subcontractor's fault, would the trial court's judgment have been affirmed? The subcontractor discontinued work on September 12, and the last payment he had received was presumably made on July 10. It is not uncommon for disputes to arise about the amount due as a progress payment, leading to a wrongful withholding of all or part of it. If the builder discontinues work, what are his rights?

In one such case where he brought an action against the other party for damages, the defendant requested an instruction that "The delay of defendant to make payments on estimates, in the absence of a positive refusal to pay anything, was not ground for a rescission or termination of the contract by plaintiff," and that plaintiff's remedy was to recover interest on the deferred payments. Instead, the court instructed the jury that if defendant failed to make payments on account as called for by the contract—"a substantial failure, amounting substantially to the withholding of the

a. Compare United States v. F. D. Rich Co., Inc., 439 F.2d 895 (8th Cir. 1971), in which a subcontractor was held to be entitled to job earnings, although there were claims against him by laborers and materialmen that exceeded the amount owing, and the contract seemed to make it clear that he was entitled to no recovery in the circumstances. The court "interpreted" the contract in the subcontractor's favor, relying on the contract provision for a payment bond, which had been supplied. The court of appeals suggested to the trial court that it enter judgment in a form assuring the defendant contractor protection against double liability.

whole payment, not necessarily the whole payment, but the bulk of the payment"—such failure constituted a breach on the part of defendant justifying plaintiff in stopping work and entitling him to recover damages (including lost profits) from defendant. A judgment for the builder was affirmed by the Supreme Court, saying: "As is usually the case with building contracts, it evidently was in the contemplation of the parties that the contractor could not be expected to finance the operation to completion without receiving the stipulated payments on account as the work progressed. In such cases a substantial compliance as to advance payments is a condition precedent to the contractor's obligation to proceed." Guerini Stone Co. v. P. J. Carlin Constr. Co., 248 U.S. 334 (1919). See also Cork Plumbing Co., Inc. v. Martin Bloom Associates, Inc., 573 S.W.2d 947 (Mo. App.1978).

For a somewhat divergent view, see Palmer v. Watson Const. Co., 265 Minn. 195, 121 N.W.2d 62 (1963): "We are committed . . . to the rule that non-payment of installment obligations is not in and of itself such prevention of performance as will make possible suit for loss of profits even though the party entitled to payment may lack working capital." On progress payments in general, see J. Sweet, Legal Aspects of Architecture, Engineering and the Construction Process, § 24.03 (1970).

(3) *Independent Covenants.* Recent cases in which a promise on one side of a bilateral contract has been held to be "independent" are exceptional. For an independent covenant in a trading-stamp contract, see Gold Bond Stamp Co. v. Gilt-Edge Stamps, Inc., 437 F.2d 27 (5th Cir. 1971).

(4) *Problem.* The defendants, who were practicing physicians and operated a hospital in X County, sold the hospital to the plaintiffs with a promise that defendants would not compete by operating any hospital in X County for 10 years, in return for which plaintiffs gave, besides the purchase price, their promise to let one of defendants practice medicine in the hospital and bring his patients to it. In a suit by plaintiffs to enjoin defendants from breaking their promise, can the latter defend on the ground that plaintiffs broke theirs? See Johnson v. Stumbo, 277 Ky. 301, 311, 126 S.W.2d 165, 176 (1939) (hospital built 300 yards outside county). See also General Billposting Co. v. Atkinson, [1909] A.C. 118 (House of Lords) (discussing Serjeant Williams' rules).

ANTICIPATORY BREACH OF CONTRACT

In Phillpotts v. Evans, 5 M. & W. 475, 151 Eng.Rep. 200 (1839), a seller sued on a contract for the sale of "wheat." The buyer had refused to take delivery. Some time before the seller was required to make delivery, the buyer had given him notice that it would not be accepted. The market price had dropped between then and the last day when the seller could have made a proper tender. The question was whether the damages should be calculated with reference to the market price at the time of the buyer's repudiation, or to the price at the later time. Naturally, the buyer preferred the earlier date. The same issue was presented in Roehm v. Horst, 178 U.S. 1 (1900), which is perhaps the leading American case on anticipatory breach of contract. For a case of a seller's repudiation in a rising market, see Leigh v. Paterson, 8 Taunt. 540, 129 Eng.Rep. 493 (1818).

In the Restatement Second the term "anticipatory breach" is called an elliptical expression for a "breach by anticipatory repudiation, because it occurs before there is any breach by non-performance." Section 253, Comment a. By the better usage, an anticipatory repudiation occurs when a promisor wrongfully signifies, in advance of the time for his performance, that it will not be forthcoming. The notice given by the buyer in Phillpotts v. Evans was a repudiation in this sense. See also UCC 2–609(4); Restatement Second, § 251.

What are the effects of an anticipatory repudiation? This is the question to be considered next. Sometimes it is assumed that if an anticipatory repudiation has one effect similar to that of a breach it must have other consequences as well.[a] The leading case on the subject, Hochster v. De la Tour, has been criticized for reasoning in that way. After reading the opinion, which follows, consider whether or not the criticism is a fair one.

In any event, the problem of calculating damages that was raised in Phillpotts v. Evans is separable from other issues relating to anticipatory repudiation. More recent materials addressing that problem are presented in Section 5, infra.

NOTE

Definitions. Repudiation has been defined as an " 'overt communication of intention' not to perform (UCC 2–610, Comment 2); a positive and unequivocal announcement of an intention not to perform." Tenavision, Inc. v. Neuman, 45 N.Y.2d 145, 408 N.Y.S.2d 36, 379 N.E.2d 1166 (1978). Compare the definition in Restatement Second, § 250.[b]

How was the word used in Walker & Co. v. Harrison, p. 816 supra? Compare UCC 2–106(4).

HOCHSTER v. DE LA TOUR

Queen's Bench, 1853.
2 E. & B. 678, 118 Eng.Rep. 922.

[Action of assumpsit.] Declaration: "for that, heretofore, to wit, on 12th April 1852, in consideration that plaintiff, at the request of defendant would agree with the defendant to enter into the service

a. For a treatment of the rather odd submission that the mailbox rule (see p. 265 supra) determines the place of breach in the form of a repudiating message, see Missouri Public Service Co. v. Peabody Coal Co., 583 S.W.2d 721 (Mo.App.1979).

b. Quoted: In re Estate of Weinberger, 203 Neb. 674, 279 N.W.2d 849 (1979).

For a lawyer's incautious use of the word see Glass v. Anderson, 596 S.W. 2d 507 (Tex.1980).

and employ of the defendant in capacity of a courier, on a certain day then to come, to wit, the 1st day of June, 1852, and to serve the defendant in that capacity, and travel with him on the continent of Europe as a courier for three months certain from the day and year last aforesaid, and to be ready to start with the defendant on such travels on the day and year last aforesaid, at and for certain wages or salary, to wit," £10 per month of such service, "the defendant then agreed with the plaintiff, and then promised him, that he, the defendant, would engage and employ the plaintiff in the capacity of a courier on and from the said 1st day of June, 1852, for three months" on these terms; "and to start on such travels with the plaintiff on the day and year last aforesaid, and to pay the plaintiff" on these terms. Averment that plaintiff, confiding in the said agreement and promise of the defendant "agreed with the defendant" to fulfill these terms on his part, "and to be ready to start with the defendant on such travels on the day and year last aforesaid, at and for the wages and salary aforesaid." That, "from the time of the making of said agreement of the said promise of the defendant until the time when the defendant wrongfully refused to perform and broke his said promise, and absolved, exonerated, and discharged the plaintiff from the performance of his agreement as hereinafter mentioned, he, the plaintiff, was always ready and willing to enter the service and employ of the defendant, in the capacity aforesaid, on the said 1st day of June, 1852, and to serve the defendant in that capacity, and to travel with him on the continent of Europe as a courier for three months certain from the day and year last aforesaid, and to start with the defendant on such travels on the day and year last aforesaid, at and for the wages and salary aforesaid; and the plaintiff, but for the breach by the defendant of his said promise as hereinafter mentioned, would, on the said 1st day of June, 1852, have entered into the said service and employ of the defendant in the capacity and upon the terms and for the time aforesaid; of all which several premises the defendant always had notice and knowledge; yet the defendant, not regarding the said agreement, nor his said promise, afterwards and before the said 1st June, 1852, wrongfully wholly refused and declined to engage or employ the defendant in the capacity and for the purpose aforesaid, on or from the said 1st June, 1852, for three months, or on, from, or for, any other time, or to start on such travels with the plaintiff on the day and year last aforesaid, or in any manner whatsoever to perform or fulfill his said promise, and then wrongfully wholly absolved, exonerated, and discharged the plaintiff from his said agreement, and from the performance of the same agreement on his the plaintiff's part, and from being ready and willing to perform the same on the plaintiff's part; and the defendant then wrongfully wholly broke, put an end to, and determined his said promise and engagement," to the damage of the plaintiff. The writ was dated on the 22d of May, 1852.

Pleas: 1. That defendant did not agree or promise in manner, and form, &c.: conclusion to the country. Issue thereon.

2. That plaintiff did not agree with defendant in manner and form, &c.: conclusion to the country. Issue thereon.

3. That plaintiff was not ready and willing, nor did defendant absolve, exonerate, or discharge plaintiff from being ready and willing, in manner and form, &c.: conclusion to the country. Issue thereon.

4. That defendant did not refuse or decline, nor wrongfully absolve, exonerate, or discharge, nor wrongfully break, put an end to, or determine, in manner and form, &c.: conclusion to the country. Issue thereon.

On the trial before Erle, J., at the London sittings in last Easter term, it appeared that plaintiff was a courier, who in April, 1852, was engaged by defendant to accompany him on a tour, to commence on 1st June, 1852, on the terms mentioned in the declaration. On the 11th May, 1852, defendant wrote to plaintiff that he had changed his mind, and declined his services. He refused to make him any compensation. The action was commenced on 22d May. The plaintiff, between the commencement of the action and the 1st of June, obtained an engagement with Lord Ashburton, on equally good terms, but not commencing till 4th July. The defendant's counsel objected that there could be no breach of the contract before the 1st of June. The learned judge was of contrary opinion, but reserved leave to enter a nonsuit on this objection. The other questions were left to the jury, who found for plaintiff.

Lord CAMPBELL, C. J.,[a] now delivered the judgment of the court:

On this motion in arrest of judgment, the question arises whether if there be an engagement between A. and B. whereby B. engages to employ A. on and from a future day for a given period of time, to travel with him into a foreign country as a courier, and to start with him in that capacity on that day, A. being to receive a monthly salary during the continuance of such service, B. may, before the day, refuse to perform the agreement and break and renounce it, so as to entitle

a. John Campbell (1779–1861), a Scotsman of ancient lineage, matriculated at St. Andrews University at the age of eleven. Upon entering the English bar he predicted that he would become Lord Chancellor. His name is associated with a number of law reform statutes which he pressed as a member of Parliament, as Attorney General, and in the House of Lords. As a reward for his services to the government, he was made the first Baron Campbell. He won literary fame with his "Lives of the Lord Chancellors," followed by the "Lives of the Chief Justices." These works are full of good stories, inaccuracies, and harsh judgments; it was said that they had added a new sting to death. He held judicial office briefly as Lord Chancellor of Ireland, where he was not popular, and as Chief Justice of England from 1850 to 1859. Then he became Lord Chancellor of England, at the age of eighty.

A. before the day to commence an action against B. to recover damages for breach of the agreement, A. having been ready and willing to perform it, till it was broken and renounced by B. The defendant's counsel very powerfully contended that, if the plaintiff was not contented to dissolve the contract, and to abandon all remedy upon it, he was bound to remain ready and willing to perform it till the day when the actual employment as courier in the service of the defendant was to begin; and that there could be no breach of the agreement, before that day, to give a right of action. But it cannot be laid down as a universal rule that, where by agreement an act is to be done on a future day, no action can be brought for a breach of the agreement till the day for doing the act has arrived. If a man promises to marry a woman on a future day, and before that day marries another woman, he is instantly liable to an action for breach of promise of marriage. Short v. Stone, 8 Q.B. 358. If a man contracts to execute a lease on and from a future day for a certain term, and, before that day, executes a lease to another for the same term, he may be immediately sued for breaking the contract. Ford v. Tiley, 6 B. & C. 325. So if a man contracts to sell and deliver specific goods on a future day, and before the day he sells and delivers them to another he is immediately liable to an action at the suit of the person with whom he first contracted to sell and deliver them. Bowdell v. Parsons, 10 East, 359. One reason alleged in support of such an action is, that the defendant has, before the day, rendered it impossible for him to perform the contract at the day; but this does not necessarily follow; for, prior to the day fixed for doing the act, the first wife may have died, a surrender of the lease executed might be obtained, and the defendant might have repurchased the goods so as to be in a situation to sell and deliver them to the plaintiff. Another reason may be that, where there is a contract to do an act on a future day, there is a relation constituted between the parties in the meantime by the contract, and that they impliedly promise that in the meantime neither will do anything to the prejudice of the other inconsistent with that relation. As an example, a man and woman engaged to marry are affianced to one another during the period between the time of the engagement and the celebration of the marriage. In this very case of traveller and courier, from the day of the hiring till the day when the employment was to begin, they were engaged to each other; and it seems to be a breach of an implied contract if either of them renounced the engagement. This reasoning seems in accordance with the unanimous decisions of the Exchequer Chamber in Elderton v. Emmens, 6 C.B. 160, which we have followed in subsequent cases in this court. The declaration in the present case, in alleging a breach, states a great deal more than a passing intention on the part of the defendant which he may repent of, and could only be proved by evidence that he had utterly renounced the contract, or done some act which rendered it impossible for him to perform it. If the plaintiff has no remedy for breach of the contract unless he treats the contract as in force, and acts upon it down to the 1st June, 1852, it follows that, till then, he must enter into no employment which will interfere with his promise "to start with the defendant on such travels on the day and year," and that he must then be properly equipped in all respects as a courier for a three months' tour on the continent of Europe. But it is surely much more rational, and more for the benefit of both parties, that, after the renunciation of the agreement by the defendant, the plaintiff should be at liberty to consider himself absolved from any future performance of it, retaining his right to sue for any damage he has suffered from the breach of it. Thus, instead of remaining idle and laying out money in preparations which must be useless, he is at liberty to seek service under another employer, which would go in mitigation of the damages to which he would otherwise be entitled for a breach of the contract. It seems strange that the defendant, after renouncing the contract, and absolutely declaring that he will never act under it, should be permitted to object that faith is given to his assertion, and that an opportunity is not left to him of changing his mind. If the plaintiff is barred of any remedy by entering into an engagement inconsistent with starting as a courier with the defendant on the 1st June, he is prejudiced by putting faith in the defendant's assertion; and it would be more consistent with principle if the defendant were precluded from saying that he had not broken the contract when he declared that he entirely renounced it. Suppose that the defendant, at the time of his renunciation, had embarked on a voyage for Australia, so as to render it physically impossible for him to employ the plaintiff as a courier on the continent of Europe in the months of June, July and August, 1852; according to decided cases, the action might have been brought before the 1st June; but the renunciation may have been founded on other facts, to be given in evidence, which would equally have rendered the defendant's performance of the contract impossible. The man who wrongfully renounces a contract into which he has deliberately entered cannot justly complain if he is immediately sued for a compensation in damages by the man whom he has injured; and it seems reasonable to allow an option to the injured party, either to sue immediately, or to wait till the time when the act was to be done, still holding it as prospectively binding for the exercise of this option, which may be advantageous to the innocent party, and cannot be prejudicial to the wrongdoer. An argument against the action before the 1st of June is urged from the difficulty of calculating the damages; but this argument is equally strong against an action before the 1st of September, when the three months would expire. In either case, the jury in assessing the damages would be justified in looking to all that happened, or was likely to happen, to increase or mitigate the loss of the plaintiff down to the day of trial. We do not find any decision contrary to the view we are taking of this case. Leigh v.

Paterson, 8 Taunt, 540, only shows that upon a sale of goods to be delivered at a certain time, if the vendor before the time gives information to the vendee that he cannot deliver them, having sold them, the vendee may calculate the damages according to the state of the market when they ought to have been delivered. . . .

If it should be held that, upon a contract to do an act on a future day, a renunciation of the contract by one party dispenses with a condition to be performed in the meantime by the other, there seems no reason for requiring that other to wait till the day arrives before seeking his remedy by action; and the only ground on which the condition can be dispensed with seems to be, that the renunciation may be treated as a breach of contract.

Upon the whole, we think that the declaration in this case is sufficient. It gives us great satisfaction to reflect that, the question being on the record, our opinion may be reviewed in a Court of Error. In the meantime, we must give judgment for the plaintiff.

Judgment for plaintiff.

NOTES

(1) *The Victim's Option.* The implication of the opinion seems to be that the victim of a repudiation may treat it as a breach, or not, as he likes: "the renunciation may be treated as a breach." The element of choice appears in many anticipatory breach cases. Sometimes it is said that the injured party has an election, sometimes that the repudiation amounts to an "offer" of breach to him.

If the injured party disregards the repudiation altogether, will his rights later be determined as if it had never occurred? An English decision of 1872 contains reasoning that is well-known in this country, and indicates that they will. However, that reasoning has also been rejected, at least where it would permit the injured party to pile up damages by proceeding with performance. See Rockingham County v. Luten Bridge Co., p. 592 supra, where the English case (Frost v. Knight) is criticized.

Nevertheless, it is a persistent idea that the injured party has a choice, upon receiving a repudiation, and that he may "keep the contract alive," to use Lord Cockburn's expression, for the benefit of both parties. As an example, see Dunn v. Reliance Life & Accident Ins. Co., 405 S.W.2d 389 (Tex. Civ.App.1966), where the court observed that the injured party did not *accept* the repudiation. The question was whether the statute of limitations began to run on the date the performance was promised, or earlier at repudiation. See also Brewer v. Simpson, 53 Cal.2d 567, 349 P.2d 289 (1960). Could this question be answered without regard to the decision in the *Luten Bridge* case? To the effect that no acceptance is requisite for a breach by anticipatory repudiation, see Stefanowicz Corp. v. Harris, 36 Md.App. 136, 373 A.2d 54 (1977); and to the contrary effect see William B. Tanner Co., Inc. v. WIOO, Inc., 528 F.2d 262 (3d Cir. 1975).

(2) *Retraction.* An offer to contract and an anticipatory repudiation have virtually nothing in common, except this: each may be withdrawn. In the case of an offer, the appropriate word is "revoke"; in the case of a re-

pudiation the appropriate word is "retract". See UCC 2–611. Inasmuch as a present breach of contract cannot be undone, the view has been expressed that the conception of breach by anticipatory repudiation is anomalous, and cannot be accounted for on "normal contract analysis." G. E. J. Corp. v. Uranium Aire, Inc., 311 F.2d 749, 754 n. 3 (9th Cir. 1963). In the case of an ordinary breach of contract, nothing the defaulting party may do can deprive the injured party of a right of action—although the breach may be so slight that only nominal damages would be granted.

The matter of retraction will be further considered below.

(3) *Laredo Hides Rebuffed.* The first case in this book, Laredo Hides Co. v. H & H Meat Products Co., reports that a seller of cattle hides gave an "ultimatum" to the buyer about payment for hides that had been delivered. Liborio Hinojosa acted for H & H, the seller, in this matter. The deadline he set for payment (March 21) passed without action satisfactory to him, and he refused payment when it was later tendered. The following delivery of hides was scheduled under the contract for Saturday, April 1. On the Thursday before that (March 30), an agent for Laredo Hides, the buyer, telephoned Hinojosa to ask if Saturday's shipment would be ready for pickup. "Hinojosa unequivocally told him that he was not going to sell him any more hides, and further advised that it was useless for him to send a truck for the hides, since at 4:30 p. m., Tuesday, March 21st, he had made up his mind to terminate the contract." The suit by Laredo Hides followed.

When the plaintiff appealed from the trial court judgment against it, the point seems to have been made, on behalf of H & H, that Laredo Hides had taken no further action in performance of the contract. Before confronting the issue of damages, the court disposed of that point briefly, as follows:

"An anticipatory breach of the entire contract exists if one party thereto, either before the time for performance, or after partial but before full performance, in positive and unconditional terms, refuses to perform further thereunder. Where one of the parties repudiates the contract and absolutely refuses to perform the duties and obligations required of him, the other party need not go through the useless act of tendering performance. Under the record before us, H & H repudiated the contract with Laredo Hides on March 30, 1972. That repudiation relieved Laredo Hides of itself tendering performance during the remaining months covered by the contract. It would have been useless and futile for Laredo Hides to have made such a tender twice in each of the months remaining." (Citations in this paragraph omitted.) See also Tenavision, Inc. v. Neuman, 45 N.Y.2d 145, 408 N.Y.S.2d 36, 379 N.E.2d 1166 (1978). *Question:* Was anything more than this decided in Hochster v. De la Tour?

PHELPS v. HERRO, 215 Md. 223, 137 A.2d 159 (1957). [In 1955 Herro contracted to sell certain interests, in realty and corporate stock, to Phelps for a price of $37,500. Phelps agreed to pay $5,000 by January 1, 1956, and to give a promissory note for the remainder. This note was to be payable in $5,000 installments, with interest, on the first of each succeeding year until paid in full. The first $5,000 was paid, and in September of 1956 Herro made the transfers called for in the contract. Later he was notified that the rest of the price would not be paid. He had never received the note. On December 7, 1956, he sued for $32,500. A judgment in his favor is the subject of this appeal. *Held:* For Phelps.

The court acknowledged that Herro might have sued Phelps for failure to give the note within a reasonable time, and recovered at least nominal damages, but it held that he was not entitled to installments due after December 7. (Not even the one due on January 1, 1957, apparently, although it was overdue at the time of judgment.)]

PRESCOTT, Judge. . . . We think the proper rule is that the doctrine of anticipatory breach of a contract has no application to money contracts, pure and simple, where one party has fully performed his undertaking, and all that remains for the opposite party to do is to pay a certain sum of money at a certain time or times, and, under the circumstances of this case, this is as far as we need to rule, although some of the cases cited hold that the doctrine of anticipatory breach has no application whatsoever in unilateral contracts, or bilateral contracts that have become unilateral by full performance on one side.

[The court said that a different rule would apply if the contract had required the giving of a note *with security.*]

The appellees argued further that a promise to give a negotiable note stands on the same footing as a promise to furnish security. We find it unnecessary to decide this question; because we think the promise to give a note in this case contemplated a non-negotiable one. . . .

HAMMOND, Judge (dissenting). . . . I could not bring myself . . . to saddle Maryland needlessly with what I consider to be illogical and unsound law—a doctrine that is more apparent than real, and one that has been repudiated by the ablest judges and scholars. [Judge Hammond conceded that Williston favored an exception to the doctrine of anticipatory breach—"perhaps because of his dislike of the doctrine." However, he quoted from Corbin and others to sustain his view.]

NOTES

(1) *The Rose Bowl Affair.* The Southern California football team played in the Rose Bowl on January 1, 1969. Tickets sold for $20 on the "black market." Before the season began, Roger Diamond had bought an "economy season ticket" from the University, on the promise that he could have a Rose Bowl ticket if the team played there. When it was selected to do so, however, the Tournament of Roses Association allotted to the University fewer tickets than it needed to meet its commitments to season ticket holders, by about 3,500. Early in December, 1968, the University notified Diamond that he and other first-time holders of economy season tickets

could not be accommodated. The notice thanked him for his support of Trojan football.

On December 9 Diamond, a lawyer, brought a class action against the University on behalf of himself and others similarly situated, holders of 3,000 tickets. About a week later the University altered its stance and began distributing applications for Rose Bowl tickets to members of the plaintiff's class. In January, the trial court gave summary judgment for the defendant. The plaintiff appealed, for the purpose of establishing his right to an attorney's fee. *Held:* Affirmed. Diamond v. University of Southern California, 11 Cal.App.3d 49, 89 Cal.Rptr. 302 (1970).[a]

The court found several unanswered questions about class actions in the appeal, but passed them by and pinned its result on the rule that "the doctrine of anticipatory repudiation does not apply to contracts which are unilateral in their inception or have become so by complete performance by one party. . . . The action was, therefore, premature. . . . We have, admittedly, taken the easy way out and decided to affirm on the basis of a simple principle of contract law. The day may come when that principle, which already is not universally admired . . . will be successfully questioned in another class action, similar in structure, but which presents major considerations of public policy which outweigh the social utility of a technical exception to the doctrine of anticipatory breach. When that day comes, the court concerned with the case can easily confine this decision to its own peculiar facts by noting that easy cases make bad law."

(2) *The Restatement.* The American Law Institute has vacillated over the effect of full performance on one side. See Comment and Reason for Changes in Restatement of the Law, 1948 Supplement 252–53 (1949). What is the difference between the rule of Phelps v. Herro and the present Institute position? See Restatement Second, §§ 243(3), 253.

(3) *The Code.* It has been suggested that the Code "demands discontinuance of the artificial distinction between contracts which have been fully performed by one party and those which are completely executory." Taylor, The Impact of Article 2 of the U.C.C. on the Doctrine of Anticipatory Repudiation, 9 Bost.Coll.Ind. & Comm.L.Rev. 917, 926–27 (1968). What Code sections are incompatible with the distinction? 2–609 or 2–610? Do any Code sections support it? 2–709?

INSTALLMENT PAYMENT CONTRACTS

In several important classes of contracts there is a commitment to pay money in installments over an extended period of time. Long-term leases are examples. In the event of repudiation by the tenant, what may the landlord recover on account of future payments? A possible answer is nothing, according to the "usual rule that contracts to pay money in installments are breached one installment at a time." Quick v. American Steel and Pump Corp., 397 F.2d

a. The trial court made a finding that the University's "sudden affluence in the matter of tickets" was not caused by the plaintiff's suit. Does this affect your judgment about the case? It did not seem to affect the court's.

561 (2d Cir. 1968). There are other answers, which cannot be examined here, except to note that anticipatory breach law has not worked in favor of lessors so well as it has worked for others. The lessor's performance is regarded as complete at the time of the lease; for by the niceties of ancient property law it is a conveyance.[a] If the rent is therefore an independent obligation, the lessor is handicapped in claiming damages. "There must be some dependency of performance in order to make anticipatory breach possible." Sagamore Corp. v. Willcutt, 120 Conn. 315, 180 A. 464 (1935). Yet this rule may not, in practice, handicap lessors so much as it seems to do, as is shown by the case cited.

Like leases, annuity contracts call for long-term installment payments. In a suit for such payments, it is generally accepted that a judgment for the payee should be limited to money owing when the action is brought,[b] or when it reaches trial,[c] or when the judgment is entered, at the latest. The consequence may be that the payee has to assert his rights in successive actions. Dissatisfaction with this state of affairs has suggested at least two remedial measures. One is to apply the doctrine of anticipatory breach, with the effect that the payee has judgment for the immediate recovery of the present value of all future installments. Another is that the court enter an order calling for future payments to be made as they fall due. This procedure amounts to specific performance, and for effectiveness it might require that the court retain the case until completion of the payments.

The former suggestion is plagued by doubt that the calculations would be accurate. Consider, for example, an agreement by which Henry Pollack was to pay $5,000 a year to his brother Charles (in monthly installments) for the life of Charles, except that if Henry died first his estate was to pay Charles $100,000. What is the present value of Charles' rights when Henry repudiates? Does it matter that Henry is a bit older? In Pollack v. Pollack, 39 S.W.2d 853 (Tex.Com.App.1931), the court directed a calculation on the assumption that Henry would die in 12 years, and Charles three years later.[d]

a. The covenants in real-property leases stand somewhat apart from those in other contracts: owing partly to the ancient conception of the lease as a conveyance of a "leasehold", certain material violations of the landlord's undertakings may not excuse the tenant from continuing rent payments. There has been a tendency, of late, to assimilate leases to other contracts in this respect. See Garcia v. Freeland Realty, Inc., 63 Misc.2d 937, 314 N.Y. S.2d 215 (1970). But these matters are left to courses in real-property law.

b. As in Phelps v. Herro, supra.

c. Brix v. People's Mutual Life Ins. Co., 2 Cal.2d 446, 41 P.2d 537 (1935).

d. The court said it was "impossible to actually tell, with certainty, which of these parties will die first, but such fact does not prevent the court from ascertaining such fact."

A more common sort of contract containing health contingencies is illustrated in the next main case. Still another is an ordinary life insurance contract. If the insurer repudiates while premiums are still to be paid, there is an element of dependency, and the policyholder is commonly entitled to the present value of the death benefit. That value will be relatively large if it is assumed that death is imminent. A policyholder having a serious ailment, Patterson suggested, may play on the court's sympathies to enlarge his recovery. Essentials of Insurance Law § 48 (2d ed. 1957).

NOTE

Specific Performance. For the annuitant of a life insurance company, once the company repudiates, what is the advantage of specific performance? If the installment payments are resumed, and stopped again, presumably the payee must apply again to the court for relief. This may seem a remote prospect because of the insurer's need to maintain a reputation.[e] Or because it would fear regulatory sanctions. But if that is so, the objective is gained, is it not, by awarding only accrued installments to the payee? See Fanning v. Guardian Life Ins. Co., 59 Wash.2d 101, 366 P.2d 207 (1961). This case is one of many which limit recovery to accrued installments by following the rule stated in Phelps v. Herro, supra. And this was done although the company denied the existence of the contract; compare the text of the next main case as to "complete repudiation."

"A contract for the payment of money in installments is not ordinarily specifically enforceable, the common law remedies being regarded as adequate." 5 Corbin, 663. But in a few courts an order may be granted for periodic future payments.[f] Corbin argues for more flexibility in this regard, especially in favor of an insured person claiming by right of disability.[g]

NEW YORK LIFE INS. CO. v. VIGLAS

Supreme Court of the United States, 1936.
297 U.S. 672, 56 S.Ct. 615, 80 L.Ed. 971.

On Writ of Certiorari to the United States Circuit Court of Appeals for the First Circuit.

Action by Demetrios P. Viglas against the New York Life Insurance Company. To review a judgment of the Circuit Court of Ap-

e. Cobb v. Pacific Mutual Life Ins. Co., 4 Cal.2d 565, 51 P.2d 84 (1935).

f. See Equitable Life Assur. Soc. v. Branham, 250 Ky. 472, 63 S.W.2d 498 (1933); John Hancock Mutual Life Ins. Co. v. Cohen, 254 F.2d 417 (9th Cir. Okla.1958); cf. Wild v. Wild, 360 Mich. 270, 103 N.W.2d 607 (1960). In Crouch v. Crouch, 566 F.2d 486 (5th Cir. 1978), a preference was shown for immediate valuation of the plaintiff's entitlement. It was not an insurance case.

g. If a recovery of the present value of promised future payments is likely to enhance the aggregate income-tax liability of the payee, is that a loss he may charge to the party guilty of breach? See Stopford v. Boonton Molding Co., 56 N.J. 169, 265 A.2d 657 (1970).

peals [78 F.2d 829] reversing a judgment of the District Court for defendant, the defendant brings certiorari.

Judgment of the Circuit Court of Appeals reversed, and judgment of the District Court affirmed.

Mr. Justice CARDOZO delivered the opinion of the Court.

The case, which is here upon demurrer to a declaration, depends for its solution upon the nature of the breach of contract imputed to the defendant, the petitioner in this court, and upon the measure of the damages recoverable therefor.

From the declaration we learn the following: Respondent received from petitioner on February 7, 1927, a policy of insurance for $2,000 payable at his death. The consideration was a semiannual premium of $38 payable during his life, but for not more than twenty years. If, however, the insured became totally and permanently disabled before the age of sixty, the company, petitioner, was to pay him a monthly income at an agreed rate and was to waive the payment of any premium that would otherwise be due. Disability was to be considered total when the insured was so affected by bodily injury or disease as to be wholly prevented from performing any work, from following any occupation, or from engaging in any business for remuneration or profit. In particular, "the total and irrecoverable loss of the sight of both eyes or of the use of both hands or of both feet or of one hand and one foot" was to constitute "total disability for life." Before making any income payment or waiving any premium, the company might demand due proof of the continuance of total disability, not oftener, however, than once a year after such disability had continued for two full years. Upon failure to furnish such proof, or if the insured performed any work, or followed any occupation, or engaged in any business for remuneration or profit, "no further income payments" were to be made, "nor premiums waived." If, at the time of a default in the payment of a premium, the insured was disabled within the definition of the policy, the insurance was to be reinstated, provided, however, that within six months after the default proofs of such disability were received by the insurer. In any event, reinstatement would be permitted at any time within five years upon evidence of insurability satisfactory to the insurer and upon payment of overdue premiums with interest at 5 per cent. Finally, the insured, though in default, was to have the benefit of surrender values in the form either of cash or of temporary insurance or of participating paid-up insurance according to his choice.

On September 11, 1931, the insured, according to the declaration, lost "the total and irrecoverable use" of one hand and one foot, and became totally and permanently disabled. Upon proof of his condition the company paid him the monthly benefits called for by the policy from October 11, 1931, to July 11, 1933, and during the same period waived the payment of semiannual premiums. It refused to make a monthly payment in August, 1933, and refused the same month to waive a semiannual premium, "asserting to the plaintiff as its ground for such refusal that since it appeared to the defendant that for some time past the plaintiff had not been continuously totally disabled within the meaning of the disability benefit provision of the policy, the defendant would make no further monthly disability payments, and that the premiums due on and after August 7, 1933, would be payable in conformity with the terms of the contract." Later, upon the expiration of a term of grace, "the defendant, on or about September 19, 1933, declared the policy as lapsed upon its records." Plaintiff has elected to treat the defendant's acts "as a repudiation and denunciation of the entire contract," relieving him on his part from any further obligation.

There are two counts to his declaration. In the first, after stating the foregoing facts, he claims the cash surrender value that the policy will have in February, 1969, if he lives until that time, the date being chosen with reference to his expectancy of life under the American Table of Mortality. This value, $1,408, is less than the amount necessary to give jurisdiction in accordance with the Judicial Code. Judicial Code, sec. 24, 28 U.S.C. sec. 41, 28 U.S.C.A. sec. 41. In the second count, after stating the same facts, he claims for damages the total benefits that will be payable to him during the same period of expectancy, if he lives that long and his disability continues. The damages so computed are $15,900. No deduction is made on account of future premiums, for by hypothesis the disability will continue during life. The defendant demurred to both counts, stating in the demurrer that the declaration sets forth a cause of action for the benefits and premiums accruing prior to the date of the writ, and for nothing in excess thereof. In that view the recovery will be only $98, which is less than the jurisdictional amount. The District Court sustained the demurrer, and gave judgment for the defendant. The Circuit Court of Appeals for the First Circuit reversed. 78 F.2d 829. A writ of certiorari issued to resolve a claim of conflict with a decision of this court. 296 U.S. 571, 56 S.Ct. 370, 80 L.Ed. 403.

Upon the showing made in the complaint there was neither a repudiation of the policy nor such a breach of its provisions as to make conditional and future benefits the measure of recovery.

Repudiation there was none as the term is known to the law. Petitioner did not disclaim the intention or the duty to shape its conduct in accordance with the provisions of the contract. Far from repudiating those provisions, it appealed to their authority and endeavored to apply them. If the insured was still disabled, monthly benefits were payable, and there should have been a waiver of the premium. If he had recovered the use of hand or foot and was not otherwise disabled, his right to benefits had ceased, and the payment of the premium was again a contractual condition. There is nothing to show that the insurer was not acting in good faith in giving notice of its contention that the disability was over. Mobley v. New York Life Insurance Co., 295 U.S. 632, 638, 55 S.Ct. 876, 79 L.Ed. 1621, 99 A.L.R. 1166. If it made a mistake, there was a breach of a provision of the policy with liability for any damages appropriate thereto. We do not pause at the moment to fix the proper measure. Enough in this connection that at that stage of the transaction there had been no renunciation or abandonment of the contract as a whole. Mobley v. New York Life Insurance Co., supra; Dingley v. Oler, 117 U.S. 490, 503, 6 S.Ct. 850, 29 L.Ed. 984; Roehm v. Horst, 178 U.S. 1, 14, 15, 20 S.Ct. 780, 44 L.Ed. 953; Pierce v. Tennessee Coal, Iron & R. Co., 173 U.S. 1, 3, 11, 19 S.Ct. 335, 43 L.Ed. 591.

Renunciation or abandonment, if not effected at that stage, became consummate in the plaintiff's view at the end of the period of grace when the company declared the policy "lapsed upon its records." Throughout the plaintiff's argument the declaration of a lapse is treated as equivalent to a declaration that the contract is a nullity. But the two are widely different under such a policy as this.[1] The policy survived for many purposes as an enforceable obligation, though default in the payment of premiums had brought about a change of rights and liabilities. The insurer was still subject to a duty to give the insured the benefit of the stipulated surrender privileges, cash or new insurance. It was still subject to a duty upon proof within six months that the disability continued to reinstate the policy as if no default had occurred. None of these duties was renounced. None of them was questioned. Indeed, there is lacking an allegation that notice of the entry on the records was given to the plaintiff, or that what was recorded amounted to more than a private memorandum. In that respect the case is weaker for the plaintiff than Mobley v. New York Life Insurance Co., supra, decided at the last term. . . .

What the damages would be if there had been complete repudiation we do not now decide. Cf. Kelly v. Security Mutual Life Insurance Co., 186 N.Y. 16, 78 N.E. 584, 9 Ann.Cas. 661; O'Neill v. Supreme Council, A.L. of H., 70 N.J.Law, 410, 415, 57 A. 463, 1 Ann. Cas. 422. For breach short of repudiation or an intentional abandonment equivalent thereto, the damages under such a policy as this do not exceed the benefits in default at the commencement of the suit. Full justice will thus be done alike to insured and to insurer. The insured, if he proves that the benefits are due, will have a judgment effective to reinstate his policy. The insurer will be saved from a heavy, perhaps a crushing, liability as the consequence of a claim of right not charged to have been made as a disingenuous pretense. Cf. Armstrong v. Ross, 61 W.Va. 38, 48, 55 S.E. 895. So the courts have held with an impressive concord of opinion.[2] Federal Life Insurance

1. See the cases collected in Vance on Insurance, 2d Ed., pp. 283, 301, 302.

2. [Twenty two cases cited.]

Co. v. Rascoe (C.C.A.) 12 F.2d 693, one of the few decisions to the contrary, was disapproved in Mobley's Case, 295 U.S. 632, at page 639, 55 S.Ct. 876, 878, 79 L.Ed. 1621, 99 A.L.R. 1166, and is now disapproved again.

We have no thought to suggest an invariable rule whereby the full value of a bargain may never be recovered for any breach of contract falling short of repudiation or intentional abandonment. All depends upon the circumstances. Helgar Corporation v. Warner's Features, Inc., 222 N.Y. 449, 452, 453, 454, 119 N.E. 113.[3] There may be times when justice requires that, irrespective of repudiation or abandonment, the sufferer from the breach shall be relieved of a duty to treat the contract as subsisting or to hold himself in readiness to perform it in the future. Roehm v. Horst, supra, 178 U.S. 1, at pages 17, 18, 20 S.Ct. 780, 44 L.Ed. 953; Nichols v. Scranton Steel Co., 137 N.Y. 471, 487, 33 N.E. 561. Generally this is so where the contract is a bilateral one with continuing obligations, as where a manufacturer has undertaken to deliver merchandise in instalments. Norrington v. Wright, 115 U.S. 188, 6 S.Ct. 12, 29 L.Ed. 366; Wolfert v. Caledonia Springs Ice Co., 195 N.Y. 118, 88 N.E. 24, 21 L.R. A.,N.S., 864. Even then, the rights that are his may depend upon the grounds of the rejection or the nature of the default, whether unintentional or wilful. Helgar Corporation v. Warner's Features, Inc., supra. On the other hand, a party to a contract who has no longer any obligation of performance on his side, but is in the position of an annuitant or a creditor exacting payment from a debtor, may be compelled to wait for the instalments as they severally mature, just as a landlord may not accelerate the rent for the residue of the term because the rent is in default for a month or for a year. McCready v. Lindenborn, 172 N.Y. 400, 408, 65 N.E. 208; cf. National Machine & Tool Co. v. Standard Shoe Machinery Co., 181 Mass. 275, 279, 63 N.E. 900; Wharton & Co. v. Winch, 140 N.Y. 287, 35 N.E. 589. With the aid of this analysis, one discovers the rationale of the cases which have stated at times, though with needless generality, that by reason of the subject-matter of the undertaking the rule applicable to contracts for the payment of money is not the same as that applicable for the performance of services or the delivery of merchandise.[a] Cf. Roehm v. Horst, supra, 178 U.S. 1, at page 17, 20 S.Ct. 780, 44 L.Ed. 953; Moore v. Security Trust & Life Insurance Co. (C.C.A.) 168 F. 496, 503; Howard v. Benefit Association of Railway Employees, 239 Ky. 465, 470, 39 S.W.2d 657, 81 A.L.R. 375; Washington County v. Williams (C.C.A.) 111 F. 801, 810; Restatement, Law of Contracts, section 316. The root of any valid distinction is not in the difference

3. For a collection of the cases, see Williston, Contracts, vol. 2, secs. 864, 866, 867, 870, vol. 3, sec. 1290, and cf. Restatement, Law of Contracts, vol. 1, sec. 275.

a. In a later case, Cardozo said that the doctrine of anticipatory breach is not applicable to unilateral contracts, especially those for the payment of money. Smyth v. U. S., 302 U.S. 329, 356 (1937).

between money and merchandise or between money and services. What counts decisively is the relation between the maintenance of the contract and the frustration of the end it was expected to subserve. The ascertainment of this relation calls for something more than the mechanical application of a uniform formula. To determine whether a breach avoids the contract as a whole one must consider what is necessary to work out reparation in varying conditions.

If that test be applied, the declaration will not stand. The plaintiff does not need redress in respect of unmatured instalments in order to put himself in a position to shape his conduct for the future.[b] If he is already in default for the nonpayment of a premium, he will not be in any worse predicament by multiplying the defaults thereafter. On the other hand, if his default is unreal because the premiums had been waived, the insurer will be estopped from insisting upon later premiums until the declaration of a lapse has been canceled or withdrawn. Besides, if the disability is permanent, there will be nothing more to pay. The law will be able to offer appropriate relief "where compensation is willfully and contumaciously withheld." Cobb v. Pacific Mutual Life Insurance Co., 4 Cal.2d 565, 51 P.2d 84, 88.

We have refrained in what has been written from developing the distinction between an anticipatory breach and others. The line of division between the two has not always been preserved with consistency or clearness. To blur it is prejudicial to accuracy of thought as well as precision of terminology. Strictly an anticipatory breach is one committed before the time has come when there is a present duty of performance. Roehm v. Horst, supra; Pollock on Contracts, 9th Ed., p. 293; Williston, Contracts, vol. 3, sec. 1296, et seq., collecting the decisions. It is the outcome of words or acts evincing an intention to refuse performance in the future. On the other hand, there are times, as we have seen, when the breach of a present duty, though only partial in its extension, may confer upon the injured party the privilege at his election to deal with the contract as if broken altogether. A loose practice has been growing up whereby the breach on such occasions is spoken of as anticipatory, whereas in truth it is strictly present, though with consequences effective upon performance in the future. The declaration in the case at hand makes a showing of a present breach. It does not make a showing of a breach so wilful and material as to make acceleration of future benefits essential to the attainment of present reparation. Helgar Corporation v. Warner's Features, Inc., supra.

The judgment of the Court of Appeals should be reversed and that of the District Court affirmed.

It is so ordered.

b. Does this statement sufficiently take account of the requirement that the insured submit himself to a periodical examination?

NOTES

(1) *Insurance Obligations and Anticipatory Breach.* In many cases where there was a showing of present breach as there was in Viglas, the extent of an insurer's liability has been said to turn on the scope of the doctrine of anticipatory breach. See Mabery v. Western Casualty & Surety Co., 173 Kan. 586, 250 P.2d 824 (1952) (monthly payments promised in settlement of tort claim). In that case the court expressed concern, as others have done, about the difficulty of valuing plaintiff's right to future payments. "Damages are not to be based upon mere conjecture or speculation, and we think plaintiff cannot be heard to claim serious physical permanent disability on the one hand, which condition existed at the time the alleged agreement was made, and at the same time to claim damages based on a normal life expectancy. Suppose he were to die a year or two from now."

In Greguhn v. Mutual of Omaha Ins. Co., 23 Utah 2d 214, 461 P.2d 285 (1969), the Viglas case was followed, by a divided court, but as to the future it said:

"The verdict and the decision of the trial court amounts to a determination that the plaintiff is entitled to the monthly payments as specified in the insurance policies so long as he is totally and permanently disabled. Defendants are not relieved of the obligation of making the payments unless the plaintiff should recover or die. Should the defendants fail in the future to make payment in accordance with the terms of the policies without just cause or excuse and the plaintiff is compelled to file another action for delinquent installments, the court at that time should be able to fashion such relief as will compel performance."

Texas courts prefer to award the present value of future benefits, but the computation presents some difficulty. In Republic Bankers Life Ins. Co. v. Jaeger, 551 S.W.2d 30 (Tex.Civ.App.1976), the trial court gave judgment for $18,000 on a disability contract. It derived that amount from the maximum recovery provided in the policy: $300 a month for 60 months. At the time of judgment the claimant had been disabled for 15 months and the insurer had paid nothing. On appeal by the insurer, held: *Reversed.* The court directed a more complex valuation of the benefits, taking into account a reasonable rate of interest. *Question:* Is it clear that no interest assumption would yield $18,000 as the present value of the maximum benefit?

(2) *Problem.* Oil companies commonly make "dry hole contributions" to the drillers of test, or wildcat, wells. Having minerals in the neighborhood, the company will be enriched if oil is found. But so will the wildcatter, who has his own minerals; and no payment is called for in that event. If no oil is found, he is a loser, but the company will reimburse part of his costs. For a few thousand dollars, it may thereby save itself the expense of drilling its own well to prove (or disprove) its holdings.

Placid Oil Company made a dry hole contribution contract with a driller, by which it agreed to pay him $25,000 if he put a test well down to 10,000 feet and it proved to be dry hole. The driller was required to prove compliance with Texas law in plugging the hole; this would have cost $2,000. He spent more than $100,000 and drilled to 10,025 feet without finding more than a trace of oil. He then asked Placid what to do. Placid answered with the following telegram: "You are obligated to test all horizons which appear promising. To do so you must set pipe and conduct tests by perforating and sandfacing the following zones [naming eight zones]. The failure of which will be a material breach of agreement and a forfeiture of all your rights." Compliance with this demand would have cost $75,000, and was not required by the contract. Instead the driller went on down a short distance (indicated by the dissenting judge to be three feet) and struck oil. (Fortune smiled on him, said the court, "albeit wanly.") Then he brought an action against Placid for $25,000.

Consider the following issues: (a) Did Placid repudiate the contract? (b) At the time of the telegram, was there an "element of dependency" in the contract? (c) What is the effect on the driller's claim of his failure to plug the well? See Placid Oil Co. v. Humphrey, 244 F.2d 184 (5th Cir. 1957).

WAIVER, ESTOPPEL, AND ELECTION

Contract obligations may be imposed or eliminated, and so may conditions attending them, by agreement between the parties. All these effects may also result from waiver, estoppel, and election. These conceptions function as junior partners, in a sense, to modification agreements. Illustrations and standard definitions are provided in cases to follow. Briefly, a *waiver* is said to be "the intentional relinquishment of a known right";[a] and an *estoppel*, the preclusion of a contestant to take some position of right when his words or actions have brought another into a changed position. "*Election* [Holmes wrote] is simply what its name imports; a choice, shown by an overt act, between two inconsistent rights, either of which may be asserted at the will of the chooser alone."[b] In expressing any of these principles there are unusual difficulties because they are applied with more stringency to some factual patterns than to others. They apply over the whole range of contract relations, and in other contexts as well. Probably their most frequent applications are in aid of suits on insurance policies, by excusing the failure of a policyholder or other claimant to comply with some condition of the contract.[c]

Elections are not always called by that name. Quite often, when a contracting party has made a necessary choice between opposing courses of action or legal positions that were open to him, a court will say that he has "waived" one of them. It has been argued that a dif-

a. Lee v. Casualty Co., 90 Conn. 202, 96 A. 952 (1916).

b. Bierce v. Hutchins, 205 U.S. 340, 346 (1907). Other standard formulations appear in Dahl v. Brunswick Corp., p. 861 infra, and New England Structures, Inc. v. Loranger, p. 902 infra.

c. See R. Keeton, Insurance Law (Basic Text) 343–45, 423–27 (1971); Morris, Waiver and Estoppel in Insurance Policy Litigation, 105 U.Pa.L.Rev. 925 (1957); E. Patterson, Essentials of Insurance Law, Ch. 11 (2d ed. 1957).

ferent kind of waiver occurs when a party submits himself voluntarily to a legal burden in the absence of pressure to do so. Yet the difference between an ordinary, "intentional" waiver and an election-waiver is a subtle one, at best.

In one respect, an intentional waiver seems to be different from both election and estoppel: there are times when it may be withdrawn. A landlord might say, for example, that he waived prompt payment of the rent, without committing himself indefinitely. If the succeeding installments of rent were not paid on time, the landlord would hardly be permitted to take immediate eviction proceedings. (Is that because he has waived prompt payment? Or because he is estopped to act on the delay?) Yet he would probably be permitted, after some experience of aggravated delays, to reinstate the requirement of prompt payment by saying, in good time, that future installments must be timely. The waiver would be withdrawn.[d] (On closer analysis, it might appear that what is withdrawn is not a waiver, which occurs month by month, but a notice of *intent* to waive. But close analysis of the word "waiver" is not usual in the cases.)

An estoppel, like an election, may sometimes be discerned in a case where the opinion speaks only of waiver. An estoppel is thought to arise only when there has been reliance—a change of position, or at least detrimental inaction—in response to conduct or expressions of the party said to be estopped. The reliance must be manifest in some form: it is not enough that the party asserting estoppel has had his expectations aroused, or that "some secret operation of his own mind" was set in motion. Wood v. State, 12 N.Y.2d 25, 186 N.E.2d 406 (1962). An estoppel may be illustrated by these facts: a buyer contracts for goods "to be shipped in wooden crates." Thereafter, he writes the seller: "you may ship in cardboard cartons, instead." After the goods are packed in cardboard, the buyer may not insist on repacking in crates.[e]

d. Compare Charles Rickards, Ltd. v. Oppenheim, 1950 1 K.B. 616, 1950, 1 All.E.R. 420. But cf. Lee v. Cas. Co., footnote a supra, saying that "rights once waived cannot be regained by revoking the waiver." See Restatement Second, § 84(2).

e. Not even this case fits within all definitions of estoppel, apparently. Does it fit within this one?—"Estoppel arises where 1) a party, by representations, admissions or silence, intentionally or negligently induces another party to believe facts, 2) the other party justifiably relies and acts on this belief, and 3) the other party will be prejudiced if the first party is permitted to deny the existence of the facts." Dimmitt & Owens Financial, Inc. v. Realtek Industries Inc., 90 Mich.App. 429, 280 N.W.2d 827 (1979).

Professor Gilmore appears to think the idea of estoppel is formless. He has said that estoppel is "simply a way of saying that, for reasons which the court does not care to discuss, there must be judgment for plaintiff." The Death of Contract 64 (1974). Another view might be that the idea is simply Protean, not formless. Compare Town & Country Bank of Springfield v. James M. Canfield Contracting Co., Inc., 55 Ill.App.3d 91, 12 Ill.Dec. 826, 370 N.E.2d 630 (1977): "In recent times, 'estoppel' has become a sort of a legal catch-all, rivaling 'res gestae' as one of the least-understood but most often used refuges when all else fails. Notwithstanding its frequent

Sometimes it is difficult to distinguish an estoppel from a modification of the contract. If the buyer in the foregoing example had *requested* the seller to pack the goods in cardboard, and the seller had begun to do so, it might be inferred that the parties had formed a new contract for a different performance. The distinction is especially difficult to maintain for contracts within Article 2 of the Code because it provides that "An agreement modifying a contract within this Article needs no consideration to be binding." UCC 2–209(1).[f] Under this rule, the buyer supposed above might be bound by an agreement to pay for the goods packed in either way the seller chooses, and be bound whether or not the seller has begun to pack them. The same section of the Code also recognizes the principle of estoppel, however, in subsection (5), by limiting the power to retract a waiver, "in view of a material change of position. . . ." What does the word "waiver" mean in this context?

The efficacy of waivers, estoppels, and elections is limited, in a way not easy to summarize, by a perception that they ought not to be allowed to displace the necessity of a bargain altogether. As an extreme example, a buyer of goods would not be held bound by waiver if he said to the seller, "I will pay for the goods promised whether they are delivered or not." The point is discussed in Corbin, § 752, and in Rennie & Laughlin, Inc. v. Chrysler Corp., 242 F.2d 208 (9th Cir. 1957): "Where substantial rights are involved, it is frequently said that waiver must be supported by either an agreed consideration or by acts amounting to estoppel."[g] Even the principle of estoppel may be impotent to achieve some of the results that are regularly accomplished by bargaining. Cf. Restatement Second, § 90, suggesting a limitation on the remedy in a case of *promissory* estoppel. An important example is the rule often stated that "estoppel cannot be used to enlarge the coverage of an insurance policy." Madgett v. Monroe County Mutual Tornado Ins. Co., 46 Wis.2d 708, 176 N.W.2d 314 (1970) ("Estoppel can block, but it cannot create. It is a barricade . . . . not a bulldozer.")[h] The rule is open to serious challenge,[i] but it indicates that estoppel, like waiver, is still only an ancillary source of contract rights.

allegations, it is a highly technical and restrictive principle of law."

For a sportsmanlike use of estoppel see Trustees of State Colleges and Universities v. National Collegiate Athletic Ass'n, 82 Cal.App.3d 461, 147 Cal.Rptr. 187 (1978), in which there was reliance by a college on a pronouncement by the National Collegiate Athletic Association about its rules, in the form of fielding some students who were "sub-predictors."

f. See also UCC 2–208, 2–209(4).

g. See also Rose v. Mitsubishi Int'l Corp., 423 F.Supp. 1162 (E.D.Pa.1976).

h. See also Mercado v. Mitchell, 83 Wis.2d 17, 264 N.W.2d 532 (1978).

i. See Keeton, op. cit. supra n. c., § 6.-6(b).

NOTES

(1) *Waiver Distributed.* It has not been possible to regard waiver as a single-valued concept since a Canadian lawyer, Ewart, published a volume called "Waiver Distributed Among the Departments Election, Estoppel, Contract, Release" in 1917.[j] "The explanation of the somewhat curious title of the present volume is that although the author commenced to write a book about 'waiver,' he very soon ascertained that there was not enough 'waiver' to write a book about." Id. at p. 3. "For the simple statement that, upon breach of a policy-condition, the insurance company may elect whether to continue or discontinue its liability, substitute that the company has a right to 'waive the forfeiture,' and you have made clear reasoning impossible. . . . The case is purely one of election." Id. at p. 25. Ewart found that waiver was also a common alias for estoppel: "The doctrine of waiver, as asserted against insurance companies to avoid the strict enforcement of conditions contained in their policies, is only another name for the doctrine of estoppel." Insurance Co. v. Wolff, 95 U.S. 326 (1877). However, he granted that waiver is sometimes a serviceable word, even if some other will usually serve the purpose better, and he approved the following proposition: "While one party has time and opportunity to comply with a condition precedent, if the other party does or says anything to put him off his guard, and to induce him to believe that the condition is waived, or that a strict compliance with it will not be insisted on, he is afterward estopped from claiming non-performance of the condition." Underwood v. Farmers' Joint Stock Ins. Co., 57 N.Y. 500, 505 (1874).[k]

(2) *Rights Upon Breach.* The discharge of a "claim or right arising out of an alleged breach" cannot be effected by a simple waiver, although the Code provides a mechanism for discharge that does not require a consideration. UCC 1–107.

(3) *Jarbeau's Case.* In Bernstein v. Meech, 130 N.Y. 354, 29 N.E. 255 (1891), a party charged with repudiation was permitted to recover on the contract because the other party had "elected" to disregard the plaintiff's apparent misconduct. The plaintiff represented a performing troupe, the Jarbeau Comedy Company. It had incurred expenses for the purpose of appearing at the Buffalo Academy of Music, but was not allowed to appear. The agreement was for a period in December, and called for an equal division of the gross receipts. The plaintiff's offense, committed in August, was to send a draft contract increasing his share: he could not think of playing for less than 60%, he said. The defendants returned the contract unsigned "for the reason that we have a contract signed by you and do not need any other for the appearance of Vernona Jarbeau and company at our Academy." On November 17 the plaintiff wrote again, sending advertising material and saying, "Please keep Miss Jarbeau before the public as much as

j. He was thinking of changing the title as early as 1905; see Waiver in Insurance Law, 18 Harv.L.Rev. 365, 378. See also Election in Insurance Law, 12 Colum.L.Rev. 619 (1912).

k. The author of this opinion also said:
"The doctrine of estoppel lays at the foundation of the law, as to waiver. . . . I think there can be no waiver of a condition precedent, except there be in the case an element of estoppel. . . . But my brethren are unwilling to express an opinion upon the doctrine of waiver as I have stated it." Id., pp. 505–7.

possible. I want to see her turn them away in your town." Owing to the itinerant habits of both parties, the plaintiff did not receive the defendants' response for about a month. It expressed surprise that Miss Jarbeau intended to play the Academy; the house was booked to other performers. The plaintiff's damage action produced a judgment favorable to him, and the defendants appealed. The Court of Appeals affirmed. For one thing, the court reasoned, it was open to the jury to conclude that the plaintiff's August letter did not justify the defendants in treating the contract as at an end and acting on that assumption. In addition, however that might be, the defendants' answer "disposed of that question."

> By this it appeared that the defendants elected to keep the contract in force for the purposes for which it was made. This operated alike upon the rights of both parties, and the plaintiff was justified in so understanding it. In that view the contract was kept alive until the time arrived for performance . . . .

Can you give an explanation of this decision which assumes (a) that the plaintiff repudiated the contract, and (b) that the defendants did not make an irrevocable "choice between two inconsistent rights" (i. e., an election)? Would some additional facts help with your explanation? On the facts given, is the decision clearly right?

McKENNA v. VERNON, 258 Pa. 18, 101 A. 919 (1917). [The plaintiff undertook to build a moving picture theatre in Philadelphia for the defendant. The contract price, $8,750, was to be paid in installments of 80% of the work set in place, and the final installment within 30 days after completion of the work. The work was to be done under the direction of an architect, whose certificate of work done was to be the condition of each payment by the defendant. The plaintiff received several payments, amounting in all to $6,000, and brought this action for the remainder of the contract price. The defendant asserted that the work was defective; but the architect testified that there were no unauthorized departures from the specifications, and the plaintiff received a judgment for $2,500. The defendant appealed on the theory that no right of action existed in the absence of a certificate from the architect of final completion of the building. *Held:* Affirmed.]

STEWART, Justice. . . . All payments were to be made only on certificate of the architect, and yet with a single exception each of the seven payments made as the work progressed was made without a certificate being asked for. With such constant and repeated disregard on the part of the owner to exact compliance with this provision in the contract, it is too late now for him to insist that failure on the part of the plaintiff to secure such certificate before suit defeats his right of action. . . . If he waived it repeatedly, as he did here, during the progress of the work, he cannot complain if he be held to have waived it when he seeks to defend against a final payment for work shown to have been honestly and substantially performed, especially when almost daily he has had the work under his own observation, without remonstrance or complaint at any time with respect to either the work done or materials employed.

NOTES

(1) *The Rationale.* How many payments might the defendant have made before losing, as to the future, the right to insist that the architect's certificates be given? Is it clear that the decision was not based on facts creating an estoppel? If the plaintiff had asked for and received, early in the course of performance, the defendant's promise that he would not insist on compliance with the condition, enforcement of the promise would present an obvious problem of consideration. Was there any problem of consideration on the facts of McKenna v. Vernon?

(2) *Waiving Without Prejudice.* "You can waive or delay enforcing any of your rights without losing them." This sentence appears in a form proposed for the installment purchase of an automobile; it purports to be addressed by a retail buyer to the dealer. (See the Supplement.) Would you advise a dealer, on the strength of this provision, that leniency in accepting late payments from the buyer will not prejudice his right to repossess the car?[a] The form is meant to be especially intelligible to consumers. Do you foresee any injury they may suffer from a form that caters to their appreciation of the word "waive"? What is needed to show that an anti-waiver clause is unconscionable? See Fontaine v. Industrial Nat. Bank of Rhode Island, 111 R.I. 6, 298 A.2d 521 (1973). See also Berger, Hard Leases Make Bad Law, 74 Colum.L.Rev. 791, 806–809 (1974).

(3) *Good Faith.* Do the instances of waiver given above support the general proposition that "Every contract imposes upon each party a duty of good faith and fair dealing in its performance and its enforcement"? Restatement Second, § 205. Two illustrations given for the section (8 and 10) are situations in which the courts would normally reason in terms of waiver and the like.

DAHL v. BRUNSWICK CORP.

Court of Appeals of Maryland, 1976.
277 Md. 471, 356 A.2d 221.

[Some employees of the Brunswick Corporation were told in mid-September, 1970, that they could not remain with Brunswick past the end of the month. The Test Corporation had contracted to purchase the division in which they worked (Concorde Yacht), and the employees were told that from October 1 forward they would be employed by a Test subsidiary in the same positions, at the same salaries, and with the same or better benefits. Their conditions of em-

a. See Few v. Automobile Financing, Inc., 101 Ga.App. 783, 115 S.E.2d 196 (1960) (note the statute). Cf. Dempsey v. Stauffer, 312 F.2d 360 (3d Cir. 1962).

ployment remained the same until August 27, 1972, when the new employer closed its doors for insolvency. Twenty one of the employees (including Antoinette Dahl) then sued Brunswick for varying amounts, alleging contracts with it for severance pay and other benefits. A Brunswick Corporate Manual provided, at the time of the buy-out, for a payment upon "any separation from the payroll for an indefinite period for actions not within the direct control of the employee when no other suitable opening is available."

[The trial court gave judgment for Brunswick and the plaintiffs appealed. The Court of Appeals concluded that "other suitable opening" did not refer to a position with an employer other than Brunswick; hence that the plaintiffs were "separated from the payroll" so as to make severance pay due in 1970. The trial court had reasoned that a novation occurred, releasing Brunswick, because the plaintiffs stayed on their jobs; but the Court of Appeals held that fact to be insufficient support for the conclusion. (As to novation see further p. 1100] infra.)

On another topic the opinion continued as follows.]

DIGGS, Judge.

. . .

As its next line of defense, Brunswick asserts that the employees' claim for severance pay is barred by waiver and equitable estoppel; we, like the trial judge, find neither to have been established. As we said in BarGale Indus. v. Robert Realty, supra, 275 Md. at 643–44, 343 A.2d at 533:

> A waiver is the intentional relinquishment of a known right, or such conduct as warrants an inference of the relinquishment of such right, and may result from an express agreement or be inferred from circumstances. '[A]cts relied upon as constituting a waiver of the provisions' of a contract must be inconsistent with an intention to insist upon enforcing such provisions. . . .

Brunswick contends that the employees' failure to demand severance pay within a reasonable time of their termination by Brunswick manifested an intent to waive any right to such pay. We, however, do not think the employees' procrastination can be said to be inconsistent with an intention to enforce their contractual right to severance pay. As stated by the trial judge: "In this case there has been no evidence offered or testimony produced to show that the [petitioners] in any way voluntarily surrendered their right to maintain this cause of action. There is no question that the action was filed within the limitations period. A lapse of time coupled with no further evidence does not constitute a waiver."

As for equitable estoppel, the definition which we have repeatedly approved and applied, see Savonis v. Burke, 241 Md. 316, 319, 216 A.2d

521 (1966) and cases cited therein, is that contained in 3 J. Pomeroy, Equity Jurisprudence § 804, at 189 (5th ed. 1941):

> Equitable estoppel is the effect of the voluntary conduct of a party whereby he is absolutely precluded, both at law and in equity, from asserting rights which might perhaps have otherwise existed, either of property, of contract, or of remedy, as against another person, who has in good faith relied upon such conduct, and has been led thereby to change his position for the worse, and who on his part acquires some corresponding right, either of property, of contract, or of remedy.

As we said in Savonis v. Burke, supra, 241 Md. at 319, 216 A.2d at 523: "It is essential for the application of the doctrine of equitable estoppel that the party claiming the benefit of the estoppel must have been misled to his injury and changed his position for the worse, having believed and relied on the representations of the party sought to be estopped."

Brunswick's contention with respect to this defense, as we understand it, is that—since (1) Brunswick, under its contract with Test, was entitled to reimbursement from Test for any money it had to pay out as severance pay to the employees of the Concorde Yacht Division; (2) the petitioners, with one exception, did not make any claim for severance pay until Test Concorde was in bankruptcy; (3) Brunswick relied on the petitioners' failure to make a claim to the extent of not demanding reimbursement while Test Concorde was solvent; and (4) Brunswick is now precluded by Test Concorde's bankruptcy from successfully obtaining repayment—the respondent was misled to its detriment by the petitioners' inaction and silence, and therefore these employees should be equitably estopped from seeking severance pay. The trial judge concluded, however, that Brunswick failed to establish either that it relied on the employees' procrastination or, since it was not precluded by Test Concorde's bankruptcy from seeking recompense from Test, that it suffered detriment. We will add that, as we have often said, silence will not raise an estoppel where there is no duty to speak or act, see, e. g., id. at 320, 216 A.2d 521; Mohr v. Universal C. I. T. Corp., 216 Md. 197, 205–06, 140 A.2d 49 (1958), and it does not appear that the employees had any such duty. Furthermore, we mention that Brunswick's knowledge of the facts and circumstances surrounding the transaction in question was at least equal to, if not greater than, that of the employees. Cf. M. & C. C. v. Chesapeake, 233 Md. 559, 581, 197 A.2d 821 (1964). We conclude that neither waiver nor estoppel bar [sic] the petitioners' claim for severance pay.[a]

. . .

a. The Maryland court is a leading producer of opinions clarifying the confusion connected with the terms waiver and estoppel. See also Evelyn v. Raven Realty, Inc., 215 Md. 467, 138 A.2d 898 (1958); Canaras v. Lift Truck Services, Inc., 272 Md. 337, 322 A.2d 866 (1974).

In sum, and as noted earlier, we hold that the employees are entitled to a judgment in their favor for severance pay and, depending on the factual determination to be made by the trial court, possibly pay in lieu of notice, but not vacation pay.

. . .

NOTES

(1) *Test as a Target.* Read closely what the trial court envisaged as recourse for Brunswick. The court did not pretend that by establishing a claim against a bankrupt corporation—the Test subsidiary—Brunswick could escape "detriment," for that would be a sophistry. Instead it envisaged a claim—presumably collectible—against the parent corporation.

Severance-pay claims have a high priority in the allocation of the assets of employers in bankruptcy proceedings. However, such claims qualify for the priority only if they arise in a brief period before the bankruptcy occurs. If the plaintiffs had lost their suit against Brunswick, they could probably have recovered little if anything from the bankruptcy estate. But there is yet one other possible target for their claims. Might they have recovered from the (parent) Test Corporation? See Chapter 10 and Chapter 11, Section 2, infra.

(2) *Question.* What does the Dahl case add on the subject of "soft" responses to breach, p. 823 supra?

PHOENIX INS. CO. v. ROSS JEWELERS, INC., 362 F.2d 985 (5th Cir. 1966). [Burglars cut their way into a retail store operated by Ross Jewelers, Inc., and made away with merchandise worth more than $60,000. All but about $10,000-worth was taken from a vault in the store. The vault had a protective alarm system, as required by insurance on the goods, but the manager's habit was to leave the key in the lock. The policy also required the insured to maintain a "detailed and itemized inventory" of its property. A report was given to the insurer's home office by the General Adjustment Bureau showing that "a detailed and itemized inventory was not kept," "the internal control over the stock was inadequate," and "the detail stock records were not up to date." A week later the supervisor of the insurer's Inland Marine Claim Department wrote to the Bureau, saying that nothing would be paid for contents of the vault, but authorizing a settlement offer for the remainder of the loss. The offer was declined. In a suit brought by Ross Jewelers on the policy, the insurer disclaimed liability altogether, relying on the inventory provision. The trial court gave judgment for the plaintiff for the merchandise lost both from the vault and elsewhere. The insurer appealed.]

JONES, Circuit Judge: . . . We are in agreement with the district court's holding that the denial of liability by Phoenix upon the sole ground that Ross Jewelers had breached the condition that it would maintain the protective devices . . . operated as a waiver of the defense of the failure of Ross Jewelers to maintain an inventory. . . . The writer of the Phoenix letter stated in an affidavit that he did not, at the time the letter was written, intend to waive the inventory defense. [He testified that he had prepared the letter in haste, without thought of the inventory question.] While it may be said that waiver depends upon intention, the intention may be inferred from acts and conduct. Such inference is fully warranted under the facts here established. [Judgment reversed, however, for redetermination of the amount, so as to eliminate the contents of the vault.]

NOTES

(1) *Waiver-Estoppel.* "Ordinarily, when an insurer, with knowledge of all pertinent facts, denies liability upon a specific ground, all other grounds are deemed to be waived. This waiver is conditioned, however, upon a showing of detriment or prejudice. . . . We find nothing in this case to indicate that the insured acted upon the announced ground or incurred any expense, loss or detriment in reliance upon it." Larson v. Occidental Fire & Cas. Co., 79 N.M. 562, 446 P.2d 210 (1968). Is it possible to reconcile this passage with the foregoing decision? If not which do you prefer?

(2) *Unfair Advantage?* Waiver and like doctrines produce results at variance with the terms of standardized contracts, determined by particular variations in patterns of facts. Does this consideration reinforce the need for caution in applying theories of waiver and estoppel? In relation to insurance contracts, Professor Keeton observes that they "may produce exceptionally favored treatment for limited numbers of policyholders, giving some a far better bargain than others with the same class of coverage. Moreover, this inequity is not mitigated by broader considerations of fairness, as when a knowledgeable policyholder benefits by an objectively reasonable construction of an onerous provision." R. Keeton, Insurance Law (Basic Text) 415 (1971).

SECTION 3. RESTITUTION FOR A DEFAULTING PLAINTIFF

Restitutionary relief, such as recovery in quasi contract, is sometimes available as between persons who have not dealt with one another (see Chapter 1). As between the parties to an agreement, it is sometimes granted when their agreement proves to be unenforceable for one reason or another: because of the statute of frauds (see Chapter 2, Section 4); or because the contract is illegal (see Chapter 5, Section 5). Sometimes restitutionary claims arise from negotiations that fall short of a contract (see Chapters 3 and 4). When there is a breach of an enforceable agreement, the aggrieved party may prefer restitution to other forms of relief, and it is commonly available to him (see Chapter 6, Section 2). It is often available also when an agreement has become unenforceable by reason of impossibility of performance or frustration (see Chapter 9).

But what of restitution for a party in breach of an enforceable agreement? If he has performed in part, and is unable to enforce the contract because he has failed to complete his performance, may he resort to an action in quasi contract? Such claims have met serious resistance, especially when the plaintiff's breach may be characterized as "willful." The following remarks represent a traditional response of the courts:

> It would be an alarming doctrine, to hold, that the plaintiffs might violate the contract, and because they chose to do so, make their own infraction of the agreement the basis of an action for money had and received. (Ketchum & Sweet v. Evertson, 13 Johns. (N.Y.) 358 (1816).) To allow a recovery of this money would be to sustain an action by a party on his own breach of his own contract, which the law does not allow. . . . That would be ill doctrine. (Lawrence v. Miller, 86 N.Y. 131 (1881).)

Some other responses are shown in this section. The following case is a watershed.

NOTE

Officious Performance. A builder was given notice of cancellation of his contract, prompted by his unreasonable delay on the job constituting a material breach. Nevertheless he continued with his work and subsequently made a restitutionary claim against his employer for its value. In denying recovery, the court observed that such a claim does not lie in favor of one who is guilty of willful breach. Trachsel v. Barney, 264 Or. 29, 503 P.2d 696 (1972). This decision was cited in Wasserburger's case, at p. 787 supra. What similarities and differences do you see between the quasi-contract aspects of the two cases?

BRITTON v. TURNER

Supreme Court of Judicature of New Hampshire, 1834.
6 N.H. 481.

Assumpsit, for work and labor, performed by the plaintiff, in the service of the defendant, from March 9, 1831, to December 27, 1831.

The declaration contained the common counts, and among them a count in quantum meruit, for the labor, averring it to be worth $100.

At the trial in the C. C. Pleas, the plaintiff proved the performance of the labor as set forth in the declaration.

The defense was that it was performed under a special contract; that the plaintiff agreed to work one year, from some time in March, 1831, to March, 1832, and that the defendant was to pay him for said year's labor the sum of $120; and the defendant offered evidence tending to show that such was the contract under which the work was done. Evidence was also offered to show that the plaintiff left the defendant's service without his consent, and it was contended by the defendant that the plaintiff had no good cause for not continuing in his employment. There was no evidence offered of any damage arising from the plaintiff's departure, farther than was to be inferred from his nonfulfillment of the entire contract.

The court instructed the jury that, if they were satisfied from the evidence that the labor was performed under a contract to labor a year, for the sum of $120, and if they were satisfied that the plaintiff labored only the time specified in the declaration, and then left the defendant's service, against his consent, and without any good cause, yet the plaintiff was entitled to recover, under his quantum meruit count, as much as the labor he performed was reasonably worth, and under this direction the jury gave a verdict for the plaintiff for the sum of $95.

The defendant excepted to the instructions thus given to the jury.

PARKER, J., delivered the opinion of the court.

It may be assumed that the labor performed by the plaintiff, and for which he seeks to recover a compensation in this action, was commenced under a special contract to labor for the defendant the term of one year, for the sum of $120, and that the plaintiff has labored but a portion of that time, and has voluntarily failed to complete the entire contract.

It is clear, then, that he is not entitled to recover upon the contract itself, because the service, which was to entitle him to the sum agreed upon, has never been performed.

But the question arises: Can the plaintiff, under these circumstances, recover a reasonable sum for the service he has actually performed, under the count in quantum meruit? Upon this, and questions of a similar nature, the decisions to be found in the books are not easily reconciled.

It has been held, upon contracts of this kind for labor to be performed at a specified price, that the party who voluntarily fails to fulfill the contract by performing the whole labor contracted for, is not entitled to recover anything for the labor actually performed, however much he may have done towards the performance, and this has been considered the settled rule of law upon this subject. [Citations of Massachusetts, New York and English cases omitted.]

That such rule in its operation may be very unequal, not to say unjust, is apparent. A party who contracts to perform certain specified labor, and who breaks his contract in the first instance, without any attempt to perform it, can only be made liable to pay the damages which the other party has sustained by reason of such non-performance, which in many instances may be trifling; whereas a party who in good faith has entered upon the performance of his contract, and nearly completed it, and then abandoned the further performance, although the other party has had the full benefit of all that has been done, and has perhaps sustained no actual damage, is in fact subjected to a loss of all which has been performed, in the nature of damages for the non-fulfillment of the remainder, upon the technical rule, that the contract must be fully performed in order to [sustain] a recovery of any part of the compensation.

By the operation of this rule, then, the party who attempts performance may be placed in a much worse situation than he who wholly disregards his contract, and the other party may receive much more, by the breach of the contract, than the injury which he has sustained by such breach, and more than he could be entitled to were he seeking to recover damages by an action.

The case before us presents an illustration. Had the plaintiff in this case never entered upon the performance of his contract, the damage could not probably have been greater than some small expense and trouble incurred in procuring another to do the labor which he had contracted to perform. But having entered upon the performance, and labored nine and a half months, the value of which labor to the defendant as found by the jury is $95, if the defendant can succeed in this defense, he in fact receives nearly five-sixths of the value of a whole year's labor, by reason of the breach of contract by the plaintiff, a sum not only utterly disproportionate to any probable, not to say possible damage which could have resulted from the neglect of the plaintiff to continue the remaining two and a half months, but altogether beyond any damage which could have been recovered by the defendant, had the plaintiff done nothing towards the fulfillment of his contract.

Another illustration is furnished in Lantry v. Parks, 8 Cow., N. Y., 63. There the defendant hired the plaintiff for a year, at ten dollars per month. The plaintiff worked ten and a half months, and then left saying he would work no more for him. This was on Saturday—on Monday the plaintiff returned, and offered to resume his work, but the defendant said he would employ him no longer. The court held that the refusal of the defendant on Saturday was a violation of his contract, and that he could recover nothing for the labor performed.

There are other cases, however, in which principles have been adopted leading to a different result.

It is said, that where a party contracts to perform certain work, and to furnish materials, as, for instance, to build a house, and the work is done, but with some variations from the mode prescribed by the contract, yet if the other party has the benefit of the labor and materials he should be bound to pay so much as they are reasonably worth. 2 Stark.Ev. 97, 98; Hayward v. Leonard, 7 Pick., Mass., 181. . . .

A different doctrine seems to have been holden in Ellis v. Hamlen, 3 Taunt. 52, and it is apparent, in such cases, that if the house has not been built in the manner specified in the contract, the work has not been done. The party has no more performed what he contracted to perform, than he who has contracted to labor for a certain period, and failed to complete the time.

It is in truth virtually conceded in such cases that the work has not been done, for, if it had been, the party performing it would be entitled to recover upon the contract itself, which it is held he cannot do.

Those cases are not to be distinguished, in principle, from the present, unless it be in the circumstance, that where the party has contracted to furnish materials, and do certain labor, as to build a house in a specified manner, if it is not done according to the contract, the party for whom it is built may refuse to receive it—elect to take no benefit from what has been performed—and therefore, if he does receive, he shall be bound to pay the value; whereas in a contract for labor, merely, from day to day, the party is continually receiving the benefit of the contract under an expectation that it will be fulfilled, and cannot, upon the breach of it, have an election to refuse to receive what has been done, and thus discharge himself from payment.

But we think this difference in the nature of the contracts does not justify the application of a different rule in relation to them.[a] The party who contracts for labor merely, for a certain period, does so with full knowledge that he must, from the nature of the case, be accepting part performance from day to day, if the other party commences the performance, and with knowledge also that the other may eventually fail of completing the entire term. If under such circumstances he actually receives a benefit from the labor performed, over and above the damage occasioned by the failure to complete, there is as much reason why he should pay the reasonable worth of what has thus been done for his benefit, as there is when he enters and occupies the house which has been built for him, but not according to the stipulations of the contract, and which he perhaps enters, not because he is satisfied with what has been done, but because circumstances compel him to accept it such as it is, that he should pay for the value of the house.

Where goods are sold upon a special contract as to their nature, quality, and price, and have been used before their inferiority has

a. The court reaffirmed this principle in Berke & Co., Inc. v. Griffin, Inc., 116 N.H. 760, 367 A.2d 583 (1976), a building contract case.

been discovered, or other circumstances have concurred which have rendered it impracticable or inconvenient for the vendee to rescind the contract in toto, it seems to have been the practice formerly to allow the vendor to recover the stipulated price, and the vendee recovered by a cross-action damages for the breach of the contract. "But according to the later and more convenient practice, the vendee in such case is allowed, in an action for the price, to give evidence of the inferiority of the goods in reduction of damages, and the plaintiff who has broken his contract is not entitled to recover more than the value of the benefits which the defendant has actually derived from the goods; and where the latter has derived no benefit, the plaintiff cannot recover at all." 2 Stark.Ev. 640, 642; Okell v. Smith, 1 Starkie's Rep. 107. . . .

There is a close analogy between all these classes of cases, in which such diverse decisions have been made.

If the party who has contracted to receive merchandise takes a part and uses it, in expectation that the whole will be delivered, which is never done, there seems to be no greater reason that he should pay for what he has received than there is that the party who has received labor in part, under similar circumstances, should pay the value of what has been done for his benefit.

It is said that in those cases where the plaintiff has been permitted to recover there was an acceptance of what had been done. The answer is that where the contract is to labor from day to day, for a certain period, the party for whom the labor is done in truth stipulates to receive it from day to day, as it is performed, and although the other may not eventually do all he has contracted to do, there has been, necessarily, an acceptance of what has been done in pursuance of the contract, and the party must have understood when he made the contract that there was to be such acceptance.

If, then, the party stipulates in the outset to receive part performance from time to time, with a knowledge that the whole may not be completed, we see no reason why he should not equally be holden to pay for the amount of value received, as where he afterwards takes the benefit of what has been done, with a knowledge that the whole which was contracted for has not been performed. In neither case has the contract been performed. In neither can an action be sustained on the original contract. In both the party has assented to receive what is done. The only difference is that in the one case the assent is prior, with a knowledge that all may not be performed; in the other it is subsequent, with a knowledge that the whole has not been accomplished.

We have no hesitation in holding that the same rule should be applied to both classes of cases, especially as the operation of the rule will be to make the party who has failed to fulfill his contract liable to such amount of damages as the other party has sustained, instead of subjecting him to an entire loss for a partial failure, and thus making the amount received in many cases wholly disproportionate to the injury. 1 Saund. 320, c; 2 Stark.Ev. 643. It is as "hard upon the plaintiff to preclude him from recovering at all, because he has failed as to part of his entire undertaking," where his contract is to labor for a certain period, as it can be in any other description of contract, provided the defendant has received a benefit and value from the labor actually performed.

We hold, then, that where a party undertakes to pay upon a special contract for the performance of labor, or the furnishing of materials, he is not to be charged upon such special agreement until the money is earned according to the terms of it, and where the parties have made an express contract the law will not imply and raise a contract different from that which the parties have entered into, except upon some farther transaction between the parties.

In case of a failure to perform such special contract, by the default of the party contracting to do the service, if the money is not due by the terms of the special agreement he is not entitled to recover for his labor, or for the materials furnished, unless the other party receives what has been done, or furnished, and upon the whole case derives a benefit from it. Taft v. Montague, 14 Mass. 282; 2 Stark. Ev. 644.

But if, where a contract is made of such a character, a party actually receives labor, or materials, and thereby derives a benefit and advantage, over and above the damage which has resulted from the breach of the contract by the other party, the labor actually done, and the value received, furnish a new consideration, and the law thereupon raises a promise to pay to the extent of the reasonable worth of such excess.[b] This may be considered as making a new case, one not within the original agreement, and the party is entitled to "recover on his new case, for the work done, not as agreed, but yet accepted by the defendant." 1 Dane's Abr. 224.

If on such failure to perform the whole, the nature of the contract be such that the employer can reject what has been done, and refuse to receive any benefit from the part performance, he is entitled so to do, and in such case is not liable to be charged, unless he has before assented to and accepted of what has been done, however much the other party may have done towards the performance. He has in such case received nothing, and having contracted to receive nothing but the entire matter contracted for, he is not bound to pay, because his express promise was only to pay on receiving the whole, and having actually received nothing the law cannot and ought not to raise an implied promise to pay. But where the party receives value —takes and uses the materials, or has advantage from the labor, he is

b. This passage exemplifies the earlier attempts to squeeze a quasi-contractual duty into the Procrustean bed of contract.

liable to pay the reasonable worth of what he has received. Farnsworth v. Garrard, 1 Camp. 38. And the rule is the same whether it was received and accepted by the assent of the party prior to the breach, under a contract by which, from its nature, he was to receive labor, from time to time until the completion of the whole contract, or whether it was received and accepted by an assent subsequent to the performance of all which was in fact done. If he received it under such circumstances as precluded him from rejecting it afterwards, that does not alter the case—it has still been received by his assent.

In fact, we think the technical reasoning—that the performance of the whole labor is a condition precedent, and the right to recover anything dependent upon it; that, the contract being entire, there can be no apportionment; and that, there being an express contract, no other can be implied, even upon the subsequent performance of service—is not properly applicable to this species of contract, where a beneficial service has been actually performed; for we have abundant reason to believe, that the general understanding of the community is that the hired laborer shall be entitled to compensation for the service actually performed, though he do not continue the entire term contracted for, and such contracts must be presumed to be made with reference to that understanding, unless an express stipulation shows the contrary. . . .

It is easy, if parties so choose, to provide by an express agreement that nothing shall be earned, if the laborer leaves his employer without having performed the whole service contemplated, and then there can be no pretense for a recovery if he voluntarily deserts the service before the expiration of the time.

The amount, however, for which the employer ought to be charged, where the laborer abandons his contract, is only the reasonable worth, or the amount of advantage he receives upon the whole transaction (Wadleigh v. Sutton, 6 N.H. 15), and, in estimating the value of the labor, the contract price for the service cannot be exceeded. . . .

If a person makes a contract fairly, he is entitled to have it fully performed; and, if this is not done, he is entitled to damages. He may maintain a suit to recover the amount of damage sustained by the non-performance. The benefit and advantage which the party takes by the labor, therefore, is the amount of value which he receives, if any, after deducting the amount of damage; and if he elects to put this in defense he is entitled so to do, and the implied promise which the law will raise, in such case, is to pay such amount of the stipulated price for the whole labor, as remains after deducting what it would cost to procure a completion of the residue of the service and also any damage which has been sustained by reason of the nonfulfillment of the contract. If in such case it be found that the damages are equal to or greater than the amount of the labor performed, so that the employer, having a right to the full performance of the contract, has not upon the whole case received a beneficial service, the plaintiff cannot recover. . . .

Applying the principles thus laid down, to this case, the plaintiff is entitled to judgment on the verdict. The defendant sets up a mere breach of the contract in defense of the action, but this cannot avail him. He does not appear to have offered evidence to show that he was damnified by such breach, or to have asked that a deduction should be made upon that account. The direction to the jury was therefore correct, that the plaintiff was entitled to recover as much as the labor performed was reasonably worth, and the jury appear to have allowed a pro rata compensation, for the time which the plaintiff labored in the defendant's service.

As the defendant has not claimed or had any adjustment of damages, for the breach of the contract, in this action, if he has actually sustained damage he is still entitled to a suit to recover the amount. . . .

Judgment on the verdict.

NOTES

(1) *Restitution for an Employer.* Melbourne Henry studied for a graduate degree with the aid of his former employer, a non-profit medical agency. The parties to the "loan" agreed that Henry would resume the employment at the end of his studies, that the agency would provide him with an appropriate position, and that the advances would be repaid through a specified payroll deduction. On concluding his studies Henry took a job elsewhere, and the agency sued for its advances. The jury returned a verdict for the defendant, finding that the agency had broken the contract by offering him only a subordinate position. On appeal from a judgment for Henry, *held:* Reversed. Appalachian Regional Hospitals, Inc. v. Henry, 287 Or. 151, 597 P.2d 1247 (1979). The trial court had improperly failed to instruct, as requested by the plaintiff, that it was entitled to the amount loaned less the defendant's damages—even if the plaintiff's breach went to the essence of the contract. "The reason plaintiff is not barred is the same as that underlying equitable rules against the enforcement of penalties and forfeitures . . . ."

Question: How is this ruling different from a decision that the covenants in the contract were independent ones?

(2) *References.* Each time the American Law Institute has taken up the subject it seems to have moved somewhat in advance of the cases at large, in favor of restitution. According to the first Restatement § 357 a plaintiff was barred from restitution if his breach or non-performance was "wilful and deliberate." For the present position, assimilating the rule to the law of liquidated damages, see § 374. Examine the cases in this section with a view to finding those affected by the change. How might it affect Wasserburger's case, p. 787 supra?

In 1978 Professor Palmer reported that the doctrine of Britton v. Turner was still a minority position. Law of Restitution, Vol. 1, § 5.13. The conflicting but rather faded precedents are reviewed in Birmingham, Breach of Contract, Damage Measures, and Economic Efficiency, 24 Rutgers L.Rev. 273, 286–89 (1970). The author approves the ruling, with qualifications, as conducive to "proper functioning of the market mechanism." [b]

(3) *Lawyer-Client Relations.* Begovich was charged with murder. He retained Murphy to defend him and paid $2,500. Later Murphy was paid another $4,000 as an advance for legal services to be rendered for Begovich. He consulted with his client, and made two appearances in his behalf, these services not being worth more than $2,500. At that point Begovich committed suicide. The administrator of the estate sued Murphy for $4,000, and Murphy demurred. What decision? See Begovich v. Murphy, 359 Mich. 156, 101 N.W.2d 278 (1960).

For an interesting and difficult question of compensation for a lawyer who quit (i. e., refused to conduct litigation for his client to a conclusion as he had agreed), see Moore v. Fellner, 50 Cal.2d 330, 325 P.2d 857 (1958). Part of an intermediate court's opinion in this case was as follows: "The question is whether an attorney who undertakes to render an entire service may quit when an important part of the work remains undone and deserve to be paid for partial performance. As well might a surgeon claim compensation when he had quit in the middle of an operation, or a barber when he had shaved half of a customer's face." The judgment of this court was reversed.

KIRKLAND v. ARCHBOLD

Court of Appeals of Ohio, Cuyahoga County, 1953.
113 N.E.2d 496.

[The plaintiff contracted to make alterations and repairs on a dwelling house owned by the defendant. Paragraph 20 of the contract provided: "The Owner agrees to pay the Contractor, as follows: $1,000 when satisfactory work has been done for ten days; an additional $1,000 when twenty days work has been completed; an additional $1,000 when thirty days work has been completed, and $1,000 on completion of the contract. $2,000 shall be paid within thirty days after the completion of the contract." After the plaintiff had worked for two months on the job he was prevented from proceeding further. He claims that he and his sub-contractors had reasonably expended $2,985 at that point; he has been paid only $800; and he sues for damages in the amount of the difference.

The trial court found that the plaintiff was in default in attempting to plaster the house over wood lath instead of rock lath, and without the use of rock wool. Paragraph 4 of the contract provided: "All outside walls are to be lined with rock wool and rock lathe, su-

b. For a general review of the problems of this section, see Lee, The Plaintiff in Default, 19 Vand.L.Rev. 1023 (1966); and for a view from abroad see Pecuniary Restitution on Breach of Contract 8–38, 64–65 (The English Law Commission, Law of Contract, Working Paper No. 65, 1975).

perimposed thereon." Thus the defendant was within her rights in preventing the plaintiff from proceeding. However, the court held that her payment of $800 was an admission that the first installment of the price was earned, and gave the plaintiff judgment for $200. The plaintiff appealed.]

SKEEL, Presiding Judge. . . . The court committed error prejudicial to the rights of plaintiff in holding that the provisions of the contract were severable. The plaintiff agreed to make certain repairs and improvements on the defendant's property for which he was to be paid $6,000. The total consideration was to be paid for the total work specified in the contract. The fact that a schedule of payments was set up based on the progress of the work does not change the character of the agreement. Newman Lumber Co. v. Purdum, 41 Ohio St. 373.

The court found that the plaintiff and not the defendant breached the agreement, leaving the job without just cause, when the work agreed upon was far from completed. In fact, the plaintiff by his pleadings and evidence does not attempt to claim substantial performance on his part. The question is, therefore, clearly presented on the facts as the court found them to be, as to whether or not the plaintiff being found in default can maintain a cause of action for only part performance of his contract.

The earlier case law of Ohio has refused to permit a plaintiff to found an action on the provisions of a contract where he himself is in default. The only exception to the rule recognized is where the plaintiff has substantially performed his part of the agreement. . . .

The result of decisions which deny a defaulting contractor all right of recovery even though his work has enriched the estate of the other party to the contract is to penalize the defaulting contractor to the extent of the value of all benefit conferred by his work and materials upon the property of the other party. This result comes from unduly emphasizing the technical unity and entirety of contracts. Some decisions permit such result only when the defaulting contractor's conduct was wilful or malicious.

An ever-increasing number of decisions of courts of last resort now modify the severity of this rule and permit defaulting contractors, where their work has contributed substantial value to the other contracting party's property, to recover the value of the work and materials expended on a quantum meruit basis, the recovery being diminished, however, to the extent of such damage as the contractor's breach causes the other party. These decisions are based on the theory of unjust enrichment. The action is not founded on the broken contract but on a quasi-contract to pay for the benefits received, which cannot be returned, diminished by the damages sustained because of the contractor's breach of his contract.

The leading case supporting this theory of the law is Britton v. Turner, 6 N.H. 481, 26 Am.Dec. 713. . . .

Williston on Contracts, Vol. 5, p. 4123, par. 1475, says:

"The element of forfeiture in wholly denying recovery to a plaintiff who is materially in default is most strikingly exemplified in building contracts. It has already been seen how, under the name of substantial performance,[a] many courts have gone beyond the usual principles governing contracts in allowing relief in an action on the contract. But many cases of hardship cannot be brought within the doctrine of substantial performance, even if it is liberally interpreted; and the weight of authority strongly supports the statement that a builder, whose breach of contract is merely negligent, can recover the value of his work less the damages caused by his default; but that one who has wilfully abandoned or broken his contract cannot recover. The classical English doctrine, it is true, has denied recovery altogether where there has been a material breach even though it was due to negligence rather than wilfulness; and a few decisions in the United States follow this rule, where the builder has not substantially performed. But the English court has itself abandoned it and now holds that where a builder has supplied work and labor for the erection or repair of a house under a lump sum contract, but has departed from the terms of the contract, he is entitled to recover for his services and materials, unless (1) the work that he has done has been of no benefit to the owner; (2) the work he has done is entirely different from the work which he has contracted to do; or (3) he has abandoned the work and left it unfinished. The courts often do not discuss the question whether one who has intentionally abandoned the contract did so merely to get out of a bad bargain or whether he acted in a mistaken belief that a just cause existed for the abandonment. Where the latter situation exists, however, it would seem that the defaulter might properly be given recovery for his part performance. It seems probable that the tendency of decisions will favor a builder who has not been guilty of conscious moral fault in abandoning the contract or in its performance."

The drastic rule of forfeiture against a defaulting contractor who has by his labor and materials materially enriched the estate of the other party should in natural justice, be afforded relief to the reasonable value of the work done, less whatever damage the other party has suffered. Such a rule has been clearly recognized in the law of bailment where a defaulting bailee has enhanced the property of the bailor (Dobie on Bailments, Page 139 (1914)) and also by statute a defaulting vendee in a conditional sales contract, where the vendor retakes the property, is entitled to a return of a just proportion of the money paid. G.C. Sec. 8570.

a. The following section of the casebook presents this doctrine.

We conclude, therefore, that the judgment is contrary to law as to the method by which the right to judgment was determined. . . .

For the foregoing reasons the judgment is reversed and the cause is remanded for further proceedings.

NOTES

(1) *Severability.* Would the trial court's treatment of the contract in Kirkland as severable, or divisible, have been justified if the *defendant* had broken the contract rather than the plaintiff? See Fuller v. United Electric Co., 70 Nev. 448, 273 P.2d 136 (1954). The Electric Company sued Fuller for 80% of the contract price of doing the wiring in his new home, which became payable "on the completion of rough-in and inspection thereof." Fuller unjustifiably replaced the Electric Company with another contractor at that point, and apparently the cost of completing the work was well above 20% of the contract price. *Held:* The damages must be ascertained upon the entire contract. "The breach was a total breach and was so treated by plaintiff. The contract was thereby terminated."

(2) *The Case of the Driller's Bond.* J. L. McBride contracted to drill seven well holes at a test site in Nevada for the Atomic Energy Commission. He subcontracted part of the drilling work to the B & B Drilling Company at a stated price per linear foot. The subcontract required B & B to furnish a performance and payment bond. It called for payments on the 15th of each month for progress made to the end of the preceding month. B & B began drilling on May 24 with McBride's approval, although no bond had been posted. About two months later B & B learned that it could not secure a bond, because surety companies will not issue one on a job that is under way. McBride was so informed. B & B continued to drill until August 10, and stopped because no progress payments had been made. McBride refused a demand for payment on August 15, and ordered B & B off the site.

In a suit by B & B against McBride, the trial court gave judgment for some $16,000, based upon the prices and rates of payment stated in the contract. On an appeal by McBride, *held:* Affirmed. Passing the question whether the plaintiff's breach was material and substantial, the court relied on the first Restatement, § 357. The proper measure of recovery was the "price fixed by the contract for [the] part performance" because the defendant assented to it with knowledge of the plaintiff's inability to procure the bond. American Surety Company v. United States, 368 F.2d 475 (9th Cir. 1966). What other measure of recovery might have been adopted? In Restatement Second, § 374, Comment b, it is said: "Since the party seeking restitution is responsible for posing the problem of measurement of benefit, doubts will be resolved against him and his recovery will not exceed the less generous of the two measures stated in § 370, that of the other party's increase in wealth." Is this consistent with the judgment for B & B?

THE CODE

When a buyer of goods defaults under a contract of sale, after he has paid all or part of the purchase price, may the seller retain the

prepayment? Prior to the enactment of the Code, the law was in some disarray on the point. In Amtorg Trading Corp. v. Miehle Printing Press & Mfg. Co., 206 F.2d 103 (2d Cir. 1953), the court examined the common law of New York, and found no convincing precedent for restitution in favor of the buyer; however, it noted "several trends away from this harsh rule in situations deemed exceptional. . . ." In 1952 the New York legislature provided a generalized right of restitution. This statute was influential in the formulation of UCC 2–718, which replaced it.

In the case cited above, Amtorg contracted to buy 20 printing presses, and made an advance payment of nearly $60,000, or 25% of the total price. It wrongfully refused to take delivery, owing to a change in federal export laws which prevented export of the presses to Russia. Miehle, the seller, then disposed of them to the Bureau of Engraving and Printing for more than Amtorg had contracted to pay. Amtorg sued Miehle for the amount of the down payment, and for the resale profit. If the case had been governed by UCC 2–718, what would Amtorg have recovered, if anything? [a]

NOTE

Seller's Default. If a seller delivers part of the goods contracted for, and defaults as to the rest, and has received no payment, is he entitled to the price fixed by the contract for the goods delivered, or to the amount by which the buyer is enriched? See UCC 2–607(1).

INSTALLMENT LAND SALES

In Sebastian v. Floyd, 585 S.W.2d 381 (Ky.1979), the court distinguished three transactions creating interests in land: (a) the ordinary short-term real estate contract, often requiring the buyer to sacrifice his down payment, or "earnest money," if he fails to consummate the purchase; (b) a conveyance to a buyer accompanied by a mortgage that he gives the seller to secure an unpaid part of the price, commonly payable over an extended period; and (c) an installment sale contract committing the buyer to pay the price over an extended period and the seller to convey when payment is complete. In some states the latter arrangement is widely used as a surrogate for the deed-and-mortgage-back. Two important results, unfavorable to the buyer, may follow: On default in payment the seller may reclaim his property without resort to whatever judicial proceeding is required for foreclosing a mortgage; and any payments the buyer has made are lost to him, though they may far exceed the value of his occupancy. Lawrence v. Miller, quoted at p. 866 supra, was an action

a. The court found a basis for recovery in federal law, and directed "refund of the prepayment, subject to deduction of any expenses proven by defendant if and only so far as they may exceed its profit of $18,765."

for restitution by a defaulting land buyer, and the result illustrates the possibilities of forfeiture.

The potential for harsh effects on buyers under installment land sales has occasioned much disquiet and widespread law reform. Statutes in some states have provided relief at least to the extent of creating a grace period in which a buyer may escape a forfeiture. Without legislative direction some courts have held that a seller must proceed against a defaulting buyer by seeking a judicial sale of the property. One such decision is Sebastian v. Floyd, supra, where the court said: "There is no practical distinction between the land sale contract and a purchase money mortgage . . . ." There are some statutory measures of like effect; but in most states the measures taken to prevent forfeitures have been more tentative. Some courts have developed doctrines of restitution in favor of defaulting buyers, and others have applied the doctrines of waiver and estoppel liberally in their favor.[a]

Professor Corbin pointed out a special reason for denying restitution to a defaulting land buyer: the seller is generally entitled to specific performance of the contract.[b] As long as he continues ready and willing to convey the property as promised, "the defaulting vendee has no right of restitution; he cannot recover back money that he has paid if it is money that the vendor could still compel him to pay if as yet unpaid." Corbin observed that a contract for the sale of land "differs in several material respects from other contracts." The Right of a Defaulting Vendee to the Restitution of Instalments Paid, 40 Yale L.J. 1013, 1016–18 (1931).[c] Naturally there are some less technical arguments against recasting the accounts under an installment land sale, in favor of a defaulting buyer. What is the most persuasive one that occurs to you?

Further consideration of the problem must be left for a real-property course. However, it may be said that default under an "ordinary short-term real estate contract"—the first transaction mentioned above—is a distinguishable problem. The Kentucky opinion cited above makes no pronouncement about that.

a. On the various measures mentioned here, and others, see Nelson & Whitman, The Installment Land Contract —A National Viewpoint, 1977 Brig. Young L.Rev. 541; Comment, 41 Alb.L.Rev. 71 (1977). As to specific performance based on waiver and a balancing of the equities, see Aden v. Alwardt, 76 Ill.App.3d 54, 31 Ill. Dec. 514, 394 N.E.2d 716 (1979).

b. For some complications in reconciling this right with a "clumsy" default provision, see Glacier Campground v. Wild Rivers, Inc., —— Mont. ——, 597 P.2d 689 (1978) ("purchasers advance a most curious request, that being to *impose* a forfeiture on them").

c. But see Maxey v. Glindmeyer, 379 So.2d 297 (Miss.1980), where an aggrieved seller sought a decree of forfeiture and the court directed a remedy on an analogy to UCC 2–718(1).

NOTES

(1) *Sales of Goods.* Are there circumstances in which the claim of a buyer of goods for restitution under UCC 2–718(2) might be denied on the ground suggested by Professor Corbin? See UCC 2–709.

(2) *Statute of Frauds.* "A makes an oral contract to buy a tract of land from B for $100,000 (§ 125). Payment is to be made in $10,000 installments, conveyance to be made on the payment of the third installment. A pays $10,000 and then refuses to pay any more and sues B to recover in restitution the $10,000 that he has paid. . . . If B refuses to sign a sufficient memorandum, A's refusal to pay is not a defense under the rule stated in § 141(2) and A can get restitution." Restatement Second, § 375, Illustration 4.

Should A be put in a better position, with respect to restitution, than he would have been in if the contract had been in writing? Does the Restatement rule do that? For variant positions see G. Palmer, 2 The Law of Restitution, § 6.2 (1978).

SECTION 4. CONSTRUCTION CONTRACTS

UNITED STATES v. SPEARIN

Supreme Court of the United States, 1918.
248 U.S. 132, 39 S.Ct. 59, 63 L.Ed. 166.

The case is stated in the opinion.

Mr. Justice BRANDEIS [a] delivered the opinion of the court.

Spearin brought this suit in the Court of Claims, demanding a balance alleged to be due for work done under a contract to construct a dry-dock and also damages for its annulment. Judgment was entered for him in the sum of $141,180.86; (51 Ct.Cl. 155) and both parties appealed to this court. The Government contends that Spearin is entitled to recover only $7,907.98. Spearin claims the additional sum of $63,658.70.

a. Louis Dembitz Brandeis (1856–1941) developed a lucrative Boston practice in corporate matters, and at the same time took a reformer's interest in public affairs. The cause of trade unionism was among those he espoused. His nomination to the Supreme Court in 1916 engendered a lengthy controversy; seven former presidents of the American Bar Association declared that he was "not a fit person to be a member" of the Court. On the Court he was frequently associated with Holmes in dissent, although his efforts to educate his older friend in economic and social conditions met with a "fastidious disrelish." The so-called "Brandeis brief" is one that seeks to inform the court of such conditions as bearing on the issue before it. He resigned in 1939. The ideal of personal moral responsibility was central to his thought, and led him to oppose insurance in certain forms, such as bank deposit insurance.

First. The decision to be made on the Government's appeal depends upon whether or not it was entitled to annul the contract. The facts essential to a determination of the question are these:

Spearin contracted to build for $757,800 a dry-dock at the Brooklyn Navy Yard in accordance with plans and specifications which had been prepared by the Government. The site selected by it was intersected by a 6-foot brick sewer; and it was necessary to divert and relocate a section thereof before the work of constructing the dry-dock could begin. The plans and specifications provided that the contractor should do the work and prescribed the dimensions, material, and location of the section to be substituted. All the prescribed requirements were fully complied with by Spearin; and the substituted section was accepted by the Government as satisfactory. It was located about 37 to 50 feet from the proposed excavation for the dry-dock; but a large part of the new section was within the area set aside as space within which the contractor's operations were to be carried on. Both before and after the diversion of the 6-foot sewer, it connected, within the Navy Yard but outside the space reserved for work on the dry-dock, with a 7-foot sewer which emptied into Wallabout Basin.

About a year after this relocation of the 6-foot sewer there occurred a sudden and heavy downpour of rain coincident with a high tide. This forced the water up the sewer for a considerable distance to a depth of 2 feet or more. Internal pressure broke the 6-foot sewer as so relocated, at several places; and the excavation of the dry-dock was flooded. Upon investigation, it was discovered that there was a dam from 5 to 5½ feet high in the 7-foot sewer; and that dam, by diverting to the 6-foot sewer the greater part of the water, had caused the internal pressure which broke it. Both sewers were a part of the city sewerage system; but the dam was not shown either on the city's plan, nor on the Government's plans and blue-prints, which were submitted to Spearin. On them the 7-foot sewer appeared as unobstructed. The Government officials concerned with the letting of the contract and construction of the dry-dock did not know of the existence of the dam. The site selected for the dry-dock was low ground; and during some years prior to making the contract sued on, the sewers had, from time to time, overflowed to the knowledge of these Government officials and others. But the fact had not been communicated to Spearin by anyone. He had, before entering into the contract, made a superficial examination of the premises and sought from the civil engineer's office at the Navy Yard information concerning the conditions and probable cost of the work; but he had made no special examination of the sewers nor special enquiry into the possibility of the work being flooded thereby; and had no information on the subject.

Promptly after the breaking of the sewer Spearin notified the Government that he considered the sewers under existing plans a menace to the work and that he would not resume operations unless the Government either made good or assumed responsibility for the damage that had already occurred and either made such changes in the sewer system as would remove the danger or assumed responsibility for the damage which might thereafter be occasioned by the insufficient capacity and the location and design of the existing sewers. The estimated cost of restoring the sewer was $3,875. But it was unsafe to both Spearin and the Government's property to proceed with the work with the 6-foot sewer in its then condition. The Government insisted that the responsibility for remedying existing conditions rested with the contractor. After fifteen months spent in investigations and fruitless correspondence, the Secretary of the Navy annulled the contract and took possession of the plant and materials on the site. Later the dry-dock, under radically changed and enlarged plans, was completed by other contractors, the Government having first discontinued the use of the 6-foot intersecting sewer and then reconstructed it by modifying size, shape and material so as to remove all danger of its breaking from internal pressure. Up to that time $210,939.18 had been expended by Spearin on the work; and he had received from the Government on account thereof $129,758.32. The court found that if he had been allowed to complete the contract he would have earned a profit of $60,000, and its judgment included that sum.

The general rules of law applicable to these facts are well settled. Where one agrees to do, for a fixed sum, a thing possible to be performed, he will not be excused or become entitled to additional compensation, because unforeseen difficulties are encountered. Day v. United States, 245 U.S. 159, 38 S.Ct. 57; Phoenix Bridge Co. v. United States, 211 U.S. 188, 29 S.Ct. 81. Thus one who undertakes to erect a structure upon a particular site assumes ordinarily the risk of subsidence of the soil. Simpson v. United States, 172 U.S. 372, 19 S. Ct. 222; Dermott v. Jones, 2 Wall., U.S., 1. But if the contractor is bound to build according to plans and specifications prepared by the owner the contractor will not be responsible for the consequences of defects in the plans and specifications. MacKnight Flintic Stone Co. v. The Mayor, 160 N.Y. 72, 54 N.E. 61; Filbert v. Philadelphia, 181 Pa.St. 530, 37 A. 545; Bentley v. State, 73 Wis. 416, 41 N.W. 338. See Sundstrom v. New York, 213 N.Y. 68, 106 N.E. 924. This responsibility of the owner is not overcome by the usual clauses requiring builders to visit the site, to check the plans, and to inform themselves of the requirements of the work, as is shown by Christie v. United States, 237 U.S. 234, 35 S.Ct. 565; Hollerbach v. United States, 233 U.S. 165, 34 S.Ct. 553, and United States v. Utah &c. Stage Co., 199 U.S. 414, 424, 26 S.Ct. 69, where it was held that the contractor should be relieved, if he was misled by erroneous statements in the specifications.

In the case at bar, the sewer, as well as the other structures, was to be built in accordance with the plans and specifications furnished by the Government. The construction of the sewer constituted as much an integral part of the contract as did the construction of any part of the dry-dock proper. It was as necessary as any other work in the preparation for the foundation. It involved no separate contract and no separate consideration. The contention of the Government that the present case is to be distinguished from the Bentley case, supra, and other similar cases, on the ground that the contract with reference to the sewer is purely collateral, is clearly without merit. The risk of the existing system proving adequate might have rested upon Spearin, if the contract for the dry-dock had not contained the provision for relocation of the 6-foot sewer. But the insertion of the articles prescribing the character, dimensions and location of the sewer imported a warranty that, if the specifications were complied with, the sewer would be adequate. This implied warranty is not overcome by the general clauses requiring the contractor to examine the site, to check up the plans, and to assume responsibility for the work until completion and acceptance. The obligation to examine the site did not impose upon him the duty of making a diligent enquiry into the history of the locality with a view to determining, at his peril, whether the sewer specifically prescribed by the Government would prove adequate. The duty to check plans did not impose the obligation to pass upon their adequacy to accomplish the purpose in view. And the provision concerning contractor's responsibility cannot be construed as abridging rights arising under specific provisions of the contract.

Neither sec. 3744 of the Revised Statutes, which provides that contracts of the Navy Department shall be reduced to writing, nor the parol evidence rule, precludes reliance upon a warranty implied by law. See Kellogg Bridge Co. v. Hamilton, 110 U.S. 108, 3 S.Ct. 537. The breach of warranty, followed by the Government's repudiation of all responsibility for the past and for making working conditions safe in the future, justified Spearin in refusing to resume the work. He was not obliged to restore the sewer and to proceed, at his peril, with the construction of the dry-dock. When the Government refused to assume the responsibility, he might have terminated the contract himself, Anvil Mining Co. v. Humble, 153 U.S. 540, 551–552, 14 S.Ct. 876; but he did not. When the Government annulled the contract without justification, it became liable for all damages resulting from its breach.

Second. Both the main and the cross-appeal raise questions as to the amount recoverable. [The Court ruled that Spearin should be, and had been, allowed recovery of all his losses resulting from the breach, including his proper expenditures, less receipts, and his lost profit.]

The judgment of the Court of Claims is, therefore,

Affirmed.[b]

NOTES

(1) *A Bit of Boilerplate.* The following provision figured in litigation over delays in highway building. It was part of the Standard Specifications of the New Jersey Department of Transportation, and it represents attempts to place responsibilities on builders through what Brandeis referred to (in the *Spearin* case) as "usual" and "general" clauses.

Article 1.2.11:

It is the obligation of the Bidder to ascertain for himself all the facts concerning conditions to be found at the location of the Project including all physical characteristics above, on and below the surface of the ground, to fully examine the Plans and read the Specifications, to consider fully these and all other matters which can in any way affect the work under the Contract and to make the necessary investigations relating thereto, and he agrees to this obligation in the signing of the Contract. The State assumes no responsibility whatsoever with respect to ascertaining for the Contractor such facts concerning physical characteristics at the site of the Project. The Contractor agrees that he will make no claim for additional payment or extension of time for completion of the work or any other concession because of any misinterpretation or misunderstanding of the Contract, on his part, or any failure to fully acquaint himself with all conditions relating to the work.

Notwithstanding this provision, in the case cited[c] the court charged the Highway Department with responsibility for faulty plans, and cited the Spearin case. Does that result signal a failure of drafting skill?

(2) *"Changed Conditions."* Government construction contracts now generally contain a "changed (or differing site) conditions" clause, more or less standard in terms, which would probably require an "equitable adjustment" of the price in circumstances such as those appearing in United States v. Spearin. As to subsoil conditions, in particular, bidders receive data on test borings by the government, and if it proves to be inaccurate an adjustment is called for. The contractor's right to rely on such information cannot be impaired by the government's disclaimer, it is said, in a broadly worded standard term, though the language is unmistakable. Foster Constr. C. A. & Williams Bros. Co. v. United States, 435 F.2d 873 (Ct.Cl. 1970; commissioner's opinion). The court said there that the government takes the risk of inaccuracy by long-established procurement policy. "The purpose of the changed conditions clause is thus to take at least some of the gamble on subsurface conditions out of bidding."[d] What calculation of benefits might have led the government to adopt such a policy?

b. For a collection of authorities related to this case, see Anno., 6 A.L.R.3d 1394 (1966). As to an agency's effort to disclaim accountability for specifications, see Grossbaum, Procedural Fairness in Public Contracts: The Procurement Regulations, 57 Va.L. Rev. 171, 211–12, 224 (1971).

c. Buckley & Co., Inc. v. State, 140 N.J.Super. 289, 356 A.2d 56 (1975).

For the simpler drafting of an earlier day, see Hollerbach v. United States, 233 U.S. 165, 167 (1914).

d. As to the important and intricate effect of the changed conditions clause on the doctrine of the *Spearin*

(3) *Aims and Achievement.* Many performances are contracted for in a way that calls for evaluation by reference to more or less general standards of behavior (e. g., workmanlike) and not to particular achievements. That is so even of an attorney employed to prepare a will.[e] A contrasting case is that of a plumber directed to connect a building to a sewer line in the street. His is an achievement contract. If by mischance he makes connection with an abandoned sewer nearby, though he has used the skill and judgment that prevail in the trade he cannot be said to have performed.[f] Professional persons, such as clergymen, are more likely to be judged by their demeanor and endeavors: though the standards of performance may be very high in their callings (e. g., upright, fervent) they do not usually promise achievements.

The line is not that between professional and nonprofessional work. A contract for delivery service probably calls for best efforts only—as is observed when snow coats the roads.[g] Moreover, an attorney who represents a client for a contingent fee is naturally like the plumber, so far as rights go. His talent and zeal as a litigator will not earn him a reward unless they are crowned with success. As we have seen, the law condemns contracts for achievement in some lines (see Note, p. 545 supra: lobbying contracts); but in general the contracting parties are free to choose between best-efforts contracts and achievement contracts. What they have chosen may be unclear in a given case. As for what amounts to performance under a contract to drill a water well, see Thiem v. Thomas, —— N.H. ——, 406 A.2d 115 (1979).[h] But the classification problem is not often severe: compare the best-effort requirement of a jockey in racing a horse with the horse owner's obligation to pay him if he rides. *Questions:* What assumptions about market pricing might affect the classification? Is the process of implying a promise likely to yield a duty of achievement? See Wood v. Lucy, p. 81 supra.

STEES v. LEONARD

Supreme Court of Minnesota, 1874.
20 Minn. 494, 20 Gil. 448.[a]

Appeal by defendants from an order of the district court, Ramsey county, denying a new trial.

case, see Jefferson Constr. Co. v. United States, 392 F.2d 1006 (Ct.Cl. 1968), cert. denied, 393 U.S. 842 (1968). Contrast the risk as to subsoil conditions placed on a contractor in private work, in P & Z Pacific, Inc. v. Panorama Apartments, Inc., 372 F. 2d 759 (9th Cir. 1967).

e. Heyer v. Flaig, 70 Cal.2d 223, 74 Cal.Rptr. 225, 449 P.2d 161 (1969): "must perform in such manner as 'lawyers of ordinary skill and capacity commonly possess and exercise.' "

f. Hennington v. Valuch, 27 Wis.2d 130, 133 N.W.2d 824 (1965).

g. See Buffalo & L. Land Co. v. Bellevue Land & Improvement Co., 165 N. Y. 247, 59 N.E. 5 (1901); Whelan v. Griffith Consumers Co., 170 A.2d 229 (D.C.Mun.App.1961) ("impossibility").

h. In this case the agreement actually mentioned two achievements, and the question was whether or not they were cumulative conditions of the driller's right to payment.

a. The statement of facts is taken in part from the 1882 edition by Gilfillan of 20 Minnesota Reports.

The action was brought to recover damages for a failure of defendants to erect and complete a building on a lot of plaintiffs, on Minnesota street, between Third and Fourth streets, in the city of St. Paul, which, by an agreement under seal between them and plaintiffs the defendants had agreed to build, erect, and complete, according to plans and specifications annexed to and made part of the agreement. The defendants commenced the construction of the building, and had carried it to the height of three stories when it fell to the ground. The next year, 1869, they began again and carried it to the height as before, when it again fell to the ground, whereupon defendants refused to perform the contract. They claimed that in their attempts to erect the building they did the work in all respects according to the plans and specifications and that the failure to complete the building and its fall on the two occasions was due to the fact that the soil upon which it was to be constructed was composed of quicksand, and when water flowed into it, was incapable of sustaining the building. . . . The specifications annexed to the contract are very full, and provide, (among other things,) that "All the walls shall be of the following thickness: foundation walls, two feet thick, and shall have footings six inches thick, which shall run clear across walls and project six inches on each side of wall above it." The specifications contain no other provisions relating to the character of the foundation for the building. [The plaintiffs alleged that the specifications, signed by both parties to the contract, had been prepared by a firm of architects named Sheire & Bro. Two persons named Sheire were named as defendants along with Leonard.]

The plaintiffs allege . . . that the fall of the building was owing to the negligence and unskilful work of the defendants, and the poor quality of the material furnished by them. Judgment is demanded for the sum of $5,214.80, with interest, as the damages sustained by the plaintiffs; being $3,745.80 paid, pursuant to the contract, during the progress of the work, $1,000 as damages for loss of the use of the lot on which the building was to be erected, and $469, as damages, occasioned by the fall of the building, to an adjacent house of plaintiffs, and property stored therein. . . .

The jury found for the plaintiffs. The defendants moved, upon a bill of exceptions, for a new trial, and appeal from the order denying their motion.

YOUNG, J. The general principle of law which underlies this case is well established. If a man bind himself, by a positive, express contract, to do an act in itself possible, he must perform his engagement, unless prevented by the act of God, the law, or the other party to the contract. No hardship, no unforeseen hindrance, no difficulty short of absolute impossibility, will excuse him from doing what he has expressly agreed to do. This doctrine may sometimes seem to bear heavily upon contractors; but, in such cases, the hardship is attributable, not to the law, but to the contractor himself, who has improvidently assumed an absolute, when he might have undertaken only a qualified, liability. The law does no more than enforce the contract as the parties themselves have made it. Many cases illustrating the application of the doctrine to every variety of contract are collected in the note to Cutter v. Powell, 2 Smith, Lead.Cas. 1 [p. 1005 infra]. . . .

School Trustees v. Bennett, 3 Dutcher, N.J., 513, is almost identical, in its material facts, with the present case. The contractors agreed to build and complete a schoolhouse, and find all materials therefor, according to specifications annexed to the contract; the building to be located on a lot owned by plaintiff, and designated in the contract. When the building was nearly completed it was blown down by a sudden and violent gale of wind. The contractors again began to erect the building, when it fell, solely on account of the soil on which it stood having become soft and miry, and unable to sustain the weight of the building; although, when the foundations were laid, the soil was so hard as to be penetrated with difficulty by a pickax, and its defects were latent. The plaintiff had a verdict for the amount of the installments paid under the contract as the work progressed. The verdict was sustained by the supreme court, which held that the loss, although arising solely from a latent defect in the soil, and not from a faulty construction of the building, must fall on the contractor. . . .

In Dermott v. Jones, 2 Wall., U.S., 1, the foundation of the building sank, owing to a latent defect in the soil, and the owner was compelled to take down and rebuild a portion of the work. The contractor having sued for his pay, it was held that the owner might recoup the damages sustained by his deviation from the contract. The court refer with approval to the cases cited, and say: "The principle which controlled them rests upon a solid foundation of reason and justice. It regards the sanctity of contracts. It requires a party to do what he has agreed to do. If unexpected impediments lie in the way, and a loss ensue, it leaves the loss where the contract places it. If the parties have made no provision for a dispensation, the rule of law gives none. It does not allow a contract fairly made to be annulled, and it does not permit to be interpolated what the parties themselves have not stipulated."

Nothing can be added to the clear and cogent arguments we have quoted in vindication of the wisdom and justice of the rule which must govern this case, unless it is in some way distinguishable from the cases cited.

It is argued that the spot on which the building is to be erected is not designated with precision in the contract, but is left to be selected by the owner; that, under the contract, the right to designate the particular spot being reserved to plaintiffs they must select one that will sustain the building described in the specifications, and if the spot they select is not, in its natural state, suitable, they must make it so; that in this respect the present case differs from School Trustees v. Bennett.

The contract does not, perhaps, designate the site of the proposed building with absolute certainty; but in this particular it is aided by the pleadings. The complaint states that defendants contracted to erect the proposed building on "*a certain piece* of land, of which the plaintiffs then were, and now are, the owners in fee, fronting on Minnesota street, between Third and Fourth streets, in the city of St. Paul." The answer expressly admits that the defendants entered into a contract to erect the building, according to the plans, etc., "on that certain piece of land in said complaint described," and that they "entered upon the performance of said contract and proceeded with the erection of said building," etc. This is an express admission that the contract was made with reference to the identical piece of land on which the defendants afterwards attempted to perform it, and leaves no foundation in fact for the defendants' argument.

It is no defense to the action that the specifications directed that "footings" should be used as the foundation of the building, and that the defendants, in the construction of those footings, as well as in all other particulars, conformed to the specifications. The defendants contracted to "erect and complete the building." Whatever was necessary to be done in order to complete the building, they were bound by the contract to do. If the building could not be completed without other or stronger foundations than the footings specified, they were bound to furnish such other foundations. If the building could not be erected without draining the land, then they must drain the land, "because they have agreed to do everything necessary to erect and complete the building." (3 Dutcher, N.J., 520; and see Dermott v. Jones, supra, where the same point was made by the contractor, but ruled against him by the court.)

As the draining of the land was, in fact, necessary to the erection and completion of the building, it was a thing to be done, under the contract, by the defendants. The prior parol agreement that plaintiffs should drain the land, related therefore, to a matter embraced within the terms of the written contract, and was not, as claimed by defendants' counsel, collateral thereto. It was, accordingly under the familiar rule, inadmissible in evidence to vary the terms of the written contract, and was properly excluded.

[In the remainder of the opinion the court considered evidence offered by the defendants that *after* the work was begun the plaintiffs made promises to drain the site of the building, and that the failure to do so caused the collapse. The court held that the evidence was properly excluded because the defendants had failed to allege consideration for the promises, or justifiable reliance upon them.]

There was, therefore, no error in the exclusion of the evidence offered, and the order appealed from is affirmed.

NOTES

(1) *Loss Questions.* The opinion in Stees seems to proceed on the assumption that a loss traceable to a latent soil condition must fall on either the owner or the builder. If the builder discovers the difficulty when he begins work, and refuses to proceed, what kinds of loss have to be considered? One may be the additional price the owner must pay to have the work done as projected. Evidently the plaintiffs did not claim this type of loss in Stees v. Leonard. Would it have been granted, if such an amount had been proved and claimed?

(2) *Mistake.* There is authority for avoiding a construction contract that the parties made without sufficient information about soil conditions, on the ground of mutual mistake. See Restatement, Restitution, § 9; but see Watkins & Son v. Carrig, p. 394 supra. If a builder has made test borings at the site before contracting, is he in a good position to plead mistake? Should he be allowed to make this defense if the agreement requires him to test the soil, and he has not done so? Compare the reference, in United States v. Spearin, to the "usual clauses requiring builders to visit the site," and so on.

If the contract in Stees v. Leonard had been held voidable for mutual mistake, which elements in the plaintiffs' recovery could have been granted, if any?

(3) *Case Comparisons.* Were the specifications in Stees v. Leonard adequate for the construction of the building on the site specified? Can the decision be distinguished from that in United States v. Spearin? Compare Ridley Investment Co. v. Croll, 192 A.2d 925, 6 A.L.R.3d 1389 (Del. 1963), a "soft soil" case in which the contractor prevailed. The court observed that "plans and specifications do not exist in a vacuum; they are made for a particular building at a particular place. The defect in the plans and specifications for the building in question was the failure to make provision for adequate pilings and other support for the floor; the fact that these plans and specifications might provide for an adequate building in some other place does not render the plans and specifications less defective for the location in question."

See also Patterson, Constructive Conditions in Contracts, 42 Colum.L. Rev. 903, 938–39 (1942), where it is said: "The owner ordinarily employs an architect or engineer to prepare the plans and specifications, and thus has control of their adequacy; moreoever, the builder's promise requires him to adhere to the plans furnished by the owner. The rub comes when the defective performance is due to a combination of sub-soil obstacles *and* the inadequacy of the owner's plans and specifications in relation to those obstacles. The marked tendency in recent years is to throw the loss on the owner, especially where the owner is the government." [b]

The usual way of distinguishing cases like Stees v. Leonard is to say that "in most, if not all of these, there was a positive and unequivocal undertaking by the contractor to furnish a completed building. Such is not the

b. See also J. Sweet, Legal Aspects of Architecture, Engineering and the Construction Process, ch. 22 (1970). In Ridley Investment Co. v. Croll, supra, the court rejected an attempted distinction between public works and private construction projects.

case here." Blue Bell, Inc. v. Cassidy, 200 F.Supp. 443 (N.D.Miss.1961). In Friederick v. Redwood County, 153 Minn. 450, 190 N.W. 801 (1922), the Minnesota court used precisely this formula without bothering to cite its prior decision in Stees v. Leonard. But see Mayville-Portland School Dist. No. 10 v. C. L. Linfoot Co., 261 N.W.2d 907 (N.D.1978), where expressions in the Friederick case were disapproved. The court was insistent on a showing by the contractor that the plans were defective, in light of certain "general clauses."

JACOB & YOUNGS v. KENT

[For the report of this case, see p. 606 supra.]

NOTES

(1) *Question.* Would it have been possible for the parties, using a tightly-drawn provision in the contract, to preclude a recovery by the contractor such as this? Consider the provisions that the contract contained, set out in footnote a, p. 607 supra. How could they have been improved upon, as a means of protecting the defendant?

In Am. Continental Life Ins. Co. v. Ranier Const. Co., 607 P.2d 372 (Ariz.1980), a builder's arguments of prevention, substantial performance, and waiver failed to overcome the condition of an architect's final certificate for payment (requirement not "procedural chaff").

(2) *Conclusive Third-Party Approval.* It has been held that a contractor is exempted from liability for misperformance by a contract provision for the approval of his work by an architect or engineer, when such approval has been certified. If the approval is stated as a condition of payment to the contractor, his failure to obtain it is not necessarily fatal to his claim for payment, as we have seen earlier in this chapter. Given identical terms in the contract about approval, are these rulings consistent? Might the difference be explained in terms of an architect's disposition to side with the owner? See Arc Electrical Constr. Co. v. George A. Fuller Co., 24 N.Y.2d 99, 247 N.E.2d 111 (1969).

For one reason or another, it seems that an architect's final certificate is not often helpful to the contractor defensively.[a] The rule of exemption was applied, however, in City of Granville v. Kovash, Incorporated, 118 N.W.2d 354 (N.D.1962). There the city sued the contractor who had laid some water mains for it, after they froze, for failure to place them at the depth required by the contract. It provided for supervision and control of the work by a project engineer, and that after an inspection by him final payment would be made upon his certificate that the work had been "com-

a. It is normally binding on the owner only to the extent of establishing the "actual final completion" of the work. Board of Education v. A. Barbaresi & Son, Inc., 25 A.D.2d 855, 269 N.Y.S.2d 823 (2d Dept.1966). So understood, it may serve to foreclose a claim upon a performance bond, yet leave the contractor open to a claim for latent defects. See City of Midland v. Waller, 430 S.W.2d 473 (Tex. 1968) (note the A.I.A. standard form provision construed in that sense). Furthermore, a certificate is open to challenge on the ground that its issuance was the result of "fraud", loosely understood, or gross mistake. James I. Barnes Const. Co. v. Washington Township, 184 N.E.2d 763 (Ind.App.1962).

pleted in a satisfactory manner and in accordance with the terms of the contract." The engineer had issued such a certificate, and it was held to bar the city's claim. As to a "final payment conclusive" provision see John Price Associates, Inc. v. Davis, 588 P.2d 713 (Utah, 1978).

(3) *Substantial Performance and Quasi Contract.* The function of the rule of substantial performance, as Cardozo explains it, is to "mitigate the rigor of implied conditions." That is also the function of quasi contract, as applied in cases like Kirkland v. Archbold, p. 874 supra. What is the difference in effect between applying the one remedy or the other? If Cardozo had accepted the principle of Kirkland, could he have said that the "willful transgressor must accept the penalty of his transgression?" In Massachusetts, the rule of substantial performance is thought not to prevail; yet the court there permits a quantum meruit recovery modelled closely on the principle of Jacob & Youngs v. Kent.[b] In some cases it is difficult to tell whether the court is proceeding on the basis of substantial performance or of quasi contract, in giving relief to a defaulting plaintiff. Should the problems in all cases of deviating builders be allowed to "blend into one problem with but one answer?" See Nordstrom & Woodland, Recovery by Building Contractor in Default, 20 Ohio St.L.J. 193, 217 (1959). In some cases the builder's measure of recovery seems to be more generous if he has failed of substantial performance than if he has achieved it.[c] Does that make any sense?

SUBSTANTIAL PERFORMANCE IN CONTEXT

The rule of substantial performance is uniquely associated with building and improvement contracts. It is applied sporadically, however, in litigation over other types of contracts. Indeed, the origin of the rule has been traced to a decision by Mansfield about the sale of a plantation in the West Indies, including land and slaves. Boone v. Eyre, 1 H.Bl. 273, 126 Eng.Rep. 160, Note (K.B. 1777). A leading English case on the subject concerned an indenture of apprenticeship. Ellen v. Topp, 9 Exch. 424, 155 Eng.Rep. 609 (1851). Nevertheless, the rule has found its chief proving ground in suits on construction contracts.[d]

Why should this be so? Several considerations suggest the answer. As for employment contracts, it is usual for an employer to pay wages at short intervals, and to reserve the power of termination at will. Leases of real property have traditionally been regarded as exempt from the usual contract rules of constructive conditions. As for contracts for the sale of goods, the party who is denied a remedy does not suffer an investment loss, ordinarily, in the same degree as a builder whose earnings prove uncollectible. As for land sale con-

b. Dodge v. Kimball, 203 Mass. 364, 89 N.E. 542 (1909).

c. See Fuller v. Rosinski, 79 Wash.2d 719, 488 P.2d 1061 (1971); Forrester v. Craddock, 51 Wash.2d 315, 317 P. 2d 1077 (1957); cf. White v. Mitchell, 123 Wash. 630, 213 P. 10 (1923); Nordin Constr. Co. v. City of Nome, 489 P.2d 455 (Alaska, 1971).

d. Its relation to contracts for the sale of goods is considered in Section 5, infra.

tracts, enforcement is regularly sought in a court of equity, in which there are specialized rules serving some of the same objects as the doctrine of substantial performance.

Ordinarily neither party to a construction contract has access to specific performance as a remedy. On the one side, there is an undertaking to pay money, which may be adequately enforced at law. On the other, there is an undertaking to make improvements. As a rule, courts will not undertake the supervision of such work. For this reason, largely, they will not make a decree requiring performance by a builder—or a painter, repairman, excavator, or the like—any more than they will order performance by an actor or singer. (Exceptions are made, but only in exceptional circumstances, such as the presence of an overriding public interest.) The result is that controversies over imperfect performance by a builder are usually transmuted into money claims, when presented in court.

"Through the doctrine of substantial performance," it is said, "the judges installed themselves as administrators of the execution and discharge of contracts. They freed themselves from rigid rules and adopted a broad standard under which they could apply a policy of making contract effective." [e] This must not be understood to mean that the courts will directly administer the performance of a contract; it means that practical judgments about performance figure in their decisions about money claims. Should the courts undertake a more active role as to construction contracts? Having become "administrators of execution" indirectly, would they find it a short and easy step beyond to order the correction of defective work?

NOTES

(1) *Judicial Barn Building.* An Idaho case illustrates the courts' reluctance to supervise builders' work. It concerned a contract to put up a barn for a dairyman. Not being paid in full, the builder sued the dairyman. The trial court ordered "that the plaintiff shall make the following changes, alterations and repairs in the barn and milk house . . . within thirty days from the date of this Order:—," and specified 14 items for attention. When the work was properly done, the court ruled, "the plaintiff will then be deemed to have substantially complied with the terms of the building contracts between the parties. . . ." Thirty days later the parties were still in contention, and the court appointed a referee to make an inspection and report. He found "minor items that still need some attention," but gave his opinion that the court's order had been substantially complied with. Further controversy ensued, and an appeal. The Idaho Supreme Court manifested extreme displeasure with the trial court's management of the suit. Mackey v. Eva, 80 Idaho 260, 328 P.2d 66 (1958).[f]

e. J. Corry, Law and Policy 41–43 (1959).

f. See also Eldred v. C. L. Folkman Co., 93 Idaho 131, 456 P.2d 775 (1969); Niagara Mohawk Power Corp. v. Graver Tank & Mfg. Co., 470 F. Supp. 1308, 1326 (N.D.N.Y.1979) (contract to build and install a nuclear containment liner). But see Link v.

(2) *Willful Breach.* What are the cases of a builder's deviation from the plans agreed upon that should be regarded as intentional or willful misconduct? The use of inferior materials for the purpose of filching a profit?

Professor Corbin has objected to the use of the word *willful* on the ground that it "indicates a childlike faith in the existence of a plain and obvious line between the good and the bad, between unfortunate virtue and unforgivable sin. . . . [T]he enrichment of even an injured man may become unjust." [g] What word is better than "willful" to describe conduct of a builder that will bar him from claiming on the theory of substantial performance? In Restatement Second, § 241, the absence of that word is noteworthy. But does subsection (e) bring the sense of it in by the back door? See Comment f.[h]

What if the builder departs from the plans for the purpose of enhancing the value of the structure? To meet unforeseen construction problems? [i] What if it is *impossible* to follow the plans literally? Compare a builder who cannot pay all his laborers and materialmen, as the contract requires him to do, because he lacks funds.[j]

It has been generally held—or at least said—that a "willful" or "intentional" deviation from the terms of the contract will always preclude a finding of substantial performance.[k] This is often said when the facts seem to show a deviation that would be material in any case.

(3) *Problem.* Contractor installs a heating system in a building, and does such poor work that he is accountable to Owner for his loss of $25,000, calculated on the "diminished value" rule. The misperformance was willful. Owner has withheld $15,000 of the contract price, and Contractor believes he should be held liable only for the difference, $10,000. Should the unpaid price be allowed as a credit upon his liability? See Kirk Reid Company v. Fine, 205 Va. 778, 139 S.E.2d 829 (1965). Compare Di Mare v. Capaldi, 336 Mass. 497, 146 N.E.2d 517 (1957). Willfulness aside, if the cost of correcting the work is greater than $25,000, Jacob & Youngs v. Kent is not an authority for limiting the contractor's liability to that amount, is it? See Bellizzi v. Huntley Estates, 3 N.Y.2d 112, 143 N.E.2d 802 (1957).

State Dept. of Fish & Game, — Mont. —, 591 P.2d 214 (1979) (contract to run a railroad).

g. Section 1123; cf. § 1254. And see Shapiro, Inc. v. Bimblich, 101 A.2d 890 (D.C.Mun.App.1954) (petty vengeance).

h. For an illustration of a purchase of iron rails that is a breach because "malicious", see § 237, Illustration 7.

i. See Shell v. Schmidt, 164 Cal.App.2d 350, 330 P.2d 817 (1958), cert. denied, 359 U.S. 959 (1959).

j. Cf. Witherell v. Lasky, 286 App.Div. 533, 145 N.Y.S.2d 624 (1955).

k. In Samuel J. Creswell I. Wks. v. Housing Auth. of Camden, 449 F.2d 557 (3d Cir. 1971), a vice-president of the plaintiff contractor testified that it did not intend to comply with the specifications of the contract when bidding for it; the plaintiff was held to be "estopped" from asserting substantial performance.

PLANTE v. JACOBS

Supreme Court of Wisconsin, 1960.
10 Wis.2d 567, 103 N.W.2d 296.

[Eugene Plante contracted with Frank and Carol Jacobs to furnish the materials and construct a house upon their lot in Brookfield, in accordance with plans and specifications, for the sum of $26,765. During the course of construction Plante was paid $20,000. Disputes arose between the parties, the Jacobs refused to continue payment, and Plante did not complete the house. He sued to establish a lien on the property as a way of recovering the unpaid balance of the contract price, plus extras. The owners—who are the appellants—answered with allegations of faulty workmanship and incomplete construction.]

HALLOWS, Justice. The defendants argue the plaintiff cannot recover any amount because he has failed to substantially perform the contract. The plaintiff conceded he failed to furnish the kitchen cabinets, gutters and downspouts, sidewalk, closet clothes poles, and entrance seat amounting to $1,601.95. This amount was allowed to the defendants. The defendants claim some 20 other items of incomplete or faulty performance by the plaintiff and no substantial performance because the cost of completing the house in strict compliance with the plans and specifications would amount to 25 or 30 per cent of the contract price. The defendants especially stress the misplacing of the wall between the living room and the kitchen, which narrowed the living room in excess of one foot. The cost of tearing down this wall and rebuilding it would be approximately $4,000. The record is not clear why and when this wall was misplaced, but the wall is completely built and the house decorated and the defendants are living therein. Real estate experts testified that the smaller width of the living room would not affect the market price of the house.

The defendants rely on Manitowoc Steam Boiler Works v. Manitowoc Glue Co., 1903, 120 Wis. 1, 97 N.W. 515, for the proposition there can be no recovery on the contract as distinguished from *quantum meruit* unless there is substantial performance. This is undoubtedly the correct rule at common law. For recovery on *quantum meruit*, see Valentine v. Patrick Warren Construction Co., 1953, 263 Wis. 143, 56 N.W.2d 860. The question here is whether there has been substantial performance. The test of what amounts to substantial performance seems to be whether the performance meets the essential purpose of the contract. In the Manitowoc case the contract called for a boiler having a capacity of 150 per cent of the existing boiler. The court held there was no substantial performance because the boiler furnished had a capacity of only 82 per cent of the old boiler and only approximately one-half of the boiler capacity contemplated by the contract. In Houlahan v. Clark, 1901, 110 Wis. 43, 85 N.W. 676, the contract provided the plaintiff was to drive pilings in the lake and place a boat house thereon parallel and in line with a neighbor's dock. This was not done and the contractor so positioned the boat house that it was practically useless to the owner. Manthey v. Stock, 1907, 133 Wis. 107, 113 N.W. 443, involved a contract to paint a house and to do a good job, including the removal of the old paint where necessary. The plaintiff did not remove the old paint, and blistering and roughness of the new paint resulted. The court held that the plaintiff failed to show substantial performance. The defendants also cite Manning v. School District No. 6, 1905, 124 Wis. 84, 102 N.W. 356. However, this case involved a contract to install a heating and ventilating plant in the school building which would meet certain tests which the heating apparatus failed to do. The heating plant was practically a total failure to accomplish the purposes of the contract. See also Nees v. Weaver, 1936, 222 Wis. 492, 269 N.W. 266, 107 A.L.R. 1405 (roof on a garage).

Substantial performance as applied to construction of a house does not mean that every detail must be in strict compliance with the specifications and the plans. Something less than perfection is the test of specific performance unless all details are made the essence of the contract. This was not done here. There may be situations in which features or details of construction of special or of great personal importance, if not performed, would prevent a finding of substantial performance of the contract. In this case the plan was a stock floor plan. No detailed construction of the house was shown on the plan. There were no blueprints. The specifications were standard printed forms with some modifications and additions written in by the parties. Many of the problems that arose during the construction had to be solved on the basis of practical experience. No mathematical rule relating to the percentage of the price, of cost of completion, or of completeness can be laid down to determine substantial performance of a building contract. Although the defendants received a house with which they are dissatisfied in many respects, the trial court was not in error in finding the contract was substantially performed.

The next question is what is the amount of recovery when the plaintiff has substantially, but incompletely, performed. For substantial performance the plaintiff should recover the contract price less the damages caused the defendant by the incomplete performance. Both parties agree. Venzke v. Magdanz, 1943, 243 Wis. 155, 9 N.W.2d 604, states the correct rule for damages due to faulty construction amounting to such incomplete performance, which is the difference between the value of the house as it stands with faulty and incomplete construction and the value of the house if it had been constructed in strict accordance with the plans and specifications. This is the diminished-value rule. The cost of replacement or repair is not the measure of such damage, but is an element to take into consideration in arriving at value under some circumstances. The cost of replacement or the cost to make whole the omissions may equal or be less than the difference in value in some cases and, likewise, the cost to rectify a defect may greatly exceed the added value to the structure as corrected. The defendants argue that under the Venzke rule their damages are $10,000. The plaintiff on review argues the defendants' damages are only $650. Both parties agree the trial court applied the wrong rule to the facts.

The trial court applied the cost-of-repair or replacement rule as to several items, relying on Stern v. Schlafer, 1943, 244 Wis. 183, 11 N.W.2d 640, 12 N.W.2d 678, wherein it was stated that when there are a number of small items of defect or omission which can be remedied without the reconstruction of a substantial part of the building or a great sacrifice of work or material already wrought in the building, the reasonable cost of correcting the defect should be allowed. However, in Mohs v. Quarton, 1950, 257 Wis. 544, 44 N.W.2d 580, the court held when the separation of defects would lead to confusion, the rule of diminished value could apply to all defects.

In this case no such confusion arises in separating the defects. The trial court disallowed certain claimed defects because they were not proven. This finding was not against the great weight and clear preponderance of the evidence and will not be disturbed on appeal. Of the remaining defects claimed by the defendants, the court allowed the cost of replacement or repair except as to the misplacement of the living-room wall. Whether a defect should fall under the cost-of-replacement rule or be considered under the diminished-value rule depends upon the nature and magnitude of the defect. This court has not allowed items of such magnitude under the cost-of-repair rule as the trial court did. Viewing the construction of the house as a whole and its cost we cannot say, however, that the trial court was in error in allowing the cost of repairing the plaster cracks in the ceilings, the cost of mud jacking and repairing the patio floor, and the cost of reconstructing the non-weight-bearing and nonstructural patio wall. Such reconstruction did not involve an unreasonable economic waste.

The item of misplacing the living-room wall under the facts of this case was clearly under the diminished-value rule. There is no evidence that defendants requested or demanded the replacement of the wall in the place called for by the specifications during the course of construction. To tear down the wall now and rebuild it in its proper place would involve a substantial destruction of the work, if not all of it, which was put into the wall and would cause additional damage to other parts of the house and require replastering and redecorating the walls and ceilings of at least two rooms. Such economic waste is unreasonable and unjustified. The rule of diminished value contemplates the wall is not going to be moved. Expert witnesses for both parties, testifying as to the value of the house, agreed that the misplacement of the wall had no effect on the market price.

The trial court properly found that the defendants suffered no legal damage, although the defendants' particular desire for specified room size was not satisfied. For a discussion of these rules of damages for defective or unfinished construction and their application see Restatement, 1 Contracts, pp. 572–573, sec. 346(1)(a) and illustrations. . . .

Judgment affirmed.[a]

NOTES

(1) *Question.* In what ways does the New York version of the substantial performance rule appear to differ from the Wisconsin court's approach in Plante v. Jacobs?

(2) *Restitution Compared.* In Kreyer v. Driscoll, 39 Wis.2d 540, 159 N.W.2d 680 (1968), a contractor had agreed to build a home for a family for about $47,000. Controversies arose, apparently over progress payments, and the parties "reached an impasse." Stopping work, the contractor sued the owners. He had done only half the work on each of the following items: plumbing, electrical work, heating, and tile work. He had placed none of the linoleum, and had done only about a quarter of the decorating. The cost of completing these items was $4,650. The trial court gave judgment for the plaintiff for nearly $11,000. It allowed credits to the owners of $740 for imperfect workmanship, and $1,233 for delay in completion. The theory of the recovery was that the plaintiff had substantially performed. The owners appealed. *Held:* Affirmed. "[T]he amount of the judgment found by the lower court was not justified on the theory of substantial performance but is justified on the theory of *quantum meruit* or restitution." Was this consistent with the principles of Plante v. Jacobs? When a builder pulls off the job in Wisconsin, does it make any difference to his rights whether or not he is justified by the conduct of the owner? The court did not discuss the issue of justification in the Kreyer case.

(3) *Problem.* Suppose this case: Once the owners have complained about the situation of the living-room wall, Plante hires another builder to put it in the proper place, for the contract price of $4,500. Plante goes about his other work. When he comes to inspect the new wall at the Jacobs home he finds that it has been moved about *two* feet—contrary to his directions. The living room is larger, but the kitchen is now narrower than it should have been. That does not affect the market price of the house. What, if anything, must Plante pay for having the wall relocated? If your answer is "nothing", how do you explain that so minor a point as the misplacement of a wall by one foot could matter so greatly to Plante?

(4) *Limitations on the Rule.* Real or apparent exceptions to the rule of substantial performance are abundant. In builders' cases, however, none of them seems to command general assent. A short list is as follows:

(a) "The doctrine is essentially a rule of damages . . . [I]ts purpose is not to compel the unwilling acceptance of tendered work that fails to

a. On the use of court-appointed experts for valuations—a building contractor for certain costs of correction and a real-estate appraiser for diminution of value—see Reith v. Wynhoff, 28 Wis.2d 336, 137 N.W.2d 33 (1965).

meet contract specifications." Ballou v. Basis Constr. Co., 407 F.2d 1137, 1140 (4th Cir. 1969).

(b) "[S]ubstantial performance relates to the degree of completion rather than the date of completion." Todd Shipyards Corp. v. Jasper Electric Service Co., 414 F.2d 8 (5th Cir. 1969).

(c) The rule does not temporize with "structural defects." See Spence v. Ham, 163 N.Y. 220, 57 N.E. 412 (1900), in which the size and placement of girders was faulty, affecting the solidity of the building: these were "deviations from the general plan of so essential a character that they cannot be remedied without partially reconstructing the building, and hence do not come within the rule of substantial performance . . . ." Compare Kizziar v. Dollar, 268 F.2d 914 (10th Cir. 1959) ("standard and adequate" foundation for the building, though not equal to that specified).

(d) "Under ordinary circumstances . . . a failure to perform 10 percent of the contract price will not admit of the claim of substantial performance." Rochkind v. Jacobson, 126 App.Div. 347, 110 N.Y.S. 583 (1908). But see Jardine Estates v. Donna Brook Corp., 42 N.J.Super. 332, 126 A.2d 372 (1956) ("The matter is not to be determined on a percentage basis, for the cost of remedying defects may sometimes even exceed the outlay for original construction.").

(5) *The Brick Veneer Problem.* A homeowner, Roper, agreed to pay $535.25 to Armstead for installing brick veneer at Roper's home. Armstead agreed to use new brick matching as closely as possible the color and appearance of Roper's existing brickwork. When the work was done, Roper refused to pay. In an action by Armstead, the trial court found that his work was functionally acceptable, but not esthetically so. On hearing testimony about Roper's "damages," the court assessed them at 50% of the contract price, and gave judgment for Armstead for $267.62. On an appeal by Roper, what decision? See Reynolds v. Armstead, 166 Colo. 372, 443 P.2d 990 (1968).

STEWART v. NEWBURY

Court of Appeals of New York, 1917.
220 N.Y. 379, 115 N.E. 984, 2 A.L.R. 519.

[Plaintiff, a builder, offered to do the excavation work for defendant's new foundry building at 65 cents per cubic yard; to furnish labor and forms for the concrete work at $2.05 per cubic yard, and to furnish labor to put in re-enforcing (of the concrete) at $4.00 per ton. The defendant accepted this offer. Other necessary facts are stated in the opinion. In the trial court judgment was entered upon a verdict for the plaintiff; this judgment was affirmed in the Appellate Division, and the defendant appealed by permission.]

CRANE, J. Nothing was said in writing about the time or manner of payment. The plaintiff, however, claims that after sending his letter and before receiving that of the defendant he had a telephone communication with Mr. Newbury and said: "I will expect my payments in the usual manner," and Newbury said, "All right, we have got the money to pay for the building." This conversation over the telephone was denied by the defendants.

The custom, the plaintiff testified, was to pay 85 per cent every thirty days or at the end of each month, 15 per cent being retained till the work was completed.

In July the plaintiff commenced work and continued until September 29th, at which time he had progressed with the construction as far as the first floor. He then sent a bill for the work done up to that date for $896.35. The defendants refused to pay the bill and work was discontinued.

The plaintiff claims that the defendants refused to permit him to perform the rest of his contract, they insisting that the work already done was not in accordance with the specifications. The defendants claimed upon the trial that the plaintiff voluntarily abandoned the work after their refusal to pay his bill.

On October 5, 1911, the defendants wrote the plaintiff a letter containing the following: "Notwithstanding you promised to let us know on Monday whether you would complete the job or throw up the contract, you have not up to this time advised us of your intention. . . . . Under the circumstances we are compelled to accept your action as being an abandonment of your contract and of every effort upon your part to complete your work on our building. As you know, the bill which you sent us and which we declined to pay is not correct, either in items or amount, nor is there anything due you under our contract as we understand it until you have completed your work on our building."

To this letter the plaintiff replied the following day. In it he makes no reference to the telephone communication agreeing, as he testified, to make "the usual payments," but does say this: "There is nothing in our agreement which says that I shall wait until the job is completed before any payment is due, nor can this be reasonably implied. . . . As to having given you positive date as to when I should let you know what I proposed doing, I did not do so; on the contrary I told you that I would not tell you positively what I would do until I had visited the job, and I promised that I would do this at my earliest convenience. . . . ."

The defendant Herbert Newbury testified that the plaintiff "ran away and left the whole thing." And the defendant F. E. Newbury testified that he was told by Mr. Stewart's man that Stewart was going to abandon the job; that he thereupon telephoned Mr. Stewart, who replied that he would let him know about it the next day, but did not.

In this action, which is brought to recover the amount of the bill presented as the agreed price and $95.68 damages for breach of contract, the plaintiff had a verdict for the amount stated in the bill, but not for the other damages claimed, and the judgment entered thereon has been affirmed by the Appellate Division.

The appeal to us is upon exceptions to the judge's charge. The court charged the jury as follows: "Plaintiff says that he was excused from completely performing the contract by the defendant's unreasonable failure to pay him for the work he had done during the months of August and September. . . . Was it understood that the payments were to be made monthly? If it was not so understood the defendant's only obligation was to make payments at reasonable periods, in view of the character of the work, the amount of work being done and the value of it. In other words, if there was no agreement between the parties respecting the payments, the defendants' obligation was to make payments at reasonable times. . . . But whether there was such an agreement or not, you may consider whether it was reasonable or unreasonable for him to exact payment at that time and in that amount."

The court further said, in reply to a request to charge:

"I will say in that connection, if there was no agreement respecting the time of payment, and if there was no custom that was understood by both parties, and with respect to which they made the contract, then the plaintiff was entitled to payments at reasonable times."

The defendants' counsel thereupon made the following request, which was refused: "I ask your Honor to instruct the jury that if the circumstances existed as your Honor stated in your last instruction, then the plaintiff was not entitled to any payment until the contract was completed."

The jury was plainly told that if there were no agreement as to payments, yet the plaintiff would be entitled to part payment at reasonable times as the work progressed, and if such payments were refused he could abandon the work and recover the amount due for the work performed.

This is not the law. Counsel for the plaintiff omits to call our attention to any authority sustaining such a proposition and our search reveals none. In fact the law is very well settled to the contrary. This was an entire contract. (Ming v. Corbin, 142 N.Y. 334, 340, 341, 37 N.E. 105.) Where a contract is made to perform work and no agreement is made as to payment, the work must be substantially performed before payment can be demanded. [Citations omitted.]

This case was also submitted to the jury upon the ground that there may have been a breach of contract by the defendants in their refusal to permit the plaintiff to continue with his work, claiming that he had departed from the specifications, and there was some evidence justifying this view of the case, but it is impossible to say upon which of these two theories the jury arrived at its conclusion. The above errors, therefore, cannot be considered as harmless and immaterial. [Citations omitted.] As the verdict was for the amount of the bill presented and did not include the damages for a breach of contract, which would be the loss of profits, it may well be presumed that the jury adopted the first ground of recovery charged by the court as above quoted and decided that the plaintiff was justified in abandoning work for nonpayment of the installment.

The judgment should be reversed, and a new trial ordered, costs to abide the event.

NOTES

(1) *Questions.* If the jury believed the plaintiff's evidence about the telephone conversation with Mr. Newbury, does it follow that he was justified in abandoning the work? Would it matter whether this conversation occurred before or after the contract was concluded? If it occurred afterward, what was the consideration for Newbury's promise to pay "in the usual manner"?

(2) *Work Before Pay.* "When the performance of a contract consists in doing (faciendo) on one side, and in giving (dando) on the other side, the doing must take place before the giving. (Langdell's Summary of Law of Contracts, sec. 125.)" Kellogg, J., in Coletti v. Knox Hat Co., Inc., 252 N.Y. 468, 472, 169 N.E. 648, 649–650 (1930). "Centuries ago, the principle became settled that where work is to be done by one party and payment is to be made by the other, the performance of the work must precede payment, in the absence of a showing of a contrary intention. It is sometimes supposed, that this principle grew out of employment contracts, and reflects a conviction that employers as a class are more likely to be responsible than are workmen paid in advance. Whether or not the explanation is correct, most parties today contract with reference to the principle, and unless they have evidenced a contrary intention it is at least as fair as the opposite rule would be." Restatement Second, § 234, Comment e.

ALLOCATING CREDIT RISKS

In a schematic analysis of contract policy by Professor Macaulay, he offers support for the rule that "in the typical employment contract the employee must work before the employer must pay for the service—the employer's duty to pay is constructively conditional on the employee's performance." One justification for the rule that he gives is that employers are, as a class, "probably better credit risks than employees paid in advance." [a] In a sale of goods for cash there is no credit risk in the standard sense. However, Professor Leff has described the buyer's risk that the goods will prove to be defective as being in the nature of a credit risk.[b] The rule placing this

a. Macaulay, Justice Traynor and the Law of Contracts, 13 Stan.L.Rev. 812, 815–16 (1961).

b. Leff, Injury, Ignorance and Spite—The Dynamics of Coercive Collection, 80 Yale L.J. 1, 20–22 (1970).

risk on the buyer "unless otherwise agreed" is reflected in UCC 2–310(a). Can this rule be justified on the ground that, as a class, sellers are probably better credit risks than buyers who obtain goods on credit?

Does the same consideration tend to justify the rule in Stewart v. Newbury? For repair work on buildings and chattels, and similar modest jobs, payment is commonly withheld until completion. But for sizable construction work it is well-nigh universal practice to agree upon periodic progress payments, or "draws," in favor of the contractor. As security for completion, the owner retains a fraction (usual 10–20%) of the amount earned each month by the contractor, and the sums withheld (sometimes called the "retent") are payable only upon completion. Does this practice indicate that contractors are dissatisfied with the rule in Stewart v. Newbury? Is it a reason for discarding the rule?

NOTE

Security Against Credit Risks. Buyers of land and goods who contract to pay in installments, after possession is transferred, are to some extent secured, as Professor Leff noted, against the "credit risk" that the property will prove to be defective. In Chapter 11, Section 3, it will be seen that credit sellers and financing institutions have attempted to deprive buyers of the privilege of stopping payment when they are disappointed. In part, the law has frustrated these attempts, showing its concern to minimize the buyer's risk. Securing payment for contractors (and laborers and materialmen) is a function of mechanics' lien laws and of payment bonds that are commonly required by statute on public projects.

Obviously the doctrine of constructive conditions has not succeeded alone in making a satisfactory allocation of credit risks; but perhaps it has played a useful part in doing so, as Professor Macaulay suggests. Reconsider Kingston v. Preston, p. 813 supra. Does it appear that Lord Mansfield was cognizant of the utility of implied conditions for allocating credit risks?

NEW ENGLAND STRUCTURES, INC. v. LORANGER

Supreme Judicial Court of Massachusetts, 1968.
354 Mass. 62, 234 N.E.2d 888.

CUTTER, Justice. In one case the plaintiffs, doing business as Theodore Loranger & Sons (Loranger), the general contractor on a school project, seeks to recover from New England Structures, Inc., a subcontractor (New England), damages caused by an alleged breach of the subcontract. Loranger avers that the breach made it necessary for Loranger at greater expense to engage another subcontractor to complete work on a roof deck. In a cross action, New England seeks to recover for breach of the subcontract by Loranger alleged to have taken place when Loranger terminated New England's right to proceed. The actions were consolidated for trial. A jury returned a verdict for New England in the action brought by Loranger, and a verdict for New England in the sum of $16,860.25 in the action brought by New England against Loranger. The cases are before us on Loranger's exceptions to the judge's charge.

Loranger, under date of July 11, 1961, entered into a subcontract with New England by which New England undertook to install a gypsum roof deck in a school, then being built by Loranger. New England began work on November 24, 1961. On December 18, 1961, New England received a telegram from Loranger which read, "Because of your . . . repeated refusal . . . or inability to provide enough properly skilled workmen to maintain satisfactory progress, we . . . terminate your right to proceed with work at the . . . school as of December 26, 1961, in accordance with Article . . . 5 of our contract. We intend to complete the work . . . with other forces and charge its costs and any additional damages resulting from your repeated delays to your account." New England replied, "Failure on your [Loranger's] part to provide . . . approved drawings is the cause of the delay." The telegram also referred to various allegedly inappropriate changes in instructions.

The pertinent portions of art. 5 of the subcontract are set out in the margin.[1] Article 5 stated grounds on which Loranger might terminate New England's right to proceed with the subcontract.

There was conflicting evidence concerning (a) how New England had done certain work; (b) whether certain metal cross pieces (called bulb tees) had been properly "staggered" and whether joints had been welded on both sides by certified welders, as called for by the specifications; (c) whether New England had supplied an adequate number of certified welders on certain days; (d) whether and to what extent Loranger had waived certain specifications; and (e) whether New England had complied with good trade practices. The architect testified that on December 14, 1961, he had made certain complaints to New England's president. The work was completed by

1. "The Subcontractor agrees to furnish sufficient labor, materials, tools and equipment to maintain its work in accordance with the progress of the general construction work by the General Contractor. Should the Subcontractor fail to keep up with . . . [such] progress . . . then he shall work overtime with no additional compensation, if directed to do so by the General Contractor. If the Subcontractor should be adjudged a bankrupt . . . or *if he should persistently . . . fail to supply enough properly skilled workmen* . . . or . . . disregard instructions of the General Contractor or fail to observe or perform the provisions of the Contract, then the General Contractor may, by *at least five . . . days prior written notice to the Subcontractor* without prejudice to any other rights or remedies, *terminate the Subcontractor's right to proceed with the work.* In such event, the General Contractor may . . . prosecute the work to completion . . . and the Subcontractor shall be liable to the General Contractor for any excess cost occasioned . . . thereby . . ." (emphasis supplied).

another company at a cost in excess of New England's bid. There was also testimony (1) that Loranger's job foreman told one of New England's welders "to do no work at the job site during the five day period following the date of Loranger's termination telegram," and (2) that, "if New England had been permitted to continue its work, it could have completed the entire subcontract . . . within five days following the date of the termination telegram."

The trial judge ruled, as matter of law, that Loranger, by its termination telegram confined the justification for its notice of termination to New England's "repeated refusal . . . or inability to provide enough properly skilled workmen to maintain satisfactory progress." He then gave the following instructions: "If you should find that New England . . . did not furnish a sufficient number of men to perform the required work under the contract within a reasonable time . . . then you would be warranted in finding that Loranger was justified in terminating its contract; and it may recover in its suit against New England . . .. [T]he termination . . . cannot, as . . . matter of law, be justified for any . . . reason not stated in the telegram of December 18 . . . including failure to stagger the joints of the bulb tees or failure to weld properly . . . or any other reason, unless you find that inherent in the reasons stated in the telegram, namely, failure to provide enough skilled workmen to maintain satisfactory progress, are these aspects. Nevertheless, these allegations by Loranger of deficiency of work on the part of New England Structures may be considered by you, if you find that Loranger was justified in terminating the contract for the reason enumerated in the telegram. You may consider it or them as an element of damages sustained by Loranger . . .."[2] Counsel for Loranger claimed exceptions to the portion of the judge's charge quoted above in the body of this opinion.[3]

1. Some authority supports the judge's ruling, in effect, that Loranger, having specified in its telegram one ground for termination of the subcontract, cannot rely in litigation upon other grounds, except to the extent that the other grounds may directly affect the

2. The judge also instructed, "[I]f you find that on the day following the sending of this telegram . . . employees of New England . . . were refused permission to continue that work, then you may consider that as a breach of the contract by Loranger, for Loranger's telegram terminated the contract . . . as of December 26th [by] the giving of five days notice . . . . [I]f you find that [employees of] New England . . . reported for work and were only informed that they were to call their office and were not prevented from working then . . . you would be warranted in finding that this was not a refusal on the part of Loranger to permit them to work for the period between the receipt of the telegram and the date of the termination, December 26th."

3. No exception appears to have been claimed to the portion of the charge (see fn. 2) relating to whether Loranger prevented New England from performing work on the subcontract during the period from December 19 to December 26.

first ground asserted. See Railway Co. v. McCarthy, 96 U.S. 258, 267–268, 24 L.Ed. 693 ("Where a party gives a reason for his conduct and decision touching . . . a controversy, he cannot, after litigation has begun, change his ground, and put his conduct upon . . . a different consideration. He is not permitted thus to mend his hold. He is *estopped* from doing it by a settled principle of law" [emphasis supplied]); Luckenbach S.S. Co. Inc. v. W. R. Grace & Co. Inc., 267 F. 676, 679 (4th Cir.); Chevrolet Motor Co. v. Gladding, 42 F.2d 440 (4th Cir.), cert. den. 282 U.S. 872, 51 S.Ct. 78, 75 L.Ed. 770. See also Rode & Brand v. Kamm Games, Inc., 181 F.2d 584, 587 (2d Cir.); Cummings v. Connecticut Gen. Life Ins. Co., 102 Vt. 351, 359–362, 148 A. 484. In each of these cases, there is reference to estoppel or "waiver" as the legal ground behind the principle.

Our cases somewhat more definitely require reliance or change of position based upon the assertion of the particular reason or defence before treating a person, giving one reason for his action, as estopped later to give a different reason. See Bates v. Cashman, 230 Mass. 167, 168–169, 119 N.E. 663, 664. There it was said, "The defendant is not prevented from setting up this defense. Although he wrote respecting other reasons for declining to perform the contract, he expressly reserved different grounds for his refusal.[4] While of course one cannot fail in good faith in presenting his reasons as to his conduct touching a controversy he is not prevented from relying upon one good defense among others urged simply because he has not always put it forward, when it does not appear that he has acted dishonestly or that the other party has been misled to his harm, or that he is estopped on any other ground." See Brown v. Henry, 172 Mass. 559, 567, 52 N.E. 1073; St. John Bros. Co. v. Falkson, 237 Mass. 399, 402–403, 130 N.E. 51; Moss v. Old Colony Trust Co., 246 Mass. 139, 150, 140 N.E. 803; Sheehan v. Commercial Travelers Mut. Acc. Assn. of America, 283 Mass. 543, 551–553, 186 N.E. 627, 88 A.L.R. 975; Restatement: Contracts, § 304; Williston, Contracts (3d ed.) § 742 (and also §§ 678, 679, 691); Corbin, Contracts, §§ 762, 1218, 1266 and also §§ 265, 721, 727, 744, 756). See also Randall v. Peerless Motor Car Co., 212 Mass. 352, 376, 99 N.E. 221.

We think Loranger is not barred from asserting grounds not mentioned in its telegram unless New England establishes that, in some manner, it relied to its detriment upon the circumstance that only one ground was so asserted. Even if some evidence tended to show such reliance, the jury did not have to believe this evidence. They should have received instructions that they might consider

4. The original papers show (record, p. 22) that the reservation was, "The statement of the foregoing [reason] is not to be taken as waiving any other reason for . . . Cashman's refusal to proceed further with the agreement." This distinction from the present case, in our opinion, does not affect the principle that any estoppel to assert a different reason must rest on actual reliance.

grounds for termination of the subcontract and defences to New England's claim (that Loranger by the telegram had committed a breach of the subcontract), other than the ground raised in the telegram, unless they found as a fact that New England had relied to its detriment upon the fact that only one particular ground for termination was mentioned in the telegram.

2. As there must be a new trial, we consider whether art. 5 of the subcontract (fn. 1) afforded New England any right during the five-day notice period to attempt to cure its default, and, in doing so, to rely on the particular ground stated in the telegram. Some evidence summarized above may suggest that such an attempt was made. Article 5 required Loranger to give "at least five . . . days prior written notice to the Subcontractor" of termination.

If a longer notice period had been specified, one might perhaps infer that the notice period was designed to give New England an opportunity to cure its defaults. An English text writer (Hudson's, Building and Engineering Contracts, 9th ed. p. 530) says, "Where a previous warning notice of specified duration is expressly required by the contract before . . . termination [in case of dissatisfaction], the notice should be explicit as to the grounds of dissatisfaction, so that during the time mentioned in the notice the builder may have the opportunity of removing the cause of objection. . . . " This view was taken of a three-day notice provision in Valentine v. Patrick Warren Constr. Co., 263 Wis. 143, 164, 56 N.W.2d 860, without, however, very full consideration of the provision's purpose. In Corbin, Contracts, § 1266, p. 66, it is said of a reserved power to terminate a contract, "If a period of notice is required, the contract remains in force and must continue to be performed according to its terms during the specified period after receipt of the notice of termination." See Simons v. American Dry Ginger Ale Co. Inc., 335 Mass. 521, 524–525, 140 N.E.2d 649.

Whether the short five-day notice period was intended to give New England an opportunity to cure any specified breach requires interpretation (see Valentine v. Patrick Warren Constr. Co., 263 Wis. 143, 155, 56 N.W.2d 860) of art. 5,[5] a matter of law for the court. See Charles L. Hazelton & Son, Inc. v. Teel, 349 Mass. 617, 621, 211 N.E.2d 352. It would have been natural for the parties to have provided expressly that a default might be cured within the five-day period if that had been the purpose. See e. g. Mad River Lumber Sales, Inc. v. Willburn, 205 Cal.App.2d 321, 322, 325, 22 Cal.Rptr. 918 (contract specifically gave period in which to cure default).[6]

5. Article 5 of this subcontract (which is part of a printed form of contract) appears to be based to some extent upon the American Institute of Architects, standard contract, Form Al, art. 22. See Parker and Adams, The A.I.A. Standard Contract Forms and the Law. The purpose of the notice period under this A.I.A. form is not clarified by any commentary.

[See also Supplement, Owner-Contractor Agreement, Art. 20.2.]

6. Somewhat analogous provisions sometimes appear in real estate purchase agreements, expressly giving a

Strong practical considerations support the view that as short a notice period as five days in connection with terminating a substantial building contract cannot be intended to afford opportunity to cure defaults major enough (even under art. 5) to justify termination of a contract. Such a short period suggests that its purpose is at most to give the defaulting party time to lay off employees, remove equipment from the premises, cancel orders, and for similar matters.

Although the intention of the notice provision of art. 5 is obscure, we interpret it as giving New England no period in which to cure continuing defaults, but merely as directing that New England be told when it must quit the premises and as giving it an opportunity to take steps during the five-day period to protect itself from injury. Nothing in art. 5 suggests that a termination pursuant to its provisions was not to be effective in any event at the conclusion of the five-day period, even if New England should change its conduct.

If Loranger in fact was not justified by New England's conduct in giving the termination notice, it may have subjected itself to liability for breach of the subcontract. The reason stated in the notice, however, for giving the notice cannot be advanced as the basis of any reliance by New England in action taken by it to cure defaults. After the receipt of the notice, as we interpret art. 5, New England had no further opportunity to cure defaults.

Exceptions sustained.

NOTES

(1) *Offense and Defense.* A waiver or estoppel foreclosing a ground for recovery is not uncommon (e. g., Loranger v. New England). The more usual case, however, is a waiver or estoppel foreclosing a line of defense (New England v. Loranger). Compare Jarbeau's case, p. 859 supra, and Phoenix Ins. Co. v. Ross Jewelers, Inc., p. 777 supra. What new light does this case throw on the doctrines of waiver and estoppel? See text at p. 856 supra.

(2) *The Notice Term.* As the court interpreted the five-day notice provision of article 5 (footnote 1), did it have any effect on New England's claim against Loranger? Notice that Loranger's telegram of December 18 stated: "we terminate your right to proceed . . . as of December 26." Was the provision intended to limit what New England might recover, if the termination was wrongful, to damages that such advance notice would not have permitted it to prevent? Was it intended to prevent or limit Loranger's recovery, if its termination was rightful but was not given upon sufficient notice? What other effect might it have? On the purposes of such a provision, see J. Sweet, Legal Aspects of Architecture, Engineering and the Construction Process, § 26.07 (1970).

(3) *Seriatim Objections.* A builder has put up a dwelling, under contract with the owner of the lot, and considers that he has complied with all

vendor an extension of time for performance in order to cure title defects. See Swaim, Crocker's Notes on Common Forms (7th ed.) § 814, p. 435, § 852.

the specifications, leaving no defects. If, however, the owner disagrees, the builder hopes to satisfy him with corrective work. The builder wishes to do all such work at one time, before moving his crew and equipment away. How can he elicit a definitive list of the owner's objections? (Compare Sears, Roebuck and Co. v. Jardel Co., p. 436 supra.)

In Cawley v. Weiner, 236 N.Y. 357, 140 N.E. 724 (1923), the owners of a new bungalow moved in before the builder had stopped work, and handed him a list of 17 items that they considered necessary by way of change in or addition to the structure. For about a week after that, apparently, the builder continued work. Not being paid in full, he brought suit against the owners for the price. At the trial, they offered to prove three particulars, not specified in the earlier list, in which the plaintiff had failed of performance. The trial court excluded the evidence on grounds of waiver and estoppel, and gave the plaintiff judgment for virtually the whole amount he claimed. On appeal by the owners, *held:* Reversed. "Unless the plaintiff were in some way harmed by the action of these defendants in furnishing him with a list of the defects, how are they estopped from showing the departures from the plans and specifications?" Compare Phoenix Ins. Co. v. Ross Jewelers, Inc., p. 777 supra.

In preparing a construction contract, what provision might be made to prevent the owner from raising new objections seriatim? Is this the answer?—"Owner agrees not to move into the house until Contractor receives final payment." See Creith Lumber v. Cummins, 163 Ohio St. 264, 126 N.E.2d 323 (1955).

(4) *Problem.* In Michel v. Efferson, 223 La. 136, 65 So.2d 115 (1953), the owner prepared a list of defects for the builder which he seems to have made some effort to correct. He then told the owner, who needed a place to live, that she could not have the keys unless she accepted the house in its then condition. Finally she accepted the house "as is," saying she guessed she would have to "swallow the plaster." At the time she did not know the extent of the defects in the plaster (as she now says), not having gone upstairs in the house on account of illness. She subsequently brought an action against the builder on account of defective construction. What result?

McCLOSKEY & CO. v. MINWELD STEEL CO.

United States Court of Appeals, Third Circuit, 1955.
220 F.2d 101.

Suit by contractor against subcontractor alleging anticipatory breach of three contracts entered into by parties. The United States District Court for the Western District of Pennsylvania, Joseph P. Willson, J., granted defendant's motion for judgment on ground that plaintiff had not made out prima facie case, and entered order denying plaintiff's motion for findings of fact, to vacate judgments and for new trial, and plaintiff appealed. . . .

Order affirmed.

McLAUGHLIN, Circuit Judge. Plaintiff-appellant, a general contractor, sued on three contracts alleging an anticipatory breach as to each. At the close of the plaintiff's case the district judge granted the defense motions for judgment on the ground that plaintiff had not made out a cause of action.

By the contracts involved the principal defendant,[1] a fabricator and erector of steel, agreed to furnish and erect all of the structural steel required on two buildings to be built on the grounds of the Hollidaysburg State Hospital, Hollidaysburg, Pa. and to furnish all of the long span steel joists required in the construction of one of the two buildings. Two of the contracts were dated May 1, 1950 and the third May 26, 1950. By Article V of each of the contracts "Should the Sub-Contractor [the defendant herein] . . . . at any time refuse or neglect to supply a sufficiency . . . . of materials of the proper quality, ... in and about the performance of the work required to be done pursuant to the provisions of this agreement . . . ., or fail, in the performance of any of the agreements herein contained, the Contractor shall be at liberty, without prejudice, to any other right or remedy, on two days' written notice to the Sub-Contractor, either to provide any such . . . . materials and to deduct the cost thereof from any payments then or thereafter due the Sub-Contractor, or to terminate the employment of the Sub-Contractor for the said work and to enter upon the premises . . . .."

There was no stated date in the contracts for performance by the defendant subcontractor. Article VI provided for completion by the subcontractor of its contract work "by and at the time or times hereafter stated to-wit:

"Samples, Shop Drawings and Schedules are to be submitted in the quantities and manner required by the Specifications, for the approval of the Architects, immediately upon receipt by the Sub-Contractor of the contract drawings, or as may be directed by the Contractor. All expense involved in the submission and approval of these Samples, Shop Drawings and Schedules shall be borne by the Sub-Contractor.

"All labor, materials and equipment required under this contract are to be furnished at such times as may be directed by the Contractor, and in such a manner so as to at no time delay the final completion of the building.

"It being mutually understood and agreed that prompt delivery and installation of all materials required to be furnished under this contract is to be the essence of this Agreement."

Appellee Minweld Steel Co., Inc., the subcontractor, received contract drawings and specifications for both buildings in May, 1950. On June 8, 1950, plaintiff McCloskey & Co. wrote appellee asking when it might "expect delivery of the structural steel" for the build-

1. The Travelers Indemnity Co., which posted performance bonds on two of the contracts, is a co-defendant in No. 11,422.

ings and "also the time estimated to complete erection." Minweld replied on June 13, 1950, submitting a schedule estimate of expecting to begin delivery of the steel by September 1, and to complete erection approximately November 15. On July 20, 1950 plaintiff wrote Minweld threatening to terminate the contracts unless the latter gave unqualified assurances that it had effected definite arrangements for the procurement, fabrication and delivery within thirty days of the required materials. On July 24, 1950 Minweld wrote McCloskey & Co. explaining its difficulty in obtaining the necessary steel. It asked McCloskey's assistance in procuring it and stated that "We are as anxious as you are that there be no delay in the final completion of the buildings or in the performance of our contract, ..."[2]

Plaintiff-appellant claims that by this last letter, read against the relevant facts, defendant gave notice of its positive intention not

2. This letter in full is as follows:

Minweld Steel Company
Incorporated
Shaler and Wabash Streets
Pittsburgh 20, Pa.

July 24, 1950.

McClosky & Company
1620 Thompson Street
Philadelphia 21, Penna.

In re: New Hospital Buildings
Hollidaysburg State Hospital
Hollidaysburg, Pennsylvania

Attention of J. C. McCloskey,
Vice President

Dear Sir:

This will acknowledge receipt of your letter of July 20th, 1950, which was received by us today.

Upon receipt of the architect's specifications, we completed the engineering and erection plans on the said specifications. Immediately after those details were available, we attempted to place orders for the steel with the Bethlehem Steel Company. Our order was held in the offices of the Bethlehem Steel Company for two weeks before we were notified that it could not be supplied. Since that time, we have tried the U. S. Steel Corporation and Carnegie-Illinois, both companies informing us that they were under contract for approximately one year and could not fulfill the order.

The recent directive by the President of the United States, with which we assume you are familiar, has further tightened up the steel market so that at the present writing we cannot give you any positive promise as to our ability to obtain the steel or delivery dates.

In view of the directive from Washington and the tightening up of the entire steel industry, we solicit your help and that of the General State Authority in aiding us to obtain the steel for these contracts.

We are as anxious as you are that there be no delay in the final completion of the buildings or in the performance of our contract, but we have nowhere else to turn at the present time for the supply of steel necessary under said contracts, unless through your aid and assistance, and that of the General State Authority, a supplier can be induced to give us the materials needed.

The U.S. Steel Corporation informs us that you have discussed this matter with them and are presently aware of our present difficulties.

If steel is to be supplied to these hospital buildings by governmental directive, we feel that the steel should be supplied to us for completion under our contract.

Very truly yours,
Minweld Steel Company, Inc.
J. A. Roberts
Sales Manager

JAR/fs

c/c Travelers Indemnity Co.,
Hartford, Conn.
General State Authority,
Harrisburg, Penna.

to perform its contracts and thereby violated same.[3] Some reference has already been made to the background of the July 24th letter. It concerned Minweld's trouble in securing the steel essential for performance of its contract. Minweld had tried unsuccessfully to purchase this from Bethlehem Steel, U. S. Steel and Carnegie-Illinois. It is true as appellant urges that Minweld knew and was concerned about the tightening up of the steel market.[4] And as is evident from the letter it, being a fabricator and not a producer, realized that without the help of the general contractor on this hospital project particularly by it enlisting the assistance of the General State Authority,[5] Minweld was in a bad way for the needed steel. However, the letter conveys no idea of contract repudiation by Minweld. That company admittedly was in a desperate situation. Perhaps if it had moved earlier to seek the steel its effort might have been successful. But that is mere speculation for there is no showing that the mentioned producers had they been solicited sooner would have been willing to provide the material.

Minweld from its written statement did, we think, realistically face the problem confronting it. As a result it asked its general contractor for the aid which the latter, by the nature of the construction, should have been willing to give. Despite the circumstances there is no indication in the letter that Minweld had definitely abandoned all hope of otherwise receiving the steel and so finishing its undertaking. One of the mentioned producers might have relented. Some other supplier might have turned up. It was McCloskey & Co. who eliminated whatever chance there was. That concern instead of aiding Minweld by urging its plea for the hospital construction materials to the State Authority which represented the Commonwealth of Pennsylvania took the position that the subcontractor had repudiated its agreement and then moved quickly to have the work completed. Shortly thereafter, and without the slightest trouble as far as appears, McCloskey & Co. procured the steel from Bethlehem[6] and brought in new subcontractors to do the work contemplated by the agreement with Minweld.

Under the applicable law Minweld's letter was not a breach of the agreement. The suit is in the federal court by reason of diversity of citizenship of the parties. Though there is no express statement to

3. Plaintiff cancelled the contracts on July 26, 1950 on the ground that the July 24th letter constituted an admission of defendant's inability to perform the required work.

4. The Korean War broke out on June 24, 1950.

5. The Pennsylvania state agency which represented and owned the Hollidaysburg State Hospital.

6. Bethlehem had originally submitted a bid in competition with Minweld. Its new proposals were dated July 28, 1950 and were finally accepted by McCloskey & Co. on August 7, 1950. The long span steel joists required by the third contract were procured from the Frederick Grundy Iron Works.

that effect the contracts between the parties would seem to have been executed in Pennsylvania with the law of that state applicable. In McClelland v. New Amsterdam Cas. Co., 1936, 322 Pa. 429, 433, 185 A. 198, 200, the Pennsylvania Supreme Court held in a case where the subcontractor had asked for assistance in obtaining credit, "In order to give rise to a renunciation amounting to a breach of contract there must be an absolute and unequivocal refusal to perform or a distinct and positive statement of an inability to do so." Minweld's conduct is plainly not that of a contract breaker under that test. See also Dingley v. Oler, 1886, 117 U.S. 490, 6 S.Ct. 850, 29 L.Ed. 984. Restatement of Contracts, Comment (i) to Sec. 318 (1932) speaks clearly on the point saying:

"Though where affirmative action is promised mere failure to act, at the time when action has been promised, is a breach, failure to take preparatory action before the time when any performance is promised is not an anticipatory breach, even though such failure makes it impossible that performance shall take place, and though the promisor at the time of the failure intends not to perform his promise." See Williston on Contracts, Vol. 5, Sec. 1324 (1937), Corbin on Contracts, Vol. 4, Sec. 973 (1951).

Appellant contends that its letter of July 20, requiring assurances of arrangements which would enable appellee to complete delivery in thirty days, constituted a fixing of a date under Article VI of the contracts. The short answer to this is that the thirty day date, if fixed, was never repudiated. Appellee merely stated that it was unable to give assurances as to the preparatory arrangements. There is nothing in the contracts which authorized appellant to demand or receive such assurances.

The district court acted properly in dismissing the actions as a matter of law on the ground that plaintiff had not made out a prima facie case.

The order of the district court of July 14, 1954 denying the plaintiff's motions for findings of facts, to vacate the judgments and for new trials will be affirmed.

NOTES

(1) *A Pair of Newer Rules.* Compare Restatement Second, § 251, with UCC 2–609. Under the former, is there necessarily a repudiation if the obligor fails to provide "adequate assurance" when it is properly demanded? Under either rule, would McCloskey's letters of June 8 and July 20 be regarded as demands for assurance of due performance? If so, would the responses be regarded as adequate?

If both the rules cited are authoritative, within their respective spheres, does the contract in the main case lie clearly in the sphere of general contract law, as opposed to that of the Code? It seems the possibility cannot be ruled out that if this case were to recur it would be governed by the statute.

(2) *Indubitable Repudiation.* "In order to constitute a repudiation, a party's language must be sufficiently positive to be reasonably interpreted to mean that the party will not or cannot perform. . . . [L]anguage that under a fair reading 'amounts to a statement of intention not to perform except on conditions which go beyond the contract' constitutes a repudiation. Comment 2 to Uniform Commercial Code § 2–610." Restatement Second, § 250, Comment b. See also Comment d as to a party's insistence on a minor enhancement of his contract rights. And see again the Note at p. 839 supra.

(3) *Questionable Repudiation.* Can you envisage a repudiation by a party who is content with his bargain and willing to perform it? See Philadelphia Eagles, Inc. v. Armstrong, [1952] 1 D.L.R. 332 (Manitoba).[a] Can you envisage a communication that would be called a repudiation if made in bad faith, and not otherwise? Consider again the reasoning in *Viglas*, p. 849 supra. Do you see a reason not to require a party receiving a disclaimer to judge whether or not it was made in good faith? Compare Williston, § 1325, and Corbin, § 973, on this point. Can you envisage a repudiation that does no more than express doubt about a party's ability or willingness to perform? See J. K. Welding Co. v. W. J. Halloran Steel Erection Co., 178 F.Supp. 584 (D.R.I.1959).[b]

If the test for determining what is a repudiation is an objective one, it is surely no better to say "I cannot perform the contract" than to say "I will not perform it." Is it any better to say, "I will try to perform, though I see no prospect of succeeding?"[c] How does that differ from what Minweld wrote to McCloskey, in the main case?[d]

In formulating tests for repudiation, what bearing might it have that a party having grounds to expect a breach by the other may (if he may) demand assurance of due performance?

(4) *Problem.* Refer to the facts in Stewart v. Newbury, p. 898 supra. Assuming that the plaintiff did not abandon the job, did he repudiate the contract at any time? By sending the bill on September 29? By writing the letter of October 5? Compare Menako v. Kassien, 265 Wis. 269, 61 N.W.2d 332 (1953).

(5) *Forcing the Issue.* A party who is delinquent in performance, or threatened with inability, can surely plead with the other for leniency without being guilty of a repudiation. If pressed, he may hope to skirt a repudiation with cautiously written letters, perhaps drafted with the aid of counsel. How may the other party force the issue? Would it be easier to do so in a face-to-face encounter than by correspondence? Which party is

a. Compare Campos v. Olson, 241 F.2d 661 (9th Cir. 1957), another sporting case.

b. This court, applying Massachusetts law, conceived of an expression of doubt which warrants rescission by the recipient, but not a damage claim. The Restatement Second appears to reject this conception; see § 253. (But see § 243(4).) What are the merits?

c. Compare Avery v. Bowden, 5 El. & Bl. 714, 119 Eng.Rep. 647 (Q.B.1855), aff'd, 6 El. & Bl. 953, 119 Eng.Rep. 1119 (Ex.Ch.).

d. For an unusual attempt to "manufacture" a sizeable claim for damages by seizing on a supposed anticipatory repudiation, see Bowes v. Saks & Co., 397 F.2d 113 (7th Cir. 1968).

likely to call for a conference? See Plunkett v. Comstock-Cheney Co., 211 App.Div. 737, 208 N.Y.S. 93 (1st Dept. 1925).

For a remarkable balancing act by the Washington Metropolitan Area Transit Authority, while developing a rapid-transit system, see City of Fairfax, Va. v. Washington Metropolitan Area Transit Authority, 582 F.2d 1321 (4th Cir. 1978), cert. denied, 440 U.S. 914 (1979). On the one hand, the City of Fairfax had been led to expect, in return for its contribution to construction of the "Metro", that a branch would extend nearly to its border. On the other hand, action by the Secretary of Transportation, concerned about rising federal costs, compelled the design of a curtailed system. As redesigned, the system did not include the Fairfax route. Given that the Authority had to seek further contributions from other municipalities even for the scaled-down system, do you see the problem it faced in avoiding repayment of the Fairfax contribution?

(6) *An Irishman's Temper.* Sean Barron had some discussions about joining forces on an apartment-building project with a construction firm headed by L. E. Spitzer. A bid was made by the firm (Spitzer Company) and it was awarded the contract. Spitzer then informed Barron that they had no agreement. This produced a "heated debate," and Spitzer agreed to settle their differences by paying Barron $10,000. Four weeks went by, and Spitzer called on Barron to appeal for help with problems on the project. Spitzer had written out a joint-venture agreement in longhand. Whether or not they agreed orally on its terms was later disputed; but they did agree that Spitzer would have his attorney put something in "proper legal form." Barron undertook supervision of the work at once and continued for several weeks. Then he received the attorney's work product. It was substantially different from what Spitzer had written. Barron proceeded directly to the job site and shut it down (leaving a building exposed to the elements). Within an hour Spitzer telephoned, and an "explosive discussion" ensued. Spitzer protested that the new document embodied their agreement. "At that point," Barron testified, "we had very little more to talk about."

The Spitzer Company completed the project for a substantial profit. Barron sued it for breach of an oral contract, and obtained a jury verdict, and judgment, for $192,000. On appeal by the company, the court referred —approvingly—to Restatement Second, § 251; it also concluded that there was sufficient evidence of a repudiation by Spitzer. L. E. Spitzer Co., Inc. v. Barron, 581 P.2d 213 (Alaska, 1978). *Questions:* Does the Restatement section support the judgment? Was this the sort of case for which a demand for assurance is appropriate?

(7) *Case Comparisons.* Compare Spitzer's behavior with that of the plaintiff in Jarbeau's case (Note 3, p. 859 supra). Was it more opprobrious? More injurious to the other contracting party? These cases tend to show that juries have a free rein in deciding what amounts to a repudiation. Should they? How can these cases be reconciled with the decisive action of the trial court in the main case? In this connection, New York Life Ins. Co. v. Viglas (p. 849 supra) should also be reviewed. Was Spitzer's conduct like that of the insurance company in an important way?

SECTION 5. SALE CONTRACTS

INTERNATIO-ROTTERDAM, INC. v. RIVER BRAND RICE MILLS, INC.

United States Court of Appeals, Second Circuit, 1958.
259 F.2d 137.
Certiorari denied 358 U.S. 946 (1959).

HINCKS, Circuit Judge. Appeal from the United States District Court, Southern District of New York, Walsh, Judge, upon the dismissal of the complaint after plaintiff's case was in.

The defendant-appellee, a processor of rice, in July 1952 entered into an agreement with the plaintiff-appellant, an exporter, for the sale of 95,600 pockets of rice. The terms of the agreement, evidenced by a purchase memorandum, indicated that the price per pocket was to be "$8.25 F.A.S. Lake Charles and/or Houston, Texas"; that shipment was to be "December, 1952, with two weeks call from buyer" and that payment was to be by "irrevocable letter of credit to be opened immediately payable against" dock receipts and other specified documents.[a] In the fall, the appellant, which had already committed itself to supplying this rice to a Japanese buyer, was unexpectedly confronted with United States export restrictions upon its December shipments and was attempting to get an export license from the government. December is a peak month in the rice and cotton seasons in Louisiana and Texas, and the appellee became concerned about shipping instructions under the contract, since congested conditions prevailed at both the mills and the docks. The appellee seasonably elected to deliver 50,000 pockets at Lake Charles and on Decem-

a. A letter of credit is a binding undertaking by a bank that is used in the following manner. Seller in Neartown and Buyer in Farville agree upon the sale of goods, but Seller is reluctant to rely upon the promise of a distant merchant. If Buyer should fail to pay after the shipment had reached Farville, Seller might sustain a substantial loss, even though he might still have the right to the goods. This would be particularly true if they were not readily resaleable or if the market price should drop so that their resale would bring little. Furthermore, suit against a buyer on his home ground is not an attractive possibility for a seller. These difficulties for a seller are of course compounded in international trade, to which letters of credit are an indispensable adjunct.

Seller may, therefore, require Buyer to obtain a letter of credit from a Farville bank. The bank, by issuing its letter of credit at Buyer's request, undertakes with Seller that it will pay against Seller's orders in an amount equal to the purchase price, on condition that the orders, known as "drafts" or "bills of exchange," are accompanied by documents affording control over the goods. The documents specified are commonly bills of lading, issued by a carrier. Less commonly they may be documents of other sorts, such as the dock receipts in the present case, that also carry with them power over the goods. When Seller ships the goods, it forwards to the Farville bank its draft together with the specified document covering the goods. The bank then pays the draft and takes up the document. As soon as Buyer reimburses the bank, he may have the document and use it to obtain the goods from the carrier.

ber 10 it received from the appellant instructions for the Lake Charles shipments. Thereupon it promptly began shipments to Lake Charles which continued until December 23, the last car at Lake Charles being unloaded on December 31. December 17 was the last date in December which would allow appellee the two week period provided in the contract for delivery of the rice to the ports and ships designated. Prior thereto, the appellant had been having difficulty obtaining either a ship or a dock in this busy season in Houston. On December 17, the appellee had still received no shipping instructions for the 45,600 pockets destined for Houston. On the morning of the 18th, the appellee rescinded the contract for the Houston shipments, although continuing to make the Lake Charles deliveries. It is clear that one of the reasons for the prompt cancellation of the contract was the rise in market price of rice from $8.25 per pocket, the contract price, to $9.75. The appellant brought this suit for refusal to deliver the Houston quota.

The trial court, in a reasoned but unreported opinion which dealt with all phases of the case, held that New York would apply Texas law. Auten v. Auten, 308 N.Y. 155, 124 N.E.2d 99, 50 A.L.R.2d 246. We think this ruling right, but will not discuss the point because it is conceded that no different result would follow from the choice of Louisiana law.

The area of contest is also considerably reduced by the appellant's candid concession that the appellee's duty to ship, by virtue of the two-week notice provision, did not arise until two weeks after complete shipping instructions had been given by the appellant. Thus on brief the appellant says: "[w]e concede (as we have done from the beginning) that on a fair interpretation of the contract appellant had a duty to instruct appellee by December 17, 1952 as to the place to which it desired appellee to ship—at both ports, and that, being late with its instructions in this respect, appellant could not have demanded delivery (at either port) until sometime after December 31, 1952." This position was taken, of course, with a view to the contract provision for shipment "December, 1952": a two-week period ending December 31 would begin to run on December 17. But although appellant concedes that the two weeks' notice to which appellee was entitled could not be shortened by the failure to give shipping instructions on or before December 17, it stoutly insists that upon receipt of shipping instructions subsequent to December 17 the appellee thereupon became obligated to deliver within two weeks thereafter. We do not agree.

It is plain that a giving of the notice by the appellant was a condition precedent to the appellee's duty to ship. Corbin on Contracts, Vol. 3, § 640. Id. § 724. Obviously, the appellee could not deliver free alongside ship, as the contract required, until the appellant identified its ship and its location. Jacksboro Stone Co. v. Fairbanks Co., 48 Tex.Civ.App. 639, 107 S.W. 567; Fortson Grocery Co. v. Pritchard

Rice Milling Co., Tex.Civ.App., 220 S.W. 1116. Thus the giving of shipping instructions was what Professor Corbin would classify as a "promissory condition": the appellant promised to give the notice and the appellee's duty to ship was conditioned on the receipt of the notice. Op. cit. § 633, p. 523, § 634, footnote 38. The crucial question is whether that condition was performed. And that depends on whether the appellee's duty of shipment was conditioned on notice *on or before December 17,* so that the appellee would have two weeks wholly within December within which to perform, or whether, as we understand the appellant to contend, the appellant could perform the condition by giving the notice later in December, in which case the appellee would be under a duty to ship within two weeks thereafter. The answer depends upon the proper interpretation of the contract: if the contract properly interpreted made shipment *in December* of the essence then the failure to give the notice on or before December 17 was nonperformance by the appellant of a condition upon which the appellee's duty to ship in December depended.

In the setting of this case, we hold that the provision for December delivery went to the essence of the contract. In support of the plainly stated provision of the contract there was evidence that the appellee's mills and the facilities appurtenant thereto were working at full capacity in December when the rice market was at peak activity and that appellee had numerous other contracts in January as well as in December to fill. It is reasonable to infer that in July, when the contract was made, each party wanted the protection of the specified delivery period; the appellee so that it could schedule its production without undue congestion of its storage facilities and the appellant so that it could surely meet commitments which it in turn should make to its customers. There was also evidence that prices on the rice market were fluctuating. In view of this factor it is not reasonable to infer that when the contract was made in July for December delivery, the parties intended that the appellant should have an option exercisable subsequent to December 17 to postpone delivery until January. United Irr. Co. v. Carson Petroleum Co., Tex.Civ. App., 283 S.W. 692; Steiner v. United States, D.C., 36 F.Supp. 496. That in effect would have given the appellant an option to postpone its breach of the contract, if one should then be in prospect, to a time when, so far as could have been foreseen when the contract was made, the price of rice might be falling. A postponement in such circumstances would inure to the disadvantage of the appellee who was given no reciprocal option. Further indication that December delivery was of the essence is found in the letter of credit which was provided for in the contract and established by the appellant. Under this letter, the bank was authorized to pay appellee only for deliveries "during December, 1952." It thus appears that the appellant's interpretation of the contract, under which the appellee would be obligated, upon receipt of shipping instructions subsequent to December 17, to deliver in January, would deprive the appellee of the security for payment of the purchase price for which it had contracted.[b]

Since, as we hold, December delivery was of the essence, notice of shipping instructions *on or before December 17* was not merely a "duty" of the appellant—as it concedes: it was a condition precedent to the performance which might be required of the appellee. The non-occurrence of that condition entitled the appellee to rescind or to treat its contractual obligations as discharged. Corbin on Contracts, §§ 640, 724 and 1252; Williston on Sales, §§ 452, 457; Restatement, Contracts, § 262; . . . On December 18th the appellant unequivocally exercised its right to rescind. Having done so, its obligations as to the Houston deliveries under the contract were at an end. And of course its obligations would not revive thereafter when the appellant finally succeeded in obtaining an export permit, a ship and a dock and then gave shipping instructions; when it expressed willingness to accept deliveries in January; or when it accomplished a "liberalization" of the outstanding letter of credit whereby payments might be made against simple forwarder's receipts instead of dock receipts.[1]

The appellant urges that by reason of substantial part performance on its part prior to December 17th, it may not be held to have been in default for its failure sooner to give shipping instructions. The contention has no basis on the facts. As to the Houston shipments the appellant's activities prior to December 17th were not in performance of its contract: they were merely preparatory to its expectation to perform at a later time. The mere establishment of the letter of credit was not an act of performance: it was merely an arrangement made by the appellant for future performance which as to the Houston deliveries because of appellant's failure to give shipping instructions were never made. From these preparatory activities the appellee had no benefit whatever.

The appellant also maintains that the contract was single and "indivisible" and that consequently appellee's continuing shipments to Lake Charles after December 17 constituted an election to reaffirm its total obligation under the contract. This position also, we hold untenable. Under the contract, the appellee concededly had an option to split the deliveries betwixt Lake Charles and Houston. The price had been fixed on a per pocket basis, and payment, under the letter of credit, was to be made upon the presentation of dock receipts which normally would be issued both at Lake Charles or Houston at different times. The fact that there was a world market for rice and that in December the market price substantially exceeded the contract

b. For critical comment on this passage, see Childres, Conditions in the Law of Contracts, 45 N.Y.U.L.Rev. 33, 56–57 (1970).

1. The appellee was not informed that the letter of credit had "liberalized" until after it had rescinded. Moreover, even the liberalized letter did not call for payment of deliveries not made until January.

price suggests that it would be more to the appellants' advantage to obtain the Lake Charles delivery than to obtain no delivery at all. The same considerations suggest that by continuing with the Lake Charles delivery the appellee did not deliberately intend to waive its right to cancel the Houston deliveries. Conclusions to the contrary would be so greatly against self-interest as to be completely unrealistic. The only reasonable inference from the totality of the facts is that the duties of the parties as to the Lake Charles shipment were not at all dependent on the Houston shipments. We conclude their duties as to shipments at each port were paired and reciprocal and that performance by the parties as to Lake Charles did not preclude the appellee's right of cancellation as to Houston. Cf. Corbin on Contracts §§ 688, 695; Simms-Wylie Co. v. City of Ranger, Tex.Civ. App., 224 S.W.2d 265.

Finally, we hold that the appellant's claims of estoppel and waiver have no basis in fact or in law.

Affirmed.

NOTES

(1) *The Uses of Divisibility.* What was the significance in this decision of the finding of divisibility? Would the rice seller have been *justified* in withholding further shipments to Lake Charles after December 17th? If the seller had done so, how would you compare the merits of the buyer's claim with that presented in Gill v. Johnstown Lumber Co., p. 826 supra?

As the Gill case shows, the notion of divisibility of contract sometimes serves to mitigate the rigorous effects that might otherwise follow from the doctrine of constructive conditions. Refer again to Shapiro Engineering Corporation v. Francis O. Day Co., Note 3, p. 590 supra. In that case the question was whether or not damages for a breach of contract must be calculated with reference to the whole performance called for. Corbin lists fourteen questions which have been answered by reference to the distinction between entirety and divisibility, concluding that they cannot be answered by "the application of some simple and uniform test." Section 695. See also Karpinski v. Ingrasci, p. 536 supra; United States v. Clementon Sewerage Authority, 365 F.2d 609 (3d Cir. 1966). As to a right to arbitration reinforced by divisibility, see Prima Paint Corp. v. Flood & Conklin Mfg. Co., 388 U.S. 395 (1967).

(2) *A Corn Case.* In July 1973 Chester Brandau, a corn grower, stopped making deliveries as contracted for with an elevator, the Nora Springs Co-op Co. (Co-op), and thereupon began delivering his corn to another elevator company. By various agreements he had made with Co-op the corn he delivered to it should have been received before the preceding February; and the corn he delivered elsewhere was due by the end of July. All through the first part of the year Co-op's manager, Arndt, resisted and postponed deliveries, pleading a shortage of railroad cars for shipping it out. The delays caused "blue-eye damage" to Brandau's corn. When Arndt learned of the deliveries elsewhere he telephoned Brandau to say he could then take more grain; to which Brandau answered that he was through

hauling corn to Co-op. Co-op sued Brandau for damages, and appealed from an adverse judgment. *Held:* Affirmed. Nora Springs Co-op Co. v. Brandau, 247 N.W.2d 744 (Iowa, 1976).

Co-op argued that its breach of the contract was too insubstantial to warrant cancellation by Brandau. The court referred to UCC 2–106(4) and 2–703(f) and observed: "Nothing is mentioned about *materiality* of the breach . . . ." Quoting UCC 1–106, the court added: "we might very well hold that materiality need not be shown to warrant cancellation of the corn contracts.

"However, even if, arguendo, materiality is a requirement for cancellation under the theory that the general principles of law merchant supplement the specific provisions of the Uniform Commercial Code [§ 1–103], plaintiff's contention is still unconvincing."

(3) *A Popcorn Case.* Baker, a dealer in popcorn, contracted to buy the 1974 crop grown by Ratzlaff, to give orders for delivery from time to time, and to pay upon delivery. Baker was to order the final delivery by the end of September. In the first week of February Ratzlaff made two deliveries as ordered and received weight tickets from Baker's plant manager. Two phone calls about further deliveries followed soon after. On February 11 Ratzlaff sent Baker notice of termination for the failure to pay on delivery. Ratzlaff then sold the remainder of his crop to another buyer for the going price: $8 a hundredweight. Baker's contract price was $4.75. By the end of September the market price was $14.

In the case from which these facts are taken—with some adaptation—the question chiefly presented grew out of the trial court's ruling that Ratzlaff terminated the contract on a technical pretense and so violated his duty to deal with Baker in good faith. The contract contained a provision, inserted at Ratzlaff's request, that "if Baker, for any reason, fails to pay Grower at the time of delivery, then the undelivered popcorn shall, at Grower's option, be released for Grower to dispose of as he sees fit." Further findings were that Baker's plant manager periodically sent weight tickets to his disbursing office in batches, that Ratzlaff could conveniently have stopped there on his delivery route, that any request for payment would have been promptly handled, and that Ratzlaff did not mention payment at any time between his first delivery and his termination, nine days later. A judgment in favor of Baker as plaintiff for $52,000 was affirmed on appeal. Baker v. Ratzlaff, 1 Kan.App.2d 285, 564 P.2d 153 (1977). *Question:* In support of the judgment might the court have used any of the principles expressed in Wasserburger v. American Scientific Chemical, Inc., p. 787 supra?

On these facts, if the buyer is found to have broken the contract, the damages might be determined to be either (a) $52,000 or (b) $148,000, since the quantity in question was 1,600,000 pounds. (Some uncertainty in the law prevails, owing to different interpretations of UCC 2–713. This matter is presented in Reliance Cooperage Corp. v. Treat, p. 931 infra, and the notes thereafter.)

CONTINENTAL GRAIN CO. v. SIMPSON FEED CO., INC.

United States District Court, E. D. Arkansas, 1951.
102 F.Supp. 354.
Affirmed 199 F.2d 284 (8th Cir. 1952).

Action by the Continental Grain Company against the Simpson Feed Company, Inc., for breach of a contract for the sale of soybeans wherein defendant filed a cross complaint. On motion of plaintiff for a judgment in accordance with its motion for a directed verdict. . . .

Judgment for plaintiff in accordance with the opinion.

LEMLEY, District Judge. [The price of soybeans rose steadily from September 14, 1950, to November 30. On September 14 Continental contracted to buy 10,000 bushels (about 5 carloads) of soybeans from Simpson. Delivery was to be made at any time Simpson named during October or November. As the beans were loaded, Continental was to furnish shipping instructions.

One car was shipped on October 30. Another car was loaded the following day, and Simpson called for shipping instructions. Continental did not give them until November 2, about 48 hours later. (Its testimony indicates trouble getting "clearance" from New Orleans, where it intended to send the beans for export.) Meanwhile, Simpson was under pressure from the railroad to move the car or unload it, and had billed the car to another customer. When the instructions were received, Simpson informed Continental that no more beans would be shipped under the contract.

On December 1, Continental bought four carloads of beans from another supplier, and later brought an action for the difference between the contract price and what it paid. The case was tried to a jury, which was unable to agree on a verdict. Continental moved for a judgment in its favor. The court assumed that the delay in furnishing shipping instructions was a breach of contract, and proceeded to discuss the question of materiality.]

The question of the materiality of a breach of the contract under the sections of the Uniform Sales Act just cited [45(2) and 65] is ordinarily one of fact for the jury, but where the facts are undisputed with respect to the breach, the question becomes one of law for the Court. 46 Am.Jur., "Sales", Section 270; 3 Williston on Contracts, Section 866; Helgar Corporation v. Warner Features, Inc. [222 N.Y. 449, 119 N.E. 113] . . .

In determining whether or not a breach on the part of a buyer, with respect to one installment of a contract for the sale of goods to be delivered and paid for in installments, is so material as to justify the seller in refusing to perform further, numerous factors are to be considered. In the Helgar case, supra, the Court was concerned with whether or not a failure on the part of the buyer to pay for certain installments within the time fixed by the contract for such payments justified the seller in refusing to make further deliveries; and the Court said: "The vendor who fails to receive payment of an installment the very day that it is due may sue at once for the price. But it does not follow that he may be equally precipitate in his election to declare the contract at an end. (Citing cases.) That depends upon the question whether the default is so substantial and important as in truth and in fairness to defeat the essential purpose of the parties. Whatever the rule may once have been, this is the test that is now prescribed by statute. The failure to make punctual payment may be material or trivial according to the circumstances. We must know the cause of the default, the length of the delay, the needs of the vendor, and the expectations of the vendee. If the default is the result of accident or misfortune, if there is a reasonable assurance that it will be promptly repaired, and if immediate payment is not necessary to enable the vendor to proceed with performance, there may be one conclusion. If the breach is willful, if there is no just ground to look for prompt reparation, if the delay has been substantial, or if the needs of the vendor are urgent so that timely performance is imperiled, in these and in other circumstances, there may be another conclusion. Sometimes the conclusion will follow from all the circumstances as an inference of law to be drawn by the judge; sometimes, as an inference of fact to be drawn by the jury."

[The court referred to First Restatement, § 275,[a] and then concluded "as a matter of law" that the breach was insubstantial; that "neither party was in a particular hurry;" and that Simpson "simply seized upon what was at most an inconsequential breach" as an excuse for release from a disadvantageous contract.]

NOTES

(1) *Question.* What decision in each of the two foregoing cases under the Code? The following sections might be relevant, among others: UCC 2–311(3)(b), 2–319(2), (3), 2–612(3), 2–703(f).

(2) *How to Assert Rights Upon Breach by the Other Party.* There is some hazard for a party complaining of a breach in saying that he elects to rescind the contract. Do you see what it is? See Plunkett v. Comstock-Cheney Co., 211 App.Div. 737, 208 N.Y.S. 93 (1st Dept. 1925). Compare such an announcement with what was said by the injured sellers in the rice case and the bean case. For obvious reasons it is better to announce a *default* than to announce a *rescission.* But see UCC 2–720. The meaning of rescission is discussed in Corbin, §§ 1236–1237.

Would any case appearing so far in this Section have been affected by UCC 2–309(3)?

(3) *When Time is of the Essence.* Whether or not a delay of performance on one side will excuse performance on the other depends largely on

a. As to the provisions of the section, see Walker & Co. v. Harrison, p. 816 supra.

the nature of the contract, and on the seriousness of the consequences of the delay. See Restatement Second, § 242. The matter is treated in Corbin, §§ 713–23; Williston, §§ 845–55; and see Stoljar, Untimely Performance in the Law of Contract, 71 Law Q.Rev. 527 (1955). "Courts of equity have treated stipulations as to time as subsidiary and of comparatively little importance, unless either the language of the parties or the nature of the case imperatively indicated that the date of performance was vital. In courts of common law, however, and especially in mercantile contracts, it is held that time is of the essence of the contract." Williston, § 845. The reference to equity has special application to land sale contracts, specific performance of which may be granted, to prevent injustice, in spite of "considerable delay" on the part of the plaintiff, either buyer or seller, in tendering his own performance. Restatement Second, § 242, Comment c.[b] General statements that "time is of the essence," even in reference to mercantile contracts, and even when so provided in the agreement, need not be taken at face value. See Fairchild Stratos Corp. v. Lear Siegler, Inc., 337 F.2d 785 (4th Cir. 1964). "By the blind eye of the common law, it would seem, 'time' is read as a master word in the contract jungle, absolute and uncompromising in its significance and power. It can be asserted with confidence that never were the common law judges so blind as this. . . . [T]here is no absolute and universal rule." Corbin, § 713. There are statutes in some states providing that time is not of the essence unless the contract expressly makes it so. They have been denied application to option contracts. Williston, § 855.

BUYERS' REMEDIES: FAIRNESS AND EFFICIENCY

The case to follow concerns a buyer's attempt under UCC 2–608 to revoke his acceptance of toys he had contracted for. ("Acceptance" of goods tendered usually occurs upon receipt of the goods or not long thereafter: UCC 2–606. Acceptance precludes rejection: 2–607(2).) It is requisite to revocation that the nonconformity of the unit accepted "substantially impairs its value to him"—the buyer. In this respect the remedy is to be contrasted with the buyer's right (subject to important qualifications) to reject goods when tendered if they "fail in any respect to conform to the contract." UCC 2–601. Under this rule, the seller's tender must be perfect, so to speak.

Consider the case of a gelding sold at auction as a colt. Presumably the buyer is entitled to reject the horse if he detects the "nonconformity" before his acceptance of it occurs; no question could arise about what he intended to do with it. But what if he detects the nonconformity after receipt, yet still in time to revoke acceptance? If he means to race the horse, and not to use it for breeding, should he be permitted to revoke? And what if he means to use it for breeding, but the seller has no reason to know that? What an-

b. See also Stefanowicz Corp. v. Harris, 36 Md.App. 136, 373 A.2d 54 (1977); Tanenbaum v. Sears, Roebuck & Co., —— Pa.Super. ——, 401 A.2d 809 (1979) (on abrogating the distinction between law and equity).

swers are suggested by UCC 2–608?[a] The phrase "value to him" may import a measure of subjectivity in extending or limiting the remedy authorized there. One critic of the Code applauds that element: she would be sorry if it were to "invoke . . . that mythical character, the good faith objective observer, as the reference for injury" in this context. Peters, Remedies for Breach of Contracts Relating to the Sale of Goods Under the UCC, 73 Yale L.J. 199, 225 (1963). But another critic, while believing that the test is largely objective, regrets that it indulges the buyer's "subjective" requirements in any degree: to do so impairs the reliability of sale contracts. Priest, Breach and Remedy for the Tender of Nonconforming Goods Under the UCC, 91 Harv.L.Rev. 960, 978–79 (1978).

As a legislative matter, what grounds are there for choosing between a perfect-tender rule and one less stringent? Consider the case of a feigned objection to goods: either they are not defective or they are defective in a way that does not matter to the buyer. Sometimes it is apparent that a buyer is moved to reject goods not because they are nonconforming, but because of a drop in the market.[b] Compare the buyer's invocation of the "mirror image" rule, discussed at p. 281 supra. Under the perfect-tender rule, a defect may require the seller to incur the expenses involved in retrieving and reselling the goods for no reason except the buyer's regret over the bargain. Apart from any question of fairness, this inefficiency is a drawback of the rule. The usual costs of resolving a dispute would presumably be heavier under a more flexible rule; but it may be, as some surmise, that under such a rule fewer instances of feigned objections and subterfuge would arise.

Professor Peters predicted that few situations in modern commercial transactions would be governed by the rule, owing to various Code limitations on a buyer's right to reject.[c] Her prediction has been borne out, it seems. But the appellate courts, at least, have applied the rule forthrightly in the apposite cases.

Is it possible, from what has been said, to pass judgment on the wisdom of the Code standards in question?

NOTES

(1) *The Shoemaker's Last.* In Moulton Cavity & Mold, Inc. v. Lyn-Flex Industries, Inc., 396 A.2d 1024 (Me.1979), a maker of molds for shoe

a. For a pair of horse-sale cases concerning the timeliness of revocation of acceptance, see Miron v. Yonkers Raceway, Inc., 400 F.2d 112 (2d Cir. 1968); Brodsky v. Nerud, 25 UCC Rep. 1266 (N.Y.App.Div. 2d Dept. 1979). Compare Greenberg v. Resnick, 29 UCC Rep. 1270 (N.Y.Sup.Ct. Kings Co., 1979).

b. Compare Fulwiler v. Beddoe, p. 945 infra; Center Garment Co., Inc. v. United Refrigerator Co., 369 Mass. 633, 341 N.E.2d 669 (1976) ("The record suggests that the plaintiff may have seized the chance for terminating the contract with some enthusiasm . . . ; but . . . we are not at liberty to analyze possible ulterior motives.").

c. Peters, as cited in the text, at 209.

soles sued for the contract price of molds it had prepared at a manufacturer's order, less adjustments for acknowledged defects. The buyer had rejected them. (According to the plaintiff's evidence it should have been given an opportunity to cure the defects.) In charging the jury the trial court said:

> Ladies and gentlemen, in considering whether the contract has been performed there is a doctrine that you should be aware of. That is the doctrine of substantial performance. It is not required that performance be in any case one hundred percent complete in order to entitle a party to enforcement of their contractual rights. Probably if we took any contract you could always find something of no substance that was not so complete. It is for you to determine what in fact constitutes substantial performance.[d]

From a judgment for the plaintiff, the defendant appealed. *Held:* Reversed. Speaking of UCC 2–601, the court observed that the section rejects the views of Professor Llewellyn—"recognized as the primum mobile of the Code's tender provisions."

(2) *Questions.* How would you arrange the remedies of a buyer—cancellation, damages, revocation of acceptance, and so on—with a view to maximizing the salvage value of defective goods? Would you accept it "as a matter of law" that, in a car sold for $5,700 as new some small dents and paint overspray, repairable for $100 or less, do not "substantially impair" its value? See Freeman Oldsmobile Mazda Co. v. Pinson, 580 S.W.2d 112 (Tex. Civ.App.1979), writ ref. n. r. e.[e] Would you differentiate between a manufacturer's purchase of equipment (e. g., molds for shoe soles) and a dealer's purchase of crops (e. g., off-grade cotton sold by a farmer)? For an evaluation of the courts' performance from this viewpoint see Priest, op. cit. supra. Consider a consumer's purchase of a defective car: when does it become "efficient" to limit his remedy to damages? See UCC 2–608(2), and compare UCC 2–607(3)(a).

HAYS MERCHANDISE, INC. v. DEWEY

Supreme Court of Washington, 1970.
78 Wash.2d 343, 474 P.2d 270.

FINLEY, Associate Justice. This is an appeal from a judgment for the sale price of a number of toys delivered by the Hays Merchandise, Inc., to the appellants Dewey.

d. Instructions edited in detail.

e. See C. Reitz, Consumer Protection Under the Magnuson-Moss Warranty Act 74–75 (1978): revocation of acceptance is "part of a remedy so powerful that even a credible threat to revoke acceptance can be a strong bargaining tool toward achieving satisfactory settlement of a buyer's grievance." As to UCC 2–608(2) Professor Reitz puts the case of a new car in which a fairly serious defect is discovered after six months of use. "Although the 'condition' of the car may not have changed very much in a physical sense as yet, its value on the marketplace will already have declined appreciably. Since it is now a second-hand car, even without a defect its market value will be substantially below the market price of a new car."

Mr. Dewey operated Dewey's Fuller Paint Store in Bremerton, Washington. In the autumn of 1967, he decided to establish and stock a "Toyland" in his store for Christmas trade. Pursuant to this plan, he and his wife and children visited Hays Merchandise, a wholesale toy company, in Seattle. Mr. Woodring, an employee of Hays, met Mr. Dewey and his family at the company's display rooms, where they together selected toys. Almost all of the toys selected at that time were stuffed animals; Mr. Dewey was apparently particularly interested in having a good stock of stuffed or "plush" animals. Mr. Dewey and Mr. Woodring then discussed the purchase of other toy items which Mr. Woodring was to select. It was agreed that the estimated cost for all of the toys, including the stuffed animals, would be approximately $2,500.00 to $3,500.00.

Several shipments of toys were sent to Dewey's Fuller Paint Store during October and November. The number of stuffed animals included in these shipments fell well below the expectations of the Deweys. Indeed, although the question was disputed at trial, the trial court found that less than half of the stuffed animals anticipated by the Deweys were in fact delivered. The purchase price of the animals ordered was found to be a sum not exceeding $500.00. There is substantial evidence in the record to support this finding and it will not be disturbed on appeal.

Mr. Dewey repeatedly called Hays Merchandise, complaining that they were not receiving all of the stuffed animals ordered. He also complained personally to Mr. Woodring on the two occasions that autumn and winter when Mr. Woodring made periodic sales visits to the store. Mr. Dewey was assured each time that the items in question had been "back ordered," and would be forthcoming. Finally, shortly before December 1, Mr. Dewey called Mr. Woodring about the stuffed-animal order. Mr. Woodring gave approximately the same reply, at which point an exasperated Mr. Dewey said that they wanted no more toys.

Apparently this call was too late to stop another shipment of toys which arrived several days thereafter. Mr. Dewey was advised by Mr. Woodring that there would be no problem with this one late unopened shipment which should be sent back. Mr. Dewey kept this shipment, along with a number of other unopened and unmarked boxes of toys. Other toys were priced and put on display for sale.

Several months later, another Hays salesman, Mr. Osterholt, visited the Dewey's store. (Mr. Woodring had been away from work for some time because of illness.) According to the unchallenged finding of fact of the trial court, Mr. Dewey advised Mr. Osterholt that they had authority from Hays Merchandise to return a considerable quantity of unmarked toys, amounting to a value of almost $2,000.00. Mr. Dewey then shipped these toys to Seattle, whereupon Hays Merchandise refused the shipment, and it was returned to Mr. Dewey.

Hays had earlier billed Dewey for $3,598.11, the amount outstanding on the account. When no payment was forthcoming this action was commenced. After trial, judgment was rendered for $3,436.36. The difference in the two sums reflects a minor accounting error by Hays and the freight charges for the shipment of the toys back to Seattle and thence back again to Bremerton. In addition, the judgment provides for an additional $299.98 credit upon the return of the one shipment received after the cancellation. The Deweys appeal from that judgment.

All of the transactions involved took place after the effective date of the Uniform Commercial Code in Washington and, hence, are governed by the provisions of RCW 62A. The trial court held that the delivery of less than one half of the stuffed animals was not a "material breach" of the sales contract. Appellant Dewey contends that this finding is in error. His contention is based largely upon RCW 62A.2–608, which provides as follows: [Here the court set out UCC 2–608.]

There is no question but that Dewey accepted the toys in question. The issue before this court is whether there was an effective revocation of acceptance. This, in turn, is dependent upon (1) whether the nonconformity substantially impaired the value of the total order to Dewey, and (2) whether notice of the revocation took place within a reasonable time.

Appellant presents an ingenious argument on the first of the above questions. He argues that he would have been entitled to initially reject the toys if they failed "in any respect to conform to the contract . . . ." RCW 62A.2–601. He chose not to reject the toys, but rather reasonably assumed "that its non-conformity would be cured . . . ." RCW 62A.2–608. Since the nonconformity was not seasonably cured, he argues that he should be entitled to revoke acceptance on, generally, the same basis for which he could have rejected the toys. Consequently, he contends that the emphasis in RCW 62A.2–608 is properly upon "impairs its value *to him*" rather than upon "*substantially* impairs." In short, appellant would have this court adopt a largely subjective test; i. e., Did the buyer *believe* that the value was substantially impaired?

The question is one of first impression in this court. Indeed, few, if any, appellate courts have considered this precise issue under UCC § 2–608.

Appellant's argument, based upon the need for a logical consistency between RCW 62A.2–608 and RCW 62A.2–601, is not persuasive. We are convicted [sic] that the emphasis is properly upon "substantially impairs . . . value" rather than upon ". . . impairs its value to him." This does not mean that "substantial impairment" is to be determined without reference to the objective needs and expectations of the buyer. See RCWA 62A.2–608, Official

Comment 2.[a] But it is an objective factual determination of the buyer's particular circumstances rather than some unarticulated desires.

The question of whether or not there is such a substantial impairment is a factual determination to be made by the trial court. This is in accord with the result of most of the few cases which have considered the interpretation of UCC § 2–608. See, e. g., Campbell v. Pollack, 101 R.I. 223, 221 A.2d 615 (1966) (evidence warranted trial court finding that omission of key equipment in sale of car-wash was substantial impairment); Rozmus v. Thompson's Lincoln-Mercury Co., 209 Pa.Super. 120, 224 A.2d 782 (1966) (remanded for factual finding by trial court as to whether defect in car was substantial impairment); L. & N. Sales Co. v. Stuski, 188 Pa.Super. 117, 146 A.2d 154 (1958) (case remanded to allow jury determination of factual question of whether defect in beverage dispensers was substantial impairment). But see Lanners v. Whitney, 247 Or. 223, 428 P.2d 398 (1967) (Supreme Court made factual finding of substantial impairment after required de novo review of record in suit in equity).

There are some similarities between the contract in the instant case and a contract which could be clearly described as an installment contract. For example, the trial court found that multiple lot deliveries were contemplated by the parties; and, delivery was in fact made in multiple installments. It is of some passing interest in this connection, by analogy, that RCW 62A.2–612, governing procedures applicable in the event of breach of an installment contract, uses similar language. Under that section, when delivery in separate lots is authorized, to be separately accepted, a nonconforming lot may be rejected only "if the non-conformity *substantially impairs the value* of that installment . . . ." As noted by Wash.L.Rev., The Uniform Commercial Code in Washington 156 (1967), "This differs from the approach taken in non-installment contracts wherein the buyer may reject 'for any reason.'" The phrase, "substantially impairs . . . value," is also used in RCW 62A.2–616; it obviously is a term chosen with care.

We are convinced that the question of "substantial impairment of value to [the buyer]" is best determined as a factual question by the trial court based upon all objective evidence properly before that court. In the instant case, the trial court's finding that there was no "material breach," while perhaps inartfully phrased, is in essence a finding that there was no substantial impairment. Our general rule is that findings of fact must be accepted as verities unless there is no substantial evidence in the record to support them. Friedlander v.

a. "Revocation of acceptance is possible only where the non-conformity substantially impairs the value of the goods to the buyer. For this purpose the test is not what the seller had reason to know at the time of contracting; the question is whether the non-conformity is such as will in fact cause a substantial impairment of value to the buyer though the seller had no advance knowledge as to the buyer's particular circumstances."

Friedlander, 58 Wash.2d 288, 362 P.2d 352 (1961). Appellant has not presented any considerations in the instant case which would lead this court to depart from that rule.

There remains the question of whether the notice of revocation was given within a reasonable time. Under the code, there is a distinction between notice of breach (RCW 62A.2–607(3)) and notice of revocation of acceptance (RCW 62A.2–608(2)). There is no question but that there was adequate and timely notice of breach. That, however, is not the question before this court. The notice of revocation of acceptance need not be in any particular form, but it must at least inform the seller that the buyer does not want the goods and does not desire to retain them. With the exception of the last small lot, there is no indication that the Deweys gave this notice prior to mid-February, when they attempted to return the unmarked and unsold toys. Indeed, the Deweys advertised the "Toyland" and attempted to sell the toys during December. It was not until a considerable time after Christmas that they attempted to return the toys. In view of the seasonal nature of the toy business and the somewhat faddish demand for certain toys, this delay in giving notice was unreasonable.

Even if the notice of revocation had been given in early December and if this were considered timely, the buyer's subsequent acts of dominion over the goods are inconsistent with such claimed revocation. The buyer's acts of pricing, displaying, advertising and selling were for his own account and were not in keeping with his duty to use reasonable care in holding the goods at the seller's disposition for a reasonable time. See RCW 62A.2–606(1)(c); Holland Furnace Co. v. Korth, 43 Wash.2d 618, 262 P.2d 772, 41 A.L.R.2d 1166 (1953).

The judgment of the trial court is affirmed.

NOTES

(1) *Question.* The court's remark, in the final paragraph, about Dewey's "acts of dominion over the goods" has been questioned: "no such limit on the right to revoke is present in the Code." Priest, Breach and Remedy for the Tender of Nonconforming Goods Under the UCC, 91 Harv.L.Rev. 960, 992 (1978). If not present there, might it be found among the principles of law and equity that are to "supplement" its provisions (UCC 1–103)? If such a principle could be identified, do the particular provisions of section 2–608 rule it out of consideration under the "displacement" idea of 1–103? See section 2–606(1)(c).

(2) *Waiver?* Would Dewey have been permitted to show, in the defense of this action, or as a ground for damages, that the toys were not of contract quality, not having mentioned that point before?

If a buyer *rejects* goods he will be well advised to use caution in stating the reason for doing so. If he states that the goods are not of merchantable quality, for example, it may not be open to him to take the position in litigation that they were not properly packaged. In a famous and controversial case it was said: "The principle is plain, and needs no argument in support of it, that if a particular objection is taken to the performance and the party is silent as to all others, they are deemed to be waived." Littlejohn v. Shaw, 159 N.Y. 188, 53 N.E. 810 (1899); see Eno, Price Movement and Unstated Objections, 44 Yale L.J. 782 (1935).

Consult UCC 2–605; cf. UCC 2–508. What is an example of a case that would be decided one way under these rules and another under the "plain principle" of Littlejohn v. Shaw?

(3) *Timely Notice.* What, if anything, was to prevent Dewey from making a counterclaim for damages arising from Hays' failure to supply as many stuffed animals as the contract called for? See UCC 2–714. Dewey gave timely notice of breach, the court says.

Notice the drastic consequence of a failure to give such notice: UCC 2–607(3)(a). By contrast, in the event of a serious default by a *buyer*, there is little incentive under the Code for the seller to give any notice of his intentions. (See UCC 2–703, 2–706(3); cf. 2–609.) How might this difference be explained? Consider the position of a Seattle seller with respect to toys in Bremerton (or farther away) when a controversy arises shortly before Christmas.

(4) *Installment Contracts.* The court's reference to UCC 2–612 for an analogy may raise more questions than it answers. Why was not the toy sale contract an "installment contract" in the strict sense of that section? Do you agree with the following comment on the section?—"[It is] a law professor's delight . . . [It] guarantees at least two class hours of wandering through a maze of inconsistent statutory standards and elliptical cross references." Peters, Remedies for Breach of Contracts Relating to the Sale of Goods Under the UCC, 73 Yale L.J. 199, 227 (1963).

Professor (now Justice) Peters comments on the absence of "to him" in UCC 2–612, and she seems to hope that it will be read in. As you understand the main case, does it read the words "to him" *out* of 2–608?

Regarding the toy sale contract as an "installment contract," does it seem that the deficiency of stuffed animals did not substantially impair the value of the whole contract, but would have permitted Dewey to demand an assurance of "cure" under UCC 2–612(2)? (See UCC 2–508.) On that situation Professor Peters said: "But if 'assurances of cure' do not mature into a realization of cure, what then? After the expiration of a reasonable —or unreasonable—period of time, the buyer should be entitled to a belated revocation of his acceptance, as 2–608(1) indicates, which would eventually put him into the same position as to remedies as if he had initially been permitted to reject. In the interim, pending the actual tender of cure, the buyer may invoke the powers given him under 2–609 to suspend his own performance." Id. at 226–27. How can this be squared with UCC 2–608(2): "Revocation of acceptance must occur within a reasonable time after the buyer discovers . . . the ground for it . . . ."?

(5) *Problem.* Seller contracts to supply a quantity of stuffed animals for Buyer's Christmas trade, for $5,000. Ten days before Christmas Seller telephones Buyer to apologize for not shipping the goods earlier, and he adds, "I can ship them today if you still want them." Buyer answers: "Your delay has cost me $2,000. I am going to pay you $3,000 for the goods, and you had better ship them at once." If the buyer is right about his damages, must the seller comply with his demand? See UCC 2–717. If the Code supports the demand, does it open up the possibility of overreaching by buyers?

RELIANCE COOPERAGE CORP. v. TREAT

United States Court of Appeals, Eighth Circuit, 1952.
195 F.2d 977.

Action by Reliance Cooperage Corp. against A. R. Treat for damages for breach of executory contract for sale of goods. The United States District Court for the Western District of Arkansas, John E. Miller, J., entered judgment on verdict of $500 for plaintiff, and plaintiff appealed. . . .

Reversed, and case remanded with directions to grant new trial limited to issue of amount of damages.

SANBORN, Circuit Judge. The question for decision is whether the measure of the general damages recoverable by a purchaser for the nonperformance by a seller of an executory contract for the sale of goods is changed or affected by an unaccepted anticipatory repudiation of the contract by the seller.

[Plaintiff, Reliance, on July 12, 1950, entered into a written contract with Treat, whereby Reliance agreed to buy and Treat to sell a quantity of staves "sufficient to aggregate 300,000 white oak bourbon staves of four and one-half average width, to be produced or purchased by seller in Arkansas, Missouri or Oklahoma; 90% of staves when shipped to be 'of bourbon grade' ". "Production shall commence as soon as possible and shall be completed not later than December 31, 1950." The price was $450 per thousand for bourbon grade staves of 4½ in. average width, and $40 per thousand for oil grade staves, same width; all to be delivered f. o. b. freight cars where produced. On August 12, 1950, Treat wrote Reliance a letter in which he stated in substance that he would be unable to produce and deliver staves at the contract price since the market price had risen to $475 or $500 per thousand (for the bourbon grade). (At the trial, however, Treat stated that the fair market value of bourbon staves was, during August, 1950, $400 to $450 per thousand.) At the end of August (or September, as Reliance's witness testified) Treat by telephone informed Reliance that no staves would be delivered at the contract price. On October 6, 1950, Reliance formally notified Treat that "we [Reliance] are looking forward to your strict compliance with all of the obligations which you have undertaken in your agreement with us", and requested a reply from Treat. No reply was shown. The evidence as to the market price of (bourbon) staves on December 31, 1950, would have sustained a finding of not more than $750 per thousand. No staves were ever delivered by Treat. Reliance brought this action against Treat to recover damages.

At the trial the court refused plaintiff's request to instruct the jury that the plaintiff was entitled to recover the difference between the contract price and the market price on December 31, 1950. Instead the Court charged that if defendant proved that he repudiated the contract prior to December 31, 1950, and that plaintiff by a reasonable effort could have mitigated its damages by the purchase of staves on the open market, without undue risk and expense, at a price in excess of the contract price, then it was plaintiff's duty to do so and mitigate its damages so far as possible, and plaintiff would then be entitled to recover only the difference between the market price at that time and the contract price. The jury returned a verdict for plaintiff for $500. Plaintiff appealed. The Court here summarizes the trial court's instruction and states that the applicable law is that of Missouri. After discussing Missouri cases the Court continues:]

There is no doubt that a party to an executory contract such as that in suit may refuse to accede to an anticipatory repudiation of it and insist upon performance, and, if he does so, the contract remains in existence and is binding on both parties, and no actionable claim for damages arises until the time for performance expires. . . .

It is our opinion that, under the undisputed facts in this case, the unaccepted anticipatory renunciation by the defendant of his obligation to produce and deliver staves under the contract did not impair that obligation or affect his liability for damages for the nonperformance of the contract, and that the measure of those damages was no different than it would have been had no notice of renunciation been given by the defendant to the plaintiff. If there had been no anticipatory repudiation of the contract, the measure of damages for nonperformance by the seller would have been the difference between the contract price and the market price of the staves on the date when delivery was due, and that is the measure which should have been applied in assessing damages in this case.

Moreover, the measure of damages would have been the same had the plaintiff accepted the anticipatory repudiation as an actionable breach of the contract. The plaintiff would still have been entitled to recover what it had lost by reason of the defendant's failure to produce and deliver by December 31, 1950, the staves contracted for, namely, the difference between the market price and the contract price of the staves on that date. The Comment in Restatement of the Law of Contracts, § 338, Measure of Damages for Anticipatory Breach, contains the following statement (page 549): "The fact that an anticipatory repudiation is a breach of contract (see § 318) does not cause the repudiated promise to be treated as if it were a promise to render performance at the date of the repudiation. Repudiation does not accelerate the time fixed for performance; nor does it change the damages to be awarded as the equivalent of the promised performance." See, also, Williston on Contracts, Rev.Ed. Vol. 5, § 1397; 46 Am.Jur., Sales, § 688.

It seems safe to say that ordinarily no obligation to mitigate damages arises until there are damages to mitigate. No damages for the nonperformance of the contract in suit accrued before December 31, 1950. Until that time the defendant, notwithstanding his anticipatory repudiation of the contract, was obligated and was at liberty to produce and deliver the staves, and had he done so the plaintiff would have been required to take and to pay for them. There is no justification for ruling that, after the plaintiff was advised that the defendant did not intend to perform, it must hold itself in readiness to accept performance from him and at the same time, at its own risk and expense, buy the staves contracted for upon the open market in the hope of reducing the defendant's liability for damages in case he persisted in his refusal to fulfill his obligations. The plaintiff did nothing to enhance its damages and seeks no special damages.

This same question as to mitigation of damages by a purchaser who insisted upon performance of a contract after a seller's anticipatory repudiation, arose in Continental Grain Co. v. Simpson Feed Co., D.C.E.D.Ark., 102 F.Supp. 354 [reprinted in part, p. 921 infra.] In that case Judge Lemley, we think, correctly decided that the purchaser was not required to attempt to mitigate his damages by buying the commodity contracted for upon the open market. Judge Lemley said [after enunciating the rule just stated by the present court], page 363 of 102 F.Supp.:

"There are two reasons for this rule. First, to require the innocent party to make an immediate purchase or sale upon receipt of notice of the other's repudiation would encourage such repudiation on the part of the seller or of the buyer as the market rose or fell. See Fahey v. Updike Elevator Co. [102 Neb. 249, 166 N.W. 622]. Second, the immediate action of the innocent party might not have the effect of mitigating his damages, but might, on the other hand, enhance them. Williston On Contracts, Section 1397, Callan v. Andrews [48 F.2d 118, 120], and Missouri Furnace Co. v. Cochran [8 F. 463] both supra."

The doctrine of anticipatory breach by repudiation is intended to aid a party injured as a result of the other party's refusal to perform his contractual obligations, by giving to the injured party an election to accept or to reject the refusal of performance without impairing his rights or increasing his burdens. Any effort to convert the doctrine into one for the benefit of the party who, without legal excuse, has renounced his agreement should be resisted.

The plaintiff is entitled to recover as damages the amount by which on December 31, 1950, the market price of the staves contracted for exceeded their contract price. What the market price of such staves was on that date is a question of fact which has not as yet been determined.

The judgment is reversed and the case is remanded with directions to grant a new trial limited to the issue of the amount of damages.

NOTES

(1) *The Code Problem.* Suppose that the market price of staves had dropped rather than risen in the latter part of 1950, and that the buyer rather than the seller had repudiated late in the summer. For that case the Code provides (subject to certain qualifications and adjustments) that the seller may recover, as damages, the unpaid contract price less the market price "at the time and place for tender." UCC 2–708(1). In view of prior law, this formula did not astound anyone, although it may produce a recovery markedly different from the seller's loss. See Peters, Remedies for Breach of Contracts, 73 Yale L.J. 199, 257–61 (1963). What has caused some wonderment is the analogous rule for the case of a seller's breach, such as Treat committed: 2–713(1) ("market price at the time when the buyer learned of the breach"). This provision has received diverse interpretations by scholars. Professor Peters (as she then was) concluded that the Code changed the rule of the main case, and Professor Taylor has offered some justification for the change.[a] On the other hand, Professors White and Summers offer five "elegant" arguments for believing that a buyer cannot—in the Code sense—learn of the seller's breach before the time for tender.[b] As will be seen, the courts are similarly divided.

Several other Code sections figure in the arguments. One is section 2–610, to the effect that a party aggrieved by a repudiation may "for a commercially reasonable time await performance by the repudiating party." Another is section 2–712, permitting the buyer to effect cover after a "breach within the preceding section." If this privilege arises upon repudiation by the seller, a cognate issue is presented: may the buyer, at his pleasure, contract for substitute goods on a spot market or make a forward contract for delivery on the schedule promised by the seller? And there are further perplexities, as the following notes will show.

(2) *Illustrations.*

(a) *Seller's Breach.* A dealer in cotton contracts to deliver a stated quantity to a mill, in a single lot, on the last day of September. On August 24 the dealer declares that he will not deliver. At first the buyer urges him to "retract." (Note that under UCC 2–610(b) this does not foreclose any remedy for breach as provided there.) On September 6 the buyer declares the contract cancelled. (Note that under UCC 2–611(1) the seller cannot effectively retract his repudiation thereafter.) The market price of cotton has advanced daily from August 24 through September 30. How should damages be computed for the dealer's breach?

UCC 2–723(1) states a rule which, owing to the delays of justice, is not likely to be applied often. By implication, however, it suggests that the price prevailing on August 24 should *not* control in the ordinary case of trial following the date fixed for delivery. Compare the expression there—"time when the aggrieved party learned of the repudiation"—with that in UCC 2–713(1). Some readers of the Code suppose that an anticipatory repudiation is not a "breach", in Code terms. Do you agree? See again sec-

a. Taylor, The Impact of Article 2 of the UCC on the Doctrine of Anticipatory Repudiation, 9 Bost.Coll.Ind. & Comm.L.Rev. 917, 928–32 (1968).

b. The Uniform Commercial Code, 197–202 (1972).

tion 2–610(b): party aggrieved may "resort to any remedy for breach." But see section 2–711(1).

(b) *Buyer's Breach.* Assume the dealer-to-mill contract as above, and suppose now that on August 24 the *mill* declares that it will not accept delivery. May the dealer claim the remedy provided in UCC 2–706 (Seller's Resale . . .)? Is it clear that the conditions stated in 2–703 prevail? As an alternative, damages may be measured under UCC 2–708(1). That makes market price on the delivery date a determinant of damages owing to the seller, in a repudiation case, just as it was a determinant of damages owing to the buyer in the main case. Yet it remains problematical under the Code how the delivery date may affect the recovery for an aggrieved buyer.

(3) *"Quick Draw"* Rules. For convenience we may say that certain rules for fixing damages in repudiation cases are "quick draw" rules—those that preclude reference to a price prevailing on or after the time fixed for performance. The foregoing note gives some reasons to believe that the Code is not committed to such rules. The Code suggests that resale is not a mandatory remedy for a seller aggrieved by a repudiation, and that cover is not mandatory for an aggrieved buyer. Indeed, it *says* that a buyer's failure to effect cover "does not bar him from any other remedy." UCC 2–712(3). Moreover, Comment 1 to that section says that cover is "the buyer's equivalent of the seller's right to resell." Yet the Code remedy provisions admit of some manipulation.

The dates August 24 and September 30 in the note above are taken from a wheat-sale case in which the seller repudiated: Cargill, Inc. v. Stafford, 553 F.2d 1222 (10th Cir. 1977). The trial court assessed damages against him by reference to the price of wheat on September 6, the day on which the buyer cancelled. On an appeal by the buyer, *held:* Remanded for a redetermination of damages. The court interpreted the phrase "learned of the breach" in UCC 2–713(1) to mean "time of performance." Hence it authorized the trial court to fix damages as the buyer asked, by reference to the September 30 price—but only if the buyer made a better case. The court indicated that the buyer should have covered in late August or early September unless it had a "valid reason" not to do so. The only excuse suggested by the court was that substitute wheat might not have been available.

For a different interpretation of "learned of the breach," see First Nat. Bank of Chicago v. Jefferson Mortgage Co., 576 F.2d 479 (3d Cir. 1978).

(4) *Quick-Draw Advocates.* Heroic efforts have been made to extract quick-draw rules both from the text of the Code and from economic analysis. A favorite Code reference is 2–610(a), which mentions "a commercially reasonable time." To that, one court added a reference to the obligation of good faith: UCC 1–203. Oloffson v. Coomer, 11 Ill.App.3d 918, 296 N.E.2d 871 (1973) (in favor of a corn grower, the day for the aggrieved dealer-buyer to cover was the very day of repudiation).[c] On the economic side, it has been pointed out that if an aggrieved buyer may delay cover indefinite-

c. See Restatement Second, § 350, Comment f; Liebson, Anticipatory Breach and Buyer's Damages, 7 UCC L.J. 252 (1975).

ly, the seller has more to fear from making an early repudiation than from committing a breach at the end. (That is so because, absent any cover requirement, the extent of his "upside" risk is unknowable and unlimited at the time of repudiation.) But the damages rule should be framed—so the argument runs—to make the seller indifferent to the time of breach: an early one may accomplish a more efficient allocation of resources. Jackson, "Anticipatory Repudiation" and the Temporal Element of Contract Law, 31 Stan.L.Rev. 69 (1978).[d]

(5) *Anomalous Cover Contracts.* On August 24, when a cotton mill learns that a supplier will default in September, it buys substitute cotton on the "spot" market and claims cover damages under UCC 2–712. If the mill could have made a (forward) contract for September delivery instead, is the claim questionable? Suppose the mill contracts for substitute cotton to be delivered in September at the price *then prevailing*, and claims cover damages. Allowable? If so, does it make any sense to impose a quick-draw rule on buyers aggrieved by repudiation?

UNITED STATES v. SEACOAST GAS CO.

United States Court of Appeals, Fifth Circuit, 1953.
204 F.2d 709.
Certiorari denied 346 U.S. 866 (1953).

Suit against gas company and its surety on gas company's performance bond, for damages alleged to have resulted from an anticipatory breach of contract in nature of notice of intent to cancel contract as of November 15, 1947. The United States District Court for the Southern District of Georgia entered judgment in favor of gas company and surety, and plaintiff appealed. . . .

Judgment reversed, cause remanded with directions.

HUTCHESON, Chief Judge. Brought against Seacoast Gas Company and the surety on its performance bond, the suit was for damages alleged to have resulted from the anticipatory breach by the Gas Company of its contract with plaintiff to supply gas to a federal housing project during the period from April 15, 1947, to June 15, 1948. The claim was: that on October 7, 1947, while performance of the contract was in progress, Seacoast anticipatorily breached the contract by writing plaintiff unequivocally that, because of plaintiff's breach of the contract, Seacoast intended to cancel same as of November 15, 1947; that the plaintiff immediately notified Seacoast that it did not recognize any right in it to cease performance and that it proposed to advertise for bids to insure a continued supply of gas if Seacoast's breach persisted; that, thereafter, having advertised for bids

d. Compare Taylor, op. cit. supra n. a. (The buyer should "pay a price" for the opportunity to convert his contract into a direct monetary gain prior to the date for delivery.) For further support for a quick-draw rule see Note, 19 Wm. & Mary L.Rev. 253 (1977).

and on November 6th, having received the low bid from Trion Company, it on that date notified Seacoast by letter that unless it retracted its repudiation of the contract within three days from the letter date, Trion's bid would be accepted and Seacoast and its surety would be held liable for breach of contract; and that thereafter Seacoast not having retracted within the time fixed, plaintiff on November 10, accepted Trion's bid, and, pursuant thereto, began its preparations to execute with Trion a contract for a price in excess of that provided in the Seacoast contract, and Seacoast is liable to plaintiff for this excess.

Defendant Seacoast, admitting in its pleading and its testimony that the facts were substantially as claimed by plaintiff, defended on the ground: that it had retracted its notice of repudiation and given assurance of its intention to continue to perform before the plaintiff had actually signed the new contract; and that, since, as it claimed, plaintiff had not then substantially changed its position or suffered any damages as a result of Seacoast's notice to terminate the contract and cease performance under it, the retraction was timely and healed the breach.

Upon the issue thus joined, the cause was tried to the court without a jury, and the court stating the question for decision thus, "The question in this case is as to whether Seacoast Gas Company, Inc. withdrew its notice of cancellation of its contract prior to the rendering of the contract to the Trion Gas Company," found that it had done so. On the basis of this finding and a further finding that on November 13, two days before the termination date which Seacoast had fixed in its notice, Zell, who was president both of Seacoast and of Trion Company, to whom the new contract was awarded, notified the regional counsel for the Public Housing Authority that Seacoast admitted it had no right to cancel the contract and was rescinding its notice, the court held that the anticipatory breach had been healed and plaintiff could not recover.

Appealing from this judgment, plaintiff is here insisting that under the settled law governing anticipatory breaches not only as it is laid down in Georgia but generally, Seacoast's retraction came too late to heal the breach, and the judgment must be reversed.

Appellees, on their part, insist that the judgment appealed from was soundly based in law and in fact and must be affirmed.

We do not think so. The undisputed facts establish: that Zell, president of both companies, was present at the opening of the new bids on November 6, 1947, and upon being asked to withdraw Seacoast's notice that it would cease performing the contract, refused to do so; that on that date the Public Housing Administration regional counsel wrote Seacoast by registered mail, addressed "Attention Zell", advising of the steps the government had taken and stating that unless Seacoast retracted its repudiation within three days from the date of the letter, Trion's bid would be accepted and Seacoast and its sureties would be held liable for breach of contract; and that having received no response from Seacoast within the three days specified, and Zell again asked on November 10th, to retract the notice of repudiation having refused to do so, the government accepted Trion's bid and proceeded with the execution of the contract. The record standing thus, under settled law [1] not only of Georgia but generally elsewhere, the breach was not healed, the judgment was wrong, and it must be reversed.

A comparison of the briefs and arguments of appellant and appellees will show that the case is in quite small compass. Both agree that Seacoast's letter of October 24th [sic] operated as an anticipatory breach and that unless effectively withdrawn during the *locus poenitentiae* it operated to put Seacoast in default and to render it liable for the loss to the government of the difference in price between the old and the new contract.

Appellees, after quoting from Anson on Contracts, 6th Ed., Sec. 385, p. 444:

> "The repudiator has the power of retraction prior to any change of position by the other party, but not afterwards."

go on to say:

> "So we see that the authorities seem to be unanimous that a person who gives notice of his intention not to perform a contract may withdraw such notice and offer to perform prior to the time the other party acted or relied thereon."

Based upon these premises, they insist that "the undisputed evidence is that appellant did not 'accept the bid of Trion Gas' until November 17th, which was after the notice of cancellation had been withdrawn in writing."

We think: that this statement is erroneous; that it represents the crucial difference between the parties; and that the error of the statement lies in the fact that it confuses the acceptance of the bid with the signing of the contract.

It is true that the contract was not signed until the 17th, after Seacoast had retracted its notice and if appellees were correct in its position that the date of the signing of the new contract was determi-

1. Baker v. Corbin, 148 Ga. 267, 96 S.E. 428; Bu-Vi-Bar Petroleum Corp. v. Krow, 10 Cir., 40 F.2d 488, 69 A.L.R. 1295; Finch v. Sprague, 117 Wash. 650, 202 P. 257; Parker v. King, 68 Ga.App. 672, 23 S.E.2d 575; Roehm v. Horst, 178 U.S. 1, 20 S.Ct. 780, 44 L.Ed. 953; United Press Ass'n v. National Newspaper Ass'n, 10 Cir., 237 F. 547; 12 Am.Jur., "Contracts" Sec. 392; Ballantine, Anticipatory Breach and the Enforcement of Contractual Duties, 22 Mich.L.Rev. 329; 17 C.J.S., Contracts, § 472, p. 973; Vold, Withdrawal of Repudiation after Anticipatory Breach of Contract, 5 Tex.L.Rev. 9, 10; Williston on Contracts (Rev. Ed.1936) Sec. 1323, Vol. 5, pp. 3710–3711.

native of this case, they would be correct in their conclusion that the judgment should be affirmed.

But that position is not correct. In fact and in law, when the government took bids and notified Seacoast that unless it retracted within three days it would proceed to accept the Trion bid and award the contract to it, the *locus poenitentiae* ended with these three days. The fact that Seacoast claims that it did not receive the notice is completely immaterial both because it was not necessary for the government to give any notice or fix any time and because Zell, on November 10th, repeated to the Regional Counsel his refusal to retract.

All that is required to close the door to repentance is definite action indicating that the anticipatory breach has been accepted as final, and this requisite can be supplied either by the filing of a suit or a firm declaration, as here, that unless within a fixed time the breach is repudiated, it will be accepted.

Here, in addition to this firm declaration, the record shows the taking of bids and the awarding of the contract to the lowest bidder. The error of the district judge lies, we think, in holding that the *locus poenitentiae* was extended until the 17th, when the contract was signed, and that Seacoast having repented before the signing of the contract, had healed the breach and restored the contract to its original vitality.

Whatever of doubt there may be, and we have none with respect to this view, as a matter of strict law, there can be none with respect to the justice or equity of this determination when it is considered; that Zell, the president and practically sole owner of Seacoast, was the organizer, the president and practically sole owner of Trion; that he organized Trion for the sole purpose of the bidding; and that on the date the bids were opened and later on the date the contract was awarded, he, though requested to do so, refused to withdraw Seacoast's repudiation and continued in that refusal until a day or two before the contract was signed.

The evidence showing, as it does, without contradiction, that the signing of the contract was not delayed because of a purpose on the part of the government to extend the time for Seacoast's repentance, but because until that date Trion had not furnished his bond, we think it clear that, in entering judgment for the defendants, the court erred. The judgment is, therefore, reversed and the cause is remanded with directions to enter judgment for plaintiff for the loss Seacoast's breach of contract has caused it.

NOTES

(1) *Alternative Explanations.* The error of the trial court was in supposing that timely action by Seacoast had "healed the breach and restored the contract to its original vitality." One way of interpreting the appellate opinion is that the United States had *elected* to treat the repudiation as conclusive before Zell recanted. In the alternative, the decision may rest on

a change of position by the United States such that Seacoast was *estopped* to retract its repudiation. Finally, it might have been said that Seacoast *waived* its power to retract through delay while the bidding procedure went forward. It is mildly surprising that the court did not use any of these terms to justify its ruling, for they are tempting ways to explain how expectations are altered over the life of a contract through behavior of the parties that does not amount to a fresh bargain.

(2) *The Door to Repentance.* There was a substantial change of position by the Government, was there not, on November 10 when it accepted Trion's bid? The filing of a suit against Seacoast would have been such a change of position. The question remaining, then, is whether *without any such step* the Government's firm declaration "accepting" the repudiation would "close the door to repentance." Why should it? See Restatement Second, § 256.

Cases which assimilate a repudiation to an offer, in that each may be made irrevocable by acceptance, are not uncommon in this country. The other side of the coin is that a repudiation can be ignored by the innocent party: "I have never been able to understand what effect the repudiation of one party has unless the other party accepts the repudiation." (Lord Scrutton) "An unaccepted repudiation is a thing writ in water and of no value to anybody: it confers no legal rights of any sort or kind." (Lord Asquith)[a] Such expressions are not consistent with American law, however. See Note 1, p. 844 supra. They overstate the difference between an "actual breach" and a breach by anticipation. For various differences between an anticipatory repudiation and an offer to rescind, see Corbin, §§ 980–81.

American cases are somewhat more compatible with the view that a repudiation puts the injured party to an election of cancelling the contract or of keeping it alive, as Lord Cockburn indicated (see the Note referred to). However, the better view is that the injured party may urge that the repudiation be withdrawn—that repentance be made—without committing himself to further performance if it is not. (Note the October notice by plaintiff in Reliance Cooperage Corp. v. Treat, p. 931 supra.) If a seller of goods repudiates his obligation, as in the Reliance Cooperage case, and then seeks to retract after a rise in market prices, should the buyer be privileged to disregard the retraction?[b]

What position does the Code take on these problems? See UCC 2–610(b), 2–611.

a. These observations were quoted and commented on in White and Carter (Councils) Ltd. v. McGregor, [1962] A.C. 413 (H.L.), at 438 and 444.

b. Is the retraction some evidence that market price equals contract price? See Goldfarb v. Campe Corp., 99 Misc. 475, 164 N.Y.S. 583 (City Ct. 1917).

For the proposition that a repudiation may be retracted see Quivirian Development Co. v. Poteet, 268 F.2d 433 (8th Cir. 1959); but see Glass v. Anderson, p. 950 infra. In the former case an ingenious argument was made —and rejected—for an exception on the ground that stipulated damages were provided for and had become payable upon the repudiation.

(3) *Summary.* "Repudiation and its effects [from Restatement Second, § 329, Comment a]. In some cases a repudiation by one party to a contract discharges the duty of the other party; in some cases it requires the other to treat as total a breach which might otherwise be partial, or it may itself be a total breach. See Chapter 10; Uniform Commercial Code § 2–610. For these purposes repudiation includes a positive statement by [a promisor] that he will not or cannot substantially perform his duties, or any voluntary affirmative action which renders substantial performance apparently impossible. In some circumstances a statement that he doubts whether he will substantially perform, or that he takes no responsibility for performance, or even a failure to give adequate assurance of performance may have a similar effect."

Reconsider the cases in this chapter with a view to finding support for each of these propositions. Where do you find indications that this pattern is not consistently followed?

SITLINGTON v. FULTON

United States Court of Appeals, Tenth Circuit, 1960.
281 F.2d 552.

SAVAGE, District Judge. . . . Sarah Sitlington and her husband, Thomas O. Sitlington, of Baxter, Kansas, were the joint owners of a farm situated in Grady County, Oklahoma. For some time prior to January, 1956, Jack Ledbetter had been in possession of this farm as a tenant operating a dairy business in partnership with Sarah Sitlington. On or about January 8, 1956, Mr. and Mrs. Sitlington entered into a written contract of sale of the farm to Robert and Ruby May Fulton, husband and wife.[1] The agreed consideration was $81,000. The sum of $3,000 as earnest money was to be placed in escrow with the contract of sale and the deed.[a] An additional $17,000 was to be paid when the sale was closed, and the balance of the purchase price was to be financed by a note secured by a mortgage. The contract also provided:

"It is further agreed between the parties hereto that as soon as the title has been approved by the second party as acceptable this transaction shall be closed and the second parties shall be entitled to full and complete possession. . . ."

The title was approved on January 17, 1956. The purchaser went into partial possession of the farm on January 10, but the ten-

1. Sarah Sitlington will be referred to as the Seller; Sarah and Thomas O. Sitlington will be referred to either as Appellants or Sellers; Robert Fulton will be referred to as Purchaser and Robert and Ruby May Fulton will be referred to as Appellees or Purchasers.

a. "Escrow" has been defined as "the deposit of any written instrument, evidence of title, or thing of value in the hands of a third person, with an instruction to deliver it on the performance of stated conditions in the effectuation of a sale, transfer, leasing, or encumbering of property. In simple terms it may be defined as a title closing mechanism." Aran, Chapter 14 in "California Real Estate Sales Transactions" 506 (1967).

ant retained possession of the improvements. The seller was unable to deliver complete possession because of the tenant's refusal to vacate the premises and the sale for that reason could not be promptly closed.

Despite the sellers' inability to close the sale, the purchaser continued in partial possession. He purchased 53 steers and placed them on the farm and 30 dairy cows which, because he did not have access to the barns, were put on leased land; he planted 33 acres of barley and arranged for the Soil Conservation Service to fill a canyon, build a pond and fell trees on the farm.

An escrow arrangement provided for in the contract was concluded on February 6, 1956. The sellers delivered to Owen Vaughn, attorney for purchaser, the contract of sale and a warranty deed properly executed. The purchasers delivered to Vaughn a check for $3,000 and a note for $61,000 with a mortgage covering the farm as security therefor. The dates on the note and mortgage were left blank with the understanding that the date of closing would be inserted. The escrow agent upon the closing of the transaction was to deliver the deed to the purchasers, the check, note and mortgage to sellers, and at the same time, purchasers were to make the additional down payment of $17,000.

The seller endeavored in good faith to perform the contract. Unable to settle her difficulties with the tenant, she brought appropriate legal proceedings to oust him. The purchaser was aware of the effort being made by the seller to remove the tenant in order that the sale could be consummated and told her, "to get Ledbetter out just as quickly as you can and I will go ahead and take over."

Finally on May 22, the tenant under compulsion of a court order vacated the premises. Promptly thereafter seller tendered full performance of the contract but purchaser insisted as a condition of closing the sale that he be paid $2,400 in damages occasioned by the delay. Upon sellers' refusal to accede to this demand, purchaser repudiated the contract. Sellers thereupon elected to treat the renunciation of the contract as a breach and in due course were restored to possession of the farm.

Some eight months thereafter and on February 25, 1957, the purchasers brought this action seeking specific performance and recovery of damages for breach of the contract. The sellers by counterclaim alleged that the contract had been breached by the purchasers and sought a judgment for damages resulting from such breach. The trial court denied specific performance of the contract but entered judgment for damages against the sellers for "failure to give up possession when agreed" in the sum of $7,675, itemized as follows: $2,500 for loss on steers, $3,750 for loss on dairy cattle, $1,300 soil conservation expense, and $125 barley planting expense.

The appellants complain of the judgment for damages and the denial of relief to them on their counterclaim. The appellees at the hearing on the motions for new trial abandoned their claim for specific performance.

The obligation of the sellers to close the sale and put the purchasers in full and complete possession of the property as soon as the title had been approved is clearly stated in the contract. It is undisputed that the title was approved on January 17, 1956. The sellers' inability to perform the contract by giving complete possession precluded the closing of the sale and constituted a breach of the contract. The purchasers thereupon had a choice of rights or remedies. They could either rescind the contract and bring an action to recover damages for its breach or they could require performance and retain a cause of action for damages suffered by the delay in performance.[2] The rights are inconsistent and the choice of one amounts to an election to surrender the other.[3]

In Oklahoma it is a statutory requirement that, if an injured party elects to rescind, he must do so promptly upon discovering facts which entitle him to do so, and he must restore to the other party everything of value which he received under the contract.[4] Any act by the injured party indicating an intent to continue performance is deemed a conclusive election.[5] But by the election to continue performance he does not forego his right of action to recover damages caused by the breach.[6]

The purchasers did not promptly rescind the contract. They remained in partial possession of the farm and thus failed to restore something of value which they had received under the contract. The escrow arrangement stipulated for in the contract was completed after the breach and on February 6, 1956. The purchaser encouraged the seller to resort to legal proceedings for eviction of the tenant in order that the contract could be performed. These acts are all indicia of an election upon the part of the purchaser to continue performance of the contract.

The trial court was apparently of the view that the purchasers had the right to rescind the contract in May because of the breach of

2. 12 Am.Jur. § 390 at p. 968; Bu-Vi-Bar Petroleum Corp. v. Krow, 10 Cir., 40 F.2d 488, 69 A.L.R. 1295; Kentucky Natural Gas Corp. v. Indiana Gas & Chemical Corp., 7 Cir., 129 F.2d 17, 143 A.L.R. 484, certiorari denied 317 U.S. 678, 63 S.Ct. 161, 87 L.Ed. 544.

3. Williston on Contracts, Vol. 3, § 683, at p. 1969; Bierce v. Hutchins, 205 U.S. 340, 346, 27 S.Ct. 524, 51 L. Ed. 828.

4. 15 O.S.A. § 235; Commercial Finance Co. v. Patterson, 182 Okl. 411, 77 P.2d 133; Smith v. Reinauer, 178 Okl. 4, 61 P.2d 1039; Appliance Distributors v. Mercury Electric Corp., 10 Cir., 202 F.2d 651.

5. Kentucky Natural Gas Corp. v. Indiana Gas & Chemical Corp., supra; 12 Am.Jur. § 390 at p. 968.

6. Williston on Contracts, Vol. 5, § 1334 at p. 3749; 12 Am.Jur. § 390 at p. 968.

the contract by the sellers in January. But the purchasers were bound by their election to continue performance and thereby lost their right to stop performance. Conceding a meritorious claim for damages, the purchaser did not have a right to compel payment of any specified amount as a condition of closing the sale. The refusal to close the sale until the unwarranted condition imposed should be satisfied was a breach of the contract by the purchasers.[7]

Thus, it is our conclusion that the purchasers had a right of action for damages for the delay in performance of the contract by sellers, and the sellers had a cause of action for damages for breach of the contract by the purchasers.

We agree with appellants, however, that the trial court did not apply the proper measure of damages. The established measure of damages in Oklahoma for delay in delivering possession of real estate is the value of the use of the land during the time that possession was wrongfully withheld. Special damages could not be recovered unless in contemplation of the parties at the time the contract was executed. The sellers could not have foreseen that the purchaser would buy cattle or incur expenses in planting crops and making improvements on the farm before obtaining complete possession. Moreover the items of damage found by the trial court to have been sustained by the purchaser obviously resulted from his repudiation of the contract when the late performance was tendered by the sellers.

At a new trial the damages suffered by the appellees should be ascertained in conformity with the views herein stated and damages should be awarded to the appellants on their counterclaim for breach of the contract by the appellees.

Reversed and remanded.[b]

NOTES

(1) *Remedies.* If Sitlington had chosen to demand specific performance, would it have been granted? Would she have been entitled to damages as well? Damages may be awarded in connection with a decree of specific performance, in an appropriate case. However, "the injured party should not be allowed to enforce and receive specific performance and at the

7. Page on Contracts, Vol. 5, § 2904; Rest.Contracts, §§ 309, 310; Also see 12 Am.Jur. § 387 at p. 963 where it is said: "Accordingly, the refusal of one party to perform an executory contract unless the other party consents to a modification amounts to a total breach of the agreement. Similarly, refusal to accept title tendered in accordance with the terms of sale constitutes a breach by the purchaser of land of his contract to purchase. . . ."

b. On retrial the trial court found that the Fultons had suffered damages in the sum of $1500, the value of the use of the land during the time that they were wrongfully deprived of its possession. It found that the Sitlingtons had suffered damages in the sum of $2504, the amount they expended in removing Ledbetter and providing complete possession for the Fultons. It gave judgment against the Fultons for $1004. On a second appeal by the Sitlingtons the judgment was affirmed. Sitlington v. Fulton, 297 F.2d 458 (10th Cir. 1961).

same time get judgment for damages for a total breach. Specific performance actually rendered, even though under the compulsion of court decree, prevents the breach from being total." 5 Corbin, 913–14. See Karpinski v. Ingrasci, p. 536 supra.

If specific performance were granted on the facts of the main case, would it be consistent to award damages in addition to *Fulton*?

Was Fulton entitled to specific performance, if he had pressed his claim for that remedy? He was awarded damages, be it noted, although he had wrongfully refused a tender of full performance by the seller.

(2) *Question.* Note the court's view that Fulton "did not have the right to compel payment of any specified amount as a condition of closing the sale." Compare the problem in Note 5, p. 930 supra. Is there a liberty for buyers of goods, in this respect, that land purchasers do not have?

(3) *Election.* The election made by Fulton was a choice between two remedies for the seller's breach. Another kind of election is sometimes required between inconsistent *judicial* remedies, to be made when litigation is begun, or as it proceeds. Are there different reasons for these different sorts of election? [c] If Fulton wished to call off the purchase unless it could be completed in the early spring, could he safely have urged the seller to start eviction proceedings against the tenant? What might he have said, if anything, to avoid making a conclusive election to continue performance?

FULWILER v. BEDDOE

Court of Appeals of Oregon, 1979.
38 Or.App. 279, 589 P.2d 1197.

[In an agreement for the sale of a home, the purchase price was stated as $116,000 payable in three parts. Upon signing the agreement (July 7) the buyers paid $5,000 as "earnest money." The agreement made a further sum payable on the date fixed for closing (September 1)—an amount which together with the earnest money equalled 20% of the price. The balance, $92,800, was made "payable as follows:"

> Purchaser will immediately apply for and obtain a minimum 80% Loan in the amount of the balance.

On July 23 the seller, Gladys Beddoe, told the buyers, Mr. and Mrs. James Fulwiler, that she was not going to complete the sale unless the purchase price was adjusted. Since signing the agreement she had learned that she had undervalued her property by at least $25,000. She had also learned—what Fulwiler did not tell her—that he was a debtor in bankruptcy proceedings, in which he was threatened with a large, nondischargeable claim. (In August that claim was determined to be subject to a bankruptcy discharge.)

c. For some various meanings of election see Corbin, §§ 755, 766, 1214.

The Fulwilers had advertised their home for sale before Beddoe balked. Thereafter they took it off the market for a time, on an attorney's advice. (In the opinion quoted below, the court said: "This would have been the logical thing to do under the circumstances.") By early in September, however, the Fulwilers had negotiated an agreement to sell their home for an amount which would net them about 50% of the price of the Beddoe house. This agreement was made subject to success for the Fulwilers in a suit for specific performance that they brought against Beddoe.

Meanwhile, the Fulwilers had begun negotiation for a secured loan on the Beddoe home with the Benjamin Franklin Savings and Loan Association. Shortly after Beddoe signed the earnest-money agreement an appraiser for the Association came to her home; on July 26 the Fulwilers made a formal loan application; and on August 3 the application was approved. However, the loan applied for was for only $75,000: not 80% of $116,000 but only some 65%.

In the specific performance suit the Fulwilers obtained a decree, and Beddoe appealed.]

HOLMAN, Judge Pro Tem.

. . . .

Defendant first contends that plaintiffs are not entitled to performance because they did not perform their obligations under the contract to "immediately" apply for and be granted a loan in a sum which was a "minimum 80%" of the purchase price. It is our conclusion that plaintiffs did prosecute the loan with dispatch. . . .

It is also our conclusion, as it was of the trial judge, that the provision for the amount of the loan was not a provision the noncompliance with which would justify defendant's repudiation of the agreement. Defendant attempted to make it such a provision by her testimony that she was getting married in August and that she put the provision for the 80 per cent loan in the agreement because she did not want to wait until the closing date and then find that plaintiffs had insufficient funds to complete the transaction. She said she did not want to take her house off the market and then find plaintiffs could not complete the deal.

[Here the court recited contrary evidence, indicating that the 80% figure was inserted for the convenience of the Fulwilers; and it said that the parol evidence rule did not bar the testimony because it was "explanatory of the reason" for the provision.] Plaintiffs' failure to secure a loan in the amount of 80 per cent was insufficient, in our opinion, to justify defendant's repudiation of the contract.

Defendant also contends that plaintiffs' failure to disclose to her their insecure financial standing arising out of Mr. Fulwiler's bankruptcy and the pendency against him of the claim that was not dischargeable in bankruptcy justified her repudiation of the contract.

Defendant made no inquiry concerning plaintiffs' financial situation and there is no evidence that any statements they made to her concerning their financial situation were untrue.[1] Again, we do not believe this failure justifies repudiation of the agreement or that it was the real reason for defendant's attempted repudiation. Plaintiffs were either going to "come up" with the money on September 1, the day for performance, or they were not.

The real question in this case is whether plaintiffs have proved that as of September 1 they were financially able to complete the transaction. Despite defendant's repudiation of the contract plaintiffs must prove that they were able to perform the transaction upon the closing date before they are entitled to the remedy of specific performance, although by her repudiation they are relieved from making a tender of the purchase price. Gaffi v. Burns, 278 Or. 327, 333, 563 P.2d 726, 728 (1977).

Plaintiffs . . . claimed they had a receivable of $10,000 but there is no evidence of its liquidity as of September 1, 1977. They had $4,000 in a bank account. To the bank account must be added the $75,000 loan from Benjamin Franklin and their equity in their present home if these amounts can be considered as being available on the required date.

. . .

Defendant claims the equity in plaintiffs' home cannot be taken into consideration because no sale had been completed by September 1, the closing date for the present transaction. This contention presents a problem because we have no way of knowing whether plaintiffs would have made a sale of their home by September 1 which would have liquidated sufficient of their equity to make up the balance of the purchase price of defendant's property. . . .

It is our conclusion that defendant is in no position to complain that the equity was unavailable to plaintiffs on September 1 because her wrongful repudiation was the cause of their taking their property off the market. Plaintiffs have demonstrated that they had adequate assets, if liquidated, to complete the transaction, and defendant is in no position to complain about the lack of liquidity because she was responsible for their lack of a full opportunity to liquidate their principal asset.

The decree of the trial judge is affirmed.

1. Defendant contends plaintiffs' statements that they might need a loan of only $65,000 was a misrepresentation of their financial situation because they did not presently have enough money in liquid funds to complete the transaction if they secured that small a loan. We do not consider it a misrepresentation because, as subsequently indicated, they had assets which, if converted to cash, were adequate for the purpose.

NOTES

(1) *Rewriting the Term.* Can you draft the loan provision in such a way that noncompliance would have justified Beddoe in refusing to complete the deal?

(2) *Rewriting the Opinion.* Might the court have derived its conclusion from the duty of good faith and fair dealing that the contract imposed on Beddoe? Would a brief opinion based on that principle have been equally persuasive, or more so? What facts would be emphasized in such an opinion? (Beddoe gave evidence which—the court said—was "capable of the construction that the reason for the 80 per cent figure was to make it sufficiently large to permit plaintiffs to borrow up to that amount if they needed it.")

(3) *Disability.* Changing the facts in Hochster v. De la Tour, p. 839 supra, suppose it appeared that between May 22, when the action was commenced, and June 1, when the employment was to begin, the plaintiff had suffered a crippling injury that would have prevented his serving the defendant for any part of the summer. Does it seem that that would have precluded a recovery? In that case the court said that "renunciation may be treated as a breach." At times it has been said that a repudiation presents the injured party with an election, or option. Is your answer consistent with these expressions?

Do you understand the main case as a holding that the capacity to perform of a party injured by repudiation is of little moment? See Farmers & Bankers Life Ins. Co. v. St. Regis Paper Co., 456 F.2d 347 (5th Cir. 1972), and cases cited at 352 n. 4.

(4) *Excuse of Tender.* In what sense were the Fulwilers "relieved from making a tender of the purchase price" by Beddoe's repudiation? Did it relieve them of the duty of paying? Of the necessity of finding the purchase money when they decided to claim specific performance?

Because the Fulwilers did claim specific performance, it seems the requirement that they tender the unpaid purchase price might not in any event have stood in the way of the action: as the note to follow shows, a tender in equity does not have quite the same significance as it has in "law" actions. Does this help to explain the contract provision about a "minimum 80% loan"?

SPECIFIC PERFORMANCE

In actions for specific performance, and especially those based on land sale contracts, constructive conditions of exchange sometimes do not operate with the same effect as in ordinary damage actions. Furthermore, courts of equity have devised some distinctive methods of securing contract expectations in specific performance cases. This is not to say that the conceptions of performance and breach are radically different in equity and at law, for it is a long-established principle that in determining whether or not a right to performance exists, "equity follows the law."

An example of the equitable standard for tender as a condition is found in McMillan v. Smith, 363 S.W.2d 437 (Tex.1962). The plaintiffs had contracted to buy a ranch, and tendered what they regarded as the correct price, on a per-acre basis, to the defendants. The defendants refused to convey, and the plaintiffs sought specific performance. They deposited in court the amount they believed to be due, and declared that they were ready and able to pay "such further sum as the Court may order." Ultimately it was decided that the sellers were entitled, upon giving a deed, to a large additional amount —some $28,000. The court directed that the buyers be given 30 days to deposit the full price, upon which the sellers were to make a conveyance. Failing full payment, judgment was to be entered for the sellers. The court said: "Historically, in a suit for specific performance, the question as to the necessity for a tender of performance by a purchaser has been determined according to equitable rules rather than to those applicable to an action at law. The latter requires the purchaser, as a condition precedent, to tender performance. Courts of equity, on the other hand, have not been bound by strict and inflexible rules."

Another doctrine peculiar to equity is known as the requirement of "mutuality of remedy." According to this doctrine, broadly stated, a plaintiff is not entitled to specific performance of his contract unless his own undertaking was such that, if the parties had been reversed, he could have been compelled to render specific performance. The requirement may be regarded as a means of securing the expectation of performance that the contract conferred on the defendant. However, it has often been observed that the requirement is unnecessary for that purpose in many instances, and the doctrine has been largely discredited, at least in the broad form stated above.[a] Nevertheless, if a plaintiff seeking specific performance has not completed his own performance, the court may hesitate to compel performance by the defendant and expose him to the risk of a later default by the plaintiff. According to the Restatement Second, § 363, the court may properly deny the remedy if the plaintiff's performance "is not secured to the satisfaction of the court." In the comments to this section various forms of decrees are suggested as means of reducing the defendant's risk, including specific performance decrees conditioned on the plaintiff's giving a mortgage or other security.

Partly because specific performance is a flexible remedy, and partly because of its history, then, in an action for specific performance the court is not required to follow the analysis of the promises as dependent or not that a court of law might make. This observation is pertinent especially to land sale contracts because equity courts have made a specialty of enforcing them.[b] Nevertheless, as

a. Gould v. Stelter, 14 Ill.2d 376, 152 N.E.2d 869 (1958); but see Rego v. Decker, 482 P.2d 834 (Alaska 1971).

b. Indeed, the making of such a contract is regarded in equity as a transfer of the beneficial ownership of the

the foregoing cases have shown, such contracts are also governed, in part, by general conceptions of performance and breach, including that of constructive conditions.

In Glass v. Anderson, 596 S.W.2d 507 (Tex.1980), the buyer of six houses in Houston told the seller, before the title reports were made, that "the deal was off." But the seller provided the buyer with satisfactory title reports and gave notice that the buyer's deposits would be retained if he did not consummate the transaction within a reasonable time. The buyer responded, through his attorney, with an unjustified demand for his deposits. About ten days later the buyer announced that he was ready to close. Now it was the seller's turn to declare the deal off. In an action by the buyer for specific performance, the trial court found that the buyer had withdrawn his repudiation before the seller accepted it or materially changed his position. From an order of specific performance the seller (Glass) appealed. *Held*: Reversed. "We hold that when the buyer repudiates the contracts after time for performance arrives the contractual obligations of the non-defaulting party are ended, and the repudiating party cannot obtain specific performance of the contracts." Compare Glass v. Anderson with United States v. Seacoast Gas Co., p. 936 supra. Do the cases suggest that the courts take a specially critical view of repudiation by one who is seeking specific performance?

NOTES

(1) *Title Defects.* In the Case of the Cool Customer, p. 816 supra, the contract recognized want of title in the seller (Dwyer) when it was made. More often the parties to a land sale assume that the seller is vested with title, and discover that it is subject to some cloud or limitation only when a title search is made. In that case what is the buyer's remedy? A possibility recognized in many equity cases is specific performance, with an abatement of the purchase price. If the buyer prefers instead to withdraw from the agreement, how should he proceed? In Cohen v. Kranz, 12 N.Y.2d 242, 238 N.Y.S.2d 928, 189 N.E.2d 473 (1963), the court said: "While a vendee can recover his money paid on the contract from a vendor who defaults on law day without a showing of tender or even of willingness and ability to perform where the vendor's title is incurably defective, a tender and demand are required to put the vendor in default where his title could be cleared without difficulty in a reasonable time. Further, the vendor in such a case is entitled to a reasonable time beyond law day to make his title good." See Restatement Second, § 237.

If a timely conveyance is important to the buyer, and he learns in advance of imperfections in the seller's title, how would you advise him to act? If the quality of the seller's title prior to "law day" is important to

property, by a principle known as "equitable conversion." Its significance cannot be appreciated fully apart from the context of a course on equity or on real estate transactions.

him, how would you advise him to contract? See Mountain View Corp. v. Horne, 74 N.M. 541, 395 P.2d 676 (1964).

(2) *Dependency in Installment Sale Contracts.* In Kane v. Hood, 13 Pick. (30 Mass.) 281 (1832), the question was said to be "whether, in a contract between parties relative to the same subject matter, some stipulations may be mutual and independent, and others dependent and mutually conditional." And it was held that they may. The contract was one for the sale of land, to be paid for in three installments, "the deed to be executed at the completing of the last payment." The buyer paid the first two installments. The court said, in dictum, that if he had not the seller might have recovered them without tender of performance or averment of readiness. But the suit was for the third installment. The seller alleged that he had always been ready to convey the land, and offered in court to do so upon payment. Yet he was nonsuited, for failure to allege or prove any tender of the deed. The promise of the final installment was dependent on the seller's promise to convey.

If no payment had been made, and the seller waited to sue until all were due, would the court's dictum still hold good? Or would a tender have been required for *any* recovery? This problem has aroused differences of opinion. See Beecher v. Conradt, 13 N.Y. 108 (1855); Restatement Second, § 234, Comment d.

(3) *Problem.* Developer lays out housing lots and a grid of streets on a tract of suburban land he owns, and grades the streets. He contracts to sell a lot to Buyer for $1,000, to be paid in monthly installments over five years. The contract requires Developer to "cinderize" the street in front of the lot, and to give Buyer a deed when his payments are complete. At the end of five years nothing has been done to the streets in the subdivision, and Buyer has paid only half the price. Developer sues Buyer for the balance, tendering a deed, and shows that the stretch of street in front of the lot could be cinderized for less than $50. What result? See Palmer v. Fox, 274 Mich. 252, 264 N.W. 361, 104 A.L.R. 1057 (1936).[c]

c. The facts in this case suggested no less than four illustrations appearing in the Restatement Second; they are appended to §§ 232, 241, and 243.

Chapter 9

IMPOSSIBILITY OF PERFORMANCE AND FRUSTRATION OF PURPOSE

In a case presented earlier, it was said that hardship, hindrance, and difficulty do not excuse a man from doing what he has agreed to do by a "positive, express contract." That case is Stees v. Leonard, p. 885 supra, in which damages were assessed against a builder for failure to put up a structure on what appeared to be quicksand. Of course there are many contractual undertakings that are not absolute in this sense. See Note 3, p. 885 supra. Even in Stees v. Leonard the court acknowledged that eventualities beyond the control of the parties will sometimes excuse the performance of a positive contract. We are now to explore the limits of "absolute" undertakings.

In this chapter, great historical events make their appearance. There is war in the Middle East, leading to closing of the Suez. There is the illness of a king. There is an OPEC embargo. And we begin with Prince Rupert's invasion of England, in the reign of Charles I. But there is also local and private distress: the death of a seaman, the burning of a theater, a crop failure. The aspect of these events that concerns us here is that each of them caused a dislocation of some agreement, and so occasioned a request for relief from an obligation that would otherwise be enforced. Hardship arising from an unexpected event, or at least a plea of hardship, is a common element in the cases that follow. They have some similarities to cases in Chapter 5, Policing the Bargain. Yet the emphasis in that chapter is on harsh and unsavory effects of contracts that are *intended,* by one of the parties at least; whereas in this one the emphasis is on unexpected effects. Of course there are several reasons for refusing to enforce an agreement as it was expressed when an extraneous event has upset a fundamental assumption on which it rested. One is simply to relieve a party from a loss that seems unjust. Another is to prevent an unmerited gain for the other party. More broadly, the object may be to mitigate the disruptive effects of an abrupt change of conditions, when, from the standpoint of the contracting parties, the change is relatively uncontrollable.

The other side of the coin is that agreements must be enforced —*pacta sunt servanda.* For this principle, also, several reasons may be given. Two of them appear in a well-known judgment of the Kings Bench, in 1647: Paradine v. Jane.[a] The plaintiff sued on a lease, for three years' back rent on a place of business. The defendant's plea was that he had been dispossessed by a hostile army under

a. Aleyn 26, 82 Eng.Rep. 897 (K.B.).

Rupert—"a German prince, an alien born, enemy to the King and kingdom"—and that during his ouster he could not take income from the premises. The court's conclusion was that he ought to pay his rent; the plea was bad. For one reason, the court said that, though the defendant was unable to prevent his eviction, "he might have provided against it in his contract." For another reason, the court added that "as the lessee is to have the advantage of casual profits, so he must run the hazard of casual losses." Evidently the court contemplated that some fortuitous event ("casualty") might have occurred during the term of the lease that would have increased markedly the value of the premises to the defendant. Nothing of that sort would have permitted the lessor to relet the premises, or to charge a higher rent. Hence—to draw out the court's reasoning—the contract imposed matching burdens on the parties. Both of these reasons are echoed in later cases and continue to be effective as argument, on occasion.

Paradine v. Jane has regularly been taken to mean that contract duties are "absolute," in the sense that no excuse based on change of conditions will be recognized.[b] If that was ever the rule, it has long been subject to some important qualifications. The scope and grounds of those qualifications are the subject of this chapter.

NOTE

Extraordinary Circumstances. In Chapter 11 of the Restatement Second, the Introductory Note has this to say: "An extraordinary circumstance may make performance so vitally different from what was reasonably to be expected as to alter the essential nature of that performance. In such a case the court must determine whether justice requires a departure from the general rule that the obligor bears the risk that the contract may become more burdensome or less desirable. This Chapter is concerned with the principles that guide that determination. . . . In recent years courts have shown increasing liberality in discharging obligors on the basis of such extraordinary circumstances."

Compare Restatement Second, § 152 with § 266. What common theme do you detect?

TAYLOR v. CALDWELL

King's Bench, 1863.
3 B. & S. 826, 122 Eng.Rep. 309.

[Action for breach of a written agreement by which defendants contracted to "let" the Surrey Gardens and Music Hall, at Newington, Surrey, to plaintiffs, for four days, for the purpose of giving four "grand concerts" and "day and night fêtes" in the hall; plain-

b. Whether the case could have been understood that way when it was decided, or ever, is questionable; but as with many an early text its importance resides chiefly in its interpretations.

tiffs agreeing to pay £100 at the close of each day. The defendants agreed to furnish a band and certain other amusements in connection with plaintiffs' entertainments, but the plaintiffs were to have all moneys paid for entrance to the music hall and gardens. The plaintiffs alleged the defendants' breach, "Whereby the plaintiffs lost divers moneys paid by them for printing advertisements of and in advertising the concerts, and also lost divers sums expended and expenses incurred by them in preparing for the concerts and otherwise in relation thereto, and on the faith of the performance by the defendants of the agreement on their part". The defendants pleaded that the Gardens and Music Hall were accidentally destroyed by fire on June 11, 1861, without the default of the defendants or either of them. A verdict was returned for the plaintiffs, with leave reserved to enter a verdict for defendants. Further facts are stated in the opinion.]

The judgment of the Court was now delivered by

BLACKBURN, J. In this case the plaintiffs and defendants had, on the 27th May, 1861, entered into a contract by which the defendants agreed to let the plaintiffs have the use of The Surrey Gardens and Music Hall on four days then to come, viz., the 17th June, 15th July, 5th August and 19th August, for the purpose of giving a series of four grand concerts, and day and night fetes at the Gardens and Hall on those days respectively; and the plaintiffs agreed to take the Gardens and Hall on those days, and pay £100 for each day.

[The court interprets the agreement not to be a lease, and concludes that the entertainments provided for in the agreement could not be given without the existence of the Music Hall.]

After the making of the agreement, and before the first day on which a concert was to be given, the Hall was destroyed by fire. This destruction, we must take it on the evidence, was without the fault of either party, and was so complete that in consequence the concerts could not be given as intended. And the question we have to decide is whether, under these circumstances, the loss which the plaintiffs have sustained is to fall upon the defendants. The parties when framing their agreement evidently had not present to their minds the possibility of such a disaster, and have made no express stipulation with reference to it, so that the answer to the question must depend upon the general rules of law applicable to such a contract.

There seems no doubt that where there is a positive contract to do a thing, not in itself unlawful, the contractor must perform it or pay damages for not doing it, although in consequence of unforeseen accidents, the performance of his contract has become unexpectedly burthensome or even impossible. The law is so laid down in 1 Roll. Abr. 450, Condition (G), and in the note (2) to Walton v. Waterhouse, 2 Wms.Saund. 421a. 6th Ed., and is recognised as the general rule by all the Judges in the much discussed case of Hall v. Wright (E. B. & E. 746). But this rule is only applicable when the contract is positive and absolute, and not subject to any condition either express or implied: and there are authorities which, as we think, establish the principle that where, from the nature of the contract, it appears that the parties must from the beginning have known that it could not be fulfilled unless when the time for the fulfillment of the contract arrived some particular specified thing continued to exist, so that, when entering into the contract, they must have contemplated such continuing existence as the foundation of what was to be done; there, in the absence of any express or implied warranty that the thing shall exist, the contract is not to be construed as a positive contract, but as subject to an implied condition that the parties shall be excused in case, before breach, performance becomes impossible from the perishing of the thing without default of the contractor.

There seems little doubt that this implication tends to further the great object of making the legal construction such as to fulfil the intention of those who entered into the contract. For in the course of affairs men in making such contracts in general would if it were brought to their minds, say that there should be such a condition.

Accordingly, in the Civil law, such an exception is implied in every obligation of the class which they call obligatio de certo corpore. The rule is laid down in the Digest, lib. XLV, tit. 1, de verborum obligationibus, 1.33. "Si Stichus certo die dari promissus, ante diem moriatur: non tenetur promissor." The principle is more fully developed in 1.23. "Si ex legati causa, aut ex stipulatu hominem certum mihi debeas: non aliter post mortem ejus tenearis mihi, quam si per te steterit, quominus vivo eo eum mihi dares: quod ita fit, si aut interpellatus non dedisti, aut occidisti eum." The examples are of contracts respecting a slave, which was the common illustration of a certain subject used by the Roman lawyers, just as we are apt to take a horse; and no doubt the propriety, one might almost say necessity, of the implied condition is more obvious when the contract relates to a living animal, whether man or brute, than when it relates to some inanimate thing (such as in the present case a theatre) the existence of which is not so obviously precarious as that of the live animal, but the principle is adopted in the Civil law as applicable to every obligation of which the subject is a certain thing. The general subject is treated of by Pothier, who in his Traite des Obligations, partie 3, chap. 6, art. 3, sec. 668, states the result to be that the debtor corporis certi is freed from his obligation when the thing has perished, neither by his act, nor his neglect, and before he is in default, unless by some stipulation he has taken on himself the risk of the particular misfortune which has occurred.[a]

a. For a criticism of the Roman law authorities relied upon by Blackburn, J., see Buckland, *Casus* and Frustration in Roman and Common Law, 46 Harv.L.Rev. 1281, 1287–89 (1933).

Although the Civil law is not of itself authority in an English Court, it affords great assistance in investigating the principles on which the law is grounded. And it seems to us that the common law authorities establish that in such a contract the same condition of the continued existence of the thing is implied by English law.

There is a class of contracts in which a person binds himself to do something which requires to be performed by him in person; and such promises, e. g. promises to marry, or promises to serve for a certain time, are never in practice qualified by an express exception of the death of the party; and therefore in such cases the contract is in terms broken if the promisor dies before fulfilment. Yet it was very early determined that, if the performance is personal, the executors are not liable; Hyde v. The Dean of Windsor (Cro.Eliz. 552, 553). See 2 Wms.Exors. 1560, 5th Ed., where a very apt illustration is given. "Thus," says the learned author, "if an author undertakes to compose a work, and dies before completing it, his executors are discharged from this contract: for the undertaking is merely personal in its nature, and, by the intervention of the contractor's death, has become impossible to be performed." . . .

These are instances where the implied condition is of the life of a human being, but there are others in which the same implication is made as to the continued existence of a thing. For example, where a contract of sale is made amounting to a bargain and sale, transferring presently the property in specific chattels, which are to be delivered by the vendor at a future day; there, if the chattels, without the fault of the vendor, perish in the interval, the purchaser must pay the price and the vendor is excused from performing his contract to deliver, which has thus become impossible.

[In Williams v. Lloyd, W. Jones, 179] the count, which was in assumpsit, alleged that the plaintiff had delivered a horse to the defendant, who promised to redeliver it on request. Breach, that though requested to redeliver the horse he refused. Plea, that the horse was sick and died, and the plaintiff made the request after its death; and on demurrer it was held a good plea, as the bailee was discharged from his promise by the death of the horse without default or negligence on the part of the defendant. "Let it be admitted," say the Court "that he promised to deliver it on request, if the horse die before, that is become impossible by the act of God, so the party shall be discharged as much as if an obligation were made conditioned to deliver the horse on request, and he died before it." [b]

It may, we think, be safely asserted to be now English law, that in all contracts of loan of chattels or bailments if the performance of the promise of the borrower or bailee to return the things lent or bailed, becomes impossible because it [sic] has perished, this impossi-

b. But at an earlier period the bailee was not excused. Holmes, The Common Law (1881) 176 et seq.

bility (if not arising from the fault of the borrower or bailee from some risk which he has taken upon himself) excuses the borrower or bailee from the performance of his promise to redeliver the chattel.

The great case of Coggs v. Bernard (1 Smith's L.C. 171, 5th ed.; 2 L.Raym. 909) is now the leading case on the law of bailments, and Lord Holt, in that case, referred so much to the Civil law that it might perhaps be thought that this principle was there derived direct from the civilians, and was not generally applicable in English law except in the case of bailments; but the case of Williams v. Lloyd (W. Jones, 179), above cited, shows that the same law had been already adopted by the English law as early as The Book of Assizes. The principle seems to us to be that, in contracts in which the performance depends on the continued existence of a given person or thing, a condition is implied that the impossibility of performance arising from the perishing of the person or thing shall excuse the performance.

In none of these cases is the promise in words other than positive, nor is there any express stipulation that the destruction of the person or thing shall excuse the performance; but that excuse is by law implied, because from the nature of the contract it is apparent that the parties contracted on the basis of the continued existence of the particular person or chattel. In the present case, looking at the whole contract, we find that the parties contracted on the basis of the continued existence of the Music Hall at the time when the concerts were to be given; that being essential to their performance.

We think, therefore, that the Music Hall having ceased to exist, without fault of either party, both parties are excused, the plaintiffs from taking the gardens and paying the money, the defendants from performing their promise to give the use of the Hall and Gardens and other things. Consequently the rule must be absolute to enter the verdict for the defendants.

Rule absolute.

NOTE

The Doctrine of Implied Conditions. A seller of jute contended that his contracts had become impossible of performance because of a wartime order prohibiting the shipments he had promised. One clause in the contracts was: "Any dispute that may arise under this contract to be settled by arbitration in Dundee." Arbiters were appointed and the question of impossibility was taken up before them. The seller brought an action for a "declarator" that this issue was not within the jurisdiction of the arbiters. Lord Sands [Lord Ordinary of the Court of Sessions] wrote an opinion in which he observed that the House of Lords had steadily expounded the law of impossibility by reference to an express or implied condition in the contract itself. He continued as follows: "Mr. Chree [counsel for the pursuers, or plaintiff] argued that this is a pious fiction—a fiction because it does not correspond with anything that was in the minds of parties at the time; pious because it seeks to do homage to a very sacred legal principle, the sanctity of contract. I confess I have some sympathy with Mr. Chree. It does seem to me somewhat far-fetched to hold that the non-occurrence of some event, which was not within the contemplation or even the imagination of the parties, was an implied term of the contract.[c] . . . No doubt this theory has been developed to square with the rule of the English common law in regard to supervening impossibility. A tiger has escaped from a travelling menagerie. The milkgirl fails to deliver the milk. Possibly the milkman may be exonerated from any breach of contract; but, even so, it would seem hardly reasonable to base that exoneration on the ground that 'tiger days excepted' must be held as if written into the milk contract. But though I sympathise with Mr. Chree's difficulty I am unable to adopt his reasoning." Lord Sands concluded that a question about an implied term was one which "arose under" the contracts, so that the arbiters had jurisdiction. Scott & Sons v. Del Sel, 1922 S.C. [Session Cases] 592, 596–97, aff'd, 1923 S.C. (H.L.) 37.

TRANSATLANTIC FINANCING CORPORATION v. UNITED STATES

United States Court of Appeals, D. C. Circuit, 1966.
363 F.2d 312.

J. SKELLY WRIGHT, Circuit Judge. This appeal involves a voyage charter between Transatlantic Financing Corporation, operator of the SS CHRISTOS, and the United States covering carriage of a full cargo of wheat from a United States Gulf port to a safe port in Iran. The District Court dismissed a libel filed by Transatlantic against the United States for costs attributable to the ship's diversion from the normal sea route caused by the closing of the Suez Canal. We affirm.

On July 26, 1956, the Government of Egypt nationalized the Suez Canal Company and took over operation of the Canal. On October 2, 1956, during the international crisis which resulted from the seizure, the voyage charter in suit was executed between representatives of Transatlantic and the United States. The charter indicated the termini of the voyage but not the route. On October 27, 1956, the SS CHRISTOS sailed from Galveston for Bandar Shapur, Iran, on a course which would have taken her through Gibraltar and the Suez Canal. On October 29, 1956, Israel invaded Egypt. On October 31, 1956, Great Britain and France invaded the Suez Canal Zone. On November 2, 1956, the Egyptian Government obstructed the Suez Canal with sunken vessels and closed it to traffic.

On or about November 7, 1956, Beckmann, representing Transatlantic, contacted Potosky, an employee of the United States Depart-

c. Cf. L. Hand: "As courts become increasingly sure of themselves, interpretation more and more involves an imaginative projection of the expressed purpose upon situations arising later, for which the parties did not provide and which they did not have in mind." L. N. Jackson & Co. v. Royal Norwegian Government, 177 F.2d 694, 702 (2d Cir. 1949), cert. denied, 339 U.S. 914 (1950) (dissent).

ment of Agriculture, who appellant concedes was unauthorized to bind the Government, requesting instructions concerning disposition of the cargo and seeking an agreement for payment of additional compensation for a voyage around the Cape of Good Hope. Potosky advised Beckmann that Transatlantic was expected to perform the charter according to its terms, that he did not believe Transatlantic was entitled to additional compensation for a voyage around the Cape, but that Transatlantic was free to file such a claim. Following this discussion, the CHRISTOS changed course for the Cape of Good Hope and eventually arrived in Bandar Shapur on December 30, 1956.

Transatlantic's claim is based on the following train of argument. The charter was a contract for a voyage from a Gulf port to Iran. Admiralty principles and practices, especially stemming from the doctrine of deviation, require us to imply into the contract the term that the voyage was to be performed by the "usual and customary" route. The usual and customary route from Texas to Iran was, at the time of contract, via Suez, so the contract was for a voyage from Texas to Iran via Suez. When Suez was closed this contract became impossible to perform. Consequently, appellant's argument continues, when Transatlantic delivered the cargo by going around the Cape of Good Hope, in compliance with the Government's demand under claim of right, it conferred a benefit upon the United States for which it should be paid in *quantum meruit*.

The doctrine of impossibility of performance has gradually been freed from the earlier fictional and unrealistic strictures of such tests as the "implied term" and the parties' "contemplation." Page, The Development of the Doctrine of Impossibility of Performance, 18 Mich.L.Rev. 589, 596 (1920). See generally 6 Corbin, Contracts §§ 1320–1372 (rev. ed. 1962); 6 Williston, Contracts §§ 1931–1979 (rev. ed. 1938). It is now recognized that " 'A thing is impossible in legal contemplation when it is not practicable; and a thing is impracticable when it can only be done at an excessive and unreasonable cost.' " Mineral Park Land Co. v. Howard, 172 Cal. 289, 293, 156 P. 458, 460, L.R.A.1916F, 1 (1916). *Accord,* Whelan v. Griffith Consumers Company, D.C.Mun.App., 170 A.2d 229 (1961); Restatement, Contracts § 454 (1932); Uniform Commercial Code (U.L.A.) § 2–615, comment 3. [The section is reproduced at p. 969 infra.] The doctrine ultimately represents the ever-shifting line, drawn by courts hopefully responsive to commercial practices and mores, at which the community's interest in having contracts enforced according to their terms is outweighed by the commercial senselessness of requiring performance.[1] When the issue is raised, the court is asked to con-

1. While the impossibility issue rarely arises, as it has here, in a suit to recover the cost of an alternative method of performance, compare Annot., 84 A.L.R.2d 12, 19 (1962), there is nothing necessarily inconsistent in claiming commercial impracticability for the method of performance actually adopted; the concept of impracticability assumes performance

struct a condition of performance [2] based on the changed circumstances, a process which involves at least three reasonably definable steps. First, a contingency—something unexpected—must have occurred. Second, the risk of the unexpected occurrence must not have been allocated either by agreement or by custom. Finally, occurrence of the contingency must have rendered performance commercially impracticable.[3] Unless the court finds these three requirements satisfied, the plea of impossibility must fail.

The first requirement was met here. It seems reasonable, where no route is mentioned in a contract, to assume the parties expected performance by the usual and customary route at the time of contract.[4] Since the usual and customary route from Texas to Iran at the time of contract [5] was through Suez, closure of the Canal made

was physically possible. Moreover, a rule making nonperformance a condition precedent to recovery would unjustifiably encourage disappointment of expectations.

2. Patterson, Constructive Conditions in Contracts, 42 Colum.L.Rev. 903, 943–954 (1942).

3. Compare Uniform Commercial Code § 2–615(a), which provides that, in the absence of an assumption of greater liability, delay or non-delivery by a seller is not a breach if performance as agreed is made "impracticable" by the occurrence of a "contingency" the non-occurrence of which was a "basic assumption on which the contract was made." To the extent this limits relief to "unforeseen" circumstances, comment 1, see the discussion below, and compare Uniform Commercial Code § 2–614(1). There may be a point beyond which agreement cannot go, Uniform Commercial Code § 2–615, comment 8, presumably the point at which the obligation would be "manifestly unreasonable," § 1–102(3), in bad faith, § 1–203, or unconscionable, § 2–302. For an application of these provisions see Judge Friendly's opinion in United States v. Wegematic Corporation, 2 Cir., 360 F.2d 674 (1966) [p. 972 infra].

4. Uniform Commercial Code § 2–614, comment 1, states: "Under this Article, in the absence of specific agreement, the normal or usual facilities enter into the agreement either through the circumstances, usage of trade or prior course of dealing." So long as this sort of assumption does not necessarily result in construction of a condition of performance, it is idle to argue over whether the usual and customary route is an "implied term." The issue of impracticability must eventually be met. One court refused to imply the Suez route as a contract term, but went on to rule the contract had been "frustrated." Carapanayoti & Co. Ltd. v. E. T. Green Ltd., [1959] 1 Q.B. 131. The holding was later rejected by the House of Lords. Tsakiroglou & Co. Ltd. v. Noblee Thorl G.m.b.H., [1960] 2 Q.B. 348.

5. The parties have spent considerable energy in disputing whether the "usual and customary" route by which performance was anticipated is defined as of the time of contract or of performance. If we were automatically to treat the expected route as a condition of performance, this matter would be crucial, and we would be compelled to choose between unacceptable alternatives. If we assume as a constructive condition the usual and customary course always to mean the one in use at the time of contract, any substantial diversion (we assume the diversion would have to be substantial) would nullify the contract even though its effect upon the rights and obligations of the parties is insignificant. Nor would it be desirable, on the other hand, to assume performance is conditioned on the availability of *any* usual and customary route at the time of performance. It may be that very often the availability of a customary route at the time of performance other than the route expected to be used at the time of contract should result in denial of relief under the impossibility

impossible the expected method of performance. But this unexpected development raises rather than resolves the impossibility issue, which turns additionally on whether the risk of the contingency's occurrence had been allocated and, if not, whether performance by alternative routes was rendered impracticable.[6]

Proof that the risk of a contingency's occurrence has been allocated may be expressed in or implied from the agreement. Such proof may also be found in the surrounding circumstances, including custom and usages of the trade. See 6 Corbin, supra, § 1339, at 394–397; 6 Williston, supra, § 1948, at 5457–5458. The contract in this case does not expressly condition performance upon availability of the Suez route. Nor does it specify "via Suez" or, on the other hand, "via Suez or Cape of Good Hope." [7] Nor are there provisions

theory; certainly if *no* customary route is available at the time of performance the contract is rendered impossible. But the same customarily used alternative route may be practicable in one set of circumstances and impracticable in another, as where the goods are unable to survive the extra journey. Moreover, the "time of performance" is no special point in time; it is every moment in a performance. Thus the alternative route, in our case around the Cape, may be practicable at some time during performance, for example while the vessel is still in the Atlantic Ocean, and impracticable at another time during performance, for example after the vessel has traversed most of the Mediterranean Sea. Both alternatives, therefore, have their shortcomings, and we avoid choosing between them by refusing automatically to treat the usual and customary route as of any time as a condition of performance.

6. In criticizing the "contemplation" test for impossibility Professor Patterson pointed out:

" 'Contemplation' is appropriate to describe the mental state of philosophers but is scarcely descriptive of the mental state of business men making a bargain. It seems preferable to say that the promisee *expects* performance by [the] means . . . the promisor expects to (or which on the facts known to the promisee it is probable that he will) use. It does not follow as an inference of fact that the promisee expects performance by *only* that means . . . ." Patterson, supra Note 2, at 947.

7. In Glidden Company v. Hellenic Lines, Limited, 2 Cir., 275 F.2d 253 (1960), the charter was for transportation of materials from India to America "via Suez Canal or Cape of Good Hope, or Panama Canal," and the court held performance was not "frustrated." In his discussion of this case, Professor Corbin states: "Except for the provision for an alternative route, the defendant would have been discharged, for the reason that the parties contemplated an open Suez Canal as a specific condition or means of performance." 6 Corbin, supra, § 1339, at 399 n. 57. Appellant claims this supports its argument, since the Suez route was contemplated as usual and customary. But there is obviously a difference, in deciding whether a contract allocates the risk of a contingency's occurrence, between a contract specifying no route and a contract specifying Suez. We think that when Professor Corbin said, "Except for the provision for an alternative route," he was referring, not to the entire *provision*—"via Suez Canal or Cape of Good Hope" etc.—but to the fact that *an alternative route* had been provided for. Moreover, in determining what Corbin meant when he said "the parties contemplated an open Suez Canal as a specific condition or means of performance," consideration must be given to the fact, recited by Corbin, that in *Glidden* the parties were specifically aware when the contract was made the Canal might be closed, and the promisee had refused to include a clause excusing performance in the event of closure. Corbin's statement, therefore, is most accurately read as referring to cases

in the contract from which we may properly imply that the continued availability of Suez was a condition of performance.[8] Nor is there anything in custom or trade usage, or in the surrounding circumstances generally, which would support our constructing a condition of performance. The numerous cases requiring performance around the Cape when Suez was closed, see e. g., Ocean Tramp Tankers Corp. v. V/O Sovfracht (The Eugenia), [1964] 2 Q.B. 226, and cases cited therein, indicate that the Cape route is generally regarded as an alternative means of performance. So the implied expectation that the route would be via Suez is hardly adequate proof of an allocation to the promisee of the risk of closure. In some cases, even an express expectation may not amount to a condition of performance.[9] The doctrine of deviation supports our assumption that parties normally expect performance by the usual and customary route, but it adds nothing beyond this that is probative of an allocation of the risk.[10]

in which a route is specified after negotiations reflecting the parties' awareness that the usual and customary route might become unavailable. Compare Held v. Goldsmith, 153 La. 598, 96 So. 272 (1919).

8. The charter provides that the vessel is "in every way fitted for *the voyage*" (emphasis added), and the "P. & I. Bunker Deviation Clause" refers to "the contract voyage" and the "direct and/or customary route." Appellant argues that these provisions require implication of a voyage by the direct and customary route. Actually they prove only what we are willing to accept—that the parties expected the usual and customary route would be used. The provisions in no way condition performance upon nonoccurrence of this contingency.

There are two clauses which allegedly demonstrate that time is of importance in this contract. One clause computes the remuneration "in steaming time" for diversions to other countries ordered by the charterer in emergencies. This proves only that the United States wished to reserve power to send the goods to another country. It does not imply in any way that either was in a rush about the matter. The other clause concerns demurrage and despatch. The charterer agreed to pay Transatlantic demurrage of $1,200 per day for all time in excess of the period agreed upon for loading and unloading, and Transatlantic was to pay despatch of $600 per day for any saving in time. Of course this provision shows the parties were concerned about time, see Gilmore & Black, The Law of Admiralty § 4–8 (1957), but the fact that they arranged so minutely the consequences of any delay or speed-up of loading and unloading operates against the argument that they were similarly allocating the risk of delay or speed-up of the voyage.

9. Uniform Commercial Code § 2–614 (1) provides: "Where without fault of either party . . . the *agreed* manner of delivery . . . becomes commercially impracticable but a commercially reasonable substitute is available, such substitute performance must be tendered and accepted." (Emphasis added.) Compare Mr. Justice Holmes' observation: "You can give any conclusion a logical form. You always can imply a condition in a contract. But why do you imply it? It is because of some belief as to the practice of the community or of a class, or because of some opinion as to policy . . .." Holmes, The Path of the Law, 10 Harv.L.Rev. 457, 466 (1897).

10. The deviation doctrine, drawn principally from admiralty insurance practice, implies into all relevant commercial instruments naming the termini of voyages the usual and customary route between those points. 1 Arnould, Marine Insurance and Average § 376, at 522 (10th ed. 1921). Insurance is cancelled when a ship unreasonably "deviates" from this course, for example by extending a

If anything, the circumstances surrounding this contract indicate that the risk of the Canal's closure may be deemed to have been allocated to Transatlantic. We know or may safely assume that the parties were aware, as were most commercial men with interests affected by the Suez situation, see The Eugenia, supra, that the Canal might become a dangerous area. No doubt the tension affected freight rates, and it is arguable that the risk of closure became part of the dickered terms. Uniform Commercial Code § 2–615, comment 8. We do not deem the risk of closure so allocated, however. Foreseeability or even recognition of a risk does not necessarily prove its allocation.[11] Compare Uniform Commercial Code § 2–615, Comment 1; Restatement, Contracts § 457 (1932). Parties to a contract are not always able to provide for all the possibilities of which they are aware, sometimes because they cannot agree, often simply because they are too busy. Moreover, that some abnormal risk was contemplated is probative but does not necessarily establish an allocation of the risk of the contingency which actually occurs. In this case, for example, nationalization by Egypt of the Canal Corporation and formation of the Suez Users Group did not necessarily indicate that the Canal would be blocked even if a confrontation resulted.[12] The surrounding circumstances do indicate, however, a willingness by Transatlantic to assume abnormal risks, and this fact should legitimately

voyage or by putting in at an irregular port, and the shipowner forfeits the protection of clauses of exception which might otherwise have protected him from his common law insurer's liability to cargo. See Gilmore & Black, supra Note 8, § 2–6, at 59–60. This practice, properly qualified, see id. § 3–41, makes good sense, since insurance rates are computed on the basis of the implied course, and deviations in the course increasing the anticipated risk make the insurer's calculations meaningless. Arnould, supra, § 14, at 26. Thus the route, so far as insurance contracts are concerned, is crucial, whether express or implied. But even here, the implied term is not inflexible. Reasonable deviations do not result in loss of insurance, at least so long as established practice is followed. See Carriage of Goods by Sea Act § 4(4), 49 Stat. 1210, 46 U.S.C.A. § 1304(4); and discussion of "held covered" clauses in Gilmore & Black, supra, § 3–41, at 161. Some "deviations" are required. E. g., Hirsch Lumber Co. v. Weyerhaeuser Steamship Co., 233 F.2d 791 (2d Cir. 1956), cert. denied, 352 U.S. 880, 77 S.Ct. 102, 1 L.Ed.2d 80. The doctrine's only relevance, therefore, is that it provides additional support for the assumption we willingly make that merchants agreeing to a voyage between two points expect that the usual and customary route between those points will be used. The doctrine provides no evidence of an allocation of the risk of the route's unavailability.

11. See Note, The Fetish of Impossibility in the Law of Contracts, 53 Colum. L.Rev. 94, 98 n. 23 (1953), suggesting that foreseeability is properly used "as a *factor* probative of assumption of the risk of impossibility." (Emphasis added.)

12. Sources cited in the briefs indicate formation of the Suez Canal Users Association on October 1, 1956, was viewed in some quarters as an implied threat of force. See N.Y. Times, Oct. 2, 1956, p. 1, col. 1, noting, on the day the charter in this case was executed, that "Britain has declared her freedom to use force as a last resort if peaceful methods fail to achieve a satisfactory settlement." Secretary of State Dulles was able, however, to view the statement as evidence of the canal users' "dedication to a just and peaceful solution." The Suez Problem 369–370 (Department of State Pub. 1956).

cause us to judge the impracticability of performance by an alternative route in stricter terms than we would were the contingency unforeseen.

We turn then to the question whether occurrence of the contingency rendered performance commercially impracticable under the circumstances of this case. The goods shipped were not subject to harm from the longer, less temperate Southern route. The vessel and crew were fit to proceed around the Cape.[13] Transatlantic was no less able than the United States to purchase insurance to cover the contingency's occurrence. If anything, it is more reasonable to expect owner-operators of vessels to insure against the hazards of war. They are in the best position to calculate the cost of performance by alternative routes (and therefore to estimate the amount of insurance required), and are undoubtedly sensitive to international troubles which uniquely affect the demand for and cost of their services. The only factor operating here in appellant's favor is the added expense, allegedly $43,972.00 above and beyond the contract price of $305,842.-92, of extending a 10,000 mile voyage by approximately 3,000 miles. While it may be an overstatement to say that increased cost and difficulty of performance never constitute impracticability, to justify relief there must be more of a variation between expected cost and the cost of performing by an available alternative than is present in this case,[14] where the promisor can legitimately be presumed to have ac-

13. The issue of impracticability should no doubt be "an objective determination of whether the promise can reasonably be performed rather than a subjective inquiry into the promisor's capability of performing as agreed." Symposium, The Uniform Commercial Code and Contract Law: Some Selected Problems, 105 U.Pa.L.Rev. 836, 880, 887 (1957). Dealers should not be excused because of less than normal capabilities. But if both parties are aware of a dealer's limited capabilities, no objective determination would be complete without taking into account this fact.

14. Two leading English cases support this conclusion. The Eugenia, supra, involved a time charter for a trip from Genoa to India via the Black Sea. The charterers were held in breach of the charter's war clause by entering the Suez Canal after the outbreak of hostilities, but sought to avoid paying for the time the vessel was trapped in the Canal by arguing that, even if they had not entered the Canal, it would have been blocked and the vessel would have had to go around the Cape to India, a trip which "frustrated" the contract because it constituted an entirely different venture from the one originally contemplated. The lower court agreed, but the House of Lords (see Lord Denning's admirable treatment, [1964] 2 Q.B. at 233), "swallowing" the difficulty of applying the frustration doctrine to hypothetical facts, reversed, holding that the contract had to be performed. Especially relevant is the fact that the case expressly overruled Societe Franco Tunisienne D'Armement v. Sidermar S.P.A. (The Massalia), [1961] 2 Q.B. 278, where a voyage charter was deemed frustrated because the Cape route was "highly circuitous" and cost 195s. per long ton to ship iron ore, rather than 134s. via Suez, a difference well in excess of the difference in this case.

In Tsakiroglou & Co. Ltd. v. Noblee Thorl G.m.b.H., supra Note 4, the difference to the seller under a C.I.F. contract in freight costs caused by the Canal's closure was £15 per ton instead of £7.10s. per ton—precisely twice the cost. The House of Lords found no frustration.

cepted some degree of abnormal risk, and where impracticability is urged on the basis of added expense alone.[15]

We conclude, therefore, as have most other courts considering related issues arising out of the Suez closure,[16] that performance of this contract was not rendered legally impossible. Even if we agreed with appellant, its theory of relief seems untenable. When performance of a contract is deemed impossible it is a nullity. In the case of a charter party involving carriage of goods, the carrier may return to an appropriate port and unload its cargo, The Malcolm Baxter, Jr., 277 U.S. 323, 48 S.Ct. 516, 72 L.Ed. 901 (1928), subject of course to required steps to minimize damages. If the performance rendered has value, recovery in *quantum meruit* for the entire performance is proper. But here Transatlantic has collected its contract price, and now seeks *quantum meruit* relief for the additional expense of the trip around the Cape. If the contract is a nullity, Transatlantic's theory of relief should have been *quantum meruit* for the entire trip, rather than only for the extra expense. Transatlantic attempts to take its profit on the contract, and then force the Government to absorb the cost of the additional voyage.[17] When impracticability with-

15. See Uniform Commercial Code § 2–615, comment 4: "Increased cost alone does not excuse performance unless the rise in cost is due to some unforeseen contingency which alters the essential nature of the performance." See also 6 Corbin, supra, § 1333; 6 Williston, supra, § 1952, at 5468.

16. Appellant seeks to distinguish the English cases supporting our view. The Eugenia, supra, appellant argues, involved a time charter. True, but it overruled The Massalia, supra Note 14, which involved a voyage charter. Indeed, when the time charter is for a voyage the difference is only verbal. See Carver, Carriage of Goods by Sea 256–257 (10th ed. 1957). More convincing is the argument that Tsakiroglou & Co. Ltd., supra Note 4, involved a contract for the sale of goods, where the seller agreed to a C.I.F. clause requiring him to ship the goods to the buyer. There is a significant difference between a C.I.F. contract and voyage or time charters. The effect of delay in the former due to longer sea voyages is minimized, since the seller can raise money on the goods he has shipped almost at once, and the buyer, once he takes up the documents, can deal with the goods by transferring the documents before the goods arrive. See Tsakiroglou & Co. Ltd., supra Note 4, [1960] 2 Q.B. at 361. But this difference is not so material that impossibility in C.I.F. contracts is unrelated to impossibility in charter parties. It would raise serious questions for a court to require sellers under C.I.F. contracts to perform in circumstances under which the sellers could be refused performance by carriers with whom they have entered into charter parties for affreightment. See The Eugenia, supra, [1964] 2 Q.B. at 241. Where the time of the voyage is unimportant, a charter party should be treated the same as a C.I.F. contract in determining impossibility of performance.

These cases certainly are not distinguishable, as appellant suggests, on the ground that they refer to "frustration" rather than to "impossibility." The English regard "frustration" as substantially identical with "impossibility." 6 Corbin, supra, § 1322, at 327 n. 9.

17. The argument that the Uniform Commercial Code requires the buyer to pay the additional cost of performance by a commercially reasonable substitute was advanced and rejected in Symposium, supra Note 13, 105 U.Pa.L.Rev. at 884 n. 205. In Dillon v. United States, 156 F.Supp. 719, 140 Ct.Cl. 508 (1957), relief was afforded for some of the cost of delivering hay from a commercially unreasonable

out fault occurs, the law seeks an equitable solution, see 6 Corbin, supra, § 1321, and *quantum meruit* is one of its potent devices to achieve this end. There is no interest in casting the entire burden of commercial disaster on one party in order to preserve the other's profit. Apparently the contract price in this case was advantageous enough to deter appellant from taking a stance on damages consistent with its theory of liability. In any event, there is no basis for relief.

Affirmed.

NOTES

(1) *Shipment via Suez.* Suppose the charter had given the Government a right to notice of the progress of the vessel by requiring the master to send it a telegram "on passing Suez." Such a provision appeared in "The Massalia," one of the more controversial of the Suez cases. The charter was for a voyage from India to Genoa. Note the court's reference to the case (and to its overruling) in footnote 14.

In footnote 7 the court uses the *Glidden* case, in the Second Circuit, for support. The charter there gave the shipper power to designate a destination (on the Atlantic seaboard) "not later than on Vessel's passing Gibraltar." But a more interesting feature of this case was that the shipowner had asked for a clause excusing it in the event the Canal was closed, and that the shipper had rejected any such term. These facts, taken together, make the case a near-perfect example of the type described in the last sentence of footnote 7, do they not? Do you agree with the court that the doctrine of impossibility is better applicable in that situation than in the case before it?

As the court notes, all of these cases were rather different from the problem in Tsakiroglou, mentioned in footnotes 4, 16 and 17, where the contract was one of *sale*. The seller had agreed to ship groundnuts from the Sudan to Hamburg, paying the cost, insurance and freight (c.i.f.). The contract was entered into on October 4, and called for shipment in November or December. The House of Lords sustained an award of damages for his failure to perform. As regards the custom of shipment via Suez, Lord Radcliffe said: "A man may habitually leave his house by the front door to keep his appointments; but, if the front door is stuck, he would hardly be excused for not leaving by the back."

Professor Harold Berman has argued that the doctrines of impossibility and frustration are out of place in relation to international trade transactions. Examining the standard terms they employ, he infers that the parties rely not on the peculiar doctrines which might excuse performance in this or that country, but on the sanctity of contract, "their surest defense," plus their own precautionary drafting of special clauses. A charter party, for instance, is not a "hit-or-miss effort to foresee the future," but a "serious attempt to exhaust the possible allocations of risks." [a] Berman,

distance, but the suit was one in which the plaintiff had suffered losses far in excess of the relief given.

a. Compare Lord Sumner's opinion in Larrinaga & Co. v. Société Franco-Americaine des Phosphates de Medulla, [1923] 92 L.J.K.B. 455, 464; 39 T.L.R. 316: "In effect most forward contracts can be regarded as a form of commercial insurance, in which every event is intended to be at the risk of one party or another."

Excuse for Nonperformance in the Light of Contract Practices in International Trade, 63 Colum.L.Rev. 1413 (1963).[b] Does the court reject that view in the main case?

(2) *Reprise.* The Canal was closed again on June 5, 1967. At that time the tanker Washington Trader was about 84 miles from Port Said, on a voyage from Beaumont to Bombay. As in the main case, the claimant (owner of the vessel) sought to charge the charterer with the additional cost of the voyage around the Cape: about $132,000. This sum was almost a third of the freight paid at the agreed rate, as compared with the 14% overrun in Transatlantic. The closing took the Washington Trader more than 8,000 miles out of her way. (Note the example used in footnote 5 of the main case, of a vessel that has "traversed most of the Mediterranean Sea.") These figures did not persuade the court that the charterer should pay more than it had contracted for.

The owner sought to distinguish Transatlantic on the ground that a flat rate was contracted for there, whereas in the present case the freight was calculated on the basis of a prevailing rate (per ton) applicable to transport through the Canal. Again the court was unpersuaded. American Trading & Pro. Corp. v. Shell Internat'l Marine Ltd., 453 F.2d 939 (2d Cir. 1972).

INTERNATIONAL PAPER CO. v. ROCKEFELLER, New York Supreme Court, Third Dept., 1914. 161 A.D. 180, 146 N.Y.S. 371. [Action for breach of contract to deliver pulpwood to plaintiff. Defense, that the pulpwood was to be cut from green spruce wood growing on a particular tract of land, and that the uncut spruce wood on this land was in 1903 destroyed by fire, except about 550 cords upon the top of a high mountain, which could be cut and delivered only at an expense of $20 per cord, as compared with the contract price of $5.50 per cord. The evidence to support defendant's contention that the parties "contemplated" delivery from this land was: The written contract, the one sued upon, referred to this tract of land and recited that the buyer "is desirous of purchasing wood now on said lands from [the seller] which the latter is willing to sell if he acquires the title to said lands under" a certain contract with the Kingsley Lumber Company; the contract sued upon was made as a result of the negotiations of one Hibbard for the purchase of these lands from the Kingsley company; and although the contract called for delivery of 6000 cords the first year and 10,000 cords in each of the next five years (ending in 1905), the plaintiff wrote defendant protesting against the cutting of spruce on this tract for any other purposes. The trial court held the defendant was bound unconditionally to deliv-

b. For less stringent views, see Birmingham, A Second Look at the Suez Canal Cases, 20 Hast.L.J. 1393 (1969) (providing an economic analysis), and Schlegel, Of Nuts, and Ships, and Sealing Wax, Suez, and Frustrating Things, 23 Rutgers L.Rev. 419 (1969), both suggesting a graduated response to differing equities.

er the entire quantity of pulpwood, and plaintiff recovered judgment for the difference between the contract price and the market price of the quantity not delivered, amounting to $48,000. Defendant appealed.]

KELLOGG, J. (after stating the facts): While not free from doubt, it seems to me that it was contemplated that the wood to be furnished was to be cut on the Kingsley lands. The statement that the plaintiff was desirous of purchasing the wood now on the lands and that the defendant was willing to sell it if he acquired the lands; the fact that the contract was conditional upon the purchase and that the first deliveries in 1899 were dependent upon the connection with the Chateaugay road which came within a very short distance but would not immediately serve any other woodlands, and the fact that Hibbard was the moving spirit in the matter, was understood to be the party getting out the wood and apparently had no other relations with the defendant than in lumbering this tract, indicate that the parties had in mind, in making the contract, the lumbering of this tract. We need not say that the defendant could not have furnished like wood of equal quality from other lands, but the contract, read in connection with the known facts, shows the source from which the parties contemplated the wood should be furnished, and when the source is destroyed the defendant is excused from further performance. The defendant did not contract to deliver the wood unless he acquired the Kingsley lands. If all the wood upon the Kingsley lands had been destroyed by fire immediately after the contract was executed, the parties would have been in substantially the same position they would have occupied if the defendant had not acquired the lands. The real reason which induced the contract and upon which it depended would have failed.

. . . The defendant is not excused from delivering the live spruce suitable for pulpwood which survived the fire by the mere fact that its location upon the tract is such that it would be very expensive for him to deliver it.

The judgment and orders are reversed on law and facts and a new trial granted, with costs to the appellant to abide the event.

NOTES

(1) *Parol Evidence.* If the seller had offered to prove an oral agreement, at the time the written one was executed, that all of the pulpwood was to come from the Kingsley lands, would the evidence have been admissible? What if the seller had offered evidence that the buyer had agreed not to hold him bound in the event of a fire consuming the timber in question? The admission of such evidence was held not to be prejudicial error in Ontario Deciduous Fruit Growers' Association v. Cutting Fruit-Packing Co., 134 Cal. 21, 66 P. 28 (1901). Other authorities on these questions, not all in accord, are cited in the text at p. 992 infra.

In the case as it stands, notice the sources, in and out of the written contract, from which the court drew the conclusion that "the parties had in mind, in making the contract, the lumbering of this tract." If the writing had made no reference to the Kingsley lands, should the court have reached a different result?

(2) *The Reverse Claim.* Suppose that the market price of pulpwood had declined, that the seller had tendered pulpwood from another tract, and that the buyer had declined to take it. Would that have been a breach by the buyer? See Patterson, The Restatement of the Law of Contracts, 33 Colum.L.Rev. 397, 423 (1933).

UCC 2–615

Among the problems of this chapter, applications of this section have come to occupy center stage. It is set out in the footnote for convenient reference.[a] Note that the court looked to it for guidance in the Transatlantic Financing case, and that it would have applied, if enacted then, to the International Paper case.[b] The questions below open a discussion of the section, which is continued on other pages to follow.

The comments after 2–615 begin: "This section excuses a seller from timely delivery of goods contracted for, where his performance has become commercially impracticable because of unforeseen supervening circumstances not within the contemplation of the parties at the time of contracting." The "restatement" of the section most frequently found in the cases expresses three conditions for excusing a seller's performance under the Code:

> (1) a contingency must occur, (2) performance must thereby be made "impracticable" and (3) the nonoccurrence of the contingency must have been a basic assumption on which the contract was made.[c]

a. **Excuse by Failure of Presupposed Conditions**

Except so far as a seller may have assumed a greater obligation and subject to the preceding section on substituted performance:

(a) Delay in delivery or non-delivery in whole or in part by a seller who complies with paragraphs (b) and (c) is not a breach of his duty under a contract for sale if performance as agreed has been made impracticable by the occurrence of a contingency the non-occurrence of which was a basic assumption on which the contract was made or by compliance in good faith with any applicable foreign or domestic governmental regulation or order whether or not it later proves to be invalid.

(b) Where the causes mentioned in paragraph (a) affect only a part of the seller's capacity to perform, he must allocate production and deliveries among his customers but may at his option include regular customers not then under contract as well as his own requirements for further manufacture. He may so allocate in any manner which is fair and reasonable.

(c) The seller must notify the buyer seasonably that there will be delay or non-delivery and, when allocation is required under paragraph (b), of the estimated quota thus made available for the buyer.

b. UCC 2–107(2).

c. Neal-Cooper Grain Co. v. Texas Gulf Sulphur Co., 508 F.2d 283, 298 (7th Cir. 1974). See also Luria Bros. & Co. v. Pielet Bros. Scrap Iron & Metal, Inc., 600 F.2d 103, 111 (7th Cir. 1979) ("Three conditions must be met . . . .")

This formula does not of course capture every nuance of section 2–615.

QUESTIONS

(1) Is the section unnecessarily vague or obscure in expression? A number of writers have urged that it be revised.[d] Does it give the courts undue discretion to relieve sellers of their undertakings?

(2) Is it clear that a seller may commit himself to a performance notwithstanding that it becomes "commercially impracticable"? Is it clear that he may, by suitable limiting language, exempt himself from obligation in an event "the non-occurrence of which" is *not* a "basic assumption on which the contract [is] made"?

In this connection, reference is often made to Comment 8, which states: "Generally, express agreements as to exemptions designed to enlarge upon or supplant the provisions of this section are to be read in the light of mercantile sense and reason, for this section itself sets up the commercial standard for normal and reasonable interpretation and provides a minimum beyond which agreement may not go." (Is the "minimum" here one of obligation, or one of exemption from obligation?)

(3) Consult UCC 1–102(3) and (4), set out in the footnote.[e] Do these provisions help to answer, or only complicate, the foregoing questions?

(4) Does paragraph (b) embody clear and workable principles? Sound ones? In cases arising under paragraph (a) much attention

d. A brief bibliography of recent items on the section is as follows:

Deusenberg, Contract Impossibility: Courts Begin to Shape § 2–615, 32 Bus.Law. 1089 (1977);

Hurst, Freedom of Contract in an Unstable Economy, 54 N.C.L.Rev. 545 (1976). Like Dean Hawkland, Professor Hurst would revive the qualification, "unless otherwise agreed," which appeared in an early draft of the section. He would revise the section also to relieve the courts of unwarranted appeals to discretion that it apparently gives them to relieve against hardship.

Macaulay, Elegant Models, Empirical Pictures and the Complexities of Contract, 11 Law & Soc.Rev. 507, 515 ff. (1977). Professor Macaulay presents the utilities of decisive legal norms and judgments, even for cases where settlements eventuate, and those of *partial* resort to litigation.

Posner & Rosenfield, Impossibility and Related Doctrines in Contract Law: An Economic Analysis, 6 J.Leg. Studies 83 (1977);

Note, 5 Hofstra L.Rev. 167 (1976) (proposing revision);

Comment, 72 Nw.U.L.Rev. 1032 (1978) (sharply critical of the Transatlantic Financing case).

For other sources, and for legislative history, see Comment, UCC Section 2–615, 51 Temp.L.Q. 518, 521, n. 8 (1978).

e. (3) The effect of provisions of this Act may be varied by agreement, except as otherwise provided in this Act and except that the obligations of good faith, diligence, reasonableness and care prescribed by this Act may not be disclaimed by agreement but the parties may by agreement determine the standards by which the performance of such obligations is to be measured if such standards are not manifestly unreasonable.

(4) The presence in certain provisions of this Act of the words "unless otherwise agreed" or words of similar import does not imply that the effect of other provisions may not be varied by agreement under subsection (3).

has been given to the extent of loss a seller would incur through performance as promised. If the "basic assumptions" of a contract are to be determined by reference to costs that the seller encounters, is there any reason to compel him to perform in part? Assuming that allocation is required, what counts in determining a "fair and reasonable" manner? The differing capacities of the customers to absorb losses? Differences among them of efficiency in serving some "ultimate" market?

For valuable legislative history of the section, see Hawkland, The Energy Crisis and Section 2–615, 79 Comm.L.J. 75 (1974).

NOTES

(1) *Assumption of Greater Liability.* In Harvey v. Fearless Farris Wholesale, Inc., 589 F.2d 451 (9th Cir. 1979), a wholesale supplier of gasoline was affected by commercial impracticability; so the court assumed. It made allocations of its supplies among its retailing customers. One of them, the plaintiff, complained that it should have received a more favorable allocation. (For a time Wholesale distributed all its supplies to gas stations owned by Farris Lind, who also owned Wholesale.) The plaintiff alleged that Wholesale had agreed to keep it supplied in the event of a shortage. The parties, it seems, had not agreed on a price for continued supplies, and the plaintiff was free, as before, to take gas from any supplier at the best available price. For this reason, the court concluded, the "shortage" agreement—if one was made—was unenforceable: nothing in the Code dispenses with the requirement of mutuality of obligation. The court affirmed a summary judgment for Wholesale.[f] Consult again the questions in the foregoing text; is any of them implicated in this case?

Comment 8 after 2–615 begins: "The provisions of this section are made subject to assumption of greater liability by agreement . . . ." Can the Harvey case be squared with this?

The statement just quoted seems to give a categorical answer to one of the questions in the text; but other comments suggest reservations. They speak of "adjustments" required by other sections and by equitable principles when the flat decision, "no excuse" (or "excuse"), is opposed by sense and justice (Comment 6).[g] They also indicate that 2–615 is not meant as an "exhaustive expression" of the underlying principle (Comment 2). See also footnote 3 in Transatlantic Financing Corporation v. United States, p. 960 supra.

(2) *Allocation Problem.* Steel Company produces steel, liquid oxygen (LOX), and gaseous oxygen (GO). It sells steel and LOX and uses GO in the production of steel. A compressor explosion reduces its capacity to produce oxygen and makes the performance of its contracts commercially impracticable. The company can maintain its production of GO only by reducing its production of LOX. Its choices are: (a) allocating its production of steel among steel customers, (b) allocating that of LOX among its LOX customers, and (c) allocating among all its customers. If it makes forward

f. Compare American Oil Co. v. Columbia Oil Co., Inc., 88 Wash.2d 835, 567 P.2d 637 (1977).

g. Set out in Note 1, p. 983 infra.

contracts for LOX, and makes only spot sales of steel, does that dictate choice (a)? If steel is its most profitable line, does that permit choice (b)? See Chemetron Corp. v. McLouth Steel Corp., 381 F.Supp. 245 (N.D.Ill.1974) (suggesting that McLouth might have maintained its production levels for both liquid oxygen *and* steel).[h]

In Campbell v. Hostetter Farms, Inc., 251 Pa.Super. 232, 380 A.2d 463 (1977), a farmer whose corn crop fell short withheld some of it from a buyer in order to feed his livestock. Is that equivalent to choice (b) above? Compare Mansfield Propane Gas Co., Inc. v. Folger Gas Co., 231 Ga. 868, 204 S.E.2d 625 (1974).

(3) *Excuses for Buyers?* The general understanding is that the Code states no general rule excusing a fixed-quantity buyer in the event of commercial impracticability for him. Can it be faulted for that? What would amount to impracticability of a buyer's performance? Comment 9 after section 2–615 states that "the reason of the present section may well apply" so as to excuse a buyer in a certain situation. See G. Gilmore, 2 Security Interests in Personal Property, § 41.7 (1965). One court has translated the comment into the following dictum: "While the section expressly mentions *sellers*, the explanations . . . make it evident the provisions should also be equally applicable to buyers." Nora Springs Co-op Co. v. Brandau, 247 N.W.2d 744 (Iowa, 1976). See Comment, 51 Temple L.Q. 518 (1978).

UNITED STATES v. WEGEMATIC CORP.

United States Court of Appeals, Second Circuit, 1966.
360 F.2d 674.

FRIENDLY, Circuit Judge. The facts developed at trial in the District Court for the Southern District of New York, fully set forth in a memorandum by Judge Graven, can be briefly summarized: In June 1956 the Federal Reserve Board invited five electronics manufacturers to submit proposals for an intermediate-type, general-purpose electronic digital computing system or systems; the invitation stressed the importance of early delivery as a consideration in determining the Board's choice. Defendant, a relative newcomer in the field, which had enjoyed considerable success with a smaller computer known as the ALWAC III–E, submitted a detailed proposal for the sale or lease of a new computer designated as the ALWAC 800. It characterized the machine as "a truly revolutionary system utilizing all of the latest technical advances," and featured that "maintenance problems are minimized by the use of highly reliable magnetic cores for not only the high speed memory but also logical elements and registers." Delivery was offered nine months from the date the contract or purchase order was received. In September the Board acted favorably on the defendant's proposal, ordering components of the ALWAC 800 with an aggregate cost of $231,800. Delivery was to be made on June 30, 1957, with liquidated damages of $100 per day for

h. Aff'd, 522 F.2d 469 (7th Cir. 1975).

delay. The order also provided that in the event the defendant failed to comply "with any provision" of the agreement, "the Board may procure the services described in the contract from other sources and hold the Contractor responsible for any excess cost occasioned thereby." Defendant accepted the order with enthusiasm.

The first storm warning was a suggestion by the defendant in March 1957 that the delivery date be postponed. In April it informed the Board by letter that delivery would be made on or before October 30 rather than as agreed, the delay being due to the necessity of "a redesign which we feel has greatly improved this equipment"; waiver of the stipulated damages for delay was requested. The Board took the request under advisement. On August 30 defendant wrote that delivery would be delayed "possibly into 1959"; it suggested use of ALWAC III–E equipment in the interim and waiver of the $100 per day "penalty." The Board also took this request under advisement but made clear it was waiving no rights. In mid-October defendant announced that "due to engineering difficulties it has become impracticable to deliver the ALWAC 800 Computing System at this time"; it requested cancellation of the contract without damages. The Board set about procuring comparable equipment from another manufacturer; on October 6, 1958, International Business Machines Corporation delivered an IBM 650 computer, serving substantially the same purpose as the ALWAC 800, at a rental of $102,000 a year with an option to purchase for $410,450.

In July 1958 the Board advised defendant of its intention to press its claim for damages; this suit followed. The court awarded the United States $46,300 for delay under the liquidated damages clause, $179,450 for the excess cost of the IBM equipment, and $10,056 for preparatory expenses useless in operating the IBM system—a total of $235,806, with 6% interest from October 6, 1958.

The principal point of the defense, which is the sole ground of this appeal, is that delivery was made impossible by "basic engineering difficulties" whose correction would have taken between one and two years and would have cost a million to a million and a half dollars, with success likely but not certain. Although the record does not give an entirely clear notion what the difficulties were, two experts suggested that they may have stemmed from the magnetic cores, used instead of transistors to achieve a solid state machine, which did not have sufficient uniformity at this stage of their development. Defendant contends that under federal law, which both parties concede to govern, see Cargill, Inc. v. Commodity Credit Corp., 275 F.2d 745, 751–753 (2 Cir. 1960), the "practical impossibility" of completing the contract excused its defaults in performance.

We agree with the defendant that the decisions most strongly relied on by the Government are not controlling; much of the seeming confusion in this field of law stems from failure to make necessary distinctions as to who is suing whom for what. Thus Day v. United

States, 245 U.S. 159, 38 S.Ct. 57, 62 L.Ed. 219 (1917), and Fritz-Rumer-Cooke Co. v. United States, 279 F.2d 200, 6 Cir. (1960), involved no question of nonperformance but an attempt by a contractor who had fully performed to secure added compensation for surmounting unexpected difficulties. While Austin Co. v. United States, 314 F.2d 518, 161 Ct.Cl. 76, cert. denied, 375 U.S. 830, 84 S.Ct. 75, 11 L.Ed.2d 62 (1963), did involve failure by a manufacturer to perform because of engineering problems, it was not an effort to resist damages, which the Government did not seek; the contractor was attempting to recover costs incurred prior to termination under a special clause in the contract without which, as Professor Corbin has noted, it "would not have had the shadow of a claim." 6 Corbin, Contracts § 1328 n. 40 (1964 Pocket Part). Consolidated Airborne Systems, Inc. v. United States, 348 F.2d 941 (Ct.Cl.1965), was a case of financial inability peculiar to the contractor and is distinguishable under the doctrine of "subjective impossibility," that a promisor's duty is never discharged "by the mere fact that supervening events deprive him of the ability to perform, if they are not such as to deprive other persons, likewise, of ability to render such a performance." 6 Corbin, Contracts § 1332, at 361 (1962). And in Carnegie Steel Co. v. United States, 240 U.S. 156, 36 S.Ct. 342, 60 L.Ed. 576 (1916), which is most nearly apposite in that it concerned a claim by the promisee for delay occasioned by an unanticipated technological problem encountered by the promisor, the precise issue was whether the difficulty came within a clause excusing delays resulting from "unavoidable causes, such as fires, storms, labor strikes, action of the United States, etc." 240 U.S. at 163, 36 S.Ct. at 344. On the other hand, the mere fact that the Government's cases do not dictate decision in its favor does not mean that defendant wins; it means only that we must seek guidance elsewhere.

We find persuasive the defendant's suggestion of looking to the Uniform Commercial Code as a source for the "federal" law of sales. The Code has been adopted by Congress for the District of Columbia, 77 Stat. 630 (1963), has been enacted in over forty states, and is thus well on its way to becoming a truly national law of commerce, which, as Judge L. Hand said of the Negotiable Instruments Law, is "more complete and more certain, than any other which can conceivably be drawn from those sources of 'general law' to which we were accustomed to resort in the days of Swift v. Tyson." New York, N. H. & H. R. Co. v. Reconstruction Finance Corp., 180 F.2d 241, 244 (2 Cir. 1950). When the states have gone so far in achieving the desirable goal of a uniform law governing commercial transactions, it would be a distinct disservice to insist on a different one for the segment of commerce, important but still small in relation to the total, consisting of transactions with the United States.

Section 2–615 of the UCC, entitled "Excuse by failure of presupposed conditions," provides that:

"Except so far as a seller may have assumed a greater obligation . . . delay in delivery or non-delivery . . . is not a breach of his duty under a contract for sale if performance as agreed has been made impracticable by the occurrence of a contingency the non-occurrence of which was a basic assumption on which the contract was made . . ."

The latter part of the test seems a somewhat complicated way of putting Professor Corbin's question of how much risk the promisor assumed. Recent Developments in the Law of Contracts, 50 Harv.L. Rev. 449, 465–66 (1937); 2 Corbin, Contracts § 1333, at 371. We see no basis for thinking that when an electronics system is promoted by its manufacturer as a revolutionary breakthrough, the risk of the revolution's occurrence falls on the purchaser; the reasonable supposition is that it has already occurred or, at least, that the manufacturer is assuring the purchaser that it will be found to have when the machine is assembled. As Judge Graven said: "The Board in its invitation for bids did not request invitations to conduct a development program for it. The Board requested invitations from manufacturers for the furnishing of a computer machine." Acceptance of defendant's argument would mean that though a purchaser makes his choice because of the attractiveness of a manufacturer's representation and will be bound by it, the manufacturer is free to express what are only aspirations and gamble on mere probabilities of fulfillment without any risk of liability. In fields of developing technology, the manufacturer would thus enjoy a wide degree of latitude with respect to performance while holding an option to compel the buyer to pay if the gamble should pan out. See Austin Co. v. United States, 314 F.2d 518, 521, 161 Ct.Cl. 76, cert. denied, 375 U.S. 830, 84 S.Ct. 75, 11 L. Ed.2d 62 (1963). We do not think this the common understanding—above all as to a contract where the manufacturer expressly agreed to liquidated damages for delay and authorized the purchaser to resort to other sources in the event of non-delivery. Contrast National Presto Industries, Inc. v. United States, 338 F.2d 99, 106–112, 167 Ct.Cl. 749 (1964), cert. denied, 380 U.S. 962 (1965). If a manufacturer wishes to be relieved of the risk that what looks good on paper may not prove so good in hardware, the appropriate exculpatory language is well known and often used.

Beyond this the evidence of true impracticability was far from compelling. The large sums predicted by defendant's witnesses must be appraised in relation not to the single computer ordered by the Federal Reserve Board, evidently for a bargain price, but to the entire ALWAC 800 program as originally contemplated. Although the record gives no idea what this was, even twenty-five machines would gross $10,000,000 if priced at the level of the comparable IBM equipment. While the unanticipated need for expending $1,000,000 or

$1,500,000 on redesign might have made such a venture unattractive, as defendant's management evidently decided, the sums are thus not so clearly prohibitive as it would have them appear. What seemingly did become impossible was on-time performance; the issue whether if defendant had offered prompt rectification of the design, the Government could have refused to give it a chance and still recover not merely damages for delay but also the higher cost of replacement equipment, is not before us.

Affirmed.

NOTES

(1) *Government Procurement.* Special cadres of judicial officers occupy a strategic position in dealing with mishaps in government procurement, notably the boards of contract appeals and the Court of Claims. Under their administration the doctrines of impracticability and the like have developed some distinctive features. Decisions about high-technology government contracts and more ordinary commercial cases maintain a certain influence on one another, but it is somewhat unpredictable.[a]

Government contractors have had unusual success in recouping unexpected costs of performance. If government specifications are found to require a technical achievement "beyond the state of the art," that showing may be enough, at least when the government provides some of the know-how.[b] Or it may be enough that the contractor tried very hard, suffered a cost overrun, and made a contribution to the government's stock of information. "Economic impossibility" has been developed as a basis for relief in such cases, supplemented by imaginative uses of mutual mistake doctrine.[c] (In one influential case the court directed that the government be charged with half the supplier's unexpected costs attributable to a "mistake." [d]) Yet it seems possible for a contractor to commit himself to making a technological breakthrough.[e] Naturally, when his performance is something so prosaic as providing foodstuff, an unexpected difficulty is the more likely to be called an assumed risk.[f]

(2) *Questions.* Does it seem more likely that (say) the Air Force would be willing to bear development costs for its equipment than that the Federal Reserve Board would? If so, why?

a. See Northern Corp. v. Chugach Electric Ass'n, 518 P.2d 76 (Alaska, 1974), vacated on rehearing, 523 P.2d 1243 (1974); Jennie-O Foods, Inc. v. United States, 580 F.2d 400 (Ct.Cl. 1978).

b. See Foster-Wheeler Corp. v. United States, 513 F.2d 588 (Ct.Cl.1975).

c. See Vogel, Impossibility of Performance—A Closer Look, 9 Pub.Contract L.J. 110 (1977). These cases are especially likely to concern Restatement Second, § 266.

d. National Presto Industries, Inc. v. United States, 338 F.2d 99 (Ct.Cl. 1964), cert. denied, 380 U.S. 962 (1965).

e. Aerosonic Instrument Corp., 1959–1 Board of Contract Appeals ¶ 2115 (contract to produce a lightweight tachometer for the Air Force). But see Smith Engineering Co. v. Rice, 102 F.2d 492 (9th Cir. 1938), cert. denied, 307 U.S. 637 (1939) (private contract; note the statute); Natus Corp. v. United States, 371 F.2d 450 (Ct.Cl. 1967).

f. Jennie-O Foods, Inc. v. United States, n. a supra.

Refer again to the Suez-closing case, p. 958 supra. Would the claimant there have made a more appealing case if it had limited its claim to *half* the additional expense of the long haul 'round the Cape?

(3) *Law or Fact?* When, if ever, should a jury be consulted about the basic assumptions of a contract? Although something like that has been attempted,[g] in the Restatement Second, the Reporter's Note on Chapter 11 states that the question of excuse by impracticability and the like "is one of law, for the court," citing Mitchell v. Ceazan Tires, Ltd., 25 Cal.2d 45, 153 P.2d 53 (1944).[h]

MINERAL PARK LAND CO. v. HOWARD, Supreme Court of California, 1916. 172 Cal. 289, 156 P. 458. [Action for breach of contract. Defendants agreed to take from plaintiff's land all the gravel and earth necessary in the construction of a bridge, and to pay for it at a stated rate. Defendants actually used 101,000 cubic yards of earth and gravel, only 50,131 of which they took from plaintiff's land, having procured the rest elsewhere. The court found this was all the material on plaintiff's land which was above water level; that defendants removed "all that could have been taken advantageously to defendants, or all that was practical to take and remove from a financial standpoint"; and ruled that this fact did not excuse defendant's failure. Defendants appealed.]

SLOSS, J. . . . The parties were contracting for the right to take earth and gravel to be used in the construction of the bridge. When they stipulated that all of the earth and gravel needed for this purpose should be taken from plaintiff's land they contemplated and assumed that the land contained the requisite quantity, available for use. . . . And, in determining whether the earth and gravel were "available," we must view the conditions in a practical and reasonable way. Although there was gravel on the land, it was so situated that the defendants could not take it by ordinary means, nor except at prohibitive cost. To all fair intents then, it was impossible for defendants to take. . . . We do not mean to intimate that the defendants could excuse themselves by showing the existence of conditions which would make the performance of their obligation more expensive than they had anticipated, or which would entail a loss upon them. But where the difference in cost is so great as here, and has the effect, as found, of making performance impracticable, the situation is not different from that of a total absence of earth and gravel.

Judgment reversed.

g. See Housing Authority v. East Tennessee Light & Power Co., 183 Va. 64, 31 S.E.2d 273 (1944).

h. But see Oosten v. Hay Haulers Dairy Employees & Helpers Union, 45 Cal.2d 784, 291 P.2d 17 (1955), cert. denied, 351 U.S. 937 (1956).

NOTES

(1) *The Case of the Rock Trap.* The State of New York contracted to pay $6 million for the construction of a hospital building, including rock excavation. The contract price was to be adjusted, however, in the event that more than specified yardages of rock was required to be excavated: the additional amount was to be either 10 or 22 dollars a cubic yard of excess, depending on the location. The builder was required to excavate as much as 1,100 yards without additional compensation. Test borings at the site by the State were relied on for estimates, but the State carefully disclaimed any representation about the amount of rock there. As it turned out the rock excavation required amounted to 2,982 yards. The builder made a claim for this work in an amount based on its reasonable value, which was found to be greater than the unit prices would yield. Accepting this basis, the Court of Claims awarded almost $88,000 for additional rock excavation. On an appeal by the State, the Appellate Division found a "mere quantitative change" and reduced this element of the award to $9,017. The builder then appealed. *Held:* Affirmed. Depot Constr. Corp. v. State, 19 N.Y.2d 109, 224 N.E.2d 866 (1967).[a] Does it seem that the builder might have been well advised to omit the unit-price feature from its bid on the job? Did the builder's claim violate the principle stated in the final paragraph of the opinion in Transatlantic Financing Corporation v. United States, p. 958 supra?

(2) *Gravel v. Gold.* In Smith v. Zepp, 173 Mont. 358, 567 P.2d 923 (1977), the defendants had contracted to develop mining properties for the benefit of both themselves and the plaintiff by processing "material" at the rate of 300 yards a day in search of gold. Failing to do so, the defendants claimed an excuse on the ground that the properties contained "so trifling an amount of gold that further mining would be economically disastrous." Assuming that to be true, the court rejected the excuse, saying that the defendants should have made geological tests.

(3) *Question.* What distinctions make it possible to justify the main case in light of the decisions reported in the foregoing notes?

CANADIAN INDUSTRIAL ALCOHOL CO. v. DUNBAR MOLASSES CO., New York Court of Appeals, 1932. 258 N.Y. 194, 179 N.E. 383, 80 A.L.R. 1173. [At the end of 1927 the plaintiff Alcohol Co. contracted with Dunbar to purchase a quantity of molasses, shipments to begin after the following April 1, and to be spread out during the warm weather. The goods were described as "approximately 1,500,-

a. The Court of Claims had found that the borings were taken haphazardly. The contract referred to them as follows:

"Test holes have been drilled on the site, at locations shown on the Plot Plan drawing. The test hole data shown on the plans are not guaranteed by the State in any respect, nor represented by it as being worthy of reliance. They are made available to the Bidders, who shall make their own independent determination as to what value to assign to them. The State makes them available as information in its possession without intent or attempt to induce the Bidders to rely thereon."

For the court's animadversions on this paragraph, see Depot Construction Corp. v. State, 41 Misc.2d 764, 246 N.Y.S.2d 527 (1964).

000 wine gallons Refined Blackstrap (Molasses) of the usual run from the National Sugar Refinery, Yonkers, N.Y., to test around 60 per cent sugars." While the contract was in force that refinery produced much less molasses than its capacity—less than half a million gallons. Dunbar shipped to the Alcohol Co. its entire allotment of the refinery's output (344,083 gallons), but failed to deliver any more molasses. Upon being sued for damages, Dunbar contended that its duty was conditioned, by an implied term, on the refinery's producing enough molasses to fill the plaintiff's order. From a judgment for the buyer, Dunbar appealed.]

CARDOZO, Ch. J. . . . The contract, read in the light of the circumstances existing at its making, or more accurately in the light of any such circumstances apparent from this record, does not keep the defendant's duty within boundaries so narrow. . . . The defendant does not even show that it tried to get a contract from the refinery during the months that intervened between the acceptance of the plaintiff's order and the time when shipments were begun. It has wholly failed to relieve itself of the imputation of contributory fault (3 Williston on Contracts, sec. 1959). So far as the record shows, it put its faith in the mere chance that the output of the refinery would be the same from year to year, and finding its faith vain, it tells us that its customer must have expected to take a chance as great. We see no reason for importing into the bargain this aleatory element. The defendant is in no better position than a factor who undertakes in his own name to sell for future delivery a special grade of merchandise to be manufactured by a special mill. The duty will be discharged if the mill is destroyed before delivery is due. The duty will subsist if the output is reduced because times turn out to be hard and labor charges high. . . . [Affirmed.]

NOTE

Subjective Impossibility. A difference in legal force is often noticed between the excuses, "The thing cannot be done," and "I cannot do it." Financial disability is the prototype of so-called subjective impossibility: a debt is not extinguished by the debtor's plea—though true—"I cannot pay." [a] The Restatement Second retains the requirement of *objective* impossibility or impracticability, in other diction. See § 261, Comment e. What of UCC 2–615? According to Comment 5, "There is no excuse under this sec-

a. Financial disability need not preclude even a decree of specific performance, in relation to an obligation to pay. Christy v. Pilkinton, 224 Ark. 407, 273 S.W.2d 533 (1954). But see Valley Associates Corp. v. Rogers, 4 Misc.2d 382, 158 N.Y.S.2d 231 (1956). The buyer there sought an order that the seller convey property as he had contracted to do. He had only a half interest. His sister had the other, she had refused to go along with the contract, and she was not a party to the action. The court said it was "not in a position" to direct the seller to convey the entire title: "The court will not attempt to decree the impossible." The serious issue in the case was whether or not the buyer could obtain a *half* interest upon paying *part* of the price. The subject of "specific performance with abatement" is not apposite to a basic contracts course.

tion unless the seller has employed all due measures to assure himself that the source will not fail"—citing the main case.

Yet it must be supposed that financial stress on a promisor has its influence with a court when it is determining, in light of changed circumstances, what it is commercially practicable for him to do. An English judge has speculated that changed circumstances may make even a loan contract unenforceable against the debtor.[b] Certainly the financial difficulties of a promisor ought not to *preclude* giving him relief for impossibility or the like: they may be traceable directly to an "objective" development contrary to a basic assumption of the contract. Even so, performances have often been required on the general view that a promise should be honored regardless of financial hardship. See Twin Harbors Lumber Co. v. Carrico, 92 Idaho 343, 442 P.2d 753 (1968); 407 E. 61st Garage, Inc. v. Savoy Fifth Avenue Corp., 23 N.Y.2d 275, 296 N.Y.S.2d 338, 244 N.E.2d 37 (1968).

THE WESTINGHOUSE LITIGATION

The most widely observed litigation over UCC 2–615 has been that concerning contracts for supplies of uranium that the Westinghouse Electric Corporation entered into with a number of electric utility companies. For honoring these contracts Westinghouse would have required some 80 million pounds of uranium. On September 8, 1975, it wrote to seventeen customers, advising them that its performance was excused under the doctrine of commercial impracticability. It proposed to prorate among them the quantity it could command—about 15 million pounds.[a] From this event a fountain of litigation flowed, and the end is not in sight. Many of the rulings so far made, including one in the House of Lords, are peripheral to contract law. For contracts students the most momentous one has been announced, but not yet explained: Judge Robert Merhige's interim decision in the "Richmond" case. Some Swedish utilities sought a remedy in a Stockholm court and another action against Westinghouse proceeded through trial in Pittsburgh; both of these actions were settled. The center ring then became the Eastern District of Virginia, in which the suits of several domestic utilities were ultimately consolidated for trial. Westinghouse has made some settlement arrangement with each of the plaintiffs there, at one stage or another of the

b. "[An] example considered in argument was a loan of money advanced to a businessman on the terms that it was to be repaid out of the profits of his business. Such a term should not automatically preclude an award in the event of frustration [impracticability?], for example if the businessman is incapacitated the day after the loan is made; but if the business consists for example of a ship, which strikes a reef and sinks, then it may be that the court, having regard to the terms of the contract and the risk taken thereunder by the lender, would make no award." B. P. Exploration Co. (Libya) Ltd. v. Hunt, [1979] 1 W.L.R. 783 (Q.B.D.) at 807.

a. Some of them had not contracted formally for their supplies, but had negotiated extensively with Westinghouse for contracts.

proceedings. Very early the company arranged, with the court's approval, to deliver the uranium available to it, subject to later determination of terms. Following some nine months of hearings, Judge Merhige (E.D.Va.) ruled that Westinghouse was not wholly excused from performance by commercial impracticability.[b] However, he expressed willingness to hear argument that a judicial limitation of the remedy is appropriate; and submissions on issues of damages and an "equitable adjustment" have been made. Meanwhile, the court

b. From the Westinghouse Annual Report, 1979:

"Among other things, the Court noted that one provision of the Uniform Commercial Code provides that the measure of damages is the difference between the market price at the time when the buyer learned of the breach and the contract price, which contract price on average for all of the alleged contracts in the original litigation was approximately $9.50 per pound and has, with respect to the pounds still in dispute, since escalated to approximately $12 per pound. It further noted that Westinghouse had introduced evidence that the market price was approximately $26 per pound at the time it notified the utilities of its inability to perform in September 1975. [T]he utilities have argued that uranium was in limited supply at that time and that the true market price might be as high as $43 per pound . . . ."

Some of Judge Merhige's observations from the bench were as follows:

"I must say that consideration [was not, I believe] ever given to the appropriateness of any specific equitable adjustment, due to the severance of the relief-related issues, and the liability-related issues at the outset.

"The Plaintiffs should not be misled . . . . If anything, the Court is disposed to believe that just as Westinghouse is not entitled to excuse from its contractual obligations, the Plaintiffs aren't entitled to anything near the full measure of their prayers for relief.

"The Court has previously stated its belief that [the position of some of the plaintiffs] does not take realistic account of the litigation risks either before this Court or on appeal, nor does it take account of the equitable considerations which weigh in favor of compromise.

"Even if the Court concludes . . . that no equitable adjustment may properly be made, and I have tended to come to that conclusion, . . . if it gets out of hand, I'll make whatever rulings I have to. I'm going to try to cut down the expense of this case, as ridiculous as that may sound.

". . . the Court feels constrained to state its decision that Westinghouse did not meet its burden of establishing that it is entitled to excuse . . . either by reason of Section 2–615 . . . or the force majuere [sic] clauses in its contracts with Plaintiffs.

"A serious issue of limitation of liability awaits further proceedings.

"In some senses the questions that still remain unanswered are perhaps more important and perhaps more difficult of resolution than those the Court has already addressed. . . . Plaintiffs do have the burden [on the issue of market price of uranium at the time Westinghouse notified them of its inability to perform] and must show that they acted reasonably in my view to limit their damages.

"[T]hese are cases which I think everybody admits should be settled if at all possible, in the public interest, and they are really business problems, and should be settled as business problems by businessmen, as I have been urging from the very first.

"I expect the utilities and Westinghouse to enter into serious and intense negotiations . . . ."

[The foregoing excerpts are drawn from the Record, pp. 22320–31 (not in sequence), as supplied by the courtesy of William R. Jentes, Esq. of Chicago, who appeared for Westinghouse.]

The court made reference, passim, to UCC 2–209, 2–713(1), 2–716, and—"as Mr. Jentes has repeatedly urged"—to Comment 6 after UCC 2–615.

sought to facilitate settlements through the appointment of a special master to deal with issues arising during negotiations.[c]

The parties to the Richmond trial appeared to agree on a number of points: that the world price of uranium had increased dramatically; that Westinghouse had promoted its nuclear steam supply system (NSSS) by offering long-term fuel supplies with it; and that its Power Systems Division would incur major losses through performance. They were agreed also that the causes of the price increases included various governmental actions about uranium stocks, and others about oil exports (owing to cross-elasticity of demand, the OPEC embargo of 1973 had its effect). The causes included also the 1975 announcement by Westinghouse itself, and the machinations of a uranium producers' "club." In a separate action, Westinghouse charged dozens of producers with anti-competitive conduct; and some of them made countercharges (e. g., tying sales of its NSSS to "predatory" pricing of yellowcake).[d] The list of related actions also includes, of course, shareholders' actions against Westinghouse, its accounting firm, investment banker, and so on.

One Westinghouse contention was that it was hoodwinked by a bid-rigging scheme of competing producers: they concealed it by arranging for some bids that were in-the-money and others that were also-rans. Details of the scheme were not known to it, according to Westinghouse, until about a year after its celebrated letter to customers—and then only through the efforts of the "Australian Friends of the Earth." *Question:* Does this timing tend to justify the letter, or to condemn it?

Suppliers of uranium on which Westinghouse relied for delivering on a reduced scale have become restive about their contracts, and the company is engaged in litigation to establish its rights as a buyer.[e] For other repercussions of the Westinghouse default and of

c. Settlements made by Westinghouse require it to give discounts, or to make no charge, for various goods (such as equipment) and services (such as power-plant inspection) and warranties, and of course require uranium deliveries and cash payments. Full performance will require the rest of this century.

The settlement costs, as estimated in the notes to the company's financial statements, are large. Figures were given as follows in the second-quarter report for 1979: "The 10 settlements to date, commencing with the first settlement in 1977, account for over 55 per cent of the total uranium originally claimed by all the plaintiffs [in 17 suits], including the uranium originally involved in the court-ordered allocation plan, and have resulted in a recorded cumulative extraordinary loss before income taxes of $497.8 million and of $258.4 million after income taxes." An opposing party to one of the settlements may have reason to assign a higher value to it than Westinghouse does. See "The New York Times," Sept. 27, 1979, D–5. Other settlements have since been reached.

d. One of these defendants, the Gulf Oil Corp., was charged by the United States with a misdemeanor under the Sherman Act; and it accepted a fine of $40,000 rather (as it said) than burden itself with a defense.

e. Litigation history is collected in Comment, The International Uranium Cartel: Litigation and Legal Implica-

the escalating cost of yellowcake (U_3O_8) see Iowa Electric Light & Power Co. v. Atlas Corp., 23 UCC Rep.Serv. 1171, 25 UCC Rep.Serv. 163 (N.D.Iowa, 1978).

NOTES

(1) *A Cloudy Comment.* Judge Merhige's management of the Westinghouse litigation concentrated the lawyers' attention on Comment 6 to UCC 2–615. After reading the comment, as follows, consider whether the law owes more decisive judgments to businessmen in their contract disputes.

> In situations in which neither sense nor justice is served by either answer when the issue is posed in flat terms of "excuse" or "no excuse," adjustment under the various provisions of this Article is necessary, especially the sections on good faith, on insecurity and assurance and on the reading of all provisions in the light of their purposes, and the general policy of this Act to use equitable principles in furtherance of commercial standards and good faith.

(2) *Strategy.* In the dealings between Westinghouse and its customers, some special factors may have affected the decisions made, at various stages, whether to litigate or to settle. See Macauley, op. cit. supra p. 970 n. d. What influences can you imagine from the following facts?—The parties have a common interest in increasing nuclear power capacity, and are opposed in that aim by numbers of articulate critics (and litigators). The utilities may not obtain approval for new rates of charge without justifying their costs to state regulatory agencies. However, fuel-cost adjustments, already approved, permit the utilities to charge their customers for increases in fossil-fuel costs without changing "rates".

DRAFTING EXCUSING CLAUSES

An exculpation provision written with special reference to events beyond either party's control is often called a *force majeure* clause. One way of summarizing such events is "act of God"—an expression still used though it would not now be chosen if the slate were clean. An excusable-delay clause used by McDonnell Douglas, the aircraft manufacturer, is given in the footnote.[a] For a term in older style,

tions, 14 Tex.Internat.L.J. 59 (1979). (See also Comment, op. cit. at 277.) For an economist's case against Westinghouse, see Joskow, Commercial Impossibility, the Uranium Market and the Westinghouse Case, 6 J. Leg.Studies 119 (1977). See also Jennings, Commercial Impracticability, 2 Whittier L.Rev. 241 (1980); Note, 47 UMKC L.Rev. 650 (1979).

a. The clause read, in part:

> EXCUSABLE DELAY
>
> Seller shall not be responsible nor deemed to be in default on account of delays in performance of this Agreement due to causes beyond Seller's control and not occasioned by its fault or negligence, including but not being limited to civil war . . . any act of government, governmental priorities, allocation regulations or orders affecting materials, equipment, facilities or completed aircraft . . . , failure of vendors (due to causes similar to those within the scope of this clause) to perform their contracts or labor troubles causing cessation, slow-down, or interruption of work, provided such cause is beyond Seller's control.

used in international sale transactions, see Cartoon, Drafting an Acceptable Force Majeure Clause, 1978 J.Bus.L. 230. Consider the position of a dealer in goods who has commitments from suppliers and to customers, all for fixed quantities and prices. If all his contracts are written so as to excuse the party on either side—seller or buyer—for acts of God, are the dealer's risks properly cared for? See id. at 232.[b] In preparing a force majeure clause for a client, his insurance coverages may well be taken into account (and perhaps revised).

In an aircraft-sale case where McDonnell Douglas was charged with delays, the court said: "if the promisor desires to broaden the protections available under the excuse doctrine he should provide for the excusing contingencies with particularity and not in general language." The court accepted a distinction between references to specific excusing events (e. g., government allocation orders, labor troubles) and general excusing language (e. g., causes beyond seller's control). How does the enactment of UCC 2–615 affect the draftsman's responsibility? The court said: "Although the Uniform Commercial Code has ostensibly eliminated the need for such clauses, lawyers, either through an abundance of caution or by force of habit, continue to write them into contracts." Eastern Air Lines, Inc. v. McDonnell Douglas Corp., 532 F.2d 957 (5th Cir. 1976).

NOTES

(1) *Old Law Replaced?* Section 2–615 has perplexed its readers because it can be perceived either as carrying forward a doctrine of sellers' excuse expressed in pre-Code cases or as implanting a new one. The case last cited, an influential one, appears to have it both ways. On the one hand, for its distinction between specific and general language the court relied on pre-Code precedents. To this it added that the Code imposes "certain strictures" on the interpretation of excusing clauses (drawing partly on its reading of Comment 8 after 2–615), as if to say that tighter drafting is required to establish a non-statutory excuse. Yet on the other hand the court said: "The Code establishes no absolute requirement that any agreement purporting to enlarge upon section 2–615 must do so in plain and specific language." How the statute affects the interpretation of general excusing provisions remains unclear.

(2) *A Case of Jet Lag.* In the case just referred to the buyer and plaintiff was Eastern Air Lines. Being the last of the major trunk carriers to make a commitment to jet aircraft, it had contracted with a single manufacturer for 99 of them, and was anxious about prompt delivery. The manufacturer was overtaken (it contended) by competing demands for military production, and incurred thousands of plane-days of delay on the Eastern orders. Sharply rising production for military use in Vietnam was a root cause. However, dealings between the government and the airline industry never led to a general pre-emption of civilian production: that was avoided

b. In Mississippi the legislature has tried its hand in writing a force majeure clause, applicable to sellers and buyers alike, in (non-uniform) § 2–617 of the Code.

through exhortation, informal agreements for expediting military production, and "jawboning." The trial court agreed with the plaintiff that the excusable-delays clause did not apply in this situation, and entered a judgment against the defendant, McDonnell, for about $24.5 million. On appeal the judgment was reversed, owing to errors such as (a) ruling that McDonnell "assumed a greater obligation" than that contemplated by section 2–615, through listing specific causes of delay in the excusing clause, (b) charging the jury that McDonnell had the burden of proving that any cause asserted as excusing "was not reasonably foreseeable at the time the contract was entered into," and (c) failing to rule "as a matter of law" that any delay proximately resulting from the government's informal procurement program was excused.[c]

(3) *A Fact of Life.* In Eastern Air Lines, Inc. v. Gulf Oil Corp., 415 F.Supp. 429 (S.D.Fla.1975), a seller of jet aviation fuel (Gulf) complained of losses it suffered as a result of actions of the United States, in 1973, which amounted to a partial decontrol of the prices for domestically produced oil. Gulf sought to prove that these actions, together with an embargo by other oil-producing nations (OPEC), caused a dramatic increase in its cost of crude: from about $5 to $11 in some four months. Gulf claimed an excuse from its contract to supply the fuel requirements of Eastern Air Lines at certain terminals. The contract provided for passing on increases in the cost of crude, through indexing to a published market price. From Gulf's point of view, the difficulty was that the cost of decontrolled ("new") domestic oil—and of imported oil—raced ahead, whereas the index basis remained the price of still-controlled "old" oil. In rejecting Gulf's appeal to UCC 2–615, the court made two main points. First, Gulf had failed to establish great hardship in performing the contract. The court observed that Gulf had power to shift profits from its domestic to its overseas subsidiaries through an intra-company pricing system, so that its evidence of cost failed to show profit or loss on the Eastern contract. Moreover, Gulf had its best profit years, overall, as the energy crisis deepened. Second, "the events associated with the so-called energy crises were reasonably foreseeable at the time the contract was executed"—June of 1972. As for decontrol, the evidence was that Gulf was constantly urging the government to decontrol crude prices at all material times. As for the OPEC action, the court was prepared to take judicial notice of the long-standing political uses of oil pricing: Gulf "assumed the risk." The court was obviously impressed by evidence that, for both parties, oil-price increases had become "a fact of life for the future." [d]

c. A settlement was reached in the case. See Macauley, op.cit. supra p. 970, n. d.

d. Some of the same factors operated in Missouri Public Service Co. v. Peabody Coal Co., 583 S.W.2d 721 (Mo. App.1979). The case concerned a contract by Peabody to supply the coal requirements of a power plant for ten years. One of several price-adjustment provisions included was an inflation escalator based on the Industrial Commodities Index of the Labor Department. In part, Peabody's claim of an excuse rested on the fact that this index became insensitive to inflation. (In negotiations, the plant operator had won the use of this index in lieu of the Consumer Price Index.) In part, the excuse rested on the OPEC oil embargo. Do you see a reason why a major coal producer might have trouble claiming that as an excuse? A decree of specific performance against Peabody was entered and affirmed on appeal.

(4) *Output and Requirements Contracts.* If a buyer of all a seller's output is asked to take an unusual volume of goods, owing to an uncontemplated event increasing the seller's production, section 2–615 seems not to be an avenue to relief. (In principle, however, it may sometimes afford relief to a seller in relation to a requirements contract; perhaps also in relation to an output contract.) "Exemption of the buyer in the case of a 'requirements' contract is covered by the 'Output and Requirements' section both as to assumption and allocation of the relevant risks." UCC 2–615, Comment 9.

In a requirements contract, such as that of Eastern Air Lines with Gulf Oil, are the risk-bearing capacities of a buyer likely to be especially good? The opinion describes an interesting technique of airlines for offsetting higher costs at certain terminals, called fuel freighting. In essence, it is to "top up" where prices are low. Gulf contended that Eastern had broken the contract by indulging in this practice.

Would the decontrol of air fares affect Eastern's risk-bearing capacity?

PRECAUTIONS COMPARED

Negotiating with a view to an unwelcome change of circumstances that cannot be forecast accurately, if at all, presents some nice choices. Take for example the concern of an airline that wants an assured supply of fuel at a terminal it hopes to serve, and the concern of the supplier negotiating with it. A way of casting the risks of the venture sharply one way or the other is to set up an option contract: either an option in the airline to buy or one in the supplier to sell. (The latter would serve a purpose of the supplier, of course, but not meet the airline's need.) Either way the option runs, one would expect a price to be exacted of the party holding it. If the concern is more particular, and relates (say) to a sharp change in the market for fuel, the parties may be more disposed to exchange commitments and to adopt some flexible pricing mechanism. Of course, if the prospective buyer is uncertain that it will be able to extend its air route, it will wish to restrict its undertaking to make any purchase at all. That might be accomplished by imposing a suitable condition, or by giving the buyer a power of cancellation, or by arranging a requirements contract. (Similarly the prospective seller may have reason for proposing restrictions on its obligation to deliver.) Or the parties may choose to curtail many of the risks on one side or both—including the risk of price fluctuation—through a liquidated damages provision.

Given all these possibilities for allocating risks, it may be wondered what considerations would lead the parties to agree on a *force majeure* clause. A partial answer lies in the materials of earlier chapters, showing that there are distinctive legal problems associated with each of the other arrangements mentioned. Some of them are bedevilled by problems of drafting and of measuring recovery. If an unrestricted power of cancellation is used, the notion of illusory promise may surface;[a] and other one-sided terms suggest grounds for caution.

Of course the parties may be led to select one form of risk-sharing or another by their habits of contracting or by trade practice. They may simply be actuated by a sense of fair play. Sometimes an excessively trustful party will assume that if he encounters severe hardship the other will consent to a concession in his favor. (For an instance of concession as to price, recall Watkins & Son v. Carrig, p. 394 supra.) Moreover, it must be understood that an astute bargainer will rarely insist on the most risk-free position that the law allows: after all, he must allow for sales resistance. The point was made in Canadian Alcohol Co. v. Molasses Co., p. 978 supra. The case concerned a middleman whose supplier—a refinery—failed him. Cardozo observed that if the middleman's customer had been asked to assume that risk he "would very likely have preferred to deal with the refinery directly."

An extreme of flexible pricing is represented by a cost-plus contract. Contrast the unit-pricing term in the Case of the Rock Trap, Note 1 p. 978 supra. Traders in goods are more likely to use some moving index of market conditions. Even that does not rule out the possibility of a serious price dislocation. The choice of an index may reflect a "basic assumption" of the contract that the reference data will continue to reflect market conditions, or at least will continue to be available. On that point the following cases make an instructive comparison: Interstate Plywood Sales Co. v. Interstate Container Corp., 331 F.2d 449 (9th Cir. 1964) (plywood distributor to pay for inventory on a "five-mill formula"); and North Central Airlines, Inc. v. Continental Oil Co., 574 F.2d 582 (D.C.Cir. 1978) (posted oil prices). In the former case the court ruled that when the formula became indeterminable the contract became unenforceable. In the latter, when the posted prices became wholly unrepresentative it was determined to enforce the contract as one having an open price term (UCC 2–305). *Questions:* Is each of these rulings compatible with UCC 2–615? Should it matter which party made the claim for continuing performance—buyer or seller?

NOTES

(1) *Economic Analyses.* For buying "insurance" of a sort against cost increases, a seller may bargain with his customer for a flexible-pricing term, as Gulf Oil attempted to do with Eastern Air Lines (see Note 3, p. 985 supra). Sometimes either the seller or the buyer may dispose of the risk of certain price changes through arrangements with third parties. These reflections have led economists to one conclusion or another about how best to deal with events of "impossibility" and the like, on the criterion of effi-

a. See Sylvan Crest Sand & Gravel Co. v. United States, p. 83 supra.

ciency. One of them suggests that the prevalence of flexible-pricing terms tends to give government a handle on the problem of price inflation. He reasons that the use of such terms would be discouraged by free-handed applications of commercial impracticability. (Do you see why?) He argues for imposing on sellers the risk of large, general price rises associated with management—or mismanagement—of the economy (i.e., inflation). Schwartz, Sales Law and Inflations, 50 So.Cal.L.Rev. 1 (1976).

Others argue that an "impossibility" of performance or a like event should excuse a promisor when it is determined that the promisee is the "superior risk bearer"—after ruling out the capacity on either side to forestall the event at reasonable cost. This test comes down, for most practical purposes, to the question which party is best situated to protect against the contingency through insuring, making hedge contracts, and the like. Posner & Rosenfield, op.cit. supra, p. 970 n. d. Was this the mainspring of the decision in Transatlantic Financing Corp. v. United States, p. 958 supra? (For an application of the analysis to facts suggested by the Westinghouse litigation, see id. at pp. 94–95.)

(2) *Remarks on Foreseeability.* The "foreseeability test" has been excoriated in academic literature; e. g. Smit, Frustration of Contract: A Comparative Attempt at Consolidation, 58 Colum.L.Rev. 287 (1958); Comment, 72 Nw.U.L.Rev. 1032 (1978). One economist appears to tolerate the test, at least, as imposing a penalty on the "suboptimal use of available information." Joskow, Commercial Impossibility, the Uranium Market and the Westinghouse Case, 6 J.Leg.Studies 119, 173 (1977). Others, however, conclude that it is "nonoperational"—at least in the form usually stated—"for it fails to indicate which contracting party is the superior bearer of the foreseeable risk. The test," they say, "is disappearing, and although occasionally mentioned is seldom applied." Posner & Rosenfield, op.cit.supra, p. 970, n. d. Does Eastern Air Lines v. Gulf Oil Corp. bear out this observation? Compare Deusenberg, loc.cit. at 1095: "Foreseeability has been central to impossibility cases for as long as they have been around. It is proving no less important under section 2–615 . . . ;" and see Robberson Steel, Inc. v. J. D. Abrams, Inc., 582 S.W.2d 558 (Tex.Civ.App.1979).

For the purpose of limiting the excuse of commercial impracticability, can you think of standards that imply the test of foreseeability without using the word? Are there examples in the foregoing cases?

(3) *The Endowed Bed Case.* In 1927 a private hospital in Oregon contracted to furnish accommodations and care, without charge, for a succession of patients—one at a time—in perpetuity. The consideration was $5,000 paid by the Council of Jewish Women (Portland Section), which was to nominate the beneficiaries. In 1971 the payor sued the hospital to compel a resumption of its performance, which had lapsed. The hospital's principal defense was based on the "vastly inflated costs of medical care"—its per-patient cost having doubled many times in the interim. A decree for the plaintiff was affirmed on appeal. Portland Section of Council of Jewish Women v. Sisters of Charity of Providence in Oregon, 266 Or. 448, 513 P.2d 1183 (1973).[b] As to rising costs, the court relied on what the parties

b. Compare the effect of rising costs on a life-care contract: Onderdonk v. Presbyterian Homes of New Jersey, 171 N.J.Super. 529, 410 A.2d 252 (1979).

"must have contemplated" in 1927; and it rejected the hospital's argument of unfairness to the community. "The expenses . . . and benefits . . . are merely being distributed through the community in a different way." *Questions:* What economic analysis, if any, is implicit in the court's reasoning? Economists build on the assumption that many people are "risk-averse," as shown by their willingness to pay for insurance. How might it be shown that a contracting party—such as a hospital accepting an endowed bed—is not risk-averse, but is (on the contrary) risk-acquisitive?

What might be said for giving the women's group a claim on a hospital bed (for an indigent patient) on the condition of their paying (say) half the current cost of maintaining it? Several cost-sharing proposals—generally more discriminating than this—have been advanced. (As to these, see pp. 1010 and 1015, infra.) One of the economic studies cited above (Posner & Rosenfield) resist such notions in favor of all-or-nothing determinations, *ex ante*, of risk-bearing capacity. *Question:* Is it possible to assess risk-bearing capacity without foreknowledge of the eventuality that presents the issue of discharge, i. e., without a definition of the risk?

MONEY MOVEMENTS

A general decline in price levels—deflation—seems rarely to have been presented, much less recognized, as an unstated contingency directly excusing a contract performance. (Periods of depression have left their mark on the law, of course, chiefly in the form of debtor-relief legislation such as bankruptcy statutes.) A claim for relief against deflation would naturally be expected to come from a payor, or "seller", of money. Occasionally a general *rise* in price levels—inflation—seems to have figured in a claim for relief on the creditor side: when over time his performance comes to seem unduly dear for the money paid or to be paid in exchange. At times, in other countries (Germany, most notably) the courts have excused or adjusted a performance on that ground; but in this country even a claim for such relief is unusual. For historical references on these matters see 6 Williston §§ 1931 (n. 10) and 1932 (n. 3).

In Kuhn v. Kuhn, 281 N.W.2d 230 (N.D.1979), a suit for specific performance was resisted partly on the ground that money had depreciated (in relation to land) over a quarter of a century. The parties were the children of Wendelin and Rosa Kuhn. At a family reunion in 1952 a family agreement was made, by which the parents' property was to be apportioned at the death of the survivor. The agreement provided that son John (the plaintiff) would receive two quarters of land, as well as an even share of the cattle and money the parents might leave. Other properties were appointed to other children, but only John and Leo were to receive so much land. Nothing was appointed to Sister M. Judith, except that John and Leo "will each pay [to her] $200 per year plus interest 2% for 5 years." In the 60's, after her husband's death, Rosa made two wills inconsistent with the agreement, and presumably less favorable to John. When she died, nearly 25 years after making the agreement, he sought specific performance and contested probate of the later will. When his complaint was dismissed, he appealed. *Held:* Reversed. (Because none of John's siblings claimed under the agreement, most of Rosa's property was distributed under her will.)[a]

In contrast, the seller of a house obtained relief when, a quarter of a century after the terms of sale were fixed, they had become absurdly favorable to the buyer. He had occupied the house all the while, making regular installment payments; but taxes and other charges against the payments had increased to the point where it appeared that the unpaid balance of the price would never be satisfied. Rather than leave the buyer in possession indefinitely, as if the payments were a kind of interminable rent, the court summarily turned the sale agreement into a 30-day option contract. Miller v. Campello Co-op. Bank, 344 Mass. 76, 181 N.E.2d 345 (1962).[b]

Is the house-sale case incompatible with Kuhn v. Kuhn? With the Endowed Bed Case? What do these cases signify, if anything, about commercial impracticability in the form of inflation, as an excuse for a seller of goods?

NOTES

(1) *Case Comparison.* Like Ruby Tuckwiller in the case at p. 371 supra, John Kuhn profited from the precept that the fairness of an exchange must be judged as of the time it was made. Yet the nature of Ruby's gain might be thought to exemplify the purpose of the contracting parties more nearly than John's did. (An object of the family-reunion agreement was to forestall family discord; but that is perhaps beside the point.) John's gain was attributable largely to advances in land prices; so his siblings argued. If so, the precept about fairness as applied in the Tuckwiller case does not require the court's decision in Kuhn v. Kuhn, does it?

(2) *Negotiations.* Your client calls on you to assist in negotiating a contract (such as a long-term lease) that calls for dollar payments to him over a period of several years. What terms can you suggest to allow for potential inflation? See Rosenn, Protecting Contracts from Inflation, 33 Bus.Law. 729 (1978).

CASUALTY LOSS IN RELATION TO SALES

One of the parties to a contract of sale must usually absorb a loss, on account of physical injury to the subject of the sale, if it is injured (or destroyed) by casualty before the contract is consummated. (For this note it will be assumed that the loss is not traceable to

a. See also Matter of Estate of Frederick, 599 P.2d 550 (Wyo.1979): "The risk of the effects of inflation, however, is inherent in any contract which includes an option to purchase in the future."

b. But see John J. Duane Realty Corp. v. Great Atlantic & Pacific Tea Co., — Mass.App. —, 394 N.E.2d 964 (1979). Compare Columbia Broadcasting v. Am. Soc. of Composers, Etc., 483 F.Supp. 616 (1980).

the fault of someone who can be held accountable.) It is common to insure against the risk of such loss. Insurance aside, how does the law allocate a casualty loss occurring while a sale of the property is executory? For real property, an answer was developed under the aegis of equity courts, which conceived of the purchaser as "owner" of the property from the time of contracting. As such, he is required to pay the purchase price without abatement for the casualty. In a number of jurisdictions, however, the classical rule no longer holds, whether by judicial [a] or legislative [b] reform.

For sales of goods, the answers are codified in the Uniform Commercial Code, §§ 2–509, 2–510, and 2–613, with possible supplementation from §§ 2–615 and 2–616. Pre-Code law asserted that a buyer was accountable for the price of damaged goods if, and only if, title in them had passed to him prior to the casualty; and the Uniform Sales Act contained elaborate rules and presumptions for locating title. In dissociating risk of loss and "title," the Code worked a major change.

Two aspects of UCC 2–613 may be noted here. First, since it assumes that the risk of loss is on the seller, the relief it affords is for his benefit, in the main. Second, it cannot apply to the usual contract for a sale of goods to be produced or procured by the seller, or even of goods to be selected from his stock of merchandise: e. g., a contract to sell a carload of alfalfa seed. Until a carload is "identified" to the contract, that is, the destruction by flood of all the seed in the vicinity would leave the seller obligated to make delivery. This proposition has its soft spots, as will be seen, and the Code states a qualification in § 2–615. But none of the other Code sections purports to relieve such a seller. (For rules about when "identification" of goods occurs, see UCC 2–501(1)—noting the provision about crops.)

A fuller treatment of these topics must be deferred to other courses.

NOTE

Insurance Spreading. In UCC 2–510 there is a Code innovation designed to spread the advantages of insurance, in special circumstances, where it is held by the "wrong" party to the sale. The treatment of insurance here has been criticized thoughtfully in McCoid, Allocation of Loss and Property Insurance, 39 Ind.L.J. 647 (1964). However, there is a strong and supportive doctrine of equity, having somewhat the same effect in relation to real property sales. If a building subject to a sale contract burns before the deed is given, and the seller is provided with fire insurance, many courts will abate the purchase price to the extent of the insurance

a. E. g., Anderson v. Yaworski, 120 Conn. 390, 181 A. 205, 101 A.L.R. 1232 (1935).

b. E. g., Cal.Civ.Code, § 1662; N.Y. Real Prop.L. § 240–a.

proceeds.[c] The seller's insurance claim is said to be held in constructive trust for the purchaser. The doctrine is discordant with the personal character of fire insurance generally, and has been ascribed to "layman's ideas of equity."[d]

A VISIT TO THE FARM

Ray Colley, an experienced wheat farmer, contracted in April 1974 to deliver 25,000 bushels of wheat to Bi-State, Inc. in July or August. He believed that prices, then high, would drop by harvest time, and he expected a bumper crop from his spring planting. Both expectations failed. June was particularly hot and dry, and his deliveries fell nearly 20,000 bushels short. Bi-State had committed the wheat to an exporter, and it incurred substantial expense, including the cost of cover, to extricate itself. When Colley sued it for the price of wheat he had delivered, Bi-State counterclaimed for this expense. Its buying agent testified that he felt Colley was probably selling wheat he planned to harvest from his farm, but that he (the agent) would not agree to buy wheat grown on specified property. Farmers and grain dealers from the area testified that, "under existing custom and trade usage, such agreements were never contingent upon the success of the seller's crop." The trial court gave judgment in favor of Bi-State on the counterclaim and it was affirmed on appeal. Colley v. Bi-State, Inc., 21 Wash.App. 769, 586 P.2d 908 (1978).

In another crop-failure case, Unke v. Thorpe, 75 S.D. 65, 59 N.W. 2d 419 (1953), the contract was for the sale of 600–800 bushels of alfalfa seed. The seller-farmer offered testimony that the agreement was executed at his farm, after the buyer had inspected his opera-

c. Or impose a constructive trust on the seller's insurance proceeds for the buyer's benefit. See Vogel v. Northern Assur. Co., 219 F.2d 409 (3d Cir. 1955).

d. Brownell v. Board of Education, 239 N.Y. 369, 146 N.E. 630, 37 A.L.R. 1319 (1925).

The seller of improved land may have his fire insurance policy endorsed with the name of the purchaser, usually without charge, so that the purchaser's interest is also insured until he arranges his own insurance. In the event of loss in the interim, the proceeds will be allocated between the parties "as their interests may appear." Similarly, a dealer in personal property sometimes insures not only his unsold inventory, but also goods "sold but not removed." So written, the policy amounts to a contract for the benefit of unnamed third parties, his customers, to the extent that they bear the risk of damage to the goods. In the absence of some policy provision of this character, it is the general rule that insurance held by one of the contracting parties is not available to the other. Insurance on property is "personal" to the named insured. Therefore a buyer may find that he must pay the agreed price for goods or improvements he has contracted for, even if they are no longer in existence and the seller has been compensated for their loss through his insurance. In that event, part or all of the payment goes to reimburse the insurer, through "subrogation" to the seller's claim. A certain number of buyers are unaware of the threat of loss that these rules impose on them, and are grievously surprised when it eventuates.

tions. The buyer testified to a conversation between the parties in which he insisted on a quantity term and explained that he intended to resell against the contract.

Should any of this testimony be excluded? If so, how does it differ from the testimony in Colley's case? Each item might shed light on the "basic assumptions" of the contract in issue, might it not? Nevertheless, in Unke v. Thorpe, evidence of the conversation was thought to be inadmissible, at least in part, in the face of the written agreement.[a]

An interesting case for comparison is Snipes Mountain Co. v. Benz Brothers & Co., 162 Wash. 334, 298 P. 714, 74 A.L.R. 1287 (1931), which involved the sale of a hundred tons of potatoes. The court effected a reformation of the writing, in order to deny the buyer's claim. After the word "potatoes," it wrote in the words "grown during the year 1929 on the following described premises: [here describing the seller's crop land]." Some courts would regard equitable relief as unnecessary; e. g., Barkemeyer Grain & Seed Co. v. Hannant, 66 Mont. 120, 213 P. 208 (1923).

NOTES

(1) *Farmers, Dealers, and the Code.* Comment 9 after UCC 2–615 is as follows: "The case of a farmer who has contracted to sell crops to be grown on designated land may be regarded as falling either within the section on casualty to identified goods or this section, and he may be excused, when there is a failure of the specific crop, either on the basis of the destruction of identified goods or because of the failure of a basic assumption of the contract." Is this assertion incompatible with any of the cases mentioned above?

If the seller is a dealer in the product being sold, a crop failure is somewhat less likely to afford him an excuse for non-delivery. As an explanation it has been said that a dealer is "in a position to spread the risk of a single crop failure among his customers." Note, 53 Colum.L.Rev. 94, 102 (1953). Presumably a farmer is less able to adjust his prices to allow for a liability he might suffer, when his crop fails. On this reasoning, does it follow that a farmer who has insured his crop against the destruction it suffered should be liable for non-delivery, whereas his uninsured neighbor, contracting on the same terms, should not?

As for excusing a dealer in case of crop failure, see Pearce-Young-Angel Co. v. Charles R. Allen, Inc., 213 S.C. 578, 50 S.E.2d 698 (1948), Jennie-O Foods, Inc. v. United States, 580 F.2d 400 (Ct.Cl.1978), and UCC 2–615, Comment 4.

(2) *Unassumable Risk?* If the possibility of a widespread crop failure arises in negotiations for the sale of a carload of corn, may the parties agree that any such risk lies with the seller?

a. See also Ralston Purina Co. v. Rooker, 346 So.2d 901 (Miss.1977); Bunge Corporation v. Recker, 519 F.2d 449 (8th Cir. 1975); and compare Campbell v. Hostetter Farms, Inc., 251 Pa.Super. 232, 380 A.2d 463 (1977). For a review of crop-failure cases endorsing Unke v. Thorpe, see Comment, 22 S.D.L.Rev. 529 (1977).

If a grower of corn, in disposing of his expected harvest, guarantees its quantity and quality, is the contract subject to avoidance under UCC 2–613, by reason of casualty? See §§ 1–102(3), (4), and 2–509(4). What evidence would be helpful in determining whether or not the guarantee is unconscionable (UCC 2–302)?

(3) *A Poultry Problem.* Edicts from Washington and great natural disasters may have much in common, but for a supplier to the government a marked distinction exists. So it was observed in Tony Downs Foods Co. v. United States, 530 F.2d 367 (Ct.Cl.1976). For about a month in 1973 the President imposed a "price freeze" affecting (inter alia) turkey and chicken parts. During that period the Department of Agriculture contracted for large quantities of these items from Tony Downs, and received its offer to supply still more. It accepted the offer two days after the price controls were removed. The removal caused a swift and immediate rise in poultry prices, according to Tony Downs, and in consequence it faced losses on the contracts of more than $300,000. What arguments might be made for relieving the supplier from the contract prices? How good are they?

KRELL v. HENRY

Court of Appeal, 1903.
2 K.B. 740.

[By a contract in writing of June 20, 1902, the defendant agreed to hire from the plaintiff a flat in Pall Mall, London, for June 26 and 27, on which days it had been officially announced that the coronation processions (i. e., to be held in connection with the coronation of Edward VII) would take place and pass along Pall Mall. The contract contained no express reference to the coronation processions, or to any other purpose for which the flat was taken. A deposit was paid when the contract was entered into. As, owing to the serious illness of the King, the processions did not take place on the days originally fixed, the defendant declined to pay the balance of the rent.]

VAUGHN WILLIAMS, L. J. The real question in this case is the extent of the application in English law of the principle of the Roman law which has been adopted and acted on in many English decisions, and notably in the case of Taylor v. Caldwell, (3 B. & S. 826). . . . I do not think that the principle of the civil law as introduced into the English law is limited to cases in which the event causing the impossibility of performance is the destruction or non-existence of some thing which is the subject matter of the contract or of some condition or state of things expressly specified as a condition of it. I think that you first have to ascertain, not necessarily from the terms of the contract, but, if required, from necessary inferences, drawn from surrounding circumstances recognized by both contracting parties, what is the substance of the contract, and then to ask the question whether that substantial contract needs for its foundation the assumption of the existence of a particular state of things. If it does, this will limit the operation of the general words, and in such case, if the contract becomes impossible of performance by reason of the non-existence of the state of things assumed by both contracting parties as the foundation of the contract, there will be no breach of the contract thus limited. Now what are the facts of the present case? The contract is contained in two letters of June 20 which passed between the defendant and the plaintiff's agent, Mr. Cecil Bisgood. These letters do not mention the coronation, but speak merely of the taking of Mr. Krell's chambers, or, rather, of the use of them, in the daytime of June 26 and 27, for the sum of 75*l.*, 25*l.* then paid, balance 50*l.* to be paid on the 24th. But the affidavits, which by agreement between the parties are to be taken as stating the facts of the case, show that the plaintiff exhibited on his premises, third floor, 56A, Pall Mall, an announcement to the effect that windows to view the Royal coronation procession were to be let, and that the defendant was induced by that announcement to apply to the housekeeper on the premises, who said that the owner was willing to let the suite of rooms for the purpose of seeing the Royal procession for both days, but not nights, of June 26 and 27.[a] In my judgment the use of the rooms was let and taken for the purpose of seeing the Royal procession. It was not a demise of the rooms, or even an agreement to let and take the rooms. It is a license to use rooms for a particular purpose and none other. And in my judgment the taking place of those processions on the days proclaimed along the proclaimed route, which passed 56A, Pall Mall, was regarded by both contracting parties as the foundation of the contract; and I think that it cannot reasonably be supposed to have been in the contemplation of the contracting parties, when the contract was made, that the coronation would not be held on the proclaimed days, or the processions not take place on those days along the proclaimed route; and I think that the words

a. Two processions were planned in connection with the coronation: that of Coronation Day, and a "Pageant" on the following day. Experience of the Diamond Jubilee (1897) provided some guidance for the pricing of space to see the processions. At that time a club-house had been "let to a speculator for £200, who realised £500 by his bargain." C. Pascoe, The Pageant & Ceremony of The Coronation 213 (1902). But there were complications in the early summer of 1902, in that the routes of the processions had not been determined. Pall Mall—"club-land of the empire"—was thought to be a certainty for the Pageant procession; but for Coronation Day two shorter routes, not including Pall Mall, were thought to be under consideration. One writer of the time estimated that prices for the Pageant ought not to exceed those paid for Victoria's Jubilee—"that is to say, if the Route be not [curtailed]. Of course, the lesser the opportunity of seeing the Pageant, the higher will be the prices asked for accommodation." Id. at 212.

On June 22 Commons was informed that the King had just undergone an operation for appendicitis, and that the Coronation was indefinitely postponed. V. Cowles, Edward VII and His Circle 240 (1956). It was performed on August 9. Though some of the captains and the princes (kings were not invited) had departed London, the splendor of the ceremony was "scarcely dimmed." Pall Mall was on the coronation route. London Illustrated News, Aug. 14, 1902.

imposing on the defendant the obligation to accept and pay for the use of the rooms for the named days, although general and unconditional, were not used with reference to the possibility of the particular contingency which afterwards occurred. It was suggested in the course of the argument that if the occurrence, on the proclaimed days, of the coronation and the procession in this case were the foundation of the contract, and if the general words are thereby limited or qualified, so that in the event of the non-occurrence of the coronation and procession along the proclaimed route they would discharge both parties from further performance of the contract, it would follow that if a cabman was engaged to take someone to Epsom on Derby Day at a suitable enhanced price for such a journey, say 10*l.*, both parties to the contract would be discharged in the contingency of the race at Epsom for some reason becoming impossible; but I do not think this follows, for I do not think that in the cab case the happening of the race would be the foundation of the contract. No doubt the purpose of the engager would be to go to see the Derby, and the price would be proportionately high; but the cab had no special qualification for this particular occasion. Any other cab would have done as well.

Appeal dismissed.

NOTES

(1) *The Doctrine.* The foregoing decision is the best-known example of a doctrine known as "frustration of purpose," or commercial frustration. As opposed to impossibility, the label *frustration* signifies that nothing has happened to impede performance of the defendant's undertaking. After the King's illness, as before, it was perfectly possible for the defendant to pay the agreed price—and indeed for him to occupy the rooms. Other instances of frustration claims are given below. Was the issue raised in Paradine v. Jane (p. 952 supra) one of impossibility or of frustration?

"Whether the basis for commercial frustration rests on failure of consideration as suggested by 6 Williston, Contracts (Rev. ed.) § 1954, p. 5480, note 14, or on equitable principles of allocation of risks as suggested by Corbin is not made entirely clear by the decided cases. Thus in 6 Corbin, Contracts, § 1322, p. 256 (1951) it is said that the 'problem is that of allocating, in the most generally satisfactory way, the risks of harm and disappointment that result from supervening events.' " Perry v. Champlain Oil Co., 101 N.H. 97, 134 A.2d 65 (1957). Compare Patterson, The Apportionment of Business Risks, 24 Colum.L.Rev. 335, 345 (1924). Does the choice of one basis or the other suggest any difference in the scope of the doctrine?

(2) *Problems.*

(a) For a promise of $500 P promises to provide a wedding dress for D by June 1. D's marriage to X is scheduled for a week after that. When the dress is all but ready, X dies by accident. Is D bound to pay anything? Would it make a difference if X had died just after P put the finishing touch on the dress?

(b) In Krell v. Henry did the opinion of Vaughn Williams succeed in distinguishing the case of the cabman engaged for Derby Day? Why not concede frustration in that case? Could the wedding-dress case be distinguished?

(c) Is either of the problem cases within section 265 of the Restatement Second?

SWIFT CANADIAN CO. v. BANET

United States Court of Appeals, Third Circuit, 1955.
224 F.2d 36.

Action to recover from buyer of goods, for breach of contract. In the United States District Court for the Eastern District of Pennsylvania, George A. Welsh, District Judge, each party moved for summary judgment upon stipulated facts, and the buyer's motion was granted. The seller appealed to the Court of Appeals. . . .

Judgment reversed with instructions to enter judgment for plaintiff.

GOODRICH, Circuit Judge.[a] This is an action on the part of a seller of goods to recover against the buyer for breach of contract. In the trial court each party, following the filing of a stipulation of facts, moved for summary judgment. The court granted the motion of the defendant. Plaintiff here says that it should have had the summary judgment or, at the worst, that the case should be remanded for trial on the facts.

The one point presented is both interesting and elusive. The seller is a Canadian corporation. It entered into an agreement with defendant buyers who do business as Keystone Wool Pullers in Philadelphia. By this contract Keystone agreed to purchase a quantity of lamb pelts at a stipulated price. Part of the quantity was delivered on board railroad cars at Toronto and shipped to Keystone in Philadelphia. On or about March 12, 1952, Swift advised Keystone of its readiness to deliver the remaining pelts to the buyer on board railroad cars in Toronto for shipment to Philadelphia. The parties have stipulated that on or about that day the government of the United States by its agency, the Bureau of Animal Industry, had issued stricter regulations for the importation of lamb pelts into the United States. The parties have stipulated that "pursuant to these regulations, the importation into the United States of these lamb pelts by Keystone was prevented." They have also stipulated that for the reasons just stated Keystone then and thereafter refused to accept deliv-

a. Herbert F. Goodrich (1889–1962) taught law for twenty-five years at Iowa, Michigan and Pennsylvania, where he also served as dean. Beginning in 1940 he served as judge on the United States Court of Appeals for the Third Circuit, and beginning in 1947 he served as director of the American Law Institute. His best-known book is a text on the conflict of laws.

ery of the pelts and the loading and shipment of the car did not occur.

From an inspection of the contract made between the parties it appears that the seller agreed to sell the pelts:

"all at $3.80 each U. S. Funds
F. O. B. Toronto."

Below this an approximate time was stipulated for shipment and then there were shipping directions in the following form:

"Note -- Frankford
Via: Buffalo-Penna. R. R. to
~~Broad & Washington Ave.~~
Freight Sta. Penna. R. R. Delivery."

Following this appears the terms and method of payment.

Two additional conditions of sale should be stated. There was a provision that neither party is to be liable for "orders or acts of any government or governmental agency . . ." And there was a provision that "when pelts are sold F.O.B. seller's plant title and risk of loss shall pass to buyer when product is loaded on cars at seller's plant."

The one question in this case is the legal effect of this agreement between the parties. If the seller's obligation was performed when it delivered, or offered to deliver, the pelts to the railroad company in Toronto, we think it is entitled to recovery. If the seller did fulfill its obligation, when it did so deliver, of course it is clear that when it failed to load the pelts because the buyer had signified his refusal to accept them, the seller may assert the same rights as though he had loaded them. A party is not obligated to do the vain thing of performing, assuming that he is ready to perform, when the other party has given notice of refusal to accept performance. 3 Williston on Sales, § 586 (Rev. ed., 1948); Restatement, Contracts, §§ 280, 306; Leonard Seed Co. v. Lustig Burgerhoff Co., 1923, 81 Pa.Super. 499. See also Uniform Commercial Code, § 2–610(c); Pa.Stat.Ann. tit. 12A, § 2–610(c) (1954).

The argument for the buyer must rest on the fact that the shipping directions in the contract showed that what the parties had in mind was such kind of performance by the seller as would start the goods to the buyer in Philadelphia. This coupled with the stipulation that, in consequence of the stiffening of federal regulations, "the importation into the United States of these lamb pelts by Keystone was prevented," forms the basis for the argument that the carrying out of the agreement was prevented by governmental agency and the buyer is therefore excused.

The validity of this argument depends upon what effect we give to a provision for shipment of the goods to the buyer via Pennsylvania R. R., destination Philadelphia. We do not think that this is any more than a shipping direction which the buyer could have changed to any other destination in the world had it so desired. Suppose the buyer had found that it wanted the goods in New York, could it not have directed such a change in destination without any violation of the contract? Could the seller have insisted that it would ship to Philadelphia and nowhere else? We think that authority in general regards these shipping directions as simply inserted for the convenience of the buyer and subject to change by him. Dwight v. Eckert, 1888, 117 Pa. 490, 12 A. 32; Hocking v. Hamilton, 1893, 158 Pa. 107, 27 A. 836; Richter v. Zoccoli, 1930, 150 A. 1, 8 N.J.Misc. 289; 1 & 2 Williston on Sales, §§ 190, 457 (Rev. ed., 1948). See also Uniform Commercial Code, § 2–319(3); Pa.Stat.Ann. tit. 12A, § 2–319(3) (1954).

If the contract in this case had called for performance "F.O.B. seller's plant" a provision of the contract itself would clearly have indicated when the seller's responsibility was finished and the buyer's had begun.[1] Here the provision in the earlier part of the contract was simply "F.O.B. Toronto" and it was not specifically provided that the sale was delivery at the seller's plant. We think the provision shows what the parties meant by "F.O.B." and can see no difference, so far as this expressed meaning goes, between F.O.B. at seller's plant and F.O.B. Toronto.

The general rule on this subject is pretty clear. Williston points out that when goods are delivered "free on board" pursuant to contract the presumption is that the property passes thereupon. Williston on Sales, § 280(b) (Rev. ed., 1948). It is agreed that this is a presumption and that the phrase F.O.B. is not one of iron-clad meaning. Seabrook Farms Co. v. Commodity Credit Corp., 206 F.2d 93 (C.A. 3, 1953). There is nothing in this case, however, to counteract the effect of such a presumption. When the shipper had made his delivery he was to send bill of lading and draft through a Philadelphia bank. His part of the agreement would have been fully performed when the goods were delivered F.O.B. at Toronto. We think both the risk of loss and the possibility of profit if the market advanced, were in the buyer from then on. Even if the goods could not be imported into the United States under the then existing regulations, the rest of the world was free to the buyer, so far as we know, as destination for the shipment. If he did not care to accept them under the circumstances and his expectation of a profitable transaction was disappointed, nevertheless, the seller having performed or being ready, able and willing to perform, was entitled to the value of his bargain.

[The court finds that the law of Pennsylvania and that of Ontario were identical on the issue involved here, and that the seller's damages were sufficiently proved.]

1. See the second additional condition of sale quoted in the text above.

The judgment of the district court will be reversed with instructions to enter judgment for the plaintiff for the difference between the contract price and the price at which the goods were sold.

QUESTIONS

(1) If the Code has a bearing on the question in this case—see Note 3, p. 972 supra—what effect does it have?

(2) Would the decision have been different if the sale contract had provided for delivery f.o.b. Philadelphia rather than Toronto? As to the seller's obligation in that case see UCC 2–319(1)(b). If the seller failed to deliver in accordance with such a contract because of United States import regulations, would that necessarily be a breach of his duty?

(3) If Canada had regulated the *export* of lamb pelts, so as to require a license, would the Canadian seller have borne the risk that one could not be obtained? See Amtorg Trading Corp. v. Miehle Printing Press & Mfg. Co., 206 F.2d 103 (2d Cir. 1953).

NOTE

Offshore Oil Risk. Early in 1969 an offshore well of Union Oil "blew out," causing an immense slick. Nearby, on tracts leased from the United States by other operators, they had drilled eight exploratory wells at a cost of some $3.8 million without achieving production (a fact that "had to be discouraging" to them). From the blow-out ensued a public outcry, an Interior Department regulation restating and probably augmenting liabilities for oil spills, and a collapse of the relevant insurance market. Forty days after the blow-out, the operators (not including Union) sued the United States for a determination that their leases were at an end and for a money recovery at least equal to their entire investment. None but the "major" oil companies, they contended, could afford the risk of drilling in the changed circumstances. Under their hypothesis, "it was the conjunction of a strict liability standard and the absence of procurable insurance that made the risks of drilling unacceptably high." Their claims were based on frustration of contract by the Government and on mutual mistake, among other grounds. *Held:* Petition dismissed. Pauley Petroleum Inc. v. United States, 591 F.2d 1308 (Ct.Cl.1979), cert. denied, 100 S.Ct. 206 (1979). *Question:* How was the operators' argument of "frustration" by the United States different from the buyer's claim of excuse by government action in the main case?

ENFORCEMENT *CY PRES* AFTER IMPOSSIBILITY OR FRUSTRATION

When it appears that a promisor's undertaking will no longer be enforced in full measure, owing to a change of circumstances, what alternatives are there to excusing further performance by the promisor altogether? May the promisee salvage something of his bargain by offering a suitable concession to the promisor? Or would that be to infringe the principle that one contracting party may not impose new terms on the other without his consent?

The question is closely connected with the matter of contract revision by the courts. In some instances, when an agreement has been disrupted by events, the court has directed that the parties fulfill its general objects on terms that the court dictates. That is not the customary judicial practice, certainly; but the doctrine of *cy pres* has a certain place in contract law. An instance is a suit on a contract for the cutting of timber on a large tract over 35 years. The seller had agreed to share the cost of measuring (scaling) the cut timber if the buyer had that service done by an official scaler "in Puget Sound waters." Through technological advance, water transport and scaling gave way to a more efficient dry-land method. The court charged the seller with costs of that method, as adopted by an official scaler.[a] See also Miller v. Campello Co-op. Bank, p. 990 supra.

Other instances may be classified as cases of "partial" and "temporary" impossibility. See Restatement Second, §§ 269 and 270; UCC 2–615(b); Patterson, Temporary Impossibility of Performance of Contract, 47 Va.L.Rev. 798 (1961). In a case of the latter type, the decision may be to extend the time allowed for full performance, or to postpone the scheduled dates for performance. There are good reasons, however, for courts to be cautious in choosing to enforce part of an agreement and not others, or to give other partial relief. When a builder meets with unanticipated difficulty, performing under a fixed-price contract, would circumstances ever justify a court in directing him to continue work, and the owner to receive it, on a cost-plus basis?

Returning to the original question, it seems there is even more reason for caution in permitting a promisee to determine what parts of his agreement remain effective in a case of temporary or partial impossibility. That is the tendency, however, of the reasoning in some cases. See, for example, Lloyd v. Murphy, 25 Cal.2d 48, 153 P.2d 47 (1944). In that case a dealer in new cars suffered from wartime restrictions, and ultimately vacated his Wilshire Boulevard location. Before that, however, the landlords had offered to reduce the rent and to waive prohibitions in the lease against uses they had not consented to, and against subletting. In ruling that the lease was not "frustrated," Justice Traynor emphasized the value of the landlords' concession.[b] The inference might be that the defendant (promisor) was bound to his lease or not, as the promisee might choose to refashion its terms or not. See also UCC 2–613(b) for a rule of "buyer's option."

a. Scott Paper Co. v. Burlington Northern, Inc., 13 Wash.App. 341, 534 P.2d 1031 (1975).

b. This opinion is a major statement in the law of commercial frustration. As to Justice Traynor's supposed conservatism on that subject, see Macaulay, Justice Traynor and the Law of Contract, 13 Stan.L.Rev. 812, 833–38 (1961).

PROBLEMS

(1) A, an inventor, licensed B, a manufacturer, to produce and sell his patented washing machine, on paying a royalty of 20¢ each. A agreed not to license any other producer of the machine, and B agreed to pay a royalty of at least $5,000 a year, after the first three years. Five years into the term of the contract, the Government prohibited further manufacture of washing machines for an indefinite term, as part of a program of total mobilization for war. (Nine years thereafter, when A's patent will expire, his permission will no longer be required for exploiting his invention.) Does the Government's order terminate the license contract, or does it only suspend B's duty to pay the minimum royalty? Or should the war-caused loss be divided between A and B in some more imaginative way? See Patch v. Solar Corp., 149 F.2d 558 (7th Cir. 1945), cert. denied, 326 U.S. 741 (1945).

(2) The owner of a waste-collection business sold out after suffering a severe heart attack. He contracted not to compete with the buyer for a five-year period. Two years into this period he died. The price of the covenant, as embodied in a document separate from those of sale, was $95,000, payable monthly over five years. The business assets (equipment and the like) were priced at $97,000, and the seller received this sum during his lifetime. In letters of offer and acceptance preceding the formal documents the "total purchase price" was stated as $192,000. Must the buyer continue making payments to the seller's estate? See Rudd v. Parks, 588 P.2d 709 (Utah, 1978); Griffeth v. Sawyer Clothing, Inc., 202 Neb. 631, 276 N.W.2d 652 (1979); Siegfried v. I. G. W. T., Inc., 592 S.W.2d 248 (Mo.App.1979). Is an answer offered by Restatement Second, § 242?

(3) How would you argue for price relief for the Aluminum Company of America (ALCOA) in the following circumstances? Over a period of six months ALCOA negotiated with the Essex Group for converting Essex's alumina into molten aluminum by an electrolytic process. Late in 1967 ALCOA committed itself to providing this service over 16 years for a flexible price. (Dr. Alan Greenspan, the economist, assisted in devising the pricing formula.) One of the variables in the formula represented changing production costs other than labor; for this the Wholesale Price Index (WPI) was used as a proxy. At all events the charge to Essex was limited to 65% of an aluminum market price periodically published (the "65% cap"). The general assumption was that WPI variations would permit ALCOA's net income per pound of aluminum produced to vary between one and seven cents. In each of the first six years of operations ALCOA's profit exceeded 4¢ a pound. By the tenth year, however, ALCOA was incurring losses that threatened to mount into many millions of dollars. Other than the labor cost, that of electricity is the chief outlay in converting alumina. Since energy costs are a relatively small component of the WPI, electricity rates had begun swiftly to outpace that index, owing to OPEC's influence on oil prices and to anti-pollution regulations.

In litigation between ALCOA and Essex, a trial court order of April 1980 restated the price so as to yield ALCOA not less than a 1¢ per pound profit (unless the 65% cap should be less). Aluminum Company of America v. Essex Group (W.D.Pa.Civ.No.78–598).[a] What authorities cast doubt

a. On appeal at this writing.

on this solution? What authorities tend to support it? Consider mistake, commercial impracticability, and frustration as grounds for the decision.

GOLD v. SALEM LUTHERAN HOME ASS'N, Supreme Court of California, 1959, 53 Cal.2d 289, 1 Cal.Rptr. 343, 347 P.2d 687. [The defendant Association maintained a home for the aged, for whom it would agree to provide lifetime care. On August 1, 1956, it admitted Nicholas Chouvaldjy for a trial period of two months. Toward the end of September, he and the Association executed a life care contract dated October 1, for which he paid $8,500. He died on September 28. His executors brought an action against the Association to recover the sum paid.]

McCOMB, Justice. . . .

Question: *Since performance of the contract was not to commence until October 1, 1956, and Mr. Chouvaldjy died before performance was to commence, (a) was there a failure of consideration for the contract, or (b) was the doctrine of frustration applicable?*

No. (a) . . . Defendant's promise to furnish food, lodging, and care to decedent "for the remainder of his life" constituted consideration for the agreement, and the fact that decedent died before performance of the contract was to commence did not give his estate the right to recover the amount paid under the agreement on the ground that there was a failure of consideration. . . .

(b) The doctrine of frustration is not applicable to the facts in the present case . . . .

That death may at any unexpected time overcome a man of decedent's age, 84 years, is by common observation readily classified as "reasonably foreseeable." In the present case each party to the contract had clearly assumed the risk of variation of the life span from that predicted by the mortality tables. Therefore, the doctrine of frustration is not applicable here. (Cf. Coyne v. Pacific Mut. Ins. Co., supra, 8 Cal.App.2d at page 109, 47 P.2d at page 1081.)

[A judgment for the Association was affirmed. PETERS, J., dissented on the ground that no "annuity relationship" was to exist until October 1. The contract was "subject to an implied condition that decedent be able to become a life member" on that date.]

NOTES

(1) *Mistake.* If Chouvaldjy's life had been threatened by a fatal illness, unknown to him, when he contracted with the Association, his executors would presumably have based their claim on an additional ground: mistake. (In fact he suffered a stroke the day before his death.) Would the claim have been materially stronger if based on that fact? See Woodworth v. Prudential Ins. Co., 258 App.Div. 103, 15 N.Y.S.2d 541 (1939), aff'd 282 N.Y. 704, 26 N.E.2d 820 (1940), and comment on that case in G. Palmer, Mistake and Unjust Enrichment 53–57 (1962).

(2) *Death and Illness.* The duty to pay for services that are "personal" (non-delegable) is usually excused when the performer suffers death or disabling illness—not to mention the duty of performing. So, in Oneal v. Colton Consolidated School Dist. No. 306, 16 Wash.App. 488, 557 P.2d 11 (1976), a schoolteacher's contract was discharged by deterioration of his vision. In such a case it may prove confusing to speak of excuse by impossibility, for salary payments might readily be continued: calling the defense "frustration of purpose" may help an understanding of it.

Not only illness, but the "apprehension" of illness, may excuse a performer from making an appearance. See Wasserman Theatrical Enterprise, Inc. v. Harris, 137 Conn. 371, 77 A.2d 329 (1950) (Walter Huston, the actor, suffered a minor throat ailment). But of course under a contract for the services of a famous performer, his illness does not excuse either party if suitable provision is made for an understudy. See Terry v. Variety Theatres Co., 44 T.L.R. 451 (1928). In regulating a type of employment, such as marketing insurance, legislatures sometimes provide for "widows' licenses" and the like; e. g., N.Y.Ins.L. § 120 et seq. *Question:* Under an ordinary agreement made between a property owner and a real estate broker, would it be possible for the broker's executor, by finding a buyer, to earn the commission? See Phoenix Title and Trust Co. v. Grimes, 101 Ariz. 182, 416 P.2d 979 (1966); Thomas Yates & Co. v. American Legion Dept. of Miss., Ass'n Group Ins. Administrators, 370 So.2d 700 (Miss.1979) (insurance sale).

(3) *Self-Induced Impossibility.* A party who willfully disables himself from performing an undertaking is in no position to assert impossibility as a defense. To some extent, not fully examined, his carelessness in permitting a disabling event to occur may have a similar effect. "Some day it may have to be finally determined whether a prima donna is excused by complete loss of voice from an executory contract to sing if it is proved that her condition was caused by her carelessness in not changing her wet clothes after being out in the rain." Viscount Simon, in Joseph Constantine S. S. Line v. Imperial Smelting Corp., [1942] A.C. 154, [1941] 2 All Eng. 165.

If a disabling event has been proved, must the promisor go further, to make good his defense, and establish that it was no fault of his? Or is it then for the promisee to come forward with evidence on the fault issue? In Carlson v. Nelson, 204 Neb. 765, 285 N.W.2d 505 (1979), each element of a partial loss described in UCC 2–613 was proved, except that no evidence was introduced on the "without fault" element. In an action by the buyer for damages under UCC 9–713, should there be judgment for the defendant seller, based on the former section? What of section 2–615? According to Comment 5 (reproduced in the Supplement) there is no excuse under this section "unless the seller has employed all due measures to assure himself that his source will not fail." Who has the burden of persuasion? On the latter point, see Blount-Midyette & Co. v. Aeroglide Corporation, 254 N.C. 484, 119 S.E.2d 225 (1961), disagreeing with the rule of the English case cited above. See also Arnold v. Ray Charles Enterprises, Inc., 264 N.C. 92, 141 S.E.2d 14 (1965); 6 Corbin, § 1329.

CUTTER v. POWELL

Court of King's Bench, 1795.
6 T.R. 320, 101 Eng. Reprint 573.

[Assumpsit for work and labour performed by plaintiff's intestate. Defendant had given the following note: "Ten days after the ship 'Governor Parry,' myself master, arrives at Liverpool, I promise to pay Mr. T. Cutter the sum of thirty guineas, provided he proceeds, continues and does his duty as second mate in the said ship from hence to the port of Liverpool. . . ." The ship sailed from Kingston on August 2, with T. Cutter on board, and arrived at Liverpool on October 9. Before this, on September 20, Cutter had died. The usual wage for a second mate on such a voyage was £4 per month.]

LORD KENYON, Ch. J. . . . But it seems to me at present that the decision of this case may proceed on the particular words of this contract, and the precise facts here stated, without touching marine contracts in general. That where the parties have come to an express contract none can be implied has prevailed so long as to be reduced to an axiom in the law. Here the defendant expressly promised to pay the intestate thirty guineas, provided he proceeded, continued and did his duty as second mate in the ship from Jamaica to Liverpool; and the accompanying circumstances disclosed in the case are that the common rate of wages is four pounds per month, when the party is paid in proportion to the time he serves; and that this voyage is generally performed in two months. Therefore if there had been no contract between these parties, all that the intestate could have recovered on a quantum meruit for the voyage would have been eight pounds; whereas here the defendant contracted to pay thirty guineas provided the mate continued to do his duty as mate during the whole voyage, in which case the latter would have received nearly four times as much as if he were paid for the number of months he served. He stipulated to receive the larger sum if the whole duty were performed, and nothing unless the whole of that duty were performed; it was a kind of insurance.

[Judgment for defendant.]

NOTES

(1) *Restitution.* In Cutter v. Powell, Lord Kenyon said that the employment contract was "a kind of insurance." An annuity contract and a lifetime care contract are also comparable to insurance contracts. "An ordinary annuity contract provides for the payment of a fixed-dollar annual benefit commencing at a specified date and continuing as long as the annuitant lives. Such a contract is in many contexts treated as a form of insurance." R. Keeton, Insurance Law (Basic Text) 18 (1971).

Seaman Cutter's contract was arguably different, in that his death cut short performance of a *duty* on his part. Ordinarily a recipient of personal services must pay their value, even though he does not receive the full performance he was promised by reason of "impossibility" such as the death or illness of the promisor. A recovery for the promisor (or his estate) is an instance of a general rule of restitution: see Restatement Second, § 272(1). Of course, the decision in Cutter v. Powell must be an exception to that rule, if it is sound. Do the words of the contract there show that the rule was not meant to apply? For criticism of the case see Stoljar, The Great Case of Cutter v. Powell, 34 Can.Bar.Rev. 288, 298–9 (1956). Professor Palmer is apparently content with the decision. 2 Law of Restitution 118–19 (1978). [For his views on other restitution cases to follow, see id. at 145–56.]

(2) *Problem.* A lawyer agrees to defend a client's title to Blackacre for $25,000 if successful, and for $5,000 if not. At a trial, the client's title is vindicated, through the lawyer's efforts. The adverse claimant takes an appeal, and the lawyer dies before the appeal is heard. In an action by the lawyer's estate against the client, how should the recovery be measured? Should the amount depend on how the appellate decision goes? See Morton v. Forsee, 249 Mo. 409, 155 S.W. 765 (1913) (4–3 decision). How should the recovery be measured if the controversy is compromised without a decision on appeal?

See also Clark v. Gilbert, 26 N.Y. 279 (1863) ("The recovery in such a case cannot exceed the contract price, or the rate of it for the part of the service performed"), and Matter of Buccini v. Paterno Construction Co., 253 N.Y. 256, 170 N.E. 910 (1930) ("The question to be determined is the benefit to the owner in advancement of the ends to be promoted by the contract").

YOUNG v. CITY OF CHICOPEE

Supreme Judicial Court of Massachusetts, 1904.
186 Mass. 518, 72 N.E. 63.

HAMMOND, J. This is an action to recover for work and materials furnished under a written contract providing for the repair of a wooden bridge forming a part of the highway across the Connecticut river. While the work was in progress the bridge was totally destroyed by fire without the fault of either party, so that the contract could not be performed. The specifications required that the timber and other woodwork of the carriageway, wherever decayed, should be replaced by sound material, securely fastened, so that the way should be in "a complete and substantial condition." As full compensation both for work and materials, the plaintiff was to receive a certain sum per thousand feet for the lumber used "on measurements made after laying and certified by the engineers"; or, in other words, the amount of the plaintiff's compensation was measured by the number of feet of new material wrought into the bridge. That the public travel might not be interfered with more than was reasonably necessary, the contract provided that no work should be begun until material for at least one-half of the repairs contemplated should be "upon the job." With this condition the plaintiff complied, the lumber, which, at the time of the fire had not been used, being distributed "all along the bridge" and upon the river banks. Some of this lumber was destroyed by the fire. At the trial the defendant did not dispute its liability to pay for the work done upon and materials wrought into the structure at the time of the fire (Angus v. Scully, 176 Mass. 357, 57 N.E. 674, 49 L.R.A. 562, 79 Am.St.Rep. 318, and cases there cited), and the only question before us is whether it was liable for the damage to the lumber which was distributed as above stated and had not been used. It is to be noted that there had been no delivery of this lumber to the defendant. It was brought "upon the job," and kept there as the lumber of the plaintiff. The title to it was in him, and not in the defendant. Nor did the defendant have any care or control over it. No part of it belonged to the defendant until wrought into the bridge. The plaintiff could have exchanged it for other lumber. If at any time during the progress of the work before the fire the plaintiff had refused to proceed, the defendant, against his consent, could not lawfully have used it. Indeed, had it not been destroyed, it would have remained the property of the plaintiff after the fire. Nor is the situation changed, so far as respects the question before us, by the fact that the lumber was brought there in compliance with the condition relating to the commencement of the work. This condition manifestly was inserted to insure the rapid progress of the work, and it has no material bearing upon the rights of the parties in relation to the lumber. It is also to be borne in mind in this connection that the compensation for the whole job was to be determined by the amount of lumber wrought into the bridge. The contract was entire. By the destruction of the bridge each party was excused from further performance, and the plaintiff could recover for partial performance. The principle upon which the plaintiff can do this is sometimes said to rest upon the doctrine that there is an implied contract upon the owner of the structure upon which the work is to be done that it shall continue to exist, and therefore, if it is destroyed, even without his fault, still he must be regarded as in default, and so liable to pay for what has been done. Niblo v. Binsse, 40 N.Y. 476; Whelen v. Ansonia Clock Co., 97 N.Y. 293. In Butterfield v. Byron, 153 Mass. 523, 27 N.E. 669, 12 L.R.A. 571, 25 Am.St. Rep. 654, it was said by Knowlton, J., that there was "an implied assumpsit for what has properly been done by either [of the parties], the law dealing with it as done at the request of the other, and creating a liability to pay for it its value." In whatever way the principle may be stated, it would seem that the liability of the owner in a case like this should be measured by the amount of the contract work done which at the time of the destruction of the structure had become so far identified with it as that, but for the destruction, it would have inured to him as contemplated by the contract. In the present case the defendant, in accordance with this doctrine, should be held liable for the labor and materials actually wrought into the bridge. To that extent it insured the plaintiff. But it did not insure the plaintiff against the loss of lumber owned by him at the time of the fire, which had not then come into such relations with the bridge as, but for the fire, to inure to the benefit of the defendant, as contemplated by the contract. The cases of Haynes v. Second Baptist Church, 88 Mo. 285, 57 Am.Rep. 413, and Rawson v. Clark, 70 Ill. 656, cited by the plaintiff, seem to us to be distinguishable from this case.

The exceptions therefore must be sustained, and the verdict set aside. In accordance with the terms of the statement contained in the bill of exceptions, judgment should be entered for the plaintiff in the sum of $584 damages, and it is so ordered.

NOTES

(1) *Repair v. Building.* If Young had contracted to erect a bridge from scratch, rather than to repair one, the risk of its destruction by casualty, before completion, would have rested entirely on him, in the absence of an agreement to the contrary.[a] So far from recovering for a part performance, he would have been accountable for breach if he did not begin again. "It is well established law, that, where one contracts to furnish labor and materials, and construct a chattel or build a house on land of another, he will not ordinarily be excused from performance of his contract by the destruction of the chattel or building, without his fault, before the time fixed for the delivery of it." Butterfield v. Byron, 153 Mass. 517, 27 N.E. 667 (1891). According to Corbin: "This is the rule that is applied to contracts for the erection of buildings and bridges, the driving of tunnels, the building of dams, the manufacture of goods." 6 Corbin, § 1338. What might account for the difference, in this respect, between construction contracts and repair contracts?

(2) *The Case of the House Halfway.* Owner contracted with Mover to have his building on Third Street relocated on First Street, at a fixed price. When Mover had gotten it about halfway, and quit work for the night, it was consumed by fire, through no fault of his. Owner disclaimed any liability, and Mover sued for the fair value of his services rendered in the work down to the time of the fire. Mover obtained a judgment on a jury

a. For a collection of cases, indicating a minor strain of dissent, see Anno., 28 A.L.R.3d 788 (1969).

For a striking example see Hartford Fire Ins. v. Riefolo Constr. Co., Inc., 81 N.J. 514, 410 A.2d 658 (1980). On August 8, when the construction of a public school was 90% complete, the board of education obtained insurance on it from the Hartford Fire Ins. Co. On August 9 a fire loss occurred, requiring restoration of the building at a cost of more than $250,000. Of the several prime contractors on the job, some had permitted their policies of builder's risk on the structure to lapse. Hartford Fire paid the board for the work, and claimed reimbursement from the contractors and their insurers, all of whom refused to pay. The building contracts made the contractors responsible for "all damage up to the time the building is accepted by the Owner," and required them to maintain builder's risk insurance. In a suit by Hartford, the trial court found that any such insurance would have been uncollectible because offices in the building had been occupied by school employees prior to the loss. The court gave judgment for the defendants, and Hartford appealed. *Held:* Reversed. The plaintiff was subrogated to the contract right of its policyholder, the board, that the defendants "repair and replace any damage or loss" to the project—an obligation of the contractors distinct from that to maintain insurance.

verdict (amount unspecified), and Owner appealed. *Held:* Affirmed. Angus v. Scully, 176 Mass. 357, 57 N.E. 674 (1900).

RESTITUTION IN ENGLISH LAW

In English law an accrued obligation—that is, a duty of performance owing at the time of the event discharging the contract—has always been treated as absolute to the same extent as a prior payment would be regarded as final. Chandler v. Webster, [1904] 1 K.B. 493 (one of the so-called "coronation cases," to be compared with Krell v. Henry, p. 994 supra). However, sums are recoverable from a party who has received payment under the contract, or has obtained a valuable benefit by reason of another party's performance, before the time of the discharge by impossibility or frustration. This doctrine dates from 1943, when the House of Lords permitted a Polish company to recover £ 1,000 which it had paid to an English maker of textile machinery, in the summer of 1939. When Poland was invaded it became impossible for the seller to make delivery of the machines as required by the contract. Fibrosa Spolka Akcyjna v. Fairbairn Lawson Combe Barbour, Ltd., [1943] A.C. 32, 144 A.L.R. 1298. If the seller had done any fruitless work on the machines, it was said that no offset could be allowed for that.

The case suggested to Parliament that a more equitable solution might be achieved, and the response was the Law Reform (Frustrated Contracts) Act, 1943. One of its chief effects was to alter the position of one who has received an advance payment, but has also incurred expenses going toward his own performance: "the court may, if it considers it just to do so having regard to all the circumstances of the case, allow him to retain [part of the prepayment], not being an amount in excess of the expenses so incurred." Section 1(2).

The first case decided under the Act was B. P. Exploration Co. (Libya) Ltd. v. Hunt, [1979] 1 W.L.R. 783 (Q.B.D.), at p. 788, growing out of the expropriation by Libya of interests in an oil concession.[b] The court made a provisional award of more than $20 million as a "just sum" to be paid by the Texas concessionnaire (H. L. Hunt) to the operating party (B. P.).

NOTES

(1) *Equal Division?* In the Fibrosa case, how much of the prepayment could the seller justly retain, if it had expended £800 in manufacturing the machines (now unsalable) before the contract was discharged? The proponents of the Act thought he should have to repay £200. The Lord Chancellor (Simon) said, "I think that will commend itself to everybody as good sense," in giving such an example. But Professor Glanville Williams has argued that he should have to return £600, shouldering half of the una-

b. It happened that the judge, Sir Robert Goff, had prepared a treatise on the law of restitution. The second edition features his opinion as an appendix. R. Goff & G. Jones, The Law of Restitution (1978).

voidable loss. "Either natural justice, on my understanding of it, is altogether silent on a case of this sort, or it decrees that the distribution of loss shall be equal. Equal division of loss is also economically sounder than the placing of loss on one party only, for each of the two parties may be able to bear half the loss without serious consequences when the whole loss might come close to ruining him." See G. Williams, Law Reform (Frustrated Contracts) Act, 35–6 (1944).

This argument assumes that the seller did not contract for the early payment of £1,000 in order to protect himself against discharge of the contract by the law of impossibility, but rather against the risk of insolvency: "It is not often that parties contemplate that performance of their contract will become impossible. If they do contemplate the latter event, their usual reaction is to take out a policy of insurance, not to provide for payment in advance." Id. at 36.

(2) *Loss Apportionment.* Statutes apportioning the consideration "according to the benefit" appear in some states (e. g., Cal.Civ.Code, § 1514). Is it sensible to apportion benefits under contracts discharged by extraordinary circumstances, and not losses? And if that is done, should losses compensated by insurance be apportioned? For an elaborate proposal to divide "apportionable" losses, see Note, 69 Yale L.J. 1054 (1960). See also Note, 5 Hofstra L.Rev. 167 (1976). Some courts have proceeded inventively along this line without statutory support, especially in government-contract cases.[c] Compare Restatement Second, §§ 158 and 272. But some students are dubious about loss-sharing systems; see Posner & Rosenfield, op. cit. supra p. 970 n. d.

M. AHERN CO. v. JOHN BOWEN CO.

Supreme Judicial Court of Massachusetts, 1956.
334 Mass. 36, 133 N.E.2d 484.

WHITTEMORE, Justice. This is an action of contract to recover for labor and materials furnished by the plaintiff as a subcontractor, to the defendant as general contractor, in connection with the construction in Boston, by the Commonwealth, of the Chronic Disease Hospital and Nurses' Home. The case was tried in the Superior Court without a jury and the judge found for the plaintiff. The defendant excepted (1) to the refusal of the trial judge to rule that upon all the evidence the defendant was entitled to judgment, (2) to

c. In certain procurement situations the United States Court of Claims is prepared to work "jury verdict" equity, and apply a cost-sharing formula as if the parties had been engaged in a joint venture. Dynalectron Corp. (Pacific Div.) v. United States, 518 F. 2d 594 (Ct.Cl.1975). See also Kinzer Constr. Co. v. State, 125 N.Y.S. 46 (1910), aff'd 145 App.Div. 41, 129 N. Y.S. 567 (1911), aff'd 204 N.Y. 381, 97 N.E. 871 (1912). The federal procurement contracts were influential in the first opinion in Northern Corp. v. Chugach Electric Ass'n, 518 P.2d 76 (Alaska, 1974), a private-contract case featuring tragic events and divergent opinions. For the court's reconsideration see Id. at 523 P.2d 1234 (1974); and see Note, 6 UCLA-Alaska L.Rev. 338 (1977).

the finding for the plaintiff, and (3) to the exclusion of certain evidence. There was no error.

The essential facts are not in dispute. The labor and materials had been furnished under a partially performed contract, the further performance of which had become impossible because of the decision of this court in Gifford v. Commissioner of Public Health, 328 Mass. 608, 105 N.E.2d 476, declaring void the underlying general contract between the defendant and the Commonwealth. The amount claimed due, apart from interest, was the difference between the value of the materials and labor furnished and the sums paid by the defendant to the plaintiff under the terms of the contract prior to the Gifford decision.

The subject contract provided in part for the plaintiff's "furnishing all labor, material, equipment, insurance, etc., to do all plumbing as called for in . . . [stated parts of the general contract and contract documents] all in accordance with the plans and specifications . . . and perform all work to the satisfaction of the governing authorities and John Bowen Co., Inc. [the defendant]"; also that "You as subcontractor, further agree to be bound to us, the general contractor, by the terms of the special form of construction contract for projects under jurisdiction of Mass. Public Building Commission, the general conditions, drawings and specifications, and to assume toward us all the obligations and responsibilities that we, by those documents, assume toward the owner. . . . Terms of payment are to be the same as our terms of payment with the owner, all as outlined under . . . [the relevant part of the construction contract]. It is understood . . . that we [the defendant] accept no clause, reservation, or agreement other than those herein mentioned."

Prior to learning that it had no contract under which it could continue work, the defendant had been paid by the Commonwealth the amounts called for in three requisitions, less ten per cent as provided in the contract, and the defendant had paid the plaintiff the amount allowed in these requisitions for plumbing work less ten per cent. The amount found due represents, as to principal, the retained ten per cent plus additional work done and materials furnished, not covered in the honored requisitions.

The evidence to the exclusion of which the defendant excepted consisted of certain papers in two cross actions between the defendant here and the Commonwealth. The defendant offered to show that these cross actions had been tried together, and that the judge had ruled that neither party could recover from the other, that is, the defendant could not recover from the Commonwealth for the fair value of materials and labor furnished up to the time work ceased, including materials and labor furnished by the plaintiff here, and the Commonwealth could not recover the amounts paid to the defendant on the honored requisitions; also that following the findings by the judge there was "in each case . . . an agreement . . . of the parties to accept his decision" evidenced by the filing of the agreements for judgment.

It is plain that the defendant does not owe the plaintiff any sum under the contract and that the plaintiff after the Gifford decision could have done nothing to mature an obligation of the defendant under its terms. But the absence of an express provision in the contract to cover the unexpected contingency has not deterred this court or other American courts from giving recovery in cases of excusable impossibility for such performance as has been received. Butterfield v. Byron, 153 Mass. 517, 521, 522, 27 N.E. 667, 12 L.R.A. 571; Angus v. Scully, 176 Mass. 357, 358, 57 N.E. 674, 49 L.R.A. 562; Young v. Chicopee, 186 Mass. 518, 72 N.E. 63; Herbert v. Dewey, 191 Mass. 403, 411, 77 N.E. 822; Eastern Expanded Metal Co. v. Webb Granite & Construction Co., 195 Mass. 356, 362–363, 81 N.E. 251; Vickery v. Ritchie, 202 Mass. 247, 250–251, 88 N.E. 835, 26 L.R.A.,N.S., 810; Williston, Contracts (Rev.Ed.) §§ 1975–1977. Restatement: Contracts, § 468.

These decisions are not, as the defendant argues, based in the ultimate analysis on the principle of unjust enrichment which underlies restitution cases wherein recovery is limited to benefits received. Restatement: Contracts, § 348; Restatement: Restitution, § 155. Our decisions have spoken of "an implication that what was furnished was to be paid for", Vickery v. Ritchie [supra], or have indulged the fiction of an implied contract that the subject matter will continue to exist so that even though the defendant is without fault in fact he is to be regarded as in default and hence liable to pay. Young v. Chicopee [supra]. In commenting upon the "benefit" theory Williston (Contracts [Rev.Ed.] § 1977, pages 5553–5554) says, "It is sometimes said that the defendant is liable for the benefit which he has received, but unless the word 'benefit' is given a meaning wider than is natural, the statement is inadequate. In the first place, the word 'benefit' suggests that the matter is to be examined as it exists after the impossibility has supervened; but . . . the American law seems clear that where the defendant has received part performance regarded as valuable under the contract between the parties, the fact that this value has been destroyed by the very circumstances which make full performance of the contract impossible will not preclude recovery. A second reason for discarding the use of the word 'benefit,' in this connection, is because it suggests that what has been received by the defendant must be of pecuniary advantage to him. This seems unnecessary. . . . Accordingly, it is well settled that a recovery on a quantum meruit or quantum valebat should prima facie be such a proportion of the price as the work which the plaintiff has done bears to the full amount of the work for which the contract provided." And see idem, § 1972A, page 5541. Restatement: Contracts, § 468(3), gives "benefit" an appropriately limited meaning in saying, "The value of performance within the meaning of Subsections (1, 2) is the benefit derived from the performance in advancing the object of the contract, not exceeding, however, a ratable portion of the contract price." . . .

In Gillis v. Cobe, 177 Mass. 584, 59 N.E. 455, on which the defendant relies, the plaintiff did not show himself free of fault in respect to his nonperformance of the contract, 177 Mass. at page 597, 59 N.E. at page 459. The distinction between that case and the line with which this case stands was noted by the court in that opinion, 177 Mass. at page 592, 59 N.E. at page 457 and reaffirmed in Vickery v. Ritchie [supra].

It is no longer necessary to find implications of a contract to support recovery. The implications are undoubtedly found in each case in accordance with what the court holds to be fair and just in the unanticipated circumstances and it is in order to proceed at once to that issue.

This is not a case where the defendant stands fully apart, as the plaintiff does, from the circumstances which caused the unexpected destruction of the subject matter of the contract. The defendant did those things with respect to the subbids discussed in Gifford v. Commissioner of Public Health [supra], which caused its bid to appear the lowest, although in fact it was not. The Gifford decision has held that what the defendant did was not properly done. Even though we assume, as the defendant urges here, that it acted in good faith, and in respects as to which the prescribed course was not clear, the fact is that its actions, in a field where it had a choice, had a significant part in bringing about the subsequent critical events—the awarding to it of an apparent contract which turned out to be void and the ensuing decision of this court. In the circumstances it is plain that this is not a case of fully excusable impossibility. The defendant's part in the train of events is amply sufficient to offset the consideration that it has suffered uncompensable loss. Whatever might be said against the application of our established rule (and we do not intend any suggestion) to a case where the contract subject matter is destroyed by an event completely unconnected with either party and where both parties were equally interested in making the contract for mutual profit, and neither, by insurance or otherwise, could have provided against the risk of the unexpected loss and there is no final benefit, it is clearly fair and just to say in the instant case that "It is enough that the defendant has actually received in part performance of the contract something for which when completed he had agreed to pay a price." Williston, Contracts (Rev. ed.) § 1976, page 5551.

The plaintiff's contract was with the defendant, not with the Commonwealth. East Side Construction Co., Inc., v. Town of Adams,

329 Mass. 347, 353, 108 N.E.2d 659. There are in it necessarily, important references to the underlying contract. And it is clear that, while the contract continued, the plaintiff would become entitled to payment only as the defendant was paid by the Commonwealth under the general contract. But there is no express provision that the plaintiff is to be paid only if the defendant is paid, regardless of what happens to the general contract. There is no basis for saying what the parties would have done if they had thought of the matter. But the implication of the circumstances (that is, fairness in the circumstances) is against such a construction.

What has been said disposes of the exception to the exclusion of evidence. The liability of the defendant did not depend upon whether the defendant had or would receive payment from the Commonwealth for the labor and materials for which the plaintiff here makes claim.

Exceptions overruled.

NOTES

(1) *Subsequent Litigation.* The Boston Plate & Window Glass Company contracted to do the glass and glazing work on the same hospital. Before the work was actually begun, it was advised by the John Bowen Company not to proceed, for the reason given in the main case. The Glass Company had incurred some expenses in preparing to do the work, and it brought an action against Bowen on the contract. The trial court concluded that it should recover the "cost of estimates, drawings, labor and all other expenses inclusive of allocable overhead charges relative to plaintiff's contract with the defendant, but exclusive of any profit."

On appeal, the court rendered judgment for Bowen, holding that it was not liable for breach of the contract. It said: "We need not consider—and intend no intimation—whether and to what extent, under appropriate pleadings, in an extension of the principle established in M. Ahern Co. v. John Bowen Co. . . . , recovery may be had for payments made or obligations reasonably incurred in preparation for performance of a contract after it has been executed and delivered and is reasonably understood to be in effect. See Williston on Contracts (Rev. ed.) § 1976. . . . [T]he damages awarded included items outside such categories." Boston Plate & Window Glass Co. v. John Bowen Co., 335 Mass. 697, 141 N.E.2d 715 (1957).

The Albre Marble and Tile Company was in a position much like that of the Glass Company. It brought an action against Bowen for the value of work and labor furnished at Bowen's request. Their contract provided that Albre would "furnish and submit all necessary or required samples, shop drawings, tests, affidavits, etc., for approval, all as ordered or specified. . . ." The court decided that Albre should recover the "fair value of those acts done in conformity with the specific request of the defendant as contained in the contract", and justified the decision by reference to a "combination of circumstances peculiar to this case". Two excerpts from its decision follow:

"Although the matter of denial of reliance expenditures in impossibility situations seems to have been discussed but little in judicial opinions, it has, however, been the subject of critical comment by scholars. See Fuller and Perdue, The Reliance Interest in Contract Damages, 46 Yale L.J. 52, 373, 379–383. Note, 46 Mich.L.Rev. 401. In England the recent frustrated contracts legislation provides that the court may grant recovery for expenditures in reliance on the contract or in preparation to perform it where it appears *'just to do so having regard to all the circumstances of the case'* (emphasis supplied). 6 & 7 George VI, c. 40." [a]

". . . We are mindful that in Young v. Chicopee [p. 1006 supra], recovery of the value of materials brought to the construction site at the specific request of the defendant therein was denied. But in that case the supervening act rendering further performance impossible was a fire not shown to have been caused by the fault of either party. We are not disposed to extend that holding to a situation in which the defendant's fault is greater than the plaintiff's.

"Moreover, the acts requested here by their very nature could not be 'wrought into' the structure. In Angus v. Scully [Note 2, p. 1008 supra], recovery for the value of services rendered by house movers was allowed although the house was destroyed midway in the moving. The present case comes nearer to the rationale of the Angus case than to that of the Young case." Albre Marble and Tile Co. v. John Bowen Co., 338 Mass. 394, 155 N.E.2d 437 (1959); 343 Mass. 777, 179 N.E.2d 321 (1962) (second appeal).

(2) *Reliance Expenditures.* Do the cases show a "covert influence of the desire to reimburse detrimental reliance"? Certain decisions that a promised performance was not excused by unforeseen circumstances may be explained this way. Cases are collected by Fuller and Perdue at 46 Yale L. J. 373, pp. 379–82. However, they could find no case in a common-law jurisdiction where a fair sharing of the loss was expressly said to require recovery of the plaintiff's reliance interest. The decision in Albre Marble and Tile Co. v. John Bowen Co., Note 1 supra, has met that description, and confirmed their analysis.

(3) *Problem.* James Moore was indicted for passing counterfeit money. Robinson, a lawyer, contracted with Thomas, James' brother, to defend him for $1,000, of which $600 was paid. Thomas gave a note to Robinson for the remainder of his fee, not to be enforced if he did not win an acquittal in 1875. James was never tried, apparently having "skipped bail," but not until Robinson had spent some time on the case. What is the legal position of the contracting parties? See Moore v. Robinson, 92 Ill. 491 (1879).

(4) *Restatement Reform.* An innovative rule is stated in Restatement Second, § 272(2): supplying a term, reasonable in the circumstances, to avoid injustice. Under this rule is there danger of meddlesome interference by the courts with the privilege of a contracting party to conduct his own affairs? See Van Dusen Aircraft Supplies v. Massachusetts Port Authority, 361 Mass. 131, 279 N.E.2d 717 (1972). Do you find decisions in this chapter that the rule helps to explain? Decisions that it would alter?

a. This is not accurate. See p. 1009 supra.

Chapter 10

THIRD PARTY BENEFICIARIES

The modern development of third party beneficiary law, at least in this country, is usually dated from Lawrence v. Fox, decided in 1859 (see p. 1018 infra). Long before then, however, claims on contracts had been made by persons who were not parties to them. The results were mixed. In 17th century England it was successfully argued that a promise to pay a woman £1,000 was enforceable by her, although it was made to her father, and although she gave nothing in exchange for the promise. Later this case was disapproved. According to a 19th century English judge, "It would be a monstrous proposition to say that a person was a party to the contract for the purpose of suing upon it for his own advantage, and not for the purpose of being sued." [a]

As the case law has developed in this country, it is generally accepted that an action may be maintained on a contract, in an appropriate case, by one who had no part in creating it. The contract in such a case is said to be a "third party beneficiary contract." Probably the class of these contracts most familiar to the public at large is contracts of life insurance. It is perfectly well understood that the beneficiary of a life insurance policy may enforce his right to the death benefits even though he did not apply for it, pay for it, or have any other connection with it.

Of course, many contracts are not in this category, and often a claimant's attempt to seize an advantage under a contract between other parties meets with failure. The Restatement of Contracts has popularized the term "incidental beneficiary" for a third party who, though he may enjoy an advantage through the performance of a contract, has no enforceable interest in its performance. A clear—though admittedly bizarre—example may be helpful. Blake and Sullivan were colleagues in an attempt at armed robbery, and were apprehended. Blake pleaded guilty to a charge of assault, by agreement with the district attorney. Part of the agreement (it was said) was that the D.A. would not call Blake to testify against Sullivan. In the prosecution against Sullivan it was held that he could not claim the benefit of this agreement. If it was a contract at all, Sullivan was only an incidental beneficiary of it.[b]

a. Crompton, J., in Tweddle v. Atkinson, 1 B. & S. 393, 121 Eng.Rep. 762 (Q.B.1861).

b. People v. Sullivan, 271 Cal.App.2d 531, 77 Cal.Rptr. 25 (1969), cert. denied, 396 U.S. 973 (1969). Blake was called to the stand, but refused to say who his companion was. Sullivan was of course convicted.

A beneficiary who has an enforceable interest in performance of the contract may be variously known as a "donee beneficiary," a "creditor beneficiary," or simply as an "intended beneficiary."

Several bodies of law exist, apart from third party beneficiary law, by which a contract may create such an interest in a party who is not named or addressed in it. By the law of agency, for example, an undisclosed principal of one of the named parties may enforce a contract made on his behalf. In some situations various doctrinal ideas work in tandem to the same end. The following example is given in the Restatement Second: "the rights of employees under a collective bargaining agreement are sometimes treated as rights of contract beneficiaries, sometimes as rights based on agency principles, sometimes as rights analogous to the rights of trust beneficiaries. Or the collective bargaining agreement may be treated as establishing a usage incorporated in individual employment contracts, or as analogous to legislation." [c]

The Restatement Second also refers to certain "overriding social policies" that may determine the stake of third parties in an agreement. Such policies are beyond the scope of the Restatement and of this book. For instance, the range of warranties accompanying sales of goods is not explored here. The business of this chapter is to identify third party interests in performance, as determined by the general law of agreements, and to indicate some qualities of those interests.

Through the power of contracting parties to create rights in others many needs have been met, some commercial in nature, others not; and there are "procedural" conveniences as well in recognizing third party claims in contracts. Nevertheless, there are complications and inconveniences in the law of third party beneficiaries. It will be well, in going through the chapter, to consider both aspects of the subject. When disadvantages are encountered in granting a third-party claim, it may be possible to think of an alternate arrangement that would serve the purpose better. And in many of the cases there is a challenge to skill in drafting, so as to remove doubts and to promote the objects of the agreement.

NOTES

(1) *Advocacy.* Advocates too will find a challenge in third party law. It is their part to conceive of new applications, and to make good claims on that basis which would otherwise be problematical or even hopeless. As an example of inventiveness, consider the suggestion that oil and gas producers may be compelled to develop their reserves on public lands with diligence, in a fuel-short age, through third-party actions. Their duty in this respect stems from lease contracts with the United States. The third parties who (it is urged) may enforce the duty are the states where the minerals lie: by Congressional command the contracts provide for these states to share in

c. Chapter 14, Introductory Note.

any production revenues. See Note, State Enforcement of Federal Oil and Gas Leases, 21 Ariz.L.Rev. 111 (1979).

One inventive use of third party beneficiary doctrine was in aid of school desegregation. The school board serving the children of black servicemen had made commitments to the United States in return for financial aid; the court recognized the parents' claim, in part, as beneficiaries of these "contractual assurances." [d]

(2) *Express Trust.* An express trust is defined as "a fiduciary relationship with respect to property, subjecting the person by whom the property is held to equitable duties to deal with the property for the benefit of another person, which arises as a result of a manifestation of an intention to create it." The requisite to be noticed here is that there be some property—a *res*—as the subject matter of the trust. An instance that is given in the next main case is a quantity of lead: X has promised a pig of lead to A, and he entrusts lead to B who undertakes to make it into a pig and deliver it to A. In such a case A has a property interest in the lead which will be recognized and vindicated by special procedures in equity, chancery courts being the historic guardians of trusts. The property may be a bag of money as well as a pig of lead; or it may be an intangible such as a contract right. But in any event, in the case of a trust "there is always some property which is the subject matter of the trust, and which is held by the trustee for the benefit of the cestui que trust." 1 Scott on Trusts, § 2.6 (3d ed. 1967).[e]

LAWRENCE v. FOX

Court of Appeals of New York, 1859.
20 N.Y. 268.

Appeal from the Superior Court of the City of Buffalo. On the trial before Mr. Justice Masten, it appeared by the evidence of a bystander that one Holly, in November, 1857, at the request of the defendant, loaned and advanced to him $300, stating at the time that he owed that sum to the plaintiff for money borrowed of him, and had agreed to pay it to him the then next day; that the defendant, in consideration thereof, at the time of receiving the money, promised to pay it to the plaintiff the then next day. Upon this state of facts the

d. Bossier Parish School Bd. v. Lemon, 370 F.2d 847 (5th Cir. 1967), cert. denied, 388 U.S. 911 (1967). The result may be a mix-up in the law, of course. The case has been carelessly cited in a purely commercial context, even though the court did not rely primarily on third party beneficiary, and though it said: "Contract rights are not involved in this case."

e. Instructive comparisons can be made also between the entitlement of a third party beneficiary and that of a person on a contract made by an agent on his behalf. Sometimes the entitlements are virtually interchangeable. See Coast Trading Co., Inc. v. Parmac, Inc., 21 Wash.App. 896, 587 P.2d 1071 (1978); Riegel Fiber Corp. v. Anderson Gin Co., p. 235 supra.

For a comparison of agency and trust relationships with those growing out of third party beneficiary contracts, see Restatement Second, § 302, Comment f.

defendant moved for a nonsuit, upon three several grounds, viz.: That there was no proof tending to show that Holly was indebted to the plaintiff, that the agreement by the defendant with Holly to pay the plaintiff was void for want of consideration, and that there was no privity between the plaintiff and defendant. The court overruled the motion, and the counsel for the defendant excepted. The cause was then submitted to the jury, and they found a verdict for the plaintiff for the amount of the loan and interest, $344.66, upon which judgment was entered, from which the defendant appealed to the Superior Court, at General Term, where the judgment was affirmed, and the defendant appealed to this court. The cause was submitted on printed argument.

H. GRAY, J. The first objection raised on the trial amounts to this: That the evidence of the person present, who heard the declarations of Holly giving directions as to the payment of the money he was then advancing to the defendant, was mere hearsay and, therefore, not competent. Had the plaintiff sued Holly for this sum of money no objection to the competency of this evidence would have been thought of; and if the defendant had performed his promise by paying the sum loaned to him to the plaintiff, and Holly had afterwards sued him for its recovery, and the evidence had been offered by the defendant, it would doubtless have been received without an objection from any source. All the defendant had the right to demand in this case was evidence which, as between Holly and the plaintiff, was competent to establish the relation between them of debtor and creditor. For that purpose the evidence was clearly competent; it covered the whole ground and warranted the verdict of the jury.

But it is claimed that notwithstanding this promise was established by competent evidence, it was void for the want of consideration. It is now more than a quarter of a century since it was settled by the supreme court of this state—in an able and painstaking opinion by the late Chief Justice Savage, in which the authorities were fully examined and carefully analyzed—that a promise in all material respects like the one under consideration was valid; and the judgment of that court was unanimously affirmed by the court for the correction of errors. Farley v. Cleveland, 4 Cow. 432, 15 Am.Dec. 387; s. c. in error, 9 Cow. 639. In that case one Moon owed Farley and sold to Cleveland a quantity of hay, in consideration of which Cleveland promised to pay Moon's debt to Farley; and the decision in favor of Farley's right to recover was placed upon the ground that the hay received by Cleveland from Moon was a valid consideration for Cleveland's promise to pay Farley, and that the subsisting liability of Moon to pay Farley was no objection to the recovery. The fact that the money advanced by Holly to the defendant was a loan to him for a day, and that it thereby became the property of the defendant, seemed to impress the defendant's counsel with the idea that because the defendant's promise was not a trust fund placed by the plaintiff in the defendant's hands, out of which he was to realize money as from the sale of a chattel or the collection of a debt, the promise although made for the benefit of the plaintiff could not inure to his benefit. The hay which Cleveland bought of Moon was not to be paid to Farley, but the debt incurred by Cleveland for the purchase of the hay, like the debt incurred by the defendant for money borrowed, was what was to be paid.

That case has been often referred to by the courts of this state, and has never been doubted as sound authority for the principle upheld by it. Barker v. Bucklin, 2 Denio 45, 43 Am.Dec. 726; Canal Co. v. Westchester County Bank, 4 Denio 97. It puts to rest the objection that the defendant's promise was void for want of consideration. The report of that case shows that the promise was not only made to Moon but to the plaintiff Farley. In this case the promise was made to Holly and not expressly to the plaintiff; and this difference between the two cases presents the question, raised by the defendant's objection, as to the want of privity between the plaintiff and defendant. . . .

But it is urged that because the defendant was not in any sense a trustee of the property of Holly for the benefit of the plaintiff, the law will not imply a promise. I agree that many of the cases where a promise was implied were cases of trusts, created for the benefit of the promisor. The case of Felton v. Dickinson, 10 Mass. 287, and others that might be cited are of that class; but concede them all to have been cases of trusts, and it proves nothing against the application of the rule to this case. The duty of the trustee to pay the cestui que trust, according to the terms of the trust, implies his promise to the latter to do so. In this case the defendant, upon ample consideration received from Holly, promised Holly to pay his debt to the plaintiff; the consideration received and the promise to Holly made it as plainly his duty to pay the plaintiff as if the money had been remitted to him for that purpose, and as well implied a promise to do so as if he had been made a trustee of property to be converted into cash with which to pay. The fact that a breach of the duty imposed in the one case may be visited, and justly, with more serious consequences than in the other, by no means disproves the payment to be a duty in both. The principle illustrated by the example so frequently quoted (which concisely states the case in hand) "that a promise made to one for the benefit of another, he for whose benefit it is made may bring an action for its breach," has been applied to trust cases, not because it was exclusively applicable to those cases, but because it was a principle of law, and as such applicable to those cases.

It was also insisted that Holly could have discharged the defendant from his promise, though it was intended by both parties for the benefit of the plaintiff, and, therefore, the plaintiff was not entitled to maintain this suit for the recovery of a demand over which he had no control. It is enough that the plaintiff did not release the defendant from his promise, and whether he could or not is a question not now necessarily involved; but if it was, I think it would be found difficult to maintain the right of Holly to discharge a judgment recovered by the plaintiff upon confession or otherwise, for the breach of the defendant's promise; and if he could not, how could he discharge the suit before judgment, or the promise before suit, made as it was for the plaintiff's benefit and in accordance with legal presumption accepted by him (Berly v. Taylor, 5 Hill, 577–584 et seq.), until his dissent was shown?

The cases cited and especially that of Farley v. Cleveland, established the validity of a parol promise; it stands then upon the footing of a written one. Suppose the defendant had given his note in which for value received of Holly, he had promised to pay the plaintiff and the plaintiff had accepted the promise, retaining Holly's liability. Very clearly Holly could not have discharged that promise, be the right to release the defendant as it may. No one can doubt that he owes the sum of money demanded of him or that in accordance with his promise it was his duty to have paid it to the plaintiff; nor can it be doubted that whatever may be the diversity of opinion elsewhere, the adjudications in this state, from a very early period, approved by experience, have established the defendant's liability; if, therefore, it could be shown that a more strict and technically accurate application of the rules applied, would lead to a different result (which I by no means concede), the effort should not be made in the face of manifest justice.

The judgment should be affirmed.

JOHNSON, Ch. J., DENIO, SELDEN, ALLEN and STRONG, JJ., concurred. JOHNSON, Ch. J., and DENIO, J., were of opinion that the promise was to be regarded as made to the plaintiff through the medium of his agent, whose action he could ratify when it came to his knowledge, though taken without his being privy thereto.

COMSTOCK, J. (dissenting). The plaintiff had nothing to do with the promise on which he brought this action. It was not made to him, nor did the consideration proceed from him. If he can maintain the suit, it is because an anomaly has found its way into the law on this subject. In general, there must be privity of contract. The party who sues upon a promise must be the promisee, or he must have some legal interest in the undertaking. In this case, it is plain that Holly who loaned the money to the defendant, and to whom the promise in question was made, could at any time have claimed that it should be performed to himself personally. He had lent the money to the defendant, and at the same time directed the latter to pay the sum to the plaintiff. This direction he could countermand, and if he had done so, manifestly the defendant's promise to pay according to the direction would have ceased to exist. The plaintiff would receive a benefit by a complete execution of the arrangement, but the arrangement itself was between other parties, and was under their exclusive control. If the defendant had paid the money to Holly, his debt would have been discharged thereby. So Holly might have released the demand or assigned it to another person, or the parties might have annulled the promise now in question, and designated some other creditor of Holly as the party to whom the money should be paid. It has never been claimed that in a case thus situated the right of a third person to sue upon the promise rested on any sound principle of law. We are to inquire whether the rule has been so established by positive authority. . . .

If A. delivers money or property to B., which the latter accepts upon a trust for the benefit of C., the latter can enforce the trust by an appropriate action for that purpose. Berly v. Taylor, 5 Hill, 577. If the trust be of money, I think the beneficiary may assent to it and bring the action for money had and received to his use. If it be of something else than money, the trustee must account for it according to the terms of the trust, and upon principles of equity. There is some authority even for saying that an express promise founded on the possession of a trust fund may be enforced by an action at law in the name of the beneficiary, although it was made to the creator of the trust. Thus, in Comyn, Dig. "Action on the Case upon Assumpsit," B. 15, it is laid down that if a man promise a pig of lead to A. and his executor give lead to make a pig to B., who assumes to deliver it to A., an assumpsit lies by A. against him. The case of Delaware & H. Canal Co. v. Westchester County Bank, 4 Denio 97, involved a trust because the defendants had received from a third party a bill of exchange under an agreement that they would endeavor to collect it and would pay over the proceeds when collected to the plaintiffs. A fund received under such an agreement does not belong to the person who receives it. He must account for it specifically; and perhaps there is no gross violation of principle in permitting the equitable owner of it to sue upon an express promise to pay it over. Having a specific interest in the thing, the undertaking to account for it may be regarded as in some sense made with him through the author of the trust. But further than this we cannot go without violating plain rules of law. In the case before us there was nothing in the nature of a trust or agency. The defendant borrowed the money of Holly and received it as his own. The plaintiff had no right in the fund, legal or equitable. The promise to repay the money created an obligation in favor of the lender to whom it was made and not in favor of any one else. . . .

The judgment of the court below should, therefore, be reversed, and a new trial granted.

GROVER, J., also dissented.

Judgment affirmed.

NOTES

(1) *Restatement Terminology.* In the diction of the first Restatement, Lawrence would be known as a "creditor beneficiary." Section 133 established a threefold classification: donee, creditor and incidental beneficiaries. "An incidental beneficiary acquires by virtue of the promise no right against the promisor or the promisee." Section 147, carried forward as Restatement Second, § 315. Because the diction of the first Restatement lingers in the courts, most of the definitional section (133) is reproduced below at p. 1029.

Restatement Second introduces the term "intended" beneficiary to designate claimants who (like the plaintiff in Lawrence v. Fox) are permitted to enforce contracts to which they are not party. Section 302. It discards the terms "creditor" and "donee" in this connection. What is gained by the new diction is not altogether clear. The new text begins: "(1) Unless otherwise agreed between promisor and promisee, a beneficiary of a promise is an intended beneficiary if recognition of a right to performance in the beneficiary is appropriate to effectuate the intention of the parties and . . . (a) the performance of the promise will satisfy a duty of the promisee to the beneficiary. . . ." In the new lexicon, it seems, Lawrence may be called a "subsection (1)(a) intended beneficiary."

Sometimes one encounters a third party beneficiary contract in which each of the immediate parties is a promisor and each is a promisee. For present purposes "the promisor" is the maker of the promise sought to be enforced by the third party, and "the promisee" is its recipient. A firm grip on this convention will speed the discussion of cases in this chapter.

(2) *An Indemnity Agreement.* Jose and Lillie Gonzalez sold the assets of their music publishing company, Bego Enterprises, to Royalco International Corporation. Part of the sellers' agreement was "to be responsible for all . . . taxes . . . and for all royalties owing . . . under mechanical licenses, and does hereby agree to indemnify and hold Buyers harmless from any liability, obligation, cost or expense arising out of or related to any action for the collection of any of the said items that accrued prior to October 24, 1970. However, after October 24, 1970, Buyers will be responsible for any such payment due therefore [sic]." Earlier, Bego had been licensed to publish some compositions under an agreement to pay royalties to Ramms Music Company. Long after the sale Ramms brought an action against the Gonzalezes, and Bego, for unpaid royalties. The trial court gave judgment for the defendants, ruling that a four-year statute of limitations precluded collection of the royalties under the licensing agreement. They had accrued more than four years before the suit was brought. On appeal, the plaintiff contended that the Gonzalezes were liable to it under their contract with Royalco, which had been made less than four years before the suit. *Held:* Affirmed. House of Falcon, Inc. v. Gonzalez, 583 S.W.2d 902 (Tex.Civ.App.1979).[a]

a. Ramms was a division of House of Falcon, Inc. By the time of the action, House of Falcon had also acquired the assets of Royalco. For another case distinguishing indemnity contracts from third-party-beneficiary contract, see Jett v. Phillips & Associates, 439 F.2d 987 (10th Cir. 1971).

The court rejected the plaintiff's contention that it was a third party beneficiary of the sale contract, under the provision quoted above. Apart from apportioning obligations between the sellers and the buyers, all the clause purported to do, the court said, was to *indemnify* the buyers. A promise to indemnify "does not create any liability until the promisee . . . have [sic] incurred a liability, loss, or expense."

(3) *Problem.* Vendor contracts to sell a parcel of land for $100,000. The contract recites that Vendor has retained the services of Broker in arranging the sale, and continues: "Vendor covenants that he will pay Broker any fee or commission to which he may be entitled by reason of this sale, and further covenants to hold Purchaser harmless from any liability to said Broker for such fee or commission." Broker sues Vendor for a commission of $5,000, alleging that to be a reasonable and customary compensation for his services. He has no writing signed by Vendor, other than the sale contract, to support his claim, and a statute makes a promise of a commission to a real estate broker unenforceable unless it is expressed in writing. What result? See Robertson v. Hansen, 89 Idaho 107, 403 P.2d 585 (1965).

(4) *Statute of Frauds.* Following the decision in Lawrence v. Fox, the situation appears to be this: two persons (Holly and Fox) are bound to pay a single debt, and as between them the person primarily accountable is Fox. This effect could have been accomplished also by an initial agreement among all three persons concerned whereby Fox became indebted to Lawrence, and Holly became *surety* for payment of the debt. Observe that for enforcing that (differing) agreement against Holly the statute of frauds would require that his undertaking be in writing. However, the suretyship clause of the statute has no application to the agreements actually made among Lawrence, Holly, and Fox. See Note 3, p. 129 supra.

In the case that follows, no section of the original statute of frauds would be applicable. (The agreement in question was oral.) In some states, however, extensions of the statute have been enacted which would in terms preclude enforcement. New York is one: if an identical case were to arise today, a different result might be compelled.[b] Consider whether or not this is a desirable "reform" in the law.

SEAVER v. RANSOM

Court of Appeals of New York, 1918.
224 N.Y. 233, 120 N.E. 639, 2 A.L.R. 1187.

Action by Marion E. Seaver against Matt. C. Ransom and another, as executors, etc., of Samuel A. Beman, deceased. From a judgment of the Appellate Division (180 App.Div. 734, 168 N.Y.S. 454), affirming judgment for plaintiff, defendants appeal. Affirmed.

b. "Every agreement, promise or undertaking is void unless [represented in a writing] if such agreement, promise or undertaking:

1. By its terms is not to be performed within one year from the making thereof *or the performance of which is not to be completed before the end of a lifetime;* . . ." N.Y.Gen.Obl.L. § 5–701[a](1) (emphasis supplied).

See also Note 2, p. 131 supra; Redke v. Silvertrust, 6 Cal.3d 94, 98 Cal.Rptr. 293, 490 P.2d 805 (1971).

POUND, J. Judge Beman and his wife were advanced in years. Mrs. Beman was about to die. She had a small estate consisting of a house and lot in Malone and little else. Judge Beman drew his wife's will according to her instruction. It gave $1,000 to plaintiff, $500 to one sister, plaintiff's mother, and $100 each to another sister and her son, the use of the house to her husband for life, and remainder to the American Society for the Prevention of Cruelty to Animals. She named her husband as residuary legatee and executor. Plaintiff was her niece, 34 years old, in ill health, sometimes a member of the Beman household. When the will was read to Mrs. Beman, she said that it was not as she wanted it. She wanted to leave the house to the plaintiff. She had no other objection to the will, but her strength was waning, and, although the judge offered to write another will for her, she said she was afraid she would not hold out long enough to enable her to sign it. So the judge said, if she would sign the will, he would leave plaintiff enough in his will to make up the difference. He avouched the promise by his uplifted hand with all solemnity and his wife then executed the will. When he came to die, it was found that his will made no provision for the plaintiff.

This action was brought, and plaintiff recovered judgment in the trial court, on the theory that Beman had obtained property from his wife and induced her to execute the will in the form prepared by him by his promise to give plaintiff $6,000, the value of the house, and that thereby equity impressed his property with a trust in favor of the plaintiff. Where a legatee promises the testator that he will use property given him by the will for a particular purpose, a trust arises. O'Hara v. Dudley, 95 N.Y. 403, 47 Am.Rep. 53; Trustees of Amherst College v. Ritch, 151 N.Y. 282, 45 N.E. 876, 37 L.R.A. 305; Aherns v. Jones, 169 N.Y. 555, 62 N.E. 666, 88 Am.St.Rep. 620. Beman received nothing under his wife's will but the use of the house in Malone for life. Equity compels the application of property thus obtained to the purpose of the testator, but equity cannot so impress a trust, except on property obtained by the promise. Beman was bound by his promise, but no property was bound by it; no trust in plaintiff's favor can be spelled out.

An action on the contract for damages, or to make the executors trustees for performance, stands on different ground. Farmers' Loan & Trust Co. v. Mortimer, 219 N.Y. 290, 294, 295, 114 N.E. 389. The Appellate Division properly passed to the consideration of the question whether the judgment could stand upon the promise made to the wife, upon a valid consideration, for the sole benefit of plaintiff. The judgment of the trial court was affirmed by a return to the general doctrine laid down in the great case of Lawrence v. Fox, 20 N.Y. 268, which has since been limited as herein indicated.

Contracts for the benefit of third persons have been the prolific source of judicial and academic discussion. Williston, Contracts for the Benefit of a Third Person, 15 Harvard Law Review, 767; Corbin,

Contracts for the Benefit of Third Persons, 27 Yale Law Review, 1008. The general rule, both in law and equity (Phalen v. United States Trust Co., 186 N.Y. 178, 186, 78 N.E. 943, 7 L.R.A.,N.S., 734, 9 Ann.Cas. 595), was that privity between a plaintiff and a defendant is necessary to the maintenance of an action on the contract. The consideration must be furnished by the party to whom the promise was made. The contract cannot be enforced against the third party, and therefore it cannot be enforced by him. On the other hand, the right of the beneficiary to sue on a contract made expressly for his benefit has been fully recognized in many American jurisdictions, either by judicial decision or by legislation, and is said to be "the prevailing rule in this country." Hendrick v. Lindsay, 93 U.S. 143, 23 L.Ed. 855; Lehow v. Simonton, 3 Colo. 346. It has been said that "the establishment of this doctrine has been gradual, and is a victory of practical utility over theory, of equity over technical subtlety." Brantly on Contracts, 2d Ed., p. 253. The reasons for this view are that it is just and practical to permit the person for whose benefit the contract is made to enforce it against one whose duty it is to pay. Other jurisdictions still adhere to the present English Rule (7 Halsbury's Laws of England, 342, 343; Jenks' Digest of English Civil Law, sec. 229) that a contract cannot be enforced by or against a person who is not a party. Exchange Bank v. Rice, 107 Mass. 37, 9 Am. Rep. 1. But see, also, Forbes v. Thorpe, 209 Mass. 570, 95 N.E. 955; Gardner v. Denison, 217 Mass. 492, 105 N.E. 359, 51 L.R.A.,N.S., 1108.

In New York the right of the beneficiary to sue on contracts made for his benefit is not clearly or simply defined. It is at present confined: First. To cases where there is a pecuniary obligation running from the promisee to the beneficiary, "a legal right founded upon some obligation of the promisee in the third party to adopt and claim the promise as made for his benefit." [Cases cited.] Secondly. To cases where the contract is made for the benefit of the wife (Buchanan v. Tilden,[a] 158 N.Y. 109, 52 N.E. 724, 44 L.R.A. 170, 70 Am.St.Rep. 454; Benton v. Welch, 170 N.Y. 554, 63 N.E. 539), affianced wife (De Cicco v. Schweizer, 221 N.Y. 431, 117 N.E. 807, Ann. Cas.1918C, 816), or child (Todd v. Weber, 95 N.Y. 181, 193, 47 Am. Rep. 20; Matter of Kidd, 188 N.Y. 274, 80 N.E. 924) of a party to the contract. The close relationship cases go back to the early King's Bench case (1677), long since repudiated in England, of Dutton v. Poole, 2 Lev. 211 (s.c., 1 Ventris, 318, 332). See Schemerhorn v. Vanderheyden, 1 Johns, 139, 3 Am.Dec. 304. The natural and moral duty of the husband or parent to provide for the future of wife or

a. The defendant in this case was the nephew of Samuel J. Tilden, who succeeded in "breaking" a portion of his uncle's will. He had promised to share the recovery with the plaintiff, who was, by adoption, a niece of Governor Tilden. The promise was made to her husband in return for arranging advances for use in prosecuting the will contest.

child sustains the action on the contract made for their benefit. "This is the furthest the cases in this state have gone," says Cullen, J., in the marriage settlement case of Borland v. Welch, 162 N.Y. 104, 110, 56 N.E. 556.

The right of the third party is also upheld in, thirdly, the public contract cases [cases cited] where the municipality seeks to protect its inhabitants by covenants for their benefit; and, fourthly, the cases where, at the request of a party to the contract, the promise runs directly to the beneficiary although he does not furnish the consideration [cases cited]. It may be safely said that a general rule sustaining recovery at the suit of the third party would include but few classes of cases not included in these groups, either categorically or in principle.

The desire of the childless aunt to make provisions for a beloved and favorite niece differs imperceptibly in law or in equity from the moral duty of the parent to make testamentary provision for a child. The contract was made for the plaintiff's benefit. She alone is substantially damaged by its breach. The representatives of the wife's estate have no interest in enforcing it specifically. It is said in Buchanan v. Tilden that the common law imposes moral and legal obligations upon the husband and the parent not measured by the necessaries of life. It was, however, the love and affection or the moral sense of the husband and the parent that imposed such obligations in the cases cited, rather than any common-law duty of husband and parent to wife and child. If plaintiff had been a child of Mrs. Beman, legal obligation would have required no testamentary provision for her, yet the child could have enforced a covenant in her favor identical with the covenant of Judge Beman in this case. De Cicco v. Schweizer, supra. The constraining power of conscience is not regulated by the degree of relationship alone. The dependent or faithful niece may have a stronger claim than the affluent or unworthy son. No sensible theory of moral obligation denies arbitrarily to the former what would be conceded to the latter. We might consistently either refuse or allow the claim of both, but I cannot reconcile a decision in favor of the wife in Buchanan v. Tilden, based on the moral obligations arising out of near relationship, with a decision against the niece here on the ground that the relationship is too remote for equity's ken. No controlling authority depends upon so absolute a rule. In Sullivan v. Sullivan, 161 N.Y. 554, 56 N.E. 116, the grandniece lost in a litigation with the aunt's estate, founded on a certificate of deposit payable to the aunt "or in case of her death to her niece;" but what was said in that case of the relations of plaintiff's intestate and defendant does not control here, any more than what was said in Durnherr v. Rau [135 N.Y. 219, 32 N.E. 49], on the relation of husband and wife, and the inadequacy of mere moral duty, as distinguished from legal or equitable obligation, controlled the decision in Buchanan v. Tilden. Borland v. Welch, supra, deals only with the rights of volunteers under a marriage settlement not made for the benefit of collaterals. Kellogg, P. J., writing for the court below, well said:

"The doctrine of Lawrence v. Fox is progressive, not retrograde. The course of the late decisions is to enlarge, not limit, the effect of that case."

The court in that leading case attempted to adopt the general doctrine that any third person, for whose direct benefit a contract was intended, could sue on it. [Next the court referred to a number of later New York precedents, some stating the doctrine in general terms, and others narrowing its application.]

But, on principle, a sound conclusion may be reached. If Mrs. Beman had left her husband the house on condition that he pay the plaintiff $6,000, and he had accepted the devise, he would have become personally liable to pay the legacy, and plaintiff could have recovered in an action at law against him, whatever the value of the house. . . . That would be because the testatrix had in substance bequeathed the promise to plaintiff, and not because close relationship or moral obligation sustained the contract. The distinction between an implied promise to a testator for the benefit of a third party to pay a legacy and an unqualified promise on a valuable consideration to make provision for the third party by will is discernible, but not obvious. The tendency of American authority is to sustain the gift in all such cases and to permit the donee beneficiary to recover on the contract. Matter of Edmundson's Estate (1918) 259 Pa. 429, 103 A. 277. The equities are with the plaintiff, and they may be enforced in this action, whether it be regarded as an action for damages or an action for specific performance to convert the defendants into trustees for plaintiff's benefit under the agreement.

The judgment should be affirmed, with costs.

Judgment affirmed.[b]

NOTES

(1) *English Law.* Though there were early precedents to the contrary, it seems to have become settled in the common law of England that contracts may not confer enforceable rights on third parties as such.[c] For discussion of the rule, see Beswick v. Beswick, [1967] 3 W.L.R. 932, [1967] 2 All E.R. 1197, in which a widow sued on a promise of payments to her that the defendant had made to her husband. The House of Lords ruled that she was entitled to specific performance, in her capacity as administratrix of her husband's estate, but it was conceded that she had no claim as an

b. For an extraordinary (alleged) agreement concerning succession to property, in which the court was divided over the entitlement of the plaintiffs as third party beneficiaries—and other matters—see White v. Mulvania, 575 S.W.2d 184 (Mo.1978).

c. Statutory exceptions have been made in relation to certain insurance contracts.

individual.[d] Lord Reid hinted that he would be prepared to reconsider the common-law rule, except that Parliamentary reform may be anticipated.

An American scholar has said that the English courts are "very ready to torture a contract into a trust" because they feel the injustice of denying a remedy to the beneficiary of a contract. Scott on Trusts, Vol. 1, § 14.4 (3d ed. 1967).

For a promise such as the one made to Mr. Beswick, specific performance may be especially appropriate in a suit by the promisee. Do you see why? See Restatement Second, § 307, Comment d; Thorpe v. Collins, 263 S.E.2d 115 (Ga.1980).

(2) *The Couples Team.* Stephen and Orise, man and wife, each brought an action against the insurance company for which Stephen had formerly worked. He established the company's liability for discharging him with malicious motives (though his employment was terminable at will). Among the benefits of his employment were medical insurance for his wife and survivorship benefits for her under a pension plan. Orise then sued the company as third party beneficiary of its obligation not to discharge Stephen out of malice. From a dismissal, she appealed. *Held:* Affirmed. Pstragowski v. Metropolitan Life Ins. Co., 553 F.2d 1 (1st Cir. 1977). The court observed that Stephen's suit could have accomplished all that Orise's could, so that to entertain her suit was not the "least cost" form of redress. *Question:* What would be the effect on third party beneficiary law if everyone claiming under it had to show that his was the least-cost remedy?

FIRST RESTATEMENT

Because the extant cases on third party beneficiary law rely largely on the first Restatement, its chief provision on the subject is reproduced here, in part.

§ 133. Definition of Donee Beneficiary, Creditor Beneficiary, Incidental Beneficiary

(1) Where performance of a promise in a contract will benefit a person other than the promisee, that person is [exception omitted [e]]:

(a) a donee beneficiary if it appears from the terms of the promise in view of the accompanying circumstances that the purpose of the promisee in obtaining the promise of all or part of the performance thereof is to make a gift to the beneficiary or to confer upon him a right

d. Much of the law lords' discussion was directed to a "consolidation act" of 1925, and they concluded that it did not make a sweeping alteration in the rights of third parties.

For discussion prompted by the case, see Baker, Note, 83 Law Q.Rev. 465 (1967); Comment, Third Party Beneficiary Contracts in England, 35 U.Chi. L.Rev. 544 (1968).

e. (3) Where it appears from the terms of the promise in view of the accompanying circumstances that the purpose of the promisee is to benefit a beneficiary under a trust and the promise is to render performance to the trustee, the trustee, and not the beneficiary under the trust, is a beneficiary within the meaning of this Section.

against the promisor to some performance neither due nor supposed or asserted to be due from the promisee to the beneficiary;

(b) a creditor beneficiary if no purpose to make a gift appears from the terms of the promise in view of the accompanying circumstances and performance of the promise will satisfy an actual or supposed or asserted duty of the promisee to the beneficiary, or a right of the beneficiary against the promisee which has been barred by the Statute of Limitations or by a discharge in bankruptcy, or which is unenforceable because of the Statute of Frauds;

(c) an incidental beneficiary if neither the facts stated in Clause (a) nor those stated in Clause (b) exist.

PROBLEMS

Consider the following cases in light of the foregoing materials and of Restatement Second, § 302:

(a) The owner of a commercial building arranges to lease it to a newspaper publisher, upon building an addition to it. A builder contracts with the owner to construct the addition in less than 80 days, knowing that the tenant expects occupancy after that. The builder completes the work more than six months late. The owner recovers from him the reasonable rental value of the structure for the period of the delay. The publisher also makes a claim against the builder, as third party beneficiary of the construction contract, for loss of anticipated profits. What result? See McDonald Constr. Co. v. Murray, 5 Wash.App. 68, 485 P.2d 626 (1971).

(b) The Exercycle Corporation contracts with a dealer in Michigan, giving him the exclusive right to sell its product there. Similarly, it contracts with a dealer in Illinois. Each of the dealers undertakes "not to sell Exercycles in any territory other than that assigned to him by the Company." The Illinois dealer violates this promise by making sales in Michigan. Does the Michigan dealer have a remedy under the Illinois dealer's contract? If the Illinois dealer had been appointed first, would that make a difference? See Exercycle of Michigan, Inc. v. Wayson, 341 F.2d 335 (7th Cir. 1965).

LUCAS v. HAMM

Supreme Court of California, 1961.
56 Cal.2d 583, 15 Cal.Rptr. 821, 364 P.2d 685.

[In a complaint against a lawyer, L. S. Hamm, some plaintiffs made the following allegations: They were designated as beneficiaries in a will prepared by the defendant for Eugene Emmick, deceased. The will had placed certain assets in trust, and specified that the plaintiffs were to have a 15% interest in it. After the will was probated, the lawyer had advised the plaintiffs that the trust provision was invalid under the California Civil Code. The plaintiffs were compelled to enter into a settlement with Emmick's blood relatives, by which they received a share of his estate that was $75,000 less than what they would have received if the will had been properly prepared. They sought recovery from the lawyer in that amount, basing the claim on his negligence, and on breach of his contract with Emmick. The action was dismissed, and the plaintiffs appealed.]

GIBSON, Chief Justice. . . . It was held in Buckley v. Gray, 110 Cal. 339, 42 P. 900, 31 L.R.A. 862, that an attorney who made a mistake in drafting a will was not liable for negligence or breach of contract to a person named in the will who was deprived of benefits as a result of the error. . . . For the reasons hereinafter stated the case is overruled. [The court's discussion of the tort claim is omitted.]

Neither do we agree with the holding in Buckley that beneficiaries damaged by an error in the drafting of a will cannot recover from the draftsman on the theory that they are third-party beneficiaries of the contract between him and the testator.[1] Obviously the main purpose of a contract for the drafting of a will is to accomplish the future transfer of the estate of the testator to the beneficiaries named in the will, and therefore it seems improper to hold, as was done in Buckley, that the testator intended only "remotely" to benefit those persons. It is true that under a contract for the benefit of a third person performance is usually to be rendered directly to the beneficiary, but this is not necessarily the case. (See Rest., Contracts, § 133, com. d; 2 Williston on Contracts (3rd ed. 1959) 829.) For example, where a life insurance policy lapsed because a bank failed to perform its agreement to pay the premiums out of the insured's bank account, it was held that after the insured's death the beneficiaries could recover against the bank as third-party beneficiaries. Walker Bank & Trust Co. v. First Security Corp., 9 Utah 2d 215, 341 P.2d 944, 945 et seq. Persons who had agreed to procure liability insurance for the protection of the promisees but did not do so were also held liable to injured persons who would have been covered by the insurance, the courts stating that all persons who might be injured were third-party beneficiaries of the contracts to procure insurance.

1. It has been recognized in other jurisdictions that the *client* may recover in a contract action for failure of the attorney to carry out his agreement. (See 5 Am.Jur. 331; 49 A.L.R. 2d 1216, 1219–1221; Prosser, Selected Topics on the Law of Torts (1954) pp. 438, 442.) This is in accord with the general rule stated in Comunale v. Traders & General Ins. Co., 50 Cal.2d 654, 663, 328 P.2d 198, 68 A.L.R.2d 883, that where a case sounds in both tort and contract, the plaintiff will ordinarily have freedom of election between the two actions.

[In Schirmer v. Nethercutt, 157 Wash. 172, 288 P. 265 (1930), S was a student of law in N's office. He employed N to draw up a will for his grandmother, for which S paid. The grandmother instructed N to provide a substantial legacy for S. N prepared the will and had it witnessed by S—thereby costing him the legacy. S recovered his loss from N.—Eds.]

Johnson v. Holmes Tuttle Lincoln-Merc., Inc., 160 Cal.App.2d 290, 296 et seq., 325 P.2d 193; James Stewart & Co. v. Law, 149 Tex. 392, 233 S.W.2d 558, 561–562, 22 A.L.R.2d 639. Since, in a situation like those presented here and in the Buckley case, the main purpose of the testator in making his agreement with the attorney is to benefit the persons named in his will and this intent can be effectuated, in the event of a breach by the attorney, only by giving the beneficiaries a right of action, we should recognize, as a matter of policy, that they are entitled to recover as third-party beneficiaries. See 2 Williston on Contracts (3rd ed. 1959) pp. 843–844; 4 Corbin on Contracts (1951) pp. 8, 20.

Section 1559 of the Civil Code, which provides for enforcement by a third person of a contract made "expressly" for his benefit, does not preclude this result. The effect of the section is to exclude enforcement by persons who are only incidentally or remotely benefited. See Hartman Ranch Co. v. Associated Oil Co., 10 Cal.2d 232, 244, 73 P.2d 1163; cf. 4 Corbin on Contracts (1951) pp. 23–24. As we have seen, a contract for the drafting of a will unmistakably shows the intent of the testator to benefit the persons to be named in the will, and the attorney must necessarily understand this.

Defendant relies on language in Smith v. Anglo-California Trust Co., 205 Cal. 496, 502, 271 P. 898, and Fruitvale Canning Co. v. Cotton, 115 Cal.App.2d 622, 625, 252 P.2d 953, that to permit a third person to bring an action on a contract there must be "an intent clearly manifested by the promisor" to secure some benefit to the third person. This language, which was not necessary to the decision in either of the cases, is unfortunate. Insofar as intent to benefit a third person is important in determining his right to bring an action under a contract, it is sufficient that the promisor must have understood that the promisee had such intent. (Cf. Rest., Contracts, § 133, subds. 1(a) and 1(b); 4 Corbin on Contracts (1951) pp. 16–18; 2 Williston on Contracts (3rd ed. 1959) pp. 836–839.) No specific manifestation by the promisor of an intent to benefit the third person is required. The language relied on by defendant is disapproved to the extent that it is inconsistent with these views.

We conclude that intended beneficiaries of a will who lose their testamentary rights because of failure of the attorney who drew the will to properly fulfill his obligations under his contract with the testator may recover as third-party beneficiaries.[a]

[The court went on to rule, however, that the complaint did not allege any error by Hamm that was not excusable in a well-informed lawyer. The supposed invalidity of the trust depended on rules about perpetuities and restraints on alienation—subjects which "have long perplexed the courts and the bar." In view of the state of the law,

a. See also McAbee v. Edwards, 340 So.2d 1167 (Fla.App.1976).

and the nature of the supposed error, "it would not be proper to hold that defendant failed to use such skill, prudence, and diligence as lawyers of ordinary skill and capacity commonly exercise." Judgment affirmed.]

NOTES

(1) *Lucas v. Hamm Revisited.* In Heyer v. Flaig, 70 Cal.2d 223, 449 P.2d 161 (1969), the court had to decide when the statute of limitations began to run on a claim such as that in the foregoing case: when the will was prepared, or when the testator died. In choosing the latter date, the court said that, under Lucas, the third party can recover on a tort theory. Of the third party beneficiary theory, it said: "This latter theory of recovery, however, is conceptually superfluous since the crux of the action must lie in tort in any case; there can be no recovery without negligence." Does this mean that a lawyer cannot contract with his client to achieve a given result, even though a careful effort might fail? See Note 3, p. 885 supra.

(2) *Parol Evidence.* Professor Corbin, no friend to the parol evidence rule, thought it should permit an extrinsic showing that a written contract was intended for the benefit of a third party. But his view has been characterized as more "liberal" in that respect than that of the New York courts. Hylte Bruks Aktiebolag v. Babcock & Wilcox Co., 399 F.2d 289 (2d Cir. 1968) (footnote 6).

In Ridder v. Blethen, 24 Wash.2d 552, 166 P.2d 834 (1946), the curious question was whether or not parol evidence was admissible to establish that one of the plaintiffs was *not* a third party beneficiary of a contract his father had made, by the express terms of which he appeared to be a donee beneficiary. The court indicated that such evidence is commonly required to show whether or not the parties had a donative purpose. It referred to the Restatement, § 133(1)(a). That section speaks of the promisee's purpose, as it appears "from the terms of the promise in view of the accompanying circumstances." Would it be proper, under this test, to take testimony from the promisee about his purpose? Compare Restatement Second, § 302. What forms of parol evidence are admissible under that rule?

(3) *A Medical Case.* For about 25 years no physician had practiced in the community of Booker, Texas, despite vigorous efforts by the Booker Booster Club to attract one. Ultimately the efforts had a limited success. A corporate Scholarship Fund was created and it received public subscriptions. It contributed $1,800 to help defray the expense of a medical education for Neal K. Suthers. In 1966 Suthers contracted to use his best efforts to become a licensed physician, and thereafter immediately move to Booker, and to remain in practice there for at least ten years. In breach of this agreement, he practiced for only about five weeks in Booker, during 1974, before moving from the state. Meanwhile, in 1973, the citizens of Booker voted to create a Hospital District, floated a bond issue, and built a clinic, all as "contemplated" by the 1966 agreement.

Dr. Suthers was sued by the Scholarship Fund for the amount of its subvention, together with a 50% "penalty," as prescribed by the agreement. Additional plaintiffs claimed further sums as third party beneficiaries: the Hospital District and some of its residents, claiming to represent both a class of taxpayers and a larger class of residents deprived of medical services. The trial court asked the jury, "Was the agreement [of 1966] intended for the direct benefit of the Plaintiff class of residents . . . ?"; to which the jury answered Yes. The court entered judgment for the Fund, and for the other claimants awarded a sum for loss of value in the clinic ($110,000) and another thousand dollars found by the jury to represent the loss to residents at large. On appeal, *held:* Reversed as to the non-Fund claimants. Suthers v. Booker Hospital Dist., 543 S.W.2d 723 (Tex.Civ.App. 1976), error ref'd, n. r. e.

Each of the three appellate judges wrote an opinion. One of them, speaking for the court, quoted testimony of the attorney who drafted the agreement, to the effect that he had tried to cover the "major points". This judge observed that Suthers' assuming an obligation to third parties would be a major point. One judge, dissenting, observed that the Scholarship Fund would derive no benefit from the promise to practice in Booker for ten years: "this contract was executed primarily to benefit the citizens."

If it were feasible to grant specific performance in such a case, and otherwise consistent with public interests, should the taxpayers and residents of Booker have been allowed to claim that remedy? If the draftsman had provided in the contract for all the recoveries allowed by the trial court, could it fairly have been questioned on the ground of unconscionability? In Restatement Second, § 302(1), what language supports the conclusion in Dr. Suthers' case?

STATUTORY ACTIONS

In several "Field Code" states there are provisions that "a contract made expressly for the benefit of a third person may be enforced by him at any time before the parties thereto rescind it." [a] In a few other states there are general statutory provisions recognizing third-party actions; the following provision of the Virginia Code is an instance.[b]

When person not a party, etc., may take or sue under instrument.

> . . . [I]f a covenant or promise be made for the benefit, in whole or in part, of a person with whom it is not made, or with whom it is made jointly with others, such person, whether named in the instrument or not, may maintain in his own name any action thereon which he might maintain in case it had been made with him only and the consideration had moved from him to the party making such covenant or promise. In such action the covenantor or promisor shall be permitted to make all defenses he may have, not only against the covenantee or promisee, but against such beneficiary as well.

a. E. g., Cal.Civ.Code, § 1559 (1954); Idaho Code § 29–102 (1967).

b. Va.Code § 55–22 (Repl.Vol.1974).

"In addition to these general provisions, statutes of limited substantive coverage frequently give rights of action to beneficiaries of three general types: beneficiaries of life insurance policies, laborers and materialmen on statutory bonds posted by public contractors, and persons injured by the negligence of a bonded public official." [c]

NOTE

Brokers' Claims. The Virginia statute quoted above was relied on by the plaintiff in Professional Realty Corp. v. Bender, a case stated in Note 1, p. 797 supra. The plaintiff was a broker, suing for the amount of a commission promised in a land-sale contract. The court denied that the statute made the buyers accountable. It said: "Clearly, both the sellers' covenant to sell to the buyers and the sellers' covenant to pay a commission for services rendered by the broker ran in favor of the broker; together, they evince the sellers' intent to confer a benefit upon the broker. But the buyers' promise to purchase ran in favor of the sellers; that promise was made in consideration of the sellers' promise to sell, not in consideration of brokerage services rendered, and cannot fairly be construed to evince an intent by the buyers to confer a gratuitous benefit upon the broker. Indeed, in the presence of the sellers' express covenant to pay the commission, the absence of a covenant by the buyers evinces a contrary intent." [d]

A Michigan statute provides: "A promise shall be construed to have been made for the benefit of a person whenever the promisor of said promise has undertaken to give or to do or refrain from doing something directly to or for said person." Does this *preclude* a third-party action that another statute would allow, in any situation you can think of?

H. R. MOCH CO., INC. v. RENSSELAER WATER CO.

Court of Appeals of New York, 1928.
247 N.Y. 160, 159 N.E. 896, 62 A.L.R. 1199.

Appeal from Supreme Court, Appellate Division, Third Department.

Action by the H. R. Moch Company, Inc., against the Rensselaer Water Company. From a judgment of the Appellate Division (219 App.Div. 673, 220 N.Y.S. 557), reversing an order of the Special Term, and granting defendant's motion for judgment dismissing the complaint for failure to state facts sufficient to constitute a cause of action, plaintiff appeals. Affirmed.

See, also, 127 Misc. 545, 217 N.Y.S. 426.

CARDOZO, C. J. The defendant, a waterworks company under the laws of this state, made a contract with the city of Rensselaer for

c. Note, The Third Party Beneficiary Concept, 57 Colum.L.Rev. 406, 414–15 (1957).

d. Compare David v. J. Elrod Realtors on Devon, Inc., 75 Ill.App.3d 449, 31 Ill.Dec. 381, 394 N.E.2d 583 (1979). With the Virginia statute compare W.Va.Code § 55–8–12 (1966) ("sole benefit").

the supply of water during a term of years. Water was to be furnished to the city for sewer flushing and street sprinkling; for service to schools and public buildings; and for service at fire hydrants, the latter service at the rate of $42.50 a year for each hydrant. Water was to be furnished to private takers within the city at their homes and factories and other industries at reasonable rates, not exceeding a stated schedule. While this contract was in force, a building caught fire. The flames, spreading to the plaintiff's warehouse near by, destroyed it and its contents. The defendant, according to the complaint, was promptly notified of the fire, "but omitted and neglected after such notice, to supply or furnish sufficient or adequate quantity of water, with adequate pressure to stay, suppress, or extinguish the fire before it reached the warehouse of the plaintiff, although the pressure and supply which the defendant was equipped to supply and furnish, and had agreed by said contract to supply and furnish, was adequate and sufficient to prevent the spread of the fire to and the destruction of the plaintiff's warehouse and its contents." By reason of the failure of the defendant to "fulfill the provisions of the contract between it and the city of Rensselaer," the plaintiff is said to have suffered damage, for which judgment is demanded. A motion, in the nature of a demurrer, to dismiss the complaint, was denied at Special Term. The Appellate Division reversed by a divided court.

Liability in the plaintiff's argument is placed on one or other of three grounds. The complaint, we are told, is to be viewed as stating: (1) A cause of action for breach of contract within Lawrence v. Fox, 20 N.Y. 268; (2) a cause of action for a common-law tort, within MacPherson v. Buick Motor Co., 217 N.Y. 382, 111 N.E. 1050, L.R.A.1916F, 696, Ann.Cas.1916C, 440; or (3) a cause of action for the breach of a statutory duty. These several grounds of liability will be considered in succession.

(1) We think the action is not maintainable as one for breach of contract.

No legal duty rests upon a city to supply its inhabitants with protection against fire. Springfield Fire & Marine Ins. Co. v. Village of Keeseville, 148 N.Y. 46, 42 N.E. 405, 30 L.R.A. 660, 51 Am.St.Rep. 667. That being so, a member of the public may not maintain an action under Lawrence v. Fox against one contracting with the city to furnish water at the hydrants, unless an intention appears that the promisor is to be answerable to individual members of the public as well as to the city for any loss ensuing from the failure to fulfill the promise. No such intention is discernible here. On the contrary, the contract is significantly divided into two branches: One a promise to the city for the benefit of the city in its corporate capacity, in which branch is included the service at the hydrants; and the other a promise to the city for the benefit of private takers, in which branch is included the service at their homes and factories. In a broad sense it is true that every city contract, not improvident or wasteful, is for the benefit of the public. More than this, however, must be shown to give a right of action to a member of the public not formally a party. The benefit, as it is sometimes said, must be one that is not merely incidental and secondary. Cf. Fosmire v. National Surety Co., 229 N.Y. 44, 127 N.E. 472. It must be primary and immediate in such a sense and to such a degree as to bespeak the assumption of a duty to make reparation directly to the individual members of the public if the benefit is lost. The field of obligation would be expanded beyond reasonable limits if less than this were to be demanded as a condition of liability. A promisor undertakes to supply fuel for heating a public building. He is not liable for breach of contract to a visitor who finds the building without fuel, and thus contracts a cold. The list of illustrations can be indefinitely extended. The carrier of the mails under contract with the government is not answerable to the merchant who has lost the benefit of a bargain through negligent delay. The householder is without a remedy against manufacturers of hose and engines though prompt performance of their contracts would have stayed the ravages of fire. "The law does not spread its protection so far." Robins Dry Dock & Repair Co. v. Flint, 275 U.S. 303, 48 S. Ct. 134.

So with the case at hand. By the vast preponderance of authority, a contract between a city and a water company to furnish water at the city hydrants has in view a benefit to the public that is incidental rather than immediate, an assumption of duty to the city and not to its inhabitants. Such is the ruling of the Supreme Court of the United States. German Alliance Ins. Co. v. Homewater Supply Co., 226 U.S. 220, 33 S.Ct. 32, 57 L.Ed. 195, 42 L.R.A.,N.S., 1000. Such has been the ruling in this state . . . though the question is still open in this court. Such with few exceptions has been the ruling in other jurisdictions. Williston, Contracts, sec. 373, and cases there cited; Dillon, Municipal Corporations (5th Ed.) sec. 1340. The diligence of counsel has brought together decisions to that effect from 26 states. [Cases cited.] Only a few states have held otherwise. Page, Contracts, sec. 2401. An intention to assume an obligation of indefinite extension to every member of the public is seen to be the more improbable when we recall the crushing burden that the obligation would impose. Cf. Hone v. Presque Isle Water Co., 104 Me. 217, at p. 232, 71 A. 769, 21 L.R.A.,N.S., 1021. The consequences invited would bear no reasonable proportion to those attached by law to defaults not greatly different. A wrongdoer who by negligence sets fire to a building is liable in damages to the owner where the fire has its origin, but not to other owners who are injured when it spreads. The rule in our state is settled to that effect, whether wisely or unwisely. . . . If the plaintiff is to prevail, one who negligently omits to supply sufficient pressure to extinguish a fire started by another assumes an obligation to pay the ensuing damage, though the whole city is laid low. A promisor will not be deemed to have had in mind the assumption of a risk so overwhelming for any trivial reward.

The cases that have applied the rule of Lawrence v. Fox to contracts made by a city for the benefit of the public are not at war with this conclusion. Through them all there runs as a unifying principle the presence of an intention to compensate the individual members of the public in the event of a default. For example, in Pond v. New Rochelle Water Co., 183 N.Y. 330, 76 N.E. 211, 1 L.R.A.,N.S., 958, 5 Ann.Cas. 504, the contract with the city fixed a schedule of rates to be supplied, not to public buildings, but to private takers at their homes. In Matter of International R. Co. v. Rann, 224 N.Y. 83, 85, 120 N.E. 153, the contract was by street railroads to carry passengers for a stated fare. In Smyth v. City of New York, 203 N.Y. 106, 96 N.E. 409, and Rigney v. New York Cent. & H. R. R. Co., 217 N.Y. 31, 111 N.E. 226, covenants were made by contractors upon public works, not merely to indemnify the city, but to assume its liabilities. These and like cases come within the third group stated in the comprehensive opinion in Seaver v. Ransom, 224 N.Y. 233, 238, 120 N.E. 639, 2 L.R.A. 1187. The municipality was contracting in behalf of its inhabitants by covenants intended to be enforced by any of them severally as occasion should arise.

(2) We think the action is not maintainable as one for a common-law tort. . . .

(3) We think the action is not maintainable as one for the breach of a statutory duty. . . .

The judgment should be affirmed with costs.

NOTES

(1) *Problem.* The Southwestern Bell Telephone Co. relocated a cable in connection with highway reconstruction, and carelessly laid it closer to the surface than was authorized. In consequence it was cut by a contractor's bulldozer. The following term appeared in the highway excavator's contract with the state; does it require him to compensate Southwestern for its loss?

> Contractor shall be responsible for all damage to any utility facility due directly to his operations regardless of location and shall repair and replace as necessary any such damaged facility or make payment to the owner for repair or replacement.

See Southwestern Bell Telephone Co. v. J. A. Tobin Constr., 536 S.W.2d 881 (Mo.App.1976).

See also St. Joseph Light & Power Co. v. Kaw Valley Tunneling, 589 S.W.2d 260 (Mo.1979). Here the court noted that "municipal contracts with water companies have historically received different treatment." Why might that be so?

(2) *Ma Bell's Case.* Is it possible that, if Southwestern Bell is barred from claiming as above, for a reason peculiar to it, the American Telephone and Telegraph Co. may make a contract claim against the excavator? The broken cable was part of an integrated communications system—so the argument might run—that was important to AT&T, as the excavator must have known. Even though Southwestern is an independent corporate entity, it is a subsidiary of AT&T; and it is treated for some purposes as an operating unit of the parent company.

A comparable problem arose in American Electric Power Co., Inc. v. Westinghouse Electric Corp., 418 F.Supp. 435 (S.D.N.Y.1976). The plaintiff, American Electric Power, made a third party beneficiary claim on a generator contract between a subsidiary company and Westinghouse. The court ruled that the claim would survive summary judgment if governed by the law of New York, but not if governed by the law of Pennsylvania. "The law of New York is somewhat more liberal . . . , and does not require that the intent to confer a benefit affirmatively appear within the four corners of the agreement." (Under the law of either state, the court thought, the plaintiff might maintain a claim as a party to the contract, made with Westinghouse by its subsidiary as an agent.) [a]

(3) *Exculpation Claim.* One of the benefits that C may derive from a contract between A and B is exculpation from a loss that A might have

a. In Pennsylvania, the law of third party beneficiaries has been more than ordinarily unstable, owing partly to the view sometimes expressed there that a third party's right depends on a showing of intent to benefit him on the part of *both* the promisee and the promisor. See General State Authority v. Sutter Corp., 403 A.2d 1022 (Pa.Comm.Ct.1979).

For advocacy of the "policy of honoring shared expectations" see Jones, Legal Protection of Third Party Beneficiaries, 46 U.Cinn.L.Rev. 313 (1977).

As the following Georgia case shows dramatically, a third-party claim may depend heavily on a choice-of-law issue.

In Miree v. United States, twenty three federal judges and seven state judges considered the responsibility of DeKalb County, Georgia, for injuries alleged to have been caused by the swarming of birds to the county garbage dump. The county was charged with breach of its contract with the Federal Aviation Administration for the safe maintenance of the DeKalb-Peachtree Airport; and the birds were said to have caused the crash of a jet on takeoff. One issue was whether state or federal law was the proper reference for determining the plaintiffs' rights as third party beneficiaries. On this issue the federal judges favored state law by a margin of 14 to 9. (A unanimous Supreme Court tipped the balance. 433 U.S. 25 (1977).)

On the second appearance of the case in the Fifth Circuit Court of Appeals, that court certified questions to the Georgia Supreme Court; its opinion was sought, *inter alia,* on whether the plaintiffs were intended or incidental beneficiaries of the county's covenants. 565 F.2d 1354 (5th Cir. 1978). The Georgia court answered that they were incidental beneficiaries only (and that the county was immune from certain tort claims made against it). Three justices dissented. As the case did not come to that court in the usual way, the majority said that their conclusions were "not necessarily binding" on the federal courts. 242 Ga. 126, 249 S.E. 2d 573 (1978). However, a panel of the court of appeals adopted the Georgia court's views of Georgia law, when they came to consider the case for the third time. 588 F.2d 453 (5th Cir. 1979). (When they first considered it, none of them had thought both that Georgia law governed the contract claim and that it required dismissal. 526 F.2d 679 (5th Cir. 1976).)

charged to C in the absence of a suitable term barring A's claim. So it was, for example, when A bought an item from B, manufactured by C. The sale contract provided: "Warranties by manufacturers are limited to repair and replacement." In K & C, Inc. v. Westinghouse Electric Corp., 437 Pa. 303, 263 A.2d 390 (1970), A claimed consequential damages from C, alleging a defect in the goods. Rejecting the claim, the court said: "A clearer case of a contract made for the benefit of another would be hard to imagine . . . ." But see Weems v. Nanticoke Homes, Inc., 37 Md.App. 544, 378 A.2d 190 (1977) (comparing the first and second Restatement provisions on third party beneficiary contracts).[b]

VISINTINE & CO. v. NEW YORK, CHICAGO & ST. LOUIS R. CO.

Supreme Court of Ohio, 1959.
169 Ohio St. 505, 160 N.E.2d 311.

The amended petition of the plaintiff, Visintine & Company, to which a demurrer was filed by each of the defendants, alleges two causes of action, one for breach of contract and one for negligence. The demurrers were sustained by the Court of Common Pleas.

The Court of Appeals reversed the judgment of sustention as to the contract cause and affirmed such judgment as to the tort cause.

Plaintiff's amended petition, containing as it does extended quotations from the contracts involved, is too long to set out in full here. The allegations of the petition are very fairly and succinctly summarized in the opinion of the Court of Appeals, as follows [155 N.E.2d 683]:

"Prior to 1950 railroad tracks of each of the defendant companies, The New York, Chicago & St. Louis Railroad Company and The Baltimore & Ohio Railroad Company, crossed United States Route 23 at grade on Wood Street in the City of Fostoria, Ohio. In August, 1949, the City of Fostoria passed an ordinance giving its consent to the grade crossing elimination and agreed to bear certain costs of the improvement. In May of 1950 the Director of Highways for the State of Ohio, by official entry, declared that the separation of grades was reasonably necessary and expedient. Following this, on the 17th day of July, 1950, the Director of Highways entered into a contract with the City of Fostoria and the defendant railroad companies, which contract set up the proportion of costs of the grade crossing elimination to be borne by each of the parties thereto, and also provided for certain work to be performed by the defendant companies. These contracts with the City of Fostoria and the railroads did not cover all the necessary work to be done on the project, the bal-

b. In this case "C" was a subcontractor on a job B had done for A. Note that if C and B had had a closer business connection the court might have ruled for C. These parties had no intercorporate relationship. See also Ison v. Daniel Crisp Corp., 146 W.Va. 786, 122 S.E.2d 553 (1961).

ance of which was to be performed under a separate contract and which was accordingly entered into at a later date, between the plaintiff-appellant Visintine Company, and the State of Ohio. Each of the separate contracts provided that the work should be performed in accordance with the plans and specifications submitted for the project and in the sequence designated. The nature of the work was such that none of the parties could perform its part in a single operation, but numerous ones were required and the time when each was to be performed was specified and spelled out in the plans and specifications agreed upon. These contracts were subsequently carried out and the project completed. Plaintiff now claims damages against the railroad companies as the result of said project and claims in the amended petition that the defendant railroad companies failed to perform their work as required by their contract with the State of Ohio."

The cause is before this court upon the allowance of motions to certify the record filed on behalf of both defendants and plaintiff.

PER CURIAM. It is conceded that there was no actual contract between the plaintiff and either of the defendants. The theory of plaintiff upon which it seeks to recover is that it was a third party beneficiary to the contracts of July 17, 1950, between the state of Ohio and each of the defendants.

[Here the court referred to the first Restatement, § 133 (p. 1029 supra).]

Although this Restatement definition distinguishes between a creditor beneficiary and a donee beneficiary, such distinction has little materiality so far as liability to the beneficiary is concerned because it is generally held that either type of beneficiary may recover. 11 Ohio Jurisprudence (2d), 429, 431. Familiar examples of recovery by third party beneficiaries, without any attempt to distinguish between creditor or donee, are by the beneficiary of a life insurance policy, by a person injured by the holder of a liability insurance policy, and by a materialman from a surety indemnifying an owner of a construction project against the defaults of a contractor.

The most frequent examples of the creditor-beneficiary situation outlined in the texts are those where one person contracts to pay the debts of another. But such need not always be the case. It is pointed out, as follows, in 4 Corbin on Contracts, 97, Section 787:

"The promises on which a creditor beneficiary has been given judgment are nearly all cases where the consideration was executed and the promisor is a money debtor. The term 'creditor,' however, may properly be used broadly to include any obligee to whom the promisee owes a duty. There seems to be no good reason for restricting the rule to cases where the third party is a creditor in the narrow sense of one to whom the promisee owes a liquidated debt. Thus, if the promise is to perform labor or deliver goods instead of to pay money, or is to pay claims for unliquidated damages, the obligee should be able to maintain suit against a promisor who has assumed the duty."

The state of Ohio owed certain duties to plaintiff under the contract entered into between them. Among those duties was that of providing plaintiff with a site on which it could perform its work without hindrance or delay and of doing those things which it promised to do at such time and in such manner as would not hinder or delay the plaintiff. Even though the state, because of governmental immunity, can not be sued for its failure to perform those duties, the duties nevertheless existed. The performance of those duties was undertaken by the defendants under their contracts with the state of Ohio. Since the contracts between defendants and the state, in addition to the performance of certain obligations assumed by the defendants for the benefit of the state, provided, also, for the performance of certain obligations owed by the state to the plaintiff, it would seem that plaintiff falls squarely within the definition of "creditor beneficiary."

Plaintiff's petition alleges that the contracts between defendants and the state of Ohio set out the standard specifications of the state of Ohio which specifically stated that those contracts and that between the state and plaintiff were entered into pursuant to the accomplishment of a single project, and that it was the duty of all contractors to co-operate and to co-ordinate their work. The petition alleges also and sets out in detail a schedule of construction contained in all contracts, whereby mutual and reciprocal obligations were placed on the defendants and plaintiff to perform their respective portions of the work on time and in sequence.

It is urged by the defendants that the contracts between them and the state of Ohio do not clearly show an intent to benefit the plaintiff, and that such an intent cannot be implied. And several cases from outside Ohio to that effect are cited to us by the defendants. However, there appears to be no unanimity of opinion on this subject. In 4 Corbin on Contracts, 20, Section 776, the following is said about the intention to benefit the third party:

"It is clear that if the 'primary' and 'paramount' purpose seems to be to benefit the third person, as in the case of all sole and donee beneficiaries, he should have an enforceable right as the court says. But rights have not been limited so narrowly as this. In the case of most creditor beneficiaries, it is the purpose and intent of the promisee to procure the discharge of his obligation. The attainment of this end involves benefit both to himself and to his creditor. This 'benefit' he intends to bring about as an entirety, having no idea in his own mind as to its division between the persons receiving it or as to 'primary' or 'paramount' purpose. Neither should the court make such a division. It should content itself with bringing about the entire result that the promised performance would attain. That result was the 'paramount' object of desire and that result was the 'primarily' intended result, including not only the ultimate end in view but also the means used to bring it about. The great majority of the courts attain this desired result in full by giving a remedy to the creditor against the promisor. The question is not 'whose interest and benefit are primarily subserved,' but what was the performance contracted for and what is the best way to bring it about."

In the light of that statement, we concur in the analysis by the Court of Appeals, where, in the opinion by Judge Miller, it is said: ". . . We are of the opinion that in considering the railroad contracts and the plans and specifications and sequence of work specifications it is apparent that it was intended to benefit the contractor, as they all provided for cooperation in order that the job might be completed as scheduled. . . . Throughout all contracts it was made plain that the work of Visintine was dependent upon the performance by the railroads of their contractual obligations and vice versa. By each performing their obligations in the proper sequence a benefit was incurred upon the other by permitting them to complete their work in accordance with the terms of their various contracts."

Taken altogether, we believe the allegations of the petition are sufficient, as against demurrer, to qualify plaintiff as a beneficiary under the contracts between the defendants and the state of Ohio, particularly in view of the fact that the state is immune from suit for any alleged violations of the duties it assumed under its contract with plaintiff.

We agree with the Court of Appeals in its affirmance of the sustaining of the demurrer to the tort cause of action. Tort is based on a duty owed by one party to another. The duty owed here by the defendants was to the state of Ohio, not to the plaintiff. The duty arising out of contract upon which plaintiff may rely in its first cause of action was that owed to it by the state. If defendants are liable to plaintiff it is due to a breach of the contracts they made with the state of Ohio and not to the violation of any duty owed directly to the plaintiff upon which a tort action may be based. Wymer-Harris Construction Co. v. Glass, 122 Ohio St. 398, 171 N.E. 857, 69 A.L.R. 517.

Judgment affirmed.

TAFT, Justice (dissenting). See Brotherton v. Merritt-Chapman & Scott Corp., 2 Cir., 1954, 213 F.2d 477; . . . Restatement of the Law of Contracts illustration under Section 147,[a] 12 American Jurisprudence, 834, Section 281.

a. This illustration is as follows: "A, an owner of land enters into a contract with B, a contractor, by which B contracts to erect a building containing certain vats. C contracts with B to build the vats according to the specifications in the contract. The vats are installed in the building,

NOTES

(1) *Cautionary Considerations.* At what point would it be too late for the state, city, and railroads to modify their contract, so as to reduce the obligations of the railroads to the Visintine Company? Such a modification would occur, for example, if the state undertook to do some of the work previously assigned to the railroads, and the costs were reapportioned accordingly. Another kind of "modification" would occur if disputes arose between the state and the railroads in the course of performance, and they agreed to a settlement on which the work might go forward in the spirit of letting bygones be bygones. If the rights of the Visintine Company were held to be unaffected by subsequent agreements such as these, the state and city might well find themselves locked into unsatisfactory contracts with the railroads—contracts that would be variable to fit changing circumstances except for the necessity of Visintine's consent. The termination of a beneficiary's right by agreement between the parties who created it in the first place is not always permitted; see Restatement Second, § 311.

One of the reasons given for caution in recognizing third party beneficiary claims on government contracts on behalf of members of the public is that it may upset "arrangements for governmental control over the litigation and settlement of claims." Restatement Second, § 313, Comment a. To some extent the same consideration makes it doubtful that Visintine should be recognized as a third party beneficiary. The decision does not have impressive support in many other courts, and has been distinguished on comparable facts. See C. H. Leavell & Co. v. Glantz Contracting Corp., 322 F.Supp. 779 (E.D.La.1971).

(2) *Question.* Might the contract between the railroads and the state have been written in such a way as to make it certain that Visintine was *not* a third party beneficiary? What language would you suggest? See Richmond Shopping Center v. Wiley N. Jackson Co., —— Va. ——, 255 S.E.2d 518 (1979).

PROMOTING A COMMON CAUSE

One of the undoubted merits of third party beneficiary theory is that it permits a group of persons to give legal backing to a common interest that they have. One such arrangement was created by a provision of the leases in a shopping center requiring each tenant to pay dues to a governing association formed to promote the center and foster ethical business practices. The association was granted specific performance of this term, as a third party beneficiary, against some disgruntled tenants. (They had been outvoted by other members.) [a]

but, owing to defective construction, leak and cause harm to A. C is under no duty to A who is only an incidental beneficiary of the contract between B and C, since C's performance is not given or received in discharge of B's duty to A."

Is there a substantial difference between this example and the situation in the main case? See also 4 Corbin, pp. 102–105.

a. Moorestown Management, Inc. v. Moorestown Bookshop, Inc., 104 N.J. Super. 250, 249 A.2d 623 (1969).

A more usual illustration is a composition among creditors. Frequently the creditors of a debtor who is unable to pay his debts as they mature are willing to scale down their claims, or extend the time for paying them, or both. A voluntary agreement among them to such an effect is called a "composition." It is enforceable by the debtor (absent any vitiating circumstance such as fraud or nonperformance on his part), and an explanation often given is that he is a third party beneficiary of the mutual promises of his creditors. On this theory, he need not have joined in the agreement. (If he is a party to the agreement, what consideration does he give for the creditors' promises of forbearance? See Massey v. Del-Valley Corp., 46 N.J.Super. 400, 134 A.2d 802 (1957).)

QUESTION

Refer to the Note, "An Industry Agreement" at p. 477 above. The writer cited there asks, "What sanctions exist, other than adverse publicity and the consequences of that, if the *Statement* is not adhered to?" Evidently this is a rhetorical question, with reference to English law. Is there a self-evident answer under American law?

BLAIR v. ANDERSON

Supreme Court of Delaware, 1974.
325 A.2d 94.

DUFFY, Justice.

This appeal submits for decision a sovereign immunity defense by the State of Delaware to a claim arising out of incarceration in a Delaware Correctional institution.

I

Plaintiff, formerly a Federal prisoner, alleges that while incarcerated in the New Castle County Correctional Institution he was attacked by a fellow prisoner and that defendants, including the State, were negligent in permitting such assault. The Superior Court granted the State's motion to dismiss the action on the ground that it is barred by the doctrine of sovereign immunity whether the claim be regarded as based on contract or in tort. 314 A.2d 919 (1973). Our analysis of the legal issues in the case persuades us that the Court's conclusion was correct as to tort but not as to the contract claim.

II

By statute, 11 Del.C. § 6505(a)(13), the Department of Correction is authorized:

"To agree with the proper authorities of the United States for payment to the General Fund of the State of such sums as shall be fixed by the Department for the maintenance and support of offenders committed to the Department by authority of the United States."

Under that statute the Department, on December 8, 1968, entered into a contract with the United States Department of Justice (Bureau of Prisons); [1] the service to be performed by the State is described therein as "[s]afekeeping, care and subsistence of persons held under authority of any United States statute . . ." and among the rules and regulations governing custody and treatment of such persons is this:

"1. Responsibility for Prisoners' Custody. It is the responsibility of the sheriff, jailer, or other official responsible for the administration of the institution to keep the prisoners in safe custody and to maintain proper discipline and control."

The State argues that it may not be sued by plaintiff because the doctrine of sovereign immunity permits such suit only after waiver by a legislative act and the General Assembly has not passed such an act.

III

The Delaware Constitution provides that "[s]uits may be brought against the State, according to such regulations as shall be made by law", Art. 1, § 9, Del.C.Ann., and the judicial history of the provision makes it plain that the defense of sovereign immunity may be "waived by legislative act and only by legislative act". George & Lynch, Inc. v. State, Del.Supr., 197 A.2d 734 (1964); Shellhorn & Hill, Inc. v. State, Del.Supr., 187 A.2d 71 (1962). It is clear, however, that waiver need not be made in express statutory language. Specifically, when the General Assembly authorizes a contract to be made it implicitly and necessarily waives immunity to suit for breach by the State of that contract. George & Lynch, Inc. v. State, supra. While the justice of that proposition stands on its own merit, we do note also that there is a tendency (recognized by the Court below) to narrow the doctrine of sovereign immunity. Cf. Wilmington Housing Authority v. Williamson, Del.Supr., 228 A.2d 782 (1967); Holden v. Bundek, Del.Super., 317 A.2d 29 (1972).

IV

First, as to plaintiff's claim in tort, a suit by a Federal prisoner for injury caused by a fellow prisoner is apparently within the scope of the Federal Tort Claims Act, 28 U.S.C.A. §§ 1346(b), 2671–2680; United States v. Muniz, 374 U.S. 150, 83 S.Ct. 1850, 10 L.Ed.2d 805 (1963). But we find no basis, in statutory waiver or otherwise, for departing from the well established Delaware law as to immunity. Therefore, so much of the decision below as accords that defense to the State against a tort claim by plaintiff will be affirmed. Shellhorn & Hill, Inc. v. State, supra.

1. The Bureau of Prisons is required to provide, *inter alia*, for the "[s]afekeeping, care, and subsistence" of a prisoner and for his "protection". 18 U.S.C.A. § 4042.

V

Considering now plaintiff's second theory, it is clear that to the extent of the contract with the United States the State has waived sovereign immunity in a suit for its own breach of that contract. Beyond doubt that is true as to any claim by the United States (which is the other contracting party), but we are concerned here, not with a suit by the Federal Government, but by a claimant who was committed to the State facility by authority of the United States (pursuant to the contract).

Upon examining the agreement the Superior Court concluded that plaintiff was a donee or incidental beneficiary thereof without standing to sue. In our view, he is a creditor beneficiary.

It is established Delaware law that a third party beneficiary of a contract may sue on it. Astle v. Wenke, Del.Supr., 297 A.2d 45 (1972).[2] Generally, the rights of third-party beneficiaries are those specified in the contract; but if performance of the promise will satisfy a legal obligation which a promisee owes a beneficiary, the latter is a creditor beneficiary with standing to sue. Restatement of Contracts § 133(1)(b). Compare Astle v. Wenke, supra.

Here, the United States obviously owed a duty of care and subsistence to a person it caused to be committed and it owed him a statutory duty of "safekeeping" and "protection". 18 U.S.C.A. § 4042. By the contract Delaware agreed to perform that duty. And the terms of the agreement show that the duty amounts to more than the "room and board" minimum which the State argued; the duty included "safekeeping" and care as well.

While there may be semantic concerns about calling a prisoner a "creditor" or "beneficiary" (or both) of a Federal-State incarceration contract, the point is that plaintiff was the very subject of the agreement between governments. He was the person (for present purposes) whom the State contracted to safekeep, to care for and to provide with subsistence. Under these circumstances he has not only a direct interest in the contract but a right to enforce it as against the State if it fails to provide the requisite minimums.

In sum, we hold that the State, by entering into the contract with the United States, waived any defense available to it based upon the principle of sovereign immunity and that plaintiff is in law a creditor beneficiary of the agreement. It should be emphasized that we make no judgment as to any alleged breach of contract by the State nor as to any measure of damages to be applied. We decide

2. See also Royal Indemnity Co. v. Alexander Industries, Inc., Del.Supr., 211 A.2d 919 (1965); Wilmington Housing Authority v. Fidelity & Deposit Co., Del.Supr., 4 Terry 381, 47 A.2d 524 (1946); Bryant, Griffith & Brunson v. General Newspapers, Del. Super., 6 W.W.Harr. 468, 178 A. 645 (1935).

only that the State may not avail itself to a defense of sovereign immunity to defeat plaintiff's contract claim.

. . .

In conclusion we note that under the present state of the law a basic unfairness may result which the judiciary cannot correct. We hold here that plaintiff may sue the State and such a right may be denied by virtue of the sovereign immunity doctrine to State prisoners held in the same institution. But a different result would mean that plaintiff would be without a remedy which is available under the Federal Tort Claims Act, 28 U.S.C.A. § 1346(b), etc., to other prisoners in a Federal prison. We can only suggest that the General Assembly and responsible officers in the Executive Branch consider the problem.

Reversed as to the contract claim.[a]

NOTES

(1) *The Privacy Case.* A state's department of social services obtained confidential information about a family receiving welfare benefits, and allowed dissemination of it. The state received federal funds for the program under a statute requiring it to take precautions against such disclosure. So it was alleged in a contract action brought by members of the family against the state. The trial court refused to dismiss, relying on the foregoing decision. On appeal, *held:* Reversed. Pajewski v. Perry, 363 A.2d 429 (Del.Super.1976). What is the distinction?

(2) *Public Law* v. *Contract Law.* For deciding whether to allow a third-party action on a government contract, a method has been suggested "analogous to that followed by courts in deciding whether to imply a private right of action from a statute." Note, 88 Harv.L.Rev. 646, 653 (1975). However, the method is said to yield an indeterminate result in the case noted, Martinez v. Socoma Companies, Inc., 11 Cal.3d 394, 113 Cal.Rptr. 585, 521 P.2d 841 (1974). That was a class action on behalf of residents of East Los Angeles who were eligible for training and employment under contracts for assistance to the area (designated a "special impact area" pursuant to the Economic Opportunity Act, as amended). The defendant companies had contracted with the United States Department of Labor to create and operate a factory there, and they failed (it was alleged) to provide jobs as promised. The California Supreme Court approved, 4–3, the dismissal of the complaint. It relied on the first Restatement, § 145.

Is it desirable, in such a case, to consult the "contractual purpose" of the governmental agency that made the contract? So the Reporter for the Restatement Second suggested, in discussing section 313, which succeeds 145. See 44 ALI Proc. 332–33 (1967) (Professor Braucher). But see the Note cited above. He also observed that the leading case, H. R. Moch Co. v. Rensselaer Water Co. (p. 1035 supra) was decided simply by reference to common-law principle. Which of the following cases most nearly resembles *Moch?*—Blair v. Anderson; the privacy case; the *Martinez* case?

a. See also Owens v. Haas, 601 F.2d 1242 (2d Cir. 1979).

(3) *This Unhappy Breed, Set in the Silver Sea.* The Washington [State] Toll Bridge Authority provides ferry service as the only link to some island communities, of whose economies the tourist trade is a main prop. Over a Labor Day weekend the islands were cut off by a seamen's strike, imposing much inconvenience and financial loss. The strike was in violation of a collective bargaining agreement between the seamen's union and the Bridge Authority. May the island residents maintain an action against the union on alleging these facts? If so, what situations of comparable liability occur to you? See Burke & Thomas, Inc. v. International Organization of Masters, 92 Wash.2d 762, 600 P.2d 1282 (1979). (Should the court be guided in its ruling by concern for peaceable labor relations in public service? If so, what ruling is indicated?)

INSURANCE STATUTES PROVIDING THIRD PARTY CLAIMS

In most states, until recently, it has been a choice for each motorist whether or not to insure himself against liability for road injuries. If he chooses to insure, however, he must usually insure not only against his own liabilities, but also against those of "permittees"—drivers to whom he entrusts his car. This requirement results partly from statutes, and partly from the manner in which insurers choose to designate the persons insured in their standard contracts. The so-called *omnibus clause* has been the chief instrument for extending protection to permittees. The clause was initially developed to serve the self-interest of the premium payer, and his altruistic interest in friends and relations. But the object of legislation on the subject is doubtless to increase the prospect that *victims* of road injuries —not permittees—will have access to insurance benefits.[a] The object of such a statute, it has been said, is to protect "that ever changing and tragically large group of persons who while lawfully using the highways themselves suffer grave injury through the negligent use of the highways by others." Atlantic National Ins. Co. v. Armstrong, 65 Cal.2d 100, 416 P.2d 801 (1966). Even in the absence of such a statute it has been argued that an insurer should not offer automobile insurance lacking an omnibus clause; but see the note case at p. 473 supra.

Other forms of legislation designed for the same broad purpose are directed to situations in which a liability insurer is entitled to rescind the contract, or otherwise resist a claim within its coverage, because of some act or neglect of the insured person. The insurer may find that it is nevertheless obliged to respond to a victim's claim against the insured. See Allstate Ins. Co. v. Dorr, 411 F.2d 198 (9th Cir. 1969), where a constitutional objection to such a statute was overcome. Automobile policies recite, in a "compliance" paragraph, that they are to be applied in accordance with such a law. And they

a. See Keeton, Insurance Law (Basic Text) § 4.7(a) (1971).

further provide: "The insured agrees to reimburse the insurer for any payment it is required to make by such law, if it would not have had to pay except for the agreement in this paragraph." The net effect is that compensation for the third party, having been provided by the "promisor" company, may be recouped from the "promisee" insured.[b]

In a number of states it is now enacted that motorists must insure themselves, and various groups such as their passengers, against certain losses caused by motoring generally, including those caused by the torts of other motorists. The shift is from a system of compensation based on fault to a "no fault" system—although there are many forms of compromise.

Incontestability. Life insurance contracts are another class of contracts in which third party benefits are commonly mandated by statute. When the policy has been in force for a certain period, usually two years, it is no longer open to the insurer to contend that it is unenforceable by reason of fraud in procuring it or the like. Furthermore, the insurer may lose the advantage of certain qualifications on its promise that may have been written into the policy. All ordinary life policies express this intention in the form of an "incontestability clause;" but the policy claimant may assert a right broader than the one stated if it is supported by an applicable statute. The policy claimant is usually a third party beneficiary, of course, but is sometimes the person who procured the policy. For debatable decisions on this topic, see Simpson v. Phoenix Mut. Life Ins. Co., 24 N.Y.2d 262, 247 N.E.2d 655 (1969), and First Pennsylvania Bank & Trust Co. v. United States Life Ins. Co., 421 F.2d 959 (3d Cir. 1969).

The Barrera Case. In California, an analogue to the incontestability clause has been announced by the supreme court for application against automobile liability insurers. They have a duty to investigate the insured person's insurability with reasonable promptness after the issuance of the policy, not waiting until the occasion of an accident. Under this doctrine, the policy may be enforced even though the insured deceitfully misrepresented his driving record in applying for insurance. The insurer's duty of investigation inures, of course, "directly to the benefit of third persons injured by the insured." And the court hinted that the insured might be held ultimately accountable for the claim. Barrera v. State Farm Mutual Automobile Ins. Co., 71 Cal.2d 659, 456 P.2d 674 (1969).

NOTE

Problems. Victims of road injuries have sought compensation through an interesting variety of contracts other than insurance policies. What

b. As to the effectiveness of such a provision, however, see the California case quoted above.

merit do you see in the following *contract* claims?—(a) Against an insurance broker, who had agreed to effect liability insurance for a customer; the customer negligently injured the claimant, and proved to be uninsured. See Gothberg v. Nemerovski, 58 Ill.App.2d 372, 208 N.E.2d 12 (1965). (b) Against a road repair firm, which had undertaken in its contract with the state to place appropriate warning signs at the site; the claimant was injured when he failed to notice an unmarked detour. See Davis v. Nelson-Deppe, Inc., 91 Idaho 463, 424 P.2d 733 (1967). (c) Against a driver for injury he caused to the claimant when he violated a traffic law; the supposed contract arose at an interview he had with a state official about possible withdrawal of his license to drive; in the course of it he agreed to abide by the traffic laws. See Hayrynen v. White Pine Copper Company, 9 Mich.App. 452, 157 N.W.2d 502 (1968).

Note that the latter two situations suggest an alternate claim for negligence. What reasons for pressing a contract claim can you envisage?

SUPPLIERS FOR CONTRACTORS

The ordinary construction contract, it is said, does not exhibit the intention to benefit third parties on which they can found actions against the promisor. Yet for sizable projects a number of contracts are required, the documents regularly refer to third-party claims, and "performance ultimately, if indirectly, runs to each party of the several contracts. Hence, interpretational difficulties prevalent in third-party beneficiary contracts are compounded as a result of the peculiar problems presented by construction contracts." [c] Whatever the "ordinary" case may be, a long list of interests connected with construction work could be compiled, conflicts among which have been mediated by third-party beneficiary law. The effects are sometimes surprising, as witness a notable decision refusing to grant preference to a federal tax claim, upon the insolvency of a contractor-taxpayer, as against claims for labor and material supplied to him.[d]

c. And the related problems of architects' contracts. See Valley Landscape Co., Inc. v. Rolland, 218 Va. 257, 237 S.E.2d 120 (1977). Careful, professional work by an architect in the performance of his contract for the design and supervision of an improvement will enure, it is conceded, to the benefit of the contractor employed for the job. Yet it is generally held that such a contractor is an incidental beneficiary, only, of the architect's undertaking. "The reason is obvious when the adverse interests of the parties are considered. The owner employs an architect, to a degree, to protect himself from the contractor." Id.

d. Avco Delta Corp. Canada Ltd. v. United States, 484 F.2d 692 (7th Cir. 1973), cert. denied, 415 U.S. 931 (1974).

The result was that the retainage was distributed pro rata among the claimants. (As an alternative ground the court developed an equitable-lien theory in their favor.) The United States was, in part, the loser. Its lien as provided for in the Internal Revenue Code (26 U.S.C.A. § 6321 et seq.) was bested, in effect, by a commonplace provision about lien-waivers in a construction contract.

The case was cited in Town & Country Bank v. James M. Canfield, Etc., 55 Ill.App.3d 91, 12 Ill.Dec. 826, 370 N.E.2d 630 (1977), as representing one of two opposing lines of authority "as to the nature and function of lien provisions in construction contracts and/or performance bonds."

A critical term in such contests is often the undertaking by a contractor (or subcontractor) to satisfy suppliers' claims. The undertaking is regularly reinforced in one of two main ways, or both:

(1) The other party withholds an agreed fraction of payments scheduled under the contract—the so-called retent, or retainage—for securing this (and other) obligations. Full disbursement of the retent is made to await the production of certificates of satisfaction given by suppliers to the contractor. These papers commonly take the form of lien-waivers, the title having reference to mechanics' lien statutes.[e]

(2) The contractor is required to procure the bond of a licensed surety ("bonding company") to assure the payment of debts he incurs on the job. This may be a separate "payment bond"; or it may be conditioned simply on his performance due under the contract; or it may speak to payment in addition to performance.

Are these arrangements intended for the benefit of claimants (suppliers of labor and materials, subcontractors, and perhaps holders of other job-related claims)? Or are they intended for the benefit of the promisee only? In third party beneficiary parlance, the promisee is the recipient of the undertaking to pay—perhaps an owner, perhaps a contractor himself (with respect to a subcontract). The promisor, with reference to the first arrangement described above, is the contractor (subcontractor) who undertakes to pay; and with reference to the second arrangement the bonding company is the promisor.

Unpaid suppliers have encountered some difficulty establishing their status as third party beneficiaries. A natural purpose to ascribe to the undertaking is to protect the promisee's individual interest. In truth, he is often fearful that an unpaid supplier will establish a mechanic's lien on the improvement, or that (if he is a contractor) he will be charged with lower-tier claims under his own contract. In answering unpaid suppliers, the promisor may plausibly argue that the promisee's sole object in extracting the undertaking was his own protection.

Often, however, the argument has been rebutted with success on one ground or another. The variety of the rebuttals is striking. In the case mentioned in the first paragraph above it was a subtle one. The contractor's undertaking was to pay not only claims for services and supplies but also tax claims such as the United States held. This fact showed that the undertaking was at least substantially for the benefit of claimants at large, for the tax claim could not have been

e. See D. Epstein & J. Landers, Debtors and Creditors, Cases & Materials 313–23 (1978).

asserted against the promisee or his property. (The promisee was a Canadian pipeline company. Is it fanciful to suppose that it negotiated a contract having the Internal Revenue Service as an "intended beneficiary"?) Hence unpaid subcontractors had claims, the court ruled, enforceable against the construction earnings that the pipeline company withheld for breach of the contractor's undertaking to pay. Otherwise the tax claim would have preempted theirs, by statute; the court's ruling required the United States to share the fund with them pro rata. On comparable reasoning, bonds on public-work contracts have been held to create third-party beneficiary claims for laborers and materialmen: since they are not permitted to establish mechanics' liens on municipal property, a payment bond must be designed for their protection rather than the owner's.

Some courts have taken a more straightforward tack: it is an *intention* that must be determined, and not the promisee's *motivation*. (As Corbin repeatedly insisted, it is not necessary for the claimant to demonstrate that the promisee had an altruistic or philanthropic purpose in obtaining the promise sued upon.) And the intention requisite to constitute rights in a third party is sometimes said to be apparent on "the face of the contract."

Finally, some judges are willing to suppose that a person hiring a builder is moved by benevolence in requiring him to make downstream payments. (Does any reason to doubt that occur to you? Is the supposition more plausible for public-work contracts than for others?)

The Thrust-Bed Case: A Hypothetical. Airline Company has paid $350,000 to Engineering Company for an instrument for gauging the thrust of a jet engine (called a thrust bed). Another $40,000 of the contract price remains unpaid. A subcontractor, Tool Company, did much of the work on the thrust bed, for a contract price of $100,000. Of that amount, $20,000 remains to be paid. Although Tool Company did its work well, the balance will not be paid by Engineering Company, for it is in receivership. Moreover, that company's failure to meet contract specifications (the thrust bed will not measure thrust as great as 100,000 pounds) has reduced the value of the product to the airline by a quarter of the contract price.

The prime contract contains this provision (referring to Engineering Company as "contractor"):

> Before making any progress or final payment, the airline may require the contractor to satisfy its architect in charge that all claims against contractor for things employed, hired or supplied upon and for the thrust bed (labor, services, plant, equipment, materials or other) have been paid or satisfied, or, if any such claims are found to exist, contractor

shall pay the same forthwith. [Do you see any signs in this term of inattentive drafting?]

Beside the part of the contract price it has withheld, Airline Company has protection in the form of a performance bond. The issuer, an insurance company, is committed to paying as much as $200,000 on account of defaults by Engineering Company in its performance of the thrust-bed contract. The only obligee designated in this bond is Airline Company.

For Tool Company the problem is to fix liability for $20,000 upon a solvent party. What is to prevent it from recovering on the bond? If that is not a good prospect, what is to prevent it from recovering from the airline? If it brings suit against the airline, do you think it possible that the defendant can obtain help in defending the suit from the insurance company?

On facts much like those above, a subcontractor *did* sue an airline, and lost. Votaw Precision Tool Co., Inc. v. Air Canada, 60 Cal. App.3d 54, 131 Cal.Rptr. 335 (1976).[f]

NOTES

(1) *Words* v. *Intent.* In Alabama, it seems, when suppliers of labor and materials on a construction project make claims on a financial instrument as third party beneficiaries, the "crucial inquiry" is the intent of the parties to the instrument. Given a bond conditioned on the payment of suppliers, the court has assumed that the payee (owner) does not require it for self-interest alone: "He may require it simply as a just protection to those whose labor and materials enter into his building." Fidelity & Deposit Co. v. Rainer, 220 Ala. 262, 125 So. 55 (1929). But this speculation has been curbed in later cases. One of them concludes that "words of payment in the document sought to be enforced by a third party are essential to his action." Ross v. Imperial Constr. Co., Inc., 572 F.2d 518 (5th Cir. 1978). In that case the document sought to be enforced was a guarantee of "timely and faithful completion of the construction free from any and all liens." For want of proper words in the document, unpaid suppliers failed in their claims against the guarantor. If these cases represent state law accurately, is the courts' talk of intention anything more than decoration of their opinions?

(2) *The Case of the Trustful Attorney.* Visor Builders, Inc. did some work as subcontractor on a public-school addition. Not being paid, it brought an action against everyone in sight: the school district, the prime contractor (Tranter) and Tranter's bonding company. As against the latter, the action failed because it was brought more than a year from the day "on which the last of the labor was performed and material was supplied for the payment of which such action is brought by the claimant." (The limitation appeared in the bond, and also in the state Public Works Contrac-

f. A letter from counsel indicates that the trial court suggested an action on the bond. The insurer was not timely notified of the claim. That may explain why no such action was brought, and why the insurer took no part in the defense of Air Canada.

tor's Bond Law.) The year began in April, 1975. In the following summer, through an exchange of letters between attorneys for Visor Builders and the school district, Visor was assured that the amount of its claim was being withheld from Tranter. This would have been required of some owners—though not school districts—if the state Mechanics' Lien Law were invoked. Visor's attorney had threatened to invoke it. Later, but well within the year allowed, he presented a claim to the bonding company. The answer was, in part: "I am a claim representative of the Aetna Casualty Company and have discussed . . . your letter . . . with our principal Devon E. Tranter. [He] explained this situation in detail to me. We . . . have no reason as his bond carrier to believe that Mr. Tranter and his company are responsible people ["are not" was intended]." The amount withheld from Tranter by the school district was released to him when his attorney pointed out that the Mechanics' Lien Law did not apply.

On these facts, chiefly, Visor based several claims against the school district: it was unjustly enriched; it caused Visor to forbear suing on the bond, and so became bound to pay by a promissory estoppel; and Visor was a third party beneficiary of the prime contract. *Held:* Dismissed. Visor Builders, Inc. v. Devon E. Tranter, Inc., 470 F.Supp. 911 (M.D.Pa.1978).[g] The prime contract provided: "Neither the owner or the architect shall have any obligation to pay or to see to the payment of any monies to any subcontractor except as may be otherwise required by law." Moreover, the court said, Visor's remedy under the bond law would "normally" be exclusive.

(3) *Upstream Liability.* Consider a reversal of the thrust-bed case as follows: performance by the prime contractor (Engineering Company) meets the contract specifications, but that of the subcontractor (Tool Company) is defective. May the airline, as third party beneficiary of the subcontract, claim damages from Tool Company? Or is it confined to a remedy against the prime contractor? A supplier of materials to a contractor does not as a rule incur liability to the owner for defects in them—not even when he undertakes to install them. Vogel v. Reed Supply Co., 277 N.C. 119, 177 S.E.2d 273 (1970). But exceptional features of the subcontract may take the case out of the rule. What features would you look for? See Oliver B. Cannon & Son, Inc. v. Dorr-Oliver, Inc., 336 A.2d 211 (Del. 1975), and the opinion below at 312 A.2d 322 (Del.Super.1973).[h]

RELIANCE AND BENEFICIARY CLAIMS

Reliance on a promise may serve to validate a claim by a person other than the promisee, according to some authority. On an extensive view of estoppel the reliance may count in situations of several types, and the distinctions among them need to be carefully observed.

g. The court said little about Tranter. Early in 1976 Visor knew that the school district was no longer withholding funds, and that Tranter was in severe financial difficulty. The court said: "Plaintiff has not lost any remedies against Tranter (whatever practical value they may have)." The court noted that Visor had obtained new counsel to succeed the one who conducted its first collection efforts.

h. For further proceedings see Oliver B. Cannon & Son, Inc. v. Dorr-Oliver, Inc., 394 A.2d 1160 (Del.Super.1978).

First, there is reliance by the promisee on a gratuitous promise, on which a third party seeks to found a claim. Second, there is the bargained-for promise on which a third party seeks to found a claim by reason of *his* reliance on it. And there may be still other situations in which a third-party claim rests on reliance.

An apparent illustration of the second type is the claim of the hospital district in Dr. Suther's case, Note 3, p. 1033 supra. According to the opinion there the non-Fund claimants made no contention that the agreement was meant to confer a gift on them, or to satisfy a duty owed to them by the Fund. Rather, they contended that once they provided the clinic they became entitled to enforce Suther's promise to practice in Booker.

In the first Restatement of Contracts the section on "promissory estoppel"—section 90—specified "action or forbearance . . . on the part of the promisee" as a requisite. The Restatement Second adds, "or a third person." This variation rejects a position taken by Professor Boyer: "It asks too much of a promisor to require that he consider whether or not his promise will induce action by a *third party*." Boyer, Promissory Estoppel: Requirements and Limitations of the Doctrine, 98 U.Pa.L.Rev. 459, 465 (1950). What sort of claim does this statement seem to address?

NOTES

(1) *The Case of Charity Chilled.* In Overlock v. Central Vermont Public Service Corp., 126 Vt. 549, 237 A.2d 356 (1967), the plaintiff was a workman injured on the job, and the defendant was his employer. Friends of the plaintiff had decided, he alleged, to "take up a collection" for his benefit. But the defendant, "in order to induce these persons not to take up the collection, promised them that there was no need . . . because the Defendant would take care of the Plaintiff for the rest of the Plaintiff's life." The suit was based on the defendant's failure to keep this promise. The court ruled that no cause of action was alleged, speaking of the abandonment of the friends' campaign as an "illusory" reliance.[a] Does the addition to section 90 speak to this case? Or is the situation different from all those sketched above?[b]

(2) *Problem.* A dealer in equipment learns that a construction job will require a certain item and solicits bids from firms that manufacture it. Taking the best bid, he adds a markup and offers to supply the item to contractors bidding for the job. The contractor who is selected has relied on the dealer's price in making up his bid. Now the manufacturer demands a higher price for the equipment and the dealer withdraws his offer. Does the contractor have a claim against the *manufacturer?* What other facts would help to sustain such a claim? See C. R. Fedrick, Inc. v. Sterling-Salem Corp., 507 F.2d 319 (9th Cir. 1974).[c]

a. The court referred to Professor Boyer's view, as quoted above.

b. As to this see Restatement Second, § 90, Comment d; the case is noted at 30 U.Pitt.L.Rev. 174 (1968).

c. See also Aronowicz v. Nalley's, Inc., 30 Cal.App.3d 27, 106 Cal.Rptr. 424 (1972).

SALE OF BUSINESS

The sale of a business enterprise commonly requires reconstitution of its charter, which may raise questions about its contract relations with third persons: suppliers, customers, employees and others. Even if the enterprise is incorporated, and its sale is effected by a simple transfer of shares, complications may occur in these relations. Some of these matters are attended to in the following chapter, especially in Section 2. One instance described already concerned the sale by the Brunswick Corporation of its Concorde Yacht division to the Test Corporation: see p. 861 supra. The rights of some employees against their former employer came into question. The new employer had contracted, in the sale agreement, to honor the commitments made to them by Brunswick. Given that fact, they were doubtless entitled to claim against the new employer as third party beneficiaries of the sale contract. (They preferred to proceed against Brunswick because the new employer shortly invoked bankruptcy proceedings.)

If the seller of the business defaults on its obligations to the buyer, what is the consequence for third-party claims such as those of the transferred employees? And what if the buyer shows that it was imposed upon in the negotiations, as through overstatement by the seller of the assets of the enterprise? Are the claims of third parties against the buyer likely to be impaired by substandard conduct on the part of the seller? Although the business situation just described occurs frequently, these questions are not often litigated. In reading the materials to follow, you should try to extrapolate answers based on third party beneficiary law.

NOTE

Election? One reason the cases are few may be that the buyer senses he is faced with an election: if he wishes to escape liability to the third party he must renounce the underlying transaction—rescind or cancel his purchase. A damage claim against the seller may serve his purpose better.

In the next case, Rouse v. United States, the United States made a claim (vice Associated Contractors) as third party "creditor" beneficiary of a contract for the sale of a house by Bessie Winston to John W. Rouse. It was faced with a defense based on misrepresentation by Winston about the condition of a home furnace (the first defense). Consider what evidence would have shown an election by Rouse not to assert this defense. Would the case be materially different if Winston had made a misrepresentation about the condition of (say) the foundation rather than about the furnace?

ROUSE v. UNITED STATES

United States Court of Appeals for the District of Columbia, 1954.
94 U.S.App.D.C. 386, 215 F.2d 872.

Action by United States, which had taken assignment of F.H.A. note which was in default, to recover from purchaser who had bought house from maker of note. The United States District Court for the District of Columbia, Burnita Shelton Matthews, J., struck purchaser's defenses and granted summary judgment for plaintiff and purchaser appealed.

EDGERTON, Circuit Judge. Bessie Winston gave Associated Contractors, Inc., her promissory note for $1,008.37, payable in monthly installments of $28.01, for a heating plant in her house. The Federal Housing Administration guaranteed the note and the payee endorsed it for value to the lending bank, the Union Trust Company.

Winston sold the house to Rouse. In the contract of sale Rouse agreed to assume debts secured by deeds of trust and also "to assume payment of $850 for heating plant payable $28 per Mo." Nothing was said about the note.

Winston defaulted on her note. The United States paid the bank, took an assignment of the note, demanded payment from Rouse, and sued him for $850 and interest.

Rouse alleged as defenses (1) that Winston fraudulently misrepresented the condition of the heating plant and (2) that Associated Contractors did not install it satisfactorily. The District Court struck these defenses and granted summary judgment for the plaintiff. The defendant Rouse appeals.

Since Rouse did not sign the note he is not liable on it. D.C.Code 1951, § 28–119; N.I.L. Sec. 18.[a] He is not liable to the United States at all unless his contract with Winston makes him so. The contract says the parties to it are not "bound by any terms, conditions, statements, warranties or representations, oral or written" not contained in it. But this means only that the written contract contains the entire agreement. It does not mean that fraud cannot be set up as a defense to a suit on the contract. [3 Williston, Contracts § 811A (Rev.Ed.1936).] Rouse's promise to "assume payment of $850 for heating plant" made him liable to Associated Contractors, Inc., only if and so far as it made him liable to Winston; one who promises to make a payment to the promisee's creditor can assert against the creditor any defense that the promisor could assert against the promisee. [2 Williston, § 394.] Accordingly Rouse, if he had been sued by the corporation, would have been entitled to show fraud on the part of Winston. He is equally entitled to do so in this suit by an assignee

a. "No person is liable on the instrument whose signature does not appear thereon, except. . . ." UCC 3–401(1): "No person is liable on an instrument unless his signature appears thereon."

of the corporation's claim. It follows that the court erred in striking the first defense. We do not consider whether Winston's alleged fraud, if shown, would be a complete or only a partial defense to this suit, since that question has not arisen and may not arise.

We think the court was right in striking the second defense. "If the promisor's agreement is to be interpreted as a promise to discharge whatever liability the promisee is under, the promisor must certainly be allowed to show that the promisee was under no enforceable liability. . . . On the other hand, if the promise means that the promisor agrees to pay a sum of money to A, to whom the promisee says he is indebted, it is immaterial whether the promisee is actually indebted to that amount or at all. . . . Where the promise is to pay a specific debt . . . this interpretation will generally be the true one." [2 Williston, § 399.]

The judgment is reversed and the cause remanded with instructions to reinstate the first defense.

Reversed and remanded.

NOTES

(1) *Question.* Is the first defense in Rouse's case the answer to Tool Company's claim against Airline Co., in the thrust-bed case, p. 1053 supra?

(2) *Problems.* An employer arranges with a health insurance company to provide coverage under a group policy, as a fringe benefit for his full-time employees. His employment contracts commit him to pay the premium for each eligible employee. As issued to the employer, the policy makes it a condition of payment to any employee that the premium on his account have been paid. When an eligible employee falls ill, may the insurer refuse payment on the ground that the employer classified him as a part-timer and paid no premium for him? That the employer has failed altogether to pay two monthly premiums? On somewhat comparable facts, a life insurer was held accountable in Bass v. John Hancock Mutual Life Ins. Co., 10 Cal. 3d 792, 112 Cal.Rptr. 195, 518 P.2d 1147 (1974) (note additional issue of acceptance of benefit by employee).

If this case and the judgment on the first defense in Rouse have to be explained by reference to the differing commercial roles of insurance companies and home buyers, how would the explanation run?

(3) *An Artificial Price.* You represent the executor of an estate. He wishes to sell a million-dollar property and pay a 5% fee to the broker who found the buyer for him. The probate court has denounced the payment of any fee by the estate. You prepare a sale contract requiring the buyer to pay the fee and to pay your client $950,000 as the "price". Your contract recites that the consideration for the fee is services rendered by the broker to the buyer. Will you be easy in your conscience about your handiwork? If not, would it make you easier to know that the court's attitude is misguided? Now suppose that the broker has previously threatened to claim a fee from your client, and all parties have agreed to a settlement: $25,000 for the broker, and a "price" of $975,000. If you write up that transaction in the same manner, are the ethical considerations different?

The buyer pays the executor and takes title, but refuses to pay the broker. Is he liable to the broker—in either case—as third party beneficiary? See Peters Grazing Ass'n v. Legerski, 544 P.2d 449 (Wyo., 1975) (divided court), citing Rouse v. United States.[b] Is the broker's claim stronger than that of the United States in any respect? Weaker?

THE COAL STRIKE CASE

In the early 50's, the United Mine Workers struck the nation's coal operators, including the Benedict Coal Company. Considering that the union had violated a collective bargaining agreement, Benedict claimed damages. It also withheld certain royalties that the agreement would have required it to make, if performed, to the UMW Welfare and Retirement Fund. Although the Fund was created by the collective bargaining agreement, it was administered by its own trustees. They sued Benedict for the sums withheld. In defense, Benedict contended that the duty to pay royalties to the trustees was conditioned on performance by the union of its promises, or at least that the amount of the company's damage claim against the union should be set off against the trustees' recovery. In Lewis v. Benedict Coal Corp., 361 U.S. 459 (1960), the Supreme Court rejected both of these contentions. Its reasoning emphasized the peculiar character of an industry-wide collective bargaining agreement. Under a more "typical" third party beneficiary contract, it indicated, when the promisor has a damage claim against the promisee it may be fair to assume that the beneficiary's claim should be correspondingly reduced. But such a design, the Court ruled, must have been expressed in "unequivocal words" before it could be applied to the agreement in question. For one of its grounds, the Court found an expression of "national labor policy" in the Taft-Hartley Act, indicating that a union, like a corporation, should be the "sole source of recovery for injury inflicted by it."

In one interesting passage the Court remarked: "Using terms like 'counterclaim' or 'setoff' in a third-party beneficiary context may be confusing." What is confusing about it? The Restatement Second describes a setoff situation (§ 309, Illustration 9), and it says: "Partial defenses by way of recoupment for breach by the promisee may be asserted against the beneficiary, unless precluded by the terms of the agreement or considerations of fairness or public policy." (Comment c)

NOTES

(1) *Collective Agreements as Contracts.* Students of labor law have often commented on the interplay, or lack of it, between the law of collective bargaining agreements and the law of contracts as represented in the

b. Rehearing denied, 546 P.2d 189 (Wyo.1976) (divided court).

treatises and the Restatements. One such comment advances these conclusions, among others: "contract rules which attempt to define with some specificity or detail rights and duties of parties are largely useless and often misleading when applied to collective agreements.[a] . . . [W]hile we may gain little insight into collective agreements by looking upon them as contracts, we can achieve significant insights into the nature of the law of contracts by viewing it from the perspective of collective agreements." [b] Compare the emphasis in Cox, The Legal Nature of Collective Bargaining Agreements, 57 Mich.L.Rev. 1 (1958).

(2) *Invincible Third Parties.* Is it possible for A to make an agreement with B such that C may claim a benefit from A under the agreement even if (as it turns out) B has procured A's assent by fraud? As a rule, the beneficiary's right, "like that of an assignee, is subject to limitations inherent in the contract, and to supervening defenses arising by virtue of its terms." Restatement Second, § 309, Comment c. But are the contracting parties free to make the third party's right invincible?

Comment b to the same section states: "The agreement may effectively provide that the right of the beneficiary is not to be affected by the act or neglect of the promisee." This statement reflects a provision commonly found in policies of insurance on buildings, entitled Standard Mortgagee Clause. The clause provides that if a mortgagee or other lienholder is named in the policy no act or neglect of the policyholder (owner) invalidates the insurance, as to the lienholder's interest. A usual case in which the mortgagee may enforce the policy, and the owner may not, is one in which the owner has "neglected" to pay a premium.[c] A more extreme case is one in which the policyholder has committed arson.

If the policy has been procured by an imposter, it might seem that the standard mortgagee clause must be voidable along with the rest of the contract. The right of a third party beneficiary is "created by contract, and in the absence of contract there is no such right." [d] Restatement Second, § 309, Comment a. Yet this is not a safe supposition. The courts have given literal force to the clause, sometimes speaking of it as an "independent contract" between the insurer and the mortgagee. As to the imposter case see Great American Ins. Co. v. Southwestern Finance Co., 297 P.2d 403 (Okl. 1956).

a. Summers, Collective Bargaining and the Law of Contracts, 78 Yale L.J. 525, 538 (1969). On the third-party aspect of collective agreements, see pp. 538–41.

b. Id., 527.

c. It is a condition of the mortgagee's continuing protection under the clause that he respond in due time to the insurer's demand on him for payment of the premium. See General Credit Corp. v. Imperial Casualty & Indemnity Co., 167 Neb. 833, 95 N.W.2d 145 (1959).

d. The clause has statutory backing in some states.

SEARS, ROEBUCK AND CO. v. JARDEL CO.

United States Court of Appeals, Third Circuit, 1970.
421 F.2d 1048.

[For a partial report, including the facts, of this case, see p. 436 supra. The opinion continues as follows.]

VAN DUSEN, Circuit Judge. . . .

Having correctly found the release to cover the claim involved here as to Robbins, Inc., the District Court held the release binding upon Jardel by disregarding the separate entities of the two corporations. . . .

Courts of Pennsylvania and Delaware do not easily pierce the corporate veil. [But the court avoided a decision on the District Court ruling, and found another reason for affirmance.]

Even if the corporate veil of Jardel were not disregarded, it cannot entirely separate itself, for the purpose of this suit, from the activities of Robbins, Inc. Jardel's claim against Hirsch is based upon Hirsch's duties arising out of Robbins, Inc.'s subcontract with it. In its third-party complaint, Jardel alleged the contract as the basis for its suit: "Defendant is informed and believes and thereon alleges that Hirsch breached its agreement with the contractor [Robbins, Inc.] . . . .." But just as Jardel did not sign the release, so too it was not a signatory to the underlying Robbins, Inc.-Hirsch contract.

Because the contract explicitly contemplated the provision of services by Hirsch to Jardel,[1] Jardel has rights under the contract as a third-party creditor beneficiary. See, e. g., Van Cor, Inc. v. American Cas. Co., 417 Pa. 408, 413, 208 A.2d 267, 269 (1965). Professor Williston defines a third-party creditor beneficiary contract as one in which:

" 'no purpose to make a gift appears from the terms of the promise in view of the accompanying circumstances and performance of the promise will satisfy an actual or supposed or asserted duty of the promisee to the beneficiary . . . .'

"The promisee's object in the contract to discharge his debt must always be primarily, and generally solely, to secure his own advantage. He wishes to be relieved from liability, and he exacts a promise to pay the third person only because that is a way of relieving himself."

2 S. Williston, Law of Contracts, § 361, at 863 (3rd Ed., 1959) [quoting Restatement of Contracts § 131(1)(b)(1932)] (footnotes omitted).[2] As general contractor, Robbins, Inc. had a duty to provide

1. Article I of the Robbins, Inc.-Hirsch contract provided:
"The word 'Owner' shall mean JARDEL CO., INC., the Owner of the building [or buildings, Art. XXIV] of which the Sub-Contractor's [Hirsch's] work forms a part."

2. Also see 4 A. Corbin, Contracts § 787, at 95 (1951):

Jardel with certain specified services; it chose to fulfill part of that duty by subcontracting with Hirsch, Hirsch thereby promising to complete the plumbing, heating and air-conditioning work. Because courts have "instinctively recogniz[ed] the creditor's [Jardel's] interest in such a promise," Williston, supra, § 361, at 864–65, the third-party creditor beneficiary can sue the promisor (in this case, Hirsch) directly.[3]

Once a third-party beneficiary contract has been made however, the beneficiary's rights are not unlimited.[4] In this case, the terms of § 143 of the Restatement of Contracts require the conclusion that the release satisfied the promisor's obligation to the creditor beneficiary (Jardel) as well as to the promisee (Robbins, Inc.):

"A discharge of the promisor by the promisee in a contract or a variation thereof by them is effective against a creditor beneficiary if,

(a) the creditor beneficiary does not bring suit upon the promise or otherwise materially change his position in reliance thereon before he knows of the discharge or variation, and

(b) the promisee's action is not a fraud on creditors." [5]

"If the promisee in a contract contemplates the present or future existence of a duty or liability to a third party and enters into the contract with the expressed intent that the performance contracted for is to satisfy and discharge that duty or liability, the third party is a creditor beneficiary."

3. Article XIV of the Robbins, Inc.-Hirsch contract provided that Hirsch "shall indemnify and save harmless the Owner . . . against all claims of damage to persons or property growing out of the execution of [Hirsch's] work." Hirsch also agreed to "indemnify and save harmless" Jardel from any damage arising out of Hirsch's work that could be asserted against the general contractor, Robbins, Inc. The parties' intention that Hirsch's performance was to carry out the obligations of Robbins, Inc. to Jardel also appears in Articles I, II, XVI, XVIII, and XXIV. These provisions make clear that "'both parties to the contract . . . [intended that Jardel be a beneficiary] . . . and [indicated] that intention in the contract . . . .'" See Van Cor, Inc. v. American Cas. Co., supra, at 413, 208 A.2d at 269.

4. For example, since the beneficiary's rights depend on the contract, if for some reason the contract is invalid, "no rights can arise in favor of anyone." Id. § 364A, at 873; accord, Restatement of Contracts § 140 (1932). See, also, Williston, supra, § 395, at 1066. Thus, in Williams v. Paxson Coal Co., 346 Pa. 468, 31 A.2d 69 (1943), a promisor agreed to look only to the dividends of three named shareholders for enforcement of a demand note given him in exchange for the transfer of property to the corporation. After the named shareholders sold their entire interest in the corporation, the promisor sued the corporation to enforce the note. The corporation argued that it was obligated to satisfy the note only if it should declare dividends to the original shareholders. Treating the corporation under its new owners as a donee beneficiary and the original shareholders as promisees to the agreement, the court held that because the promisees had made enforcement of the agreement impossible by removing their names from the shareholder list, there was a failure of consideration by the promisees, and thus the corporation, as third-party beneficiary, could not enforce the agreement.

5. Illustration 1, accompanying § 143, provides:

"B contracts with A to pay C $200 which A owes C. C learns of this

Professor Williston has adopted the Restatement rule, distinguishing the creditor beneficiary situation from that of the donee beneficiary,[6] reasoning that the creditor beneficiary's right "is purely derivative." Williston, supra, § 397, at 1074.[7]

This is the rule that Pennsylvania would adopt. Not only do Pennsylvania courts rely upon the Restatement and Professor Williston in establishing the law of third-party beneficiary contracts, e. g., Williams v. Paxson Coal Co., 346 Pa. 468, 470, 471, 472, 31 A.2d 69, 70, 71 (1943),[8] but they apparently have adopted § 143. In Clardy v. Barco Construction Co., 205 Pa.Super. 218, 224–225, 208 A.2d 793, 796 (1965), the court found that a release did not bar the third-party creditor beneficiary's claim by reason of § 143, because the creditor had relied on the contract in completing his duties. In Miller v. Travelers Insurance Co., 143 Pa.Super. 270, 17 A.2d 907 (1941), the court adopted the rule of § 143, although it actually cited § 140 [9] as au-

contract and expresses satisfaction but does not make a novation with B, or begin an action to enforce a right against B, or change his position in reliance on the contract. Later, in consideration of a horse worth $200 given him by B, A releases B from his contract. C, after learning of the release, cannot enforce a right against B. . . ."

[See Restatement Second, § 311.]

6. The distinction between a creditor and donee beneficiary, restricting the right of the promisor in the donee situation to be released, is based on the theory that only the donee beneficiary (and not the promisee) has so substantial an interest in the contract that he can enforce it. See, e. g., Tasin v. Bastress, 284 Pa. 47, 57, 130 A. 417, 421 (1925). Professor Corbin, however, argues that the creditor beneficiary's rights are similar to those of the donee beneficiary, since the creditor beneficiary is "given" the right to look not only to the promisee for enforcement of his contract, for which he had originally bargained, but also to the promisor. "It seems best, therefore, that the discharge by the promisee should be operative as against the beneficiary only in case he learns of the discharge before he has assented to the contract or has acted in reliance upon it." Corbin, supra, note 19, § 815, at 260; see e. g., Hughes v. Gibbs, 55 Wash.2d 791, 350 P.2d 475 (1960).

The proposed Second Restatement of Contracts, to which Professor Corbin served as Consultant, adopts his view that the promisee and promisor have no power to modify or release the promisor's duties to the beneficiary after the beneficiary has assented to their contract. Restatement (Second) of Contracts § 142 (Tent. Draft No. 3, 1967). However, this tentative draft has been adopted by neither the American Law Institute nor the courts of Pennsylvania.

[For the position adopted see Restatement Second, § 311.]

7. Also see R. J. Cardinal Co. v. Ritchie, 218 Cal.App.2d 124, 32 Cal.Rptr. 545, 552–553, 561 (1963); Davis v. Nelson-Deppe, Inc., 91 Idaho 463, 424 P.2d 733, 737 (1967); Britton v. Groom, 373 P.2d 1012, 1015–1016 (Okl.1962); Morstain v. Kircher, 190 Minn. 78, 250 N.W. 727 (1933). In commenting on Morstain, one student authority relied on § 143: "Since the [creditor beneficiary's] right seems only derivative, . . . it appears better to permit a release if the creditor has not materially changed his position in reliance on the [promisor's] agreement." 47 Harv.L. Rev. 1065, 1066 (1934).

8. Also see note [4], supra.

9. Restatement of Contracts § 140 provides:

"There can be no donee beneficiary or creditor beneficiary unless a contract has been formed between

thority. Plaintiff's husband contracted with his employer to have deductions taken from his wages to support a group life insurance policy that the employer took out with the defendant insurance company. After giving notice to the employees, the employer cancelled the policy. Upon her husband's death, the plaintiff sued the insurance company as a third-party beneficiary, arguing that the contract between the employer and the insurance company could not have been cancelled without her husband's consent. The court held:

"The insured employee or his beneficiary have no greater rights than are provided in the policy, certainly no vested right which would prevent cancellation by mutual agreement between the insurer and the employer, especially where reasonable notice of cancellation is given to the employee. A third party beneficiary in an ordinary contract is subject to the limitation of its terms as he has no greater rights under it than are provided in the contract itself: Restatement of the Law, Contracts, § 140 . . . ." Id. at 273, 17 A.2d at 908.[10]

Application of § 143 to this case bars not only the recovery by Jardel under a contractual theory, but its suit in negligence as well. Under § 143 the release was also a "variation," expressly precluding "all, and all manner of, actions and causes of action" arising from the contract between Robbins and Hirsch. Pennsylvania courts have uniformly honored such contractual provisions where they are entered into by "free bargaining agents,". . . .

Applying the above-stated rule to Jardel would not work an "injustice," as Jardel has argued.[11] Should Jardel not have an actionable claim against Hirsch, it can still sue the general contractor, Robbins, Inc., whose obligation to Jardel remained unchanged by the sub-

a promisor and promisee; and if a contract is conditional, voidable, or unenforceable at the time of its formation, or subsequently ceases to be binding in whole or in part because of impossibility, illegality or the present or prospective failure of the promisee to perform a return promise which was the consideration for the promisor's promise, the right of a donee beneficiary or creditor beneficiary under the contract is subject to the same limitation."

[See Restatement Second, § 309.]

10. Another bar to the recovery of the creditor beneficiary occurs in the situation where the promisee recovers a judgment under the contract against the promisor:

"Whatever the hardship upon the promisor may be in being liable to two persons when he promised but one, most courts have found it the simpler alternative, a recovery by either party being a bar to an action by the other."

Williston, supra, § 392, at 1057 (footnotes omitted); cf. Parker v. London Guar. & Accident Co., 30 F.2d 464 (E.D.Pa.1927) (federal common law). We need not reach the question whether the rule would be accepted by Pennsylvania or whether it applies to the facts of this case.

11. Of course, the parties can contract that a release given the promisor shall not be binding on the creditor beneficiary. See Beaver Falls B. & L. Ass'n v. Allemania Fire Ins. Co., 305 Pa. 290, 157 A. 616 (1931).

contract or the release. See, e. g., National Fire Ins. Co. of Hartford v. Westgate Constr. Co., 227 F.Supp. 835 (D.Del.1964). Indeed, Jardel's separate existence was justified in part by the necessity of keeping its assets apart from those of its parent, and thus suit against its parent would be more than a futile gesture in this instance.[12]

Accordingly, we hold that Jardel is bound by the release, since the record does not show any material change of position by it in reliance on the promise prior to the variation of the contract by the release.[13] See Morstain v. Kircher, 190 Minn. 78, 250 N.W. 727, 728 (1933),[14] where the court said:

". . . [The plaintiff] paid no consideration for defendant's agreement to pay the mortgage debt, nor had she in reliance on the assumption contract placed herself in a position from which she could not retreat without loss. [citing § 143] . . ."

For the foregoing reasons, the District Court order of December 9, 1968, will be affirmed.

NOTES

(1) *Questions.* Does the court's footnote 6 indicate that the result would be different under Restatement Second, § 311? If so, which rule seems preferable? Compare Christian v. Metropolitan Life Ins. Co., 566 P.2d 445 (Okl.1977).[a]

(2) *Problem.* John Sunday and his wife contracted to sell a house for $37,500, to be paid by George Rheims. The contract document named Mrs. Annette Oman as purchaser, however, rather than Rheims, for he intended to give the house to her. All the parties mentioned signed the document. Rheims gave a check for earnest money (10% of the contract price) to a lawyer acting for the other parties. The check was presented for payment, but was returned marked "NSF" (not sufficient funds). About a month after the agreement was made, Rheims died. The Sundays refused to convey to Mrs. Oman, and made a settlement with the Rheims estate, whereby

12. It is irrelevant that Jardel's action against Robbins, Inc. may now be barred by the applicable statute of limitations. It seems reasonable to surmise that Jardel would not have let the statute of limitations run had not Robbins, Inc. been its sole stockholder.

13. In a supplemental brief to this court, Jardel claims that it paid Robbins, Inc. in reliance on the Robbins, Inc.-Hirsch contract, so that Robbins, Inc. could pay Hirsch. Such an allegation, if proved, might well be a defense to a claim by Hirsch against Jardel for payments owed to Hirsch by Robbins, Inc. Cf. Clardy v. Barco Constr. Co., supra. We do not believe, however, that in the posture of this case such a payment represents a material change of position, as contemplated by § 143.

Since Robbins was the president of Jardel when he signed the release on behalf of Robbins, Inc., Jardel simultaneously had knowledge. Jardel did not bring suit on the contract before the release was signed, nor can we find any evidence that Robbins, Inc.'s action in executing the release was a fraud upon its creditors.

14. See, also, Britton v. Groom, supra, note [7], 373 P.2d at 1016.

a. For cases compatible with either rule, see Wiley v. Berg, 282 Or. 9, 578 P.2d 384 (1978); Greenway Park Townhomes Condominium Ass'n v. Brookfield Municipal Utility Dist., 575 S.W.2d 90 (Tex.Civ.App.1978).

the executor allowed their claim for $3,750 as liquidated damages. Does Mrs. Oman have a claim against either Rheims' estate or the Sundays? See Oman v. Yates, 70 Wash.2d 181, 422 P.2d 489 (1967).

(3) *A Tale of Two States.* The case to follow was decided by reference to Minnesota law, though it arose in Massachusetts. The geography of the case is interesting because of the dates on which third party beneficiary theory was embraced in the two states. In Massachusetts it was maintained for 125 years that a "stranger to the consideration" cannot recover on a contract though it was made for his benefit. As late as 1978 the Supreme Judicial Court refused to discard this doctrine—though it took note of numerous "exceptions" established by statute or decision. Falmouth Hospital v. Lopes, 382 N.E.2d 1042. In Minnesota the Supreme Court rejected the (then) Massachusetts doctrine in 1940. The decisive case, La Mourea v. Rhude, is relied on in the opinion to follow; it applied the principles of the first Restatement, § 133, to a public works contract.

In 1979 the Massachusetts court at length subscribed to what it called the general rule: "American courts, under the inspiration of *Lawrence v. Fox* . . ., have held quite generally that 'creditor' beneficiaries may sue on contracts to which they were not parties." Choate, Hall & Stewart v. SCA Serv., Inc., 392 N.E.2d 1045.

MASSENGALE v. TRANSITRON ELECTRONIC CORPORATION

United States Court of Appeals, First Circuit, 1967.
385 F.2d 83.

[Prior to 1962, McClellan and Burck, Inc. was a New York corporation engaged in the business of planning and effecting mergers of business corporations. One of its clients was a Minnesota firm, Thermo King Corporation. Ultimately, in August, 1961, many efforts it had made on behalf of Thermo King resulted in its acquisition by the Westinghouse Electric Corporation. At that time, Thermo King paid McClellan and Burck $325,000 for its services.

The present action is one against Transitron Electronic Corporation, which had been interested in acquiring Thermo King in 1960. It was brought by McClellan and Burck, and continued by Massengale, as trustee for the stockholders of the firm after its dissolution. That firm is referred to hereafter as "Burck". (The court's opinion also refers to the plaintiff as "Burck".)

In July, 1960, both Westinghouse and Transitron had become interested, through Burck's efforts, in acquiring Thermo King. Burck and Thermo King entered into a letter agreement about Burck's compensation, which was fixed as a percentage of the sale price, not to exceed $325,000. The fee was expected to be paid by the acquiring company, and its amount was to be approved (at Thermo King's insistence) by the acquiring company. The compensation was agreed upon, in Burck's words, "in the event a transaction is consummated with any company where our firm has originated the transaction."

A month later, negotiations had focussed on Transitron. Burck wrote to Thermo King stating its willingness to accept a reduced fee of $300,000—only in connection with the Transitron purchase—"to be due and payable when and if the proposed transaction with Transitron is consummated."

In October Transitron and Thermo King entered into an agreement for the sale of Thermo King's assets. The price was to be paid in Transitron stock, Thermo King was to be dissolved, and the stock distributed to its shareholders. The execution of the sale was subjected to various conditions, including the taking of certain corporate actions such as a favorable vote by the seller's stockholders. The agreement recited Thermo King's agreement to pay Burck's fee "in the event that the said transactions are consummated, but not otherwise. Such fee shall be paid by Transitron if and when such transactions are effected."

In December Transitron sent Thermo King a notice terminating the agreement on the grounds of a material adverse change in Thermo King's business, and the failure of Thermo King to call a stockholders' meeting.

Several years later, the present action was brought to recover the $300,000 fee from Transitron. The plaintiff alleged that the termination was without justification, and was a willful breach of the agreement, and was a violation of Transitron's obligation to Burck; also that Transitron "wrongfully prevented the effecting and consummation of the transaction." [a]

The trial court, though sitting in Massachusetts, gave effect to a provision in the Transitron agreement that it should be "governed by Minnesota law." In the present appeal, this ruling was approved. The court said that to apply Minnesota law, including its recognition of third party beneficiary claims, did not offend substantial Massachusetts public policy.[b]

The trial court nevertheless granted a motion by Transitron for summary judgment, on two grounds. One was that Burck's receipt of $325,000 on account of the Westinghouse transaction discharged any claim it may have had against Transitron. (In this connection the court attempted to distinguish Olds v. Mapes-Reeve Construction Co., herein at p. 574 supra.) The other ground was that none of the agreements contemplated payment of a fee to Burck, in relation to the Transitron sale, if it was not consummated. In this connection the court refused to accept an implication drawn from two Minnesota cases: Huntley v. Smith and Flower v. Davidson. According to the

a. Immediately after the termination, Burck wrote to Westinghouse, seeking to revive its interest in Thermo King. This letter stated that the Transitron sale was aborted by a precipitous drop in the market value of Transitron stock, which eroded the price by almost 40%.

b. Citing Restatement Second, of Conflict of Laws, §§ 332(2), 332a (and comment g), and 346 (and comment c).

appellate court, these cases "allowed recovery to a broker of a fee contingent on consummation when his seller-principal arbitrarily refused to consummate a transaction." The trial court refused to extend the principle of these cases to the present one, finding no Minnesota case that had applied it in favor of a third party beneficiary. The plaintiff appealed.]

COFFIN, Circuit Judge.

. . . [W]e cannot say that Burck has advanced no cause of action. Appellee acknowledges that Minnesota law confers upon a third party beneficiary the right to assert such claims against a promisor as he has against a promisee. The district court recognized this when it declared that Transitron's obligation to Burck was co-extensive with Thermo King's. Appellee implicitly and the court explicitly accepted the principle of La Mourea v. Rhude, 209 Minn. 53, 295 N.W. 304 (1940) [see Note 3, p. 1067 supra]. But both failed to pursue the implications of this landmark case.

The court read *La Mourea* as merely giving Burck the right to maintain an action, without shedding light on the nature of its rights. It therefore, as we have noted, refused to apply Huntley v. Smith, supra, and Flower v. Davidson, supra, because ". . . in this case [Burck] and [Transitron] had no relationship apart from the Transitron-Thermo King agreement." In similar vein appellee relied heavily on Kramer v. Gardner, 104 Minn. 370, 116 N.W. 925, 22 L.R.A.,N.S., 492 (1908), which held that a promise by the purchaser of a business to a second mortgagee to pay off the first mortgage gave no rights to the first mortgagee, there being no privity between the two mortgagees, no obligation on the part of the second mortgagee to the first mortgagee, nor any consideration moving from the beneficiary (first mortgagee) to the promisor.

Leaving aside the factual differences between *Kramer* and the case at bar, *La Mourea* specifically overruled the "outmoded" doctrine of Kramer v. Gardner and in so doing, dealt fatal blows to the traditional concepts of both consideration and privity. . . .

La Mourea was not an accident. It was foreshadowed by the concurring opinion of Justice Royal Stone in Peterson v. Parviainen, 174 Minn. 297, 219 N.W. 180 (1928), who, twelve years later, wrote the opinion in *La Mourea* for a unanimous court. See de Werff, Third Party Beneficiary Contracts in Minnesota, 29 Minn.L.Rev. 436, 441–45 (1945).[1] See also 25 Minn.L.Rev. 523 (1941); Mitchell v. Rende, 225 Minn. 145, 147, 30 N.W.2d 27, 29 (1947).

1. We are told that in the valedictory of Justice Stone, his last opinion—a dissent—he wrote of the third party beneficiary contract doctrine: "It illustrates the fact that the common law is not a matured, rigid, and inert mass. It is rather a live and growing organism, self-adapting to new problems and new truths. While avowing respect for precedent, it owes no allegiance either to ancient error or any concept invalidated by progress." Farmers State Bank v. Burns, 212 Minn. 455, 472, 5 N.W.2d 589, 591 (1942), quoted in 29 Minn.L.Rev., supra at 436, n. 3.

To use the language of *La Mourea*, Burck in the case before us "has come directly into legal relationship with" Transitron. This is no surprise to anyone, for Burck drafted its fee agreement letter knowing it would be shown to the acquiring company; Thermo King accepted the fee agreement only on condition that Transitron approve; in fact subsequent discussions between Thermo King and Transitron resulted in a reduction in fee for that transaction; and Transitron in its contract with Thermo King assumed the obligation to pay Burck's commission. But, apart from the express characterization of the direct relationship just quoted, the entire import of *La Mourea* is that, regardless of such labels as "consideration" and "privity", Transitron stands in the same position toward Burck as does Thermo King. The district court, while formally accepting this concept in referring to Transitron's obligation as "co-extensive" with Thermo King's, for all practical purposes diminished it by applying traditional concepts of consideration and privity when it refused to extend to Transitron the principle that arbitrary refusal to consummate a transaction could mature its obligation as fully as could consummation.

This principle is to be distinguished from the undertaking by Thermo King and Transitron in their contract to use "best efforts" to bring about the transaction. We do not reach the issue whether, as the district court said, this obligation was reciprocal only, for there is a large difference between the positive duty to use best efforts and the negative duty to refrain from termination for unjustifiable cause.

On what basis of reason should there be a difference between the liability of a seller and a buyer, each of whom had undertaken to pay a brokerage fee in the event of consummation and each of whom wrongfully refuses to consummate a transaction? Or, to put it more concretely, why should Thermo King be obliged to pay Burck if it captiously aborted the transaction while Transitron would be under no such obligation for the same conduct leading to the same result? We cannot see any basis—other than "privity"—for making a distinction.[2] Nor can we see the distinction drawn by the district court between a fee agreement contingent on "consummation" and one contingent on specified preconditions to consummation as well as final consummation itself. . . .

We recognize that the Minnesota courts, so far as we are aware, have not had occasion to rule on the obligation of an arbitrarily defaulting promisor to a third party beneficiary in such a case as that at bar. But we feel that they would today be constrained to recog-

2. That a broker's right to his commission should not turn on whether the sale falls through because of the default of the seller or buyer seems clear from Blanken v. Bechtel Properties, Inc., 194 F.Supp. 638 (D.D.C. 1961) in which Judge Holtzoff thoughtfully reviews a wide range of authorities, citing, among others, Restatement (Second) of Agency § 445, comment d, ill. 1, and 4 Williston, Contracts § 1030A (1936).

nize a cause of action.[3] The most pertinent case that has been cited to us is Chipley v. Morrell, 228 N.C. 240, 45 S.E.2d 129 (1947), where, on demurrer, a broker hired by a seller, was held entitled to sue an arbitrarily reneging buyer despite the absence of any undertaking to pay the fee on the part of the buyer. This case is, a fortiori, persuasive authority for that at bar since we have here an explicit undertaking by the buyer to pay the fee. . . .

The second ground of the district court's decision—that Thermo King's payment for the Westinghouse transaction satisfied any liability of Transitron—is based on the concept that all that was bargained for was one fee for one transaction. In a sense this is true. Prospectively, Burck and Thermo King contemplated only one completed transaction. There obviously could be only one completed merger. But what is alleged by the complaint to have happened is something beyond the contemplation of the parties, i. e., the unjustifiable refusal by Transitron to consummate the first transaction. This, as we have concluded, gives rise to an obligation. The broker has in such case earned a commission just as if the merger had been completed. When its subsequent services, which it was under no compulsion to render, resulted in a completed transaction, a second commission was earned. This is not, as appellant properly notes, an action against an employer for damages caused by wrongful discharge, in which damages would be mitigated by plaintiff's subsequent earnings.

In sum, while only one transaction was originally contemplated, the allegedly wrongful withdrawal of Transitron matured one commission-producing occurrence and the completion of the Westinghouse transaction matured another. Appellant therefore does not seek double compensation for a single debt but one payment for each of two separate debts.

Judgment will be entered reversing the judgment of the District Court and remanding the action for further proceedings not inconsistent herewith.

NOTES

(1) *Release and Modification.* Suppose that Transitron had not declared a termination of its agreement with Thermo King, but had obtained Thermo King's consent to a rescission, on the eve of consummating the agreement. Would Burck have had a claim against either of them for its fee? If they had agreed to reduce the purchase price by a substantial

3. We are conscious of the fact that both Huntley v. Smith, supra, and Flower v. Davidson, supra, contain dicta that a broker is not entitled to a commission if the failure to complete the sale rested on the purchaser's refusal to carry out the contract of sale. While no underlying reason was given in either case, the concepts of privity and consideration, so unequivocally laid low by *La Mourea*, supra, must have made the proposition appear too obvious to warrant discussion. We cannot believe that these dicta would today be accepted as law in Minnesota.

amount, would that have affected Burck's right to the fee? On this controversial point, a comment in the Restatement Second has this to say: "Even though there is no novation and no change of position by the beneficiary, the power of promisor and promisee to vary the promisor's duty to an intended beneficiary is terminated when the beneficiary manifests assent to the promise in a manner invited by the promisor or promisee." (Comment h to § 311) This proposition marks a retreat from the original Restatement position taken in § 142; but it strengthens the hand of a *creditor* beneficiary as stated in the first Restatement, § 143. On both points, see McCulloch v. Canadian Pacific Railway Co., 53 F.Supp. 534 (D.Minn.1943).

The proposition does not quite answer the questions posed above, however. Was it Thermo King's duty to Burck not to release Transitron from its undertaking to pay the fee? Nothing in the main case indicates that a release would not be effective, except that both parties contracted to use their "best efforts" to bring about the transaction. Possibly this provision created a duty to Burck that could not be altered without its consent. According to the Restatement Second a duty to an intended beneficiary is *irrevocable* if it is created by a promise prohibiting its discharge or modification through subsequent agreement of the parties. See § 311, Comment a.[a]

(2) *Questions.* Refer to Professional Realty Corp. v. Bender, Note 1, p. 797 supra. Why was the tripartite signing of the contract in that case not enough to bring the plaintiff broker "directly into legal relationship" with the defendant buyers? Or if there was such a relationship why were the buyers not liable—as Transitron would have been—for termination for no good cause?

(3) *Mortgagee as Third Party Beneficiary.* Note the facts in Kramer v. Gardner, as stated in the main case. (And note that the doctrine of the case was rejected.) That case is one variant of a problem which has been a proving-ground for the law of third party beneficiaries. The more usual instance concerns a purchase of mortgaged property, in which the buyer undertakes to maintain the scheduled mortgage payments. Whether or not he does so, he stands to lose the property in case of default. (The case of a sale in which the seller's mortgage is retired is excluded from this discussion.) The mortgagee is entitled to a "deficiency judgment" if, upon foreclosure, the proceeds of the property do not satisfy his claim. If the buyer does not assume the mortgage, but takes the property only "subject to" it, the deficiency judgment may run against the seller, but cannot run against the buyer. Mortgage assumption agreements are regularly implemented, and a usual ground has been that the mortgagee is a third party creditor beneficiary.

There may indeed be a "chain" of assumptions: A buys the property (assuming the mortgage), and B buys from him (assuming the mortgage). The A–B contract is enforceable by the mortgagee: A is the promisee, just as the original mortgagor was the recipient of A's promise. But suppose there is a break in the chain: A did *not* assume the mortgage, but required B to do so. Is B personally subject to the mortgagee's claim? The Restatement has always taken a position generally favorable to the mortgagee.[b] But in some states there are crystallized rules that may be ex-

a. But another comment (§ 309, Comment c) hints that the promisor's duty may not be so irrefragable as this one indicates. Compare § 338(2).

b. See Restatement Second, § 312, Illustration 3.

empt from general argumentation about third party rights. The topic is not further noticed here, partly because it is dealt with in other courses. See G. Osborne, G. Nelson & D. Whitman, Real Estate Finance Law, Ch. 5, Part A, especially § 5.11 et seq. (1979).

Chapter 11

ASSIGNMENT AND DELEGATION

Today most contract rights having commercial value are transferable. The proposition is, indeed, something of a truism, for commercial worth is attributable to a right largely *because* of its transferability. Broad recognition of the principle is commonly found in statutes, as for instance in § 13–101 of the New York General Obligations Law which begins, "Any claim or demand can be transferred, except in one of the following cases. . . ." [a]

Section 1 of this chapter presents some fundamental propositions about assignments of contract rights, including the necessity of taking certain simple steps in order to effect the transfer of such a right. The topic of non-commercial (i. e., gift) assignments is featured here. The section demonstrates the primary function of an assignment: by this means a creditor may institute a duty running directly from his debtor to a third party, the assignee.

Section 2 focusses on sales of businesses, although lessons learned from other types of transaction are brought to bear on this one. When a business is sold, the buyer commonly acquires not only its tangible properties, such as plant and equipment, but also its intangibles, including accounts receivable. In addition, the buyer commonly undertakes to perform the duties of the seller under contracts that the seller has made, but not yet performed. From the seller's point of view, this transaction amounts to a delegation of his duties, which may be to render service to his customers, or to supply goods to them, or to render some other variety of performance. Of course, the right to be paid for such a performance is also transferred to the buyer—assigned to him. With respect to an executory contract, then, a seller of a business typically makes both an assignment of the contract rights and a delegation of its duties. The section considers the limits of assignability and delegability in this context.

Section 3 concentrates on a problem loosely described as the "holder in due course" problem. May a credit sale transaction be so arranged that, upon an assignment by the seller of the right to be paid, the assignee can override defenses of the buyer that would have

a. "1. Where it is to recover damages for a personal injury;

"2. Where it is founded upon a grant, which is made void by a statute of the state; or upon a claim to or interest in real property, a grant of which, by the transferrer, would be void by such a statute;

"3. Where a transfer thereof is expressly forbidden by a statute of the state, or of the United States, or would contravene public policy."

Cal.Civ.Code, § 1458: "A right arising out of an obligation is the property of the person to whom it is due, and may be transferred as such."

defeated or limited a claim against him by the seller? (Not only contracts for the sale of goods, but services contracts and others present the problem.) The issue has been highly controversial, especially in relation to "consumer" transactions. Banks and finance companies provide financing for consumer credit, backed by assignments purporting to give them a specialized legal advantage. Successes and failures in this attempt are examined here.

Section 4 turns to the role of financing institutions in relation to commercial credit. Manufacturers and merchants obtain financing on the strength of assigning their accounts receivable. Contractors obtain financing through assigning their anticipated job earnings. Farmers assign anticipated crop earnings. A large and complex body of law bears on the value of these assignments. In part it is case law; in part it is the Code and other state legislation; in part it is federal law, particularly the Bankruptcy Code. The financer (and its counsel) have to think of multiple risks, in addition to the prospect that the person expected to pay may be financially unable to do so. For one thing, he and the assignor may indulge in dealings without regard to the financer's interest, and prejudicial to it. For another, the payment may be intercepted by other creditors of the assignor, or his bankruptcy trustee, or someone else claiming under him. These risks, and the measures available to limit them, are examined in this section.

NOTES

(1) *Evolution of Assignments.* Contract rights of many kinds, known as "choses in action," were not transferable in an early stage of English law. Legal historians have delighted in tracing the process by which this rule was overthrown. As usually recounted, it employed the device called a "power of attorney." That device is still in use to enable lawyers and collection agencies to proceed against debtors on claims turned over to them by their creditor-clients, for collection only. Characteristically the agent suing on the claim does so in the name of the client, his principal. So used, the device does not involve an assignment of a claim. There was a time, however, when the device was employed to implement assignments indirectly, apparently to circumvent the rule that a chose in action is not transferable. The critical point in this evolution was passed when the creditor, having given a power of attorney for that purpose, could no longer prevent his "agent" from using his name in the agent's suit.

"Although a person to whom a contract right was owed could not transfer it to one to whom the obligor was not bound in privity, he could appoint an agent or attorney to collect in his place or stead. In time the fictitious agency became irrevocable and the nominal owner, after notice of the assignment to the obligor, lost any power to interfere with the assignee's rights. Thus by the typically muddle-headed process of thinking known as the genius of the common law, assignments of intangibles were made effective in fact while basic theory still proclaimed them to be legal impossibilities." G. Gilmore, 1 Security Interests in Personal Property 202 (1965).

Sections 7.3 and 7.4 of this work provide references to the historical studies, and an entertaining account of their differences.

(2) *Banking Receivables in Volume.* About the first of August, 1979, credit-rating agencies withdrew their approval from debt instruments issued by the Chrysler Financial Corporation. Within three weeks that company arranged for two other financial institutions (Household Finance and General Motors Acceptance) to supply it with hundreds of millions of dollars through purchasing receivables. The payment rights to be assigned grew out of sales by Chrysler automobile dealers and had been assigned by them to Chrysler Financial. An officer of that firm was quoted as saying, "The positive thing about the sales is that they enable Chrysler Financial to continue to provide the kind of financing support to Chrysler dealers that it has in the past." [b] Another large transaction in receivables occurred in 1978, when a group of banks agreed with Sears, Roebuck & Company to supply it with more than a billion dollars, over a period of years, for part of its receivables (not the major part, by any means).

In such a transaction careful attention is paid to the possibility that the rate of default, including non-payment by retail buyers of the goods, will increase markedly. Any number of provisions might be made against that possibility. For one hypothetical example, the purchaser of the receivables might withhold (say) 5% of the purchase price and agree to release it only as the record of collections shows a default rate not greater than twice what the seller has experienced historically. In such an agreement, the idea of default would be carefully defined so as to suit the circumstances. In relation to payment rights acquired by Chrysler Financial from dealers who make themselves responsible for ultimate collection (i. e., sell the paper "with recourse"), default may be confined to the case of non-paying customers of dealers who themselves fail to make good. So conceived, a characteristic default rate experienced by Chrysler Financial prior to the transactions mentioned above is said to have been .0012.[c]

SECTION 1. GENERAL PRINCIPLES

What is the effect of an assignment? Consider the following example:

> A has a right to $100 against B. A assigns his right to C. A's right is thereby extinguished, and C acquires a right against B to receive $100. (Restatement Second, § 317, Illustration 1)

On these facts alone, the Restatement goes on to say, C's right does not amount to much, except the power to enforce the claim without the cooperation of A.[d] For C's right is subject to extinction by any of the following events: revocation of the assignment by A; death of A; re-assignment by A of the same right to D. Revocability is char-

b. "The New York Times," August 19, 1979, Section 3.

c. Ibid.

d. On the historical antecedents of this proposition, see Restatement Second, § 332, Comment a.

acteristic of many assignments. (Until revocation, however, C may disable A from giving an effective discharge to B, by notifying B of the assignment.)

Assignments that are not "gratuitous" are not revocable, as a rule. And only some gift assignments are revocable. In Restatement terms, the issue in the following case was whether or not a gratuitous assignment was made irrevocable.

ADAMS v. MERCED STONE CO.

Supreme Court of California, 1917.
176 Cal. 415, 178 P. 498, 3 A.L.R. 928.

Suit by Edson F. Adams, as executor of the estate of Thomas Prather, deceased, against the Merced Stone Company. From a judgment for defendant and order denying new trial plaintiff appeals. Reversed.

SHAW, J. . . . The court found that during the last sickness of Thomas Prather, to wit, on April 17, 1913, said Thomas Prather made a gift to his brother Samuel D. Prather, of all of the indebtedness due from the defendant to said Thomas, being the indebtedness sued for by the plaintiff herein. That at that time Samuel was the president, the general manager, and a member of the board of directors of the defendant, said defendant being a corporation, and Thomas Prather knew that Samuel held said offices and by reason thereof had full and exclusive charge and control of defendant's books of account, including power to make or direct the making of entries and transfers in said books, and knew that by reason thereof Samuel D. Prather had the means of obtaining possession and control of the said indebtedness so given to him. . . . It is admitted that the asserted gift was made during the last sickness of Thomas Prather, two days before his death, which event occurred on April 19, 1913, and was therefore a gift in view of death. It is also admitted that no change was made upon the books of the defendant regarding said indebtedness, up to the time of the trial of this action, and that when the action was begun the account books of the defendant showed it to be indebted to the said Thomas Prather in the sum claimed in the complaint.

The only evidence of the gift asserted in the answer is found in the testimony of Samuel D. Prather, and is as follows: "In talking business matters my brother said to me, 'Now, in reference to the account of Thomas Prather in the Merced Stone Company, I want to give you that account, all that is due me from that account. I don't know just how to do this, but I give it to you.' . . . A little further in the conversation my brother said to me, 'I give you the keys to my office, the combination of my safe and keys to my desk, and with these I give you all accounts, books, papers, letters, documents, furnishings, pictures, everything that belongs to me in that office. It is yours.' "

[The court quoted California Civil Code, § 1147: "A verbal gift is not valid, unless the means of obtaining possession and control of the thing are given, nor, if it is capable of delivery, unless there is an actual or symbolical delivery of the thing to the donee." The court rejected defendant's construction of the section.] It contemplates that the donor shall do something at the time of making the gift which has the effect of placing in the hands of the donee the means of obtaining the control and possession of the thing given. That the fact that the thing was already in possession of the donee at the time of declaring the gift is not enough, is well settled by the authorities. . . .

In order to comply with the section the "means" must be "given." In the connection in which these words occur the effect is that such means must be given by the donor to the donee. This giving of the means is authorized, where the thing given is not capable of delivery, as a substitute for the actual or symbolical delivery of the thing by the donor to the donee required in cases where such thing is capable of delivery. No good reason can be given for supposing that a transmission or delivery by the donor to the donee of the means was not intended to be as essential in the case of intangible property, as the delivery, actual or symbolical of the thing itself, where it is tangible.

In the case of a chose in action not evidenced by a written instrument, the only means of obtaining control that is recognized by the authorities is an assignment in writing, or some equivalent thereof. . . .

In the present case it is true that Samuel D. Prather was possessed of the physical power and of the official authority, by reason of his relation to the defendant, to make the necessary changes on its books to show that the indebtedness was due to him and not to the decedent. But this power did not emanate from the decedent. Samuel possessed it before the asserted gift as well as after. The decedent did not even authorize him to make such changes, nor suggest that the gift might be effected in that way. It was not shown that such method was in the mind of the donor. The fact that it was a book account, or that a change might be made in the name of the debtor, was not even mentioned in the conversation. The law intends something more than a mere power to make physical entries in the books of the debtor in such a case. The authority to make the change, or cause it to be made, must be vested in the debtor by reason of some act or direction of the creditor. If verbal gifts could be made in such loose manner as this it would open the door to innumerable frauds and perjuries. . . . For this reason the authorities hold that something more than mere physical power is necessary; something more than the previous possession of the property or of the means of obtaining it; something emanating from the donor which operates to give to the donee the means of obtaining such possession and control. . . .

The conclusion of the court below upon the facts found was not in accordance with the law, and its finding of the ultimate fact that Thomas Prather transferred the debt to Samuel D. Prather by way of a verbal gift is not supported by the evidence. Consequently the judgment and order cannot be upheld.

The judgment and order are reversed and the cause is remanded, with directions to the court below to enter judgment upon the findings in favor of the plaintiff for the amount prayed for.

NOTES

(1) *Death-Bed Gifts.* If there had been other witnesses to the conversation between Thomas and Samuel, does it seem that the result would have been different? Would the court have been satisfied with anything less than a writing, containing the decedent's signature? "Speaking for myself," said a lord chancellor of England, "I do not look with any particular favor on these death-bed gifts." [a] The Restatement Second agrees with the ruling in the main case; see § 332.

Suppose that Thomas Prather wishes to make the gift to his other brother, Paul. Instead of speaking to Paul about it, Thomas says to Samuel: "I want you, as president of the Merced Stone Company, to agree that after my death the Company will pay to Paul all that it owes me. In exchange for your promise, I will release the company from its indebtedness to me." Samuel agrees, acting as the company's authorized agent. After Thomas' death, may his executor (Adams) made a successful claim for the amount owing? What arguments would you make in favor of Paul? Is there anything more about the transaction that tends to remove the suspicion commonly surrounding an oral death-bed gift?

(2) *Writing and Revocability.* The Uniform Commercial Code provides that certain assignments are not enforceable against the assignor or third parties unless he has signed a "security agreement." Section 9–203(1)(a). This section does not speak of assignments in terms, but it clearly applies to all transactions that are "financing" assignments, in a broad sense. For certain "sale" assignments, other than those effected by security agreements, the Code requires a signed writing in Section 1–206. Nothing in the Code applies to a gift assignment. By statute in New York, the absence of consideration does not entail the conclusion that an assignment is revocable, if it is in writing and signed by the assignor.[b]

As to "symbolic" documents referred to in subsection (1)(b), see Comment c. Representative examples are savings-bank account books and certain life insurance policies. See also Restatement Second, § 342(b).

(3) *A Case of Two Wives.* After his second marriage, John Cassiday brought home from the office a folder containing two certificates of insur-

a. Ashbourne, quoted in Williston, Gifts of Rights, 40 Yale L.J. 1 (1930).

b. Gen.Obl.L. § 5–1107. Compare § 5–708[a](9).

ance on his life, and placed it in a dresser drawer. His former wife, Margaret, was named as beneficiary on these certificates, and that designation was never changed. Yet when he brought them home John said to his wife, Edytha: "the beneficiaries are changed . . . and he also said he didn't want that woman [Margaret] to have any more of his money." After John died, a contest arose between the two women over the proceeds, and the insurer brought an interpleader action. From a judgment for Margaret, Edytha appealed. *Held:* Affirmed. It was found that John had made no parol assignment or gift of the two policies in question to Edytha. "He did not say: 'Edytha, I give you these policies.' He did not say: 'Edytha, these policies are yours.' . . . [H]e exhibited no intention either to give or assign the policies to Edytha." Cassiday v. Cassiday, 256 Md. 5, 259 A.2d 299 (1969).

Even if John had said what the court suggested, Edytha's claim would probably have failed in some courts, for want of delivery of the certificates to her. On the other hand, a symbolic or a "constructive" delivery sometimes meets the requirement. In the attempt to apply these conceptions, especially to intangible assets, the courts have made some refined distinctions. See Brooks v. Mitchell, 163 Md. 1, 161 A. 261, 84 A.L.R. 547 (1932); Rohan, Delivery in the Law of Gifts, 38 Ind.L.J. 1 (1962), 470 (1963). If John had handed the insurance certificates to Edytha for her to place in the dresser drawer, should that be regarded as a sufficient delivery?

FORM OF ASSIGNMENT

For making an assignment, it is agreed, no particular expression or form of words is required. However, it may be helpful to consider an excerpt from a form of assignment prepared by the American Bankers Association. The form is designed for use by a bank in taking an assignment of a life insurance policy from a borrower, as security for a loan: [a]

> For Value Received the undersigned hereby assign, transfer and set over to ______, its successors and assigns, (herein called the "Assignee") Policy No. ______ issued by ______ (herein called the "Insurer") . . . and any supplementary contracts issued in connection therewith . . . ., upon the life of ______ . . . and all claims, options, privileges, rights, title and interest therein and thereunder . . . .

According to Restatement Second, § 324, "It is essential to an assignment of a right that the obligee manifest an intention to transfer the right to another person without further action or manifestation of intention." The manifestation is usually made to the "other person," but it may also be made to a third person on his behalf; e. g., a borrower might make an assignment of an insurance claim to a bank by a suitable indication to the insurer. However, in such a case, special problems arise in characterizing the terms used. If obligee (A) says

a. Reprinted with permission of the Association.

to obligor (B), "I direct you to pay what you owe me to C," is that an assignment? If he says, "I authorize you to discharge your debt to me by paying C," is that an assignment? The Restatement Second states that an order to pay may be an assignment, but only in special circumstances. See section 325. The following illustration is given:

> A writes to B, "Please pay to C the balance due me." This is insufficient to establish an assignment . . . But the letter would be an effective assignment if delivered to C to pay or secure a debt owed by A to C.

Assignments have often been contrasted with promises to make payments. See Christmas v. Russell's Executors, 81 U.S. 69, 84 (1871): "An agreement to pay out of a particular fund, however clear in its terms, is not an equitable assignment . . . ."

PROBLEM

Which of the following documents most clearly effects an assignment? How would you redraft the others so as to make it clear that an assignment is being given?

(a) The owner of a store suffers a large loss when a Navy jet crashes into it. As a result he has a claim against his insurance company and also a tort claim against the United States. The insurer makes a loan to him for immediate repairs, in the amount of $100,000, and he gives it a document in this form: "In consideration of the loan, I will pay you all sums paid to me by the United States on account of my loss up to the amount of $100,000." See Arkwright Mutual Ins. Co. v. Bargain City, U. S. A., Inc., 251 F.Supp. 221 (E.D.Pa.1966).

(b) A real estate broker (A) earns a commission, with the help of another (C), and before it is paid gives him this signed document: "In consideration of $1 I hereby agree with C that he is entitled to one-half of the commission earned from the sale of Blackacre." See Donovan v. Middlebrook, 95 App.Div. 365, 88 N.Y.S. 607 (Sup.Ct.1904).

(c) A sends a signed document to his tailor (C) reading: "First Bank. Pay to the order of C $100 (One Hundred) Dollars." A has a large checking account in First Bank. See UCC 3–409(1): "A check or other draft does not of itself operate as an assignment . . ." (For an assignment in the form of a computer entry see Delbrueck & Co. v. Mfrs. Hanover Trust Co., 609 F.2d 1047 (2d Cir. 1979).)

(d) Siler obtains a contract for work on a telephone-company project. Before starting, he obtains a bank loan and executes this document: "I, Vernon Siler, do hereby sell, assign and transfer to the First National Bank . . . my right, title and interest in the funds due me from Mountain States Telephone Company on Job No. N–3–0868 . . . ." See First Nat. Bank v. Mountain States Telephone & Telegraph Co., 91 N.M. 126, 571 P.2d 118 (1977).

NOTE

Legal Effect Without Assignment. If any of the documents set out in the preceding note is not an assignment, it does not follow that the document is legally insignificant. It is clear, for instance, that a bank may charge the checking account of a customer upon payment of a check properly drawn by him, issued, and indorsed and presented by the payee. Do you find the elements of a contract in any of the transactions described above? [a]

FUTURITY

"Concededly the courts have encountered some difficulty in defining the contours of a future right or interest for purposes of assignment law." [b] For one advancing a claim on the strength of an assignment, this means that his hopes may be dashed if the claim has a quality that may be called *futurity*. According to the Restatement Second, a right expected to arise in the future can be effectively assigned, but the rule is qualified in important ways. See section 321.[c]

The problem may be illustrated by the facts in Shiro v. Drew, 174 F.Supp. 495 (D.Me.1959), which grew out of the financial difficulties of the American Fiberlast Company. Fiberlast borrowed some $2,000 from Drew on or about November 1, 1956, and gave him the following letter: "To Gordon L. Drew: Whereas the American Fiberlast Co. has received a contract for a 21′ Radome from Hazeltine Electronics Corp. totaling $4900 but is unable to finance the purchase of the necessary materials and labor to construct the dome—the American Fiberlast Co. agrees that any money advanced by Mr. Drew for the specific expense of manufacturing the Radome will be paid immediately to Mr. Drew upon receipt of Hazeltine's remittance irrespective of any other demands from other creditors."

This letter was not needed to establish Drew's right to repayment of the loan. Its object was, rather, to provide him with a right

a. There is even a possibility that a right to payment may become subject to a security interest, of sorts, by an agreement between its owner and a creditor of his, though it does not embody an assignment. At best, such an interest, known as an equitable lien, is of limited value to the creditor; and the precedents supporting it are unstable. For an elaborate essay on the doctrine, see Warren Tool Co. v. Stephenson, 11 Mich.App. 274, 161 N.W.2d 133 (1968).

Constructive trust doctrine has also been used to bridge a chasm between the entitlement of a claimant and the source of the right which is claimed. Simonds v. Simonds, 45 N.Y.2d 233, 408 N.Y.S.2d 359, 380 N.E.2d 189 (1978); see Gegan, Constructive Trusts: A New Basis for Tracing Equities, 53 St. John's L.Rev. 593 (1979).

b. Law Research Service, Inc. v. Martin Lutz Appellate Printers, Inc., 498 F.2d 836 (2d Cir. 1974).

c. See especially Illustration 5.

Assignments of rights to payment yet to become due were recognized in du-Pont de-Bie v. Vredenburgh, 490 F.2d 1057 (4th Cir. 1974) (separation agreement), and In re Freeman, 489 F.2d 431 (9th Cir. 1973) (income-tax refund).

For a case concerning the musical "My Fair Lady" and a covey of celebrities see Speelman v. Pascal, 10 N.Y.2d 313, 222 N.Y.S.2d 324, 178 N.E.2d 723 (1961). Cf. Summers v. Freishstat, 274 Md. 404, 335 A.2d 89 (1975).

of repayment out of the proceeds of the Radome contract, to the exclusion of other creditors of Fiberlast. In other words, it was designed to give Drew a security interest. The enactment of the Uniform Commercial Code has removed any doubt that a lender can achieve that object by complying with Article 9, on Secured Transactions. As late as 1942, however, a New York lender very nearly came to grief in relying on the security of the borrower's executory contracts.[d] In that case the court first ruled that the security agreement was ineffectual. The lender's petition for rehearing was supported by several New York banks, as amici curiae. According to Corbin, the banks "showed the court that in the period of one week the banks had lent to wartime contractors the amount of $600 million on no other security than an assignment of the contractors' rights to future payments by the Government, all of the rights so assigned being conditional on performances still to be rendered by the assignors. . . . The shock produced by this showing caused the two majority judges (men of the very highest honor and ability) to reverse their decision." Corbin, § 903, Supp.

A creditor may seize his debtor's right to a contract payment through the process of garnishment or (as it is known in some states) attachment, creating a lien on it for the satisfaction of his claim. Unless an assignment of the right is effectual in foreclosing garnishment of it, it fails of its essential purpose. Before the Code was widely enacted, an enormous volume of financing was subject to a certain risk owing to the doubts that courts entertained about assignments of "future" rights. When Fiberlast borrowed from Drew, of course, it had already contracted with Hazeltine, and had an existing "contract right." This term has been defined as a right to payment not yet earned by performance.[e] Subsequently, Fiberlast completed construction of the Radome, thereby acquiring a right to payment. Such a right might be called an earned account,[f] and the power to assign it has long been established. Obviously Fiberlast could not wait until it had an account to make an assignment, for it needed loan money to turn its contract right into an account.

A more acute problem of "futurity" is presented when funds are obtained on the strength of contracts not in existence, but which the borrower expects to make later. There is a deep-seated conceptual difficulty about recognizing a present transfer of a non-existent right. However, there is a commercial need for obtaining funds in reliance on anticipated contracts. Many merchants who extend

d. Rockmore v. Lehman, 128 F.2d 564 (2d Cir. 1942), reversed on rehearing 129 F.2d 892 (1942), cert. denied, 317 U.S. 700 (1943).

e. UCC 9–106, 1962 Official Text. The 1972 Text retains the conception in other terms. See note *o* infra.

f. This is the only sort of right called an "account" in the 1962 version of the Code.

short-term credit to their customers have accounts receivable on their books at all times, which may be large and fairly constant in amount. From month to month, however, the specific accounts outstanding are different. Many merchants, both dealers and manufacturers, obtain liquid capital from financial institutions which rely, for security, on assignments of such accounts. If an assignment had no prospective effect, the security would rapidly be depleted by payments of the accounts outstanding at the time of the assignment. Rather than taking a new assignment each month, or oftener, the lender will wish to be secured by new accounts as they arise, so that the security is continually replenished. The following form of "assignment" is suggested in the Restatement Second: Merchant assigns as security "all the book debts due and owing or which may during the continuance of this security become due and owing" to the merchant.[g] The Restatement uses quotation marks on the word "assignment" to indicate that the lender is not truly an assignee at the time of the agreement, as to accounts yet to arise. "Strictly there cannot be an effective assignment of a right not yet in existence." [h]

If that were the whole story, the lender could not be effectively protected against creditors of the merchant who might levy writs of garnishment on the "future" accounts. However, means have been found to make the assignment effectual, under both judicial and legislative auspices. The judicial approach is to treat the "assignment" as a contract to make an assignment of each account as it arises, and to implement the contract as if it had been performed. According to Restatement Second, § 330, the effect of a contract to make an assignment is "determined by the rules relating to specific performance . . . ." If the promisee is entitled to specific performance, his right "resembles that of an assignee, and it is sometimes referred to as an 'equitable assignment' or 'equitable lien.' " [i]

The Uniform Commercial Code appears to renounce this approach.[j] In any event, it provides a mechanism by which an agreement for a security interest in an account or contract right not yet in existence may preempt the claims of creditors of the assignor. Some features of this mechanism are described in the Note, Assignments, Bankruptcy, and Creditors, p. 1172 infra. The result is that, for transactions within the Code, it is both unnecessary and undesirable to rely on the equity doctrine referred to above. According to an official report made on Article 9 in 1971, "This Article rejects any lingering common law notion that only rights already earned can be assigned." [k]

g. Section 330, Illustration 7.

h. Restatement Second, § 331, Comment b.

i. Id., § 330, Comment c.

j. Yet there is controversy about the extent to which equitable liens are compatible with the Code. See the first case cited in n. a supra.

k. Final Report, Review Committee for Article 9, Permanent Editorial Board for the UCC, 46.

The unstable effects of an "assignment" of rights not yet in existence are partly traceable to historical factors and to conceptual difficulties. But a more suitable ground for giving it a limited effect may sometimes be found in a "public policy which seeks to protect the assignor and third parties against transfers which may be improvident or fraudulent." Restatement Second, § 321, Comment b. Such a policy is especially prominent in relation to an employee's assignment of earnings that are not matured claims.[l]

NOTES

(1) *Assigning Proceeds.* Refer again to the terms of Fiberlast's letter to Drew: it agreed that "any money advanced by Mr. Drew . . . will be paid immediately to Mr. Drew upon receipt of Hazeltine's remittance . . . ." Could better language have been chosen to express an assignment of the contract right? Consider the following rule: "the assignment of after-acquired proceeds of a claim is generally considered an assignment only of a future right and, therefore, the assignment does not give the assignee priority over lienors who have attached before the proceeds have come into existence." Harold Moorstein & Co. v. Excelsior Ins. Co., 25 N.Y.2d 651, 254 N.E.2d 766 (1969).

The court that stated the foregoing rule also adheres to the view that an effective transfer of a "present" claim is possible, although it has not yet matured, or is disputed, or is dependent upon future conditions.[m] Do you see a way of reconciling these views?[n] Outside the range of the Code, the subject continues to defy understanding. For an impressive essay on the subject, see the opinion of Justice Breitel, in Stathos v. Murphy, 26 A.D.2d 500, 276 N.Y.S.2d 727 (1st Dept.1966), aff'd, 19 N.Y.2d 883, 227 N.E.2d 880 (1967).

(2) *Problem.* After Fiberlast has completed construction of the Radome, and before Hazeltine has paid it the price, a bank sues Fiberlast on an overdue loan and serves a writ of garnishment on Hazeltine. Drew intervenes, asserting a superior interest in the proceeds of the contract. Should the court direct Hazeltine to pay Drew or the bank? Garnishment is a lien-producing legal proceeding. Does Restatement Second, § 341 answer the question? (The phrasing of subsection (2) is based on the final case in this book.)

l. See Commodore v. Armour & Co., 201 Kan. 412, 441 P.2d 815 (1968); New England Merchants Nat. Bank v. Herron, 243 A.2d 722 (Me.1968).

Assignments of future wages are generally prohibited in some states, and are regulated in one way or another in almost all others, especially as they may be used as security for small loans. A compilation of statutes appears in Introductory Note to Chapter 15 of Restatement Second.

m. Note the court's reliance, in the case last cited, on Stathos v. Murphy, cited below.

n. See State Farm Mutual Automobile Ins. Co. v. Pohl, 255 Or. 46, 464 P.2d 321 (1970).

UCC 9–318

INTRODUCTION

Meet next a provision about assignments found in Article 9 of the Uniform Commercial Code: section 9–318. It has a bearing on nearly all the rest of this book. Almost every phrase of the statute offers a challenge to understanding; but for the moment you need be concerned with only a part of it. In the case following the statute, the plaintiff sued to enforce an assigned right to payment, and one of the defenses made was that payment had already been made—properly—to the assignor. A defense of that character is governed by subsection (1)(b)—assuming that the assignment is one within Article 9. (A note on scope appears at p. 1155 infra below.) For the moment, attention may be focussed on that and on subsection (3).

Defenses Against Assignee; Modification of Contract After Notification of Assignment; Term Prohibiting Assignment Ineffective; Identification and Proof of Assignment.

(1) Unless an account debtor has made an enforceable agreement not to assert defenses or claims arising out of a sale as provided in Section 9–206 the rights of an assignee are subject to

(a) all the terms of the contract between the account debtor and assignor and any defense or claim arising therefrom; and

(b) any other defense or claim of the account debtor against the assignor which accrues before the account debtor receives notification of the assignment.

(2) So far as the right to payment or a part thereof under an assigned contract has not been fully earned by performance,[o] and

o. In 1972 the sponsors of the UCC proposed amendments to the previous Official Text—that of 1962. By all odds the most extensive amendments were made in Article 9, and they did not leave section 9–318 untouched. However, the principal change there may fairly be called editorial in character. (One that cannot was an alteration in subsection (4) so as to add the material about a general intangible and about a requirement of the debtor's consent.) The editorial changes are reflected in subsection (2) by the "not fully earned" passage, and in subsection (3) by the phrase "amount due or to become due." Unlike the current Official Text, the 1962 version contained a definition of "contract right," which embraced most payment rights "not yet earned by performance." In that version the definition of "account" seems to have been restricted to *earned* payment rights; the thought was that a contract right (usually) turns into an account when an executory contract is performed on the payee's side. The revisers considered that the expression "contract right" could be dispensed with. By broadening the definition of account they simplified some parts of Article 9. But in section 9–318 the distinction had to be reintroduced. In subsection (2) that was accomplished by putting a

notwithstanding notification of the assignment, any modification of or substitution for the contract made in good faith and in accordance with reasonable commercial standards is effective against an assignee unless the account debtor has otherwise agreed but the assignee acquires corresponding rights under the modified or substituted contract. The assignment may provide that such modification or substitution is a breach by the assignor.

(3) The account debtor is authorized to pay the assignor until the account debtor receives notification that the amount due or to become due has been assigned and that payment is to be made to the assignee. A notification which does not reasonably identify the rights assigned is ineffective. If requested by the account debtor, the assignee must seasonably furnish reasonable proof that the assignment has been made and unless he does so the account debtor may pay the assignor.

(4) A term in any contract between an account debtor and an assignor is ineffective if it prohibits assignment of an account . . . or requires the account debtor's consent to such assignment or security interest.[p]

NOTES

(1) *Perfection.* The efficacy of an assignment of accounts as against creditors of the assignor is largely determined by Article 9 of the Code. For that purpose the assignee must not only take steps to make the assignment enforceable against the assignor, by putting it in proper form, but must also file a paper known as a "financing statement" in an appropriate public office. The indispensable contents of a financing statement do little more than advise an inquirer that there is, or may be, a transaction in accounts between the assignor and the assignee. (A mechanism is provided whereby he may obtain further particulars by directing a quiz to the assignee who has filed: UCC 9–208.) The form commonly prescribed for filing is known as the "UCC-1." The essentials are stated in UCC 9–402(3). The filing is one step required for accomplishing a technical condition known as "perfection" of the assignee's interest. Some consequences of non-perfection are indicated at p. 1174 infra.[q]

qualification on the term "assigned contract;" and in subsection (3) where the word "account" had been used it was deleted in favor of "amount due or to become due." The 1972 amendments had been enacted in most states by 1979.

p. Several definitional provisions of the Code are germane to UCC 9–318. Some of them are as follows:

"'Account' means any right to payment for goods sold or leased or for services rendered which is not evidenced by an instrument or chattel paper, whether or not it has been earned by performance." UCC 9–106.

"'Account debtor' means the person who is obligated on an account [or] chattel paper . . . ." UCC 9–105(1)(a). [Chattel paper is illustrated by the conditional sale contract described at p. 1114 infra.]

As to notification see UCC 1–201(26). [The definitional references are to the 1972 Official Text.]

q. This note concerns only assignments affected by Article 9 of the Code. Some are not: see Note, p. 1155 infra.

Under Article 9 perfection is critical to the efficacy not only of security interests in (and sales of) accounts but

The point now to be noticed is that the filing of a UCC–1 does not effect notification of the account debtor under UCC 9–318. Chase Manhattan Bank (N.A.) v. State, 40 N.Y.2d 590, 388 N.Y.S.2d 896, 357 N.E.2d 366 (1976) (state as account debtor); see Restatement Second, § 338, Comment e.

(2) *Timing and Diction.* The notification condition in UCC 9–318(3) was pre-destined to cause controversy: "That the amount due . . . *has been* assigned and that payment *is to be made* to the assignee." First, there is the case of the financer who writes, "I intend to take an assignment from X of his rights against you," and gets an acknowledgement. Right kind of notification? See C.I.T. Corp. v. Glennan, 137 Cal.App. 636, 31 P.2d 430 (1934); Time Finance Corp. v. Johnson Trucking Co., 23 Utah 2d 115, 458 P.2d 873 (1969). (What of amounts becoming due under contracts not yet made at the time of the assignment?) Second, there is the case of the assignment simply presented to the obligor without a special instruction to redirect his payments. See First Nat. Bank v. Mountain States Telephone & Telegraph Co., 91 N.M. 126, 571 P.2d 118 (1977). Should the Code language be read with indulgence for the assignee whose timing or diction is imperfect?

ERTEL v. RADIO CORP. OF AMERICA

Supreme Court of Indiana, 1974.
261 Ind. 573, 307 N.E.2d 471.

[The Delta Engineering Corporation obtained a loan from the Economy Finance Corporation, and to secure it assigned some accounts receivable to Economy. From time to time Delta made shipments of its products to RCA, giving rise to payment rights which were the subject of assignment. The loan to Delta was represented by a note, and its payment was guaranteed by two officers of Delta: its president and general manager, John Dugan, and its secretary-treasurer, John Ertel. When Delta defaulted on payment of the note, Economy sued all three. The only one having an apparent ability to pay was Ertel (Dugan had disappeared). Ertel made a third-party complaint against RCA; his theory was that upon paying Economy he would be subrogated to its rights as assignee. (A surety who satisfies the obligation of the principal debtor—here Delta—is entitled to the benefit of a security interest held by the creditor, such as the accounts assigned to Economy in this case.) RCA contested its liability on two grounds: (1) that it had paid Delta for the machinery delivered to it before receiving notification of the assignment, and (2) that one set of goods delivered by Delta failed to conform to

also of security interests in a wide range of other personal property, including inventory and equipment. There are means other than filing under Article 9 for perfecting security interests in goods: for another, the Code allows for perfection by possession in the secured party. That is not feasible for collateral in the form of pure intangibles such as accounts, of course.

the contract, and that the default caused expense which RCA was entitled to offset against the assigned accounts.[a]

The trial court gave judgment for Economy on its claim against Ertel, and he paid it. His claim against RCA was denied. However this part of the judgment was reversed on appeal; the Indiana Court of Appeals ruled that neither of RCA's defenses was good.[b] On further review in the Supreme Court of the state, Ertel was less successful. As will be seen, that court decided the case by reference to UCC 9–318. It concluded that the defense of payment was defective, but that RCA had a setoff defense under subsection (1)(b) of 9–318. The court's discussion of setoff appears below at p. 1159. At this point only its treatment of the "wrongful payment" issue is given.]

HUNTER, Justice.

. . .

There are three major issues presented for our consideration:

1. Does Economy have a claim against RCA for wrongful payments?

2. Is Ertel, as guarantor of the note, subrogated to Economy's rights against RCA?

3. Does RCA have rights of set-off against Economy and, therefore, against Ertel?

I *Economy's claim against RCA*

[The court set out UCC 9–318(3), and continued:]

Section 9–318(3) clearly delineates the legal relationship between the account debtor (RCA) and the assignee (Economy) once the account debtor receives adequate notification of an assignment. The account debtor, upon receipt of said notification, is duty-bound to pay the assignee and not the assignor. Payment to an assignor, after notification of assignment, does not relieve the account debtor of his obligation to pay the assignee unless the assignee consents to such a collection process. (See official Comment #3, 9–318.) The account debtor's failure to pay the assignee after receiving due notification gives rise to an assignee's claim for wrongful payment.

In order to determine liability for wrongful payment, we must ascertain whether or not RCA received adequate notification as required by 9–318(3). Notification is nowhere defined in 9–318(3), but is defined in 1–201(26).

a. RCA pleaded both *setoff* and *counterclaim* in this respect. It also contested Ertel's right of subrogation as a guarantor. Both of the two appellate courts considering that issue resolved it in Ertel's favor; their reasoning on the issue is not represented here.

b. Ertel v. Radio Corp. of America, 297 N.E.2d 446 (1973).

[Here the court set out that provision.]

The following facts are stipulated in the record:

1. On or about May 12, 1969, Economy Finance Corp. mailed written notice of assignment to the RCA Magnetic Products Division, Indianapolis.

2. Notice was sent by certified mail.

3. A dock employee of RCA Magnetic Products Division receipted for said notice by signature on May 14, 1969.

4. The mail was normally delivered by the post office to the receiving dock.

5. Dock employees were authorized to sign receipts for certified mail.

6. The notice was never received by the accounting department.[c]

The above facts, in our judgment, demonstrate receipt of notification as contemplated by 1–201(26). The fact that the accounting department never received the notice is of no consequence in this case. The notice was duly delivered and received at the appropriate place by an authorized agent of RCA. The negligence of RCA employees after the initial receipt at the dock should not be charged to Economy Finance, but rather to RCA. To hold otherwise is to circumvent the obvious policy behind 1–201(26). Therefore, we hold, as the Court of Appeals held, that RCA was notified of the assignment and that, as a consequence, Economy has a claim for wrongful payment.

NOTES

(1) *Acceptance.* The Arrow Construction Co., general contractors for a building, subcontracted the glass work to the Border Glass Co. Border assigned its expected earnings on the job to the Bank of Yuma as security for loans. The bank presented the assignment to Arrow, which signed an "acceptance" in these words: "the undersigned agrees to pay all moneys due under said [glass] contract, to the Bank of Yuma . . . with the understanding that acceptance of this assignment places no greater burden upon the undersigned than if this assignment had not been accepted . . ." Arrow received checks for the glass work from time to time, which it endorsed in such a way that Border could use them to pay the firm supplying it with glass. As a result, the bank's loans were not repaid, and it sued Arrow. From judgment for the defendant, the plaintiff appealed. *Held:* Reversed. Arrow argued that the terms of its acceptance relieved it of the necessity of indorsing the checks specially, so that they could not be

c. From the Court of Appeals opinion: "Economy notified RCA by registered mail of the assignment prior to any payments by RCA; said notice . . . identified the rights assigned, and required payment be made to Economy; RCA has stipulated that the assignment was valid and that the notice was received at its shipping dock . . . . RCA contends that although it may have had technical 'notice' it did not have knowledge since the notice sent by Economy never reached the accounting department at RCA. RCA offers no factual explanation as to why this mix-up occurred."

cashed without the bank's signature. The court said: "This argument is fallacious. When notice of an assignment is given to and received by the debtor, he becomes liable to pay the assignee, whether he accepts the assignment or not." Arrow was held liable to pay the bank the amount of its unpaid loans. Bank of Yuma v. Arrow Constr. Co., 106 Ariz. 582, 480 P.2d 338 (1971).

(2) *Discharge After Assignment.* "Except as stated in this Section, notwithstanding an assignment, the assignor retains his power to discharge or modify the duty of the obligor to the extent that the obligor performs or otherwise gives value until but not after the obligor receives notification that the right has been assigned and that performance is to be rendered to the assignee." Restatement Second, § 338(1). Ensuing subsections state some qualifications, one of which has to do with possession of "symbolic documents." [d]

(3) *Relief for Mistake.* For whatever it might be worth, RCA has a claim against Delta Engineering for the amount of its "wrongful payment," if Delta was unjustly enriched thereby. Is there any doubt that this is so? As for restitutionary claims as affected by a statute, see Great American Ins. Co. v. United States, 492 F.2d 821 (Ct.Cl.1974).

KEEPING THE 9–318 RULES IN BOUNDS

The principle of estoppel is to supplement the provisions of the Uniform Commercial Code, unless it is "displaced by the particular provisions" thereof. UCC 1–103. Is the following rule one that displaces estoppel?—"the rights of an assignee are subject to . . . any defense or claim arising" from the contract between the account debtor and the assignor. UCC 9–318(1)(a). Note the "unless" clause preceding the rule as quoted.

In Dimmit & Owens Financial, Inc. v. Realtek Ind., Inc., 90 Mich.App. 429, 280 N.W.2d 827 (1979), the court gave an answer favorable to the assignee, Financial, Inc. The right assigned represented earnings of Art Clover for masonry work on an apartment project. Officers of the builder, Realtek, executed an acknowledgement that the amount of Clover's invoice was just and correct, due and approved, and not contingent on any past or future performance by Clover. One who signed testified that he did so because he needed Clover to continue on the job and knew he did not have enough money to pay his materialmen. Another testified that he expected Financial, Inc. to make an advance to Clover after he signed; and in fact it did

d. If a claim is represented by a symbolic document, it is not safe for the obligor to render performance to the original obligee without requiring him to produce it: "Non-production has the same effect as receipt of notification of assignment . . . . In addition, the obligor who performs without surrender or cancellation of or appropriate notation on the writing takes the risk of further obligation to an assignee who takes possession of the writing as a bona fide purchaser. The latter rule may be regarded as an application of a broader doctrine of estoppel." Restatement Second, § 338, Comment h. See also § 342, Comment f.

issue checks to Realtek for delivery to Clover. Apparently Clover did not do what he should have done with the funds advanced, and so left Realtek exposed to loss. Realtek contended that Financial, Inc. should bear that loss, pointing to section 9–318(1)(a). The court concluded that the acknowledgement, and the assignee's reliance on it, gave rise to an estoppel against Realtek.[a]

Would it be possible, on these facts, to find an enforceable agreement by Realtek not to assert claims or defenses arising out of its contract with Clover against Financial, Inc. as assignee? If so, perhaps the court need not have addressed the estoppel problem. (Even so, there was probably no such agreement as that mentioned in the opening clause of UCC 9–318, for two reasons. First, section 9–206 concerns agreements by buyers and lessees (only); and second it appears *not* to concern agreements made between such a party *and an assignee.*) Possibly section 9–318(1) should be understood as if it incorporated a further limitation something like this: "Unless . . . and unless the assignee establishes a ground of recovery from the account debtor based on dealings directly between them . . . ."

Consider subsections (2) through (4) of 9–318: May any or all of these rules be freely varied by arrangements that an account debtor and an assignee agree upon between themselves? If not, why not?

NOTES

(1) *Battle of the Forms: Further Skirmishes.* A life insurance company received an "assignment questionnaire" from a bank. The paper described a policy on the life of Lionel Birkeland, called for particulars about premiums, and concluded, "In the event of premium default, will you notify assignee in ample time for assignee to protect its collateral?" The assignee was the bank, of course: it had made a loan to Birkeland and taken an assignment from him of his rights in the policy ("collateral") to the extent necessary to protect the loan. With the questionnaire the bank sent a copy of the assignment.

In answer to the question, the insurance company wrote "No." The bank did not take this for an answer, however, and after a time sent another questionnaire. This time the answer was "Yes." After about three years the policy lapsed because an annual premium went unpaid. Another three years passed, and Birkeland died, leaving the bank loan unpaid. What more facts are needed to establish a claim against the insurance company based on promissory estoppel? The bank showed that after receiving the answer to its second questionnaire it continued to lend money to Birkeland and did not seek other collateral. See Northwestern Bank of Commerce v. Employers' Life Ins. Co., 281 N.W.2d 164 (Minn.1979). (On recovery by the bank, subrogation to its claim against the Birkeland estate, in favor of the insurance company, is presumably in order.)

a. But see Bank of Commerce v. Intermountain Gas Co., 96 Idaho 29, 523 P.2d 1375 (1974).

At least an equal hazard for an insurer, probably, is that its contract will remain in force and that (forgetting the assignment) it will pay the wrong party (e. g., the policy beneficiary instead of the bank). The seriousness of this risk for payors of various types appears in many cases, some of them cited below. The payor may sometimes hope to get control of the paperwork of an assignment—even to the point of providing a form for the assignment—with a view to limiting the risk. How would you write a form for minimizing the payor's risks? [b]

(2) *Problem.* What is the best way, on the following facts, to arrive at the conclusion that Milk Producers, Inc. (MPI) is *not* accountable to Edith Raley (ER)?

ER gave credit to a dairyman (N) on an agreement for payment, in monthly installments, from the proceeds on N's milk sales. MPI was N's selling agent. ER's lawyer wrote to MPI, saying, "By the terms of the contract you are to mail $2,000 to ER on the 20th day of each month from the proceeds of sales of N's milk." He enclosed this form for MPI to sign:

> N does hereby authorize MPI to pay to ER, from the proceeds of milk sold, $2,000 on or before the 20th day of each month until $60,000 has been paid.

MPI answered that the "authorization" was unacceptable. It cited a federal regulation permitting it, as selling agent, to make deductions from a producer's checks only as "authorized in writing" by him. MPI said it would accept an assignment only on a form that it provided. For a reason not explained, MPI was then provided with an authorization on its form, signed by N, to pay *$1,000* a month to ER; and it made payments accordingly over a period of eight months. Unable to collect more of her claim from N, ER sues MPI for the amount it has disbursed to N in violation of the attorney's direction.

Among the possible answers to the question above are these:

—The papers prepared by the attorney only *authorized* payments as ER desired, and did not accomplish an assignment to her.

—ER failed to furnish proof of the assignment as she was required to do upon request made by MPI, the "account debtor." See UCC 9–318(3).

—Contrary to these conclusions, MPI was at first bound to pay ER $2,000 a month; but that direction was superseded by the authorization to pay the lesser amount in the form later executed by N.

—None of the conclusions above is correct. However, ER's failure to protest shortfalls in the payments made by MPI over a period of eight months is a basis for holding her estopped to claim against MPI.

For some support for three of these answers, see Raley v. Milk Producers, Inc., 90 N.M. 720, 568 P.2d 246 (1977).[c]

b. See Federal Nat. Bank & Trust Co. v. Owen, 389 F.2d 457 (10th Cir. 1968); Worthen Bank & Trust Co. v. Franklin Life Ins. Co., 370 F.2d 97 (8th Cir. 1966).

c. It is a remarkable discovery, having considerable commercial potential, that UCC 3–306(b) expresses an implied limitation on the reach of UCC 9–318. Citizens Nat. Bank of Orlando v. Bornstein, 27 UCC Rep. 242 (Fla.1979) (assignment of bank certificate of deposit).

In connection with point 3, consider UCC 9–318(1). Was the suggested defense one which arose from the contract between N and ER? If the answer appears uncertain, what further facts would clarify the matter?

SECTION 2. ASSIGNMENT AND DELEGATION IN CONNECTION WITH THE SALE OF A BUSINESS

THE BRITISH WAGGON CO. AND THE PARKGATE WAGGON CO. v. LEA & CO.

Queen's Bench Division, 1880.
5 Q.B.D. 149.

COCKBURN, C. J. This was an action brought by the plaintiffs to recover rent for the hire of certain railway waggons, alleged to be payable by the defendants to the plaintiffs, or one of them, under the following circumstances:

By an agreement in writing of February 10th, 1874, the Parkgate Waggon Company let to the defendants, who are coal merchants, fifty railway waggons for a term of seven years, at a yearly rent of £600 a year, payable by equal quarterly payments. By a second agreement of June 13th, 1874, the company in like manner let to the defendants fifty other waggons, at a yearly rent of £625, payable quarterly like the former.

Each of these agreements contained the following clause: "The owners, their executors, or administrators, will at all times during the said term, except as herein provided, keep the said waggons in good and substantial repair and working order, and, on receiving notice from the tenant of any want of repairs, and the number or numbers of the waggons requiring to be repaired, and the place or places where it or they then is or are, will, with all reasonable despatch, cause the same to be repaired and put into good working order."

On October 24th, 1874, the Parkgate Company passed a resolution, under the 129th section of the Companies Act, 1862, for the voluntary winding up of the company. Liquidators were appointed, and by an order of the Chancery Division of the High Court of Justice, it was ordered that the winding up of the company should be continued under the supervision of the Court.

By an indenture of April 1st, 1878, the Parkgate Company assigned and transferred, and the liquidators confirmed to the British Company and their assigns, among other things, all sums of money, whether payable by way of rent, hire, interest, penalty, or damage, then due, or thereafter to become due, to the Parkgate Company, by virtue of the two contracts, and all the interest of the Parkgate Company and the said liquidators therein; the British Company, on the other hand covenanting with the Parkgate Company "to observe and perform such of the stipulations, conditions, provisions, and agreements contained in the said contracts as, according to the terms thereof were stipulated to be observed and performed by the Parkgate Company." On the execution of this assignment the British Company took over from the Parkgate Company the repairing stations, which had previously been used by the Parkgate Company for the repair of the waggons let to the defendants, and also the staff of workmen employed by the latter company in executing such repairs. It was expressly found that the British Company have ever since been ready and willing to execute, and have, with all due diligence, executed all necessary repairs to the said waggons. . . .

The main contention on the part of the defendants, however, was that, as the Parkgate Company had, by assigning the contracts, and by making over their repairing stations to the British Company, incapacitated themselves to fulfill their obligation to keep the waggons in repair, that company had no right, as between themselves and the defendants, to substitute a third party to do the work they had engaged to perform, nor were the defendants bound to accept the party so substituted as the one to whom they were to look for performance of the contract; the contract was therefore at an end.

The authority principally relied on in support of this contention was the case of Robson v. Drummond, 2 B. & Ad. 303, approved by this court in Humble v. Hunter, 12 Q.B. 310. In Robson v. Drummond a carriage having been hired by the defendant of one Sharp, a coachmaker, for five years, at a yearly rent, payable in advance each year, the carriage to be kept in repair and painted once a year by the maker—Robson being then a partner in the business, but unknown to the defendant—on Sharp retiring from the business after three years had expired, and making over all interest in the business and property in the goods to Robson, it was held, that the defendant could not be sued on the contract—by Lord Tenterden on the ground that "the defendant might have been induced to enter into the contract by reason of the personal confidence which he reposed in Sharp, and therefore have agreed to pay money in advance, for which reason the defendant had a right to object to its being performed by any other person"; and by Littledale and Parke, JJ., on the additional ground that the defendant had a right to the personal services of Sharp, and to the benefit of his judgment and taste, to the end of the contract.

In like manner, where goods are ordered of a particular manufacturer, another, who has succeeded to his business, cannot execute the order, so as to bind the customer, who has not been made aware of the transfer of the business, to accept the goods. The latter is entitled to refuse to deal with any other than the manufacturer whose goods he intended to buy. For this Boulton v. Jones, 2 H. & N. 564, is a sufficient authority. The case of Robson v. Drummond comes nearer to the present case, but is, we think, distinguishable from it. We entirely concur in the principle on which the decision in Robson v. Drummond rests, namely, that where a person contracts with another to do work or perform service, and it can be inferred that the person employed has been selected with reference to his individual skill, competency, or other personal qualification, the inability or unwillingness of the party so employed to execute the work or perform the service is a sufficient answer to any demand by a stranger to the original contract of the performance of it by the other party, and entitles the latter to treat the contract as at an end, notwithstanding that the person tendered to take the place of the contracting party may be equally well qualified to do the service. Personal performance is in such a case of the essence of the contract, which, consequently, cannot in its absence be enforced against an unwilling party. But this principle appears to us inapplicable in the present instance, inasmuch as we cannot suppose that in stipulating for the repair of these waggons by the company—a rough description of work which ordinary workmen conversant with the business would be perfectly able to execute—the defendants attached any importance to whether the repairs were done by the company, or by any one with whom the company might enter into a subsidiary contract to do the work. All that the hirers, the defendants, cared for in this stipulation was that the waggons should be kept in repair; it was indifferent to them by whom the repairs should be done. Thus if, without going into liquidation, or assigning these contracts, the company had entered into a contract with any competent party to do the repairs, and so had procured them to be done, we cannot think that this would have been a departure from the terms of the contract to keep the waggons in repair. While fully acquiescing in the general principle just referred to, we must take care not to push it beyond reasonable limits. And we cannot but think that, in applying the principle, the Court of Queen's Bench in Robson v. Drummond went to the utmost length to which it can be carried, as it is difficult to see how in repairing a carriage when necessary, or painting it once a year, preference would be given to one coachmaker over another. Much work is contracted for, which it is known can only be executed by means of subcontracts; much is contracted for as to which it is indifferent to the party for whom it is to be done, whether it is done by the immediate party to the contract, or by some one on his behalf. In all these cases the maxim Qui facit per alium facit per se applies.

In the view we take of the case, therefore, the repair of the waggons, undertaken and done by the British Company under their contract with the Parkgate Company, is a sufficient performance by the latter of their engagement to repair under their contract with the defendants. Consequently, so long as the Parkgate Company continues to exist, and, through the British Company, continues to fulfill its obligation to keep the waggons in repair, the defendants cannot, in our opinion, be heard to say that the former company is not entitled to the performance of the contract by them, on the ground that the company have incapacitated themselves from performing their obligations under it, or that, by transferring the performance thereof to others, they have absolved the defendants from further performance on their part.

That a debt accruing due under a contract can, since the passing of the Judicature Acts, be assigned at law as well as equity, cannot since the decision in Brice v. Bannister, 3 Q.B.D. 569, be disputed.

We are therefore of opinion that our judgment must be for the plaintiffs for the amount claimed.

NOTES

(1) *Offer to the Wrong Person.* The court distinguishes Boulton v. Jones, the case of the leather pipe hose stated in Note 3, p. 68 supra, and Robson v. Drummond, the case of the carriage, admitting that the latter "comes nearer to the present case." It should be noticed that the two cases cited are analytically quite different. In the former the court held that there was no contract. In the latter there was an unquestioned contract between the coachmaker and his customer. Might the outcome in Boulton v. Jones have been different if Jones' order for hose had been handled differently?

Suppose that A, wishing to buy a used truck that he has seen, writes an offer to B, whose name is painted on it. The truck belongs in fact to "B Corporation," a company wholly owned by B. B likes the offer, and does not want to give A a chance to change his mind. Advise B. Would there be any advantage in having A readdress his offer to the company, if he will do it?

In connection with the analytical difference between the cases referred to, compare what was said in United States v. Braunstein, Note 2, p. 282 supra: "It is true that there is much room for interpretation once the parties are inside the framework of a contract, but it seems that there is less in the field of offer and acceptance."

(2) *The Boston Ice Case.* An old and well-known case about a buyer of ice for home use has recently been restated as follows: "Potter, who had dealt with the Boston Ice Co., and found its service unsatisfactory, transferred his business to Citizens' Ice Co. Later, Citizens' sold out to Boston, unbeknown to Potter, and Potter was served by Boston for a full year. When Boston attempted to collect its ice bill, the Massachusetts court sustained Potter's demurrer on the ground that there was no privity of contract, since Potter had a right to choose with whom he would deal and could not have another supplier thrust upon him." The case is Boston Ice Co. v. Potter, 123 Mass. 28 (1877).

The case has been "roundly criticized" by Corbin, and it is said that modern authorities do not support the result. Macke Co. v. Pizza of Gaithersburg, Inc., 259 Md. 479, 270 A.2d 645 (1970) (source of the quotation above). Would you support a quasi-contract claim against Potter? A contract claim? On the facts, which of the following cases does this one resemble most?—the British Waggon case, Boulton v. Jones, or Robson v. Drummond?

(3) *The Pizza Shop Case.* In the case last cited the defendants operated a chain of pizza shops. The plaintiff, Macke, bought the assets of the Virginia Coffee Service, Inc., including vending machines it had installed in the pizza shops. Virginia Coffee Service had one-year agreements with Pizza to "maintain the equipment in good operating order and stocked with merchandise." Pizza Shops attempted to terminate the contracts after Virginia assigned them to the Macke Company, saying they preferred the way Virginia conducted its business: that "the president of Virginia kept the machines in working order, that commissions were paid in cash, and that Virginia permitted them to keep keys to the machines so that minor adjustments could be made when needed." The trial court denied recovery for Macke, in a suit against the Pizza Shops; but the judgment was reversed on appeal. The court relied on the British Waggon case. Also, it seemed to disapprove the Boston Ice case. Should the court have distinguished the latter case? Would you have advised the Pizza Shops, given their strong preference for Virginia, not to repudiate the contracts abruptly, but to wait and see what quality of service Macke would provide?

In part, the court relied on the following excerpt from a California case:

"All painters do not paint portraits like Sir Joshua Reynolds, nor landscapes like Claude Lorraine, nor do all writers write dramas like Shakespeare or fiction like Dickens. Rare genius and extraordinary skill are not transferable, and contracts for their employment are therefore personal, and cannot be assigned. But rare genius and extraordinary skill are not indispensable to the workmanlike digging down of a sand hill or the filling up of a depression to a given level, or the construction of brick sewers with manholes and covers, and contracts for such work are not personal, and may be assigned." Taylor v. Palmer, 31 Cal. 240, at 247–248 (1866).

(4) *Code Influence.* The British Waggon case is the basis for an illustration after Restatement Second, § 320. The original Restatement standard of a permissible delegation—§ 160(3)(a)—has been made more congruent with the Code standard in the Second Restatement: see UCC 2–210(1) and § 318 of the latter. Which of the foregoing cases would be affected by the Code provision?

WESTERN OIL SALES CORP. v. BLISS & WETHERBEE, 299 S.W. 637 (Tex.Com.App.1927). [A contract was executed by a partnership of oil well owners (McCamey, Sheerin and Dumas) and the Western Corporation. Western undertook to connect certain wells with tanks by laying gathering lines. All the oil produced from the wells for six months after they were connected up was to be sold to Western, which agreed to pay a "posted" price for crude oil, plus 25 cents per barrel premium. "This agreement shall extend to and be binding on the parties hereto, their heirs, executors, administrators, successors, and assigns." After about three months Western assigned the contract to the American Oil Company, American acquiring all rights and assuming all obligations of Western under the contract. Western notified the partnership of the assignment, declaring that American would be responsible to pay for future deliveries of oil and that Western would not. American made demand for deliveries (it was then solvent), but the sellers refused to deliver except on condition that Western should recognize its liability under the contract. When Western refused to do so, the sellers treated the contract as terminated. They assigned all claims growing out of the contract to Bliss & Wetherbee, who brought suit against Western for damages. Damages of $4,420.25 were awarded, and Western brought error.]

HARVEY, P. J. . . . The mere fact that a contract is invested, by consent of the parties or otherwise, with the quality of assignability, does not signify that either party may, by assigning the contract, release himself from liability under it. When a contract is assignable, a party may assign the benefits of his contract to another, and delegate to his assignee the performance of his obligations under the contract; but he remains liable for the proper performance of those obligations, unless the other party to the contract consents for the assignment to have the effect of releasing him. 5 C.J. § 45, p. 878, and authorities there cited.

The Western Corporation was not released from its contract by the assignment to the American Oil Company. The unexecuted portion of the contract remained constituted, as it was in the beginning, of the mutual promises of the contracting parties. When, therefore, the corporation repudiated all liability for future deliveries of oil, it committed an anticipatory breach, and the sellers thereupon became entitled to terminate the contract. . . .

The contract having been thus terminated, the sellers' obligation to make future deliveries of oil under it was released; and the sellers were under no obligation which required them to substitute the promise of the American Oil Company for that of the Western Corporation which had been repudiated. Nor was it the duty of the sellers, in order to minimize their damage, to waive the breach and continue to deliver oil to the oil company under the contract. Nor is the evidence such as to establish, as a matter of law, that the sellers, or the plaintiffs, failed to exercise ordinary prudence and diligence to mitigate the damage flowing from said breach.

We recommend that the judgment of the Court of Civil Appeals affirming the judgment of the trial court be affirmed.

CURETON, C. J. Judgments of the district court and Court of Civil Appeals both affirmed, as recommended by the Commission of Appeals.

NOTES

(1) *Question.* If the partnership had made deliveries to American as demanded, after notice of the assignment, what would the legal position of

the parties have been? See Dowling v. Parker, 221 Ala. 63, 127 So. 813 (1930).

(2) *Novation.* When an agreement is made for the substitution of one obligor for another, such that the obligee is entitled to the same performance, but the original obligor is released, the agreement is one of a class called "novations".[a] The assent of the obligee is indispensable. It may be inferred from his conduct, of course. When an obligor delegates performance of his duty, and the obligee does no more than indicate that he will "go along" with it, as a rule he is not understood as agreeing to release of the original obligor. See Bank of Fairbanks v. Kaye, 227 F.2d 566 (9th Cir. 1955).[b] In Barton v. Perryman, 265 Ark. 228, 577 S.W.2d 596 (1979), the sellers of a house trailer (plaintiffs) took a much more active part in transactions in which the "purchase agreement" was sold and resold. On each sale the plaintiffs had required new financing terms and had made a charge for preparing the forms. Over a sharp dissent, these transactions were classified as novations. Compare Dahl v. Brunswick Corp., p. 861 supra, where the trial court ruled for Brunswick on the ground of novation. In a part of the opinion not reproduced, the Court of Appeals disapproved that ruling.

(3) *The Case of the Dancers' Faux Pas.* Mr. and Mrs. Philip Seale signed up with the Dale Dance Studio, a corporation, for a series of lessons, paying some $200. They became dissatisfied, and Dale arranged for them to complete the lessons at the Bates Dance Studio, also a corporation. At the end of this series they contracted with Bates for another series of 600 lessons. These lessons were interrupted by illness, and when the Seales returned they found that Bates had assigned the contract to the Dale Studio which undertook to complete performance for Bates. They were told that the entire Bates organization was transferred to Dale, and that they would have the same instructors and instruction as before. However, the Seales found the lessons unsatisfactory and made unsuccessful complaints: the rooms were small, crowded and noisy, and the couple had to share an instructor, a Mr. Ritchie. After some 30 sessions at the Dale Studio they stopped attending, and subsequently sued Bates and Dale to recover the cost of the lessons. *Held:* For the defendants.

"The argument of plaintiffs that this was a personal service contract and therefore non-assignable without their consent is valid. . . . Had they refused to receive instruction from Dale and had they taken the position that their contract was with Bates and no other, there would be substance to their present contention that this violation justified the rescission. [But they accepted the assignment.] While we sympathize with Mr. Seale's preference for Miss Valie over Mr. Ritchie, we do not consider this a breach

a. Sometimes novation is defined to embrace not only the substitution of one debtor for another, but a substitution of creditors as well, and even the substitution of a new debt or obligation for an existing one between the same parties. But it is said that in any of these situations "the old debt must be extinguished." Davenport v. Dickson, 211 Kan. 306, 507 P. 2d 301 (1973). See also Elliott v. Whitney, 215 Kan. 256, 524 P.2d 699 (1974).

b. "Mere assignment of the obligation from one debtor to another even with the creditor's knowledge of that assignment will not suffice to release the original debtor unless there is the crucial intent to substitute." Ingalls Iron Works Co. v. Fruehauf Corp., 518 F.2d 966, 969 (5th Cir. 1975).

of a promise implicit in the contract. . . . It is probable that Mrs. Seale preferred to be taught by Mr. Ritchie. It thus appears to us that the proper remedy for this problem is an express stipulation in the contract requiring a partner of the opposite sex." Seale v. Bates, 145 Colo. 430, 359 P.2d 356 (1961).

DELEGATION DISPUTED

The making of an assignment "in general terms" may invite an unnecessary dispute. An illustration suggested in the Restatement Second concerns a contract for the sale of oil by the Ace Oil Company to Buyer. Before delivery is made, Ace sells its refinery to the Deuce Company. Referring to Buyer's contract, this sale agreement provides that "Ace assigns all its right, title and interest in said contract to Deuce." Buyer does not receive the oil he has contracted for, and sues Deuce for nondelivery.[a] Is it a sufficient defense for Deuce that it made no promise to deliver the oil?

For this simple problem an answer may be found in UCC 2–210(4). (The provision is set out on p. 1143 infra.) According to Comment 5, this subsection "lays down a general rule of construction . . ." A comparable rule, expressed as one of interpretation, is stated in the first Restatement, § 164. However, even before the Restatement was promulgated it became evident that some courts might not accede to it. In Langel v. Betz, 250 N.Y. 159, 164 N.E. 890 (1928), the court quoted from the rule (in draft), giving it emphasis as follows: "Acceptance by the assignee of such an assignment is interpreted . . . as a promise *to the assignor to assume the performance of the assignor's duties.*" The court said: "This promise to the assignor would then be available to the other party to the contract. Lawrence v. Fox [p. 1018 supra]." It also cited Seaver v. Ransom, p. 1024 supra, and seemed sympathetic to the draftsmen's purpose. Perhaps, it said, the proposed rule is "more in harmony with modern ideas of contractual relations than is 'the archaic view of a contract as creating a strictly personal obligation between the creditor and debtor' (Pollock on Contracts, 9th Ed., 232), which prohibited the assignee from suing at law in his own name and which denied a remedy to third party beneficiaries." Nevertheless, the court said, "The proposed change is a complete reversal of our present rule of interpretation as to the probable intention of both parties. . . . [T]he law remains that no promise of the assignee to assume the assignor's duties is to be inferred from the acceptance of an assignment of a bilateral contract, in the absence of circumstances surrounding the assignment itself which indicate a contrary intention."

a. The illustration referred to is Restatement Second, § 328, Illustration 1. The facts given here are a free adaptation.

The facts in Langel v. Betz were notably different from the illustration of a refinery sale, given above, and it would be possible for any court to make an intelligible distinction between the two situations. Langel, the plaintiff, had contracted to sell certain real property to two individuals. They assigned the contract to Benedict, who in turn assigned it to Betz, the defendant. In form, these were assignments of the assignors' "right, title and interest in and to the said contract." Betz refused to perform on the date set for closing, and Langel brought an action against him for specific performance. From a judgment for the plaintiff, defendant appealed. *Held:* Reversed. "The mere assignment of a bilateral executory contract may not be interpreted as a promise by the assignee to the assignor to assume the performance of the assignor's duties, so as to have the effect of creating a new liability on the part of the assignee to the other party to the contract assigned." Langel v. Betz, supra.[b] In the case of the oil-sale contract, how would you argue for Buyer, distinguishing Langel v. Betz?

The rule of the case has had continuing recognition in New York and elsewhere, and is not always confined to land-sale cases. However, the revisers of the Restatement considered that contracts for the sale of land may be regarded as distinctive for this purpose. (For possible justification, see Chapter 5, Section 2, and Chapter 8, Section 5, supra.) In preparing the Restatement Second, they were agreed that the original Restatement rule should be carried forward, as rephrased to parallel the language of UCC 2–210(4), except in relation to such contracts. As limited to land-sale contracts, the rule of Langel v. Betz presented the revisers with a dilemma. They found much authority to support it, and none directly contrary. A draft subsection (in new § 328) was therefore prepared to reflect the case-law rule. On the other hand, they were not in sympathy with it, and would have preferred to state a single rule embracing all types of contracts. Further consideration led to the drafting of a "caveat."[c] In using this technique, the Restatement simply avoids pronouncement on a debatable point. In 1967 the American Law Institute voted on the choice between the caveat and the draft embodying the

b. Additional facts in the case were these: "The date for performance of the contract was originally set for October 2d, 1925. This was extended to October 15th, 1925, at the request of the defendant, the last assignee of the vendees. The ground upon which the adjournment was asked for by defendant was that the title company had not completed its search and report on the title to the property." The plaintiff based an argument on this request, which the court also rejected.

The case was followed in Peterson v. Johnson, 56 Wis.2d 145, 201 N.W.2d 507 (1972). But see Rose v. Vulcan Materials Co., 282 N.C. 643, 194 S.E. 2d 521 (1973).

For the continuing preference in New York for strict construction see Davies, Hardy, Ives & Lawther v. Abbott, 38 N.Y.2d 216, 379 N.Y.S.2d 686, 342 N.E.2d 490 (1975).

c. See Reporter's Notes to § 328.

(land sale) rule of Langel v. Betz. The caveat won, 47–44. It reads: "The Institute expresses no opinion as to whether the rule stated in Subsection (2) applies to an assignment by a purchaser of his rights under a contract for the sale of land."

In both UCC 2–210(4) and Restatement Second, § 328(2), the undertaking imputed to assignees is qualified by this phrase: "unless the language or the circumstances indicate the contrary." By this language it is possible to explain why, when a contractor obtains funds from a bank for a house-building job, and assigns it "the contract," the owner may not hold the bank accountable to put up the house. It explains also why, when a merchant assigns his sale contracts as security for a loan, his customers may not hold the lender accountable for nondelivery of the goods. Something more than a "financing assignment" in general terms would be required to charge a financial institution with such a duty.

Naturally, cases arise in which the indications of a financing assignment are ambiguous. An example is Chatham Pharmaceuticals, Inc. v. Angier Chemical Co., 347 Mass. 208, 196 N.E.2d 852 (1964). Angier (the company) had given an exclusive license to Chatham for the making of a product patented by the company. The contract permitted Chatham to give up the license and resell to the company, at an agreed price, all the product it had on hand. The company owed large sums to some of its stockholders, and it gave them an assignment of "all of its right, title and interest" in the Chatham contract. Evidently this entitled the assignees to royalties under the Chatham contract. When Chatham gave up the license and called for performance under its sale option, the company refused to perform. In an action against the company and its assignees, Chatham obtained a favorable decree, and the assignees appealed. (What does this suggest about the solvency of the company?) *Held:* Decree modified by dismissing the bill against the assignees. What circumstances, if any, indicated that the assignees were not to pay for the left-over inventory? If the company were shown to have been insolvent at the time of the assignment, would that fact tend to reinforce the court's conclusion? If the assignees had paid the company a substantial sum for the assignment, what inference might be drawn from that fact?

NOTES

(1) *Exercise.* Prepare a form of assignment making it clear that the assignees of the Chatham contract are not obliged to pay for the inventory. Prepare one making it clear that they *are.* If the contract to be assigned is one governed by UCC 2–210, and the assignee means to undertake the assignor's duties of performance, what practical value is there in including a statement to that effect in the assignment?

(2) *The Code.* Consult UCC 2–210(4) in relation to the following case: "A sells and delivers an automobile to B, the price to be paid in installments, and assigns to C for value 'all A's rights under the contract.' After B has made all the payments, the automobile is discovered to have

been stolen and is retaken by the owner. C is not liable to B for breach of warranty of title; A is." Restatement Second, § 328, Illustration 3. How can it be explained, under the Code, that C is not liable to B? Note the parenthesis in the Code section. The Restatement comment, to which the illustration is appended, directs attention (via other sections) to UCC 1-201(37), the third sentence.

(3) *Problem.* For more than twenty years the Southwest Distributing Co. was the exclusive distributor for Hamm's beer in New Mexico. In 1975 the Olympia Brewing Co. bought the chief assets of the Theodore Hamm Co. (brewery and trademark), and within two months it notified Southwest that it would no longer accept orders for Hamm's beer. What additional facts are required to make a case for Southwest against Olympia? See Southwest Distributing Co. v. Olympia Brewing Co., 90 N.M. 502, 565 P.2d 1019 (1977).

CRANE ICE CREAM CO. v. TERMINAL FREEZING & HEATING CO.

Court of Appeals of Maryland, 1925.
147 Md. 588, 128 A. 280, 39 A.L.R. 1184.

Action by the Crane Ice Cream Company against the Terminal Freezing & Heating Company. Demurrer to the declaration was sustained, and from the judgment entered thereon against plaintiff, it appeals. Judgment affirmed.

PARKE, J. The appellee and one W. C. Frederick entered into a contract for the delivery of ice by the appellee to Frederick, and, before the expiration of the contract, Frederick executed an assignment of the contract to the appellant; and on the refusal of the appellee to deliver ice to the assignee it brought an action on the contract against the appellee to recover damages for the alleged breach. . . .

The contract imposed upon the appellee the liability to sell and deliver to Frederick such quantities of ice as he might use in his business as an ice cream manufacturer to the extent of 250 tons per week, at and for the price of $3.25 a ton of 2,000 pounds on the loading platform of Frederick. The contractual rights of the appellee were (a) to be paid on every Tuesday during the continuation of the contract, for all ice purchased by Frederick during the week ending at midnight upon the next preceding Saturday; (b) to require Frederick not to buy or accept any ice from any other source than the appellee, except in excess of the weekly maximum of 250 tons. . . .

Before the first year of the second term of the contract had expired Frederick, without the consent or knowledge of the appellee, executed and delivered to the appellant, for a valuable consideration, a written assignment dated February 15, 1921, of the modified agreement between him and the appellee. The attempted transfer of the contract was a part of the transaction between Frederick and the appellant whereby the appellant acquired by purchase the plant, equipment, rights, and credits, choses in action, "good will, trade, custom, patronage, rights, contracts," and other assets of Frederick's ice cream business which had been established and conducted by him in Baltimore. The purchaser took full possession and continued the former business carried on by Frederick. It was then and is now a corporation "engaged in the ice cream business upon a large and extensive scale in the city of Philadelphia, as well as in the city of Baltimore, and state of Maryland," and had a large capitalization, ample resources, and credit to meet any of its obligations "and all and singular the terms and provisions" of the contract; and it was prepared to pay cash for all ice deliverable under the contract.

As soon as the appellee learned of this purported assignment and the absorption of the business of Frederick by the appellant, it notified Frederick that the contract was at an end, and declined to deliver any ice to the appellant. Until the day of the assignment the obligations of both original parties had been fully performed and discharged. . . .

The basic facts upon which the question for solution depends must be sought in the effect of the attempted assignment of this executory bilateral contract on both the rights and the liabilities of the contracting parties, as every bilateral contract includes both rights and duties on each side while both sides remain executory. Williston on Contracts, sec. 407. If the assignment of rights and the assignment of duties by Frederick are separated, they fall into these two divisions: (1) The rights of the assignor were (a) to take no ice, if the assignor used none in his business, but if he did (b) to require the appellee to deliver, on the loading platform of the assignor, all the ice he might need in his business to the extent of 250 tons a week, and (c) to buy any ice he might need in excess of the weekly 250 tons from any other person; and (2) the liabilities of the assignor were (a) to pay to the appellee on every Tuesday during the continuance of the contract the stipulated price for all ice purchased and weighed by the assignor during the week ending at midnight upon the next preceding Saturday, and (b) not directly or indirectly, during the existence of this agreement, to buy or accept any ice from any other person, firm, or corporation than the said Terminal Freezing & Heating Company, except such amounts as might be in excess of the weekly limit of 250 tons.

Whether the attempted assignment of these rights, or the attempted delegation of these duties must fail because the rights or duties are of too personal a character, is a question of construction to be resolved from the nature of the contract and the express or presumed intention of the parties. Williston on Contracts, sec. 431.

The contract was made by a corporation with an individual, William C. Frederick, an ice cream manufacturer, with whom the corporation had dealt for 3 years, before it executed a renewal contract for a second like period. The character, credit, and resources of Frederick had been tried and tested by the appellee before it renewed the contract. Not only had his ability to pay as agreed been established, but his fidelity to his obligation not to buy or accept any ice from any other source up to 250 tons a week had been ascertained. In addition, the appellee had not asked in the beginning, nor on entering into the second period of the contract, for Frederick to undertake to buy a specific quantity of ice or even to take any. Frederick simply engaged himself during a definite term to accept and pay for such quantities of ice as he might use in his business to the extent of 250 tons a week. If he used no ice in his business, he was under no obligation to pay for a pound. In any week, the quantity could vary from zero to 250 tons, and its weekly fluctuation, throughout the life of the contract, could irregularly range between these limits. The weekly payment might be nothing or as much as $812.50; and for every week a credit was extended to the eighth day from the beginning of every week's delivery. From the time of the beginning of every weekly delivery of the ice to the date of the payment therefor the title to the ice was in the purchaser, and the seller had no security for its payment except in the integrity and solvency of Frederick. The performances, therefore, were not concurrent, but the performance of the nonassigning party to the contract was to precede the payments by the assignor.

When it is also considered that the ice was to be supplied and paid for, according to its weight on the loading platform of Frederick, at an unvarying price without any reference either to the quantity used, or to the fluctuations in the cost of production or to market changes in the selling price, throughout 3 years, the conclusion is inevitable that the inducement for the appellee to enter into the original contract and into the renewal lay outside the bare terms of the contract, but was implicit in them, and was the appellee's reliance upon its knowledge of an average quantity of ice consumed, and probably to be needed, in the usual course of Frederick's business, at all times throughout the year, and its confidence in the stability of his enterprise, in his competency in commercial affairs, in his probity, personal judgment, and in his continuing financial responsibility. The contract itself emphasized the personal equation by specifying that the ice was to be bought for "use in his business as an ice cream manufacturer," and was to be paid for according to its weight "on the loading platform of the said W. C. Frederick."

When Frederick went out of business as an ice cream manufacturer, and turned over his plant and everything constituting his business to the appellant, it was no longer his business, or his loading platform, or subject to his care, control, or maintenance, but it was the business of a stranger, whose skill, competency, and requirements of ice were altogether different from those of Frederick. The assignor had his simple plant in Baltimore. The assignee, in its purchase, simply added another unit to its ice cream business which it had been, and is now, carrying on "upon a large and extensive scale in the city of Philadelphia and state of Pennsylvania, as well as in the city of Baltimore and state of Maryland." The appellee knew that Frederick could not carry on his business without ice wherewith to manufacture ice cream at his plant for his trade. It also was familiar with the quantities of ice he would require, from time to time, in his business at his plant in Baltimore, and it consequently could make its other commitments for ice with this knowledge as a basis.

The appellant, on the other hand, might wholly supply its increased trade acquired in the purchase of Frederick's business with its ice cream produced upon a large and extensive scale by its manufactory in Philadelphia, which would result in no ice being bought by the assignee of the appellee, and so the appellee would be deprived of the benefit of its contract by the introduction of a different personal relation or element which was never contemplated by the original contracting parties. Again, should the price of ice be relatively high in Philadelphia in comparison with the stipulated price, the assignee could run its business in Baltimore and furnish its patrons, or a portion of them, in Philadelphia with its product from the weekly maximum consumption of 250 tons of ice throughout the year. There can be no denial that the uniform delivery of the maximum quantity of 250 tons a week would be a consequence not within the normal scope of the contract, and would impose a greater liability on the appellee than was anticipated. 7 Halsbury's Laws of England, sec. 1015, p. 501. . . .

While a party to a contract may as a general rule assign all his beneficial rights, except where a personal relation is involved, his liability under the contract is not assignable inter vivos, because any one who is bound to any performance whatever or who owes money cannot by any act of his own, or by any act in agreement with any other person than his creditor or the one to whom his performance is due, cast off his own liability and substitute another's liability. If this were not true, obligors could free themselves of their obligations by the simple expedient of assigning them. A further ground for the rule, is that, not only is a party entitled to know to whom he must look for the satisfaction of his rights under the contract, but in the familiar words of Lord Denman in Humble v. Hunter, 12 Q.B. 317, "you have a right to the benefit you contemplate from the character, credit, and substance of the person with whom you contract." For these reasons it has been uniformly held that a man cannot assign his liabilities under a contract, but one who is bound so as to bear an unescapable liability may delegate the performance of his obligation to another, if the liability be of such a nature that its performance by another will be substantially the same thing as performance by the promisor himself. In such circumstances the performance of the third party is the act of the promisor, who remains liable under the contract and answerable in damages if the performance be not in strict fulfillment of the contract. . . .

However, the analysis of the facts on this appeal leaves no room for doubt that the case at bar falls into the category of those assignments where an attempt is made both to transfer the rights and to delegate the duties of the assignor under an executory bilateral contract whose terms and the circumstances make plain that the personal qualification and action of the assignor, with respect to both his benefits and burdens under the contract, were essential inducements in the formation of the contract, and further, that the assignment was a repudiation of any future liability of the assignor. The attempted assignment before us altered the conditions and obligations of the undertaking. The appellee would here be obliged not only to perform the subsequent stipulations of the contract for the benefit of a stranger and in conformity with his will, but also to accept the performance of the stranger in place of that of the assignor with whom it contracted, and upon whose personal integrity, capacity, and management in the course of a particular business he must be assumed to have relied by reason of the very nature of the provisions of the contract and of the circumstances of the contracting parties. . . .

Judgment affirmed.

NOTES

(1) *Question.* Suppose that Terminal's contract with Frederick had provided that, upon demand by Terminal Freezing, he would pay cash for any ice he ordered, not later than its delivery at his loading platform. And suppose it provided that Terminal might terminate the contract immediately, upon discovering that Frederick had bought ice from another source (without having taken 250 tons from Terminal that week).[a] Given these provisions, would the decision have been different?

(2) *The Code.* Would the reasoning or the result of the case be any different now that Maryland has adopted the Code? See UCC 2–210. According to Comment 4, "This Article and this section are intended to clarify [the problem of assignability of rights], particularly in cases dealing with output, requirement and exclusive dealing contracts. In the first place the section on requirements and exclusive dealing removes from the construction of the original contract most of the 'personal discretion' element by substituting the reasonably objective standard of good faith operation of the plant or business to be supplied. Secondly, the section on insecurity and assurances . . . frees the other party from the doubts and uncertainty which may afflict him under an assignment of the character in question by permitting him to demand adequate assurance of due performance without which he may suspend his own performance. [In subsection 5] the word 'performance' includes the giving of orders under a requirements contract. Of course, in any case where a material personal discretion is sought

a. Would this provision be enforceable as written? See UCC 1–208.

to be transferred, effective assignment is barred by subsection (2)." Cf. Robbins v. Hunts Food & Industries, Inc., 64 Wash.2d 304, 391 P.2d 713 (1964).

With slight alterations, the phrasing of subsection (2) has been copied into Restatement Second, § 317(2)(a).

(3) *The Reverse Action.* Does the court hold, in the main case, that Frederick committed a breach of his contract with Terminal Freezing? Suppose, for example, that after the sale of his business Terminal could find no buyer for its ice for more than $3 a ton, and that (for some reason) it preferred not to sell to Crane. Aside from any "duty" to mitigate damages by dealing with Crane, would Terminal be permitted to hold Frederick accountable for its damages?

Whatever the case implies about this problem, the Code rather clearly indicates a way for Terminal to establish a damage claim against Frederick. See UCC 2–210(5) and the final clause of 2–609: ". . . is a repudiation of the contract." (The Western Oil Sales case, p. 1098 supra—a pre-Code case—is exceptional in that the assignor did not wait for a demand for assurances; it was in haste to repudiate.)

The Code sections cited above permit the non-assigning party to demand assurances from *both* the assignee and the assignor in a proper case, do they not? If only one of them responds, but he is unquestionably willing and able to perform, should that count as an "adequate assurance" on behalf of both?

(4) *New Entitlement for Terminal?* Did Frederick's attempt to transfer the contract to Crane, and its acceptance, create any new obligation to purchase Terminal's ice? (The question assumes that Terminal is eager to keep a customer and that Crane has other ice available.) If so, what would Terminal's new entitlement have in common with the right of Antoinette Dahl—see p. 861 supra—to wages and other employment benefits from the Test Concorde Company?

BUSINESS PERSONALITY

There is an idea in the law that "in dealing with a corporation a party cannot rely on what may be termed the human equation in the company." New York Bank-Note Co. v. Hamilton Bank Note Engraving & Printing Co., 180 N.Y. 280, 293, 73 N.E. 48, 52 (1905). Does this suggest that if, in the *Crane Ice Cream* case, p. 1104 supra, Frederick had conducted his business through a corporate form the result would have been different? Or suppose that Frederick, instead of selling his business to Crane, had transferred it—plant, contract and all—to a corporation he formed, of which he was the principal officer and the sole stockholders were himself and his wife. Would the court have said, in that case, that the assignment was a "repudiation of any future liability" by Frederick? A reading of cases from New York courts has raised a doubt that they "would impose the same implied duty of personal service upon a contracting corporation as [they] would on an individual under the same circumstances." Arnold Productions, Inc. v. Favorite Films Corp., 298 F.2d 540 (2d Cir. 1962) [p. 1170 infra].

In contrast, when there is change in the membership of a professional partnership, having ongoing services contracts with clients, there is often good reason to doubt that the "new firm" may maintain the entitlements of the former partnership as of right. In legal principle, there is a gulf between the reformation of a partnership and a rearrangement of corporate ownership.

Yet the decisions relating to delegation of contract obligations do not insist on a sharp dichotomy. Something of a "personal character" has been ascribed to a corporation, owing to its distinctive charter powers and the applicable laws governing the liabilities of its officers and stockholders. ("These are matters of great importance when, as at present, many states and territories seem to have entered into the keenest competition in granting charters; each seeking to outbid the other by offering to directors and stockholders the greatest immunity from liability at the lowest cash price." [a]) For partnership cases an illustration is City of North Kansas City v. Sharp, 414 F.2d 359 (8th Cir. 1969). The city had contracted for the services of the engineering firm, Riddle & Sharp. When Riddle withdrew and Sharp brought in a new partner, the city declared the contract terminated and relet the work to another firm. (The findings told a sorry story, said the reviewing court: the replacement firm had agreed to take Riddle in; he was a friend of the mayor's; and the mayor had advised giving the work to that firm at a higher fee.) The Sharp firm sued the city and won a judgment, partly on evidence that Riddle would, if asked, have worked with the plaintiff on the city contract. On appeal by the city, *held:* Affirmed. "The essence of the professional service cases is that the critical partner, for one reason or another, is no longer available to render those services. Here the critical partners were available and the record indicates . . . that they were able to, and did function collectively." [b]

NOTES

(1) *Big Fish, Little Fish.* Should a contracting party be permitted to object to an assignment that makes him beholden to a new firm, as assignee, on the ground that he is a financial weakling in relation to that firm? In Schultze v. Chevron Oil Co., 579 F.2d 776 (3d Cir. 1978), an industry giant (Chevron) obtained rights under a lease from a lesser firm (Morris Oil Co.). One of the judges speculated as follows on the consequences for the obligors: "If Morris' bargaining position was significantly less powerful than that of a major oil company, it would follow that the Schultzes could expect that in enforcing its right of first refusal, Morris would be

a. New York Bank Note Co. v. Hamilton Bank-Note Engraving & Printing Co., 180 N.Y. 280, 73 N.E. 48 (1905).

b. Compare Rossetti v. City of New Britain, 163 Conn. 283, 303 A.2d 714 (1972) (partnership of architects).

forced to be more accommodating than a major oil company, since its position would not be as strong." (Adams, J., dissenting at 780, 783, n. 20) Is this reasoning questionable on the ground that it tends to make the assets of the Morris Company less marketable?

Do you find an indication that the power, position or personality of the assignee counts, in this matter, in the provisions on assignability of the Code—2–210—or the Restatement—§ 317?

(2) *Clean Hands.* In August, 1969, the owners of the Oakland "Oaks" basketball club contracted to sell all its assets to the Washington Capitols Basketball Club, Inc. One of its assets, valued at three-quarters of a million dollars, was a contract for the services of their star player Richard "Rick" Barry. He had signed with the Oaks for a three-year term in 1967. The day after the sale, Barry contracted to play for the San Francisco "Warriors." The Washington club brought an action against him in equity, seeking an injunction against his playing for the Warriors.

One of the defenses was based on the curious events of 1967, leading up to Barry's contract with the Oaks. It appears that he had previously had a contract with the Warriors club, and that the owners of the Oaks had induced him to play for them in violation of that contract. An objection to the injunction, then, was based on the maxim: "He who comes into equity must come with clean hands." (See Note at p. 563 supra.) The court granted a preliminary injunction, ruling that the suitor, Washington, should not be barred by the offense of its assignor, the Oakland Club. The relation between an assignee and his assignor is relatively remote, the court said, for purposes of the maxim. Washington Capitols Basketball Club, Inc. v. Barry, 304 F.Supp. 1193 (N.D.Cal.1969). (The court observed that the Warriors club had had Barry enjoined from playing with the Oaks in 1967–68.)

How can it be supposed that a contract so "personal" as this one was assignable at all? The opinion discusses the point.

EVENING NEWS ASS'N v. PETERSON

United States District Court, District of Columbia, 1979.
477 F.Supp. 77.

[Gordon Peterson performed as a newscaster-anchorman for Channel 9, in the District of Columbia, over several yeras when it was owned by Post-Newsweek Stations, Inc. In June 1978 the station was acquired by the Evening News Association. At that time Peterson had served for nearly a year under a contract of employment for three years, which was renewable for two additional one-year terms by Post-Newsweek. The sale to Evening News included an assignment of Post-Newsweek's rights in this contract. In August 1979, having negotiated for employment with a competing station, Peterson tendered his resignation to Evening News, which thereupon sued Peterson for an injunction against taking the other employment. Peterson testified that he had had "almost a family relationship" with program executives for Post-Newsweek, who no longer worked for Channel 9. He also expressed disappointment with the plaintiff's broadcasting activities: "less agressive," failure to seize opportunities for live in-depth coverage of current events, and the like. On the other hand, the court heard evidence of the continued high ratings and quality of Channel 9 broadcasts, including recognition such as Peabody and Emmy awards.]

BARRINGTON D. PARKER, District Judge.

. . .

A.

The distinction between the assignment of a right to receive services and the obligation to provide them is critical in this proceeding. This is so because duties under a personal services contract involving special skill or ability are generally not delegable by the one obligated to perform, absent the consent of the other party. The issue, however, is not whether the personal services Peterson is to perform are delegable but whether Post-Newsweek's right to receive them is assignable.

Contract rights as a general rule are assignable. Munchak Corp. v. Cunningham, 457 F.2d 721 (4th Cir. 1972); Meyer v. Washington Times Co., 64 App.D.C. 218, 76 F.2d 988 (D.C.Cir.) cert. denied, 295 U.S. 734, 55 S.Ct. 646, 79 L.Ed. 1682 (1935); 4 A. Corbin, Contracts § 865 (1951); Restatement (First) of Contracts § 151 (1932). This rule, however, is subject to exception where the assignment would vary materially the duty of the obligor, increase materially the burden of risk imposed by the contract, or impair materially the obligor's chance of obtaining return performance. Corbin § 868; Restatement § 152. There has been no showing, however, that the services required of Peterson by the Post-Newsweek contract have changed in any material way since the Evening News entered the picture. Both before and after, he anchored the same news programs. Similarly he has had essentially the same number of special assignments since the transfer as before. Any additional policy-making role that he formerly enjoyed and is now denied was neither a condition of his contract nor factually supported by other than his own subjective testimony.

The general rule of assignability is also subject to exception where the contract calls for the rendition of personal services based on a relationship of confidence between the parties. Munchak, 457 F.2d at 725; Meyer, 64 App.D.C. at 219, 76 F.2d at 989. As Corbin has explained this limitation on assignment:

> In almost all cases where a "contract" is said to be non-assignable because it is "personal," what is meant is not that the contractor's right is not assignable, but that the performance required by his duty is a personal performance and that an attempt to perform by a substituted person would not discharge the contractor's duty.

Corbin § 865. In *Munchak,* the Court concluded that a basketball player's personal services contract could be assigned by the owner of the club to a new owner, despite a contractual prohibition on assignment to another club, on the basis that the services were to the club. The Court found it "inconceivable" that the player's services "could be affected by the personalities of successive corporate owners." 457 F. 2d at 725. The policy against the assignment of personal service contracts, as the Court noted, "is to prohibit an assignment of a contract in which the obligor undertakes to serve only the original obligee." 457 F.2d at 726.

Given the silence of the contract on assignability, its merger clause, and the usual rule that contract rights are assignable, the Court cannot but conclude on the facts of this case that defendant's contract was assignable. Mr. Peterson's contract with Post-Newsweek gives no hint that he was to perform as other than a newscaster-anchorman for their stations. Nor is there any hint that he was to work with particular Post-Newsweek employees or was assured a policy-making role in concert with any given employees. Defendant's employer was a corporation, and it was for Post-Newsweek Stations, Inc. that he contracted to perform. The corporation's duties under the contract did not involve the rendition of personal services to defendant; essentially they were to compensate him. Nor does the contract give any suggestion of a relation of special confidence between the two or that defendant was expected to serve the Post-Newsweek stations only so long as the latter had the license for them.

. . .

C.

Plaintiff's argument that defendant has waived any objection to the assignment by accepting the contract benefits and continuing to perform for the Evening News for over a year has perhaps some merit. If defendant has doubts about assignability, he should have voiced them when he learned of the planned transfer [December, 1977] or at least at the time of transfer. . . . The Court, however, concludes that the contract was assignable in the first instance and thus it is not necessary to determine whether defendant's continued performance constitutes a waiver of objection to the assignment.

[The court directed the preparation of an order consistent with its opinion.]

NOTES

(1) *The Chautauqua Case.* Citizens of Mankato, Kansas, formed a committee to present programs of instruction and entertainment. A talent bureau, Midland Chautauqua, contracted with them to supply performers, a tent, advertising matter and the like. (The bluestocking community on the shores of Lake Chautauqua, New York, provided the model for such assemblies across the country.) Not long before the scheduled assembly the com-

mittee was notified that Midland's offices would be performed by the Standard Chautauqua System and was advised that Standard's program would be of at least equal quality to that of Midland. (Among the events proposed were appearances of the St. Cecilia Singing Orchestra and a troupe playing "The Gorilla.") The committee had promised Midland their hearty support and cooperation, and payments of at least $750. When Standard tendered its services, the committee defaulted. All this being alleged in an action by Standard, the trial court sustained a demurrer by the defendants, members of the committee. On appeal, *held:* Affirmed. Midland's "rights" were not assignable. Standard Chautauqua System v. Gift, 120 Kan. 101, 242 P. 145 (1926). The court's view was unshaken by the fact that the contract with Midland referred to the parties and "their successors and assigns."

(2) *Drafting.* When referring to John Doe in drafting a contract, would you expect to convey much meaning by adding "and his assigns"? "Contracts often refer to the 'assigns' of one or both parties. A purported promise by a promisor 'and his assigns' does not mean that the promisor can terminate his duty by making an assignment, nor does it of itself show an assumption of duties by any assignee. It tends to indicate that the promised performance is not personal, just as a promise to a promisee 'and his assigns' tends to indicate that the promisor is willing to render performance to an assignee. Whether there is a manifestation of assent to assignment or delegation, however, depends on the interpretation of the contract as a whole." Restatement Second, § 323, Comment b.

(3) *Personal Services Contracts.* It is frequently said that contracts for personal services are not assignable. The following questions may suggest some limitations on that proposition: (a) Would the Chautauqua decision necessarily have been the same if the Midland bureau had delegated only *part* of its duties to Standard? (b) If Midland had transferred only its rights to payment under the contract, and had tendered its own performance, would the assignee's claim be objectionable? (c) Is it clear that the defendants—members of the committee—could not delegate their duties without the consent of the bureau?

SECTION 3. FINANCING CONSUMER CREDIT

Mr. John Q. Public buys a new Thunderwagen car from the Potluck Motor Company. The purchase is on "time," because John does not have cash enough to pay the full price at once. He signs a promissory note in favor of the Motor Company for the price of the car, interest, and certain other charges, less the down payment. It calls for equal monthly payments over the course of four years. At the same time both the Motor Company (as Seller) and John (as Customer) sign a "Conditional Sale Contract." The critical feature of the contract is this sentence: "Title to the car is retained by Seller until said time balance is fully paid in money to the holder hereof (meaning Seller or its assignee if this contract is assigned) when title shall pass to Customer." The contract is lengthy, and contains many clauses in rather fine print. Permission for the Seller to seize the car in the event of John's default is expressly reserved.

The Motor Company wishes to maintain a full inventory of cars. Since it has to pay cash to the manufacturer before delivery, it does not have the additional funds necessary to finance its customers. For this purpose it has a long-standing arrangement with a finance company, the Thunderwagen Acceptance Corporation (TACO). In accordance with this agreement, TACO credits the Motor Company with all of the time balance owing under the conditional sale contract, less a "discount." In return, the Motor Company executes a "Dealer's Assignment" form appearing on the back of the contract, indorses John's note, and delivers both instruments to TACO. The first sentence of the assignment form is as follows: "We hereby sell and assign the contract on the reverse side and all interest in the car . . . to you . . . with full power to you in your or our name to collect and discharge the same and to take all such legal or other proceedings as we might take, save for this assignment." TACO sends notice to John that he should make the monthly payments directly to it. It encloses a handy coupon book for keeping the account straight. Steps may be taken, depending on local law, to reflect the fact that the car is subject to an encumbrance, or security interest. (Ordinarily a notation to that effect would be made on the buyer's certificate of title.) When John completes his payments, he then has the car free of TACO's security interest and can obtain a suitable record of his unencumbered title.

A transaction more or less like the one described occurs in connection with most consumer purchases of cars in this country, and the volume of credit generated is enormous. Sometimes the security agreement taken by the dealer and assigned to the finance company takes the form of a chattel mortgage rather than a conditional sale contract. Not only automobile purchases, but also purchases of many kinds of durable consumer goods (furniture, appliances, etc.) are similarly financed. And so it is with the purchase of items of business equipment ranging from barber chairs to drilling rigs. Some finance companies specialize in particular lines of business—the name TACO suggests an affiliation with the manufacturer of Thunderwagen cars. Others are not specialized, and commercial banks generally engage in financing on the same basis.

NOTES

(1) *Another Version.* In a "plain language" form of John's contract with the dealer, set out in the Supplement, there is no title-reservation provision, but this instead: "I agree to give you a security interest under the Uniform Commercial Code in the purchased vehicle . . . . I give you permission to file a financing statement covering your security interest without my signature on it." See also the Assignment clause therein. The form is titled "Retail Instalment Contract (Automobiles)."

(2) *Dealer's Finance Agreement.* By the agreement between the Motor Company and TACO, the assignment of John's contract might be made "without recourse," so that the Motor Company would be under no liability to TACO in the event of the customer's default in making payments. However, certainly with respect to a new-car sale, it would more probably be agreed that the Motor Company would repurchase the car from TACO if it be repossessed as a result of the customer's default. The amount credited to the Motor Company in connection with the assignment of John's contract would depend on that and a number of other factors. "In automobile financing under a repurchase arrangement, the financing agency ordinarily pays into a reserve account a portion of the finance charge on paper purchased from a particular dealer. Such payments continue until the account reaches either a minimum dollar amount or, more commonly, a percentage of the dealer's outstanding paper (usually three percent). Upon default by a buyer and repossession by the financer, the dealer is obligated to repurchase the vehicle, and the unpaid balance of the note is charged to the reserve account. . . . Once the stipulated reserve account balance is attained, subsequent sums payable under the dealer-participation agreement are periodically distributed to the dealer. Since the dealer's share of the finance charges typically ranges from one-fifth to one-third, dealer participation constitutes a major element of his income." Warren, Regulation of Finance Charges, 68 Yale L.J. 839, 859 (1959).

(3) *Assignee's Rights.* The principal problem of this section may be stated as follows: after the assignment, is the contract, in the hands of TACO, subject to the defenses that John might have made against the dealer? On the facts so far given, the answer is certainly "yes." When sued by the assignee, the buyer's defense is most often based on breach of warranty by the seller, or other non-performance, or on a misrepresentation inducing the buyer to contract. All these and many other defenses are available to the buyer to the same extent they would be if the dealer itself were suing for the purchase price.

If an assignee bank or finance company finds that the contract is unenforceable by reason of the seller's conduct it will invariably have a claim against him. The claim may be based on an implied warranty of the assignor; see Restatement Second, § 333. Or it may be based on express warranties accompanying the assignment. For examples of such warranties see Warner v. Seaboard Finance Company, 75 Nev. 470, 345 P.2d 759 (1959), concerning the assignment of an installment contract for storm windows and awnings. Among other things, the dealer warranted to the finance company that the contracts he assigned would be valid and enforceable obligations of the customer, signed by him, and that "ethical and proper selling practice will be followed."

The assignee must consider the possibility, however, that the dealer will be unable to respond to such a claim, by reason of insolvency, when the time comes to enforce it. For this reason, chiefly, financing institutions have not been content to take assignments of contracts "subject to defenses" that the customer, or obligor, may have against the assignor. The law has traditionally provided means for them to "take free" of such defenses, and the efficacy of these means is to be considered in this section. In most of the cases presenting the issue there is a loss attributable to substandard performance by a dealer in goods or services, and it must be allocated either to the customer or to the financing assignee. If the dealer is available for suit, and able to pay a judgment, the problem is not an acute one. In considering the materials to follow, you should assume that that is not the case.

WAIVING DEFENSES AND HOLDING IN DUE COURSE

Two principal arrangements are available for permitting an assignee to take free of an obligor's defenses against the assignor. Each requires a specialized form of expression for the obligor's undertaking. One relies upon the law of negotiable instruments, and the object is to give the assignee status as a "holder in due course." This arrangement is illustrated in the "Participation Case," p. 1119 infra, and the basic rules of negotiability are important to an understanding of that case. The other arrangement relies on a term in the assigned contract known as a "waiver of defense" clause. For consumer transactions, such clauses are now more commonly used than negotiable instruments. However, the issues they raise are similar to those associated with negotiability. The second arrangement is illustrated in Holt v. First Nat. Bank of Minneapolis, p. 1123 infra, and in the Merediths' Case, p. 1130 infra.

Both arrangements are illustrated in Unico v. Owen, 50 N.J. 101, 232 A.2d 405 (1967), which concerned the sale of 140 record albums, to be delivered and paid for in installments (with a "free" record player thrown in). That sale contract is the source of the following waiver-of-defense clause:

> Buyer hereby acknowledges notice that the contract may be assigned and that assignees will rely upon the agreements contained in this paragraph, and agrees that the liability of the Buyer to any assignee shall be immediate and absolute and not affected by any default whatsoever of the Seller signing this contract; and in order to induce assignees to purchase this contract, the Buyer further agrees not to set up any claim against such Seller as a defense, counterclaim or offset to any action by an assignee for the unpaid balance of the purchase price or for possession of the property.

The buyers received the record player, and 12 albums; but the remainder were never received because the seller became insolvent. The buyers stopped their monthly payments after a year, and were then sued by a finance company as assignee of their contract.

The same buyers had also signed a promissory note, negotiable in form, for the entire purchase price of the albums, payable in installments. The note had also been transferred to the finance company, and it sought to recover on the note as a holder in due course, in the technical sense. The case is unusual in that the documents were designed to give the finance company the advantages both of a waiver clause and of negotiability; but the object was the same: to deprive the buyers of defenses such as failure of consideration.

The definition and effects of negotiable instruments are now stated in Article 3 of the Uniform Commercial Code. For about half a century before the Code was drafted, the subject was governed by the Negotiable Instruments Law (NIL), the first of the "uniform laws." And for perhaps two centuries before that the essential characteristics of negotiable instruments were established in the common law.

When the obligation on the instrument takes the form of a promise, the instrument is known as a *promissory note* or simply a *note.* UCC 3–104(2)(d). In order to be *negotiable,* however, the note must meet a number of other requirements: it must be signed by the maker, it must contain an unconditional promise to pay a sum certain in money, it must be payable on demand or at a definite time, and it must be payable to order or to bearer. UCC 3–104(1). Only if it meets these requirements is the note invested with the special characteristics of a negotiable instrument.

Chief among these characteristics is the protection of a good faith purchaser against defenses. When a negotiable instrument payable to bearer is transferred by delivery or when a negotiable instrument payable to order is transferred by a valid indorsement followed by delivery, the transfer is known as *negotiation* and the transferee is known as a *holder* of the instrument. UCC 3–202. The holder will qualify as a *holder in due course* if, in addition, he takes the instrument for value, in good faith, and without notice that it is overdue or has been dishonored or of any defense against or claim to it. UCC 3–302(1). Thus in order to be a holder in due course, he must show: first, that the instrument is negotiable; second, that he took by negotiation, as a holder; and third, that he took in due course. If he can do all this, then he "takes the instrument free from . . . all defenses of any party to the instrument with whom the holder has not dealt," with the exception of certain rare defenses know as *real* defenses, such as incapacity, duress, and some types of fraud. UCC 3–305. He takes free of all other defenses, known as *personal* defenses, including such common matters as want of consideration, failure of condition, breach of warranty in the sale of goods, and most cases of fraud. See UCC 3–306.

NOTES

(1) *Multiple-Choice Question.* You have bought a refrigerator under a credit contract containing a waiver-of-defense clause. Given this assumption, a group of laymen were asked to read the "contract" and then, without referring to it, to answer the following question:

> If the seller assigns the contract to another party, say a bank, you will make your payments to the bank rather than to the seller.

If, then, the refrigerator stops working and the seller wrongfully fails to honor the warranty:

(a) You will still have to make the payments to the bank.

(b) You will be excused from making payments to the bank until the seller honors the warranty.

(c) . . .

(d) Don't know/unsure.

Actually, two groups were given the test, based on different contracts. One contract—not the other—contained a notice, in a form mandated by the Federal Trade Commission, indicating that (b) is the most nearly correct answer. (For the FTC Rule see p. 1132 infra.) The group that did not see the notice scored markedly better than the group that did. Davis, Protecting Consumers from Overdisclosure and Gobbledygook, 63 Va.L.Rev. 841, 884 n. 119 (1977).[a]

(2) *Three of a Kind.* In each of the three cases presented next—in summary or in text—a buyer of goods contested his or her duty to pay for them in litigation with a financial institution: bank or finance company. In the first case the financer claimed holder-in-due-course status; in each of the others it claimed the benefit of a waiver-of-defense clause. After these cases are considered, the more recent pronouncement of the FTC, affecting one or more of these situations, should be examined.

The first case is an excursion into commercial financing, lying outside the literal scope of this section. However, this and a number of comparable cases have had a pronounced influence on consumer-credit cases, as will be seen.

A Participation Case

Whelan and Williams, partners, did business as the Coin Operated Laundry Sales Company, selling machines to cleaning establishments. (At the time of the trial to be mentioned, their whereabouts was unknown.) Customers of the sales company—dealer—who did not pay cash were asked to sign documents in three forms: (1) a promissory note for the unpaid part of the purchase price, together with a finance charge;[b] (2) a conditional sale contract describing the goods sold and creating in the seller a security interest for assuring payment of the unpaid balance; and (3) a certificate that the goods had been delivered and installed to the customer's satisfaction. The practice of the dealer was not to retain the rights so expressed, but to assign them, with delivery of the documents, to a finance company. The forms were supplied to the dealer by the International Finance Corporation. The name of that corporation was printed on the forms, as the prospective assignee. However, before purchasing a note and contract from the dealer the finance company made investi-

a. Professor Davis appears to conclude that the FTC has failed signally in an attempt at informing consumers of their rights. At best, however, this is only a secondary object of the notice requirement; see p. 1136 infra.

b. Actually a time-price differential, so-called.

gation into the credit of the goods buyer. Also, it required the dealer to present the installation certificate, signed by the buyer, before making such a purchase.

LeRoy Rieger bought two dry-cleaning machines from the dealer, for use in his laundry business. He signed a note for $24,190, payable to the dealer, and a conditional sale contract. The contract recited a purchase price of $26,000, a finance charge of $3,690, and an initial payment of $5,500. In fact, Rieger made no payment for the machines; the contract indicated such a payment "so that the amount due for the purchase of the machines could be more readily financed" with International. Moreoever, the machines were not installed at once, owing to objections by the city building inspector. The dealer sold the note and contract to International and delivered to it an installation certificate on which Rieger's signature had been forged.

After the machines were installed Rieger made various complaints about them to the dealer and to International, and ultimately demanded that they be "picked up" and that the note and contract be returned to him. Instead, International sued Rieger on his note. One of his defenses was that the note and contract were not to become effective, according to his agreement with the dealer, until he acknowledged that the machines were satisfactorily installed. Another was that the dealer had falsely represented that the machines would carry an 8 to 10 pound load. The trial court made no finding that International had knowledge of any wrongdoing by the dealer. It gave judgment against Rieger for less than the amount of the note, and he appealed.

The Supreme Court of Minnesota reversed for a new trial. International Finance Corp. v. Rieger, 272 Minn. 192, 137 N.W.2d 172 (1965). Most of the court's discussion was devoted to the question whether or not International qualified as a holder in due course of the note. It sustained the trial court's apparent ruling on that issue, in favor of Rieger. The court cited a dozen cases for the proposition that when an assignee "has participated in the transaction from its origin so as to have acquired knowledge of the conditional liability of the purchaser or maker of the note," it does not qualify as a holder in due course. The evidence showing "participation" was that the assignment was not meant to be consummated in the absence of an installation certificate, that the certificate was to manifest proper performance of the sale contract—as all the parties understood—and that International had furnished the forms to the dealer, complete with instructions for their execution.

The court recognized precedents apparently to the contrary. As to them it said: "These decisions for the most part have reference to situations where an assignee of a note has knowledge of the executory consideration for it rather than knowledge that conditions are to be performed by the payee before liability on the note attaches to the maker."

NOTES

(1) *Policy Question.* Is there any social utility in a rule that places a risk on a financial institution because it provides prepared forms, in mass, to the dealers whose retail trade it finances?

(2) *Estoppel.* Suppose that, though the machines were not ever installed, Rieger had trustingly signed the installation certificate which was presented to International Finance. Would you expect the court to permit Rieger to prove, in an action by the latter, that Sales Company had not installed the machines? Estoppel arguments have not been well received in somewhat comparable cases. See Parker v. Funk, 185 Cal. 347, 197 P. 83 (1921).

(3) *Statutory Reform.* In 1966 the Uniform Commercial Code became effective in Minnesota. Section 9–206, part of which is set out next, thereupon became applicable to transactions like those in the Participation Case.

UCC 9–206

Agreement Not to Assert Defenses Against Assignee; . . .

(1) Subject to any statute or decision which establishes a different rule for buyers or lessees of consumer goods, an agreement by a buyer or lessee that he will not assert against an assignee any claim or defense which he may have against the seller or lessor is enforceable by an assignee who takes his assignment for value, in good faith and without notice of a claim or defense, except as to defenses of a type which may be asserted against a holder in due course of a negotiable instrument under the Article on Commercial Paper (Article 3).[a] A buyer who as part of one transaction signs both a negotiable instrument and a security agreement makes such an agreement.

NOTES

(1) *The Code and Business Buyers.* How would the Participation Case have been decided if the Code had been applicable? Observe that according to the final sentence of the Code excerpt Rieger made a "will not assert" agreement by signing the note and the contract. Observe that the "except" clause of the statute would not seem to help Rieger, if the Code

a. As to the exceptional "real" defenses, see the Note on Waiving Defenses and Holding in Due Course, p. 1117 supra.

In reading the subsection it may be helpful to see it as having three main parts. First, the section broadly validates waiver of defense clauses, in favor of certain assignees. Second, in the concluding sentence the section places a transferee of a negotiable instrument on at least as strong a footing as an assignee relying on a waiver of defense clause. (Note that the section does not require that the transferee be a holder taking the instrument by negotiation.) Third, the section begins with a curious qualification referring to non-Code law. This phrase is explained in Comment 2 as follows: "This Article takes no position on the controversial question whether a buyer of consumer goods may effectively waive defenses by contractual clause or by execution of a negotiable note." Early drafts of the Code show that this formula was achieved only after intense debate.

would otherwise bind him to pay. To be sure, forgery is a "real" defense, i. e., one assertable against a holder in due course. But his defense was not that the *note* was forged—only that the dealer had not performed as asserted in a (forged) statement.

Under the Code, it seems, the argument for Rieger must be that International Finance did not take its assignment "in good faith and without notice of a claim or defense." Would you expect the Minnesota court to agree with that? International had had no direct contact with Rieger until some time after it purchased his contract, of course. Suppose that the installation certificate was accurate and genuine, Rieger's only defense being that the machines did not have the load capacity he had been led to expect. Would you expect the court to allow that defense? [b]

For assignees of commercial contracts, at least, the elements of "good faith" and "notice" are critical. Consult the definitions in UCC 1–201(19) and (27). Are they generally helpful to assignees? Does the context of these terms in UCC 9–206(1) require that they be given special meanings there? (See the opening lines of UCC 1–201.) If the textual context does not, does the *business* context permit the courts to take liberties with the definitions?

(2) *The Code and Consumer Buyers.* Now suppose that all the foregoing questions are decided against Rieger, as a business buyer. If we also suppose that he bought the machines for household use, a further question arises. Note the opening phrase of UCC 9–206: "Subject to any statute or decision which establishes a different rule for buyers or lessees of consumer goods . . . ." Was *International Finance Corp. v. Rieger* a decision establishing that, against a consumer buyer, holder-in-due-course status may not be claimed by a financer which supplies forms to the seller, or otherwise "participates" in the sale transaction from its origin? See Rehurek v. Chrysler Credit Corp., 262 So.2d 452 (Fla.App.1972), relying on commercial-credit cases.

(3) *More Statutory Reform.* As the next main case will show, there is now in Minnesota a statute which "establishes a different rule" for consumer buyers. However, the transactions before the court occurred before that statute took effect.[c]

(4) *The Litton Leases.* Regent Leasing Corporation supplied photocopiers to Litton under leases which permitted Regent to assign its payment rights and provided that Litton would not assert against an assignee any defense it might have against Regent. The payment rights were assigned, for value, to banks which were without notice of any defense. When Litton ceased to pay, the banks sued it. (What is called "Litton" here was actually a set of lessees and defendants, all of them subsidiaries of Litton Industries, Inc.) In defense, Litton contended that the leases were affected by illegality. For arranging the agreements Regent had secretly agreed with a Litton employee to pay him "service fees," which for purposes of the decision the court regarded as bribes. On an appeal by Litton from a judgment

b. For an application of UCC 9–206(1) against a "business buyer," see Credit Alliance Corp. v. David O. Crump Sand & Fill Co., 470 F.Supp. 489 (S.D.N.Y.1979).

c. A description and compilation of retail installment sales statutes as they affect assignment law appear in Introductory Note to Chapter 15 of Restatement Second.

against it, *held:* Affirmed. Bankers Trust Co. v. Litton Systems, Inc., 599 F.2d 488 (2d Cir. 1979).

The court referred to the "except" clause in UCC 9–206(1) and to UCC 3–305(2)(b), whereby "nullifying" illegality in a transaction is made a defense against a holder in due course. The court concluded that, according to New York law, the illegality was not of that character. In this connection it examined Sirkin v. Fourteenth Street Store (p. 546 supra) and McConnell v. Commonwealth Pictures Corp. (p. 553 supra).

HOLT v. FIRST NAT. BANK OF MINNEAPOLIS

Supreme Court of Minnesota, 1973.
297 Minn. 457, 214 N.W.2d 698.

PER CURIAM.

This appeal deals with the validity of a provision in an installment sales contract whereby the purchaser of an automobile waived as against the assignee of the contract defenses which could have been asserted against the assignor-seller. The trial court held that the assignment of the contract containing the waiver provision was unrelated to the actual sale of the automobile "in the usual sense" and that it was not "unconscionable" to enforce the waiver in the peculiar circumstances of the case. We agree and affirm.

In May 1967, plaintiff, Gail Holt, purchased a Dodge Charger automobile from Herzog Dodge, Inc. (Herzog). The purchase price was $4,046.65 and was to be paid by cash in the sum of $3,415.15 and by the equity of $631.50 in a Dodge Dart which plaintiff traded for the balance. At the time of the sale, plaintiff's Dart was subject to a mortgage held by her credit union in the sum of $1,345.15.

Plaintiff looked to Herzog for assistance in financing the purchase of her new Charger. Herzog made appropriate arrangements with Drovers State Bank. The sale was consummated by plaintiff's executing an installment contract for $3,906. The contract was thereupon assigned to Drovers bank which issued its money order to Herzog for $3,415.15, the balance of the purchase price less the equity in the Dart.

Critical to the disposition of this case is the fact that plaintiff and Herzog, by prearrangement, agreed that Drovers bank was to pay Herzog an amount which included the full value of the Dart without any deduction for the balance of the mortgage owed plaintiff's credit union. Under its agreement with plaintiff Herzog was to satisfy the chattel mortgage on plaintiff's Dart. That arrangement, however, was not communicated to Drovers bank and they had no knowledge of the existence of the mortgage.

In performance of their agreement, Herzog drew a check to plaintiff's credit union in the sum of $1,345.15 and delivered it to the credit union. After it was deposited by the credit union, the check was dishonored by the First National Bank of Minneapolis on which it was drawn because that bank had unsecured loans made to Herzog which it believed to be in jeopardy. Consequently, the bank retained Herzog's deposits to secure its loans. Herzog thereafter was rendered insolvent and the chattel mortgage on plaintiff's Dart in the sum of $1,345.15, held by plaintiff's credit union, remained unsatisfied.

[Being sued for the amount due on that mortgage, Holt brought this action against several parties, including the Drovers Bank.]

The issue presented by the parties is whether the following language in the installment contract running from plaintiff to Herzog and assigned to Drovers bank is contrary to public policy and unenforceable:

"No agreement, promise or warranty not expressed herein and no defect in condition or quality of the Property shall bind or afford a defense against any assignee hereof."

Minn.St. 336.9–206(1) of the Uniform Commercial Code provides as follows: [1] [See p. 1121 supra].

If the waiver is invalid, the Uniform Commercial Code makes the following section effective (§ 336.9–318[1][a]):

"(1) Unless an account debtor has made an enforceable agreement not to assert defenses or claims arising out of a sale as provided in section 336.9–206 the rights of an assignee are subject to

"(a) all the terms of the contract between the account debtor and the assignor and any defense or claim arising therefrom; . . ."

Finally, the Uniform Commercial Code makes this provision for dealing with unconscionable contracts (§ 336.2–302[1]): [omitted]

Plaintiff cites as authority for reversal a number of cases which have held waivers to be contrary to public policy. . . .

Although plaintiff sought relief against all of the parties to whom we have alluded, the issue has been narrowed to her right to deduct from the installment contract held by Drovers the sum of $1,345.15 included in that contract to satisfy her mortgage with the credit union.

Plaintiff seeks in these proceedings to invalidate application of Minn.St. 336.9–206 to consumer goods transactions as contrary to public policy. As we have indicated, the legislature has now made that portion of the Uniform Commercial Code inapplicable, in certain instances, in the following language (§ 325.941, subd. 2[a]):

"No contract or obligation relating to a consumer credit sale shall contain any provision by which:

"(a) The consumer agrees not to assert against an assignee any claim or defense arising out of the transaction".

1. That statute has been made inapplicable to consumer credit transactions by L.1971, c. 275, § 2.

Since July 1, 1971, the effective date of § 325.941, subd. 2(a), lending agencies have been on notice of their obligation to scrutinize assignments in consumer transactions with the same degree of caution they would exercise in dealing directly with consumers were such agencies vendors. Drovers bank, in the instant case, had no such duty. Nor is there any evidence that Drovers and Herzog entertained the kind of relationship we held in International Finance Corp. v. Rieger, 272 Minn. 192, 137 N.W.2d 172 (1965), deprived the lending agency of the protections accorded a holder in due course. We are not disposed to hold the statute contrary to public policy for all purposes. There may be fact situations which will justify that conclusion in particular cases. This is not one of them. Indeed, the claims of plaintiff are not directly related to a "consumer credit sale" on which the statutes focus.

The cases which are cited by plaintiff deal with a variety of contract breaches pertaining to goods sold. The conduct of the seller in each instance was manifestly "unconscionable." The waiver provisions which were set aside in those cases would have protected the assignees from defenses based on conduct which approached fraud. That is not the situation before us in this case. There is no suggestion that either Herzog or Drovers bank did not act in good faith. The bank had no information which should have put it on notice that plaintiff had delegated to Herzog the responsibility for satisfying her mortgage to the credit union out of the proceeds of the loan. While, of course, we recognize the hardship which has resulted to plaintiff, it was brought about by a collateral arrangement which she herself made with Herzog in which the bank took no part and for which it had no responsibility. In effect, she designated Herzog her agent to satisfy an outstanding mortgage. Herzog became as to her simply a creditor in a fiduciary capacity. The situation is no different from what it would have been had the bank paid plaintiff the $1,345.15 and she had turned that sum over to Herzog with directions to satisfy the mortgage out of it. Where one of two innocent persons must assume the loss, it is not unconscionable to permit the person to suffer the loss who had knowledge of all the facts and was in a position to protect against the loss.

For the reasons indicated, we have concluded that the waiver-of-defenses clause in the case at hand is not unconscionable, and it was proper for the trial court to give it effect.

Affirmed.

MacLAUGHLIN, Justice (dissenting).

I believe that this court should declare a waiver-of-defense clause such as the one involved in this case to be against the public policy of the State of Minnesota. The pertinent statute, Minn.St. 336.9–206(1), makes such clauses enforceable, subject however "to any statute or decision which establishes a different rule for buyers or lessees of consumer goods." I would accept the invitation to issue a decision of this court declaring such provisions in consumer transactions to be against public policy.

While some courts have upheld waiver-of-defense clauses, others have regarded such waivers to be at variance with state public policy. Annotation, 39 A.L.R.3d 518, 522. Among those cases invalidating waiver-of-defense clauses in consumer transactions are Quality Finance Co. v. Hurley, 337 Mass. 150, 148 N.E.2d 385 (1958); Unico v. Owen, 50 N.J. 101, 232 A.2d 405 (1967); Toker v. Perl, 108 N.J.Super. 129, 260 A.2d 244 (1970); Fairfield Credit Corp. v. Donnelly, 158 Conn. 543, 264 A.2d 547, 39 A.L.R.3d 509 (1969). Cf. Rehurek v. Chrysler Credit Corp., 262 So.2d 452 (Fla.App.1972). In Fairfield Credit Corp. v. Donnelly, supra, the Connecticut Supreme Court held that a waiver-of-defense clause in an installment contract for a television set was void as against public policy and stated (158 Conn. 550, 264 A.2d 550, 39 A.L.R.3d 515):

". . . [T]he use of a waiver of defense clause is an attempt to impart the attributes of negotiability to an otherwise nonnegotiable instrument. [Uniform Commercial Code, § 3–104]. An attempt to evade the clear prerequisites of negotiability by the use of such clauses (often, as here, in fine print and couched in technical language the significance of which is difficult for the ordinary consumer to appreciate) is opposed to the policy and spirit of [Uniform Commercial Code, § 3–306], which provides that one not a holder in due course of an instrument is subject to all claims and defenses which would have been available against the original holder."

The Donnelly case also points out the policy of the Connecticut Legislature to protect purchasers of consumer goods from the impositions of overreaching sellers. I believe the same legislative goal exists in Minnesota. See, e. g., Minn.St. 325.78 to 325.80 (prevention of consumer fraud); 45.15 and 45.16 (establishing a consumer services section of the department of commerce); 325.92 (unsolicited goods deemed gifts); 325.94 and 325.941 (consumer credit sales). See, generally, c. 325.[1] Since there exists in Minnesota a strong public policy in favor of protecting purchasers of consumer goods, it is contrary to that policy for us to enforce a waiver-of-defense clause in a consumer-goods transaction.

The majority opinion states that the claims of plaintiff do not relate directly to a consumer credit sale. Inasmuch as her claims arise from an agreement made incident to the purchase of a new automobile pursuant to an installment sales credit contract which con-

1. The most recent legislative session resulted in laws protecting a wide range of consumer interests. See, e. g., L.1973, c. 264 (prohibiting odometer tampering); c. 383 (regulating hearing aid sales); c. 442 (requiring itemizing of funeral costs); c. 443 (regarding sales not made at seller's place of business); c. 467 (banning dangerous toys); c. 687 (requiring display of octane ratings); c. 692 (limiting disclaimer of implied warranties).

tained the waiver-of-defense clause, it seems clear to me that the sale was a consumer credit sale within the meaning of the code.

Further, I do not believe it is relevant that neither Herzog nor Drovers State Bank acted in bad faith or that Drovers bank did not have information which would have put it on notice that plaintiff delegated to Herzog the responsibility for satisfying her mortgage to the credit union out of the proceeds of the loan. Had the bank been on notice of the agreement, or acted in other than good faith, the waiver-of-defense clause would have been unenforceable under the express terms of Minn.St. 336.9–206(1), set forth in the majority opinion. The issue to be decided in this case is whether waiver-of-defense clauses should be against public policy in transactions involving consumer goods where the assignee takes his assignment for value, "in good faith and without notice of a claim or defense . . . ." § 336.9–206(1).

Rather than decide this question on a case-by-case basis, I would take the prerogative left to this court by the legislature and abolish waiver-of-defense clauses in any transaction involving a buyer or lessee of consumer goods.

Because this case is nonprecedential in that our legislature has passed a statute invalidating a waiver of this kind,[2] I will not further enlarge upon my reasons for believing that we should declare such waivers against public policy. I would reverse.[a]

NOTES

(1) *Degrees of Intimacy.* Note that the Dodge dealer assisted Gail Holt in obtaining financing, by making "arrangements" with the Drovers Bank. Yet the court said that the dealer-bank relationship was critically different from that in the Participation Case (p. 1119 supra) between Laundry Sales and International Finance. What important difference might the court have had in mind?

(2) *Degrees of Unfairness.* In what other circumstances might the court have held that the waiver-of-defense clause was unconscionable? On a showing that the car she bought was defective? That Herzog had misrepresented its condition? How would you expect the court to treat such a clause if it appeared in a contract for the sale of a grossly overpriced food freezer, foisted on the buyer at his home through high-pressure sale tactics? If the court were to decide such a case differently, would it be confusing the propriety of the clause with the impropriety of the bargaining?

(3) *Gaps in the Fictional Fence.* Unico v. Owen, cited in both the foregoing opinions, has been partially stated at p. 1117 supra. Unico, the assignee of the contract, sued Owen, the buyer, and lost in the trial court. On successive appeals, the judgment was twice affirmed. The Supreme

2. Minn.St. 325.941, subd. 3, which makes an assignee subject to any defenses the consumer has against the seller, is effective as to any consumer credit sale entered into on or after July 1, 1971. L.1971, c. 275, § 3. The instant sale was in 1967.

a. Mr. Justice Olson concurred in the dissent.

Court of New Jersey wrote an elaborate opinion, referring to Henningsen v. Bloomfield Motors (p. 457 supra) and Williams v. Walker-Thomas Furniture Co. (p. 504 supra), among other cases. It summarized some of them as follows:

"The courts have recognized that the basic problem in consumer goods sales and financing is that of balancing the interest of the commercial community in unrestricted negotiability of commercial paper against the interest of installment buyers of such goods in the preservation of their normal remedy of withholding payment when, as in this case, the seller fails to deliver as agreed, and thus the consideration for his obligation fails. Many courts have solved the problem by denying to the holder of the paper the status of holder in due course where the financer maintains a close relationship with the dealer whose paper he buys; where the financer is closely connected with the dealer's business operations or with the particular credit transaction; or where the financer furnishes the form of sale contract and note for use by the dealer, the buyer signs the contract and note concurrently, and the dealer endorses the note and assigns the contract immediately thereafter or within the period prescribed by the financer. . . . Other courts have said that when the financer supplies or prescribes or approves the form of sales contract, or conditional sale agreement, or chattel mortgage as well as the installment payment note (particularly if it has the financer's name printed on the face or in the endorsement), and all the documents are executed by the buyer at one time and the contract assigned and note endorsed to the financer and delivered to the financer together (whether or not attached or part of a single instrument), the holder takes subject to the rights and obligations of the seller. The transaction is looked upon as a species of tripartite proceeding, and the tenor of the cases is that the financer should not be permitted 'to isolate itself behind the fictional fence' of the Negotiable Instruments Law, and thereby achieve an unfair advantage over the buyer."

In this case the New Jersey court also considered the effect of a negotiable note given by Mr. Owen, on which Unico asserted rights as a holder in due course.[b]

POLICY CONSIDERATIONS

Are there distinctive considerations of policy that underlie the decision in Unico v. Owen (preceding note) and the Minnesota stat-

b. On this point see also Jones v. Approved Bancredit Corp., 256 A.2d 739 (Del.1969), a case said to be "especially analogous" to Unico v. Owen, and Rosenthal, Negotiability—Who Needs It?, 71 Colum.L.Rev. 375, 378–80 (1971). The Unico case was successfully defended for the Owens by private counsel, who accepted a "small fee" for representing them in the trial court. Unico appealed to an intermediate court, and then to the state supreme court. (What would justify this expense to a finance company? Was it worth it?) The Owens could not pay for appellate representation, but their lawyers espoused their cause through both appeals, plus supplementary briefing and argument requested by the supreme court. "We, of course, did not realize what we were getting into; however, once we were involved we had no choice but to proceed to the ultimate conclusion." During the proceedings Mr. Owen died, leaving his family without means, and they moved back to their former home in another state. The foregoing incidents are as reported in a letter to the editors from counsel for the Owens.

ute described in n. 2, p. 1127 supra? To some extent these rules reflect only concern about the more general problems of standard form contracts. However, there have been attempts to show that the "holder in due course problem" is a singular one, deserving of specialized treatment. The following considerations figure in the argument.

(1) Financing institutions are in a superior position, by comparison with ordinary consumers, to evaluate a merchant's responsibility. The prospect of disappointment in dealing with a merchant is partly a function of his usual business practices, his reputation for fair dealing, and the risk of his becoming insolvent. On all these matters a bank or finance company supplying him with funds is equipped to make judgments more accurately than his ordinary customers.

(2) A merchant's customers are poorly situated to exercise discipline against him for substandard business practices, whereas corrective measures may readily be forced on him by a financer if his retail operations give rise to an undue number of complaints. Hence a rule imposing on financers the risk of customer disappointment will effectively engage them in the function of "policing" against irresponsible merchandising.

(3) Pooling of information is an effective means of reducing substandard performance by merchants. Financing institutions are capable of organizing exchanges of information, such that a merchant who proves unworthy of trust will be promptly foreclosed from the credit market. By contrast, information exchanges among consumers are feebly organized, so that a merchant may maintain a certain reputation with the public even though many of his customers suffer from his delinquencies. Not only so, but he may also be able to escape their wrath by a change of business name, or of location. Financing institutions can more easily penetrate disguises. Furthermore, when such an institution undertakes collections for a merchant the wrath of a disappointed customer is likely to be deflected from the merchant to his assignee.[a] Hence, the argument runs, it is appropriate to align the assignee with the customer as a party aggrieved by the merchant's delinquency. That is the effect when the assignee is deprived of holder-in-due-course status, and deprived of the benefit of a waiver-of-defense clause.[b]

None of these arguments need be taken at face value, of course. What countervailing considerations are there? It has been forcefully argued that, if merchants cannot give the assurances to financing institutions described as holder-in-due-course status, they will find

a. See Leff, Injury, Ignorance and Spite—The Dynamics of Coercive Collection, 80 Yale L.J. 1, 35 (1970).

b. An extensive statement of policy arguments tending in the same direction as these appears in a paper of the Federal Trade Commission published as an addendum to the F.T.C. Rule set out at p. 1132 infra: Statement of Basis and Purpose, 40 Fed. Reg. 5306 (1975).

credit more expensive, or inaccessible, and that the cost to merchants must be reflected in retail prices. How do you appraise this argument? If a rule against cutting off defenses has any such consequence, would you expect it to affect only credit prices, or cash prices as well? Suppose that the buyers in Unico v. Owen (preceding note) had paid cash in advance for the merchandise. What would their remedy have been? Presumably any remedy you suggest would have been available to them on the facts as they were. Do you conclude that a disappointed cash buyer never has a better prospect of relief than one who pays by a negotiable note, and often has a worse one? Does this state of affairs make any sense? You should reconsider these questions after reading further in this section.

The Merediths' Case

Bennie and Joyce Meredith purchased a food freezer and some foodstuffs from the Tri-State Foods Company under two installment contracts. The contracts contained waiver-of-defense clauses, and were assigned to the Personal Finance Company. When the finance company sued the Merediths for payments, the trial court struck certain defenses they sought to make as insufficient in law, and they appealed. *Held*: Reversed for an erroneous exclusion of evidence. Personal Finance Co. v. Meredith, 39 Ill.App.3d 695, 350 N.E.2d 781 (1976).

According to the Illinois Retail Installment Sales Act, an assignee is not protected by a waiver-of-defense clause if it has knowledge of "certain facts regarding the seller-assignor's history of complaints for its failure to fulfill its contractual obligations . . . ."[c] The Merediths should have been allowed to probe for complaints, known to the finance company, by other customers of Tri-State Foods. On the other hand, the statute was used to refute the Merediths' contention that the clause was ineffective by virtue of the business relationship between Tri-State and the finance company. The statute specifies certain relationships having that effect: e. g., parent-subsidiary corporations. The record failed to show any closer connection than an agreement by the financer to purchase Tri-State's contracts.

Another Illinois statute, the Consumer Fraud Act, was also applicable to the Merediths' contracts.[d] It prescribes a notice, in 10-point bold type, in the absence of which an assignment of the contract, or a transfer of a negotiable instrument, "does not bar [the] consumer from asserting . . . any defense or right of action he

c. This is the court's paraphrase of Ill.Rev.Stat. ch. 12½, § 517. See also § 576.

d. Although this statute is in terms addressed to negotiable instruments, it has been construed as applicable also to non-negotiable contracts containing waiver-of-defense clauses.

For a decision by a divided court on an analogous statute see Stevwing v. Western Pennsylvania Nat. Bank, 468 Pa. 24, 359 A.2d 793 (1976).

may have against the seller." The Merediths' contracts contained such a notice as follows:

NOTICE TO BUYER

> You have the right to give the assignee named (or if no assignee is named, to give the seller) written notice of any defense or right of action which you may have against the seller within 5 days of delivery of the merchandise described herein. If a notice is not received within that time, you may not assert such defense or right of action against the assignee.

Finally, the court considered at length whether or not the waiver-of-defense clauses were unconscionable in relation to the Merediths, and concluded they were not. By the Merediths' own testimony, the court said, "their failure to examine the contract . . . was not caused by the salesman's alleged unfair techniques but by their haste to get to their bowling game." No claim was made of a failure by Tri-State to deliver satisfactory merchandise.[e]

NOTES

(1) *Unconscionability.* The point has been made that UCC 9–206(1) explicitly yields to opposing non-Code rules favoring buyers of consumer goods (Note 2, p. 1122 supra). And that Article 9 defers generally to legislation of that character: "it does not prescribe regulations and controls which may be necessary to curb abuses arising in the small loan business or in the financing of consumer purchases on credit." Note to UCC 9–102.[f] But may the rule of section 9–206(1) itself amount to such an abuse, so far as it is not overridden by non-Code "different rules"? For an intimation that it may, see United States Leasing Corp. v. Franklin Plaza Apartments, Inc., 8 UCC Rep. 1026 (N.Y.Civ.Ct.1971), where the court found support in UCC 2–302, on unconscionability.

Is it proper to regard these two Code sections as being at war with one another? And if so which should be the victor?

In Equico Lessors, Inc. v. Mines, 84 Cal.App.3d 374, 148 Cal.Rptr. 554 (1978), a physician was charged with rentals for oil-well drilling equipment which (he alleged) was never delivered, by reason of UCC 9–206(1). He had not known he was signing a lease (he said), much less one that might require him to pay when the consideration failed.[g] He objected that the re-

e. A Truth-in-Lending claim was made in the case. An assignee may be fitted within the definition of "creditor" for the purpose of fixing liability under that statute, it is held. See A. Charles & Co. v. Bishop, 75 Ill.App.3d 556, 31 Ill.Dec. 448, 394 N.E.2d 650 (1979). This does not signify, of course, that the assignee is chargeable with the assignor's shortcomings.

f. As to the Code's neutrality on consumer credit issues, see Skilton & Helstad, Protection of the Installment Buyer of Goods under the UCC, 65 Mich.L.Rev. 1465 (1967).

g. Perhaps all he knew was that he expected an income-tax advantage from the transaction. He stopped paying the rentals when they were disallowed as deductions.

sult was harsh. To that the court answered: "the Legislature, in order to avoid mischief in the commercial world, requires participants to proceed with some modicum of prudence."

(2) *Variant State Rules.* The formulation of UCC 9–206(1) was sharply debated in the councils of the Code sponsors. The decision, of course, was not to strive for uniformity on the issue of consumer protection. (Does that fact suggest any attitude that should be taken toward the business buyer?) The issue of consumer protection has also been hard-fought in the legislatures and the courts. A number of statutes virtually deprive waiver-of-defense clauses—and holder-in-due-course status, with respect to notes—of their efficacy in ordinary consumer transactions.[h] Other statutes embody the principle of the Illinois Consumer Fraud Act: they provide the consumer with a limited period for raising objections against paying the assignee. (In states of this persuasion, the inception and the duration of this period are variables.[i])

(3) *"More than a Mere Assignee."* An assignee is not subject, it is said, to the "contract or tort liabilities imposed by the contract on the assignor, in the absence of an assumption of such liabilities." Farmers Acceptance Corp. v. DeLozier, 178 Colo. 291, 496 P.2d 1016 (1972).

Yet it has been held, under a consumer-protection statute, that an assignee is subject, as such, to the assignor's liability to the extent of what the assignee received through the assignment. (See Vasquez v. Superior Court, p. 1138 infra.) Beyond that, one must watch for an *implied* assumption of the assignor's liabilities. In Massey-Ferguson Credit Corp. v. Brown, 173 Mont. 253, 567 P.2d 440 (1977), the assignment was of rights under a contract for the sale of a combine. An agent of the assignee had signed the contract as a witness, and had made certain representations to the buyer about the combine. On these facts, and a finding of breach by the seller, the buyer was not only absolved from making any payments to the assignee but was also given judgment against it for the value of a trade-in combine. On appeal by the assignee, ***held:*** Affirmed. The court called it "more than a mere assignee," in relation to the sale. *Question:* How far must a finance company withdraw itself from a dealer's business to avoid this characterization? For a sharply debated case concerning the financing of a real-estate development, see Senn v. Manchester Bank of St. Louis, 583 S.W.2d 119 (Mo.1979).

PRESERVATION OF CONSUMERS' CLAIMS AND DEFENSES

Effective May 14, 1976, the Federal Trade Commission promulgated a new rule under the title above. It has the form of two sections, in a new Part (433) of Trade Regulations Rules, Subchapter D (16 CFR, Chapter I). As promulgated in November, 1975, the new

h. See UCCC 3.307 and other sections cited in the Comment.

i. E. g., 60 days from mailing of notice of assignment, with warning. Ind. Code 1971, 24–4.5–2–404. For difficulty in binding an unresponsive consumer, see Insurance Agency Managers v. Gonzales, 578 S.W.2d 803 (Tex.Civ.App.1979).

Part appears at 40 Fed.Reg. 53506, and is followed by a "Statement of Basis and Purpose."

§ 433.1 Definitions.

(a) *Person.* An individual, corporation, or any other business organization.

(b) *Consumer.* A natural person who seeks or acquires goods or services for personal, family, or household use.

(c) *Creditor.* A person who, in the ordinary course of business, lends purchase money or finances the sale of goods or services to consumers on a deferred payment basis; *Provided,* such person is not acting, for the purposes of a particular transaction, in the capacity of a credit card issuer.

(d) *Purchase money loan.* A cash advance which is received by a consumer in return for a "Finance Charge" within the meaning of the Truth in Lending Act and Regulation Z, which is applied, in whole or substantial part, to a purchase of goods or services from a seller who (1) refers consumers to the creditor or (2) is affiliated with the creditor by common control, contract, or business arrangement.

(e) *Financing a sale.* Extending credit to a consumer in connection with a "Credit Sale" within the meaning of the Truth in Lending Act and Regulation Z.

(f) *Contract.* Any oral or written agreement, formal or informal, between a creditor and a seller, which contemplates or provides for cooperative or concerted activity in connection with the sale of goods or services to consumers or the financing thereof.

(g) *Business arrangement.* Any understanding, procedure, course of dealing, or arrangement, formal or informal, between a creditor and a seller, in connection with the sale of goods or services to consumers or the financing thereof.

(h) *Credit card issuer.* A person who extends to cardholders the right to use a credit card in connection with purchases of goods or services.

(i) *Consumer credit contract.* Any instrument which evidences or embodies a debt arising from a "Purchase Money Loan" transaction or a "financed sale" as defined in paragraphs (d) and (e).

(j) *Seller.* A person who, in the ordinary course of business, sells or leases goods or services to consumers.

§ 433.2 Preservation of Consumers' Claims and Defenses, Unfair or Deceptive Acts or Practices.

In connection with any sale or lease of goods or services to consumers, in or affecting commerce as "commerce" is defined in the Federal Trade Commission Act, it is an unfair or deceptive act or practice within the meaning of Section 5 of that Act for a seller, directly or indirectly, to:

(a) Take or receive a consumer credit contract which fails to contain the following provision in at least ten point, bold face, type:

NOTICE

ANY HOLDER OF THIS CONSUMER CREDIT CONTRACT IS SUBJECT TO ALL CLAIMS AND DEFENSES WHICH THE DEBTOR COULD ASSERT AGAINST THE SELLER OF GOODS OR SERVICES OBTAINED PURSUANT HERETO OR WITH THE PROCEEDS HEREOF. RECOVERY HEREUNDER BY THE DEBTOR SHALL NOT EXCEED AMOUNTS PAID BY THE DEBTOR HEREUNDER.

or, (b) Accept, as full or partial payment for such sale or lease, the proceeds of any purchase money loan (as purchase money loan is defined herein), unless any consumer credit contract made in connection with such purchase money loan contains the following provision in at least ten point, bold face, type:

NOTICE

ANY HOLDER OF THIS CONSUMER CREDIT CONTRACT IS SUBJECT TO ALL CLAIMS AND DEFENSES WHICH THE DEBTOR COULD ASSERT AGAINST THE SELLER OF GOODS OR SERVICES OBTAINED WITH THE PROCEEDS HEREOF. RECOVERY HEREUNDER BY THE DEBTOR SHALL NOT EXCEED AMOUNTS PAID BY THE DEBTOR HEREUNDER.

NOTES

(1) *Problem.* If the contract between Holt and Herzog Dodge (see case at p. 1123 supra) had contained the first notice term set out in the Rule, is there a serious doubt that she could have asserted against the bank (as holder) the claim or defense that she could have asserted (as debtor) in an action brought by Herzog (as seller)? In that case the court said that Holt's claim against Herzog was not directly related to a consumer credit sale. But observe that the notice is not confined to claims and defenses assertable against the seller *as seller*. Should that restriction be read in?

(2) *Reading the Rule.* In the three cases last presented, which of the buyers was *not* a "consumer"? In the two consumer-buyer cases the sellers and financial institutions concerned were "creditors" in the sense of the Rule. In at least one of the three cases there was evidently a "contract" between a seller and a financial institution, as well as a "business arrangement." (Do you see which one?)

The application of the Rule, depends, however, on the presence of either a "consumer credit contract"—paragraph 2(a)—or a "purchase money loan" —paragraph 2(b). None of the three cases concerned the latter (for there was no "cash advance received by a consumer"). But in the two consumer-buyer cases there were doubtless "consumer credit contracts." This conclusion rests on the following premises:

(a) Credit sales occurred, "within the meaning of the Truth in Lending Act and Regulation Z." This statute[a] is the charter for federal disclosure requirements respecting consumer credit, and Regulation Z (of the Federal Reserve Board) implements it. Few extensions of credit to a consumer escape it.[b]

(b) As credit was extended to a consumer in connection with such a sale, the debt arose "from . . . a 'financed sale' as defined in paragraph (e)."

(Note some exclusions that are not applicable to these cases. The definition of "seller" rules out casual, consumer-to-consumer sales, for the word "seller" is central to both the prohibitions of clause 2. In that clause there is a jurisdictional reference to "commerce." But that restriction may be disregarded for present purposes. It imposes no limit short of the constitutional authority of Congress—broad indeed—with respect to commerce. Finally, credit card transactions are excluded by paragraphs (c) and (h) of clause 1.)

Hence we arrive at the conclusion, under the Rule, that if the notice prescribed in paragraph 2(a) does not appear in "any instrument which evidences or embodies a debt" such as the debts incurred by Holt or the Merediths, the seller has violated section 5 of the FTC Act.

(3) *Consequences.* For a violation of the Act, the Commission may claim a civil penalty or invoke other sanctions. That is not the intended thrust of the Rule, however. The effect intended is to deprive an assignee (such as Drovers Bank) of the power to override the buyer's defenses by virtue of either negotiability or a waiver-of-defense clause. If the required notice does appear, the assignee is hardly in a position to assert the immunity provided by those mechanisms.

But what if the seller flouts the law, omits the notice, and transfers a "clean" embodiment of debt? So far as the Rule goes, its purpose is not attained in that event (assuming that the transferee purchases "in good faith and without notice . . ."). The buyer seems to be remitted to whatever protection applicable state law may afford him. However, this prospect is probably negligible in practice. A transferee such as Drovers Bank knows the law—or should know it. If it knowingly purchases a "consumer credit contract" from which the notice is omitted, its good faith will be suspect, to say the least. There is the possibility, of course, that it will purchase a consumer credit contract supposing it to be something else. But the case of a financial institution doing that—as the initial transferee—is probably so exceptional as to deserve little notice. One who is troubled about it may take some comfort from Stewart v. Thornton, 116 Ariz. 107,

a. Part of the Consumer Credit Protection Act, 15 U.S.C.A. § 1601 et seq.

b. 12 C.F.R. § 226.2(s).
Regulation Z exempts most transactions, other than real property transactions, in which the amount to be financed exceeds $25,000. Section 226.3 (15 U.S.C.A. following § 1700). In § 433.3 the FTC Rule itself exempts certain transactions not of moment here.

568 P.2d 414 (1977), concerning the Interstate Land Sales Full Disclosure Act [c] and a note issuing out of a non-complying transaction.

Of course one may wonder why the Commission took so roundabout an approach to the holder-in-due-course matter as the Rule represents. And the answer is that as between writing "disclosure" requirements—such as the Rule imposes—and recasting the law of commercial paper, the tradition of the agency, and some question about its authority for the latter action, commit it to the former.[d]

SPECIOUS CASH SALES

Having agreed to buy a new car from Herzog Dodge, Inc., Gail Holt asks it for assistance in financing the purchase. After making appropriate arrangements with Drovers State Bank, Herzog advises her to go there for a loan. At the bank she gives an installment-payment note, naming it as payee, and receives cash or its equivalent. (In practice, she would probably not receive quite the equivalent, but a draft made payable jointly to her and to Herzog. Because such a draft will not clear without the indorsements of both, it commits the borrower to the car purchase, in a sense.) The car-sale then goes through, the dealer receiving payment in full. If Holt now has a ground for revoking her acceptance of the car, and does so, may she withhold payment from the bank?

That question translates into some questions about the FTC Rule: Is the note a "consumer credit contract"? And was the loan a "purchase money loan," as defined? Certainly if there was such a loan there was such a contract; and the answer to all three questions is Yes. Given a purchase money loan, if the notice prescribed in clause 2(b) does not appear in the note the seller (*sic*) is in violation of the FTC Act. Any bank that believes it is making a purchase money loan will see to the notice; by omitting it the bank has nothing to gain and something to lose: the good will of the seller, a probable

c. 15 U.S.C.A. § 1707–20. See also Salter v. Vanotti, 26 UCC Rep. 964 (Colo.App.1979). But see Sherrill v. Frank Morris, Etc., 366 So.2d 251 (Ala. 1978).

d. For a Comment highly critical of the Rule see 25 UCLA L.Rev. 821 (1978). "[N]ot only do the Rule's poorly worded definitions and limited coverage lead to a misallocation of resources, they also contain great danger for the consumer." Id. at 854.

Here and elsewhere proposals to reform the relations between consumer-credit suppliers and users have met with objections based on suppositions about what the costs will be and who will bear them. These suppositions are questioned in Wallace, The Logic of Consumer Credit Reform, 82 Yale L.J. 461 (1973), where it is argued that some such reforms, at least, may effect gains in both market efficiency and distributive justice. For an attempt at empirical research on "holder in due course" reform, and a comment on its methodology, see Note, A Case Study, etc., 78 Yale L.J. 618 (1969), and Schuchman, Empirical Studies in Commercial Law, 23 J.Leg.Ed. 181 (1970).

For valuable studies see Rohner, Holder in Due Course in Consumer Transactions, 60 Corn.L.Rev. 503 (1975), and Garner & Dunham, FTC Rule 433 and the Uniform Commercial Code, 43 Mo. L.Rev. 122 (1978).

customer. For other financial institutions, similar incentives will doubtless hold.

Then what makes a "purchase money loan"? A consumer loan carrying no finance charge (as defined) is outside the conception—and outside of common experience as well. The important point is that Holt's loan does not fit the description if

(1) all other customers of Herzog who borrowed at Drovers Bank found their own way there; *and*

(2) Herzog is not "affiliated with the [bank] by common control, contract [defined], or business arrangement [defined]."

Many merchants would, if not restrained by off-premises laws,[a] maintain finance-company offices adjacent to their sales floors, for the convenience of "cash" customers. Under the Rule, when that occurs it behooves the finance company to take heed of the quality of the merchant's goods and services. In such a case "purchase money loans" are bound to be the rule, both because there is affiliation and because proximity amounts to referral.

When there is one referral, there is usually a series. The more interesting question is where the outer boundary of "affiliation" lies. As counsel to a bank or finance company, how would you advise it to act, so as to keep its distance from the merchants in the community? When would you advise the client not to try, but rather to clasp a merchant in a "business arrangement" as close as possible?

NOTES

(1) *State Statutes.* The expression "specious cash sale" fits very well the situation in which a merchant ostensibly makes only cash sales, but most of the cash is provided by a lender under common ownership. However, the several statutes addressing this situation go well beyond such intimate seller-lender connections (as does the FTC Rule). For example, under a Massachusetts statute a creditor is "deemed to have participated" in a sale if it was "specifically recommended" to the borrower by the seller and if the proceeds of as many as two loans made by the creditor in any calendar year have been used in transactions with the same seller (and in other circumstances as well)[b]. Note that as an evidentiary matter it may be easier for a disappointed buyer to establish participation under that statute than to establish that his note is a "consumer credit contract" within the definition of the FTC Rule (and should therefore have contained the notice prescribed in clause 2(b)). A comparable New York statute erects a presumption (rebuttable) that a lender was "directly connected" with a consumer sale on proofs of certain circumstances—e. g., that forms used to evidence the loan were prepared by the seller.[c] State legislatures entering the field have not contented themselves with notice requirements, as the FTC

a. E. g., N.Y.Bank.L. § 351.

b. Mass.Gen.L.Ann. c. 255 § 12F.

c. Gen.Bus.L. §§ 252–255.

has done, but have driven directly to the conclusion.[d] For example, the New York statute declares that, given the requisite participation or connection, "A creditor, who made a consumer loan the proceeds of which were primarily used in a consumer sale, shall be subject to all of the defenses of a consumer arising from such consumer sale . . . ."

Does the use of a presumption make a nice compromise between the stiffness of the Massachusetts statute (two loans a year) and the flaccidity of the FTC Rule ("business arrangement")? If so, the New York approach lost its appeal when the federal rule was put in place alongside it, did it not?

(2) *Fraud as an Offense.* In Commercial Credit Corp. v. Orange County Machine Works, 34 Cal.2d 766, 214 P.2d 819 (1950), the court held that "since the assignee of a contract and note advanced money to the seller with the understanding that these instruments would be assigned to it, supplied the contract forms to the seller, and actively participated in the transaction from its inception, it could not claim holder-in-due-course status." [e] The buyer, Machine Works, was in the commercial arena. Thereafter the California legislature enacted broad consumer-protection provisions (the Unruh Act [f]), including one which subjected an assignee to "all claims and defenses of the buyer against the seller arising out of the sale notwithstanding an agreement to the contrary . . . ." [g] In Vasquez v. Superior Court of San Joaquin County, 4 Cal.3d 800, 94 Cal.Rptr. 796, 484 P.2d 964 (1971), the State Supreme Court took occasion to instruct the trial court about potential liabilities under the statute. According to the provision mentioned above,

> . . . the assignee's liability may not exceed the amount of the debt owing to the assignee at the time that the defense is asserted against the assignee. The rights of the buyer under this section can only be asserted as a matter of defense to a claim by the assignee.

The court concluded that these limitations "are not applicable if an assignee has taken the contract with notice of defenses of the buyer against the assignor or if the assignee's relationship with the assignor comes within the rule set forth in *Commercial Credit.*" [h] Compare Meyers v. Postal Finance Co., 287 N.W.2d 614 (Minn.1979).

Vasquez dealt with charges of fraud and of violation of the Unruh Act which had been made in connection with sales of freezers and frozen food by the Bay Area Meat Company. In addition to Bay Area, three finance companies, assignees of its contracts, were made defendants in an action brought by consumer buyers. The finance companies were alleged to have been aware of the fraud. Because the case had not proceeded beyond de-

d. But not always. See Conn.Gen. Stats. § 42–136—part of the Home Solicitation Sales Act.

e. The quotation is from the case next cited.

f. Civil Code, § 1801 et seq.

g. Civil Code, § 1804.2.

h. Another important ruling in *Vasquez* was that certain customers of Bay Area Meat Company should be permitted to press the claims of its customers in a class action, with respect not only to the Unruh Act but to the asserted fraud as well, against Bay Area and the several finance-company defendants.

For a symposium on the case see 18 U.C.L.A.L.Rev. 1041 (1971).

murrers, it is not certain what remedies the buyers might have had. The position *rejected* by the court was as follows:

> The finance companies contend that under [the statute] plaintiffs may not bring an affirmative action against them for rescission but may only assert their defense of fraud in an action by the finance companies to collect on the contracts and then only to the extent of the amount still owing.

The court said: "It would be ironic indeed if a provision in an act intended to benefit consumers could be invoked to [place them] in a less advantageous position than others in the commercial arena."

PROBLEMS OF REMEDY

A firm operating a burglar-alarm system assigns one of its contracts during the second year of service to the subscriber. All the firm's contracts are for a one-year term, but they are renewable "automatically" for like terms if no contrary sign is given. Ten months later, when a burglary loss occurs, the subscriber has paid $1,500 to the firm and $1,000 to the assignee, all at the contract rate of $100 a month. The loss—$5,000—is caused by failure of the system, but the contract purports to liquidate the subscriber's damages at $500. What may the subscriber recover from the assignee, if anything?

Under the Unruh Act, as construed in *Vasquez*, one of the questions necessary to ask is whether or not the assignee took "too active a part" in the assignor's business. If the answer is Yes, then would it matter whether the subscriber was in or out of the "commercial arena"? Whether or not the stipulation of damages would be effective in a suit against the service operator seems a natural question. (In deciding that, might it count that the subscriber was a merchant?) Might anything be said for limiting the assignee's liability to $1,000 at most?

In 1975 the California statute debated in *Vasquez* was amended to read: "but the assignee's liability may not exceed the amount . . . owing to the assignee at the time of the assignment." The sentence about "only as a matter of defense" was deleted.[a] What do these changes signify?

Consider the possibilities of relief under the following statute, treating the alarm service as the "seller," the assignee as the "creditor," and the subscriber as a "consumer." (For purposes of the statute, certain services contracts are treated as sales.)

> The creditor's liability under this article shall not exceed the amount owing to the creditor at the time the defenses of the consumer are asserted against the creditor. Rights of the consumer under this article can only be asserted as a matter

a. The amendment also added a subsection (b) as follows: "The assignee shall have recourse against the seller to the extent of any liability incurred by the assignee pursuant to this section . . ."

of defense to or set-off against a claim by the creditor. The creditor shall be subrogated to the rights of the consumer arising from the consumer sale and shall have recourse against the seller to the extent of any liability incurred by the creditor pursuant to this article.[b]

When a true sale-of-goods contract is considered, the remedy problems are more difficult even than those concerning services contracts. For a buyer wishing to revoke his acceptance of the goods, there is the practical problem where to return them. Or if that is not a real question, he may have to decide whose orders to follow with respect to the unwanted merchandise: those of the seller or those of the financer.

If the goods have caused personal injury—as spoiled frozen food might do—can that be brought home to the assignee? In the Vasquez case mention was made of a provision of the Uniform Consumer Credit Code, which contains "only as a matter of defense" language. The court relied on the recollection of Professor (now Dean) William D. Warren, of UCLA, that the discussion attending the section concerned product liability claims.[c]

What does the FTC Rule (p. 1132 supra) contribute to answering the foregoing questions? Note the language of the prescribed notice: "Recovery hereunder by the debtor shall not exceed amounts paid by the debtor hereunder." This does not mean that California must abandon any remedy it chooses to confer on a consumer debtor, does it?

NOTES

(1) *Corporate Form.* Consider the case of a merchant doing business in corporate form, and holding all the shares in the corporation. It is the received tradition that he is not accountable, as an individual, for fraud, breach of warranty, or other delinquencies of the corporation, absent a personal involvement. See F. O'Neal, Close Corporations §§ 1.09, 109a (2d ed. 1971). Does it make sense to adhere to this rule while permitting a customer of the corporation to press a complaint against a financial institution that becomes somehow involved in his transaction?

(2) *The Case of the Flimsy Franchise.* In 1967 the plaintiff, Marion Weil, paid more than $7,000 for dance lessons, pursuant to three contracts with "New York Dance, Inc.," a dance studio holding a franchise from Arthur Murray, Inc. Marion had previously taken dancing instruction, over some six years, offered by the Arthur Murray Dance Studio in the same quarters, from the same instructors. She claimed reimbursement of the sums paid under the three contracts, asserting that these contracts violated statutory prohibitions, and that the payments were for "unused" lessons.

b. N.Y.Gen.Bus.L. § 253.

c. That point was especially important in California because the Unruh Act provision was modelled on that of the UCCC. The New York statute quoted just above was not. Professor Warren was a co-reporter for the Code. He participated in preparing an amicus brief in *Vasquez*.

(It appeared that when asked to sign a new contract Marion always had an entitlement to unused instruction under a previous one.)

The whole series of contracts was in identical form, but in the three in question the name "Arthur Murray, Inc." had been stamped out, and "New York Dance Studio, Inc." stamped over it before Marion signed them. Arthur Murray contended that to hold it liable for a franchisee's dereliction "would make a continuation of a franchising system impossible." *Held:* Arthur Murray was accountable for Marion's payments. The court said: "the control maintained by this defendant over its franchisees, and their transferability from one location to another, so transcends the ordinary and normal franchisor-franchisee relationship that, in effect, the franchisees became the alter egos of this defendant in the conduct and operation of its studios." Weil v. Arthur Murray, Inc., 324 N.Y.S.2d 381 (City Court, 1971).

SECTION 4. FINANCING COMMERCIAL CREDIT

NOBLETT v. GENERAL ELECTRIC CREDIT CORPORATION

United States Court of Appeals, Tenth Circuit, 1968.
400 F.2d 442, cert. denied, 393 U.S. 935 (1968).

CHRISTENSEN, District Judge. In this diversity action General Electric Credit Corporation obtained summary judgment against Ernest V. Noblett for rentals under a bowling equipment "Rental Lease", which had been assigned to the corporation by the lessor, Bowl-Mor Company.

Whether the case was factually ripe for summary judgment and whether Noblett in the rental agreement validly waived defenses as against the assignee as a matter of law, are the problems presented by this appeal.

Noblett's answer as amended had raised among other defenses that of failure of consideration by reason of alleged breaches of an express warranty against defects, an implied warranty of fitness and the obligations of the lessor to furnish advertising and training assistance.

The rental agreement included the following provision:

"The lessor may assign all its right, title and interest under this lease, including the payments due hereunder, but the assignee shall not be held responsible for any of the lessor's obligations. The obligations of the Lessee shall, however, continue in full force and effect."

Applying Massachusetts law in accordance with the terms of the rental agreement, and being of the view that Noblett thereby had waived the pleaded defenses, General Electric Credit Corp. v. Noblett, 268 F.Supp. 984 (W.D.Okl.1967), the trial court granted summary judgment for the balance of the rentals in the sum of $64,389.91, together with interest of $3,541.45, $11,814 attorney's fees and costs of the action.

Section 9–206, Chapter 106, of the General Laws of Massachusetts, based upon the Uniform Commercial Code, provides:

[See p. 1121 supra for the text as set out here.]

The equipment did not constitute "consumer goods" within the meaning of the Act.

The appellant Noblett contends that under any view of the Massachusetts law this case was not ripe for summary judgment since there was an issue of fact whether the assignee credit corporation took the assignment "for value, in good faith, and without notice of a claim or defense"; if not, under the terms of the Code no waiver agreement would be recognized.

In support of its motion for summary judgment the credit corporation filed below an affidavit from one R. N. Lamy, who stated that he was a Credit Specialist for General Electric Credit Corporation; that on the 24th day of May, 1965, General Electric Credit Corporation took an assignment from Bowl-Mor Company, Inc., for "good and valuable consideration" of the lease in question and "that said assignment was taken by General Electric Credit Corporation in good faith and without notice of any claim or defenses which Ernest V. Noblett might have against Bowl-Mor Company, Inc.".

We are not unmindful of the practical difficulties of establishing by affidavit in strict compliance with Rule 56(e), F.R.Civ.P., a lack of notice on the part of a corporation having numerous officers, managing agents and employees. A reasonable application is all that is required. It is apparent that in any view this affidavit did not conform with the requirements that such an affidavit be made on personal knowledge, state facts which would be admissible in evidence and show affirmatively that affiant was competent to testify to the matters therein stated. [But the court ruled that the trial judge was justified in giving credit to the affidavit, as the defendant had not challenged its assertions before it was entered. The court said: "there is a more dispositive reason why the summary judgment cannot stand."]

The trial court determined that in agreeing that "the Assignee shall not be held responsible for any of the Lessor's obligations", and that "the obligations of the Lessee shall, however, continue in full force and effect", Noblett effectually indicated "that he will not assert against an assignee any claim or defense which he might have against the . . . Lessor" within the contemplation of § 9–206(1), and, hence, that he was barred from asserting against the appellee his defense of failure of consideration and related defenses.[1]

1. "Whether the allegations in the answer and amendment thereto, to-wit: breach of warranty of fitness of the machines; disregard of the agreement

Our attention has been directed to two unpublished decisions of courts in other states holding that the precise language used in the form of the lease in question is valid and binding under Massachusetts law for the purpose.[2] And we are mindful that in Straight v. James Talcott, Inc., 329 F.2d 1 (10th Cir. 1964), this court held that an agreement of a buyer that he would settle all claims against the seller directly with him and would not set up any such claim against his assignee, operated to waive defenses in a suit brought by the assignee.

No Massachusetts decision has been called to our attention, nor can we find any, defining how far from the precise language of the authorizing statute an agreement might depart and still be effective as a waiver. Neither the decision of the trial court nor any of the cases cited come to grips expressly with the most persuasive phase of appellant's argument—that the intent manifested by the quoted provision of the lease agreement was not to waive defenses as allowed by § 9–206(1) of the Uniform Commercial Code but to relieve the assignee of the duty of affirmative performance of the lessor's obligations under the lease with reference to an entirely different section of the Code. It is provided in § 2–210:

"(4) An assignment of 'the contract' or of 'all my rights under the contract' or an assignment in similar general terms is an assignment of rights and unless the language or the circumstances (as in an assignment for security) indicate the contrary, it is a delegation of performance of the duties of the assignor and its acceptance by the assignee constitutes a promise by him to perform those duties. This promise is enforceable by either the assignor or the other party to the original contract."

The provisions of the lease agreement which speaks in terms of obligations is peculiarly suited to an indication for the purposes of § 2–210(4) that there was no "delegation of the performance of the duties of the assignor" or a "promise by him to perform those duties." Indeed, more apt language for this purpose could hardly be devised than was used in the lease agreement. But with respect to waiver of defenses, the language at best is indirect and unclear and at its worst misleading or entrapping. The question of the appropriateness of

to provide 'on the job training'; and failure to make allowance for advertising and signs, be technically designated as 'defenses', 'counterclaim' or 'set-off' and regardless of whether defendant seeks rescission of the contract or affirmance with damages to him because of the alleged breach, it is clear that all of the omissions complained of by him were obligations of Bowl-Mor, not plaintiff. It seems further to be clear from the contract that plaintiff is exonerated from responsibility for all of these complaints unless the contract provision allowing same be invalid".

2. General Electric Credit Corp. v. Brick Plaza Lanes, Inc., et al., Superior Court of New Jersey Law Division, Ocean County, Docket Number L25891–64, A–13908 (1966), and Baldino v. ABC Appliance Service, 83 Pa.Dist. & Co., 305 (Philadelphia County, 1952).

language, however, is not the worst of the problem, which goes deeper into the very substance of the legal concepts involved.

An assignment in general terms under the Uniform Commercial Code, and, hence, under the present Massachusetts law, is an assignment of rights, and unless the language or the circumstances indicate the contrary, it is also a delegation of performance of the duties of the assignor and its acceptance by the assignee, constituting a promise by him to perform those duties. The promise is enforceable by either the assignor or the other party to the original contract. In general, whether there is a delegation of duties as well as rights in and of itself does not affect defenses available to the other original contracting party. If there is a delegation of obligations, failure of consideration remains a defense, and the same is true even though there is no delegation of obligation to the assignee in the absence of waiver; the assignee stands in the shoes of the assignor as far as the right to recover is concerned in either event. Moreover, if there is a delegation of obligation to the assignee, this in and of itself does not relieve the assignor from the obligation of performance. If the assignor is required to respond to the other contracting party after duties have been delegated by the assignor, the assignee may be rendered liable to the assignor, which is a reason why a nondelegation agreement may be important to the assignee in the absence of a waiver of defenses.[3]

The point of these general principles is that defenses are available against the assignee in the absence of waiver, not because of the delegation or non-delegation of duties but because the assignee in either event must claim under the original contract and is subject to the defenses allowed thereby. The fact that the lease recited that the lessee should continue to be bound to his contracted obligations despite any assignment does not suggest in context that he agreed to waive defenses any more than the agreement that responsibilities of the assignor were not to be deemed delegated had anything to do with the waiver of defenses. The intent and meaning of the lease in this respect is made all the more clear by Bowl-Mor's assignment to the credit corporation which simply provides on the point that "Assignee shall have no obligations of lessor under said lease."

Whether responsibilities of the assignor were or were not delegated pursuant to § 2–210(4), or as a matter of general law, the rule continued operative that failure of consideration could be raised as a defense either against the assignee or the assignor in the absence of a waiver as authorized by the other provision of the Code. There was no such waiver. To enlarge the agreement concerning the non-dele-

3. See generally William D. Hawkland, A Transactional Guide to the U.C.C. (A.L.I.) (1964), § 1.25 p. 150 et seq.; 6 Am.Jur.2d Assignments, § 102, p. 282; 3 Williston on Contracts (Third Ed.-Jaeger), Sec. 432, pp. 177, et seq. Cf. Nickell v. United States, etc., 355 F.2d 73 (10th Cir. 1966); Denver United States Nat. Bank v. Asbell Bros. Constr., 294 F.2d 289 (10th Cir. 1961); Imperial Refining Co. v. Kanotex Refining Co., 29 F.2d 193 (8th Cir. 1928).

gation of obligation into such a waiver would be not only unwarranted but unfair. When appellant consented to the non-delegation to the assignee of obligations of the assignor under the lease, whether viewed from the standpoint of one learned in the law and capable of appreciating these distinctions, or as one only generally aware of the meaning of the language, he reasonably could have assumed that the purpose was what it purported to be and was not to preclude his defenses should he not receive the consideration for which he bargained. We are of the opinion that as a matter of law there was no waiver of defenses.[4]

We see nothing in Straight v. James Talcott, Inc., 329 F.2d 1 (10th Cir. 1964), supra, that warrants a contrary conclusion. There Oklahoma law was involved; the language which was employed more specifically sustained the conclusion reached and was not apparently designed for another purpose; it was not expressly questioned that the provision was intended to waive defenses, and the primary issue was whether such an agreed waiver would be valid under Oklahoma law. Massachusetts law governs the result here. In view of considerations discussed above and the general policy expressed in Quality Finance Company v. Hurley, 337 Mass. 150, 148 N.E.2d 385 (1957), it is fairly to be predicted that in the interpretation of the subsequently adopted Uniform Commercial Code an agreement that an assignment would not constitute a delegation of duties would not be so broadly construed as to be accepted in that state as a waiver of defenses under § 9–206(1).

Reversed and remanded for further proceedings not inconsistent with this opinion.

On Petition for Rehearing

PER CURIAM. Appellee has filed a petition for rehearing, its only contention justifying further notice being that the court has held in effect that the "Sales" provisions of the Uniform Commercial Code govern "Secured Transactions". In other words, it is argued that "the application of Section 2–210(4) was erroneous" and would open all secured transactions to question by indicating that in the absence of specific negation the obligation of performance would be placed upon the security holder as a matter of course. It should have been enough to preclude such misunderstanding to quote, as we did, Section 2–210(4) which states among other things that there is a delegation of performance "unless the language or the circumstances (*as in*

4. Even if the contract had been ambiguous on this point, summary judgment would have been inappropriate, since the appellant would have had the right to be heard on the question of intent as a matter of fact, and to resort to intrinsic aids to establish that intent at the trial. The lease agreement bears the letterhead of the lessor and appears to be on its printed form, and the rule of interpretation that in such event ambiguities are to be resolved against the drafter could well apply.

an assignment for security) indicate the contrary" (emphasis added). We did not refer to Section 2–210(4) to indicate that the "Sales" provisions of the Code necessarily governed Secured Transactions in the absence of language so providing but rather to demonstrate that waiver of affirmative performance is not the same as waiver of defenses for non-performance by a party to the original contract.

Far from justifying the appellee's claim that we misconceived the relationship of the Sales provisions to the Secured Transactions provisions of the Code, we simply pointed up in our opinion the basic misconception implicit in appellee's argument that language in the rental agreement which would have been appropriate for purposes of Section 2–210(4) relating to Sales could serve the entirely different purpose of satisfying the waiver of defense requirements established in Section 9–206(1) concerning Secured Transactions.

Finally, appellee sees in the language of the rental agreement that "the assignee shall not be responsible for any of lessor's obligations", an enigma if it is not held to constitute a waiver of defenses by the lessee since in a secured transaction an assignment does not delegate performance in any event. Perhaps appellee is in the best position to explain this supposed enigma; in the assignment by which it took the security it was again stipulated that "assignee shall have no obligation of lessor under the lease". The same question applies—why, if there would be no such obligation anyway, was this specifically provided there? No matter the reason, such language does not operate as a waiver of defenses under Section 9–206(1) and this is the determinative point.

The petitions for rehearing and for rehearing en banc are denied.

NOTES

(1) *Problem.* Prepare a term for inclusion in a rental lease that would be operative as a "waiver of defenses" by the lessee. If your provision is used, in leases of business equipment, can the assignee (finance company) count on obtaining summary judgment in other cases like the main one?

(2) *Assignees as Third Party Beneficiaries.* When an assignee succeeds in making claim against the obligor on the strength of a waiver of defense clause, and would not have succeeded otherwise, what is the theory of the recovery? The Restatement sections on assignments skirt the issues raised by such clauses. However, in Comments f and g to § 336 of the Restatement Second, three theories are offered for their efficacy, including estoppel. Strangely, it is not suggested that the assignee may enforce the clause as a third party beneficiary. Would that construction be a sound basis for his claim, in an appropriate case?

To characterize an assignee as (also) a third party beneficiary would not be a novelty; but in the absence of a waiver of defense clause it would not contribute much to his standing. In Restatement Second § 309, Comment c, a comparison is made between a beneficiary's position and that of an assignee after notice to the obligor of the assignment. As to the effect of a waiver clause, the comparison seems incomplete. In the chapter on assignments, a comment says that "if the agreement not to assert defenses or claims is itself voidable or unenforceable, the assignee takes subject to the defect." [a] Can this be reconciled with the provisions about a beneficiary? [b]

When UCC 9–206 applies so as to override a "claim or defense" by a buyer (or lessee), the assignee need not appeal to third party beneficiary law, of course: he has *statutory* support for his claim. On that basis, however, he can succeed only if he took his assignment "for value," etc. Suppose that an assignee cannot meet the requisites of that section for enforcing a waiver of defense clause: Is it possible that he may nevertheless enforce it under the general principles of third party beneficiary law? Note that the Code is "supplemented" by the general principles of law and equity (§ 1–103)—*unless* they are "displaced by the particular provisions of this Act." The question, then, becomes how far the law of third party beneficiaries is displaced by UCC 9–206. And the answer is clear: it is so far displaced that an assignee who does not meet the requisites of that section may not enforce such a clause.

BENTON STATE BANK v. WARREN

Supreme Court of Arkansas, 1978.
263 Ark. 1, 562 S.W.2d 74.

GEORGE ROSE SMITH, Justice.

The appellees, the Warrens, are engaged in building and operating apartments in California and elsewhere in the United States. In 1974 the Warrens, as owners and general contractors, began the construction of a 111-unit apartment complex at 2000 Reservoir Road in Little Rock. Four separate subcontracts—for concrete work, rough carpentry, finish carpentry and heating and air conditioning—were let to Harps General Contractors.

Harps failed to pay its suppliers of labor and materials, even though adequate progress payments were made from time to time by the Warrens. Those progress payments were made by checks payable jointly to Harps and to the appellant, Benton State Bank, which had lent money to Harps and had taken an assignment of Harps's right to receive progress payments. Eventually the Warrens had to take over and complete Harps's four subcontracts. Various unpaid materialmen brought this suit against Harps and the Warrens, asserting liens against the apartment complex. The Warrens cross-complained against Harps and the bank for any loss that the Warrens might ultimately sustain. That loss proved to be $13,367.12, for which the chancellor entered judgment in favor of the Warrens against Harps

a. Section 336, Comment f.

b. Compare especially Illustration 10 after § 336 with Illustration 7 after § 309.

and the bank. The bank appeals. The sole question is whether the loss shold be borne by the bank or by the Warrens. As we view the case, that question in turn depends upon which was more seriously at fault in allowing the loss to occur, both being at fault to some degree.

The facts, though undisputed, are not simple. The subcontract between Harps and the Warrens for rough carpentry is typical of the four subcontracts. The agreement provides that the Warrens will pay Harps $55,080 for its performance of the subcontract. On the tenth of each month the Warrens will make a progress payment to Harps for 90% of the work done in the preceding month. If there are unpaid suppliers of labor and materials the Warrens at their option may make the progress-payment checks payable jointly to Harps and to the suppliers. The contract also provides that Harps's right to compensation under the contract is assignable. Any assignment is subject to the Warrens' rights against Harps.

Shortly before construction began, the bank made a $60,000 loan to Harps to pay a tax delinquency owed by Harps, secured by a lien on some cattle. Later on Harps, as additional security, assigned to the bank its right to the progress payments under its subcontracts with the Warrens.

The president of the bank testified that the bank agreed to make additional loans to Harps of up to 75% of the amount due upon each application by Harps for a progress payment. In practice, the matter was handled in this way: Harps signed a printed form of application for each progress payment. The form set out the amount due and requested payment of 90% of that amount. Harps certified on each form that all bills for labor and materials covered by earlier progress payments had been paid. Those certifications were false. Harps was delinquent all along in the payment of its outstanding accounts, as the bank had reason to know even if it did not have actual knowledge.

Whenever Harps submitted an application for a progress payment to the bank, the bank would advance money to Harps, as it had agreed to do. The bank president testified that he understood generally that the advances were to be used by Harps to meet its payroll. The bank sent each progress-payment application to the Warrens, with a covering letter like this one: "Enclosed is a copy of [Harps's] Application for Payment . . . ., which has been assigned to us. Please make your check payable to Benton State Bank, as per our agreement with Harps's Construction Company, and sign [an acceptance of the assignment] in the space provided at the bottom of this page, and return the original to us."

The Warrens, upon the receipt at their California office of each application for a progress payment, would send their check for the requested amount to the bank. The checks were payable jointly to Harps and to the bank and bore this statement above the payees' endorsement: "By endorsement of this check payee acknowledges payment for labor, materials, or both, in construction at the following address: 2000 Reservoir Road, Little Rock, Ark." Such progress-payment checks totaled $82,686.24. Of that amount the bank used $27,271.86 to repay itself for loans on the Warren project, used $9,393.42 to repay itself for other loans, and deposited the balance of $46,020.96 to Harps's general account at the bank.

The procedure that we have outlined was followed by the parties for several months. Finally, however, a representative of one of the unpaid materialmen visited the Warrens' superintendent at the project site and expressed concern about getting money that was overdue from Harps for materials delivered to the job. The Warrens at once made an investigation and learned that Harps was delinquent in its indebtedness to its suppliers and was unable to demonstrate its solvency. The Warrens then took over the responsibility for completing the work, and this suit followed.

In our study of the case we have been assisted not only by the briefs of opposing counsel but also by a brief, submitted at our request, by counsel for the Permanent Editorial Board for the Uniform Commercial Code.

The case falls within the general purview of the Code, which applies by its terms to any transaction which is intended to create a security interest in accounts. Ark.Stat.Ann. § 85–9–102(1) (Supp. 1977). Harps's right to progress payments from the Warrens was an "account" as that term is defined in § 85–9–106. The Warrens were "account debtors" with respect to that account. § 85–9–105. Hence Harps was the assignor of an account, and the bank the assignee, as a result of Harps's assignment to the bank of its right to progress payments.

Section 85–9–318(1)(a) provides that the rights of an assignee (the bank) are subject to all of the terms of the contract between the account debtor (the Warrens) and the assignor (Harps) and to any defense or claim arising therefrom. It follows that the bank necessarily took some risk in lending Harps up to 75% of the amount specified in each application for a progress payment. That is, if the Warrens, upon receipt of an application, had discovered that there were outstanding bills for labor and materials, the Warrens, under the subcontract, could have made their check payable jointly to the bank and to the suppliers of labor and materials. In that situation it cannot be doubted that the bank's interest in the check would have been subordinate to the suppliers' primary right to payment. That is so because the bank's rights as assignee were subject to any claim by the Warrens against the bank's assignor, Harps, who was primarily liable to its own suppliers.

That, however, is not what happened. Instead the Warrens, with no knowledge of Harps's indebtedness to its suppliers, made their checks payable to Harps and to the bank. The bank cashed the checks and applied part of the money to its own loans to Harps. The narrow question is: In that situation, are the Warrens entitled to recover from the bank their payments up to the amount of their net loss, $13,367.12?

This precise question seems to have been considered in only one case, Farmers Acceptance Corporation v. DeLozier, 178 Colo. 291, 496 P.2d 1016, 10 UCC Rep. 1099 (1972). That case was nearly identical to this one, in that a subcontractor had assigned his contract rights to a lender, the general contractor had made a progress payment to that lender, and the general contractor then sought to recover its payment when it sustained a loss as a result of the subcontractor's failure to pay its suppliers. In holding that the general contractor was entitled to recover the amount that the lender had applied to its own loan to the subcontractor, the court relied upon Code provisions that we have mentioned and upon this sentence in a law review article by Professor Grant Gilmore: "[W]here the assignor fails to perform the contract, the assignee cannot retain mistaken, or even negligent, payments made to it by the [debtor] unless there has been a subsequent change of position by the assignee." Gilmore, The Assignee of Contract Rights and His Precarious Security, 74 Yale L.J. 217, 235, n. 35 (1964–65).[a]

We need not say whether we would agree with Gilmore's statement in every case, no matter how negligent the account debtor might be or how innocent of fault the assignee might be. The issue is open to some exercise of judgment, for the precise point is not covered by any specific provision in the Uniform Commercial Code. In fact, Gilmore's sentence is, in context, merely his summary of the holding in Firestone Tire & Rubber Co. v. Central Nat. Bank, 159 Ohio St. 423, 112 N.E.2d 636 (1953), a pre-Code case.

In the case at bar the equities clearly do not stand entirely in favor of either party. No doubt the Warrens were remiss in making no apparent effort to verify Harps's representations that all previous bills for labor and materials had been paid. On the other hand, the bank was certainly not an innocent recipient of the progress payments, without notice of possible claims on the part of the Warrens against Harps.

a. In the Gilmore article, five pages before the sentence quoted, the author speaks of breach of warranty and failure of consideration suffered by a buyer. As between them, he says, the seller's default "would be available both as defenses and as claims." But in a face-off between the buyer and the seller's *assignee*, the default is available "only defensively. . . . The assignee, who comes in to finance the transaction, does not thereby become responsible for the assignor's warranties or prospective performance."

The Colorado case cited by the court (DeLozier) relied on the "general rule that an assignee stands in the shoes of the assignor." Do you see how this aphorism might be misleading?

The bank knew that Harps had been compelled to borrow a large sum to pay delinquent federal taxes. It knew that another bank had refused to make that loan. It was in close touch with Harps's financial difficulties and knew, for instance, that shortly before the last progress payment was made at least eleven checks written by Harps on the bank had been dishonored. It had solid reasons for suspecting the truth of Harps's assertions, which the bank forwarded to the Warrens, that all past-due bills for labor and materials had been paid. It was on notice that its endorsements on the progress-payment checks recited that the money was furnished to pay for labor and materials. The president of the bank, a law school graduate, knew that unpaid laborers and materialmen could file liens against the project. He knew that part of the earlier progress payments had been applied by the bank to its own loans to Harps and assumed that additional progress-payment money had been used by Harps to meet its payrolls. The question would naturally arise, How had Harps been able to pay its suppliers when it had to borrow against the progress payments to meet its payrolls? When all the circumstances are considered, we cannot say that the chancellor's decision in favor of the Warrens is clearly against the preponderance of the evidence.

Affirmed.

BYRD, Justice, dissenting.

The provisions of the Uniform Commercial Code, so far as here applicable provide:

"Ark.Stat.Ann. § 85–9–318 (Supp.1977) (1) . . . the rights of an assignee are subject to (a) all the terms of the contract between the account debtor and assignor and any defense or claim arising therefrom; . . ."

The term "rights" is defined, Ark.Stat.Ann. § 85–1–201 (Add.1961) as follows:

"(36) 'Rights' includes remedies."

Thus when we look at Ark.Stat.Ann. § 85–9–318, supra, with the definition of "rights" superimposed, we then read it as saying " . . . the [remedies] of an assignee are subject to (a) all the terms of the contract between the account debtor and assignor and any defense or claim arising therefrom; . . ."

Notwithstanding, the specific language of the Uniform Commercial Code and its specific definitions, the majority has now interpreted Ark.Stat.Ann. § 85–9–318 to place a *liability* upon the assignee. The Benton State Bank was not pursuing a remedy as to the accounts in question from which the Warrens could make any defense or claim arising from the pursuit of such remedy. The bank had no need to pursue a right (remedy) against the account debtor because all such accounts had been paid—in fact the bank was no longer an assignee as to those accounts.

The effect of the majority's view is to make every Banker, who has taken an assignment of accounts for security purposes, a deep pocket surety for every bankrupt contractor in the state to whom it has loaned money. Will the majority apply the same reasoning to product liability arising from such transactions under the innumerable warranty provisions? If so, what limitations will be applied to the bank's liability in such situations?

I also disagree with the majority that the bank had such notice of the unpaid bills that it was not a bona fide purchaser of the accounts.

For the reasons herein stated, I respectfully dissent.

NOTES

(1) *Conclusiveness of Payment.* When the court (quoting Professor Gilmore) refers to the payments by the Warrens as "mistaken, or even negligent" ones, it identifies the problem with a longstanding controversy in the law of restitution. A small but impressive set of cases hold that the recipient of a mistaken payment who receives it in satisfaction of a genuine debt (such as Harps' debt to the bank) cannot be required to reimburse the payor. The Restatement of Restitution supports the rule on the ground that the payee is a bona fide purchaser of the money: § 14(2).[b] Professor Palmer prefers the reason that the payee is not unjustly enriched by the payment: Law of Restitution, Vol. III, § 16.7 (1978). More generally, one might call the payment conclusive, when the competing equity is not compelling, in the interest of maintaining the security of transactions.

These views are of course rejected in the main case. The decision did not turn at all upon the conclusiveness of the payment, but rather upon which of the contesting parties "was more seriously at fault in allowing the loss to occur." The court says that the bank was not an innocent recipient of the payment. However, that statement cannot be given any stronger interpretation than as saying that the bank, as a creditor of the contractor, might have learned through further inquiry that the bills submitted by the contractor to the Warrens rested on false certifications. Naturally it was open also to the Warrens to investigate the accuracy of those bills; and the court concedes that to some degree both the bank and the Warrens were at fault in extending trust to the contractor.

The Warrens' brief charged the bank with misrepresentation for signing their checks under the "By endorsement" legend. Should the court have based itself on that ground?

(2) *Code Readings.* Consider Justice Byrd's recasting of UCC 9–318(1)(a): "the [remedies] of an assignee are subject to . . . any defense or claim arising [from the contract]." On his reading, what sense can be given to "*or claim*"? Subsection (1)(b) also mentions "defense or claim." In DeLozier's case, cited by the majority, the court said that

b. " . . . if the transferee made no misrepresentation and did not have notice of the defense."

"claim" includes setoffs and counterclaims. Could Justice Byrd agree to that without damaging his dissent?

The amicus brief submitted by the Permanent Editorial Board for the Code supported the bank's position. For a thorough review see Nickles, Rethinking Some UCC Article Nine Problems, 34 Ark.L.Rev. 1, 27–40 (1980).

(3) *Responsibilities of Financers.* Justice Byrd also expresses a general view about the responsibility of a creditor (the bank) to police the conduct of its debtor. It is natural, when a commercial loss occurs, for the disappointed party to cast about for a highly responsible party ("a deep pocket" party such as a financial institution) against whom to proceed. Some other cases, although they are not numerous, suggest that bankers have a special responsibility for the depredations on the public that their borrowers may be enabled to make by virtue of an extension of credit. (See Note 3, p. 1132 supra.) In this case it does not seem that the general responsibilities of banks are greatly enlarged. The pattern of construction financing as described in the case is a highly standardized one. It commonly features a considerable exchange of information and commitments among borrowers, their financers, and those who employ them. Nevertheless, it is moderately surprising that the employer of a contractor should be relieved against its error in making payment, when the payee has an undoubted claim against the builder: it is as if the employer has a second chance to verify bills submitted to him.

ASSIGNMENTS IN RELATION TO CONSTRUCTION CONTRACTS

Assignments are a customary and prominent by-product of contracts for construction, improvement, and repair work. The role of banks and other institutions financing such work is largely dependent on the effectiveness of assignments for security purposes. In general, the problems connected with such assignments arise out of the insolvency of an assigning contractor or subcontractor.

Two main types of controversy must be distinguished. One source of resistance to the financer (assignee) is the owner or contractor from whom the assigned payments are expected. (Such a person will be called an "employer" in this note, without any intention to suggest that he is empowered to direct performance of the work as a true employer is.) The other source of controversy is a set of persons who have claims derived from the contractor (assignor). This group includes a person taking a competing assignment, a surety company that has written a bond for his performance of the work, and a representative of his creditors—usually his trustee in bankruptcy.

Controversies of the first type are illustrated by Monroe Banking & Trust Company v. Allen, 286 F.Supp. 201 (N.D.Miss.1968). In that case the defendant was a builder who had subcontracted a painting job. The painter had obtained financing from a bank, assigning for security his right to payment. After notice of the assignment, the builder sold materials to the painter on credit. When the bank sought to enforce the assigned claim, the builder asserted the right to set off the unpaid price of the materials. The bank was not informed of the credit sales until it appeared that the painter could not repay the bank's advances.

Controversies of the second type are illustrated by interpleader cases, in which an employer seeks direction about how to allocate payment for a contractor's work, as between competing claimants. If the contractor is a bankrupt, one of the claimants is likely to be the trustee, who is vested with the bankrupt contractor's "title" by the Bankruptcy Code.[a] Another may be a bonding company which has had to pay claims of laborers and materialmen for their contribution to the work. The United States is frequently a contender, in its role as tax collector.[b] Banks and others who finance contractors on the strength of assignments must regularly anticipate competing claims from these quarters. As against a bankruptcy trustee, the key to victory for an assignee lies chiefly in his compliance with the filing requirements of the Uniform Commercial Code, Article 9 (see Note 1, p. 1087 supra). Social policy gives mixed signals about how to divvy up a "broke" contractor's earnings among competing claimants. In a case recited in Chapter 10 (Avco Delta Corp. Canada Ltd. v. United States, p. 1051 supra, n. d) each contestant was backed by a strong public interest.[c] The claims for services and supplies were the victors there; one doctrinal basis for their success was third party beneficiary law. Assignment law is not the only solvent for tough problems in this connection.

Bonding companies and financing banks have not been content to rely altogether on their status as assignees.[d] A technique sometimes

a. 11 U.S.C.A. § 541; see also § 544(a).

b. The statutory tax lien is provided for, and regulated by, 26 U.S.C.A. § 6321 et seq.

c. The "assignment" in question was one effected by operation of law: the United States pressed its claim by virtue of the statutory lien for taxes.

d. Bonding companies commonly do not make filings under the Code so as to perfect assignments of job earnings. For an explanation see Hoffman, *Jacobs*—Sureties' Panacea or Narcosis?, 1967 Ins.Couns.J. 387, 391–92. Financing banks have sought to exploit this situation, but have suffered a series of reverses. In their capacity as sureties for contractors, bonding companies have usually preempted bank assignments by relying on the principle of subrogation. See In re J. V. Gleason Co., 452 F.2d 1219 (8th Cir. 1971); First Vermont Bank & Trust Co. v. Village of Poultney, 134 Vt. 28, 349 A.2d 722 (1975).

Bankruptcy trustees are also subjugated to bonding companies, through subrogation, in situations to which the Code is not applicable. The leading case is Pearlman v. Reliance Ins. Co., 371 U.S. 132 (1962), involving earnings under a government contract.

See also Canter v. Schlager, 358 Mass. 789, 267 N.E.2d 492 (1971); Travelers Indemnity Co. v. Clark, 254 So. 2d 741 (Miss.1971) (receiver). Each of these cases concerns the filing problem. The former gives references to controversies between banks and sureties.

used to advantage is to procure an "acceptance" of the assignment by the contractor's employer. The acceptance may have no import except to signify prompt notification of the assignment to the obligor. But it may include terms open to a more helpful construction. For example, the employer sometimes undertakes to make progress payments by check payable jointly to the contractor and to the financer. If he fails to do so, and in consequence funds are improperly diverted by the contractor, the financer is in a position to claim indemnity from the employer. Of course, it is well for a financer to lay a careful predicate, in advance, for such a claim. Several cases concern "acceptances" addressed solely to the contractor (assignor): the employer, for example, promises him to issue checks payable to his bank. In such a case it is necessary for the bank to develop a theory to overcome the lack of privity. Can you suggest such a theory.[e]

PROBLEM

In Monroe Banking Co. v. Allen, briefed above, the bank's claim was held not to be subject to the contractor's set-off. Before advancing funds to the painter, the bank had obtained an acceptance of the assignment from the contractor. Was that fact essential to the result? Do you consider that additional facts might have dictated a different result? If so, what facts?

SCOPE PROVISIONS FOR UCC ARTICLE 9

For various reasons it may often be important to determine whether or not a given assignment is one to which the rules of Article 9 apply. First, the Article purports to nullify an assignment within its scope unless the assignor has signed a writing containing a "description of the collateral;" absent that the assignment is unenforceable against him or anyone else.[a] Second, there is the virtual necessity of filing a financing statement in a public office if Article 9 applies to the assignment.[b] Finally—what is most important for present purposes—the reach of the rules of UCC 9–206 and 9–318 is determined by the scope provisions of Article 9.

Broadly speaking, those provisions identify assignments that occur in connection with commercial financing. An example is the assignment in Benton State Bank v. Warren, p. 1147, supra. An example of a type *not* within the scope of Article 9 is that in British Waggon Co. v. Lea & Co., p. 1094, supra. (The footnote mentions other ex-

e. If so, you may wish to consider whether or not your theory offers a way for financing banks to avoid the necessity of filing financing statements under Article 9. For materials on this rather arcane subject, see G. Gilmore, 2 Security Interests in Personal Property, § 41.3 (1965). See also Wolters Village Management Co. v. Merchants & Planters Nat. Bank, 223 F.2d 793 (5th Cir. 1955). Cf. Citizens Nat. Bank of Orlando v. Vitt, 367 F.2d 541 (5th Cir. 1966).

a. UCC 9–203(1).

b. See Note 1, p. 1087 supra.

amples in this book, on each side of the line.[c]) The scope provisions proceed by stating the reach of Article 9 quite expansively, and making some specific exclusions. Two of the exclusions apply to Parkgate's assignment to British Waggon: an assignment of accounts "as part of a sale of the business out of which they arise," and an assignment of unearned payments "to an assignee who is also to do the performance under the contract." UCC 9–104(f).[d]

NOTE

Sales of Payment Rights. A financing assignment embraces more than those made for the purpose of securing debt. Article 9 is expressly written so as to apply to *sales* of accounts, subject to exclusions such as those mentioned above. The two types of transfer have differing characteristics, of course;[e] but their commercial uses are so similar that it was decided, in drafting the Code, to say that an agreement for security *or sale* is a "security agreement;" that the transferee's interest is a "security interest;" and that the subject of the transfer is—though sold—"collateral". This consolidation, with its curiosities of expression, has not been made for most types of collateral; an outright sale of goods certainly does not create a pledge, mortgage, or other security interest, for example. The consolidation affects transactions of the following types:

(1) A merchant disposes of his receivables for cash. He may and may not make some commitment as to their collectibility; but he does not promise payment as a borrower does. The collateral is "accounts" as that term is used in both the 1962 and 1972 texts of the Code.

(2) A manufacturer selling his accounts as above, includes payment rights under contracts he has made to supply merchandise in the future. Being unearned, these rights are "contract rights" according to the definitions of the 1962 text. The 1972 text discards that expression and broadens the definition of "account" so as to include unearned payment rights.[f]

c. (1) Cases which on their facts would be affected by the provisions of Article 9:

Shiro v. Drew, p. 1082 supra.
Ertel v. Radio Corp. of America
Holt v. First Nat. Bank of Minneapolis
Noblett v. General Electric Credit Corp.

(2) Cases which on their facts could not be so affected:

Adams v. Merced Stone Co.
Western Oil Sales Corp. v. Bliss & Wetherbee
Crane Ice Cream Co. v. Terminal Freezing & Heating Co.
Evening News Ass'n v. Peterson

d. The 1972 revision of Article 9 also excludes "a transfer of a single account to an assignee in whole or partial satisfaction of a pre-existing indebtedness." Ibid. This textual change had been foreshadowed in case law. See Spurlin v. Sloan Constr. Co., 368 S.W.2d 314 (Ky. 1963).

e. Therefore it is occasionally a question whether an Article 9 assignment is one in which the assignor does or does not retain an interest analogous to that of a mortgagor. E. g., Major's Furniture Mart, Inc. v. Castle Credit Corp., Inc., 602 F.2d 538 (3d Cir. 1979).

f. In a Code state where the 1972 amendments have not been enacted, of course Article 9 continues to employ the term "contract right."

(3) A dealer has generated "chattel paper" by selling goods for deferred payment and retaining a security interest in them—the payment right and the security agreement being expressed in a single writing or group of writings. He disposes of—"discounts"—the rights so expressed, after the fashion of the merchant in case (1). The transferee of the chattel paper is a "secured party" with respect to it, even though he is its owner.

In the conventional sense of a security transfer, the purpose is to make more certain the payment of a debt owed to the transferee, and the transferor retains an interest in the thing transferred. Many transfers of accounts and chattel paper fit this description. One that does is (almost) surely within Article 9. One that does not may be an excluded sale; but it is not excluded simply for being a sale.

THREE PROBLEMS OF "ACCRUAL"

UCC 9–318 is set out at p. 1086 supra, and some features of it have been noticed. Next in order is an examination of subsection (1).

In the portion of Ertel v. Radio Corp. of America reproduced above (p. 1088) the account debtor (RCA) asserted the defense of payment—to Delta, the assignor—when sued by Ertel as successor to the assignee (Economy Finance). It must be understood that that was *not* a defense based on the terms of the RCA–Delta contract, and did not "arise therefrom." Hence the payment could not give rise to a subsection (1)(a) defense. It was a separate transaction giving rise to a (1)(b) defense, if any. The court held that RCA's payment was not a defense that accrued before it received notification of the assignment. There is not usually a question about when such a defense—payment to the assignor—has "accrued". However, the term does raise questions on occasion, and these are now to be examined.

What it means to say that a defense or claim "accrues" has been discussed in only a few cases arising under UCC 9–318(1). Why the word *accrues* was chosen in subsection (1)(b) is a puzzle. One court has said, plaintively, that it would be helped in defining the word "if we could determine why the accrual of [the defense in question] was selected as the cutoff event." Apparently (the court said) accruing of the defense was selected arbitrarily. "The choice of the event of the accrual was based upon previous decisions, some of which used the phrase 'matured' rather than 'accrued' claim." [a]

The principal defenses and claims which an obligor must assert under subsection (1)(b) are prior payment—to someone other than the claiming assignee—and setoff.[b] Others that may be thought of

a. Seattle-First Nat. Bank v. Oregon Pacific Industries, Inc., 262 Ore. 578, 500 P.2d 1033 (1972).

b. The fact of setoff must be the explanation for the words "or claim" appearing in subsection (1)(b). On

are release, rescission, modification, and substituted contract. As to the latter, subsection (2) of 9–318 puts an elaborate qualification on the simple rule of (1)(b). For present purposes we need attend only to the defenses of payment and setoff. As for the time that a *payment* "accrues", no one seems to have had a doubt. Hence the three problems below center on setoff as a "defense or claim;" the time of setoff accrual was what troubled the court quoted above.

Ace Bank

The owner of a building project agrees with his prime contractor to make direct payment to a subcontractor, in a fashion making the latter a third party beneficiary. After the sub's work is done, the owner receives notification from Ace Bank that it holds an assignment from the sub of all his earnings on the job, from whatever source, as security for a loan. As a defense (or claim) against the bank, the owner now shows that unless he pays a bill for supplies that the sub used on the job the supplier will fix a materialman's lien on his property. No one but the bank or the owner is available to charge with an impending loss. Must the bank give the owner credit for the amount he has to pay the supplier—and so lose the chance of collecting its loan in full? That may depend on whether the owner's "claim" against the sub was *accrued* or not before notification of the assignment. The debt to the supplier was incurred before that, but is not paid till after. Should it matter when the bill was *payable*? [c]

Deuce Bank

A painting subcontractor reports to the prime contractor that he is unable to pay cash for paint that he needs in his work, and unable to get credit elsewhere. The prime pays the paint supplier directly, on an agreement that the sub will reimburse him from a forthcoming income tax refund. Before the refund is paid, Deuce Bank notifies the prime that it holds an assignment from the sub of his job earnings. On completion of the painting, may the prime assert a defense or claim against the bank under 9–318(1)(b)?

Credit Company

A lumber dealer accepts two purchase orders from a customer, one for a carload of plywood in June and one for a carload of studs in July. The customer receives notification from a credit company that the dealer has assigned to it his right to payment under both sale contracts. In June the plywood is delivered; in July the dealer repudiates the stud sale contract.

reflection, it might appear that those words are unneeded, for in this context the word "defense" appears to embrace setoff.

c. This case is constructed with reference to the facts in Farmers Acceptance Corp. v. DeLozier, 178 Colo. 291, 496 P.2d 1016 (1972). In that case, however, the "obligor" faced with a materialman's lien was the general contractor. That being so, the court could fairly observe that the assignee's rights were "subject to claims arising out of *the contract.*" (emphasis supplied) Does the problem case squarely locate the issue under subsection (1)(b)?

On the point of the assignee's accountability for payment made, the holding in DeLozier is not supported by the authorities cited.

In accounting to the credit company for the price of the plywood, may the customer offset his damages from the breach?

For a decision tending to favor the assignee in each of these cases, see Commercial Sav. Bank v. G & J Wood Products Co., Inc., 46 Mich.App. 133, 207 N.W.2d 401 (1973).[d] Compare Wear v. Farmers & Merchants Bank, Etc., 605 P.2d 27 (Alaska, 1980).

ERTEL v. RADIO CORP. OF AMERICA

Supreme Court of Indiana, 1974.
261 Ind. 573, 307 N.E.2d 471.

[For a statement of this case, and part of the opinion, see p. 1088 supra. Part II of the opinion, on subrogation, is omitted.]

HUNTER, Justice. . . .

III *RCA's set-off rights against Economy (Ertel).*

The assignment agreement between Delta and Economy covered Delta's present and future accounts receivable. The accounts receivable in question were created by contracts for the sale of machinery from Delta to RCA. There were three such sales and each was governed by the same standard contract. RCA now claims that machines transferred in the last sale were substantially incomplete and that RCA had to expend considerable sums of money to make the machines complete and usable. Thus, RCA claims to have a set-off right against Delta for Delta's incomplete performance of the last contract and that, *ergo*, Ertel, as subrogee of Economy, also takes subject to those rights.

Determining against whom RCA can assert its claim is governed by § 9–318(1) of the Commercial Code:

[Here the court set out that provision, emphasizing "or claim arising therefrom" in subsection (1)(a).]

The Court of Appeals concluded that RCA had no set-off rights, viewing 9–318(1)(b) as a bar. Apparently, the Court's decision was based on the fact that the last sales transaction between RCA and Delta (the one out of which RCA's claim arises) occurred after notice of the assignment was given by Economy, and that somehow the third contract was a "separate transaction." We believe that this application of 9–318(1)(b) to the facts of this case is entirely improper.

It has been held that set-off is the type of claim contemplated by 9–318(1). Farmers Acceptance Corp. v. DeLozier (1972 Colo.Sup.

d. In Libby, McNeill, and Libby v. City Nat. Bank, 592 F.2d 504 (9th Cir. 1978), a post-notification defense that appears to have been in the nature of setoff was allowed against an assignee. The court did not make it clear how the defense could have been characterized as being within UCC 9–318(1)(a).

Ct.), 496 P.2d 1016. The issue here is whether RCA's set-off is the type of claim comprehended by 9–318(1)(a) or 9–318(1)(b). Section 9–318(1)(a) is clearly the applicable provision in that RCA's claim arose from the contract between itself and Delta.

The Oregon Supreme Court has provided us with the following analysis of § 9–318(1)(a) and (b):

"The Code distinguishes 'between what might be called the contract-related and the unrelated defenses and claims. *Defenses and claims "arising" from the contract can be asserted against the assignee whether they "arise" before or after notification.* . . . Under the Code, "any other defense or claim" is available against the assignee only if it "accrues before . . . notification."' 2 Gilmore, Security Interests in Personal Property, 1090–1091, § 41.4 (1965).

"The setoff or claim the defendant seeks to assert *is an unrelated setoff because it arises out of a breach of a contract not connected with the invoice assigned to the bank.* For this reason the defendant can assert the setoff only if it accrued before the defendant was notified of Centralia's assignment to the bank." Seattle-First National Bank v. Oregon Pacific Industries, Inc. (1972), 262 Or. 578, 581, 500 P.2d 1033, 1034. (Emphasis added.)

This interpretation is entirely consistent with UCC 9–318, Official Comment, No. 1:

"When the account debtor's defenses on an assigned account, chattel paper or a contract right *arise from the contract between him and the assignor it makes no difference whether the breach giving rise to the defense occurs before or after the account debtor is notified of the assignment.*" (Emphasis added.)

In the case at bar RCA's claim arose from the subsequently assigned contract between itself and Delta. The fact that the claim arose *after* Economy gave notice of the assignment is irrelevant. Therefore, Economy's rights were subject to RCA's herein asserted claim.

Ertel, as subrogee of Economy, succeeds to the rights of Economy vis-a-vis RCA. That is to say, Ertel becomes subrogated to Economy's interest in the RCA accounts. However, the subrogee (Ertel) receives no more or no fewer rights than Economy possessed at the time Ertel satisfied the debt. . . . It follows, therefore, that Ertel has succeeded to the rights of Economy—subject to the RCA claim.

For all the foregoing reasons, transfer is hereby granted and the cause remanded to the trial court to determine liability with respect to the third-party complaint of John C. Ertel.

Transfer granted.

NOTES

(1) *One-a Defenses and One-b Defenses.* What might have led the Court of Appeals to apply subsection (1)(b) of 9–318, rather than subsection (1)(a), to this case? Compare Bank Leumi Trust Co., Etc. v. Collins Sales Serv., 47 N.Y.2d 888, 393 N.E.2d 468 (1979).

Some other particulars to which the parties stipulated were as follows: RCA's first order from Delta was given more than a year before the notice of assignment. It was for a "special fixture" valued at $325. Payment for it was made near the end of May, 1969. On June 24, 1969, RCA ordered two disc sanding machines for $4,500—order (2). On July 30 it ordered six more such machines for $29,526—order (3). RCA made payments on these orders as follows: July 29 (2) and (3); September 12 (2), and September 29 (3). In late October, being advised that Delta had ceased doing business, RCA received all materials relating to the third order. Only three of the six machines it concerned were so far advanced in fabrication as to justify further work, and the expense to RCA of completing them was nearly $20,000. The damages asserted by RCA were several times that amount.

According to counsel for RCA the subjects of the first two orders were pre-production models of the machines; only the third concerned an approved production item. He reports that RCA made a new commitment at each stage. Note the Supreme Court's observation that there were three sales, suggesting three offers, three acceptances, and three opportunities to negotiate. This might explain why the Court of Appeals regarded the third contract as a separate transaction. It stated the rule as follows: "a set-off arising out of a separate transaction subsequent to the assignment notification could not bind the assignee." Does the Supreme Court reject that rule? If so, what alternative rule fits the case?

(2) *A House Divided.* A manufacturer obtains credit from a lender by providing him with a security interest in both the manufacturer's inventory of its products and its accounts. Upon default by the borrower, the lender must expect that he will have to seek repayment by (a) disposing of the inventory at a wholesaler's auction and (b) collecting the accounts. In the manufacturer's line of business (toys) it is usual for a customer to demand, and the manufacturer to give, price protection: to agree that for a period following the purchase there will be no other wholesale transaction in goods of the same kind at a lower price. In these circumstances one lender found that it could not use collection procedure (a) without undercutting collection procedure (b). James Talcott, Inc. v. H. Corenzwit & Co., 76 N.J. 305, 387 A.2d 350 (1978). What are the causes of the lender's dilemma?

CONTRACT MODIFICATION

As a rule, an assignee's rights against the obligor are not impaired by the fact that the obligor, having notice of the assignment, makes a payment in disregard of the assignment. If the obligor is so unwise as to deal with the assignor after notice, the assignee may commonly require him to make a second payment of the assigned claim.

An important qualification on this rule is suggested by a handful of cases that may be described as involving "necessary advances." One of them is outlined in this note: Fricker v. Uddo & Taormina Co., 48 Cal.2d 696, 312 P.2d 1085 (1957). These cases are part of the legislative history of an Article 9 provision about "modification" and "substitution" respecting an assigned contract: subsection (2) of 9–318. One case construing this provision has been found, and it is also outlined here: Madden Eng. Corp. v. Major Tube Corp., 568 S.W.2d 614 (Tenn.App.1977), cert. denied, (1978). In each case a seller of goods had assigned expected earnings, and had encountered severe financial difficulty in meeting his performance requirements. In each case the buyer, knowing all this, came to the seller's aid. For the non-assigning party to do this entails a substantial risk. If the arrangement amounts to a "modification", the statute provides a limited shield against double payment. One question the cases suggest is what counts as a modification of (or substitution for) the assigned contract; and the statute itself presents issues about good faith and reasonableness, among others.

In Fricker v. Uddo & Taormina Co., supra, the parties were a canning company (defendant), a farmer (George Kikuchi), and a creditor of his (plaintiff). Kikuchi contracted to sell his 1952 tomato crop to the defendant company, and his harvest produced earnings for him of about $77,000. Unhappily the venture was unprofitable for him, inasmuch as he incurred obligations during the season of more than $84,000. Most of this was advanced to him by the canning company, as a charge against his "crop account." By early spring it had already advanced Kikuchi $27,000. Then he sought to buy soil fumigant from Fricker, on credit. The canning company was informed, and wrote to Fricker: "This will confirm that we have accepted a crop order instructing us to pay to you $4,074.91 from the return due George Kikuchi from tomatoes delivered by him to us during the 1952 season." The crop order was treated, in the subsequent litigation, as a partial assignment of Kikuchi's right to payment for the tomatoes.

Thereafter the canning company made other large advances to Kikuchi, so that the total was more than he earned by supplying tomatoes. Not being paid, Fricker sued the company. His complaint was that the latter advances were made in disregard of the assignment.

The company argued that its advances were necessary to enable Kikuchi to perform his contract; and the court accepted the view that payments by an obligor of this character, in disregard of an assignment, are justified. Such a rule, it said, is "obviously an exception to the general rule relating to assignments." But the canning company, it said, was required to make a showing of necessity. To a considerable extent, it did so. After accepting the crop order it had advanced Kikuchi some $42,000 which was actually used for producing the crop. (Installment payments on his farm machinery were thought to be among the allowable costs.) However, advances beyond this sum were held to violate Fricker's rights as assignee. Some of the advances were used by Kikuchi for living expenses of his family. The court ruled that such sums could not be treated as having been used for the purpose of tomato production. Advances by the company prior to the crop order, plus "necessary" ones thereafter, amounted to less than $70,000. Since the gross return from the crop exceeded this amount by more than the plaintiff's fumigant bill, a judgment for the plaintiff was affirmed.

The second case cited above concerns the collapse, in 1972, of the Major Tube Corporation (MT). It had earlier made a contract with RJR Archer, Inc. which produced a certain flow of earnings. Archer contracted to buy from MT all the needs of its manufacturing business for paper cores, or tubes. It also sublet building space to MT. In January a bank loaned MT $100,000 and took for security the proceeds of the supply contract. Archer consented to the assignment by letter, assuring the bank that there were then no defaults by MT under the contract.[a] However, MT proved to be unable to supply all of Archer's needs as promised. In July the contract was modified to permit Archer to buy tubes elsewhere. Moreover, since MT could not finance purchases of core paper, Archer began to stock it and dispense it to MT as required. The trial court later observed that Archer thereby "diluted payments" under the contract. MT's rent payments were also charged against its earnings. Finally, as creditors of MT began to serve Archer with garnishments, it diverted some payments to them. It handled the garnishments sloppily: "never pleaded the contract and assignment." In August Archer cancelled the contract and thereafter dealt with MT on a day-to-day basis. In November MT ceased operations. The bank sued Archer for the unpaid balance of its loan, $78,200. A master reported unpaid invoices for tubes of nearly $100,000, but gave Archer credit for core paper supplied, for unpaid rent, and for "payments to court," which virtually wiped out the account. The trial court gave judgment for the bank in the full amount claimed, and Archer appealed. *Held*: award reduced to some $12,000.

For the sums paid to court, Archer was not entitled to credit: "it does not appear that Archer made any effort to protect [the bank's] assignment." [b] As to other credits the court (Goddard, J.) referred to UCC 9–318 and said:

"As to the purchase of core paper, it is undisputed that had Archer not purchased the paper Major Tube would have gone out of

a. "and no claims or set-offs due to us at this date."

b. On petition to rehear, Archer complained that this would require it to make double payment. Conceding this, the court said it is "invariably the penalty exacted of a creditor [debtor?] who fails to protect an assignee."

business the latter part of July rather than in November, and that it was absolutely necessary for them to have the raw material to be able to operate. Consequently, we find that this was a commercially reasonable modification of the contract as contemplated by subsection (2) and should be credited against any amount owed Nassau.

"We are of the same opinion as to the rent deductions which also enabled Major Tube to continue in business."

NOTES

(1) *Restatements.* The original Restatement contains no provision comparable to UCC 9–318(2); but Restatement Second states a closely parallel rule, in § 338(2). Comment f after the section states: "Contrary agreement between obligor and assignee is effective." The inference is clear that a "contrary agreement" between obligor and assignor is *ineffective.* But Comment a after § 311 states: "The parties to a contract . . . can by agreement create a duty to a beneficiary which cannot be varied without the beneficiary's consent." How is it possible to reconcile these rules?

(2) *An Illustration.* "A Company contracts to supply electricity to B for twenty years. Later A assigns to C for value certain fixed monthly payments to be made by B under the contract. After ten years B ceases to require electricity and A and B agree in good faith to terminate all performance under the contract. B is not liable to C for payments which would have accrued thereafter." Illustration 6 to Restatement Second, § 338.

(3) *A Stand-Pat Position.* In UCC 9–318(2), the standards for a modification or substitution, effective against a notifying assignee, are that it be "made in good faith and in accordance with reasonable commercial standards." At this point there is a variance in the New York version of the Code, which adds: "and without material adverse effect upon the assignee's rights under or the assignor's ability to perform the contract."

Does this addition make a worthwhile limitation on the power of the contracting parties to alter their relations? The Permanent Editorial Board for the Code thinks not.[c]

(4) *The Case of Bannister's Boat.* A shipowner, Bannister, contracted to pay £1375 to John Gough, in installments, for the building of a vessel. On October 27, 1876, two installments of £250 each had been earned, but Bannister had already advanced sums that were necessary for Gough to pay his workmen and the cost of materials employed on the job, amounting to £1015. On that date Gough assigned to William Brice, a solicitor, £100 out of money due or to become due under the contract, and notice of the assignment was given to Bannister. Subsequently Bannister made payments to Gough of more than £100, and refused to pay anything to Brice. Gough

c. Final Report, Permanent Editorial Board for the UCC, Review Committee for Article 9, 215 (1971).

"In practice, many security agreements covering accounts and contract rights make a modification of or substitution for a contract an event of default." W. Davenport & D. Murray, Secured Transactions 111 (1978).

would not have been able to complete the vessel without these payments. Brice brought an action against Bannister upon the assignment. ***Held:*** For Brice. One of the judges expressed doubt that the decision would have been the same if Bannister had made the subsequent payments in response to a threat by Gough not to finish the vessel. Brett, L. J., dissented, saying this of the transaction between Gough and the defendant: "if what they do is done bonâ fide and in the ordinary course of business, I cannot think their dealings ought to be impeded or imperilled . . . , and it seems to me the purchaser of a ship and the builder might have cancelled the contract even after this assignment. Why may they not modify it? If they cannot modify it, it seems to me to denote a state of slavery in business that ought not to be suffered . . . ." Brice v. Bannister, L.R. 3 Q.B.D. 569 (1878). How may this case be distinguished from the one in the preceding note?

ALLHUSEN v. CARISTO CONSTRUCTION CORP.

Court of Appeals of New York, 1952.
303 N.Y. 446, 103 N.E.2d 891, 37 A.L.R.2d 1245.

Herman Allhusen, as assignee, sued the Caristo Construction Corp. for money due plaintiff's assignor under a contract with defendant. The Special Term, New York County, Botein, J., entered an order granting defendant's motion for summary judgment dismissing the complaint, and plaintiff appealed. The Appellate Division, 278 App.Div. 817, 104 N.Y.S.2d 565, by a divided court, affirmed the judgment, and plaintiff appealed. . . .

FROESSEL, Judge. Defendant, a general contractor, subcontracted with the Kroo Painting Company (hereinafter called Kroo) for the performance by the latter of certain painting work in New York City public schools. Their contracts contained the following prohibitory provision: "The assignment by the second party [Kroo] of this contract or any interest therein, or of any money due or to become due by reason of the terms hereof without the written consent of the first party [defendant] shall be void." Kroo subsequently assigned certain rights under the contracts to Marine Midland Trust Company of New York, which in turn assigned said rights to plaintiff. These rights included the "moneys due and to become due" to Kroo. The *contracts* were not assigned, and no question of improper delegation of contractual duties is involved. No written consent to the assignments was procured from defendant.

Plaintiff as assignee seeks to recover, in six causes of action, $11,650 allegedly due and owing for work done by Kroo. . . . Special Term dismissed the complaint, holding that the prohibition against assignments "must be given effect." The Appellate Division affirmed, one Justice dissenting on the ground that the "account receivable was assignable by nature, and could not be rendered otherwise without imposing an unlawful restraint upon the power of alienation of property." 278 App.Div. 817, 104 N.Y.S.2d 565, 566.

Whether an anti-assignment clause is effective is a question that has troubled the courts not only of this State but in other jurisdictions as well, Burck v. Taylor, 152 U.S. 634, 14 S.Ct. 696, 38 L.Ed. 578; State St. Furniture Co. v. Armour & Co., 345 Ill. 160, 177 N.E. 702, 76 A.L.R. 1298 [other citations omitted].

Our courts have not construed a contractual provision against assignments framed in the language of the clause now before us. Such kindred clauses as have been subject to interpretation usually have been held to be either (1) personal covenants limiting the covenantee to a claim for damages in the event of a breach as e. g., Manchester v. Kendall, 19 Jones & Sp. 460, affirmed 103 N.Y. 638; Sacks v. Neptune Meter Co., 144 Misc. 70, 258 N.Y.S. 254, affirmed 238 App.Div. 82, 263 N.Y.S. 462, or (2) ineffectual because of the use of uncertain language, State Bank v. Central Mercantile Bank, 248 N.Y. 428, 162 N.E. 475, 59 A.L.R. 1473. But these decisions are not to be read as meaning that there can be no enforcible prohibition against the assignment of a claim; indeed, they are authority only for the proposition that, in the absence of language clearly indicating that a contractual right thereunder shall be nonassignable, a prohibitory clause will be interpreted as a personal covenant not to assign.

In the Manchester case, supra, it was held, 103 N.Y. at page 463, that the words, " 'This contract not to be assigned, or any part thereof, or any installments to grow due under the same' ", must be construed as an agreement not to assign, the breach of which would give rise to a claim for damages by the covenantee. The court stated, 103 N.Y. at page 463, that the quoted words "would not make the assignment void." In the clause now before us, however, it is expressly provided that the "assignment . . . shall be void." In the State Bank case, supra, 248 N.Y. at page 431, 162 N.E. at page 476, 59 A.L.R. 1473, which involved the assignment of certificates of deposit which were "not subject to check" and were "payable only to himself [depositor] . . . on return of this Certificate properly endorsed", we held that such language did not make the certificates nonassignable, and that nonnegotiable certificates of deposit are assignable *in the absence of an agreement to the contrary.* Judge Pound, writing for a unanimous court, added, however, 248 N.Y. at page 435, 162 N.E. at page 477: "Clear language should therefore be required to lead to the conclusion that the certificates are not assignable. 1 Williston on Contracts, § 422. We cannot deduce such consequences from uncertain language. Scheffer v. Erie County Sav. Bank, 229 N.Y. 50, 127 N.E. 474. The plainest words should have been chosen so that he who runs could read, in order to limit the freedom of alienation of rights and prohibit the assignment. It might have been stipulated on the face of the certificates that they should be 'nontransferable' or 'nonassignable.' "

In Devlin v. Mayor of City of N. Y., 63 N.Y. 8 at pages 17, 20, we said: "Parties may, in terms, prohibit the assignment of any contract ["and the interest of the contractor under it"] and declare that neither personal representatives nor assignees shall succeed to any rights in virtue of it, or be bound by its obligations." In Fortunato v. Patten, 147 N.Y. 277, 41 N.E. 572, where the contract with the city provided in substance that the contractor shall not assign the contract, or any moneys payable thereunder, without the consent of the city, we noted, 147 N.Y. at page 281, 41 N.E. at page 573: "it was inserted in the contract solely for the benefit of the city, and prevents any claim being asserted against it in the absence of consent."

In the lower courts, Sacks v. Neptune Meter Co., supra, expresses the view, and Morkel v. Metropolitan Life Ins. Co., App.Term, 1st Dept., 163 Misc. 366, 297 N.Y.S. 962, and Reisler v. Cohen, 67 Misc. 67, 121 N.Y.S. 603, hold that, where the agreement provides that the claim is nonassignable the assignee may not recover. This is in harmony with Restatement of the Law of Contracts (§ 151): "A right may be the subject of effective assignment unless . . . (c) the assignment is prohibited by the contract creating the right." See, also, 2 Williston on Contracts, § 422, pp. 1217–1218.

In the light of the foregoing, we think it is reasonably clear that, while the courts have striven to uphold freedom of assignability, they have not failed to recognize the concept of freedom to contract. In large measure they agree that, where appropriate language is used, assignments of money due under contracts may be prohibited. When "clear language" is used, and the "plainest words . . . have been chosen", parties may "limit the freedom of alienation of rights and prohibit the assignment." State Bank v. Central Mercantile Bank, supra, 248 N.Y. at page 435, 162 N.E. at page 477, 59 A.L.R. 1473. We have now before us a clause embodying clear, definite and appropriate language, which may be construed in no other way but that any attempted assignment of either the contract or any rights created thereunder shall be "void" as against the obligor. One would have to do violence to the language here employed to hold that it is merely an agreement by the subcontractor not to assign. The objectivity of the language precludes such a construction. We are therefore compelled to conclude that this prohibitory clause is a valid and effective restriction of the right to assign.

Such a holding is not violative of public policy. Professor Williston, in his treatise on Contracts, states (Vol. 2, § 422, p. 1214): "The question of the free alienation of property does not seem to be involved." The New York cases do not hold otherwise, State Bank v. Central Mercantile Bank, supra, 248 N.Y. at page 435, 162 N.E. at page 477, 59 A.L.R. 1473. Plaintiff's claimed rights arise out of the very contract embodying the provision now sought to be invalidated. The right to moneys under the contracts is but a companion to other jural relations forming an aggregation of actual and potential interrelated rights and obligations. No sound reason appears why an assignee should remain unaffected by a provision in the very contract which gave life to the claim he asserts.

Nor is there any merit in plaintiff's contention that section 41 of the Personal Property Law, Consol.Laws, c. 41,[a] requires that the prohibitory clause be denied effect. Because the statute provides that a person may transfer a claim, it does not follow that he may not contract otherwise. Countless rights granted by statutes are voluntarily surrendered in the everyday affairs of individuals. In Rosenthal Paper Co. v. National Folding Box & Paper Co., 226 N.Y. 313, 325–326, 123 N.E. 766, 770, we noted: "The general rule now prevailing . . . that any property right, not necessarily personal, is assignable, *is overcome only by agreement of the contracting parties* or a principle of law or public policy. [Citing cases.] In this jurisdiction the statute, in effect, so provides [referring to the predecessor of section 41 of the Personal Property Law]." (Emphasis supplied.)

The judgment should be affirmed, with costs.

NOTES

(1) *Status of the Rule.* The Restatement Second seems to acknowledge that an assignment may be proscribed, but only in a rather grudging way: § 322.

Holmes observed that it is one thing to permit a contracting party to confine his obligation to narrow limits, but quite another to permit him to make the other party's right (such as it is) inalienable. The buyer of a horse may not contract in such a way that he may not later transfer the horse; the parties to the sale may not deprive him of the *power* of resale. According to Holmes, "it is not illogical to apply the same rule to a debt that would be applied to a horse"—and he applied it. He observed that sometimes assignability is "sustained on the ground that the provision against assignment is inserted only for the benefit of the [obligor]. Whether that form of expression is accurate or merely is an indirect recognition of the principle that we have stated, hardly is material here." Portuguese-American Bank of San Francisco v. Welles, 242 U.S. 7 (1916).

"The no assignment right is one of those peculiar legal rules which are honored almost exclusively in the breach." Gilmore, Good Faith Purchase, 63 Yale L.J. 1057, 1118 (1954). Both here and in drafting UCC comments Professor Gilmore criticized Allhusen as a monument to conceptualism and a throwback to ancient law. "The cases are legion in which courts have construed the heart out of prohibitory or restrictive terms and held the assignment good. . . . This gradual and largely unacknowledged shift in legal doctrine has taken place in response to economic need: as accounts and contract rights have become the collateral which secures an ever-increasing number of financing transactions, it has been necessary to reshape the law so that these intangibles, like negotiable instruments and negotiable documents of title, can be freely assigned." Comment to UCC 9–318(4).

a. The statute referred to has been carried forward as General Obligations Law, § 13–101. See p. 1074 supra.

Should commercial accounts receivable be accorded the quality of negotiability as a matter of law? See Gilmore, op. cit. supra, 1120.

(2) *The Code.* Delta Engineering Corporation accepts an order for machines from RCA in which it is provided that an assignment by Delta of its payment rights under the contract shall be void without RCA's prior written consent. The term is ineffective under UCC 9–318(4)—p. 1087 supra.[b] In states where the 1972 amendments to Article 9 have not been enacted, the Code section does not contain the final phrase, beginning "or require . . ." Does the absence of the phrase signify any difference in the law of those states? Do you see a reason to doubt it? [c]

In fact the orders that RCA gave Delta in the Ertel case (p. 1088 supra) contained the following "assignment" term:

> Neither this Order nor any interest under it shall be assigned by Seller without the prior written consent of RCA, except that claims for moneys due or to become due under this Order may be assigned by Seller without such consent, and subject to the provision of this paragraph, RCA shall promptly be furnished with two signed copies of any such assignment. Payment to an assignee of any such claim shall be subject to set off or recoupment for any present or future claim or claims which RCA may have against Seller except to the extent that any such claims may be expressly waived in writing by RCA. RCA reserves the right to make direct settlements and/or adjustments in price(s) with Seller notwithstanding any assignment of claims for moneys due or to become due hereunder and without notice to the assignee.

What purposes and effects can be ascribed to these provisions?

(3) *Protection for the Obligor.* Consider some of the reasons a contracting party might have for insisting upon a term prohibiting an assignment of rights by the other party: (a) He anticipates equivocal action by the other party—a questionable notice or the like—which leaves doubt about the person to whom his own performance is due. (b) He is concerned about the other party's financial needs and the risk involved in meeting those needs—after notice of an assignment—with prepayments and advances. (c) He foresees circumstances that might make it desirable to modify the contract in a way affecting the interest of the assignee adversely—a hazardous course to take without the assignee's assent. Are there other possible reasons for prohibiting an assignment?

How much does the Code do to satisfy these objectives of the obligor? Is it enough to offset the rule that a prohibition on assignment is ineffective?

(4) *Problem.* Kroo Painting Company makes an assignment of its job earnings to First Bank, without Caristo's consent. Then it makes another assignment of the same earnings—fraudulently—to Second Bank, this time obtaining written consent from Caristo. When both banks claim the pro-

b. But in the drafting of Article 2 the rule of Article 9 seems to have been overlooked. Note the first three words of section 2–210(2): what can they possibly mean?

c. For a case decided under the 1962 Official Text—and difficult to reconcile with it—see Merchants & Farmers Bank v. McClendon, 220 So.2d 815 (Miss.1969). Compare American Bank of Commerce v. City of McAlester, 555 P.2d 581 (Okla.1976).

ceeds, Caristo interpleads them and deposits the fund into the court. Does it follow from the main case that Second Bank will prevail, because the first assignment was "void"? See Fox-Greenwald Sheet Metal Co. v. Markowitz Bros., Inc., 452 F.2d 1346 (D.C.Cir. 1971); Restatement Second, § 322(d). For references on the general problem see Note 2, p. 1176 infra.

ARNOLD PRODUCTIONS, INC. v. FAVORITE FILMS CORP., 298 F.2d 540 (2d Cir. 1962). [Two motion pictures were the subject of a distribution agreement whereby Arnold, the owner, gave Favorite the exclusive right for seven years to "distribute and exploit" them through theatres and television. Favorite, as licensee, agreed to use its best efforts to obtain as many bookings and exhibitions as possible; the receipts were to be shared. The contract further provided: "This agreement is personal and cannot be assigned by the Licensee . . . without the consent in writing of the Licensor first obtained." Within two years Favorite contracted with Nationwide Television Corporation, without having Arnold's consent, making Nationwide its "sole and exclusive agent for the television distribution of the films." The actual distribution of the films was handled by corporate subsidiaries of Nationwide.

In an action brought by Arnold it charged Favorite with a breach of their distribution agreement by delegating its performance. From an adverse judgment, Arnold appealed.]

LUMBARD, Chief Judge. . . . We find no error in Judge Murphy's holding that Favorite did not assign the contract to Nationwide or abandon its duties under it, and thus committed no breach.

It is clear that Favorite did not technically "assign" its contract in its entirety, but merely delegated a part (the extent of which we shall presently discuss) of its duties. Favorite did not purport to divest itself of its ultimate responsibility to Arnold. Although it made Nationwide its "sole and exclusive agent," it maintained certain supervisory powers over it. It reserved "the right to designate . . . a Representative, to whom you agree to submit for approval or rejection, each and all of your proposed license or sub-license agreements with respect to the Photoplays," and it appointed its president as such representative. Thus there was no breach of the specific covenant against assignment. Rather the question is whether the delegation of performance deprived Arnold of any right to Favorite's own services which it may have acquired explicitly from the provision that "this agreement is personal" or implicitly from the "best efforts" clause and the inherent nature of the contract.[1]

1. "In a contract for a sales agency, the personal performance of the agent is practically always a condition precedent to the duty of the principal and employer," and the agent cannot discharge his obligation by furnishing a substitute. 4 Corbin, Contracts 444–45 (1951); see, Paige v. Faure, 229 N.Y. 114, 127 N.E. 898, 10 A.L.R. 649 (1920); cf. Nassau Hotel Co. v. Barnett & Barse Corp., 162 App.Div. 381, 147 N.Y.S. 283 (1st

We do not find it necessary to consider whether New York would impose the same implied duty of personal service upon a contracting corporation as it would on an individual under the same circumstances, or whether this contract by its explicit terms gave Arnold the right to demand Favorite's own services.[2] Even if we assume that only Favorite was to give the performance called for by the contract, which was the "exploitation" of the films and the "obtaining" of bookings, we do not believe that this performance excluded such use of Nationwide's services as Favorite made. The contract must be interpreted in light of what the record reveals about the practices of the business in which the parties were engaged, and especially what it reveals about the general understanding and course of dealings between them.

It is significant that under this contract Favorite's duties with respect to reissue of the two films to theatres were exactly the same as the television distribution duties here in question. There is no dispute that it was understood that little if any of the actual theatre distribution (possibly that in New York City, at the most) was to be done by Favorite itself; most was to be delegated to various "franchise holders" in various parts of the country, who were to do the actual work of selling films to local exhibitors. There is no indication that Favorite's supervision over these franchise holders was any greater than its supervision over Nationwide's television distribution. Favorite maintained the right to reject any agreements suggested by Nationwide, and there was sufficient evidence that on occasion its president actually did so with respect to television distribution, to justify Judge Murphy's finding that there was no abdication of responsibility. There is no suggestion that Arnold was endangered by lack of financial responsibility on Nationwide's part, or in any other way not having to do with the quality of the performance it received. In any event, the concession that under the same contract distribution through franchise holders was contemplated is sufficient to foreclose any inference that Favorite's employees were expected to do all television distribution personally. There is, indeed, testimony which would support a finding that throughout most of the term of the contract Arnold acquiesced in Favorite's delegation of sales duties.

Affirmed.[a]

Dept. 1914), aff'd mem., 212 N.Y. 568, 106 N.E. 1036 (1914). Plaintiff has made no claim that Favorite's duty should be determined by principles of actual agency, and we see no reason to treat the duty as more than contractual.

2. There is some reason to believe that the New York courts would not permit such an implication in the case of a corporation. Wetherell Bros. v. United States Steel Co., 200 F.2d 761 (1 Cir. 1953); New York Bank Note Co. v. Hamilton Bank Note Engraving & Printing Co., 180 N.Y. 280, 293, 73 N.E. 48, 52 (1905); New England Iron Co. v. Gilbert Elevated Ry. Co., 91 N.Y. 153, 166–167 (1883).

a. But see Rother-Gallagher v. Montana Power Co., 164 Mont. 360, 522 P.2d 1226 (1974).

NOTE

Demand for Assurances? Was there, in this case, any "assignment which delegates performance," as that expression is used in UCC 2–210? The exact issue could not arise in relation to a film-distribution agreement, presumably, unless it were characterized as a transaction in goods under Article 2 of the Code. But if the provision *were* applicable, the question would be whether or not it entitled Arnold to demand assurances from Nationwide (or from Favorite) under section 2–609, because of the arrangement between Favorite and Nationwide. It is risky to make a demand for assurances, of course, unless the Code clearly authorizes it; for an unwarranted demand may itself constitute a repudiation. The Code expression, "assignment which delegates performance," might be read narrowly, justifying a demand only when the contract has been assigned in its entirety—and the court says Favorite did not do that. Would you support a broader reading? How broad?

For discussion of this and other questions arising out of the Code treatment of assignments, see Note, 105 U.Pa.L.Rev. 836, 906–20 (1957). (In some respects the Code text has been altered since this study.)

ASSIGNMENTS, BANKRUPTCY, AND CREDITORS

Bankruptcy is the preeminent type of insolvency proceeding, in which the assets of a business are parcelled out among its creditors. Few creditors, except those who have effective liens and security interests, can expect to share substantially in the distribution. An assignee of accounts as collateral for advances naturally hopes not to meet the fate of an unsecured, "general" creditor if bankruptcy overtakes the assignor. For him (and for any other secured creditor) the ultimate test of his position is whether or not he can retain his collateral against a trustee in bankruptcy. The trustee, who administers the estate on behalf of general creditors, will properly appropriate collateral for their benefit so far as the law allows.

A bankruptcy case has been mentioned in which Gordon Drew made money available to the American Fiberlast Company for the purpose of building a Radome: Shiro v. Drew, p. 1082 supra. Fiberlast became a bankrupt (now officially called a bankruptcy "debtor") and Drew found himself in a contest with the bankruptcy trustee over the right to Fiberlast's earnings under the Radome contract. Drew contended that he had an assignment of the debtor's payment rights, indefeasible in bankruptcy, which assured him of repayment of his loan to the extent of the value of those rights. The opposing position of the trustee was that the Radome earnings were distributable among the creditors of Fiberlast generally (those having claims allowable in bankruptcy). That is, Drew asserted a security interest in the earnings, whereas the trustee regarded him as an unsecured, "general" creditor, entitled at best to a pro-rata distribution from the bankruptcy estate.

Both before and since that decision (in 1959) there have been repeated adjustments in the law that determines the fortunes in bankruptcy of financing assignees. The principal determinants are Article 9 of the Code and the bankruptcy statutes, each as amended from time to time. Since before World War II there has been continuing skirmishing between financing assignees and unsecured-creditor interests. It has produced an astoundingly complex body of law which must be left for the most part to development in a course in security interests or bankruptcy.

A key to success for the financer is achieving "perfection" of his security interest, a condition compounded of both state and federal elements. One of the elements of perfection—a public filing—has been mentioned in Note 1, p. 1087 supra. If this and the other requisites of perfection are not achieved by the time bankruptcy proceedings concerning the assignor are commenced, the accounts claimed by the assignee as collateral will surely be lost to him. Moreover, an assignee who makes a belated filing of a financing statement runs a serious risk of invalidation by the trustee of his interest. (A filing more than ten days after the interest attaches and within 90 days of the bankruptcy is a particular target of the anti-preference provisions of the Bankruptcy Code.) The thought is that a secured creditor should not maintain secrecy about his interest until the debtor's financial dissolution is imminent and then be permitted to save himself with a last-minute filing.

It is good practice for a financer to file a financing statement (UCC–1), as permitted by Article 9, in *anticipation* of having an interest in the debtor's accounts. The statutory system allows for the prevalent case of using an ever-changing block of short-term accounts for collateral. In the business of many a merchant-borrower his customers are expected to—and usually do—make payments within thirty days or so after their debts arise. In that case the financer must of course depend on replacement accounts to accomplish continuous replenishment of his pool of collateral. Much disputation has occurred over the bankruptcy aspects of this practice, for it could readily be depicted as infringing the anti-preference provisions of the statutes. (In other words, the attachment of the financer's interest to each account arising shortly before bankruptcy could be challenged as a preferential transfer.) In the Bankruptcy Reform Act of 1978 the Congress put this matter on a new footing. The details are too elaborate for description here. Briefly, however, it may be suggested that financing a merchant whose business is seasonal is hazardous. If his book of receivables (for, say, watch sales) is expected to swell during the pre-Christmas season, and his financer relies on this asset as collateral, the financer will be well advised to see that his advances do not outrun the value of the collateral at the beginning of the season. The Bankruptcy Code provides, in general, that any increase in the quantity of accounts within the 90-day period preceding a bankruptcy (relative to the amount of debt as it stands at the opening and closing of that period) will redound to the benefit of the bankruptcy estate.[a]

NOTES

(1) *More on the Radome Case.* If this case were to arise again today, Drew could not hope to prevail without having made timely filing of a financing statement, unless his assignment could be brought within a Code dispensation from filing built on the *de minimis* principle.[b]

More fundamentally, Drew might be thought not to have gotten to first base toward perfection of his security interest. A security interest cannot be perfected until it has attached; and attachment in the case of intangibles requires the signing of a "security agreement." Re-read the letter addressed to him by Fiberlast, and consider the argument made by the bankruptcy trustee that it fell short of an assignment. Do you agree? How would you have written the document so as to strengthen Drew's position?

(2) *Lien Creditors' Rights.* Ordinary creditors—those who have taken no steps to enforce their claims and who do not have a security interest—have no ground for objection to the debtor's assignment of a claim, even if it shows favoritism to a particular creditor by securing or satisfying his claim to the exclusion of other claims. (For this discussion the law of fraudulent conveyances is set aside.) The disfavored creditors must resort to collective proceedings such as bankruptcy to have preferential transfers reversed.

However, a "lien creditor"—one who has invoked an appropriate enforcement procedure—may very well oust an assignment. One becomes a lien creditor by taking proceedings on his claim such as directing a writ of garnishment to an "account debtor"—one who is indebted on an assigned account. Such a creditor may well oust a prior assignment under the following Code rule:

> [A]n unperfected security interest is subordinate to the rights of . . . (b) a person who becomes a lien creditor before the security interest is perfected; . . . UCC 9–301(1).

This generally signifies that an assignee is vulnerable to processes such as attachment or garnishment until he has filed a financing statement in proper form and in the appropriate office or offices. (It is largely owing to this rule that a security interest unperfected at the debtor's bankruptcy carries no weight. The Bankruptcy Code makes the trustee a sort of apotheosis of all the challenges that creditors of the debtor might have made to his

a. Statutory references apposite to this text and the following notes include:

UCC [1972 edition] 9–104, 9–106, 9–108, 9–203, and 9–301. Bankruptcy Code [U.S.C.A. 11] §§ 541, 544(a), 547, and 550.

b. UCC 9–302(1): A financing statement must be filed to perfect all security interests except the following . . .

(e) an assignment of accounts which does not alone or in conjunction with other assignments to the same assignee transfer a significant part of the outstanding accounts of the assignor; . . .

pre-bankruptcy transfers: § 544(a); see the first paragraph of these notes.)

(3) *Looking Back.* Before a filing system for assignments was thought of there were various other modes of "perfection". A usual one was for the assignee to notify the account debtor that he had an interest in the account. Looking back, one can see that this measure did not accomplish much in the way of public notoriety. Moreover, many firms borrowing on the strength of their accounts did not relish the idea of such advices to their customers. Hence in some courts a degree of indulgency was shown toward what is called "non-notification" financing. The case that follows counts as an instance. The precise question it raises is how far a creditor must proceed with collection processes in order to earn, as against an "unperfected" assignment, the favor shown to a lien creditor.

McDOWELL, PYLE & CO. v. HOPFIELD

Supreme Court of Maryland, 1925.
148 Md. 84, 128 A. 742, 52 A.L.R. 105.

[The Commercial Credit Company was in the business of purchasing accounts receivable on the "non-notification basis." In July, 1923, it purchased some accounts from the Wirth Concord Ade Company, of Rhode Island. They represented sales made to a customer in Baltimore, McDowell, Pyle & Company. On August 13, Carl Hopfield, a salesman for Wirth, brought an action against it in Maryland, claiming that his services had not been paid for. Jurisdiction was based on the "presence" of Wirth's claim in Maryland, and a writ of attachment which Hopfield served on its debtor, McDowell. The next day, McDowell answered, admitting its indebtedness. On September 20 a default judgment was entered, Wirth not appearing, to be enforced against its claim. (By Maryland practice, the judgment was entitled a "condemnation".) Not receiving payment of the accounts as it expected, Commercial Credit notified McDowell of its assignments on October 8. Ten days later it learned from McDowell of the attachment and judgment. On October 20 both Commercial Credit and McDowell filed petitions asking that the judgment be stricken. The petitions were denied, and they appealed.

The court first examined the character of a garnishor's judgment in Maryland, and concluded that equitable considerations might require it to be reconsidered, in the court's discretion, upon an application made before the close of the term.]

WALSH, J. . . . In the present case the equities of the situation are clearly with the assignee. It purchased the accounts for a valuable consideration, and in deference to the assignor, which was to collect and forward the money, it did not notify the original debtor of the assignment until after the accounts had all matured. When payment was not received through the assignor in the usual course of business the assignee within two weeks of the final maturity notified the debtor, and now both the assignee and debtor (the garnishee) are asking that the judgment in favor of the attaching creditor be stricken out. This creditor dealt with the assignor on the basis of the latter's general credit, and not with any special reference to these accounts, while the assignee advanced money on these specific accounts, and it is the almost universal rule that under such conditions the assignee has the better claim, unless the judgment of condemnation alters the rule. . . . The judgment in this case has not been paid, nor has any execution been issued on it, and the garnishee against whom it was entered applied within the term to have it stricken out. Considering all the circumstances of the case, and the legal principles which we deem properly applicable thereto, we think that the judgment should have been stricken out and the assignee allowed to intervene as claimant.[a]

NOTES

(1) *Levy and the Like.* The Uniform Commercial Code, which would now govern this case, does not specify the procedure requisite for acquiring a "lien" on a debtor's property, further than to say "by attachment, levy or the like." § 9–301(3). To serve a writ of garnishment (called attachment or trustee process in some states), as Hopfield did, is commonly regarded as a lien-creating step. However, a close examination of creditors' remedies may be required for a confident opinion about the law of a particular jurisdiction. Certainly a lien is established by an appropriate service of a writ of execution, following judgment.

Whatever the requisites may be, the essential rule of the preceding case is unquestioned: a creditor of the assignor who has taken no such step is in no position to challenge the interest of an assignee. Like other transfers, an assignment may be a fraud upon creditors of the transferor, and voidable by them. A gratuitous assignment, in particular, is open to challenge by the assignor's creditors. But a judicial process, either a levy or something comparable, is an essential step in the challenge. The "something comparable" may be filing a bankruptcy petition: that is said to amount to a general levy on the debtor's assets.

(2) *Successive Assignees from the Same Assignor.* The Restatement Second, states a complex rule for the problem of ranking conflicting assignments. (The quotations that follow are from comments to § 342.) The problem was much reduced in importance by the enactment of the Code and legislation that preceded it. "The subject is now largely governed by the Uniform Commercial Code, except in cases of wage claims, rights under insurance policies, deposit accounts, and certain other excluded types of transactions. See § 9–104." The sequence of filing is the chief factor in ranking "conflicting security interests" under the Code.[b] In this connec-

a. The original Restatement rule on an attaching creditor's position vis-a-vis the assignee has been revised to follow the rule of this case. The Reporter's Note on § 341 so indicates.

b. "An unperfected security interest is subordinate to the rights of a person who is not a secured party to the extent that he gives value for accounts or general intangibles without knowledge of the security interest

tion, it is well to observe that parties who contemplate entering into an assignment in the future (or other Code security agreement in many forms) may effect a filing before the transaction is executed. There is no name for the status that such a filing confers on the prospective assignee; it certainly gives him no present interest in anything. Yet it is an important step in practice, for it will surely warn off any wary financer who might otherwise be inclined to give value for an interest within the description of the financing statement.

The Restatement rule is known as the "four horsemen" rule. If both A and B have bought a claim from a double-dealing assignor, in that order, and B collects it, the rule permits B to retain the proceeds against A,[c] and in any one of three other circumstances it permits B to recover and retain the proceeds.

"In England and in a number of states, aside from statute, a different rule has been followed, giving priority to the assignee who first gives notice to the obligor, regardless of the order in which the assignments were made. That rule stems from the leading case of Dearle v. Hall, 3 Russ. 1, 48 (1828), involving successive assignments of the interest of a beneficiary of a trust. The English rule has consequences similar to that of a system of public filing, except that the obligor acts as the filing office; it is somewhat more convenient where a single obligor is involved such as a trustee or the owner or prime contractor on a construction project than in cases of multiple obligors, as where a business concern assigns its accounts receivable." [d]

and before it is perfected. § 9–301." But the usual contest between two assignees of the same claim is one between two *secured parties,* if it is governed by the Code at all.

c. B must have given value, in good faith.

d. Restatement Second, § 342, Comment b.

*

INDEX

References are to Pages

References are to Pages

References are to Pages

†